The Psychology of Gender
Volume II

The International Library of Critical Writings in Psychology

Series Editors: A.J. Chapman
Professor of Psychology
University of Leeds
N.P. Sheehy
Professor of Psychology
School of Psychology
The Queen's University of Belfast
Leo Goldberger
Professor of Psychology
New York University

Industrial and Organizational Psychology (Volumes I and II)
Edited by Cary L. Cooper
The Psychology of Gender (Volumes I, II, III and IV)
Edited by Carol Nagy Jacklin
Social Psychology (Volumes I, II and III)
Edited by Elliot Aronson and Anthony R. Pratkanis

Future titles will include:
Memory
Edited by Peter E. Morris and Martin Conway
Developmental Psychology
Edited by Peter E. Bryant
Ageing
Edited by Patrick Rabbitt
Cognitive Science
Edited by Noel P. Sheehy and Antony J. Chapman
Attention
Edited by Geoffrey Underwood
Ergonomics and Human Factors
Edited by David Oborne
Mathematical and Statistical Psychology
Edited by Philip Levy
Physiological Psychology
Neuropsychology
Perception
Learning
Emotion
Language
Motivation
Personality
Psychodiagnostics
Psychoanalysis and Psychotherapy

The Psychology of Gender
Volume II

Edited by

Carol Nagy Jacklin

Professor of Psychology
University of Southern California

A New York University Press Reference Collection

First published in the U.S.A. in 1992 by
NEW YORK UNIVERSITY PRESS
Washington Square
New York, N.Y. 10003

Library of Congress Cataloging in Publication Data
The Psychology of gender/edited by Carol Nagy Jacklin.
    p. cm. – (International library of critical writings in psychology)
"New York University Press reference collection".
Includes index.
    ISBN 0–8147–4185–1 (v.1). – ISBN 0–8147–4186–X (v.2).
ISBN 0–8147–4187–8 (v.3). – ISBN 0–8147–4188–6 (v.4).
ISBN 0–8147–4184–3 (set)
    1. Sex differences (Psychology) I. Jacklin, Carol Nagy.
II. Series.
    [DNLM: 1. Gender Identity. 2. Sex Behavior–psychology.
3. Sex Characteristics. BF 692 P9743]
BF 692.2.P764 1992
155.3′3–dc20
DNLM/DLC
for Library of Congress
92–16187
CIP

Manufactured in Great Britain

Contents

Acknowledgements

The editor and publishers wish to thank the following who have kindly given permission for the use of copyright material.

Academic Press, Inc. for articles: Carol Nagy Jacklin (1981), 'Methodological Issues in the Study of Sex-Related Differences', *Developmental Review*, **1**, 266–73; Beverly I. Fagot (1985), 'Changes in Thinking about Early Sex Role Development', *Developmental Review*, **5**, 83–98; Stephen J. Thoma (1986), 'Estimating Gender Differences in the Comprehension and Preference of Moral Issues', *Developmental Review*, **6**, 165–80.

American Association for the Advancement of Science for articles: Camilla Persson Benbow and Julian C. Stanley (1980), 'Sex Differences in Mathematical Ability: Fact or Artifact?', *Science*, **210**, 1262–4; Camilla Persson Benbow and Julian C. Stanley (1983), 'Sex Differences in Mathematical Reasoning Ability: More Facts', *Science*, **222**, 1029–31.

American Educational Research Association for article: Camilla Persson Benbow and Julian C. Stanley (1982), 'Consequences in High School and College of Sex Differences in Mathematical Reasoning Ability: A Longitudinal Perspective', *American Educational Research Journal*, **19** (4), 598–622.

American Psychological Association for articles: Alice H. Eagly (1987), 'Reporting Sex Differences', *American Psychologist*, **42** (7), 756–7; Alan Feingold (1988), 'Cognitive Gender Differences are Disappearing', *American Psychologist*, **43** (2), 95–103; Rachel T. Hare-Mustin and Jeanne Marecek (1988), 'The Meaning of Difference: Gender Theory, Postmodernism, and Psychology', *American Psychologist*, **43** (6), 455–64; Earl R. Carlson and Rae Carlson (1960), 'Male and Female Subjects in Personality Research', *Journal of Abnormal and Social Psychology*, **61** (3), 482–3; Inge K. Broverman, Donald M. Broverman, Frank E. Clarkson, Paul S. Rosenkrantz and Susan R. Vogel (1970), 'Sex-Role Stereotypes and Clinical Judgments of Mental Health', *Journal of Consulting and Clinical Psychology*, **34** (1), 1–7; Robert Rosenthal and Donald B. Rubin (1982), 'Further Meta-Analytic Procedures for Assessing Cognitive Gender Differences', *Journal of Educational Psychology*, **74** (5), 708–12; David G. Perry and Kay Bussey (1979), 'The Social Learning Theory of Sex Differences: Imitation is Alive and Well', *Journal of Personality and Social Psychology*, **37** (10), 1699–1712; Kay Bussey and Albert Bandura (1984), 'Influence of Gender Constancy and Social Power on Sex-Linked Modeling', *Journal of Personality and Social Psychology*, **47**, 1292–1302; Maureen Rose Ford and Carol Rotter Lowery (1986), 'Gender Differences in Moral Reasoning: A Comparison of the Use of Justice and Care Orientations', *Journal of Personality and Social Psychology*, **50** (4), 777–83; Thomas A. Widiger and Shirley A. Settle (1987), 'Broverman et al. Revisited: An Artifactual Sex Bias',

Journal of Personality and Social Psychology, **53** (3), 463–9; Janet P. Boldizar, Kenneth L. Wilson and Deborah Kay Deemer (1989), 'Gender, Life Experiences, and Moral Judgment Development: A Process-Oriented Approach', *Journal of Personality and Social Psychology*, **57** (2), 229–38; Janet Shibley Hyde and Marcia C. Linn (1988), 'Gender Differences in Verbal Ability: A Meta-Analysis', *Psychological Bulletin*, **104** (1), 53–69; Meredith M. Kimball (1989), 'A New Perspective on Women's Math Achievement', *Psychological Bulletin*, **105** (2), 198–214; Janet Shibley Hyde, Elizabeth Fennema and Susan J. Lamon (1990), 'Gender Differences in Mathematics Performance: A Meta-Analysis', *Psychological Bulletin*, **107** (2), 139–55; Sandra Lipsitz Bem (1981), 'Gender Schema Theory: A Cognitive Account of Sex Typing', *Psychological Review*, **88** (4), 354–64; Alice H. Eagly (1990), 'On the Advantages of Reporting Sex Comparisons', *American Psychologist*, **45** (4), 560–62; Hugh Lytton and David M. Romney (1991), 'Parents' Differential Socialization of Boys and Girls: A Meta-Analysis', *Psychological Bulletin*, **109** (2), 267–96.

Blackwell Publishers for article: Lorraine B. Code (1981), 'Is the Sex of the Knower Epistemologically Significant?', *Metaphilosophy*, **12** (3&4), 267–76.

Harvard Educational Review for article: Carol Gilligan (1977), 'In a Different Voice: Women's Conceptions of Self and of Morality', *Harvard Educational Review*, **47** (4), 481–517.

Plenum Publishing Corporation for articles: David C. Bellinger and Jean Berko Gleason (1982), 'Sex Differences in Parental Directives to Young Children', *Sex Roles*, **8** (11), 1123–39; Nancy Eisenberg, Karlsson Roth, Karyl A. Bryniarski and Edward Murray (1984), 'Sex Differences in the Relationship of Height to Children's Actual and Attributed Social and Cognitive Competencies', *Sex Roles*, **11** (7/8), 719–34.

Society for Research in Child Development, Inc. for articles: Lynn S. Liben and Margaret L. Signorella (1980), 'Gender-related Schemata and Constructive Memory in Children', *Child Development*, **51** (1), 11–18; Carol Lynn Martin and Charles F. Halverson, Jr. (1981), 'A Schematic Processing Model of Sex Typing and Stereotyping in Children', *Child Development*, **52** (4), 1119–34; Carol Lynn Martin and Charles F. Halverson, Jr. (1983), 'The Effects of Sex-Typing Schemas on Young Children's Memory', *Child Development*, **54** (3), 563–4; Jacquelynne Eccles Parsons, Terry F. Adler and Caroline M. Kaczala (1982), 'Socialization of Achievement Attitudes and Beliefs: Parental Influences', *Child Development*, **53** (2), 310–21; Jacquelynne Eccles Parsons, Caroline M. Kaczala and Judith L. Meece (1982), 'Socialization of Achievement Attitudes and Beliefs: Classroom Influences', *Child Development*, **53** (2), 322–39; Marcia C. Linn and Anne C. Petersen (1985), 'Emergence and Characterization of Sex Differences in Spatial Ability: A Meta-Analysis', *Child Development*, **56**, 1479–98.

Society for the Psychological Study of Social Issues for article: Inge K. Broverman, Susan Raymond Vogel, Donald M. Broverman, Frank E. Clarkson and Paul S. Rosenkrantz (1972), 'Sex-Role Stereotypes: A Current Appraisal', *Journal of Social Issues*, **28** (2), 59–78.

University of Chicago Press for articles: Sandra Lipsitz Bem (1983), 'Gender Schema Theory and Its Implications for Child Development: Raising Gender-aschematic Children in a Gender-schematic Society', *Signs: Journal of Women in Culture and Society*, **8** (4), 598–616; Nancy M. Henley (1985), 'Psychology and Gender', *Signs: Journal of Women in Culture and Society*, **11** (1), 101–19; Jacquelynne S. Eccles and Janis E. Jacobs (1986), 'Social Forces Shape Math Attitudes and Performance', *Signs: Journal of Women in Culture and Society*, **11** (2), 367–80; Linda K. Kerber, Catherine G. Greeno and Eleanor E. Maccoby, Zella Luria, Carol B. Stack, and Carol Gilligan (1986), 'On *In a Different Voice*: An Interdisciplinary Forum', *Signs: Journal of Women in Culture and Society*, **11** (2), 304–33; Micaela Di Leonardo (1987), 'The Female World of Cards and Holidays: Women, Families and the Work of Kinship', *Signs: Journal of Women in Culture and Society*, **12** (3), 440–53; Janet Shibley Hyde (1990), 'Meta-Analysis and the Psychology of Gender Differences', *Signs: Journal of Women in Culture and Soceity*, **16** (1), 55–73.

Wayne State University Press for article: Carol Gilligan and Jane Attanucci (1988), 'Two Moral Orientations: Gender Differences and Similarities', *Merrill-Palmer Quarterly*, **34** (3), 223–37.

Every effort has been made to trace all the copyright holders but if any have been inadvertently overlooked the publishers will be pleased to make the necessary arrangement at the first opportunity.

In addition the publishers wish to thank the library of the London School of Economics and Political Science, Tom Chao and Rebecca Custodio, assistants to Professor Jacklin, and many of the authors for their assistance in obtaining these articles.

Introduction

MEANS (METHODS) AND ENDS (FINDINGS)

Methodological and conceptual issues may seem esoteric. The reader might wonder what all the fuss is about. Although some methodological issues are highly technical and beyond the scope of this volume, others are straightforward with obvious biases. We will discuss only the straightforward problems. Once we understand a problem, we are likely to label it a 'bias' instead of a 'method'. 'Method' is a neutral term and 'bias' is pejorative. Bias also refers to the personal views of a researcher. I prefer to use the neutral term 'method'. We need to be reminded that even when we think we are being 'objective' or neutral, our biases remain with us.

Findings depend on methods. The particular methodology used in a study determines not only how much confidence we can have in its findings, but in what the actual findings are. That methods and findings are necessarily interrelated can be more or less obvious but always true.

In this Introduction, I will first describe some of the issues of bias that relate to the views of researchers and of society. Issues like these occur in all research but are especially salient to the study of gender. I will then examine some of the conceptual problems involved in studying and understanding any group or individual 'difference'. Finally, I will introduce the articles in this volume. This will take us to some of the specific problems of bias and method and then to some of the specifics of various substantive findings.

There are strong opinions and political issues involved in studying gender. Much of the scholarship of gender studies has been in historical parallel with the social force of the feminist movement. This parallel is described in the Introduction to Volume I, *The Gendering of Psychology*. Because of the concurrent social forces, political questions have been consciously raised alongside the scholarship. Political issues are always a part of science, even though political positions are usually neither clear nor verbalized by most scientists. (For full discussions of this issue see Hare-Mustin and Marecek, 1988[1]; Jacklin, 1987, or Harding, 1986.)

Suggestions for eliminating bias in gender research have varied widely. At one extreme, some believe that gender differences should not be reported in research findings at all. For example, Baumeister (1988) claimed that reporting differences may be detrimental to one sex. At the other extreme, it has been argued that gender must always be reported (Eagly, 1987). Still others believe that gender should only be reported in certain circumstances and in certain forms. McHugh, Koeske and Frieze (1986) claimed that routine reporting of gender effects would provide an exaggerated view of gender differences.

---

[1] I will continue to use the convention of underlining the year of articles reprinted in this volume.

What do we mean when we say that individuals are different from each other? A large part of the problem is the conception of the term 'difference'. As reported in Volume I Part III on 'Brain Organization and Brain Injury', 'difference' seems to imply deficit. Philosophers of science have recognized this conceptual difficulty. For example, Harding (1987) has shown that thinking in dichotomous terms is almost always hierarchical. That is, we are unable to conceptualize a dichotomous variable (or two ends of a continuum) without believing that one of the pair of variables has a higher value than the other. Thus, if we think about any dichotomy – light/dark, heavy/light, up/down, black/white, female/male – we give one of the pair a higher value. We will return to these issues in the description of individual papers. In the contributions that follow in Volume II, we will discuss in some depth the methodological issues that determine the substantive findings about gender. And we will cover some of the substantive findings as well.

Methodological and Conceptual Issues

In Part I some of these concerns are clear and straightforward. We will begin with some of these simpler problems. For many years, most research in Psychology used only male subjects, a bias documented in Chapter 1. If investigators were interested only in males or in generalizing to all males, this would be a legitimate course of action and not a bias at all. However, psychologists most often explicitly generalize to all of humanity (Carlson, 1971) even if their basis for generalization is very limited.

But given that both females and males need to be studied if we are truly to understand all of humanity, should gender differences be reported? We referred earlier to some psychologists of good-will who hold the political position that gender differences should not be reported. In two short chapters (2 and 3), Eagly strongly argues against these positions. She believes, first, that bias will prevail unless gender findings are reported but, second, that analysis by gender should not be reported in any particular form. By omitting such analysis and reporting, Eagly argues, we are doing a disservice to science and to both females and males. Only when gender findings are routinely reported are we able to aggregate over such individual reports in meta-analyses. Without the ability to aggregate studies, bias will persist.

Meta-analysis is the topic of Chapter 4 by Janet Hyde. When a gender or other difference is reported in a study, it is difficult to be confident of the finding. A whole array of statistics have been developed to aggregate over individual studies. Many of the contributions in the present volumes use meta-analysis methods. Hyde reviews these techniques in a non-technical style, informing the reader of the use of statistical methods and meta-analysis throughout her paper.

Two general reviews are included. The first by Henley (Chapter 5) is largely an empirical review with a thoughtful discussion of methodological issues. In an overview of gender and psychology, she covers many current topics, some of which we will discuss in detail in this and other volumes (androgyny research, moral development research, brain organization, pornography and violence towards women). In each case Henley describes some of the conceptual and methodological problems with the particular area of study; she shows how in some areas, such as fear of success research, initial findings have been tempered by methodological considerations. The second general review by Jacklin (Chapter 6) more narrowly covers bias and methodological problems, surveying common errors in gender research. Some of these problems have been described here, but there are many others as well.

Two conceptual papers are included. The first by Code (Chapter 7) is philosophical, posing the question of whether the sex of the knower is epistemologically significant. She explores issues important to knowledge in any field, but her work has particular resonance for the study of gender. The second, by Hare-Mustin and Marecek (Chapter 8), details the problems of the concept of 'difference'. Applying some of the philosophical ideas of constructivism and deconstructivism to gender research, they shed further light on the difficulty of the concept of 'difference'.

Part I also examines how findings are shaped by methods. Chapters 9 and 10 provide two classic studies in gender, followed by a methodological critique (Widiger and Settle, Chapter 11). Broverman and her colleagues gave questionnaires with instructions to describe a healthy adult, a healthy man or a healthy woman. They reported that clinical psychologists, psychiatrists and psychiatric social workers all found the healthy man to have the same characteristics as a healthy adult. However, these practising mental health clinicians described a healthy woman as an unhealthy adult. In their critique, Widiger and Settle show that these results were produced not by sexism, but by the construction of the questionnaire. If a questionnaire were composed in the same way today, it would replicate the Broverman conclusions. If, on the other hand, it were constructed in a bias-free manner, the results would differ. It is instructive to see how the findings were completely dependent on design flaws in the methodology of research. Since these errors in method were subtle, the findings were widely cited and unchallenged for over a decade. The research and the critique of the research stand as an object lesson. Specific methodology and methodological problems shape the findings of all research. Our understanding of gender is limited by our methods of investigation. A clearer understanding of our limitations will help us understand what we do and do not know.

Cognitive Abilities

Part II considers one of the most researched subjects in psychology and in the study of gender. One of the reasons for interest in this topic is the importance of cognitive test scores in our lives. Scholarships, admissions to universities, jobs, career training, fellowships, etc. often hinge on the test scores one receives. A second reason for the interest in research on cognitive testing is that large databases exist. Large national samples from many countries can be studied and compared. Moreover, since most of the testing is done in schools where both girls and boys are present, analyses by gender are possible.

In an early summary of gender differences in cognitive abilities (Maccoby and Jacklin, 1974), we concluded that there were two or possibly three cognitive ability gender differences. Verbal abilities showed small but consistent differences, with women and girls scoring slightly higher than men and boys. Spatial visualization also showed consistent divergences, with men and boys scoring slightly higher than women and girls. The size of the effects in spatial visualization was larger than that in verbal abilities. Mathematical ability was the third possible cognitive gender difference, but this seemed to be a much more elusive phenomenon. Tested mathematical ability is usually related to spatial visualization and may not be an independent domain. As we shall see, current nomenclature is more likely to discuss mathematical 'performance' or 'achievement' and less likely to use the term 'ability' when describing mathematical test scores.

Do these general conclusions still hold true? Several recent review papers are included in this volume which conduct meta-analysis for gender on large numbers of primary studies of cognitive abilities. By evaluating these review articles, we can summarize literally hundreds of studies which analyzed gender in tests of cognitive abilities, thus providing an overview of current position regarding gender similarities and differences.

Two general reviews are included in Part II. Chapter 13 describes refinements of meta-analytic techniques on which many of the other studies rest (Rosenthal and Rubin, 1982). In addition to furthering the statistical sophistication in the field, the Rosenthal and Rubin paper presents some substantive findings. Their meta-analysis demonstrates that the gender differences in cognitive ability on various kinds of tests have diminished with time. The second review in Chapter 12 confirms that most 'cognitive gender differences are disappearing' (Feingold, 1988). We will now investigate whether the lessening of gender differences holds in the specific areas (verbal, spatial visual and mathematical) identified by Maccoby and Jacklin in 1974.

Similarities and differences with regard to verbal abilities are summarized by Hyde and Linn in Chapter 14 in which they review many types of verbal abilities. In addition they are able to test several hypotheses with the data of the 165 studies they include in their meta-analysis. For example they test whether there are greater gender differences with age, and whether the sex of the experimenter is implicated in finding gender differences. Overall, however, they found 'no evidence for a substantial gender difference in any aspect of [verbal] processing'.

Gender similarities and differences in spatial visualization are summarized by Linn and Petersen in Chapter 15. They find that 'spatial' ability is not a unitary concept. Gender differences are not found in most types of spatial ability, but are confined to tests of mental rotation in which the authors do find gender differences as soon as they are measurable. However, they do not find changes in magnitude of gender differences across the life-span.

Mathematical achievement or performance is discussed in several papers. As stated earlier, there seems to be more difficulty in testing mathematical ability than verbal or spatial visualization. Perhaps this stems from that fact that mathematics is not a single domain. Or perhaps the difficulty lies in the relationship of mathematical ability to the other cognitive abilities (verbal and spatial visual) by which the former is tested. In addition to presenting a meta-analytic review of mathematics, several articles investigate some of the intricacies of both the gender difference findings and of some research on what causes the findings.

The meta-analysis of mathematical performance is presented by Hyde, Fennema and Lamon in Chapter 16. Their work demonstrates again that findings are determined according to the populations tested. In studies of the general population they find very small differences, though overall females get higher scores than males. With very selective samples, they found that gender differences were larger and that males did better than females.

A slightly different slant on the question is presented by Kimball (1989) in Chapter 17. She reviews the consistent finding that girls receive better grades in mathematics courses than boys at all levels. She then tries to understand the relationship (or lack thereof) between grades in mathematics classes and scores on standardized mathematics tests. Finally, she argues the need to understand this discrepancy and for the use of mathematics class grades in addition to achievement test scores.

When papers by Benbow and Stanley appeared in 1980 and 1982, they stirred up a controversy unusual for scientific manuscripts. This arose largely because of statements in the media which they provoked. The population of the Benbow and Stanley studies was a highly selected group of precocious junior high school students, mostly 13- and 14-year olds (Chapter 18). A further selected group of this sample was tested four to five years later (Chapter 19). The authors found large gender differences in these samples, with precocious boys outscoring precocious girls.

At the time the Benbow and Stanley findings were publicized, Eccles (Parsons) and her colleagues were studying why elective advanced mathematics courses are chosen by high school girls and boys (Chapters 21 and 22). These studies found that parent and teacher expectations of children taking advanced courses was a good predictor of whether a child actually chose such courses. A child's tested ability in mathematics, on the other hand, was not as good a predictor of whether that child did or did not take advanced mathematics courses.

Eccles and Jacobs (1986) were able to take advantage of the media attention given to the Benbow and Stanley research to create a natural experiment (see Chapter 23). Some of the parents in the Eccles study had heard the news reports of the Benbow and Stanley findings and others had not. Eccles and Jacobs were able to demonstrate that the news reports did influence mothers' expectations for their daughters: that is, if mothers had heard the news reports, they expected less of their daughters than mothers who had not heard them. Although the results are depressing from the point of view of negative influences on half the student body, the study is important in documenting the effects of the news media on people's attitudes with real-life consequences.

Gender Socialization

The question of interest in Part III is how gender roles or expectations of gender-specific behaviour are learned by children. How do little girls acquire girl-like behaviour and little boys, boy-like behaviour? There have been, for the last several decades, three theories of gender (or sex-role) socialization: Freudian theory, social learning theory and cognitive developmental theory (see Maccoby and Jacklin, 1974 for a review). Very little research has been undertaken to test Freudian theory since the classic work of the 1950s did not find any evidence to support the Freudian claims (Sears, Maccoby and Levine, 1957). Social learning theory still has advocates and work in this area continues. Cognitive development, which evolved from and kept many of the elements of social learning, now seems to have coalesced into a new theory.

In the early 1980s, this new theory was developed and labelled gender schema theory (Liben and Signorella, 1980; Martin and Halverson, 1981; Bem, 1981). It grew out of both cognitive developmental theory and the schema work being done at the time in memory research (Archer and Lloyd, 1982). Gender schema theory has come to dominate much of the thinking and new research in the socialization of gender (see Chapters 33, 34 and 30). We will confine ourselves in this section to describing only two theories – contemporary social learning theory and gender schema theory.

In its simplest form, social learning theory is the view that gender roles are learned as a result of teaching by social agents. Girls and boys are believed to be rewarded and punished for different things, or 'differentially socialized'. Little girls are rewarded for 'girl-like' behaviour and punished for 'boy-like' behaviour, while the reverse pattern is administered to boys. Much research has been undertaken to confirm differential socialization (see Maccoby and Jacklin, 1974 for a review). The problem is that it is difficult to 'catch' parents treating their young girls and boys differently. (It is easier to find differential socialization with older children.) There could be many reasons for this problem. (1) Parents may actually treat their young girls and boys similarly. (2) Researchers may not have investigated the right kinds of situations. (3) Parents may be unwilling to engage in differential socialization when researchers are studying them.

A recent meta-analysis of studies looking for differential socialization by parents appears in Chapter 24. In this study, Lytton and Romney (1991) summarize the data from 172 individual studies (these authors originally considered 1,250 studies!). The only area in which they could document parents treating girls and boys differently (in the 158 studies in North America) was in the encouragement of sex-typed activities.

Although most social learning theorists would argue that differential reinforcement and punishment do occur, the theory does not rest on differential socialization. Social learning theorists would also argue that there are other ways in which children learn in addition to direct rewards and punishments. For example, imitation of same-sex models is a form of behaviour that children engage in which teaches and reinforces the cultural sex-specific behaviours they are expected to follow.

Several research articles are included which illustrate the importance of imitation. Bellinger & Gleason (1982) did not discover parents treating their children differently, but did find children imitating same-sex parents. Greif (1980) observed parents acting differently, but also identified the importance of power differences in parents' behaviour. Bussey and Bandura (1984) and Perry and Bussey (1979) found imitation of power figures and same-sex modelling in situations where children have multiple models. All in all, as Perry and Bussey claim, research shows that 'imitation is alive and well' and, at least in part, accounts for gender socialization. (See Chapters 25, 26, 27 and 28.)

Social learning theory is summarized in an interesting paper by Fagot (1985). Describing data that has forced changes in social learning theory over the past 15 years, she demonstrates the need to conjoin a cognitive developmental theory with social learning theory. She also points out unresolved problems inherent in all of our current explanations of gender-specific behaviour.

The classic papers introducing gender schema are included in this section. Liben and Signorella (1980), Bem (1981), Martin and Halverson (1981) and Martin and Halverson (1983) – all in close time proximity – introduced a new way of understanding how children learn gender-specific behaviours. The basic idea of a schema comes from information processing and memory work. As information is processed, generalizations of that information are formed as schema. Children and adults build up schema of many kinds. Of interest here is all of the information (attitudes, feeling states, modes of behaviour) a child receives from her or his culture about gender. From this information, generalizations or schema are formed. The articles presented give many examples of studies in which a child's memory, information processing and behaviour can be understood by the notion of a gender-schema. One paper by Bem (1983) goes further, suggesting ways in which a child can be raised with limited gender-schema even in cultures such as ours where gender-schema are pervasive.

A thoughtful and thought-provoking paper concludes the discussion of gender socialization. Eisenberg, Roth, Bryniarski and Murray (1984) show that parents too have many expectations and schema not only for gender but for other attributes of their children such as height. Tall and short children are treated differently, these treatments by height interacting with those by gender. From other work (Stephan and Langlois, 1984), we know that the attractiveness of children affects how they are treated. Each child is a complex pattern of physical, mental and emotional attributes. In other words gender, complex as it is, is only part of an even more complicated milieu in which a child is raised.

Moral Development

Part IV describes the gender issues in Moral Development. The research area of moral development has been largely based on the work of Kohlberg (for instance Kohlberg and Kramer, 1969; Kohlberg, 1976). Kohlberg postulated stages of moral development that are parallel to the intellectual developmental stages of Piaget. In formulating these stages, Kohlberg based his research on the concept of justice and validated his measures on boys and men. Gender differences have been found in Kohlberg's moral stages, with girls scoring lower on the justice framework questions than boys (see Kohlberg, 1984).

Carol Gilligan and her associates (Chapters 36 and 37) have criticized Kohlberg's abstract justice framework as a male concept. They have postulated a 'different voice' of female moral development based on a morality of caring for others. Besides the classic Gilligan (1977) and Gilligan and Attanucci (1988) articles reprinted here, related work by other investigators is also included. Di Leonardo (1987) shows how caring is instantiated in the real world by women in ways thus far overlooked by scholars.

There are both empirical and conceptual problems involved in this emerging field of gendered moral development. The empirical questions revolve around whether there really are differences between females and males on justice-framework or caring-framework questions. Several papers address such empirical questions (Thoma, 1986; Ford and Lowery, 1986; Boldizar, Wilson and Deemer, 1989).

As mentioned earlier, conceptual questions include how the concept of 'difference' is understood in scholarship and in the political world we live in. These questions are partly addressed in the articles listed above. But they are more directly confronted by several authors from different disciplines in the edited series of papers by Kerber, Greeno, Maccoby, Luria, Stack and Gilligan (1986) in Chapter 42. Gilligan's response to these critiques, which concludes that chapter, shows how much the issues in moral development, in gender research and in scholarship, are conceptual rather than empirical.

References

Archer, J. and Lloyd, B. (1982), *Sex and Gender*, London: Cambridge University Press.
Baumeister, R.F. (1988), 'Should we stop studying sex differences altogether?', *American Psychologist*, **43**, 756–7.
Carlson, R. (1971), 'Where is the person in personality research?', *Psychological Bulletin*, **75**, 203–19.
Harding, S. (1986), *The Science Question in Feminism*, Ithaca, NY: Cornell University Press.

Harding, S. (1987), 'Introduction: Is there a feminist method?' in S. Harding (ed.), *Feminism and Methodology*, Bloomington, IN: Indiana University Press.

Jacklin, C.N. (1987), 'Feminist research and psychology', in C. Farnham (ed.), *From Periphery to Paradigm: The Impact of Feminist Research in the Academy*, Bloomington, IN: Indiana University Press, pp. 95–107.

Kohlberg, L. and Kramer, R. (1969), 'Continuities and discontinuities in childhood and adult moral development', *Human Development*, **12**, 93–120.

Kohlberg, L. (1976), 'Moral stages and moralization: The cognitive-developmental approach', in T. Lickona (ed.), *Moral Development and Behavior: Theory, Research, and Social Issues*, New York: Holt, Rinehart & Winston.

Kohlberg, L. (1984), *The Psychology of Moral Development*, Vol. 2, San Francisco: Harper & Row.

Maccoby, E.E. and Jacklin, C.N. (1974), *The Psychology of Sex Differences*, Stanford, CA: Stanford University Press.

McHugh, M.D. Koeske, R.D. and Frieze, I.H. (1986), 'Issues to consider in conducting non-sexist psychological·research: A guide for researchers', *American Psychologist*, **41**, 879–90.

Sears, R.R. Maccoby, E.E. and Levine, H. (1957), *Patterns of Child Rearing*, Evanston, IL: Row, Peterson.

Stephan, C.W. and Langlois, J.H. (1984), 'Baby beautiful: Adult attributions of infant competence as a function of infant attractiveness', *Child Development*, **55**, 576–85.

Part I
Methodological and Conceptual Issues

[1]

Journal of Abnormal and Social Psychology
1960, Vol. 61, No. 3, 482-483

CRITIQUE AND NOTES

MALE AND FEMALE SUBJECTS IN PERSONALITY RESEARCH

EARL R. CARLSON   AND   RAE CARLSON

Michigan State University   East Lansing, Michigan

THERE is a sizable accumulation of evidence today that males and females react differently to many social situations and differ in many personality characteristics. Not only are there mean differences on a number of psychological measures, but often a relationship appears for one sex group but not for the other. Potential sex differences are omnipresent, but are largely ignored in even the best of current research on personality and social problems.

The present report is directed to three problems we see in current research: the imbalance in sampling in research, the paucity of tests for sex differences, and the inadequacy of reporting of the sex composition of research samples. An individual investigator, of course, must select his sample to meet specific needs of the problem. Typically, a study is criticized only if the investigator states an obvious overgeneralization. Beyond this, however, it is important at times to view the research literature as a whole to note possible implied overgeneralizations as a function of consistent biases entering into the selection of samples. From such views we can often redirect our efforts, and explicitly check for the limits of generalizability of early findings.

The 298 empirical studies reported in the 14 consecutive issues of the *Journal of Abnormal and Social Psychology*, Vol. 56 (1958), Number 1 through Vol. 60 (1960), Number 2, were selected as a sample of current research on personality and social phenomena. The few studies based upon single cases, nonhuman subjects, or reanalyses of previous research data were not included in this sample. Tabulations were made of the sex composition of the samples of subjects studied, the completeness of reporting of sex composition, and the reports of tests for, and findings of, sex differences.

The results show an overwhelming use of males as compared with female subjects. Of a total of 298 studies reported, 113 (38%) used male subjects exclusively, and 15 studies (5%) used only female subjects. A total of 108 studies reported using both male and female subjects, and for 65 studies the sex of subjects was unknown. The studies using both male and female subjects were fairly well balanced; in 36 studies (33%) an equal number of males and females were used, and in

20 studies (19%) the proportions of males and females were not reported.

Obviously, sex differences could be tested in only those 108 studies using subjects of both sexes. In only 32 studies (30%) were tests of sex differences reported. But in 22 of these cases (69%) sex differences were found at a level of statistical significance.

Several implications follow from these findings. First, males are selected far more often than females as research subjects. In studies of many psychological processes this bias may lead to no problems, but on a number of personality and social measurements sex differences do occur. As readers of research reports we can say to ourselves that of course we realize that only males were used, and that generalizations to females must depend upon further research. It is not only difficult to retain such contingencies in our recollection of studies we have read, but, we venture to guess, readers are largely unaware of sex composition in reported studies—even when this information *is* reported.

How often are sex differences actually tested? If it is correct that all *tests* for differences are reported, then with 69% of these showing significant differences it would follow, with little question, that differences do in fact exist in numerous cases, but were overlooked by the researcher. If many tests were made but never reported, then the reported differences could be expected by chance alone. Either of these alternatives would seem more plausible than the possibility that unreported tests precisely parallel the sex differences reported.

Even for a reader who is cautious in generalizing results, interpretation is ambiguous when the sex composition of the sample is incompletely reported. In 20 of 108 studies reporting both male and female subjects the proportions are unknown. In 62 studies (21% of all studies) a reader is totally unaware of the sex of the subjects, although many of these studies presumably included both men and women. In several studies the N can be discerned only from a thorough reading of the tables. We suspect that all readers will assume that Yale undergraduates and naval recruits are male, as we have done in the tabulations for this paper. There may be other similar situations where the authors assume, perhaps too optimistically, that readers can infer the sex of subjects from other information given.

Mean sex differences may or may not affect tests of psychological relationships between variables. In cases where test ceilings restrict the range of scores for one group, the variance for this group may be reduced to the point where a relationship cannot be tested. In a substantial number of studies a relationship holds for one sex but not for the other. A more serious problem arises in studies using extreme groups, where mean differences between sexes may lead to an imbalance of sex in the groups selected for intensive analysis. Some studies separate sex distributions and select high and low groups separately from each (e.g., Goldstein, 1959). Other studies do not (e.g., Taylor, 1958) and the resulting findings may stem from other correlates of sex than the variable under study.

Obviously many characteristics of an individual may interact with psychological relationships under study. A researcher cannot hope to do more than control or test for the effects of more than the most significant of these factors. We suggest that for two reasons, at least, sex should be included routinely as an explicit variable in studies where such a comparison is possible. First, sex differences do run rampant through our literature, and no one can deny that they are often important. Secondly, sex is an easy factor to measure, and sex differences are easily tested and reported. There seems little excuse not to include them as a standard procedure.

REFERENCES

GOLDSTEIN, M. J. The relationship between coping and avoiding behavior and response to fear-arousing propaganda. *J. abnorm. soc. Psychol.*, 1959, **58**, 247–252.

TAYLOR, J. The effects of anxiety level and psychological stress on verbal learning. *J. abnorm. soc. Psychol.*, 1958, **57**, 55–60.

(Received May 2, 1960)

[2]

Reporting Sex Differences

Alice H. Eagly
Purdue University

The advocacy of rules to limit the reporting of sex differences in the research literature raises issues that demand attention. In a recent article, McHugh, Koeske, and Frieze (August 1986) argued that "sex-related differences that have not been replicated or have not been predicted by or grounded in a theoretical model may not be appropriate content for published research" (p. 883). They further maintained that authors should report the percentage of variance explained by sex to allow readers to discern whether a finding is "a meaningful one." I take issue with these views. Because McHugh et al. expressed the desire that their article foster debate on how to encourage nonsexist research practices in psychology, I discuss their recommendations and offer an alternative. In brief, this alternative is that investigators (a) routinely report sex comparisons, regardless of whether these findings are replicated, hypothesized, or theoretically relevant and (b) report these findings precisely, in the same metrics that they apply to their reports of other findings.

If investigators screened their reports of sex comparisons in order to exclude findings that were not replicated or theoretically meaningful, the published research literature would represent women's and men's behavior less accurately than it does at present because of increased selectivity in reporting findings. Published findings would be artificially constrained to those that fit the current theoretical fashions, and findings not readily interpretable in terms of these theories or interpretable in terms of theories that are unfashionable or not yet developed by psychologists would tend to lie buried in file drawers. Although a certain amount of such selectivity is probably inevitable in published research, it should not be encouraged.

If findings uncongenial or irrelevant to current theories were suppressed, investigators could not effectively address the question of replicability because there would be no means for comparing these findings across studies and research programs. In addition, the artificial absence of theoretically uncongenial findings would lead to retardation in the growth of new theories because new theories are frequently stimulated by puzzling and serendipitous findings.

Restricting published reports to predicted or theoretically relevant findings would also tend to eliminate reports of null findings. Most theories of gender predict sex differences, at least under certain conditions. In fact, there is little gender-relevant theory about some behaviors, because neither psychologists nor laypersons believe that such behaviors are sex-typed and therefore predictable in terms of any theories that take sex and gender into account. It is probably just such theory-irrelevant sex comparisons that are most likely to yield null findings.

Null findings, if obtained consistently across studies, would help establish that women and men are similar in many respects—a point argued by many feminist psychologists. Such conclusions can only be firmly established if theory-irrelevant findings are regularly reported and then aggregated across studies. In a recent meta-analytic survey of sex differences, Hall (1984, Table 11.3) analyzed the limited numbers of sex comparisons reported for a wide range of personal dispositions and behaviors. For some of these dispositions and behaviors, sex comparisons are irrelevant to current theories. Indeed, Hall found little evidence of sex differences in some of these domains. Only when larger numbers of such reports become available can reviewers further this work and confidently offer conclusions about the absence of many types of differences between the sexes.

McHugh et al.'s (1986) recommendation that authors include the percentage of variance explained by sex with their reports of sex comparisons has merit only in the context of a further recommendation that authors report *all* their findings in this manner. It is the comparison of sex-difference findings with the effects of other variables within the same study that is most informative—not the absolute amount of variability explained by sex. Variability accounted for is not very informative in and of itself because it is a product, not merely of the strength of the underlying relations, but also of many features of research methods. For example, one such feature is the extent to which extraneous variables are controlled through controlled settings and homogeneous samples of subjects. Because such aspects of research design have an impact on the strength of all findings for a study, the magnitude of a sex difference is best evaluated in relation to the magnitude of other findings obtained with the same methods.

Also important in influencing the magnitude of relations between independent and dependent variables is the extent to which the criteria that serve as dependent variables aggregate subjects' responses. This point has been demonstrated in research on personality traits and attitudes as predictors of behaviors (e.g., Epstein, 1979; Fishbein & Ajzen, 1974). Thus, a disposition of persons, such as a trait or general attitude, may affect an overall tendency to engage in relevant behaviors to a substantial degree, without having more than a minor impact on each of the individual behaviors that compose the overall tendency. By this logic, a relation between sex and a behavior assessed on a single occasion may appear to be tiny in terms of variance explained but may be nontrivial in terms of its cumulative impact on a set of behaviors examined over many occasions. Consequently, the percentage of variance explained by sex (which is typically less than 5% but sometimes as high as about 25%; see Hall, 1984) does not provide evidence adequate to support claims about the meaningfulness of sex differences in natural settings. Any such conclusions can follow only from a careful and detailed analysis that compares the magnitudes of sex-difference findings and other findings in the same research literature and takes important features of research methods into account.

Finally, it is debatable whether percent-variance is the most appropriate metric for helping the consumers of psychological research to understand the meaningfulness of sex differences and other findings. Statisticians concerned with interpreting and aggregating research findings (e.g., Cohen, 1977; Hedges & Olkin, 1985) have more often advocated other metrics, such as the effect size d, which for sex comparisons is defined as the difference between women and men, standardized in terms of the average of the two within-sex standard deviations. The effect size has a number of advantages, including the fact that it takes the direction of the difference into account.

If effective communication with the consumers of research reports is a primary goal, Rosenthal and Rubin's (1982) "binomial effect size display" may well be the metric of choice for interpreting findings. Rosenthal and Rubin argued that the binomial effect-size display provides an index of the practical importance of findings in terms that are easily understood by both psychologists and laypersons. To apply this technique to sex differences, an investigator determines the percentage of each sex above (and the percentage below) the average response in the combined group of women and men (see Rosenthal & Rubin, 1982, Table 2). Thus, in terms of this metric, an effect of sex accounting for 4% of the variance can be interpreted as meaning that above-average amounts of the behavior in question were enacted by approximately 40% of one sex and 60%

of the other sex. For a substantial sex difference, such as the difference in social smiling meta-analyzed by Hall (1984), which accounts for about 9% of the variability (aggregated across 15 studies of adults), the binomial effect-size display provides the interpretation that above-average amounts of smiling occurred for 65% of women and 35% of men. In agreement with Rosenthal and Rubin, I believe that this metric more readily conveys the practical meaning of sex comparisons than does the percent-variance metric advocated by McHugh et al. (1986).

If investigators ignore all advice to interpret their findings by means of such metrics, the possibility of having this information is certainly not lost to readers of research reports. Such readers can readily translate any statistically precise finding (i.e., reported in terms such as t or F statistics or means and standard deviations) to any of these alternative metrics (see Glass, McGaw, & Smith, 1981; Rosenthal & Rubin, 1982). Vague reports (e.g., "there were no significant sex differences") cannot be so translated and cannot be aggregated across studies in an informative way. Authors should strictly avoid such vague reports.

In summary, the complete and precise reporting of all sex comparisons should foster accurate scientific understanding of the importance—or unimportance—of sex and gender. Of course, this practice would not guarantee unbiased outcomes. Sexism and other kinds of bias commonly surface when reported findings are aggregated inappropriately across studies and interpreted inaccurately.

REFERENCES

Cohen, J. (1977). *Statistical power analysis for the behavioral sciences* (rev. ed.). New York: Academic Press.

Epstein, S. (1979). The stability of behavior: I. On predicting most of the people much of the time. *Journal of Personality and Social Psychology, 37,* 1097–1126.

Fishbein, M., & Ajzen, I. (1974). Attitudes toward objects as predictors of single and multiple behavioral criteria. *Psychological Review, 81,* 59–74.

Glass, G. V., McGaw, B., & Smith, M. L. (1981). *Meta-analysis in social research.* Beverly Hills, CA: Sage.

Hall, J. A. (1984). *Nonverbal sex differences: Communication accuracy and expressive style.* Baltimore, MD: Johns Hopkins University Press.

Hedges, L. V., & Olkin, I. (1985). *Statistical methods for meta-analysis.* Orlando, FL: Academic Press.

McHugh, M. D., Koeske, R. D., & Frieze, I. H. (1986). Issues to consider in conducting nonsexist psychological research: A guide for researchers. *American Psychologist, 41,* 879–890.

Rosenthal, R., & Rubin, D. B. (1982). A simple, general purpose display of the magnitude of experimental effect. *Journal of Educational Psychology, 74,* 166–169.

[3]

The Politically Liberating Consequences of Examining Sex Differences

The silence on sex differences that most psychologists maintained in their scientific writings prior to the modern women's movement surely did not counter stereotypes or promote equality between the sexes. In fact, when women were ignored in research, psychologists had no way to evaluate claims that the sexes differed and consequently could not support or reject such claims on the basis of empirical evidence. Opening up these issues to scientific inquiry in the 1970s, many feminist researchers embarked on the study of sex differences in order to show that women and men are substantially similar. Indeed, research on sex differences in cognitive abilities has shown that these differences have decreased considerably in magnitude during recent decades and that a number of these differences are now relatively small (e.g., Feingold, 1988; Hyde & Linn, 1988). The closing off of reports of sex comparisons would stop this feminist effort in its tracks. If the current sex difference in mathematical performance should recede further, for example, this important change would go unnoticed, thus perpetuating outdated beliefs about the sexes.

Somewhat to the surprise of researchers who set out to disprove sex differences in the 1970s, research has established that the social behavior of women and men *does* differ in a number of respects, primarily along gender-stereotypic lines (see Aries, 1987; Eagly, 1987b; Eagly & Wood, in press; Hall, 1984). I did not make this important point in my earlier statement (1987a), which was focused solely on countering McHugh, Koeske, and Frieze's (August 1986) arguments in favor of limiting reports of sex comparisons. In view of Baumeister's incorrect assumption that "the study of sex differences has successfully achieved its goals" (p. 1093), presumably by showing that sex differences are null or at least very small, the state of the evidence needs to be clarified. Thus, the *presence* rather than the *absence* of sex differences has been established in research data on nonverbal behavior, numerous aspects of communicative and group behavior, aggression, helping behavior, susceptibility to social influence, and other social behaviors.

Although some psychologists have maintained that such sex differences are "small" in magnitude and therefore "unimportant," comparisons of meta-analytic aggregations of sex-difference findings with aggregations of findings on other hypotheses suggest that the magnitude of these findings is fairly typical of social psychological research more generally (see

Eagly, 1987b). Thus, in terms of the strength of its impact on social behavior, sex may be a representatively strong predictive variable for gender-stereotypic behaviors. These sex differences are probably not small in comparison with most other research findings in psychology. If psychologists such as Baumeister wish to dismiss sex difference findings as trivially small, in fairness they should apply this magnitude-of-effect standard throughout psychology and thereby dismiss many (perhaps even the majority) of other research findings. Because many psychologists who write about gender have misdiagnosed the magnitude issue, it is a time for intensification of our efforts to accurately describe sex differences—not a time to rest on our laurels. The generalizations about sex differences in many of our current textbooks are seriously misleading and should be reevaluated in the light of contemporary scholarship.

Baumeister's argument that reporting such sex differences invites discrimination against women deserves careful scrutiny. His view seems to imply that sex comparisons display women's deficiencies and thus provide a ground for unfavorable treatment. In point of fact, women, as a group, manifest many behaviors that most people evaluate very favorably. For example, women engage more than men do in behaviors that demonstrate interest in other people and provide supportive involvement in their concerns (see Eagly, 1987b). In our current historical context, these communal tendencies seem to result in quite a favorable evaluation of women as a group. Recent research on gender stereotypes has shown that, at least for college student respondents, the stereotype of women is more favorable than that of men (Eagly & Mladinic, 1989). People particularly approve of the greater warmth, friendliness, and interpersonal involvement that they ascribe to women and are less approving of many behaviors, such as aggression, that they ascribe to men. These attitudes of current-day college students may reflect some cultural change—and may even explain the responsive chord hit by President Bush's call for a "kinder, gentler nation."

Other sex-difference findings have liberating consequences for women, not because they portray women especially favorably, but because they display the behavioral repertoire of male dominance. Many of the differences in the social behavior of the sexes describe in exquisite detail the ways in which men maintain their power over women. To understand the microprocess of male dominance, women need to recognize these sex differ-

On the Advantages of Reporting Sex Comparisons

Alice H. Eagly
Purdue University

In an environment in which scholarship on gender is all too often dismissed as politicized mythology,[1] research psychologists should be very cautious in recommending that research findings in this area be censored for political reasons. Yet Baumeister (December 1988) advocated that psychologists cease reporting comparisons between the sexes. This proposal was formulated in response to McHugh, Koeske, and Frieze's (August 1986) suggestion that researchers report comparisons between the sexes only under limited circumstances, and Eagly's (July 1987a) counterproposal in favor of open reporting of sex comparisons in all research. Baumeister argued that the inclusion of sex-difference findings in research reports is undesirable from both political and scientific standpoints. I take issue with Baumeister's position and argue that, on the contrary, far more advantages than disadvantages stem from the scientific scrutiny of sex differences.

---

[1] See, for example, a lead editorial in the *Wall Street Journal* ("Fundamental Fairness," 1989), in which courses in women's studies were described as "intolerantly argued propaganda" (p. A10).

April 1990 • American Psychologist

ences. In teaching the psychology of women, I have found that even the most factual description of those sex differences that have implications for dominance always receives extremely close attention. For college students, the political implications of these studies do not pass unnoticed. Having the facts enables many female students to experiment with enlarging their own behavioral repertoires to encompass the behaviors that have traditionally allowed men to dominate and to emerge as leaders in groups. If researchers now fall silent on the subject of sex differences in social behavior, this avenue for empowering women will be closed off.

To the extent that some sex differences are interpreted as deficiencies for either sex, an enlightened society should adopt the view that educational opportunities should be made available to improve the status of the disadvantaged group. I disagree with Baumeister's view that it is patronizing for social policy to allow for compensatory education. Programs that feminists have generated provide a useful model for gender-sensitive social policy that takes sex differences into account along with other individual differences. For example, the assertiveness training popular in feminist circles in the 1970s was directed almost exclusively to women and represented an important effort to teach interested women how to counter some of the cultural lessons they had learned. In addition, some feminist educators have promoted math anxiety workshops and have redesigned math and science courses. These innovative educational efforts communicate mathematical and scientific skills with methods that are especially effective for women and girls (Kahle, 1985). Without the political awareness generated by the women's movement, it is doubtful that women would have recognized the legitimacy of special programs that empower women through differential treatment. Scientific knowledge of sex differences and of the consequences of these differences could allow psychologists to evaluate various calls for compensatory education and to design and foster such education, under appropriate circumstances.

Baumeister also feared that sex-difference findings may be blown out of proportion by the media. Indeed, problems in communicating scientific information to the public are not confined to gender research. These problems are acute for all research problems that attract public interest. Rather than abandon socially relevant research and cease to publish sensitive findings, researchers should accept the challenge of communicating to the

public with clarity yet with concern for the implications that their findings have for the people who are described. Researchers' explicit censorship of their findings on the basis of their personal political philosophy damages the trust that the public has placed in the scientific community. Although it certainly cannot be claimed that science is value free, the public assumes that scientists strive to eliminate the effects of political bias and other biases from their research, and indeed, most scientists, on an individual and collective basis, do try to protect their research from recognized biases.

In summary, open and full reporting of sex comparisons should, on balance, be a political asset for women. This scientific openness should (a) allow some stereotypes to be weakened, (b) result in a portrayal of women that is favorable, on the whole, (c) empower women by revealing the microprocess of male dominance, (d) provide a basis for gender-sensitive training and education, and (e) preserve the trust that the public has placed in the scientific community.

The Scientifically Liberating Consequences of Studying Sex Differences

Baumeister (1988) argued that the study of sex differences is scientifically questionable because the causes of such differences are complex and ambiguous. Reports of sex differences invite explanation, and psychologists' explanations often invoke other, presumably more basic variables. It would be strange indeed if researchers were to accept Baumeister's idea that a scientifically worthy question must yield simple answers. Many problems that psychologists investigate are exceedingly complex (e.g., the causes of mental illness), and few researchers are daunted by the necessity of turning to other variables to develop a causal model. Complex causal models are becoming the rule rather than the exception in psychology. In studying sex differences, many psychologists quickly come to appreciate the interplay of biological, psychological, and social variables that determine human behavior.

The variables that Baumeister suggested are more worthy of scrutiny than sex or gender—introversion and intimacy motivation—are hardly basic variables in the eyes of many psychologists. What can be deemed a true causal variable depends on the scientist's theoretical perspective. For psychologists such as myself who regard societal gender roles as a fundamental cause of sex differences, the classification of people into male and female is extremely important because gender roles

apply to men and women as social categories. Normative expectations are the causal variables of primary interest, but many norms about appropriate behavior are applied to people according to their sex in many social settings. By a similar logic, a biologically inclined psychologist might point instead to the importance of hormonal levels that differ by sex. To compare the behavior of the sexes makes eminent theoretical sense from such perspectives. It would be helpful to have *all* the sex comparisons available from our research data so that theories of sex and gender could be evaluated by a maximally complete and unbiased data base.

Sex is a variable that is easily and reliably measured and is routinely included in most data sets in psychology. Taking the next steps—comparing the sexes in one's data and including the outcome of this comparison in one's research report—is a responsible contribution to psychology. By reporting sex comparisons, research psychologists contribute to a significant ongoing scientific debate about the correct description and explanation of the results of these comparisons. Because of the large body of theory about sex and gender, the reporting of sex differences is much more crucial than the reporting of other group differences for which the body of theory and existing research is relatively small. In fact, psychologists' debate about the meaning of sex differences may be one of the most important scientific debates of our time.

REFERENCES

Aries, E. (1987). Gender and communication. In P. Shaver & C. Hendrick (Eds.), *Sex and gender: Vol. 7. Review of personality and social psychology* (pp. 149–176). Newbury Park, CA: Sage.

Baumeister, R. F. (1988). Should we stop studying sex differences altogether? *American Psychologist, 43,* 1092–1095.

Eagly, A. H. (1987a). Reporting sex differences. *American Psychologist, 42,* 756–757.

Eagly, A. H. (1987b). *Sex differences in social behavior: A social-role interpretation.* Hillsdale, NJ: Erlbaum.

Eagly, A. H., & Mladinic, A. (1989). Gender stereotypes and attitudes toward women and men. *Personality and Social Psychology Bulletin, 15,* 543–558.

Eagly, A. H., & Wood, W. (in press). Explaining sex differences in social behavior: A meta-analytic perspective. *Personality and Social Psychology Bulletin.*

Feingold, A. (1988). Cognitive gender differences are disappearing. *American Psychologist, 43,* 95–103.

Fundamental fairness. (1989, January 5). *Wall Street Journal,* p. A10.

Hall, J. A. (1984). *Nonverbal sex differences: Communication accuracy and expressive style.* Baltimore, MD: Johns Hopkins University Press.

Hyde, J. S., & Linn, M. C. (1988). Gender differences in verbal ability: A meta-analysis. *Psychological Bulletin, 104,* 53–69.

Kahle, J. B. (Ed.). (1985). *Women in science: Report from the field.* Philadelphia: Falmer Press.

McHugh, M. D., Koeske, R. D., & Frieze, I. H. (1986). Issues to consider in conducting nonsexist psychological research: A guide for researchers. *American Psychologist, 41,* 879–890.

[4]

META-ANALYSIS AND THE PSYCHOLOGY OF GENDER DIFFERENCES

JANET SHIBLEY HYDE

Psychological research on gender differences has had a long, and sometimes dishonorable, history spanning more than a century.[1] The research ranges from early efforts to measure the cranial capacities of males and females to the current sophisticated meta-analyses of psychological gender differences. Here I will briefly review the history of research on gender differences, focusing particularly on the issue of gender differences in cognitive abilities, and then move to a discussion of recent meta-analyses of psychological gender differences.

Early research on gender differences in abilities

Stephanie Shields has provided an excellent analysis of the zeitgeist that influenced early research and writing on female psychol-

This research was supported by grants BNS 8508666, BNS 8696128, and MDR 8709533 from the National Science Foundation. I express my thanks for the insightful suggestions of an anonymous *Signs* reviewer.

[1] I use the term gender differences rather than sex differences throughout this essay because the data I discuss do not address the issue of whether such differences have a biological or cultural origin. I do not want to imply that the differences are biologically caused; "gender differences" allows me to focus on the existence and significance of differences regardless of origin.

[*Signs: Journal of Women in Culture and Society* 1990, vol. 16, no. 1]

ogy beginning around 1879, the date usually cited as the beginning of formal psychology.[2] Darwinism and functionalism dominated intellectual thought in the sciences. Evolutionary theory, because it highlighted the importance of variability, made it legitimate to study variations in behavior, including gender differences. Nonetheless, the outcome of such study was generally to provide further data supporting the notion of the evolutionary supremacy of the white male.

The topic of female intelligence was first investigated by phrenologists and neuroanatomists. The early belief was that male and female brains must be as different in their gross appearance as were male and female bodies in other selected areas. Franz Joseph Gall claimed that "if there had been presented to him in water, the fresh brains of two adult animals of any species, one male and the other female, he could have distinguished the two sexes."[3] The most popular argument was that females had smaller heads and smaller brains than males, that brain size was a direct indicator of intelligence, and that women must therefore be less intelligent than men.[4] Indeed, George Romanes considered brain size and its corollary, intelligence, to be among the secondary sex characteristics.[5] This argument overlooks the fact that there is a correlation between brain size and body size. The slightly larger size of male brains, on the average, is accounted for almost entirely by males' larger average body size.

Later theorizing was based on the notion of localization of function, that is, that different functions of the brain were localized in different regions. For a time it was thought that the frontal lobes of the brain were the site of the highest mental abilities; quickly, researchers claimed that males possessed larger frontal lobes.[6] Next, the parietal lobes were favored as the location of intelligence, and the parietal lobes of females were found wanting.[7]

In 1910, Helen Thompson Woolley provided the first review of psychological research on gender differences.[8] She quickly dis-

[2] Stephanie A. Shields, "Functionalism, Darwinism, and the Psychology of Women: A Study in Social Myth," *American Psychologist* 30, no. 7 (July 1975): 739–54.

[3] A. Walker, *Woman Physiologically Considered* (New York: J. & H. G. Langley, 1850), 317.

[4] A. Bain, *Mental Science* (New York: Appleton, 1875).

[5] George J. Romanes, "Mental Differences between Men and Women," *Nineteenth Century* 21, no. 123 (May 1887): 654–72.

[6] For example, P. J. Mobius, "The Physiological Mental Weakness of Woman," trans. A. McCorn, *Alienist and Neurologist* 22 (1901): 624–42.

[7] Henry Havelock Ellis, *Man and Woman: A Study of Secondary and Tertiary Sexual Characteristics*, 8th rev. ed. (London: Heinemann, 1934).

[8] Helen Thompson Woolley, "A Review of the Recent Literature on the Psychology of Sex," *Psychological Bulletin* 7, no. 18 (October 1910): 335–42.

Autumn 1990 / **SIGNS**

missed the arguments on brain size: "It is now a generally accepted belief that the smaller gross weight of the female brain has no significance other than that of the smaller average size of the female."[9] She found only a meager amount of research using psychological methods to assess gender differences. She reviewed studies that measured rate and endurance in tapping a telegraph key, handwriting (women's was judged colorless, conventional, neat, and small, whereas men's was bold, careless, experienced, and individual), and tests of association. In the last case, participants were required to write a series of associations to a given word. The investigator of tests of association interpreted his results as indicating that women showed abnormality of reaction, meager presentations, a less active flow of ideas, less variety in ideas, more concrete forms of response, a more subjective attitude, and more indecision. Woolley's methodological critique of the research was devastating.

None of these measures has survived to have importance in modern psychology. Woolley's own evaluation of the research on gender differences available at the time is telling. "There is perhaps no field aspiring to be scientific where flagrant personal bias, logic martyred in the cause of supporting a prejudice, unfounded assertions, and even sentimental rot and drivel have run riot to such an extent as here."[10]

The mental testing movement

Research on gender differences in abilities entered a new phase with the rise of the mental testing movement and the development of standardized ability tests. The first viable intelligence test was devised by the French psychologist Alfred Binet. Binet was originally commissioned by the French minister of public instruction to accomplish a practical task: to find a means of identifying in advance those children who would not be successful when taught in normal public school classrooms and who might therefore benefit from special education. Given the myriad criticisms of intelligence tests (IQ tests), it is interesting that their origins were benign and pragmatic.[11] Binet's original test, published in 1905, included many quick, practical tasks, such as counting coins, that

---

[9] Ibid., 335.

[10] Ibid., 340.

[11] See, e.g., Stephen Jay Gould, *The Mismeasure of Man* (New York: Norton, 1981).

were intended to measure basic reasoning processes.[12] Stanford psychologist Lewis Terman expanded the test and published the first American version in 1916, naming it the Stanford Binet.[13]

Remarkably, given the popular views of the time, both Binet and Terman believed that there were no gender differences in general intelligence and so attempted to construct their tests to produce equal average scores for boys and girls. Repeated large-scale testing using the Binet has yielded no gender difference in this measure of general intelligence.[14] Noting that girls scored as well as boys in IQ measures, Terman decried women's limited access to the professions as both unjust and a waste of talent.[15] There is an irony here, of course. Because of the way the tests were constructed, a finding of no gender differences does not "prove" that there are no gender differences in general intelligence; rather, it only provides evidence that the test constructors succeeded in their goal of producing a test that resulted in no gender differences, by balancing items that would give advantages to males and females.

The next chapter in the testing movement that is of relevance is L. L. Thurstone's development of the Primary Mental Abilities (PMA) test in the 1930s and 1940s.[16] Until this time intelligence tests, including the Binet, had been based on the notion of general intelligence and yielded a single score, the intelligence quotient, or IQ, for each individual. Thurstone, in contrast, believed that there were multiple intellectual abilities and that he could identify them using a statistical technique called factor analysis. The PMA assesses seven abilities: verbal comprehension, word fluency, number (numerical computation), space (spatial visualizing), memory, perceptual speed (speed and accuracy on clerical tasks), and reasoning. This conceptualization of intelligence as composed of multiple abilities laid the foundation for research on gender differences in verbal ability, mathematical ability, and spatial ability.

[12] Alfred Binet and Theophile Simon, *A Method of Measuring the Development of the Intelligence of Young Children* (Lincoln, Ill.: Courier, 1912).

[13] Lewis M. Terman, *The Measurement of Intelligence* (Boston: Houghton Mifflin, 1916).

[14] Janet Shibley Hyde, *Half the Human Experience: The Psychology of Women*, 3d ed. (Lexington, Mass.: D. C. Heath, 1985), 186.

[15] Terman, *The Measurement of Intelligence*, 72, and *The Intelligence of School Children* (Boston: Houghton Mifflin, 1919), 278, 288.

[16] L. L. Thurstone, *Primary Mental Abilities* (Chicago: University of Chicago Press, 1938); L. L. Thurstone and Thelma G. Thurstone, *Factorial Studies of Intelligence*, Psychometric Monographs, no. 2 (Chicago: University of Chicago Press, 1941).

Autumn 1990 / **SIGNS**

Reviews of research on gender differences

By the 1930s, sufficient data had begun to accumulate to do substantial reviews of research on gender differences in abilities. Some of the most authoritative and influential of these reviews were found in textbooks on differential psychology. Differential psychology as a specialty examines individual differences among humans, including differences in personality and intelligence, and group differences, including gender differences, race differences, social class differences, and age differences. Two works that present views typical of psychologists through the 1960s are Anne Anastasi's *Differential Psychology* (first published in 1937) and Leona Tyler's *The Psychology of Human Differences* (first published in 1947).[17] Anastasi concluded that females are superior in verbal and linguistic functions from infancy through adulthood; that males are superior in tests of spatial relations, although the difference is not found so early as the difference in verbal ability; and that males are superior on numerical tests, although the difference does not appear until well into elementary school and tends to be found on tests of numerical reasoning rather than computation, where girls are equal to or exceed boys in performance. Tyler's conclusions were quite similar: females are superior in verbal ability, although the difference is found on tests of verbal fluency, not vocabulary; males are superior in mathematical ability when the measure involves mathematical reasoning but not when it involves only mathematical computation; and males are superior on spatial ability tests. In her 1966 review, Eleanor Maccoby reached similar conclusions.[18]

By the publication of Eleanor Maccoby and Carol Nagy Jacklin's *The Psychology of Sex Differences,* literally thousands of studies had been published reporting data on gender differences in psychological characteristics, including not only abilities but also personality, social behavior, and memory.[19] One of the achievements of Maccoby and Jacklin's work was the systematic compilation of evidence so that a number of widely held beliefs about gender differences could be assessed for their empirical support.

[17] Anne Anastasi, *Differential Psychology: Individual and Group Differences in Behavior,* 3d ed. (New York: Macmillan, 1958); Leona E. Tyler, *The Psychology of Human Differences,* 3d ed. (New York: Appleton-Century-Crofts, 1965).

[18] Eleanor E. Maccoby, "Sex Differences in Intellectual Functioning," in *The Development of Sex Differences,* ed. E. E. Maccoby (Stanford, Calif.: Stanford University Press, 1966).

[19] Eleanor E. Maccoby and Carol Nagy Jacklin, *The Psychology of Sex Differences* (Stanford, Calif.: Stanford University Press, 1974).

Specifically, they concluded that the beliefs that girls are more social than boys, that girls are more suggestible than boys, that girls have lower self-esteem, that girls are better at rote learning and simple tasks whereas boys are better at higher-level cognitive processing, and that girls lack achievement motivation are unfounded. In contrast, they concluded that gender differences are well established in four domains: girls have greater verbal ability than boys, boys have greater visual-spatial ability, boys excel in mathematical ability, and boys are more aggressive. Thus, their conclusions, based on far more extensive evidence than were previous reviews, reaffirmed the belief in the holy trinity of gender differences in abilities: female superiority in verbal ability and male superiority in mathematical and spatial ability. Their conclusions have had a major impact on the field of psychology: they are taught to undergraduates in basic courses, and most introductory psychology and child development texts cite and discuss Maccoby and Jacklin's findings.[20]

Maccoby and Jacklin used a methodology that permitted systematic vote counting, that is, a listing of the studies according to the construct of interest (e.g., verbal ability, mathematical ability, aggressiveness). Consequently, it is possible to tally the percentage of studies that found a significant difference favoring females, the percentage that found no significant gender difference, and the percentage that found a significant difference favoring males. For example, in their analysis of mathematics performance, they located ten studies of subjects eleven years of age or younger; of those, seven found no significant gender difference and three found a significant difference favoring females. Among the remaining seventeen studies they located of older subjects, twelve found significant differences favoring males, five found no significant difference, and none found a difference favoring females (except for a few isolated findings favoring females on specific tests or in a specific age group). They concluded that the gender difference in mathematics performance emerges at twelve to thirteen years of age.[21]

In her 1976 critique of Maccoby and Jacklin's work, Jeanne Block pointed out, among other things, that Maccoby and Jacklin

---

[20] For examples, see Rita L. Atkinson, R. C. Atkinson, and E. R. Hilgard, *Introduction to Psychology*, 8th ed. (New York: Harcourt Brace Jovanovich, 1983); Henry Gleitman, *Psychology* (New York: Norton, 1981); E. Mavis Hetherington and Ross D. Parke, *Child Psychology: A Contemporary Viewpoint*, 3d ed. (New York: McGraw-Hill, 1986); and Paul H. Mussen, John J. Conger, Jerome Kagan, and Aletha C. Huston, *Child Development and Personality*, 6th ed. (New York: Harper & Row, 1984).

[21] Maccoby and Jacklin, 88–89.

Autumn 1990 / **SIGNS**

were inconsistent in the criteria they used to decide whether the percentage of studies indicating a particular difference was sufficiently large to conclude that there is a true gender difference. Criticisms of their method of vote counting have also been raised. Statisticians have pointed out that this method can lead to false conclusions, specifically, that there is no significant difference when there actually is one.[22]

Meta-analysis and the new research on gender differences in abilities

In the 1980s the development of a new statistical method called meta-analysis, which uses quantitative methods to combine evidence from different studies, has radically altered the analysis of gender differences in abilities.[23] Essentially a quantitative or statistical method for doing a literature review, a meta-analysis proceeds in several stages. First, the researchers collect as many studies as possible that report data on the question of interest. Computerized literature searches can be helpful in assuring that there is a good sampling of studies. In the area of psychological gender differences, researchers can often obtain a very large sample of studies. For example, I was able to locate 143 studies reporting data on gender differences in aggression for one meta-analysis and 165 studies of gender differences in verbal ability for another.[24]

Second, the researchers perform a statistical analysis of the statistics reported in each article. For each study, an effect size statistic, d, is computed. For analyses of gender differences, the formula is $d = (M_M - M_F)/s$, where M_M is the mean or average of

---

[22] A detailed coverage of the statistical argument behind this assertion is beyond the scope of this article. The rationale is given by John E. Hunter, Frank L. Schmidt, and Gregg B. Jackson, *Meta-Analysis: Cumulating Research Findings across Studies* (Beverly Hills, Calif.: Sage, 1982). A discussion of the problem of vote counting as applied to research on gender differences is provided by Janet Shibley Hyde, "Introduction: Meta-Analysis and the Psychology of Gender," in *The Psychology of Gender: Advances through Meta-Analysis*, ed. Janet S. Hyde and Marcia C. Linn (Baltimore: Johns Hopkins University Press, 1986), 1–13.

[23] Larry V. Hedges and Ingram Olkin, *Statistical Methods for Meta-Analysis* (New York: Academic Press, 1985), 13.

[24] Janet Shibley Hyde, "How Large Are Gender Differences in Aggression? A Developmental Meta-Analysis," *Developmental Psychology* 20, no. 4 (July 1984): 722–36; and Janet Shibley Hyde and Marcia C. Linn, "Gender Differences in Verbal Ability: A Meta-Analysis," *Psychological Bulletin* 104, no. 1 (July 1988): 53–69.

males' scores and M_F is the mean or average of females' scores; s is the within-groups standard deviation, which is a measure of the variability of scores, that is, the within-sex variability. Essentially, d indicates how far apart the means for males and females are in standard deviation units. Positive values of d mean that males scored higher than females and negative values mean that females scored higher.

From a feminist point of view, one of the virtues of the d statistic is that it takes into account not only gender differences (the difference between male and female means), but also female variability and male variability (s, the standard deviation). That is, it recognizes that each sex is not homogeneous. According to earlier methods of assessment when reviewers concluded, as Maccoby and Jacklin did, that there were indeed gender differences in verbal, mathematical, and spatial ability, readers often assumed that because the differences were well established they were large. The d statistic assesses exactly how large, or small, the difference is.

In the third stage of the meta-analysis, the researchers average the d values obtained from all studies, which allows them to draw conclusions based on the average of the results of all of the studies.[25] For example, based on 100 values of d obtained from 100 studies, the average magnitude of the gender difference in spatial ability is $d = .45$. Recent developments in meta-analysis make it possible to proceed one step further, to analyzing variations in values of d, that is, in the magnitude of the gender difference, according to various features of the studies.[26] This step is called homogeneity analysis because it analyzes the extent to which the values of d in the set are uniform or homogeneous. When there are large variations in the values of d across the studies in the set, the meta-analyst must account for the inconsistencies in the findings. By grouping the studies into subsets, the meta-analyst attempts to find a classification scheme that yields relatively homogeneous values of d within each subset of studies. For example, in an analysis of gender differences in verbal ability, one could compute a value of d for those studies that measured vocabulary, another value of d for those that measured reading comprehension, and yet a third value for those that measured higher-order reasoning on tests such as anal-

[25] For a highly readable account of these statistical methods, designed for the beginner, see Larry V. Hedges and Betsy Jane Becker, "Statistical Methods in the Meta-Analysis of Research on Gender Differences," in Hyde and Linn, eds.

[26] See, e.g., Hedges and Olkin.

ogies. Thus the investigators could determine whether the gender difference was large for some kinds of verbal ability and small or perhaps zero for other kinds.

The interpretation of the magnitude of d values remains a point of contention among researchers. Because values can be lower or higher than 1, there is no absolute standard against which to measure any particular value of d. Jacob Cohen has offered as a somewhat arbitrary guideline the suggestion that an absolute value of .20 is small, a value of .50 is medium, and a value of .80 is large.[27] Robert Rosenthal and Donald Rubin have introduced another scheme using the statistic r, which translates into $d = 2r$.[28] Their method of assessing the magnitude of effect sizes is to use the binomial effect size display (BESD), which displays the change in success rate (e.g., recovery from cancer due to a particular treatment, compared with an untreated control group) as a function of the effect size. Thus, for example, an $r = .30$ ($d = .60$) translates into an improvement in recovery from cancer from 35 percent to 65 percent of patients studied. In the study of gender differences, an effect size of $d = .40$ means that approximately 40 percent of one sex falls above the median for both sexes and 60 percent of the other sex falls above the same median.

Yet a third scheme for interpreting the magnitude of an effect size is to compare it with other effect sizes that have been obtained either for related studies in the same field or for quite different studies. Thus, for example, one might compare the value of d for gender differences in verbal ability with one for gender differences in spatial ability. Drawing a broader comparison, one might compare the magnitude of gender differences in mathematics performance with the magnitude of the effects of psychotherapy (comparison of adjustment levels following therapy with untreated controls), which has been reported to be $d = .68$.[29] Ultimately it will be valuable for feminist research to be able to compare the magnitude of gender difference effects with the magnitude of other effects on that same phenomenon. For example, in a study of

[27] Jacob Cohen, *Statistical Power Analysis for the Behavioral Sciences* (New York: Academic Press, 1969).

[28] Robert Rosenthal and Donald B. Rubin, "A Simple, General Purpose Display of the Magnitude of Experimental Effect," *Journal of Educational Psychology* 74, no. 2 (April 1982): 166–69. The formula $d = 2r$ is a good approximation so long as values of r are small or moderate. For larger values of r, the exact formula should be used, $d = 2r / (1 - r^2)$.

[29] Mary Lee Smith and Gene V Glass, "Meta-Analysis of Psychotherapy Outcome Studies," *American Psychologist* 32, no. 9 (September 1977): 752–60.

mathematics performance, the effect of gender difference could be compared to the effect of social class difference, or the effect of differences in attitudes toward mathematics.

Meta-analyses of gender differences in abilities

The first published meta-analysis of gender differences in abilities appeared in 1981.[30] For that research, I reanalyzed and computed values of d for the studies collected by Maccoby and Jacklin, with the result that on the average, $d = -.24$ for gender differences in verbal ability, .45 for spatial ability, and .43 for mathematical ability. These results indicate that gender differences in abilities are not as large as the prominence of such findings in reviews and textbooks would indicate. According to Cohen's scheme, the gender difference in verbal ability is small, and the gender differences in spatial and mathematical ability are at most moderate in size. Another statistical analysis reported in the 1981 article indicated that within-gender differences were far larger than between-gender differences.

Gender differences in abilities have sometimes been used as an explanation for lopsided gender ratios in some occupations. The above meta-analysis made it possible to determine whether such explanations are adequate. For example, fewer than 5 percent of engineers in the United States are women, and possessing a high level of spatial ability is generally considered important for success at engineering. Assuming that spatial ability at least at the 95th percentile is required to become an engineer, and that $d = .40$ for gender differences in spatial ability, about 7.35 percent of men and 3.22 percent of women would possess sufficiently high spatial ability to be engineers. That result would support a 2:1 ratio of males:females in the profession, or 67 percent men and 33 percent women.[31] Thus, if women constitute fewer than 5 percent of

[30] Janet Shibley Hyde, "How Large Are Cognitive Gender Differences? A Meta-Analysis Using ω^2 and d," *American Psychologist* 36, no. 8 (August 1981): 892–901. Maccoby and Jacklin had computed a few effect sizes for their 1974 book, but they did not do so systematically. They concluded that $d = .25$ for verbal ability, but they found the variations in values of d for gender differences in mathematical ability to be so great that they did not hazard a guess as to an average value.

[31] This analysis ignores the issue of whether spatial performance can be learned. Many studies indicate that training can be successful, which might in turn narrow the gap between males and females. See, e.g., Maryann Baenninger and Nora Newcombe, "The Role of Experience in Spatial Test Performance: A Meta-Analysis," *Sex Roles* 20, nos. 5/6 (March 1989): 327–44; M. F. Blade and W. S.

Autumn 1990 / **SIGNS**

engineers, they are seriously underrepresented in comparison with their spatial ability test performance, and other factors must be considered to account for the lopsided gender ratio.

Subsequent to my research, Marcia Linn and Anne Petersen performed a more sophisticated meta-analysis of gender differences in spatial ability, using homogeneity analyses.[32] Using studies published since 1974, they computed 172 values of d and concluded that there are actually three distinct types of spatial ability, each measured by different types of tests and each showing a different pattern of gender differences. The first type of spatial ability, which they term spatial perception (what I would call a sense of horizontality/verticality), is measured by tests such as the rod-and-frame test and the water-level task (see fig. 1). For these tests, $d = .44$, indicating a moderate advantage for males. The second type of spatial ability, which they term mental rotation, is a measure of participants' ability to rotate mentally a three-dimensional object pictured in two dimensions, to see whether it matches one of a number of other illustrations (see fig. 2). For these tests, $d = .73$. The third type of spatial ability, according to their analysis, is spatial visualization, or what I would term spatial disembedding. This type measures the participant's ability to extract visually a simpler figure from a more complex figure. Here $d = .13$. Thus, there is essentially no gender difference for spatial disembedding, a moderate difference for horizontality/verticality, and a rather large difference for mental rotation. Global statements about gender differences in spatial ability are therefore simplistic.

Linn and Petersen also analyzed the data for age trends in the magnitude of gender differences in spatial ability—an analysis motivated by Maccoby and Jacklin's previous arguments that gender differences in spatial ability do not emerge until adolescence and are therefore a result of biological changes—perhaps hormonal, perhaps brain lateralization—that occur at puberty. Their meta-analysis indicated that such assumptions are false; where gender differences were present, they were present throughout the life span. For example, for measures of horizontality/verticality, $d = .37$ for studies of persons under thirteen and $d = .37$ for studies of participants between the ages of thirteen and eighteen. Not all biological explanations of gender differences in spatial ability (e.g.,

Watson, "Increase in Spatial Visualization Test Scores during Engineering Study," *Psychological Monographs*, vol. 69, no. 397 (1955).

[32] Marcia C. Linn and Anne C. Petersen, "Emergence and Characterization of Sex Differences in Spatial Ability: A Meta-Analysis," *Child Development* 56, no. 4 (December 1985): 1479–98.

Hyde / META-ANALYSIS OF GENDER DIFFERENCES

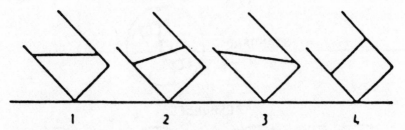

FIG. I A spatial perception item. Respondents are asked to indicate which tilted bottle has a horizontal water line.

sex-linked, genetic ones) predict a change in the pattern of gender differences at puberty, however, and the question of whether the differences in some aspects of spatial ability are rooted in biology or socialization remains an open one.

In our recently completed meta-analysis of gender differences in verbal ability, Marcia Linn and I used 165 studies that reported relevant data, and from those we were able to compute 120 values of d.[33] Over all studies, the mean $d = -.11$. This value is so small, even in comparison to Cohen's prescription, that we concluded that there is no gender difference in verbal ability. Meta-analysis is capable of yielding surprising conclusions that contradict widely held beliefs about gender differences. When we considered specific types of verbal tests, there was still no evidence of any substantial gender difference. For example, for vocabulary tests, $d = -.02$; for reading comprehension, $d = -.03$; and for essay writing, $d = -.09$.

As part of the analysis, we considered data from the SAT-Verbal, which includes a mixture of items measuring vocabulary, reading comprehension, and so on. For the 1985 administration of the SAT-Verbal, $d = +.11$, the positive value indicating superior male performance.[34] There are a number of possible explanations for why males outscore females on the test, including, for example, the test writers' selection of question topics and formats. Whatever the explanation, however, the difference is small (only about .1 standard deviation), which translates into a mean score of 437 for males and 425 for females.

One closely related project is the meta-analysis of gender differences in causal attributions done by Irene Frieze and her

[33] Hyde and Linn (n. 24 above).
[34] L. Ramist and S. Arbeiter, *Profiles, College-bound Seniors, 1985* (New York: College Entrance Examination Board, 1986).

Autumn 1990 / **SIGNS**

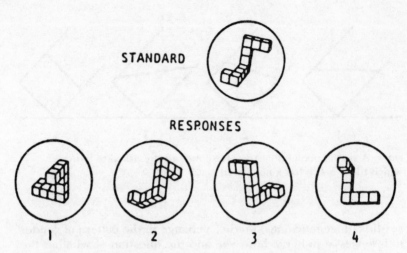

STANDARD

RESPONSES

1   2   3   4

FIG. 2 A mental rotation item. Respondents are asked to identify the two responses that show the standard in a different orientation.

colleagues.[35] Causal attributions are the mental explanations people generate for things that occur. For example, if a student gets an A on an exam, she might attribute that success to ability, to luck, to the exam's being easy, or to her own hard work. The four attributions studied most by social psychologists have been ability, luck, task ease, and effort. Ability and effort are regarded as internal attributions—that is, they involve factors in the individual—while luck and task ease are regarded as external attributions. Prior to Frieze and her colleagues' meta-analysis, the consensus in the field had been that females tend to make external attributions for their successes and internal attributions for their failures. These conclusions were used as an explanation for the lesser academic and occupational achievements of females. However, the meta-analysis indicated that gender differences were insignificant. For example, for attributions of success to ability, $d = .13$, suggesting that males are slightly more likely than females to make such attributions. For attributions of failure to (insufficient) ability, $d = .16$, indicating

[35] Irene H. Frieze, Bernard E. Whitley, Jr., Barbara H. Hanusa, and Maureen C. McHugh, "Assessing the Theoretical Models for Sex Differences in Causal Attributions for Success and Failure," *Sex Roles* 8, no. 4 (April 1982): 333–43; Bernard E. Whitley, Jr., Maureen C. McHugh, and Irene Hanson Frieze, "Assessing the Theoretical Models for Sex Differences in Causal Attributions of Success and Failure," in Hyde and Linn, eds. (n. 22 above), 102–35.

that males are also slightly more likely to make these attributions. Thus, widely held models of gender differences in attributions—which were female deficit models—were dismissed by the results of this meta-analysis, which led to a conclusion that there are no gender differences in patterns of attributions.[36]

Meta-analyses of gender differences in social behaviors

Although the present review concentrates on gender differences in cognitive abilities, a number of meta-analyses of gender differences in sociopsychological variables have been performed, and they yield interesting results.

Alice Eagly and Linda Carli performed a meta-analysis of studies of gender differences in influenceability.[37] Prior to their work, the consensus in the field of social psychology had been that women are more influenceable than men—that is, that they are more easily persuaded to change their opinion, that they are more suggestible, and that they are more conforming. Most of the relevant studies are of the laboratory experimental variety. For example, a standard measure of conformity is the Asch paradigm, in which a number of "subjects" give judgments of the length of a line, but in fact there is only one true experimental subject and the rest are confederates of the experimenter's who sometimes are unanimous in giving wrong answers: if the subject then also gives the same wrong answer, it is viewed as an indicator of conformity.[38] Eagly and Carli found that the magnitude of gender differentiation in the answers of males and females was small. For studies of influenceability, the average $d = -.16$; for studies in which there was group pressure to conform (as in Asch's paradigm), the average $d = -.32$; and for other conformity studies, in which group pressure was absent, the average $d = -.28$. Even in the set of studies

[36] Another effect-size analysis of gender differences in attributions was reported by David Sohn, "Sex Differences in Achievement Self-Attributions: An Effect-Size Analysis," *Sex Roles* 8, no. 4 (April 1982): 345–57. Although Sohn used a somewhat different statistical analysis, he reached essentially the same conclusion as Frieze and her colleagues: there was no evidence of a "consequential" relationship between sex and self-attributions.

[37] Alice H. Eagly and Linda L. Carli, "Sex of Researchers and Sex-typed Communications as Determinants of Sex Differences in Influenceability: A Meta-Analysis of Social Influence Studies," *Psychological Bulletin* 90, no. 1 (July 1981): 1–20.

[38] The original paradigm was presented in Solomon E. Asch, "Studies of Independence and Conformity: I. A Minority of One against a Unanimous Majority," *Psychological Monographs*, vol. 70, no. 416 (1956).

Autumn 1990 / **SIGNS**

in which the gender difference was largest, where there was group pressure to conform, the studies may not necessarily be evidence of greater passivity on the part of females. An alternative interpretation is that these studies reflect the tendency of females to try to preserve harmony in a group.

Eagly and Carli's exploration of the relationship between the gender of the researchers and the results of their studies illustrates the way in which meta-analysis can be used to provide empirical answers to feminist questions about research methodology.[39] Male researchers found larger gender differences and greater persuasibility and conformity among women than did female researchers. In studies authored by women, no gender difference was found. There are many possible explanations for such an effect. For example, male researchers by their presence may encourage conformity in female participants. Male researchers may design experimental settings or stimulus materials that better measure males' responses or that contain more masculine content.[40]

Judith Hall reports a number of meta-analyses, including studies of gender differences in accuracy of judging facial expressions, gender differences in gazing, and gender differences in interpersonal distance, touch, body movement, and voice.[41] Her results indicate that females are better than males at understanding others' nonverbal cues ($d = -.42$), at recognizing faces ($d = -.34$), and at expressing emotions using nonverbal communication ($d = -.50$). Females have more expressive faces ($d = -.90$, but based on only five studies), are approached more closely by others ($d = -.86$), and emit fewer speech errors ($d = -.66$). These gender differences are generally larger than the differences in spatial and verbal abilities discussed earlier.

[39] It should be noted, however, that sex-of-author effects are not found consistently in all meta-analyses; relevant studies are discussed by Alice H. Eagly, *Sex Differences in Social Behavior: A Social-Role Interpretation* (Hillsdale, N.J.: Erlbaum, 1987), 144.

[40] For a meta-analysis addressed to some of these issues, see Betsy Jane Becker, "Influence Again: An Examination of Reviews and Studies of Gender Differences in Social Influence," in Hyde and Linn, eds., 178–209.

[41] Judith A. Hall, *Nonverbal Sex Differences: Communication Accuracy and Expressive Style* (Baltimore: Johns Hopkins University Press, 1984). In her reporting, Hall uses the statistic r, or the correlation between subject sex and behavioral measures, rather than the more conventional d. For the reader's convenience in comparing the results of different studies, I have converted all her r statistics to d statistics, using the formula $d = 2r$. Judith Hall should also be recognized for having reported, in 1978, what was probably the first meta-analysis of psychological gender differences; see her "Gender Effects in Decoding Nonverbal Cues," *Psychological Bulletin* 85, no. 4 (July 1978): 845–57.

Hyde / META-ANALYSIS OF GENDER DIFFERENCES

Alice Eagly and Maureen Crowley have meta-analyzed studies on gender differences in helping behaviors.[42] Their article is particularly interesting because it is theory grounded, unlike many other meta-analyses with more applied orientations. Eagly and Crowley articulated a social-role theory of gender and helping behaviors, leading to the hypotheses that male gender roles foster helping that is heroic and chivalrous whereas female roles foster helping that is nurturant and caring. They noted that social psychologists have tended to study helping behaviors primarily in the context of short-term encounters with strangers. The consequence has been to neglect to study helping behaviors prescribed by the female role, which are most likely to occur in long-term, close relationships. In support of their theoretical formulations, the greatest differentials, in which males helped more than females, were in situations in which there was perceived danger in the testing situation and in which males feel most competent to help. For example, if the helping situation involves whether a motorist stops to help a person stopped by the roadside with a flat tire, most studies have found more helping by males because there is some danger involved to the helper and males feel more competent about automotive problems. In contrast, if the situation involves volunteering time to help a disturbed child, most studies have found more helping from females because there is little danger present for the helper and because females feel more competent in nurturing.

I and one other researcher have performed meta-analyses of studies of gender differences in aggression, with different focuses. The focus of my meta-analysis was developmental, concerning itself particularly with age trends in the patterns of gender differences in aggression.[43] Averaging over all ages and many different methods of measuring aggression, the magnitude of the gender difference was $d = .50$, indicating that males are indeed more aggressive but that the difference is moderate, not large. There was a negative correlation between participants' age and the magnitude of the gender difference; that is, gender differences were largest for studies of children and smallest for older participants. Specifically, for studies with participants six years of age or younger, $d = .58$, whereas for studies of college students, $d = .27$. One must view

[42] Alice H. Eagly and Maureen Crowley, "Gender and Helping Behavior: A Meta-analytic Review of the Social Psychological Literature," *Psychological Bulletin* 100, no. 3 (November 1986): 283–308.
[43] Janet S. Hyde, "How Large Are Gender Differences in Aggression?" (n. 24 above).

Autumn 1990 / **SIGNS**

this difference with caution, however, since the measures of aggression in different age groups often differ. Many studies of preschoolers use direct observations of physical aggression (e.g., hitting, kicking) as the measure of aggression, whereas studies of college students more often use measures such as willingness to shock another person.

It is interesting that the magnitude of the gender difference in aggression indicated by such studies has declined over time. For studies published between 1966 and 1973, $d = .53$, whereas for studies published between 1978 and 1981, $d = .41$. Similar trends have been found in meta-analyses of cognitive abilities. For example, in my analysis of gender differences in verbal ability, studies published in 1973 or earlier showed $d = -.23$, whereas studies published after 1973 showed $d = -.10$.[44] This trend toward declining gender differences may represent an increasing tendency for psychologists to publish results when the gender difference is not significant. Alice Eagly has reviewed the evidence on trends over time in the magnitude of gender differences, finding the results to be inconsistent from one meta-analysis to another.[45] Alternatively, the trend toward diminished gender differences may be a real one. If that is the case, it provides remarkable evidence of the extent to which changes in gender roles in the past two decades have led to a diminishing of gender differences in behavior.

The other meta-analysis of gender differences in aggressive behavior was performed by Alice Eagly and Valerie Steffen.[46] Their focus was on social psychologists' research, the majority of it done with college students as subjects. They again used social-role theory to predict the pattern of results. Overall, men were more aggressive than women ($d = .29$). However, the pattern of results varied considerably depending on the way in which the aggressive

[44] Rosenthal and Rubin also investigated trends over time in the magnitude of gender differences, reanalyzing my 1981 meta-analysis of cognitive gender differences. They reported that their results indicated a "substantial gain in cognitive performance by females relative to males" (708) in more recent studies. However, the nature of their data cannot possibly support such a conclusion about improved levels of female performance on some absolute scale. Their data indicate only a trend toward diminished gender differences, which is consistent with the trends for aggression and verbal ability that are noted. See Robert Rosenthal and Donald B. Rubin, "Further Meta-analytic Procedures for Assessing Cognitive Gender Differences," *Journal of Educational Psychology* 74, no. 5 (October 1982): 708–12.

[45] Alice H. Eagly, *Sex Differences in Social Behavior: A Social-Role Interpretation* (n. 39 above).

[46] Alice H. Eagly and Valerie J. Steffen, "Gender and Aggressive Behavior: A Meta-analytic Review of the Social Psychological Literature," *Psychological Bulletin* 100, no. 3 (November 1986): 309–30.

behavior was assessed. The gender difference was larger when physical aggression was involved ($d = .40$) than when psychological aggression was involved ($d = .18$).[47] When women, more than men, believe the behavior to produce harm to the victim, guilt or anxiety to oneself, or danger to oneself, gender differences are larger. The results are therefore consistent with Eagly's social-role theory.

Summary and conclusions

We have come a long way from the belief, a century ago, that women's brains, and therefore their mental abilities, are smaller than men's. In the few decades before meta-analyses, reviewers consistently concluded that there are no gender differences in general intelligence, but that there are gender differences favoring females in verbal ability and males in mathematical and spatial ability. Meta-analysis, by quantitatively cumulating results from many studies, has permitted more sophisticated and convincing probing of these patterns of gender differences. A number of conclusions emerge from these meta-analyses. Gender differences in cognitive abilities are generally not large. The largest difference is for one type of spatial ability, mental rotations ($d = .73$), but the gender difference in mathematical performance is moderate ($d = .43$), and there is no gender difference in verbal ability.

In the realm of social behaviors such as aggression and helping behavior, whether gender differences are found in a particular study, and how large they are, depends greatly on the setting of the study and the ways in which the behaviors are measured; this variation in results is consistent with social-role theory. Gender differences in nonverbal behaviors are in some cases larger than other gender differences (e.g., females are approached more closely than males are), although here, too, most differences are small or moderate. Some (though not all) meta-analyses demonstrate a trend over approximately two decades toward a decline in the magnitude of gender differences.

[47] As most meta-analysts do, the authors calculated values of d so that they would be positive if the gender difference is in the hypothesized direction (in this case, greater male than female aggression) and negative if the gender difference is opposite to the hypothesis. Thus, although the gender difference is larger for physical than psychological aggression, the value of d is still positive for psychological aggression, meaning that males showed higher levels of psychological aggression than females did.

Autumn 1990 / **SIGNS**

Meta-analysis is a useful statistical tool that allows one to perform a systematic and relatively unbiased assessment of existing research on any particular area of psychological gender differences.[48] It also allows detailed exploration of which types of tests or research settings are more likely to find gender differences and which are not. Although meta-analysis has been used in psychology and a few other disciplines such as education, it has yet to be used broadly in other social sciences, where it doubtless can contribute to feminist research. It has great promise because it cumulates large bodies of research findings and provides powerful quantitative answers to questions, thereby smashing many myths about gender differences.

Department of Psychology and Women's Studies Research Center
University of Wisconsin—Madison

[48] Meta-analysis has been used to address issues other than gender differences that are of interest to feminist psychologists. One example is Taylor and Hall's analysis of studies assessing the relation between androgyny and self-esteem. See Marylee C. Taylor and Judith A. Hall, "Psychological Androgyny: Theories, Methods, and Conclusions," *Psychological Bulletin* 92 (1982): 347–66.

[5]

REVIEW ESSAY

Psychology and Gender

Nancy M. Henley

Introduction

This review considers recent efforts within the field of psychology to understand issues involving gender—from self-concept to rape, from mathematical ability to moral development. In so doing it also seeks to demonstrate certain patterns of development within feminist psychology and in its relation to mainstream psychology. A review such as this must, for reasons of space, be selective. I have used as criteria for inclusion my own and my colleagues' judgments about the importance and interest of recent scholarship in the psychology of gender (generally that published since 1979). I have also chosen to discuss work that has not been covered previously in such reviews in *Signs*. My own familiarity with certain areas of inquiry has of course influenced the selection process as well; and the review unfortunately is limited to work published in the United States. I begin by looking briefly at the status of the field, and then present two case studies in the recent history of psychology of gender for the lessons they teach. From there I proceed to examine controversial new research dealing with sex differences in cognition, and then to survey recent

I wish to thank Deborah Burke, Kathleen Grady, Vickie Mays, and Mary Parlee for their early consultation on various aspects of this paper and Kay Deaux, Neil Malamuth, Mary Parlee, Anne Peplau, Barbara Wallston, and Michele Wittig for their excellent suggestions for revisions.

[*Signs: Journal of Women in Culture and Society* 1985, vol. 11 no. 1]

research and theory on gender in such areas as schema theory, moral development, masculine identity, pornography and aggression, and women of color.

The Field

Problems of terminology still plague the field, and most lengthy works must start with definitions of terms.[1] The railings of prominent scholars against loose and inappropriate terms such as "sex roles" and "psychology of women" seem to be cries in the wilderness; not only do those terms remain in heavy use, but also the two main journals of the field take them as their titles.[2]

Two organizations devoted to women's issues in psychology continue to exist, united by common concerns and by some overlap in membership. The Division of the Psychology of Women (Division 35) of the American Psychological Association (APA) publishes a newsletter and the journal *Psychology of Women Quarterly*, organizes convention programs, and examines critical issues through its task forces.[3] The autonomous Association for Women in Psychology (AWP), which consists of local chapters and regional networks, sponsors its own conferences, makes awards, publishes a newsletter, and facilitates information sharing at psychological conventions. The APA also has an Office for Women's Programs and a Committee on Women in Psychology, which have been gaining influence, and feminists are increasingly serving in the APA's elected offices and on its policy-making boards.

In the teaching of psychology of gender, as in other disciplines, there is sentiment in favor of "mainstreaming"[4] as well as ongoing support for specialized courses. Useful materials for both traditional and gender-

1. See, e.g., Carolyn W. Sherif, "Needed Concepts in the Study of Gender Identity," *Psychology of Women Quarterly* (hereafter cited as *PWQ*) 6, no. 4 (1982): 375–98; Joseph Pleck, *The Myth of Masculinity* (Cambridge, Mass.: MIT Press, 1981).

2. For the debate on "psychology of women," see Mary Brown Parlee, "Review Essay: Psychology," *Signs: Journal of Women in Culture and Society* 1, no. 1 (1975): 119–38, esp. 120–21; and Martha T. Shuch Mednick, "Some Thoughts on the Psychology of Women: Comment on Mary Brown Parlee's 'Review Essay: Psychology,' " *Signs* 1, no. 3, pt. 1 (1976): 763–70, esp. 766–68. Parlee ("Review Essay: Psychology and Women," *Signs* 5, no. 1 [1979]: 121–33, esp. 133) and Sherif, p. 393, have also protested the use of "sex roles." See also Helen Z. Lopata and Barrie Thorne, "On the Term 'Sex Roles,' " *Signs* 3, no. 4 (1978): 718–21.

3. An excellent task force report is "Guidelines for Nonsexist Research," available for $2.00 from Irene Frieze, Women's Studies Program, University of Pittsburgh, Pittsburgh, Pennsylvania 15260.

4. Rita J. Freedman, Sharon Golub, and Beatrice Krauss, "Mainstreaming the Psychology of Women into the Core Curriculum," *Teaching of Psychology* 9, no. 3 (1982): 165–68.

Signs Autumn 1985 103

related courses have been developed in recent years.[5] The number and quality of texts on psychology of gender are also on the rise. Excellent books by Virginia O'Leary and Bernice Lott have been honored with the AWP Publication Award. Others, such as those by Juanita Williams and by Janet Hyde, have gone into second and third editions. Sue Cox's *Female Psychology*, now in its second edition, is an especially good edited collection, apparently the most popular anthology in classroom use. A fine graduate-level text by Rhoda Unger has also been well received.[6] These texts are beginning to reflect the reevaluation of some of the early major areas of inquiry in feminist psychology, to which I now turn.

Two Case Studies: Fear of Success and Androgyny

In the late sixties and early seventies, two lines of research captured the attention of many psychologists and strongly influenced feminist scholarship: one focused on fear of success and the other on androgyny.[7] Later investigations in both areas have failed to support earlier understandings, however, and thus it is instructive to review the history of these concepts.

Fear of Success

The concept of fear of success (FOS) as a particular problem for women was developed by Matina Horner in her 1968 Ph.D. dissertation.[8]

---

5. See Nancy Russo and Natalie Malovich, "Assessing the Introductory Psychology Course," available from the Order Department, American Psychological Association, 1200 17th St., N.W., Washington, D.C. 20036; a special issue on teaching psychology of women, *PWQ*, vol. 7, no. 1 (Fall 1982); and Sharon Golub et al., "Resources for Introducing Psychology of Women Content and Methodology into the Psychology Core Curriculum," *Psychological Documents* 14, no. 1 (1984):1.

6. Virginia O'Leary, *Toward Understanding Women* (Monterey, Calif.: Brooks/Cole, 1977); Bernice Lott, *Becoming a Woman* (Springfield, Ill.: C. C. Thomas, 1981); Juanita H. Williams, *Psychology of Women: Behavior in a Biosocial Context*, 2d ed. (New York: W. W. Norton & Co., 1983); Janet S. Hyde, *Half the Human Experience*, 3d ed. (Lexington, Mass.: D. C. Heath & Co., 1985); Sue Cox, ed., *Female Psychology: The Emerging Self*, 2d ed. (New York: St. Martin's Press, 1981); Rhoda K. Unger, *Female and Male: Psychological Perspectives* (New York: Harper & Row, 1979). Information on the popularity of texts is from Nancy F. Russo, "Psychology of Women: Analysis of the Faculty and Courses of an Emerging Field," *PWQ* 7, no. 1 (1982): 18–31.

7. Matina S. Horner, "Toward an Understanding of Achievement-related Conflicts in Women," *Journal of Social Issues* 28, no. 2 (1972): 157–75; Sandra L. Bem, "The Measurement of Psychological Androgyny," *Journal of Consulting and Clinical Psychology* 42, no. 2 (1974): 155–62.

8. Matina S. Horner, "Sex Differences in Achievement Motivation and Performance in Competitive and Non-competitive Situations" (Ph.D. diss., University of Michigan, 1968).

Horner found that 62 percent of her female subjects, compared with only 9 percent of the men, incorporated negative imagery in stories written in response to success-related cues. While other women, and men, did better at word-game tasks when they were in a large, mixed-sex group, females whose stories included negative FOS imagery tended to perform better when alone. This suggested to Horner that women with FOS performed less well when in competition with men.

Other researchers attempted to replicate the experiment, with mixed results; Horner and others revised her scoring procedure and identified methodological and analytical problems in her work. All of this has been reviewed thoroughly by David Tresemer, who concludes that (1) there is no significant difference between females and males in the incidence of FOS imagery; (2) high-achievement-oriented women who also use FOS imagery do not show a performance decrement when in competition with men (reanalysis of Horner's data showed that it was FOS women with *low* achievement imagery who showed a decrement); (3) males do not write more negatively than females when cued with female success stories; (4) there has been no sex difference in the changes in FOS imagery found in stories produced over the years (there is a slight decrease in FOS imagery for both females and males); and (5) more traditional (sex-typed) women do not exhibit more FOS.[9]

In sum, the hypothesis of gross gender differences in the fear of success, in any simple form, does not stand up under examination. The definition of "success" in this research has also been too narrow, Tresemer states, reflecting traditional business and medical school visions. He concludes, however, that the concept of fear of success, as it applies to both women and men, should be retained but must be broadened to include a personal view of success and achievement.

Androgyny

When Sandra Bem first published her Sex Role Inventory (BSRI) in 1974, earlier measures of masculinity and femininity were already under fire. In particular, critics of those scales pointed out that their bipolar nature precluded the possibility of an individual's having both feminine and masculine traits. Following this reasoning, Bem developed a scale in which masculinity and femininity were independent dimensions, and the traits scored for each were positive. Individuals rated themselves for various traits previously determined to be stereotypically feminine or masculine; thus the scale is a measure of self-concept rather than an "objective" assessment of personality or behavior. The personality types

9. David W. Tresemer, *Fear of Success* (New York: Plenum Publishing Corp., 1977). See also John Condry and Sharon Dyer, "Fear of Success: Attribution of Cause to the Victim," *Journal of Social Issues* 32, no. 3 (1976): 63–83.

created by this new scale were called "Masculine," "Feminine," and "Androgynous"—the last being those whose masculinity and femininity scores did not differ significantly. In several experimental studies, Bem and her colleagues determined that in situations calling for behavior alien to one's sexual stereotype, androgynous individuals were more adaptable than those who were sex-typed.[10]

With similar principles in mind, Janet Spence, Robert Helmreich, and Joy Stapp published the Personal Attributes Questionnaire (PAQ), also a sex-role self-concept scale, the same year.[11] They reserved the term "androgynous," however, for those who scored high on both masculinity and femininity, and created the term "undifferentiated" for those who scored low on both. (This distinction was later accepted by Bem.) These researchers and their many followers began to develop a voluminous literature that examined nearly every variable of interest in psychology for its relationship to sex-role identity. As they developed and refined their procedures,[12] however, increasingly serious critiques were developing within the field.[13]

These critiques pointed out that the research findings were in fact weak and quite mixed and that the degree of masculinity in one's behavior, rather than the combination of femininity and masculinity, was the true predictor of one's behavior whether one was female or male. Others questioned research methodology—and the very relevance of the findings to gender research.[14] Conceptual criticisms were the most exten-

10. Bem (n. 7 above), and Sandra L. Bem, "Sex Role Adaptability: One Consequence of Psychological Androgyny," *Journal of Personality and Social Psychology* 31, no. 4 (1975): 634–43.

11. Janet Spence, Robert Helmreich, and Joy Stapp, "The Personal Attributes Questionnaire: A Measure of Sex Role Stereotypes and Masculinity-Femininity," *JSAS Catalog of Selected Documents in Psychology* 4 (Spring 1974): 43 (MS no. 617).

12. See, e.g., Sandra L. Bem, "On the Utility of Alternative Procedures for Assessing Psychological Androgyny," *Journal of Consulting and Clinical Psychology* 45, no. 2 (1977): 196–205.

13. Among these were Jeffrey A. Kelly and Judith Worell, "New Formulations of Sex Roles and Androgyny: A Critical Review," *Journal of Consulting and Clinical Psychology* 45, no. 6 (1977): 1101–15; "Special Section on Interpretive Controversies in Personality and Social Psychology," *Journal of Personality and Social Psychology* 37, no. 6 (1979): 996–1054; Bernice Lott, "A Feminist Critique of Androgyny: Toward the Elimination of Gender Attributions for Learned Behavior," in *Gender and Nonverbal Behavior*, ed. Clara Mayo and Nancy M. Henley (New York: Springer-Verlag, 1981).

14. On the latter point, e.g., Janet Spence and Robert Helmreich in 1979 disclaimed any attempt to develop a global measure of masculinity/femininity or sex role identity, stating that they conceived of the PAQ as a "specialized measure of socially desirable instrumental and expressive characteristics, objectively defined trait dimensions that distinguish between the sexes to some degree" and that they suspected that the personality traits measured by the PAQ and BSRI were only minimally related to many sex-associated behaviors ("The Many Faces of Androgyny: A Reply to Locksley and Colten," *Journal of Personality and Social Psychology* 37, no. 6 [1979]: 1032–45, esp. 1032).

sive, challenging the validity of the construct of androgyny as it was realized in the scales, the appropriateness of applying general perceptions of aggregate sex differences to the measurement of individual traits, the use of gender-labeling terms to designate learned behaviors that in themselves have no gender, and the view of gender as a personal attribute rather than as a structural feature of situations and life experiences. Bem has since changed her focus, although many continue to use the androgyny scales to investigate personality factors in behavior.

Androgyny and Fear of Success in Retrospect

These two fruitful areas of inquiry produced thoughtful critiques and important reconceptualizations, but the research itself could not bear the heavy weight of media attention and scholarly replication. Why were these particular themes seized on with such vigor by feminist scholars and interested bystanders alike, and why have the largely discredited ideas proved so hard to relinquish? In the past, the variable "sex" had proved a most serviceable old warhorse for psychological explanation. In the late sixties and early seventies, however, the new emphasis on sex differences, inspired by the women's movement, was making it painfully clear that sex as a variable could not account for the gross discrepancies found between the lives of men and women. Surveying hundreds of studies, Eleanor Maccoby and Carol Nagy Jacklin concluded that only four purported sex differences could be considered "fairly well established."[15] New explanatory variables had to be found. Little wonder that feminine sex typing and fear of success, to name just two, became popular explanations: the supporting research entailed fairly easy data collection, and popularized accounts of the findings pointed the finger at individual differences— back at women themselves—and away from larger social phenomena.

Some fear that the inadequacy of such variables to explain women's lives has shifted scholarly attention to timeworn and repressive biological explanations in recent research on sex differences in cognition. It is important, whether we fear such a trend or not, to understand the issues and findings in this field.

Sex-related Differences in Cognition

Mathematical Performance

A major focus of interest has been the often poorer performance of females than males on tests of mathematical skill. In 1980, Camilla Ben-

15. Eleanor Maccoby and Carol Nagy Jacklin, *The Psychology of Sex Differences* (Stanford, Calif.: Stanford University Press, 1974).

bow and Julian Stanley attracted much attention with their *Science* article, which reported higher averages for boys' scores than for girls' on the mathematics portion of the Scholastic Aptitude Test (SAT-M) over a period of eight years, with the greatest differences occurring in the upper ranges of mathematical ability. The authors concluded "that sex differences . . . result from superior male mathematical ability, which may in turn be related to greater male ability in spatial tasks. This male superiority is probably an expression of a combination of both endogenous and exogenous variables."[16]

While the popular media gave fast and broad coverage to the article, critics in the scientific community pointed to flaws in the authors' talent bank, assumptions, and reasoning and questioned the nature of their evidence, the extent of their scientific knowledge, and even the focus of their research.[17] Benbow and Stanley stuck to their guns, regretting in response that the media did not alert people "to the *magnitude* of the sex difference. The situation is far worse than most persons realize."[18] They have continued with these themes in 1982 and 1983 publications, considering briefly and inadequately some environmental explanations but rejecting them all, and concluding in 1983 that the reasons for the sex difference are unclear.[19]

The question of the magnitude of sex difference in mathematical ability is an important one: not all differences that are statistically significant are necessarily meaningful. Hyde has reviewed and reanalyzed those studies Maccoby and Jacklin cite as the evidence backing claims of well-established sex differences in verbal, quantitative, and visual-spatial abilities. Using the technique of meta-analysis, Hyde concludes that these "well-established" gender differences are very small indeed: the proportion of variance attributable to sex was only 1–5 percent of the population variance (quite small), and mean differences amounted to only .24 to .51 of a standard deviation (a small-to-medium proportion). Hyde points out that the availability of standardized test scores makes it convenient to conduct large-scale research projects on gender differences in cognitive abilities but that such research is "particularly prone to having large sample sizes that produce reliable but tiny differences."[20]

16. Camilla P. Benbow and Julian C. Stanley, "Sex Differences in Mathematical Ability: Fact or Artifact?" *Science*, no. 210 (1980), pp. 1262–64.

17. See "Letters," *Science*, no. 212 (1981), pp. 114–21.

18. Ibid., p. 121.

19. J. C. Stanley and C. P. Benbow, "Huge Sex Ratios at Upper End," *American Psychologist* 37, no. 8 (1982): 972; C. P. Benbow and J. C. Stanley, "Sex Differences in Mathematical Reasoning Ability: More Facts," *Science*, no. 222 (1983), pp. 1029–31.

20. Janet S. Hyde, "How Large Are Cognitive Gender Differences?" *American Psychologist* 36, no. 8 (1981): 892–901, quote on 900; Maccoby and Jacklin (n. 15 above). Meta-analysis tests the magnitude of differences found between two groups by looking at such factors as the difference in means as a function of the standard deviation and the proportion of variance accounted for by the differences found.

Furthermore, Joseph Rossi points out that the greater sex discrepancy that Stanley and Benbow identify at the upper ranges follows from the measure they select: the higher the cutoff score selected for a ratio, the more extreme the ratio.[21] At the same time, the higher the cutoff, the smaller the proportion of the total sample represented by the ratio. Only about 5 percent of the children tested, for example, are counted in the 5:1 boy:girl ratio for those scoring 600 or more on the SAT-M. Rossi notes that Benbow and Stanley attribute much of the sex difference to "a lack of high-scoring girls"; if this is the case, he observes, "then gender differences among the remaining 95 percent of their sample—all highly gifted students—must have been negligible."

Meanwhile, others have concentrated on the obvious social factors involved, looking particularly at the links between mathematical performance, school and home experience, and attitudes toward mathematics and self.[22] Julia Sherman has pursued the question longitudinally among junior high and high school girls, finding a relationship between a favorable attitude toward mathematics and decisions to take further courses in the subject.[23]

Most investigators would agree that there seems to be some likelihood of a small but true difference in mathematical performance favoring boys, though its source and the mechanism of its realization are not clear. Sherman had, before the Benbow and Stanley article came out, advanced the hypothesis that the sex difference in mathematical performance is related to a sex difference in spatial ability; others had linked mathematical to spatial skill, and numerous studies had found that males exhibit better spatial skills than females.[24] But in addition to attempts to understand mathematical ability, there has been interest in the sex difference in verbal ability, in which females demonstrate an advantage over males. Much research and theorizing has focused on both mathematical and verbal skills and has suggested the possibility of a relationship between the two.[25]

21. Joseph S. Rossi, "Ratios Exaggerate Gender Differences in Mathematical Ability," *American Psychologist* 38, no. 3 (1983): 348.

22. See, e.g., Marilynn B. Brewer and Myrtle W. Blum, "Sex-Role Androgyny and Patterns of Causal Attribution for Academic Achievement," *Sex Roles* 5, no. 6 (1979): 783–96, esp. 795.

23. Julia A. Sherman, "Mathematics the Critical Filter: A Look at Some Residues," *PWQ* 6, no. 4 (1982): 428–44.

24. Julia A. Sherman, "Problem of Sex Differences in Space Perception and Aspects of Intellectual Functioning," *Psychological Review* 74, no. 4 (1967): 290–99.

25. On this literature, see Julia A. Sherman, *Sex-related Cognitive Differences: An Essay on Theory and Evidence* (Springfield, Ill.: C. C. Thomas, 1978); Michele A. Wittig and Anne C. Petersen, eds., *Sex-related Differences in Cognitive Functioning: Developmental Issues* (New York: Academic Press, 1979). See also Susan L. Star, "The Politics of Right and Left: Sex Differences in Hemispheric Brain Asymmetry," in *Women Look at Biology Looking at Women*, ed.

In the physiological realm, such work has invoked genes, hormones, and brain organization as explanations. Outside that realm, social and environmental factors, neglected in research on cognitive functioning,[26] play an important part in major attempts at integrative theory.[27] There have also been theoretical and methodological challenges to the validity of sex difference findings. I examine the research on brain organization in some detail below and discuss its social, theoretical, and methodological implications as well.

Theories of Brain Organization

Studies of brain organization have attempted to identify the degree to which either hemisphere of the brain may specialize in the control of a particular ability. The left hemisphere, for example, has long been more closely associated with verbal functioning than has the right, and the right hemisphere has been similarly associated with spatial ability. This hemispheric specialization is also referred to as cerebral lateralization. (Lateralization does not mean that only one hemisphere controls a particular function but that the hemisphere predominates in mediating that function.) Not only the degree of lateralization but also the particular hemisphere of dominance for a function (right or left) and the relationship of sex to both functioning and lateralization have been of interest.

One hypothesis advanced regarding sex difference in spatial abilities has been that lateralization aids ability and that male brains are more highly lateralized than female, particularly for spatial ability. In fact, investigators repeatedly have found greater specialization for spatial ability in males,[28] while females have been considered less laterally

Ruth Hubbard, Mary Sue Henifin, and Barbara Fried (Cambridge, Mass.: Schenkman Publishing Co., 1979). While it offers less coverage of the literature, Star's article presents a valuable political critique of this research.

26. See Anne C. Petersen and Michele A. Wittig, "Sex-related Differences in Cognitive Functioning: An Overview," in Wittig and Petersen, eds., pp. 1–17, esp. p. 13.

27. See, e.g., Sherman, Sex-related Cognitive Differences, esp. pp. 172–79; J. Lauren Harris, "Sex-related Differences in Spatial Ability: A Developmental Psychological View," in Becoming Female: Perspectives on Development, ed. Claire B. Kopp (New York: Plenum Publishing Corp., 1979), pp. 133–81, esp. p. 171; Michele A. Wittig, "Genetic Influences on Sex-related Differences in Intellectual Performance: Theoretical and Methodological Issues," in Wittig and Petersen, eds. (n. 25 above), pp. 21–65; M. P. Bryden, "Evidence for Sex-related Differences in Cerebral Organization," in Wittig and Petersen, eds., pp. 121–43, esp. p. 138; Anne C. Petersen, "Hormones and Cognitive Functioning in Normal Development," in Wittig and Petersen, eds., pp. 189–214, esp. pp. 208–9.

28. Richard A. Harshman and Roger Remington, "Sex, Language, and the Brain, Part I: A Review of the Literature on Adult Sex Differences in Lateralization," Working Papers in Phonetics, no. 31 (1976), pp. 86–103; Sandra F. Witelson, "Sex and the Single Hemisphere: Specialization of the Right Hemisphere for Spatial Processing," Science, no. 193 (1976), pp. 425–27; Jerre Levy and Marylou Reid, "Variations in Cerebral Organization as a Function

differentiated.[29] (An earlier conclusion by Anthony Buffery and Jeffrey Gray that females may be *more* lateralized for verbal skill than males has sometimes been cited as an example of the chaos in this field; it seemed researchers were claiming simultaneously that females are both less and more lateralized.[30] However, Buffery and Gray's finding has not been upheld by later studies, and current reviews of the field generally discount the theory.)[31]

But the linchpin of the argument that specialization aids ability is not supported by the literature in the field. Deborah Waber cites evidence to the contrary—that early maturing adolescents (regardless of sex) are both less lateralized for and more adept at verbal functions than are late maturing young people.[32] She advances the intriguing theory that female verbal superiority results from the fact that maturation stops the process of supposedly increasing hemispheric specialization. More recent research, however, has not supported this theory.[33]

The relationship of sex to lateralization and ability is also unclear. Waber finds not sex but the rate of maturation to be significantly correlated with spatial skill. Anne Petersen found not sex but degree of physical androgyny to correlate positively with spatial ability. William Ray and his associates found the relationship between lateralization and spatial ability to be true for males of high spatial ability but not for those of low spatial ability or for females. Sherman concludes, "Degree of lateralization as a general concept is probably meaningless."[34]

Several scholars, surveying the field after some initial difficulties had been ironed out, have attempted to account for the data that indicate sex

of Handedness, Hand Posture in Writing, and Sex," *Journal of Experimental Psychology: General* 107, no. 2 (1978): 119–44; Bryden; and Harris.

29. Witelson; Levy and Reid. See also Sherman, *Sex-related Cognitive Differences* (n. 25 above).

30. Anthony W. H. Buffery and Jeffrey A. Gray, "Sex Differences in the Development of Spatial and Linguistic Skills," in *Gender Differences: Their Ontogeny and Significance*, ed. Christopher Ounsted and David C. Taylor (Edinburgh: Churchill Livingstone, 1972), pp. 123–57; Star.

31. See Harshman and Remington; Sherman, *Sex-related Cognitive Differences* (n. 25 above); Bryden; Deborah P. Waber, "Cognitive Abilities and Sex-related Variations in the Maturation of Cerebral Cortical Functions," in Wittig and Petersen, eds. (n. 25 above), pp. 161–86.

32. Deborah P. Waber, "Sex Differences in Cognition: A Function of Maturation Rate?" *Science*, no. 192 (1976), pp. 572–74.

33. See Anne C. Petersen, "Physical Androgyny and Cognitive Functioning in Adolescence," *Developmental Psychology* 12, no. 6 (1976): 524–33; Sherman, *Sex-related Cognitive Differences* (n. 25 above); William J. Ray et al., "Spatial Abilities, Sex Differences and EEG Functioning," *Neuropsychologia* 19, no. 5 (1981): 719–22. Harris (n. 27 above) states that the evidence is mixed.

34. Waber, "Sex Differences in Cognition"; Petersen, "Physical Androgyny and Cognitive Functioning in Adolescence"; Ray et al.; Sherman, *Sex-related Cognitive Differences* (n. 25 above), p. 129.

Signs   Autumn 1985   111

differences in ability. Sherman suggests that a true—though small—difference favoring female verbal precocity does exist, tied somehow to earlier female maturation. This precocity could predispose females toward verbal (left-hemisphere) approaches to problem solving. Cultural factors keep most females from developing spatial skills but emphasize verbal training, which they don't need. Males, however, typically benefit from the cultural emphasis on verbal education, and thus they catch up verbally as they mature; in addition, they receive sex-specific training that enhances visual-spatial skills. This combination of slight biological predisposition and strong cultural intervention could produce the observed sex differences in verbal and spatial performance.[35]

Like Sherman, Lauren Harris endorses a theory that takes into account both biological predisposition and cognitive strategy, adding in the assumption that language functions among females are ultimately more lateralized than they are among males.[36] M. P. Bryden presents a biological theory, a cultural theory, and a theory of interaction between the biological and cultural, without choosing among them but remarking that the interactionist position "may be quite reasonable."[37]

It is clear, as those in the field point out, that more, and more careful, research is needed; even when more is known, however, scholars do not expect a single, simple explanation of the findings. In addition to the acknowledged fact of small demonstrated differences, methodological questions, contradictory findings, neglect of work on environmental factors, problematic interpretations of data, and biased research and publication practices combine to make this a volatile field. Nevertheless, it need not be dismissed as just another attempt to pin cultural differentiation on immutable causes; phenotype does not solely determine genotype, and the observed differentiation by gender has no necessarily "good" or "bad" effects. In particular, while some suggest that greater lateralization of visual-spatial function is an aid to male mathematical performance, others propose that lesser lateralization of verbal function enhances female verbal performance (because lesser lateralization means that more areas of the brain are involved in verbal processing, a female would be less vulnerable to loss of function if the "verbal" areas of the brain were damaged). Investigation in this field includes some of the more controversial research going on today; while some argue that such work is indefensible in the current political climate, one can also maintain that, given the continued interest in this area, feminist scholars must stay informed and involved in order to keep it from being a mire of misogyny.

I turn now to other—less controversial but no less interesting—areas of inquiry in the psychology of gender.

35. Sherman, "Problem of Sex Differences" (n. 24 above), and *Sex-related Cognitive Differences* (n. 25 above), esp. pp. 172–79.
36. Harris (n. 27 above), esp. p. 171.
37. Bryden (n. 27 above), esp. p. 138.

Recent Research and Theory

Schema Theory

In recent years scholars have shifted their attention from gender-related self-concepts to the cognitive structures, or schemas, that organize our perceptions. Bem, in particular, has moved from investigating the androgynous individual to concentrating on the sex-typed individual. Like her critics, she now contends that her earlier concept of androgyny presupposed that "the concepts of masculinity and femininity have an independent and palpable reality rather than being themselves cognitive constructs derived from gender-based schematic processing."[38] As an alternative, Bem proposes "gender schema theory," which states that sex typing derives in part from "a generalized readiness to process information on the basis of sex-linked associations that constitute the gender schema" and from the fact that "the self-concept itself gets assimilated to the gender schema."[39] In her research, sex-typed individuals do indeed demonstrate greater readiness than those who are non-sex-typed to process information on the basis of gender. Bem concludes—though some will find her proposal quite mild—that the "feminist moral" of gender schema theory is "that the network of associations that constitutes the gender schema ought to become more limited in scope and that society ought to temper its insistence upon the ubiquitous functional importance of the gender dichotomy."[40]

In independent research, Hazel Markus and her colleagues have developed a similar conception of "self-schemas about gender."[41] Self-schema theory differs from gender schema theory in that self-schemas are described as influencing sex-typed individuals to organize information only as it relates to their own sex type, not to gender in general. Markus et al. find that only androgynous individuals organize information equally around both feminine and masculine concepts and thus can be called "gender schematic" in the sense that Bem uses the term.[42] Debate has ensued, and while both schools of thought offer important contributions to our understanding of the cognitive consequences of gender

---

38. Sandra L. Bem, "Gender Schema Theory: A Cognitive Account of Sex Typing," *Psychological Review* 88, no. 4 (1981): 354–64, esp. 363.

39. Ibid., p. 355.

40. Ibid., p. 363. See also Sandra Lipsitz Bem, "Gender Schema Theory and Its Implications for Child Development: Raising Gender-aschematic Children in a Gender-schematic Society," *Signs* 8, no. 4 (1983): 598–616.

41. Hazel Markus et al., "Self-Schemas and Gender," *Journal of Personality and Social Psychology* 42, no. 1 (1982): 38–50.

42. Marie Crane and Hazel Markus, "Gender Identity: The Benefits of a Self-Schema Approach," *Journal of Personality and Social Psychology* 43, no. 6 (1982): 1195–97.

Signs   Autumn 1985   113

identity, they have not explained how the divergence in their theories might lead to significantly different consequences.[43] Future work by these authors or by others may answer this question and ought to bring about some integration of the two theories.

Moral Development

Carol Gilligan's work on female moral development challenges that of some of the giants in developmental psychology.[44] Gilligan is concerned with the diverging moral conceptions that arise from the sex differences in identity development posited by Nancy Chodorow, who argues that masculinity is defined through separation while femininity is defined through attachment.[45] Gilligan points out that mainstream theories of moral development were built around masculine models and male experience, emphasizing separation as the criterion of growth and holding up a model of maturation that does not involve a progression of relationships toward a state of interdependence. Deriving her theory by starting with women and listening to them talk about their lives led to a quite different model, Gilligan claims: "In this conception, the moral problem arises from conflicting responsibilities rather than from competing rights and requires for its resolution a mode of thinking that is contextual and narrative rather than formal and abstract. This conception . . . centers moral development around the understanding of responsibility and relationships, as the conception of morality as fairness ties moral development to the understanding of rights and rules."[46]

Gilligan's criticisms of mainstream developmental psychology theories are useful and sound, and many find that her description of sex differences in moral reasoning rings true. Unfortunately, her conclusions can be taken to support traditional sex stereotypes. In the enthusiasm for her work—especially among those outside psychology, where she has had most appeal—one hears echoes of the initial uncritical acceptance given to such hypotheses as fear of success and androgyny. A full assessment of her ideas will require further research,[47] but if her perceptions have

43. Ibid.; Sandra L. Bem, "Gender Schema Theory and Self-Schema Theory Compared: A Comment on Markus, Crane, Bernstein, and Siladi's 'Self-Schemas and Gender,'" *Journal of Personality and Social Psychology* 43, no. 6 (1982): 1192–94.

44. Carol Gilligan, *In a Different Voice: Psychological Theory and Women's Development* (Cambridge, Mass.: Harvard University Press, 1982).

45. Nancy Chodorow, *The Reproduction of Mothering: Psychoanalysis and the Sociology of Gender* (Berkeley: University of California Press, 1978).

46. Gilligan, p. 19.

47. For a criticism of one basis of Gilligan's theory, see Cynthia Benton et al., "Is Hostility Linked with Affiliation among Males and with Achievement among Females? A Critique of Pollak and Gilligan," *Journal of Personality and Social Psychology* 45, no. 5 (1983): 1167–71.

brought new life and interest to a field in which humans are still unconsciously assumed to be male, we will all benefit.

Communication

Studies of language and gender, focusing on sex bias in language, on the one hand, and sex difference in language use, on the other, are slowly gaining more attention within psychology. In the recent sex-bias literature, the work of Wendy Martyna and Donald MacKay deserves special notice for demonstrating the failure of such masculine forms as "he" and "mankind" to evoke thoughts or images of females, and for examining the circumstances under which masculine or alternative forms are likely to be used as generics.[48]

In the area of sex difference in language usage, all that can be concluded at present is that the hypotheses of Robin Lakoff are still being tested;[49] research has not consistently verified the existence of a "woman's language" or "female register," although certain differences in conversational style, such as greater incidence of interruption by males, seem well demonstrated. Such topics have been covered in several essays in *Signs*, and readers should consult those essays and others for reviews of the literature.[50]

Several significant works reviewing the relation of gender to nonverbal behavior have appeared in the past few years: Erving Goffman's *Gender Advertisements*; Marianne Wex's *Let's Take Back Our Space*; and *Gender and Nonverbal Behavior*, edited by Clara Mayo and Nancy Henley.[51] Judith Hall's reviews of research in this area, as well as those of Robert Rosenthal and Bella DePaulo and of Henley and Marianne LaFrance, provide good overviews of and points of entry into this field.[52]

48. Wendy Martyna, "The Psychology of the Generic Masculine," in *Women and Language in Literature and Society*, ed. Sally McConnell-Ginet, Ruth Borker, and Nelly Furman (New York: Praeger Publishers, 1980), pp. 69–78; Donald G. MacKay, "Prescriptive Grammar and the Pronoun Problem," in *Language, Gender and Society*, ed. Barrie Thorne, Cheris Kramarae, and Nancy Henley (Rowley, Mass.: Newbury House, 1983), pp. 38–53. For a review of such studies, see Jeanette Silveira, "Generic Masculine Words and Thinking," *Women's Studies International Quarterly* 3, nos. 2/3 (1980): 165–78.

49. Robin Lakoff, *Language and Woman's Place* (New York: Harper & Row, 1975).

50. See, e.g., Cheris Kramarae, Barrie Thorne, and Nancy Henley, "Review Essay: Perspectives on Language and Communication," *Signs* 3, no. 3 (1978): 638–51; and Thorne, Kramarae and Henley, eds. (n. 48 above).

51. Erving Goffman, *Gender Advertisements* (New York: Harper & Row, 1979); Marianne Wex, *Let's Take Back Our Space: "Female" and "Male" Body Language as a Result of Patriarchal Structures* (Hamburg: Frauenliteraturverlag Hermine Fees, 1979); Clara Mayo and Nancy M. Henley, eds., *Gender and Nonverbal Behavior* (New York: Springer-Verlag, 1981).

52. Judith A. Hall, "Gender Effects in Decoding Nonverbal Cues," *Psychological Bulletin* 85 (1978): 845–57, and "Gender, Gender-Roles and Nonverbal Communication," in *Skill in*

Signs   Autumn 1985   115

Masculinity, Male Identity, and Sex Role Strain

The growing field of men's studies has generated numerous publications of interest in recent years—including the annotated bibliography of Kathleen Grady, Robert Brannon, and Joseph Pleck; the special issue of *The Family Coordinator* on "Men's Roles in the Family," edited by Robert Lewis and Pleck; James Doyle's textbook *The Male Experience*; Barbara Ehrenreich's *The Hearts of Men*; and the *Men's Studies Newsletter*.[53] Of most theoretical importance to psychology, however, is Pleck's *The Myth of Masculinity*, in which the author identifies the unstated assumptions that have guided previous work on masculinity and examines their validity.[54]

According to Pleck, these assumptions together define the "Male Sex Role Identity" (MSRI) paradigm, which primarily contends "that sex roles develop from within, rather than being arbitrarily imposed from without"; that "appropriate sex role identity" is necessary to good psychological adjustment; that males have particular difficulty with development of this identity; and that "problems of sex role identity" are used to explain such phenomena as homosexuality, exaggerated masculinity, school difficulties, the problems of Black men, and negative male attitudes and behaviors toward women. The paradigm further states that historical changes have made the risky business of developing and maintaining masculine identity more difficult.

The remainder of *The Myth of Masculinity* exposes the flimsy research, self-fulfilling prophecies, flawed logic, and wishful thinking that have largely gone to make the MSRI model. As an alternative, Pleck presents a paradigm of Sex Role Strain (SRS). Unlike the MSRI paradigm, which is based on sex-typing measures (e.g., masculinity/femininity scales), the SRS model defines sex roles by societal stereotypes and norms. According to this model, sex roles are constricting, contradictory, inconsistent, and dysfunctional. They are frequently violated; however, since violation

---

Nonverbal Communication: Individual Differences, ed. Robert Rosenthal (Cambridge, Mass.: Oelgeschlager, Gunn & Hain, 1979); Robert Rosenthal and Bella M. DePaulo, "Sex Differences in Accommodation in Nonverbal Communication," in Rosenthal, ed.; Nancy M. Henley and Marianne LaFrance, "Gender as Culture: Difference and Dominance in Nonverbal Behavior," in *Nonverbal Behavior: Perspectives, Applications, Intercultural Insights*, ed. Aaron Wolfgang (Toronto: C. J. Hogrefe, 1984), pp. 351–71.

53. Kathleen E. Grady, Robert Brannon, and Joseph H. Pleck, *The Male Sex Role: A Selected and Annotated Bibliography* (Rockville, Md.: National Institute of Mental Health, 1979); *The Family Coordinator*, vol. 28, no. 4 (October 1979), ed. Robert A. Lewis and Joseph H. Pleck; James A. Doyle, *The Male Experience* (Dubuque, Iowa: William C. Brown, 1983); Barbara Ehrenreich, *The Hearts of Men: American Dreams and the Flight from Commitment* (Garden City, N. Y.: Anchor/Doubleday, 1983). Information on the *Men's Studies Newsletter* may be obtained from Harry Brod, Editor, SWMS–THH331, University of Southern California, Los Angeles, California 90089–4352.

54. Pleck (n. 1 above), esp. pp. 4–5, 8–9.

leads to negative social and psychological consequences (more so for males than for females), people tend to overconform to them. Sex role strain is felt (by both men and women) in paid work and family roles, and is particularly exacerbated by historical change.

The SRS model has not been articulated as thoroughly as the MSRI, but this may be because of the extensive literature detailing the MSRI and its entrenched ideology. Pleck's book is valuable in that it presents these opposing viewpoints systematically and offers as well critical appendices on the biological bases of male aggression and of weak paternal involvement in child rearing and a compendium of resources for male role studies.

Pornography and Aggression against Women

Extensive research has been focused on pornography and aggression against women and the links between them. *Pornography and Sexual Aggression*, edited by Neil Malamuth and Edward Donnerstein, provides a good overview of the findings.[55] An important contribution of this research has been to clarify distinctions between forms of pornography and erotica and to differentiate their effects. Donnerstein and others have found in their research that nonaggressive erotic materials have very little influence on aggressive male attitudes and behaviors toward women.[56] However, materials that show male aggression (often rape) in the context of heterosexual activity have a very different effect.

Neil Malamuth has investigated both cultural and individual factors and has concluded that both contribute to aggression against women; that is, that some men (for whatever reason) have greater propensity to rape than others and that cultural materials such as pornography can contribute to men's aggressive tendencies toward women.[57] In his research on cultural causes, Malamuth has found, for example, that males exposed to aggressive pornography subsequently created more aggressive sexual fantasies than did those exposed to depictions of mutually consenting sex; that males' aggressiveness against women has increased after viewing aggressive pornography, especially if the woman is depicted as sexually aroused or if the male has been angered; and that exposure to commercial films showing sexual aggression with the female sexually aroused increased males' (but not females') acceptance of interpersonal violence

55. Neil M. Malamuth and Edward Donnerstein, eds., *Pornography and Sexual Aggression* (New York: Academic Press, 1984).

56. Edward Donnerstein, "Pornography: Its Effect on Violence against Women," in ibid. pp. 53–81.

57. Neil M. Malamuth, "Agression against Women: Cultural and Individual Causes," in Malamuth and Donnerstein, eds., pp. 19–52. Studies mentioned in this paragraph are described and cited fully in that chapter.

Signs   *Autumn 1985*   *117*

against women and acceptance of rape myths. Pornography's tendency to portray women enjoying rape makes all the more frightening the finding that such portrayal increases male propensity for violence against women.

The work of Pleck and that of Malamuth and Donnerstein exemplify two approaches in the growing literature on the psychology of masculinity, one predominantly theoretical and the other experimental. It is hard to find an explicit, or even implicit but nontrivial, link between them. The theory does not explain the observed behavior, nor does the behavior illustrate the theory. Future work may build stronger connections and help to develop an integrated psychology of masculinity.

Race and Ethnicity

Most of the literature examined in this review does not address issues of specific concern to women of color (and most likely was developed without their participation). The psychology of women of racial and ethnic minorities is in a stage of development similar to that of psychology of gender in its early years; there are few articles and no texts. Scholars must search far and wide for relevant publications and create their own research networks; instructors must build courses on minority women from photocopied readings from other fields as well as from psychology. Standard psychology of women texts have omitted or given small notice to concerns of minority women, although the newer texts are beginning to correct this problem: O'Leary's text includes a fine chapter by Algea Harrison on Black women; Hyde includes a chapter entitled "Black Women and Women as a Minority Group"; and Unger integrates research on minority women throughout her book. Cox's anthology gives full coverage to the diversity of women's experience, with a section including articles by and about Asian-American, Chicana, and Native-American as well as Black women.[58]

Division 35 has committees devoted to the concerns of Black, Hispanic, and Asian women, each following its own course, influenced in part by how each culture views psychology. Relevant publications include directories of Black and Hispanic women in psychology and a bibliography on Black women. A bibliography on Hispanic women is in preparation.[59] The bibliography on Black women, compiled by Vickie

58. O'Leary, pp. 131–46; Hyde, pp. 271–91; Unger; Cox, ed., pp. 108–55 (all in n. 6 above). "Black" is capitalized in this section for consistency with other racial groups.

59. Information on the "Directory of Black Women in Psychology" may be obtained from Pamela Reid, Department of Psychology, University of Tennessee, Chattanooga, Tennessee 37402. The "Directory of Hispanic Women in Psychology" may be obtained without charge by sending a self-addressed mailing label to the Women's Programs Office, American Psychological Association, 1200 17th St., N.W., Washington, D. C. 20036. See *Bibliographic Guide to Research Materials on Black Women in the Social Sciences and Mental Health* (New York: Praeger Publishers, in press).

Mays, also includes reviews of current work, lists of periodical resources, and discussion of strategies for researching Black women.

In Black feminist psychology, more sophisticated conceptualizations of the interaction between race and gender are beginning to replace earlier models that described Black women's lives as a composite of the Black and female experiences. In 1982, a special issue of *Psychology of Women Quarterly* on Black women appeared, edited by Saundra Rice Murray and Patricia Bell Scott.[60] This collection covers such topics as adolescent development, professional identity, fear of success, inter-role conflict, and political commitment.

As more networks and resources emerge, as sparsely funded research projects continue, and as scholars focusing on various ethnic groups examine the commonalities and differences among them, those surveying the field will be able to report a better developed psychology, or psychologies, of minority women.

Conclusion

As the psychology of gender matures as an area of study, much changes—its terms, its topics, its methods, its concepts.[61] Cognitive sex differences, masculinity, and ethnic minorities have entered the list of topics in the field; meta-analysis, little used several years ago, is now an

60. *PWQ*, vol. 6, no. 3 (Spring 1982).

61. Space does not permit review of the following work in important areas of the psychology of gender. On the menstrual cycle, see Alice Dan, Effie Graham, and Carol Beecher, eds., *The Menstrual Cycle*, vol. 1, *A Synthesis of Interdisciplinary Research* (New York: Springer, 1980); Pauline Komnenich, ed., *The Menstrual Cycle*, vol. 2, *Research and Implications for Women's Health* (New York: Springer-Verlag, 1981); Sharon Golub, ed., *Menarche: The Transition from Girl to Woman* (Lexington, Mass.: Lexington Books/D. C. Heath, 1983). On the history of gender issues in psychology, see Stephanie Shields, "The Variability Hypothesis: The History of a Biological Model of Sex Differences in Intelligence," *Signs* 7, no. 4 (1982): 769–97. On sex differences in influenceability, see Alice H. Eagly and Linda L. Carli, "Sex of Researchers and Sex-typed Communications as Determinants of Sex Differences in Influenceability: A Meta-Analysis of Social Influence Studies," *Psychological Bulletin* 90, no. 1 (1981): 1–20. On stereotypes, see Kay Deaux and Laurie Lewis, "Structure of Gender Stereotypes: Interrelationships among Components and Gender Labels," *Journal of Personality and Social Psychology* 46, no. 5 (1984): 991–1004. On relationships, sexuality, and gender, see Elizabeth R. Allgeier and Naomi B. McCormick, eds., *Changing Boundaries: Gender Roles and Sexual Behavior* (Palo Alto, Calif.: Mayfield Publishing Co., 1983). For other current reviews of the psychology of women, sex, and gender, see Kay Deaux, "Sex and Gender," *Annual Review of Psychology* (in press); Janet T. Spence, Kay Deaux, and Robert L. Helmreich, "Sex Roles in Contemporary American Society," in *Handbook of Social Psychology*, ed. Gardner Lindzey and Elliot Aronson (Reading, Mass.: Addison-Wesley, in press); and Barbara Strudler Wallston, "Social Psychology of Women and Gender," *Journal of Applied Social Psychology* (in press).

Signs   Autumn 1985   119

important aspect of several areas of inquiry;[62] and conceptions like masculinity, femininity, and androgyny undergo continual rethinking.

Critiques of male bias in psychology continue; but more recently psychologists of gender have cast their critical vision beyond blatant bias to seek out underlying problems in psychological methodology and positivist science itself.[63] The most recent presidents of Division 35 have joined earlier voices in the field in raising these deeper questions about values, methodology, and positivism.[64] Unger in particular argues from a feminist perspective against the unacknowledged assumptions of positivism and for a reflexive or dialectical psychology—a psychology with values that sees the reciprocal influence of "subject" and "experimenter" in research. Thus feminist psychology attempts to move from a compensatory and revisionist approach toward one that is transformative.

That there has been development within psychology is obviously true; however, that growth has been inhibited because psychologists of women and gender have seldom brought broader feminist theory into their work.[65] Discussions that have occupied the feminist scholarly community—for example, discussions of Chodorow's or Michel Foucault's theories,[66] topics that should be of interest to psychologists—get little if any attention in feminist psychological writings. We can hope that with further growth and changes in the field will come both a more rigorous testing of new concepts and greater interdisciplinary theoretical sophistication.

Department of Psychology
University of California, Los Angeles

62. See Tresemer (n. 9 above); Hyde (n. 20 above); and Eagly and Carli.

63. On this point, see also Parlee, "Review Essay: Psychology and Women" (n. 2 above).

64. Carolyn W. Sherif, "Male Bias in Psychology," in *The Prism of Sex: Essays in the Sociology of Knowledge*, ed. Julia A. Sherman and Evelyn T. Beck (Madison: University of Wisconsin Press, 1979), pp. 93–133; Barbara S. Wallston, "What Are the Questions in Psychology of Women? A Feminist Approach to Research," *PWQ* 5, no. 4 (1981): 597–617; Rhoda K. Unger, "Through the Looking Glass: No Wonderland Yet! (The Reciprocal Relationship between Methodology and Models of Reality)," *PWQ* 8, no. 1 (1983): 9–32; Michele A. Wittig, "Metatheoretical Dilemmas in the Psychology of Gender," *American Psychologist* (in press); Mary Brown Parlee, "Appropriate Control Groups in Feminist Research," *PWQ* 5, no 4 (1981): 637–44.

65. See Judith Stacey and Barrie Thorne, "The Missing Feminist Revolution in Sociology," *Social Problems* (in press), on the reasons for the failure of sociology, as well as psychology, political science, and economics, to incorporate feminist theory.

66. Chodorow (n. 45 above); Michel Foucault, *The History of Sexuality* (New York: Random House, 1978), vol. 1.

[6]

DEVELOPMENTAL REVIEW 1, 266–273 (1981)

Methodological Issues in the Study
of Sex-Related Differences

CAROL NAGY JACKLIN

Stanford University

Ten ubiquitous methodological problems are described in relation to group differences research and particularly sex-related research. Substantive issues in sex-related research are used as illustrations of the methodological problems.

A number of methodological issues arise in the study of sex-related differences, and indeed in the study of all group differences. These issues will be listed and then discussed more fully in the context of cognitive and social sex-related differences. Although substantive findings will be used to illustrate methodological points, a substantive review is not intended.

The methodological issues in the study of sex-related differences include: (1) conceptualization of the term "difference," (2) failure to distinguish the significance of an effect from the size of an effect, (3) bias toward positive findings in the publishing, abstracting, indexing, citing, and reprinting of results, (4) confusion of within-sex differences with between-sex differences, (5) assuming that all sex-related differences are expressions of genetic or innate differences, (6) confusion of sex-of-stimuli effects with sex-of-subject effects, (7) interaction of sex-of-experimenter effects with sex-of-subject effects, (8) disregard of systematic differences in self-report of males and females, (9) reliance upon a narrow data base in terms of subject characteristics from which most sex-related differences are generalized, (10) the number of variables confounded with sex which make comparisons of sex difficult.

(1) The conceptualization of "difference" poses an immediate problem. A "difference" implies a contrast, something that distinguishes individuals or groups. However, when group differences are described in the social sciences, the characteristics usually do not distinguish most of the members of one group from most of the members of the comparison group. Typically only a few subjects of one group are different from the subjects of the other group. Rough-and-tumble play is a case in point.

One of the largest sex-related differences reported is rough-and-tumble play. In one study (DiPietro, 1981), 15 to 20% of the boys scored higher

An earlier version of this paper was given as a Master Lecture at the Annual Meeting of the American Psychological Association, New York, September 1979. Special thanks to Joanne Zidek and Ruth Prehn for their careful work on this manuscript. Requests for reprints should be sent to: Dr. Carol Nagy Jacklin, Department of Psychology, Stanford University, Stanford, CA 94305.

0273-2297/81/030266-08$02.00/0

than any of the girls. Although this is an unusually large group difference, it is concurrently the case that 80 to 85% of the boys are indistinguishable from 80 to 85% of the girls. One would certainly conclude that rough-and-tumble play is a sex-related difference. Nonetheless, focusing on 80% of the two populations seems as sensible as focusing on 20% which the word "difference" demands.

(2) A related methodological issue is the lack of information given in research articles on the size of group difference effects. The significance of an effect and the size of the significance statistic are still the coin of the social science realm. However, if a group difference is a significance difference, it is largely a function of sample size. With large enough samples, any group-mean difference will be significant (some published examples are tabled in Jacklin, 1979). What we need to determine and emphasize is how large a sex-related difference is. The size of a sex-related effect tells what can be predicted about an individual's behavior if one knows that individual's gender. Unless one has a measure of the size of the difference as well as its significance, very little is gained in predictive ability.

In an attempt to measure just how much predictive power is gained by sex in some established sex-related differences, Plomin and Foch (1981) did a large-scale measurement of the size of effect for verbal and quantitative abilities. Using the Maccoby and Jacklin (1974) tables on verbal abilities, they computed point biserial correlations for 26 studies representing 85,619 scores over 67,000 children. They found that the sex difference in verbal ability accounted for only 1% of the variance. Plomin and Foch succinctly state: "If all we know about a child is the child's sex, we know next to nothing about the child's verbal ability." Similarly, for the 292,574 children's scores listed in Maccoby and Jacklin's tables on quantitative ability, sex accounts for only 4% of the variance. Clearly, effect size must be distinguished from statistical significance. Recently, some attention has been given to detailed descriptions of distributions in sex-related differences (Favreau & Lépine, 1981; Kail, Carter, & Pellegrino, 1979) and size-of-effect discussions are increasing (Hyde, in press). However, until journal editors strongly encourage size-of-effect statistics, their use is unlikely to become widespread.

(3) A third serious issue in studies of sex-related differences is the bias toward publishing, abstracting, indexing, citing, and reprinting positive findings. If a positive instance is found, it is much easier to publish; it is more likely to be reprinted; it gets into the abstracts. In short, it becomes a part of the literature. Although it is possible to get negative results (or sex similarities) into the literature, it is very difficult. The institutionalizing of a rubric like "sex similarities" or "sex-unrelated characteristics" would go a long way in rectifying this problem. If one could easily publish

findings of similarities and if they were abstracted and indexed, these
nondifferences would also become the material for summaries of sex-
related differences. However, highlighting a nondifference or null finding
is contrary to the traditional approach to science. Rejection of the null
hypothesis is used to determine whether we actually have done the study
correctly. A finding of no difference can always be attributed to problems
in the study and often should be so attributed. Unfortunately, negative
instances, particularly nonreplications, are as important in sorting out
true group differences as positive instances. Rosenthal (1979) has called
this the "file drawer problem" and has tried to quantify it. Actively retrieving negative results is difficult but necessary even before one can
determine how big the "file drawer problem" really is.

(4) A glaring, but common, error is generalizing from a *within-sex*-
difference finding to a *between-sex*-difference conclusion. One example is
overgeneralization of current laterality data. Witelson (1977) found male
dyslexics less lateralized than males who are not dyslexic. However, a
recent study has not replicated this work (Cioffi & Kondels, 1979). The
Witelson work did not demonstrate a sex-related difference; only boy
dyslexics were studied. Yet that study has been used to explain sex-
related differences (e.g., see McGee, 1979). Boys who were not dyslexic,
it is argued, have an advantage over girls, because boys, in general, are
more lateralized than girls. We have no evidence to date relating laterality
and cognitive abilities in girls. And since there are very few dyslexic girls,
the argument from general laterality differences seems prima facie absurd.
Various sources do seem to indicate that girls and women, on the average,
are less lateralized for a number of tasks than boys and men. If a female
has massive brain damage, she is much more likely to recover than a male
who has the same damage (e.g., Bryden, 1979; McGlone & Davidson,
1972). If females are somewhat more robust in surviving brain damage, it
may be (as McGlone and others have argued) that females are more likely
to have the same functions on both sides of the brain. What has not yet
been demonstrated, but continues to be alleged, is a relationship between
laterality and cognitive ability for males *and* females.

Another example of an erroneous generalization from a within-sex to a
between-sex difference comes from studies using the menstrual cycle as a
response measure. Certainly it is not possible to demonstrate a sex-
related difference (or similarity) if the menstrual cycle is the response
measure or if any response measure is used with only subjects of one sex.
However, conclusions are often drawn about women's (as opposed to
men's) hormone/mood relationships, or pheromone sensitivity, or cycle
shift. If some other response measure is used the same questions can and
have been studied in males. For example, some work has found roughly a
28-day cycle length (Doering, Brodie, Kraemer, Becker, and Hamburg,

1974; Doering, Brodie, Kraemer, Moos, Becker, and Hamburg, 1975) in male testosterone measured from plasma. In half the males hormone and mood covary.

This methodological problem is fairly obvious when studies using only one gender are used as explanations of sex-related differences. More subtle variants of the same problem exist for studies which do have data on both males and females. Inappropriate conclusions from some statistical procedures make the same within-sex/between-sex confusion. For example, in studies of intellectual performance, many current researchers (Leibowitz, 1974; Engle, Yarbrough, Townsend, Klein, & Irwin, 1979; Howell & Frese, 1979) use multivariate regression analysis on data of both boys and girls. However, all of these investigations use separate regressions for each gender. And when they obtain a significant beta weight for one sex but not the other, they erroneously conclude they have found sex differences. When a variable is found to be significantly related to the intellectual performance in the regression equation of one sex but not the other, a sex-related difference has *not* been established. In order to establish a sex-related difference, one must show that two variables (as an example, parental education and intellectual performance) have a *significantly different relation* for boys than they do for girls. This can only be established if both sexes are included in the same regression equation.

There is a simpler version of this error: demonstrating a significant correlation between two variables for one sex but not the other and then concluding that a sex-related difference has been found. For example, finding mother's behavior is significantly correlated with son's behavior but not with daughter's. Only when significant differences *between* correlations of males and females are found, can one conclude rightly that a sex-related difference has been established.

(5) A striking logical error is assuming the *cause* of a sex-related difference is genetic once the existence of a sex-related difference is established. A recent example is a study of the mathematical ability of seventh-grade boys and girls (Bendow & Stanley, 1981). In this study of children who volunteered to take an advanced math test, boys were found to have the highest scores. (The problem of sampling boys and girls from volunteers will be discussed below.) The authors state that ''sex differences in achievement in and attitude toward mathematics result from superior male mathematical ability.'' Although the definition of ''ability'' is not given, the context suggests a genetic component. This is particularly surprising since no genetic evidence has been found to be related to math and math-related abilities in direct tests of the genetic hypothesis (see Vanderberg & Kuse, 1979, for a review). Moreover, although the seventh-grade boys and girls had had the same number of mathematics classes, there is considerable work showing differences in classroom

270   CAROL NAGY JACKLIN

feedback to boys and girls from nursery school through grade school (e.g., Serbin, O'Leary, Kent, & Tonick, 1973; Dweck & Bush, 1976; Dweck, Davidson, Nelson, & Enna, 1978). Finding out whether some characteristic is or is not a sex-related difference is the first step before trying to understand the cause of the difference. However, too often the documentation of a difference is seen as evidence that a natural, genetic, unchangeable sex-related difference has been established.

(6) Sex-of-stimuli effects have often been confused with sex-of-subject effects. Blatant examples are the use of "male" and "female" versions of a test. Some versions of the Thematic Apperception Test (TAT) give stories or pictures of girls to girl subjects and stories or pictures of boys to boy subjects. A famous example using a modified TAT test is the Horner (1968) "Fear of Success" study. In that study, men are asked to complete a story which starts "John is the top of his Medical School Class," and women are asked to complete a story starting "Ann is the top of her Medical School Class." In these cases, different stimuli are presented to the sexes, yet conclusions are made about sex-related differences. If the sexes are to be compared, both stories must be given to both sexes. When this is done, there are no sex-of-subject differences, although consistent sex-of-stimuli differences are found (Monahan, Kuhn, & Shaver, 1974).

(7) The sex of the experimenter may be another confound in the design of a study. If the experimenter's sex produces an effect which happens to interact with the sex of the subject but that interaction is not measured, then there will appear to be a sex-of-subject effect when none actually exists. Classical conditioning of the eye-blink response is a case in point. A sex difference has been reported in eye-blink conditioning. However, being highly anxious produces faster eye-blink conditioning (see Spence & Spence, 1966, for a review). Eye-blink conditioning is often carried out with elaborate equipment in dark rooms with male experimenters. Some anxiety is probably produced in all subjects. If the anxiety level is raised differently for male and female subjects, a sex-related difference will be found. Attributing the difference to a conditioning difference will be a mistake.

(8) Another methodological confound exists with data obtained by self-report. In general, males are more defensive when filling out self-reports than are females (e.g., Lekarcyzk & Hill, 1969; Williams & Byars, 1968). For example, boys do not disclose their thoughts and personal feelings either to parents or peers as much as do girls (Riverbark, 1971). Since there is a sex-related difference in the willingness and/or ability to be candid on self-report measures, their use must be suspect in trying to establish sex-related differences in personal attributes. Self-report may be the only possible way to study many aspects of adult feelings and behavior, but concern for the bias that this type of data collection produces

must be taken into account. We should either attempt to estimate the defensiveness of subjects or attempt to validate the self-report measures more extensively than has been done.

(9) As in other areas of psychological research, there is a clear restrictedness of the subject characteristics used in sex-related research. White, upper-middle-class, educated, largely Anglo-Saxon populations are disproportionately used, while generalizations are erroneously made to all. The availability of college students as subjects in psychological research will probably continue the practice of nonrepresentativeness of the research population to the general population. Still, sex-related differences found for this population may not be found generally.

(10) Probably the most pervasive problem in sex-related research is the number of variables that are confounded with sex. It is difficult to find populations on which sex-only comparisons can be made. As an extreme example, if Army generals and their wives were used as subjects in a study and sex comparisons were made, they would match on many characteristics but would be unmatched on many others.

One longitudinal study of males and females, The Terman Genius Study, has been unusual in that the researchers were aware of the confounds with sex and wrote about them. In the initial identification of the gifted children, Miles (1954) notes two problems: teachers nominated more boys than girls for the tests, and gifted boys were more likely to volunteer to take the tests than gifted girls. The researchers compensated for this tendency since when all boys and girls are tested equal numbers of genii-range scores are found. (Surprisingly, Bendow and Stanley (1981) used volunteers as their subject pool and then made sex-differences comparisons.) In the Terman sample disproportionate numbers of males received college and graduate school education and in adulthood had higher-paying and higher-prestige jobs than females. However, Bayley and Oden (1955) were able to demonstrate that in the Terman data, occupation not sex accounted for IQ changes over the life span.

Problems of sampling appropriately matched males and females may be less obvious in cross-sectional studies. College students, for example, are likely to have had different numbers of high school math classes and are therefore suspect for cognitive sex-difference comparisons.

With fewer variables confounded with sex, sex will account for smaller percentages of variance. Thus, paradoxically the better the sex-related research, the less useful sex is as an explanatory variable. In the best controlled sex-related research, sex may account for no variance at all. This may force researchers to stop focusing upon and trying to explain the trivially small amounts of variance accounted for by group differences, and start trying to explain the vast variance between individuals within the groups.

272   CAROL NAGY JACKLIN

There are psychological dimensions on which one can find statistically significant differences between males and females. And findings of sex differences and interest in sex-related research may have helped change the tradition in psychology of considering individual differences as error variance. However, from all indications thus far, there are many more psychologically interesting ways in which males and females differ from other males and females. It may be time to turn our scientific attention to the search for these variables.

REFERENCES

Bayley, N., & Oden, M. The maintenance of intellectual ability in gifted adults. *Journal of Gerontology*, 1955, 10, 91–107.

Bendow, C. P., & Stanley, J. C. Sex differences in mathematical ability: Fact or artifact? *Science*, 1980, 210, 1262–1264.

Bryden, P. Evidence for sex differences in cerebral organization. In M. A. Witting & A. C. Petersen (Eds.), *Sex-related differences in cognitive functioning: Developmental issues*. New York: Academic Press, 1979.

Cioffi, J., & Kondels, G. Laterality of stereognostic accuracy of children for words, shapes, and bigrams: A sex difference for bigrams. *Science*, 1979, 204, 1432–1434.

DiPietro, J. A. Rough and tumble play: A function of gender. *Developmental Psychology*, 1981, 17, 50–58.

Doering, C. H., Brodie, H. K. H., Kraemer, H. C., Becker, H. B., & Hamburg, D. A. Plasma testosterone levels and psychologic measures in men over a 2-month period. In R. C. Friedman, R. M. Richart, & R. L. Vande Wiele (Eds.), *Sex differences in behavior*. New York: Wiley, 1974.

Doering, C. H., Brodie, H. K. H., Kraemer, H. C., Moos, R. H., Becker, H. B., & Hamburg, D. A. Negative affect and plasma testosterone: A longitudinal human study. *Psychosomatic Medicine*, 1975, 37, 484–491.

Dweck, C. S., & Bush, E. S. Sex differences in learned helplessness. I. Differential debilitation with peer and adult evaluators. *Developmental Psychology*, 1976, 12, 147–156.

Dweck, C. S., Davidson, W., Nelson, S., & Enna, B. Sex differences in learned helplessness. II. The contingencies of evaluative feedback in the classroom. III. An experimental analysis. *Developmental Psychology*, 1978, 14, 268–276.

Engle, P. L., Yarbrough, C., Townsend, J., Klein, R. E., & Irwin, M. *Sex differences in the effects of nutrition and social class on mental development in rural Guatemala*. Guatemala: INCAP, 1979.

Favreau, O. E., & Lépine, L. *Spatial abilities: What is a sex difference?* Submitted for publication, 1981.

Horner, M. S. *Sex differences in achievement motivation and performance in competitive and noncompetitive situations*. Unpublished doctoral dissertation, University of Michigan, 1968.

Howell, F. M., & Frese, W. Race, sex, and aspirations: Evidence for the "Race Convergence" hypothesis. *Sociology of Education*, 1979, 52, 34–46.

Hyde, J. S. How large are cognitive gender differences? A meta-analysis using ω^2 and *d*. *American Psychologist*, in press.

Jacklin, C. N. Epilogue. In M. Witting & A. C. Petersen (Eds.), *Sex-related differences in cognitive functioning: Developmental issues*. New York: Academic Press, 1979.

Kail, R., Carter, P., & Pellegrino, J. The locus of sex differences in spatial ability. *Perception and Psychophysics*, 1979, 26, 182–186.

METHODOLOGICAL ISSUES   273

Leibowitz, A. Home investments in children. In T. W. Schultz (Ed.), *Economics of the family.* Chicago: Univ. of Chicago Press, 1974.

Lekarczyk, D. T., & Hill, K. T. Self-esteem, test anxiety, stress, and verbal learning. *Developmental Psychology,* 1969, 1, 147–154.

Maccoby, E. E., & Jacklin, C. N. *The psychology of sex differences.* Stanford, Calif.: Stanford Univ. Press, 1974.

McGee, M. G. Human spatial abilities: Psychometric studies and environmental, genetic, hormonal and neurological influences. *Psychological Bulletin,* 1979, 86, 889–918.

McGlone, J., & Davidson, W. The relationship between cerebral speech laterality and spatial ability with special reference to sex and hand preference. *Neuropsychologia,* 1972, 11, 105–113.

Miles, C. C. Gifted children. In L. Carmichael (Ed.), *Manual of child psychology* (2nd ed.). New York: Wiley, 1954.

Monahan, L., Kuhn, D., & Shaver, P. Intrapsychic versus cultural explanations of the "Fear of success" motive. *Journal of Personality and Social Psychology,* 1974, 29, 60–64.

Plomin, R., & Foch, T. T. Sex differences and individual differences. *Child Development,* 1981, 52, 383–385.

Riverbark, W. H. Self-disclosure among adolescents. *Psychological Reports,* 1971, 28, 35–42.

Rosenthal, R. The "file drawer problem" and tolerance for null results. *Psychological Bulletin,* 1979, 86, 638–640.

Serbin, L. A., O'Leary, K. D., Kent, R. N., & Tonick, I. J. A comparison of teacher response to the preacademic and problem behavior of boys and girls. *Child Development,* 1973, 44, 796–804.

Spence, K. W., & Spence, J. T. Sex and anxiety differences in eyelid conditioning. *Psychological Bulletin,* 1966, 65, 137–142.

Vandenberg, S. G., & Kuse, A. R. Spatial ability: A critical review of the sex-linked major gene hypothesis. In M. A. Wittig, & A. C. Petersen (Eds.), *Sex-related differences in cognitive functioning: Developmental issues.* New York: Academic Press, 1979.

Williams, T. M., & Byars, H. Negro self-esteem in a transitional society. *Personnel and Guidance Journal,* 1968, 47, 120–125.

Witelson, S. F. Neural and cognitive correlates of developmental dyslexia: age and sex differences. In C. Shagass, S. Gershon, & A. J. Friedhoff (Eds.), *Psychopathology and brain dysfunction.* New York: Raven Press, 1977.

RECEIVED: October 28, 1980; REVISED: May 29, 1981.

[7]

METAPHILOSOPHY
Vol. 12, Nos. 3 & 4, July/October 1981

IS THE SEX OF THE KNOWER EPISTEMOLOGICALLY SIGNIFICANT?

LORRAINE B. CODE

The purpose of this paper is primarily exploratory. I shall designate a number of ways in which the sex of the knower might be a significant factor in the knowledge-seeking process, and shall consider, briefly, the implications for theory of knowledge if this is so. The investigation arises out of a conviction that constraints upon the process will lead to constraints in the product: if the sex of the knower is a constraint in the process, the ensuing knowledge must be differently structured by, and differently accessible to, male and female knowers. I shall suggest directions in which answers might be sought to the problems I raise. But I do not, at this point, have fully elaborated solutions. These will be the subject of future writings on this question.

Knowledge is the product of the efforts of individual human knowers. At any point in history it has the form and content that it does because of the ways in which particular cognitive enterprises have yielded results which are accommodated within a growing body of knowledge. Human individuality is an important factor in the growth of knowledge: this is recognized in references, for example, to Pythagoras' theorem, to Copernicus' revolution, and to Newtonian and Einsteinian physics. The names commemorate the individuality of scientists who stand at the culmination of a particular knowledge-seeking process. By their efforts they have made possible a quantum-leap of progress in a particular field of investigation. In less spectacular ways other individuals contribute to the growth of knowledge.

One must ask, then, what aspects of human individuality can reasonably be declared epistemologically significant in the sense that they constitute conditions for the existence of knowledge, or in some way determine the kind of knowledge that can be achieved. Presumably individuals do not succeed in contributing to human knowledge because of such accidental physical attributes as height, weight, or hair colour. We do not, for example, consider how much Archimedes weighed when we accept the general applicability of his famous discovery. Nor do we doubt that a thinner or a fatter man could have reached the same conclusions. But it is not clear that maleness or femaleness, too, can be classified as accidental physical attributes similar to height, weight and hair colour. These may well be subjective factors which are influential in determining the form and content of knowledge. The fact of being male or being female seems to be fundamental to one's way of being a person in such a way that it could have a strong influence upon one's way of

LORRAINE B. CODE

knowing. The question is, then, whether there is knowledge which is, quite simply, beyond the range of the cognitive capacity of one or other half of the human race; whether there are kinds of knowledge which only men, or only women, can acquire.

Many kinds of knowledge and many skills have, historically speaking, been inaccessible for women from a purely practical point of view. Women were simply not permitted to learn. The problem for epistemology is to determine whether these practical impossibilities are also logical impossibilities. If they are, the answer to the question this paper poses must be an unqualified "yes". Here I do not take "logical possibility" in the extreme sense, as when one asks, for example, "If there were only one person in the world would it be logically possible to act morally?" I do not mean to ask whether, if women were *different*, it would be logically possible for them to know what men know; nor do I ask whether it would be logically possible for them to become different to the extent that . . . and so on. My purpose is, given the biological nature of the female human being, to ask whether it is logically possible for her to have certain kinds of knowledge hitherto designated strictly male. It is necessary to establish the limits of the process of socialization and to distinguish them from the limits of cognitive capacity.

In such discussion as there is of this matter in the history of philosophy the consensus seems to be that there is a basic qualitative difference between the kinds of knowledge which women can acquire and that which is accessible to men. Women's knowledge seems to be of an inferior sort, less controlled by reason, more determined by emotion, than that which men possess. For Aristotle it is man who is rational. Woman may be rational, but she cannot use her rationality with authority. Kierkegaard sees the attainment of the ethical and religious levels of existence to be open to men only; women are aesthetic beings. And for Nietzsche, the Apollonian is the male preserve; women are Dionysian creatures. The nineteenth century philosopher and linguist Wilhelm von Humboldt, who has written at some length about female knowledge, remarks:

> A sense of truth exists in (women) quite literally as a sense: their nature also contains a lack or a failing of analytic capacity which draws a strict line of demarcation between ego and world; therefore, they will not come as close to the ultimate investigation of truth as man.[1]

The view which emerges is that female knowledge is more subjective, less objective, than male knowledge. If this can be established, it is clearly an epistemologically significant point.

[1] From *Humanist Without Portfolio*, An Anthology of the Writings of Wilhelm von Humboldt. Translated from the German with an Introduction by Marianne Cowan. Detroit, Wayne State University Press, 1963, p. 349.

IS THE SEX OF THE KNOWER EPISTEMOLOGICALLY SIGNIFICANT?   269

These preliminary considerations make of the sex of the knower a special instance of a central problem which, I believe, runs through all epistemological enquiry. It is the problem of reconciling the necessarily subjective factors in all human knowledge with the need for objectivity in anything that is to count as knowledge. Human knowledge is knowledge of an independently existing reality whose nature sets limits upon what can be known. Yet the knowledge itself is the product of a combination of objective and subjective factors. The objective side, which serves as the foundation of knowledge at all other levels, consists in (1) a framework of constant expectations, of common-sense knowledge about the everyday behaviour of material objects and one's ability to deal with them on a practical level; (2) the biologically-determined nature of human cognitive equipment, which is reasonably constant from knower to knower, regardless of sex, and which dictates the kind and scope of knowledge human beings can acquire.

On the subjective side, firmly grounded within this objectivity, yet leading to a considerable degree of diversity within the unity of knowledge are (1) the individual creativity of the human knower, (2) the location of every knower within a period of history, (3) the location of every knower within a linguistic and cultural setting, and (4) the affective side of human nature (contrasted with its purely intellectual side). All of these factors contribute necessarily to the end product of the knowing process: the ensuing knowledge. I call them "subjective" because of their reference to the circumstances of the knowing subject.

In the domain I have designated objective, most differences between male and female knowledge can be attributed to socialization rather than to differences in cognitive capacity. At the level of basic knowledge it is men, generally speaking, who know how to start stalled cars; women who know how to mend torn garments. But this is a result of the kinds of skill men and women have been schooled to acquire. The fact that women, or men, do not habitually possess or exercise certain skills does not mean that they cannot, except where individual, trans-sexual explanations in terms of physical strength, coordination, or mental capacity can be found. In the changing climate of modern Western society many men and women are becoming skilled in those activities traditionally seen to belong to the opposite sex. This makes it plausible to suggest that knowledge of the fundamental, common-sense kind, is sexually differentiated more by virtue of practical expectations than of logical necessity. As more women become able to build bookcases and more men to make cakes, it becomes less feasible to suggest that these are simply statistically unusual members of their sex; more feasible to attribute such differences in practical knowledge to cultural imposition.

This claim is strengthened by investigations of the nature and development of human cognitive equipment such, for example, as Jean Piaget's genetic epistemology. Throughout his research Piaget uses male and female subjects interchangeably. His assumption is, clearly, that the

270   LORRAINE B. CODE

manner in which cognitive structuring takes place is identical in male and female human beings. This may well be a tacit assumption which Piaget himself has never questioned. I think, however, that it would be clear in the results of the research if the structuring of knowledge were necessarily differentiated according to the sex of the knower. But there is no evidence of such differentiation.[2]

Recent psychological research, however, seems to suggest that the brains of men and women are not identical, but specialized and designed to perform in somewhat different ways.[3] Women, the research suggests, are, on the average, better at verbal skills and fine coordination than men; and they have a greater ability to make rapid choices. They are not as good as men at so-called spatial skills such as mathematics, and the organization and mental rotation of subjects. Researchers suggest that this is because the areas that control language-function are in the left hemisphere of the male brain; those that control spatial functions are more on the right. Thus language and spatial functions do not interfere significantly with one another. But in women the functions of the brain appear to be distributed equally between the two hemispheres with the result that language and spatial functions are more likely to conflict with one another and to inhibit certain talents. Here we seem to have evidence that the sex of the knower is epistemologically significant, and is significant in an aspect of the knowledge-seeking situation which I have designated objective: the nature of human cognitive equipment. Such a conclusion should lead to a fundamental difference between male and female knowledge at all levels. Indeed it suggests that it may well be logically impossible for women, or men, to acquire certain kinds of knowledge.

However, I am not convinced that such conclusions are unequivocally warranted. It is plausible to suggest that even these seemingly fundamental differences can be attributed to cultural causes. In the first

[2] For a basic account of Piaget's position see Jean Piaget, *Genetic Epistemology*, translated by Eleanor Duckworth. New York, W.W. Norton and Co. Inc., 1971. This position is elaborated throughout Piaget's other works. In her study, "In a Different Voice: Women's Conceptions of Self and Morality" (*Harvard Educational Review*, Vol. 47, No. 4, 1977), Carol Gilligan points out that Piaget's studies of the rules of children's games reveal girls to be 1) less explicit about agreement, less concerned with legal elaboration than boys; 2) more pragmatic in their attitude to rules than boys, willing to accept a rule if the rewards are clear; 3) more tolerant of innovation than boys. (cf. J. Piaget, *The Moral Judgement of the Child*, New York: The Free Press, 1968.) Since the question of whether moral knowledge is possible is beyond the scope of the paper, I shall not proceed to assess the significance of these findings for theory of knowledge. I mention them to indicate Piaget's awareness of sex differences as potentially significant in his research.

[3] See, for example, "Brains and Sex" by Robert Sheppard in *The Globe and Mail*, Science Section, Toronto, Ontario, March 6, 1979. This is a report of research in progress on this topic in hospitals and universities in Montreal, Toronto, Hamilton, and London, Ontario.

IS THE SEX OF THE KNOWER EPISTEMOLOGICALLY SIGNIFICANT?   271

place, scientists allow that these differences in the brain itself are not observable; that it is more a matter of brains controlling certain processes in sexually-differentiated areas and ways. Secondly, there is persuasive evidence to indicate that the brain develops its powers by practice.[4] The brain of an animal presented with a wide variety of tasks and of stimuli develops strikingly greater performance capacity than one in a more impoverished environment. Thirdly, it has been demonstrated that musical ability, for example, which was believed to be a right-hemisphere characteristic, can become a right-*and* left-hemisphere function, with increased sophistication in performance, understanding and sensitivity, if musical education is begun at an early age.[5] It is thus possible that differences in male and female brains can be attributed to cultural causes such as the sex-stereotyping of children's activities, and the likelihood that parental attitudes differ to children of different sexes, even from earliest infancy. One can argue plausibly that the nature of human cognitive equipment remains an objective factor in all human knowledge. But it may well become a sexually-differentiated factor as a result of socialization and thus, from a practical point of view, make the sex of the knower epistemologically significant in the sense I have indicated. But it is not irrevocably so.

On the subjective side, the individual creativity of the human knower is a centrally determining factor in all human knowledge. Kant's concept of the creative synthesis of the imagination is a revolutionary concept in the history of epistemology in its placing of the epistemological subject at the centre of the cognitive process. It is possible, without losing sight of its original sense, to extend the scope of the Kantian creative synthesis to a full recognition of the knowing subject as person, rather than merely as knower in a more anonymous sense. This points to the further contention that each individual's knowledge has its particular shape as much as a result of what he or she is as because of what the world is. Knowledge comes into existence as a result of a cooperative interaction of the will, feeling, thought, and perception of individual knowing subjects. This is not to deny that the objective nature of reality and of human cognitive structures determine and delimit the ways of knowing which can have validity and stand fast. Nor is it to deny that knowledge must develop according to logical principles, where contradiction and inconsistency can be recognized and eradicated. Nevertheless, within these limits there is a wide spectrum of diversity.

The person with strongly fundamentalist religious convictions, for

---

[4] In this connection see "A New View of the Brain" by Gordon Rattray Taylor, in *Encounter*, Vol. XXXVI, No. 2, 1971. Taylor points out: "If the eyelids of an animal are sewn up at birth, and freed at maturity, it cannot see and will never learn to do so. The brain has failed to develop the necessary connections at the period when it was able to do so". (p. 30)

[5] Donal Henahan makes these points in his article "Harmony in a Mind Divided?" *The Globe and Mail*, Science Section, Toronto, Ontario, January 29, 1979.

272   LORRAINE B. CODE

example, may well see and understand Darwinian theory in a manner quite different from that of the person who is not committed to any form of religious belief. (Edmund Gosse, in his work *Father and Son*, depicts his biologist father's conflict between his scientific and his religious knowledge.) The nature of an individual's contribution to knowledge on a broader level is influenced by such conflicts in knowledge acquisition. Thomas Kuhn makes this point for science in general when he writes:

> Observation and experience can and must drastically restrict the range of admissible scientific belief, else there would be no science. But they cannot alone determine a particular body of such belief. An apparently arbitrary element, compounded of personal and historical accident, is always a formative ingredient of the beliefs espoused by a given scientific community at a given time.[6]

Kuhn acknowledges that science has seemed to provide an illustration of the generalization, so important for epistemology, that truth and falsity are determined by the confrontation of statement with fact. Yet the act of judgment which leads scientists to reject a previously accepted theory, or to accept one which had seemed unacceptable, is always based upon more than a simple comparison of that theory with the world.

These considerations are relevant to the question of epistemological significance of the sex of the knower in the following way. A woman who is strongly aware of her femininity, a member of a feminist organization, for example, and a man who is self-consciously masculine, a so-called "male chauvinist", will very likely show that their possibilities of structuring experience are constrained by these facts. But a female Christian and a female atheist would be equally far apart in their ways of knowing certain kinds of things, just as would a male Marxist and a female capitalist. In an important sense, one's attitude to one's sexuality is similar to an ideological stance. Just as some people are fervently ideological and others less so, and this is significant in the acquisition of knowledge, so some people are keenly aware of sexuality and others less so, and this is a constraint upon the acquisition of knowledge. At this general level then, it is reasonable to suggest that the sex of the knower is a subjective factor similar to emotional, professional and religious orientations. It does influence the form and content of knowledge in a manner similar to these factors. But the degree of influence is by no means constant for members of one sex as opposed to members of the other sex.

The historical circumstances of the knower are closely linked with the kind and amount of knowledge which can be acquired. A fifteenth-century man could no more know about the DNA molecule or about nuclear physics than he could know about the Nazi regime in Germany.

---

[6] Thomas S. Kuhn. *The Structure of Scientific Revolutions*, 2nd edition. Chicago, The University of Chicago Press, 1970, p. 4.

IS THE SEX OF THE KNOWER EPISTEMOLOGICALLY SIGNIFICANT? 273

This is not because certain biological and physical information would not have been true in his time, but because it would constitute novelty of a degree which he could not accommodate within the body of his knowledge. The level of existing knowledge dictates what kind of knowledge it is possible (i.e. logically and practically possible) to acquire at any time in history.[7]

In periods of history when the academies are closed to women, it is difficult to the point of impossibility for women to acquire knowledge of the "academic" variety. This is not to suggest that the closed doors of the institutions of learning produce feminine stupidity. But the evidence about the adaptability of the human brain, and the need for certain skills to be acquired at an early developmental stage if they are to be acquired at all, is pertinent here. If one branch of the species is prevented, in practical terms, from developing in certain ways, higher levels of knowledge will simply be inaccessible, at least to most of these people. The rare individual will achieve the desired results by independent efforts: one might argue that any Renaissance woman *could*, by her own efforts and with great difficulty have achieved the intellectual status of the Renaissance man. Nonetheless, I think one must take seriously Christine Pierce's observation that

> . . . . certain abilities of persons can be manifested only in circumstances of cooperativeness. One cannot, for instance, manifest intelligence in an interpersonal situation with someone priorly convinced of one's stupidity.[8]

The word "cannot" is well chosen. Most women, in eras prior to the rise of feminist movements, *can* know much less than men.

Location within a particular language is a further subjective constraint upon the possibility of complete objectivity for knowledge in general. Because language is so powerful a formative force in determining the structure of knowledge, the recognition of a measure of linguistic relativism, which I urge, is equivalent to a measure of epistemological relativism. This is true not only from one natural language to another, but of various sub-languages within a particular natural language. The language of physics, for example construes reality in one way; the language of sociology in another. Apart from mathematics and the mathematically formalized branches of the natural sciences, with their precise symbolism, problems of interpretation, understanding, and evaluation attend all human speech situations. Any act of communication between human beings is, at the same time, an act of translation. The creative synthesis which leads to knowledge is shaped, to some extent, by the language in which it takes place.

[7] This is an application of Piaget's principle of equilibration at a phylogenetic level.

[8] Christine Pierce, "Philosophy", in *Signs: Journal of Women in Culture and Society*, Vol. 1, No. 2, 1975, p. 493.

274   LORRAINE B. CODE

The question arises, then, whether there are distinct male and female languages which point to a sexual relativism in knowledge. Differences of pitch and intonation, for example, which linguistic studies detect in men's and women's speech[9] are epistemologically equivocal: one might make a case for their epistemological significance by arguing that the image of self reflected in speech is indicative of the knower's way of approaching the world, and thence of knowing it. This suggestion is supported in Robin Lakoff's study of *Language and Woman's Place*[10], and in Miller and Swift's *Words and Women*.[11] Here there is persuasive evidence for woman's place in the world being linguistically defined and maintained in innumerable subtle ways: ways which determine her approach to the world and hence must have an effect upon her knowledge of it.

Furthermore, the suggestion that "in general men have been in control of determining what is labeled . . ."[12] points to a crucial epistemological difference related to the sex of the knower. If this suggestion is in any way plausible, it leads to the conclusion that men establish the limits of the conceptual structuring which is central to the growth of knowledge. Women, then, find the limits of their creativity (i.e. the limits of their knowledge) dictated by men. The kinds of knowledge available to the entire species are dictated by half of its members.[13] These conclusions, however, are extremely tentative. They are relevant more to the psychology of individual knowers than to conditions for the growth of knowledge in general. Like poets and scientists, women can make a creative leap beyond the dominant communal language. Galileo and Kepler, for example, were successful in creating new forms of scientific discourse. One can acknowledge that

> there is a problem (for women) both of concept formation within an existing male constructed framework and a problem of language use in developing and articulating an authentic understanding of the world and one's relationship to it.[14]

But one must at the same time recognize that this does not hold equally

[9] See "Intonation in a Man's World" by Sally McConnell-Ginet, in *Signs: Journal of Women in Culture and Society*, Vol. 3, No. 3, 1978, pp. 541-559.

[10] Robin Lakoff, *Language and Woman's Place*. New York, Harper and Row, 1975.

[11] Casey Miller and Kate Swift, *Words and Women*. Garden City, New York: Doubleday Anchor Books, 1977.

[12] Kramer, Thorne and Henley, "Perspectives on Language and Communication", in *Signs: Journal of Women in Culture and Society*, Vol. 3, No. 3, 1978, p. 644.

[13] The same authors suggest that "language renders females invisible" (*loc. cit.*), citing the generic "he" as evidence, e.g. "everyone take *his* seat". This may be a valid condemnation of the English language but it cannot apply to languages where the gender of the noun determines the gender of the possessive pronoun. Consider the French equivalent: "Tout le monde à *sa* place".

[14] Kramer, Thorne and Henley, *op. cit.*, p. 646.

for all women, and that feminist movements are slowly altering the epistemological significance of woman's place in language.

Finally, the affective side of human nature, the fact that human beings are as much feeling creatures as they are thinking creatures, constitutes a subjective constraint upon objectivity for knowledge in general. Susanne Langer points out that epistemology finds the entire area of feeling unmanageable because it eludes propositional formulation, yet she designates it "The generic basis of all mental experience — sensation, emotion, recollection, and reasoning, to mention only the main categories."[15] The interests, inclinations and enthusiasms of the knower have a central effect upon how and what he or she can know. This is true of the scientist and of the artist, and of the everyday knowledge of human beings in general. It is in this sense that Thomas Kuhn, in the remarks cited above, might amplify the notions of "personal and historical accident".

It is in this subjective constraint in particular that male and female knowledge differ. There is an entire range of affective experience bound up specifically with being male or being female: experiences of sexuality and of parenthood, of general self-awareness as a physical and emotional being, and some aspects of interpersonal relations, which must of necessity be different for men and for women. The experience of what it is to be male or what it is to be female (in those aspects not connected with roles imposed by society) must constitute an area where it is logically impossible for one group of human beings to know what another does.

The greater proportion of human knowledge could roughly be designated "knowledge by description".[16] But the acceptance of a knowledge claim involves the tacit assumption that what is known could be, or could have been, experienced at first hand. Such a condition does not hold for this kind of experience. In the same way that a blind person cannot really know colour, that a deaf person cannot really know sound, so it is reasonable to argue that a person who is male cannot really know what it is to be female, and vice versa.

Even here, however, the boundaries are not as clear as they may seem to be. This is knowledge which belongs to the realm where the affective side of the knower is most active, just as mathematics belongs to that area which is most purely intellectual. And I think one possible solution to the lack of vocabulary for dealing with the problem of feelings is to be found in the "vocabulary" of art. Knowledge which has its source in the

[15] Susanne, Langer, *Philosophical Sketches*. Baltimore, The Johns Hopkins Press, 1962, p. 11.

[16] Here I am adopting the spirit of Bertrand Russell's terminology as he spells it out, for example, in *The Problems of Philosophy*. Oxford, O.U.P. Paperback edition, 1970, pps. 26-28. I am using the acquaintance/description distinction in a very broad derivative sense. In this broad sense the distinction is useful for my purposes here, at least where its epistemological, as opposed to its ontological, implications are concerned.

experience of works of art falls between Russell's acquaintance/ description distinction, very broadly used. It can be designated "knowledge-by-second-hand-acquaintance". Just as a photograph displays a person's appearance more adequately than any verbal description can evoke it, so an artist's creation shows what a situation is like. The artist provides a means of letting one "see" for oneself, experience it for oneself in such a way that one is able to enter into an entire and immediate experience of "what it is like to be x"; either to be in an x kind of situation, or to be an x kind of person. As one enters into the experience in this way it becomes very close to knowledge by acquaintance. It is true that a woman can never know at first hand just what it is like to be a man. But it is possible that the reading of a novel or a poem, or the viewing of a painting or a sculpture will allow her to know some aspect of "maleness" almost as though she were experiencing it for herself. And the same can be said of a male apprehension of aspects of "femaleness". Even in this apparently clear-cut area, then, the logical impossibility is not as absolute as it might seem.

The historical accounts to which I have referred suggest that female knowledge cannot achieve the degree of objectivity male knowledge can achieve. Female knowledge is characterized as more subjective than male knowledge. And the assumption is that it is therefore inferior to male knowledge, the more objective being necessarily the "better" knowledge. But this assumption must not go unquestioned. Perhaps total objectivity in knowledge is both impossible and undesirable. One might argue that women bring a richness of feeling and a depth of understanding to cognitive activity such that the final known *Gestalt* is richer, more multi-faceted, and better. Perhaps the admission of women to the kingdom of knowers, on an equal footing, will effect a shift in the standard evaluation of knowledge claims, granting greater respectability to the contribution made by the affective side of human nature.

In any case, most of these comments refer to socially acquired characteristics rather than to cognitive capacity. As male and female roles become less rigidly specified by society, so it will become more common for men to acknowledge the affective side of their nature and for women to acknowledge their intellectual side. The differences between male and female knowledge, language, and experience will no longer be equivalent to differences between "forms of life". And the epistemological significance of being male or being female will not be so great.

YORK UNIVERSITY

[8]

The Meaning of Difference

Gender Theory, Postmodernism, and Psychology

Rachel T. Hare-Mustin   *Villanova University*
Jeanne Marecek   *Swarthmore College*

ABSTRACT: *Two recent postmodern movements, constructivism and deconstruction, challenge the idea of a single meaning of reality and suggest that meanings result from social experience. We show how these postmodern approaches can be applied to the psychology of gender. Examining gender theories from a constructivist standpoint, we note that the primary meaning of gender in psychology has been difference. The exaggeration of differences, which we call alpha bias, can be seen in approaches that focus on the contrasting experiences of men and women. The minimizing of differences, beta bias, can be seen in approaches that stress the similarity or equality of men and women. From a deconstructivist position, we examine previously hidden meanings in the discourse of therapy that reveal cultural assumptions about gender relations. Paradoxes in contemporary constructions of gender impel us to go beyond these constructions.*

Conventional meanings of gender typically focus on difference. They emphasize how women differ from men and use these differences to support the norm of male superiority. The overlooking of gender differences occurs as well. Until recently, psychology accepted the cultural meaning of gender as difference, and psychological research offered scientific justification for gender inequality (Lott, 1985a; Morawski, 1985; Shields, 1975; Weisstein, 1971). Theories of psychotherapy similarly supported the cultural meanings of gender (Hare-Mustin, 1983).

The connection between meaning and power has been a focus of postmodernist thinkers (Foucault, 1973; Jameson, 1981). Their inquiry into meaning focuses especially on language and the process of representation. Our concern here is with language as the medium of cognitive life and communication, rather than as the rules by which sentences are strung together. Language is not simply a mirror of reality or a neutral tool (Bruner, 1986; Taggart, 1985; Wittgenstein, 1960; 1953/1967). Language highlights certain features of the objects it represents, certain meanings of the situations it describes. Once designations in language become accepted, one is constrained by them. Language inevitably structures one's own experience of reality as well as the experience of those to whom one communicates.

Language and meaning making are important resources held by those in power. Indeed, Barthes (1957/1972) has called language a sign system used by the powerful to label, define, and rank. Throughout history, men

have had greater influence over language than women. This is not to say that women do not also influence language, but within social groups, males have had privileged access to education and thus have had higher rates of literacy; this remains true in developing countries today (Newland, 1979). In addition, more men are published, and men control the print and electronic media (Strainchamps, 1974). The arbiters of language usage are primarily men, from Samuel Johnson and Noah Webster to H. L. Mencken and Strunk and White. Although not all men have influence over language, for those who do, such authority confers the power to create the world from their point of view, in the image of their desires. This power is obscured when language is regarded simply as description.

Two recent postmodernist movements, constructivism and deconstruction, challenge the idea of a single meaning of reality and concern themselves with the way meaning is represented. The current interest in constructivism and deconstruction is part of a widespread skepticism about the positivist tradition in science and essentialist theories of truth and meaning (Rorty, 1979). Both constructivism and deconstruction assert that meanings are historically situated and constructed and reconstructed through the medium of language.

In this article, we apply postmodernist thought to the psychology of gender. We first take up constructivism. We examine various constructions of gender, and the problems associated with the predominant meaning of gender—that of male–female difference. We then turn to deconstruction. We show how a deconstructive approach to therapeutic discourse can reframe clients' understanding of reality by revealing alternative meanings and thus can promote change. We do not propose a new theory of gender; rather, we shift to a metatheoretical perspective on gender theorizing. Our purpose is not to answer the question of what is the meaning of gender but rather to examine the question.

The Construction of Reality

Constructivism asserts that we do not discover reality, we invent it (Watzlawick, 1984). Our experience does not directly reflect what is "out there" but is an ordering and organizing of it. Knowing is a search for "fitting" ways of behaving and thinking (Von Glaserfeld, 1984). Rather than passively observing reality, we actively construct the meanings that frame and organize our perceptions and experience. Thus, our understanding of reality is a representation, that is, a "re-presentation," not a replica, of

Copyright 1988 by the American Psychological Association, Inc. 0003-066X/88/$00.75
Vol. 43, No. 6, 455-464

what is "out there." Representations of reality are shared meanings that derive from language, history, and culture. Rorty (1979) suggests that the notion of "accurate representation" is a compliment we pay to those beliefs that are successful in helping us do what we want to do.

Constructivism challenges the scientific tradition of positivism, which holds that reality is fixed and can be observed directly, uninfluenced by the observer (Gergen, 1985; Sampson, 1985; Segal, 1986). As Heisenberg (1952) has pointed out, a truly objective world, devoid of all subjectivity, would be unobservable. Constructivism also challenges the positivist presumption that it is possible to distinguish facts and values; for constructivists, values and attitudes determine what are taken to be facts (Howard, 1985). It is not that formal laws and theories in psychology are wrong or useless, but rather, as Kuhn (1962) asserted, that they are explanations based on a set of social conventions. Thus, whereas positivism asks what are the facts, constructivism asks what are the assumptions; whereas positivism asks what are the answers, constructivism asks what are the questions.

The positivist tradition holds that science is the exemplar of the right use of reason, neutral in its methods, socially beneficial in its results (Flax, 1987). Constructivism, and postmodernism more generally, hold that scientific knowledge, like all other knowledge, cannot be disinterested or politically neutral. In psychology, constructivism, drawing on the ideas of Bateson and Maturana, has influenced epistemological developments in systems theories of the family (Dell, 1985). Constructivist views have also been put forth in developmental psychology (Bronfenbrenner, Kessel, Kessen, & White, 1986; Scarr, 1985), in the psychology of women (Unger, 1983), and in the study of human sexuality (Tiefer, 1987). Constructivist views also form the basis of the social constructionism movement in social psychology, which draws inspiration from symbolic anthropology, ethnomethodology, and related movements in sociology and anthropology (Gergen, 1985).

Theories of gender, like other scientific theories, are representations of reality organized by particular assumptive frameworks and reflecting certain interests. In the next section, we examine gender theorizing in psychology and indicate some of the issues that a constructivist approach makes apparent.

The Construction of Gender as Difference

From a constructivist standpoint, the "real" nature of male and female cannot be determined. Constructivism focuses our attention on representations of gender, rather than on gender itself. The very term *gender* illustrates the power of linguistic categories to determine what we know of the world. The use of gender in contexts other than discussions of grammar is quite recent. Gender was appropriated by American feminists to refer to the social

A portion of this article was presented at the meeting of the American Psychological Association, New York, August 1987.

Correspondence concerning this article should be addressed to Rachel T. Hare-Mustin, Villanova University, Villanova, PA 19085.

quality of distinctions between the sexes (Scott, 1985). Gender is used in contrast to terms like *sex* and *sexual difference* for the explicit purpose of creating a space in which socially mediated differences can be explored apart from biological differences (Unger, 1979). We still lack an adequate term for speaking of each gender. *Male-female* has the advantage of including the entire life span but implies biological characteristics and fails to distinguish humans from other species. *Men-women* is more restrictive, referring specifically to human adults but omitting childhood and adolescence. We use male-female, as well as men-women, especially when we wish to suggest the entire life span.

Just what constitutes "differentness" is a vexing question for the study of sex and gender. Research that focuses on mean differences may produce one conclusion, whereas research that focuses on range and overlap of distributions may produce another (Luria, 1986). Moreover, the size and direction of gender differences in any particular behavior, such as aggression or helping, will vary according to the norms and expectations for men and women made salient by the setting (Eagly & Crowley, 1986; Eagly & Steffen, 1986). Even more troubling, the very criteria for deciding what should constitute a difference as opposed to a similarity are disputed. How much difference makes a difference? Even anatomical differences between men and women can seem trivial when humans are compared with daffodils or ducks.

Psychological inquiry into gender has held to the construction of gender as difference. One recent line of inquiry reexamines gender with the goal of deemphasizing difference by sorting out "genuine" male-female differences from stereotypes. Some examples include Hyde's (1981) meta-analyses of cognitive differences, Maccoby and Jacklin's (1975) review of sex differences, and Eccles's work on math achievement (Eccles & Jacobs, 1986). The results of this work dispute that male-female differences are as universal, as dramatic, or as enduring as has been asserted (Deaux, 1984). Moreover, this line of inquiry sees the origins of difference as largely social and cultural, rather than biological. Thus, most differences between males and females are seen as culturally and historically fluid.

Another line of inquiry, exemplified in recent feminist psychodynamic theories (e.g., Chodorow, 1978; Eichenbaum & Orbach, 1983; Miller, 1976), takes as its goal establishing and reaffirming differences. Although these theories provide varying accounts of the origins of difference, they all emphasize deep-seated and enduring differences between women and men in "core self-structure," identity, and relational capacities. Other theorists have suggested that gender differences in psychic structure give rise to cognitive differences, for example, differences in moral reasoning and in acquiring and organizing knowledge (cf. Belenky, Clinchy, Goldberger, & Tarule, 1986; Gilligan, 1982; Keller, 1985). All these theorists represent differences between men and women as essential, universal (at least within contemporary Western culture), highly dichotomized, and enduring.

These two lines of inquiry have led to two widely held but incompatible representations of gender, one that sees few differences between males and females and another that sees profound differences. Both groups of theorists have offered empirical evidence, primarily quantitative in the first case and qualitative in the second. Rather than debating which representation of gender is "true," we shift to a meta-level, that provided by constructivism.

From the vantage point of constructivism, theories of gender are representations based on conventional distinctions. Such theories embody one or the other of two contrasting biases, alpha bias and beta bias (Hare-Mustin, 1987). Alpha bias is the tendency to exaggerate differences; beta bias is the tendency to minimize or ignore differences.

The alpha–beta schema is in some ways analogous to that in hypothesis testing. In hypothesis testing, alpha or Type I error involves reporting a significant difference when one does not exist; beta or Type II error involves overlooking a significant difference when one does exist. In our formulation, the term *bias* refers not to the probability of "error" (which would imply that there is a "correct" position), but rather to a systematic inclination to emphasize certain aspects of experience and overlook other aspects. This formulation of bias relates to the idea that all knowledge is influenced by the standpoint of the knower. "Taking a standpoint" has been seen by some feminist theorists as a positive strategy for generating new knowledge (Harding, 1986; Hartsock, 1985). Our use of the term bias underscores our contention that all ideas about difference are social constructs that can never perfectly mirror reality. Alpha and beta bias can be seen in representations of gender, race, class, age, and the like. Here we use the alpha–beta schema to examine recent efforts to theorize about gender.

Alpha Bias

Alpha bias is the exaggeration of differences. The view of male and female as different and opposite and thus as having mutually exclusive qualities transcends Western culture and has deep historical roots. Ideas of male-female opposition are present in Eastern philosophy and in the works of Western philosophers from Aristotle, Aquinas, Bacon, and Descartes to the liberal theory of Locke and the romanticism of Rousseau (Grimshaw, 1986). Women have been regarded as the repository of nonmasculine traits, an "otherness" men assign to women. Alpha bias has been the prevailing view in our culture and one that has also attracted many feminist theorists.

The scientific model developed by Bacon was based on the distinction between "male" reason and its "female" opposites—passion, lust, and emotion (Keller, 1985). Because women were restricted to the private sphere, they did not have knowledge available in the public realm. When women had knowledge, as in witchcraft, their knowledge was disparaged or repudiated. As Keller points out, women's knowledge was associated with insatiable

lust; men's knowledge was assumed to be chaste. In Bacon's model of science, nature was cast in the image of the female, to be subdued, subjected to the penetrating male gaze, and forced to yield up her secrets. Our purpose here is not to provide a critique of gender and science, which has been done elsewhere (cf. Keller, 1985; Merchant, 1980), but to draw attention to the long-standing association of women with nature and emotion, and men with their opposites, reason, technology, and civilization (Ortner, 1974).

In psychology, alpha bias can be seen most readily in psychodynamic theories. Freudian theory takes masculinity and male anatomy as the human standard; femininity and female anatomy are deviations from that standard. The Jungian idea of the animus and the anima places the masculine and the feminine in opposition. More recent psychodynamic theories also depict female experience as sharply divergent from male experience. For example, Erikson (1964) holds that female identity is predicated on "inner space," a somatic design that "harbors . . . a biological, psychological, and ethical commitment to take care of human infancy" (p. 586) and a sensitive indwelling. Male identity is associated with "outer space," which involves intrusiveness, excitement, and mobility, leading to achievement, political domination, and adventure-seeking. In Lacan's (1985) poststructuralist view, women are "outside" language, public discourse, culture, and the law. The female is defined not by what is, but by the absence or lack of the phallus as the prime signifier. These theories all overlook similarities between males and females and emphasize differences.

Parsons's sex role theory, which dominated the social theories of the 1950s and 1960s, also exaggerates male-female differences (Parsons & Bales, 1955). The very language of sex role theory powerfully conveys the sense that roles are fixed and dichotomous, as well as separate and reciprocal (Thorne, 1982). Parsons asserted that men were instrumental and women were expressive, that is, men were task-oriented and women were oriented toward feelings and relationships. Parsons's sex role theory was hailed as providing a scientific basis for separate spheres for men and women. Men's nature suited them for paid work and public life; women became first in "goodness" by making their own needs secondary to those of the family and altruistically donating their services to others (Lipman-Blumen, 1984). Parsons believed that separate spheres for men and women were functional in reducing competition and conflict in the family and thus preserving harmony. The role definitions that Parsons put forward became criteria for distinguishing normal individuals and families from those who were pathological or even pathogenic (cf. Broverman, Broverman, Clarkson, Rosenkrantz, & Vogel, 1970).

Alpha bias, or the inclination to emphasize differences, can also be seen in feminist psychodynamic theories such as those of Chodorow (1978), Eichenbaum and Orbach (1983), Gilligan (1982), and Miller (1976). Their emphasis on women's special nature and the richness of women's inner experience has been an important resource for cultural feminism. Cultural feminism is a movement within feminism that encourages women's culture, celebrates the special qualities of women, and values relations among women as a way to escape the sexism of the larger society.

According to Chodorow (1978), boys and girls undergo contrasting experiences of identity formation during their early years under the social arrangement in which women are the exclusive caretakers of infants. Her influential work, which is based on object relations theory, argues that girls' identity is based on similarity and attachment to their mothers whereas boys' identity is predicated on difference, separateness, and independence. These experiences are thought to result in broad-ranging gender differences in personality structures and psychic needs in adulthood. Women develop a deep-seated motivation to have children; men develop the capacity to participate in the alienating work structures of advanced capitalism. Thus, according to Chodorow, the social structure produces gendered personalities that reproduce the social structure. Although Chodorow locates the psychodynamics of personality development temporally and situationally in Western industrial capitalism, much of the work in psychology based on her ideas overlooks this point. Her work is taken to assert essential differences between women and men and to view these, rather than the social structure, as the basis for gender roles (cf. Chernin, 1986; Eichenbaum & Orbach, 1983; Jordan & Surrey, 1986; Schlachet, 1984). In any case, both Chodorow's theory and the work of her followers emphasize differences and thus exemplify alpha bias.

In her study of women's development, Gilligan (1982) harks back to Parsons's duality, viewing women as relational and men as instrumental and rational. Her theory of women's moral development echoes some of the gender differences asserted by Freud (1925/1964) and Erikson (1964). She describes female identity as rooted in connections and relationships and female morality as based on an ethic of care. However, unlike Freud, she views women's differences from men in a positive light.

A final example of alpha bias comes from the theories of certain French feminists such as Cixous and Irigaray. They have asserted that differences in the structure of the body and in early childhood experience give rise to differences in language and in the sexual desires of men and women (Donovan, 1985).

Beta Bias

Beta bias, the inclination to ignore or minimize differences, has been less prominent in psychological theory, and thus our treatment of it is necessarily briefer. Until recently, beta bias has gone unnoticed in theories of personality and adult development. Prior to the last decade, most generalizations that psychologists made about human behavior were based on observations of males (Wallston, 1981). The male was the norm against which human behavior was measured, and male experience was assumed to represent all experience. Generalizations about human development based only on the male life

course represent a partial view of humanity and overlook the many differences in men's and women's experiences.

Overlooking the social context and differences in social evaluation reflects beta bias. Women and men typically have different access to economic and social resources, and their actions have different social meanings and consequences. Beta bias can be seen in recent social policies and legislation that try to provide equal benefits for men and women, such as comparable parental leave and no-fault divorce (Weitzman, 1985). Beta bias can also be seen in educational and therapeutic programs that ignore aspects of the social context. They groom women for personal or professional success by providing training in what are deemed "male" behaviors or skills, such as assertiveness, authoritative speech patterns, or "male" managerial styles. Such programs make the presumption that a certain manner of speaking or acting will elicit the same reaction regardless of the sex of the actor. This can be questioned (Gervasio & Crawford, 1987; Marecek & Hare-Mustin, 1987). For example, asking for a date, a classic task in assertiveness training, is judged differently for a woman than a man (Muehlenhard, 1983).

Beta bias can also be seen in theories that represent male and female roles or traits as counterparts, as in the theory of psychological androgyny. When the idea of counterparts implies symmetry and equivalence, it obscures differences in power and social value. Bem's (1976) theory of psychological androgyny, which involves the creation of a more "balanced" and healthy personality by integrating positive masculine and feminine qualities, implies the equivalence of such qualities (Morawski, 1985; Worrell, 1978), but in fact, the masculine qualities she includes are more highly valued and adaptive (Bem, 1976). This is not to say that every quality associated with males is regarded as positive. Aggression, for instance, is deplored outside of combat situations.

Beta bias occurs in systems approaches to family therapy such as the systems and structural theories of Haley (1976) and Minuchin (1974). The four primary axes along which hierarchies are established in all societies are class, race, gender, and age. Within families, class and race usually are constant, but gender and age vary. However, family systems theories disregard gender and view generation (that is, age) as the central organizing principle in the family (Hare-Mustin, 1987). In so doing, they ignore the fact that mothers and fathers, though they may be of the same generation, do not necessarily hold comparable power and resources in the family. Systems theories put forward a neutered representation of family life (Libow, 1985).

The Question of Utility

Rather than debate the correctness of various representations of gender, the "true" nature of which cannot be known, constructivism examines their utility or consequences. How do representations of gender provide the meanings and symbols that organize scientific and therapeutic practice in psychology? What are the consequences of representations of gender that either emphasize or minimize male–female difference? The alpha–beta schema affords a framework for discussing the utility of gender theories.

Because alpha bias has been the prevailing representation of gender, we first examine its utility. Alpha bias has had a number of effects on our understanding of gender. The idea of gender as male–female difference and the idea of masculinity and femininity as opposite and mutually exclusive poles on a continuum of personality —as in the Terman-Miles M–F Personality Scale (Terman & Miles, 1936), the Femininity Scale of the California Psychological Inventory (Gough, 1964), and other measures (see Constantinople, 1973)—mask inequality between men and women as well as conflict between them. For example, by construing rationality as an essential male quality and relatedness as an essential female quality, theories like those of Gilligan and Parsons conceal the possibility that those qualities result from social inequities and power differences. Many differences of men and women can be seen as associated with their position in the social hierarchy (Eagly, 1983). Men's propensity to reason from principles may stem from the fact that the principles were formulated to promote their interests; women's concern with relationships can be understood as the need to please others that arises from a lack of power (Hare-Mustin & Marecek, 1986). Typically, those in power advocate rules, discipline, control, and rationality, whereas those without power espouse relatedness and compassion. Thus, in husband–wife conflicts, husbands call on rules and logic, whereas wives call on caring. When women are in the dominant position, however, as in parent–child conflicts, they emphasize rules, whereas children appeal for sympathy and understanding. Such a reversal suggests that these differences can be accounted for by an individual's position in the social hierarchy rather than by gender.

In her interpretations of women's narratives, Gilligan (1982) highlights women's concern with caring and construes it as an essential female attribute. From another point of view, this concern can be seen as the necessity for those in subordinate positions to suppress anger and placate those on whom they depend. In a careful analysis, Hayles (1986) has pointed out that the only female voice that a male world will authorize is one that does not openly express anger.

Feminist psychodynamic theories make assertions of extensive male–female personality differences throughout life. Critics have challenged the idea that a brief period in early life is responsible for broad-ranging differences in men's and women's lives and for gendering all social institutions throughout history (cf. Kagan, 1984; Lott, 1985b; Scott, 1985). Further questions have been raised as to whether changes in patterns of infant caregiving such as Chodorow (1978) and Dinnerstein (1976) have proposed are sufficient to effect social transformation. The alpha bias of feminist psychodynamic theories leads theorists to underplay the influence of economic conditions, social role conditioning, and historical change. Moreover, in focusing on the question of why *differences* exist, feminist psychodynamic theories disregard the question of why *domination* exists.

Alpha bias, the exaggerating of differences between groups, has the additional consequence of ignoring or minimizing within-group variability. Furthermore, outgroups such as women are viewed as more homogeneous than dominant groups (Park & Rothbart, 1982). Thus, men are viewed as individuals, but women are viewed as women. As a result, most psychological theories of gender have not concerned themselves with differences among women that are due to race, class, age, marital status, and social circumstances.

Another consequence of alpha bias is the tendency to view men and women as embodying opposite and mutually exclusive traits. Such a dichotomy seems a caricature of human experience. For example, to maintain the illusion of male autonomy at home and in the workplace, the contribution of women's work must be overlooked. Similarly, the portrayal of women as relational ignores the complexity of their experiences. Rearing children involves achievement, and nurturing others involves power over those in one's care (Hare-Mustin & Marecek, 1986). Gender dichotomies are historically rooted in an era, now past, when the majority of women were not part of the paid labor force (Hare-Mustin, 1988). When gender is represented as dichotomized traits, the possibility that each includes aspects of the other is overlooked.

The autonomy–relatedness dichotomy is not unique; it clearly resembles earlier gender dichotomies, such as instrumentality–expressiveness (Parsons & Bales, 1955) and agency–communion (Bakan, 1966). The idea of man/woman as a universal binary opposition is not a result of faulty definitions, but of prevailing ideology, according to Wilden (1972). He has drawn attention to the way that calling the psychosocial and economic relationships of men and women "opposition" imputes a symmetry to a relationship that is unequal. Furthermore, inequality can only be maintained if interrelationships are denied. The representation of gender as opposition has its source, not in some accidental confusion of logical typing, but in the dominant group's interest in preserving the status quo. The cultural preoccupation with gender difference may be the result (Chodorow, 1979). Dinnerstein (1976) points out that women have been discontent with the double standard, but men on the whole are satisfied with it.

In our opinion, an important positive consequence of alpha bias, or focusing on differences between women and men, is that it has allowed some theorists to assert the worth of certain "feminine" qualities. This has the positive effect of countering the cultural devaluation of women and fostering a valued sense of identity in them. The focus on women's special qualities by some feminists has also prompted a critique of cultural values that extol aggression, the pursuit of self-interest, and narrow individualism. It has furnished an impetus for the development of a feminist social ethics and for a variety of philosophical endeavors (Eisenstein, 1983).

Beta bias, or minimizing differences, also has consequences for understanding gender, but its consequences have received less attention. On the positive side, equal treatment under the law has enabled women to gain greater access to educational and occupational opportunities. This enhanced access is largely responsible for the improvement in some women's status in the last two decades.

Arguing for no differences between women and men, however, draws attention away from women's special needs and from differences in power and resources between women and men. In a society in which one group holds most of the power, seemingly neutral actions usually benefit members of that group, as in no-fault divorce or parental leave. In Weitzman's (1985) research, no-fault divorce settlements were found to have raised men's standard of living 42% while lowering that of women and children 73%. Another example is the effort to promote public policies granting comparable parental leave for men and women. Such policies overlook the biological changes in childbirth from which women need to recuperate and the demands of breastfeeding, which are met uniquely by women.

Birth is, paradoxically, both an ordinary event and an extraordinary one, as well as the only visible biological link in the kinship system. The failure of the workplace to accommodate women's special needs associated with childbirth represents beta bias, in which male needs and behaviors set the norm.

In therapy, treating men and women as if they are equal is not always equitable (Gilbert, 1980; Margolin, Talovic, Fernandez, & Onorato, 1983). In marital and family therapy, equal treatment may overlook structural inequality between husband and wife. When the social status and economic resources of the husband exceed those of the wife, quid pro quo bargaining as a strategy for resolving conflicts between partners will not lead to equitable results. "Sex-fair" or "gender-neutral" therapies that advocate nonpreferential and nondifferential treatment of women and men to achieve formal equality may inadvertently foster inequality (Marecek & Kravetz, 1977).

Our purpose in examining representations of gender has not been to catalogue every possible consequence of alpha and beta bias but rather to demonstrate that representation is never neutral. From the vantage point of constructivism, theories of gender can be seen as representations that construct our knowledge and inform social and scientific practice. Representation and meaning in language are the focus of deconstruction. We now turn to the ways in which deconstruction can be used to examine the practice of therapy.

Deconstruction

Just as constructivism denies that there is a single fixed reality, the approach to literary interpretation known as deconstruction denies that texts have a single fixed meaning. Deconstruction offers a means of examining the way language operates below our everyday level of awareness to create meaning (Culler, 1982; Segal, 1986). Deconstruction is generally applied to literary texts, but it can

be applied equally readily to scientific texts, or, as we suggest, to therapeutic discourse.

A primary tenet of deconstruction is that texts can generate a variety of meanings in excess of what is intended. In this view, language is not a stable system of correspondences of words to objects but "a sprawling limitless web where there is constant circulation of elements" (Eagleton, 1983, p. 129). The meaning of a word depends on its relation to other words, specifically, its difference from other words.

Deconstruction is based on the philosophy of Derrida, who has pointed out that Western thought is built on a series of interrelated hierarchical oppositions, such as reason–emotion, presence–absence, fact–value, good–evil, male–female (Culler, 1982). In each pair, the terms take their meaning from their opposition to (or difference from) each other; each is defined in terms of what the other is not. Moreover, the first member of each pair is considered "more valuable and a better guide to the truth" (Nehamas, 1987, p. 32). However, Derrida challenges both the opposition and the hierarchy, drawing attention to how each term contains elements of the other and depends for its meaning on the other. It is only by marginalizing their similarities that their meaning as opposites is stabilized and the value of one over the other is sustained.

Just as the meaning of a word partly depends on what the word is not, the meaning of a text partly depends on what the text does not say. Deconstructive readings thus rely on gaps, inconsistencies, and contradictions in the text, and even on metaphorical associations, to reveal meanings present in the text but outside our everyday level of awareness. Our intention here is not to provide a detailed explication of deconstruction but to demonstrate how it can be used to understand therapy and gender.

Therapy, Meaning, and Change

Therapy centers on meaning, and language is its medium. A deconstructivist view of the process of therapy draws attention to the play of meanings in the therapist–client dialogue and the way a therapist uses alternative meanings to create possibilities for change. From this standpoint, we examine the therapeutic process as one in which the client asks the therapist to reveal something about the client beyond the client's awareness, something that the client does not know.

Clients in therapy talk not about "actual" experiences but about reconstructed memories that resemble the original experiences only in certain ways. The client's story conforms to prevailing narrative conventions (Spence, 1982). This means that the client's representation of events moves further and further away from the experience and into a descriptive mode. Experience and its description are not the same. The client as narrator is a creator of his or her world, not a disinterested observer.

The therapist's task of listening and responding to the client's narratives is akin to a deconstructive reading of a text. Both seek to uncover hidden subtexts and multiple levels of meaning. The metaphor of therapy as healing is an idealization that obscures another metaphor, that therapists manipulate meanings. These metaphors are not contrary to each other; rather, as part of helping clients change, therapists change clients' meanings (Haley, 1976). Just as deconstructive readings disrupt the frame of reference within which conventional meanings of a text are organized, so a therapist's interventions disrupt the frame of reference within which the client sees the world. Providing new frames imparts new meanings (Watzlawick, Weakland, & Fisch, 1974). As a multiplicity of meanings becomes apparent through such therapist actions as questioning, explaining, and disregarding, more possibilities for change emerge. The deconstructive process is most apparent in psychoanalysis, but indeed, all therapy involves changing meaning as part of changing behavior.

Gender and Meaning in Therapy

Just as a poem can have many readings, a client's experience can have many meanings. However, as postmodernist scholars have pointed out, certain meanings are privileged because they conform to the explanatory systems of the dominant culture. As a cultural institution whose purpose is to help individuals adapt to their social condition, therapy largely reflects and promulgates privileged meanings. For therapists who bring a social critique to their work, therapy involves bringing out alternative or marginalized meanings. In what follows, we examine certain privileged and marginalized meanings in relation to gender issues, issues that have been the center of considerable debate among therapists and in society at large (Brodsky & Hare-Mustin, 1980).

When we look at Freud's classic case of Dora (Freud, 1905/1963) from a deconstructive perspective, we can see it as a therapist's attempt to adjust the meaning a client attaches to her experience to match the prevailing meanings of the patriarchal society in which she lives. Dora viewed the sexual attentions of her father's associate, Herr K., as unwanted and uninvited. She responded to them with revulsion. Freud framed the encounter with Herr K. as a desirable one for a 14-year-old girl and interpreted Dora's revulsion as disguised sexual arousal. When Dora refused to accept Freud's construction, he labeled her as vengeful and the therapy as a failure.

From our vantage point 90 years after Dora's encounter with Freud, the case shows how meanings embedded in the dominant culture often go unrecognized or unacknowledged. Freud evidently viewed Herr K.'s lecherous advances as acceptable behavior, although Herr K. was married and Dora was only 14 and the daughter of a close family friend. We might surmise that the cultural belief in the primacy of men's sexual needs prevented Freud from seeing Dora's revulsion as genuine.

Freud's analysis of Dora provides an example of how a therapist attempts to reaffirm privileged meanings and marginalize and discourage other meanings. The many meanings of Dora's behavior—and Freud's as well—are evident in the numerous reanalyses, film representations, and critical literary readings of the case.

Conventional meanings of gender are embedded in the language of therapy. Like all language, the language used in therapy can be thought of as metaphoric: it selects, emphasizes, suppresses, and organizes certain features of experience and thus, imparts meaning to experience. For example, "Oedipus complex" imposes the complexity of adult erotic feelings onto the experiences of small children and emphasizes male development and the primacy of the phallus. The metaphor of the "family ledger" in family therapy implies that family relations are (or should be) organized as mercantile exchanges and centered on male achievements (Boszormenyi-Nagy & Sparks, 1973).

Therapists can also use language and metaphor to disrupt dominant meanings. With respect to gender, for example, a therapist may "unpack" the metaphor of "family harmony" and expose the hierarchy by pointing out that accord within the family often is achieved through women's acquiescence and accommodation (Hare-Mustin, 1978, 1987). The stress generated by women's prescribed family roles is marginalized or overlooked (Baruch, Biener, & Barnett, 1987). In unpacking the metaphor of "family loyalty," the therapist may draw attention to the way the needs of some family members are subordinated to those of dominant members in the name of loyalty. Pogrebin (1983) has disrupted such metaphors as "preserving the family," or "the decline of the family," by suggesting that "the family" is a metaphor for male dominance when used in this way.

When the metaphor of "women's dependency" is disrupted, the dependency of men and boys on women as wives and mothers is revealed. Women have traditionally been characterized as dependent, but Lerner (1983) has questioned whether women have been dependent enough, that is, have been able to call on others to meet their needs. The therapist may draw attention to the way men's dependency on women is obscured while women's own dependency needs go unmet.

As we have shown, the resemblance of therapeutic discourse to narrative offers the possibility of using deconstruction as a resource for understanding meaning and the process of therapy. Therapy typically confirms privileged meanings, but deconstruction directs attention to marginalized meanings. Doing therapy from a feminist standpoint is like the deconstructivist's "reading as a woman" (Culler, 1982). The therapist exposes gender-related meanings that reside in culturally embedded metaphors such as "family harmony," but go unacknowledged in the conventional understanding of those metaphors. These examples also show how deconstruction reveals the meanings of gender embedded in the hierarchical opposition of male–female.

Conclusion

Postmodernism makes us aware of connections among meaning, power, and language. A constructivist view of gender theorizing in contemporary psychology reveals that gender is represented as a continuum of psychological difference. This representation serves to simplify and purify the concept of gender; it obscures the complexity of human action and shields both men and women from the discomforting recognition of inequality. Deconstruction focuses attention on hidden meanings in culturally embedded metaphors. Applying deconstruction to the discourse of therapy shows how metaphors also simplify gender by obscuring and marginalizing alternative meanings of gender. From a postmodernist perspective, there is no one "right" view of gender, but various views that present certain paradoxes.

Paradoxes in Gender Theorizing

Paradoxes arise because every representation conceals at the same time it reveals. For example, focusing on gender differences marginalizes and obscures the interrelatedness of women and men as well as the restricted opportunities of both. It also obscures institutional sexism and the extent of male authority.

The issue of gender differences has been a divisive one for feminist scholars. Some believe that differences affirm women's value and special nature; others are concerned that focusing on differences reinforces the status quo and supports inequality, given that the power to define remains with men. A paradox is that efforts to affirm the special value of women's experience and their "inner life" turn attention away from efforts to change the material conditions of women's lives and alleviate institutional sexism (Fine, 1985; Russ, 1986; Tobias, 1986). Another paradox arises from the assertion of a female way of knowing, involving intuition and experiential understanding, rather than logical abstraction. This assertion implies that all other thought is a male way of knowing, and if taken to an extreme, can be used to support the view that women are incapable of rational thought and of acquiring the knowledge of the culture.

There is a paradox faced by any social change movement, including feminism: Its critique is necessarily determined by the nature of the larger social system, and its meanings are embedded in that system. Moreover, feminist separatism, the attempt to avoid male influence by separating from men, leaves intact the larger system of male control in the society. In addition, as Sennett (1980) has observed, even when one's response to authority is defiance, that stance serves to confirm authority just as compliance does. In this regard, Dinnerstein (1976) has suggested that woman is not really the enemy of the system but its loyal opposition.

There is yet another paradox. Qualities such as caring, expressiveness, and concern for relationships are extolled as women's superior virtues and the wellspring of public regeneration. At the same time, however, they are seen as arising from women's subordination (Miller, 1976). When we extol such qualities, do we necessarily also extol women's subordination (Echols, 1983; Ringleheim, 1985)? If subordination makes women "better people," then the perpetuation of women's "goodness" would seem to require the perpetuation of inequality.

The assertion that women are "as good as" men is a source of pride for some women, but it is also a paradox arising from beta bias. Man is the hidden referent in our language and culture. As Spender (1984) points out, "women can only aspire to be as good as a man, there is no point in trying to be as good as a woman" (p. 201). Paradoxically, this attempt at denying differences reaffirms male behavior as the standard against which all behavior is judged.

In conclusion, difference is a problematic and paradoxical way to construe gender. What we see is that alpha and beta bias have similar assumptive frameworks, despite their diverse emphases. Both take the male as the standard of comparison and support the status quo. Both construct gender as attributes of individuals, not as the ongoing relations of men and women, particularly relations of domination. Neither effectively challenges the gender hierarchy. The representation of gender as difference frames the problem of what gender is in such a way that the solution produces "more of the same" (Watzlawick, Weakland, & Fisch, 1974).

The paradoxes we discover when we challenge the construction of gender as difference shake us loose from our conventional thought, revealing meanings that are present but obscured in the dominant view. Contradictions become apparent when we examine the play among meanings and entertain the question of the utility of various representations.

Postmodernism accepts randomness, incoherence, indeterminacy, and paradox, which positivist paradigms are designed to exclude. Postmodernism creates distance from the seemingly fixed language of established meanings and fosters skepticism about the fixed nature of reality. Constructing gender is a process, not an answer. In using a postmodernist approach, we open the possibility of theorizing gender in heretofore unimagined ways. Postmodernism allows us to see that as observers of gender we are also its creators.

REFERENCES

Bakan, D. (1966). *The duality of human existence.* Chicago: Rand McNally.

Barthes, R. (1972). *Mythologies* (A. Lavers, Trans.). New York: Hill & Wang. (Original work published 1957)

Baruch, G. K., Biener, L., & Barnett, R. C. (1987). Women and gender in research on work and family stress. *American Psychologist, 42,* 130–136.

Belenky, M. F., Clinchy, B. M., Goldberger, N. R., & Tarule, J. M. (1986). *Women's ways of knowing: Development of self, voice, and mind.* New York: Basic Books.

Bem, S. L. (1976). Probing the promise of androgyny. In A. G. Kaplan & J. P. Bean (Eds.), *Beyond sex-role stereotypes: Readings toward a psychology of androgyny* (pp. 48–62). Boston: Little, Brown.

Boszormenyi-Nagy, I., & Sparks, G. M. (1973). *Invisible loyalties.* New York: Harper & Row.

Brodsky, A. M., & Hare-Mustin, R. T. (1980). *Women and psychotherapy: An assessment of research and practice.* New York: Guilford.

Bronfenbrenner, U., Kessel, F., Kessen, W., & White, S. (1986). Toward a critical social history of developmental psychology: A propaedeutic discussion. *American Psychologist, 41,* 1218–1230.

Broverman, I. K., Broverman, D. M., Clarkson, F. E., Rosenkrantz, P., & Vogel, S. R. (1970). Sex role stereotypes and clinical judgments of mental health. *Journal of Consulting Psychology, 34,* 1–7.

Bruner, J. (1986). *Actual minds, possible worlds.* Cambridge, MA: Harvard University Press.

Chernin, K. (1986). *The hungry self: Women, eating, and identity.* New York: Perennial Library.

Chodorow, N. (1978). *The reproduction of mothering.* Berkeley: University of California Press.

Chodorow, N. (1979). Feminism and difference: Gender, relation, and difference in psychoanalytic perspective. *Socialist Review, 9*(4), 51–70.

Constantinople, A. (1973). Masculinity–femininity: An exception to a famous dictum. *Psychological Bulletin, 80,* 389–407.

Culler, J. (1982). *On deconstruction: Theory and criticism after structuralism.* Ithaca, NY: Cornell University Press.

Deaux, K. (1984). From individual differences to social categories: Analysis of a decade's research on gender. *American Psychologist, 39,* 105–116.

Dell, P. F. (1985). Understanding Bateson and Maturana: Toward a biological foundation for the social sciences. *Journal of Marital and Family Therapy, 11,* 1–20.

Dinnerstein, D. (1976). *The mermaid and the minotaur.* New York: Harper & Row.

Donovan, J. (1985). *Feminist theory: The intellectual traditions of American feminism.* New York: Ungar.

Eagleton, T. (1983). *Literary theory: An introduction.* Minneapolis: University of Minnesota Press.

Eagly, A. H. (1983). Gender and social influence: A social psychological analysis. *American Psychologist, 38,* 971–981.

Eagly, A. H., & Crowley, M. (1986). Gender and helping behavior: A meta-analytic review of the social psychological literature. *Psychological Bulletin, 100,* 283–308.

Eagly, A. H., & Steffen, V. J. (1986). Gender and aggressive behavior: A meta-analytic review of the social psychological literature. *Psychological Bulletin, 100,* 309–330.

Eccles, J., & Jacobs, J. (1986). Social forces shape math participation. *Signs, 11,* 368–380.

Echols, A. (1983). The new feminism of yin and yang. In A. Snitow, C. Stansell, & S. Thompson (Eds.), *Powers of desire: The politics of sexuality* (pp. 440–459). New York: Monthly Review Press.

Eichenbaum, L., & Orbach, S. (1983). *Understanding women: A feminist psychoanalytic approach.* New York: Basic Books.

Eisenstein, H. (1983). *Contemporary feminist thought.* Boston: G. K. Hall.

Erikson, E. H. (1964). Inner and outer space: Reflections on womanhood. *Daedelus, 93,* 582–606.

Fine, M. (1985). Reflections on a feminist psychology of women. *Psychology of Women Quarterly, 9,* 167–183.

Flax, J. (1987). Postmodernism and gender relations in feminist theory. *Signs, 12,* 621–643.

Foucault, M. (1973). *The order of things.* New York: Vintage.

Freud, S. (1963). *Dora: An analysis of a case of hysteria.* New York: Collier Books. (Original work published 1905)

Freud, S. (1964). Some psychical consequences of the anatomical distinction between the sexes. In J. Strachey (Ed. and Trans.), *Standard edition of the complete psychological works of Sigmund Freud* (Vol. 19, pp. 243–258). London: Hogarth Press. (Original work published 1925)

Gergen, K. J. (1985). The social constructionist movement in modern psychology. *American Psychologist, 40,* 266–275.

Gervasio, A. H., & Crawford, M. (1987). *Social evaluations of assertiveness: A review and reformulation.* Unpublished manuscript, Hamilton College, Clinton, NY.

Gilbert, L. A. (1980). Feminist therapy. In A. M. Brodsky & R. T. Hare-Mustin (Eds.), *Women and psychotherapy: An assessment of research and practice* (pp. 245–265). New York: Guilford.

Gilligan, C. (1982). *In a different voice: Psychological theory and women's development.* Cambridge, MA: Harvard University Press.

Gough, H. G. (1964). *California Psychological Inventory: Manual.* Palo Alto, CA: Consulting Psychologists Press.

Grimshaw, J. (1986). *Philosophy and feminist thinking.* Minneapolis: University of Minnesota Press.

Haley, J. (1976). *Problem-solving therapy.* San Francisco: Jossey-Bass.

Harding, S. (1986). *The science question in feminism.* Ithaca, NY: Cornell University Press.

Hare-Mustin, R. T. (1978). A feminist approach to family therapy. *Family Process, 17,* 181–194.

Hare-Mustin, R. T. (1983). An appraisal of the relationship of women and psychotherapy: 80 years after the case of Dora. *American Psychologist, 38,* 593–601.

Hare-Mustin, R. T. (1987). The problem of gender in family therapy theory. *Family Process, 26,* 15–27.

Hare-Mustin, R. T. (1988). Family change and gender differences: Implications for theory and practice. *Family Relations, 37,* 36–41.

Hare-Mustin, R. T., & Marecek, J. (1986). Autonomy and gender: Some questions for therapists. *Psychotherapy, 23,* 205–212.

Hartsock, N. C. M. (1985). *Money, sex, and power: Toward a feminist historical materialism.* Boston: Northeastern University Press.

Hayles, N. K. (1986). Anger in different voices: Carol Gilligan and *The Mill on the Floss. Signs, 12,* 23–39.

Heisenberg, W. (1952). Philosophic problems of nuclear science (F. C. Hayes, Trans.). New York: Pantheon.

Howard, G. (1985). The role of values in the science of psychology. *American Psychologist, 40,* 255–265.

Hyde, J. S. (1981). How large are cognitive gender differences? *American Psychologist, 36,* 892–901.

Jameson, F. (1981). *The political unconscious: Narrative as a socially symbolic act.* Ithaca, NY: Cornell University Press.

Jordan, J. V., & Surrey, J. L. (1986). The self-in-relation: Empathy and the mother–daughter relationship. In T. Bernay & D. W. Cantor (Eds.), *The psychology of today's woman: New psychoanalytic visions* (pp. 81–104). New York: Analytic Press.

Kagan, J. (1984). *The nature of the child.* New York: Basic Books.

Keller, E. F. (1985). *Reflections on gender and science.* New Haven, CT: Yale University Press.

Kuhn, T. S. (1962). *The structure of scientific revolutions.* Chicago, IL: University of Chicago Press.

Lacan, J. (1985). *Feminine sexuality* (J. Mitchell & J. Rose, Eds.; J. Rose, Trans.). New York: Norton.

Lerner, H. G. (1983). Female dependency in context: Some theoretical and technical considerations. *American Journal of Orthopsychiatry, 53,* 697–705.

Libow, J. (1985). Gender and sex role issues as family secrets. *Journal of Strategic and Systemic Therapies, 4*(2), 32–41.

Lipman-Blumen, J. (1984). *Gender roles and power.* Englewood Cliffs, NJ: Prentice-Hall.

Lott, B. (1985a). The potential enrichment of social/personality psychology through feminist research and vice versa. *American Psychologist, 40,* 155–164.

Lott, B. (1985b). *Women's lives: Themes and variations.* Belmont, CA: Brooks/Cole.

Luria, Z. (1986). A methodological critique: On "In a different voice." *Signs, 11,* 316–321.

Maccoby, E. E., & Jacklin, C. N. (1975). *The psychology of sex differences.* Stanford, CA: Stanford University Press.

Marecek, J., & Hare-Mustin, R. T. (1987, March). *Cultural and radical feminism in therapy: Divergent views of change.* Paper presented at the meeting of the American Orthopsychiatric Association, Washington, DC.

Marecek, J., & Kravetz, D. (1977). Women and mental health: A review of feminist change efforts. *Psychiatry, 40,* 323–329.

Margolin, G., Talovic, S., Fernandez, V., & Onorato, R. (1983). Sex role considerations and behavioral marital therapy: Equal does not mean identical. *Journal of Marital and Family Therapy, 9,* 131–145.

Merchant, C. (1980). *The death of nature: Women, ecology, and the scientific revolution.* San Francisco: Harper & Row.

Miller, J. B. (1976). *Toward a new psychology of women.* Boston: Beacon Press.

Minuchin, S. (1974). *Families and family therapy.* Cambridge, MA: Harvard University Press.

Morawski, J. G. (1985). The measurement of masculinity and femininity: Engendering categorical realities. *Journal of Personality, 53,* 196–223.

Muehlenhard, C. L. (1983). Women's assertion and the feminine sex-role stereotype. In V. Frank & E. D. Rothblum (Eds.), *The stereotyping of women: Its effects on mental health* (pp. 153–171). New York: Springer.

Nehamas, A. (1987, October 5). Truth and consequences: How to understand Jacques Derrida. *The New Republic,* pp. 31–36.

Newland, K. (1979). *The sisterhood of man.* New York: Norton.

Ortner, S. B. (1974). Is female to male as nature is to culture? In M. Z. Rosaldo & L. Lamphere (Eds.), *Women, culture, and society* (pp. 67–87). Stanford, CA: Stanford University Press.

Park, B., & Rothbart, M. (1982). Perception of out-group homogeneity and levels of social categorization: Memory for the subordinate attributes of in-group and out-group members. *Journal of Personality and Social Psychology, 42,* 1051–1068.

Parsons, T., & Bales, R. F. (1955). *Family, socialization, and interaction process.* Glencoe, IL: Free Press.

Pogrebin, L. C. (1983). *Family politics: Love and power on an intimate frontier.* New York: McGraw-Hill.

Ringleheim, J. (1985). Women and the Holocaust: A reconsideration of research. *Signs, 10,* 741–761.

Rorty, R. (1979). *Philosophy and the mirror of nature.* Princeton, NJ: Princeton University Press.

Russ, J. (1986). Letter to the editor. *Women's Review of Books, 3*(12), 7.

Sampson, E. E. (1985). The decentralization of identity: Toward a revised concept of personal and social order. *American Psychologist, 40,* 1203–1211.

Scarr, S. (1985). Constructing psychology: Making facts and fables for our times. *American Psychologist, 40,* 499–512.

Schlachet, B. C. (1984). Female role socialization: The analyst and the analysis. In C. M. Brody (Ed.), *Women therapists for working with women* (pp. 55–65). New York: Springer.

Scott, J. (1985, December). *Is gender a useful category of historical analysis?* Paper presented at the meeting of the American Historical Association, New York.

Segal, L. (1986). *The dream of reality: Heinz von Foerster's constructivism.* New York: Norton.

Sennett, R. (1980). *Authority.* New York: Knopf.

Shields, S. A. (1975). Functionalism, Darwinism, and the psychology of women: A study in social myth. *American Psychologist, 30,* 739–754.

Spence, D. P. (1982). *Narrative truth and historical truth.* New York: Norton.

Spender, D. (1984). Defining reality: A powerful tool. In C. Kramarae, M. Schulz, & W. M. O'Barr (Eds.), *Language and power* (pp. 194–205). Beverly Hills, CA: Sage.

Strainchamps, E. (Ed.). (1974). *Rooms with no view: A woman's guide to the man's world of the media.* New York: Harper & Row.

Taggart, M. (1985). The feminist critique in epistemological perspective:

Questions of context in family therapy. *Journal of Marital and Family Therapy, 11,* 113–126.

Terman, L. M., & Miles, C. C. (1936). *Sex and personality.* New York: McGraw Hill.

Thorne, B. (1982). Feminist rethinking of the family: An overview. In B. Thorne & M. Yalom (Eds.), *Rethinking the family: Some feminist questions* (pp. 1–24). New York: Longmans.

Tiefer, L. (1987). Social constructionism and the study of human sexuality. In P. Shaver & C. Hendrick (Eds.), *Review of Social and Personality Psychology: Vol. 7. Sex and gender* (pp. 70–94). Beverly Hills, CA: Sage.

Tobias, S. (1986). "In a different voice" and its implications for feminism. *Women's Studies in Indiana, 12*(2), 1–2, 4.

Unger, R. K. (1979). Toward a redefinition of sex and gender. *American Psychologist, 34,* 1085–1094.

Unger, R. K. (1983). Through the looking glass: No wonderland yet! (The reciprocal relationship between methodology and models of reality). *Psychology of Women Quarterly, 8,* 9–32.

Von Glaserfeld, E. (1984). An introduction to radical constructivism. In P. Watzlawick (Ed.), *The invented reality: Contributions to constructivism* (pp. 17–40). New York: Norton.

Wallston, B. S. (1981). What are the questions in psychology of women? A feminist approach to research. *Psychology of Women Quarterly, 5,* 597–617.

Watzlawick, P. (Ed.). (1984). *The invented reality: Contributions to constructivism.* New York: Norton.

Watzlawick, P., Weakland, J. H., & Fisch, R. (1974). *Change: Principles of problem formation and problem resolution.* New York: Norton.

Weisstein, N. (1971). Psychology constructs the female. In V. Gornick & B. K. Moran (Eds.), *Woman in sexist society* (pp. 133–146). New York: Basic Books.

Weitzman, L. J. (1985). *The divorce revolution: The unexpected social and economic consequences for women and children in America.* New York: Free Press.

Wilden, A. (1972). *System and structure: Essays in communication and exchange.* London: Tavistock.

Wittgenstein, L. (1960). *Preliminary studies for the "Philosophical Investigations": The blue and brown books.* Oxford: Blackwell.

Wittgenstein, L. (1967). *Philosophical investigations.* Oxford: Blackwell. (Original work published 1953)

Worrell, J. (1978). Sex roles and psychological well-being: Perspectives on methodology. *Journal of Consulting and Clinical Psychology, 46,* 777–791.

Journal of Consulting and Clinical Psychology
1970, Vol. 34, No. 1, 1-7

SEX-ROLE STEREOTYPES AND CLINICAL JUDGMENTS
OF MENTAL HEALTH

INGE K. BROVERMAN,[1] DONALD M. BROVERMAN, FRANK E. CLARKSON

Worcester State Hospital

PAUL S. ROSENKRANTZ   AND   SUSAN R. VOGEL

Holy Cross College   *Brandeis University*

A sex-role Stereotype Questionnaire consisting of 122 bipolar items was given to actively functioning clinicians with one of three sets of instructions: To describe a healthy, mature, socially competent (*a*) adult, sex unspecified, (*b*) a man, or (*c*) a woman. It was hypothesized that clinical judgments about the characteristics of healthy individuals would differ as a function of sex of person judged, and furthermore, that these differences in clinical judgments would parallel stereotypic sex-role differences. A second hypothesis predicted that behaviors and characteristics judged healthy for an adult, sex unspecified, which are presumed to reflect an ideal standard of health, will resemble behaviors judged healthy for men, but differ from behaviors judged healthy for women. Both hypotheses were confirmed. Possible reasons for and the effects of this double standard of health are discussed.

Evidence of the existence of sex-role stereotypes, that is, highly consensual norms and beliefs about the differing characteristics of men and women, is abundantly present in the literature (Anastasi & Foley, 1949; Fernberger, 1948; Komarovsky, 1950; McKee & Sherriffs, 1957; Seward, 1946; Seward & Larson, 1968; Wylie, 1961; Rosenkrantz, Vogel, Bee, Broverman, & Broverman, 1968). Similarly, the differential valuations of behaviors and characteristics stereotypically ascribed to men and women are well established (Kitay, 1940; Lynn, 1959; McKee & Sherriffs, 1959; Rosenkrantz et al., 1968; White, 1950), that is, stereotypically masculine traits are more often perceived as socially desirable than are attributes which are stereotypically feminine. The literature also indicates that the social desirabilities of behaviors are positively related to the clinical ratings of these same behaviors in terms of "normality-abnormality" (Cowen, 1961), "adjustment" (Wiener, Blumberg, Segman, & Cooper, 1959), and "health-sickness" (Kogan, Quinn, Ax, & Ripley, 1957).

Given the relationships existing between masculine versus feminine characteristics and social desirability, on the one hand, and between mental health and social desirability on the other, it seems reasonable to expect that clinicians will maintain parallel distinctions in their concepts of what, behaviorally, is healthy or pathological when considering men versus women. More specifically, particular behaviors and characteristics may be thought indicative of pathology in members of one sex, but not pathological in members of the opposite sex.

The present paper, then, tests the hypothesis that clinical judgments about the traits characterizing healthy, mature individuals will differ as a function of the sex of the person judged. Furthermore, these differences in clinical judgments are expected to parallel the stereotypic sex-role differences previously reported (Rosenkrantz et al., 1968).

Finally, the present paper hypothesizes that behavioral attributes which are regarded as healthy for an adult, sex unspecified, and thus presumably viewed from an ideal, absolute standpoint, will more often be considered by clinicians as healthy or appropriate for men than for women. This hypothesis derives from the assumption that abstract notions of health will tend to be more influenced by the greater social value of masculine stereotypic characteristics than by the lesser valued feminine stereotypic characteristics.

[1] Requests for reprints should be sent to Inge K. Broverman, Worcester State Hospital, Worcester, Massachusetts 01604.

1

The authors are suggesting, then, that a double standard of health exists wherein ideal concepts of health for a mature adult, sex unspecified, are meant primarily for men, less so for women.

METHOD

Subjects

Seventy-nine clinically-trained psychologists, psychiatrists, or social workers (46 men, 33 women) served as Ss. Of these, 31 men and 18 women had PhD or MD degrees. The Ss were all actively functioning in clinical settings. The ages varied between 23 and 55 years and experience ranged from internship to extensive professional experience.

Instrument

The authors have developed a Stereotype Questionnaire which is described in detail elsewhere (Rosenkrantz et al., 1968). Briefly, the questionnaire consists of 122 bipolar items each of which describes, with an adjective or a short phrase, a particular behavior trait or characteristic such as:

Very aggressive   Not at all aggressive
Doesn't hide emotions at all   Always hides emotions

One pole of each item can be characterized as typically masculine, the other as typically feminine (Rosenkrantz et al., 1968). On 41 items, 70% or better agreement occurred as to which pole characterizes men or women, respectively, in both a sample of college men and in a sample of college women (Rosenkrantz et al., 1968). These items have been classified as "stereotypic."

The questionnaire used in the present study differs slightly from the original questionnaire. Seven original items seemed to reflect adolescent concerns with sex, for example, "very proud of sexual ability · · · not at all concerned with sexual ability." These items were replaced by seven more general items. Since three of the discarded items were stereotypic, the present questionnaire contains only 38 stereotypic items. These items are shown in Table 1.

Finally, in a prior study, judgments have been obtained from samples of Ss as to which pole of each item represents the more socially desirable behavior or trait for an adult individual in general, regardless of sex. On 27 of the 38 stereotypic items, the masculine pole is more socially desirable, (male-valued items), and on the remaining 11 stereotypic items, the feminine pole is the more socially desirable one (female-valued items).

Instructions

The clinicians were given the 122-item questionnaire with one of three sets of instructions, "male," "female," or "adult." Seventeen men and 10 women were given the "male" instructions which stated "think of normal, adult men and then indicate on each item the pole to which a mature, healthy,

socially competent adult man would be closer." The Ss were asked to look at the opposing poles of each item in terms of directions rather than extremes of behavior. Another 14 men and 12 women were given "female" instructions, that is, they were asked to describe a "mature, healthy, socially competent adult woman." Finally, 15 men and 11 women were given "adult" instructions. These Ss were asked to describe a "healthy, mature, socially competent adult person" (sex unspecified). Responses to these "adult" instructions may be considered indicative of "ideal" health patterns, without respect to sex.

Scores

Although Ss responded to all 122 items, only the stereotypic items which reflect highly consensual, clear distinctions between men and women, as perceived by lay people were analyzed. The questionnaires were scored by counting the number of Ss that marked each pole of each stereotypic item, within each set of instructions. Since some Ss occasionally left an item blank, the proportion of Ss marking each pole was computed for each item. Two types of scores were developed: "agreement" scores and "health" scores.

The agreement scores consisted of the proportion of Ss on that pole of each item which was marked by the majority of the Ss. Three agreement scores for each item were computed; namely, a "masculinity agreement score" based on Ss receiving the "male" instructions, a "femininity agreement score," and an "adult agreement score" derived from the Ss receiving the "female" and "adult" instructions, respectively.

The health scores are based on the assumption that the pole which the majority of the clinicians consider to be healthy for an adult, independent of sex, reflects an ideal standard of health. Hence, the proportion of Ss with either male or female instructions who marked that pole of an item which was most often designated as healthy for an adult was taken as a "health" score. Thus, two health scores were computed for each of the stereotypic items: a "masculinity health score" from Ss with "male" instructions, and a "femininity health score" from Ss with "female" instructions.

RESULTS

Sex Differences in Subject Responses

The masculinity, femininity, and adult health and agreement scores of the male clinicians were first compared to the comparable scores of the female clinicians via *t* tests. None of these *t* tests were significant (the probability levels ranged from .25 to .90). Since the male and female Ss did not differ significantly in any way, all further analyses were performed with the samples of men and women combined.

CLINICAL JUDGMENTS OF MENTAL HEALTH   3

TABLE 1

MALE-VALUED AND FEMALE-VALUED STEREOTYPIC ITEMS

Feminine pole	Masculine pole
Male-valued items	
Not at all aggressive	Very aggressive
Not at all independent	Very independent
Very emotional	Not at all emotional
Does not hide emotions at all	Almost always hides emotions
Very subjective	Very objective
Very easily influenced	Not at all easily influenced
Very submissive	Very dominant
Dislikes math and science very much	Likes math and science very much
Very excitable in a minor crisis	Not at all excitable in a minor crisis
Very passive	Very active
Not at all competitive	Very competitive
Very illogical	Very logical
Very home oriented	Very worldly
Not at all skilled in business	Very skilled in business
Very sneaky	Very direct
Does not know the way of the world	Knows the way of the world
Feelings easily hurt	Feelings not easily hurt
Not at all adventurous	Very adventurous
Has difficulty making decisions	Can make decisions easily
Cries very easily	Never cries
Almost never acts as a leader	Almost always acts as a leader
Not at all self-confident	Very self-confident
Very uncomfortable about being aggressive	Not at all uncomfortable about being aggressive
Not at all ambitious	Very ambitious
Unable to separate feelings from ideas	Easily able to separate feelings from ideas
Very dependent	Not at all dependent
Very conceited about appearance	Never conceited about appearance
Female-valued items	
Very talkative	Not at all talkative
Very tactful	Very blunt
Very gentle	Very rough
Very aware of feelings of others	Not at all aware of feelings of others
Very religious	Not at all religious
Very interested in own appearance	Not at all interested in own appearance
Very neat in habits	Very sloppy in habits
Very quiet	Very loud
Very strong need for security	Very little need for security
Enjoys art and literature very much	Does not enjoy art and literature at all
Easily expresses tender feelings	Does not express tender feelings at all

Agreement Scores

The means and sigmas of the adult, masculinity, and femininity agreement scores across the 38 stereotypic items are shown in Table 2. For each of these three scores, the average proportion of *S*s agreeing as to which pole reflects the more healthy behavior or trait is significantly greater than the .50 agreement one would expect by chance. Thus, the average masculinity agreement score is .831 ($z = 3.15$, $p < .001$), the average femininity agreement score is .763 ($z = 2.68$, $p < .005$), and the average adult agreement score is .866 ($z = 3.73$, $p < .001$). These means indicate that on the stereotypic items clinicians strongly agree on the behaviors and attributes which

4   BROVERMAN, BROVERMAN, CLARKSON, ROSENKRANTZ, AND VOGEL

TABLE 2

MEANS AND STANDARD DEVIATIONS FOR ADULT,
MASCULINITY, AND FEMININITY AGREEMENT
SCORES ON 38 STEREOTYPIC ITEMS

Agreement score	M	SD	Deviation from chance	
			Z	p
Adult	.866	.116	3.73	< .001
Masculinity	.831	.122	3.15	< .001
Femininity	.763	.164	2.68	< .005

characterize a healthy man, a healthy woman, or a healthy adult independent of sex, respectively.

Relationship between Clinical Judgments of Health and Student Judgments of Social Desirability

Other studies indicate that social desirability is related to clinical judgments of mental health (Cowen, 1961; Kogan et al., 1957; Wiener et al., 1959). The relation between social desirability and clinical judgment was tested in the present data by comparing the previously established socially desirable poles of the stereotypic items (Rosenkrantz et al., 1968) to the poles of those items which the clinicians judged to be the healthier and more mature for an *adult*. Table 3 shows that the relationship is, as predicted, highly significant ($\chi^2 = 23.64$, $p < .001$). The present data, then, confirm the previously reported relationships that social desirability, as perceived by nonprofessional *Ss*, is strongly related to professional concepts of mental health.

The four items on which there is disagreement between health and social desirability ratings are: to be emotional; not to hide emotions; to be religious; to have a very strong need for security. The first two items are considered to be healthy for adults by clinicians but not by students; the second two items have the reverse pattern of ratings.

Sex-Role Stereotype and Masculinity versus Femininity Health Scores

On 27 of the 38 stereotypic items, the male pole is perceived as more socially desirable by a sample of college students (male-valued items); while on 11 items, the feminine pole is seen as more socially desirable (female-

valued items). A hypothesis of this paper is that the masculinity health scores will tend to be greater than the femininity health scores on the male-valued items, while the femininity health scores will tend to be greater than the masculinity health scores on the female-valued items. In other words, the relationship of the clinicians' judgments of health for men and women are expected to parallel the relationship between stereotypic sex-role behaviors and social desirability. The data support the hypothesis. Thus, on 25 of the 27 male-valued items, the masculinity health score exceeds the femininity health score; while 7 of the 11 female-valued items have higher femininity health scores than masculinity health scores. On four of the female-valued items, the masculinity health score exceeds the femininity health score. The chi-square derived from these data is 10.73 ($df = 1$, $p < .001$). This result indicates that clinicians tend to consider socially desirable masculine characteristics more often as healthy for men than for women. On the other hand, only about half of the socially desirable feminine characteristics are considered more often as healthy for women rather than for men.

On the face of it, the finding that clinicians tend to ascribe male-valued stereotypic traits more often to healthy men than to healthy women may seem trite. However, an examination of the content of these items suggests that this trite-seeming phenomenon conceals a powerful, negative assessment of women. For instance, among these items, clinicians are more likely to suggest that healthy women differ from healthy men by being more submissive, less independent, less adventurous, more easily influenced, less aggressive, less

TABLE 3

CHI-SQUARE ANALYSIS OF SOCIAL DESIRABILITY
VERSUS ADULT HEALTH SCORES ON
38 STEREOTYPIC ITEMS

Item	Pole elected by majority of clinicians for healthy adults
Socially desirable pole	34
Socially undesirable pole	4

Note.—$\chi^2 = 23.64$, $p < .001$.

competitive, more excitable in minor crises, having their feelings more easily hurt, being more emotional, more conceited about their appearance, less objective, and disliking math and science. This constellation seems a most unusual way of describing any mature, healthy individual.

Mean Differences between Masculinity Health Scores and Femininity Health Scores

The above chi-square analysis reports a significant pattern of differences between masculine and feminine health scores in relationship to the stereotypic items. It is possible, however, that the differences, while in a consistent, predictable direction, actually are trivial in magnitude. A t test, performed between the means of the masculinity and femininity health scores, yielded a t of 2.16 ($p < .05$), indicating that the mean masculinity health score (.827) differed significantly from the mean femininity health score (.747). Thus, despite massive agreement about the health dimension per se, men and women appear to be located at significantly different points along this well-defined dimension of health.

Concepts of the Healthy Adult versus Concepts of Healthy Men and Healthy Women

Another hypothesis of this paper is that the concepts of health for a sex-unspecified adult, and for a man, will not differ, but that the concepts of health for women will differ significantly from those of the adult.

This hypothesis was tested by performing t tests between the adult agreement scores versus the masculinity and femininity health scores. Table 4 indicates, as predicted, that the adult and masculine concepts of health do not differ significantly ($t = 1.38$, $p > .10$), whereas, a significant difference does exist between the concepts of health for adults versus females ($t = 3.33$, $p < .01$).

These results, then, confirm the hypothesis that a double standard of health exists for men and women, that is, the general standard of health is actually applied only to men, while healthy women are perceived as significantly less healthy by adult standards.

TABLE 4

RELATION OF ADULT HEALTH SCORES TO MASCULINITY HEALTH SCORES AND TO FEMININITY HEALTH SCORES ON 38 STEREOTYPIC ITEMS

Health score	M	SD
Masculinity	.827	.130
		$t = 1.38$*
Adult	.866	.115
		$t = 3.33$**
Femininity	.747	.187

* $df = 74$, $p > .05$.
** $df = 74$, $p < .01$.

DISCUSSION

The results of the present study indicate that high agreement exists among clinicians as to the attributes characterizing healthy adult men, healthy adult women, and healthy adults, sex unspecified. This agreement, furthermore, holds for both men and women clinicians. The results of this study also support the hypotheses that (*a*) clinicians have different concepts of health for men and women and (*b*) these differences parallel the sex-role stereotypes prevalent in our society.

Although no control for the theoretical orientation of the clinicians was attempted, it is unlikely that a particular theoretical orientation was disproportionately represented in the sample. A counterindication is that the clinicians' concepts of health for a mature adult are strongly related to the concepts of social desirability held by college students. This positive relationship between social desirability and concepts of health replicates findings by a number of other investigators (Cowen, 1961; Kogan et al., 1957; Wiener et al., 1959).

The clinicians' concepts of a healthy, mature man do not differ significantly from their concepts of a healthy adult. However, the clinicians' concepts of a mature healthy woman do differ significantly from their adult health concepts. Clinicians are significantly less likely to attribute traits which characterize healthy adults to a woman than they are likely to attribute these traits to a healthy man.

Speculation about the reasons for and the effects of this double standard of health and its ramifications seems appropriate. In the

6   Broverman, Broverman, Clarkson, Rosenkrantz, and Vogel

first place, men and women do differ biologically, and these biological differences appear to be reflected behaviorally, with each sex being more effective in certain behaviors (Broverman, Klaiber, Kobayashi, & Vogel, 1968). However, we know of no evidence indicating that these biologically-based behaviors are the basis of the attributes stereotypically attributed to men and to women. Even if biological factors did contribute to the formation of the sex-role stereotypes, enormous overlap undoubtedly exists between the sexes with respect to such traits as logical ability, objectivity, independence, etc., that is, a great many women undoubtedly possess these characteristics to a greater degree than do many men. In addition, variation in these traits within each sex is certainly great. In view of the within-sex variability, and the overlap between sexes, it seems inappropriate to apply different standards of health to men compared to women on purely biological grounds.

More likely, the double standard of health for men and women stems from the clinicians' acceptance of an "adjustment" notion of health, for example, health consists of a good adjustment to one's environment. In our society, men and women are systematically trained, practically from birth on, to fulfill different social roles. An adjustment notion of health, plus the existence of differential norms of male and female behavior in our society, automatically lead to a double standard of health. Thus, for a woman to be healthy, from an adjustment viewpoint, she must adjust to and accept the behavioral norms for her sex, even though these behaviors are generally less socially desirable and considered to be less healthy for the generalized competent, mature adult.

By way of analogy, one could argue that a black person who conformed to the "pre-civil rights" southern Negro stereotype, that is, a docile, unambitious, childlike, etc., person, was well adjusted to his environment and, therefore, a healthy and mature adult. Our recent history testifies to the bankruptcy of this concept. Alternative definitions of mental health and maturity are implied by concepts of innate drives toward self-actualization, toward mastery of the environment, and toward fulfillment of one's potential (Allport,

1955; Bühler, 1959; Erikson, 1950; Maslow, 1954; Rogers, 1951). Such innate drives, in both blacks and women, are certainly in conflict with becoming adjusted to a social environment with associated restrictive stereotypes. Acceptance of an adjustment notion of health, then, places women in the conflictual position of having to decide whether to exhibit those positive characteristics considered desirable for men and adults, and thus have their "femininity" questioned, that is, be deviant in terms of being a woman; or to behave in the prescribed feminine manner, accept second-class adult status, and possibly live a lie to boot.

Another problem with the adjustment notion of health lies in the conflict between the overt laws and ethics existing in our society versus the covert but real customs and mores which significantly shape an individual's behavior. Thus, while American society continually emphasizes equality of opportunity and freedom of choice, social pressures toward conformity to the sex-role stereotypes tend to restrict the actual career choices open to women, and, to a lesser extent, men. A girl who wants to become an engineer or business executive, or a boy who aspires to a career as a ballet dancer or a nurse, will at least encounter raised eyebrows. More likely, considerable obstacles will be put in the path of each by parents, teachers, and counselors.

We are not suggesting that it is the clinicians who pose this dilemma for women. Rather, we see the judgments of our sample of clinicians as merely reflecting the sex-role stereotypes, and the differing valuations of these stereotypes, prevalent in our society. It is the attitudes of our society that create the difficulty. However, the present study does provide evidence that clinicians do accept these sex-role stereotypes, at least implicitly, and, by so doing, help to perpetuate the stereotypes. Therapists should be concerned about whether the influence of the sex-role stereotypes on their professional activities acts to reinforce social and intrapsychic conflict. Clinicians undoubtedly exert an influence on social standards and attitudes beyond that of other groups. This influence arises not only from their effect on many individuals through conventional clinical functioning, but also out of their role as "expert" which leads to consultation to governmental and private agencies of all kinds, as well as guidance of the general public.

It may be worthwhile for clinicians to critically examine their attitudes concerning sex-role stereotypes, as well as their position with respect to an adjustment notion of health. The cause of mental health may be better served if both men and women are encouraged toward maximum realization of individual potential, rather than to an adjustment to existing restrictive sex roles.

REFERENCES

ALLPORT, G. W. *Becoming.* Princeton: Yale University Press, 1955.

ANASTASI, A., & FOLEY, J. P., JR. *Differential psychology.* New York: Macmillan, 1949.

BROVERMAN, D. M., KLAIBER, E. L., KOBAYASHI, Y., & VOGEL, W. Roles of activation and inhibition in sex differences in cognitive abilities. *Psychological Review,* 1968, 75, 23–50.

BÜHLER, C. Theoretical observations about life's basic tendencies. *American Journal of Psychotherapy,* 1959, 13, 561–581.

COWEN, E. L. The social desirability of trait descriptive terms: Preliminary norms and sex differences. *Journal of Social Psychology,* 1961, 53, 225–233.

ERIKSON, E. H. *Childhood and society.* New York: Norton, 1950.

FERNBERGER, S. W. Persistence of stereotypes concerning sex differences. *Journal of Abnormal and Social Psychology,* 1948, 43, 97–101.

KITAY, P. M. A comparison of the sexes in their attitudes and beliefs about women. *Sociometry,* 1940, 34, 399–407.

KOGAN, W. S., QUINN, R., AX, A. F., & RIPLEY, H. S. Some methodological problems in the quantification of clinical assessment by Q array. *Journal of Consulting Psychology,* 1957, 21, 57–62.

KOMAROVSKY, M. Functional analysis of sex roles. *American Sociological Review,* 1950, 15, 508–516.

LYNN, D. B. A note on sex differences in the development of masculine and feminine identification. *Psychological Review,* 1959, 66, 126–135.

MASLOW, A. H. *Motivation and personality.* New York: Harper, 1954.

McKEE, J. P., & SHERRIFFS, A. C. The differential evaluation of males and females. *Journal of Personality,* 1957, 25, 356–371.

McKEE, J. P., & SHERRIFFS, A. C. Men's and women's beliefs, ideals, and self-concepts. *American Journal of Sociology,* 1959, 64, 356–363.

ROGERS, C. R. *Client-centered therapy; Its current practice, implications, and theory.* Boston: Houghton, 1951.

ROSENKRANTZ, P., VOGEL, S., BEE, H., BROVERMAN, I., & BROVERMAN, D. Sex-role stereotypes and self-concepts in college students. *Journal of Consulting and Clinical Psychology,* 1968, 32, 287–295.

SEWARD, G. H. *Sex and the social order.* New York: McGraw-Hill, 1946.

SEWARD, G. H., & LARSON, W. R. Adolescent concepts of social sex roles in the United States and the two Germanies. *Human Development,* 1968, 11, 217–248.

WHITE, L., JR. *Educating our daughters.* New York: Harper, 1950.

WIENER, M., BLUMBERG, A., SEGMAN, S., & COOPER, A. A judgment of adjustment by psychologists, psychiatric social workers, and college students, and its relationship to social desirability. *Journal of Abnormal Social Psychology,* 1959, 59, 315–321.

WYLIE, R. *The self concept.* Lincoln: University of Nebraska Press, 1961.

(Received December 23, 1968)

[10]

JOURNAL OF SOCIAL ISSUES
VOLUME 28, NUMBER 2, 1972

Sex-Role Stereotypes: A Current Appraisal [1]

Inge K. Broverman

Worcester State Hospital

Susan Raymond Vogel

Brandeis University Mental Health Center

Donald M. Broverman

Worcester State Hospital

Frank E. Clarkson

Worcester State Hospital

Paul S. Rosenkrantz

College of the Holy Cross

Consensus about the differing characteristics of men and women exists across groups differing in sex, age, marital status, and educa-

[1] This work was in part supported by Contract No. N I H - 71 - 2038 with the National Institutes of Health, Department of Health, Education and Welfare.

60   INGE BROVERMAN ET AL.

tion. Masculine characteristics are positively valued more often than feminine characteristics. Positively-valued masculine traits form a cluster entailing competence; positively-valued feminine traits reflect warmth-expressiveness. Sex-role definitions are incorporated into the self-concepts of both men and women; moreover, these sex-role differences are considered desirable by college students and healthy by mental health professionals. Individual differences in sex related self-concepts are related to sex-role relevant behaviors such as achieved and ideal family size. Sex-role perceptions also vary as a function of maternal employment.

Sex-role standards can be defined as the sum of socially designated behaviors that differentiate between men and women. Traditionally, psychologists have uncritically accepted sex roles as essential to personality development and function. Thus psychopathologists have considered gender identity to be a crucial factor in personal adjustment, with disturbances in adjustment often attributed to inadequate gender identity. Developmentalists tend to focus upon the conditions and processes which facilitate successful internalization of appropriate sex-role standards. The positive values of sex-role standards have rarely been questioned.

Recently, however, investigators have expressed concern over possible detrimental effects of sex-role standards upon the full development of capabilities of men and women (Blake, 1968; Davis, 1967; Hartley, 1961; Horner, 1969; Maccoby, 1963; Rossi, 1964). Traditional sex-role patterns are also being challenged by the new feminist movement. During such a period of revaluation, there is need for a close systematic scrutiny of the actual content of sex-role standards and an examination of the influence that these standards have upon individual behaviors. For the past six years we have been engaged in programmatic research examining the nature and effects of sex-role standards in our contemporary society. As psychologists with varying theoretical backgrounds, we share the conviction that existing sex-role standards exert real pressures upon individuals to behave in prescribed ways; we share also a strong curiosity as to what these standards consist of, how they develop, and what their consequences are.

It appeared in the mid 1960s that traditional sex-role patterns were in a state of flux, and we anticipated that a corresponding fluidity would appear in definitions of sex roles. As a first step toward determining these definitions, we devised a questionnaire that assesses individual perceptions of "typical"

SEX-ROLE STEREOTYPES: A CURRENT APPRAISAL   61

masculine and feminine behavior (Rosenkrantz, Vogel, Bee, Broverman, & Broverman, 1968). This questionnaire has now been administered to almost a thousand subjects, providing normative indices of the content of sex-role standards. In addition, individual differences in sex-role perception have been related to a number of independent variables, thus providing some tentative answers to questions about the antecedents and consequents of varying perceptions of sex roles.

Our findings, culled from a number of studies, lead to the following broad conclusions:

1. A strong consensus about the differing characteristics of men and women exists across groups which differ in sex, age, religion, marital status, and educational level.

2. Characteristics ascribed to men are positively valued more often than characteristics ascribed to women. The positively-valued masculine traits form a cluster of related behaviors which entail competence, rationality, and assertion; the positively-valued feminine traits form a cluster which reflect warmth and expressiveness.

3. The sex-role definitions are implicitly and uncritically accepted to the extent that they are incorporated into the self-concepts of both men and women. Moreover, these sex-role differences are considered desirable by college students, healthy by mental health professionals, and are even seen as ideal by both men and women.

4. Individual differences in sex-role self-concepts are associated with (a) certain sex-role relevant behaviors and attitudes such as actual and desired family size, and (b) certain antecedent conditions such as mother's employment history.

These findings will be discussed in detail following a description of our instrument and its development.

DEVELOPMENT OF THE SEX-ROLE QUESTIONNAIRE

Since our concern was with measuring current sex-role perceptions, we rejected traditional masculinity-feminity scales such as the California Psychological Inventory (CPI)(Gough, 1957) precisely because these scales are based on traditional notions of sex-appropriate behaviors and interests, which we suspected might no longer be relevant. Our concern was with the traits and behaviors currently assigned to men and women. Hence we developed our own instrument. Approximately 100 men and women enrolled in three undergraduate psychology classes were asked to list all the characteristics, attributes, and behaviors on which they thought men and women differed. From these listings, all of the items which occurred at least twice ($N = 122$) were selected for inclusion in the questionnaire. These items span a wide range of content, e.g., interpersonal sensitivity, emotionality, aggressiveness, dependence-independence, maturity, intelligence, activity level, gregariousness.

Many of the earlier studies demonstrating the existence of sex-role stereotypes required subjects to select from a list those traits which characterize men and those which characterize women (Fernberger, 1948; Sherriffs & Jarrett, 1953; Sherriffs & McKee, 1957). In contrast, we conceptualized sex roles as the degree to which men and women are perceived to possess any particular trait. Therefore the 122 items were put into bipolar form with the two poles separated by 60 points.

Men and women subjects in various other samples were then given the questionnaire with instructions to indicate the extent to which each item characterized an adult man (masculinity response), an adult woman (femininity response), and themselves (self response). The order of presentation of masculinity and femininity instructions was reversed for approximately half the *Ss* within each sample; however, the self instructions were always given last in order to obtain self-descriptions within a masculinity-femininity context.

Scoring the Sex-Role Questionnaire

The scoring procedure for the instrument, developed in our first study, was based upon responses from 74 college men and 80 college women (Rosenkrantz et al., 1968). The concept of sex-role stereotype implies extensive agreement among people as to the characteristic differences between men and women. Therefore, those items on which at least 75% agreement existed among *Ss* of each sex as to which pole was more descriptive of the average man than the average woman, or vice versa, were termed "stereotypic." Forty-one items met this criterion. To determine the extent of the perceived difference, correlated *t* tests were computed between the masculinity response (average response to the male instructions) and the femininity response to each of the items; on each of the 41 stereotypic items the difference between these two responses was significant ($p <$ .001) in both the samples of men and women. The sterotypic items are listed in Table 1.

Forty-eight of the remaining items had differences between the average masculinity response and the average femininity response that were significant beyond the .05 level of confidence in each sample, but the agreement as to the direction of the differences was less than 75%. These items were termed "dif-

SEX-ROLE STEREOTYPES: A CURRENT APPRAISAL   63

TABLE 1
STEREOTYPIC SEX-ROLE ITEMS
(RESPONSES FROM 74 COLLEGE MEN AND 80 COLLEGE WOMEN)

| Competency Cluster: Masculine pole is more desirable | |
Feminine	Masculine
Not at all aggressive	Very aggressive
Not at all independent	Very independent
Very emotional	Not at all emotional
Does not hide emotions at all	Almost always hides emotions
Very subjective	Very objective
Very easily influenced	Not at all easily influenced
Very submissive	Very dominant
Dislikes math and science very much	Likes math and science very much
Very excitable in a minor crisis	Not at all excitable in a minor crisis
Very passive	Very active
Not at all competitive	Very competitive
Very illogical	Very logical
Very home oriented	Very worldly
Not at all skilled in business	Very skilled in business
Very sneaky	Very direct
Does not know the way of the world	Knows the way of the world
Feelings easily hurt	Feelings not easily hurt
Not at all adventurous	Very adventurous
Has difficulty making decisions	Can make decisions easily
Cries very easily	Never cries
Almost never acts as a leader	Almost always acts as a leader
Not at all self-confident	Very self-confident
Very uncomfortable about being aggressive	Not at all uncomfortable about being aggressive
Not at all ambitious	Very ambitious
Unable to separate feelings from ideas	Easily able to separate feelings from ideas
Very dependent	Not at all dependent
Very conceited about appearance	Never conceited about appearance
Thinks women are always superior to men	Thinks men are always superior to women
Does not talk freely about sex with men	Talks freely about sex with men

| Warmth-Expressiveness Cluster: Feminine pole is more desirable | |
Feminine	Masculine
Doesn't use harsh language at all	Uses very harsh language
Very talkative	Not at all talkative
Very tactful	Very blunt
Very gentle	Very rough
Very aware of feelings of others	Not at all aware of feelings of others
Very religious	Not at all religious
Very interested in own appearance	Not at all interested in own appearance
Very neat in habits	Very sloppy in habits
Very quiet	Very loud
Very strong need for security	Very little need for security
Enjoys art and literature	Does not enjoy art and literature at all
Easily expresses tender feelings	Does not express tender feelings at all easily

64   INGE BROVERMAN ET AL.

ferentiating" items. The remaining 33 items were termed "non-differentiating."

PERVASIVENESS OF SEX-ROLE STEREOTYPES

Numerous investigators have noted the existence of sex-role stereotypes, i.e., consensual beliefs about the differing characteristics of men and women. These stereotypes are widely held (Lunneborg, 1970; Seward, 1946), persistent (Fernberger, 1948), and highly traditional (Komarovsky, 1950; McKee & Sherriffs. 1959). Despite the apparent fluidity of sex-role definition in contemporary society as contrasted with the previous decades, our own findings to date confirm the existence of pervasive and persistent sex-role stereotypes.

In our initial study (Rosenkrantz et al., 1968) Ss were drawn from a variety of New England institutions of higher learning, e.g., a two-year community college, a four-year city college, women's and men's schools, and parochial schools. Although the subsamples clearly differed with respect to religion and social class, our analyses indicated that they did not differ substantially from each other with respect to sex-role perceptions. Furthermore, the average masculinity responses (responses to "adult man" instructions) given by the male subjects to the 122 items correlated nearly perfectly with the average masculinity responses given by the female subjects ($r = .96$). The mean femininity responses (responses to "adult woman" instructions) given by the men and those given by women were also highly correlated ($r = .95$). In addition, the means of the masculinity responses given by men and women were almost identical, as were the mean femininity responses given by the two groups. Thus, we must conclude that sex-role stereotypes cut across the sex, socioeconomic class, and religion of the respondents, at least in individuals who seek education beyond the high school level.

Responses to the sex-role questionnaire have now been obtained from 599 men and 383 women, both married and single, who range in age from 17 to 60 years and in education from the elementary school level to the advanced graduate degree level. These subjects were divided by sex and into three age groups, 17–24 years, 25–44 years, 45–56 years, making a total of six groups. Educational level varied considerably in the four older groups, while it was relatively homogeneous within the two youngest. Marital status also varied among the age groups;

the oldest groups were comprised predominantly of married individuals (most frequently, parents of college students), the middle age groups consisted of both married and single individuals (including priests and nuns), while most subjects in the youngest age groups were single.

Within each of these six groups, the proportion of subjects agreeing that a given pole was more characteristic of men, or of women, was calculated for each item. All items on which agreement differed significantly from chance at the .02 level of confidence or better were noted. Seventy-four of the items met the criterion in at least four of the six different groups; 47 of the items were significant in all six groups. Thus, although some variation exists from group to group, high consensuality about the differing characteristics of men and women was found on a considerable number of items, and this was independent of age, sex, religion, education level, or marital status.

SOCIAL DESIRABILITY OF THE STEREOTYPIC ITEMS

The literature indicates that men and masculine characteristics are more highly valued in our society than are women and feminine characteristics (Dinitz, Dynes, & Clarke, 1954; Fernberger, 1948; Kitay, 1940; Lynn, 1959; McKee & Sherriffs, 1957, 1959; Sherriffs & Jarrett, 1953; Sherriffs & McKee, 1957; Smith, 1939; White, 1950). Moreover, both boys and girls between 6 and 10 years express greater preference for masculine things and activities than for feminine activities (Brown, 1958); similarly between 5 to 12 times as many women than men recall having wished they were of the opposite sex (Gallup, 1955; Terman, 1938). Sears, Maccoby, and Levin (1957) report that mothers of daughters only are happier about a new pregnancy than are mothers of sons. Investigators have also found that the interval between the birth of the first child and conception of the second is longer when the first child is a boy than when it is a girl; and that the likelihood of having a third child is greater if the first two children are both girls than both boys (Pohlman, 1969).

The valuation, or social desirability, of the characteristics designated as masculine or feminine by the questionnaire responses follows this same pattern: The masculine poles of the various items were more often considered to be socially desirable than the feminine poles. This differential valuation of sex-related characteristics was observed in several different

66   INGE BROVERMAN ET AL.

studies. For instance, two different samples of students, one
from a Catholic liberal arts college for men and one from
an Eastern women's college, indicated the pole of each item
that they considered to be the more socially desirable behavior
for the population at large (Rosenkrantz et. al., 1968). Of the
41 items defined as stereotypic, 29 had the masculine pole
chosen as more desirable by a majority of each sample. We
have termed these "male-valued" items; the remaining 12 items
are termed "female-valued." Moreover, the men and women
showed high agreement about which poles were socially desirable
(r between men and women = .96).

Additional samples of men and women were given the
questionnaire with instructions to indicate that point on each
item scale which they considered most desirable for an adult,
sex unspecified. The average response was computed for each
item for the sexes separately. The point most desirable for
an adult was found to be closer to the masculine pole on the
same 29 stereotypic items on which the masculine pole was
considered more socially desirable by the previous samples. Also,
men and women once more showed high agreement about the
point on each stereotypic item that was most socially desirable
for an adult.

Content of the Sex-Role Stereotypes

To explore further the dimensions reflected by the
stereotypic items, factor analyses were performed separately on
the masculinity and feminity responses in both a sample of
men and a sample of women. Each analysis produced two initial
factors accounting, on the average, for 61% of the total extract-
able communality. The two factors in all four analyses divided
the stereotypic items into those on which the male pole is more
socially desirable versus those on which the female pole is more
socially desirable. These results indicated that the stereotypic
items consist of two orthogonal domains, i.e., male-valued items
and female-valued items.

The male-valued items seem to us to reflect a "competency"
cluster. Included in this cluster are attributes such as being
independent, objective, active, competitive, logical, skilled in business, worldly, adventurous, able to make decisions easily, self-
confident, always acting as a leader, ambitious. A relative *absence*
of these traits characterizes the stereotypic perception of women;
that is, relative to men, women are perceived to be dependent,
subjective, passive, noncompetitive, illogical, etc.

SEX-ROLE STEREOTYPES: A CURRENT APPRAISAL 67

The female-valued stereotypic items, on the other hand, consist of attributes such as gentle, sensitive to the feelings of others, tactful, religious, neat, quiet, interested in art and literature, able to express tender feelings. These items will be referred to as the "warmth and expressiveness" cluster. Men are stereotypically perceived as lacking in these characteristics, relative to women.

Self-Concepts and Sex-Role Stereotypes

These factorial distinctions between the male-valued and female-valued components of the sex-role stereotypes have important implications for the self-concepts of men and women.

The social desirability of an item is known to increase the likelihood of that item's being reported as self-descriptive on personality tests (Edwards, 1957). This tendency to align one's self with socially desirable behaviors, together with the fact that the feminine stereotype entails many characteristics that are less socially desirable than those of the masculine stereotype, implies that women ought to reject the negatively-valued feminine characteristics in their self-reports. However, our findings indicate that women incorporate the negative aspects of femininity (relative incompetence, irrationality, passivity, etc.) into their self-concepts along with the positive feminine aspects (warmth and expressiveness).

In a study of college men and women (Rosenkrantz et al., 1968), the mean self-concept scores of the men over the 41 stereotypic items were significantly different from the mean self-concept scores of the women ($p < .001$), indicating that male and female Ss clearly perceived themselves as differing along a dimension of stereotypic sex differences. However, the women's self-concepts were also significantly less feminine than their perceptions of women in general. Similarly, the self-concepts of the men were significantly less masculine than their perceptions of the "average" man.

Ideal Sex-Roles

Our evidence and that of others (Elman, Press, & Rosenkrantz, 1970; Fernberger, 1948; McKee & Sherriffs, 1959) suggest that the existing stereotypic differences between men and women are approved of and even idealized by large segments of our society. One hundred thirty-seven college men

68   INGE BROVERMAN ET AL.

were given the questionnaire with instructions to indicate that
point for each item which is most desirable for an adult man,
and that point which is most desirable for an adult woman.
The number of Ss who agreed that a particular pole of each
item is more desirable for men or women was first computed.
On 71 of the 122 items agreement was significantly different
from chance ($p < .001$). The masculine pole was judged more
desirable ($p < .01$) for men than women on 28 of the 29 male-
valued stereotypic items (competency cluster); similar agreement
reaches the .07 level of confidence on the remaining stereotypic
items. These data indicate that college men feel that it is desirable
for women to be less independent, less rational, less ambitious,
etc., than men.

The 12 stereotypic female-valued items (warmth-expressiveness cluster), however, present a different picture. On only
7 of the 12 items was there significant agreement ($p < .01$)
that the feminine pole is more socially desirable for women
than for men; on one item, the agreement reaches the $p <$
.07 level; on the remaining 4 items there is no significant agreement, i.e., the socially desirable adult pole is rated desirable
as often for men as for women. Thus these male Ss appear
to reserve for men those masculine traits which are socially
desirable for adults in general, and also to consider 40% of
the desirable feminine characteristics as equally desirable for
men.

Again it is important to know not only the extent of agreement among Ss as to whether a trait is more desirable for
men or for women, but also whether there is a significant
difference between the amount of each trait assigned to men
and women. Hence, the mean point at which each trait was
considered most desirable for men and women, respectively,
was computed for each of the stereotypic items. On the 29
male-valued traits, the difference between the means was 9.82;
on the female-valued characteristics, the mean difference was
4.94. The t test between these two differences was significant
($p < .01$). This sample of college men, then, perceives male-
valued traits as significantly less desirable for women than are
female-valued traits for men.

Elman et al. (1970) investigated ideal sex-role concepts of
both men and women. Using a shortened version of our questionnaire which included 10 male-valued and 10 female-valued
stereotypic items, they asked both men and women to indicate
that point on each item which is ideal for men and for women,

respectively. Their results indicate that the concepts of the ideal man and the ideal woman in both men and women subjects closely parallel the male and female sex-role stereotypes. The ideal woman is perceived as significantly less aggressive, less independent, less dominant, less active, more emotional, having greater difficulty in making decisions, etc., than the ideal man; the ideal man is perceived as significantly less religious, less neat, less gentle, less aware of the feelings of others, less expressive, etc., than the ideal woman. Both greater competence in men than in women, and greater warmth and expressiveness in women than in men, then, are apparently desirable in our contemporary society. Furthermore, Elman et. al. and our own results suggest that the college population, a group which tends to be critical of traditional social norms and conventions, nonetheless believes that the existing sex-role stereotypes are desirable.

SEX-ROLE STEREOTYPES AND JUDGMENTS OF MENTAL HEALTH

The literature consistently points to a positive relationship between the social desirability of behaviors and clinical ratings of the same behaviors in terms of normality-abnormality (Cowen, Staiman, & Wolitzky, 1961), adjustment (Wiener, Blumberg, Segman, & Cooper, 1959); and health-sickness (Kogan, Quinn, Ax, & Ripley, 1957). Given the relationship existing between masculine versus feminine characteristics and social desirability, on the one hand, and social desirability and mental health on the other, we expected that clinicians would maintain distinctions in their concepts of healthy behavior in men and women paralleling stereotypic sex differences. Secondly, we predicted that behavioral attributes which are regarded as healthy for an adult, sex unspecified, and presumably indicative of an ideal health pattern will more often be considered by clinicians as healthy for men than for women. This latter prediction was derived from the assumption that an abstract notion of health (adult, sex unspecified) will tend to be more influenced by the greater social desirability of masculine stereotypic characteristics than by the lesser desirability of feminine stereotypic traits (Broverman, Broverman, Clarkson, Rosenkrantz, & Vogel, 1970).

The sample in this study consisted of 79 practicing mental health clinicians: clinical psychologists, psychiatrists, and psychiatric social workers. There were 46 men, 31 of whom held PhD or MD degrees, and 33 women, 18 with doctoral degrees. Their

70   INGE BROVERMAN ET AL.

ages ranged from 23 to 55 years, and their experience from an internship to extensive professional practice. The clinicians were given the sex-role questionnaire with one of three sets of instructions: *male* instructions asked respondents to "think of normal, adult men, and then indicate on each item that pole to which a mature, healthy, socially competent adult man would be closer"; *female* instructions were to describe "a mature, healthy, socially competent adult woman"; finally *adult* instructions asked for the description of "a healthy, mature, socially competent adult person." Ss were asked to think of the poles of each item in terms of direction, rather than in terms of extremes of behavior.

The results of this study, concerning the stereotypic items, indicated that men and women clinicians did not differ from each other in their descriptions of adults, women, and men, respectively. Furthermore, within each set of instructions there was high agreement as to which pole reflected the more healthy behavior, indicating that these clinicians did have generalized concepts of mental health. We also found high agreement between the pole judged as more healthy for an adult by the clinicians and the pole chosen as more desirable for adults by college students ($\chi^2 = 23.64$; $p < .01$). This confirms the positive relationship between professional concepts of mental health and conceptions of social desirability held by lay people which has been reported by other investigators (Cowen et al., 1961; Kogan et al., 1957; Wiener et al., 1959).

Comparisons of the clinicians' judgments of the healthy men and the healthy women on the competency cluster indicated that the desirable masculine pole was ascribed to the healthy man significantly more often than to the healthy woman (on 25 out of 27 items). However, only about half of the socially desirable feminine characteristics (warmth-expressiveness cluster) were ascribed more often to women than to men (7 out of 11 items). On the face of it, the finding that clinicians tend to ascribe the male-valued, competency cluster traits more often to healthy men than to healthy women may seem trite. However, a consideration of the content of these items reveals a powerful, negative assessment of women. In effect, clinicians are suggesting that healthy women differ from healthy men by being more submissive, less independent, less adventurous, less objective, more easily influenced, less aggressive, less competitive, more excitable in minor crises, more emotional, more conceited about their appearance, and having their feelings more easily hurt.

The clinicians' ratings of a healthy adult and a healthy man did not differ from each other. However, a significant difference did exist between the ratings of the healthy adult and the healthy woman. Our hypothesis that a double standard of health exists for men and women was thus confirmed: the general standard of health (adult, sex-unspecified) is actually applied to men only, while healthy women are perceived as significantly *less* healthy by adult standards.

Essentially similar findings were reported by Neulinger (1968), who asked psychiatrists, psychologists, and social workers to rank 20 paragraphs descriptive of Henry Murray's manifest needs according to how descriptive they were of the Optimally Integrated Personality (OIP), i.e., the mentally healthy person. Each of his Ss completed the rankings once for the male OIP, once for the female OIP. His results showed that, although the two rankings were highly correlated, there were significant differences in the mean rankings of male and female OIP on 18 of the 20 paragraphs, 14 of them at the $p < .001$ level. Neulinger's Ss ranked dominance, achievement, autonomy, counteraction, aggression, etc., as more indicative of mental health in men than in women; sentience, nurturance, play, succorance, deference, abasement, etc., were rated as higher for the female OIP than the male OIP. These findings are strikingly similar to ours. Neulinger interprets his findings as indicating that different conceptions of mental health exist for males and females, and that "the sex orientation of this society is not only shared, but also promoted by its clinical personnel." He believes that these rankings reflect an ideal rather than an optimally functioning person, judging by the female OIP, namely: "an affiliative, nurturant, sensuous playmate who clings to the strong, supporting male [Neulinger, 1968, p. 554]."

BEHAVIORAL CORRELATES OF SEX-ROLE STEREOTYPES

Family Size

Davis (1967) and Blake (1969) have proposed that a critical psychological factor affecting the number of children a woman has is her acceptance or rejection of the feminine social role prevalent in our society. Blake (1969) has argued that most societies hold "pronatalistic" attitudes which prescribe for women the role of childbearer and rearer. Effective functioning in this feminine role encourages childbearing and earns social approval, while acceptance of an alternative role, such as gainful employ-

72   INGE BROVERMAN ET AL.

ment outside of the home, tends to reduce childbearing and earn social disapproval. Several studies have reported that working women do indeed desire (Ridley, 1959) and have (Pratt & Whelpton, 1958) fewer children than do nonworking women.

Certainly the sex-role stereotypes delineated by our research appear to be pronatalistic. Women who are perceived and perceive themselves as relatively incompetent might well feel inadequate to the challenges and stresses of employment. A less anxiety-provoking course of action would be to focus one's energies on home and family for which societal approval is certain, regardless of one's effectiveness in this role. Accordingly, we investigated the relationship between self-perception in the context of stereotypic sex roles and the number of children a woman has (Clarkson, Vogel, Broverman, Broverman, & Rosenkrantz, 1970).

Sixty Catholic mothers of male college students were studied. Their ages, 45 to 59 years, permitted the assumption that their families were completed. Only women with two or more children were included, thus excluding women with possible fertility problems. Education ranged from seven grades completed to doctoral degrees, with the median at 12 grades; the number of years employed outside the home since completion of formal education ranged from 0 to 29 years, with the median at 7.5 years.

Mothers with high competency self-concepts, as measured by our sex-role questionnaire, were found to have significantly fewer children than mothers who perceived themselves to be low on the competency items (3.12 versus 3.93 children, $p < .025$). Number of years worked was inversely related to number of children as expected, but did not reach statistical significance ($p < .10$).

Incorporation of male-valued stereotypic traits into the self-concepts of women should not be interpreted as a shift away from the positively valued characteristics of the female stereotype. The correlation between the self-concept score based on the competency cluster and the self-concept score based on the warmth-expressiveness cluster is low and not significant. Moreover, the self-concept scores on the warmth-expressiveness cluster were not related to family size. Thus, the self-concepts of mothers with relatively fewer children differed from the self-concepts of mothers with relatively more children only with respect to the negatively valued aspects of the feminine stereotype, i.e., the competency cluster, but do not differ with respect to the positively valued feminine traits, i.e., the warmth-expressiveness cluster.

Interpretation of these findings is not without ambiguity. It is not clear whether women who perceive themselves as relatively more competent chose to have fewer children; or whether a woman's estimation of her own competency diminishes as a function of her preoccupation with home and family. Preliminary analyses of new data from unmarried women attending a Catholic women's college suggest, however, that self-concept may be primary. College women with relatively high competency self-concepts perceive their ideal future family size as significantly smaller (4.16 children) than college women who see themselves as relatively less competent (4.89 children). Furthermore, those women who perceive themselves as more competent indicate that they plan to combine employment with childrearing, while women who perceive themselves as relatively less competent indicate that they plan to stop working when they become mothers. Self-concept in the context of stereotypic sex roles is thus related not only to the number of children a woman has once her family is completed, but apparently influences the plans of young women concerning their future sex roles.

These data clearly demonstrate a predictable and systematic relationship between sex-role attitudes—specifically, self-concept in a sex-role context—and concrete sex-role behaviors.

Maternal Employment

We have conceptualized sex-role stereotypes very broadly as attitudinal variables which intervene between particular antecedent conditions and sex-role behaviors. The following study demonstrates the relationship between sex-role attitudes and the specific antecedent condition of maternal employment.

We reasoned that a person's perception of societal sex roles, and of the self in this context, may be influenced by the degree of actual role differentiation that one experiences in one's own family. Maternal employment status appears to be central to the role differentiation that occurs between parents. If the father is employed outside the home while the mother remains a full-time homemaker, their roles tend to be clearly polarized for the child. But if both parents are employed outside the home, their roles are more likely to be perceived as similar—not only because the mother is employed, but also because the father is more likely to share childrearing and other family-related

74   INGE BROVERMAN ET AL.

activities with the mother. Evidence exists that husbands of working wives share more in household tasks (Hoffman, 1963) and decisions (Blood, 1963; Heer, 1963) than husbands of wives remaining at home. Moreover, a number of studies suggest that the mother's employment history and status do in fact minimize a daughter's perception of sex-role related behavioral differences (Hartley, 1964), increase the likelihood of her expectation to combine marriage and a career (Riley, 1963), and make her more likely to actually pursue a career (Graham, 1970).

Accordingly, we examined the relationship between mother's employment status and sex-role perceptions of college students (Vogel, Broverman, Broverman, Clarkson, & Rosenkrantz, 1970). The sex-role questionnaire was administered under standard instructions to 24 men and 23 women whose mothers had never been employed, and to 35 men and 38 women whose mothers were currently employed. For each S the mean masculinity, femininity, and self-response scores were computed, separately for the male-valued (competency) items and for the female-valued (warmth-expressiveness) items.

As expected, daughters of employed mothers perceived significantly smaller differences between men and women than did daughters of homemaker mothers, on both the competency cluster and the warmth-expressiveness cluster. Sons of employed mothers perceived a significantly smaller difference between women and men on the warmth-expressiveness cluster than did sons of homemaker mothers. However, the perceptions of the two groups of male Ss did not differ significantly on the competency cluster. Further analysis uncovered another significant difference: Daughters of employed mothers perceived women less negatively on the competency characteristics than did daughters of homemaker mothers. Thus, while the two groups did not differ in their perceptions of women with respect to the characteristics usually valued in women (warmth-expressiveness), daughters of employed mothers did perceive women to be more competent than did the daughters of homemaker mothers.

No significant differences were found between the mean self responses of Ss with employed mothers compared to Ss with homemaker mothers for either men or women. The self responses fall between the masculinity and the feminity responses for all Ss. However, since the difference between the masculinity and the femininity responses is significantly smaller in Ss whose

SEX-ROLE STEREOTYPES: A CURRENT APPRAISAL 75

mothers are employed compared to Ss with homemaker mothers, the meaning of the self-concepts of the two groups may differ as a function of the different contexts in which they occur.

The results of this study suggest that the stereotypic conceptions of sex roles are not immutable. Insofar as perceptions of sex roles are subject to variation as a function of the individual's experience, then societal sex-role stereotypes may also be subject to change.

SUMMARY AND CONCLUSIONS

Our research demonstrates the contemporary existence of clearly defined sex-role stereotypes for men and women contrary to the phenomenon of "unisex" currently touted in the media (Bowers, 1971). Women are perceived as relatively less competent, less independent, less objective, and less logical than men; men are perceived as lacking interpersonal sensitivity, warmth, and expressiveness in comparison to women. Moreover, stereotypically masculine traits are more often perceived to be desirable than are stereotypically feminine characteristics. Most importantly, both men and women incorporate both the positive and negative traits of the appropriate stereotype into their self-concepts. Since more feminine traits are negatively valued than are masculine traits, women tend to have more negative self-concepts than do men. The tendency for women to denigrate themselves in this manner can be seen as evidence of the powerful social pressures to conform to the sex-role standards of the society.

The stereotypic differences between men and women described above appear to be accepted by a large segment of our society. Thus college students portray the ideal woman as less competent than the ideal man, and mental health professionals tend to see mature healthy women as more submissive, less independent, etc., than either mature healthy men, or adults, sex unspecified. To the extent that these results reflect societal standards of sex-role behavior, women are clearly put in a double bind by the fact that different standards exist for women than for adults. If women adopt the behaviors specified as desirable for adults, they risk censure for their failure to be appropriately feminine; but if they adopt the behaviors that are designated as feminine, they are necessarily deficient with respect to the general standards for adult behavior.

While many individuals are aware of the prejudicial effects

76   INGE BROVERMAN ET AL.

of sex-role stereotypes both from personal experience and hear-
say, evidence from systematic empirical studies gives added
weight to this fact. The finding that sex-role stereotypes continue
to be held by large and relatively varied samples of the population and furthermore are incorporated into the self-concepts
of both men and women indicates how deeply ingrained these
attitudes are in our society. The magnitude of the phenomenon
with which individuals striving for change must cope is well
delineated.

On the other hand, the finding that antecedent conditions
are associated with individual differences in stereotypic sex-role
perceptions offers encouragement that change is possible and
points to one manner in which change can be achieved. Finally,
the finding that stereotypic sex-role self-concepts correlate with
actual and desired family size testifies to the central role in
behavior that these concepts play. One can speculate that eventual change in sex-role concepts will in fact be associated with
far reaching changes in the life styles of both women and
men.

REFERENCES

Blake, J. Are babies consumer durables? *Population Studies*, 1968, **22**, 5–25.

Blake, J. Population policy for Americans: Is the government being mis-
lead? *Science*, 1969, **164**, 522–529.

Blood, R. O., Jr. The husband-wife relationship. In F. I. Nye and L.
W. Hoffman (Eds.), *The employed mother in America*. Chicago: Rand
McNally, 1963.

Bowers, F. The sexes: Getting it all together. *Saturday Review*, 1971, **54**,
16–19.

Broverman, I. K., Broverman, D. M., Clarkson, F. E., Rosenkrantz, P.,
& Vogel, S. R. Sex-role sterotypes and clinical judgments of mental
health. *Journal of Consulting Psychology*, 1970, **34**, 1–7.

Brown, D. G. Sex role development in a changing culture. *Psychological
Bulletin*, 1958, **55**, 232–242.

Clarkson, F. E., Vogel, S. R., Broverman, I. K., Broverman, D. M., &
Rosenkrantz, P. S. Family size and sex-role stereotypes. *Science*, 1970,
167, 390–392.

Cowen, E. L., Staiman, M. G., & Wolitzky, D. L. The social desirability
of trait descriptive terms: Applications to a schizophrenic sample.
Journal of Social Psychology, 1961, **54**, 37–45.

Davis, K. Population policy: Will current programs succeed? *Science*, 1967,
158, 730–739.

Dinitz, S., Dynes, R. R., & Clarke, A. C. Preference for male or female
children: Traditional or affectional. *Marriage and Family Living*, 1954,
16, 128–130.

SEX-ROLE STEREOTYPES: A CURRENT APPRAISAL   77

Edwards, A. L. *The social desirability variable in personality assessment and research.* New York: Dryden, 1957.

Elman, J. B., Press, A., & Rosenkrantz, P. S. Sex-roles and self-concepts: Real and ideal. Paper presented at the meeting of the American Psychological Association, Miami, August 1970.

Fernberger, S. W. Persistence of stereotypes concerning sex dfferences. *Journal of Abnormal and Social Psychology*, 1948, **43**, 97-101.

Gallup, G. *Gallup poll.* Princeton: Audience Research Inc., 1955.

Gough, H. G. *California Psychological Inventory Manual.* Palo Alto: Consulting Psychologists Press, 1957.

Graham, P. A. Women in academe. *Science*, 1970, **169**, 1284-1290.

Hartley, R. E. Current patterns in sex roles: Children's perspectives. *Journal of the National Association of Women Deans and Counselors*, 1961, **25**, 3-13.

Hartley, R. E. A developmental view of female sex-role defintion and identification. *Merrill-Palmer Quarterly of Behavior and Development*, 1964, **10**, 3-16.

Heer, D. M. Dominance and the working wife. In F. I. Nye and L. W. Hoffman (Eds.), *The employed mother in America.* Chicago: Rand McNally, 1963.

Hoffman, L. W. Parental power relations and the divsion of household tasks. In F. I. Nye and L. W. Hoffman (Eds.), *The employed mother in America.* Chicago: Rand McNally, 1963.

Horner, M. Fail: Bright woman. *Psychology Today*, 1969, **3**.

Kitay, P. M. A comparison of the sexes in their attitudes and beliefs about women. *Sociometry*, 1940, **34**, 399-407.

Kogan, W. S., Quinn, R., Ax, A. F., & Ripley, H. S. Some methodological problems in the quantification of clinical assessment by Q array. *Journal of Consulting Psychology*, 1957, **21**, 57-62.

Komarovsky, M. Functional analysis of sex roles. *American Sociological Review*, 1950, **15**, 508-516.

Lunneborg, P. W. Stereotypic aspects in masculinity-femininity measurement. *Journal of Consulting and Clinical Psychology*, 1970, **34**, 113-118.

Lynn, D. B. A note on sex differences in the development of masculine and feminine identification. *Psychological Review*, 1959, **66**, 126-135.

Maccoby, E. Woman's intellect. In S. M. Farber and R. H. Wilson (Eds.), *The potential of women.* New York: McGraw-Hill, 1963.

McKee, J. P., & Sherriffs, A. C. The differential evaluation of males and females. *Journal of Personality*, 1957, **25**, 356-371.

McKee, J. P., & Sherriffs, A. C. Men's and women's beliefs, ideals, and self-concepts. *American Journal of Sociology*, 1959, **64**, 356-363.

Neulinger, J. Perceptions of the optimally integrated person: A redefinition of mental health. *Proceedings of the 76th Annual Convention of the American Psychological Association*, 1968, 553-554.

Pohlman, E. *The psychology of birth planning.* Cambridge, Mass.: Schenkman, 1969.

Pratt, L., & Whelpton, P. K. Extra-familial participation of wives in relation to interest in and liking for children, fertility planning and actual and desired family size. In P. K. Whelpton and C. V. Kiser (Eds.),

78   INGE BROVERMAN ET AL.

Social and psychological factors affecting fertility. Vol. 5. New York: Milbank Memorial Fund, 1958.
Ridley, J. Number of children expected in relation to nonfamilial activities
   of the wife. *Milbank Memorial Fund Quarterly,* 1959, **37,** 277-296.
Riley, M., Johnson, M., & Boocock, S. Womans changing occupational
   role: A research report. *The American Behavioral Scientist,* 1963, **6,**
   33-37.
Rosenkrantz, P. S., Vogel, S. R., Bee, H., Broverman, I.K., & Broverman,
   D. M. Sex-role stereotypes and self-concepts in college students. *Journal
   of Consulting and Clinical Psychology,* 1968, **32,** 287-295.
Rossi, A. S. Equality between the sexes: An immodest proposal. *Daedalus,*
   1964, **93,** 607-652.
Sears, R. R., Maccoby, E. E., & Levin, H. *Patterns of child rearing.* New
   York: Row, Peterson, 1957.
Seward, G. H. *Sex and the social order.* New York: McGraw-Hill, 1946.
Sherriffs, A. C., & Jarrett, R. F. Sex differences in attitudes about sex
   differences. *Journal of Psychology,* 1953, **35,** 161-168.
Sherriffs, A. C., & McKee, J. P. Qualitative aspects of beliefs about men
   and women. *Journal of Personality,* 1957, **25,** 451-464.
Smith, S. Age and sex differences in children's opinions concerning sex
   differences. *Journal of Genetic Psychology,* 1939, **54,** 17-25.
Terman, L. M. *Psychological factors in marital happiness.* New York: McGraw-
   Hill, 1938.
Vogel, S. R., Broverman, I. K., Broverman, D. M., Clarkson, F. E., &
   Rosenkrantz, P. S. Maternal employment and perception of sex-roles
   among college students. *Developmental Psychology,* 1970, **3,** 384-391.
White, L., Jr. *Educating our daughters.* New York: Harper, 1950.
Wiener, M., Blumberg, A., Segman, S., & Cooper, A. A judgment of
   adjustment by psychologists, psychiatric social workers, and college
   students, and its relationship to social desirability. *Journal of Abnormal
   and Social Psychology,* 1959, **59,** 315-321.

[11]

Journal of Personality and Social Psychology
1987, Vol. 53, No. 3, 463–469

Broverman et al. Revisited: An Artifactual Sex Bias

Thomas A. Widiger and Shirley A. Settle
University of Kentucky

Broverman, Broverman, Clarkson, Rosenkrantz, and Vogel (1970) is one of the most widely cited and influential studies on sex bias in the judgment of mental health. However, we demonstrate in this study that the findings were the result of an imbalanced ratio of male-valued to female-valued items in the dependent measure that forced the subjects to display a sex bias. A sex bias against women, against men, and no bias are obtained by altering the ratio of male-valued to female-valued items. The implications of the results for the measurement of sex biases and sex roles are discussed.

Broverman, Broverman, Clarkson, Rosenkrantz, and Vogel (1970) reported that "clinicians are significantly less likely to attribute traits which characterize healthy adults to a woman than they are likely to attribute these traits to a healthy man" (p. 5). Broverman et al. (1970) is widely recognized as the most influential and important study on sex bias in the judgment of mental health (Davidson & Abramowitz, 1980; Deaux, 1985; Hare-Mustin, 1983; Schaffer, 1980; Smith, 1980; Stricker, 1977; Zeldow, 1978). The study was published 17 years ago, but it is still being cited as the principal support for the hypothesis of sex bias in clinical judgments. "The implications of the stereotyping described by Broverman et al. (1970) . . . are that to be considered an unhealthy adult, women must act as women are supposed to act (conform too much to the female sex role stereotype); to be considered an unhealthy woman, women must act as men are supposed to act" (Kaplan, 1983, p. 788). "According to Broverman et al. (1970), mental health professionals, rather than challenging gender stereotypes, shared popular biases" (Person, 1983, p. 38). "Broverman and associates noted different standards of mental health for women and men, including tacit assumptions that dependency and passivity are normal for women" (Karasu, 1980, p. 1509). Many other examples are readily found (e.g., Hare-Mustin, 1983; Lemkau, 1983; LoPiccolo, Heiman, Hogan, & Roberts, 1985; Russell, 1986).

A number of methodological and conceptual limitations have been noted (Gove, 1980; Phillips & Gilroy, 1985; Smith, 1980; Stearns, Penner, & Kimmel, 1980; Stricker, 1977). The findings of Broverman et al. (1970) may not demonstrate that clinicians have a biased standard of health because (a) it was an analogue study (Smith, 1980), (b) failures to replicate tend to be unpublished (Smith, 1980), (c) the subjects' ratings may have been accurate (Gove, 1980), (d) the sex of the subject may not be important when additional information is available (Stearns et

al., 1980), and (e) changes in sex role attitudes may have occurred since (Constantinople, 1973; Phillips & Gilroy, 1985). However, these limitations and qualifications have been disputed, and the study continues to be widely cited as providing empirical support for the sex bias hypothesis (Davidson & Abramowitz, 1980; Hare-Mustin, 1983; Kaplan, 1983; Schaffer, 1980).

What has not been appreciated is that the original findings may have been artifactual. The dependent measure may have impelled the subjects to display a bias against women. It is the hypothesis of this study that the findings were not the result of a bias in the subjects but were instead the result of a bias in the Stereotype Questionnaire. This hypothesis was suggested by Stricker (1977), but it has not been demonstrated empirically and its implications have not been fully appreciated.

The Broverman et al. (1970) Study

Broverman et al. provided 79 subjects with a questionnaire of 122 items. Each item contained two poles (e.g., *very independent–not at all independent*). Subjects were given one of three sets of instructions leading them to think of either "normal, adult men," "normal, adult women," or "normal adults." They were to "indicate on each item the pole to which a mature, healthy, socially competent [adult man, adult woman, or adult person] would be closer" (Broverman et al., 1970, p. 2). They analyzed only the 38 items that had been found to contain sex role stereotypic and socially desirable poles by Rosenkrantz, Vogel, Bee, Broverman, and Broverman (1968). Of these, 27 were "male-valued" and 11 were "female-valued." For example, *very independent–not at all independent* was a male-valued item because the very-independent pole was rated as stereotypically masculine and, by another group of subjects, as socially desirable.

Broverman et al. obtained an agreement score for each item under all three sets of instructions that was the proportion of subjects who marked the pole of the item in the direction marked by a majority of the subjects. They next obtained a masculinity health score, a femininity health score, and an adult health score. The adult health score was equal to the adult agreement score. The masculinity and femininity health scores were the proportion of subjects with the male and female in-

We express our appreciation to Mike Nietzel, Juris Berzins, Tim Trull, and four anonymous reviewers for their comments on an earlier version of this article and to Tonya Scarbrough and Sonya Bonneman for their assistance in the data collection and analyses.

Correspondence concerning this article should be addressed to Thomas A. Widiger, Psychology Department, University of Kentucky, Lexington, Kentucky 40506-0044.

structions, respectively, who marked the item in the same direction as the majority had marked it under the adult instructions. For example, if 85% of the subjects under the male instructions and 40% under the female instructions marked the *very independent–not at all independent* item in the same direction as the majority of subjects marked it under the adult instructions (i.e., the very-independent pole), that item would obtain a .85 masculinity health and a .40 femininity health score.

Broverman et al. then calculated the mean of the health scores across the 38 items. The mean masculinity health score of .827 was significantly higher than the femininity health score of .747 ($t = 2.16, p < .05$). There was no significant difference between the masculinity health score and the .866 adult health score ($t = 1.38, p > .10$), but "a significant difference [did] exist between the concepts of health for adults versus females ($t = 3.33, p < .01$)" (Broverman et al., 1970, p. 5). Broverman et al. (1970) also reported that on 25 of the 27 male-valued items, the masculinity health score exceeded the femininity health score (the excess could be by any amount greater than zero), and on 7 of the 11 female-valued items the femininity health score was greater than the masculinity health score, $\chi^2(1, N = 38) = 10.73, p < .001$.

The Methodological Problem

Broverman et al. acknowledged that the chi-square results were not surprising. What has not yet been appreciated is that the differences in the mean health scores were simply the result of the fact that 71% of the items were male valued. The 38 items analyzed were selected to have only one pole be socially desirable, and for 71% of the items the socially desirable pole was a stereotypically masculine characteristic. When the socially desirable pole concerns a stereotypically masculine characteristic, one would expect less agreement regarding which pole is healthy for a woman than for which is healthy for a man. Because most of the socially desirable poles concerned a stereotypically masculine characteristic, it is not surprising that the mean masculinity health score was close to the adult health score and greater than the femininity health score. If most of the socially desirable poles concerned stereotypically feminine characteristics, one would probably find the femininity health score close to the adult health score and greater than the masculinity health score. This study demonstrates the effect of the bias in the number of male-valued items in the dependent measure by replicating Broverman et al. with 71% of the items male valued (i.e., containing a socially desirable and stereotypically masculine pole), 50% male valued, and 71% female valued (i.e., containing a socially desirable and stereotypically feminine pole).

Method and Results

We could not assume that the items determined to be male valued and female valued by Rosenkrantz et al. (1968) would still obtain comparable stereotypy and social desirability ratings. It was therefore necessary first to repeat the analyses of Rosenkrantz et al. (1968).

Subjects were introductory psychology undergraduate college students, a population comparable to that in Rosenkrantz et al. (1968) but different in age and career from that in Broverman et al. (1970). They were provided with a questionnaire of 110 items that included the 38

items from Broverman et al., items from Rosenkrantz et al. (1968), and additional items representing socially desirable, stereotypic feminine traits.

Rosenkrantz et al. Replication

Stereotypy ratings. Forty-four subjects (24 female and 20 male) were given the same instructions provided by Rosenkrantz et al. (1968) to obtain the stereotypy ratings. Half of the subjects were told to "imagine that you are going to meet a person for the first time and the only thing you know in advance is that the person is an adult male" (p. 288). The subjects were then to mark on a 7-point scale "the extent to which they expected each item to characterize the adult male" (p. 288). Following this rating, they were provided with the same items and instructions for an "adult female." The other half of the subjects was given the female instructions first.

Rosenkrantz et al. (1968) determined an item to be sex role stereotypic if 75% or more of the subjects provided a higher rating for one sex. Of the 122 items used in Rosenkrantz et al., 41 reached this criterion for both male and female subjects. The difference between the mean of the male and female ratings for these items was also statistically significant at $p < .001$. Sixty-four of the 110 items reached this criterion in our study for both male and female subjects, and 62 of these obtained mean differences at $p < .001$.

The masculine and feminine poles of each item were determined by Rosenkrantz et al. (1968) by the relative direction of the mean of the male and female ratings. For example, if the mean male rating for *very subjective–very objective* was closer to the very-objective pole than was the mean female rating, then *very objective* was considered masculine and *very subjective* was considered feminine, even if the mean female rating was closer to the very-objective pole than to the very-subjective pole.

Social desirability. Rosenkrantz et al. (1968) had a separate group of subjects indicate which pole of the 122 items "represented the more socially desirable behavior" (p. 288) without reference to sex. An item was male valued if "the masculine pole was more often perceived as more desirable" (p. 290) and female valued if the feminine pole was more often perceived as more desirable. Twenty-nine of the 41 Rosenkrantz et al. items were male valued and 12 were female valued. In our study, 36 subjects (18 female and 18 male) indicated that 33 of the stereotypic items were female valued and 29 were male valued.

Broverman et al. Replication

Broverman et al. (1970) used 38 of the 41 stereotypic items. We used 54 of the 62 stereotypic items in order to replicate the ratio of 27 male-valued to 11 female-valued items used in Broverman et al. and to analyze in addition a ratio of 27 female-valued to 11 male-valued items and 27 male-valued to 27 female-valued items. The 8 items with the lowest stereotypy ratings, desirability ratings, or both were therefore deleted (2 male valued and 6 female valued).

Table 1 presents the 54 items. Items indicated by a superscript *a* were included in Broverman et al. (1970). Fifteen of the 27 Broverman male-valued items and 3 of the 11 female-valued items were not included because their stereotypy ratings, social desirability ratings, or both did not meet the Rosenkrantz et al. criteria. One item, *very emotional–not at all emotional*, switched from a male-valued to a female-valued item because the socially desirable pole changed from *not at all emotional* to *very emotional*.

The same male, female, and adult instructions used by Broverman et al. (1970) were provided in our study to three groups of subjects of 40 (21 men and 19 women), 44 (23 men and 21 women), and 50 (23 men and 27 women) members, respectively. Each group was administered

Table 1

Agreement and Health Scores for Male-Valued and Female-Valued Items

Feminine pole	Masculine pole	MA	FA	MH	FH	AH
	Male-valued items					
Not at all independent[a,b]	Very independent	95	86	95	86	90
Does not know the way of the world[a]	Knows the way of the world	90	81	90	81	90
Very dependent[a]	Not at all dependent	50	60	50	40	71
Not at all competitive[a]	Very competitive	95	90	95	90	90
Very subjective[a,b]	Very objective	80	62	80	62	77
Not at all adventurous[a,b]	Very adventurous	95	83	95	83	71
Very passive[a,b]	Very active	95	95	95	95	90
Has difficulty making decisions[a]	Can make decisions easily	93	60	93	60	85
Unable to separate feelings from ideas[a,b]	Easily able to separate feelings from ideas	78	55	78	55	92
Very home oriented[a,b]	Very worldly	58	52	58	48	56
Very sneaky[a]	Very direct	85	67	85	67	83
Very excitable in a minor crisis[a,b]	Not at all excitable in a minor crisis	85	69	85	69	75
Does not control emotions	Controls emotions	95	69	95	69	75
Not at all authoritative	Very authoritative	85	76	85	76	71
Acts on feeling rather than logic[b]	Acts on logic rather than feeling	50	55	50	45	60
Not at all brave	Very brave	90	75	90	75	75
Does not enjoy a challenge very much[b]	Enjoys a challenge very much	90	95	90	95	90
Not at all firm	Very firm	95	81	95	81	79
Becomes upset under stress	Controls self under stress	78	57	78	43	83
Not heroic[b]	Heroic	100	60	100	40	90
Not at all industrious	Very industrious	80	81	80	81	90
Does not have a strong will	Has a strong will	85	95	85	95	85
Not at all daring	Daring	98	62	98	62	83
Weak	Strong	100	62	100	62	98
Indecisive	Decisive	93	55	93	55	83
Relies on others[b]	Relies on self	95	67	95	67	77
Very afraid to take risks	Not at all afraid to take risks	75	76	75	76	60
	Female-valued items					
Very talkative[a,b]	Not at all talkative	60	90	60	90	60
Very gentle[a,b]	Very rough	55	95	45	95	85
Very aware of feelings of others[a]	Not at all aware of feelings of others	90	100	90	100	96
Very interested in own appearance[a]	Not at all interested in own appearance	55	100	55	100	85
Very neat in habits[a,b]	Very sloppy in habits	70	86	70	86	96
Enjoys art & literature very much[a]	Does not enjoy art & literature very much	70	93	70	93	90
Very strong need for security[a]	Very little need for security	60	79	40	79	60
Easily expresses tender feelings[a]	Does not express tender feelings at all	60	86	40	86	75
Very soft	Very harsh	65	95	65	95	79
Very considerate of others[b]	Very inconsiderate of others	90	100	90	100	90
Very sensitive	Not at all sensitive	90	95	90	95	85
Very concerned about others	Not at all concerned about others	90	93	90	93	85
Very idealistic	Not at all idealistic	90	81	90	81	75
Very careful[b]	Very careless	75	90	75	90	85
Very understanding of others[b]	Not at all understanding of others	90	95	90	95	75
Very affectionate[b]	Not at all affectionate	80	100	80	100	96
Not at all uncomfortable when people express emotions	Very uncomfortable when people express emotions	55	81	55	81	65
Very emotional	Not at all emotional	60	88	40	88	67
Very soothing[b]	Not at all soothing	90	86	90	86	85
Very compassionate	Not at all compassionate	85	95	85	95	90
Very forgiving	Not at all forgiving	80	90	80	90	85
Very loving	Not at all loving	95	100	95	100	96
Very charitable	Not at all charitable	85	86	85	86	85
Very sympathetic[b]	Not at all sympathetic	75	90	75	90	96
Very sentimental	Not at all sentimental	60	95	60	95	96
Very creative	Not at all creative	83	95	83	95	90
Very warm in relations with others[b]	Very cold in relations with others	90	88	90	88	98

Note. MA = male agreement score; FA = female agreement score; MH = masculinity health score; FH = femininity health score; AH = adult health (agreement) score.
[a] Included in Broverman et al. (1970).
[b] Included in male-bias and female-bias dependent measures.

Table 2
Means and t-Test Results for Health Scores

Dependent measure (item type)	Health scores						t tests			
	Adult (A)		Male (M)		Female (F)					
	M	SD	M	SD	M	SD	A minus M	A minus F	M minus F	df
27 male, 11 female	.81	.12	.82	.16	.75	.18	−.32	1.75*	1.84*	74
27 male, 27 female	.82	.11	.79	.17	.80	.17	.94	.63	−.26	106
11 male, 27 female	.83	.12	.76	.18	.85	.16	2.06**	−.63	−2.36**	74
27 male, 0 female	.80	.11	.85	.14	.69	.17	−1.77*	3.44***	4.60***	52
0 male, 27 female	.84	.11	.73	.18	.92	.06	3.29***	−4.04***	−6.33***	52
Broverman items	.79	.14	.74	.17	.72	.18	1.44	1.94*	.51	74

* $p < .05$, one-tailed. ** $p < .05$, two-tailed. *** $p < .001$, one-tailed.

the 110 items, and the male, female, and adult agreement and health scores described earlier were calculated and are presented in Table 1. It is apparent from Table 1 that the pole chosen under the adult instructions was always the masculine pole for the male-valued items and the feminine pole for the female-valued items. This is not surprising and probably consistent with Broverman et al. (1970) because these poles were already shown to be the socially desirable ones. No significant differences were found between male and female subjects in Broverman et al. or the current study.

The male agreement score was identical to the masculinity health score on 85% of the female-valued items (and on all of the male-valued items), and the female agreement score was identical to the femininity health score on 81% of the male-valued items (and on all of the female-valued items). These results indicate that for the majority of the items, the same pole was considered optimal or descriptive for both sexes. Broverman et al. did not report these data, nor did they provide the results for each item. However, it is likely that they obtained a similar finding, because the means of the male agreement and masculinity health scores (.831 and .827, respectively) and the means of the female agreement and femininity health scores (.763 and .747, respectively) were very close. For the Broverman et al. items that were included in our study, the poles were the same for both sexes on 83% of the male-valued items and 73% of the female-valued items.

The Broverman et al. analyses were applied to three sets of items: (a) a male-bias dependent measure consisting of the 27 male-valued items and 11 female-valued items, which were indicated by a superscript *b* in Table 1 (the female-valued items were selected by a random-numbers table with the constraint that at least half of the Broverman et al. items were included); (b) a no-bias dependent measure consisting of all 54 items; and (c) a female-bias dependent measure consisting of all 27 female-valued items and 11 male-valued items, selected in the same manner as just described.

The results are presented in Table 2. The *t* tests are pair-wise comparisons with independent groups of health-score items. Matched-group *t* tests might be more appropriate because the same items were used under each set of instructions. Unmatched *t* tests are reported to ensure a faithful replication of the analyses used by Broverman et al. (Worell, 1978), but the findings are the same with matched-group *t* tests. Also, multiple *t* tests were conducted on overlapping sets of items. However, this was necessary to demonstrate the effect of altering the dependent measure.

The male-bias measure replicated the results obtained by Broverman et al. (see Table 2). Masculinity health scores were greater than femininity health scores on 22 of the 27 male-valued items, and the reverse was true on 9 of the 11 female-valued items, $\chi^2(1, N = 38) = 10.9$, $p < .001$. When the no-bias measure was used, there were no significant

differences between the means of the adult, masculinity, and femininity health scores. Masculinity health scores were greater than femininity health scores on 22 of the 27 male-valued items, and the reverse was true on 24 of the 27 female-valued items, $\chi^2(1, N = 54) = 17.6$, $p < .001$. With the female-bias measure, there was no significant difference between the means of the adult and femininity health scores, and there were significant differences between the adult and masculinity health scores and the masculinity and femininity health scores. Femininity health scores were greater than masculinity health scores on 24 of the 27 female-valued items, and the reverse was true on 9 of the 11 male-valued items, $\chi^2(1, N = 38) = 15.1$, $p < .001$.

Table 2 also presents the health scores and *t* tests when only the 27 male-valued items were used and when only the 27 female-valued items were used. This alteration magnifies the effect of the bias in the dependent measure. The analyses were also applied to the original set of Broverman et al. items (see Table 2). The failure to replicate completely the Broverman et al. results with these items is most likely the result of the fact that 18 of the items are no longer rated as male valued or female valued in the same manner.

Discussion

The results demonstrated that the findings of Broverman et al. (1970) were a result of the ratio of male-valued to female-valued items in the dependent measure. The sex bias was in the inventory, not the subjects. The illusory nature of their findings is not surprising when one understands how the data were analyzed. If most of the socially desirable poles describe stereotypically masculine behavior, then the masculinity health score is close to the adult health score and greater than the femininity health score. It is relatively easy to obtain agreement on what is healthy for a man when the items contain a pole that describes a socially desirable, stereotypically masculine characteristic, but there is less agreement concerning whether these stereotypically masculine characteristics are optimal for a woman. On the other hand, if most of the socially desirable poles describe stereotypically feminine behavior, then there is considerable agreement regarding which pole is healthy for a woman, and there is less agreement for a man.

Early, classic studies have at times continued to be misreported and exaggerated (Hare-Mustin, 1983; Harris, 1979; Kravitz & Martin, 1986). Historical and scientific accuracy necessitate corrected appreciation of Broverman et al. (1970). The study was important in generating attention and research on sex biases in the judgment of mental health, but it is not itself informative. The findings are compelling and the analyses sufficiently complex that it is understandable that the flaw has gone unrecognized, but it is time that its illusory findings are recognized as such. Clinicians may in fact possess sex biases in their judgments of mental health (Hare-Mustin, 1983; Kaplan, 1983; Widiger & Frances, 1985), but it is not in keeping with an empirical science to rely on the Broverman et al. finding to support this hypothesis.

The measurement problem is particularly important to recognize because it continues to occur. Replications using the Stereotype Questionnaire and similar measures continue to appear (Broverman, Vogel, Broverman, Clarkson, & Rosenkrantz, 1972; Davidson & Abramowitz, 1980; Smith, 1980), most recently by Phillips and Gilroy (1985) and Rosenkrantz, DeLorey, and Broverman (1985), and the sex bias in the dependent measure remains unrecognized.

One may ask, though, whether it is our study that was biased. Perhaps one should use a questionnaire that contains more male-valued items if there are more male-valued terms in the English language. The answer depends on the purpose of the study. Broverman et al. (1970) were testing the hypothesis that clinicians are less likely to attribute traits that characterize healthy adults to a woman than to a man. In this case it is important for the dependent measure not to impel the judgments to be biased against either sex, even if there are more male-valued terms in the English language. A disproportionate number of male-valued terms in the language does not require clinicians to use them more often than female-valued terms, but the dependent measure used by Broverman et al. to assess bias did require clinicians to evaluate the mental health of adults and women in terms that favored men.

In fact, one may question whether the English language is inherently biased against women. The selection of items by Rosenkrantz et al. (1968) was not comprehensive. The 122 items were obtained by asking two undergraduate classes to list behaviors, attributes, and traits they thought differentiated men and women. Items listed more than once were retained. The item list was subsequently shown to be biased in favor of men, but it was not shown to be representative or comprehensive. The item selection in our study was also not comprehensive. Items were purposely chosen to obtain an equal number of female-valued and male-valued traits, many of which were simply synonyms. It would be more informative to rate every trait term in the English language with respect to masculinity and femininity and, independently, with respect to social desirability. This seemingly monumental task is feasible, because Goldberg and Norman have already reduced the 17,953 attribute terms to a complete yet familiar set of 1,710 trait terms (Goldberg, 1982). Norman has also obtained social desirability ratings on a subset of terms (Goldberg, 1982).

Additional Measurement Issues

The results of this study suggest that it may be very difficult to assess sex bias in an unbiased manner. A questionnaire with an equal number of male-valued and female-valued items may

still fail to be unbiased because the degree of desirability and stereotypy may not be equal across items. One can also increase the agreement of the adult health scores for the male-valued or the female-valued items by making the opposite poles undesirable. For example, the pole *very competitive* obtained an adult health score of .90. It might have been lower if its opposite pole was *very cooperative* rather than *not at all competitive*. Because it is difficult to obtain items with equally desirable poles (Goldberg, 1982), it may be best for future studies to obtain unipolar ratings.

A final concern noted elsewhere (Phillips & Gilroy, 1985; Smith, 1980; Stricker, 1977; Widiger & Nietzel, 1984) is that Rosenkrantz et al. (1968) considered a pole of an item to be stereotypically masculine if the male rating was simply closer to the pole than was the female rating. But an item that is more masculine is not necessarily not feminine. The same problem occurs in the Broverman et al. (1970) health ratings. The item *very independent* received a higher masculinity than femininity rating, but 86% of the subjects considered it to be characteristic of the healthy adult woman. A large majority of the subjects in our study considered a healthy adult woman very active (95%), very adventurous (83%), and very competitive (90%). Ratings for women in the opposite direction of men were obtained on only a few of the items. A small majority of the subjects rated the adult woman very dependent (60%), very home oriented (53%), and not heroic (60%). However, comparable majorities stated that a healthy adult man does not express tender feelings at all (60%), is not at all emotional (60%), and is very rough (54%).

Further Implications

This study focused on Broverman et al. (1970), but the results are relevant to other research that uses questionnaires to assess sex role biases and attitudes. One example is the relation of masculinity, femininity, and androgyny to adjustment. This question is different from the issue of whether a particular group of subjects is sex biased, but there is again a problem with the ratio of male-valued to female-valued items, and in this case, having a balance in social desirability can be as problematic as having an imbalance.

If one's measure of masculinity contains more socially desirable traits than does the measure of femininity, masculinity will appear more highly associated with self-esteem, competence, and adjustment than will femininity. On the other hand, if the two scales are equated on social desirability, elevations on both scales will be more highly correlated with various measures of adjustment. Those who are elevated on both (e.g., androgynous persons) will have more socially desirable traits than will those who are elevated on only one.

Partialing out social desirability with a covariate is not necessarily a solution because the association of many of the masculine and feminine traits with self-esteem and adjustment is appropriately reflected in the social desirability of these traits (Nicholls, Licht, & Pearl, 1982). Some masculine and some feminine traits are desirable because they are associated with self-esteem and adjustment. However, whether the construct of masculinity, femininity, or androgyny is more desirable or more

468   THOMAS A. WIDIGER AND SHIRLEY A. SETTLE

highly associated with adjustment is unclear, because the results of any study will depend in part on the relative number and degree of the desirability of the items in the masculinity and femininity scales. Unless the items were selected to represent comprehensively the constructs of masculinity and femininity, the scales may provide a biased measure of these constructs.

Space limitations prohibit a thorough examination of the research on the relation of masculinity, femininity, and androgyny to adjustment with the Bem Sex-Role Inventory (Bem, 1974), the Personality Attributes Questionnaire (Spence, Helmreich, & Stapp, 1974), and the Personality Research Form Androgyny Scale (Berzins, Welling, & Wetter, 1978). The methodological issues and the reasons for inconsistent findings are certainly far more complicated than the relative degree of social desirability in the masculinity and femininity scales (Locksley & Colten, 1979; Nicholls et al., 1982; Spence, 1984). However, the extent to which the various masculinity and femininity scales do provide comprehensive representations of the social desirability of the respective constructs has not been considered, and we suggest that this issue should be addressed if the relation of the various inventories to adjustment is to be interpreted with respect to the constructs of masculinity, femininity, and androgyny.

Conclusions

If one wishes to know whether masculinity or femininity, or their combination, entails healthier or more desirable traits, then one should conduct a representative or comprehensive assessment of the constructs rather than arbitrarily selecting traits or constructing items in order to develop scales that are equal or unequal with respect to social desirability. Whether the language is inherently biased against masculinity or femininity is determined best by a comprehensive sampling of the masculinity and femininity trait terms in the language.

If one wishes to determine whether a particular subject group is biased, then it is necessary to use an unbiased dependent measure. One can use a biased measure if one wishes to compare groups (thereby assessing judgments relative to each other), but the presence of bias within a particular group cannot be determined unless the questionnaire is itself neutral or the degree of bias that the questionnaire would generate in a neutral subject could be determined. The difficulty in developing a neutral questionnaire or determining the degree of bias it would generate in a neutral subject suggest that a more feasible and informative methodology would be to abandon the use of questionnaires altogether and conduct naturalistic studies of the subject group's language usage. Subjects would then not be biased by the content and form of a questionnaire, and one could assess the relative degree and frequency in the use of male-valued and female-valued terms.

References

Bem, S. (1974). The measurement of psychological androgyny. *Journal of Consulting and Clinical Psychology, 42,* 155–162.

Berzins, J., Welling, M., & Wetter, R. (1978). A new measure of psychological androgyny based on the Personality Research Form. *Journal of Consulting and Clinical Psychology, 46,* 126–138.

Broverman, I., Broverman, D., Clarkson, F., Rosenkrantz, P., & Vogel, S. (1970). Sex-role stereotypes and clinical judgments of mental health. *Journal of Consulting and Clinical Psychology, 34,* 1–7.

Broverman, I., Vogel, S., Broverman, D., Clarkson, F., & Rosenkrantz, P. (1972). Sex-role stereotypes: A current appraisal. *Journal of Social Issues, 28,* 59–78.

Constantinople, A. (1973). Masculinity–femininity: An exception to a famous dictum? *Psychological Bulletin, 80,* 389–407.

Davidson, C., & Abramowitz, S. (1980). Sex bias in clinical judgment: Later empirical returns. *Psychology of Women Quarterly, 4,* 377–395.

Deaux, K. (1985). Sex and gender. *Annual Review of Psychology, 36,* 49–81.

Goldberg, L. (1982). From ace to zombie: Some explorations in the language of personality. In C. Spielberger & J. Butcher (Eds.), *Advances in personality assessment* (Vol. 1, pp. 203–234). Hillsdale, NJ: Erlbaum.

Gove, W. (1980). Mental illness and psychiatric treatment among women. *Psychology of Women Quarterly, 4,* 345–362.

Hare-Mustin, R. (1983). An appraisal of the relationship between women and psychotherapy: 80 years after the case of Dora. *American Psychologist, 38,* 593–601.

Harris, B. (1979). Whatever happened to Little Albert? *American Psychologist, 34,* 151–160.

Kaplan, H. (1983). A woman's view of DSM-III. *American Psychologist, 38,* 786–792.

Karasu, T. (1980). The ethics of psychotherapy. *American Journal of Psychiatry, 137,* 1502–1512.

Kravitz, D., & Martin, B. (1986). Ringelmann rediscovered: The original article. *Journal of Personality and Social Psychology, 50,* 936–941.

Lemkau, J. (1983). Women in male-dominated professions: Distinguishing personality and background characteristics. *Psychology of Women Quarterly, 8,* 144–165.

Locksley, A., & Colten, M. (1979). Psychological androgyny: A case for mistaken identity? *Journal of Personality and Social Psychology, 37,* 1017–1031.

LoPiccolo, J., Heiman, J., Hogan, D., & Roberts, C. (1985). Effectiveness of single therapists versus cotherapy teams in sex therapy. *Journal of Consulting and Clinical Psychology, 53,* 287–294.

Nicholls, J., Licht, B., & Pearl, R. (1982). Some dangers of using personality questionnaires to study personality. *Psychological Bulletin, 92,* 572–580.

Person, E. (1983). The influence of values in psychoanalysis: The case of female psychology. In L. Grinspoon (Ed.), *Psychiatry update: The American Psychiatric Association annual review* (Vol. 2, pp. 36–50). Washington, DC: American Psychiatric Press.

Phillips, R., & Gilroy, F. (1985). Sex-role stereotypes and clinical judgments of mental health: The Brovermans' findings reexamined. *Sex Roles, 12,* 179–193.

Rosenkrantz, P., DeLorey, C., & Broverman, I. (1985, August). *One half a generation later: Sex role stereotypes revisited.* Paper presented at the annual convention of the American Psychological Association, Los Angeles.

Rosenkrantz, P., Vogel, S., Bee, H., Broverman, I., & Broverman, D. (1968). Sex-role stereotypes and self-concepts in college students. *Journal of Consulting and Clinical Psychology, 32,* 287–295.

Russell, D. (1986). Psychiatric diagnosis and the oppression of women. *International Journal of Social Psychiatry, 31,* 298–305.

Schaffer, K. (1980). *Sex-role issues in mental health.* Reading, MA: Addison-Wesley.

Smith, M. (1980). Sex bias in counseling and psychotherapy. *Psychological Bulletin, 87,* 392–407.

Spence, J. (1984). Masculinity, femininity, and gender-related traits: A conceptual analysis and critique of current research. In B. Maher & W. Maher (Eds.), *Progress in experimental personality research* (pp. 1–97). New York: Academic Press.

Spence, J., Helmreich, R., & Stapp, J. (1974). The Personal Attributes Questionnaire: A measure of sex-role stereotypes and masculinity–femininity. JSAS: *Catalog of Selected Documents in Psychology, 4,* 43–44.

Stearns, B., Penner, L., & Kimmel, E. (1980). Sexism among psychotherapists: A case not yet proven. *Journal of Consulting and Clinical Psychology, 48,* 548–550.

Stricker, G. (1977). Implications of research for psychotherapeutic treatment of women. *American Psychologist, 32,* 14–22.

Widiger, T., & Frances, A. (1985). Axis II personality disorders: Diagnostic and treatment issues. *Hospital and Community Psychiatry, 36,* 619–627.

Widiger, T., & Nietzel, M. (1984). Kaplan's view of DSM-III: The data revisited. *American Psychologist, 39,* 1319–1320.

Worell, J. (1978). Sex roles and psychological well-being: Perspectives on methodology. *Journal of Consulting and Clinical Psychology, 46,* 777–791.

Zeldow, P. (1978). Sex differences in psychiatric evaluation and treatment: An empirical review. *Archives of General Psychiatry, 35,* 89–93.

Received July 28, 1986
Revision received February 2, 1987
Accepted February 17, 1987 ■

Part II
Cognitive Abilities

[12]

Cognitive Gender Differences Are Disappearing

Alan Feingold   *Yale University*

ABSTRACT: Gender differences in cognitive abilities were determined using the norms from the four standardizations of the Differential Aptitude Tests conducted between 1947 and 1980, and from the four standardizations of the Preliminary Scholastic Aptitude Test/Scholastic Aptitude Test conducted between 1960 and 1983. The standardized gender differences (ds) were averaged over grade of examinees and year of standardization to obtain a mean effect size for each ability, and variations among effect sizes were examined for grade, year, and Grade × Year trends. Girls scored higher than boys on scales of grammar, spelling, and perceptual speed; boys had higher means on measures of spatial visualization, high school mathematics, and mechanical ability; and no average gender differences were found on tests of verbal reasoning, arithmetic, and figural reasoning. Gender differences declined precipitously over the years surveyed, and the increases in these differences over the high school grades have diminished. The important exception to the rule of vanishing gender differences is that the well-documented gender gap at the upper levels of performance on high school mathematics has remained constant over the past 27 years.

In their pioneering review of the literature on sex differences, Maccoby and Jacklin (1974) concluded that there was a gender difference favoring girls in verbal ability, and there were differences favoring boys in quantitative and spatial abilities. Because of the implications of sex differences in cognitive abilities, the Maccoby and Jacklin findings have been widely disseminated and discussed.

Over the past decade, the quantitative or meta-analytic review (Glass, McGaw, & Smith, 1981; Light & Pillemer, 1984; Rosenthal, 1984), which focuses on effect-size summarization and on explaining variability among findings, has gradually been supplanting narrative surveys of the literature. Meta-analysis has become a popular method of reviewing work on gender differences (e.g., Eagly & Steffen, 1986; Hall, 1984; Hyde & Linn, 1986). Hyde's (1981) meta-analysis on cognitive gender differences was conducted on the set of studies reviewed by Maccoby and Jacklin (1974). Hyde used d, an effect size calculated by dividing the mean difference between two groups by their pooled within-group standard deviation (Cohen, 1977), and obtained median effects of .24, .43, and .45 for verbal, mathematical, and visual–spatial abilities, respectively, in the expected directions. Hyde contended that her findings supported Sherman's (1978) interpretation that the magnitude of cognitive gender differences is too small to be meaningful, a position shared by Caplan, MacPherson, and Tobin (1985). Others, however, disagreed (e.g., Burnett, 1986).

Rosenthal and Rubin (1982) and Becker and Hedges (1984) reexamined Hyde's (1981) data and found that the within-domain effect sizes were not homogeneous across the studies Hyde had combined. Most of the heterogeneity was accounted for by two moderator variables, year of study and selectivity (intellectual level) of sample: Girls reportedly showed gains in cognitive abilities relative to boys over years, and more selective samples yielded larger gender differences than did representative groups. The latter finding is corroborated by the work of Benbow and Stanley (1980, 1982; Stanley & Benbow, 1982), who found large gender differences in mathematical reasoning ability among mathematically gifted adolescents. Also, Benbow and Stanley (1982), Hilton and Berglund (1974), and Sherman (1980) found that the gender difference in math performance increased over the high school years. Thus, gender differences should be examined separately for representative and intellectually able groups, and the effect sizes should be calculated within combinations of year of study and grade of examinees.

Burnett (1986) has recently suggested that the most valid way to assess gender differences is to examine the norms for standardized psychometric tests because (a) such norms are based on large representative samples, (b) publication bias is eliminated because the availability of results of sex differences is independent of their statistical significance, and (c) experimenter bias is minimized because examinees in normative groups are tested in large numbers. In this article, I examine the normative data obtained from test manuals and technical reports to document past and current gender differences on the eight scales composing the Differential Aptitude Tests (DAT; Bennett, Seashore, & Wesman, 1947, 1966, 1974, 1982) and on the Verbal and Mathematical portions of the Preliminary Scholastic Aptitude Test (PSAT; Donlon, 1984) and the Scholastic Aptitude Test (SAT; Donlon, 1984).

Differential Aptitude Tests

The DAT is a battery of eight reliable group-administered paper-and-pencil tests. Three DAT scales assess verbal ability: Verbal Reasoning (an analogies test) and Spelling and Language (two tests of English skills). The other scales quantify perceptual speed (Clerical Speed and Accuracy), three-dimensional spatial visualization (Space Relations), arithmetic (Numerical Ability), mechanical aptitude (Mechanical Reasoning), and figural reasoning (Abstract Reasoning).

Each DAT aptitude is measured by a single type of item, and item types have remained constant over the standardizations of the DAT conducted in 1947, 1962, 1972, and 1980, although new forms were administered

Copyright 1988 by the American Psychological Association, Inc. 0003-066X/88/$00.75
Vol. 43, No. 2, 95-103

to each normative sample. Because the DAT standard-izations (a) span a 33-year period, (b) obtained means and standard deviations by sex for Grades 8–12, and (c) used carefully selected samples (see Bennett et al., 1947, 1966, 1974, and 1982, for details of the sampling plans used to ensure nationwide representativeness), the DAT's norms constitute an ideal data base for the assessment of gender differences—and changes in gender differences—across a wide range of cognitive abilities.

A total of 193,844 students (95,462 boys and 98,382 girls) were examined in the DAT standardizations. The sample sizes, by year, were 21,994 (1947), 48,450 (1962), 62,900 (1972), and 60,500 (1980). By grade, the sample sizes were 39,307 (8th grade), 43,345 (9th grade), 42,381 (10th grade), 36,603 (11th grade), and 32,208 (12th grade). The Grade × Year matrix of sample sizes exhib-ited proportionality, and approximately an equal number of boys and girls were tested in each Grade × Year cell, with, at minimum, about 1,500 boys and 1,500 girls per cell.

DAT Analysis

Gender differences (*d*s) were computed by grade and year of standardization for the eight DAT aptitudes, and the 20 effect sizes obtained for each ability are arrayed in matrices in Table 1. Negative signs were assigned to *d*s when female performance was higher than male perfor-mance. Grand means (underscored values) indicate av-erage gender differences (collapsed over grade and year). Also shown are the grade means and the year means, which were used to partition the sums of squares of the 20 *d*s into sources of variance for grade and year. Effect-size growths (ESG) were obtained by subtracting 8th-grade *d*s from their corresponding 12th-grade values to highlight the interaction pattern.

The sources of variance for grade and year were each partitioned into a linear trend (regression) component and a residual component. The variance for the Grade × Year interaction was partitioned into an interaction con-trast (Linear × Linear interaction) and an interaction residual.

The trends for the main effects indicate whether the gender difference increased or decreased in a linear fash-ion with grade or year. The interaction contrast indicates whether the slope of the regression of effect size on grade increased or decreased linearly across standardization years. The proportions of variance explained (eta²) by the three contrasts were summed to obtain an overall R^2 for explained variance. The total sum of squares about each *d* was divided by its *df* (19) to obtain the variance about the mean *d*. Finally, the three residual sources of variance were pooled to form an error term to test the significance of each of the three contrasts.[1]

DAT Results

Cognitive gender differences favoring girls. Exam-ination of the first three matrices in Table 1 shows that all gender differences were negative for the Spelling, Lan-guage, and Clerical Speed and Accuracy tests. Thus, for all grades and all normative years, girls scored higher than boys on these three tests. The average gender difference (the grand mean of each Grade × Year matrix), calculated for each test, appears in Table 1. The smallest mean *d* occurred on the Language test (−.43) and the largest oc-curred on the Spelling test (−.50), but this range is narrow and indicates that the higher average female performance was relatively homogeneous across these tests. The vari-ance of Clerical Speed and Accuracy *d*s (.013), however, was appreciably higher than the variances for Spelling and Language (.004 and .002, respectively).

Of particular concern in the present analyses were the effects of grade and year on the gender differences. Examination of the grade means, shown in the bottom row of each matrix, indicates no clear pattern for either Language or Clerical Speed and Accuracy. For Spelling, however, the girls' advantage over boys increased steadily to a total of 28% from Grade 8 (−.43) to Grade 12 (−.55).

Year of DAT standardization had an effect on gender differences for all three tests. Year means, shown in the next to the last column of each matrix in Table 1, indicate a consistent decrease in effect magnitude from 1947 to 1980. The largest gender difference decline occurred on Clerical Speed and Accuracy, where *d* decreased 45% from −.62 to −.34 over the 33-year period, but notable de-creases were also found for Spelling (17%) and Language (18%). Results of the statistical analysis of the *d*s for the three abilities (Table 2) showed that year of DAT stan-dardization accounted for at least 32% of the variance among effect sizes for all three tests.

The interaction of grade and year can be understood best by examining the trends of the effect-size growths (found in the last column of each matrix in Table 1) across years. The interaction contrast was significant only for the Language test, explaining about 18% of the vari-ance among its *d*s. In 1947, the female advantage declined progressively from Grade 8 (−.55) to Grade 12 (−.43), producing an ESG of .12. In subsequent years, the gender difference was constant across grades.

In summary, there was a consistent female advantage on these three tests but, most important, the gender dif-ferences declined significantly from 1947 to 1980. For Spelling, there was also an effect of grade on the gender

The author thanks Mahzarin Banaji, Robert Sternberg, and Edward Zigler for reviewing an earlier draft of this article.

Correspondence concerning this article should be addressed to Alan Feingold, Department of Psychology, Yale University, P.O. Box 11A Yale Station, New Haven, CT 06520.

[1] The variance partitioning can be accomplished by analysis of variance (ANOVA) or multiple regression analysis (Cohen & Cohen, 1983). For ANOVA, contrast weights of −2, −1, 0, 1, and 2 (for grade) and −18.25, −3.25, 6.75, and 14.75 (for year) are applied to extract the linear trends. In the regression method, effect size (*d*) is the dependent variable and grade and year are (orthogonal) independent variables, with *n* = 20. The squares of the simple correlations of *d* with grade and year equal the corresponding eta²s from a trend analysis. The increment in R^2 from the addition of the Grade × Year cross products to an equation with grade and year entered equals the eta² of the interaction contrast. The R^2 obtained from the simultaneous regression of *d* on grade, year, and the Grade × Year cross products equals the sum of the three eta²s from the contrasts.

Table 1
Cognitive Gender Differences (ds) on the DAT by Test, Grade, and Year of Standardization

Test and year		Grade				Year M	ESG
	8	9	10	11	12		

DAT tests on which girls scored higher							
Spelling							
1947	−.47	−.51	−.59	−.55	−.57	−.54	−.10
1962	−.48	−.48	−.53	−.54	−.60	−.53	−.12
1972	−.37	−.47	−.47	−.52	−.53	−.47	−.16
1980	−.39	−.41	−.48	−.47	−.51	−.45	−.12
Grade M	−.43	−.47	−.52	−.52	−.55	<u>−.50</u>	−.12
Language							
1947	−.55	−.50	−.51	−.45	−.43	−.49	.12
1962	−.44	−.38	−.40	−.41	−.43	−.41	.01
1972	−.39	−.39	−.40	−.43	−.40	−.40	−.01
1980	−.37	−.41	−.42	−.41	−.40	−.40	−.03
Grade M	−.44	−.42	−.43	−.42	−.42	<u>−.43</u>	.02
Clerical Speed and Accuracy							
1947	−.53	−.65	−.63	−.66	−.62	−.62	−.09
1962	−.59	−.54	−.51	−.52	−.49	−.53	.10
1972	−.39	−.48	−.38	−.47	−.49	−.44	−.10
1980	−.36	−.34	−.29	−.37	−.32	−.34	.04
Grade M	−.47	−.50	−.45	−.50	−.48	<u>−.48</u>	−.01
DAT tests on which boys scored higher							
Mechanical Reasoning							
1947	1.02	1.24	1.34	1.48	1.55	1.33	.53
1962	.80	.90	1.00	1.06	1.23	1.00	.43
1972	.74	.79	.84	.88	.92	.83	.18
1980	.66	.68	.75	.82	.89	.76	.23
Grade M	.80	.90	.98	1.06	1.15	<u>.98</u>	.34
Space Relations							
1947	.20	.32	.39	.42	.52	.37	.32
1962	.15	.19	.25	.33	.36	.26	.21
1972	.12	.13	.19	.22	.27	.19	.15
1980	.13	.08	.12	.20	.22	.15	.09
Grade M	.15	.18	.24	.29	.34	<u>.24</u>	.19
DAT tests showing no average sex differences							
Verbal Reasoning							
1947	−.01	.07	.12	.20	.30	.14	.31
1962	.00	.07	.04	.07	.11	.06	.11
1972	.01	−.03	.02	.02	.05	.01	.04
1980	−.03	−.03	−.04	.01	.00	−.02	.03
Grade M	−.01	.02	.04	.08	.12	<u>.05</u>	.12
Abstract Reasoning							
1947	.09	.17	.25	.27	.38	.23	.29
1962	.02	.06	.09	.10	.16	.09	.14
1972	−.04	−.01	.05	.02	.09	.02	.13
1980	−.09	−.08	−.04	.00	.02	−.04	.11
Grade M	.00	.04	.09	.10	.16	<u>.08</u>	.17
Numerical Ability							
1947	−.10	.09	.12	.36	.58	.21	.68
1962	−.04	.02	.06	.20	.27	.10	.31
1972	−.11	−.08	.00	.03	.13	−.01	.24
1980	−.16	−.15	−.15	−.04	−.01	−.10	.15
Grade M	−.10	−.03	.01	.14	.24	<u>.05</u>	.34

Note. DAT = Differential Aptitude Tests; ESG = effect-size growth (12th-grade *d* minus corresponding 8th-grade *d*). Negative *d*s denote higher female performance. Grand means for *d*s (average effect sizes) are underscored.

Table 2
Variance Partitioning of Cognitive Gender Differences for the Eight DAT Tests

Test	GL ($df = 1$)	GR ($df = 3$)	YL ($df = 1$)	YR ($df = 2$)	GL × YL ($df = 1$)	G × Y-R ($df = 11$)
DAT tests on which girls scored higher						
Spelling						
eta²	.514	.033	.325	.038	.006	.085
F	52.81**	—	33.36**	—	.58	—
Language						
eta²	.016	.017	.528	.120	.176	.143
F	.91	—	30.17**	—	10.08*	—
Clerical Speed and Accuracy						
eta²	.001	.031	.844	.030	.003	.091
F	.13	—	88.88**	—	.34	—
DAT tests on which boys scored higher						
Mechanical Reasoning						
eta²	.220	.000	.720	.017	.029	.013
F	115.63**	—	377.38**	—	15.37*	—
Space Relations						
eta²	.382	.003	.539	.005	.044	.027
F	176.63**	—	249.17**	—	20.06**	—
DAT tests showing no average sex differences						
Verbal Reasoning						
eta²	.266	.007	.491	.002	.177	.058
F	63.30**	—	117.01**	—	42.04**	—
Abstract Reasoning						
eta²	.226	.007	.715	.006	.029	.016
F	121.66**	—	384.88**	—	15.80*	—
Numerical Ability						
eta²	.437	.016	.399	.006	.122	.021
F	163.67**	—	149.48**	—	45.63**	—

Note. DAT = Differential Aptitude Tests. GL = Grade-Linear. GR = Grade-Residual. YL = Year-Linear. YR = Year-Residual. G × Y-R = G × Y-Residual. The *F* ratios were computed using error terms obtained by pooling the sums of squares and *df* from the three residual sources of variance, *df* = 1, 16.
* *p* < .01. ** *p* < .001.

difference, and for Language, a Grade × Year interaction was found. Overall, most of the variance among within-test effect sizes was explained by the two factors and by their interaction, with R^2s of .84, .72, and .85 for Spelling, Language, and Clerical Speed and Accuracy, respectively.

Cognitive gender differences favoring boys. For all grades and years, male students scored higher than their female peers on Mechanical Reasoning, which had a large mean *d* (.98), and on Space Relations, on which the average effect size was small (.24). The corresponding variances about these mean *d*s were .067 and .014.

The pattern of the effects of grade, year, and the Grade × Year interaction on the gender differences was the same for the two measures. Boys gained in these abilities across grades and years more than did girls; their higher scores diminished from 1947 to 1980, and their increases in relative performance with age declined over the 33-year period.

As indicated by the grade means at the bottom of the fourth matrix in Table 1, the 8th-grade *d* for Mechanical Reasoning was .80 and increased 44% by the senior year of high school. Similarly, the 8th-grade *d* for Space Relations was .15 (fifth matrix in Table 1) and increased to .34 by the final year of secondary school, a growth of 127%.

Although the grade effects accounted for 22% to 38% of the variances among the *d*s for these two tests, the year effects explained much more (54% to 72%) of these variances. As indicated by the year means in Table 1, the 1947 *d* associated with Mechanical Reasoning was 1.33, and it decreased 43% by 1980. The *d* for Space Relations dropped by 59% (from .37 to .15) over the same period.

Although statistically significant (see Table 2), the Grade × Year interaction contrasts explained only 3% to 4% of the variances among effect sizes, far less than the main effect trends. As can be seen by the effect-size growth in Table 1, the gender difference in Mechanical Reasoning ability increased .53 across the grades in 1947. The corresponding increase in 1980 was only .23, a decrease of 57%. In 1947, the gender difference in Space Relations increased .32 from the 8th to the 12th grade. In 1980, the increase was only .09. For both tests, the R^2s of .97

indicated that almost all of the variance was explained by the three trend components.

DAT tests showing no appreciable average gender differences. There were no notable mean gender differences on three DAT tests, Verbal Reasoning, Abstract Reasoning, and Numerical Ability, with values in the .05–.08 range. The variances about the average *d*s were .007, .015, and .035, respectively.

The pattern formed by the *d*s for each of these three tests was identical to that found previously on both the Mechanical Reasoning and Space Relations measures. Boys increased in these abilities more than did girls across grades; girls' relative performance improved over years; and the effect-size growths (indexing the magnitude of the male advantage over grade) diminished from 1947 to 1980.

The grade effects were significant for all three tests, explaining between 23% and 44% of the variances among within-test effect sizes (see Table 2). Averaged over the three tests, the 8th-grade mean *d* was −.04. By the senior year, however, the corresponding average effect size was .17, indicating small differences in these abilities favoring boys.

The year effects were also significant for all three of these tests, and the trends explained much more of the variances (40% to 70%) than did the grade trends. Boys scored higher than girls on all three tests in 1947 (*d*s = .14–.23). By 1980, the boys' advantages had completely vanished.

The Linear × Linear interactions were significant for all three tests, but explained much less of the variance than did the trends for the main effects (see Table 2). In 1947, the Verbal Reasoning, Abstract Reasoning, and Numerical Ability effect-size growths were .31, .29, and .68, respectively. The corresponding values in 1980 were .03, .11, and .15. Thus, there were strong gender difference increases (favoring boys) in these abilities in 1947, but the differences in 1980 were trivial.

The R^2s of .93, .97, and .96 for Verbal Reasoning, Abstract Reasoning, and Numerical Ability, respectively, indicate that even though these mean gender differences were trivial, the within-test effect sizes varied, and their variances were almost fully explained by the grade, year, and Grade × Year contrasts.

Preliminary Scholastic Aptitude Test/ Scholastic Aptitude Test

The PSAT and SAT of the College Entrance Examination Board (Donlon, 1984) each consist of two tests, a verbal scale (PSAT-Verbal; SAT-Verbal) and a quantitative scale (PSAT-Mathematical; SAT-Mathematical). The PSAT-Verbal and SAT-Verbal each contain antonym, analogy, sentence completion, and reading comprehension items. The PSAT-Mathematical and SAT-Mathematical both contain a roughly equal number of arithmetic, elementary algebra, and plane geometry problems, all emphasizing quantitative reasoning. The types of items in the PSAT and SAT forms have remained largely unchanged since the first norming of the PSAT in 1960.

Several parallel forms for the PSAT and SAT have been developed and equated to yield equivalent scaled scores. The PSAT and SAT scaled scores are identical after a linear transformation is performed, and represent equivalent levels of performance.

Archival normative data for the PSAT and SAT were obtained from technical reports produced by the College Entrance Examination Board (Braun, Centra, & King, 1987; *College Board Score Reports,* 1962, 1966, 1970; Donlon, 1984; Dorans & Livingston, 1987; Jackson & Shrader, 1976). The difference between the standardization data from the PSAT and that available from the SAT does not involve test content (which is identical on the two instruments), but it involves the characteristics of the groups from which the norms were obtained.

PSAT

The PSAT was the instrument used in the four standardizations conducted by the College Board in 1960, 1966, 1974, and 1983 (Donlon, 1984). These standardizations were all conducted with representative nationwide samples of high school juniors and seniors, obtained with sampling methods similar to those used for the DAT (see Braun et al., 1987, and Jackson & Shrader, 1976, for details).

A total of 99,654 high school juniors and seniors (49,326 boys, 50,328 girls) were examined. The number of juniors tested, by year, were 10,313 (1960), 18,864 (1966), 17,758 (1974), and 25,316 (1983). The number of seniors tested were 9,745 in 1960 and 17,658 in 1966. (The PSAT was not normed on seniors in the last two standardizations.) About an equal number of boys and girls were tested in each grade and year.

SAT

Normative data on the SAT are available only for self-selected high school juniors and seniors who registered for and completed the examination (usually as a requirement for college admission) and are based on yearly populations rather than on samples of examinees. The normative data for the SAT were examined for juniors and seniors for the same years in which the PSAT was normed on representative samples.[2] The sample size for the SAT was over 170,000 for each cell in the Sex × Grade × Year matrix.

Because the PSAT and the SAT are equivalent tests, any discrepancies in gender differences found between the two measures are ascribable to the different types of examinees (i.e., representative samples of high school students on the PSAT vs. the population of SAT registrants on the SAT). Although the SAT norms are based on self-selected yearly populations, it is a widely known data base that has been used in previous group comparisons (e.g., Jones, 1984). It is important to determine whether the two groups of examinees yield similar gender differences.

---

[2] Because SAT norms for 1966 were not published, 1967 norms were substituted.

PSAT and SAT Analyses and Results

Gender-difference *d*s were computed by grade, year, and test and appear in Table 3. There was a slight gender difference in PSAT-Verbal favoring girls (*d* = −.12) among high school juniors in 1960, but it had faded completely by 1974. There was no gender difference on the PSAT-Verbal in 1960 or 1966.

Although male high school juniors and seniors consistently outperformed their female peers on PSAT-Mathematical, the gender difference among juniors (the only students tested four times) decreased from .34 in 1960 to .12 in 1983, a 65% decline. The math gender difference was larger for seniors than for juniors (a grade effect), and this difference was larger in 1960 than in 1966 (.15 vs. .08, Grade × Year interaction effect).

The gender differences found on SAT-Verbal were very small for both grades in all years (see Table 3). However, a small trend for boys to be improving relative to girls on SAT-Verbal from 1960 to 1983 was observed. The norms for SAT-Mathematical showed notable gender differences (*d*s = .37–.51) favoring boys in all years, with no discernible trends among effect sizes.

Comparisons of the corresponding PSAT and SAT mean scaled scores showed that the representatively sampled PSAT examinees scored about one standard deviation lower in verbal and mathematical abilities than did the SAT registrants, indicating that the self-selected (and generally college-bound) SAT examinees are more intellectually able than the general population of high school juniors and seniors. Thus, there was an apparent correlation between SAT ability (whether measured or not) and SAT registration. The considerable discrepancies in gender differences—and in the trends of the *d*s across years—obtained with the two measures indicated that

---

Table 3
Cognitive Gender Differences (ds) on the PSAT and SAT by Test, Grade, and Year of Norms

Test and Year	Verbal		Math	
	Juniors	Seniors	Juniors	Seniors
PSAT				
1960	−.12	−.03	.34	.49
1966	−.08	−.02	.24	.32
1974	.01	NA	.17	NA
1983	−.02	NA	.12	NA
SAT				
1960	NA	−.06	NA	.51
1967[a]	−.05	−.01	.37	.38
1974	−.02	.04	.42	.42
1983	.11	.08	.42	.42

Note. PSAT = Preliminary Scholastic Aptitude Test; SAT = Scholastic Aptitude Test; NA = not available. Negative *d*s denote higher female performance. The PSAT and SAT are equivalent tests, but the PSAT norms used representative samples of high school students, whereas the SAT norms were based on the populations of self-selected SAT registrants for the given years of administration.
[a] 1966 norms for SAT examinees were not published.

---

this correlation was higher for male high school students than for their female peers, and that the difference between the correlations increased from 1960 to 1983. Therefore, gender comparisons using the SAT norms artifactually suggest that boys are less intelligent than girls, and this bias was greatest in the most recent years. In 1983, for example, the gender difference in SAT ability (averaged over verbal and math performance) was only .05 for the representative samples of juniors constituting the normative group, but was .26 for the self-selected population of juniors taking the SAT. (However, the larger effect size may be the more appropriate value if gender differences among college-bound high school students are of interest.)

Stanley and Benbow (1982, p. 972) argued that there are "huge ratios at upper end" of the mathematical reasoning continuum. The PSAT norms afford support for their conclusion. From 1960 to 1974, the gender difference on PSAT-Mathematical declined by 50%. On the separate-sex norms, however, boys needed to score about 50 points higher than girls (almost half of a standard deviation) to be at the 99th percentile in both years (*College Board Score Reports,* 1962; Jackson & Shrader, 1976). Thus, even though the overall gender difference had declined to only .17 by 1974, mathematically talented adolescents remained disproportionately boys. At the other end of the scale, a different pattern emerged. In 1960, there were 50% more girls than boys who scored very poorly (a PSAT-Mathematical score of 25—equivalent to an SAT-Mathematical score of 250—or less) in mathematics. By 1974, one half of the low-ability examinees were boys and one half were girls. Therefore, the gender difference decline was attributable to the relatively smaller proportion of low-scoring girls in 1974. The 1974 pattern was replicated in the PSAT norms for 1983 (Braun et al., 1987).

Although the normative reports for the PSAT and the SAT do not indicate the number of boys and girls earning the highest scores on these tests, Dorans and Livingston (1987) reported the number of very high scores earned by boys and girls on the SAT-Mathematics for all English-speaking examinees tested in June 1981 and May 1982. When the examinees from the two test administrations were combined, 96% of 99 scores of 800 (the highest possible scaled score), 90% of 433 scores in the 780–790 range, 81% of 1479 scores between 750 and 770, and 56% of 3,768 scores of 600 were earned by boys. Thus, the degree of male overrepresentation was directly related to the level of SAT-Math performance. However, the population of adolescents was not examined. Different percentages might be found for the subset of high-ability youths who did not take the SAT. But given the high correlation found between ability and SAT completion, it is doubtful that there were enough unrepresented youths to bias the reported percentages.

The disproportionately large percentages of mathematically able boys is attributable in part to the consistently higher standard deviations of the male examinees on the PSAT-Mathematical and the SAT-Mathematical scales. In combination with the slightly higher male means, the greater variability in math performance wiped out the gender difference at the low end of the distribution and magnified it at the high end.[3]

The average gender difference on PSAT-Mathematical was small in 1974 and 1983, in spite of the large gap at the upper end of the distribution, because mathematically gifted students composed a very small proportion of the high school students, and their data were thus not weighted heavily in the norms. These results do, however, suggest a second reason for the discrepancy found between the PSAT and SAT gender differences in math performance: High-scoring examinees make up a larger proportion of the pool of SAT registrants than of the unselected high school students sampled for the PSAT norms.

Discussion

Gender differences were found on all DAT and PSAT tests when these instruments were first normed in 1947 and 1960, respectively. Girls then scored higher on three DAT tests, Spelling, Language, and Clerical Speed and Accuracy, and (for high school juniors) on the PSAT-Verbal. Boys then scored higher on the Mechanical Reasoning, Space Relations, Verbal Reasoning, Abstract Reasoning, and Numerical Ability tests of the DAT and on PSAT-Mathematics. By 1980, boys had completely closed the gap on PSAT-Verbal and cut in half the difference in Clerical Speed and Accuracy. The gender differences favoring girls in English skills had also narrowed, but to a smaller degree. Girls have since closed the gap on three DAT aptitudes, Verbal Reasoning, Abstract Reasoning, and Numerical Ability, and cut in half the differences on DAT Mechanical Reasoning, DAT Space Relations, and PSAT-Math. The important exception to the rule of vanishing gender differences is that the well-documented gender gap at the highest levels of performance on high school mathematics has remained constant from 1960 to 1983.

The finding that boys increased in ability relative to girls over the high school years (except in the aptitudes favoring girls) may partially be attributable to a sex difference favoring girls in rate of maturation. Similar increases would be obtained if gender differences in height were examined across grades. If the grade effects obtained on the DAT could be adjusted for maturational differences, girls would show an increase in d across grades in Spelling (which would be larger than the unadjusted effect), Language, and Clerical Speed and Accuracy, and boys would still show greater increases in performance on Mechanical Reasoning and Space Relations (although the adjusted effects would be smaller than the obtained effects). Thus, grade effects would then be obtained for all abilities on which average gender differences were found, with the directions of the adjusted ds indicating a constant increase in gender differences from the 8th to the 12th grade once maturational differences are taken into consideration.

[3] Boys were also found to be more variable on the DAT Spelling test. The greater male variability in spelling performance, in combination with the lower male means, erased the gender difference at the upper tail of the distribution and augmented it at the lower tail.

The analyses of the DAT and PSAT normative data question the validity of the findings that girls outperform boys in the verbal domain and that this advantage has increased over the years (Becker & Hedges, 1984; Hyde, 1981; Maccoby & Jacklin, 1974; Rosenthal & Rubin, 1982). Although girls had higher means than boys on the tests of English skills (spelling and language), they currently perform equally with boys in verbal reasoning and may have scored lower than boys in the past. And although female high school juniors once slightly outperformed their male counterparts on PSAT-Verbal, no gender differences were found on the PSAT-Verbal norms for 1974 and 1983.

The examination of the norms for SAT-Verbal showed a small current gender difference in favor of boys, but that effect is probably spurious, an artifact of the use of a population of self-selected examinees. Interestingly, the myth that girls perform better than boys on the SAT-Verbal is prevalent among college students (Matlin & Matkoski, 1985).

The analyses of the norms from the math tests of the DAT and the PSAT, both of which suggested that girls narrowed the gender difference in quantitative abilities over the years, are in agreement with results from the reanalyses of Hyde's (1981) effect sizes by Rosenthal and Rubin (1982) and Becker and Hedges (1984). The finding from the PSAT and SAT norms that the math gender difference was more pronounced at higher levels of mathematical ability is in accord with the results obtained by Becker and Hedges (1984) and Benbow and Stanley (1980, 1982). On the 1980 norms for the DAT Numerical Ability subtest, however, there was no mean gender difference, and an examination of percentile ranks for each gender found no differences at the upper levels of performance. These discrepant results can be explained by Becker's (1983) finding that the gender difference on SAT-Mathematical is attributable to performance on the algebra items. Unlike the PSAT-Mathematical, the DAT Numerical Ability test consists exclusively of arithmetic items. Thus, boys and girls did not differ at all in basic math skills, even at the upper end of the scale, but only on performance in high school level mathematics.

Just as verbal ability and quantitative ability each can be decomposed into more homogeneous subdomains within which gender differences vary, different types of spatial tests yield different gender differences in performance. In their meta-analysis of the literature on sex differences in spatial ability, Linn and Petersen (1986) classified spatial tests into the categories of spatial perception, mental rotation, and spatial visualization. The spatial visualization category, which subsumes the DAT Space Relations test, yielded the smallest effect size in favor of boys, mean $d = .13$, a value quite similar to the mean d of .24 obtained from the examination of the norms for DAT Space Relations.

There are some possible confounding factors that may have distorted effect sizes and effect size comparisons in the present analyses. These same biasing factors may also have been present in the studies summarized by Hyde

(1981) and have not been noted in reviews of her meta-analysis (e.g., Deaux, 1985).

First, the examinees tested in the DAT and PSAT standardizations—and in most gender research—were sampled by grade rather than by age. The comparison of gender differences found on the PSAT with those obtained from the SAT norms for the same grades indicated that unrepresentative samples can yield biased effect sizes and biased trends. Yet, representative samples of high school juniors and seniors are certainly not representative of all American youths of a given age. Some students drop out of high school before reaching the higher grades, and other students are either retained or promoted across grades. Because these factors might operate differentially for boys and girls, within-grade gender differences may not accurately reflect within-age differences. For example, school promotions probably result in within-grade variances in cognitive abilities that are smaller than within-age differences, thus inflating effect sizes of gender differences, especially for the most educationally related abilities. However, as the DAT and PSAT scales do not have perfect reliability, the variances of obtained scores are larger than would be computed from "true" scores (Nunnally, 1978), thereby reducing gender differences. (An alternative way to conceptualize the problem is to realize that the correlations between gender and cognitive abilities are attenuated by measurement error in the latter.) Thus, these two opposing biases may have offset one another.

Another possible confounding relates to the fact that the same test forms were not used in the different standardizations of the DAT and PSAT. A seemingly plausible rival hypothesis for the year effects is that sex bias may have been removed from more recent forms of the tests. Removal of test bias, however, would not have engendered the obtained linear decreases over years. Instead, the temporal trends would have been flat, with the exception of steep drops in gender differences in the year that sex-related item analyses were introduced to eliminate or reduce sex differences in performance.

Finally, cohort effects can distort results in cross-sectional developmental research (Hilton & Patrick, 1970). In each DAT standardization, the 8th graders had been born four years later than the seniors. Thus, to a small degree, the grade and year effects were confounded.

This article affords an overview of cognitive gender differences but does not endeavor to explain the causes of these differences or the causes of the changes in these differences. The origins of sex differences have been attributed to childhood training and experience, to gender differences in attitudes (especially toward math), to parental and teacher expectations and behaviors, to differential course taking, and also to biological differences between the sexes. For reviews of the literature on this controversial topic, see Deaux (1985), Fausto-Sterling (1985), Sherman (1978), and Wittig and Petersen (1979).

The published research on cognitive gender differences has focused on the preadolescent and adolescent years. Yet, abilities change over the adult years. Verbal abilities, for example, increase up to the third decade,

especially for bright people, whereas spatial and other nonverbal abilities (especially perceptual speed) start to decline at this age (Feingold, 1984). Whether these developmental patterns interact with gender needs to be examined.

REFERENCES

Becker, B. J. (1983, April). *Item characteristics and sex differences on the SAT-M for mathematically able youths.* Paper presented at the annual meeting of the American Educational Research Association, Montreal.

Becker, B. J., & Hedges, L. V. (1984). Meta-analysis of cognitive gender differences: A comment on an analysis by Rosenthal and Rubin. *Journal of Educational Psychology, 76,* 583–587.

Benbow, C. P., & Stanley, J. C. (1980). Sex differences in mathematical ability: Fact or artifact? *Science, 210,* 1262–1264.

Benbow, C. P., & Stanley, J. C. (1982). Consequences in high school and college of sex differences in mathematical reasoning ability: A longitudinal perspective. *American Educational Research Journal, 19,* 598–622.

Bennett, G. K., Seashore, H. G., & Wesman, A. G. (1947). *Manual for the Differential Aptitude Tests.* New York: Psychological Corporation.

Bennett, G. K., Seashore, H. G., & Wesman, A. G. (1966). *Fourth edition manual for the Differential Aptitude Tests.* New York: Psychological Corporation.

Bennett, G. K., Seashore, H. G., & Wesman, A. G. (1974). *Fifth edition manual for the Differential Aptitude Tests.* New York: Psychological Corporation.

Bennett, G. K., Seashore, H. G., & Wesman, A. G. (1982). *Differential Aptitude Tests Form V and W: Administrator's handbook.* New York: Psychological Corporation.

Braun, H. I., Centra, J., & King, B. F. (1987). *Verbal and mathematical ability of high school juniors and seniors in 1983: A norm study of the PSAT/NMSQT and the SAT* (Research report). Princeton, NJ: Educational Testing Service.

Burnett, S. A. (1986). Sex-related differences in spatial ability: Are they trivial? *American Psychologist, 41,* 1012–1014.

Caplan, P. J., MacPherson, G. M., & Tobin, P. (1985). Do sex-related differences in spatial abilities exist? A multilevel critique with new data. *American Psychologist, 40,* 786–799.

Cohen, J. (1977). *Statistical power analysis for the behavioral sciences* (rev. ed.). New York: Academic Press.

Cohen, J., & Cohen, P. (1983). *Applied multiple regression/correlation analysis for the behavioral sciences* (2nd ed.). Hillsdale, NJ: Erlbaum.

College Board score reports: A guide for counselors. (1962). New York: College Entrance Examination Board.

College Board score reports: A guide for counselors and admissions officers. (1966). New York: College Entrance Examination Board.

College Board score reports: A guide for counselors and admissions officers. (1970). New York: College Entrance Examination Board.

Deaux, K. (1985). Sex and gender. *Annual Review of Psychology, 36,* 49–81.

Donlon, T. F. (Ed.). (1984). *The College Board technical handbook for the Scholastic Aptitude Test and Achievement Tests.* New York: College Entrance Examination Board.

Dorans, N. J., & Livingston, S. A. (1987). Male–female differences in SAT-Verbal ability among students of high SAT-Mathematical ability. *Journal of Educational Measurement, 24,* 65–71.

Eagly, A. H., & Steffen, V. J. (1986). Gender and aggressive behavior: A meta-analytic review of the social psychological literature. *Psychological Bulletin, 100,* 309–330.

Fausto-Sterling, A. (1985). *Myths of gender: Biological theories about men and women.* New York: Basic Books.

Feingold, A. (1984). The effects of differential age adjustment between the WAIS and the WAIS-R on the comparability of the two scales. *Educational and Psychological Measurement, 44,* 569–573.

Glass, G. V., McGaw, B., & Smith, M. L. (1981). *Meta-analysis in social research.* Beverly Hills, CA: Sage.

Hall, J. A. (1984). *Nonverbal sex differences: Communication accuracy and expressive style.* Baltimore, MD: Johns Hopkins University Press.

Hilton, T. L., & Berglund, G. W. (1974). Sex differences in mathematics achievement: A longitudinal study. *Journal of Educational Research, 67,* 231–237.

Hilton, T. L., & Patrick, C. (1970). Cross-sectional versus longitudinal data: An empirical comparison of mean differences in academic growth. *Journal of Educational Measurement, 7,* 15–24.

Hyde, J. S. (1981). How large are cognitive gender differences? A meta-analysis using ω^2 and *d*. *American Psychologist, 36,* 892–901.

Hyde, J. S., & Linn, M. C. (Eds.). (1986). *The psychology of gender: Advances through meta-analysis.* Baltimore, MD: Johns Hopkins University Press.

Jackson, R., & Shrader, W. B. (1976). *Verbal and mathematical ability of high school juniors in 1974: A norms study of the PSAT/NMSQT* (Research Bulletin 76-27). Princeton, NJ: Educational Testing Service.

Jones, L. V. (1984). White–black achievement differences: The narrowing gap. *American Psychologist, 39,* 1207–1213.

Light, R. J., & Pillemer, D. B. (1984). *Summing up: The science of reviewing research.* Cambridge, MA: Harvard University Press.

Linn, M. C., & Petersen, A. C. (1986). A meta-analysis of gender differences in spatial ability: Implications for mathematics and science achievement. In J. S. Hyde & M. C. Linn (Eds.), *The psychology of gender: Advances through meta-analysis* (pp. 67–101). Baltimore, MD: Johns Hopkins University Press.

Maccoby, E. E., & Jacklin, C. N. (1974). *The psychology of sex differences.* Stanford, CA: Stanford University Press.

Matlin, M. W., & Matkoski, K. M. (1985, March). *Gender-stereotyping of cognitive abilities.* Paper presented at the annual meeting of the Eastern Psychological Association, Boston. (ERIC Document Reproduction Service No. ED 261 294)

Nunnally, J. C. (1978). *Psychometric theory* (2nd ed.). New York: McGraw-Hill.

Rosenthal, R. (1984). *Meta-analytic procedures for social research.* Beverly Hills, CA: Sage.

Rosenthal, R., & Rubin, D. (1982). Further meta-analytic procedures for assessing cognitive gender differences. *Journal of Educational Psychology, 74,* 708–712.

Sherman, J. (1978). *Sex-related cognitive differences.* Springfield, IL: Charles C Thomas.

Sherman, J. (1980). Mathematics, spatial visualization, and related factors: Changes in girls and boys, grades 8–11. *Journal of Educational Psychology, 72,* 476–482.

Stanley, J. C., & Benbow, C. P. (1982). Huge sex ratios at upper end. *American Psychologist, 37,* 972.

Wittig, M., & Petersen, A. C. (Eds.). (1979). *Sex-related differences in cognitive functioning.* New York: Academic Press.

[13]

Journal of Educational Psychology
1982, Vol. 74, No. 5, 708–712

Further Meta-Analytic Procedures for Assessing Cognitive Gender Differences

Robert Rosenthal
Department of Psychology
and Social Relations
Harvard University

Donald B. Rubin
Department of Statistics
Educational Testing Service
Princeton, New Jersey

We describe procedures for (a) assessing the heterogeneity of a set of effect sizes derived from a meta-analysis, (b) testing for trends by means of contrasts among the effect sizes obtained, and (c) evaluating the practical importance of the average effect size obtained. On the basis of applying these procedures to data presented in Hyde (1981) on cognitive gender differences, we conclude the following: (a) that for all four areas of congitive skill investigated, effect sizes for gender differences differed significantly across studies (at least at $p < .001$); (b) that studies of gender differences conducted more recently show a substantial gain in cognitive performance by females relative to males (unweighted mean r across four cognitive areas = .40); (c) that studies of gender differences show male versus female effect sizes of practical importance equivalent to outcome rates of 60% versus 40%.

In an interesting and important recent article, Hyde (1981) reported the results of a meta-analysis of studies of gender differences in cognitive abilities. The general purpose of the present note is to extend Hyde's analyses by the application of procedures with general utility in meta-analyses. More specifically we address the following three questions: (a) Are the results of studies of gender differences homogeneous within each type of cognitive ability or do these results show significant heterogeneity? (b) Are the results of studies of gender differences stable over time or do more recent studies show significantly larger or smaller gender differences than do older studies? (c) Are the magnitudes of the obtained gender differences of any practical importance?

In her meta-analyses, Hyde employed both ω^2 and d as her effect size estimates. In our analyses we employed only d for the following two reasons: (a) d is by nature a directional estimate, whereas ω^2 is nondi-

rectional, and (b) d was more accurately estimated than ω^2 (two vs. one significant digit). Every study reporting both a d and the size of the sample (N) was included. The definition of d employed by Hyde was $(M_1 - M_2)/\overline{SD}$; that is, the difference between the mean scores of females and males divided by the mean of the standard deviations of the female and male samples. Since separate sample sizes for females and males were not reported, we assumed sample sizes to be equal.

It should be noted that, of all the studies summarized by Hyde, only one half (51%) yielded a reported value of d. Following the valuable suggestion of one of our reviewers, we were able to check for one type of possible bias in the availability of d. If there were no "significance level" bias, we might expect to find the same percentage (51%) of ds available for studies showing a significant gender difference and for those not showing a significant gender difference. We found, however, that of the 45 studies showing significant effects, 60% permitted a report of d, whereas of the 33 studies not showing significant effects, only 39% permitted a report of d. Since studies showing significant effects tend to yield larger ds than studies not showing significant effects (Rosenthal & Rubin, 1978; 1979), it is likely that the studies summarized quantitatively tend to

Preparation of this article was supported in part by the National Science Foundation. The order of authors was determined alphabetically.

Requests for reprints should be sent to Robert Rosenthal, Department of Psychology and Social Relations, Harvard University, 33 Kirkland Street, Cambridge, Massachusetts 02138.

Table 1
Summary of Statistics Employed in Meta-Analysis of Gender Differences in Cognitive Abilities

Statistic	Type of ability			
	Verbal	Quantitative	Visual-spatial	Field articulation
1. Number of studies	12	7	7[a]	14
2. Total number of persons	62,083	55,931	11,015	911
3. Weighted mean d ($\bar{d}$)	.30	−.35	−.50	−.51
4. Z for mean d[b]	36.54	−40.65	−25.81	−7.45
5. p for Z for mean d <	.001	.001	.001	.001
6. χ^2 for heterogeneity of ds	769	333	111	34.9
7. df for χ^2 above	11	6	6	13
8. p for χ^2 above <	.001	.001	.001	.001
9. Z for linear contrast	2.79	0.80	1.88	3.38
10. p for Z above (one-tailed)	.0026	.21[c]	.030	.00037
11. r between recency and d	.29	.21[c,d]	.46	.60
12. r corresponding to mean d	.15	−.17	−.24	−.25

[a] An 8th d was available, but because the N for that d was not available it was not included in our analysis.
[b] Computed as $\bar{d}\sqrt{\Sigma w}$.
[c] This is not a typographical error but is simply a coincidence.
[d] Although this r does not differ significantly from zero, it also does not differ significantly from the other three correlations or from their mean (all Zs < 1).

overestimate gender differences. Offsetting biases may, of course, also be operating if there were studies with large gender differences that were not reported, for example, because of fear that the results would be used to maintain traditional sex typing.

Before beginning our analyses, we want to endorse strongly Hyde's own emphasis on effect-size estimation and reporting as well as her recommendation that effect sizes be supplied with all significant results in reports of research. Indeed, we feel that any time the results of a significance test are reported, significant or not, an effect size should also be reported. If it could be arranged logistically, we would prefer basic summary data being made a part of the original article—as is now strongly encouraged for all articles involving the analysis of real data published in the *Journal of the American Statistical Association* of which one of us (D. B. R.) is currently the Coordinating and Applications Editor.

Testing for Heterogeneity of Gender Differences

Our first question asked whether the magnitudes of gender differences differed significantly from study to study for each type of cognitive ability. We have given the

details elsewhere (Rosenthal & Rubin, 1982b); here we give only the basic χ^2 test for the heterogeneity of a set of effect sizes

$$\chi^2(K - 1) = \Sigma[w(d - \bar{d})^2]$$

where K is the number of effect sizes to be assessed for heterogeneity, w is the reciprocal of the estimated variance of d in each of the K studies, d is the estimated effect size in each of the K studies, and $\bar{d}$ is the mean d weighted by w. Details on the estimation of w are in the reference just above, but when sample sizes are nearly equal and not smaller than, say, 10 it can be estimated by

$$w = \frac{2N}{8 + d^2},$$

where N is the total sample size in the study.

The first row of Table 1 shows the number of studies available for analysis and the second row shows the total number of persons upon which these studies were based. The third row gives the weighted mean ds for all four areas of cognitive skill. A positive d means that females performed better than males, whereas a negative d means that males performed better than females. For the area of verbal ability, females performed better than males; for the areas of quantitative, visual-spatial, and field articulation,

710   ROBERT ROSENTHAL AND DONALD B. RUBIN

males performed better than females. The fourth row gives the Z testing the significance of the difference of each mean d from zero, and the fifth row gives the p values associated with each of the obtained Z. Actually, all four p values are very much smaller than the ps of .001 shown.

The sixth row of Table 1 shows the χ^2 test of heterogeneity of ds for each of the four types of ability. The seventh row gives the df on which each of the χ^2s is based, and the eighth row gives the p values associated with each of the obtained χ^2s. All four of the p values are less than .001; for the areas of verbal ability, quantitative, and visual-spatial, the actual p values are very much smaller than .001. Thus, for all four areas of cognitive functioning, the effect sizes differed significantly among themselves.

The computation of these χ^2s is illustrated

in Table 2 for one of the four types of ability—visual-spatial ability. For each of the seven studies for which both d and N were available, Table 2 provides the two quantities from each study required to obtain the weighted mean $\bar{d}$—d and w, the latter being the reciprocal of the estimated variance of d. The computation of d is shown near the bottom of Table 2, followed by the computation of χ^2 for heterogeneity, which requires for its ingredients, d, w, and $\bar{d}$.

Testing for Stability of Gender Differences

Although it was useful to learn that the ds differed significantly from each other, more focused questions can be addressed. One specific question is whether gender differences were found to be stable over time or

Table 2
Illustration of Meta-Analytic Procedures: Gender Differences in Visual-Spatial Ability

Study	Date	N	d[a]	w[b]	λ[c]
1	1975	105	.04	26	4.3
2	1975	102	.48	25	4.3
3	1961	128	.60	31	-9.7
4	1967	6,167	.41	1,510	-3.7
5	1972	2,925	.83	673	1.3
6	1967	355	.52	86	-3.7
7	1978	1,233	.25	306	7.2[d]
Σ	13,795	11,015	3.13	2,657	
Unweighted M	1970.7	1573.6	.45	379.6	

Weighted mean $\bar{d}$:

$$\bar{d} = \frac{\Sigma(wd)}{\Sigma w} = \frac{26(.04) + 25(.48) + 31(.60) + 1,510(.41) + 673(.83) + 86(.52) + 306(.25)}{2,657}$$

$$= \frac{1,330.55}{2,657} = .50.$$

χ^2 *for heterogeneity of ds:*

$$\chi^2(K - 1) = \Sigma[w(d - \bar{d})^2] = 26(.04 - .50)^2 + 25(.48 - .50)^2 + 31(.60 - .50)^2 + 1510(.41 - .50)^2$$
$$+ 673(.83 - .50)^2 + 86(.52 - .50)^2 + 306(.25 - .50)^2$$
$$= 110.502, \text{ rounded to } 111.$$

Z *for linear contrast (ds predicted from date of study):*

$$Z = \frac{\Sigma(\lambda d)}{[\Sigma(\lambda^2/w)]^{1/2}} = \frac{(4.3)(.04) + (4.3)(.48) + (-9.7)(.60) + (-3.7)(.41) + (1.3)(.83) +}{[(4.3)^2/(26) + (4.3)^2/(25) + (-9.7)^2/(31) + (-3.7)^2/(1510) + (1.3)^2/(673)}$$
$$\frac{(-3.7)(.52) + (7.2)(.25)}{(-3.7)^2/(86) + (7.2)^2/(306)]^{1/2}}$$

$$= \frac{4.15}{[4.83]^{1/2}} = 1.88.$$

[a] In this table a positive d means that males performed better than females. [b] Estimated for $2N/(8 + d^2)$ and presented to nearest integer. [c] Defined as publication date minus mean year of publication. [d] Rounded down to keep $\Sigma\lambda = 0$.

whether they were found to be changing over time. If they are found to be changing over even the short span of 20 or so years covered by Hyde's meta-analyses, one should be reluctant to make strong biogenic interpretations on the basis of this evidence.

To test whether effect sizes have been changing linearly over the years, we compute a linear contrast. We give the details elsewhere (Rosenthal & Rubin, 1982b), but essentially we compute the test statistic Z from the following:

$$Z = \frac{\Sigma(\lambda d)}{[\Sigma(\lambda^2/w)]^{1/2}},$$

where λ is the contrast weight for each study and d and w are as defined earlier. Contrast weights were defined as the year of publication minus the mean year of publication.

The computation of these Z tests of linear contrasts is illustrated in Table 2 for visual-spatial ability. The last column of that table provides the weights or λs that, along with d and w, are required to compute Z. In this case, the predicted values of the contrast could be conveniently obtained as residuals from the mean year of publication. (It should be noted that the sum of the λs must equal zero.) The Table 2 note shows each step of the computation of Z.

Row 9 of Table 1 shows the Zs obtained, Row 10 shows the p levels associated with each Z; Row 11 shows the correlation (r) between the recency of the study (year of publication) and degree of female superiority (d). These results are quite striking. In all four areas of cognitive skills, including the three areas showing male superiority, as years went by, females gained in cognitive skill relative to males. The mean r, weighted by df, was .43 (unweighted mean r = .40)—quite a large effect (Cohen, 1977).

Of course we cannot say whether this marked linear trend for females to gain relative to males in cognitive skills is due to changes in the relative ability of females and males or to changes in the nature of the studies conducted over the years; for example, differential gender selection for college over the years (since disproportionately many of these studies employed college samples), or to changes in both. But we can say that whatever the reason, in these studies

Table 3
Binomial Effect Size Display for Gender Differences

Gender and Σ	Relative performance		
	Above *Mdn*	Below *Mdn*	Σ
Females	60	40	100
Males	40	60	100
Σ	100	100	200

females appear to be gaining in cognitive skill relative to males rather faster than the gene can travel!

Practical Importance of Gender Differences

Although we agree in a general way with much of Hyde's work, we are less inclined to minimize the importance of the gender differences obtained in her meta-analysis. For example we do not agree that "gender is a poor predictor of one's performance on ability tests in any of these areas" (Hyde, 1981, p. 897). To show why we disagree, we employ the Binomial Effect Size Display (BESD), a general purpose effect-size display that shows clearly the practical importance of an effect size (Rosenthal & Rubin, 1982a). The BESD is particularly easy to calculate from the effect size r, so we have shown the r that corresponds to each mean d for gender difference in the bottom row of Table 1. The mean of the absolute values of the four rs shown was .20, either weighted by df or unweighted. Table 3 shows the BESD for this correlation as though females performed better. (If males performed better we would only have to interchange the rows.) The BESD shows that a correlation of only .20 accounting for only 4% of the variance is associated with the difference between 60% and 40% of a group's performing above average. Such a difference must be seen as nontrivial. For example, if obtaining a particular job required scoring above the median on a test that correlated .20 with being female, then for every 100 females and 100 males that applied, 60 of the women but only 40 of the men would be job-eligible. Put into a different context to show the generality of the BESD, if we had a new biomedical treatment whose use correlated

712   ROBERT ROSENTHAL AND DONALD B. RUBIN

.20 with survival, that treatment would be associated with a reduction in death rate of from 60% to 40%!

Conclusion

On the basis of these analyses we conclude the following: (a) that for all four areas of cognitive skill investigated, effect sizes for gender differences differed significantly from study to study (at least at $p < .001$); (b) that studies of gender differences conducted more recently show a substantial gain in cognitive performance by females relative to males (unweighted mean $r = .40$); (c) that studies of gender differences show female versus male effect sizes of practical importance equivalent to outcome rates of 60% versus 40%.

References

Cohen, J. *Statistical power analysis for the behavioral sciences* (Rev. ed.). New York: Academic Press, 1977.

Hyde, J. S. How large are cognitive gender differences? A meta-analysis using ω^2 and d. *American Psychologist*, 1981, *36*, 892–901.

Rosenthal, R., & Rubin, D. B. Interpersonal expectancy effects: The first 345 studies. *The Behavioral and Brain Sciences*, 1978, *3*, 377–386.

Rosenthal, R., & Rubin, D. B. Comparing significance levels of independent studies. *Psychological Bulletin*, 1979, *86*, 1165–1168.

Rosenthal, R., & Rubin, D. B. A simple, general purpose display of magnitude of experimental effect. *Journal of Educational Psychology*, 1982, *74*, 166–169. (a)

Rosenthal, R., & Rubin, D. B. Comparing effect sizes of independent studies. *Psychological Bulletin*, *92*, 1982, 500–504. (b)

Received November 9, 1981 ∎

[14]

Psychological Bulletin
1988, Vol. 104, No. 1, 53–69

Gender Differences in Verbal Ability: A Meta-Analysis

Janet Shibley Hyde
University of Wisconsin-Madison

Marcia C. Linn
University of California, Berkeley

Many regard gender differences in verbal ability to be one of the well-established findings in psychology. To reassess this belief, we located 165 studies that reported data on gender differences in verbal ability. The weighted mean effect size (d) was +0.11, indicating a slight female superiority in performance. The difference is so small that we argue that gender differences in verbal ability no longer exist. Analyses of effect sizes for different measures of verbal ability showed almost all to be small in magnitude: for vocabulary, $d = 0.02$; for analogies, $d = -0.16$ (slight male superiority in performance); for reading comprehension, $d = 0.03$; for speech production, $d = 0.33$ (the largest effect size); for essay writing, $d = 0.09$; for anagrams, $d = 0.22$; and for tests of general verbal ability, $d = 0.20$. For the 1985 administration of the Scholastic Aptitude Test–Verbal, $d = -0.11$, indicating superior male performance. Analysis of tests requiring different cognitive processes involved in verbal ability yielded no evidence of substantial gender differences in any aspect of processing. Similarly, an analysis by age indicated no striking changes in the magnitude of gender differences at different ages, countering Maccoby and Jacklin's (1974) conclusion that gender differences in verbal ability emerge around age 11. For studies published in 1973 or earlier, $d = 0.23$ and for studies published after 1973, $d = 0.10$, indicating a slight decline in the magnitude of the gender difference in recent years. The implications of these findings are discussed, including their implications for theories of sex differences in brain lateralization and their relation to changing gender roles.

The existence of gender differences in verbal ability has been one of the tried and true "facts" of psychology for decades. Anastasi (1958), in her classic text on differential psychology, stated that females are superior to males in verbal and linguistic functions from infancy through adulthood. Tyler (1965), in another classic text on differential psychology, reached similar conclusions. Maccoby (1966) concluded,

> Through the preschool years and in the early school years, girls exceed boys in most aspects of verbal performance. They say their first word sooner, articulate more clearly and at an earlier age, use longer sentences, and are more fluent. By the beginning of school, however, there are no longer any consistent differences in vocabulary. Girls learn to read sooner, and there are more boys than girls who require special training in remedial reading programs; but by approximately the age of ten, a number of studies show that boys have caught up in their reading skills. Throughout the school years, girls do better on tests of grammar, spelling, and word fluency. (p. 26)

In the major contemporary review of psychological gender differences, Maccoby and Jacklin (1974) located 85 studies reporting an analysis of gender differences in verbal ability. They concluded,

This research was supported by Grants BNS 8508666 and BNS 8696128 from the National Science Foundation to Janet Shibley Hyde. The opinions expressed are ours and not the National Science Foundation's.

We thank Eleanor Maccoby and Amy Halberstadt for comments on an earlier draft of this article.

Correspondence concerning this article should be addressed to Janet Shibley Hyde, Department of Psychology, Brogden Psychology Building, University of Wisconsin, Madison, Wisconsin 53706.

It is probably true that girls' verbal abilities mature somewhat more rapidly in early life, although there are a number of recent studies in which no sex difference has been found. During the period from preschool to early adolescence, the sexes are very similar in their verbal abilities. At about age 11, the sexes begin to diverge, with female superiority increasing through high school and possibly beyond. Girls score higher on tasks involving both receptive and productive language, and on "high-level" verbal tasks (analogies, comprehension of difficult written material, creative writing) as well as upon the "lower-level" measures (fluency). The magnitude of the female advantage varies, being most commonly about one-quarter of a standard deviation. (p. 351)

Denno (1982), in another review, also concluded that females were superior in verbal ability, having a slight advantage beginning in the preschool years, with the difference becoming stronger and more reliable after age 10 or 11. And, in yet another recent review, Halpern (1986) concurred that females have better verbal abilities than males.

Thus, although there is some disagreement among the reviews on details (a point to be discussed below), there is a clear consensus that there are gender differences in verbal ability favoring females. Reflecting this consensus, most textbooks in introductory psychology and developmental psychology present this finding as one of the well-established "facts" of psychology (e.g., Atkinson, Atkinson, & Hilgard, 1983, p. 90; Gleitman, 1981, p. 516; Hetherington & Parke, 1986, p. 626; Mussen, Conger, Kagan, & Huston, 1984, p. 276).

Despite the consensus on the existence of gender differences in verbal ability, the reviews disagree on some important details regarding the nature of the differences. The disagreements fall into two categories: (a) which types of verbal ability show gender differences and which do not, and (b) the developmental timing of the appearance or disappearance of the differences. For example, Anastasi argued that gender differences are found for simpler verbal tasks, whereas Maccoby and Jacklin concluded that female superiority was found in both high-level and low-level tasks. Further, Anastasi (1958) and Maccoby (1966) agreed that females were superior to males in vocabulary in the preschool years, whereas by 1974 Maccoby and Jacklin concluded that the sexes are similar in verbal ability in the preschool and elementary school years, with female superiority emerging around age 11 and increasing through high school and possibly beyond.

We contend, then, that beyond the global statement that females have superior verbal ability to males, we know very little about the nature of the gender difference in verbal ability, either in terms of the types of abilities showing gender differences or the developmental timing of possible differences. It was the purpose of the present study to extend our knowledge of the nature of gender differences in verbal ability through a meta-analysis of existing primary research reports.

Meta-Analysis and Psychological Gender Differences

In order to understand the contributions that meta-analysis can make to clarifying the nature of psychological gender differences, it is helpful to understand the history of methods of reviewing psychological gender differences (Hyde, 1986).

The traditional reviews of psychological gender differences (e.g., Maccoby, 1966) used the method of *narrative review.* That is, the reviewer located as many studies of gender differences as possible, organized them in some fashion, and reported his or her conclusions in narrative form. The narrative review, however, is subject to some serious criticisms: It is nonquantitative, unsystematic, and subjective, and the task of reviewing 100 or more studies simply exceeds the information-processing capacities of the human mind (Hunter, Schmidt, & Jackson, 1982).

The Maccoby and Jacklin (1974) review represented a considerable advance over previous ones in that it amassed far more studies than had been done before, but also because it permitted the systematic use of the method of *vote counting.* That is, Maccoby and Jacklin provided a listing of the studies reporting analyses of gender differences in verbal ability, so that one could tally the percentage that found a significant difference favoring females, the percentage that found no significant gender difference, and the percentage that found a significant difference favoring males.

Block (1976) provided a detailed critique of the Maccoby and Jacklin review. Block pointed out that Maccoby and Jacklin were inconsistent in the criteria they applied for deciding when a sufficiently large percentage of studies found a gender difference to allow one to conclude that there is a true gender difference.

General criticisms of the method of vote counting have also been raised (e.g., Hedges & Olkin, 1985; Hunter et al., 1982). Statisticians have pointed out that vote counting can lead to false conclusions (e.g., Hunter et al., 1982). Specifically, if there is a true effect in the population, but the studies reviewed have poor statistical power (perhaps because of small sample sizes), only a minority of the studies will find a significant effect, and the reviewer is likely to conclude that there is no effect (for a detailed numerical example of this problem, see Hyde, 1986). Thus the method of vote counting can lead to false conclusions.

Meta-analysis has been defined as the application of "quantitative methods to combining evidence from different studies" (Hedges & Olkin, 1985, p. 13). Meta-analysis began, in the 1980s, to make important contributions to the literature on psychological gender differences, although it should be noted that Maccoby and Jacklin (1974) had earlier estimated effect sizes for a few studies on verbal ability and concluded that the magnitude of the gender difference was about one quarter of a standard deviation (i.e., $d = 0.25$). Hyde (1981) performed a meta-analysis on the 27 studies of the verbal ability of subjects age 11 or older (corresponding to the age at which Maccoby and Jacklin concluded that the sexes began to diverge in verbal ability) in the Maccoby and Jacklin sample of studies. Her finding of a median value of $d = 0.24$ confirmed Maccoby and Jacklin's estimate, but the median value of $\omega^2 = .01$ led her to conclude that the magnitude of the gender difference in verbal ability is not large.

Since the time of the Hyde (1981) review, statistical methods in meta-analysis have advanced considerably. Most relevant here is the development of homogeneity statistics by Hedges and others (Hedges, 1982a, 1982b, 1982c; Rosenthal & Rubin, 1982a). These statistical methods allow one to determine whether a group of studies are uniform in their outcomes. Applied to the present problem, they allow one to determine whether the magnitude of the gender difference varies according to the type of verbal task ("verbal ability" having been used as a category to include everything from quality of speech in 2-year-olds, to performance on the Peabody Picture Vocabulary Test by 5-year-olds, to essay writing by high school students, to solutions of anagrams and analogies), and whether the magnitude of the gender difference varies with age. Thus meta-analyses using these techniques can answer considerably more sophisticated questions than earlier meta-analyses could, and certainly more than earlier narrative reviews could.

The Current Study

We performed a meta-analysis of studies reporting statistics on gender differences in verbal ability, including both the Maccoby and Jacklin sample of studies and a large sample of more recent studies. Our goal was to provide answers to the following questions:

1. What is the magnitude of gender differences in verbal ability, using the d metric?

2. Is the magnitude of gender differences in verbal ability declining?

3. Are gender differences in verbal ability uniform across various measures of verbal ability, such as vocabulary, analogies, and essay writing, or does the magnitude of the gender difference vary on these tasks, perhaps being close to zero on some and large on others?

4. Developmentally, at what ages do gender differences appear or disappear, and on what tasks?

5. Combining Hedges's (1982a, 1982b) homogeneity analyses with cognitive processing analyses, are there gender differences in certain aspects of verbal information processing that produce the gender differences in tested verbal abilities?

Our model for the analysis of the last question is Linn and Petersen's (1985) meta-analysis and cognitive analysis of gender differences in spatial ability. Arguing from both a cognitive processing perspective and a "strategies" perspective, they concluded that there are three distinct categories of spatial tests: spatial perception, mental rotation, and spatial visualization. Combining this categorization with the homogeneity analyses of meta-analysis, they concluded that large gender differences are found only on measures of mental rotation.

Method

The Sample of Studies

The sample of studies came from three sources: (a) the studies listed in Maccoby and Jacklin's (1974) Table 3.3; (b) a computerized literature search of the databases PsycINFO (indexes *Psychological Abstracts*) and ERIC (indexes ERIC documents) using the key terms "verbal ability and sex differences"; and (c) inspection of 1986 issues of psychology journals that had yielded pertinent studies in the earlier searches. The result was an initial pool of 176 studies reporting at least some usable information on gender differences in verbal ability.

Glass, McGaw, and Smith (1981) discussed the problems of the sampling of studies in a meta-analysis. They contended that the sampling should be well defined and comprehensive. Computer searches of the kind described above are ideal in producing a well-defined set of studies. Glass et al. also cautioned against ignoring "hidden" studies such as dissertations or other unpublished reports, which may be of equal quality to that of published studies but which may not be published because of null findings, because such studies are essential in a meta-analysis. Dissertations were included in the present sampling because the Psyc-INFO database includes dissertations; the sample in fact included 15 dissertations. ERIC indexes many unpublished studies, and 10 of them were included in the sample of studies.

Studies were excluded from the sample if they had any of the following characteristics: (a) The sample of subjects was not from the United States or Canada. (Because gender roles and patterns of gender differences vary cross-culturally, and because it was beyond the scope of the present analysis to explore issues cross-culturally, the sample was restricted to studies of subjects from these two adjacent and similar cultures.) (b) The article did not report original data. Or (c) the sample was clinical or was purposely selected for extremes of verbal ability. No restriction on selection of studies was made according to age, because a major goal of the present research was to define age trends in the pattern of gender differences.

Because the purpose of this research was to clarify the nature of gender differences in verbal ability in the general population, studies of various defects in verbal performance (e.g., stuttering and dyslexia) were not included. Such studies typically find a preponderance of male subjects with the problem (e.g., Halpern, 1986) and are often used as evidence of female verbal superiority. However, they represent a different population of studies and a different set of hypotheses from the ones currently under investigation.

One other group of studies was excluded: those dealing with early language learning by children in the age range of 18 months to 3 years. There have been claims that girls are verbally precocious compared with boys, citing evidence that girls learn to talk earlier or produce longer utterances at earlier ages than boys do (e.g., Halpern, 1986). Again, this is a distinct set of studies representing a different set of hypotheses from the ones investigated in the present research.

In cases in which insufficient information for computation of effect sizes was provided in the original article, follow-up letters requesting further information were sent to authors at the address provided in the article or a more recent address as provided in the 1985 *Directory of the American Psychological Association*.

Studies were eliminated from the final sample if, following attempts at correspondence with the author, no information was available to permit calculation of either an effect size or a significance test for gender differences. A total of 11 studies were eliminated for this reason.

The result was 165 usable studies that reported a significance test for gender differences and/or sufficient information to compute an effect size. (See Appendix for complete citations.) These 165 studies represent the testing of 1,418,899 subjects.

Coding of the Studies

For each study, the following information was recorded: (a) all statistics on gender differences in the verbal ability measure(s), including means and standard deviations, t, F, and df; (b) the number of male and female subjects; (c) the mean age of the subjects (if the article reported no age but mentioned "undergraduates" or students in introductory psychology classes, the average age was set equal to 19); (d) the type of test (vocabulary, analogies, reading comprehension, speaking or other verbal communication, essay writing, Scholastic Aptitude Test (SAT)–Verbal, general verbal ability test such as the American College Testing Program Examination–Verbal, anagrams, or other); (e) the test's reliability; (f) the kind of sample and how selective it was, using Becker and Hedges's (1984) index of sample selectivity (1 represents unselected samples, such as national samples; 2 represents somewhat selective samples, such as college students; and 3 represents highly selective samples, such as students from prestigious colleges); (g) the sex of the first author; and (h) the sex of the experimenter or tester. Studies were also coded for the cognitive processes involved in the particular test used, as explained below.

Cognitive Processing Analysis

Our cognitive processing analysis assumed that there are five basic processes that may be involved in various tests of verbal ability: (a) retrieval of the definition of a word (as occurs in most standard vocabulary tests in which the subject is given a word and must supply the definition); (b) retrieval of the name of a picture (as occurs in vocabulary tests such as the Peabody Picture Vocabulary Test, in which the subject is given a picture and must supply the name for it); (c) analysis of the relation among words (as occurs when comparing one word with another while solving analogies); (d) selection of relevant information from extensive information (as occurs in reading comprehension tests); and (e) verbal production (as occurs in essay writing or measures of spoken language). Further, a particular task may require a combination of these processes. For example, reading comprehension requires definition retrieval, word relations analysis, and selection of relevant information. Verbal analogies require definition retrieval and word relations analysis.

Each verbal ability measure was coded for the five processes noted above. Each of the authors independently coded all studies. Disagreements occurred for 10 of the 165 studies, for an interrater agreement of 94%. Disagreements were discussed and resolved.

Statistical Analysis

The effect size computed for each study was d, defined as the mean for females minus the mean for males, divided by the pooled within-sex standard deviation. Thus positive values of d represent superior female performance and negative values represent superior male performance. Depending on the statistics available for a given study, formulas provided by Hedges and Becker (1986) and Hedges and Olkin (1985) were used for the computation of d and the homogeneity statistics. All values of d were first corrected for bias, using values tabled by Glass et al. (1981). The complete listing of all studies, with effect sizes, is provided in Tables 1 and 2.

56   JANET SHIBLEY HYDE AND MARCIA C. LINN

Table 1
Studies of Gender Differences in Verbal Ability, Maccoby and Jacklin's (1974) Sample
(in same order as Maccoby & Jacklin, Table 3.3)

Study	Mean age	N	Difference	d^a	Type of test[b]	Cognitive processes[c]	Sample selectivity[d]
Moore, 1967	7	76	None	.09	1	1	1
Clarke-Stewart, 1973	2	36	Females	NA	4	NA	1
Reppucci, 1971	2	48	None	NA	1	2	1
Rhine, Hill, & Wandruff, 1967	4	50	None	-.15	1	2	1
McCarthy & Kirk, 1963	3	50	None	0	2	5	1
Dickie, 1968	4	50	None	NA	1	2	2
Sitkei & Meyers, 1969	4	100	None	NA	1	2	1
Shipman, 1971	4	1,198	None	.07	1	2	2
Williams & Fleming, 1969	4	45	None	.10	1	2	2
Brown, 1971	4	96	None	.32	3	5	1
Friedrichs et al., 1971	4	50	None	NA	9	5	2
Mehrabian, 1970	4	127	None	.44	1	1	1
Shipman, 1972	4	82	Females	.07	3	6	2
Klaus & Gray, 1968	6	88	None	NA	9	9	2
Jeruchimowicz, Costello, & Bagur, 1971	4	79	None	NA	1	2	2
Shure, Spivack, & Jaeger, 1971	4	62	None	.31	1	2	2
Ali & Costello, 1971	4	56	None	-.14	1	2	2
Harrison & Nadelman, 1972	4	50	None	.17	1	2	1
Osser, Wang, & Zaid, 1969	5	32	None	NA	1	2	1
Suppes & Feldman, 1971	6	64	None	NA	3	5	1
James & Miller, 1973	6	32	None	NA	9	9	1
Masters, 1969	6	72	None	.19	9	1	1
Brimer, 1969	8	606	Males	-.26	1	2	1
Winitz, 1959	5	150	None	.27	4	8	1
McCarver & Ellis, 1972	6	60	None	NA	1	2	1
Milgram, Shoire, & Malasky, 1971	6	90	None	NA	4	8	1
Saltz, Soller, & Sigel, 1972	8	24	None	NA	1	5	1
Stanford Research Institute, 1972	7	3,486	Females	.01	3	6	2
Cowan, Weber, Hoddinott, & Klein, 1967	8	96	None	.16	4	8	1
Routh & Tweney, 1972	10	60	None	NA	4	8	1
Darley & Winitz, 1961	5	150	None	.08	6	7	1
Davis & Slobodian, 1967	5	238	None	.11	9	9	1
Dykstra & Tinney, 1969	6	3,283	Females	.08	3	6	1
Lesser, Fifer, & Clark, 1965	6	320	None	-.12	1	1	1
France, 1973	8	252	Males	-.44	1	2	1
Graves & Koziol, 1971	7	67	None	NA	9	9	1
Penk, 1971	9	100	Females	NA	9	8	1
Gates, 1961	7	1,826	Females	.27	3	6	1
Parsley, Powell, O'Connor, & Deutsch, 1963	9	717	None	.01	3	6	1
Harris & Hassemer, 1972	8	96	None	NA	4	8	1
Lipton & Overton, 1971	10	80	None	.16	8	9	1
Eska & Black, 1971	8	100	None	NA	6	7	2
Eisenberg, Berlin, Dill, & Frank, 1968	9	64	Females	.56	4	8	1
Corah, 1965	9	60	Males	-.66	1	1	2
Hoemann, 1972	11	40	None	NA	4	8	1
Stevenson, Hale, Klein, & Miller, 1968	13	85	Females	.42	8	9	1
Stevenson, Klein, Hale, & Miller, 1968	11	529	Females	.34	8	9	1

GENDER DIFFERENCES IN VERBAL ABILITY   57

Table 1 *(continued)*

Study	Mean age	N	Difference	d^a	Type of test[b]	Cognitive processes[c]	Sample selectivity[d]
Palmer & Masling, 1969	12	48	None	NA	1	5	2
Cohen & Klein, 1968	10	80	None	.66	4	8	1
Hopkins & Bibelheimer, 1971	10	354	None	.04	6	7	1
Cotler & Palmer, 1971	11	120	Females	.36	4	8	1
Penney, 1965	11	108	None	NA	1	2	1
Preston, 1962	11	686	Females	.22	3	6	1
Stevenson & Odom, 1965	10	318	None	.06	8	9	1
Shepard, 1970	11	137	Females	.47	1	1	1
Baldwin, McFarlane, & Garvey, 1971	10	96	None	NA	4	8	2
Heider, 1971	10	143	None	NA	4	8	1
Achenbach, 1969	12	48	Females	.50	1	1	1
Cicirelli, 1967	11	641	Females	NA	6	7	1
Weinberg & Rabinowitz, 1970	15	48	None	NA	1	1	4
Flanagan et al., 1961	14	1,545	Females	NA	3	6	2
Walberg, 1969	16	2,074	Females	.32	6	7	2
Backman, 1972	17	2,925	Females	1.43	6	7	2
American College Testing Program, 1976–1977	18	45,222	Females	.26	6	7	2
Rosenberg & Sutton-Smith, 1966	19	600	None	NA	6	7	2
Bieri, Bradburn, & Galinsky, 1958	19	76	None	.18	7	7	3
DeFazio, 1973	19	44	None	.21	1	1	2
Feather, 1968	19	60	None	NA	8	9	2
Feather, 1969	19	167	None	NA	8	9	2
Koen, 1966	19	72	None	NA	4	8	3
Laughlin, Branch, & Johnson, 1969	19	528	None	−.03	9	5	2
Marks, 1968	18	760	None	NA	7	7	2
Mendelsohn & Griswold, 1966	19	223	None	.16	1	1	3
Mendelsohn & Griswold, 1967	19	181	None	.07	8	9	3
Sarason & Minard, 1962	19	96	None	NA	1	1	2
Very, 1967	19	355	Females	.26	3	6	2
Rosenberg & Sutton-Smith, 1964	19	377	Females	NA	6	7	2
Rosenberg & Sutton-Smith, 1969	19	1,013	Females	.44	6	7	2
Sutton-Smith, Rosenberg, & Landy, 1968	19	1,055	None	.08	6	7	2
Bayley & Oden, 1955	41	1,102	Males	−.31	2	5	3
Blum, Fosshage, & Jarvik, 1972	64	54	None	.56	1	1	1

Note. NA = not available.
[a] Positive values reflect superior performance by females; negative values reflect superior performance by males. [b] 1 = vocabulary, 2 = analogies, 3 = reading comprehension, 4 = speaking or other verbal communication, 5 = essay writing, 6 = general verbal ability (mixture of items), 7 = Scholastic Aptitude Test–Verbal, 8 = anagrams, 9 = other. [c] 1 = retrieval of definition of word; 2 = retrieval of name of picture; 3 = analysis of relations among words; 4 = selection of relevant information; 5 = 1 and 3; 6 = 1, 3, and 4; 7 = mixture of all processes; 8 = verbal production (spoken or written); 9 = other. [d] 1 = general, unselected; 2 = somewhat selected; 3 = highly selected; 4 = other.

The analyses developed by Hedges assume independence of the values of d entered into them. Thus multiple measures from the same study should not be included. In cases in which an individual study reported multiple tests of gender differences—either because several ages or several measures were included—one age group and one measure were selected randomly and only that single value of d was included in subsequent computations.

Results

Magnitude of Gender Differences in Verbal Ability

The summary results of computations of mean effect size are shown in Table 3. The unweighted mean value of d, averaged over 120 available values, was small and positive, indicating

58   JANET SHIBLEY HYDE AND MARCIA C. LINN

Table 2
Studies of Gender Differences in Verbal Ability, Recent Sample (in Alphabetical Order)

Study	Mean age	N	Difference	d[a]	Type of test[b]	Cognitive processes[c]	Sample selectivity[d]
Alesandrini, 1981	19	383	Males	−.32	3	6	2
Applebee, Langer, & Mullis, 1986	13	2,000	Females	.57	5	8	1
Averitt, 1981	5	100	Females	.43	6	7	1
Baden, 1981	9	81	None	.14	5	8	1
Berry & Webb, 1985	58	119	None	.35	6	7	2
Bodner, McMillen, Greenbowe, & McDaniel, 1983	19	1,300	None	.07	7	7	2
Bristow, 1978	10	76	None	.22	3	6	1
Brownell & Smith, 1973	4	56	Females	.58	4	8	2
Buswell, 1980	8	36	None	−.41	4	8	1
Carter, 1976	33	683	None	−.03	1	1	1
Chase, 1981	18	3,839	Males	−.07	7	7	2
Clarke-Sewart, Umeh, Snow, & Pederson, 1980	2	60	Females	.54	6	7	1
Coie & Dorval, 1973	8	90	None	0	1	1	1
Cole & LaVoie, 1985	4	78	None	−.17	1	2	1
Dawson, 1981	12	40	None	NA	1	1	1
Denno, 1983	15	987	Females	.14	3	6	1
Denno, Meijs, Nachshon, & Aurand, 1981	7	3,013	None	.05	6	7	1
Dunn, 1977	8	144	None	.30	4	8	1
Elfman, 1978	4	121	None	.16	2	5	1
Enright, Manheim, Franklin, & Enright, 1980	6	22	None	−.29	1	2	1
Feely, 1975	15	304	Males	−.22	1	1	1
Fennema & Sherman, 1978	12	431	None	.07	6	7	1
Fiore, 1977	22	40	Females	NA	1	5	2
Fisher & Mandinach, 1985	13	132	None	−.16	1	1	1
Forte, Mandato, & Kayson, 1981	19	40	None	.33	1	1	2
Frederiksen & Evans, 1974	18	395	Females	.34	1	1	2
Gjerde, Block, & Block, 1985	11	59	None	−.23	6	7	1
Harris & Siebel, 1976	11	144	Females	.61	5	8	1
Hartle, Baratz, & Clark, 1983	40	34,298	Females	.22	6	7	2
Haslett, 1983	4	49	Females	NA	4	8	1
Hennessy & Merrifield, 1978	18	2,985	None	.20	6	7	2
Hertzog & Carter, 1982	49	421	None	.15	1	1	1
Hogrebe, Nist, & Newman, 1985	18	23,362	Males	−.05	3	6	1
Houtz, Montgomery, & Kirkpatrick, 1979	9	156	Females	NA	6	7	1
Hyde, Geiringer, & Yen, 1975	19	81	Females	.54	1	1	2
Ingersoll, 1978	9	7,119	None	NA	1	1	1
Ironsmith & Whitehurst, 1978	8	64	Females	.61	9	6	1
Johnson, 1974	4	40	None	−.38	6	5	1
Jordan, 1981	14	328	Males	−.33	1	2	2
Kappy, 1980	23	37,112	Females	.04	6	7	2
Khatena, 1975	13	50	None	−.24	2	5	2
Klecan-Aker, 1984	14	24	None	.37	4	8	1
Koffman & Lips, 1980	34	70	None	.18	6	7	2

Table 2 (*continued*)

Study	Mean age	N	Difference	d^a	Type of test[b]	Cognitive processes[c]	Sample selectivity[d]
Kuchler, 1983	21	97	None	NA	1	1	2
Linn & Pulos, 1983	14	778	None	−.07	1	1	1
Long, 1976	5	151	None	.08	6	7	1
Lunneborg & Lunneborg, 1985	17	632	None	.03	1	1	2
McGee, 1982	19	454	Females	.24	1	1	1
McKeever & van Deventer, 1977	19	151	None	NA	6	6	2
McLoyd, 1980	4	36	Females	.75	4	8	2
Mills, 1981	13	115	None	−.17	6	7	1
National Assessment of Educational Progress, 1985	13	22,693	Females	.12	3	6	1
Perney, Freund, & Barman, 1976	5	202	None	.16	9	9	1
Posluszny & Barton, 1981	10	42	None	−.03	6	7	1
Purdue University Measurement and Research Center, 1974	17	100	Females	.38	1	1	1
Pusser & McCandless, 1974	4	181	None	NA	1	2	2
Ramist & Arbeiter, 1986a	18	977,361	Males	−.11	7	7	2
Ramist & Arbeiter, 1986b	18	188,811	Females	.09	5	8	2
Rebecca, 1974	9	40	Males	−.87	1	2	2
Riley & Denmark, 1974	9	53	None	−.22	1	1	2
Roberge & Flexer, 1981	12	450	None	.12	3	7	2
Rock, Hilton, Pollack, Ekstrom, & Goertz, 1985	18	25,948	None	−.02	3	6	1
Sanders & Soares, 1986	19	274	Females	.32	1	1	2
Sassenrath & Maddux, 1974	5	98	None	.10	6	7	2
Sause, 1976	5	144	Males	NA	4	8	1
Schuerger, Kepner, & Lawler, 1979	17	234	None	.22	6	7	1
Schultz, Elias, Robbins, Streeten & Blakeman, 1986	40	54	None	NA	6	6	1
Searleman, Herrmann, & Coventry, 1984	18	86	None	.14	7	7	2
Sherman, 1979	14	108	None	.04	1	1	1
Signorella, 1984	19	75	None	−.07	3	6	2
Silverman & Zimmer, 1976	25	20	None	.41	4	8	2
Skanes, 1970	12	644	None	.06	6	1	1
Sobol, 1980	21	408	None	.13	1	1	1
Soriano, 1975	18	168	Females	.56	2	5	1
Stephenson, 1973	4	120	None	.19	4	8	1
Stevenson & Newman, 1986	7	136	Females	.44	3	6	1
Stoner, Panek, & Satterfield, 1982	73	50	None	.19	1	1	1
Stoner & Spencer, 1983	4	108	None	−.14	1	2	2
Tseng & Rhodes, 1973	14	99	None	.25	3	6	1
Vance, Hankins, & McGee, 1979	10	60	None	NA	3	6	1
Waber, 1977	13	40	None	.44	6	7	1
Wilkie & Eisdorfer, 1977	69	64	None	−.13	1	1	1

(*table continued*)

Table 2 (*continued*)

Study	Mean age	N	Difference	d^a	Type of test^b	Cognitive processes^c	Sample selectivity^d
Wolf & Gow, 1986	8	98	None	.05	3	6	1
Wormack, 1979	19	106	Females	.49	5	8	2

Note. NA = not available.
^{a} Positive values reflect superior performance by females; negative values reflect superior performance by males. ^{b} 1 = vocabulary, 2 = analogies, 3 = reading comprehension, 4 = speaking or other verbal communication, 5 = essay writing, 6 = general verbal ability (mixture of items), 7 = Scholastic Aptitude Test–Verbal, 8 = anagrams, 9 = other. ^{c} 1 = retrieval of definition of word; 2 = retrieval of name of picture; 3 = analysis of relations among words; 4 = selection of relevant information; 5 = 1 and 3; 6 = 1, 3, and 4; 7 = mixture of all processes; 8 = verbal production (spoken or written); 9 = other. ^{d} 1 = general, unselected; 2 = somewhat selected; 3 = highly selected.

that, overall, females outperformed males. When the weighted mean effect size was computed, weighting effect sizes by the number of subjects in the study (Hedges & Becker, 1986), the result was a very small negative value, indicating superior male performance. The shift from a positive to a negative value is largely due to a single study reported by Ramist and Arbeiter (1986), providing data for all persons—977,361 of them—taking the SAT in 1985. The study had a negative value of *d*, and because of the enormous number of subjects it overshadowed other studies in computations of weighted means and other statistics in the meta-analysis. Hence we assigned it to a separate category and deleted it in all succeeding computations. We consider the SAT–Verbal in a special section of the Discussion. With that study deleted, the weighted mean *d* is again small and positive (see Table 3).

Overall, 29 (24%) of the 120 available values of *d* were negative, reflecting superior male performance; two were exactly zero; and the remainder (75%) were positive, indicating superior female performance.

Concerning statistical significance, 44 (27%) of the 165 studies found females to perform significantly better than males, 109 (66%) found no significant gender difference, and 12 (7%) found males performing significantly better than females.

Homogeneity analyses using procedures specified by Hedges and Becker (1986) indicated that the set of 119 effect sizes is significantly nonhomogeneous, $H = 2196.08$, $p < .05$, compared against a critical value of $\chi^2(118) = 146.57$. Therefore we can conclude that the set of effect sizes is heterogeneous. We can thus seek to partition the set of studies into more homogeneous subgroups, using factors that we hypothesized would differentiate studies.

Table 3
Summary of Effect-Size Statistics for All Studies

Variable	No. studies	d
Unweighted mean *d*, all studies	120	+0.14
Weighted mean *d*, all studies	120	−0.04
Weighted mean *d*, excluding national Scholastic Aptitude Test data	119	+0.11

Varieties of Verbal Ability

The results of the analysis of effect sizes according to the type of verbal ability test are shown in Table 4. Note that, as with the overall analysis, the magnitude of the gender difference is close to zero (and in fact the 95% confidence interval covers zero) for many types of tests. The only exceptions are a modest gender difference of 0.20 standard deviations favoring females on measures of general verbal ability, a difference of similar magnitude favoring females in the solution of anagrams, and a difference of approximately one third of a standard deviation favoring females in measures of the quality of speech production.

Note that significant heterogeneity of effect sizes remains, particularly for the category of tests of general verbal ability, as might be expected. True homogeneity of effect sizes means that the studies behave as if they were replications of each other. Because of the large number of studies and the large numbers of subjects, the statistical tests for homogeneity are in a sense too

Table 4
Magnitude of Gender Differences as a Function of Type of Verbal Ability Test

Type of test	k	d	95% confidence interval for d	H
Vocabulary	40	0.02	−0.02 to 0.06	116.88*
Analogies	5	−0.16	−0.26 to −0.06	30.34*
Reading comprehension	18	0.03	0.01 to 0.04	159.84*
Speech production	12	0.33	0.20 to 0.46	11.34
Essay writing	5	0.09	0.08 to 0.10	123.77*
Scholastic Aptitude Test	4	−0.03	−0.08 to 0.03	5.69
Anagrams	5	0.22	0.10 to 0.33	5.72
General/mixed	25	0.20	0.19 to 0.21	1,217.46*
Other	5	0.08	−0.04 to 0.20	6.48
Total	119	0.11	0.10 to 0.12	2,196.08*

Note. k represents the number of studies, that is, the number of effect sizes; *H* is the within-group homogeneity statistic (Hedges & Becker, 1986).
* Significant nonhomogeneity at $p < .05$, according to χ^2 test. All other categories are homogeneous.

Table 5

Magnitude of Gender Differences as a Function of Hypothesized Types of Cognitive Processes

Cognitive process	k	d	95% confidence interval for d	H
Retrieval of definition of a word (RD)	29	0.08	0.04 to 0.13	63.46*
Retrieval of name of a picture	13	−0.12	−0.19 to 0.04	33.75*
Analysis of relations among words (A)	0	—	—	—
Selection of relevant information (S)	0	—	—	—
RD + A	8	−0.11	−0.20 to −0.03	37.04*
RD + A + S	17	0.02	0.01 to 0.04	161.99*
Production (written or oral)	17	0.09	0.08 to 0.10	148.27*
Mixture of processes	28	0.19	0.18 to 0.20	1283.42*
Other	7	0.19	0.10 to 0.29	6.37

Note. k represents the number of studies, that is, the number of effect sizes; H is the within-group homogeneity statistic.
* Significant nonhomogeneity at $p < .05$, according to χ^2 test.
All other categories are homogeneous.

powerful. Experience with meta-analysis suggests that we should tolerate a certain amount of heterogeneity.

Another way to assess these effect sizes is to test the significance of between-groups differences, between-groups homogeneity, $H_B = 518.56$, compared against a critical value of $\chi^2(8) = 15.51$, indicating significant between-groups heterogeneity. That is, there are significant differences in effect sizes (the magnitude of the gender difference) between the types of tests.

Cognitive Processes

The variations in effect size as a function of the cognitive processes used, according to our analysis, are shown in Table 5. Note that, as with the analysis for type of test, none of the effect sizes is very large. The largest ones are quite modest ($d = +0.19$) for tests requiring mixtures of processes (usually general verbal ability tests) and for the category "other," which contained, among other things, studies measuring anagram solutions. Five of seven values of d are positive, indicating superior female performance. The two negative values are for retrieval of the name of a picture ($d = -0.12$) and the combination of retrieval of a definition and analysis of relations among words ($d = -0.11$).

The homogeneity analysis indicated significant between-groups heterogeneity, $H_B = 461.78$ compared against a critical value of $\chi^2(6) = 12.59$. This indicates significant variations in effect size (magnitude of the gender difference) among the different cognitive processes. Significant heterogeneity within categories of cognitive processes also remained, although again

it must be remembered that the significance tests are extremely powerful. All categories were actually rather close to homogeneity except for the category "mixture of cognitive processes," which, as might be expected, was quite heterogeneous.

Age Trends

Studies were grouped according to the average age of subjects as follows: 5 years and younger, 6 to 10 years, 11 to 18 years, 19 to 25 years, and 26 and older. Those groupings were chosen a priori because of debates in the literature. The 5 years and younger group (preschoolers) speaks to the issue of whether there is an early advantage for girls in the development of verbal ability. The 6- to 10-year-old group encompasses the elementary school years. The 11- to 18-year-old group (adolescence) addresses Maccoby and Jacklin's (1974) assertion that the sexes begin to diverge around age 11 in verbal ability, with female superiority increasing through the high school years and possibly beyond. The 19- to 25-year-old group represents college students and other young adults. The 26 years and older group represents adults.

The effect sizes are shown in Table 6. Notice that when averaged over all tests, the effect sizes are small and positive for all age groups and do not show impressive variations. Vocabulary measures yield similar results, with the exception of a negative effect size (indicating superior male performance) for the 6 to 10 age group. Reading comprehension tests show values close to zero for all age groups, with the exception of a value of +0.31 for the 5 years and younger age group, but this is based on a single study and therefore has little generalizability. Indeed, the very measurement of reading comprehension in 5-year-olds might be questioned.

For the vocabulary studies, all the within-group (age groups) homogeneity statistics were nonsignificant (with the exception of the 11- to 18-year-old group, which was barely significant). Thus, the magnitude of gender differences on vocabulary tests was uniform within the age groups.

Selectivity of Sample

As noted above, studies were coded according to the selectivity of the sample of studies. The mean effect sizes as a function

Table 6

Magnitude of Gender Differences (d) as a Function of Age

Age group	All tests		Vocabulary		Reading comprehension tests	
	d	No. studies	d	No. studies	d	No. studies
5 years and younger	0.13	24	0.07	9	0.31	1
6 to 10	0.06	29	−0.26	9	0.09	7
11 to 18	0.11	39	0.01	10	0.02	7
19 to 25	0.06	18	0.23	7	−0.03	3
26 and older	0.20	9	0.05	5	NA	0

Note. NA = not available; no studies in this category were found.

of the selectivity of the sample were 0.05 for unselected samples (based on 74 studies), 0.13 for moderately selective samples (based on 41 studies), and −0.18 for highly selective samples (based on 4 studies). Again, the values are all small.

Year of Publication

Studies were grouped into two categories: those published in 1973 or earlier (corresponding approximately to Maccoby and Jacklin's sample of studies) and those published in 1974 or later (corresponding approximately to the sample of studies that we collected). For the pre-1973 studies $d = 0.23$, and for the post-1973 studies $d = 0.10$. Homogeneity analysis indicated that this between-groups difference is significant, $H_B = 93.71$ compared against a critical $\chi^2(1) = 3.84$. Thus the gender difference is significantly smaller in more recent studies.

Author's Sex

The mean effect size was 0.08 for the 60 studies whose first author was male and 0.15 for the 46 studies whose first author was female. This difference is statistically significant, $H_B = 102.4$ compared against a critical $\chi^2(1) = 3.84$.

Discussion

We are prepared to assert that there are no gender differences in verbal ability, at least at this time, in American culture, in the standard ways that verbal ability has been measured. We feel that we can reach this conclusion with some confidence, having surveyed 165 studies that represent the testing of 1,418,899 subjects (excluding the Ramist and Arbeiter SAT data, 441,538 subjects) and averaged 119 values of d to obtain a weighted mean value of +0.11. A gender difference of one tenth of a standard deviation is scarcely one that deserves continued attention in theory, research, or textbooks. Surely we have larger effects to pursue.

It is part of psychologists' creed that one can never accept the null hypothesis, yet here we do just that. We believe that meta-analysis furnishes the tools to allow more symmetrical decision making in research. Because the technique relies on the estimation of effect size rather than hypothesis testing, it allows us to determine that some effect sizes are so close to zero that we should conclude that there is no effect.

There has been some debate over the interpretation of effect sizes. Cohen (1969) considered a d of 0.20 small, a d of 0.50 medium, and a d of 0.80 large. Thus the effect size of 0.11 that we obtained falls short even of what he considered to be small. Rosenthal and Rubin (1982c), on the other hand, have introduced the binomial effect size display as a means of determining the practical significance of an effect size, and they have argued that many effect sizes that seem to be small are actually large in terms of their practical significance. For an example, an effect size reported as a correlation of 0.20, when measuring the success of a treatment for cancer, translates into increasing the cure rate from 40 to 60%, something that surely has practical significance. On the other hand, using the approximation formula $d = 2r$, our effect size of 0.11 translates to an r of 0.055, which yields only a 5% increase in "success rate" (e.g., from 47.5 to 52.5%); thus our effect size is so small that even the binomial effect size technique indicates little practical significance. Further, the question under consideration is gender differences in verbal ability, not curing cancer. While an effect size of 0.11 might have some practical significance if the topic is cancer, it has no significance for understanding the nature of differences between male and female verbal ability. Such a small difference does not translate into any meaningful psychological or educational implications.

The effect size for the gender difference in verbal ability reported here can also be compared with effect sizes for gender differences reported in meta-analyses of other domains. For gender differences in spatial ability tests involving mental rotations, $d = .73$ (although for other measures of spatial ability the difference is smaller) (Linn & Petersen, 1985). For gender differences in mathematics performance, $d = .43$ (Hyde, 1981). For gender differences in aggression, including studies with subjects of all ages, $d = .50$ (Hyde, 1984). For social-psychological studies of aggression by adult subjects, $d = .40$ (Eagly & Steffen, 1986). And for gender differences in helping behavior, $d = .13$ (Eagly & Crowley, 1986). Thus the magnitude of the gender difference in verbal ability is clearly one of the smallest of the gender differences. One can also compare the magnitude of the effect with effect sizes that have been computed outside the domain of gender differences. For example, the average effect of psychotherapy (comparison of treated and control groups) has been computed to be a d of .68 (Smith & Glass, 1977). Again, the gender difference in verbal ability seems small by comparison.

One caveat on sampling should be stated. Earlier we noted the preponderance of boys in various categories of verbal performance deficits such as dyslexia. If more boys than girls are removed from regular classrooms for placement in special classes (such as remedial reading), then test results from regular classrooms may have omitted more low-scoring boys than low-scoring girls. The effect would be to reduce the effect size for the gender difference in verbal performance. It remains speculative, of course, whether this disproportionate removal of low-scoring boys occurs.

Implications for Brain Lateralization Theories

Two theories have been proposed to explain cognitive gender differences on the basis of the notion that lateralization of function occurs somewhat differently in male and female brains. The Buffery and Gray hypothesis (1972) is that left hemisphere dominance for verbal functions is attained earlier in girls (consistent with their superior verbal ability), which in turn does not permit spatial processing to be as bilateral in girls as it is in boys. The second theory, which has somewhat better—though certainly not consistent—empirical support, is the Levy hypothesis (Levy, 1976; Levy-Agresti & Sperry, 1968). It states that females, like left-handed males, are more likely to be bilateral for verbal functions; this in turn inhibits the development of spatial processing capabilities, which the theory asserts will develop best with great lateralization of function. Levy also argued that bilateral verbal processing is advantageous. (For reviews of evidence regarding both theories, see Halpern, 1986; Sherman, 1978.)

Both theories assume male superiority in spatial ability and female superiority in verbal ability and then seek to explain them on the basis of differential patterns of lateralization. However, our research indicates that the belief in the superior verbal ability of females has little empirical support. Thus our research pulls out one of the two wobbly legs on which the brain lateralization theories have rested. (For a tug at the other wobbly leg, spatial ability, see Caplan, MacPherson, & Tobin, 1985.) And Hahn's (1987) extensive review of research on cerebral lateralization lead him to conclude that there was no consistent evidence of sex differences in asymmetrical organization of the brain.

The Scholastic Aptitude Test–Verbal Scale

Beginning in 1972, the traditional gender difference favoring females on the SAT–Verbal has been reversed. This can be seen in the data reported by Ramist and Arbeiter (1986) for the 1985 administration of the SAT. For males, $M = 437$ and $SD = 112$, and for females, $M = 425$ and $SD = 109$, for an effect-size d of $-.1086$. The test affects the lives of hundreds of thousands of people each year, so the finding is an important one and requires some consideration. Although many explanations are possible, we offer two. One possibility is that the content of the material—either vocabulary words or reading passages that measure comprehension—has become more technical in recent years. For example, if it is material covered in physics or chemistry classes, to which females have had less exposure, then females would be at a disadvantage in performing on the test.

A second possibility has to do with sampling. The magnitude and even the direction of gender differences can be profoundly affected by the way in which the sample of males and the sample of females are drawn (Hyde, 1981). The 1985 SAT data represent the testing of 471,992 males and 505,369 females. Substantially more females took the test. Those who take the SAT are a selected sample to begin with, and it may be that the male sample (smaller in number) is somewhat more highly selected than the female, creating higher scores for males on the test even though the difference might be nonexistent or reversed if the general population were sampled. Data from the Educational Testing Service support this hypothesis: females taking the SAT in 1985 were disadvantaged compared with males taking the test on the variables of parental income, father's education, and attendance at private schools, although all the differences are small (Ramist & Arbeiter, 1986). Further, there may be increasing numbers of women in the middle-adult years returning to college and taking the SAT to meet entrance requirements; having been out of school for many years, they are not practiced test takers, a factor that would be particularly handicapping on a timed test such as the SAT.

Developmental Trends

Meta-analysis is capable of detecting age trends in the magnitude of gender differences. For example, Hyde (1984) found that gender differences in aggression were twice as large for preschoolers ($d = .58$) as for college students ($d = .27$). The present analysis, however, found little evidence of age trends in the magnitude of gender differences, either when considering the evidence from all measures of verbal ability combined or when considering two particularly frequently studied aspects of verbal ability, vocabulary and reading comprehension (see Table 6). The majority of the effect sizes are .11 or less. The largest value is $-.26$ for vocabulary measures with 6- to 10-year-olds, based on nine studies. This finding of male superiority can be traced to four studies (Buswell, 1980; Corah, 1965; France, 1973; and Rebecca, 1974), all of which found moderate to large differences favoring males. Of those studies, two of the four were unpublished, and three of the four had rather small sample sizes (Ns = 36, 60, and 40). It is difficult to say whether there is sufficient evidence of this effect to warrant pursuing it with further research.

Year of Publication

For the group of studies published in 1973 and earlier, $d = .23$, and for the group of post-1973 studies, $d = .10$. Thus there has been some decline in the magnitude of the gender difference in verbal ability in more recent research. Hyde (1984) found a similar trend toward smaller gender differences in aggression in more recent studies. Linn and Petersen (1985) reported some decline in gender differences in spatial ability in recent years. And Chipman, Brush, and Wilson (1985) reported declines in gender differences in mathematics performance. Thus the present findings are consistent with trends in other areas (see also Rosenthal & Rubin, 1982b).

Several interpretations of this recent smaller gender difference in verbal ability are possible. It is unclear whether it results from increases in male performance or declines in female performance. These two possibilities cannot be sorted out because there is not a common metric across studies. One possibility is that with increased flexibility in gender roles beginning in the 1970s, boys have been permitted or encouraged to engage in more activities formerly reserved for girls, and these activities foster verbal ability. Similarly, girls have been permitted to engage in more activities formerly reserved for boys, and participation in these activities has fostered spatial ability and mathematics performance.

On the other hand, it may be that the trend is simply the result of changing publication practices on the part of researchers. Maccoby and Jacklin's work may have been pivotal, because it pointed out the selective tendency not to publish studies of gender differences in which no significant effect was found. Perhaps researchers now feel encouraged to report null findings about gender differences, so that more small effect sizes are uncovered in literature searches.

This trend over time also helps to reconcile the difference between our conclusions and Maccoby and Jacklin's. They computed a few effect sizes for gender differences in verbal ability, found that the effect size was typically $d = .25$, and concluded that the gender difference in verbal ability was "well established," but that it was smaller than the gender difference in quantitative ability or spatial ability. Hyde's (1981) more systematic analysis of those studies yielded a d of .24. And our current analysis of pre-1973 studies yielded a d of .23. Thus all these findings are highly congruent. The new information comes from the post-1973 studies, many of them based on large sample sizes, which yield a d of .10.

Author's Sex

Other meta-analysts have found significant fluctuations in effect sizes depending on the sex of the researchers. For example, Eagly and Carli (1981) found that male researchers obtained greater gender differences, that is, greater persuasibility among females compared with males, than female researchers did. We found a significant difference in effect sizes for those studies whose first author was male compared with those whose first author was female, with female authors reporting a larger difference and therefore greater female superiority in performance. However, both effect sizes are close to zero (0.08 and 0.15 for male and female authors, respectively), so the effect of author's sex cannot be considered substantial. It may be that social–psychological variables are more sensitive than ability variables are to the researcher's sex. Social psychology studies involve designing a social setting in which to measure the behavior, and it may be that male researchers design settings that are more comfortable for male subjects. Research on abilities, on the other hand, typically taps performance on standardized tests not designed by the researcher, so that the researcher's sex has little influence on the stimulus materials (although, of course, there may be sex-biased items on the test). In addition, the sex of the person actually collecting data from subjects has been demonstrated to have an effect in social–psychological research (e.g., Walters, Shurley, & Parsons, 1962), in part because the experimenter actually becomes a part of the social environment of the study. In contrast, measures of abilities are often collected by large-scale testing, where the experimenter has little or no contact with the individual subject.

Conclusion

Our meta-analysis provides strong evidence that the magnitude of the gender difference in verbal ability is currently so small that it can effectively be considered to be zero. More detailed analysis of various types of verbal ability (e.g., vocabulary, reading comprehension, and analogies) similarly yielded no evidence of a substantial gender difference. The one possible exception is measures of speech production, which favor females, $d = .33$. It should be noted that most of these studies used measures of the *quality* of speech. In terms of other kinds of measures, such as total talking time, males exceed females (e.g., Swacker, 1975), contrary to stereotypes.

Where do we go from here? First, we need to rewrite some textbooks. We also need to study gender differences in abilities more precisely. We need to move away from the old model of intellect that specified only three rather general cognitive abilities—verbal ability, mathematical ability, and spatial ability—toward investigating the possibility of gender differences in new, more refined, and more expansive models of intellect such as those proposed by Gardner (1983) and Sternberg (1982, 1984; Sternberg & Walter, 1982). Only then will we gain a more advanced understanding of gender differences—and similarities—in abilities.

In the meantime, we should keep in mind that even with more refined studies of gender differences based on more sophisticated models of abilities, we might still conclude that gender differences in cognitive abilities are nonexistent and that other explanations must be found for the large gender differences in earning power and career advancement in our society.

Furthermore, our results suggest a practical recommendation. The present findings might be regarded as indicating that verbal ability tests provide gender-unbiased measures of cognitive abilities, compared with mathematics tests. Verbal skills are central to virtually all academic pursuits, and male and female students have more comparable course preparation for verbal tests than for mathematics tests; thus the findings of this review lead us to recommend the use of verbal tests for the selection of students for academic programs when selection tests are used.

References

Anastasi, A. (1958). *Differential psychology* (3rd ed.). New York: Macmillan.

Atkinson, R. L., Atkinson, R. C., & Hilgard, E. R. (1983). *Introduction to psychology* (8th ed.). New York: Harcourt, Brace, Jovanovich.

Becker, B. J., & Hedges, L. V. (1984). Meta-analysis of cognitive gender differences: A comment on an analysis by Rosenthal and Rubin. *Journal of Educational Psychology, 76,* 583–587.

Block, J. H. (1976). Issues, problems, and pitfalls in assessing sex differences: A critical review of *The psychology of sex differences. Merrill-Palmer Quarterly, 22,* 283–308.

Buffery, A. W. H., & Gray, J. A. (1972). Sex differences in the development of spatial and linguistic skills. In C. Ounsted & D. C. Taylor (Eds.), *Gender differences: Their ontogeny and significance* (pp. 123–157). Edinburgh: Churchill Livingstone.

Buswell, J. H. (1980). *The relationships between oral language competency and reading achievement of second and third grade students.* Unpublished Ed.D. dissertation, University of Northern Colorado, Greeley.

Caplan, P. J., MacPherson, G. M., & Tobin, P. (1985). Do sex-related differences in spatial abilities exist? *American Psychologist, 40,* 786–799.

Chipman, S. F., Brush, L. R., & Wilson, D. M. (Eds.). (1985). *Women and mathematics: Balancing the equation.* Hillsdale, NJ: Erlbaum.

Cohen, J. (1969). *Statistical power analysis for the behavioral sciences.* New York: Academic Press.

Corah, N. L. (1965). Differentiation in children and their parents. *Journal of Personality, 33,* 300–308.

Denno, D. (1982). Sex differences in cognition: A review and critique of the longitudinal evidence. *Adolescence, 17,* 779–788.

Eagly, A. H., & Carli, L. L. (1981). Sex of researchers and sex-typed communications as determinants of sex differences in influenceability: A meta-analysis of social influence studies. *Psychological Bulletin, 90,* 1–20.

Eagly, A. H., & Crowley, M. (1986). Gender and helping behavior: A meta-analytic review of the social psychological literature. *Psychological Bulletin, 100,* 283–308.

Eagly, A. H., & Steffen, V. J. (1986). Gender and aggressive behavior: A meta-analytic review of the social psychological literature. *Psychological Bulletin, 100,* 309–330.

France, K. (1973). Effects of "white" and of "Black" examiner voices on IQ scores of children. *Developmental Psychology, 8,* 144.

Gardner, H. (1983). *Frames of mind: The theory of multiple intelligences.* New York: Basic Books.

Glass, G. V., McGaw, B., & Smith, M. L. (1981). *Meta-analysis in social research.* Beverly Hills: Sage.

Gleitman, H. (1981). *Psychology.* New York: Norton.

Hahn, W. K. (1987). Cerebral lateralization of function: From infancy through childhood. *Psychological Bulletin, 101,* 376–392.

Halpern, D. F. (1986). *Sex differences in cognitive abilities.* Hillsdale, NJ: Erlbaum.

Hedges, L. V. (1982a). Fitting categorical models to effect sizes from a series of experiments. *Journal of Educational Statistics, 7,* 119-137.

Hedges, L. V. (1982b). Fitting continuous models to effect size data. *Journal of Educational Statistics, 7,* 245-270.

Hedges, L. V. (1982c). Estimation of effect size from a series of independent experiments. *Psychological Bulletin, 92,* 490-9.

Hedges, L. V., & Becker, B. J. (1986). Statistical methods in the meta-analysis of research on gender differences. In J. S. Hyde & M. C. Linn (Eds.), *The psychology of gender: Advances through meta-analysis* (pp. 14-50). Baltimore: Johns Hopkins University Press.

Hedges, L. V., & Olkin, I. (1985). *Statistical methods for meta-analysis.* New York: Academic Press.

Hetherington, E. M., & Parke, R. D. (1986). *Child psychology: A contemporary viewpoint* (3rd ed.). New York: McGraw-Hill.

Hunter, J. E., Schmidt, F. L., & Jackson, G. B. (1982). *Meta-analysis: Cumulating research findings across studies.* Beverly Hills: Sage.

Hyde, J. S. (1981). How large are cognitive gender differences? A meta-analysis using ω^2 and d. *American Psychologist, 36,* 892-901.

Hyde, J. S. (1984). How large are gender differences in aggression? A developmental meta-analysis. *Developmental Psychology, 20,* 722-736.

Hyde, J. S. (1986). Introduction: Meta-analysis and the psychology of gender. In J. S. Hyde & M. C. Linn (Eds.), *The psychology of gender: Advances through meta-analysis* (pp. 1-13). Baltimore: Johns Hopkins University Press.

Levy, J. (1976). Cerebral lateralization and spatial ability. *Behavior Genetics, 6,* 171-188.

Levy-Agresti, J., & Sperry, R. W. (1968). Differential perceptual capacities in major and minor hemispheres. *Proceedings of the National Academy of Science U.S.A., 61,* 1151.

Linn, M. C., & Petersen, A. C. (1985). Emergence and characterization of sex differences in spatial ability: A meta-analysis. *Child Development, 56,* 1479-1498.

Maccoby, E. E. (1966). Sex differences in intellectual functioning. In E. E. Maccoby (Ed.), *The development of sex differences.* Stanford, CA: Stanford University Press.

Maccoby, E. E., & Jacklin, C. N. (1974). *The psychology of sex differences.* Stanford, CA: Stanford University Press.

Mussen, P. H., Conger, J. J., Kagan, J., & Huston, A. C. (1984). *Child development and personality* (6th ed.). New York: Harper & Row.

Ramist, L., & Arbeiter, S. (1986). *Profiles, college-bound seniors, 1985.* New York: College Entrance Examination Board.

Rebecca, M. (1974). *The relationship of creativity to field-independence and field-dependence* (Developmental Program Report No. 40). University of Michigan, Ann Arbor.

Rosenthal, R., & Rubin, D. B. (1982a). Comparing effect sizes of independent studies. *Psychological Bulletin, 92,* 500-504.

Rosenthal, R., & Rubin, D. B. (1982b). Further meta-analytic procedures for assessing cognitive gender differences. *Journal of Educational Psychology, 74,* 708-712.

Rosenthal, R., & Rubin, D. B. (1982c). A simple, general purpose display of magnitude of experimental effect. *Journal of Educational Psychology, 74,* 166-169.

Sherman, J. A. (1978). *Sex-related cognitive differences.* Springfield, IL: Charles C Thomas.

Smith, M. L., & Glass, G. V. (1977). Meta-analysis of psychotherapy outcome studies. *American Psychologist, 32,* 752-760.

Sternberg, R. J. (1982). Reasoning, problem solving, and intelligence. In R. J. Sternberg (Ed.), *Handbook of human intelligence.* New York: Cambridge University Press.

Sternberg, R. J. (1984). Testing intelligence without IQ tests. *Phi Delta Kappan, 65*(10), 694-698.

Sternberg, R. J., & Walter, W. (1982). Conceptions of intelligence. In R. J. Sternberg (Ed.), *Handbook of human intelligence.* New York: Cambridge University Press.

Swacker, M. (1975). The sex of the speaker as a sociolinguistic variable. In B. Thorne & N. Henley (Eds.), *Language and sex: Difference and dominance* (pp. 76-83). Rowley, MA: Newbury House.

Tyler, L. E. (1965). *The psychology of human differences.* New York: Appleton-Century-Crofts.

Walters, C., Shurley, J. T., & Parsons, O. A. (1962). Differences in male and female responses to underwater sensory deprivation: An exploratory study. *Journal of Nervous and Mental Disease, 135,* 302-310.

Appendix

Studies Used in the Meta-Analysis

Achenbach, T. M. (1969). Cue learning, associative responding, and school performance in children. *Developmental Psychology, 1,* 717-725.

Alesandrini, K. L. (1981). Pictorial–verbal and analytic–holistic learning strategies in science learning. *Journal of Educational Psychology, 73,* 358-368.

Ali, F., & Costello, J. (1971). Modification of the Peabody Picture Vocabulary Test. *Developmental Psychology, 5,* 86-91.

American College Testing Program. (1976-1977). *College student profiles: American College Testing Program.* Iowa City: ACT Publications.

Applebee, A. N., Langer, J. A., & Mullis, I. V. S. (1986). *The writing report card: Writing achievement in American schools* (Report No. 15-W-02). Princeton, NJ: Educational Testing Service.

Averitt, C. H. (1981). *The interrelationships between several socio-cultural variables and cognitive sex differences in preschool children.* Unpublished doctoral dissertation, North Carolina State University, Raleigh.

Backman, M. E. (1972). Patterns of mental abilities: Ethnic, socioeconomic, and sex differences. *American Educational Research Journal, 9,* 1-12.

Baden, M. J. P. (1981). *A comparison of composition scores of third-grade children with reading skills, pre-kindergarten verbal ability, self-concept, and sex.* Unpublished doctoral dissertation, University of Nebraska, Lincoln.

Baldwin, T. L., McFarlane, P. T., & Garvey, C. J. (1971). Children's communication accuracy related to race and socioeconomic status. *Child Development, 42,* 345-357.

Bayley, N., & Oden, M. (1955). The maintenance of intellectual ability in gifted adults. *Journal of Gerontology, 10,* 91-107.

Berry, D. T. R., & Webb, W. B. (1985). Sleep and cognitive functions in normal older adults. *Journal of Gerontology, 40,* 331-335.

Bieri, J., Bradburn, W., & Galinsky, M. (1958). Sex differences in perceptual behavior. *Journal of Personality, 26,* 1-12.

Blum, J. E., Fosshage, J. L., & Jarvik, L. F. (1972). Intellectual changes and sex differences in octogenarians: A twenty-year longitudinal study of aging. *Developmental Psychology, 7,* 178-187.

Bodner, G. M., McMillen, T. L. B., Greenbowe, T. J., & McDaniel, E. D. (1983, August). *Verbal, numerical, and perceptual skills related to chemistry achievement.* Paper presented at the annual meeting of the American Psychological Association. (ERIC document 238 349)

Brimer, M. A. (1969). Sex differences in listening comprehension. *Journal of Research and Development in Education, 3*, 72–79.

Bristow, P. S. (1978). *The relationship of reading ability, freedom from distractibility, verbal knowledge, and ability, and sex to amount of subvocalization during reading.* Unpublished doctoral dissertation, University of Georgia, Athens.

Brown, H. (1971). Children's comprehension of relativized English sentences. *Child Development, 42*, 1923–1936.

Brownell, W., & Smith, D. R. (1973). Communication patterns, sex, and length of verbalization in speech of four-year-old children. *Speech Monographs, 40*, 310–316.

Buswell, J. H. (1980). *The relationships between oral language competency and reading achievement of second and third grade students.* Unpublished Ed.D. dissertation, University of Northern Colorado, Greeley.

Carter, S. L. (1976). *The structure and transmission of individual differences in patterns of cognitive ability.* Unpublished doctoral dissertation, University of Minnesota, Minneapolis.

Chase, C. I. (1981). *GPA prediction procedures and normative data for freshmen* (Indiana Studies in Higher Education, No. 44). Bloomington: Bureau of Evaluative Studies and Testing, Indiana University.

Cicirelli, V. G. (1967). Sibling constellation, creativity, IQ, and academic achievement. *Child Development, 38*, 481–490.

Clarke-Stewart, K. A. (1973). Interactions between mothers and their young children: Characteristics and consequences. *Monographs of the Society for Research in Child Development, 38*(Whole No. 153).

Clarke-Stewart, K. A., Umeh, B. J., Snow, M. E., & Pederson, J. A. (1980). Development and prediction of children's sociability from 1 to 2½ years. *Developmental Psychology, 16*, 290–302.

Cohen, B. D., & Klein, J. F. (1968). Referent communication in school age children. *Child Development, 39*, 597–609.

Coie, J. D., & Dorval, B. (1973). Sex differences in the intellectual structure of social interaction skills. *Developmental Psychology, 8*, 261–267.

Cole, D., & LaVoie, J. C. (1985). Fantasy play and related cognitive development in 2- to 6-year-olds. *Developmental Psychology, 21*, 233–240.

Corah, N. L. (1965). Differentiation in children and their parents. *Journal of Personality, 33*, 300–308.

Cotler, S., & Palmer, R. J. (1971). Social reinforcement, individual difference factors, and the reading performance of elementary school children. *Journal of Personality and Social Psychology, 18*, 97–104.

Cowan, P. A., Weber, J., Hoddinott, B. A., & Klein, J. (1967). Mean length of spoken response as a function of stimulus, experimenter, and subject. *Child Development, 38*, 191–203.

Darley, F. L., & Winitz, H. (1961). Comparison of male and female kindergarten children on the WISC. *Journal of Genetic Psychology, 99*, 41–49.

Davis, O. L., & Slobodian, J. J. (1967). Teacher behavior toward boys and girls during first grade reading instruction. *American Education Research Journal, 4*, 261–270.

Dawson, G. D. (1981). Sex differences in dichaptic processing. *Perceptual and Motor Skills, 53*, 935–944.

DeFazio, V. J. (1973). Field articulation differences in language abilities. *Journal of Personality and Social Psychology, 25*, 351–356.

Denno, D. J. (1983, August). *Neuropsychological and early maturational correlates of intelligence.* Paper presented at the annual meeting of the American Psychological Association. (ERIC document 234 920)

Denno, D., Meijs, B., Nachshon, I., & Aurand, S. (1981). *Early cognitive functioning: Sex and race differences.* Paper presented at the annual

meeting of the American Psychological Association. (ERIC document 207 707)

Dickie, J. P. (1968). Effectiveness of structured and unstructured (traditional) methods of language training. *Monographs of the Society for Research in Child Development, 33*(Serial No. 124).

Dunn, J. A. (1977). *The effect of creative dramatics on the oral language abilities and self-esteem of Blacks, Chicanos, and Anglos in the second and fifth grades.* Unpublished doctoral dissertation, University of Colorado, Boulder.

Dykstra, R., & Tinney, R. (1969). Sex differences in reading readiness—first-grade achievement and second grade achievement. *Reading & Realism, 13*, 623–628.

Eisenberg, L., Berlin, C. I., Dill, A., & Frank, S. (1968). Class and race effects on the intelligibility of monosyllables. *Child Development, 39*, 1077–1089.

Elfman, J. A. (1978). *The effects of Piagetian developmental level, sex, and method of presentation on the acquisition of figurative language in young children.* Unpublished doctoral dissertation, University of Georgia, Athens.

Enright, R. D., Manheim, L. A., Franklin, C. C., & Enright, W. F. (1980, April). *Assessing young children's moral development: A standardized and objective scale.* Paper presented at the meeting of the American Educational Research Association. (ERIC document 196 963)

Eska, B., & Black, K. N. (1971). Conceptual tempo in young grade-school children. *Child Development, 42*, 505–516.

Feather, N. T. (1968). Change in confidence following success or failure as a predictor of subsequent performance. *Journal of Personality and Social Psychology, 9*, 38–46.

Feather, N. T. (1969). Attribution of responsibility and valence of success and failure in relation to initial confidence and task performance. *Journal of Personality and Social Psychology, 13*, 129–144.

Feely, T. (1975). Predicting students' use of evidence: An aspect of critical thinking. *Theory and Research in Social Education, 3*, 63–72.

Fennema, E. H., & Sherman, J. A. (1978). Sex-related differences in mathematics achievement and related factors: A further study. *Journal for Research in Mathematics Education, 9*, 189–203.

Fiore, J. (1977). *Sex and occupation differences in EEG asymmetries and cognitive abilities.* Unpublished doctoral dissertation, Emory University, Atlanta, GA.

Fisher, C., & Mandinach, E. (1985, March). *Individual differences and acquisition of computer programming skill.* Paper presented at the annual meeting of the American Educational Research Association, Chicago.

Flanagan, J. C., Dailey, J. T., Shaycoft, M. F., Gorham, W. A., Orr, D. B., Goldberg, I., & Neyman, C. A. (1961). *Counselor's technical manual for interpreting test scores.* Unpublished manuscript, Project Talent, Palo Alto, CA.

Forte, F. L., Mandato, D., & Kayson, W. A. (1981). Effect of sex of subject on recall of gender-stereotyped magazine advertisements. *Psychological Reports, 49*, 619–622.

France, K. (1973). Effects of "white" and of "Black" examiner voices on IQ scores of children. *Developmental Psychology, 8*, 144.

Frederiksen, N., & Evans, F. R. (1974). Effects of models of creative performance on ability to formulate hypotheses. *Journal of Educational Psychology, 66*, 67–82.

Friedrichs, A. G., Hertz, T. W., Moynahan, E. D., Simpson, W. E., Arnold, M. R., Christy, M. D., Cooper, C. R., & Stevenson, H. W. (1971). Interrelations among learning and performance tasks at the preschool level. *Developmental Psychology, 4*, 164–172.

Gates, A. I. (1961). Sex differences in reading ability. *Elementary School Journal, 61*, 431–434.

Gjerde, P. F., Block, J., & Block, J. H. (1985). Longitudinal consistency of Matching Familiar Figures Test performance from early childhood to preadolescence. *Developmental Psychology, 21*, 262–271.

Graves, M. F., & Koziol, S. (1971). Noun plural development in primary grade children. *Child Development, 42,* 1165–1173.

Harris, M. B., & Hassemer, W. G. (1972). Some factors affecting the complexity of children's sentences: The effects of modeling, age, sex, and bilingualism. *Journal of Experimental Child Psychology, 13,* 447–455.

Harris, M. B., & Siebel, C. E. (1976). Effects of sex, occupation, and confidence of model and sex and grade of subject on imitation of language behaviors. *Developmental Psychology, 12,* 89–90.

Harrison, A., & Nadelman, L. (1972). Conceptual tempo and inhibition of movement in black preschool children. *Child Development, 43,* 657–668.

Hartle, T., Baratz, J., & Clark, M. J. (1983). *Older students and the GRE aptitude test* (Research Report 83–20). Princeton, NJ: Educational Testing Service.

Haslett, B. J. (1983). Communicative functions and strategies in children's conversations. *Human Communication Research, 9,* 114–129.

Heider, E. R. (1971). Style and accuracy of verbal communications within and between social classes. *Journal of Personality and Social Psychology, 18,* 33–47.

Hennessy, J. J., & Merrifield, P. R. (1978). Ethnicity and sex distinctions in patterns of aptitude factor scores in a sample of urban high school seniors. *American Educational Research Journal, 15,* 385–389.

Hertzog, C., & Carter, L. (1982). Sex differences in the structure of intelligence: A confirmatory factor analysis. *Intelligence, 6,* 287–303.

Hoemann, H. W. (1972). The development of communication skills in deaf and hearing children. *Child Development, 43,* 990–1003.

Hogrebe, M. C., Nist, S. L., & Newman, I. (1985). Are there gender differences in reading achievement? An investigation using the high school and beyond data. *Journal of Educational Psychology, 77,* 716–724.

Hopkins, K. D., & Bibelheimer, M. (1971). Five-year stability of intelligence quotients from language and non-language group tests. *Child Development, 42,* 645–649.

Houtz, J. C., Montgomery, C., & Kirkpatrick, L. (1979). Relationship among measures of evaluation ability (problem solving), creative thinking, and intelligence. *Contemporary Educational Psychology, 4,* 47–54.

Hyde, J. S., Geiringer, E. R., & Yen, W. M. (1975). On the empirical relation between spatial ability and sex differences in other aspects of cognitive performance. *Multivariate Behavioral Research, 10,* 289–310.

Ingersoll, G. M. (1978, April). *A non-recursive analysis of antecedents to reading achievement.* Paper presented at the annual conference of the American Educational Research Association. (ERIC document 155 594)

Ironsmith, M., & Whitehurst, G. J. (1978). The development of listener abilities in communication: How children deal with ambiguous information. *Child Development, 49,* 348–352.

James, S. L., & Miller, J. F. (1973). Children's awareness of semantic constraints in sentences. *Child Development, 44,* 69–76.

Jeruchimowicz, R., Costello, J., & Bagur, J. S. (1971). Knowledge of action and object words: A comparison of lower and middle class Negro preschoolers. *Child Development, 42,* 455–464.

Johnson, D. L. (1974). The influence of social class and race on language test performance and spontaneous speech of preschool children. *Child Development, 45,* 517–521.

Jordan, T. J. (1981). Self-concepts, motivation, and academic achievement of black adolescents. *Journal of Educational Psychology, 73,* 509–517.

Kappy, K. A. (1980). *Differential effects of decreased testing time on the verbal and quantitative aptitude scores of males and females.* Unpublished doctoral dissertation, Fordham University, New York.

Khatena, J. (1975). Imagination imagery of children and the production of analogy. *The Gifted Child Quarterly, 19,* 310–315.

Klaus, R. A., & Gray, S. W. (1968). The early training project for disadvantaged children: A report after five years. *Monographs of the Society for Research in Child Development, 33*(Serial No. 120).

Klecan-Aker, J. S. (1984). A study of the syntactic skills of normal middle-school males and females. *Language and Speech, 27,* 205–215.

Koen, F. (1966). Codability of complex stimuli: Three modes of representation. *Journal of Personality and Social Psychology, 3,* 435–441.

Koffman, S., & Lips, H. M. (1980). Sex differences in self-esteem and performance expectancies in married couples. *Social Behavior and Personality, 8,* 57–63.

Kuchler, C. J. (1983). *Hemispheric laterality and cognitive style.* Unpublished doctoral dissertation, University of North Dakota, Grand Forks.

Laughlin, P. R., Branch, L. G., & Johnson, H. H. (1969). Individual versus triadic performance on a unidimensional complementary task as a function of initial ability level. *Journal of Personality and Social Psychology, 12,* 144–150.

Lesser, G. S., Fifer, G., & Clark, D. H. (1965). Mental abilities of children from different social-class and cultural groups. *Monographs of the Society for Research in Child Development, 30*(4, Serial No. 102).

Linn, M. C., & Pulos, S. (1983). Male–female differences in predicting displaced volume: Strategy use, aptitude relationships, and experience influences. *Journal of Educational Psychology, 75,* 86–96.

Lipton, C., & Overton, W. F. (1971). Anticipatory imagery and modified anagram solution: A developmental study. *Child Development, 42,* 615–623.

Long, M. L. (1976). *The influence of sex, race, and type of preschool experience on scores on the McCarthy scales of children's abilities.* Unpublished doctoral dissertation, University of Georgia, Athens.

Lunneborg, P. W., & Lunneborg, C. E. (1985). Nontraditional and traditional female college graduates: What separates them from the men? *Journal of College Student Personnel, 26,* 33–36.

Marks, E. (1968). Personality factors in the performance of a perceptual recognition task under competing incentives. *Journal of Personality and Social Psychology, 8,* 69–74.

Masters, J. C. (1969). Word association and the functional definition of words. *Developmental Psychology, 4,* 517–519.

McCarthy, J. J., & Kirk, S. A. (1963). *The construction, standardization, and statistical characteristics of the Illinois Test of Psycholinguistic Abilities.* Urbana: University of Illinois Press.

McCarver, R. B., & Ellis, N. R. (1972). Effect of overt verbal labeling on short-term memory in culturally deprived and nondeprived children. *Developmental Psychology, 6,* 38–41.

McGee, M. G. (1982, August). *Cognitive sex differences and their practical implications.* Paper presented at the annual meeting of the American Psychological Association. (ERIC document 229 703)

McKeever, W. F., & van Deventer, A. D. (1977). Failure to confirm a spatial ability impairment in persons with evidence of right hemisphere speech capability. *Cortex, 13,* 321–326.

McLoyd, V. C. (1980). Verbally expressed modes of transformation in the fantasy play of black preschool children. *Child Development, 51,* 1133–1139.

Mehrabian, A. (1970). Measures of vocabulary and grammatical skills for children up to age six. *Developmental Psychology, 2,* 439–446.

Mendelsohn, G. A., & Griswold, B. B. (1966). Assessed creative potential, vocabulary level, and sex as predictors of the use of incidental cues in verbal problem solving. *Journal of Personality and Social Psychology, 4,* 423–431.

Mendelsohn, G. A., & Griswold, B. B. (1967). Anxiety and repression as predictors of the use of incidental cues in problem solving. *Journal of Personality and Social Psychology, 6,* 353–359.

Milgram, N. A., Shore, M. F., & Malasky, C. (1971). Linguistic and thematic variables in recall of a story by disadvantaged children. *Child Development, 42,* 637–640.

Mills, C. J. (1981). Sex roles, personality, and intellectual abilities in adolescents. *Journal of Youth and Adolescence, 10,* 85–112.

Moore, T. (1967). Language and intelligence: A longitudinal study of the first eight years. Part 1. Patterns of development in boys and girls. *Human Development, 10,* 89–106.

National Assessment of Educational Progress. (1985). *The reading report card: Progress toward excellence in our schools* (Report No. 15-R-01). Princeton, NJ: Educational Testing Service.

Osser, H., Wang, M., & Zaid, F. (1969). The young child's ability to imitate and comprehend speech: A comparison of two subculture groups. *Child Development, 40,* 1063–1075.

Palmer, R. M., & Masling, J. (1969). Vocabulary for skin color in Negro and white children. *Developmental Psychology, 1,* 396–401.

Parsley, K. M., Powell, M., O'Connor, H. A., & Deutsch, M. (1963). Are there really sex differences in achievement? *Journal of Educational Research, 57,* 210–212.

Penk, W. (1971). Developmental changes in idiodynamic set responses of children's word associations. *Developmental Psychology, 5,* 55–63.

Penney, R. K. (1965). Reactive curiosity and manifest anxiety in children. *Child Development, 36,* 697–702.

Perney, J., Freund, J., & Barman, A. (1976). *Television viewing: Its relationship to early school achievement.* Unpublished manuscript. (ERIC Document Reproduction Service No. 153 723)

Posluszny, R., & Barton, K. (1981). Dichaptic task performance as a function of ability pattern, sex, and hand preference. *Perceptual and Motor Skills, 53,* 435–438.

Preston, R. C. (1962). Reading achievement of German and American children. *School and Society, 90,* 350–354.

Purdue University Measurement and Research Center. (1974). Freedom to read issues (Purdue Opinion Panel Poll Report No. 100). West Lafayette, IN: Author.

Pusser, H. E., & McCandless, B. R. (1974). Socialization dimensions among inner-city five-year-olds and later school success: A follow-up. *Journal of Educational Psychology, 66,* 285–290.

Ramist, L., & Arbeiter, S. (1986a). *Profiles, college-bound seniors, 1985.* New York: College Entrance Examination Board.

Ramist, L., & Arbeiter, S. (1986b). *Profiles, college-bound seniors, 1985.* New York: College Entrance Examination Board.

Rebecca, M. (1974). *The relationship of creativity to field-independence and field-dependence* (Developmental Program Report No. 40). University of Michigan, Ann Arbor.

Reppucci, N. D. (1971). Parental education, sex differences, and performance on cognitive tasks among two-year-old children. *Developmental Psychology, 4,* 248–253.

Rhine, R. J., Hill, S. J., & Wandruff, S. E. (1967). Evaluative responses of preschool children. *Child Development, 38,* 1035–1042.

Riley, R. T., & Denmark, F. L. (1974). Field independence and measures of intelligence: Some reconsiderations. *Social Behavior and Personality, 2,* 25–29.

Roberge, J. J., & Flexer, B. K. (1981). Re-examination of the covariation of field independence, intelligence, and achievement. *British Journal of Educational Psychology, 51,* 235–236.

Rock, D., Hilton, T., Pollack, J., Ekstrom, R., & Goertz, M. (1985). *Psychometric analysis of the NLS and the High School and Beyond Test Batteries* (NCES 85-218). Washington, DC: National Center for Education Statistics.

Rosenberg, B. G., & Sutton-Smith, B. (1964). The relationship of ordinal position and sibling sex status to cognitive abilities. *Psychonomic Science, 1,* 81–82.

Rosenberg, B. G., & Sutton-Smith, B. (1966). Sibling association, family size, and cognitive abilities. *Journal of Genetic Psychology, 109,* 271–279.

Rosenberg, B. G., & Sutton-Smith, B. (1969). Sibling age spacing effects upon cognition. *Developmental Psychology, 1,* 661–668.

Routh, D. K., & Tweney, R. D. (1972). Effects of paradigmatic response training on children's word associations. *Journal of Experimental Child Psychology, 14,* 398–407.

Saltz, E., Soller, E., & Sigel, I. E. (1972). The development of natural language concepts. *Child Development, 43,* 1191–1202.

Sanders, B., & Soares, M. P. (1986). Sexual maturation and spatial ability in college students. *Developmental Psychology, 22,* 199–203.

Sarason, I. G., & Minard, J. (1962). Test anxiety, experimental instructions and the Wechsler Adult Intelligence Scale. *Journal of Educational Psychology, 53,* 299–302.

Sassenrath, J. M., & Maddux, R. E. (1974). Language instruction, background, and development of disadvantaged kindergarten children. *California Journal of Educational Research, 25,* 61–68.

Sause, E. F. (1976). Computer content analysis of sex differences in the language of children. *Journal of Psycholinguistic Research, 5,* 311–324.

Schuerger, J. M., Kepner, J., & Lawler, B. (1979). Verbal–quantitative differential as indicator of temperamental differences. *Multivariate Experimental Clinical Research, 4,* 57–66.

Schultz, N. R., Elias, M. F., Robbins, M. A., Streeten, D. H. P., & Blakeman, N. (1986). A longitudinal comparison of hypertensives and normotensives on the Wechsler Adult Intelligence Scale: Initial findings. *Journal of Gerontology, 41,* 169–175.

Searleman, A., Herrmann, D. J., & Coventry, A. K. (1984). Cognitive abilities and left-handedness: An interaction between familial sinistrality and strength of handedness. *Intelligence, 8,* 295–304.

Shepard, W. O. (1970). Word association and definition in middle childhood. *Developmental Psychology, 3,* 412.

Sherman, J. (1979). Cognitive performance as a function of sex and handedness: An evaluation of the Levy hypothesis. *Psychology of Women Quarterly, 3,* 378–390.

Shipman, V. C. (1971). *Disadvantaged children and their first school experiences* (Educational Testing Service Head Start Longitudinal Study). Princeton, NJ: Educational Testing Service.

Shipman, V. C. (1972). *Disadvantaged children and their first school experiences* (Educational Testing Service Head Start Longitudinal Study, Report No. PR-72-18). Princeton, NJ: Educational Testing Service.

Shure, M. B., Spivack, G., & Jaeger, M. (1971). Problem-solving thinking and adjustment among disadvantaged preschool children. *Child Development, 42,* 1791–1803.

Signorella, M. L. (1984). Cognitive consequences of personal involvement in gender identity. *Sex Roles, 11,* 923–939.

Silverman, E., & Zimmer, C. H. (1976, January). *The fluency of women's speech.* Paper presented at the Conference on the Sociology of the Languages of American Women. (ERIC document 126 547)

Sitkei, E. G., & Meyers, C. E. (1969). Comparative structure of intellect in middle- and lower-class four-year-olds of two ethnic groups. *Developmental Psychology, 1,* 592–604.

Skanes, G. R. (1970). *Ability changes in children moving from small to large isolated communities.* Institute for Research in Human Abilities Research Bulletin No. 70-003. (ERIC document 157 647)

Sobol, D. R. (1980). *Academic performance of community college students as a function of method of instruction, personality, and verbal ability.* Unpublished doctoral dissertation, University of Michigan, Ann Arbor.

Soriano, L. V. (1975). *Sex differences in analogy test performance.* Unpublished doctoral dissertation, University of Minnesota, Minneapolis.

Stanford Research Institute. (1972). Follow-through pupil tests, parent interviews, and teacher questionnaires. Unpublished manuscript.

Stephenson, T. R. (1973). *Task persistence in early childhood educa-*

tion. Unpublished doctoral dissertation, Utah State University, Logan.

Stevenson, H. W., Hale, G. A., Klein, R. E., & Miller, L. K. (1968). Interrelations and correlates in children's learning and problem solving. *Monographs of the Society for Research in Child Development, 33*(7, Serial No. 123).

Stevenson, H. W., Klein, R. E., Hale, G. A., & Miller, L. K. (1968). Solution of anagrams: A developmental study. *Child Development, 39,* 905–912.

Stevenson, H. W., & Newman, R. S. (1986). Long-term prediction of achievement and attitudes in mathematics and reading. *Child Development, 57,* 646–659.

Stevenson, H. W., & Odom, R. D. (1965). The relation of anxiety to children's performance on learning and problem-solving tasks. *Child Development, 36,* 1003–1012.

Stoner, S., Panek, P., & Satterfield, G. T. (1982). Age and sex differences on the Hand Test. *Journal of Personality Assessment, 46,* 260–264.

Stoner, S. B., & Spencer, W. B. (1983). Sex differences in expressive vocabulary of Head Start children. *Perceptual and Motor Skills, 56,* 1008.

Suppes, P., & Feldman, S. (1971). Young children's comprehension of logical connectives. *Journal of Experimental Child Psychology, 12,* 304–317.

Sutton-Smith, B., Rosenberg, B. G., & Landy, F. (1968). Father-absence effects in families of different sibling compositions. *Child Development, 39,* 1213–1221.

Tseng, M. S., & Rhodes, C. I. (1973). Correlates of the perception of occupational prestige. *Journal of Counseling Psychology, 20,* 522–527.

Vance, H. B., Hankins, N., & McGee, H. (1979). A preliminary study of black and white differences on the revised Wechsler Intelligence Scale for Children. *Journal of Clinical Psychology, 35,* 815–819.

Very, P. S. (1967). Differential factor structures in mathematical abilities. *Genetic Psychology Monographs, 75,* 169–207.

Waber, D. P. (1977). Sex differences in mental abilities, hemispheric lateralization, and rate of physical growth at adolescence. *Developmental Psychology, 13,* 29–38.

Walberg, H. J. (1969). Physics, femininity, and creativity. *Developmental Psychology, 1,* 47–54.

Weinberg, S., & Rabinowitz, J. A. (1970). A sex difference in the Wechsler IQ vocabulary scores as a predictor of strategy in a probability-learning task performed by adolescents. *Developmental Psychology, 3,* 218–224.

Wilkie, F. L., & Eisdorfer, C. (1977). Sex, verbal ability, and pacing differences in serial learning. *Journal of Gerontology, 32,* 63–67.

Williams, T. M., & Fleming, J. W. (1969). Methodological study of the relationship between associative fluency and intelligence. *Developmental Psychology, 1,* 155–162.

Winitz, H. (1959). Language skills of male and female kindergarten children. *Journal of Speech and Hearing Research, 2,* 377–386.

Wolf, M., & Gow, D. (1986). A longitudinal investigation of gender differences in language and reading development. *First Language.*

Wormack, L. (1979). Cognitive predictors of articulation in writing. *Perceptual and Motor Skills, 48,* 1151–1156.

Received April 27, 1987
Revision received October 9, 1987
Accepted October 19, 1987 ∎

[15]

Emergence and Characterization of Sex Differences in Spatial Ability: A Meta-Analysis

Marcia C. Linn

University of California, Berkeley, and Weizmann Institute of Science, Israel

Anne C. Petersen

Pennsylvania State University

LINN, MARCIA C., and PETERSEN, ANNE C. *Emergence and Characterization of Sex Differences in Spatial Ability: A Meta-Analysis.* CHILD DEVELOPMENT, 1985, **56**, 1479–1498. Sex differences in spatial ability are widely acknowledged, yet considerable dispute surrounds the magnitude, nature, and age of first occurrence of these differences. This article focuses on 3 questions about sex differences in spatial ability: (*a*) What is the magnitude of sex differences in spatial ability? (*b*) On which aspects of spatial ability are sex differences found? and (*c*) When, in the life span, are sex differences in spatial ability first detected? Implications for clarifying the linkage between sex differences in spatial ability and other differences between males and females are discussed. We use meta-analysis, a method for synthesizing empirical studies, to investigate these questions. Results of the meta-analysis suggest (*a*) that sex differences arise on some types of spatial ability but not others, (*b*) that large sex differences are found only on measures of mental rotation, (*c*) that smaller sex differences are found on measures of spatial perception, and (*d*) that, when sex differences are found, they can be detected across the life span.

Differences between males and females in spatial ability are widely acknowledged, yet considerable dispute surrounds the magnitude, nature, and age of first occurrence of these differences (Harris, 1982; Hyde, 1981; Liben, Patterson, & Newcombe, 1981; Linn & Petersen, in press; Maccoby & Jacklin, 1974; McGee, 1979). To establish the magnitude of sex differences in spatial ability, meta-analysis has proved useful for studies published prior to 1974 (Hyde, 1981).[1] In this article we review studies reported since 1974 using recent refinements of the meta-analysis technique.

It is generally agreed that spatial ability is an important component of intellectual ability, yet its nature remains to be clarified. Activities as disparate as perception of horizontality, mental rotation of objects, and location of simple figures within complex figures have all been referred to as measures of spatial ability. No consensus exists for categorization of measures of spatial ability, although many different schemes have been presented. The only view achieving agreement is that spatial ability involves multiple processes. In this article we draw on recent psychometric studies, information-processing investiga-

The authors greatly appreciate the advice about meta-analysis procedures provided by Ingram Olkin, Larry Hedges, and Betsy Becker; their contributions are reflected throughout the article. We thank Kevin Delucchi for providing important assistance with statistical analysis of the data. The assistance of Maryse Tobin-Richards and Lisa Crockett in gathering information about effect sizes is gratefully acknowledged. Discussions of these findings with Lee Cronbach, Roger Shepard, Alice Eagly, and Lynn Cooper fostered our thinking and are much appreciated. This work was completed while Linn was a Fulbright Professor Abroad at the Weizmann Institute of Science, Israel. Support from the Fulbright program and the Weizmann Institute is appreciated. This material is based partially on research supported by the National Science Foundation under grant no. 81-12631, by the National Institute of Mental Health under grant MH30252/38142, and by the Spencer Foundation. Any opinions, findings and conclusions, or recommendations expressed here are those of the authors and do not necessarily reflect the views of the supporting agencies. A version of this article was presented at the meeting of the American Psychological Association, Anaheim, CA, August 1983. Send requests for reprints to the first author at Lawrence Hall of Science, University of California, Berkeley, CA 94720.

[1] Note that the term "sex" is used to reflect that individuals are assigned to groups on the basis of being males or females. This choice of term does *not* imply that biological differences account for the observed performance of the group. Clearly, different socialization experiences are also associated with membership in the two groups.

1480   Child Development

tions, and theories of sex differences. These views, as well as meta-analysis techniques, are used to partition the measures of spatial ability into meaningful categories.

Explanations of sex differences in spatial ability depend, to some extent, on when these differences first occur. The hypothesized emergence of sex differences in spatial ability in early adolescence had led researchers to suggest explanations linked to pubertal change (e.g., Petersen, 1980; Waber, 1976). If, instead, sex differences in spatial ability are found to emerge prior to adolescence, then a biological explanation for the sex differences based on genetic factors (see Wittig & Petersen, 1979) or prenatal hormonal influences (see Reinisch, Gandelman, & Spiegal, 1979) would be preferred.

For example, Waber (1979) has indicated that spatial tests on which males have shown a consistent superiority have several common characteristics: the sex differences do not appear reliably until adolescence, and the mechanisms that mature during that period and permit children to perform the task are sexually differentiated. Maccoby and Jacklin (1974) cited some evidence for emergence of sex differences in adolescence. However, subsequent writers (e.g., Newcombe, Bandura, & Taylor, 1983) identify studies suggesting that male-female differences in spatial ability emerge prior to adolescence. The speculative link of sex differences in spatial ability to the biological changes in adolescence may have been based more on the limited number of convincing studies with preadolescent subjects than on a lack of differences between boys and girls on spatial ability tasks prior to adolescence. In this article we examine the magnitude of sex differences in spatial ability prior to, during, and after adolescence.

Clarification of the character and timing of emergence of sex differences in spatial ability has implications for areas such as science and mathematics education (Linn & Petersen, in press). For example, the possible emergence of sex differences in science and mathematics performance in adolescence has been linked to the emergence of sex differences in spatial ability (Benbow & Stanley, 1980, 1984). This linkage, however, may reflect sex differences in mathematics course experience, which, until recently, often first occurred during adolescence. Recent increases in mathematics course enrollment patterns for females have paralleled delays in the emergence of sex differences in mathematics performance among males and females (e.g., Armstrong, 1979; Chipman, Brush, & Wilson, 1985; Fennema & Sherman, 1978).

Thus we address three questions about sex differences in spatial ability: (*a*) What is the magnitude of sex differences in spatial ability? (*b*) On which aspects of spatial ability are sex differences found? and (*c*) When, in the life span, are sex differences in spatial ability first detected? Implications for clarifying the linkage between sex differences in spatial ability and other differences between males and females are discussed. We use meta-analysis, a method for synthesizing empirical studies, to investigate these questions.

Research on Spatial Ability

Results from meta-analysis depend inexorably on the approach, methodology, and quality of available primary analyses. The research perspectives that motivated those conducting primary analyses of spatial ability provide both the opportunities and the constraints of meta-analysis. Thus we briefly summarize the major research perspectives for investigating spatial ability that influenced our secondary analysis.

Four research perspectives have generated most studies of spatial ability: (*a*) the *differential* perspective, involving comparison of spatial ability for different populations (such as males and females); (*b*) the *psychometric* perspective, involving comparison of correlations between different spatial tasks in order to define "factors" in spatial ability; (*c*) the *cognitive* perspective, involving the identification of the processes used universally to solve a particular spatial ability task, albeit with quantitatively different efficiency; and (*d*) the *strategic* perspective, involving identification of the qualitatively different strategies used to solve a given spatial ability task by different respondents.

These four perspectives illustrate the complexity of this field. Researchers from each of these perspectives consider information at different levels of detail and take qualitatively different approaches. All four influence the planning and interpretation of our meta-analysis. Our meta-analysis, drawing on the differential perspective, focuses on group mean differences. We draw on the psychometric and cognitive perspectives to partition the many studies of spatial ability into homogeneous groups. To interpret variations in performance on the same task we rely on the strategic perspective.

Meta-Analysis

Recent advances in meta-analysis procedures make this a preferred tool for research synthesis (Hedges, 1982a, 1982b). Meta-analysis procedures offer more opportunities for valid inference from empirical studies than "eyeball analysis" or "vote counting" methods do (e.g., Glass, 1976; Hedges & Olkin, 1980; Pillemer & Light, 1980). As mentioned above, the results of a meta-analysis are only as valid as the studies that go into it. Furthermore, the research perspectives in the field influence what researchers study and, therefore, constrain the meta-analysis.

In the meta-analysis we synthesized effect sizes or standardized mean differences between males and females on spatial ability tasks. Using the recently developed methods of Hedges (1982a, 1982b), we computed unbiased estimates of effect size. We computed unbiased effect sizes from ANOVA and *t* test data as well as from means and standard deviations using the methods of Cohen (1977). Unbiased estimates of effect sizes have lower standard deviations than biased estimates and, therefore, are more precise.

Testing for homogeneity is essential to ensure that effect sizes are drawn from a uniform population. When effect sizes are homogeneous, a pooled estimate of effect size provides a summary of the results of a series of studies. However, when effect sizes are not homogeneous, pooled estimates may be misleading. Hedges (1982a) reports a statistical test for homogeneity of effect size within groups and a strategy for fitting a model to effect sizes divided into a priori classes. Hedges's homogeneity test assesses whether studies in the sample can be viewed as replicates of each other. Thus findings that studies are nearly homogeneous imply that they come close to being replications. Since studies entering meta-analysis do differ on many dimensions, near homogeneity may be appropriate (e.g., Class, McGaw, & Smith, 1981). As a wide range of meta-analyses reveal, homogeneity is infrequently achieved (e.g., Hyde & Linn, in press). More experience with these measures is needed to clarify how the statistic behaves when studies are similar but not exact replicates. For further discussion of these issues, see Linn (in press).

Implementing the Hedges (1982a, 1982b) approach in this study, we tested all the spatial ability effect sizes for homogeneity. When an acceptable level of homogeneity was not found, we partitioned the studies into smaller groups following a model derived from the psychometric and cognitive research perspectives. We tested the partitioned studies for homogeneity and basically continued until we located homogeneous or nearly homogeneous groups of studies.

In summary, through meta-analysis we offer a promising method for research synthesis. Advances in methodology, including procedures for computing unbiased estimates of effect size and for testing homogeneity of effects, increase the accuracy of conclusions. Ultimately we expect that meta-analysis techniques will encourage progress from one set of studies to another in ways that vote counting or informal comparisons are not able to accomplish.

Study Selection
In our meta-analysis we included studies of spatial ability published since Maccoby and Jacklin's (1974) review and before June 1982. We searched journals likely to publish studies focused on spatial ability as well as *Psychological Abstracts, Child Development Abstracts,* and the *Index Medicus.* Sources of studies included *Behavioral Genetics, Psychological Bulletin, Journal of Early Adolescence, Developmental Psychology,* and *Child Development.* In addition, papers presented at recent meetings of the American Educational Research Association, the American Psychological Association, and the Society for Research in Child Development were included. Inclusion of unpublished studies as well as studies of topics other than sex differences (where sex differences are reported whether or not significant differences are found) offsets, to some extent, the concern that available studies are biased toward significant effects while other studies remain in the file drawer (Rosenthal, 1979).

Initially we identified over 200 effect sizes; 172 entered our meta-analysis. (The studies and effect sizes are cataloged in Hyde & Linn, in press.) Studies were eliminated because they (a) had samples of fewer than 40 volunteers selected haphazardly, (b) reported insufficient information to compute effect sizes, or (c) had text presentations that did not coincide with the data reported in the tables. (These events were clarified with the author when possible, and several typographical errors were detected.) Furthermore, to avoid dependence among the effect sizes in the data, we randomly selected one effect size from studies that used the same subjects to measure the same category of spatial ability.

Analysis Procedure
The analysis plan involved using a branching procedure governed by a criterion of homogeneity following Hedges (1982a). First, all 172 effect sizes were tested to see whether they could be from a uniform popu-

1482   Child Development

lation. As described in detail below, when homogeneity was not achieved, the psychometric and cognitive perspectives were used to identify three categories of spatial ability, and the effect sizes were partitioned into those categories. When homogeneity did not result, effect sizes within a particular category of spatial ability were partitioned according to the age of the respondents and again tested for homogeneity. Partitioning by age reflected both the differential perspective, because different age groups are hypothesized to have different levels of spatial ability, and the cognitive perspective, because tests of spatial ability can tap different processes at different points in development. If homogeneity was still not achieved, we investigated other partitions for the effect sizes.

Categories of Spatial Ability

Spatial ability generally refers to skill in representing, transforming, generating, and recalling symbolic, nonlinguistic information. Given the uncertainty about categories of spatial ability, we first formed broad categories that could be further partitioned if meta-analysis of the effect sizes failed to yield homogeneity. Considerable dispute surrounds the identification of specific spatial abilities and the characterization of the processes used to solve spatial items (e.g., Caplan, MacPherson, & Tobin, in press).

Categorizations of spatial ability, stemming from the psychometric perspective, have frequently used factor analysis (e.g., Lohman, 1979; McGee, 1979). Thurstone and Thurstone (1941) identified space as a prominent aspect of the primary mental abilities. In the 1940s, Air Force researchers partitioned Thurstone's concept of spatial ability into four separate dimensions. The French kit of reference tests (French, Ekstrom, & Price, 1963) identifies three types of spatial ability. Hierarchical models, such as those of Cattell (1971) and Vernon (1965), generally locate spatial ability near the top of the hierarchy and include two or more subabilities in the general category.

Since the psychometric perspective yields categorizations that depend on the tests used for the investigation, this approach will never yield a general answer. In contrast, research from the cognitive perspective, identifying processes used to solve the tasks thought to measure spatial ability, offers some promise for identifying general categories of spatial ability (e.g., Carpenter & Just, 1981; Cooper & Regan, 1982; Guilford, 1969; Shepard & Cooper, 1982). In this research we

focus on similarities in the processes that respondents use for individual items, a different level of analysis from the correlational approach used in the psychometric perspective. Informed by these perspectives, the categories we describe are labeled *spatial perception, mental rotation,* and *spatial visualization.*

Spatial Perception

In spatial perception tests, subjects are required to determine spatial relationships with respect to the orientation of their own bodies, in spite of distracting information. One example is the Rod and Frame Test (RFT), in which subjects must place a rod vertically while viewing a frame oriented at 22° (Witkin, Dyk, & Faterson, 1962). Another is water level, a task that requires subjects to draw or identify a horizontal line in a tilted bottle (e.g., DeAvila, Havassy, & Pascual-Leone, 1976; Harris, Hanley, & Best, 1978; Inhelder & Piaget, 1958). An example appears in Figure 1.

Cognitive rationale.—What processes characterize spatial perception tasks? Some process analyses of spatial perception tasks suggest that subjects use the gravitational vertical to locate the correct orientation. Corballis and colleagues (Corballis & Roldan, 1975; Corballis, Zbrodoff, & Roldan, 1976) here demonstrated that participants in studies of symmetry detection rotate the stimuli to achieve either visual (consistent with head tilt) or gravitational upright. Respondents may rely on kinesthetic cues for locating the gravitational horizontal or vertical (e.g., Goodenough, Oltman, & Cox, 1984; Linn & Kyllonen, 1981; Sigman, Goodenough, & Flanagan, 1978, 1979). For example, respondents to the RFT report relying on whether the position "feels" upright (Linn & Kyllonen, 1981) and respondents to water level report relying on whether the water "feels" level (Petersen & Gitelson, in press). The other feature of spatial perception tasks is a focus on disembedding or overcoming distracting cues. Respondents can either ignore or correct for the possibly misleading cues from tilted objects

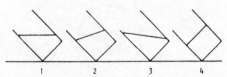

Fig. 1.—A spatial perception item. Respondents are asked to indicate which tilted bottle has a horizontal water line.

in their visual field. Reliance on kinesthetic cues may accompany a decision to ignore the distracting cues in the situation.

Although RFT and water level are certainly not identical in their task demands, they share important features. They both depend on locating the gravitational upright; they both present distracting perceptual information; and they both provide a series of items requiring the same response with slight variation in the distractors.

Psychometric rationale.—Historically, the RFT was introduced by Witkin (1949) to measure what he called Field-Dependence Independence (FDI). Subsequently, high correlations between RFT and the Embedded Figures Test (EFT) were noted, as were similarities in task demands (both included distracting information). Both RFT and EFT became accepted measures of FDI. Recently, however, Witkin and Goodenough (1981) reviewed the work on FDI and concluded that RFT represents FDI better than EFT does and that the two abilities are distinct. Furthermore, they indicated that the role of kinesthetic cues distinguished the RFT from the EFT. In a correlational study, Linn and Kyllonen (1981) supported the distinction between RFT and EFT. Linn and Kyllonen, using both factor analysis and structured equation approaches, showed that measures of spatial orientation could be separated from measures such as EFT, thus providing a psychometric rationale for two distinct categories. Lohman's (1979) identification of an orientation factor in measures of spatial ability corresponds to this distinction. Correlational evidence suggests that RFT and water level are more similar to each other than they are to other measures of spatial ability (Goodenough et al., 1984; Linn & Kyllonen, 1981). Goodenough et al. found

that, in a group of spatial tasks, water level had the highest correlation with RFT and that both had their highest loadings on a factor labeled "vestibular."

In summary, the potential advantage of using gravitational kinesthetic processes may differentiate spatial perception tasks from other tasks that require disembedding such as the EFT. The psychometric perspective is consistent with this process analysis, demonstrating that spatial perception tasks are distinct from other tasks requiring disembedding.

Mental Rotation

Shepard and his colleagues (Shepard & Cooper, 1982; Shepard & Metzler, 1971) have studied the ability to rotate a two or three dimensional figure rapidly and accurately. They devised individually administered tasks to measure the speed of response to different amounts of rotation (Cooper & Shepard, 1973; Shepard & Metzler, 1971). Subsequently Vandenberg and Kuse (1978) modified the Shepard-Metzler Mental Rotation Test for group administration (see example in Fig. 2). Other potential measures of this dimension are Flags and Cards from the French kit (French et al., 1963) and Primary Mental Abilities (PMA) space (Thurstone & Thurstone, 1941).

Cognitive rationale.—Shepard and his colleagues (e.g., Shepard & Cooper, 1982) sought to substantiate an analogue process for mental rotation. They hypothesized that during a mental rotation the respondent's internal cognitive processes have a one-to-one correspondence with the external rotation of the object (Shepard & Cooper, 1982). Thus they infer that a Gestalt-like process governs the rotation of objects. Controversy centers on

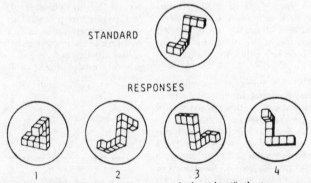

STANDARD

RESPONSES

1   2   3   4

Fig. 2.—A mental rotation item. Respondents are asked to identify the two responses that show the standard in a different orientation.

1484   Child Development

whether mental rotation is analogous to physical rotation or is subject to analytic processing strategies (e.g., Carpenter & Just, 1978; Just & Carpenter, 1976; Pylsyshyn, 1979, 1981; Shepard & Cooper, 1982).

Evidence for the Gestalt-like process comes from research by Shepard and his coworkers (e.g., Shepard & Cooper, 1982) showing that the reaction time to solution for mental rotation items reflects the number of degrees through which the item must be rotated. Shepard finds that individuals take longer to rotate objects through a larger angle, supporting an analogue process for rotation of the figure. Those attempting to demonstrate that mental rotation is subject to analytic processing have sought to demonstrate effects for stimulus complexity (e.g., Pylsyshyn, 1979, 1981). Taken together, however, the various studies of mental rotation provide a strong case for the availability of Gestalt-like analogue mental rotation processes.

Mental rotation items are used to measure the time required for solution rather than the accuracy of solution (which is extremely high). Conditions of measurement encourage an analogue process. The possibility remains that respondents could use analytic processes to rotate figures when mental rotation is part of a more complex task such as Surface Development (French et al., 1963). When individually administered mental rotation items are translated into a group administered format, different processes may contribute to performance. Thus processes required for mental rotation may vary with the mode of task presentation. Furthermore, since the primary dimension is speed of response, such tasks have not been used successfully with young children because the level of concentration required is often limited in the young.

Some researchers suggest that mental rotation in two dimensions is easier and may reflect a different process than mental rotation in three dimensions (e.g., Rosser, 1980). Shepard and Cooper (1982) question this assertion, finding no effect of dimension when rotation of two- and three-dimensional objects is compared. Another factor differentiating two- and three-dimensional stimuli is complexity. Possibly, when respondents encounter complex stimuli, some find that the strategies they used for simple stimuli are no longer effective. Cooper (1983) suggests that the longer response times for three-dimensional stimuli result from some subjects whose inefficient strategies interfere with success. Thus all subjects may use a process analogous to physical rotation, but some sub-

jects may apply the strategy inefficiently. Such inefficiency would be more apparent for complex stimuli.

Psychometric rationale.—The primary psychometric question is whether mental rotation can be differentiated from other measures of spatial ability. Thurstone's original space factor included mental rotation. French (1951), Fruchter (1954), Smith (1964), and Thurstone and Thurstone (1941) generally concur that two major factors characterize spatial ability: perception and visualization. None of these earlier systems differentiated mental rotation from spatial visualization.

Recently, DeFries et al. (1974) and Wilson and Vandenberg (1978) factor analyzed a group of 15 cognitive tests and found the same factor structure for different ethnic groups, for males and females, and for different age cohorts. In all cases a spatial factor was characterized by the Vandenberg and Kuse (1978) mental rotations test (subsequently called the Vandenberg) and by Cards (French et al., 1963) but also included spatial visualization tasks such as Hidden Patterns, Paper Form Board, and Progressive Matrices. However, the Vandenberg test had a low relationship to the other factors, which were identified as verbal, perceptual speed, and visual memory. In contrast, the spatial visualization tasks were more strongly related to the verbal factor than was the Vandenberg. Thus psychometrically, the Vandenberg test may identify a spatial ability independent of verbal ability and may be differentiated from spatial visualization in this respect.

In summary, results from the process analysis suggest that mental rotation tasks are distinct and involve a Gestalt-like analogue process. Factor analyses using mental rotation tasks have sometimes been used to identify a factor independent from spatial visualization. Our initial categorization of spatial ability separates mental rotation from spatial visualization, but our analysis procedures provide an opportunity to combine the two if effect sizes are similar.

Spatial Visualization

Spatial visualization is the label commonly associated with those spatial ability tasks that involve complicated, multistep manipulations of spatially presented information. These tasks may involve the processes required for spatial perception and mental rotations but are distinguished by the possibility of multiple solution strategies. Spatial visualization tasks include EFT, Hidden Figures, Paper Folding (see Fig. 3), Paper Form

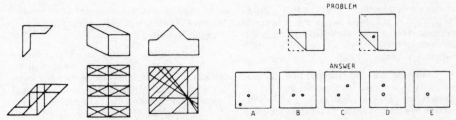

FIG. 3.—Spatial visualization items. Left, Embedded Figures: respondents are asked to find the simple shape shown on the top in the complex shape shown on the bottom. Right, Paper Folding: respondents are asked to indicate how the paper would look when unfolded.

Board, Surface Development, Differential Aptitude Test (spatial relations subtest), Block Design, and Guilford-Zimmerman spatial visualization. As many researchers have noted (Cattell, 1971; Guay & McDaniel, 1977; Shepard & Feng, 1972), an analytic strategy is required to solve these complex tasks. Mental rotation and spatial perception may or may not be elements of that strategy.

Cognitive rationale.—Process analyses of spatial visualization tasks stress that multistep, analytic procedures are required to solve the tasks. Consider Paper Folding (Fig. 3). Subjects must represent the paper and transform their representations by examining pictures that show (*a*) the folding of a piece of paper, (*b*) the punching of a hole through the folded paper, and (*c*) the resulting pattern of holes when the paper is unfolded. As is characteristic of spatial visualization tests, the student is required to work quickly (many fail to finish), rotate figures, and keep track of multistep operations.

Successful performance on spatial visualization tasks involves flexibility in selecting the optimal strategy for each item. As Kyllonen, Woltz, and Lohman (1981) have shown, respondents rapidly adjust their strategies to the unique features of new items. Successful respondents have a repertoire of strategies for these items.

Psychometric rationale.—Correlational studies often, but not always, identify spatial visualization. Guilford (1969) places these tests on a dimension called Cognition of Figural Transformation. Horn and Cattell (1966) identified spatial visualization using factor analysis with oblique rotation. Snow, Kyllonen, and Marshalek (in press) attempted to separate spatial visualization from Horn and Cattell's (1966) construct of general fluid ability, which is defined as the ability to form relationships among symbols, and is measured by tests such as Letter Series (French et

al., 1963). They were unable to separate the two constructs in an orthogonal factor analysis, so they defined a construct called general fluid visualization that included both. Thus the distinction between spatial visualization and fluid ability requires further clarification. As discussed above, spatial visualization has sometimes but not always been distinguished from mental rotation but has been distinguished from spatial perception.

In summary, it appears that processes used for spatial visualization are distinct from those used for other spatial abilities. Success on spatial visualization requires analysis of task demands and flexible adaptation of a repertoire of solution procedures. Those conducting psychometric studies suggest that spatial visualization might be distinguished from other spatial abilities but not necessarily from nonspatial tasks such as measures of general fluid ability.

Thus we found three spatial ability categories: (*a*) spatial perception, which can be done efficiently using a gravitational/kinesthetic process; (*b*) mental rotation, which can be done efficiently using a Gestalt-like mental rotation process analogous to physical rotation of the stimuli; and (*c*) spatial visualization, which can be done efficiently using an analytic process. Other categorizations are, of course, possible. Our approach to research synthesis helps us decide whether this categorization is appropriate.

Meta-Analysis Results

As mentioned in the description of our meta-analysis procedure, we first tested to see whether all our effect sizes were homogeneous; they were not. Thus we partitioned the effect sizes using the three spatial ability categories described above.

Spatial Perception

The 62 spatial perception unbiased effect sizes were not homogeneous. Using Hedges's

1486   Child Development

TABLE 1

EFFECT SIZES (ES) AND HOMOGENEITY FOR SPATIAL ABILITY META-ANALYSIS

Group	ES (N)	Weighted Estimator of ES	95% Confidence Interval for ES	Homogeneity Statistic (Critical Value)
Spatial perception:				
All ages	62	.44	.04–.84	110(80)[a]
Under 13	26	.37	−.06–.81	45(38)[a]
13–18	23	.37	−.11–.85	19(34)[b]
Over 18	13	.64	.31–.97	26(21)[a]
Mental rotation:				
All ages	29	.73	.50–.96	247(43)
Vandenberg[c]	18	.94	.77–1.12	28(20)[b]
PMA space[d]	11	.26	.002–.54	18(16)[a]
Spatial visualization				
All ages	81	.13	−.24–.50	98(101)[b]

[a] Close to homogeneity.
[b] Homogeneity achieved with $p < .95$ confidence.
[c] Effect sizes for the Vandenberg version of the Shepard-Metzler figures.
[d] Effect sizes for the PMA-space subtest and other similar tests.

(1982a) methods for fitting categorical models, we partitioned by age of the subjects as shown in Table 1. After partitioning, the within-class homogeneity was reduced (from $\chi^2[62] = 110$ to $\chi^2[61] = 90$) but still high, indicating that heterogeneity remained. The between-class homogeneity was significant ($\chi^2[1] = 20$, $p < .05$), indicating that the observed differences in effect sizes between groups were significant. Partitioning resulted in homogeneity for the 12–18-year-old age range and near homogeneity for the other ages. As discussed above, near homogeneity implies the studies are similar but not exact replicates of each other. The fit was improved by partitioning because the weighted estimator for the over-18 age group exceeded the estimates for younger individuals.

Unbiased effect sizes for sex on spatial perception range between −.27 and 1.00. The weighted estimator is one-third of a standard deviation (favoring males) for those 18 and under and two-thirds of a standard deviation for those over 18 years of age. Only the effect size for those over 18 is significantly different from zero, as indicated by the 95% confidence interval in Table 1.

Why is the effect size for those over 18 years of age larger than for the others? Sex differences in spatial perception may accelerate with age, or they may be larger for one test than for another. We computed separate effect sizes for RFT and water level but found no difference in pattern. Alternatively, this difference could reflect a cohort influence: perhaps older individuals (studied since 1974) have had less access to relevant spatial experi-

ences than younger individuals (e.g., science instruction emphasizing the physical principles involved in water level). A recent study by Liben and Golbeck (1984) suggests that substantial amounts of instruction can reduce or eliminate sex differences on these tasks. Also, the over-18 samples may be drawn from a different population than the other samples (e.g., particular occupation groups). Thus the postadolescent effect size may reflect acceleration in sex differences after 18 years, a cohort effect, or sampling biases that differentiate that group from the other two groups. No clear support for a single hypothesis emerged from review of the 13 studies involved.

When in the life span are sex differences in spatial perception first detected? We consider studies involving young respondents as well as a longitudinal study to answer this question.

First, can this dimension be measured reliably across the life span? Spatial perception can be measured reliably in 4-year-olds (Block & Block, 1982; Foorman, 1979), although the task may measure a different dimension than that assessed in older children. Piaget and Inhelder's (1967) study of water level suggested that younger children view the task as a memory task, whereas older children can reason about the variables.

The youngest respondents to a spatial perception measure entering the meta-analysis were also part of a longitudinal sample. The 4-year-olds in the meta-analysis came from the Block and Block (1982) longitudinal study. These individuals were given the RFT at ages 4, 5, 7, and 11. At age 4, girls outperformed boys. At ages 5 and 7, boys slightly outperformed girls. By 11 years, boys performed significantly better than girls. Between age 7 and 11 the difference between boys' and girls' scores increased threefold. Thus the Block and Block (1982) longitudinal study suggests that sex differences in spatial perception favoring males are first detected around age 7 and accelerate to adult levels by age 11. These differences could account for the slight heterogeneity of effect sizes.

The remaining subjects in the meta-analysis were 8 years of age or older. For those from 8 to 18 years, the analysis reveals homogeneous sex differences in performance on spatial perception favoring males. There is no evidence for a change in the magnitude of sex differences in spatial perception at adolescence. As noted above, the larger effect size for those over 18 years, together with the longitudinal data described suggests the possibility that sex differences in spatial perception may accelerate beyond adolescence.

Maccoby and Jacklin's (1974) review included 21 studies of RFT and no studies of water level (possibly because the few available studies at that time failed to report data by sex). In 16 of their 21 studies, there are significant effects favoring males, including all the youngest groups (age 7 or 8). Thus the conclusions in the studies reviewed by Maccoby and Jacklin (1974) concur with our finding that sex differences in spatial perception exist by age 8 and persist across the life span.

Cognitive and strategic perspective.— The meta-analysis results imply that sex differences in spatial perception can be detected from age 8 onward, although they are only significant, as a group, for those age 18 and older. We turn to the cognitive and strategic research perspectives for some insight into the mechanisms that might govern these differences. Our investigations suggest that knowledge about physical principles, propensity to rely on gravitational/kinesthetic cues, and propensity to combine task features analytically are dimensions that influence spatial perception performance.

A number of researchers (e.g., Liben & Golbeck, 1980; Linn & Delucchi, 1983) have investigated the role of knowledge of physical principles (e.g., that water is horizontal in tilted bottles) in water level performance. They found that the task was easier when knowledge of physical principles was not required for solution but that this knowledge did not interact with sex differences.

In the water level task, instructions that encourage analytic attention to task features also influence performance. Harris et al. (1978) report that sex differences are eliminated when the instructions indicate "the water is in motion" and "the water is at rest." When the instructions indicate that the "water is in motion," males find the task more difficult than they find the standard task. When the instuctions indicate that the "water is at rest," females find the task easier than they find the standard task. However, when the instructions are changed to describe the "container at rest" and the "container in motion," the usual sex differences occur just as they do in the standard version where the illustration suggests that the container is at rest. These results may indicate a sex difference in propensity to rely on cues from the task situation.

Certain visual task features may inhibit reliance on distracting cues. In some studies, but not others, the shape of the container in the water level task influences performance (Thomas & Jamison, 1975, 1981). In another example, reducing the size of the retinal image of the frame in RFT inhibits reliance on the frame (Dichgans, Young, & Brandt, 1972; Sigman et al., 1978, 1979) and fosters performance.

In summary, spatial perception items typically include task features that encourage or discourage analytic solutions to the items. Errors probably reflect inappropriate weighing of these features. In the standard version, reasoners who depend more or primarily on gravitational/kinesthetic cues may well outperform those who use an analytic procedure and rely on visual features.

Mental Rotation

The second category of spatial ability, mental rotation, yielded 29 effect sizes. The effect sizes were not homogeneous, so we partitioned them by age. Homogeneity was not achieved for the separate age groups.

Most of the studies of mental rotation involved either PMA space or the Vandenberg. To investigate whether lack of homogeneity reflected a task effect, we plotted the effect sizes by age and task, as shown in Figure 4. We found larger effects at all ages for the Vandenberg and Kuse (1978) version of the Shepard-Metzler Mental Rotation Test than for the other measures of mental rotation. Thus we partitioned all the effect estimates into two groups: (*a*) Vandenberg and Kuse (1978) and (*b*) PMA space or Coordinated Viewpoints (Guay & McDaniel, 1977) or

1488   Child Development

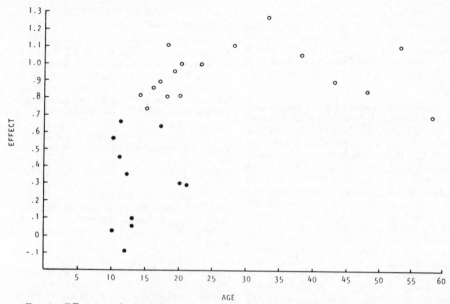

FIG. 4.—Effect sizes for mental rotations tests by age. ○ = Vandenberg (1971). ● = PMA space (Thurstone & Thurstone, 1941), Cards (French et al., 1963), Flags (French et al., 1963).

Cards (French et al., 1963). (Cards and Coordinated Viewpoints were each represented by a single effect estimator.) The resulting partition yielded homogeneity or near homogeneity for each group (Table 1). As discussed above, near homogeneity suggests that the studies are similar but are not perfect replicates of each other. In fact, as can be seen, most effect sizes on the Vandenberg and Kuse (1978) exceeded those on the other tests.

There were no changes in effect size with age over the ages studied. Sex differences are detected as soon as mental rotation could be measured. The two studies with the youngest respondents using PMA space (age 10–11) have means favoring males, but only one is significant. Wilson and Vandenberg (1978) found sex differences on mental rotation from their youngest (age 13) to their oldest (age 60+) subjects. For studies prior to 1974, Maccoby (1966) and Maccoby and Jacklin (1974) report studies of PMA space that detect sex differences at whatever age it is measured.

In summary, the effect sizes for the mental rotation category lacked homogeneity because the tests included have systematically different magnitudes of sex differences. Across ages, we found large homogeneous effects for sex on mental rotation as measured by the Vandenberg test. Similarly, across age we found moderately sized and fairly homogeneous effects for sex on mental rotation as measured by PMA space (Thurstone & Thurstone, 1941). Both types of mental rotation tasks yield consistent sex differences across ages, although the magnitude of the difference depends on the test used, and the Vandenberg and Kuse (1978) task has not been used with those younger than 13.

Cognitive and strategic perspective.— From the process analysis described above we see that mental rotation may often occur as a cognitive process analogous to the physical rotation of an object. Of course, the analogue process can be applied inefficiently, or an analytic process can also be used to rotate figures, but these approaches are less efficient for highly speeded mental rotation tests. As discussed above, the research program of Shepard and his colleagues has verified the existence of an analogue process (Cooper & Regan, 1982; Shepard & Cooper, 1982). Conditions under which the process is applied require investigation.

What differentiates the Vandenberg from PMA space? The Vandenberg items are in three dimensions and are more complex than the two-dimensional PMA-space items (see Figure 2). Research suggests that both the additional complexity and the additional dimension lead to slower reaction times for all subjects (Cooper, 1975; Pylsyshyn, 1979; Shepard & Metzler, 1971). In contrast, in both tests the respondents are required to locate two instances of the rotated stimulus figure and to work quickly. These task characteristics encourage use of an efficient rotation strategy.

Analysis of studies in the cognitive perspective can shed light on this finding. These studies use small numbers of volunteer subjects but assess their performance individually rather than through the use of group-administered paper and pencil tests. Such studies were not entered in the meta-analysis because of nonsystematic subject selection but can help us clarify our results. Comparison of male and female performance on individually administered mental rotation items yields surprisingly consistent results for error rates and for response times for unrotated figures (the intercept from an equation fitted to the responses gives the response time) (Kail, Carter, & Pellegrino, 1979; Metzler & Shepard, 1974; Tapley & Bryden, 1977). Differences are found only in the slopes of the regression lines, which reflect the response times to solution as items are rotated through greater angles.

Essentially, each respondent takes longer to rotate a figure angle than through a larger angle than through a smaller angle, but the rate of increase (or slope of the regression line) differs widely. Females have longer response times than do males. The most comprehensive study (Kail et al., 1979) showed that sex differences in speed of rotation were dramatic (30% of the females were slower than all the males). Besides these group differences, variability in response times for females was greater than for males because of a bimodal distribution of scores for females. Some females performed just like the males; others formed a separate group with longer response times.

If performance on the Vandenberg and the PMA-space measure is based primarily on rate of mental rotation, then the greater magnitude of sex differences on the Vandenberg relative to the PMA space could reflect slower rotation rates for a subgroup of females. Research on rate of eye tracking suggests that females, as a group, track more slowly than males (Kuechenmeister, Linton, Mueller, & White, 1977). Eye tracking, however, has not been linked to mental rotation performance and could be used to investigate this hypothesis. At present, it would be prohibitively expensive to study samples large

enough for conclusions to be reached (e.g., Carpenter & Just, 1978).

Another hypothesis to explain the differences between the Vandenberg test and the PMA-space test is based on students selecting inefficient solution strategies. Since all the stimuli are presented simultaneously, subjects could select part-by-part rotation and comparison rather than rotation of a whole integrated figure (e.g., Carpenter & Just, 1978). For the more complex figures in the Vandenberg test, several part-by-part rotations may be necessary to get enough information to choose a response. In contrast, fewer part-by-part rotations may be necessary to get enough information to choose a response for the simpler PMA-space figures. If females, more than males, adopt a part-by-part strategy, then the sex differences should be more apparent on more complex figures.

More generally, a part-by-part strategy could be mediated by an analytic meta-strategy that guides part selection. For the relatively straightforward PMA-space items, such an approach may be as efficient as mental rotation; for the complex Vandenberg items, such an approach may be inefficient. Thus if females adopt an analytic strategy more often than males, then, in situations where the meta-strategy for analytic solution is efficient, few sex differences would be detected. Thus for PMA space, reliance on an analytic meta-strategy may yield small sex differences, whereas for the Vandenberg test, reliance on an analytic meta-strategy may yield large sex differences.

Slower performance on mental rotation may reflect greater caution on the part of females (since few errors are made by either sex) rather than lack of ability to perform quickly. Female caution in testing situations has been documented for tests administered across a wide range of ages such as the National Assessment of Educational Progress (de-Benedictis, Delucchi, Harris, Linn, & Stage, 1982; Wheeler & Harris, 1981). The slower performance of females relative to males on mental rotations may reflect a tendency to double check an answer by rotating twice or by rotating additional parts of the figure (when using a part-by-part strategy) rather than slower rotation of a single figure.

In summary, males tend to outperform females on mental rotation at any age where measurement is possible. Then sex differences may result from differential rate of rotation, differential efficiency in strategy application, differential use of analytic processes, or differential caution.

1490   Child Development

Spatial Visualization

In the meta-analysis of the 81 effect estimators for spatial visualization we found that effects were small and homogeneous across the life span. Individual studies had effect sizes ranging from −.91 to .71. The average effect size was .13 of a standard deviation unit. The effects were not partitioned since they were homogeneous. A confidence interval for the mean effect included zero, indicating that the average effect size did not differ from zero (see Table 1).

Furthermore, sex differences in spatial visualization do not change across the life span. For most of the studies, no significant differences between males and females were found. Therefore sex differences in spatial visualization are not detected at any point in the life span.

Other research is consistent with this finding. Maccoby and Jacklin (1974) summarized 32 studies of an aspect of spatial visualization: the EFT. In five studies there were significant differences favoring males, and in three there were significant differences favoring females. Thus for the studies reviewed by Maccoby and Jacklin (1974) no consistent sex differences on this aspect of spatial visualization emerged.

One longitudinal study deserves special mention because it illustrates consistency in performance on spatial visualization. Block and Block (1982) administered a version of embedded figures at ages 3, 4, 5, and 11 and found a sex difference at age 4 favoring females but no differences at other ages. This longitudinal study lends further support to the conclusion that spatial visualization is equally difficult for both sexes.

Cognitive and strategic perspective.— Process analyses of performance on spatial visualization items conducted recently show that these items require an analytic procedure. For example, Kyllonen et al. (1981), in a study analyzing performance on paper folding, found that the item characteristics were more likely to determine the strategies used to solve the item than were the characteristics of the individuals responding to the items. Thus individuals tend to select different strategies for different items, rather than performing similarly from item to item. Individuals who do well on spatial visualization items do so because they have an appropriate repertoire of strategies and because they have effective meta-strategies to govern the selection of a strategy for each item.

As we mentioned above, both spatial perception and many of the spatial visualization items require disembedding. In spatial perception the subject may rely on gravitational/kinesthetic cues instead of correcting for distracting cues. In contrast, kinesthetic cues are rarely helpful in spatial visualization disembedding. Thus spatial perception may be uniquely characterized by the possibility of relying on gravitational/kinesthetic cues.

The analogue mental rotation process studied by Shepard and his colleagues could be employed for many spatial visualization items. Recall, however, that males and females differ primarily on speed of mental rotation, not accuracy. The strategy of rotation exists for both groups. Speed of rotation is probably less critical in spatial visualization than in mental rotation because it constitutes much less of the total solution time. Alternatively, consider the hypothesis that speed of rotation reflects caution on the part of females. Caution in the form of double-checking responses may hinder performance on mental rotations but not on the more analytic spatial visualization items.

The repertoire of strategies for spatial visualization items thus probably includes the propensity to rely on gravitational/kinesthetic cues hypothesized to characterize spatial perception performance as well as analogue mental rotation speed hypothesized to characterize mental rotations. These may account for the slight tendency of males to perform better than females on spatial visualization. Tasks requiring reliance on either of these strategies may yield larger sex differences than shown in this meta-analysis. Our investigation does not include sufficient numbers of such tasks to allow a test of this hypothesis, but a larger pool of effect sizes might permit partitioning of the studies by test and provide a more detailed picture of performance. Sex differences in strategy selection might be revealed if the solutions used by males and females for spatial visualization items were studied.

Spatial visualization performance probably reflects the meta-strategy for selecting processes for each item rather than the individual's relative proficiency in using any particular process. Spatial visualization items can be solved using a range of processes besides those associated with spatial perception and mental rotation. Thus the spatial processes that yield sex differences could be among those from which the reasoner flexibly selects to solve spatial visualization items. Reasoners, therefore, could select optimal processes for their own performance and minimize effects of sex differences on total score.

That males and females may differ in the processes they select for solving spatial problems is reflected in correlations between aptitudes and performance for males and females. Kyllonen, Lohman, and Snow (1984) found that for females verbal aptitude correlated with paper folding performance whereas for males spatial aptitude correlated with this task. Similarly, Sternberg and Weil (1980) found that those using a spatial strategy on linear syllogisms showed a relationship between spatial but not verbal aptitude and solution time, whereas those using a verbal strategy showed a relationship between verbal but not spatial aptitude and solution time.

Given the lack of sex differences in spatial visualization and the process analysis reported above, it appears that spatial visualization performance depends on use of meta-strategies. Furthermore, as Lohman (1979) suggests, much of the variance in complex spatial tasks is explained by variation in general ability. These strategies are more characteristic of general ability than of spatial ability. Recall also that Snow et al. (in press) could not separate spatial visualization from fluid ability in factor analysis. Certainly these meta-strategies resemble processes thought to be components of intelligence (e.g., Sternberg, 1982). Spatial visualization performance may depend, in large part, on general abilities that do not exhibit sex differences.

Thus, sex differences in spatial ability may influence which processes reasoners select for spatial visualization items. Flexible selection of the most efficient processes may mean that females select different processes than males for some items. The meta-strategies governing selection appear more similar to general ability than to other spatial ability processes. Further research is needed to establish how or whether sex differences in spatial perception and mental rotations influence spatial visualization performance and how or whether spatial visualization can be distinguished from general ability.

Summary and Discussion

In summary, we identified homogeneous sex differences in two of the three aspects of spatial ability. Spatial perception is easier for males than females. Differences range between one-third of a standard deviation unit for those under 18 to two-thirds of a standard deviation unit for those over 18. Mental rotation is also easier for males than for females;

differences range from about one-quarter of a standard deviation unit for PMA space to almost an entire standard deviation unit for the Vandenberg. Spatial visualization, which is characterized by analytic combination of both visual and nonvisual strategies, is about equally difficult for males and females.

Our categorization of spatial ability resulted in nearly homogeneous effect sizes for sex within categories. However, these findings do not imply that this is the only or even the best way to partition spatial ability. For example, the spatial perception effect size for those under 18 is statistically similar to the mental rotation effect size for PMA space. Statistical similarity does not, of course, imply similarity in processes or strategies required to solve the items; such similarity simply raises possibilities.

Originally, we combined diverse measures such as PMA space and the Vandenberg test, both of which seemed to require mental rotation, on the basis of process analysis. Statistical procedures in meta-analysis demonstrated that task features can have large effects on performance even when tasks appear superficially similar. This finding illustrates the advantages of combining ideas from varied research perspectives and the power of recent advances in meta-analysis. This finding also suggests some unanswered questions about spatial ability performance.

Our categories reflect the nature of measures chosen for research study. Measures represented by few studies in recent research receive less emphasis than widely studied measures. For example, two tests are used to establish nearly all the effect sizes for spatial perception. Mental rotation is also primarily assessed by two measures that proved to have effect sizes of different magnitude. In contrast, spatial visualization has a variety of measures, some of which, if sampled more widely, might form a separate category. In particular, spatial visualization tests with many items that could be efficiently solved using a mental rotation strategy might yield small but consistent sex differences.

Magnitude of sex differences in spatial ability.—Sex differences in spatial ability are large only for mental rotation, medium for spatial perception, and small for spatial visualization. Linn and Pulos (1982, 1983) report that approximately 5% of the variance in the water level task is attributable to sex. Hyde (1981) and Plomin and Foch (1982) both report that between 1% and 5% of the variance

1492   Child Development

in performance in the studies of spatial ability reported by Maccoby and Jacklin (1974) can be attributed to sex. In most studies, sex accounts for up to 5% of all the individual differences in performance on spatial tasks, excluding mental rotation.

Our meta-analysis results contradict the assertion that sex differences in spatial ability are first detected in adolescence. For spatial perception, differences are detected in individual studies at about age 8 and, for grouped studies, emerge statistically only at age 18. For mental rotation, sex differences are detected whenever measurement is possible, although some versions of the test are inappropriate for those under 13. For spatial visualization, there are no differences. Thus sex differences in spatial ability are detected prior to adolescence for some categories of spatial ability and not at all for others.

The nature of spatial ability sex differences.—Sex differences in spatial ability appear on tasks for which efficient solution requires rapid manipulation of symbolic information and on tasks that require recognition of the vertical or horizontal. Spatial visualization tasks, where efficient solution depends on effective use of analytic procedures to select strategies for manipulating symbolic information, do not appear to yield sex differences.

Our explanation of the observed sex differences on these tasks centers on selection and efficient application of solution strategies. For both mental rotations and spatial perception, inefficient or inaccurate strategies have been identified. For mental rotations, the less efficient analytic strategy can be used, or an inefficient use of the process analogous to the physical rotation of the object might be employed rather than a process analogous to rotation of the entire physical object. For spatial perception, the less accurate strategy of attempting to correct for distracting information could be used rather than a strategy of reliance on gravitational/kinesthetic cues.

The pattern of sex differences could result from a propensity of females to select and consistently use less efficient or less accurate strategies for these tasks. Cooper (1983) provides evidence for the view that respondents choose from a variety of strategies even for tasks involving mental rotations that seem to encourage use of a single strategy. Cooper (1983) suggests that, for mental rotation, once a respondent has selected a strategy, the same strategy is used for all the items. Since mental rotation items are all very similar to each

other, there would be little in the situation to encourage strategy shifting. Linn and Pulos (1983) report similar patterns of consistent strategy use for spatial perception tasks. In contrast, spatial visualization tasks, because of the complexity of their items, may encourage strategy shifting. Further investigation is needed to determine whether tasks that encourage strategy shifting have fewer sex differences than other spatial tasks.

Another explanation centers on acquisition of appropriate strategies for these tasks. If females are less likely to acquire the efficient or accurate strategies, then no amount of skill in strategy selection will help.

Both these explanations for the observed differences could reflect different experiences of males and females relevant to each of these tasks. Inefficient strategy selection for these tasks may reflect a lack of attention to the cues governing strategy selection or lack of opportunity to acquire the strategy. Those conducting training studies have shown that instruction improves performance on spatial perception items for both sexes (Liben & Golbeck, 1980). In addition, the experiences of males and females differ in areas thought relevant to spatial performance (e.g., Newcombe et al., 1983; Petersen & Gitelson, in press). More precise investigations of these questions are needed.

It appears that spatial visualization performance depends, in large part, on meta-strategies used to select an approach for each item, so that in this sense spatial visualization resembles general ability. Furthermore, it may be that, as the mental rotation strategy analogous to the physical rotation of the object becomes more central to task performance, sex differences become more pronounced. Further research using tasks that demand more mental rotation skill than those we classified as spatial visualization and less than those classified with PMA space would help to clarify the performance of males and females on spatial ability tasks. Further study of the repertoire of strategies available to reasoners, of the cues used by reasoners to select a particular strategy, and of the efficiency with which reasoners apply strategies would also be illuminating.

Relationship to mathematics and science performance.—The pattern of sex differences in spatial ability and the process analysis hypothesized to account for this pattern do not correspond to the pattern of sex differences found in mathematics and in science performance (e.g., Armstrong, 1979; Malone &

Fleming, 1983; Meehan, 1984; Steinkamp & Maehr, 1983). Processes of speed of mental rotation, most strongly implicated in spatial ability sex differences, do not correspond to processes likely to contribute to mathematics and science performance (see Linn & Petersen, in press, for a more detailed discussion). Correlational studies show a strong relationship between spatial abilities and scientific and mathematical reasoning, probably reflecting the role of general ability in performance in each area. Sex differences in spatial ability do not generally account for sex differences in mathematics and science (e.g., Fennema & Sherman, 1977; Karplus, Pulos, & Stage, 1980; Kreinberg & Stage, 1981; Linn & Pulos, 1982, 1983). Studies that separate each type of spatial ability are needed to clarify these relationships further.

Biological mechanisms for sex differences in spatial ability.—Many hypothesize that sex differences in spatial ability result from hormonal changes at puberty. Since the meta-analysis showed no change in the magnitude of spatial ability sex differences in early adolescence, a pubertal mechanism for sex differences would seem unlikely. Furthermore, although many factors governing the emergence of sex differences in spatial ability at puberty have been proposed, the research evidence is inconsistent (e.g., Carey, Diamond, & Woods, 1980; Newcombe et al., 1983; Petersen, 1983; Waber, 1976, 1977).

For example, Waber originally (1976, 1977) proposed a relationship between spatial ability and the timing of pubertal maturation. She suggested that later maturers would be better spatial visualizers than earlier maturers because of the effects of maturational timing on the development of hemispheric specialization in the brain. This hypothesis, that the brain functioning of later maturers becomes more laterally specialized for spatial ability, would explain sex differences in spatial ability since boys mature 1–2 years later than girls, on the average (e.g., Petersen & Taylor, 1980). The association between maturational timing and spatial ability was supported in some studies (Carey et al., 1980; Newcombe et al., 1983; Petersen & Gitelson, in press) and not supported in several others (Herbst & Petersen, 1979; Petersen, 1976; Roach, 1979; Strauss & Kinsbourne, 1981). Studies supporting the hypothesis generally utilized designs in which extreme maturation groups (earlier and late maturers) were contrasted. The fact that support has been found mainly in such "extreme groups" studies suggests that the effect of maturational timing may be a weak one

in the whole population. Waber's subsequent research (Waber, Bauermeister, Cohen, Ferber, & Wolff, 1981) yielded support for the hypothesis only among upper-middle-class students. Furthermore, even when late maturers are found to outperform early maturers on spatial tasks, they usually do not show greater lateralization. Thus the hypothesized proximal cause underlying the association between timing of maturation and spatial ability has not been supported (e.g., Herbst & Petersen, 1979; Newcombe et al., 1983; Waber et al., 1981), and the role for timing of maturation in sex differences is more complex than originally thought. Timing of maturation may be involved with sex differences in spatial ability, but more research with appropriate measures (e.g., mental rotation) is needed at this point.

Genetic factors constitute the other major biological mechanism used to explain sex differences in spatial ability. There is ample evidence that spatial ability, like other cognitive abilities, is highly heritable (e.g., DeFries et al., 1976; Spuhler & Vandenberg, 1980). Some special genetic mechanism, however, is needed to explain sex differences in spatial ability. The primary plausible mechanism is that a spatial gene is carried on the X chromosome (Wittig & Petersen, 1979). Bock and Kolakowski (1973) initially proposed an X-linked recessive major gene for spatial ability.

The evidence for a genetic mechanism for sex differences could be obscured by lumping together studies of diverse forms of spatial ability, only some of which show consistent sex differences. The meta-analysis suggests that mental rotations would be the best task to use to identify a genetic mechanism since it yields the largest sex differences. Indeed, Vandenberg and Kuse (1979) reviewed the evidence for a genetic explanation for sex differences in mental rotations and found that evidence fails to support this explanation.

The total body of research examining the X-linked hypothesis offers contradictory findings. Some researchers have found evidence for X linkage using spatial visualization measures (e.g., Hartlage, 1970; Stafford, 1961), mental rotations (Bock & Kolakowski, 1973), and water level (Thomas & Jamison, 1981). Conversely, other studies fail to support the hypothesis using spatial visualization measures (Corely, DeFries, Kuse, & Vandenberg, 1980) and mental rotations (e.g., McGee, 1978, 1979). Additional studies on all three categories of spatial ability have produced mixed results (Fralley, Eliot, & Dayton, 1978; Goodenough et al., 1977; Loehlin, Sharan, &

1494   Child Development

Jacoby, 1978; Walker, Krasnoff, & Peaco, 1981; Yen, 1975). Thus no consistent evidence for the X-linked hypothesis has been found.

A biological mechanism for observed sex differences in spatial ability may be expressed through a hormonal mechanism occurring earlier than puberty. Just prior to and after birth, prenatal hormones reach adult levels, with the related sex difference. There is some evidence that brain organization is affected by hormones at this time (Hines & Shipley, 1984; Reinisch et al., 1979). However, no evidence linking this hypothesis to spatial ability has been put forth.

To the extent that any biological factors affect spatial ability they would interact with sex-typed experiences and sex-role expectations to produce the observed patterns of performance (e.g., Newcombe et al., 1983; Tobin-Richards & Petersen, 1981). Males and females have differing experiences across the life span (e.g, Bem & Bem, 1970; Cordua, McGraw, & Drabman, 1979; Haugh, Hoffman, & Cowan, 1980; Papalia & Tennent, 1975). The relationship between these experiences and documented sex differences in spatial ability has not been established but may eventually offer an explanation for sex differences in spatial ability (e.g., those in mental rotations) and for the success of training programs aimed at reducing the differences (Connor, Schackman, & Serbin, 1978; Goodenough et al., 1984; Newcombe et al., 1983; Liben & Golbeck, 1984).

In conclusion, sex differences in spatial ability are now more specifically described. The mechanisms that lead to these differences remain to be established, as do the possible influence of these differences on other behaviors. Individuals probably have an assortment of spatial skills rather than a single ability. Furthermore, several mechanisms may contribute to the observed sex differences. Researchers attempting to characterize the nature and origin of these differences and their potential influence on other behavior need to differentiate the types of spatial ability and the processes respondents use for each item type.

References

Armstrong, J. (1979). *A national assessment of achievement and participation of women in mathematics* (ERIC Document Reproduction Service No. ED 187562). Denver, CO: Education Commission of the States.

Bem, S. L., & Bem, D. J. (1970). Case study of a nonconscious ideology: Training the woman to know her place. In D. J. Bem (Ed.), *Beliefs, attitudes and human affairs* (pp. 89–99). Monterey, CA: Brooks-Cole.

Benbow, C. P., & Stanley, J. C. (1980). Sex differences in mathematical ability: Fact or artifact? *Science*, **210**, 1262–1264.

Benbow, C. P., & Stanley, J. C. (Eds.). (1984). *Academic precocity: Aspects of its development*. Baltimore: Johns Hopkins University Press.

Block, J., & Block, J. (1982). *Cognitive development from childhood and adolescence* (NIMA Research Grant MH16080). Unpublished manuscript.

Bock, R. D., & Kolakowski, D. (1973). Further evidence of sex-linked major-gene influence on human spatial visualizing ability. *American Journal of Human Genetics*, **25**, 1–14.

Caplan, P. J., MacPherson, G. M., & Tobin, P. (in press). Do sex-related differences in spatial abilities exist? *American Psychologist*.

Carey, S. E., Diamond, R., & Woods, B. (1980). Development of face recognition—a maturational component? *Developmental Psychology*, **16**, 257–269.

Carpenter, P. A., & Just, M. A. (1978). Eye fixations during mental rotation. In J. W. Senders, D. F. Fisher, & R. A. Monty (Eds.), *Eye movements and the higher psychological functions* (pp. 128–136). Hillsdale, NJ: Erlbaum.

Carpenter, P. A., & Just, M. A. (1981). *Spatial ability: An information-processing approach to psychometrics*. Unpublished manuscript, Carnegie-Mellon University.

Cattell, R. B. (1971). *Abilities: Their structure, growth, and action*. Boston: Houghton Mifflin.

Chipman, S., Brush, L., & Wilson, D. (1985). *Women and mathematics: Balancing the equation*. New York: Erlbaum.

Cohen, J. (1977). *Statistical power analogies for the behavioral sciences* (2d ed.). New York: Academic Press.

Connor, J. M., Schackman, M., & Serbin, L. A. (1978). Sex-related differences in response to practice on a visual-spatial test and generalization to a related test. *Child Development*, **49**, 24–29.

Cooper, L. A. (1975). Mental rotation of random two-dimensional shapes. *Cognitive Psychology*, **7**, 20–43.

Cooper, L. A. (1983, April). Spatial information processing: The nature of strategic variation. In M. J. Farr (Chair), *Individual differences in spatial ability and information processing*. Symposium conducted at the annual meeting of the American Educational Research Association, Montreal.

Cooper, L. A., & Regan, D. T. (1982). Attention, perception, and intelligence. In R. J. Sternberg (Ed.), *Handbook of human intelligence* (pp.

123–169). New York: Cambridge University Press.

Cooper, L. A., & Shepard, R. N. (1973). The time required to prepare for a rotated stimulus. *Memory and Cognition,* 1, 246–250.

Corballis, M. C., & Roldan, C. E. (1975). Detection of symmetry as a function of angular orientation: Human perception and performance. *Journal of Experimental Psychology,* 1, 221–230.

Corballis, M. C., Zbrodoff, J., & Roldan, C. E. (1976). What's up in mental rotation? *Perception and Psychophysics,* 19, 525–530.

Cordua, G. D., McGraw, K. O., & Drabman, R. S. (1979). Doctor or nurse: Children's perception of sex typed occupations. *Child Development,* 50, 590–593.

Corely, R. P., DeFries, J. C., Kuse, A. R., & Vandenberg, S. G. (1980). Familial resemblance for the Identical Blocks Test of spatial ability: No evidence for X linkage. *Behavior Genetics,* 10, 211–215.

DeAvila, E. A., Havassy, B., & Pascual-Leone, J. (1976). *Mexican-American school children: A neo-Piagetian analysis.* Washington, DC: Georgetown University Press.

de-Benedictis, T., Delucchi, K., Harris, A., Linn, M., & Stage, E. (1982, March). Sex differences in science: "I don't know." In M. L. Maehr (Chair), *Sex-related differences in science.* Symposium conducted at the meeting of the American Educational Research Association, New York.

DeFries, J. C., Ashton, G. C., Johnson, R. C., Kuse, A. R., McClearn, G. E., Mi, M. P., Rashad, M. N., Vandenberg, S. G., & Wilson, J. R. (1976). Parent off-spring resemblance for specific cognitive abilities in two ethnic groups. *Nature,* 261, 131–133.

DeFries, J. C., Vandenberg, S. G., McClearn, G. E., Kuse, A. R., Wilson, J. R., Ashton, G. C., & Johnson, R. C. (1974). Near identity of cognitive structure in two ethnic groups. *Science,* 183, 338–339.

Dichgans, J., Young, L. R., & Brandt, T. (1972). Moving visual scenes influence the apparent direction of gravity. *Science,* 178, 1217–1219.

Fennema, E., & Sherman, J. (1977). Sex-related differences in mathematics achievement, spatial visualization and affective factors. *American Educational Research Journal,* 14, 51–71.

Fennema, E. H., & Sherman, J. A. (1978). Sex-related differences in mathematics achievement and related factors: A further study. *Journal of Research in Mathematics Education,* 9, 189–203.

Fooman, B. R. (1979, February). *4 year olds' performance on Piaget's water level task: The contribution of maturation and experience.* Paper presented at the Ninth Annual International

Interdisciplinary University Affiliated Professionals Conference on Piagetian Theory and Its Implications for the Helping Professions, University of Southern California.

Fralley, J. S., Eliot, J., & Dayton, C. M. (1978). Further study of the X-linked recessive gene hypotheses for inheritance of spatial abilities. *Perceptual and Motor Skills,* 47, 1023–1029.

French, J. W. (1951). The description of aptitude and achievement tests in terms of rotated factors. *Psychometric Monographs,* 5.

French, J. W., Ekstrom, R. B., & Price, L. A. (1963). *Manual for kit of reference tests for cognitive factors* (rev. ed.). Princeton, NJ: Educational Testing Service.

Fruchter, B. (1954). Measurement of spatial abilities: History and background. *Educational and Psychological Measurement,* 14, 387–395.

Glass, G. V. (1976). Primary, secondary, and meta-analysis of research. *Educational Researcher,* 5, 3–8.

Glass, G., McGaw, B., & Smith, M. L. (1981). *Meta-analysis in social research.* Beverly Hills, CA: Sage.

Goodenough, D. R., Gandini, E., Olkin, I., Pizzamiglio, L., Thayer, D., & Witkin, H. A. (1977). A study of X chromosome linkage with field dependence and spatial visualization. *Behavior Genetics,* 7, 373–413.

Goodenough, D. R., Oltman, P. K., & Cox, P. W. (1984). *The nature of individual differences in field dependence.* Princeton, NJ: Educational Testing Service.

Guay, R. B., & McDaniel, E. D. (1977). The relationship of mathematical achievement and spatial abilities among elementary school children. *Journal of Research in Mathematics Education,* 8, 211–215.

Guilford, J. P. (1969). *The nature of human intelligence.* New York: McGraw-Hill.

Harris, L. J. (1982). Sex related variations in spatial skill. In L. S. Liben, A. H. Patterson, & N. Newcombe (Eds.), *Spatial representation and behavior across the life span* (pp. 83–128). New York: Academic Press.

Harris, L. J., Hanley, C., & Best, C. T. (1978). Conservation of horizontality: Sex differences in sixth graders and college students. In M. S. Smart & R. C. Smart (Eds.), *Adolescence: Development and relationships* (pp. 95–107). New York: Macmillan.

Hartlage, L. C. (1970). Sex-linked inheritance of spatial ability. *Perceptual and Motor Skills,* 31, 610.

Haugh, S. S., Hoffman, C. D., & Cowan, G. (1980). The eye of a very young beholder: Sex typing of infants by young children. *Child Development,* 51, 598–600.

Hedges, L. V. (1982a). Fitting categorical models to effect sizes from a series of experiments. *Journal of Educational Statistics,* 7, 119–137.

1496   Child Development

Hedges, L. V. (1982b). Fitting continuous models to effect size data. *Journal of Educational Statistics*, **7**, 245–270.

Hedges, L. V., & Olkin, I. (1980). Vote counting methods in research synthesis. *Psychological Bulletin*, **88**, 359–369.

Herbst, L., & Petersen, A. C. (1979, November). *Timing of maturation, brain lateralization, and cognitive performance in adolescent females*. Paper presented at the meeting of the Fifth Annual Conference on Research on Women and Education, Cleveland, OH.

Hines, M., & Shipley, C. (1984). Prenatal exposure to diethylstilbestrol (DES) and the development of sexually dimorphic cognitive abilities and cerebral lateralization. *Developmental Psychology*, **20**, 81–94.

Horn, J. L., & Cattell, R. B. (1966). Refinement and test of the theory of fluid and crystallized general intelligences. *Journal of Educational Psychology*, **57**(5), 253–270.

Hyde, J. S. (1981). How large are cognitive gender differences? A meta-analysis using w and d. *American Psychologist*, **36**, 892–901.

Hyde, J. S., & Linn, M. C. (in press). *The psychology of gender: Advances through meta-analysis*. Baltimore: Johns Hopkins University Press.

Inhelder, B., & Piaget, J. (1958). *The growth of logical thinking from childhood to adolescence*. New York: Basic.

Just, M. A., & Carpenter, P. A. (1976). Eye fixations and cognitive processes. *Cognitive Psychology*, **8**, 441–480.

Kail, R., Carter, P., & Pellegrino, J. (1979). The locus of sex differences in spatial ability. *Perception and Psychophysics*, **26**, 182–186.

Karplus, R., Pulos, S., & Stage, E. K. (1980, August). Early adolescents' structure of proportional reasoning. In R. Karplus (Ed.), *Proceedings of the Fourth International Conference for the Psychology of Mathematics Education* (pp. 136–142). Berkeley: University of California.

Kreinberg, N., & Stage, E. K. (1981, April). *The equals teacher education program*. Paper presented at the annual meeting of the American Educational Research Association, Los Angeles.

Kuechenmeister, C. A., Linton, P. H., Mueller, T. V., & White, H. B. (1977). Eye tracking in relation to age, sex, and illness. *Archives of General Psychiatry*, **34**, 578–579.

Kyllonen, P. C., Lohman, D. F., & Snow, R. E. (1984). Effects of aptitudes, strategy training, and task facets on spatial task performance. *Journal of Educational Psychology*, **76**, 130–145.

Kyllonen, P. C., Woltz, D. J., & Lohman, D. F. (1981). Models of strategy and strategy-shifting in spatial visualization performance (Technical Report No. 17). Stanford, CA: Stanford University, School of Education, Aptitude Research Project. (NTIS No. AD-A108003)

Liben, L. S., & Golbeck, S. L. (1980). Sex differences in performance on Piagetian spatial tasks: Differences in competence or performance? *Child Development*, **51**, 594–597.

Liben, L. S., & Golbeck, S. L. (1984). Performance on Piagetian horizontality and verticality tasks: Sex-related differences in knowledge of relevant physical phenomena. *Developmental Psychology*, **20**, 595–606.

Liben, L. S., Patterson, A. H., & Newcombe, N. (Eds.). (1981). *Spatial representation and behavior across the life span: Theory and application*. New York: Academic Press.

Linn, M. C., (in press). Meta-analysis of studies of gender differences: Implications and future directions. In J. Hyde & M. C. Linn (Eds.), *The psychology of gender: Advances through meta-analysis*. Baltimore: Johns Hopkins University Press.

Linn, M. C., & Delucchi, K. (1983). *The water level: Influences of task features on gender differences in performance*. Berkeley: University of California, Berkeley, Lawrence Hall of Science, Adolescent Reasoning Project.

Linn, M. C., & Kyllonen, P. (1981). The field dependency construct: Some, one, or none. *Journal of Educational Psychology*, **73**, 261–273.

Linn, M. C., & Petersen, A. C. (in press). Gender differences in spatial ability: Implications for mathematics and science performance. In J. Hyde & M. C. Linn (Eds.), *The psychology of gender: Advances through meta-analysis*. Baltimore: Johns Hopkins University Press.

Linn, M. C., & Pulos, S. (1982). Aptitude and experience influences on proportional reasoning during adolescence: Focus on male-female differences. *Journal of Research in Mathematics Education*, **14**, 30–46.

Linn, M. C., & Pulos, S. (1983). Male-female differences in predicting displaced volume strategy usage, aptitude relationships, and experience influences. *Journal of Educational Psychology*, **75**, 86–96.

Loehlin, J. C., Sharan, S., & Jacoby, R. (1978). In pursuit of the "spatial gene": A family study. *Behavior Genetics*, **8**, 27–41.

Lohman, D. F. (1979). *Spatial ability: A review and re-analysis of the correlational literature* (Technical Report No. 8). Stanford CA: Stanford University, School of Education, Aptitude Research Project. (NTIS No. AD-A075972)

Maccoby, E. E. (Ed.). (1966). *The development of sex differences*. Stanford, CA: Stanford University Press.

Maccoby, E. E., & Jacklin, C. N. (1974). *The psychology of sex differences*. Stanford, CA: Stanford University Press.

Malone, M. R., & Fleming, M. L. (1983, May). The relationship of student characteristics and student performance in science as viewed by meta-analysis research. *Journal of Research in Science Teaching, 20*(5), 481–495.

McGee, M. G. (1978). Intrafamilial correlations and heritability estimates for spatial ability in a Minnesota sample. *Behavior Genetics, 8,* 77–80.

McGee, M. G. (1979). Human spatial abilities: Psychometric studies and environmental, genetic, hormonal, and neurological influences. *Psychological Bulletin, 86,* 899–918.

Meehan, A. M. (1984). A meta-analysis of sex differences in formal operational thought. *Child Development, 55,* 1110–1124.

Metzler, J., & Shepard, R. N. (1974). Transformational studies of the internal representation of three-dimensional objects. In R. L. Solso (Ed.), *Theories of cognitive psychology: The Loyola symposium* (pp. 147–202). Potomac, MD: Erlbaum.

Newcombe, N., Bandura, M., & Taylor, D. G. (1983). Sex differences in spatial ability and spatial activities. *Sex Roles, 9,* 377–386.

Papalia, D. E., & Tennent, S. S. (1975). Vocational aspirations in preschoolers: A manifestation of early sex-role stereo-typing. *Sex Roles, 1,* 197–199.

Petersen, A. C. (1976). Physical androgyny and cognitive functioning in adolescence. *Developmental Psychology, 12,* 524–533.

Petersen, A. C. (1980). Biopsychosocial processes in the development of sex-related differences. In J. Parsons (Ed.), *The psychobiology of sex differences and sex roles* (pp. 31–55). Washington, DC: Hemisphere.

Petersen, A. C. (1983). Pubertal change and cognition. In J. Brooks-Gunn & A. C. Petersen (Eds.), *Girls at puberty: Biological and psychosocial perspectives* (pp. 179–198). New York: Plenum.

Petersen, A. C., & Gitelson, I. B. (in press). *Toward understanding sex-related differences in cognitive performance.* New York: Academic Press.

Petersen, A. C., & Taylor, B. C. (1980). The biological approach to adolescence: Biological change and psychological adaptations. In J. Adelson (Ed.), *Handbook of adolescent psychology* (pp. 117–155). New York: Wiley.

Piaget, J., & Inhelder, B. (1967). *The child's conception of space* (pp. 375–418). New York: Norton.

Pillemer, D. B., & Light, R. J. (1980, May). Synthesizing outcomes: How to use research evidence from many studies. *Harvard Educational Review, 50*(2), 176–195.

Plomin, R., & Foch, T. T. (1982). Sex differences and individual differences. *Child Development, 52,* 383–385.

Pylsyshyn, Z. W. (1979). The rate of "mental rotation" of images: A test of a holistic analogue hypothesis. *Memory and Cognition, 7,* 19–28.

Pylsyshyn, Z. W. (1981). The imagery debate: Analogue media versus tactic knowledge. *Psychological Review, 87,* 16–45.

Reinisch, J. M., Gandelman, R., & Spiegal, F. S. (1979). Prenatal influences on cognitive abilities: Data from experimental animals and human genetic and endocrine syndromes. In M. S. Wittig & A. C. Petersen (Eds.), *Sex-related differences in cognitive functioning: Developmental issues* (pp. 215–239). New York: Academic Press.

Roach, D. H. (1979). The effects of conceptual style preference, related cognitive variables, and sex on achievement in mathematics. *British Journal of Educational Psychology, 49,* 79–82.

Rosenthal, R. (1979). The "file drawer problem" and tolerance for null results. *Psychological Bulletin, 86,* 638–641.

Rosser, R. (1980). Acquisition of spatial concepts in relation to age and sex (Final Report on Grant No. NIE-6-79-0091 from the National Institute of Education, Department of Education). Tucson: University of Arizona.

Shepard, R. N., & Cooper, L. A. (1982). *Mental images and their transformations.* Cambridge: Massachusetts Institute of Technology.

Shepard, R. N., & Feng, C. (1972). A chronometric study of mental paper folding. *Cognitive Psychology, 3,* 228–243.

Shepard, R. N., & Metzler, J. (1971). Mental rotation of three-dimensional objects. *Science, 171,* 701–703.

Sigman, E., Goodenough, D. R., & Flanagan, M. (1978). Subjective estimates of body tilt and the rod-and-frame test. *Perceptual and Motor Skills, 47,* 1051–1056.

Sigman, E., Goodenough, D. R., & Flanagan, M. (1979). Instructions, illusory self-tilt and the rod-and-frame test. *Quarterly Journal of Experimental Psychology, 31,* 155–165.

Smith, I. (1964). *Spatial Ability.* London: University of London Press.

Snow, R. E., Kyllonen, P. C., & Marshalek, B. (in press). The topography of ability and learning correlations. In R. J. Sternberg (Ed.), *Advances in the psychology of human intelligence* (Vol. 2). Hillsdale, NJ: Erlbaum.

Spuhler, K. P., & Vandenberg, S. G. (1980). Comparison of parent-offspring resemblance in specific cognitive abilities. *Behavior Genetics, 10,* 413–418.

Stafford, R. E. (1961). Sex differences in spatial visualization as evidence of sex-linked inheritance. *Perceptual and Motor Skills, 13,* 428.

Steinkamp, M. W., & Maehr, M. L. (1983). Affect, ability, and science achievement: A quantita-

1498   Child Development

tive synthesis of correlational research. *Review of Educational Research*, **53**(3), 369–396.

Sternberg, R. J. (1982). Reasoning, problem solving, and intelligence. In *Handbook of human intelligence* (pp. 227–351). Cambridge: Cambridge University Press.

Sternberg, R. J., & Weil, E. M. (1980). An aptitude-strategy interaction in linear syllogistic reasoning. *Journal of Educational Psychology*, **72**, 226–234.

Strauss, E., & Kinsbourne, M. (1981). Does age of menarche affect the ultimate level of verbal and spatial skills? *Cortex*, **17**, 323–325.

Tapley, S. M., & Bryden, M. P. (1977). An investigation of sex differences in spatial ability: Mental rotation of three-dimensional objects. *Canadian Journal of Psychology*, **31**, 122–130.

Thomas, H., & Jamison, W. (1975). On the acquisition of understanding that still water is horizontal. *Merrill-Palmer Quarterly*, **21**, 31–44.

Thomas, H., & Jamison, W. (1981). A test of the X-linked genetic hypothesis for sex differences on Piaget's water-level task. *Developmental Review*, **1**, 274–283.

Thurstone, L. L., & Thurstone, T. G. (1941). Factorial studies of intelligence. *Psychometric Monographs*, **2**.

Tobin-Richards, M. H., & Petersen, A. C. (1981, August). *Spatial and sex-appropriate activities: Spatial visual ability during adolescence.* Paper presented at the meetings of the American Psychological Association, Los Angeles.

Vandenberg, S. G., & Kuse, A. R. (1978). Mental rotations: A group test of three-dimensional spatial visualization. *Perceptual and Motor Skills*, **47**, 599–604.

Vandenberg, S. G., & Kuse, A. R. (1979). Spatial ability: A critical review of the sex-linked major gene hypothesis. In M. A. Wittig & A. C. Petersen (Eds.), *Sex-related differences in cognitive functioning: Developmental issues* (pp. 67–95). New York: Academic Press.

Vernon, P. E. (1965). Ability factors and environmental influences. *American Psychologist*, **20**, 723–733.

Waber, D. P. (1976). Sex differences in cognition: A

function of maturation rate? *Science*, **192**, 572–574.

Waber, D. P. (1977). Sex differences in mental abilities, hemispheric lateralization, and rate of physical growth at adolescence. *Developmental Psychology*, **13**, 29–38.

Waber, D. P. (1979). The ontogeny of higher cortical functions: Implications for sex differences in cognition. In M. A. Wittig & A. C. Petersen (Eds.), *Sex-related differences in cognitive functioning: Developmental issues* (pp. 161–186). New York: Academic Press.

Waber, D. P., Bauermeister, M., Cohen, C., Ferber, R., & Wolff, P. H. (1981). Behavioral correlates of physical and neuromotor maturity in adolescence from different environments. *Developmental Psychobiology*, **14**(6), 513–522.

Walker, J. T., Krasnoff, A. G., & Peaco, D. (1981). Visual spatial perception in adolescents and their parents: The X-linked recessive hypothesis. *Behavior Genetics*, **11**, 403–413.

Wheeler, R., & Harris, B. (1981). *Comparison of male and female performance on the AP physics test.* New York: College Entrance Examination Board.

Wilson, J. R., & Vandenberg, S. G. (1978). Sex differences in cognition: Evidence from the Hawaii family study. In T. E. McGill, D. A. Dewsbury, & B. D. Sachs (Eds.), *Sex and behavior: Stages and prospectus* (pp. 317–335). New York: Plenum.

Witkin, H. A. (1949). The nature and importance of individual differences in perception. *Journal of Personality*, **18**, 145–170.

Witkin, H. A., Dyk, R. B., & Faterson, H. F. (1962). *Psychological differentiation.* New York: Wiley.

Witkin, H. A., & Goodenough, D. R. (1981). *Cognitive styles: Essence and origins.* New York: International Universities Press.

Wittig, M. A., & Petersen, A. C. (Eds.). (1979). *Sex-related differences in cognitive functioning: Developmental issues.* New York: Academic Press.

Yen, W. M. (1975). Sex-linked major-gene influences on selected types of spatial performance. *Behavior Genetics*, **5**, 281–298.

[16]

Psychological Bulletin
1990, Vol. 107, No. 2, 139–155

Gender Differences in Mathematics Performance: A Meta-Analysis

Janet Shibley Hyde, Elizabeth Fennema, and Susan J. Lamon
University of Wisconsin—Madison

Reviewers have consistently concluded that males perform better on mathematics tests than females do. To make a refined assessment of the magnitude of gender differences in mathematics performance, we performed a meta-analysis of 100 studies. They yielded 254 independent effect sizes, representing the testing of 3,175,188 Ss. Averaged over all effect sizes based on samples of the general population, d was −0.05, indicating that females outperformed males by only a negligible amount. For computation, d was −0.14 (the negative value indicating superior performance by females). For understanding of mathematical concepts, d was −0.03; for complex problem solving, d was 0.08. An examination of age trends indicated that girls showed a slight superiority in computation in elementary school and middle school. There were no gender differences in problem solving in elementary or middle school; differences favoring men emerged in high school ($d = 0.29$) and in college ($d = 0.32$). Gender differences were smallest and actually favored females in samples of the general population, grew larger with increasingly selective samples, and were largest for highly selected samples and samples of highly precocious persons. The magnitude of the gender difference has declined over the years; for studies published in 1973 or earlier d was 0.31, whereas it was 0.14 for studies published in 1974 or later. We conclude that gender differences in mathematics performance are small. Nonetheless, the lower performance of women in problem solving that is evident in high school requires attention.

During the past 15 years, there has been much concern about women and mathematics. Since Lucy Sells (1973) identified mathematics as the "critical filter" that prevented many women from having access to higher paying, prestigious occupations, there has been much rhetoric and many investigations focused on gender differences in mathematics performance.

Particularly within the fields of psychology and education, gender differences in mathematics performance have been studied intensively, and there has been some consensus on the pattern of differences. Anastasi (1958), in her classic differential psychology test, stated that although differences in numerical aptitude favored boys, these differences did not appear until well into the elementary school years. Furthermore, she stated that if gender differences in computation did appear, they favored females, whereas males excelled on tests of numerical reasoning. Concurring with this, Maccoby and Jacklin (1974) concluded that one of four sex differences that "were fairly well established" was that "boys excel in mathematical ability" (p. 352). They also noted that there were few sex differences until about ages 12–13, when boys' "mathematical skills increase faster than girls' " (p. 352).

This research was supported by National Science Foundation Grant MDR 8709533. The opinions expressed are our own and not those of the National Science Foundation.

We thank Marilyn Ryan for her assistance in conducting the meta-analysis. We thank researchers at the Educational Testing Service, especially Carol Dwyer and Eldon Park, for their help in providing Educational Testing Service data.

Correspondence concerning this article should be addressed to Janet Shibley Hyde, Department of Psychology, Brogden Psychology Building, University of Wisconsin, Madison, Wisconsin 53706.

Most recently, Halpern (1986) concluded that "the finding that males outperform females in tests of quantitative or mathematical ability is robust" (p. 57). She stated that the differences emerge reliably between 13–16 years of age.

The literature in education has reported conclusions that are basically in agreement with the psychological literature. In 1974, Fennema reviewed published studies and concluded that

> No significant differences between boys' and girls' mathematics achievement were found before boys and girls entered elementary school or during early elementary years. In upper elementary and early high school years significant differences were not always apparent. However, when significant differences did appear they were more apt to be in the boys' favor when higher-level cognitive tasks were being measured and in the girls' favor when lower-level cognitive tasks were being measured. (Fennema, 1974, pp. 136–137)

In the Fennema review, no conclusions were made about high school learners because of the scarcity of studies of subjects of that age. However, a few years later, Fennema and Carpenter (1981) reported that the National Assessment of Educational Progress showed that there were gender differences in high school, with males outperforming females, particularly in high cognitive-level tasks. This conclusion has been reported by each succeeding National Assessment (Meyer, in press).

Stage, Kreinberg, Eccles, and Becker (1985), in a thorough review of the major studies that had been reported up to 1985, concluded that

> The following results are fairly consistent across studies using a variety of achievement tests: 1) high school boys perform a little better than high school girls on tests of mathematical reasoning (primarily solving word problems); 2) boys and girls perform similarly on tests of algebra and basic mathematical knowledge; and 3) girls occasionally outperform boys on tests of computational skills. . . . Among normal populations, achievement differences favoring

boys do not emerge with any consistency prior to the 10th grade, are typically not very large, and are not universally found, even in advanced high school populations. There is some evidence, however, that the general pattern of sex differences may emerge somewhat earlier among gifted and talented students. (p. 240)

Thus, although there are some variations, there is a consensus that, overall, gender differences in mathematics performance have existed in the past and are still present. Global conclusions tend to assert simply that males outperform females on mathematics tests. More refined discussions generally conclude that the overall differences in mathematics performance are not apparent in early childhood; they appear in adolescence and usually favor boys in tasks involving high cognitive complexity (problem solving) and favor girls in tasks of less complexity (computation).

Theoretical Models of Gender and Mathematics Performance

Theoretical models concerning gender and mathematics performance generally begin with the assumption that males outperform females in mathematics. The models are designed to explain the causes of that phenomenon. For example, Eccles and her colleagues (e.g., Eccles, 1987; Meece, [Eccles] Parsons, Kaczala, Goff, & Futterman, 1982) have built an Expectation × Value model to explain differential selection of mathematics courses in high school. Fennema and Peterson (1985) proposed an autonomous learning behavior model that suggested that failure to participate in independent learning in mathematics contributes to the development of gender differences in mathematics performance. Others have proposed biological theories focusing, for example, on brain lateralization (reviewed by Halpern, 1986).

This model building may be premature because the basic phenomenon that the models seek to explain—the gender difference in mathematics performance—is in need of reassessment, using the modern tools of meta-analysis.

Meta-Analysis and Psychological Gender Differences

The reviews cited previously have all used the method of *narrative review.* That is, the reviewers located studies of gender differences, organized them in some fashion, and reported their conclusions in narrative form. The narrative review, however, has been criticized on several grounds: It is nonquantitative, unsystematic, and subjective, and the task of reviewing 100 or more studies simply exceeds the human mind's information-processing capacity (Hunter, Schmidt, & Jackson, 1982).

Meta-analysis has been defined as the application of "quantitative methods to combining evidence from different studies" (Hedges & Olkin, 1985, p. 13). In the 1980s, meta-analysis began to make important contributions to the literature on psychological gender differences (e.g., Hyde & Linn, 1986). Hyde (1981) performed a meta-analysis on the 16 studies of quantitative ability of subjects aged 12 or older that were included in Maccoby and Jacklin's (1974) review (12 being the age at which Maccoby and Jacklin concluded that the sexes begin to diverge in mathematics performance). Hyde found a median effect size of .43 and noted that this difference was not as large as one

might have expected given the widely held view that the difference is well established.

The Hyde (1981) meta-analysis included only studies reported through 1973, and thus there is a need to update it with recent research. Furthermore, the median value of *d* was computed on the basis of only seven values. In addition, statistical methods have advanced considerably since the time of the Hyde review. Hedges and his colleagues have developed homogeneity statistics that allow one to determine whether a group of studies is uniform in its outcomes (Hedges & Olkin, 1985; Rosenthal & Rubin, 1982a). Applied to the topic of gender differences in mathematics performance, these statistical techniques allow one to determine whether the magnitude of the gender difference varies according to the cognitive level of the task, the age group, and so on. Thus, modern techniques of meta-analysis can answer considerably more sophisticated questions than could the earlier meta-analyses and certainly more than could earlier narrative reviews.

Current Study

We performed a meta-analysis of studies of gender differences in mathematics performance. Our goal was to provide answers to the following questions:

1. What is the magnitude of gender differences in mathematics performance, using the *d* metric? We were chiefly interested in answering this question for the general population. However, we also provide analyses for selective samples.

2. Does the magnitude or direction of the gender difference vary as a function of the cognitive level of the task?

3. Does the magnitude or direction of the gender difference vary as a function of the mathematics content of the test (arithmetic, geometry, algebra, and so on)?

4. Developmentally, at what ages do gender differences appear or disappear, and for what cognitive levels?

5. Are there variations across ethnic groups in the magnitude or direction of the gender difference?

6. Does the magnitude of the gender difference vary depending on the selectivity of the sample, whether the sample is of the general population or of a population that is selected for high performance?

7. Has the magnitude of gender differences in mathematics performance increased or declined over the years?

Method

Sample of Studies

The sample of studies came from seven sources: (a) a computerized data base search of PsycINFO for the years 1967–1987, using the key terms *human–sex–differences* crossed with (*mathematics* or *mathematics-concepts* or *mathematics-achievement* or *standardized tests*), which yielded 198 citations; (b) a computerized data base search of ERIC, using the key terms *sex-differences* crossed with (*mathematics* or *mathematics achievement* or *mathematics-tests*), which yielded 435 citations; (c) inspection of all articles in *Journal for Research in Mathematics Education* and *Educational Studies in Mathematics;* (d) the bibliography of Maccoby and Jacklin (1974); (e) the bibliography of Fennema (1974); (f) norming data from widely used standardized tests; and (g) state assessments of mathematics performance.

In the case of the computerized literature searches, abstracts were printed for each citation. The abstracts were inspected, and citations that did not promise to yield relevant data (e.g., review articles or nonempirical articles) were excluded. All relevant articles were photocopied. Doctoral dissertations were obtained through interlibrary loan and were then inspected for the data necessary to compute effect sizes.

Only studies reporting psychometrically developed mathematics tests were included. Specifically, we excluded studies using Piagetian measures (e.g., the concept of conservation of number) because they assess a much different construct than do standardized tests. Grades, too, were excluded because they may measure a different construct, and because they are assigned more subjectively and may therefore be more subject to bias than are standardized tests. (See Kimball, 1989, for a review of gender differences in classroom grades; girls consistently outperform boys in mathematics grades.)

If an article appeared to have relevant data but the data were not presented in a form that permitted computation of an effect size, a letter was sent to the author at the address specified for reprints or at a more recent address found in the American Psychological Association *Membership Register* or the American Educational Research Association *Directory.*

Large-sample, normative data were obtained for the following widely used tests: American College Testing Program test (ACT), Graduate Management Admissions Test (GMAT), Scholastic Aptitude Test (SAT-Q), SAT Mathematics Level 1 and Level 2, Differential Aptitude Test (DAT), Graduate Record Examination (GRE-Q), GRE-Mathematics, California Achievement Test, and the Iowa Test of Basic Skills (ITBS).[1] Data from the National Assessment of Educational Progress (NAEP; Dossey, Mullis, Lindquist, & Chambers, 1988) were also included.

To obtain data from additional large-scale assessments, a letter was sent to one official of each state department of education and of the departments of education of the District of Columbia and the Canadian provinces of Manitoba, Nova Scotia, Ontario, and Saskatchewan (based on the 1987–1988 membership list of the Association of State Supervisors of Mathematics), for a total of 55 letters. There were 29 responses, and nine states provided usable data: Alabama, Connecticut, Michigan, North Carolina, Oregon, Pennsylvania, South Carolina, Texas, and Wisconsin.

It is possible to obtain several independent effect sizes from a single article if, for example, data from several age groups (in a cross-sectional design) or several ethnic groups are reported. These groups can essentially be regarded as separate samples (Hedges, 1987, personal communication).

The result was 100 usable sources, yielding 259 independent effect sizes. This represents the testing of 3,985,682 subjects (1,968,846 males and 2,016,836 females). When data from the SATs were excluded (for reasons discussed later), there were 254 effect sizes, representing the testing of 3,175,188 subjects (1,585,712 males and 1,589,476 females).

Coding the Studies

For each study, the following information was recorded: (a) all statistics on gender differences in mathematics performance measure(s), including means and standard deviations or t, F, and df; (b) the number of female and male subjects; (c) the cognitive level of the measure (computation,[2] concepts, problem solving, and general–mixed); (d) the mathematics content of the test (arithmetic, algebra, geometry, calculus, and mixed–unreported); (e) the age(s) of the subjects (if the article reported no age but reported "undergraduates" or students in an introductory college course, the age was set equal to 19; if a grade level was reported, 5 years was added to that level to yield the age: e.g., third graders were recorded as 8-year-olds); (f) the ethnicity of the sample (Black, Hispanic, Asian American, American Indian, White, Australian, Canadian, or mixed–unreported); (g) the selectivity of the sample (general samples, such as national samples or classrooms; moderately

selected samples, such as college students or college-bound students; highly selected samples, such as students at highly selective colleges; samples selected for extreme precocity, such as the Study of Mathematically Precocious Youth; samples selected for poor performance, such as Headstart samples, low socioeconomic status samples, or remedial college samples; and adult nonstudent samples); and (h) the year of publication.

Interrater Reliability

Interrater agreement was computed for ratings of ethnicity, sample selectivity, cognitive level of the test, and mathematics content of the test. The formula used was Scott's (1955) pi coefficient, as recommended by Zwick (1988).

Pi was 1.00 for ethnicity, .90 for sample selectivity, .88 for cognitive level, and 1.00 for mathematics content. Thus, these categories were coded with high reliability.

Statistical Analysis

The effect size computed was d, defined as the mean for males minus the mean for females, divided by the mean within-sexes standard deviation. Thus, positive values of d represent superior male performance and negative values represent superior female performance. Depending on the statistics available for a given study, formulas provided by Hedges and Becker (1986) were used for the computation of d and the homogeneity statistics. All effect sizes were computed independently by two researchers, Janet Shibley Hyde and an advanced graduate student. There were discrepancies in fewer than 4% of the d values; these were resolved. All values of d were corrected for bias in estimation of the population effect size, using the formula provided by Hedges (1981). The complete listing of all studies, with effect sizes, is provided in Table 1.

Results

Magnitude of Gender Differences in Mathematics Performance

Averaged over 259 values, the weighted mean effect size was 0.20. When data from the SATs (Ramist & Arbeiter, 1986) were

---

[1] Although we tried to sample broadly over the major standardized tests, the number of these tests is great and it was not feasible to report data for all. In some cases, the test publisher was not able to provide the needed data. In other cases, we did not wish to include too many tests by the same publisher with the same format, thereby weighting those tests too greatly. For example, we include the GMAT but not the Law School Admission Test (LSAT) or the Medical College Admission Test (MCAT). All are published by Educational Testing Service and are similar, in the quantitative portion, in content and format. Furthermore, all include selective samples, although it is difficult to assess the degree of selection for mathematics performance. Therefore, we included the GMAT but not the LSAT or MCAT. Because our major interest was in assessing the magnitude of gender differences in mathematics performance in the general population, inclusion of data from tests (e.g., the MCAT) based on very selective samples was counterproductive.

[2] The definitions of the cognitive levels were as follows: *Computation* refers to a test that requires the use of only algorithmic procedures to find a single numerical answer. *Conceptual* refers to a test that involves analysis or comprehension of mathematical ideas. *Problem solving* refers to a test that involves extending knowledge or applying it to new situations. *Mixed tests* include a combination of items from these categories.

(text continues on page 146)

142   J. HYDE, E. FENNEMA, AND S. LAMON

Table 1
Studies of Gender Differences in Mathematics Performance (in Alphabetical Order)

Study	Mean age	Male subjects	Female subjects	d[a]	Ethnic group[b]	Selectivity of sample[c]	Cognitive level[d]	Mathematics content[e]
Advanced Placement Calculus, 1988 (personal communication, Carol Dwyer, January 20, 1989)	18	31,280	22,115	0.20	6	5	4	4
Alabama Department of Education, 1986–1987	6	34,250	31,336	−0.02	6	1	4	5
Alabama Department of Education, 1986–1987	7	30,419	28,573	−0.03	6	1	4	5
Alabama Department of Education, 1986–1987	9	27,307	26,872	−0.06	6	1	4	5
Alabama Department of Education, 1986–1987	10	25,845	25,095	−0.07	6	1	4	5
Alabama Department of Education, 1986–1987	13	26,657	25,889	−0.02	6	1	4	5
Alabama Department of Education, 1986–1987	15	24,427	25,388	0.00	6	1	4	5
American College Testing Program, 1970 (American College Testing Program, 1987)	18	11,994	11,664	0.36	6	2	4	5
American College Testing Program, 1987	18	356,704	420,740	0.32	6	2	4	5
Backman, 1972	18	1,406	1,519	0.92	6	4	4	5
Behrens & Verron, 1978	12	155	137	−0.12	8	1	4	5
Bell & Ward, 1980	12	31	41	−0.10	6	1	4	5
Benbow & Stanley, 1980	12	90	77	0.41	6	4	4	5
Benbow & Stanley, 1980	14	133	96	0.76	6	4	4	5
Benbow & Stanley, 1980	12	135	88	0.73	6	4	4	5
Benbow & Stanley, 1980	14	286	158	0.54	6	4	4	5
Benbow & Stanley, 1980	12	372	222	0.43	6	4	4	5
Benbow & Stanely, 1980	14	556	369	0.48	6	4	4	5
Benbow & Stanley, 1980	12	495	356	0.46	6	4	4	5
Benbow & Stanley, 1980	13	1,549	1,249	0.44	6	4	4	5
Benbow & Stanley, 1980	13	2,046	1,628	0.39	6	4	4	5
Benbow & Stanley, 1983	12	19,883	19,937	0.37	6	4	4	5
Boli, Allen, & Payne, 1985	18	689	465	0.55	6	3	4	5
Brandon et al., 1985	9	1,237	1,207	−0.10	5	1	3	5
Brandon et al., 1985	11	1,259	1,176	0.02	5	1	3	5
Brandon et al., 1985	13	1,137	1,107	−0.06	5	1	3	5
Brandon et al., 1985	9	891	857	−0.07	3	1	3	5
Brandon et al., 1985	11	1,000	953	−0.11	3	1	3	5
Brandon et al., 1985	13	1,122	1,087	−0.15	3	1	3	5
California Achievement Test (Green, 1987)	6	959	858	−0.02	1	1	1	5
California Achievement Test (Green, 1987)	5	377	419	−0.13	1	1	2	5
California Achievement Test (Green, 1987)	7	1,953	2,001	−0.11	1	1	2	5
California Achievement Test (Green, 1987)	8	476	529	−0.32	1	1	1	5
California Achievement Test (Green, 1987)	9	304	331	−0.16	1	1	2	5
California Achievement Test (Green, 1987)	10	351	389	−0.28	1	1	1	5
California Achievement Test (Green, 1987)	11	369	378	−0.09	1	1	2	5
California Achievement Test (Green, 1987)	12	472	465	−0.38	1	1	1	5
California Achievement Test (Green, 1987)	13	411	402	−0.07	1	1	2	5
California Achievement Test (Green, 1987)	14	283	329	−0.14	1	1	1	5
California Achievement Test (Green, 1987)	15	224	275	−0.08	1	1	2	5
California Achievement Test (Green, 1987)	5	374	367	−0.18	2	1	2	5
California Achievement Test (Green, 1987)	6	553	540	0.09	2	1	1	5
California Achievement Test (Green, 1987)	7	1,316	1,228	0.04	2	1	2	5
California Achievement Test (Green, 1987)	8	280	277	−0.12	2	1	1	5
California Achievement Test (Green, 1987)	9	229	228	−0.23	2	1	2	5
California Achievement Test (Green, 1987)	10	224	212	−0.45	2	1	1	5
California Achievement Test (Green, 1987)	11	217	207	−0.07	2	1	2	5
California Achievement Test (Green, 1987)	12	379	332	−0.15	2	1	1	5
California Achievement Test (Green, 1987)	13	278	314	−0.10	2	1	2	5
California Achievement Test (Green, 1987)	14	188	227	−0.30	2	1	1	5
California Achievement Test (Green, 1987)	15	112	132	0.04	2	1	2	5
California Achievement Test (Green, 1987)	5	2,507	2,425	−0.09	6	1	2	5
California Achievement Test (Green, 1987)	6	3,649	3,377	−0.03	6	1	1	5
California Achievement Test (Green, 1987)	7	7,486	7,353	0.01	6	1	2	5

Table 1 (*continued*)

Study	Mean age	Male subjects	Female subjects	d^a	Ethnic group[b]	Selectivity of sample[c]	Cognitive level[d]	Mathematics content[e]
California Achievement Test (Green, 1987)	8	2,035	1,925	−0.11	6	1	1	5
California Achievement Test (Green, 1987)	9	1,266	1,175	−0.06	6	1	2	5
California Achievement Test (Green, 1987)	10	1,402	1,279	−0.32	6	1	1	5
California Achievement Test (Green, 1987)	11	1,547	1,429	−0.08	6	1	2	5
California Achievement Test (Green, 1987)	12	2,178	1,967	−0.35	6	1	1	5
California Achievement Test (Green, 1987)	13	2,010	1,947	−0.08	6	1	2	5
California Achievement Test (Green, 1987)	14	1,646	1,748	−0.32	6	1	1	5
California Achievement Test (Green, 1987)	15	1,121	1,170	0.05	6	1	2	5
Carrier, Post, & Heck, 1985	9	65	79	−0.43	6	1	1	1
Connecticut Department of Education, 1987	9	15,465	15,462	0.02	6	1	4	5
Connecticut Department of Education, 1987	11	14,504	14,722	−0.02	6	1	4	5
Connecticut Department of Education, 1987	13	15,009	14,919	0.06	6	1	4	5
Connor & Serbin, 1980	12	71	63	0.04	6	1	4	3
Connor & Serbin, 1980	15	108	97	0.23	6	1	4	2
Differential Aptitude Test (Bennett, Seashore, & Wesman, 1979)	13	7,000	6,900	−0.11	6	1	1	1
Differential Aptitude Test (Bennett et al., 1979)	14	7,000	7,350	−0.08	6	1	1	1
Differential Aptitude Test (Bennett et al., 1979)	15	6,400	6,750	0.00	6	1	1	1
Differential Aptitude Test (Bennett et al., 1979)	16	5,350	5,800	0.03	6	1	1	1
Differential Aptitude Test (Bennett et al., 1979)	17	5,000	5,350	0.13	6	1	1	1
D'Augustine, 1966	10	29	31	−0.59	6	1	4	3
D'Augustine, 1966	11	33	27	0.15	6	1	4	3
D'Augustine, 1966	12	34	26	−0.09	6	1	4	3
Davis, 1973	13	45	45	0.81	6	1	3	3
Dees, 1982	15	1,053	962	0.14	6	1	4	3
deWolf, 1981	16	962	1,131	0.38	6	1	3	5
Dick & Balomenos, 1984	19	72	62	0.09	6	2	4	2
Edge & Friedberg, 1984	19	74	51	−0.15	6	2	1	2
Edge & Friedberg, 1984	19	158	207	−0.05	6	2	1	2
Engle & Lerch, 1971	6	67	63	−0.35	6	1	1	1
Ethington & Wolfle, 1986	15	3,610	4,226	0.21	6	1	4	5
Ethington & Wolfle, 1984	18	2,306	2,807	0.27	6	1	4	5
Exezidis, 1982	11	80	80	0.06	5	1	3	5
Exezidis, 1982	11	80	80	−0.11	1	1	3	5
Exezidis, 1982	11	80	80	−0.18	2	1	3	5
Exezidis, 1982	12	80	80	−0.09	5	1	3	5
Exezidis, 1982	12	80	80	−0.15	1	1	3	5
Exezidis, 1982	12	80	80	−0.21	2	1	3	5
Exezidis, 1982	13	80	80	0.00	5	1	2	5
Exezidis, 1982	13	80	80	−0.66	1	1	2	5
Exezidis, 1982	13	80	80	−0.03	2	1	2	5
Fendrich-Salowey, Buchanan, & Drew, 1982	11	12	12	0.18	6	0	1	1
Fennema & Sherman, 1978	11	203	203	0.30	6	1	3	5
Fennema & Sherman, 1978	12	206	225	−0.05	6	1	2	5
Fennema & Sherman, 1978	13	223	260	−0.11	6	1	1	5
Fennema & Sherman, 1977	14	194	219	0.23	6	1	4	5
Fennema & Sherman, 1977	15	181	169	0.35	6	1	4	5
Fennema & Sherman, 1977	16	199	167	0.41	6	1	4	5
Fennema & Sherman, 1977	17	70	34	0.22	6	1	4	5
Ferrini-Mundy, 1987	19	127	122	0.06	6	2	4	2
Flaugher, 1971	16	1,211	1,923	0.29	1	1	4	5
Flaugher, 1971	16	155	151	0.28	5	1	4	5
Flaugher, 1971	16	207	200	0.27	3	1	4	5
Flaugher, 1971	16	512	562	0.49	2	1	4	5
Flaugher, 1971	16	1,120	1,614	0.18	1	1	4	5
Flaugher, 1971	16	864	950	0.33	5	1	4	5
Flexer, 1984	13	61	63	0.18	6	3	1	5
Graduate Management Admission Council, 1987	21	2,952	2,392	0.45	6	3	4	5
Graduate Management Admission Council, 1987	23	25,048	17,687	0.43	6	3	4	5

(*Table continues*)

144   J. HYDE, E. FENNEMA, AND S. LAMON

Table 1 (*continued*)

Study	Mean age	N Male subjects	N Female subjects	d^a	Ethnic group[b]	Selectivity of sample[c]	Cognitive level[d]	Mathematics content[e]
Graduate Management Admission Council, 1987	25	25,855	15,681	0.41	6	3	4	5
Graduate Management Admission Council, 1987	27	19,246	10,078	0.42	6	3	4	5
Graduate Management Admission Council, 1987	29	19,233	8,704	0.44	6	3	4	5
Graduate Management Admission Council, 1987	33	14,088	6,633	0.42	6	3	4	5
Graduate Management Admission Council, 1987	37	8,967	4,570	0.39	6	3	4	5
Graduate Management Admission Council, 1987	45	4,445	2,419	0.51	6	3	4	5
Graduate Management Admission Council, 1987	55	954	397	0.47	6	3	4	5
GRE-Mathematics, 1978 (personal communication, Eldon Park, January 9, 1989)	27	1,813	734	0.77	6	9	3	5
GRE-Q (Educational Testing Service, 1987)	27	92,722	104,922	0.67	6	3	4	5
Hancock, 1975	14	65	54	0.20	6	1	4	5
Hanna, 1986	13	1,773	1,750	0.17	8	1	4	3
Harnisch & Ryan, 1983	17	4,791	4,791	0.06	6	1	4	5
Harris & Romberg, 1974	10	195	196	−0.25	6	1	2	3
Hawn et al., 1981	7	324	272	−0.12	6	1	4	5
Hawn et al., 1981	8	324	301	−0.13	6	1	4	5
Henderson, Landesman, & Kachuck, 1985	15	45	36	−0.28	6	1	4	1
Hilton & Berglund, 1974	16	632	688	0.40	6	3	3	5
Hilton & Berglund, 1974	16	249	290	0.33	6	0	3	5
Howe, 1982	13	40	40	−0.01	6	1	4	5
Iowa Test of Basic Skills, 1984 (Lewis & Hoover, 1987)	7	4,623	4,712	0.00	6	1	1	5
Iowa Test of Basic Skills, 1984 (Lewis & Hoover, 1987)	10	5,088	5,152	0.00	6	1	2	5
Iowa Test of Basic Skills, 1984 (Lewis & Hoover, 1987)	13	5,085	5,148	0.00	6	1	3	5
Iowa Test of Basic Skills, 1978 (Lewis & Hoover, 1987)	8	4,497	4,875	−0.04	6	1	3	5
Jacobs, 1973	12	40	40	0.20	6	1	4	5
Jacobs, 1973	17	40	40	0.67	6	1	4	5
Jarvis, 1964	11	366	347	0.10	6	1	3	1
Jerman, 1973	10	107	133	−0.06	6	1	1	1
Johnson, 1984	19	97	97	0.36	6	2	3	5
Johnson, 1984	19	99	104	0.66	6	2	3	5
Johnson, 1984	19	58	67	0.37	6	2	3	5
Johnson, 1984	19	42	44	0.81	6	2	3	5
Johnson, 1984	19	46	42	0.56	6	2	3	5
Johnson, 1984	19	49	58	0.88	6	2	3	5
Kaczala, 1983	10	50	46	−0.06	6	1	4	5
Kaczala, 1983	11	36	43	−0.47	6	1	4	5
Kaczala, 1983	12	52	53	−0.21	6	1	4	5
Kaczala, 1983	13	46	52	0.20	6	1	4	5
Kaczala, 1983	14	48	45	−0.27	6	1	4	5
Kaplan & Plake, 1982	19	18	76	0.74	6	2	4	5
Kissane, 1986	13	52	46	0.66	7	3	3	5
Kissane, 1986	16	50	20	0.49	7	3	3	5
Kloosterman, 1985	15	63	61	0.24	6	1	2	5
Koffman & Lips, 1980	30	35	35	0.10	6	NA	4	5
Lee & Coffman, 1974	13	76	74	0.09	6	1	4	5
Lee & Coffman, 1974	10	93	61	0.13	6	1	4	5
Leinhardt, Seewald, & Engel, 1979	7	372	354	−0.12	6	1	4	5
Lewis & Hoover, 1983	11	223	234	0.14	6	1	4	5
Lloyd, 1983	10	497	466	0.10	6	1	4	3
Marjoribanks, 1987	11	472	456	0.11	7	1	4	5
Marsh, Smith, & Barnes, 1985	10	422	137	−0.30	7	1	4	5

(*Table continues*)

GENDER DIFFERENCES IN MATHEMATICS PERFORMANCE   145

Table 1 (*continued*)

		N						
Study	Mean age	Male subjects	Female subjects	d[a]	Ethnic group[b]	Selectivity of sample[c]	Cognitive level[d]	Mathematics content[e]
Marshall & Smith, 1987	11	3,750	3,650	−0.12	6	1	1	1
Meyer, 1978	9	97	82	−0.14	6	1	3	5
Michigan Department of Education, 1987	9	2,486	2,479	−0.15	6	1	1	5
Michigan Department of Education, 1987	12	2,391	2,563	−0.09	6	1	1	5
Michigan Department of Education, 1987	15	2,435	2,520	−0.15	6	1	1	5
Mills, 1981	13	42	73	0.18	6	1	4	5
Moore & Smith, 1987	19	316	247	−0.04	1	0	3	1
Moore & Smith, 1987	19	668	553	0.11	5	0	3	1
Moore & Smith, 1987	19	212	207	0.08	2	0	3	1
Moore & Smith, 1987	19	314	365	0.31	1	1	3	1
Moore & Smith, 1987	19	971	1078	0.41	5	1	3	1
Moore & Smith, 1987	19	118	137	0.45	2	1	3	1
Moore & Smith, 1987	19	95	161	0.28	1	2	3	1
Moore & Smith, 1987	19	454	532	0.48	5	2	3	1
Moore & Smith, 1987	19	57	62	0.76	2	2	3	1
Muscio, 1962	11	206	207	0.21	6	1	4	5
National Assessment of Educational Progress [NAEP], 1978 (Dossey, Mullis, Lindquist, & Chambers, 1988)	9	3,688	3,688	−0.08	6	1	4	5
NAEP, 1978 (Dossey et al., 1988)	13	6,052	6,052	−0.03	6	1	4	5
NAEP, 1978 (Dossey et al., 1988)	17	6,689	6,689	0.22	6	1	4	5
NAEP, 1986 (Dossey et al., 1988)	9	1,733	1,733	0.00	6	1	4	5
NAEP, 1986 (Dossey et al., 1988)	13	1,550	1,550	0.07	6	1	4	5
NAEP, 1986 (Dossey et al., 1988)	17	967	967	0.18	6	1	4	5
Newman, 1984	7	82	61	−0.20	6	1	1	1
North Carolina Department of Public Instruction, 1987	8	41,053	38,439	−0.12	6	1	4	5
North Carolina Department of Public Instruction, 1987	11	41,279	38,855	−0.24	6	1	4	5
North Carolina Department of Public Instruction, 1987	13	42,817	40,938	−0.26	6	1	4	5
Oregon Department of Education, 1987	13	1,027	1,028	0.06	6	1	4	5
Parsley, Powell, O'Connor, & Deutsch, 1963	7	379	338	0.00	6	1	4	1
Parsley et al., 1963	8	379	338	0.00	6	1	4	1
Parsley et al., 1963	9	379	383	0.00	6	1	4	1
Parsley et al., 1963	10	379	383	0.00	6	1	4	1
Parsley et al., 1963	11	379	383	0.00	6	1	4	1
Parsley et al., 1963	12	379	338	0.00	6	1	4	1
Parsley et al., 1963	13	379	338	0.00	6	1	4	1
Pattison & Grieve, 1984	15	192	156	0.29	7	1	3	3
Pattison & Grieve, 1984	18	31	11	0.05	7	1	3	3
Pattison & Grieve, 1984	18	91	95	0.33	7	1	3	3
Pederson, Shinedling, & Johnson, 1968	8	12	12	−0.70	6	1	1	1
Pennsylvania Department of Education, 1987	8	52,228	52,150	−0.02	6	1	4	5
Pennsylvania Department of Education, 1987	10	49,851	50,184	−0.06	6	1	4	5
Pennsylvania Department of Education, 1987	13	55,384	54,309	0.00	6	1	4	5
Plake, Ansorge, Parker, & Lowry, 1982	19	26	31	0.53	6	2	4	5
Powell & Steelman, 1983	21	30	21	0.83	6	3	4	5
Randhawa & Hunt, 1987	9	675	654	0.16	8	1	2	5
Randhawa & Hunt, 1987	12	790	706	0.06	8	1	3	5
Randhawa & Hunt, 1987	15	859	900	−0.06	8	1	1	5
Rosenberg & Sutton-Smith, 1969	20	355	658	0.16	6	2	4	5
Saltzen, 1982	7	92	75	−0.13	6	1	1	5
Saltzen, 1982	10	104	80	−0.39	6	1	1	5
Saltzen, 1982	7	76	77	0.08	6	1	2	5
Saltzen, 1982	10	122	144	0.15	6	1	2	5
SAT Mathematics Level 1 (Ramist & Arbeiter, 1986)	18	71,881	76,373	0.40	6	2	4	5
SAT Mathematics Level 2 (Ramist & Arbeiter, 1986)	18	28,890	17,000	0.38	6	2	4	5
Schonberger, 1981	19	34	23	0.48	6	0	2	2
Schratz, 1978	9	20	20	−0.34	2	0	2	5
Schratz, 1978	9	20	20	0.03	1	0	2	5

(*Table continues*)

146   J. HYDE, E. FENNEMA, AND S. LAMON

Table 1 (*continued*)

Study	Mean age	N Male subjects	N Female subjects	d^a	Ethnic group[b]	Selectivity of sample[c]	Cognitive level[d]	Mathematics content[e]
Schratz, 1978	9	20	20	0.08	5	0	2	5
Schratz, 1978	14	20	20	−0.89	2	0	2	5
Schratz, 1978	14	20	20	−0.05	1	0	2	5
Schratz, 1978	14	20	20	0.45	5	0	2	5
Senk & Usiskin, 1983	16	674	690	0.05	6	1	4	3
Senk, 1982	16	266	240	0.04	6	1	3	3
Senk, 1982	16	268	240	0.12	6	1	3	3
Senk, 1982	16	245	261	−0.03	6	1	3	3
Sheehan, 1968	14	57	50	−0.04	6	1	3	2
South Carolina Department of Education, 1987	9	22,531	22,313	−0.26	6	1	1	5
South Carolina Department of Education, 1987	10	21,622	21,076	−0.01	6	1	2	5
South Carolina Department of Education, 1987	12	23,390	22,513	−0.29	6	1	1	5
South Carolina Department of Education, 1987	14	25,559	24,370	−0.04	6	1	2	5
South Carolina Department of Education, 1987	16	18,778	19,627	−0.02	6	1	1	5
Steel, 1978	18	546	621	0.01	6	1	4	5
Swafford, 1980	14	294	329	−0.09	6	1	1	1
Texas Education Agency, 1987	NA	95,168	97,366	0.03	6	1	4	5
Todd, 1985	9	63	60	−0.21	6	1	4	5
Usiskin, 1972	15	87	67	0.33	6	1	2	3
Usiskin, 1972	15	74	75	0.30	6	1	2	3
Verbeke, 1982	13	17	23	−0.49	6	4	4	5
Verbeke, 1982	15	14	12	0.46	6	4	4	5
Verbeke, 1982	16	10	14	0.00	6	4	4	5
Webb, 1984	13	44	33	0.15	6	2	4	5
Weiner, 1983	13	43	27	0.32	6	4	4	5
Whigham, 1985	20	63	54	−0.19	6	2	4	2
Whigham, 1985	20	123	115	−0.05	6	2	4	2
Whigham, 1985	20	88	89	−0.09	6	2	4	3
Whigham, 1985	20	20	26	0.08	6	2	4	4
Wisconsin Department of Public Instruction, 1984	9	871	867	−0.10	6	1	1	5
Wisconsin Department of Public Instruction, 1984	13	783	761	0.06	6	1	2	5
Wisconsin Department of Public Instruction, 1984	17	691	750	−0.17	6	1	1	5
Wozencraft, 1963	8	282	282	−0.23	6	1	3	1
Wozencraft, 1963	11	301	302	−0.15	6	1	1	1
Wrabel, 1985	15	99	103	−0.06	6	1	4	5
Yawkey, 1981	5	48	48	−0.42	6	1	4	1
Zahn, 1966	13	14	13	0.86	6	1	2	1

[a] Positive values reflect better performance by males; negative values reflect better performance by females.
[b] 1 = Black, 2 = Hispanic, 3 = Asian American, 5 = White, 6 = mixed or unreported, 7 = Australian, 8 = Canadian, 9 = American Indian.
[c] 0 = Selected for low performance, 1 = general samples, 2 = moderately selected, 3 = highly selected, 4 = highly precocious samples.
[d] 1 = computation, 2 = understanding of concepts, 3 = problem solving, 4 = mixed or unreported.
[e] 1 = arithmetic, 2 = algebra, 3 = geometry, 4 = calculus, 5 = mixed or unreported.

excluded, the remaining 254 effect sizes yielded a weighted mean *d* of 0.15. In both cases, this small positive value indicates that, overall, males outperformed females by a small amount. When one looks just at samples of the general population, *d* was −0.05, reflecting a superiority in female performance, but of negligible magnitude.

We excluded the SAT data from the remainder of the meta-

analysis for the following reason. The number of subjects in this group was so enormous (810,494) that they accounted for 20% of all subjects and, in a weighted means analysis, they exerted a disproportionate effect. We reserve a separate section of the discussion for the SAT data.

Overall, 131 (51%) of the 259 effect sizes were positive, reflecting superior male performance; 17 (6%) were exactly zero;

Table 2
Magnitude of Gender Differences as a Function of the Cognitive Level of the Test

Cognitive level	k	d	95% confidence interval for d	H
Computation	45	−0.14	−0.14 to −0.13	1,144*
Concepts	41	−0.03	−0.04 to −0.02	118*
Problem solving	48	0.08	0.07 to 0.10	703*
Mixed or unreported	120	0.19	0.18 to 0.19	39,557*

Note. k represents the number of effect sizes; H is the within-groups homogeneity statistic (Hedges & Becker, 1986).
* Significant nonhomogeneity at $p < .05$, according to chi-square test. All other categories are homogeneous.

and 111 (43%) were negative, reflecting superior female performance.

Homogeneity analyses using procedures specified by Hedges and Becker (1986) indicated that the set of 254 effect sizes was significantly nonhomogeneous, $H = 49,001.09$, compared with a critical value of $\chi^2(253) = 300$ (approximation), $p < .0001$. Therefore, we concluded that the set of effect sizes is heterogeneous and we sought to partition the set of studies into more homogeneous subgroups, using factors that we hypothesized would predict effect size. These factors are ones that have previously been shown to be important moderators of gender differences in mathematics performance (e.g., Fennema, 1974; Stage et al., 1985). Subsequently, we performed regression analyses to determine which variables are the best predictors of variations in d.

Cognitive Level

The results of the analysis of effect sizes, arranged according to the cognitive level of the test, are shown in Table 2. As in the overall analysis, the effect sizes are small. There is a slight female superiority in computation, no gender difference in understanding of concepts, and a slight male superiority in problem solving. Oddly, the gender difference for tests with a mixture of cognitive levels (or no report of cognitive level) is largest, although still less than 0.25 standard deviation.

Homogeneity analyses indicate that there are significant differences between the four effect sizes shown in Table 2; the between-groups homogeneity statistic (H_B) was 7,479 compared with a critical $\chi^2(3) = 7.81$. However, it should be noted that the number of subjects and the number of effect sizes in this analysis is so great that small differences can be significant. In the succeeding analyses, H_Bs can be compared to see which between-groups effects are strongest. The cognitive-level effect is a large one compared with the others.

Mathematics Content of the Tests

The analysis according to the mathematics content of the tests was less successful because so many studies failed to report the mathematics content or used tests with a mixture of con-

tent. The results of the analysis are shown in Table 3. They indicate that there was no gender difference in arithmetic or algebra performance. The male superiority in geometry was small (0.13), and the tests with mixed content showed the largest gender difference.

Homogeneity analyses indicated that there was a significant difference between the effect sizes for the different types of math content, $H_B = 548$ compared against a critical $\chi^2(4) = 9.49$. This between-groups difference was smaller than most of the others.

Age Differences

The ages were divided into five subgroups: (a) 5- to 10-year-olds, (b) 11- to 14-year-olds, (c) 15- to 18-year-olds, (d) 19- to 25-year-olds, and (e) those 26 and older. These age groupings were chosen for two reasons. First, they correspond roughly to elementary school, middle or junior high school, high school, college, and adulthood. Second, some reviewers have asserted that there is no gender difference in mathematics performance until the age of 12, when it begins to emerge (e.g., Maccoby & Jacklin, 1974). Other reviewers believe that the difference does not emerge until the last 2 or 3 years of high school (e.g., Meece et al., 1982; Stage et al., 1985). Thus, it was important to have age categories reflecting these two hypotheses.

The results of the analysis for age categories are shown in Table 4. Overall, there was a small female superiority in the elementary and middle school years. There was a more substantial male superiority in the high school years, the college years, and beyond, although this last finding is based on relatively few effect sizes, most of them from the GRE.

Homogeneity analyses indicate that there are significant differences in the magnitude of the gender difference as a function of age group, $H_B = 37,669$ compared with a critical $\chi^2(4) = 9.49$. The age effect is strong.

The results of the analysis of Age × Cognitive Level of the Test interaction are also shown in Table 4. Females were superior in computation in elementary school and middle school, although all differences were small. There was essentially no gender difference at any age level in understanding of mathematical concepts. Problem solving, on the other hand, presents

Table 3
Magnitude of Gender Differences as a Function of the Mathematics Content of the Test

Mathematics content	k	d	95% confidence interval for d	H
Arithmetic	35	0.00	−0.02 to 0.01	368*
Algebra	9	0.02	−0.08 to 0.11	8
Geometry	19	0.13	0.09 to 0.16	47*
Calculus	2	0.20	0.18 to 0.22	0.17
Mixed or unreported	190	0.15	0.15 to 0.15	48,064*

Note. k represents the number of effect sizes; H is the within-groups homogeneity statistic (Hedges & Becker, 1986).
* Significant nonhomogeneity at $p < .05$, according to chi-square test. All other categories are homogeneous.

148   J. HYDE, E. FENNEMA, AND S. LAMON

Table 4
Magnitude of Gender Differences as a Function of Age and Cognitive Level of the Test

Age group	All studies	Cognitive level		
		Computation	Concepts	Problem solving
5–10	−0.06 (67)	−0.20 (30)	−0.02 (33)	0.00 (11)
11–14	−0.07 (93)	−0.22 (38)	−0.06 (28)	−0.02 (21)
15–18	0.29* (53)	0.00 (12)	0.07 (9)	0.29 (10)
19–25	0.41 (31)	NA	NA	0.32 (15)
26 and older	0.59 (9)	NA	NA	NA

Note. NA = not available; there were two or fewer effect sizes, so a mean could not be computed. k is shown in parentheses, where k = number of effect sizes on which the computation of the mean was based.
* Data for the Scholastic Aptitude Test were excluded in the computation of this effect size.

a different picture. There was a slight female superiority or no gender difference in the elementary and middle school groups; however, a moderate gender difference favoring males was found in the high school and college groups.

Ethnicity

The results for the analysis of gender differences as a function of ethnicity are shown in Table 5. Data for the SAT are provided by ethnic group and were coded in that manner for the present meta-analysis. Two effect sizes are provided: d_1 is the mean of all effect sizes including the SAT, and d_2 is the mean of effect sizes excluding the SAT.

When the SAT data were excluded, there was essentially no gender difference in mathematics performance for Blacks, Hispanics, and Asian Americans. Indeed, the 95% confidence inter-

Table 5
Magnitude of Gender Differences as a Function of Ethnicity

Ethnic group	d_1	d_2	H
Black	0.23 (22)	−0.02 (21)	219*
Hispanic	0.30 (21)	0.00 (20)	157*
Asian American	0.29 (5)	−0.09 (4)	15*
White	0.41 (14)	0.13 (13)	152*
Australian	0.11 (7)	0.11 (7)	31*
Canadian	0.09 (5)	0.09 (5)	21*
American Indian	0.44 (1)	NA	
Mixed or unreported	0.15 (184)	0.15 (184)	48,114*

Note. NA = Not available; no effect size was available in this category. d_1 = the mean for all effect sizes, d_2 = the mean effect size excluding Scholastic Aptitude Test (SAT) data, H = homogeneity statistic based on data excluding the SAT. All samples are from the United States unless otherwise indicated. k, the number of effect sizes on which each mean is based, is shown in parentheses.
* Significant nonhomogeneity at $p < .05$ according to chi-square test.

Table 6
Magnitude of the Gender Difference as a Function of the Selectivity of the Sample

Sample	k	d	95% confidence interval for d	H
General	184	−0.05	−0.06 to −0.05	5,461*
Moderately selective	24	0.33	0.33 to 0.34	290*
Highly selective	18	0.54	0.53 to 0.54	1,674*
Precocious	15	0.41	0.39 to 0.43	211*
Selected for low performance	12	0.11	0.04 to 0.18	24*

Note. k represents the number of effect sizes; H is the within-groups homogeneity statistic (Hedges & Becker, 1986).
* Significant nonhomogeneity at $p < .05$, according to chi-square test.

val for d covers 0 for both Blacks and Hispanics. The slight difference for Asian Americans favored females. Only for White Americans was there evidence of superior male performance, and the difference was still small. The mean effect size for American Indians should not be taken too seriously because it is based on a single value.

Homogeneity analyses, using the data set excluding the SAT, indicated that there were significant differences between ethnic groups in the magnitude of the gender difference, H_B = 293 compared with a critical $\chi^2(6)$ = 12.59. Ethnicity was not one of the stronger effects.

Selectivity of the Sample

The analysis for the magnitude of the gender difference as a function of the selectivity of the sample is shown in Table 6. Notice that the gender difference was close to zero (favoring females slightly) for general samples; a larger gender difference favoring males was found for each successive level of selection for higher ability. The gender difference was moderate to large for highly selected samples (d = 0.54) and for samples selected for extreme precocity (d = 0.41). Also note that the great majority of samples (184) in this meta-analysis were general and unselected. Not surprisingly, the greatest heterogeneity of effect sizes was for the general samples.

Homogeneity analyses indicated that there were significant differences in effect size depending on how selective the sample was, H_B = 41,341 compared with a critical $\chi^2(4)$ = 9.49. Sample selectivity was one of the large effects.

When the interaction of sample selectivity and cognitive level was examined, it was apparent that the effects of sample selectivity were found most strongly for problem solving. For such measures, the magnitude of the gender difference varied from 0.02 for general samples to 0.43 for highly selected samples.

Year of Publication

Studies were divided into two subgroups depending on the year of publication: those published in 1973 or earlier and those published after 1973. We chose 1973 as a divider between older studies and more recent ones because it marked the last year that was included in the Maccoby and Jacklin (1974) and Fennema (1974) reviews.

For studies published in 1973 and earlier, d was 0.31, based on 37 effect sizes. For studies published in 1974 or later, d was 0.14, based on 217 effect sizes. Thus, the data show both the increase in research on gender and mathematics and a substantial trend for smaller gender differences in more recent studies.

Regression Analysis

In view of the fact that the first homogeneity analysis indicated that, overall, the set of effect sizes was nonhomogeneous, multiple regression analysis was used to construct a model of the sources of variation in effect sizes (Hedges & Becker, 1986). The effect size was the criterion variable. On the basis of the results of the categorical analyses reported previously, we performed an initial regression analysis using the following predictors: age of subjects, year of publication, ethnicity of sample, selectivity of sample, cognitive level of the test, mathematics content of the test, and the Age × Cognitive Level interaction. The regression analyses were conducted by using the GLM procedure in the SAS statistics program. Repeated regression analyses indicated that the SAT data were having a disproportionate effect on the results, particularly in terms of the strength of the ethnicity variable, because of the large sample size. Thus, the SAT data were deleted in the final multiple regression analysis. In addition, those few studies in which the sample had been selected for poor performance were also deleted, because they did not fit conceptually with the ratings of samples for increasingly greater selectivity for high performance. For the final regression analysis, predictors that were nonsignificant in previous analyses were deleted.

The result was a simple, well-defined equation in which 87% of the variance in d was predicted by three variables: subjects' age, selectivity of the sample, and cognitive level of the test. All three were significant predictors; Age was the strongest predictor, $F(1, 232) = 1,171.04$, $p < .0001$, followed by sample selectivity, $F(3, 232) = 113.22$, $p < .0001$, which was followed by cognitive level, $F(3, 232) = 7.88$, $p < .0001$. (Sample selectivity and cognitive level were coded as class variables.)

Discussion

Averaged over all studies, the mean magnitude of the gender difference in mathematics performance was 0.20. When SAT data were excluded, d was 0.15. The positive value indicates better performance by males on the average, but the magnitude of the effect size is small. Figure 1 shows two normal distributions that are 0.15 standard deviation apart. If one looks only at samples of the general population (excluding selective samples), d was −0.05, indicating a female superiority in performance, but one of negligible magnitude. We can place considerable confidence in these results because they are based on testing literally millions of subjects, on more than 200 effect sizes, and on many well-sampled, large studies such as the state assessments.

These findings are in contrast to the results of Hyde's (1981) earlier meta-analysis, in which she reported a d of 0.43 for quantitative ability. The discrepancy may be accounted for in two ways. First, her computation was based on a small sample of studies taken from the Maccoby and Jacklin (1974) review;

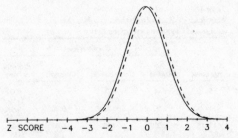

Figure 1. Two normal distributions that are 0.15 standard deviations apart (i.e., $d = 0.15$. This is the approximate magnitude of the gender difference in mathematics performance, averaging over all samples.)

sufficient information was available for the computation of only seven values of d. In addition, to test Maccoby and Jacklin's hypothesis that gender differences in mathematics performance emerge around the age of 12 or 13, only studies with subjects 12 years old or older were included. Using only that set of studies probably produced a larger gender difference than if studies with younger subjects had also been included. Second, the present meta-analysis provides evidence that the magnitude of gender differences has declined over the past three decades. We found that d was 0.31 for studies published in 1973 or earlier and 0.14 for studies published in 1974 or later. Thus, there probably has been a decline in the gender difference since 1973. These findings are consistent with those of Feingold (1988), who documented a decline in the magnitude of gender differences in abilities as measured by several standardized tests.

It is important to recognize that the set of effect sizes is not homogeneous. It is therefore essential to consider variations in the magnitude of the gender difference as a function of the three variables that were significant predictors in the multiple regression analyses: age, selectivity of the sample, and cognitive level of the test.

Age Trends and Cognitive Level

Age trends in the magnitude of the gender difference in mathematics performance are important. Averaging over all studies, there was a slight female superiority in performance in the elementary and middle school years. A moderate male superiority emerged in the high school years ($d = 0.29$) and continued in the college years ($d = 0.41$), as well as in adulthood ($d = 0.59$).

However, the age trends were a function of the cognitive level tapped by the test. Females were superior in computation in elementary and middle school, and the difference was essentially zero in the high school years. The gender difference was essentially zero for understanding of mathematical concepts at all ages for which data were available. It was in problem solving that dramatic age trends emerged. The gender difference in problem solving favored females slightly (effect size essentially zero) in the elementary and middle school years, but in the high school and college years there was a moderate effect size favoring males. These are precisely the years when students are permitted to select their own courses, and females elect somewhat fewer mathematics courses than do males (Meece et al., 1982). Differences in course selection appear to account for some but not all of the gender difference in performance on standardized tests in the high school and college years (Kimball, 1989).

We are puzzled by the fact that tests with mixed or unreported cognitive levels had a slightly larger gender difference (0.19) than tests of problem solving (0.08). One possible explanation is that there may be some feature of the format or administration of these tests, about which we lacked information, that produced a male advantage on the tests. For example, the content of problem-solving items on those tests may have heavy representation of masculine-stereotyped content, which has been shown to produce better performance by males in some studies, although results on the issue are mixed (e.g., Donlon, 1973; Selkow, 1984).

Sample Selectivity

Sample selectivity was one of the three most powerful predictors of effect size in the multiple regression analysis. When all effect sizes (excluding the SAT) were averaged, d was 0.15. Yet when only those 184 effect sizes based on general, unselected populations were averaged, d was -0.05. That is, there was a shift to a slight female advantage, although the difference was essentially zero. The magnitude of the gender difference favoring males grew larger as the sample was more highly selected: d was 0.33 for moderately selected samples (such as college students), 0.54 for highly selected samples (such as students at highly selective colleges, or graduate students), and 0.41 for samples selected for exceptional mathematical precocity.

These findings are very helpful in interpreting the results of Benbow and Stanley's (1980, 1983) study of mathematically precocious youth. Their research has found large gender differences favoring males in mathematics performance, and the results have been widely publicized. Often the secondary reports fail to acknowledge the specialized sampling in the study, implying that the large gender differences are true of the general population. The results of the present meta-analysis demonstrate empirically exactly what would be expected from a consideration of normal distributions (Hyde, 1981): Large gender differences can be found at the extreme tails of distributions even though the gender difference for the entire population is small. Certainly it is important to study gifted populations, but it is essential to remember that results from studies like Benbow and Stanley's do not generalize to the rest of the population.

We must raise one caveat about studies that were coded as unselected samples of the general population. In high school, males have a higher dropout rate than females (Ekstrom, Goertz, Pollack, & Rock, 1986). Dropouts tend to be low scorers, and they are not included in data based on the testing of high school students. Thus, male advantages in performance in high school and later may in part result from the selective loss of low-scoring males from the samples.

The SAT–Math

A recent meta-analysis of gender differences in verbal ability (Hyde & Linn, 1988) indicated that the SAT-Verbal produced idiosyncratic results. The average of all effect sizes yielded a d

of 0.11, indicating a slight female superiority in performance, although the authors concluded that the gender difference had essentially become zero. Yet the SAT-Verbal produced a d of $-.11$ (the negative sign reflecting superior male performance in that meta-analysis). That is, the SAT yielded superior male performance when the pattern over all other tests was a slight female superiority in performance.

The SAT-Math also yielded discrepant results in the present analysis. The overall effect size, excluding the SAT, was 0.15. Yet, according to the data from the 1985 administration of the SAT (Ramist & Arbeiter, 1986), for males the mean was 499 ($SD = 121$), and for females the mean was 452 ($SD = 112$), resulting in a d of .40. That is, the SAT produced a considerably larger gender difference than our overall meta-analysis found. The larger gender difference favoring males on the SAT may be due to several factors:

1. The SAT data are based on a moderately selected sample, those who are college-bound. As we indicated earlier, sample selectivity increases the magnitude of the gender difference. For moderately selected samples excluding the SAT, d was 0.33.

2. As Hyde and Linn (1988) pointed out, a larger number of females take the SAT, and the males appear to be a somewhat more advantaged sample in terms of parental income, father's education, and attendance at private schools (Ramist & Arbeiter, 1986). In short, the male SAT sample may be more highly selected than the female sample.

3. There may be features of the content of the test itself or of its administration that enlarge the difference between males and females. For example, the present meta-analysis indicates that gender differences are larger in the high school years for measures of problem solving but not for computation. Although the SAT includes many items that tap problem solving, there also are some purely computational items.[3] The SAT was coded as "mixed" in our cognitive-level analysis. The mixture of problem solving and computational items should produce a gender difference favoring males, but it should be smaller than 0.40.

How Large Are the Gender Differences in Mathematics Performance?

The interpretation of the magnitude of effect sizes has been debated. Cohen (1969) considered a d of 0.20 small, a d of 0.50 medium, and a d of 0.80 large. On the other hand, Rosenthal and Rubin (1982b) have introduced the binomial effect size display as a means of translating effect sizes into practical significance. For example, an effect size reported for success in curing cancer, reported as a correlation of .20, translates into increasing the cure rate from 40% to 60%, surely an important practical effect. Our overall value for samples of the general population, a d of -0.05, translates into a correlation of $-.025$, which yields only a 3% increase in success rate (from 48.5% to 51.5%). Applied to the analysis of gender differences, it means that approximately 51.5% of females score above the mean for the gen-

---

[3] An example of a computational item from the SAT is the following: The test taker is asked to tell which of the following quantities is greater or whether the two are equal: $(\frac{1}{3} - \frac{1}{5})$ and $\frac{2}{15}$ (College Entrance Examination Board, 1986).

eral population, whereas 48.5% of males score above the mean. Thus, the overall effect size is so small that even the binomial effect size display indicates little practical significance.

The effect size of 0.29 for problem solving in high school-aged students translates into 43% of females and 57% of males falling above the mean of the overall distribution, using the binomial effect size display.

Some idea of the magnitude of the overall effect size of -0.05 for general populations or the effect size of 0.29 for problem solving in high school students can also be gained by comparing them with effect sizes found in other meta-analyses. For example, a meta-analysis of gender differences in verbal ability found d to be .11, and the authors concluded that the value was so small as to indicate no difference (Hyde & Linn, 1988). A meta-analysis of gender differences in spatial ability indicated that the magnitude of the gender difference depended considerably on the type of spatial ability tested (Linn & Petersen, 1985). For measures of spatial perception (e.g., the rod-and-frame test), d was 0.44. For measures of spatial visualization (e.g., Hidden Figures Test), d was 0.13. For measures of mental rotation (e.g., PMA Space or the Vandenberg), d was 0.73. In all cases the differences favored males. Linn and Petersen concluded that the only substantial gender difference was in measures of mental rotation.

Meta-analyses in the realm of social behavior have indicated that d was .50 for gender differences in aggression, including studies with subjects of all ages (Hyde, 1984). For social-psychological studies of aggression by adult subjects, d was .40 (Eagly & Steffen, 1986). For gender differences in helping behavior, d was .13, although the effect sizes were extremely heterogeneous and d varied, for example, from -0.18 for studies conducted in the laboratory to 0.50 for studies conducted off campus (Eagly & Crowley, 1986).

One can also compare the magnitude of the gender difference with effects that have been obtained outside the realm of gender differences. For example, the average effect of psychotherapy, comparing treated with control groups, is .68 (Smith & Glass, 1977).

Thus, the overall effect size of 0.15 (or -0.05 for samples of only the general population) for gender differences in mathematics performance can surely be called small. The largest effect sizes we obtained were 0.29 and 0.32 for problem solving in the high school and college years, respectively. These are moderate differences that are comparable, for example, to the gender difference in aggressive behavior, yet they are smaller than the effects of psychotherapy.

Implications

This meta-analysis provided little support for the global conclusions that "boys excel in mathematical ability" (Maccoby & Jacklin, 1974, p. 352) or "the finding that males outperform females in tests of quantitative or mathematical ability is robust" (Halpern, 1986, p. 57). The overall gender difference is small at most ($d = 0.15$ for all samples or -0.05 for general samples). Furthermore, a general statement about gender differences is misleading because it masks the complexity of the pattern. For example, females are superior in computation, there are no gender differences in understanding of mathemati-

cal concepts, and gender differences favoring males in problem solving do not emerge until the high school years.

However, where gender differences do exist, they are in critical areas. It is important for us to know that females begin in high school to perform less well than males on mathematical problem-solving tasks. Problem solving is critical for success in many mathematics-related fields, such as engineering and physics. In this sense, mathematics skills may continue to be a critical filter. The curriculum in mathematics, beginning well before high school, should emphasize problem solving for all students (National Council of Teachers of Mathematics, 1988). Currently, it emphasizes computation, and girls seem to learn that very well. The schools must take more responsibility in the teaching of problem solving, both because it is an important area of mathematics and because it is an issue of gender equity.

Boys may have more access to problem-solving experiences outside the mathematics classroom than do girls, creating boys' pattern of better performance (Kimball, 1989). For example, data from California high schools from 1983 to 1987 indicate that girls made up only about 38% of physics students, 34% of advanced physics students, and 42% of chemistry students (Linn & Hyde, in press). These science courses are likely to provide extensive experience with problem solving, and fewer girls than boys gain that experience.

The gender difference that was found on the SAT-Math also has significant implications. Scores on the SAT are used as criteria for college admission and for selection of scholarship recipients. Thus, lower SAT-Math scores may influence these critical decisions about female students. The format and items of the SAT-Math should continue to be inspected for two purposes: (a) to determine whether some items are gender-biased and should be eliminated from the test, and (b) to determine whether certain items tap important problem-solving skills that are not taught adequately in the mathematics curriculum of the schools. Then schools will be able to take positive steps to improve the teaching of the mathematics required to solve such problems.

One frustration that occurred in the process of conducting this meta-analysis was the difficulty of analyzing the results according to the mathematics content of the test. Few authors specified the content clearly, probably because the content was mixed. We must know if there are large gender gaps for certain types of content. That can be determined only when researchers construct tests and report results that assess the various kinds of mathematics content separately.

Nonetheless, the gender differences in mathematics performance, even among college students or college-bound students, are at most moderate. Thus, in explaining the lesser presence of women in college-level mathematics courses and in mathematics-related occupations, we must look to other factors, such as internalized belief systems about mathematics, external factors such as sex discrimination in education and in employment (Kimball, 1989), and the mathematics curriculum at the precollege level.

References

Anastasi, A. (1958). *Differential psychology* (3rd ed.). New York: Macmillan.

152   J. HYDE, E. FENNEMA, AND S. LAMON

Benbow, C. P., & Stanley, J. C. (1980). Sex differences in mathematical ability: Fact or artifact? *Science, 210,* 1262–1264.

Benbow, C. P., & Stanley, J. C. (1983). Sex differences in mathematical reasoning ability: More facts. *Science, 222,* 1029–1031.

Cohen, J. (1969). *Statistical power analysis for the behavioral sciences.* New York: Academic Press.

College Entrance Examination Board. (1986). *10 SATs.* New York: Author.

Donlon, T. F. (1973). *Content factors in sex differences on test questions* (ETS RB 73-28). Princeton, NJ: Educational Testing Service.

Dossey, J. A., Mullis, I. V. S., Lindquist, M. M., & Chambers, D. L. (1988). *The mathematics report card: Are we measuring up?* (1986 National Assessment of Educational Progress Report No. 17-M-01). Princeton, NJ: Educational Testing Service.

Eagly, A. H., & Crowley, M. (1986). Gender and helping behavior: A meta-analytic review of the social psychological literature. *Psychological Bulletin, 100,* 283–308.

Eagly, A. H., & Steffen, V. J. (1986). Gender and aggressive behavior: A meta-analytic review of the social psychological literature. *Psychological Bulletin, 100,* 309–330.

Eccles, J. S. (1987). Gender roles and women's achievement-related decisions. *Psychology of Women Quarterly, 11,* 135–172.

Ekstrom, R., Goertz, M. E., Pollack, J. M., & Rock, D. A. (1986). Who drops out of high school and why? Findings from a national study. *Teachers College Record, 87,* 356–373.

Feingold, A. (1988). Cognitive gender differences are disappearing. *American Psychologist, 43,* 95–103.

Fennema, E. (1974). Mathematics learning and the sexes. *Journal for Research in Mathematics Education, 5,* 126–129.

Fennema, E., & Carpenter, T. P. (1981). Sex-related differences in mathematics: Results from the National Assessment. *Mathematics Teacher, 74,* 554–559.

Fennema, E., & Peterson, P. (1985). Autonomous learning behavior: A possible explanation of gender-related differences in mathematics. In L. S. Wilkinson & C. B. Marrett (Eds.), *Gender influences in classroom interaction* (pp. 17–36). New York: Academic Press.

Halpern, D. F. (1986). *Sex differences in cognitive abilities.* Hillsdale, NJ: Erlbaum.

Hedges, L. V. (1981). Distribution theory for Glass's estimator of effect size and related estimators. *Journal of Educational Statistics, 7,* 119–137.

Hedges, L. V., & Becker, B. J. (1986). Statistical methods in the meta-analysis of research on gender differences. In J. S. Hyde & M. C. Linn (Eds.), *The psychology of gender: Advances through meta-analysis* (pp. 14–50). Baltimore: Johns Hopkins University Press.

Hedges, L. V., & Olkin, I. (1985). *Statistical methods for meta-analysis.* New York: Academic Press.

Hunter, J. E., Schmidt, F. L., & Jackson, G. B. (1982). *Meta-analysis: Cumulating research findings across studies.* Beverly Hills, CA: Sage.

Hyde, J. S. (1981). How large are cognitive gender differences? A meta-analysis using ω^2 and *d. American Psychologist, 36,* 892–901.

Hyde, J. S. (1984). How large are gender differences in aggression? A

developmental meta-analysis. *Developmental Psychology, 20,* 722–736.

Hyde, J. S., & Linn, M. C. (Eds.). (1986). *The psychology of gender: Advances through meta-analysis.* Baltimore: Johns Hopkins University Press.

Hyde, J. S., & Linn, M. C. (1988). Gender differences in verbal ability: A meta-analysis. *Psychological Bulletin, 104,* 53–69.

Kimball, M. M. (1989). A new perspective on women's math achievement. *Psychological Bulletin, 105,* 198–214.

Linn, M. C., & Hyde, J. S. (in press). Trends in cognitive and psychosocial gender differences. In R. M. Lerner, A. C. Petersen, & J. Brooks-Gunn (Eds.), *The encyclopedia of adolescence.* New York: Garland Publishing.

Linn, M. C., & Petersen, A. C. (1985). Emergence and characterization of sex differences in spatial ability: A meta-analysis. *Child Development, 56,* 1479–1498.

Maccoby, E. E., & Jacklin, C. N. (1974). *The psychology of sex differences.* Stanford, CA: Stanford University Press.

Meece, J. L., (Eccles) Parsons, J., Kaczala, C. M., Goff, S. B., & Futterman, R. (1982). Sex differences in math achievement: Toward a model of academic choice. *Psychological Bulletin, 91,* 324–348.

Meyer, M. R. (in press). Gender differences in mathematics. In M. M. Lindquist (Ed.), *Results from the fourth mathematics assessment of the National Assessment of Educational Progress.* Reston, VA: National Council of Teachers of Mathematics.

National Council of Teachers of Mathematics. (1988). *Curriculum and evaluation standards for school mathematics.* Reston, VA: Author.

Ramist, L., & Arbeiter, S. (1986). *Profiles, college-bound seniors, 1985.* New York: College Entrance Examination Board.

Rosenthal, R., & Rubin, D. B. (1982a). Comparing effect sizes of independent studies. *Psychological Bulletin, 92,* 500–504.

Rosenthal, R., & Rubin, D. B. (1982b). A simple, general purpose display of magnitude of experimental effect. *Journal of Educational Psychology, 74,* 166–169.

Scott, W. A. (1955). Reliability of content analysis: The case of nominal scale coding. *Public Opinion Quarterly, 19,* 321–325.

Selkow, P. (1984). *Assessing sex bias in testing.* Westport, CT: Greenwood Press.

Sells, L. W. (1973). High school mathematics as the critical filter in the job market. In R. T. Thomas (Ed.), *Developing opportunities for minorities in graduate education* (pp. 37–39). Berkeley: University of California Press.

Smith, M. L., & Glass, G. V. (1977). Meta-analysis of psychotherapy outcome studies. *American Psychologist, 32,* 752–760.

Stage, E. K., Kreinberg, N., Eccles, J. R., & Becker, J. R. (1985). Increasing the participation and achievement of girls and women in mathematics, science, and engineering. In S. S. Klein (Ed.), *Handbook for achieving sex equity through education* (pp. 237–269). Baltimore: Johns Hopkins University Press.

Zwick, R. (1988). Another look at interrater agreement. *Psychological Bulletin, 103,* 374–378.

Appendix

Studies Used in the Meta-Analysis

Alabama Department of Education. (1986–1987). [*State mathematics assessment*]. Personal communication: Rex C. Jones.

American College Testing Program. (1987). *State and national trend data for students who take the ACT assessment.* Iowa City, Iowa: Author.

Backman, M. E. (1972). Patterns of mental abilities: Ethnic, socioeconomic, and sex differences. *American Educational Research Journal, 9,* 1–12.

Behrens, L. T., & Vernon, P. E. (1978). Personality correlates of over-achievement and under-achievement. *British Journal of Educational Psychology, 48,* 290–297.

Bell, C., & Ward, G. R. (1980). An investigation of the relationship between dimensions of self concept (DOSC) and achievement in mathematics. *Adolescence, 15,* 895–901.

Benbow, C. P., & Stanley, J. C. (1980). Sex differences in mathematical ability: Fact or artifact? *Science, 210,* 1262–1264.

Benbow, C. P., & Stanley, J. C. (1983). Sex differences in mathematical reasoning ability: More facts. *Science, 222,* 1029–1031.

Bennett, G. K., Seashore, H. G., & Wesman, A. G. (1979). *Differential aptitude tests: Fifth edition manual.* New York: Psychological Corporation.

Boli, J., Allen, M. L., & Payne, A. (1985). High-ability women and men in undergraduate mathematics and chemistry courses. *American Educational Research Journal, 22,* 605–626.

Brandon, P. R. (1985, April). *The superiority of girls over boys in mathematics achievement in Hawaii.* Paper presented at the 69th annual meeting of the American Educational Research Association, Chicago, IL. (ERIC Document Reproduction Service No. 260 906)

Carrier, C., Post, T. R., & Heck, W. (1985). Using microcomputers with fourth-grade students to reinforce arithmetic skills. *Journal for Research in Mathematics Education, 16,* 45–51.

Connecticut Department of Education. (1987). [State mathematics assessment data]. Unpublished raw data.

Connor, J. M., & Serbin, L. A. (1980). *Mathematics, visual-spatial ability, and sex roles* (Final Report). Washington, DC: National Institute of Education. (ERIC Document Reproduction Service No. 205 385)

D'Augustine, C. H. (1966). Factors relating to achievement with selected topics in geometry and topology. *The Arithmetic Teacher, 13,* 192–197.

Davis, E. J. (1973). A study of the ability of school pupils to perceive and identify the plane sections of selected solid figures. *Journal for Research in Mathematics Education, 4,* 132–140.

Dees, R. L. (1982). *Sex differences in geometry achievement.* Paper presented at the annual meeting of the American Educational Research Association, New York, NY. (ERIC Document Reproduction Service No. 215 873)

De Wolf, V. A. (1981). High school mathematics preparation and sex differences in quantitative abilities. *Psychology of Women Quarterly, 5,* 555–567.

Dick, T. P., & Balomenos, R. H. (1984). *An investigation of calculus learning using factorial modeling.* Paper presented at the 68th annual meeting of the American Educational Research Association, New Orleans, LA. (ERIC Document Reproduction Service No. 245 033)

Dossey, J. A., Mullis, I. V. S., Lindquist, M. M., & Chambers, D. L. (1988). *The mathematics report card: Are we measuring up?* (1986 National Assessment of Educational Progress Report No. 17-M-01). Princeton, NJ: Educational Testing Service.

Edge, O. P., & Friedberg, S. H. (1984). Factors affecting achievement in the first course in calculus. *Journal of Experimental Education, 52,* 136–140.

Educational Testing Service. (1987). *A summary of data collected from Graduate Record Examinations test-takers during 1985–86.* Princeton, NJ: Author.

Engle, C. D., & Lerch, H. H. (1971). A comparison of first-grade children's abilities on two types of arithmetical practice exercises. *School Science and Mathematics, 71,* 327–334.

Ethington, C. A., & Wolfle, L. M. (1984). Sex differences in a causal model of mathematics achievement. *Journal for Research in Mathematics Education, 15,* 361–377.

Ethington, C. A., & Wolfle, L. M. (1986). A structural model of mathematics achievement for men and women. *American Educational Research Journal, 23,* 65–75.

Exezidis, R. H. D. (1982, May). *An investigation of the relationship of reading comprehension, vocabulary, mathematical concepts, and computation on problem solving among Anglo, Black, and Chicano male and female middle school adolescents.* Unpublished doctoral dissertation, University of Houston, Houston, TX.

Fendrich-Salowey, G., Buchanan, M., & Drew, C. J. (1982). Mathematics, quantitative and attitudinal measures for elementary school boys and girls. *Psychological Reports, 51,* 155–162.

Fennema, E., & Sherman, J. (1977). Sex-related differences in mathematics achievement, spatial visualization and affective factors. *American Educational Research Journal, 14,* 51–71.

Fennema, E. H., & Sherman, J. A. (1978). Sex-related differences in mathematics achievement and related factors: A further study. *Journal for Research in Mathematics Education, 9,* 189–203.

Ferrini-Mundy, J. (1987). Spatial training for calculus students: Sex differences in achievement and in visualization ability. *Journal for Research in Mathematics Education, 18,* 126–140.

Flaugher, R. L. (1971). *Minority versus majority group performance on an aptitude test battery* (Project Access Research Report No. 3). Princeton, NJ: Educational Testing Service. (ERIC Document Reproduction Service No. 056 081)

Flexer, B. K. (1984). Predicting eighth-grade algebra achievement. *Journal for Research in Mathematics Education, 15,* 352–360.

Graduate Management Admission Council. (1987). *A demographic profile of candidates taking the graduate management admission test during 1986–1987.* New York: College Entrance Examination Board.

Green, D. (1987, August). *Sex differences in item performance on a standardized achievement battery.* Paper presented at the 95th annual meeting of the American Psychological Association, New York.

Hancock, R. R. (1975). Cognitive factors and their interaction with instructional mode. *Journal for Research in Mathematics Education, 6,* 37–50.

Hanna, G. (1986). Sex differences in the mathematics achievement of eighth graders in Ontario. *Journal for Research in Mathematics Education, 17,* 231–237.

Harnisch, D. L., & Ryan, K. E. (1983, September). *An investigation of the relationship of achievement motivation with achievement in mathematics for students in the United States and Japan.* Paper presented at the annual meeting of the Midwestern Educational Research Association, Kansas City, MO. (ERIC Document Reproduction Service No. 235 886)

Harris, M. L., & Romberg, T. A. (1974). An analysis of content and task dimensions of mathematics items designed to measure level of concept attainment. *Journal for Research in Mathematics Education, 5,* 72–86.

Hawn, H. C., et al. (1981). *Differences in mathematics achievement between males and females in grades 1–3.* Paper presented at the annual

154 J. HYDE, E. FENNEMA, AND S. LAMON

meeting of the Eastern Educational Research Association, Philadelphia, PA. (ERIC Document Reproduction Service No. 209 094)

Henderson, R. W., Landesman, E. M., & Kachuck, I. (1985). Computer-video instruction in mathematics: Field test of an interactive approach. *Journal for Research in Mathematics Education, 16,* 207–224.

Hilton, T. L., & Berglund, G. W. (1974). Sex differences in mathematics achievement: A longitudinal study. *Journal of Educational Research, 67,* 231–237.

Howe, A. C. (1982). *Classroom process variables in urban integrated junior high school individualized science programs* (Final Report). (ERIC Document Reproduction Service No. 220 283)

Jacobs, J. E. (1973). *A comparison of the relationships between the level of acceptance of sex-role stereotyping and achievement and attitudes toward mathematics of seventh graders and eleventh graders in a suburban metropolitan New York community.* Unpublished doctoral dissertation, New York University.

Jarvis, O. T. (1964). Boy-girl ability differences in elementary school arithmetic. *School Science and Mathematics, 64,* 657–659.

Jerman, M. (1973). Individualized instruction in problem solving in elementary school mathematics. *Journal for Research in Mathematics Education, 4,* 6–19.

Johnson, E. S. (1984). Sex differences in problem solving. *Journal of Educational Psychology, 76,* 1359–1371.

Kaczala, C. M. (1983). *Sex role identity and its effect on achievement attitudes and behaviors.* Unpublished doctoral dissertation, University of Michigan, Ann Arbor.

Kaplan, B. J., & Plake, B. S. (1982). Sex differences in mathematics: Differences in basic logical skills? *Educational Studies, 8,* 31–36.

Kissane, B. V. (1986). Selection of mathematically talented students. *Educational Studies in Mathematics, 17,* 221–241.

Kloosterman, P. (1985, March). *Sex-related differences in students' reactions to failure on algebra word problems.* Paper presented at the 69th annual meeting of the American Educational Research Association, Chicago, IL. (ERIC Document Reproduction Service No. 258 829)

Koffman, S., & Lips, H. M. (1980). Sex differences in self-esteem and performance expectancies in married couples. *Social Behavior and Personality, 8,* 57–63.

Lee, L-M. P., & Coffman, W. E. (1974). *A study of the "I don't know" response in multiple choice tests* (Iowa Testing Programs Occasional Papers No. 5). Iowa City, IA: Iowa Testing Programs.

Leinhardt, G., Seewald, A. M., & Engel, M. (1979). Learning what's taught: Sex differences in instruction. *Journal of Educational Psychology, 71,* 432–439.

Lewis, J., & Hoover, H. D. (1983, April). *Sex differences on standardized academic achievement tests.* Paper presented at the annual convention of the American Educational Research Association, Montreal, Quebec, Canada.

Lewis, J. C., & Hoover, H. D. (1987). Differential prediction of academic achievement in elementary and junior high school by sex. *Journal of Early Adolescence, 7,* 107–115.

Lloyd, B. H. (1983). *The impact of sex, ability, and item type on mathematics performance.* Paper presented at the 67th annual meeting of the American Educational Research Association, Montreal, Quebec, Canada. (ERIC Document Reproduction Service 245 935)

Marjoribanks, K. (1987). Ability and attitude correlates of academic achievement: Family-group differences. *Journal of Educational Psychology, 79,* 171–178.

Marsh, H. W., Smith, I. D., & Barnes, J. (1985). Multidimensional self-concepts: Relations with sex and academic achievement. *Journal of Educational Psychology, 77,* 581–596.

Marshall, S. P., & Smith, J. D. (1987). Sex differences in learning mathematics: A longitudinal study with item and error analysis. *Journal of Educational Psychology, 79,* 372–383.

Martin, D. J., & Hoover, H. D. (1987). Sex differences in educational achievement: A longitudinal study. *Journal of Early Adolescence, 7,* 65–83.

Meyer, R. A. (1978). *Sex-related differences in mathematical problem solving performance and intellectual abilities.* (ERIC Document Reproduction Service No. 166 023)

Michigan Department of Education. (1987). [*Michigan Educational Assessment Program*]. Personal communication: Edward R. Roeber.

Mills, C. J. (1981). Sex roles, personality, and intellectual abilities in adolescents. *Journal of Youth and Adolescence, 10,* 85–111.

Moore, E. G. J., & Smith, A. W. (1987). Sex and ethnic group differences in mathematics achievement: Results from the National Longitudinal Study. *Journal for Research in Mathematics Education, 18,* 25–36.

Muscio, R. D. (1962). Factors related to quantitative understanding in the sixth grade. *The Arithmetic Teacher, 9,* 258–262.

Newman, R. S. (1984). Children's achievement and self-evaluations in mathematics: A longitudinal study. *Journal of Educational Psychology, 76,* 857–873.

North Carolina Department of Public Instruction. (1987). [*State mathematics assessment*]. Personal communication: Cleo M. Meek.

Oregon Department of Education. (1987). [*Oregon state mathematics assessment*]. Personal communication: Wayne Newburger.

Parsley, K. M., Powell, M., O'Connor, H., & Deutsch, M. (1963). Are there really sex differences in achievement? *Journal of Educational Research, 57,* 210–212.

Pattison, P., & Grieve, N. (1984). Do spatial skills contribute to sex differences in different types of mathematical problems? *Journal of Educational Psychology, 76,* 678–689.

Pederson, D. M., Shinedling, M. M., & Johnson, D. L. (1968). Effects of sex of examiner and subject on children's quantitative test performance. *Journal of Personality and Social Psychology, 10,* 251–254.

Pennsylvania Department of Education. (1987). Personal communication, Francis J. Reardon.

Plake, B. S., Ansorge, C. J., Parker, C. S., & Lowry, S. R. (1982). Effects of item arrangement, knowledge of arrangement, test anxiety and sex on test performance. *Journal of Educational Measurement, 19,* 49–57.

Powell, B., & Steelman, L. C. (1983). Testing for sex inequality in standardized admission exams: The case for open access. *Integrated Education, 20,* 86–88.

Ramist, L., & Arbeiter, S. (1986). *Profiles, college-bound seniors, 1985.* New York: College Entrance Examination Board.

Randhawa, B. S., & Hunt, D. (1987). Sex and rural-urban differences in standardized achievement scores and mathematics subskills. *Canadian Journal of Education, 12,* 137–151.

Rosenberg, B. G., & Sutton-Smith, B. (1969). Sibling age spacing effects upon cognition. *Developmental Psychology, 1,* 661–668.

Saltzen, J. A. (1982, June). *Sex differences in mathematics performance and the organization of instruction in the elementary school.* Unpublished doctoral dissertation, University of Oregon, Eugene.

Schonberger, A. K. (1981). *Gender differences in solving mathematics problems among two-year college students in a developmental algebra class and related factors.* Paper presented at the midyear meeting of the American Education Research Association Special Interest Group on Women in Education, Washington, DC. (ERIC Document Reproduction Service 214 602)

Schratz, M. M. (1978). A developmental investigation of sex differences in spatial (visual-analytic) and mathematical skills in three ethnic groups. *Developmental Psychology, 14,* 263–267.

Senk, S. L. (1982). *Achievement in writing geometry proofs.* Paper presented at the annual meeting of the American Educational Research

Association, New York. (ERIC Document Reproduction Service No. 218 091)

Senk, S., & Usiskin, Z. (1983). Geometry proof writing: A new view of sex differences in mathematics ability. *American Journal of Education, 187*–201.

Sheehan, T. J. (1968). Patterns of sex differences in learning mathematical problem-solving. *Journal of Experimental Education, 36,* 84–87.

South Carolina Department of Education. (1987). [*State mathematics assessment*]. Personal communication: Joseph C. Saunders.

Steel, L. (1978). *Origins of sex differences in high school mathematics achievement and participation.* (ERIC Document Reproduction Service No. 176 947)

Swafford, J. O. (1980). Sex differences in first-year algebra. *Journal for Research in Mathematics Education, 11,* 335–346.

Texas Education Agency. (1987). [*Texas educational assessment of minimum skills*]. Personal communication: Ramona Jo DeValcourt.

Todd, W. E. (1985). *Effects of computer-assisted instruction on attitudes and achievement of fourth grade students in reading and mathematics.* Unpublished doctoral dissertation, North Texas State University, Denton, TX.

Usiskin, Z. P. (1972). The effects of teaching Euclidean geometry via transformations on student achievement and attitudes in tenth-grade geometry. *Journal for Research in Mathematics Education, 3,* 249–259.

Verbeke, K. A. (1982). *Sex-related differences in mathematically gifted secondary students: An investigation of selected cognitive, affective, and educational factors.* Unpublished doctoral dissertation, University of Maryland.

Webb, N. M. (1984). Sex differences in interaction and achievement in cooperative small groups. *Journal of Educational Psychology, 76,* 33–44.

Weiner, N. C. (1983). *Cognitive aptitudes, personality variables, and gender difference effects on mathematical achievement for mathematically gifted students.* Unpublished doctoral dissertation, Arizona State University, Tempe.

Whigham, M. A. (1985). *Variables related to the academic success of women engineering students.* Unpublished doctoral dissertation, Iowa State University, Ames.

Wisconsin Department of Public Instruction. (1984). [*State mathematics assessment*]. Personal communication: Russ Allen.

Wozencraft, M. (1963). Are boys better than girls in arithmetic? *Arithmetic Teacher, 10,* 486–490.

Wrabel, T. J. (1985). Ego identity, cognitive ability, and academic achievement: Variances, relationships, and gender differences among high school sophomores. (ERIC Document Reproduction Service No. ED 263 185)

Yawkey, T. D. (1981). Sociodramatic play effects on mathematical learning and adult ratings of playfulness in five year olds. *Journal of Research and Development in Education, 14,* 30–39.

Zahn, K. G. (1966). Use of class time in eighth-grade arithmetic. *The Arithmetic Teacher, 13,* 113–120.

Received September 21, 1988
Revision received May 23, 1989
Accepted June 16, 1989 ■

Psychological Bulletin
1989, Vol. 105, No. 2, 198–214

A New Perspective on Women's Math Achievement

Meredith M. Kimball
Simon Fraser University

This article presents an examination of the little noted sex-related difference in classroom grades. In contrast to standardized measures of mathematics achievement, girls receive better math grades than do boys. Three hypotheses are proposed to account for this difference. The first hypothesis proposes that boys' greater math experience facilitates their performance on standardized tests. The second hypothesis proposes that math learning styles account for the observed differences. Autonomous learning behavior is presumed to facilitate performance on standardized tests, whereas rote learning is presumed to facilitate performance on classroom exams. The third hypothesis proposes that boys and girls respond differently to novel and familiar achievement situations. It is hypothesized that girls do better when dealing with familiar situations such as classroom exams, whereas boys do better when dealing with novel situations such as standardized tests. Theoretical and empirical evidence consistent with each hypothesis is reviewed, and directions for further research are explored.

The traditional view of sex-related differences in mathematics achievement has focused on nonclassroom measures of mathematics achievement, usually a standardized test. The conclusions from this literature are reasonably consistent. Sex-related differences do not reliably appear until the junior high school years; when they appear, they almost always favor boys, and differences are greater for very bright adolescents.

One question has been thoroughly explored in the literature: When do sex-related differences favoring boys appear? Up until junior high school, sex-related differences are rare. The most common finding is that sex-related differences do not occur (Armstrong, 1981; Boswell, 1985; Connor & Serbin, 1985; Fennema, 1974, 1980, 1983; Fennema & Carpenter, 1981; Fennema & Sherman, 1978; Holloway, 1986; Moore & Smith, 1987; Pallas & Alexander, 1983; Parsons, Adler, & Kaczala, 1982; Sherman & Fennema, 1978; Swafford, 1980). When sex-related differences occur in samples of young children, girls often score better on tests of computation (Armstrong, 1981; Fennema, 1974; Fennema & Carpenter, 1981; Fennema & Sherman, 1978; Fennema & Tartre, 1985; Marshall, 1984; Threadgill-Sowder, Sowder, Moyer, & Moyer, 1985), and boys score better on tests of problem solving, applications of mathematics, and math reasoning (Armstrong, 1981; Fennema, 1974; Fennema & Sherman, 1978; Marshall, 1984). In one study, Grade 8 girls did better than boys on a test of math concepts (Sherman, 1983). Occasionally, one sex will do better on an overall math test. Hilton and Bergland (1974) found that Grade 5 girls did better on one test, whereas Grade 7 boys did better on another test. Using the highly select Study of Mathematically Precocious Youth (SMPY) sample, the Johns Hopkins research group found that boys consistently did better in Grades 7 and 8 on the

Scholastic Aptitudes Test—Quantitative Subscale (SAT—M; Benbow & Stanley, 1980, 1983b; Fox & Cohn, 1980).

Beginning in Grade 8 or 9, sex-related differences occur fairly consistently, and when they occur they almost always favor boys (Armstrong, 1981; Backman, 1972; Benbow & Stanley, 1982a; Burnett, Lane, & Dratt, 1979; Connor & Serbin, 1985; deWolf, 1981; Fennema, 1980; Fennema & Carpenter, 1981; Fennema & Sherman, 1977; Fox, Brody, & Tobin, 1985; Hanna, 1986; Hilton & Bergland, 1974; Kissane, 1986; Moore & Smith, 1987; Mura et al., 1985; Pallas & Alexander, 1983; Pattison & Grieve, 1984; Perl, 1982; Sawada, Olson, & Sigurdson, 1981; Weiner & Robinson, 1986; Wise, 1985). Male superiority does not appear in all samples, however. Most studies (Armstrong, 1981; Fox et al., 1985; Hanna, 1986; Hanna & Sonnenschein, 1985; Perl, 1982) report no differences on tests of algebra skills using high school students. Sometimes sex-related differences are found for some but not all of the classrooms or schools studied. Fennema and Sherman (1977) found no sex-related differences in math achievement in two of the four schools they studied, and Mura et al. (1985) found a significant sex difference for only one of three schools studied. Collins (1985) found no sex-related differences in math achievement for a highly select sample of Grade 12 students comparable to the Benbow and Stanley sample. Occasionally, differences are found that favor girls. Pattison and Grieve (1984) found that Grade 10 and 12 girls performed significantly better on tests of logic and geometric reasoning, whereas boys performed better on tests of scale and three-dimensional solid geometry.

Sex-related differences vary among different ethnic and national samples. Schratz (1978) found that among Black and Hispanic high school students, girls scored higher than boys. In a recent study (Brandon, Newton, & Hammond, 1987) of Grade 4–10 students in Hawaii, girls outperformed boys in all groups, although the female advantage was significantly larger in Filipino, Hawaiian, and Japanese samples than in the Caucasian sample. In contrast, Jones (1987) found that for both Black

Correspondence concerning this article should be addressed to Meredith M. Kimball, Psychology Department, Simon Fraser University, Burnaby, British Columbia V5A 1S6 Canada.

and White students, girls scored lower than boys at all levels of mathematics course taking. Moore and Smith (1987) found the largest sex-related differences favoring boys among White and Hispanic students and the smallest among Black students. Wagner and Zimmerman (1986) found somewhat smaller sex-related differences for a high-achieving German sample than have been found for similar U.S. (Benbow & Stanley, 1980) or Australian (Kissane, 1986) samples.

The presence of a significant sex-related difference does not necessarily mean that the difference is large or meaningful. In an attempt to examine the size of sex differences in the area of quantitative skills, Hyde (1981) found that the percentage of variance accounted for by sex ranged from .5% to 17%. She also used d or the proportion of the standard deviation by which the sexes differed as a measure of the size of the sex difference. The median d for math studies was .43. From this review, Hyde concluded that sex-related differences in math were relatively small. Rosenthal and Rubin (1982) analyzed the same data base and noted that d values were more likely to be available for studies that reported a significant difference than for those reporting no difference. Thus the average d reported by Hyde (1981) would be biased toward overestimating the size of the sex difference. Furthermore, the d values for quantitative skills differed significantly among themselves. In a further analysis of effect size, B. J. Becker and Hedges (1984) found that the size of sex-related differences in quantitative ability reported by Maccoby and Jacklin (1974) varied by both date of publication and sample selectivity. Larger differences were reported in older studies and in studies with more select samples. That the size of the difference should increase with an increase in sample selectivity is not surprising, because even small mean differences will generate larger differences at the tails of the distribution (Hyde, 1981). The difference related to date of publication is more puzzling; however, it might reflect an increase in the number of courses taken by young women or a lessening of the tendency on the part of young women to stereotype math as a male domain with the result that they are more motivated when taking the tests. It is also possible that this decrease reflects a change in publication policy. With the recent increase in the reporting of analyses for nonsignificant as well as significant sex-related differences, there would be a decrease in average effect size. However, because the research considered in all of the meta-analysis studies (B. J. Becker & Hedges, 1984; Hyde, 1981; Rosenthal & Rubin, 1982) was published between 1966 and 1974 (Maccoby & Jacklin, 1974), it is less likely that changes in reporting of data would account for the difference than if the studies considered were a more recent sample.

Several specific studies that use comparable samples report smaller sex differences over time. None of them report significance tests for these differences, so they must be treated as descriptive data. Feingold (1988) reported a decrease in the effect size of the male advantage on Preliminary Scholastic Aptitudes Test—Quantitative Subscale (PSAT—M) scores for Grade 11 students from .34 in 1960 to .12 in 1983. However, the effect size for SAT—M scores for both Grade 11 and Grade 12 students has remained constant (around .40) since 1960. It is interesting to note that the PSAT—M norms are based on representative national samples in contrast to the SAT—M norms,

which represent a volunteer college-bound sample. Fennema (1980), in comparing a 1960 sample with a 1975 sample, found that the difference between the boys' and girls' scores was smaller in 1975. Fennema and Carpenter (1981) found that although there were no clear patterns for 9- and 13-year-old children, for 17-year-old adolescents, sex-related differences were smaller in a large national sample tested in 1978 than they were in a similar sample tested in 1973.

A similar decrease occurred in the highly select SMPY sample over the same time period. In 1972, 19% of the boys scored higher than the highest scoring girl on the SAT—M. By 1976 this figure was 2%, and in 1979 only one boy scored higher than the highest scoring girl (Fox & Cohn, 1980). This decrease in differences between the highest scoring boys and girls is also shown by comparing the highest scoring individual of each sex. In 1972 the highest boy's score was 790, and the highest girl's score was 600. In 1976 the highest girl's and boy's scores were 610 and 780, respectively. However, by 1979 this gap had narrowed considerably, with the highest scoring girl receiving 760 and the highest scoring boy 790 (Benbow & Stanley, 1980). Group measures of the size of the sex-related difference also tend to decrease. For example, using w^2 for the combined samples for the years 1972, 1976, and 1979 shows values of .08, .05, and .04, respectively. Similarly, the d values for the 1972, 1976, and 1979 samples were .61, .46, and .39, respectively.[1] Benbow and Stanley (1983b) reported data for samples of select junior high students tested with the SAT—M in 1980, 1981, and 1982. The size of the sex-related difference with these samples (d = .37 and w^2 = .034) is quite similar to that reported for the 1979 sample (Benbow & Stanley, 1980). The Fox and Cohn (1980) figures for percentage of boys scoring higher than the highest scoring girl and the Benbow and Stanley reports of the highest scoring individuals show the most dramatic decrease. This may reflect an increasing willingness on the part of the most gifted girls to participate in these math contests.

Sex-Related Differences: Alternative View

When sex-related differences in mathematics achievement are measured using grades in mathematics classes, the results are opposite to those found using standardized achievement tests. When differences are found, they almost always favor girls, and these differences are quite consistent across samples of varying selectivity for junior high through university mathematics courses.

During the junior high and high school years, the most common finding is that girls achieve significantly better math grades than do boys. This is true for specific courses (Benbow & Stanley, 1982a; Hanna & Sonnenschein, 1985) and for overall mathematics grade point averages (Benbow & Stanley, 1982a; Casserly, 1980; Deboer, 1984; deWolf, 1981; Pallas & Alexander, 1983; Stockard & Wood, 1984). Other studies have found no

---

[1] The original data from Benbow and Stanley (1980) were used. Means and standard deviations were combined for the Grade 7 and Grade 8 samples in 1972 and 1976. The formulas for d and w^2 were the same as those used by Hyde (1981) except that the correction factor for d reported by Hedges and Becker (1986) was used.

differences in mathematics grades (Collins, 1985; Parsons, Adler, et al., 1982; K. Peterson, Burton, & Baker, 1984). Either female superiority or no sex-related differences in mathematics grades continues at the university level. Female superiority has been reported both for precalculus courses (Llabre & Suarez, 1985; MacDonald, 1980; Struik & Flexer, 1984) and for overall math grade point averages (Deboer, 1984). For calculus the results are more mixed. Some studies (Ernest, 1976; Struik & Flexer, 1977) report no sex-related differences in elementary calculus courses. Ferrini-Mundy (1987) reported no difference in an overall calculus grade but reported female superiority on one unit requiring high visualization. Boli, Allen, and Payne (1985) found that boys received higher grades than girls in an introductory calculus course. However, when subsamples of students from the course were compared, it was found that boys' and girls' grades did not differ when students were equated on the SAT—M (high or low) or on high school calculus (taken or not taken). In two studies of graduate statistics courses, either no sex-related differences were found in final grades (Woehlke & Leitner, 1980) or women received higher grades (Elmore & Vasu, 1986).

The contrast between sex-related differences in performance on standardized tests and classroom grades is best illustrated with the studies that report both kinds of measures for the same samples. These studies illustrate for specific samples the same pattern that is found in the preceding comparisons among different studies. Using the highly select SMPY sample, Benbow and Stanley (1982a) found a significant sex-related difference favoring boys on the SAT—M taken in both Grade 7 and Grade 12. They also reported significant sex-related differences in high school math grades in favor of girls. Using less select samples, deWolf (1981) and Pallas and Alexander (1983) also reported that girls receive higher grades, whereas boys score higher on standardized mathematics achievement tests.

The size of the sex-related difference favoring girls is difficult to assess, because 53% (9 out of 17) of the studies reporting either no sex-related difference or female superiority in grades do not report sufficient descriptive data to determine effect size. Of those that do, the size of the female advantage ranges from .09 to .35. The male advantage in the one study reporting boys' significantly higher calculus grades was .21. From the available literature it would appear that the size of the female advantage in grades is smaller than that of the male advantage in standardized tests. However, the study of sex-related differences in grades has until this point been very unsystematic, whereas the study of sex-related differences in standardized tests has been highly systematic. Thus the size of the female advantage in math grades cannot be determined with the same degree of accuracy as the size of the male advantage in standardized tests. It may also make a difference how the sex-related differences in grades are calculated. For example, Benbow and Stanley (1982a) reported in the text of their article that the female advantage in grades resulted mainly from the greater tendency of girls to receive A grades. The chi-square testing of this difference results in a large effect size ($q = .41$). I calculated effect sizes from the tables reported in their study that give an average grade for three cohorts of boys and girls in 10 high school math classes. These 28 effect sizes range from $-.10$ to $.77$.[2] The weighted average

(Hedges & Becker, 1986) for all 28 comparisons was .09 ($Z = 4.8$, $p < .001$). Calculated in this way, the effect sizes, although consistently favoring girls and significantly different from zero, would be considered small.

Other questions of interest—in particular, the possible variation of effect sizes over dates of publication, age of the sample, or selectivity of the sample—are similarly difficult to determine. Of studies reporting sufficient data to calculate effect sizes, the range of publication dates is 1980–1987, a small time range with no consistent pattern of results. Whether the effect sizes change with age or selectivity of the sample is also difficult to determine from the small sample of studies reporting sufficient data. Some of the largest differences are found with university samples (.35 for college algebra and trigonometry [Struik & Flexer, 1984]; .34 for college algebra [Llabre & Suarez, 1985]). However, these are studies of precalculus courses. The most general finding for calculus is that of no difference (Ernest, 1976; .12, Ferrini-Mundy, 1987; Struik & Flexer, 1977) and the one finding of male superiority is for calculus (.21; Boli et al., 1985). An analysis of the effect sizes for grades reported by Benbow and Stanley (1982a) reveals some support for a relationship between effect size and level of high school mathematics course for a highly talented sample. The effect sizes across all the courses do not form a homogeneous group ($H_T = 41.28$, $p < .05$).[3] However, if the courses are divided into lower level courses (algebra, plane geometry, and trigonometry) and higher level courses (analytical geometry, calculus, probability and statistics, and elementary functions), a clear difference emerges. The average effect sizes for the lower level courses ($x = .05$) and the higher level courses ($x = .19$) are both significantly different from zero (lower, $Z = 2.18$, $p < .02$; higher, $Z = 5.33$, $p < .001$), and they are also significantly different from each other ($H_B = 23.089$, $p < .001$). Furthermore, the effect sizes are homogeneous within each of the subgroups (lower, $H_W = 7.47$, $p > .05$; higher, $H_W = 10.71$, $p > .05$). Thus for these data the girls' advantage in course grades is significantly greater for more advanced courses.

It is difficult from these data to conclude whether effect size increases with age or not. Although the Benbow and Stanley (1982a) data would suggest that it might, one confounding variable is that for more advanced students, especially those in a university, men may have had more math courses than women. Thus if women achieve better grades, it would be relevant to calculate effect sizes not only for the raw scores but also with math background held constant. By systematically examining sex-related differences in classroom achievement, researchers should be able in the future to answer a number of these important questions concerning the variability of effect sizes across

---

[2] Because the numbers of students in Cohorts 1 and 2 taking elementary functions were so small (seven boys in Cohort 1 and three boys in Cohort 2; six girls in Cohort 1 and two girls in Cohort 2), the three cohorts were combined, and a single effect size was calculated for this course. Computer science was not included as a mathematics course for this analysis.

[3] Formulas for all effect size calculations reported here are from Hedges and Becker (1986).

ages, types of samples, types of math courses, or differing class-room instructional styles.

Are Girls a More Select Sample?

One possible explanation of girls' higher math grades is that because fewer girls continue in math, they may constitute a more select sample. Logically, if this were true, one would expect girls not only to receive better grades but also to perform better on standardized tests if they had taken the same number of elective math courses. However, as will be shown below, controlling for number of advanced math courses taken does not produce female superiority on standardized math tests (Armstrong, 1981; deWolf, 1981; Ethington & Wolfe, 1984; Fennema & Sherman, 1977; Pallas & Alexander, 1983; Wise, 1985). One would also expect that earlier achievement measures should relate to later mathematics course taking for girls, that is, the brightest girls should take the most courses. Wise (1985) did find that girls taking more math had higher Grade 9 achievement scores. In contrast, other studies have found that girls who continue to take math in high school (Sherman, 1981) or who plan to take advanced math (Stallings, 1985) do not constitute a more select sample on the basis of earlier achievement measures. In addition to this indirect evidence, a number of the studies demonstrating female superiority in grades offer direct evidence that argues against this explanation. In one case, female superiority occurred for Grade 9 algebra grades (Hanna & Sonnenschein, 1985). Because all students at this level are required to take algebra, greater female selectivity could not account for the difference in grades. In studies involving more advanced mathematics, several authors report that girls receive better grades even though there are no sex-related differences on SAT—M scores (Llabre & Suarez, 1985; Struik & Flexer, 1984) for the same sample. Other studies find that female superiority in grades remains after performance on various standardized tests or number of courses taken have been covaried out or controlled for in regression equations (Deboer, 1984; Ferrini-Mundy, 1987; Pallas & Alexander, 1983). Thus the balance of evidence clearly does not support the explanation that female superiority in math grades is due to greater sample selectivity.

Sex-Related Differences in the Classroom

Girls receive their better grades in classroom situations that are less than conducive to their learning math. Although teachers do not play an active role in the generation of stereotypes in their classrooms, they do passively reinforce the different behaviors that boys and girls bring to the classroom (Brophy, 1985; Eccles & Blumenfeld, 1985). Boys receive more of the teacher's attention; teachers interact with boys, particularly high achievement boys, more than with girls, and boys are more active in providing answers, particularly unsolicited answers, than are girls (Brophy, 1985, 1986; Eccles & Blumenfeld, 1985; Fennema & Peterson, 1985; Good, Sikes, & Brophy, 1973).

Although there are very few studies of elementary and secondary school mathematics classes, differential treatment of the sexes appears to increase with age (Brophy, 1985). Beginning with studies of elementary school mathematics classrooms, re-

sults are mixed. Leinhardt, Seewald, and Engel (1979) found that Grade 2 girls received less academic contact than boys during math lessons. The authors estimated that over a year, this difference amounted to 6 hours of instruction. Examining a Grade 6 classroom, Leder (1987) found that girls received more engagement and attention time than did boys on product questions and that the reverse was true for process questions. In a study of academic feedback, Dweck and her colleagues (Dweck, Davidson, Nelson, & Enna, 1978) found that Grade 4 and 5 girls received a higher percentage than did boys of negative feedback related to the intellectual aspects of their work. This study examined student–teacher interaction over a range of subjects, and results are not reported separately for mathematics instruction.

Other studies involving elementary and middle school children (Grades 5 to 9) have found very few overall differences in mathematics classrooms either in the way boys and girls were treated or in the way teachers responded to them (Heller & Parsons, 1981; Hudgings, 1985/1986; Parsons, Kaczala, & Meece, 1982). However, when Parsons and her colleagues looked at classrooms in which boys' math expectancies were higher than those of girls and compared these classrooms to those where there was no sex-related difference, interesting results emerged. In classrooms where students' expectancies did not differ, girls interacted more with the teacher than did boys and received more praise. The reverse was true in the classrooms where boys had higher math expectancies than girls. Even more importantly in the classrooms with no differences, high-achievement (as measured by teacher expectancies) boys and girls received more attention and praise than low-achievement students of each sex. However, in the classes with sex-related differences in student expectancies, high-achievement boys and low-achievement girls received the most attention, with high-achievement girls receiving the least (Eccles & Blumenfeld, 1985). Furthermore, in classrooms where boys had higher math expectancies than girls, there was a more competitive atmosphere with greater teacher criticism, more public recitation, and less private teacher–student interaction (Eccles & Blumenfeld, 1985). P. L. Peterson and Fennema (1985) also found results that suggested that a competitive classroom environment was not advantageous for Grade 4 girls' achievement in math.

With older students in high school classes, differences are consistently found. Koehler (1985/1986), in a study of algebra classes, found that boys engaged in or received more of all types of interactions. Stallings (1985) found small but consistent differences in favor of boys. Boys were spoken to more; were called on more (even though the numbers of volunteered answers were equal across the sexes); and received more corrective feedback, social interaction, individual instruction, praise, and encouragement. J. R. Becker (1981) found similar results with another sample of geometry classes. Male students answered open questions, process questions, and call-outs more often than female students, though there were no differences in student-initiated interactions, answers to direct questions, and answers to product questions. Although there was no difference in student-initiated interactions, 63% of the teacher-initiated academic contacts were with boys. In nonacademic contacts, boys also predominated, taking part in 74% of the conversations and

72% of the joking and receiving 61% of the praise and 54% of the discipline. There was also a large sex-related difference in the teachers' use of comments that encouraged or discouraged academic abilities and pursuits. Girls received 30% of the encouraging comments and 84% of the discouraging comments. Furthermore, teachers showed a strong tendency to persist longer with boys than with girls. Boys received 70% of the persistent interactions, and all of the contacts lasting more than 5 min were with boys. Clearly, the girls in these geometry classes experienced a different learning environment and one that would not encourage their math achievement. In classroom observations in high schools in Quebec, Mura and her colleagues (Mura et al., 1985) found that in one of the three classrooms studied, the teacher engaged in more nonacademic contact with the boys, particularly in discussions of hockey. In all of the above studies in which both male and female teachers were studied, there were no effects of the sex of the teacher; that is, both male and female teachers gave more attention to boys.

Girls also do not receive as much information from peers, particularly male peers, in small work groups within math classes. Wilkinson, Lindow, and Chiang (1985) studied Grade 2 and 3 students working in small groups on money and time problems. When there were disagreements about who had the right answer, boys' answers were more likely to prevail than were girls' answers even though there were no sex-related differences on the achievement tests over the assigned information. Boys were more likely to make requests to other boys for action or information, whereas girls did not discriminate in their requests. Webb and her colleagues (Webb, 1984; Webb & Kenderski, 1985) found that for high-achievement Grade 8 students, girls were at a significant disadvantage in working on math problems in small mixed-sex groups. In particular, the girls were less likely to receive information and explanations in response to their requests, especially the requests they directed to boys. When the behavior of the students was analyzed according to the balance within the groups (one girl and three boys; two girls and two boys; three girls and one boy), the unbalanced groups were found to provide the least information to girls because of the girls' tendency to direct attention and information disproportionately toward the boy or boys present and to receive disproportionately less help from the boy or boys present.

Girls' experience in the classroom appears from the preceding review to be one of relative deprivation when compared with boys' experience. Given that girls receive better math grades, it would appear that they do so in spite of classroom experiences that might be expected to correlate negatively with their performance. However, it is important to look more closely at possible relationships between what happens in the classroom and students' math achievement. Most of the studies examining teacher–student interaction do not also correlate interaction patterns with math achievement. Dweck et al. (1978), in an experimental study examining the effect of differential feedback on verbal tasks, found that failure feedback similar to that given to boys in the classroom produced different attributions than the failure feedback that girls more typically received. It would be interesting to see if this generalized to a mathematics task. In a more direct test of the relationship between interaction pat-

terns and math performance, P. L. Peterson and Fennema (1985) found that Grade 4 girls' and boys' math achievement was related to classroom variables. In general they concluded that girls' math achievement was positively related to a cooperative atmosphere and negatively related to a competitive one, and boys' high-level math achievement was negatively related to a cooperative classroom atmosphere. Koehler (1985/1986) found no relationship between the differential treatment of the sexes in algebra classrooms and algebra achievement. Reuman (1986) found that within-classroom ability grouping in mathematics was particularly detrimental to the math self-concept of high-ability girls.

In a study of peer-helping behavior, Webb and Kenderski (1985) found that both sexes' math achievement was positively related to receiving explanations and information and negatively related to the failure to receive explanations and information. Furthermore, in Webb's (1984) analysis of small group composition, the only groups in which boys did significantly better than girls were those consisting of three girls and one boy. In these groups the single boy received more explanations and information and was asked more questions than would have been expected by chance.

Overall it appears that when classroom interactions and achievement are studied with the same sample, patterns of interaction are related to math achievement. Sometimes the pattern is similar for both sexes (Webb, 1984; Webb & Kenderski, 1985), whereas in other studies the pattern of relationships is different for girls and boys (P. L. Peterson & Fennema, 1985). More work is needed, particularly in more advanced math courses, that directly relates classroom interaction patterns with achievement on a variety of achievement measures, including classroom exams and standardized tests.

Explanations of Sex-Related Differences in Grades

The female superiority in math grades is often ignored or dismissed in the literature on sex-related differences in mathematics achievement. Usually, math grades are not reported, and if they are, the differences are often downplayed. For example, in discussing the superiority of the SMPY girls' math grades, Benbow and Stanley (1982a) reported that girls receive more As in their coursework. They reported a chi-square of 20.5, $p < .001$, with a large effect size. They went on to say of this difference: "Thus, it was accepted that SMPY girls reported receiving somewhat better grades in their mathematics classes than their male counterparts reported" (p. 604). In contrast, the sex-related difference in Grade 7 and 8 SAT—M scores, which they state revealed on average medium effect sizes, is described as follows: "Thus the sex difference on SAT—M was considered important" (p. 603). A large effect size for grades is reduced to "somewhat better," and a medium effect size for SAT—M scores is "important."

When differences in mathematics grades are reported, they most often go unexplained. If they are explained, it is usually in terms of girls' better behavior in the classroom. Benbow and Stanley (1982a) explained the SMPY girls' better math grades as due to "sex differences favoring girls that have been found in conduct and demeanor in school" (p. 617). The references used to support this assumption are to research with young elementary school children. It is hard to believe that receiving more As in advanced high school mathematics is solely or even primarily due to these highly talented girls' better conduct and demeanor. Several authors propose that girls' greater dependency in the classroom, or their presumed greater reliance on rote learning of mathematics, is responsible for their lesser achievement on standardized tests (Fennema & Peterson, 1985; Ridley & Novak, 1983). Although these authors do not deal directly with girls' better math grades, one might hypothesize that if math grades reflect rote learning more than standardized tests do, such learning patterns might be used to explain women's better math grades. This possibility is discussed in more detail below in the section dealing with explanations of the differing achievement patterns of boys and girls.

Another possible explanation of the sex-related differences in mathematics grades may be differential teacher expectations. If math teachers expect less of their female students than of their male students, then it may be easier for girls to surpass these expectations when their actual performance is equal to or even below that of the boys. This possibility is not likely, given that teachers do not have lower expectations of their female students in their current math classes (Eccles, Adler, & Meece 1984; Lorenz, 1982; Mura et al., 1985), although they do expect female students to do less well in future math courses (Mura et al., 1985). However, it would be interesting to know how teachers' expectations do relate to grades they give as well as to achievement on standardized tests. Kissane (1986) found that teachers were much less accurate in nominating girls who would do well on the SAT—M than they were in nominating boys who would do well.

Although there is ample evidence of young women's superior math achievement when grades are used to measure achievement, they have not been considered seriously in the literature on mathematics achievement. I am proposing that it is important to begin to take them seriously. Although I am not arguing that grades can or should replace standardized achievement tests, I would urge researchers and educators to consider examining and using grades as well as standardized achievement tests to evaluate knowledge of math. There are a number of reasons why this is important. First, as scientists, we are interested in puzzles. The reversal of sex-related differences using the differing measures is an interesting puzzle, but only if we take young women's superior grades seriously. I have proposed in the following section three possible explanations for the different findings using standardized achievement tests and classroom grades. All of these are testable and may reveal different aspects of the process of learning mathematics that are not revealed by a focus on standardized measures only.

Currently, there is very little evidence that examines correlates of classroom measures of achievement. Two studies provide some evidence about the relationship of math grades to other attitudes or performance. Eccles et al. (1984) found that earlier math grades did not predict enrollment plans but did predict actual Grade 12 enrollment for both sexes. Value of math, which was a strong predictor of both enrollment plans and actual enrollment, was significantly related to the previous year's math grade for boys but not for girls. Sherman (1979)

examined the reverse relationship, that is, how attitudes and achievement measures in Grade 9 predicted later math grades. She found that Grade 9 achievement measures and confidence predicted grades in Grade 10 geometry classes for girls. For boys, achievement measures and usefulness were predictors. Interestingly, usefulness was negatively correlated with geometry grades. For Grade 11 math grades, there were no predictors. For Grade 12 girls, Grade 9 attitude toward success in math was negatively related to their math grade.

By systematically examining sex-related differences both in classroom achievement and on standardized exams, researchers will be able to answer a number of important questions that cannot be answered at this time because of the unsystematic inclusion of grades as an achievement measure in the existing literature. These questions include, (a) How do grades compare with standardized tests in predicting later course enrollment and career choices in math and science? (b) How do grades and standardized test performance correlate with or predict attitudes toward math, particularly confidence and attributions? (c) Do sex-related differences in grades differ by student age or content of math classes? Each of these questions should be examined separately by sex.

The second reason for taking sex-related differences in mathematics classroom grades seriously is that grades offer one of the best ways to ensure that boys and girls have comparable prior experience. Because only classroom learning is tested, experiences in other courses or outside the classroom potentially do not influence the results as much as when a standardized test is used. The third reason is a practical one. The information that girls are not at a disadvantage and actually have an advantage in many courses in terms of class grades could be most useful in increasing girls' confidence in their own math abilities. Furthermore, counselors could use this material to encourage individual girls to go on to advanced math courses without fear of lowering their grade point average. If more young women are to enter the scientific professions, they must first take math courses. Doing well in math courses is ultimately more important for scientific career training than is one's score on the SAT—M.

Hypotheses to Explain Differences Between Traditional and Alternative Views

Differential Experience Hypothesis

Using grades as a measure of mathematics achievement minimizes sex-related differences in experience with math. Using course grades partially controls for number of math courses taken and reduces the importance of math-related experience outside the classroom. The greater number of courses that boys take and their more extensive experience with math outside the classroom may give them an advantage both in knowledge of math and in confidence when taking standardized tests that include information that may or may not have been covered in class. In contrast, grades reflect knowledge of a body of material that has been presented in class. Although extracurricular mathematics activities may facilitate class learning, they are not critical for such learning to occur. Having more mathematics-related experience may increase boys' performance on standardized tests either directly or indirectly. Directly, greater experience with math may provide specific knowledge such as algorithms that can be used to solve problems. Indirectly, greater experience may facilitate performance through general familiarity with mathematical thinking and increased confidence. For example, although calculus is not specifically covered on the SAT—M, having taken calculus may facilitate performance on the SAT—M by allowing one to work more quickly on what seem to be relatively simple problems, to generalize knowledge learned in calculus to individual problems, and to increase confidence that comes from knowledge that one has solved much more complicated problems.

That boys take more math courses has been well documented (Armstrong, 1981; Benbow & Stanley, 1982a; Brush, 1980; Collins, 1985; Elmore & Vasu, 1986; Ernest, 1976; Fennema & Carpenter, 1981; Fennema & Sherman, 1977; Mura, 1982; Perl, 1982; Sells, 1980; Wiggins, 1982). Mathematics experience outside the classroom has not been nearly as extensively studied. However, the studies that have examined it consistently show that boys have more science- and mathematics-related experience than girls (Hilton & Bergland, 1974; Kahle, Matyas, & Cho, 1985; Linn & Petersen, 1986). Even among mathematically gifted students, boys report more math experiences outside the classroom (Benbow & Stanley, 1982b). When the SMPY students were asked a number of questions about their math experience, boys were more likely to report learning math on their own. Specifically, 74% of the boys and 81% of the girls reported learning most of their math in the regular classroom and 23% of the boys and 17% of the girls reported engaging in independent study of math outside of school. Among a group of girls taking accelerated math and science classes, a commonly remembered experience was trouble convincing their parents to buy them toys such as Legos (Casserly, 1980). In particular, chemistry sets had been much desired with little success unless they were only children, the oldest of several girls, or separated from their brothers by a large age span. Although these findings indicate that boys have more math-related experience than girls, much more specific research is needed to determine the range and extent of students' mathematics experiences outside the classroom, the sex-related differences in these experiences, and the relationship of such experiences to mathematics achievement.

A partial test of the differential experience hypothesis is to relate number of courses taken or experience outside the classroom to performance on standardized tests. If sex-related differences disappear or are reduced, then the greater experience of boys may be assumed to account for part or all of the male superiority on standardized tests. Although no one has examined the relationship of experience outside the classroom to performance on standardized tests, several studies have looked at the effect of number of courses taken on performance on standardized tests. The results from these studies offer some support for the hypothesis. In only one sample (Armstrong, 1981, National Assessment of Educational Progress [NAEP] sample) did controlling for the number of courses taken lead to no reduction in the sex-related differences on standardized tests. On the other hand, no study has reported the complete elimination of sex-related differences when number of math courses is controlled. The most common finding is that controlling for courses taken eliminates some but not all of the sex-related differences studied. For example, the difference is eliminated in some subsamples but not in others (Armstrong, 1981, women in mathematics sample; Fennema & Sherman, 1977), or on some tests but not on others (deWolf, 1981). Two regression studies found that controlling for courses taken reduced a preexisting sex-related difference by either about one third (Ethington & Wolfe, 1984) or almost two thirds (Pallas & Alexander, 1983). A failure to control for prior quantitative aptitude has been cited as an important flaw in these studies (Benbow & Stanley, 1983a); that is, if greater aptitude leads to greater course taking, especially on the part of girls, the finding that controlling for courses taken reduces sex-related differences on achievement tests would be spurious (Benbow & Stanley, 1983a). Thus Wise (1985) reported an elimination of the sex-related difference in mathematics achievement in a national sample of Grade 12 students when courses taken were controlled. However, because the girls taking more math had higher Grade 9 achievement scores, when Grade 9 achievement was controlled as a covariate, a significant sex-related difference reappeared. Other studies, however, do not report a relationship between prior aptitude and mathematics course taking (Benbow & Stanley, 1982a; Sherman, 1981). Furthermore, Pallas and Alexander (1983) found a relationship between course taking and SAT—M scores even after prior aptitude was controlled for in the regression equation (Alexander & Pallas, 1983). Thus it does not appear that a failure to control for prior aptitude can be used to discount the reduction in sex-related differences that occurs when course taking is controlled.

Even though controlling for courses taken does reduce some of the sex-related difference, it does not in any study eliminate all of the sex-related differences. It is possible that courses other than math courses, in particular science courses, also may be related to differential performance (deWolf, 1981). In support of this, Pallas and Alexander (1983) found that having taken a physics course was positively related to performance on the SAT—M. Also, it is quite possible that experiences outside the classroom could be related to the remaining differential performance.

Although the differential experience hypothesis appears to be able to explain at least some of the male superiority on standardized tests, it is much less clear how it might be applied to female superiority in grades. It would be logical to expect that boys' greater experience outside the classroom would facilitate their interest in classroom material and their performance on classroom exams in relation to that of girls, and it is puzzling to say the least to see how girls' lesser experience outside the classroom can be used to explain their better performance in the classroom. Perhaps girls do work harder in the classroom because they have less confidence and this lesser confidence is somehow related to their lack of mathematics-related experience. Or perhaps boys find classroom material more boring in comparison to their outside experience, and thus their motivation to perform well in the class is decreased. In order to test these or related possibilities, we need to know a great deal more about the nature of children's experience with math outside the

The Psychology of Gender II

classroom and how this experience relates to both classroom and standardized measures of achievement. It would be particularly interesting if experience outside the classroom was related to performance on standardized tests but not to classroom grades.

It is clear that an adequate explanation of female superiority on classroom measures as well as of male superiority on standardized measures will require the consideration of factors other than differential mathematics experience. In an attempt to do this, I will next examine the nature of the potentially different learning styles of the sexes and possible differential responses to familiar and novel testing materials.

Rote Versus Autonomous Learning Hypothesis

According to this hypothesis, boys have a more autonomous approach to learning math that facilitates performance on standardized tests, which require one to apply or generalize mathematics knowledge to new or unfamiliar problems. Girls, on the other hand, take a rote learning approach to mathematics that proves an advantage in classroom exams, which are based on the more routine use of rules or algorithms learned in class.

In order to evaluate this hypothesis, I will first review the evidence that girls learn math in a rote fashion, whereas boys are more autonomous in their approach. Then I will examine the evidence that these differing styles of learning facilitate performance on different kinds of achievement measures. There is no direct evidence for a sex-related difference in mathematics learning style. However, several authors have hypothesized that girls' greater dependence, teacher orientation, and focus on being good in the classroom are related to a rote learning style (Fennema & Peterson, 1985; Grant, 1985; Ridley & Novak, 1983). In addition, it is assumed that girls are less encouraged to engage in math and science activities outside the classroom, which makes the material they are learning in class more arbitrary and increases the chances that they will rely on rote learning and memorization (Ridley & Novak, 1983). Boys are thought to rebel against the teacher, resist the solutions provided by teachers, and develop their own independent solutions to math problems, which leads to further autonomous learning (Grieb & Easley, 1984). Furthermore, these sex-related differences are thought to accumulate over time in the fashion of compound interest so that even though girls may continue to take math courses, the material becomes increasingly arbitrary to them and they increasingly approach math learning in a rote fashion (Grieb & Easley, 1984; Ridley & Novak, 1983).

Girls' greater orientation to good behavior and boys' greater rebellion and independence in the classroom are processes assumed to underlie the differences in learning styles. Teachers are assumed to respond differentially to these student behaviors by directing more of their negative remarks and criticisms, especially procedural criticisms, to boys (Brophy, 1985). Several studies have shown that teachers direct more negative comments to boys even in the absence of greater male misbehavior (Eccles & Blumenfeld, 1985; Pintrich & Blumenfeld, 1985). Teachers' specific encouragement of autonomy may be more necessary for girls than for boys. Green and Foster (1987) compared control-oriented and autonomy-oriented elementary

classrooms. The children answered questions concerning their preferences for challenging work in the classroom. The preference for challenging work revealed a Sex $\times$ Orientation interaction. Specifically, boys did not differ across the two kinds of classrooms, but girls had significantly higher challenge scores in the autonomy-oriented classrooms than in the control-oriented classrooms.

In order for this hypothesis to work, not only must girls and boys differ in their learning styles, but the learning styles must be related to differential performance on classroom and standardized measures of achievement. A major theoretical explanation (Fennema, 1985b; Fennema & Peterson, 1985) of sex-related differences in mathematics achievement has proposed that differences in autonomous learning behaviors directly cause sex-related differences in mathematics achievement (as defined by performance on standardized tests). Both internal and external factors are assumed to lead to differences in autonomous learning behaviors that in turn lead to differences in achievement. Autonomous learning behavior is defined as working independently on high-level tasks, persisting with difficult problems, choosing high-level tasks, and achieving at these tasks (Fennema & Peterson, 1985). Fennema and Peterson (1985) argue that autonomous learning behavior may be a particularly important skill for success at high-level mathematics. One of the internal beliefs that is hypothesized to relate to autonomous learning behavior is the congruency of sex-role identity with achievement in math. The perception that achievement in math is incongruent with femininity is thought to decrease autonomous learning behavior. In terms of my hypothesis, a further distinction may be useful. It may be that memorization or rote learning of mathematics is perceived to be less incongruent with femininity than a more autonomous, independent, and even perhaps aggressive approach to the subject.

Empirical evidence linking specific learning styles to performance on specific achievement measures is meager and mostly indirect. Koehler (1985/1986) related teaching styles that foster autonomous learning behavior to gains in algebra achievement for both boys and girls. A common finding that is consistent with the hypothesis is that girls tend to do better on tests of computation (Armstrong, 1981; Fennema, 1974; Fennema & Carpenter, 1981; Fennema & Sherman, 1978; Fennema & Tartre, 1985; Marshall, 1984; Threadgill-Sowder et al., 1985), whereas boys score better on tests of problem solving, applications of mathematics, and math reasoning (Armstrong, 1981; Fennema, 1974; Fennema & Sherman, 1978; Marshall, 1984). Ridley and Novak (1983) reported that in a university-level science course there was no sex-related difference on recall of information but that men did better on problems that required application of knowledge. P. L. Peterson and Fennema (1985) found that elementary boys and girls both did equally well on low-level math problems but that the boys did better than the girls ($p < .10$) on high-level problems. Furthermore, different teacher–student interaction factors influenced boys' and girls' performance on low-level and high-level problems. Boys' achievement on both kinds of problems (with prior achievement controlled for) was negatively related to time spent with the teacher and help by the teacher. For girls, high-level perfor-

206   MEREDITH M. KIMBALL

mance was related negatively to amount of social activity and time spent waiting for the teacher. These findings are consistent with a view of a more autonomous style in boys.

The autonomous versus rote learning hypothesis is consistent with much theory and some data in the literature. However, much further evidence is required before we can evaluate its potential to explain sex-related differences in classroom and standardized achievement measures. First, it is necessary to operationalize autonomous and rote learning styles. Although the theoretical formulations in this area are interesting and useful, we must also be able to reliably observe behaviors that relate to the concepts. Fennema and her colleagues (Fennema & Peterson, 1985; Koehler, 1985/1986) have begun the work of operationalizing autonomous learning behaviors and teacher styles that encourage autonomous learning behavior. Second, it is necessary to demonstrate that boys and girls do approach the study of math differently. Third, the link between learning styles, performance on classroom measures, and performance on standardized measures needs to be demonstrated. Specifically, better performance on classroom measures and worse performance on standardized measures should be related to rote learning styles, and the reverse achievement pattern should be related to autonomous learning styles. Furthermore, if more advanced math courses require a more autonomous approach in order to learn the material and girls use a less autonomous approach, then the sex-related difference favoring girls in classroom achievement should decrease with age. Although we do not have sufficient information to draw a conclusion one way or the other, it certainly is not clear that sex-related differences favoring girls decrease with age.

Novelty Versus Familiarity Hypothesis

According to this hypothesis, girls are motivated to do well and are confident when dealing with familiar material but are less confident and sometimes debilitated when dealing with novel material. Thus they do better on classroom math exams that cover relatively more familiar material, but they do less well on standardized tests that are more likely to contain novel material and are a more unusual testing situation. On the other hand, boys are motivated to do well and are more confident when dealing with novel or challenging material or situations but are less motivated to perform well when faced with familiar material. Thus they do better on standardized tests, which offer more of a challenge, but do less well on classroom exams, which appear to be less of a challenge and perhaps not worth the effort.

This hypothesis rests on the assumption that standardized tests are relatively more novel or unfamiliar than classroom exams. They are more novel in two ways. First, the standardized test is a more novel situation in that it occurs less often, sometimes a stranger comes into the classroom to administer the test, and occasionally (SATs) the test is given outside of class time and in a strange environment. On the other hand, exams are taken several times within a course with the same group of people, are given by the same person, and occur in the same physical environment. Second, the material or problems on a standardized test are more likely to be novel or unfamiliar to the student taking the test. Standardized exams are not designed to

cover what has been learned in class, but exams are. A "fair test" in the classroom emphasizes what has been emphasized in class. Furthermore, the student may be given hints or information about how to prepare for a classroom exam, told what kind of problems will be on the exam, or told what the exam format will be.

Why should girls do less well than boys on the relatively more novel standardized tests and do better than boys on the relatively more familiar classroom exams? The work of Dweck and her colleagues (Dweck, 1986; Elliot & Dweck, 1988; Licht & Dweck, 1983) on achievement goals provides some possible answers to this question. Two different achievement goals are proposed by Dweck. If performance is the goal, then achievement tasks are approached as a test of one's ability. Because any failure reflects negatively on one's ability, the goal is to choose tasks to maximize success and minimize failure. If learning is the goal, then achievement tasks are approached as a learning opportunity. Success and failure are not important per se but rather are cues that one has or has not mastered what one wants to learn. Because one would expect and does find (Diener & Dweck, 1978, 1980; Dweck, 1986) large within-sex differences in achievement orientation and because any one person may vary in achievement orientation or goals over different achievement tasks, I do not predict a sex difference in overall orientation. However, Dweck's model includes different predictions for people with high or low confidence within the performance orientation. A person with a performance goal and high confidence will choose moderately difficult tasks to demonstrate his or her ability and will respond to a difficult task with a mastery orientation. The person with a performance goal and low confidence will be most concerned with avoiding failure, which would demonstrate low ability, and thus will avoid confusing, difficult, or novel tasks and will respond to a difficult task with negative affect and deterioration of performance. For the learning orientation, people with both high and low confidence will choose tasks that are perceived to provide good learning opportunities, even if mistakes are likely, and will respond to a difficult task with persistence and mastery behavior (Dweck, 1986; Elliot & Dweck, 1988).

Although girls may be no more likely to be performance oriented toward math than boys, I would predict that for math there may be more girls than boys who fall in the category of performance orientation and low confidence. The evidence to support this prediction comes from the consistent finding that girls are less confident of their math ability than are boys (Eccles et al., 1984; Fennema & Sherman, 1977, 1978; Meece, Parsons, Kaczala, Goff, & Futterman, 1982; Mura, Kimball, & Cloutier, 1987; Perl, 1982; Sherman, 1983). Thus among children who are performance oriented, girls more than boys should show avoidance of confusing, novel, or difficult tasks and negative affect and deterioration of performance in difficult achievement situations. Hudson (1986) asked junior high students to verbalize while solving NAEP math problems. Girls more than boys verbalized difficulty in solving the problems, lower confidence, and more negative affect and were less confident that their final solutions were correct. The girls' verbalizations in this study were similar to those made by the helpless children in Diener and Dweck's (1978) study. Eccles et al. (1984) found that only among low-expectancy children and only on a number sequence task did girls more than boys attribute their failure to ability.

Direct evidence that more girls than boys approach math with a performance orientation and low confidence is not available from the literature. Dweck and Licht (1980) argued that more girls than boys express a helpless orientation as opposed to a mastery orientation with adult but not with peer evaluators. Other studies found that women more than men respond to failure in a verbal task with attributions and expectancies that are consistent with a performance plus low confidence orientation (Hughes, Sullivan, & Beaird, 1986; La Noue & Curtis, 1985; Miller, 1986). Also there is evidence that it is among the highest ability girls that this response to failure is the strongest (Dweck, 1986; Michael, 1983; Stipek & Hoffman, 1980). Licht and Dweck (1984) found a positive relationship ($r = .47$) between self-estimates of intelligence and performance of girls in the straightforward condition but found a negative (and significantly lower) correlation ($r = -.38$) in the confusing condition. On the other hand, several studies found no sex-related differences in orientation (Diener & Dweck, 1978, 1980; Eccles et al., 1984; Elliot & Dweck, 1988). However, because of the design of these latter studies, it is often difficult to infer that sex-related differences do not exist. Some match boys and girls on achievement orientation (Diener & Dweck, 1978, 1980), and others create experimental conditions designed to enhance different orientations (Elliot & Dweck, 1988). Thus any naturally occurring sex-related differences may be masked. Another problem with the work in this area is that primarily verbal or discrimination learning and not mathematics achievement tasks have been used. Thus we do not know how results might vary if math problems were used. Most of the studies finding no sex-related differences have used elementary school children for whom sex-related differences in mathematics performance do not exist. The exception to this pattern is the work of Eccles (Eccles et al., 1984), who found very few sex-related differences in the achievement-related behaviors of Grade 8, 9, and 10 children working on either anagrams or number sequence problems. In order to know if sex-related differences in achievement orientation exist for mathematics, much more research must be done that uses math problems, does not experimentally induce achievement orientations, and studies older as well as younger children.

Math more than verbal subjects may create difficulties for students with a performance orientation and low confidence. Mathematics, especially in junior high and beyond, is more likely than verbal subjects to present students with new concepts and confusing material. Each new area (algebra, geometry, trigonometry, calculus) begins with the introduction of new concepts. Even the fact that each area has a new name may increase the sense that one is dealing with a new and different learning task. Math also is an area in which there is a high probability of error, and one's errors are highly visible (Dweck & Licht, 1980; Licht & Dweck, 1983). These characteristics make math a subject that children with a performance orientation and low confidence will tend to avoid. Verbal subjects on the other hand have a more subjective component and errors or weaknesses in one area may be compensated for in other ways

(Dweck & Licht, 1980; Licht & Dweck, 1983). Students with a performance orientation and high confidence, on the other hand, actually may prefer math to verbal subjects because of the high probability of demonstrating one's ability with clear successful solutions to problems.

I would add a further distinction within math between different types of achievement measures. The standardized test with its greater likelihood of novel problems and confusing material will lead to greater debilitation of girls in comparison with boys because of the greater probability that girls with a performance orientation will approach the task with low confidence in their own ability. In contrast, in classroom exams the greater familiarity of content and context and the possibility of preparation may lead these same girls to overprepare in order to avoid failure and the resulting implication of low ability.

In addition to the possible sex-related differences in achievement orientations, it is also probable that the two achievement situations differ in the extent to which they induce performance concerns in the students who take them. Given that math is seen to be more ability-dependent than English (Eccles et al., 1984; Ruthvan, 1987) or even than science subjects (Ruthvan, 1987), any math test may be perceived as more of an ability test than exams or tests in other academic areas. However, I would argue that the standardized math test in relation to the classroom exam is more likely to be perceived as a measure of one's ability. The isolated and special nature of the standardized test may contribute to the perception that it is an ability measure. Mention or knowledge of national norms may also lead students to think of standardized tests as particularly good or important measures of ability. Receiving feedback in which one's score is presented in terms of a percentile among all those taking the test (SATs) would certainly contribute to the perception of an ability measure. On the other hand, exams may be presented by teachers as a measure of how hard one has studied. They can be viewed more easily as a measure of how much one has mastered or learned the material presented in class. To the extent that standardized exams induce relatively more of a performance orientation and classroom exams relatively more of a learning orientation, girls' lower confidence should put them at more of a disadvantage on the standardized exam. On the other hand, to the extent that the classroom exam induces relatively more of a learning orientation, girls' assumption that their effort is primarily responsible for their success (Deboer, 1986; Fennema, 1985a; Lyons-Lepke, 1986; Mura et al., 1987; Ryckman & Peckham, 1987; Wooleat, Pedro, Becker, & Fennema, 1980) and their resulting hard work may give them a relative advantage.

The empirical evidence that is consistent with this hypothesis falls into three areas: (a) evidence that girls are not disadvantaged on standardized tests that are designed to reflect classroom content; (b) evidence that girls' confidence and math achievement behaviors are consistent with an avoidance of or lack of confidence in novel situations; and (c) evidence from classroom observation studies that girls are more forthcoming when dealing with well-prepared or familiar material and do not learn math as well in classrooms that emphasize competition.

The first category of evidence comes from studies that have

used a standardized testing format but have purposely designed the content of the tests to reflect material covered in classrooms. Senk and Usiskin (1983) compared sex-related differences on a standardized geometry achievement test to those found on a test that required students to generate geometric proofs. The authors found that boys did better on the standardized test but that there were no significant sex-related differences on the proofs tests. They argued that geometric proofs are a high-level cognitive task that are unlikely to be encountered outside the geometry classroom. Galbraith (1986) designed mathematics achievement tests using "thoroughly familiar mathematical content" (p. 423). Grade 8, 9, and 10 students' performance was scored both on the correctness of their answers and on the validity of their mathematical reasoning used to explain their answer. Girls scored significantly higher than boys. Smith and Walker (1988) analyzed sex-related differences on the New York Regents examinations. These exams are designed to reflect the content of the high school curriculum, and teachers design their math classes to cover what will be on the exams. They found no sex-related differences for Grades 9 and 11 and a sex-related difference favoring girls for Grade 10. Hudson (1986) in an analysis of sex-related differences on NAEP items found that the male advantage was larger on more unfamiliar items, more difficult items, and items assessing spatially related topics. Perhaps the most extreme example of standardized tests that contain unfamiliar or novel material is Benbow and Stanley's (1980) use of the SAT—M tests with Grade 7 students, a procedure that results in large differences favoring boys.

The second category of evidence consistent with the hypothesis involves girls' avoidance or lack of confidence in novel situations. One finding is that there is no sex-related difference in confidence that one can do well in a current math course but that girls are less confident that they can do well in future math courses (Meece et al., 1982; Mura, 1987; Parsons, Adler et al., 1982). Hanna and Sonnenschein (1985) also found that although Grade 8 girls scored as well as boys on three prealgebra tests, they predicted lower algebra grades for themselves. The following year, they actually achieved higher algebra grades than the boys. A related kind of evidence is that girls, if given the option, make more omission errors than boys on standardized math tests (Hanna, 1986) or use "I don't know" choices in responding to math or science items (Hudson, 1986; Linn, De Benedictis, Delucchi, Harris, & Stage, 1987). In working in small groups of peers in mathematics classes, girls tend, especially of boys, to ask general questions (How do you do this?) or make general statements (I can't get this one; Webb & Kenderski, 1985). These kinds of statements as opposed to more specific questions (Does x = 64 in the first problem?) may represent a lack of confidence in dealing with novel or difficult material.

The third category of evidence comes from studies of classrooms. Within the classroom, boys and girls are differentially active in ways that would be predicted by the hypothesis. Boys consistently are more active in giving unsolicited answers or call-outs (J. R. Becker, 1981; Brophy, 1985, 1986; Eccles & Blumenfeld, 1985; Fennema & Peterson, 1985; Good et al., 1973; Stallings, 1985). No differences are found in the number of volunteered answers (Stallings, 1985) or student-initiated interactions (J. R. Becker, 1981) in geometry classes. Girls do not often dominate in classroom participation, but Morse and Handley (1985) found that girls in Grade 7 and 8 science classes dominated in only one class of responses, those based on prepared homework or reports. Furthermore, girls' and boys' achievement and confidence in math classrooms is related to classroom teaching styles. Eccles and Blumenfeld (1985) found that girls had the lowest math expectations in relation to boys in classrooms that involved high teacher criticism and a public teaching style. P. L. Peterson and Fennema (1985) found that girls' math achievement was negatively related to a competitive classroom style and positively related to a cooperative one. The competitive classroom is likely to require the student to respond on the spot to novel math problems. Peterson and Fennema gave the example from one math classroom of a game that the teacher called "around the world." In this game, Student A stood by Student B's desk, the teacher presented a math problem, and whoever answered first went on to Student C's desk. Under this or similar competitive situations, not only must the student deal quickly with novel (in the sense that one cannot prepare them beforehand) math problems but also she or he must do so in an atmosphere that emphasizes social comparison cues. Thus a competitive classroom atmosphere in relation to a more cooperative one may be more likely to induce a performance orientation. Under these conditions, girls' lower confidence in their math ability would put them at a disadvantage in comparison with boys. The cooperative classroom, in contrast, is more likely to involve the teacher working privately with a single student or with small groups of students, a situation that may induce more of a learning orientation and allow students time to prepare their answers before sharing them with an evaluator.

Although there is some theoretical and empirical support for this hypothesis, more empirical evidence is necessary to evaluate it. How sex-related differences in math performance vary with changes in novelty is a critical test of the hypothesis. Not only should sex-related differences vary between standardized tests and classroom measures of achievement, but variations in novelty and familiarity within standardized tests and within the classroom should relate in predictable ways to patterns of girls' and boys' performance. The relationship between classroom performance and performance on standardized tests for both boys and girls is also of interest. Kissane (1986) found that teachers were much less accurate in nominating high math achievement girls (measured by the SAT—M) than in nominating high math achievement boys. Benbow and Stanley (1982a) found that the correlations between SAT—M and grades were somewhat higher for boys (.31 to .41) than for girls (.17 to .27). Correlations among standardized tests also might vary depending on the degree to which novel material was incorporated. Another important area to investigate empirically is that of the perceptions of boys and girls of standardized tests and classroom exams. Do students' perceptions of standardized and classroom measures of math achievement vary in terms of novelty, the degree to which they measure ability, and the degree to which they reflect performance or learning goals? As was mentioned earlier, it is also important to test with mathematics material the possible existence of sex-related differences in achievement orientation, particularly the incidence of performance orientation and low confidence in both sexes.

Conclusions and Future Directions

Given girls' better math grades, why do they take advanced math classes at lower rates? In other words, why do girls' better grades not make a difference in their mathematics participation? Each of the hypotheses in the previous section can be applied to these questions. Girls' lesser experience with extracurricular math and science as well as a presumed rote approach to learning math may reduce both their confidence and their motivation for choosing math courses. Also, future math classes may be viewed as novel tasks with a high risk of failure, so even though one has done well in current courses, this experience may not seem applicable to future courses.

Two factors may mediate the process whereby high grades in current math courses do not lead to taking future math courses. The first is the tendency of girls more than boys to attribute success in math to effort rather than to ability (Deboer, 1986; Fennema, 1985a; Lyons-Lepke, 1986; Mura et al., 1987; Ryckman & Peckham, 1987; Stipek, 1984; Wooleat et al., 1980), especially among high-achieving girls (Licht & Shapiro, 1982, cited in Licht & Dweck, 1983). One result of attributing success to effort is that although one can be sure that the effort was enough in this situation, it may be difficult to believe it will be enough for novel situations such as future math courses. Furthermore, perceptions of high effort in an achievement situation that involves comparison of one's performance to that of others implies that one has lower ability in that area, at least in relation to someone who does as well or better with less effort (Nicholls, 1976, 1984). Ability, on the other hand, is popularly thought of as a quality that is sufficient to deal with present as well as with future situations. The consequences of making effort attributions for success may be more debilitating for girls' mathematics confidence than for their confidence in other academic areas. Girls are more likely to use effort attributions for success in math than in language arts (Ryckman & Peckham, 1987). Furthermore, math more than English (Eccles et al., 1984; Ruthvan, 1987) and more than science (Ruthvan, 1987) is perceived as a subject in which success is linked to ability more than to effort. What happens as a result is that girls' experience with success does not increase their confidence for future challenges. Singer and Stake (1986) found that men's but not women's general performance self-esteem was enhanced by participation and success in math courses in high school and college. Eccles (1986) found that math-able college women who were pursuing math-related careers were more likely to attribute their math success to stable internal causes than were equally math-able women pursuing other careers.

The second factor is sex-role conflict. Sex-role conflict can result both from discrimination against girls' and women's participation in math and from perceived or experienced conflict between parental and career goals. Discrimination occurs at many levels and in both subtle and not-so-subtle forms. Girls are sometimes directly discouraged from gaining mathematics training. For example, half of the girls participating in a special SMPY accelerated program encountered resistance to their request to enroll early in Algebra II (Fox, Benbow, & Perkins, 1983). Women mathematicians report that as they engaged in more advanced levels of study in mathematics, they were more likely to be actively discouraged from pursuing math as a career (Luchins & Luchins, 1980). Women's achievement is sometimes treated in a trivializing manner. For example, adults asked different questions of a gifted Grade 6 girl who had built a robot. Women asked questions about her design, where she had gotten the parts, and where she got the idea. In contrast, the first or second question asked by all male visitors (and never by a female visitor) was, Did you build it to do housework? (Reis, 1987). Discrimination may also take more subtle forms. The finding that boys more than girls experience more social, joking, and nonacademic conversations in the high school mathematics classroom (J. R. Becker, 1981; Mura et al., 1985) may communicate to young men and women that this is an environment where men belong more than women do. Although neither sex highly stereotypes math as a male domain, men typically stereotype it more than women (Collis & Williams, 1987; Fennema, 1980, 1983; Fennema & Sherman, 1977; Sherman & Fennema, 1977; Swafford, 1980). That their male peers stereotype math more than they do may create in women an uncertainty about their place as women and as mathematics achievers (Fennema, 1980). Women mathematicians report that a common sexist attitude they encounter is the idea that women mathematicians are not feminine (Ernest, 1976).

The second source of sex-role conflict is in the perceived or experienced conflict between career and parental goals. Young women continue to expect to be employed part-time or not at all when their children are young, and young men expect that they but not their wives will be employed full-time when they are fathers of young children (Mura et al., 1987; Sherman, 1983; Tittle, 1986). College women value their future roles as mothers very highly. When asked to rate a series of occupations including mothering, they rate mothering in comparison to other occupations as being moderately difficult, having the highest probability of success, the highest importance of success, highest effort required, highest positive affect associated with success, and the highest negative affect associated with failure (Eccles, 1986). Mothering is an extremely important role, and an occupation that is perceived to be threatening to the success of mothering will probably not be attractive. Careers that require many mathematics courses may be perceived as requiring a full-time involvement, and that may be perceived to threaten success at mothering. Young women planning careers who are concerned about possible conflict between mothering and scientific career goals are not being unrealistic. Female mathematicians report more conflict between family and career than do male mathematicians (Luchins & Luchins, 1980). Women in mathematics doctoral programs worry most that their graduate training may take away from their involvement with family, friends, and other interests. In contrast, their male peers worry most about professional status and their mentor's estimates of their ability (Maines, 1983, cited in Eccles, 1987). Older female engineers are twice as likely to be childless as older male engineers (Jagacinski, 1987). Highly creative female mathematicians in comparison with female mathematicians of average creativity are distinguished by their willingness to subordinate other activities to professional goals. Highly creative male mathematicians differ from their average counterparts in their desire to accomplish great things and achieve fame (Helson, 1980). Perceptions of future conflict may well lower the perceived usefulness of future math courses to women even though they have high grades in current math courses.

What action can be taken on the basis of girls' higher math grades? It is important that teachers, parents, researchers, and young women themselves take their good math grades seriously. This article is, I hope, a first step in this process. Grades are an important measure of achievement. They cannot replace standardized tests that allow comparisons across populations, but they can be used in addition to standardized tests. Furthermore, they can be interpreted as an indicator of young women's future potential to do well in math and succeed in math-related careers. It may be particularly important to use girls' better math grades to change parents' attitudes about the value of math for their daughters and their daughters' ability to do math. Parents' attitudes about their daughters' and sons' mathematics participation and skill vary systematically. Given equal mathematics performance, parents of daughters more than parents of sons believe that their daughters must work harder at math, that math is more difficult for them, and that math is less important for them (Parsons, Adler et al., 1982). Similarly, mothers of daughters in comparison with mothers of sons are more satisfied with their daughters' math performance (given equal performance) but expect less of their daughters in terms of future schooling (Holloway, 1986). Parents' expectations for their daughters' and sons' future career plans also reinforce the expectation on the part of girls that they will pursue careers parttime or not at all when they have young children (Brody & Fox, 1980). Parental attitudes are significantly correlated with their child's self-perception of math ability as well as with their child's math performance (Parsons, Adler et al., 1982). Thus it appears that grades affect subsequent math performance through their effect on parental attitudes, which in turn affect student attitudes and behavior (Eccles & Jacobs, 1986).

Furthermore, parental attitudes are influenced by media reports. Mothers of daughters who read popular media reports of the Benbow and Stanley (1980) study in comparison with mothers who had not seen such reports felt that their daughters had less math ability and a lower chance of future success in math, that math was more difficult for their daughters, and that their daughters had to work harder to do well in math. In contrast, fathers of daughters who had read popular reports perceived their daughters' math ability as higher than when they had rated it prior to media exposure. On the other hand, fathers of sons exposed to media reports were more likely to rate math as more important for boys and to perceive girls as less able in math than were fathers of sons who had not seen the media coverage (Eccles & Jacobs, 1986; Jacobs & Eccles, 1985). Thus it may be possible to use information about girls' superior math grades to convince parents of their daughters' math potential, which may in turn increase girls' self-perceived math ability, performance, and course taking.

Girls' higher math grades may also lead to a reevaluation of some common underlying assumptions in the area of sex-related differences in mathematics achievement. Because the literature has focused on girls' poorer performance on standardized tests, it has also been assumed that girls' presumed preference for a rote learning style or familiar performance situation is disadvantageous. However, if these preferences facilitate girls' performance on classroom exams, perhaps we should reevaluate our judgments. Indeed, boys' autonomous learning style or lack of motivation to do well on familiar tasks may be problematic in some situations. Perhaps what is most needed is an increased flexibility on the part of both boys and girls so that they may perform optimally across a wide range of achievement situations, as well as increased flexibility in our views of mathematics achievement in order to accommodate the different strengths that each sex brings to the study of math.

References

Alexander, K. L., & Pallas, A. M. (1983). Reply to Benbow and Stanley. *American Educational Research Journal, 20*, 475–477.

Armstrong, J. M. (1981). Achievement and participation of women in mathematics: Results of two national surveys. *Journal for Research in Mathematics Education, 12*, 356–372.

Backman, M. E. (1972). Patterns of mental abilities: Ethnic, socioeconomic, and sex differences. *American Educational Research Journal, 9*, 1–12.

Becker, B. J., & Hedges, L. V. (1984). Meta-analysis of cognitive gender differences: A comment on an analysis by Rosenthal and Rubin. *Journal of Educational Psychology, 76*, 583–587.

Becker, J. R. (1981). Differential treatment of females and males in mathematics classes. *Journal for Research in Mathematics Education, 12*, 40–53.

Benbow, C. P., & Stanley, J. C. (1980). Sex differences in mathematical ability: Fact or artifact? *Science, 210*, 1262–1264.

Benbow, C. P., & Stanley, J. C. (1982a). Consequences in high school and college of sex differences in mathematical reasoning ability: A longitudinal perspective. *American Educational Research Journal, 19*, 598–622.

Benbow, C. P., & Stanley, J. C. (1982b). Intellectually talented boys and girls: Educational profiles. *Gifted Child Quarterly, 26*, 82–88.

Benbow, C. P., & Stanley, J. C. (1983a). Differential course-taking hypothesis revisited. *American Educational Research Journal, 20*, 469–473.

Benbow, C. P., & Stanley, J. C. (1983b). Sex differences in mathematical reasoning ability: More facts. *Science, 222*, 1029–1030.

Boli, J., Allen, M. L., & Payne, A. (1985). High ability women and men in undergraduate mathematics and chemistry courses. *American Educational Research Journal, 22*, 605–626.

Boswell, S. L. (1985). The influence of sex-role stereotyping on women's attitudes and achievement in mathematics. In S. F. Chipman, L. R. Brush, & D. M. Wilson (Eds.), *Women and mathematics: Balancing the equation* (pp. 175–197). Hillsdale, NJ: Erlbaum.

Brandon, P. R., Newton, B. J., & Hammond, O. W. (1987). Children's mathematics achievement in Hawaii: Sex differences favoring girls. *American Educational Research Journal, 24*, 437–461.

Brody, L., & Fox, L. H. (1980). An accelerative intervention program for mathematically gifted girls. In L. H. Fox, L. Brody, & D. Tobin (Eds.), *Women and the mathematical mystique* (pp. 164–192). Baltimore, MD: Johns Hopkins University Press.

Brophy, J. (1985). Interactions of male and female students with male and female teachers. In L. C. Wilkinson & C. B. Marrett (Eds.), *Gender influences in classroom interaction* (pp. 115–142). Orlando, FL: Academic Press.

Brophy, J. (1986). Teaching and learning mathematics: Where research should be going. *Journal for Research in Mathematics Education, 17,* 323–346.

Brush, L. R. (1980). *Encouraging girls in mathematics: The problem and the solution.* Cambridge, MA: Abt Books.

Burnett, S. A., Lane, D. M., & Dratt, L. M. (1979). Spatial visualization and sex differences in quantitative ability. *Intelligence, 3,* 345–354.

Casserly, P. L. (1980). Factors affecting female participation in advanced placement programs in mathematics, chemistry, and physics. In L. H. Fox, L. Brody, & D. Tobin (Eds.), *Women and the mathematical mystique* (pp. 138–163). Baltimore, MD: Johns Hopkins University Press.

Collins, E. L. (1985). Ability, academic achievement, and aspiration of mathematically gifted males and females. (Doctoral dissertation, University of Maryland, 1985). *Dissertation Abstracts International, 46,* 2219A–2220A.

Collis, B., & Williams, R. L. (1987). Cross cultural comparison of gender differences in adolescents' attitudes toward computers and selected school subjects. *Journal of Educational Research, 81,* 17–27.

Connor, J. M., & Serbin, L. A. (1985). Visual-spatial skill: Is it important for mathematics? Can it be taught? In S. F. Chipman, L. R. Brush, & D. M. Wilson (Eds.), *Women and mathematics: Balancing the equation* (pp. 151–174). Hillsdale, NJ: Erlbaum.

Deboer, G. E. (1984). A study of gender effects in the science and mathematics course-taking behavior of a group of students who graduated from college in the late 1970s. *Journal of Research in Science Teaching, 21,* 95–103.

Deboer, G. E. (1986). Perceived science ability as a factor in the course selections of men and women in college. *Journal of Research in Science Teaching, 23,* 343–352.

deWolf, V. A. (1981). High school mathematics preparation and sex differences in quantitative abilities. *Psychology of Women Quarterly, 5,* 555–567.

Diener, C. I., & Dweck, C. S. (1978). An analysis of learned helplessness: Continuous changes in performance, strategy, and achievement cognitions following failure. *Journal of Personality and Social Psychology, 36,* 451–462.

Diener, C. I., & Dweck, C. S. (1980). An analysis of learned helplessness: II. The processing of success. *Journal of Personality and Social Psychology, 39,* 940–952.

Dweck, C. S. (1986). Motivational processes affecting learning. *American Psychologist, 41,* 1040–1048.

Dweck, C. S., Davidson, W., Nelson, S., & Enna, B. (1978). Sex differences in learned helplessness: II. The contingencies of evaluative feedback in the classroom and III. An experimental analysis. *Developmental Psychology, 14,* 268–276.

Dweck, C. S., & Licht, B. G. (1980). Learned helplessness and intellectual achievement. In J. Garber & M. Seligman (Eds.), *Human helplessness: Theory and applications* (pp. 197–221). New York: Academic Press.

Eccles, J. S. (1986). Gender roles and women's achievement. *Educational Researcher, 15*(6), 15–19.

Eccles, J. S. (1987). Gender roles and women's achievement-related decisions. *Psychology of Women Quarterly, 11,* 135–171.

Eccles, J. (Parsons), Adler, T., & Meece, J. L. (1984). Sex differences in achievement: A test of alternate theories. *Journal of Personality and Social Psychology, 46,* 26–43.

Eccles, J. S., & Blumenfeld, P. (1985). Classroom experiences and student gender: Are there differences and do they matter? In L. C. Wilkinson & C. B. Marrett (Eds.), *Gender influences in the classroom* (pp. 79–114). Orlando, FL: Academic Press.

Eccles, J. S., & Jacobs, J. E. (1986). Social forces shape math attitudes and performance. *Signs, 11,* 367–380.

Elliot, E. S., & Dweck, C. S. (1988). Goals: An approach to motivation

and achievement. *Journal of Personality and Social Psychology, 54,* 5–12.

Elmore, P. B., & Vasu, E. S. (1986). A model of statistics achievement using spatial ability, feminist attitudes and mathematics-related variables as predictors. *Educational and Psychological Measurement, 46,* 215–222.

Ernest, J. (1976). Mathematics and sex. *American Mathematical Monthly, 83,* 595–614.

Ethington, C. A., & Wolfe, L. M. (1984). Sex differences in a causal model of mathematics achievement. *Journal for Research in Mathematics Education, 15,* 361–377.

Feingold, A. (1988). Cognitive gender differences are disappearing. *American Psychologist, 43,* 95–103.

Fennema, E. (1974). Mathematics learning and the sexes: A review. *Journal of Research in Mathematics Education, 5,* 126–139.

Fennema, E. (1980). Sex-related differences in mathematics achievement: Where and why. In L. H. Fox, L. Brody, & D. Tobin (Eds.), *Women and the mathematical mystique* (pp. 76–93). Baltimore, MD: Johns Hopkins University Press.

Fennema, E. (1983). Success in mathematics. In M. Marland (Ed.), *Sex differentiation and schooling* (pp. 163–180). London: Heinemann Educational Books.

Fennema, E. (1985a). Attribution theory and achievement in mathematics. In S. R. Yussen (Ed.), *The growth of reflection in children* (pp. 245–265). New York: Academic Press.

Fennema, E. (Ed.). (1985b). Explaining sex-related differences in mathematics: Theoretical models. *Educational Studies in Mathematics, 16,* 303–320.

Fennema, E., & Carpenter, T. P. (1981). Sex-related differences in mathematics: Results from the national assessment. *Mathematics Teacher, 74,* 554–559.

Fennema, E., & Peterson, P. (1985). Autonomous learning behavior: A possible explanation of gender-related differences in mathematics. In L. C. Wilkinson & C. B. Marrett (Eds.), *Gender influences in classroom interaction* (pp. 17–35). Orlando, FL: Academic Press.

Fennema, E., & Sherman, J. (1977). Sex related differences in mathematics achievement, spatial visualization and affective factors. *American Educational Research Journal, 14,* 51–71.

Fennema, E., & Sherman, J. (1978). Sex related differences in mathematics achievement and related factors: A further study. *Journal for Research in Mathematics Education, 9,* 189–203.

Fennema, E., & Tartre, L. A. (1985). The use of spatial visualization in mathematics by girls and boys. *Journal for Research in Mathematics Education, 16,* 184–206.

Ferrini-Mundy, J. (1987). Spatial training for calculus students: Sex differences in achievement and in visualization ability. *Journal for Research in Mathematics Education, 18,* 126–140.

Fox, L. H., Benbow, C. P., & Perkins, S. (1983). An accelerated mathematics program for girls: A longitudinal evaluation. In C. P. Benbow & J. C. Stanley (Eds.), *Academic precocity: Aspects of its development* (pp. 113–139). Baltimore, MD: Johns Hopkins University Press.

Fox, L. H., Brody, L., & Tobin, L. (1985). The impact of early intervention upon course-taking and attitudes in high school. In S. F. Chipman, L. R. Brush, & D. M. Wilson (Eds.), *Women and mathematics: Balancing the equation* (pp. 249–274). Hillsdale, NJ: Erlbaum.

Fox, L. H., & Cohn, S. J. (1980). Sex differences in the development of precocious mathematical talent. In L. H. Fox, L. Brody, & D. Tobin (Eds.), *Women and the mathematical mystique* (pp. 94–112). Baltimore, MD: Johns Hopkins University Press.

Galbraith, P. L. (1986). The use of mathematical strategies: Factors and features affecting performance. *Educational Studies in Mathematics, 17,* 413–441.

Good, R., Sikes, J. N., & Brophy, J. (1973). Effects of teacher sex and student sex on classroom interaction. *Journal of Educational Psychology, 65,* 74–87.

Grant, L. (1985). Race-gender status, classroom interaction, and children's socialization in elementary school. In L. C. Wilkinson & C. B. Marrett (Eds.), *Gender influences in classroom interaction* (pp. 57–77). Orlando, FL: Academic Press.

Green, L., & Foster, D. (1987). Classroom intrinsic motivation: Effects of scholastic level, teacher orientation, and gender. *Journal of Educational Research, 80,* 34–39.

Grieb, A., & Easley, J. (1984). A primary school impediment to mathematical equity: Case studies in rule-dependent socialization. In M. W. Steinkamp & M. L. Maehr (Eds.), *Advances in motivation and achievement: Women in science* (Vol. 2, pp. 317–362). Greenwich, CT: JAI Press.

Hanna, G. S. (1986). Sex differences in the mathematics achievement of eighth graders in Ontario. *Journal for Research in Mathematics Education, 17,* 231–237.

Hanna, G. S., & Sonnenschein, J. L. (1985). Relative validity of the Orleans-Hanna Algebra Prognosis Test in the prediction of girls' and boys' grades in first-year algebra. *Educational and Psychological Measurement, 45,* 361–367.

Hedges, L. V., & Becker, B. J. (1986). Statistical methods in the meta-analysis of research on gender differences. In J. S. Hyde & M. C. Linn (Eds.), *The psychology of gender: Advances through meta-analysis* (pp. 14–50). Baltimore, MD: Johns Hopkins University Press.

Heller, K. A., & Parsons, J. E. (1981). Sex differences in teachers' evaluative feedback and students' expectancies for success in mathematics. *Child Development, 52,* 1015–1019.

Helson, R. (1980). The creative woman mathematician. In L. H. Fox, L. Brody, & D. Tobin (Eds.), *Women and the mathematical mystique* (pp. 23–54). Baltimore, MD: Johns Hopkins University Press.

Hilton, T. L., & Bergland, G. W. (1974). Sex differences in mathematics achievement: A longitudinal study. *Journal of Educational Research, 67,* 231–237.

Holloway, S. D. (1986). The relationship of mothers' beliefs to children's mathematics achievement: Some effects of sex differences. *Merrill-Palmer Quarterly, 32,* 231–250.

Hudgings, M. W. (1986). Girls and mathematics: An analysis of middle school mathematics classroom environments (Doctoral dissertation, Bryn Mawr College, 1985). *Dissertation Abstracts International, 46,* 3657A.

Hudson, L. (1986). Item-level analysis of sex differences in mathematics achievement test performance (Doctoral dissertation, Cornell University, 1986). *Dissertation Abstracts International, 47,* 850B–851B.

Hughes, B. J., Sullivan, H. J., & Beaird, J. (1986). Continuing motivation of boys and girls under differing evaluation conditions and achievement levels. *American Educational Research Journal, 23,* 660–667.

Hyde, J. S. (1981). How large are cognitive gender differences? A meta-analysis using w^2 and d. *American Psychologist, 36,* 892–901.

Jacobs, J., & Eccles, J. S. (1985). Gender differences in math ability: The impact of media reports on parents. *Educational Researcher, 14*(3), 20–25.

Jagacinski, C. M. (1987). Engineering careers: Women in a male-dominated field. *Psychology of Women Quarterly, 11,* 97–110.

Jones, L. V. (1987). The influence on mathematics test scores, by ethnicity and sex, of prior achievement and high school mathematics courses. *Journal for Research in Mathematics Education, 18,* 180–186.

Kahle, J. B., Matyas, M. L., & Cho, H. (1985). An assessment of the impact of science experiences on the career choices of male and female biology students. *Journal of Research in Science Teaching, 22,* 385–394.

Kissane, B. V. (1986). Selection of mathematically talented students. *Educational Studies in Mathematics, 17,* 221–241.

Koehler, M. C. S. (1986). Effective mathematics teaching and sex-related differences in algebra one classes (Doctoral dissertation, University of Wisconsin, 1985). *Dissertation Abstracts International, 46,* 2953A.

La Noue, J. B., & Curtis, R. C. (1985). Improving women's performance in mixed-sex situations by effort attributions. *Psychology of Women Quarterly, 9,* 337–356.

Leder, G. C. (1987). Teacher student interaction: A case study. *Educational Studies in Mathematics, 18,* 255–271.

Leinhardt, G., Seewald, A., & Engel, M. (1979). Learning what's taught: Sex differences in instruction. *Journal of Educational Psychology, 71,* 432–439.

Licht, B. G., & Dweck, C. S. (1983). Sex differences in achievement orientations: Consequences for academic choices and attainments. In M. Marland (Ed.), *Sex differentiation and schooling* (pp. 72–97). London: Heinemann Educational Books.

Licht, B. G., & Dweck, C. S. (1984). Determinants of academic achievement: The interaction of children's achievement orientations with skill area. *Developmental Psychology, 20,* 628–636.

Linn, M. C., De Benedictis, T., Delucchi, K., Harris, A., & Stage, E. (1987). Gender differences in national assessment of educational progress science items: What does "I don't know" really mean? *Journal of Research in Science Teaching, 24,* 267–278.

Linn, M. C., & Petersen, A. C. (1986). A meta-analysis of gender differences in spatial ability: Implications for mathematics and science achievement. In J. S. Hyde & M. C. Linn (Eds.), *The psychology of gender: Advances through meta-analysis* (pp. 67–101). Baltimore, MD: Johns Hopkins University Press.

Llabre, M. M., & Suarez, E. (1985). Predicting math anxiety and course performance in women and men. *Journal of Counseling Psychology, 32,* 283–287.

Lorenz, J. H. (1982). On some psychological aspects of mathematics achievement assessment and classroom interaction. *Educational Studies in Mathematics, 13,* 1–19.

Luchins, E. H., & Luchins, A. S. (1980). Female mathematicians: A contemporary appraisal. In L. H. Fox, L. Brody, & D. Tobin (Eds.), *Women and the mathematical mystique* (pp. 7–22). Baltimore, MD: Johns Hopkins University Press.

Lyons-Lepke, E. M. (1986). Choosing majors and careers: An investigation of women persisters and defectors in mathematics and science majors in college (Doctoral dissertation, Rutgers–The State University of New Jersey, 1986). *Dissertation Abstracts International, 47,* 2325A.

Maccoby, E. E., & Jacklin, C. N. (1974). *The psychology of sex differences.* Stanford, CA: Stanford University Press.

MacDonald, C. T. (1980). An experiment in mathematics education at the college level. In L. H. Fox, L. Brody, & D. Tobin (Eds.), *Women and the mathematical mystique* (pp. 115–137). Baltimore, MD: Johns Hopkins University Press.

Marshall, S. P. (1984). Sex differences in children's mathematics achievement: Solving computations and story problems. *Journal of Educational Psychology, 76,* 194–204.

Meece, J. L., Parsons, J. E., Kaczala, M., Goff, S. B., & Futterman, R. (1982). Sex differences in math achievement: Toward a model of academic choice. *Psychological Bulletin, 91,* 324–348.

Michael, W. B. (1983). Manifestation of creative behaviors by maturing participants in the study of mathematically precocious youth. In C. P. Benbow & J. C. Stanley (Eds.), *Academic precocity: Aspects of its development* (pp. 38–50). Baltimore, MD: Johns Hopkins University Press.

Miller, A. (1986). Performance impairment after failure: Mechanism and sex differences. *Journal of Educational Psychology, 78,* 486–491.

Moore, E. G. J., & Smith, A. W. (1987). Sex and ethnic group differences in mathematics achievement: Results from the national longitudinal study. *Journal for Research in Mathematics Education, 18,* 25–36.

Morse, L. W., & Handley, H. M. (1985). Listening to adolescents: Gender differences in the science classroom interaction. In L. C. Wilkinson & C. B. Marrett (Eds.), *Gender influences in classroom interactions* (pp. 37–56). Orlando, FL: Academic Press.

Mura, R. (1982). Gender and mathematics in Canada. In E. Schildkamp-Kuendiger (Ed.), *An international review of gender and mathematics* (pp. 32–43). Columbus, OH: Ohio State University, The ERIC Science, Mathematics and Environmental Educational Clearinghouse.

Mura, R. (1987). Sex-related differences in expectations of success in undergraduate mathematics. *Journal for Research in Mathematics Education, 18,* 15–24.

Mura, R., Cloutier, R., Kimball, M., Braconne, A., Caron, L., & Gagnon, F. (1985). *Attitudes, expériences et performance en mathématique d'étudiantes et d'étudiants de cinquième secondaire selon leur choix scolaire* [Attitudes, experiences, and performance in fifth-form secondary mathematics students according to their scholastic choice] (Cahier 9). Quebec: Université Laval, Les cahiers de recherche du GREMF.

Mura, R., Kimball, M. M., & Cloutier, R. (1987). Girls and science programs: Two steps forward, one step back. In J. Gaskell & A. McLaren (Eds.), *Women and education: A Canadian perspective* (pp. 133–149). Calgary, Alberta, Canada: Detselig.

Nicholls, J. G. (1976). Effort is virtuous but it's better to have ability: Evaluative responses to perceptions of effort and ability. *Journal of Research in Personality, 10,* 306–315.

Nicholls, J. G. (1984). Achievement motivation: Conceptions of ability, subjective experience, task choice, and performance. *Psychological Review, 91,* 328–346.

Pallas, A. M., & Alexander, K. L. (1983). Sex differences in quantitative SAT performance: New evidence on the differential coursework hypothesis. *American Educational Research Journal, 20,* 165–182.

Parsons, J. E., Adler, T. F., & Kaczala, C. M. (1982). Socialization of achievement attitudes and beliefs: Parental influences. *Child Development, 53,* 310–321.

Parsons, J. E., Kaczala, C. M., & Meece, J. L. (1982). Socialization of achievement attitudes and beliefs: Classroom influences. *Child Development, 53,* 322–339.

Pattison, P., & Grieve, N. (1984). Do spatial skills contribute to sex differences in different types of mathematical problems? *Journal of Educational Psychology, 76,* 678–689.

Perl, T. H. (1982). Discriminating factors and sex differences in electing mathematics. *Journal for Research in Mathematics Education, 12,* 66–74.

Peterson, K., Burton, G., & Baker, D. (1984). Geometry students' role-specific self concept: Success, teacher, and sex differences. *The Journal of Educational Research, 77,* 122–126.

Peterson, P. L., & Fennema, E. (1985). Effective teaching, student engagement in classroom activities, and sex-related differences in learning mathematics. *American Educational Research Journal, 22,* 309–336.

Pintrich, P. R., & Blumenfeld, P. C. (1985). Classroom experience and children's self-perceptions of ability, effort, and conduct. *Journal of Educational Psychology, 77,* 646–657.

Reis, S. M. (1987). We can't change what we don't recognize: Understanding the special needs of gifted females. *Gifted Child Quarterly, 31,* 83–89.

Reuman, D. A. (1986). Motivational implications of ability grouping in sixth-grade mathematics: A strong inference approach to theories of achievement motivation (Doctoral dissertation, University of Michigan, 1986). *Dissertation Abstracts International, 47,* 1315B.

Ridley, D. R., & Novak, J. D. (1983). Sex-related differences in high school science and mathematics enrollments: Do they give males a critical headstart toward science- and math-related careers? *Alberta Journal of Educational Research, 29,* 308–318.

Rosenthal, R., & Rubin, D. B. (1982). Further meta-analytic procedures for assessing cognitive gender differences. *Journal of Educational Psychology, 74,* 708–712.

Ruthvan, K. (1987). Ability stereotyping in mathematics. *Educational Studies in Mathematics, 18,* 243–253.

Ryckman, D. B., & Peckham, P. (1987). Gender differences in attributions for success and failure situations across subject areas. *Journal of Educational Research, 81,* 120–125.

Sawada, D., Olson, A. T., & Sigurdson, S. E. (1981). Sex differences in mathematics learning in a Canadian setting. *Canadian Journal of Education, 6*(2), 5–19.

Schratz, M. M. (1978). A developmental investigation of sex differences in spatial (visual-analytic) and mathematical skills in three ethnic groups. *Developmental Psychology, 14,* 263–267.

Sells, L. W. (1980). The mathematical filter and the education of women and minorities. In L. H. Fox, L. Brody, & D. Tobin (Eds.), *Women and the mathematical mystique* (pp. 66–75). Baltimore, MD: Johns Hopkins University Press.

Senk, S., & Usiskin, Z. (1983). Geometry proof writing: A new view of sex differences in mathematics ability. *American Journal of Education, 91,* 187–201.

Sherman, J. (1979). Predicting mathematics performance in high school girls and boys. *Journal of Educational Psychology, 71,* 242–249.

Sherman, J. (1981). Girls' and boys' enrollments in theoretical math courses: A longitudinal study. *Psychology of Women Quarterly, 5,* 681–689.

Sherman, J. (1983). Factors predicting girls' and boys' enrollment in college preparatory mathematics. *Psychology of Women Quarterly, 7,* 272–281.

Sherman, J., & Fennema, E. (1977). The study of mathematics by high school girls and boys: Related variables. *American Educational Research Journal, 14,* 159–168.

Sherman, J., & Fennema, E. (1978). Distribution of spatial visualization and mathematical problem solving scores: A test of Stafford's x-linked hypothesis. *Psychology of Women Quarterly, 3,* 157–167.

Singer, J. M., & Stake, J. E. (1986). Mathematics and self esteem: Implications for women's career choices. *Psychology of Women Quarterly, 10,* 339–352.

Smith, S. E., & Walker, W. J. (1988). Sex differences on New York state regents examinations: Support for the differential course-taking hypothesis. *Journal for Research in Mathematics Education, 19,* 81–85.

Stallings, J. (1985). School, classroom, and home influences on women's decisions to enroll in advanced mathematics courses. In S. F. Chipman, L. R. Brush, & D. M. Wilson (Eds.), *Women and mathematics: Balancing the equation* (pp. 199–223). Hillsdale, NJ: Erlbaum.

Stipek, D. J. (1984). Sex differences in children's attributions for success and failure on math and spelling tests. *Sex Roles, 11,* 969–981.

Stipek, D. J., & Hoffman, J. M. (1980). Children's achievement-related expectancies as a function of academic performance histories and sex. *Journal of Educational Psychology, 72,* 861–865.

Stockard, J., & Wood, J. W. (1984). The myth of female underachievement: A re-examination of sex differences in academic achievement. *American Educational Research Journal, 21,* 825–838.

214   MEREDITH M. KIMBALL

Struik, R. R., & Flexer, R. J. (1977). Self-paced calculus: A preliminary examination. *American Mathematic Monthly, 84,* 129–134.

Struik, R. R., & Flexer, R. J. (1984). Sex differences in mathematical achievement: Adding data to the debate. *International Journal of Women's Studies, 7,* 336–342.

Swafford, J. (1980). Sex differences in first year algebra. *Journal for Research in Mathematics Education, 11,* 335–345.

Threadgill-Sowder, J., Sowder, L., Moyer, J. C., & Moyer, M. B. (1985). Cognitive variables and performance on mathematical story problems. *Journal of Experimental Education, 54,* 56–62.

Tittle, C. K. (1986). Gender research and education. *American Psychologist, 41,* 1161–1168.

Wagner, H., & Zimmerman, B. (1986). Identification and fostering of mathematically gifted students. *Educational Studies in Mathematics, 17,* 243–259.

Webb, N. M. (1984). Sex differences in interaction and achievement in cooperative small groups. *Journal of Educational Psychology, 76,* 33–44.

Webb, N. M., & Kenderski, C. M. (1985). Gender differences in small-group interaction and achievement in high- and low-achieving classes. In L. C. Wilkinson & C. B. Marrett (Eds.), *Gender influences in classroom interaction* (pp. 209–236). Orlando, FL: Academic Press.

Weiner, N. C., & Robinson, S. E. (1986). Cognitive abilities, personality and gender differences in math achievement of gifted adolescents. *Gifted Child Quarterly, 30,* 83–87.

Wiggins, W. (1982). *Mathematics: The invisible filter: A report on math avoidance, math anxiety and career choices.* Toronto, Ontario, Canada: Toronto Board of Education.

Wilkinson, L. C., Lindow, J., & Chiang, C. P. (1985). Sex differences and sex segregation in students' small-group communication. In L. C. Wilkinson & C. B. Marrett (Eds.), *Gender influences in classroom interaction* (pp. 185–207). Orlando, FL: Academic Press.

Wise, L. L. (1985). Project TALENT: Mathematics course participation in the 1960s and its career consequences. In S. F. Chipman, L. R. Brush, & D. M. Wilson (Eds.), *Women and mathematics: Balancing the equation* (pp. 25–50). Hillsdale, NJ: Erlbaum.

Woehlke, P. L., & Leitner, D. W. (1980). Gender differences in performance on variables related to achievement in graduate-level educational statistics. *Psychological Reports, 47,* 1119–1125.

Wooleat, P. L., Pedro, J. D., Becker, J. D., & Fennema, E. (1980). Sex differences in high school students' causal attributions of performance in mathematics. *Journal for Research in Mathematics Education, 11,* 356–366.

Received November 16, 1987
Revision received May 9, 1988
Accepted July 8, 1988 ■

[18]

Sex Differences in Mathematical Ability: Fact or Artifact?

Abstract. *A substantial sex difference in mathematical reasoning ability (score on the mathematics test of the Scholastic Aptitude Test) in favor of boys was found in a study of 9927 intellectually gifted junior high school students. Our data contradict the hypothesis that differential course-taking accounts for observed sex differences in mathematical ability, but support the hypothesis that these differences are somewhat increased by environmental influences.*

Huge sex differences have been reported in mathematical aptitude and achievement (*1*). In junior high school, this sex difference is quite obvious: girls excel in computation, while boys excel on tasks requiring mathematical reasoning ability (*1*). Some investigators believe that differential course-taking gives rise to the apparently inferior mathematical reasoning ability of girls (*2*). One alternative, however, could be that less well-developed mathematical reasoning ability contributes to girls' taking fewer mathematics courses and achieving less than boys.

We now present extensive data collected by the Study of Mathematically Precocious Youth (SMPY) for the past 8 years to examine mathematical aptitude in approximately 10,000 males and females prior to the onset of differential course-taking. These data show that large sex differences in mathematical aptitude are observed in boys and girls with essentially identical formal educational experiences.

Six separate SMPY talent searches were conducted (*3*). In the first three searches, 7th and 8th graders, as well as accelerated 9th and 10th graders, were eligible; for the last three, only 7th graders and accelerated students of 7th grade age were eligible. In addition, in the 1976, 1978, and 1979 searches, the stu-

dents had also to be in the upper 3 percent in mathematical ability as judged by a standardized achievement test, in 1972 in the upper 5 percent, and in 1973 and 1974 in the upper 2 percent. Thus, both male and female talent-search participants were selected by equal criteria for high mathematical ability before entering. Girls constituted 43 percent of the participants in these searches.

As part of each talent search the students took both parts of the College Board's Scholastic Aptitude Test (SAT)—the mathematics (SAT-M) and the verbal (SAT-V) tests (*4*). The SAT is designed for able juniors and seniors in high school, who are an average of 4 to 5 years older than the students in the talent searches. The mathematical section is particularly designed to measure mathematical reasoning ability (*5*). For this reason, scores on the SAT-M achieved by 7th and 8th graders provided an excellent opportunity to test the Fennema and Sherman differential course-taking hypothesis (*2*), since until then all students had received essentially identical formal instruction in mathematics (*6*). If their hypothesis is correct, little difference in mathematical aptitude should be seen between able boys and girls in our talent searches.

Results from the six talent searches are shown in Table 1. Most students

Table 1. Performance of students in the Study of Mathematically Precocious Youth in each talent search (N = 9927).

| Test date | Grade | Number | | SAT-V score* ($\overline{X} \pm$ S.D.) | | SAT-M scores† | | | | Percentage scoring above 600 on SAT-M | |
| | | Boys | Girls | Boys | Girls | $\overline{X} \pm$ S.D. | | Highest score | | Boys | Girls |
						Boys	Girls	Boys	Girls		
March 1972	7	90	77			460 ± 104	423 ± 75	740	590	7.8	0
	8+	133	96			528 ± 105	458 ± 88	790	600	27.1	0
January 1973	7	135	88	385 ± 71	374 ± 74	495 ± 85	440 ± 66	800	620	8.1	1.1
	8+	286	158	431 ± 89	442 ± 83	551 ± 85	511 ± 63	800	650	22.7	8.2
January 1974	7	372	222			473 ± 85	440 ± 68	760	630	6.5	1.8
	8+	556	369			540 ± 82	503 ± 72	750	700	21.6	7.9
December 1976	7	495	356	370 ± 73	368 ± 70	455 ± 84	421 ± 64	780	610	5.5	0.6
	8‡	12	10	487 ± 129	390 ± 61	598 ± 126	482 ± 83	750	600	58.3	0
January 1978	7 and 8‡	1549	1249	375 ± 80	372 ± 78	448 ± 87	413 ± 71	790	760	5.3	0.8
January 1979	7 and 8‡	2046	1628	370 ± 76	370 ± 77	436 ± 87	404 ± 77	790	760	3.2	0.9

*Mean score for a random sample of high school juniors and seniors was 368 for males and females (*8*).   †Mean for juniors and seniors: males, 416; females, 390 (*8*).   ‡These rare 8th graders were accelerated at least 1 year in school grade placement.

scored high on both the SAT-M and SAT-V. On the SAT-V, the boys and girls performed about equally well (*7*). The overall performance of 7th grade students on SAT-V was at or above the average of a random sample of high school students, whose mean score is 368 (*8*), or at about the 30th percentile of college-bound 12th graders. The 8th graders, regular and accelerated, scored at about the 50th percentile of college-bound seniors. This was a high level of performance.

A large sex difference in mathematical ability in favor of boys was observed in every talent search. The smallest mean difference in the six talent searches was 32 points in 1979 in favor of boys. The statistically significant *t*-tests of mean differences ranged from 2.5 to 11.6 (*9*). Thus, on the average, the boys scored about one-half of the females' standard deviation (S.D.) better than did the girls in each talent search, even though all students had been certified initially to be in the top 2nd, 3rd, or 5th percentiles in mathematical reasoning ability (depending on which search was entered).

One might suspect that the SMPY talent search selected for abler boys than girls. In all comparisons except for two (8th graders in 1972 and 1976), however, the girls performed better on SAT-M relative to female college-bound seniors than the boys did on SAT-M relative to male college-bound seniors. Furthermore, in all searches, the girls were equal verbally to the boys. Thus, even though the talent-search girls were at least as able compared to girls in general as the talent-search boys were compared to boys in general, the boys still averaged considerably higher on SAT-M than the girls did.

Moreover, the greatest disparity between the girls and boys is in the upper ranges of mathematical reasoning ability. Differences between the top-scoring

boys and girls have been as large as 190 points (1972 8th graders) and as low as 30 points (1978 and 1979). When one looks further at students who scored above 600 on SAT-M, Table 1 shows a great difference in the percentage of boys and girls. To take the extreme (not including the 1976 8th graders), among the 1972 8th graders, 27.1 percent of the boys scored higher than 600, whereas not one of the girls did. Over all talent searches, boys outnumbered girls more than 2 to 1 (1817 boys versus 675 girls) in SAT-M scores over 500. In not one of the six talent searches was the top SAT-M score earned by a girl. It is clear that much of the sex difference on SAT-M can be accounted for by a lack of high-scoring girls.

A few highly mathematically able girls have been found, particularly in the latest two talent searches. The latter talent searches, however, were by far the largest, making it more likely that we could identify females of high mathematical ability. Alternatively, even if highly able girls have felt more confident to enter the mathematics talent search in recent years, our general conclusions would not be altered unless all of the girls with the highest ability had stayed away for more than 5 years. We consider that unlikely. In this context, three-fourths as many girls have participated as boys each year; the relative percentages have not varied over the years.

It is notable that we observed sizable sex differences in mathematical reasoning ability in 7th grade students. Until that grade, boys and girls have presumably had essentially the same amount of formal training in mathematics. This assumption is supported by the fact that in the 1976 talent search no substantial sex differences were found in either participation in special mathematics programs or in mathematical learning processes (*6*). Thus, the sex difference in mathe-

matical reasoning ability we found was observed before girls and boys started to differ significantly in the number and types of mathematics courses taken. It is therefore obvious that differential course-taking in mathematics cannot alone explain the sex difference we observed in mathematical reasoning ability, although other environmental explanations have not been ruled out.

The sex difference in favor of boys found at the time of the talent search was sustained and even increased through the high school years. In a follow-up survey of talent-search participants who had graduated from high school in 1977 (*10*), the 40-point mean difference on SAT-M in favor of boys at the time of that group's talent search had increased to a 50-point mean difference at the time of high school graduation. This subsequent increase is consistent with the hypothesis that differential course-taking can affect mathematical ability (*2*). The increase was rather small, however. Our data also show a sex difference in the number of mathematics courses taken in favor of boys but not a large one. The difference stemmed mainly from the fact that approximately 35 percent fewer girls than boys took calculus in high school (*10*). An equal proportion of girls and boys took mathematics in the 11th grade (83 percent), however, which is actually the last grade completed before taking the SAT in high school. It, therefore, cannot be argued that these boys received substantially more formal practice in mathematics and therefore scored better. Instead, it is more likely that mathematical reasoning ability influences subsequent differential course-taking in mathematics. There were also no significant sex differences in the grades earned in the various mathematics courses (*10*).

A possible criticism of our results is that only selected mathematically able, highly motivated students were tested. Are the SMPY results indicative of the general population? Lowering qualifications for the talent search did not result in more high-scoring individuals (except in 1972, which was a small and not widely known search), suggesting that the same results in the high range would be observed even if a broader population were tested. In addition, most of the concern about the lack of participation of females in mathematics expressed by Ernest (*11*) and others has been about intellectually able girls, rather than those of average or below average intellectual ability.

To what extent do girls with high mathematical reasoning ability opt out of the SMPY talent searches? More boys than girls (57 percent versus 43 percent) enter the talent search each year. For this to change our conclusions, however, it would be necessary to postulate that the most highly talented girls were the least likely to enter each search. On both empirical and logical grounds this seems improbable.

It is hard to dissect out the influences of societal expectations and attitudes on mathematical reasoning ability. For example, rated liking of mathematics and rated importance of mathematics in future careers had no substantial relationship with SAT-M scores (*6*). Our results suggest that these environmental influences are more significant for achievement in mathematics than for mathematical aptitude.

We favor the hypothesis that sex differences in achievement in and attitude toward mathematics result from superior male mathematical ability, which may in turn be related to greater male ability in spatial tasks (*12*). This male superiority is probably an expression of a combination of both endogenous and exogenous variables. We recognize, however, that our data are consistent with numerous alternative hypotheses. Nonetheless, the hypothesis of differential course-taking was not supported. It also seems likely that putting one's faith in boy-versus-girl socialization processes as the only permissible explanation of the sex difference in mathematics is premature.

CAMILLA PERSSON BENBOW
JULIAN C. STANLEY
Department of Psychology,
Johns Hopkins University,
Baltimore, Maryland 21218

References and Notes

1. E. Fennema, *J. Res. Math. Educ.* **5**, 126 (1974); "National assessment for educational progress," *NAEP Newsl.* **8** (No. 5), insert (1975); L. Fox, in *Intellectual Talent: Research and Development,* D. Keating, Ed. (Johns Hopkins Univ. Press, Baltimore, 1976), p. 183.
2. For example, E. Fennema and J. Sherman, *Am. Educ. Res. J.* **14**, 51 (1977).
3. W. George and C. Solano, in *Intellectual Talent: Research and Development,* D. Keating, Ed. (Johns Hopkins Univ. Press, Baltimore, 1976), p. 55.
4. The SAT-V was not administered in 1972 and 1974, and the Test of Standard Written English was required in 1978 and 1979.
5. W. Angoff, Ed., *The College Board Admissions Testing Program* (College Entrance Examination Board, Princeton, N.J., 1971), p. 15.
6. C. Benbow and J. Stanley, manuscript in preparation.
7. This was not true for the accelerated 8th graders in 1976. The *N* for the latter comparison is only 22.
8. College Entrance Examination Board, *Guide to the Admissions Testing Service* (Educational Testing Service, Princeton, N.J., 1978), p. 15.
9. The *t*-tests and *P* values for 7th and 8th graders, respectively, in the six talent searches were 2.6, $P < .01$; 5.3, $P < .001$; 5.1, $P < .001$; 5.2, $P < .001$; 4.9, $P < .001$; 7.1, $P < .001$; 6.6, $P < .001$; 2.5, $P < .05$; 11.6, $P < .001$; and 11.5, $P < .001$.
10. C. Benbow and J. Stanley, in preparation.
11. J. Ernest, *Am. Math. Mon.* **83**, 595 (1976).
12. I. MacFarlane-Smith, *Spatial Ability* (Univ. of London Press, London, 1964); J. Sherman, *Psychol. Rev.* **74**, 290 (1967).
13. We thank R. Benbow, C. Breaux, and L. Fox for their comments and help in preparing this manuscript. Supported in part by grants from the Spencer Foundation and the Educational Foundation of America.

21 March 1980; revised 14 August 1980

[19]

American Educational Research Journal
Winter 1982, Vol. 19, No. 4, Pp. 598-622

Consequences in High School and College of Sex Differences in Mathematical Reasoning Ability: A Longitudinal Perspective

CAMILLA PERSSON BENBOW and JULIAN C. STANLEY
The Johns Hopkins University

Between 1972 and 1974 the Study of Mathematically Precocious Youth (SMPY) identified over 2,000 7th and 8th graders who scored as well as a national sample of 11th and 12th grade females on the College Board's Scholastic Aptitude Test (SAT) Mathematics or Verbal tests. A substantial sex difference in mathematical reasoning ability was found (Benbow & Stanley, 1980b, 1981). The consequences and development of this sex difference over the following 5 years were investigated longitudinally. Over 91 percent (1,996 out of 2,188 SMPY students) participated. This study established that the sex difference persisted over several years and was related to subsequent sex differences in mathematics achievement. The sex difference in mathematics did not reflect differential mathematics course taking. The abilities of males developed more rapidly than those of females. Sex differences favoring males were found in participation in mathematics, performance on the SAT-M, and taking of and performance on mathematics achievement and Advanced Placement Program examinations. SMPY females received better grades in their mathematics courses than SMPY males did. Few significant sex differences were found in attitudes toward mathematics.

The Study of Mathematically Precocious Youth (SMPY) was begun in 1971 to study and facilitate the education of mathematically precocious junior high school students. It was designed to be longitudinal, involving successive follow-ups throughout the adult lives of the students identified and helped by SMPY.

We thank Robert A. Gordon, Lynn H. Fox, David P. Baker, and the anonymous reviewers for helpful comments and suggestions concerning earlier drafts of this article.

One of SMPY's most controversial and unexpected findings was the large and consistent sex difference in mathematical reasoning ability favoring boys (Benbow & Stanley, 1980b, 1981). In six talent searches conducted over an 8-year interval in the mid-Atlantic states and involving almost 10,000 students, the gifted seventh or eighth grade boys, who had previously been matched with gifted seventh or eighth grade girls in mathematical ability on standardized achievement tests, scored substantially better than their female counterparts on a difficult test of mathematical reasoning ability. No sex differences were seen, however, on the equally difficult verbal reasoning test.

This finding was consistent with numerous other studies of sex differences in mathematical ability and achievement (Backman, 1972; Bieri, Bradburn, & Galinsky, 1958; Ernest, 1976; Fennema, 1974; Fox, 1976; Fox, Brody, & Tobin, 1980; Garai & Scheinfeld, 1968; Glennon & Callahan, 1968; Keating, 1974; Maccoby & Jacklin, 1974; National Assessment of Educational Progress, 1975; Suydam & Weaver, 1970; Very, 1967; Wilson, 1972). The significance of the Benbow and Stanley (1980b, 1981) results was that they found the sex difference at the seventh-grade level, when formal mathematics is similar for boys and girls, and were able to rule out the hypothesis (e.g., see Fennema & Sherman, 1977) that differential course taking by boys and girls in mathematics causes the sex difference in mathematical reasoning ability. The expected sex differences in attitudes toward mathematics were also not found by these investigators (Benbow & Stanley, 1980b, 1982), and now others (Fox, Brody, & Tobin, 1982). This, along with other observations, prompted the statement that it "seems likely that putting one's faith in boy-versus-girl socialization processes as the only permissible explanation of the sex difference in mathematics is premature" (Benbow & Stanley, 1980b, p. 1264).

This investigation studied the development and consequences during junior and senior high school of the sex difference found in the seventh grade among a certain subpopulation of the students studied by Benbow and Stanley (1980b). Of special interest was the determination of what additional sex differences emerged over this 5-year interval and how they related to the initial sex difference in mathematical reasoning ability at seventh grade. We hypothesized that sex differences in mathematics participation and achievement favoring boys would develop during the high school years and that they could be partly accounted for by the sex difference in mathematical reasoning ability found several years earlier. Moreover, it was hypothesized that the sex difference on SAT-M favoring males would increase during the high school years, partly because of environmental influences and because the mathematical reasoning ability of the boys might have been increasing at a faster rate all along than the girls' was.

SUBJECTS

The special subpopulation of subjects consisted of students from SMPY's first three talent searches. In those, seventh and eighth grade students (some *accelerated* 9th and 10th-graders were eligible also) attending schools in Maryland were eligible to participate if they scored in the upper 5 percent (March 1972) or the upper 2 percent (January-February 1973 or January 1974) in mathematical ability on the national norms for a standardized achievement test administered in the regular testing program of the students' schools. As part of the talent search itself, qualifying students then took the College Board's *Scholastic Aptitude Test-Mathematics* (SAT-M) and also, in 1973, the SAT-Verbal. These tests measure mathematical and verbal reasoning ability, respectively (Angoff, 1971; Messick & Jungeblut, 1981; also see Benbow & Stanley, 1981). The participants in the talent search also completed a background questionnaire. It has been shown that these students tend to come from homes where the parents had been rather highly educated (Benbow & Stanley, 1980a; Keating, 1974).

To be part of this study, which followed up the talent search participants at high school graduation, the student had to have scored at least 390 on SAT-M *or* 370 on SAT-V during the talent search as a 7th or 8th grader. These SAT criteria selected students who as 7th or 8th graders scored as well as the average 11th and 12th grade female does on SAT-M and SAT-V (Admission Testing Program [ATP], 1979).

A sample size of 2,188 was obtained of which approximately 61 percent were males. (In the initial talent searches, approximately 57 percent were males.) When the subjects were contacted (between 1976 and 1980), most were college freshmen. This was approximately 4 to 5 years after participation in one or more of SMPY's talent searches.

INSTRUMENTATION

The initial talent-search questionnaire of the students, their talent-search SAT scores, and an eight-page questionnaire assessing their achievements in high school are the three main sources for the results of this study. The initial talent-search questionnaire was designed to assess the characteristics of the students at the time of talent search participation. The purpose of the follow-up questionnaire was to determine this group's achievement in high school, particularly in mathematics and science.

PROCEDURES

The subjects were mailed the eight-page follow-up questionnaire with an offer of monetary compensation ($5.00, or in some cases $6.00) as an incentive to return the questionnaire. The questionnaires were mailed to students at a time when they should have completed high school without educational acceleration or deceleration since talent search participation. Usually, the questionnaire was completed by the students while they were freshmen in college. Because the students were sampled from the three talent searches held in 1972, 1973, and 1974, and they could have participated in the talent searches as either seventh or eighth graders, the follow-up questionnaires were sent out in four different waves: in December 1976 (N = 214, Cohn, Note 1),[1] 1977 (594), 1978 (881), and 1979 (499). After 6 weeks, students who still had not completed the questionnaire were sent a reminder letter, including an additional questionnaire. Six weeks later a postal card reminder was sent. Finally, subjects were telephoned and urged to provide the questionnaire responses orally.

The response rates for each wave of the follow-up were 94 (Cohn, Note 1), 90, 93, and 90 percent, respectively, of the total sample. If unlocatable persons are omitted, the response rates become 98 (Cohn, Note 1), 94, 96, and 93 percent, respectively. Across all waves, the overall response rate exceeded 91 percent of the total sample of 2,188 students. There were 1,996 students in the analyses, 62 percent of whom were males. Because the response rate was so high, it seems likely that the findings accurately reflect the development in high school of the sex difference in mathematical reasoning ability among the talent search participants.

Nonrespondents: The nonresponse rate for males and females was approximately 9 percent in both cases. Nonrespondent males were not significantly less able mathematically or verbally than the males who did return their questionnaires. Nonrespondent females were, however, significantly less able mathematically, but not verbally, than those who returned questionnaires. The effect size (Cohen, 1977) for the difference on SAT-M for the girls was considered small. Thus, this difference was not judged important. (The meaning of effect size will be discussed below.)

Data Analysis

Statistical analyses, performed with the SPSS program (Nie et al., 1975), were done separately for the first wave, second wave, and combined third and fourth waves of the follow-ups.[2] Analyses using talent-search SAT scores were also performed separately by grade at talent search.[3]

Because the numbers for all the tests were large, effect sizes (Cohen, 1977) were computed to test whether a significant difference was important. Effect sizes are computed differently, depending on which statistic is used. Thus, the values for the various effect sizes are not equivalent. Cohen (1977) arbitrarily classified effect sizes as being either small, medium, or large. In this study a medium or large effect size was considered important.

---

[1] It was Cohn and Stanley's (Cohn, Note 1) responsibility for conducting the first wave of the follow-ups, with 214 students who had either met a science criterion or had scored greater than 420 on SAT-M as an eighth grader. The data collection and analysis for the remaining three waves, with N = 1,974, was our responsibility.

[2] The first and second wave data could not be combined with the third and fourth waves, because the questions on the questionnaire were slightly different in some cases.

[3] This was done to reduce confounding; in the talent search, most eighth-grade participants received higher scores on the SAT than did the seventh-grade participants.

BENBOW AND STANLEY

TABLE I

SAT Scores at the Time of the Talent Search and in High School of the Participants in Follow-up by Wave, versus High School Performance of a National Sample of College-Bound Seniors

	Talent Search					
	First Wave[a]		Second Wave		Third and Fourth Waves	
	M	SD	M	SD	M	SD
SAT-M						
Boys	567	91	549	74	526	76
Girls	505	58	510	58	498	61
t of mean difference	5.1		6.7		6.9	
	p < .001		*p* < .001		*p* < .001	
SAT-V[b]						
Boys	—		443	86	400	65
Girls	—		468	86	411	74
t of mean difference			−3.1		*ns*	
			p < .01			

	High School							
	First Wave[a]		Second Wave		Third and Fourth Waves		National Sample of College-Bound Seniors	
	M	SD	M	SD	M	SD	M	SD
SAT-M								
Boys	691	75	693	72	695	67	493	121
Girls	652	72	643	68	650	75	443	109
t of mean difference	3.5		7.9		10.6			
	p < .001		*p* < .001		*p* < .001			
SAT-V								
Boys	596	100	602	82	590	88	431	110
Girls	594	115	612	83	592	91	423	110
t of mean difference	*ns*		*ns*		*ns*			

Note. N = 1,996

[a] Taken from Cohn (Note 1).

[b] SAT-V was administered only in the 1973 Talent Search. Thus SAT-V scores were available for the 1973 Talent Search eighth graders, all in the second wave of the follow-ups, and for the 1973 Talent Search seventh graders, all in the third wave of the follow-ups.

RESULTS

Initial Sex Difference

Mean SAT scores of the follow-up group at the time of the talent search are shown in Table I. Because of the additional selection criteria, mean scores are much higher than the average from SMPY's six talent searches.

The groups' scores were also far superior to the means of a national sample of college-bound seniors (ATP, 1979). On SAT-M, boys in each wave scored significantly higher than the girls by at least 28 points, whereas girls scored higher on the SAT–V—significantly so for the second-wave.[4] The effect size for the sex difference on SAT-M in the talent search on the average was medium (i.e., .82, .59, and .41, respectively), while for the difference on SAT-V it was small (i.e., .29 and .16, respectively). Thus, the sex difference on SAT-M was considered important, but not the difference on SAT-V. Below we investigate the consequences in high school of this important difference on SAT-M in the seventh or eighth grade.

SAT Scores in High School

In the follow-up questionnaire the students were asked to report the SAT scores they received in high school. By the end of high school the boys' and girls' mean score on SAT-M had increased an average of 155 and 145 points, respectively, from the time of talent search participation (see Table I). Both boys and girls in the follow-up scored approximately 200 points better than their respective norm group of college-bound seniors (see the lower half of Table I). The sex difference on SAT-M in high school was significant beyond the $p < .001$ level. Effect sizes ranged from .52 to .71, all of which are in the medium range. Thus, the sex difference found in the seventh grade clearly persisted.

On SAT-V in the second wave of the follow-up males improved by 159 points and females by 144 points (see Table I). For the combined third and fourth waves males increased their scores by 190 points and females by 181 points. The mean scores on SAT-V were approximately 170 points above the mean for a national sample of college-bound seniors. It can be seen in Table I that the initial sex difference on SAT-V favoring girls at the time of talent search participation diminished in high school, and for the second wave was no longer statistically significant. On both SAT-M and SAT-V SMPY males improved more than SMPY females. The sex differences in the two-point growth curve on SAT-M and SAT-V were found to be statistically significant ($p < .05$ for SAT-M and $p < .01$ for SAT-V) by two separate multivariate analysis of variance procedures (Finn & Bock, 1981). Relative to Johns Hopkins undergraduates, whose means are 626V and 677M, SMPY students at the end of high school score somewhat higher on SAT-M but somewhat lower on SAT-V.

---

[4] The first wave of the follow-up consisted only of students who had been at least eighth graders in the talent search, the second wave consisted mainly of former eighth graders but of some former seventh graders in the talent searches, and the combined third and fourth waves consisted mainly of former seventh graders but also of some former eighth graders. The talent search mean score difference on SAT-M and SAT-V for the waves is probably accounted for by this difference in composition of the groups.

BENBOW AND STANLEY

Mathematics Course Taking

SMPY males took significantly more semesters of high school mathematics than did SMPY females (i.e., 9.2 vs. 8.4). By a t-test this difference was statistically significant beyond the .001 level. The effect size, d, was approximately .33. Thus, the effect was considered to be small and therefore not important.

Self-reported achievement in mathematics courses taken is shown by sex in Table II. The mean grades were high, with girls receiving marginally better grades. Although the overall mean mathematics grades for boys and girls were not much different (i.e., on a scale where $A = 4$, $B = 3$, etc., boys had a mathematics grade point average of 3.5 and girls 3.6), it becomes apparent from Table II that in almost every comparison by course and sex girls receive slightly better grades. The difference resulted from more SMPY girls than boys reporting that they received A's in their coursework. A sign test was employed to test the statistical significance of this difference in grades by sex. It yielded chi-square $= 20.5, p < .001$, with a large effect size, $g = .41$. Thus, it was accepted that SMPY girls reported receiving somewhat better grades in their mathematics classes than their male counterparts reported.

The correlations between talent search SAT-M score and overall grade point average in high school mathematics courses, computed separately for follow-up wave and grade, ranged between .31 and .41 (medium effect size range) for the boys and .17 and .27 (small effect size range) for the girls. Verbal ability did not relate much to mathematics grades. Thus, for boys, mathematical ability exhibited in the seventh grade does relate importantly to grades received in their mathematics coursework.

SMPY males reported taking their mathematics in a significantly earlier school grade than SMPY females. The mean school grades when SMPY students took each of their mathematics courses are also shown in Table II. In almost every comparison by sex, SMPY males took the course in a slightly earlier grade. A sign test indicated that the difference was significant (chi-square $= 22.1, p < .001$). The effect size was large ($g = .42$).

It is apparent from Table II that differential course taking in mathematics by the SMPY males and females occurred at the upper levels. About the same percentage of girls and boys took each mathematics course up through trigonometry. But then approximately 10 percent more boys than girls took college algebra and analytic geometry. This difference in proportions was significant at the $p < .05$ level, but the computed effect size was small. With respect to calculus, approximately two-thirds of SMPY boys took at least one calculus course, compared to 40 percent of the girls (see Table II). This difference in proportions was significant ($p < .01$), with a medium effect size ($h = .53$). We conclude that the gender difference in taking calculus in high school was important.

TABLE II

Reported Mathematics Course Taking in High School by SMPY Students, Their Mean Course Grades, and Their Mean School Grades When Enrolled, Shown by Sex and Follow-up Wave for Those Courses Where at Least 5% Had Been Enrolled*

Follow-up Wave	First		Second		Third & Fourth	
	Male (133)	Female (69)	Male (310)	Female (221)	Male (785)	Female (478)
Algebra I						
Mean course grade	3.74	3.85	3.65	3.70	3.69	3.75
SD	0.51	0.36	0.60	0.58	0.55	0.51
Mean school grade	8.10	8.16	8.13	8.19	8.11	8.11
SD	0.62	0.44	0.58	0.50	0.51	0.46
Percentage enrolled	96	100	93	94	92	94
Algebra II						
Mean course grade	3.61	3.67	3.57	3.60	3.60	3.62
SD	0.65	0.59	0.68	0.66	0.63	0.61
Mean school grade	9.39	9.49	9.49	9.53	9.48	9.58
SD	0.08	0.68	0.82	0.83	0.84	0.91
Percentage enrolled	94	100	92	94	92	95
Plane Geometry						
Mean course grade	3.66	3.72	3.64	3.64	3.68	3.65
SD	0.65	0.51	0.62	0.57	0.59	0.59
Mean school grade	9.61	9.82	9.54	9.74	9.34	9.47
SD	0.71	0.62	0.67	0.58	0.65	0.63
Percentage enrolled	93	99	93	94	92	94
College Algebra						
Mean course grade	3.61	3.67	3.60	3.53	3.49	3.53
SD	0.73	0.57	0.63	0.74	0.73	0.68
Mean school grade	10.87	11.33	10.68	10.97	10.70	10.89
SD	0.99	0.57	0.90	0.86	0.90	0.79
Percentage enrolled	53	35	49	40	43	35

(Continued on next page)

TABLE II
(continued)

Follow-up Wave	First		Second		Third & Fourth	
	Male (133)	Female (69)	Male (310)	Female (221)	Male (785)	Female (478)
Trigonometry						
Mean course grade	3.51	3.56	3.55	3.60	3.54	3.58
SD	0.75	0.65	0.66	0.66	0.67	0.66
Mean school grade	10.52	11.19	10.60	10.96	10.50	10.79
SD	0.77	0.54	0.75	0.64	0.77	0.67
Percentage enrolled	87	86	81	80	83	80
Analytical Geometry						
Mean course grade	3.51	3.65	3.49	3.62	3.49	3.55
SD	0.75	0.53	0.72	0.62	0.74	0.68
Mean school grade	10.93	11.15	10.87	11.08	10.74	10.92
SD	0.71	0.56	0.75	0.56	0.97	0.63
Percentage enrolled	80	67	71	61	70	60
Calculus I						
Mean course grade	3.47	3.62	3.44	3.55	3.40	3.59
SD	0.85	0.56	0.78	0.69	0.77	0.61
Mean school grade	11.42	11.93	11.65	11.82	11.60	11.82
SD	0.77	0.26	0.61	0.42	0.63	0.45
Percentage enrolled	61	42	69	34	66	43
Calculus II						
Mean course grade	3.56	3.59	3.42	3.63	3.39	3.50
SD	0.71	0.57	0.76	0.60	0.81	0.73
Mean school grade	11.67	11.93	11.73	11.87	11.73	11.85
SD	0.71	0.27	0.57	0.34	0.60	0.47
Percentage enrolled	55	39	61	30	53	29

Probability & Statistics						
Mean course grade	3.62	3.90	3.59	3.87	3.69	3.84
SD	0.56	0.32	0.53	0.34	0.54	0.42
Mean school grade	11.28	11.80	11.47	11.30	11.17	11.55
SD	0.96	0.63	0.93	1.19	1.05	0.63
Percentage enrolled	22	15	18	10	17	12
Elementary Functions						
Mean course grade	3.50	3.50	4.00	3.50	3.25	3.51
SD	0.55	0.55	0	0.71	0.90	0.66
Mean school grade	10.83	11.33	11.33	11.33	10.92	11.11
SD	0.40	0.52	0.58	0.58	0.57	0.47
Percentage enrolled	5	9	1	1	6	8
Computer Science						
Mean course grade	3.64	3.75	3.65	3.88	3.66	3.68
SD	0.50	0.50	0.58	0.34	0.63	0.59
Mean school grade	11.00	11.00	11.32	11.33	11.21	11.53
SD	0.95	1.41	0.96	1.11	0.93	0.80
Percentage enrolled	9	6	19	7	23	17

[a] The differences between males and females in course grades and school grades were significant. Females received better grades ($\chi^2 = 20.5$, $p < .001$, $g = .41$), and males took their mathematics in an earlier grade ($\chi^2 = 22.1$, $p < .001$, $g = .42$).

BENBOW AND STANLEY

Mathematics "enrichment" courses also were taken more frequently by boys than by girls. The difference in proportions was significant ($p < .05$), but with a small effect size.

Because SMPY girls took their mathematics later than SMPY boys, they had less time to take calculus and other advanced mathematics courses in high school. This difference accounts for some of the disparity in the number of mathematics courses taken. For example, the same proportion of girls and boys took mathematics up to and including 11th grade; that is, in the 11th grade, 83 percent of both boys and girls took mathematics. In the 12th grade, however, more SMPY boys than girls took mathematics (68% vs. 60%). This difference was statistically significant, but its effect size was not large enough to be considered even small ($h = .17$). Thus, it was not judged important.

It is of interest what the possible predictors of high school mathematics course taking are. We hypothesized that it was probably a combination of ability, family background variables, and attitudes. Our best measures of ability were the talent search SAT-M score and, if available, talent search SAT-V score. For family background variables our best available measures were parents' education, fathers' occupational status,[5] number of siblings, and sibling position. Finally, our best measures of attitudes were rated liking for mathematics in talent search, if available (otherwise in high school), rated importance of mathematics for future career (in seventh or eighth grade), and having rated mathematics as the favorite course in high school. The "dummy" variable sex was also added to the equation to see what weight it would have. Stepwise multiple regression analyses were performed separately by follow-up wave and grade. In the analyses, only relatively small amounts of variance in mathematics course taking (between 9 and 16%) could be accounted for by the predictor variables. The actual R^2 s, respectively by follow-up wave and grade, were .12 (N = 177), .16 (N = 329), .09 (N = 682), and .10 (N = 448). (Further data are available upon request from the authors.) The effect size values, f^2, ranged from .10 to .19. One was in the medium range, while the other three were in the small range.

Having rated mathematics as the favorite course in high school appeared to be the overall best predictor of mathematics course taking. This was followed by sex and mathematical ability in talent search. Least important among the set of variables appeared to be the family background characteristics. It can be argued that having rated mathematics as the favorite course in high school is not a predictor because this rating was done at the end of high school, not before. It becomes of interest, then, that liking for math in the seventh grade was not a stronger predictor of course taking than the ability measures.

---

[5] Occupational status was assessed by the National Opinion Research Center (NORC) transform of the Duncan Socioeconomic Index (Hodge, Siegel, & Rossi, 1964; Reiss, 1961).

Comparing the standard error of estimate with the standard deviation of the criterion variable revealed the numbers to be almost identical. On account of this and the effect sizes, it was concluded that the independent variables, which included sex and ability measures, could not accurately predict subsequent mathematics course taking in this population of able young students.

In a separate analysis it was found that talent search SAT-M and SAT-V scores, liking for mathematics, and sex could not discriminate between students who took mathematics in the 12th grade and the ones who did not (although the discriminant functions comprised of these variables were mostly significant). These same variables, however, could significantly and somewhat better discriminate between students who took calculus and those who did not. For the first set of analyses in which we tried to discriminate between students taking mathematics in the 12th grade and the ones not doing so, done separately by follow-up wave and grade, the first canonical correlation ranged in value from .11 to .32. Classification of students on whether or not they took mathematics in the 12th grade, based on the discriminant function, was correct approximately 59 percent of the time. The same analyses used to discriminate between students who took calculus and the ones who did not resulted in canonical correlations ranging from .30 to .47. Classification based on the discriminant function was correct approximately 65 percent of the time. Clearly, among a highly able group of students, other factors, such as availability of calculus in the high school, probably are also important in determining whether a student takes mathematics, especially calculus, in the 12th grade.

In a further analysis the difference between talent search SAT-M and SAT-V was computed. This variable was considered important because, independent of SAT-M level, it determines the hierarchy of preference for mathematics versus verbal tasks (Gordon, 1981). The difference was correlated with the number of semesters of mathematics taken. For girls a significant relationship was not found. For boys, one was found ($r = .19$, N = 270), with a small effect size. The larger V-M was, the (slightly) more mathematics the student tended to take.

AP-Level Mathematics Courses

Of the mathematics courses offered in high school, the most advanced and difficult are the ones that prepare students for taking the College Board's Advanced Placement Program (AP) examinations. Students can take either the AP Mathematics, Level AB, or the more advanced Level BC. A high grade on the Level AB examination usually yields credit for a one-semester college course in calculus, while two semesters of credit can usually be gained by means of a high grade on the BC examination. Grades reported on these examinations range from 1 to 5, where 3, 4, and 5 are considered high scores.

609

TABLE III

Reported Performance on the Advanced Placement Program (AP) Examinations and the College Board's High-School Level Achievement Tests in Mathematics by Follow-up Wave

AP Scores	First Wave (202)		Second Wave (531)		Third & Fourth Waves (1263)		AP Examination Distribution of Candidate Grades May 1980
	Male	Female	Male	Female	Male	Female	
Calculus AB							
M Score	4.1	3.0	3.8	3.0	3.7	3.7	3.0
SD	0.8	1.4	1.2	1.3	1.1	1.1	1.2
N	11	4	33	15	98	43	20,096
Calculus BC							
M Score	3.6	2.3	3.7	4.0	3.8	3.6	3.2
SD	1.2	0.6	1.2	0.9	1.2	1.1	1.3
N	26	3	51	6	132	26	7,783

Achievement Test Scores							National Sample of 1978 College-Bound H.S. Students (ATP, 1979)
Math Level I							
M Score	692	664	698	656	695	644	541
SD	81	99	74	70	65	76	99
N	34	19	60	58	149	100	146,426
Math Level II							
M Score	742	676	751	724	748	705	665
SD	67	93	60	57	59	71	95
N	46	7	91	29	281	99	32,743

Table III shows that, although many more boys than girls took these examinations, no significant differences in grades earned were seen.

Approximately 12 percent of the males and 8 percent of the females took the AP Calculus AB examination. Although the difference in proportions was significant at the $p < .01$ level, the effect size did not even reach the criterion for being considered small. The more difficult BC examination was taken by 17 percent of the males and 5 percent of the females, a difference significant at the $p < .01$ level. The effect size was small ($h = .40$), even though the ratio of boys to girls taking the test is more than 3-to-1. We believe that these ratios are not negligible. Moreover, the harder the mathematics criterion becomes, the greater the ratio of boys to girls.

Mathematics Achievement Tests

Significantly more SMPY males than females reported that they took the College Board's mathematics achievement tests (see Table III). The difference in proportions between males and females taking the Math Level I achievement test, which is less advanced than Math Level 2, was not significant (i.e., 20% of the boys vs. 23% of the girls). The difference on Math Level 2 was, however, significant ($p < .01$). Approximately 34 percent of the boys took this test, while only 18 percent of the girls did. The effect size was in the small range ($h = .37$).

SMPY males did score higher than the females on the mathematics achievement tests (Table III). On the Math Level 1 boys scored on the average 695, while girls scored around 650. The difference was significant beyond the $p < .01$ level, except for the first wave of the follow-up (see Table III). The associated effect sizes equaled .58 for the second wave and .73 for the combined third and fourth waves, which are considered to be in the medium range.

On the more difficult Math Level 2 the boys scored on the average 748 and the girls approximately 708, significantly different beyond the $p < .05$ level. The effect sizes ranged from .47 to .86, which is in the medium to large range.

It was hypothesized that perhaps the sex difference in mathematical reasoning ability, detected as early as the 7th grade, may be related to why SMPY females received lower scores than SMPY males on the mathematics achievement tests. An analysis of covariance was, thus, computed on Math Level 1 and 2 achievement test scores by follow-up wave and grade. The effect of sex was tested after controlling for talent search SAT-M. Because there was no significant sex difference on Math Level 1 for the first wave of the follow-up, the first wave was excluded from this analysis. When mathematical reasoning ability was controlled for, the effect of sex was reduced (except in one of the seven analyses). The ANCOVA F's ranged in value from .3 to 15.9, while the ANOVA F's ranged from 3.5 to 19.2. Yet sex still remained a significant effect for four of the seven analyses performed. Because the effect of sex was reduced, a relationship may exist between the sex difference on the Math Level 1 and 2 achievement tests and the less well-developed mathematical reasoning ability of SMPY girls compared to SMPY boys. But other factors also seem to be operating that make girls perform less well on the mathematics achievement test. Obviously, it could hardly be performance in class, because girls reported receiving better grades for their course work. Furthermore, it could not be that boys had taken more mathematics. The big gender difference in mathematics course taking occurs in calculus, which is not covered on the achievement tests and was taken by the students only after these tests were completed. More research is needed to discover possible causes for this discrepancy. Our present work can tell us only which factors are not likely to be involved.

Stepwise multiple regression analyses performed separately by follow-up wave and grade were also employed to see if talent search SAT scores and sex can predict the number of science and/or mathematics achievement or AP examinations taken in high school. There was a significant sex difference

($p < .001$) in the total number taken (1.45 for boys vs. 0.81 for girls) and the effect sizes were in the small to medium range (.68, .47, and .43 for the three waves).

Between 16 and 23 percent of the variance in the taking of these examinations could be accounted for by the talent search SAT scores and sex. The associated effect sizes ranged in value from .19 to .30, which are considered to be medium.

By itself talent search SAT-M, the overall best predictor, could account for between 15 and 21 percent of the variance. Sex was a significant predictor in some but not all equations, accounting for .6 to 3.6 percent additional variance. Therefore, it was accepted that talent search SAT scores could predict fairly accurately the number of science and/or mathematics achievement or AP examinations taken, and the contribution of sex was negligible.

The difference between talent search SAT-M and SAT-V scores (i.e., SAT-M minus SAT-V) was computed and then correlated with the number of science and/or mathematics achievement or AP examinations taken in high school. The negative correlations, computed separately by follow-up wave, for the girls were not significant, but the positive r's for the boys were. The r's for the boys were .10 (N = 270, small effect size) and .35 (N = 35, medium effect size).

College Major

Students were asked to report their intended college majors. The percentage of males reporting that they intended to major in the mathematical sciences was 15 percent, while for the females this was 17 percent. The difference favoring the girls was not significant, however. Because some of these intended majors will probably change during the college experience, this may not be a reliable predictor. It does, however, indicate that initially in college the girls were at least as interested in mathematics as the boys and perhaps find it as important for their careers. Thus, this variable may be an indicator of attitudes. Benbow and Stanley (Note 2) investigated the sex difference in college majors in this group and possible causes. No strong explanations for the sex difference were found.

College Mathematics

The students also reported whether they took mathematics during their first semester of college. Of the students in college, 81 percent of the males and 68 percent of the females reported that they took at least one mathematics course during their first semester. This difference was significant beyond the $p < .01$ level, with a small effect size ($h = .30$). Because the difference was not considered important, perhaps it is not worthwhile to ponder on reasons for the discrepancy that, even though slightly more girls were planning to major in the mathematical sciences, the boys took more mathematics during the first semester of college; however, it is of interest.

Mathematics Contests

Several students in the follow-up reported that they had participated in mathematics contests in high school. Approximately 23 percent of the boys and 12 percent of the girls had participated in at least one, significantly different beyond the $p < .01$ level. The effect size was small ($h = .29$), even though the ratio was almost two boys to every one girl.

Attitudes Toward Mathematics

Students in the follow-up were asked to rate their liking for mathematics on a 5-point scale, ranging from strong disliking (1) to strong liking (5). As a group, both girls and boys expressed moderate liking. The males' means in the three waves ranged from 4.28 to 4.44. The females' means ranged from 4.12 to 4.36. Clearly, the difference between the sexes was extremely small. For the combined third and fourth waves of the follow-up, however, the sex difference was significant ($p < .05$) because of the large N. Yet the effect size equaled only .13, which is not even considered small by Cohen (1977). Thus, this statistically significant difference was ignored.

Students also were asked to rank their preference for mathematics relative to biology, chemistry, and physics. Mathematics was most highly ranked by both SMPY males and females. No significant difference occurred.

The favorite courses of SMPY students in high school were mathematics and science. Their favorite courses were grouped into five categories, by sex and total (see Table IV). The favorite subject for both the boys and girls was mathematics. The difference between the SMPY males and females was significant ($p < .01$) because of the large N. When an effect size was calculated, however, it did not reach the criterion for even being considered small ($h = .11$). Thus, this significant difference was ignored. SMPY boys and girls prefer mathematics the most and to an essentially equal degree in high school in comparison with their other high school subjects.

Hence, it cannot be that these girls like mathematics less than boys, causing them to participate at a lower level in mathematics than boys. Perhaps instead girls prefer verbal areas more than boys, which would then tend to lower their participation in mathematics.[6] A chi-square was computed between rated favorite course being verbal or quantitative and sex. The "other" category in Table IV was omitted. The chi-square equaled 26.8 and was significant. The effect size was small ($w = .14$), indicating a weak association.

This possibility was investigated in another way and supported. Students were classified into two groups on the basis of whether they had indicated a

---

[6] Robert A. Gordon suggested this idea to us.

TABLE IV

The Reported Favorite Courses of SMPY Students in High School by Sex and for 17-Year-Olds

Favorite Course	Percent		
	Males (1228)	Females (768)	17-Year-Olds (NAEP, 1979)
Mathematics	36	31	18
Science	34	25	12
Social Studies	11	9	13
English	7	17	16
Other	13	17	41

verbal subject in high school as their favorite course or whether a quantitative one (i.e., science or mathematics) had been reported. Students not fitting into either category were excluded from the analysis. A discriminant analysis was performed, separately by follow-up wave, using these variables as indicators of participation in mathematics: number of semesters of mathematics taken in high school, whether a mathematics course was taken during the first semester of college, the quantitative index of the student's intended college major on a scale of 1 to 5 (see Benbow & Stanley, Note 2), number of science or mathematics achievement or AP examinations taken, and number of mathematics contests participated in. For the first wave of the follow-up, two variables, mathematics course-taking in college and the quantitative index of intended college major, were not available. Thus, the analysis for the first wave is slightly different from the other two. All analyses presented here were performed on a combined group of boys and girls, because no differences were apparent between the groups that would warrant separate analyses. The results of the discriminant analysis are shown in Table V.

Before the first function was removed the Wilks' Lambda values for the three waves equaled .76, .88, and .80, respectively. This indicated that there existed some discriminating power between the groups in the variables being used (see Table V). The one and only discriminant function for each analysis was, therefore, significant. Its associated canonical correlation values equaled .49, .35, and .45 (see Table V). The contributions of the discriminating variables to the function can be seen in the lower half of Table V. No one variable appeared to be consistently best in discriminating between the groups.

Classification based on the discriminating function was correct for approximately 73 percent of the students, compared to 50 percent expected by chance (see Table V). Thus, there is considerable overlap between the groups. Yet the function does aid in classifying students. Therefore, it was accepted that measures of participation in mathematics can discriminate between students preferring verbal areas in high school and those preferring

TABLE V

Discriminant Analyses Between SMPY Students Preferring Verbal Areas in High School and Students Preferring Quantitative Areas on Several Measures of Mathematics Participation

Follow-up Wave (N)	Eigen value	Canonical Correlation	Wilks' Lambda	Chi-Square	df	Sig.
1 (100)[a]	.32	.49	.76	26.7	3	.001
2 (433)	.14	.35	.88	56.5	5	.001
3 and 4 (1048)	.26	.45	.80	237.7	5	.001

Standardized Discriminant Function Coefficients:	First Wave	Second Wave	Third and Fourth Waves
College Math[b]		.67	.15
Semesters of Math in High School	.69	.43	.20
Choice[c]		.12	.87
Number of Science and Math Tests	.45	.31	.16
Number of Math Contests	.32	.05	.09
Percent Classified Correctly	75	67	75

[a] The analysis for the first wave of the follow-up was performed differently, using only semesters of mathematics in high school, number of science and mathematics tests taken, and number of mathematics contests.

[b] College Math is a measure of whether or not a student took mathematics in his or her first semester of college.

[c] Choice is an indicator of quantitative orientation of a student's college major on a scale of 1 to 5 (see Benbow & Stanley, Note 2).

the quantitative areas. Because slightly more girls than boys prefer the verbal areas, although no differences were seen in the quantitative areas, these findings support the hypothesis that the lower female participation in mathematics in high school can be accounted for to some extent by the greater female than male preference for the verbal areas.

DISCUSSION

In all six SMPY talent searches a large sex difference favoring males was found on the SAT-M, a test of mathematical reasoning ability (Benbow & Stanley, 1980b, 1981). This study followed up at high school graduation the students studied by Benbow and Stanley (1980b) who, as 7th or 8th graders, had participated in any of the first three talent searches and had scored as well as a national sample of 11th and 12th grade females do on the SAT. The objective was to investigate the development and consequences of this initial sex difference. Many consequences were found.

This study and the Benbow and Stanley (1980b, 1981) paper demonstrate that (1) sex differences in mathematical reasoning ability are found at an early age among mathematically talented students; (2) they persist over several years and are related to subsequent differences in mathematics achievement; and (3) the differences in mathematical reasoning ability and achievement do not reflect differential mathematics course taking, at least not among mathematically talented adolescents.

One of the more interesting findings was that the mathematical abilities of SMPY males appeared to develop significantly more rapidly or to improve more during high school than the abilities of SMPY females. Males improved significantly more than females on both SAT-M and SAT-V by about 10 points. This finding partly contradicts a previous study, which showed that the sex with the initial superior ability improved more in that ability during high school (Shaycoft, 1967).

Fennema and Sherman (1977) postulated that sex differences in mathematical ability commence in high school because boys take more semesters of mathematics than girls (i.e., differential course taking). Because SMPY boys did take marginally more mathematics in high school than SMPY girls, this might appear to be the reason why the boys improved more on the SAT-M in high school. But this hypothesis cannot explain why the boys improved more on the SAT-V also. Furthermore, the differential course-taking hypothesis cannot explain why there is a sex difference on the SAT-M earlier than senior high school and, for the following reasons which were derived from this and two other studies, cannot even account for the increase in the sex difference in high school: (1) The initial sex difference on SAT-M was found in the 7th or 8th grade, before differential course taking took effect (Benbow & Stanley, 1980b); (2) equal percentages of girls and boys took mathematics in high school up to the 12th grade, when the SATs are normally taken; (3) SMPY boys took only about one semester more of mathematics than SMPY girls, which was mostly accounted for by the larger number of SMPY boys than girls taking calculus (calculus items do not appear on the SAT); and (4) in a separate study it was found that the best predictor of high school SAT-M score was talent search SAT-M, not the number of semesters of mathematics taken in high school, which accounted for little additional variance in high school SAT-M (Benbow, Note 3).

Clearly, the differential course-taking hypothesis does not explain the ability differences found in this population. More research is needed to discover possible reasons why SMPY males improved more than SMPY females in both mathematical and verbal reasoning ability during high school. Perhaps SMPY males are proceeding at a faster developmental rate than SMPY females.

Can ability differences explain differential course taking? When students taking calculus and students not taking calculus in high school were compared, three variables could discriminate somewhat between them: talent search SAT-M and SAT-V, liking for mathematics in talent search, and sex. The most typical student to take calculus in high school was a male who was able and liked mathematics. The significance of the sex difference will be discussed later. It is also of interest to note that the 10-point increase in the sex difference on SAT-M during high school made the mean sex difference for the SMPY group equal the mean difference found for college-bound seniors in high school (ATP, 1979).[7]

Sex differences in mathematical achievement were widely noted. Some of these differences appeared to be related to the sex difference on SAT-M in the talent search. When ability on the SAT-M at talent search was controlled, the significant sex differences in performance on the mathematics achievement tests were either no longer significant or reduced. With regard to taking mathematics and/or science achievement or AP examinations, talent search SAT-M score was the best predictor. Sex accounted for little additional variance. It appears then that the sex difference in mathematical reasoning ability found as early as the seventh or eighth grade may later contribute to sex differences in mathematics achievement.

Slightly (but not significantly) more females than males were planning to major specifically in the mathematical sciences in college, and SMPY females received better grades in their high school mathematics courses than did SMPY males. The mathematics course grade differences can probably be explained by the sex differences favoring girls that have been found in conduct and demeanor in school (Baker, 1981; see Entwisle & Hayduk, 1981, in press). Girls have better conduct and demeanor. This possibility is consistent with the stronger relationship between mathematical reasoning ability and mathematics course grades for boys than girls. Unfortunately, we could not control for conduct or demeanor.

With regard to attitudes toward mathematics, few of the expected sex differences were found. SMPY boys and girls reported that they liked mathematics equally. Furthermore, reported attitudes toward mathematics had little relationship with achievement in mathematics. Attitudes toward mathematics at time of the talent search and in high school could not predict the number of semesters of mathematics taken. In a separate study, attitudes toward mathematics could not predict high school SAT-M score and score on the College Board's Math Level 1 achievement test (Benbow, Note 3). Expressed liking for mathematics, however, could somewhat discriminate between students taking calculus in high school and the ones not doing so. Furthermore, there were some indications that girls participate in mathematics less than boys not because they like it less, but partly because they like verbal areas, especially English, more than boys do.

Therefore, there does not appear to be much relationship between attitudes toward mathematics and achievement in mathematics in a high-aptitude group, unless the variables measured in this study were inadequate indicators of attitudes toward mathematics (i.e., mathematics liking, importance of mathematics for future job, and having rated mathematics a favorite course

---

[7] ATP (1981) shows the mean score of college-bound 12th-grade males on SAT-M to be 492, versus the analogous female mean of 443. That 49-point difference occurs among much more heterogeneous groups than the SMPY talent search participants constituted.

in high school). For example, Fennema and Sherman (1976) demonstrated that attitude toward mathematics involves several distinct components. Although our measures of attitudes might have been too global, it is hard to imagine that they failed to capture some information that was useful overall.

We tentatively conclude that mathematical reasoning ability by itself seems to be a better predictor of achievement in mathematics, even in this intellectually rather homogeneous group, than attitudes toward mathematics.

Yet mathematical reasoning ability cannot be the sole reason why girls perform less well than boys in high school, because it could not totally account for the sex difference in the mathematics achievement tests. Other factors must be operating. Performance in the class and having taken more courses in the subject matter were ruled out because: (1) SMPY females received better grades than the SMPY males in their mathematics course work; (2) the same proportion of females and males took mathematics up through the 11th grade, which is right before or when these achievement tests are taken; and (3) most of the sex difference in the taking of mathematics can be accounted for by the higher percentage of males taking calculus (calculus items do not appear on these achievement tests). What factors are involved in the performance differential between the sexes needs to be investigated. This study suggests strongly what these factors are not likely to be.

Along this line, Fox, Brody, and Tobin (1982) investigated the family background of the SMPY talent participants. They found few differences. Especially, no indications of differential training or encouragement of boys and girls were discovered.

A study of sex differences in science achievement among this population has also been conducted (Benbow & Stanley, Note 2). The sex difference in mathematical reasoning ability also related to the sex difference in science achievement, but could not account for the sex difference in intended college majors of the group.

Large sex differences were found in taking higher level mathematics. Among the SMPY group, almost twice as many boys as girls took calculus in high school. In college fewer females than males took mathematics during their first semester. Actually, the time when less SMPY females than males were taking mathematics seemed to begin in the 12th grade. Thus, if one wants to increase the participation of able women in mathematics, earlier than the 12th grade would seem to be the time to use some intervention strategies. As Sells (1980) pointed out, women are closed out of certain career options because they do not take enough mathematics in high school.

In 1973 such a program was implemented at SMPY (Fox, 1976). Moderately gifted seventh grade SMPY girls were invited to an accelerated mathematics program in algebra during the summer of 1973. The program, in addition to emphasizing algebra, catered to the social needs of girls, provided interaction with female role models who had careers in the mathematical sciences, and encouraged the girls to study a number of years of mathematics. The girls who successfully completed the program (i.e., those who were placed in Algebra II that fall) did take more advanced mathematics in high school and college (Fox, Benbow, & Perkins, Note 4). That was, however, the only major difference between this group of girls and an equally able group of girls not invited to attend the program. No effects were found for the girls who attended the accelerated algebra program but were not successful. Clearly, an early intervention strategy can improve the participation of girls in higher level mathematics, but the girls have to be successful in such a program. Unfortunately, many of the girls in this study may not have been able enough to benefit sufficiently from such intensive training.

A potential problem with our study is that it is based on self-reported data. Moreover, there is the possibility of differential accuracy (sex-related) in recall. Hamilton (1981) found, however, that females tend to exaggerate (positively) more than males. If this is the case, then our results might be underestimating the magnitude of the sex differences favoring males.

A further limitation of the study is that the students involved are mathematically able and highly motivated. Therefore, we urge caution when generalizing to the total population.[8] If one is interested in the question of why women do not pursue careers in mathematics and science as frequently as men do, however, the students whom we studied are an appropriate nonprobability sample of the population. Because all of them are intellectually (especially mathematically) talented, they are the most likely to enter the sciences at those academically difficult colleges where most top-level scientists received their undergraduate education (Davis, 1965; Werts, 1967).

Another problem was our use of Cohen's (1977) effect sizes to evaluate the importance of a difference found. Values of effect sizes have been classified as being either small, medium, or large. This classification is arbitrary. We choose to accept as important a difference classified as being either medium or large. As Cohen warns, however, in some areas even small differences can be important. Thus, we may have been too rigid in adhering to this standard. Many differences were found that we felt were important despite the small effect size. Readers should evaluate whether a small effect size might be important in some cases.

We conclude that sex differences in mathematical reasoning ability and achievement are widely noted in this highly able group of students, they persist over several years, and they are better accounted for by the sex difference in mathematical reasoning ability than by sex differences in expressed attitudes toward mathematics and mathematics course taking in junior and senior high school. The slightly greater female than male prefer-

---

[8] The influence of the researchers' expectations on these students' responses was probably minimal, because there was little personal contact and the SMPY study was not conducted primarily to find sex differences in this population.

ence for the verbal areas in high school might also explain some of the sex difference in participation in mathematics. The reason for this difference in preference for verbal areas is not clear and needs to be investigated. Moreover, why boys tend to reason better than girls from at least as early as second grade (Dougherty et al., Note 5) onward is also, of course, not clear. What interactions of factors such as environment, female versus male hormones during prenatal development, physiologically induced differences in activity levels, and different brain-hemisphere lateralization (Goy & McEwen, 1980; Harris, 1979; Levy, 1981; Wittig & Petersen, 1979) might be responsible cannot be ascertained yet. It "seems likely that putting one's faith in boy-versus-girl socialization processes as the only permissible explanation of the sex difference in mathematics is premature" (Benbow & Stanley, 1980b, p. 1264).

REFERENCE NOTES

1. COHN, S. J. *Two components of the Study of Mathematically Precocious Youth's intervention studies of educational facilitation and longitudinal follow-up.* Unpublished doctoral dissertation, Johns Hopkins University, 1980.
2. BENBOW, C. P., & STANLEY, J. C. Gender and the science major. To appear in M. W. Steinkamp & M. L. Maehr (Eds.), *Women in science.* Greenwich, Conn.: JAI Press.
3. BENBOW, C. P. *Development of superior mathematical ability during adolescence.* Unpublished doctoral dissertation, Johns Hopkins University, 1981.
4. FOX, L. H., BENBOW, C. P., & PERKINS, S. *An accelerated mathematics program for girls: A longitudinal evaluation.* Unpublished manuscript, 1982.
5. DOUGHERTY, K., HERBERT, M., EDENHART-PEPE, M., & SMALL, A. *Sex-related differences in mathematics, grades 2-5.* Unpublished manuscript, 1980.

REFERENCES

Admissions Testing Program. *National report, college bound seniors, 1979.* Princeton, N.J.: Educational Testing Service, 1979.

Admissions Testing Program. *National report on college-bound seniors, 1981.* Princeton, N.J.: Educational Testing Service, 1981.

ANGOFF, W. (ED.). *The College Board admissions testing program.* Princeton, N.J.: College Entrance Examination Board, 1971.

BACKMAN, M. E. Patterns of mental abilities: Ethnic, socioeconomic, and sex differences. *American Educational Research Journal,* 1972, *9,* 1-12.

BAKER, D. P. Personal communication, September 1981.

BENBOW, C. P., & STANLEY, J. C. Intellectually talented students: Family profiles. *Gifted Child Quarterly,* 1980, *24,* 119-122. (a)

BENBOW, C. P., & STANLEY, J. C. Sex differences in mathematical ability: Fact or artifact? *Science,* 1980, *210,* 1262-1264. (b)

BENBOW, C. P., & STANLEY, J. C. Mathematical ability: Is sex a factor? *Science,* 1981, *212,* pp. 118, 121.

SEX DIFFERENCES IN MATHEMATICS

BENBOW, C. P., & STANLEY, J. C. Intellectually talented boys and girls: Educational profiles. *Gifted Child Quarterly,* 1982, *26,* 82–88.

BIERI, J., BRADBURN, W., & GALINSKY, M. Sex differences in perceptual behavior. *Journal of Personality,* 1958, *26,* 1–12.

COHEN, J. *Statistical power analysis for the behavioral sciences.* New York: Academic Press, 1977.

DAVIS, J. A. Undergraduate career decisions: Correlates of academic choice. *NORC Monographs in Social Research.* 1965 (Serial No. 2).

ENTWISLE, D. R., & HAYDUK, L. A. Academic expectations and the school attainment of young children. *Sociology of Education,* 1981, *54,* 34–50.

ENTWISLE, D. R., & HAYDUK, L. A. *Schooling of young children.* Baltimore, Md.: Johns Hopkins University Press, in press.

ERNEST, J. Mathematics and sex. *American Mathematical Monthly,* 1976, *83*(8), 595–612.

FENNEMA, E. Mathematics learning and the sexes: A review. *Journal for Research in Mathematics Education,* 1974, *5,* 126–139.

FENNEMA, E., & SHERMAN, J. Fennema-Sherman mathematics attitude scales: Instruments designed to measure attitudes toward the learning of mathematics by females and males. JSAS *Catalog of Selected Documents in Psychology,* 1976, *6,* 31–32. (Ms. No. 1225)

FENNEMA, E., & SHERMAN, J. Sex-related differences in mathematics achievement, spatial visualization, and sociocultural factors. *American Educational Research Journal,* 1977, *14,* 51–71.

FINN, J. D., & BOCK, R. D. *Multistat/multivariance manual.* Chicago, Ill.: International Educational Services, 1981.

FOX, L. H. Sex differences in mathematical precocity: Bridging the gap. In D. P. Keating (Ed.), *Intellectual talent: Research and development.* Baltimore, Md.: Johns Hopkins University Press, 1976.

FOX, L. H., BRODY, L., & TOBIN, D. (EDS.). *Women and the mathematical mystique.* Baltimore, Md.: Johns Hopkins University Press, 1980.

FOX, L. H., BRODY, L., & TOBIN, D. *The study of social processes that inhibit or enhance the development of competence and interest in mathematics among highly able young women.* Report to the National Institute of Education (NIE-G-79-0113), January 1982.

GARAI, J. E., & SCHEINFELD, A. Sex differences in mental and behavioral traits. *Genetic Psychology Monographs,* 1968, *77,* 169–229.

GLENNON, V. J., & CALLAHAN, L. G. *A guide to current research: Elementary school mathematics.* Washington, D.C.: Association for Supervision and Curriculum Development, 1968.

GORDON, R. A. Personal communication, September 1981.

GOY, R. W., & MCEWEN, B. S. *Sexual differentiation of the brain.* Cambridge, Mass.: Massachusetts Institute of Technology Press, 1980.

HAMILTON, L. C. Sex differences in self-report errors: A note of caution. *Journal of Educational Measurement,* 1981, *18*(4), 221–228.

HARRIS, L. J. Sex-related differences in cognitive functioning. *Science,* 1979, *206,* 50–52.

HODGE, R. W., SIEGEL, P. M., & ROSSI, P. H. Occupational prestige in the United States, 1925–1963. *American Journal of Sociology,* 1964, *70,* 286–302.

BENBOW AND STANLEY

KEATING, D. P. The Study of Mathematically Precocious Youth. In J. C. Stanley, D. P. Keating, & L. H. Fox (Eds.), *Mathematical talent: Discovery, description, and development.* Baltimore, Md.: Johns Hopkins University Press, 1974.

LEVY, J. Sex and the brain. *The Sciences,* 1981, *21*(3), 20–28.

MACCOBY, E. E., & JACKLIN, C. N. *The psychology of sex differences.* Stanford, Calif.: Stanford University Press, 1974.

MESSICK, S., & JUNGEBLUT, A. Time and method in coaching for the SAT. *Psychological Bulletin,* 1981, *89*(2), 191–216.

National Assessment of Educational Progress. Males dominate in educational success. *National Assessment of Educational Progress Newsletter,* 1975, *8*(5), insert.

National Assessment of Educational Progress. *Attitudes toward science.* Report to the National Institute of Education (#08-5-02), 1979.

NIE, N. H., HULL, C. H., JENKINS, J. G., STEINBRENNER, K., & BENT, D. H. *Statistical package for the social sciences, 2nd edition.* New York: McGraw-Hill, 1975.

REISS, A. J. *Occupations and social status.* New York: Free Press of Glencoe, 1961.

SELLS, L. W. The mathematics filter and the education of women and minorities. In L. H. Fox, L. Brody, & D. Tobin (Eds.), *Women and the mathematical mystique.* Baltimore, Md.: Johns Hopkins University Press, 1980.

SHAYCOFT, M. F. *The high school years: Growth in cognitive skills.* Palo Alto, Calif.: American Institutes for Research, 1967.

SUYDAM, M. N., & WEAVER, J. F. *Individualizing instruction.* Washington, D.C.: U.S. Office of Education, 1970.

VERY, P. S. Differential factor structures in mathematical ability. *Genetic Psychology Monographs,* 1967, *75*(2), 169–207.

WERTS, C. E. Career changes in college. *Sociology of Education,* 1967, *40*(1), 90–95.

WILSON, J. W. *Patterns of mathematics achievement in grade 11: Z population.* Stanford, Calif.: School Mathematics Study Group, 1972.

WITTIG, M. A., & PETERSON, A. (EDS.). *Sex-related differences in cognitive functioning: Developmental issues.* New York: Academic Press, 1979.

AUTHORS

CAMILLA PERSSON BENBOW, Associate Research Scientist in Psychology, Johns Hopkins University, Baltimore, MD 21218. *Specializations:* Individual differences; psychometrics; intellectual precocity; sex differences.

JULIAN C. STANLEY, Professor, Dept. of Psychology, Johns Hopkins University, Baltimore, MD 21218. *Specializations:* Individual differences; psychometrics; intellectual precocity; sex differences.

[20]

Sex Differences in Mathematical Reasoning Ability: More Facts

Abstract. *Almost 40,000 selected seventh-grade students from the Middle Atlantic region of the United States took the College Board Scholastic Aptitude Test as part of the Johns Hopkins regional talent search in 1980, 1981, and 1982. A separate nationwide talent search was conducted in which any student under age 13 who was willing to take the test was eligible. The results obtained by both procedures establish that by age 13 a large sex difference in mathematical reasoning ability exists and that it is especially pronounced at the high end of the distribution: among students who scored ≥ 700, boys outnumbered girls 13 to 1. Some hypothesized explanations of such differences were not supported by the data.*

In 1980 we reported large sex differences in mean scores on a test of mathematical reasoning ability for 9927 mathematically talented seventh and eighth graders who entered the Johns Hopkins regional talent search from 1972 through 1979 (*1, 2*). One prediction from those results was that there would be a preponderance of males at the high end of the distribution of mathematical reasoning ability. In this report we investigate sex differences at the highest levels of that ability. New groups of students under age 13 with exceptional mathematical aptitude were identified by means of two separate procedures. In the first, the Johns Hopkins regional talent searches in 1980, 1981, and 1982 (*3*), 39,820 seventh graders from the Middle Atlantic region of the United States who were selected for high intellectual ability were given the College Board Scholastic Aptitude Test (SAT). In the second, a nationwide talent search was conducted for which any student under 13 years of age who was willing to take the SAT was eligible. The results of both procedures substantiated our prediction that before age 13 far more males than females would score extremely high on SAT–M, the mathematical part of SAT.

The test items of SAT–M require numerical judgment, relational thinking, or insightful and logical reasoning. This test is designed to measure the developed mathematical reasoning ability of 11th and 12th graders (*4*). Most students in our study were in the middle of the seventh grade. Few had had formal opportunities to study algebra and beyond (*5, 6*). Our rationale is that most of these students were unfamiliar with mathematics from algebra onward, and that most who scored high did so because of extraordinary reasoning ability (*7*).

In 1980, 1981, and 1982, as in the earlier study (*1*), participants in the Johns Hopkins talent search were seventh graders, or boys and girls of typical seventh-grade age in the Middle Atlantic area. Before 1980, applicants had been required to be in the top 3 percent nationally on the mathematics section of any standardized achievement test. Beginning in 1980, students in the top 3 percent in verbal or overall intellectual ability were also eligible. During that and the next 2 years 19,883 boys and 19,937 girls applied and were tested. Even though this sample was more general and had equal representation by sex, the mean sex difference on SAT-M remained constant at 30 points favoring males (males' $\overline{X}$ = 416, S.D. = 87; females' $\overline{X}$ = 386, S.D. = 74; t = 37; $P < 0.001$). No important difference in verbal ability as measured by SAT-V was found (males' $\overline{X}$ = 367, females' $\overline{X}$ = 365).

The major point, however, is not the mean difference in SAT-M scores but the ratios of boys to girls among the high scorers (Table 1). The ratio of boys to girls scoring above the mean of talent-search males was 1.5:1. The ratio among those who scored ≥ 500 (493 was the mean of 1981–82 college-bound 12th-grade males) was 2.1:1. Among those who scored ≥ 600 (600 was the 79th percentile of the 12th-grade males) the ratio was 4.1:1. These ratios are similar to those previously reported (*1*) but are derived from a broader and much larger data base.

Scoring 700 or more on the SAT-M before age 13 is rare. We estimate that students who reach this criterion (the 95th percentile of college-bound 12th-grade males) before their 13th birthday represent the top one in 10,000 of their age group. It was because of their rarity that the nationwide talent search was created in November 1980 in order to locate such students who were born after 1967 and facilitate their education (*8*). In that talent search applicants could take the SAT at any time and place at which it was administered by the Educational Testing Service or through one of five regional talent searches that cover the

Table 1. Number of high scorers on SAT-M among selected seventh graders—19,883 boys and 19,937 girls—tested in the Johns Hopkins regional talent search in 1980, 1981, and 1982, and of scorers of ≥ 700 prior to age 13 in the national search (*9*).

Score	Number	Percent	Ratio of boys to girls
Johns Hopkins regional search			
420 or more*			
Boys	9119	45.9	1.5:1
Girls	6220	31.2	
500 or more			
Boys	3618	18.2	2.1:1
Girls	1707	8.6	
600 or more			
Boys	648	3.3	4.1:1
Girls	158	0.8	
National search			
In Johns Hopkins talent search region			
700 or more			
Boys	113	†	12.6:1
Girls	9	†	
Outside Johns Hopkins talent search region			
700 or more			
Boys	147	†	13.4:1
Girls	11	†	

*Mean score of the boys was 416. The highest possible score is 800.   †Total number tested is unknown (*9*).

United States (*9*). Extensive nationwide efforts were made to inform school personnel and parents about our search. The new procedure (unrestricted by geography or previous ability) was successful in obtaining a large national sample of this exceedingly rare population. As of September 1983, the number of such boys identified was 260 and the number of girls 20, a ratio of 13.0:1 (*10*). This ratio is remarkable in view of the fact that the available evidence suggests there was essentially equal participation of boys and girls in the talent searches.

The total number of students tested in the Johns Hopkins regional annual talent searches and reported so far is 49,747 (9,927 in the initial study and 39,820 in the present study). Preliminary reports from the 1983 talent search based on some 15,000 cases yield essentially identical results. In the ten Middle Atlantic regional talent searches from 1972 through 1983 we have therefore tested about 65,000 students. It is abundantly clear that far more boys than girls (chiefly 12-year-olds) scored in the highest ranges on SAT-M, even though girls were matched with boys by intellectual ability, age, grade, and voluntary participation. In the original study (*1*) students were required to meet a qualifying mathematics criterion. Since we observed the same sex difference then as now, the current results cannot be explained sole-

ly on the grounds that the girls may have qualified by the verbal criterion. Moreover, if that were the case, we should expect the girls to have scored higher than the boys on SAT-V. They did not.

Several "environmental" hypotheses have been proposed to account for sex differences in mathematical ability. Fox *et al.* and Meece *et al.* (*11*) have found support for a social-reinforcement hypothesis which, in essence, states that sex-related differences in mathematical achievement are due to differences in social conditioning and expectations for boys and girls. The validity of this hypothesis has been evaluated for the population we studied earlier (*1*) and for a subsample of the students in this study. Substantial differences between boys' and girls' attitudes or backgrounds were not found (*5, 6, 12*). Admittedly, some of the measures used were broadly defined and may not have been able to detect subtle social influences that affect a child from birth. But it is not obvious how social conditioning could affect mathematical reasoning ability so adversely and significantly, yet have little detectable effect on stated interest in mathematics, the taking of mathematics courses during the high school years before the SAT's are normally taken, and mathematics-course grades (*5, 6*).

An alternative hypothesis, that sex differences in mathematical reasoning ability arise mainly from differential course-taking (*13*), was also not validated, either by the data in our 1980 study (*1*) or by the data in the present study. In both studies the boys and girls were shown to have had similar formal training in mathematics (*5, 6*).

It is also of interest that sex differences in mean SAT-M scores observed in our early talent searches became only slightly larger during high school. In the selected subsample of participants studied, males improved their scores an average of 10 points more than females (the mean difference went from 40 to 50 points). They also increased their scores on the SAT-V by at least 10 points more than females (*6*). Previously, other researchers have postulated that profound differences in socialization during adolescence caused the well-documented sex differences in 11th- and 12th-grade SAT-M scores (*11*), but that idea is not supported in our data. For socialization to account for our results, it would seem necessary to postulate (ad hoc) that chiefly early socialization pressures significantly influence the sex difference in SAT-M scores—that is, that the intensive social pressures during adolescence have little such effect.

It is important to emphasize that we are dealing with intellectually highly able students and that these findings may not generalize to average students. Moreover, these results are of course not generalizable to particular individuals. Finally, it should be noted that the boys' SAT–M scores had a larger variance than the girls'. This is obviously related to the fact that more mathematically talented boys than girls were found (*14*). Nonetheless, the environmental hypotheses outlined above attempt to explain mean differences, not differences in variability. Thus, even if one concludes that our findings result primarily from greater male variability, one must still explain why.

Our principal conclusion is that males dominate the highest ranges of mathematical reasoning ability before they enter adolescence. Reasons for this sex difference are unclear (*15*).

CAMILLA PERSSON BENBOW
JULIAN C. STANLEY
*Study of Mathematically Precocious
Youth, Johns Hopkins University,
Baltimore, Maryland 21218*

References and Notes

1. C. Benbow and J. Stanley, *Science* 210, 1262 (1980).
2. Also see letters by C. Tomizuka and S. Tobias; E. Stage and R. Karplus; S. Chipman; E. Egelman *et al.*; D. Moran; E. Luchins and A. Luchins; A. Kelly; C. Benbow and J. Stanley, *ibid.* 212, 114 (1981).
3. The Johns Hopkins Center for the Advancement of Academically Talented Youth (CTY) conducts talent searches during January in Delaware, the District of Columbia, Maryland, New Jersey (added in 1980), Pennsylvania, Virginia, and West Virginia. In 1983 coverage expanded northeast to include Connecticut, Maine, Massachusetts, New Hampshire, Rhode Island, and Vermont.
4. T. Donlon and W. Angoff, in *The College Board Admissions Testing Program*, W. Angoff, Ed. (College Board, Princeton, N.J., 1971), pp. 24–25; S. Messick and A. Jungeblut, *Psychol. Bull.* 89, 191 (1982).
5. C. Benbow and J. Stanley, *Gifted Child Q.* 26, 82 (1982).
6. _____, *Am. Educ. Res. J.* 19, 598 (1982).
7. We have found that among the top 10 percent of these students (who are eligible for our fast-paced summer programs in mathematics) a majority do not know even first-year algebra well.
8. J. Stanley, "Searches under way for youths *exceptionally* talented mathematically or verbally," *Roeper Rev.*, in press.
9. The regional talent searches are conducted by Johns Hopkins (begun in 1972), Duke (1981), Arizona State–Tempe (1981), Northwestern (1982), and the University of Denver (1982). Because there was no logical way to separate students who entered through the regional programs from those who entered through the national channel, results were combined. Most students fit into both categories but at different time points, since the SAT could be taken more than once to qualify or could be retaken in the regional talent search programs. The SAT is not administered by the Educational Testing Service between June and October or November of each year. Therefore, entrants who had passed their 13th birthday before taking the test were included if they scored 10 additional points for each excess month or a fraction of a month.
10. There is a remarkably high incidence of left-handedness or ambidexterity (20 percent), immune disorders (55 percent), and myopia (55 percent) in this group (manuscript in preparation).
11. L. Fox, D. Tobin, L. Brody, in *Sex-Related Differences in Cognitive Functioning*, M. Wittig and A. Petersen, Eds. (Academic Press, New York, 1979); J. Meece, J. Parsons, C. Kaczala, S. Goff, R. Futterman, *Psychol. Bull.* 91, 324 (1982).
12. L. Fox, L. Brody, D. Tobin, *The Study of Social Processes that Inhibit or Enhance the Development of Competence and Interest in Mathematics Among Highly Able Young Women* (National Institute of Education, Washington, D.C., 1982); C. Benbow and J. Stanley, in *Women in Science*, M. Steinkamp and M. Maehr, Eds. (JAI Press, Greenwich, Conn., in press); L. Fox, C. Benbow, S. Perkins, in *Academic Precocity*, C. Benbow and J. Stanley, Eds. (Johns Hopkins Univ. Press, Baltimore, 1983).
13. For example, E. Fennema and J. Sherman, *Am. Educ. Res. J.* 14, 51 (1977).
14. Why boys are generally more variable has been addressed by H. Eysenck and L. Kamin [*The Intelligence Controversy* (Wiley, New York, 1981)] and others.
15. For possible endogenous influences see, for example, R. Goy and B. McEwen, *Sexual Differentiation of the Brain* (MIT Press, Cambridge, Mass., 1980); J. Levy, *The Sciences* 21 (No. 3), 20 (1981); T. Bouchard and M. McGue, *Science* 212, 1055 (1981); D. Hier and W. Crawley, Jr., *N. Engl. J. Med.* 306, 1202 (1982); C. De Lacoste-Utamsing and R. Holloway, *Science* 216, 1431 (1982); L. Harris, in *Asymmetrical Function of the Brain*, M. Kinsbourne, Ed. (Cambridge Univ. Press, London, 1978); M. McGee, *Psychol. Bull.* 86, 889 (1979); S. Witelsen, *Science* 193, 425 (1976); J. McGlone, *Behav. Brain Sci.* 3, 215 (1980); D. McGuiness, *Hum. Nat.* 2 (No. 2), 82 (1979); R. Meisel and I. Ward, *Science* 213, 239 (1981); F. Naftolin, *ibid.* 211, 1263 (1981); A. Ehrhardt and H. Meyer-Bahlburg, *ibid.*, p. 1312; J. Inglis and J. Lawson, *ibid.* 212, 693 (1981); M. Wittig and A. Petersen, Eds., *Sex-Related Differences in Cognitive Functioning* (Academic Press, New York, 1979).
16. We thank K. Alexander, L. Barnett, R. Benbow, R. Gordon, P. Hines, L. Minor, B. Persson, B. Polkes, D. Powers, B. Stanley, Z. Usiskin, and P. Zak. This study was supported by grants from the Spencer and Donner Foundations.

8 November 1982; accepted 17 May 1983

[21]

Socialization of Achievement Attitudes and Beliefs: Parental Influences

Jacquelynne Eccles Parsons, Terry F. Adler, and
Caroline M. Kaczala
University of Michigan

PARSONS, JACQUELYNNE ECCLES; ADLER, TERRY F.; and KACZALA, CAROLINE M. *Socialization of Achievement Attitudes and Beliefs: Parental Influences.* CHILD DEVELOPMENT, 1982, **53,** 310–321. To assess the impact of parents on children's achievement self-concept and related beliefs, extensive questionnaires measuring attitudes and beliefs regarding mathematics achievement were administered to children in grades 5–11 and their parents. The potential influence of parents both as role models and as expectancy socializers was investigated. Both mothers and fathers held sex-differentiated perceptions of their children's math aptitude despite the similarity of the actual performance of boys and girls. The difference was most marked for parents' estimates of how hard their children had to try to do well in math. Parents of daughters believed their child had to work harder to do well in math than parents of sons. Parents of sons thought advanced math was more important for their child than parents of daughters. Parents' perceptions of and expectations for their children were related to both the children's perceptions of their parents' beliefs and to the children's self- and task perceptions. Further, parents' beliefs were more directly related to children's self-concepts and expectancies than were the children's past performances in math. Path analysis supported our hypothesis that the children's attitudes were influenced more by their parents' attitudes about their abilities than by their own past performances. Finally, parents as role models of sex-differentiated math behaviors did not have a direct effect on their children's self-concepts, expectations, or course plans.

The existence of a sex difference in expectancies for success and in self-concept of ability from middle childhood on is well documented (see Frieze, Fisher, Hanusa, McHugh, & Valle [1978]; Lenney [1977]; Parsons, Ruble, Hodges, & Small [1976]; and Stein & Bailey [1973] for reviews). However, the developmental origins of this difference are unclear. Parsons et al. (1976) suggested several ways in which teachers and parents might be perpetuating, if not creating, this sex difference. While several recent studies of possible teacher influences have emerged (e.g., Brophy & Good 1974; Dweck, Davidson, Nelson, & Enna 1978), there have been virtually no recent studies of parental influences. The study reported herein was designed to assess parental influences on children's achievement expectancies and self-concepts of ability with a particular focus on the contributions of parents to the commonly reported sex differences. The roles of parents both as models and as expectancy socializers were investigated.

Parents as Role Models

The importance of role models in socialization is a recurring theme throughout the sex-difference literature. The process of "observational learning" has been suggested as one of the ways in which children absorb social norms, especially those associated with sex-appropriate qualities of behavior (see Bandura & Walters 1963; Maccoby & Jacklin 1974). According to this hypothesis, models, parents in particular, exhibit behaviors which children imitate and later adopt as part of their own behavioral repertoire; if important female models exhibit different behavior patterns than comparable male models, then girls and boys

Copies of this paper can be obtained from the first author at the Psychology Department, University of Michigan, Ann Arbor, Michigan 48109. This research was funded by grants from the National Institute of Education (NIE-G-78-0022) and the National Institute of Mental Health (5R01-MH31724-01). We wish to thank Robert Futterman, Kirby Heller, Julie D. Karabenick, Judy Mecce, Carol Midgley, Margaret Peterson, Linda Murray, the many undergraduate students who helped collect and code these data, and the Ann Arbor Public Schools for their assistance throughout the project.

[*Child Development*, 1982, 53, 310–321. © 1982 by the Society for Research in Child Development, Inc.

will exhibit different behavioral patterns. In regard to mathematics in particular, Ernest (1976) reported that after sixth grade, fathers are more likely than mothers to help their children with their math homework, and Fox (Note 1) has reported a tendency for more advanced courses to be taught by males. This underrepresentation of appropriate female role models could influence girls' decisions to engage in mathematical activities. The success of intervention programs which have increased female math participation through exposure to female models supports this line of reasoning (e.g., Brody & Fox 1980; Tobin & Fox 1980).

Role models may also influence children's achievement behaviors through the messages they provide regarding their beliefs about their own abilities. If male and female socializers hold different beliefs about their own math abilities and competence, then it would be expected that boys and girls would develop different beliefs about their own abilities. While relevant research on parents is sparse, Aiken (1970), in his review, cited data indicating that female student teachers have lower estimates of their math ability and openly admit they are less comfortable teaching math than do their male peers.

In summary, the role-modeling hypothesis takes the following form with regard to expectancies for general achievement: girls exhibit different achievement choices and have lower expectancies than boys because mothers exhibit different achievement behaviors and have lower achievement expectancies than fathers. To assess this hypothesis, two tests are needed: (*a*) a demonstration that mothers and fathers differ on key variables, and (*b*) a demonstration that these differences predict individual differences in children's responses to related variables. If parents' behaviors and self-concepts do not predict children's behaviors and self-concepts, then role modeling is not a tenable causal explanation for the sex differences found in the child sample, even if the predicted sex differences exist in the parent sample. Furthermore, even if parent behaviors and self-concepts were predictive of children's behaviors, this would only support a correlational hypothesis and would not provide definitive evidence of causality.

Parents as Expectancy Socializers

The role of parents as expectancy socializers has received less attention. Previous work (e.g., Crandall 1969; Rosen & D'Andrade 1959; Winterbottom 1958) related both parents' in-

dependence training and parental expectancies to children's need-achievement motives and related achievement behaviors. This body of work established a positive relation between parents' expectations for their children's achievement behaviors and children's actual behaviors. However, this work did not address directly the issue of parental socialization of sex differences in expectancies. Several studies suggest that, in general, parents and teachers have higher educational expectancies for boys than for girls (e.g., Sears, Maccoby, & Levin 1957), although these biases do not emerge consistently until children are older. During the elementary school years parents generally expect girls to do better than boys (see Maccoby & Jacklin 1974). In their review of socialization influences, Parsons et al. (1976) concluded that, while studies are not entirely consistent, there is some evidence that parents do have lower achievement expectancies for adolescent girls than for adolescent boys. However, the relation of these expectancies to children's expectancies and self-concepts of ability for achievement activities and the exact nature of the expectancy messages themselves have not been adequately explored.

How might parental expectancies for their children be manifested? First and foremost, parents may form specific expectancies regarding their child's probable performance in a particular course. Parents may convey these expectations in the messages they give regarding their beliefs about their child's abilities, about the difficulty of various achievement tasks, and about the importance of various achievement activities. For example, parents may stress the difficulty or the importance of certain courses more to their daughters than to their sons; they may acknowledge their sons' abilities more than they acknowledge their daughters'; they may encourage their sons to tackle difficult tasks more than they encourage their daughters. In basic agreement with this suggestion, Hoffman (1972) concluded that parents encourage independence in their sons more than in their daughters. Whether this tendency characterizes parents' behavior regarding specific achievement tasks has not been studied.

To assess the validity of the hypothesized relation of expectancy messages to sex differences in children's expectancies and achievement self-concepts, the following tests are needed: (*a*) a demonstration that parents have different expectancies and beliefs regarding the abilities of their sons and daughters, and (*b*) a demonstration that these parental beliefs predict individual differences in the children's ex-

312   Child Development

pectancies, self-concepts of their abilities, and conceptions of the difficulty of the subject matter. Again, it should be stressed that a significant relation between these parental beliefs and children's attitudes would provide correlational rather than causal support for this hypothesis.

Math as the Domain of Study

To investigate these parental influences on sex-differentiated expectancies and self-concepts of ability, a domain was needed that met the following criteria: (a) sex differences in expectancies and self-concepts of ability had to exist among school-age children, (b) congruent sex differences in both attitudinal and related achievement behaviors had to exist among adults, and (c) these sex differences should not relate isomorphically to the assessment of "actual" ability differences. Additionally, to increase the relevance of the study, it was decided that the domain should be one in which the sex difference has significant long-range consequences for the children. Mathematics is one area that meets all of these criteria. Boys have both higher expectancies and self-concepts of their math abilities than girls. Men are much more likely to be involved in math-related careers. Boys and girls do equally well in the math courses in which they are enrolled. And, finally, the failure to take advanced high school math severely limits the career options of females in exactly those areas of employment that offer some of the highest and least sex-discriminatory salaries (see Parsons, Adler, Futterman, Goff, Kaczala, Meece, & Midgley [in press] for discussion of these differences).

Method

Sample

The student sample consisted of volunteering children from 22 fifth- through eleventh-grade classrooms chosen randomly from those made available by volunteering teachers. The school district was in a small midwestern city populated primarily by middle- to upper-class families. Two fifth-grade classes, one sixth-

grade class, eight seventh-grade classes, three eighth-grade classes, six ninth-grade classes, one tenth-grade class, and one eleventh-grade class were selected. The larger numbers of seventh- and ninth-grade classes were chosen because past research has suggested that the early adolescence years are critical in the formation of sex-differentiated expectancies in math. The overall participation rate was 57%; participation rates varied somewhat between grades and seemed to be a function primarily of the teacher's interest in the study. The total sample included approximately the same number of boys and girls (53% of the sample being female).

The parent sample consisted of the mothers and fathers of these student subjects. Both parents of 62% of the participating students and one parent of an additional 18% of the students completed the questionnaire.

Measures

Student questionnaire.—The questionnaire was developed in two steps. Initially, nine-point bipolar rating scales anchored at the extremes with short verbal descriptors were designed and pilot tested in a school district comparable to the district in which the study was to be run. Based on these students' comments and on their responses to the items, the nine-point scale was reduced to a seven-point scale, several items were eliminated or reworded, and scales were formed using Cronbach's coefficient α. The final student questionnaire contained several scales.[1] The following were used for ᵗhis study: (a) difficulty of current math course: absolute and comparative ratings of difficulty of current mathematics course ($\alpha = .81$); (b) difficulty of future math courses: absolute and comparative ratings of difficulty of future mathematics courses ($\alpha = .77$); (c) current expectancies: ratings of students' expected performance in current mathematics course ($\alpha = .83$); (d) future expectancies: ratings of students' expected performance in future mathematics courses ($\alpha = .79$); (e) self-concept of ability and performance in math: ratings of ability in current and advanced mathematics ($\alpha = .80$); (f) perception of effort involved in

---

[1] The full questionnaire is discussed in more detail in Parsons, Adler, Futterman, Goff, Kaczala, Meece, and Midgley (Note 3), available from the first author. The full questionnaire contained the PAQ and the following six additional constructed scales: a shortened version of the IAR, a measure of sex-role identity, sex typing of ability in math, utility of math for one's own goals, incentive value of math, cost of effort needed to do well, perceptions of parents' use of and liking of math, perceptions of parents' beliefs regarding one's math abilities, and the importance of math.

math: ratings of the effort perceived to be necessary to do well in math $(\alpha = .76)$.

There were also a number of single-item scales for which alpha coefficients were not available. These include child's perception of mothers' use of math, mothers' and fathers' enjoyment of math, mothers' and fathers' beliefs regarding both child's math ability and their expectancies for the child's performance.

Parent questionnaire.—A questionnaire consisting of both seven-point Likert items and open-ended questions was employed to assess parents' attitudes and expectancies. The parents' questionnaire was constructed to parallel the children's questionnaire as much as possible. It was developed and pilot tested in a manner similar to that used in constructing the student questionnaire.

The parents' questionnaire contained items tapping three categories of information: (1) the parents' perceptions of their own experiences in math and their own attitudes regarding mathematics, (2) parents' beliefs about their children's attitudes toward math, and (3) parents' beliefs about their children's math abilities and their children's math experiences. For purposes of this paper, only items from categories 1 and 3 were included for analysis; each of these two sets of items is described in more detail below.

Referring first to parental attitudes about mathematics, parents were asked to reflect back on their years in high school and to report their experiences and attitudes at that time. Given the inaccuracies often associated with retrospection, this information was intended not so much to inform us about past conditions as to inform us about parents' current views of their past high school experiences with mathematics. This section of the questionnaire contained the following scales: (a) parents' perception of past math ability (mothers' $\alpha = .90$, fathers' $\alpha = .87$); (b) importance of math for parents in the past (mothers' $\alpha = .73$, fathers' $\alpha = .75$); (c) effort required by parents to do well in math in the past (mothers' $\alpha = .77$, fathers' $\alpha = .71$); (d) difficulty of math for parents in the past (mothers' $\alpha = .84$, fathers' $\alpha = .81$).

Current parental attitudes were also assessed. In particular, parents were asked about the following: (a) parents' perceptions of their current math ability (assessed with a single item; thus, α is not available); (b) usefulness of math for parents in the present (mothers'

$\alpha = .59$, fathers' $\alpha = .73$); (c) difficulty of math for parents in the present (mothers' $\alpha = .75$, fathers' $\alpha = .55$); (d) parents' current enjoyment of math (assessed with a single item; thus, α is not available).

In addition, parents were asked to report the number of math courses they had taken in high school and college, their level of education, who presently does the household math, and their current occupation.

The second set of items from the parent questionnaire of relevance to this paper tapped parental beliefs and attitudes about their children. This section of the questionnaire included the following scales: (a) parents' perception of child's math ability (mothers' $\alpha = .61$, fathers' $\alpha = .58$); (b) parents' perception of importance of math for child (mothers' $\alpha = .49$, fathers' $\alpha = .47$); (c) parents' perception of effort needed by child to do well in math (mothers' $\alpha = .74$, fathers' $\alpha = .65$); (d) parents' perception of the difficulty of math for child (mothers' $\alpha = .79$, fathers' $\alpha = .76$); (e) parents' expectations for child's performance in future math courses (mothers' $\alpha = .66$, fathers' $\alpha = .83$). This section of the questionnaire also contained several single items which assessed parents' perceptions of their child's general school performance and their enjoyment of math, the amount of encouragement they have given their children to continue in math, and the amount of importance they placed on various school subjects.

School record data.—In addition to the questionnaires, several measures were taken directly from the children's school files. These measures included the children's grades in mathematics for the 2 previous years and all available absolute scores on the Michigan Educational Assessment Program and California Achievement Test. Given that teachers vary in reporting procedures, that not all children had all three scores, and that no one measure of past performance is perfectly reliable, these measures were standardized within grade and averaged to form an estimate of each child's past performance in mathematics.

Procedures

The student questionnaire was administered in two 30-min sessions in the child's math classroom in the spring of 1978. The parent questionnaires were mailed to participants' homes and returned by mail during the summer of 1978.

314   Child Development

Results and Discussion

Parents as Role Models

To test for the hypothesized differences between mothers and fathers, the mathematics-relevant self-concepts of the mothers and fathers were compared. In comparison to mothers' responses, fathers reported that they were ($t = 5.40$, $p < .001$) and are currently better at math ($t = 8.30$, $p < .001$), that math was ($t = 5.73$, $p < .001$) and is currently easier for them ($t = 4.87$, $p < .001$), that they needed to expend less effort to do well at math ($t = 4.39$, $p < .001$), that they have enjoyed math more in the past ($t = 4.12$, $p < .001$) as well as in the present ($t = 6.67$, $p < .001$), that math has always been more useful ($t = 5.11$, $p < .001$), and that it is currently more important to them ($t = 3.31$, $p < .01$). Only two items yielded nonsignificant differences: past importance of math and the current importance of basic math skills. In sum, fathers were more positive toward math and had a more positive self-concept regarding their math abilities. Furthermore, these sex-differentiated beliefs were specific to math. Consistent with the fact that girls on the average outperform boys in school, mothers rated their general high school performance higher than did fathers ($t = 2.58$, $p < .05$).

In line with the modeling hypothesis, one might conclude at this point that boys and girls differ because their parents' beliefs and behaviors are sex differentiated. But one needs to demonstrate a relation between parents' beliefs and their children's beliefs before this conclusion is justified.

To test the modeling hypothesis more directly, the parent self-concept variables, measures of the number of math courses taken in high school and college, occupation and work patterns, and the number of years of education of both parents were correlated with their children's responses to the student questionnaire and with the measure of their children's past performance in math. Mother and father variables were correlated separately with both son and daughter variables. Two criteria were used to determine which of these relationships was meaningful: correlation coefficients had to attain a significance level of $p < .01$ and a magnitude of at least .30. These criteria were based on the fact that our large sample size made it possible to have correlation coefficients which were statistically significant from zero but did not reflect a psychologically meaningful relationship between the two variables. The rela-

tionship between those variables which did attain a significance level of $p < .01$ but did not have a magnitude of at least .30 was further examined by the use of scatter plots. None of the more than 400 correlations met our initial criteria. Thus, while parents' self-concepts do differ in the predicted direction, there was no strong relation between these differences and their children's math self-concepts and expectancies.

Parents were also asked who did the math-related tasks in the household. According to their own reports, mothers were not less likely to do the math-related tasks (58 reported that both parents did the math, 97 reported that their husbands did the math, and 91 reported that they did the math). In contrast, fathers reported that they were more likely to do the math-related tasks (53 reported that both parents did the math, 45 reported that their wives did the math, and 121 reported that they did the math). Analyses of variance using the parental reports of who did the math as the independent variable indicated that parental division of math-related tasks at home had no effect on the children's self-concept, task-concept, and performance measures ($p > .05$ for all tests).

Before ruling out the parental modeling hypothesis, two additional tests were performed. It is possible that children are not accurate in their perceptions of their parents. If children are inaccurate, then one would not expect parents' self-reported math attitudes and behaviors to correlate significantly with the children's self-perceptions, task perceptions, and performance. Instead, one would predict significant correlations between measures of children's perceptions of their parents and measures of children's self-perceptions. To test for these possibilities, the children's perceptions of their parents' attitudes and behaviors were correlated with the parents' self-reports and both the children's math ability self-concept and task-concept measures.

While the children's perceptions of their parents' use and enjoyment of math were not correlated with any of the parental occupation or schooling variables, the children's perceptions of their parents' enjoyment of math were, by and large, significantly correlated with the parents' self-reports of past and present math ability, math difficulty, and effort needed to do well in math. Of the 24 correlations tested, 19 were both significant at the $p < .01$ level and larger than .30; four more were significant at the $p < .01$ level but fell between .24 and

.29. Additionally, analyses of variance using the children's perceptions of the parents' liking and use of math as the dependent variables, and maternal reports of the sex division of math-related tasks in the household as the independent variable, yielded significant F's. Children whose fathers did the household math felt their fathers liked math more than did children whose mothers or both parents did the math, $F(2) = 5.25$, $p < .01$. Similarly, children whose mothers did the household math, either alone or in conjunction with the father, felt that their mothers liked and used math more than did children whose fathers did the household math, $F(2) = 3.3$, $p > .05$. Thus, children had fairly accurate perceptions of their parents' math attitudes and behaviors; the failure to find significant correlations between parents' self-reports and children's self-perceptions was not due to children's inaccurate perceptions of their parents' use of or liking of mathematics.

Were children's perceptions of their parents' use and enjoyment of math significant predictors of the children's ratings of their own math abilities, and of the difficulty and usefulness of mathematics? No. As with the correlation between parent self-reports and the children's self-ratings, none of the 30 correlations met our criteria. Twelve of these relationships were significant at the $p < .01$ level but did not attain a magnitude of .30 (they ranged in magnitude from .19 to .28; eight of these fell below .25). These relationships were further examined by scatter plot; weak linear relationships were found. In sum, neither parents' self-reports nor children's perceptions of their parents' math use were strong predictors of children's self-perceptions, task perceptions, or actual performance. Thus, it seems clear that parental role modeling of mathematical skills does not exert a very strong influence on children's math-related self-perceptions, task perceptions, actual performance, or plans to continue in mathematics courses.

Parents as Expectancy Socializers

Parental beliefs.—Parents may contribute to the sex differences in math expectancies through the messages they provide to their children regarding their beliefs about their children's math abilities, the difficulty of math itself, and the importance of taking math courses. That is, girls may have lower self-concepts and expectations because parents think daughters are not as good in math as are sons. To assess this hypothesis, the perceptions of boys' parents regarding their sons' math ability and effort, their expectancies for their sons' future performance in math, their perceptions of the relative importance of a variety of courses for their sons, and their estimates of the difficulty of math for their sons were compared to similar beliefs of the parents of girls. The data are summarized in table 1.

Despite the fact that boys and girls in this sample had performed equally well in math the previous year and on their most re-

TABLE 1

MEAN RATING OF PARENTS' PERCEPTIONS OF AND VALUES FOR THEIR CHILDREN

	MOTHERS			FATHERS		
VARIABLE	Sons	Daughters	F value	Sons	Daughters	F value
Math ability............................	10.16	9.94	.51	9.97	9.60	1.85
Effort needed to do well in math.......	8.50	9.59	9.07**	8.73	9.67	9.32**
Task difficulty of math...............	7.75	8.73	7.77**	7.64	8.78	13.53**
Future expectancies in math..........	10.98	10.67	.89	10.83	10.08	2.38
Importance of math..................	11.10	10.65	4.46*	10.84	10.64	.94
Relative importance of math..........	4.88	4.67	1.90	4.76	4.48	3.93*
Importance of English...............	5.91	6.14	2.07	5.32	5.97	14.61**
Importance of geometry..............	6.20	5.55	18.33**	5.84	5.62	1.88
Importance of trig/calculus...........	5.42	4.65	12.37**	5.54	4.99	6.94**
Importance of chemistry.............	5.89	5.47	6.08*	5.63	5.45	1.10
Importance of American history.......	6.05	5.96	.44	5.32	5.84	9.11**
Encouragement to continue in math...	5.55	5.46	.14	5.86	5.29	5.20*
Enjoyment of math..................	5.18	4.83	2.87	5.01	4.53	6.49*
Perception of school performance......	5.65	5.96	3.91*	5.64	5.97	4.60*

NOTE.—The first five variables represent summary scales; all other variables represent single items; $df = 1,250$ with the exception of the twelfth mother variable and the fourth and twelfth father variables ($1,106 \leq df \geq 1,128$).

* $p < .05$.

** $p < .01$.

316   Child Development

cent standardized math test ($p > .05$), the sex of the child had a significant effect on parents' perceptions of their child's math ability and on parents' perceptions of the relative importance of various high school courses. While parents of daughters did not rate their child's math abilities as significantly lower than did parents of sons, parents of daughters reported that math was harder for their child and that their child had to work harder to do well in math. Their daughters' general school performance was better than their sons. In addition, parents of sons as compared to parents of daughters felt that math was more important than other subjects for their child. In general, these sex-differentiated beliefs held primarily for math and science. Parents of daughters felt that their child's general school performance was better than parents of sons, and fathers of daughters rated both English and American history as more important for their children than fathers of sons.

That parents feel their daughters have to try harder to do well in math is of particular interest in light of both our previous findings and a common finding in the attribution literature. In previous work we have found that girls think they have to try harder than boys to do well in math even though they report spending equivalent amounts of time on their math homework (Parsons et al., in press; Kaczala, Parsons, Futterman, & Meece, Note 2; Parsons, Adler, Futterman, Goff, Kaczala, Meece, & Midgley, Note 3); and on an experimental task, girls rated their efforts as greater even though an objective measure of effort did not reveal a sex difference (Parsons, Note 4). Similarly, women have been shown to attribute their successes more to effort than do men (see Frieze et al. 1978). Taken together these findings suggest that females think they will have to try harder to receive a good grade than males think they will have to try. The present data suggest that parents are reinforcing this tendency. Whether parents initiate the bias or merely echo it is not clear, but they certainly are not providing their daughters with a counterinterpretation.

Is it necessarily harmful that both girls and their parents think girls have to try harder to do well in math? It has been argued in the attribution literature that because attributions to effort do not contribute to a stable notion of one's ability in a particular domain, attributing one's success to effort is not as ego enhancing as attributing it to ability (Frieze et al. 1978). Attributing one's successes to effort may

also leave doubt about one's future performance on increasingly difficult tasks. If one is having to try very hard to do well now and one expects next year's math course to be even harder, one may not expect to do as well next year. In support of this suggestion, perceptions of how hard one is trying in the present have been found to be negatively correlated with future expectancies and with one's estimates of one's ability and the difficulty of the task (Parsons et al., Note 3). In addition, using cross-lagged panel analyses, Parsons et al. (in press) found that perceptions of how hard one is trying in the present are causally related to children's self-concepts of their math ability 1 year later. If one adds to this dynamic the fact that both girls and their parents think that continuing in math is less important for them than do boys and their parents, then a cognitive set could emerge that would decrease the tendency in girls to continue in advanced math courses.

Relation of parental beliefs to children's attitudes.—Having demonstrated that parental beliefs about their children's abilities and plans are sex related, the next step is to test whether these parental beliefs are predictive of the children's self- and task perceptions. As hypothesized, children's self-perceptions, expectancies, and perceptions of task difficulty related consistently to both their perceptions of their parents' beliefs and expectancies and to the parents' actual estimates of their children's abilities (see table 2). Parents who think that math is hard for their children and who think their children are not very good at math have children who also possess a low self-concept of their math ability, see math as difficult, and have low expectancies for their future performances in math. In addition, the magnitude of the relations between parental perceptions of their child and their child's beliefs and behaviors did not vary as a function of the child's sex.

Path analysis.—As hypothesized, then, parents' beliefs about their children were related to their children's self- and task perceptions. It is possible, however, that this relation represents the shared knowledge parents and children have of the child's past math performance rather than the child's incorporation of the parents' beliefs. It is our contention that parental beliefs are causally related to children's self- and task concepts. We predict that parents' beliefs influence children's self-concepts rather than both sets of beliefs resulting from the child's past performance.

TABLE 2

ZERO-ORDER CORRELATION OF MOTHER AND FATHER ATTITUDES TOWARD CHILD AND CHILD ATTITUDES AND PERCEPTIONS OF PARENTS' ATTITUDES

Mother Attitudes

	Past Math Performance	Intention to Take More Math	Current Expectancies in Math	Future Expectancies in Math	Self-Concept of Math Ability	Perception of Task Difficulty	Value of Math	Perception of Parents' Perception of Child's Math Ability	Perception of Parents' Future Expectancies for Child	Perception of Parents' Perception of Task Difficulty for Child	Perception of Parents' Aspirations for Child
Mother's perception of importance of math for child	.41**	.35**	.41**	.44**	.46**	-.11	.42**	.46**	.25**	-.17**	.12
	.42**	.40**	.43**	.44**	.47**	-.09	.43**	.46**	.28**	-.20*	.11
	.39**	.29**	.40**	.50**	.47**	-.16	.43**	.48**	.21*	-.16	.15
Mother's perception of child's math ability	.40**	.34**	.44**	.46**	.54**	-.31**	.33**	.54**	.33**	-.23**	.16*
	.38**	.38**	.45**	.49**	.58**	-.37**	.32**	.58**	.36**	-.29**	.14
	.43**	.27*	.44**	.42**	.49**	-.23*	.35**	.50**	.28**	-.15	.19
Mother's perception of child's effort in math	-.32**	-.21**	-.32**	-.35**	-.47**	.49**	-.20**	-.38**	-.27**	.41**	-.18**
	-.20*	-.26**	-.25**	-.35**	-.44**	.48**	-.19*	-.34**	-.26**	.45**	-.11
	-.47**	-.15	-.40**	-.31**	-.48**	.47**	-.18	-.42**	-.29**	.33**	-.26*
Mother's perception of task difficulty for child	-.35**	-.27**	-.42**	-.47**	-.58**	.52**	-.29**	-.46**ᵃ	-.31**	.43**	-.19**ᵃ
	-.28**	-.27**	-.35**	-.45**	-.53**	.50**	-.23**	-.38**	-.27**	.42**	-.07
	-.46**	-.26**	-.51**	-.48**	-.64**	.51**	-.38**	-.58**	-.38**	.40**	-.37**
Mother's perception of child's perception of importance of math	-.03	.02	.13*	.15*	.14*	-.08	.17**	.18**	.17**	.07	.21**
	.09	.11	.09	.10	.09	-.05	.20*	.13	.18*	.03	.22**
	.04	-.12	.17	.18	.18	-.09	.09	.24*	.17	.09	.17
Mother's future expectancies for child	.51**	.29**	.48**	.50**	.56**	-.33**	.28**	.55**	.36**	-.35**	.19**
	.53**	.28**	.45**	.50**	.56**	-.41**	.18*	.49**	.37**	-.34**	.17*
	.49**	.29**	.51**	.50**	.56**	-.22*	.41**	.63**	.34**	-.35*	.21*

NOTE.—Within each row there are three sets of correlations. The top set contains the correlations for all subjects. The middle set contains the correlations for females. The bottom set contains the correlations for males.

ᵃ Boxed correlations contain a set of correlations in which the male and female correlations differ p < .05.

* p < .05.
** p < .01.

TABLE 2—*Continued*

	Past Math Perfor- mance	Intention to Take More Math	Current Expec- tancies in Math	Future Expec- tancies in Math	Self- Concept of Math Ability	Perception of Task Difficulty	Value of Math	Perception of Parents' Perception of Child's Math Ability	Perception of Parents' Future Expec- tancies for Child	Perception of Parents' Perception of Task Difficulty for Child	Perception of Parents' Aspira- tions for Child
Father Attitudes											
Father's perception of importance of math for child	.41** .48** .32**	.34** .38** .28**	.26** .30** .21*	.37** .36** .40**	.31** .34** .27**	-.02 -.06 .03	.26** .22* .35**	.34** .38** .28**	.19** .15 .25*	-.10 -.19* -.00	.07 .02 .17
Father's perception of child's math ability	.46** .47** .44**	.27** .25** .31**	.36** .36** .34**	.43** .41** .45**	.47** .48** .45**	-.28** -.33** -.20	.26** .18* .38**	.48** .43** .55**	.24** .19* .29**	-.28** -.35** -.16	.07 -.01 .19
Father's perception of child's effort in math	-.31** -.28** -.34**	-.20** -.22** -.17	-.35** -.34** -.33**	-.39** -.38** -.37**	-.45** -.43** -.43**	.38** .32** .41**	-.25** -.17* -.33**	-.37** -.30** -.43**	-.21** -.17* -.25*	.34** .33** .33**	-.16* -.11 -.18
Father's perception of task difficulty for child	-.36** -.37** -.35**	-.19** -.17* -.21	-.43** -.37** -.48**	-.43** -.35** -.49**	-.53** -.47** -.58**	.40** .35** .40**	-.25** -.14 -.38**	-.50** -.42** -.59**	-.29** -.21* -.37**	.32** .33** .27**	.12[a] .01 .27*
Father's perception of child's perception of importance of math	-.02 -.07 .03	.11 .10 .11	.06 .05 .06	.12 .08 .15	.03 -.01 -.06	.10 .13 .12	.17** .18* .10	.06 .04 .09	.16* .21* .04	.01 .04 .01	.18** .25** .00
Father's future expectancies for child	.53** .57** .49**	.22** .21* .24*	.30** .30** .30**	.40** .40** .42**	.39** .38** .40**	-.21** -.28** -.12	.20** .10 .34**	.35** .28** .43**	.18** .15 .22*	-.21** -.22** -.19	.09 .07 .11
Child Perceptions											
Perception of parents' perception of child's math ability	.34** .27** .42**	.32** .34** .29**	.61** .58** .64**	.64** .62** .65**	.72** .74** .69**	-.38** -.44** -.28**	.42** .35** .51**	1.00 1.00 1.00	.49** .45** .55**	-.36** -.36** -.36**	.25** .19** .33**
Perception of parents' future expectancies for child	.10 .04 .17	.26** .26** .27**	.47** .52** .42**	.58** .59** .58**	.52** .55** .48**	-.21** -.21** -.21*	.45** .41** .50**	.49** .45** .55**	1.00 1.00 1.00	-.26** -.25** -.28**	.73** .73** .75**
Perception of parents' perception of task difficulty for child	-.13* -.06 -.22**	-.11 -.15 -.06	-.37** -.38** -.35**	-.32** -.29** -.34**	-.44** -.45** -.42**	.51** .46** .57**	-.15** -.16* -.13	-.36** -.36** -.36**	-.26** -.25** -.28**	1.00 1.00 1.00	-.12* -.07 -.18

Recursive path analysis (Duncan 1966) was used to assess this hypothesis. This statistical technique allows one to estimate both direct and indirect relationships among variables. The coefficients of the relations between the predictor and criterion variables provide the test of significance.

Before performing the path analysis, parent scores were factored using the exploratory factor-analytic procedures developed by Joreskog, Sorbom, and Magidson (1979). Factor analysis was performed to reduce the number of parent variables and to reduce the multicollinearity in the parent variable set. Using criteria suggested by Joreskog and Sorbom (1978), it was determined that a four-factor structure best described the underlying relationships. The four factors were (a) both parents' perceptions of the importance of math for their child, (b) fathers' perceptions of the difficulty of math for their child, (c) mothers' perceptions of the difficulty of math for their child, and (d) both parents' perceptions of their child's math ability.

A model based on the above predictions and on the model proposed by Parsons et al. (in press) was then specified. Referring to figure 1, we predicted that the variables in the first (far-left) column would have a direct

effect only on the variables in column 2; the variables in column 2 would have direct effects on the variables in column 3; and finally, that children's expectancies in math would be directly predicted by the variables in column 3.

The path coefficients were estimated using a series of multiple-regression equations. At each step the criterion variables in a given level (or column) of the model were regressed on the prediction variables from all previous levels (or columns). The coefficients were standardized; thus their size provides an estimate of the relative strength of the relations specified by each path. However, since these estimates are based on multiple regressions, they are dependent on the set of variables used in each analysis and should not be taken as absolute estimates of any given relationship.

In an initial path analysis the one father factor (father's perception of the difficulty of math for his child) did not emerge as a significant predictor of anything. Rather than limit our sample to two-parent families, we omitted this father variable and used the mother's response as an indicator variable for the two-parent factors for children in one-parent households. We then repeated the path analysis. The results of this analysis are depicted in figure 1. The basic path structure was equivalent to the

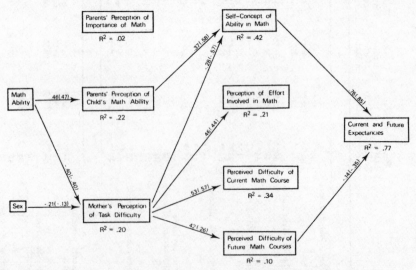

Fig. 1.—Path analysis of parent and student attitudes. All paths significant at $p < .01$; $N = 201$; standardized beta weights are shown on path; zero order correlations are shown in parentheses; R^2 = percent of variance accounted for on each criterion measure by all preceding predictor variables; each R^2 is listed under its criterion measure.

320   Child Development

structure which emerged in the initial analysis. The results depicted in figure 1, however, are representative of a broader population of family types.

The path analysis was collapsed across our male and female samples so that sex could be used as an independent variable. To make sure that this collapsed analysis was equally representative of boys and girls, within-sex correlations of the predictor and criterion variables were compared. The only correlation which was not comparable for boys and girls at the $p <$ .05 level was that of child's math ability and parents' perception of child's math ability. However, further examination showed that both the magnitude and direction of the path coefficient of this relationship were virtually identical when within-sex path analyses were compared. We thus are confident that our path analysis applies to both boys and girls.

In support of our predictions, the children's self-concepts and task concepts were more directly related to their parents' beliefs about their math aptitude and potential than to their own past performance or their sex. While these results do not demonstrate causality, they are congruent with the hypothesized causal model.

With regard to the differential effectiveness of various socializers, the two-path analyses and the factor analysis suggest that mothers have the stronger influence on children's achievement beliefs and attitudes; fathers appear to have little independent effect over and above that which they share with mothers.

Conclusions

In conclusion, parents had sex-differentiated perceptions of their children's math aptitude despite the similarity of the actual performance of boys and girls. This difference was most marked for parents' estimates of how hard their children have to try to do well in math. Parents of sons also thought advanced math was more important for their child than parents of daughters, perhaps reflecting a tendency to encourage children to develop skills which are assumed to be "natural" for the child. Parents' perceptions of and expectations for their children were related to both the children's perception of parents' beliefs and to the children's self- and task perceptions. Further, parents' beliefs were more directly related to children's self-concepts and expectancies than were the children's own past performances in math. Path

analysis supported our hypothesis that the children's attitudes are influenced more by their parents' attitudes about their children's abilities than by their own past performances. Finally, parents as role models of sex-differentiated math behaviors did not have a direct effect on their children's self-concepts, expectations, and course plans.

In line with Popper's comments (1979) on the importance of negative observations for scientific understanding, these data also indicate that parents do not influence their children's achievement attitudes and beliefs through their power as role models. Instead, parents have their major impact as conveyors of expectancies regarding their children's abilities. Unfortunately, parents hold sex-stereotyped beliefs regarding their children's achievement potential, and these beliefs appear to be the critical parental mediators of the sex differences we find in children's achievement self-concepts. Parental beliefs are even more critical mediators than the children's own math performance. While we do not have, as yet, the necessary longitudinal data to test the hypothesis, it seems probable that parents are exerting this influence through their role as interpreters of reality. By attributing their daughters' achievements to hard work and their sons' to high ability, parents may be teaching their sons and daughters to draw different inferences regarding their achievement abilities from equivalent achievement experiences.

Reference Notes

1. Fox, L. The effects of sex role socialization on mathematics participation and achievement (Paper No. 8). Washington, D.C.: National Institute of Education, 1977.

2. Kaczala, C.; Parsons, J.; Futterman, R.; & Meece, J. Developmental shifts in expectancies and attributions for performance in mathematics. Paper presented at the meeting of the American Educational Research Association, San Francisco, April 1979.

3. Parsons, J. E.; Adler, T. F.; Futterman, R.; Goff, S. B.; Kaczala, C. M.; Meece, J. L.; & Midgley, C. Self-perceptions, task perceptions and academic choice: origins and change. Final report to the National Institute of Education, Washington, D.C., 1980.

4. Parsons, J. Cognitive mediation of the effects of evaluative feedback on children's affect and expectancy for success. Symposium paper presented at the annual meeting of the American Educational Research Association, Toronto, April 1978.

References

Aiken, L. Attitudes toward mathematics. *Review of Educational Research,* 1970, **40,** 551–596.

Bandura, A., & Walters, R. H. *Social learning and personality development.* New York: Holt, Rinehart & Winston, 1963.

Brody, L., & Fox, L. H. An accelerated intervention program for mathematically gifted girls. In L. H. Fox, L. Brody, & D. Tobin (Eds.), *Women and the mathematical mystique.* Baltimore: Johns Hopkins University Press, 1980.

Brophy, J. E., & Good, T. *Teacher-student relationships: causes and consequences.* New York: Holt, Rinehart & Winston, 1974.

Crandall, V. C. Sex differences in expectancy of intellectual and academic reinforcement. In C. P. Smith (Ed.), *Achievement-related behaviors in children.* New York: Russell Sage, 1969.

Duncan, O. D. Path analysis: sociological examples. *American Journal of Sociology,* 1966, **72,** 1–16.

Dweck, C. S.; Davidson, W.; Nelson, S.; & Enna, B. Sex differences in learned helplessness. II. The contingencies of evaluative feedback in the classroom. III. An experimental analysis. *Developmental Psychology,* 1978, **14,** 268–276.

Ernest, J. *Mathematics and sex.* Santa Barbara: University of California, 1976.

Frieze, I. H.; Fisher, J.; Hanusa, B.; McHugh, M.; & Valle, V. Attributing the causes of success and failure: internal and external barriers to achievement in women. In J. Sherman & F. Denmard (Eds.), *Psychology of women: future directions of research.* New York: Psychological Dimensions, 1978.

Hoffman, L. W. Early childhood experiences and women's achievement motives. *Journal of Social Issues,* 1972, **28,** 129–155.

Joreskog, K. G., & Sorbom, D. *EFAP: exploratory factor analysis program: user's guide.* Chicago: National Educational Resources, 1978.

Joreskog, K. G.; Sorbom, D.; & Magidson, J. (Eds.). *Advances in factor analysis and structural equation models.* Cambridge, Mass.: Abt, 1979.

Lenney, E. Women's self-confidence in achievement settings. *Psychological Bulletin,* 1977, **84,** 1–13.

Maccoby, E. E., & Jacklin, C. N. *Psychology of sex differences.* Palo Alto, Calif.: Stanford University Press, 1974.

Parsons, J. E.; Adler, T. F.; Futterman, R.; Goff, S. B.; Kaczala, C. M.; Meece, J. L.; & Midgley, C. Expectancies, values, and academic behaviors. In J. T. Spence (Ed.), *Perspectives on achievement and achievement motivation.* San Francisco: Freeman, in press.

Parsons, J. E.; Ruble, D. N.; Hodges, K. L.; & Small, A. W. Cognitive-developmental factors in emerging sex differences in achievement-related expectancies. *Journal of Social Issues,* 1976, **32,** 47–61.

Popper, K. R. *Objective knowledge: an evolutionary approach.* London: Oxford University Press, 1979.

Rosen, B., & D'Andrade, R. The psychosocial origins of achievement motivation. *Sociometry,* 1959, **22,** 185–218.

Sears, R. R.; Maccoby, E. E.; & Levin, H. *Patterns of child rearing.* Evanston, Ill.: Row & Peterson, 1957.

Stein, A. H., & Bailey, M. M. The socialization of achievement orientation in females. *Psychological Bulletin,* 1973, **80,** 345–366.

Tobin, D., & Fox, L. H. Career interests and career education: a key to change. In L. H. Fox, L. Brody, & D. Tobin (Eds.), *Women and the mathematical mystique.* Baltimore: Johns Hopkins University Press, 1980.

Winterbottom, M. R. The relation of need for achievement to learning experiences in independence and mastery. In J. W. Atkinson (Ed.), *Motives in fantasy, action, and society.* Princeton, N.J.: Van Nostrand, 1958.

[22]

Socialization of Achievement Attitudes and Beliefs: Classroom Influences

Jacquelynne Eccles Parsons, Caroline M. Kaczala, and Judith L. Meece

University of Michigan

PARSONS, JACQUELYNNE ECCLES; KACZALA, CAROLINE M.; and MEECE, JUDITH L. *Socialization of Achievement Attitudes and Beliefs: Classroom Influences.* CHILD DEVELOPMENT, 1982, **53**, 322–339. The relation between classroom experiences and individual differences in expectations for future success in mathematics courses, self-concept of math abilities and perceptions of the difficulty of math were investigated in an observational study of 17 math classrooms for grades 5–9. 2 questions were addressed: (1) Does the sex of the student or the teacher's expectation for the student influence the nature of student-teacher interactions? (2) Do variations in teacher-student interaction patterns affect student attitudes? Although few sex differences emerged, girls received less criticism than boys, especially low-teacher-expectancy boys, and high-teacher-expectancy females received less praise than other groups. No support was found for sex differences in teacher discriminant use of praise and criticism. Some support was found for more general sex differences and teacher expectation differences in teacher behavior. Multiple-regression analyses, with the students' past grades used as a control variable, showed that teacher behaviors influence children's attitudes but the effects differ for males and females; for example, self-concept of ability for boys, but not for girls, was predicted by relatively high levels of both teacher criticism and praise. In general, past grades and student-teacher interaction variables accounted for a larger percentage of the variation in boys' attitudes than in girls'. In the second set of analyses 2 types of classrooms were compared: classrooms in which boys and girls had equally high future expectations and classrooms in which boys have higher future expectations. Boys and girls were treated differently in these 2 classroom types. The data suggest that boys and girls have equivalent expectations when the relative distribution of praise and criticism within a class across high- and low-teacher-expectancy groups is similar for both sexes.

Introduction

The link between achievement expectancies and performance has been amply documented in the achievement literature (see Crandall 1969; Dweck & Bush 1976; Parsons, Ruble, Hodges, & Small 1976). Within this literature females often are found to have lower expectancies than males. This sex difference in expectancies has been suggested as an important mediator of the sex differences we observe in the achievement patterns of adolescents and adults. The developmental origin of this sex difference in expectation has come under recent investigation. For example, Parsons et al. (1976) suggested several ways in which teachers and parents might be perpetuating, if not creating,

this sex difference. The research reported in this paper is concerned with the socialization of expectancies in classrooms. While it focuses primarily on student gender differences, it also explores more generally the relation between classroom experiences and individual differences in expectancies.

In assessing socialization processes within classrooms, two separable questions need to be addressed: (1) Are there characteristics of either the teachers or the students that influence the nature of the student-teacher interaction (e.g., does the sex of the student or the expectancy of the teacher influence teacher-student interaction patterns?); and (2) Do variations in teacher-student interaction patterns affect

This research was partially supported by grants from the National Institute of Education, U.S. Department of Education (NIE-G-78-0022), and the National Institute of Mental Health (1 R01 MH 31724-0) awarded to the first author. Grateful acknowledgments are extended to Kirby Heller, who was involved in the development of the observation system and initial data collection, and to the project staff who have been involved with this research throughout. Thanks are also extended to the classroom observers who collected these data and to all the students and teachers who allowed us to observe in their classrooms. Address reprint requests to Jacquelynne Eccles Parsons, Department of Psychology, 3441 Mason Hall, University of Michigan, Ann Arbor, Michigan 48109.

students' self-concepts of ability and expectations for their own future performance? It is quite possible that a given variable might yield sex differences but be unrelated to students' expectancies. Similarly, it is possible that a variable might yield no significant sex differences but have a strong relation to the expectancies of either boys or girls or both. Both of these questions are addressed in this study. Two additional concerns guided this investigation. First, we assessed the possibility that some teachers might have a potentially depressing effect on girls' expectancies while others might not. Second, in interpreting the meaning of various interaction patterns, we distinguished between those interactional variables that are under the control of the student and those which are under the control of the teacher.

GENERAL TEACHER-STUDENT INTERACTION PATTERNS AND THEIR RELATION TO EXPECTATION

Teachers' expectations for their students' performance have been shown to affect not only teacher-student interactions but also student performance (see Brophy & Good 1974; Cooper 1979). Moreover, while teachers do not typically have lower expectations for girls, teacher-student interaction patterns have been found to vary as a function of the sex of the student (see Brophy & Good 1974). While girls are rated by teachers as being more effective learners and more hardworking than boys, boys have the most interactions of all kinds with their teachers. In fact, it is the boys for whom the teacher has high expectations who have the most favorable interactions with their teachers; low-expectancy boys are criticized the most, while girls of all achievement levels are treated similarly to one another. As a consequence, the way teachers treat girls for whom they have high expectations may facilitate achievement less than the way they treat comparable groups of boys.

These findings suggest that teacher-student interaction patterns may be important mediators of the sex differences in expectancies. But the link between teacher-student interaction patterns and students' achievement attitudes (e.g., expectancies, self-concepts of academic ability, and perceptions of task difficulty) has received very little direct attention. The only study which attempted to assess the effects of teacher-student interaction patterns on student expectations (Dweck, Davidson, Nelson, & Enna 1978) failed to test for the relationship directly in the classroom setting. Given the strong

relation between expectancies and achievement, those teacher behaviors which vary across types of children and which have been found to be critical mediators of the teacher-expectancy effects ought to be related to student expectations as well. Based on past literature and on our general belief that cognition mediates behavior, two separate sets of hypotheses were generated for the first set of analysis.

Hypotheses Relating Teacher and/or Student Characteristics to Student-Teacher Interaction Patterns

Dweck et al. (1978) predicted and found that the boys in the fourth and fifth grade (a total of three classrooms) received more indiscriminate criticism (criticism focused on conduct and the form of the students' work rather than the academic quality) than girls, while the girls received more indiscriminate praise. This differential pattern of feedback, they argued, should result in girls having lower expectancies than boys. While data from a laboratory study of the feedback patterns supported their suggestion, no attempt was made to test the relation between the feedback patterns and students' expectancies in the classroom. Based on this work, it is predicted that boys will receive more indiscriminate criticism and more ability-relevant discriminate praise, while girls will receive more indiscriminate praise and more ability-relevant discriminate criticism.

Cooper (1979) argued that teachers use praise and criticism to shape student questioning behavior. In particular, he proposed that teachers use criticism to reduce the number of student-initiated questions asked by low-ability children so that the teacher maintains control of his or her interactions with these children. Consequently, it is predicted that teachers' expectations for the students will be negatively related to the amount of criticism given for student-initiated questions.

Based on the work on teacher-expectancy effects (see, e.g., Brophy & Good 1974; Cooper 1979), the following relations are expected to hold: teachers will praise, interact with, and encourage continued responses from high-expectancy (high) students more than low-expectancy (low) students and will criticize "lows" more than "highs"; these differences will be more marked for boys than girls. Consequently, "high" boys will receive more praise and will interact more than "high" girls.

Students who have done well previously should be more confident of their abilities, and consequently should initiate more student-

324   Child Development

teacher interactions than students who have done less well in the past.

Hypotheses Relating Student-Teacher Interaction Patterns to Students' Expectations and Self-Concepts of Ability

There has been little research directly related to this issue. Most existing teacher-expectancy work has focused on establishing relations between student-teacher interaction patterns and students' academic performance. Consequently, some hypotheses in this section represent what we consider to be logical extensions of the research findings reported in the performance literature. Two hypotheses are taken directly from the work of Dweck et al. (1978). Other hypotheses grew out of our analysis of the possible self-concept-relevant inferences or attributions a student might make from various classroom interaction patterns.

Since causality cannot be inferred from our data set, the hypotheses are stated as relationships rather than causal predictions. But, to the extent that a predicted relationship is not found, the causal relation implied is also called into question. Significant predicted relations indicate a possible causal relation that warrants further laboratory investigation. Nonsignificance suggests that the implied causal relation is not operative in the natural classroom setting even though such relations may have been demonstrated in the laboratory. Our specific hypotheses are listed below.

1. Based on the analysis by Dweck et al. (1978) reviewed earlier, it is predicted that the percentage of total criticism directed at the academic content of one's work will be negatively related to both self-concept of ability and expectations for future performance, while the percentage of total praise directed at the academic content of one's work will be positively related to both one's self-concept of ability and one's expectations.

2. Extending the findings relating teacher-expectancy effects to student performance (see Brophy & Good 1974; Cooper 1979), it is predicted that the following student-teacher interaction variables will be positively related to both students' self-concept of ability and expectations: frequency of interaction, encouragement to continue responding, high praise, and low criticism.

3. Based on general principles of reinforcement, it is predicted that rewarding experiences will have a positive effect on measures of self-concept of ability and expectancies, while

punishing experiences such as criticism will have a negative effect. Consequently the frequency of praise one receives, and of being called on, and of being correct should be positively related to self-concepts of ability and expectations, while the frequency of criticism and being incorrect in public responses should be negatively related to self-concepts of ability and expectations. Alternatively, it may be the subjective meaning of the feedback that is more critical. If students are engaging in attributional analyses, then they should interpret teacher feedback in terms of the possible hidden messages regarding the teacher's expectations for them. Consequently, frequency of being called upon, criticism for incorrect answers, sustaining feedback following an incorrect response, and lack of praise for correct response may all convey the message that the teacher expects one to both participate and do well. Conversely, both praise following correct response and low frequency of being called upon may convey the opposite message. Both sets of hypotheses will be tested.

In addition, since students' past performance is related to their current self-concept, to the teacher's expectations regarding their performance, and potentially to the student-teacher interaction patterns, any relations emerging between teacher-student interaction patterns and students' self-concepts could very well reflect the concomitant effect of past performance on both. Thus, analyses will be performed with the effects of past performance partialed out.

CLASSROOM TYPE AND ITS MEDIATING ROLE

The possibility that not all teachers have a detrimental effect on girls' expectancies is the focus of our second set of analyses. As Brophy and Good (1974) have pointed out, not all teachers produce expectancy effects in their classrooms. Consequently, we were concerned with identifying a parameter that would allow us to discriminate between those classrooms in which teachers were most likely to have a detrimental effect on girls' expectations and those in which teachers were least likely to have such an effect. The presence or absence of a sex difference in the students' expectations within the classroom is the parameter we chose. In Analysis II, interaction variables that discriminate between these two classroom types, particularly in terms of the treatment of boys and girls, are identified and related to students' expectations. In keeping wtih the results reported by Brophy and Good (1974), independent comparisons within classroom type are made for children who have been nominated by their teacher as "highs" and "lows." It is predicted that the interactional patterns which vary across these classroom types will differ most markedly for "high" girls and boys.

Method

Sample

The student sample consisted of 428 children from 17 math classrooms in grades 5, 6, 7, and 9. All of these children are included in the descriptive analyses of classroom interactive patterns. Only the 275 children who volunteered (57% of the available population) to complete the student questionnaire are represented in the analyses involving the attitudinal scales taken from the questionnaire. Eight seventh-grade and six ninth-grade classes were chosen since past research has indicated that the early adolescent years might be critical in the formation of sex-differentiated expectancies in math. Three upper elementary school classrooms were included to provide a comparison sample for the Dweck et al. (1978) study. Participation varied across classes primarily due to variations in the individual teacher's commitment to the study.

Given the tremendous variability in teaching styles (Hearn & Moos 1978) across subject areas, observations were made in only one subject area. Math was chosen because it has recently come under intensive investigation due to a fairly clear developmental pattern associated with emerging sex difference in self-expectations, confidence in one's ability, and actual course enrollments (see Parsons, Adler, Futterman, Goff, Kaczala, Meece, & Midgley, in press).

Instruments

Student questionnaire and school record data.—Students' expectancies, self-concepts of ability, and concepts of task difficulty were measured by questionnaires. The questionnaire consisted of a long series of items each containing a seven-point Likert-type scale anchored at the extremes. Summary scales composed of two or more items were formed using

Cronbach's coefficient α as a measure of internal consistency. These scales were then factored using the exploratory factor analysis program designed by Joreskog and Sorbom (1978). Two factors emerged: one related to self-concept of math ability and the other related to perception of the difficulty of math. Since expectancies loaded on the self-concept factor, it is most comparable to the expectancy measures used in past research. However, given both our interest in the determinants of sex differences in expectancies and previous findings suggesting that the sex difference in performance expectations is most marked for future math course or less familiar tasks (Heller & Parsons 1981), the scale composed of the three items asking for expectancies in future math courses and in a math-related career was included as a dependent variable. (Details on these analyses and the specific items used can be obtained from the first author.)[1]

Past grades and performance scores on the Michigan Educational Assessment Program (MEAP) and California Achievement Test (CAT) were obtained from the students' school records. A measure of past performance in math was created using the data obtained from the students' school records. Most recent math grade and any available scores on the MEAP or CAT were standardized within the population as a whole. The mean of the available standardized scores for each student was used as an estimate of past performance. A constant of 3 was added to make all scores positive. In addition to these scales, students were asked to rate how well they thought their teacher expected them to do in math.

Teacher questionnaire.—Each teacher filled out a six-item questionnaire regarding each of his or her participating students. Each item was a seven-point Likert-type scale anchored at the extremes. Teacher expectancies for each child were calculated using the mean of two items: "How well will ———— do in advanced math course?" and "How good is ———— at math?" Since the teachers varied in their use of these scales, a second teacher-expectancy score was created by standardizing the initial teacher-expectancy scores within each classroom. This standardized score was used to assign children

[1] The full questionnaire is discussed in more detail in Parsons, Adler, Futterman, Goff, Kaczala, Meece, & Midgley (Note 1), available from the first author. The full questionnaire contained the PAQ and the following six additional constructed scales: a shortened version of the IAR, a measure of sex-role identity, sex typing of the ability of math, utility of math for one's goals, incentive value of math, cost of effort needed to do well, perceptions of parents' use of and liking of math, perceptions of parents' beliefs regarding one's math abilities, and the importance of math.

326   Child Development

to the high-expectancy ("high") and low-expectancy ("low") categories: children above the mean in each classroom were categorized as "highs," children below the mean were categorized as "lows."

Observational system.—The observational system used was a modified version of those used by Brophy and Good (Note 2) and Dweck (Dweck et al. 1978). Sequences of teacher-student interactions were coded in a variety of settings, such as public question-and-answer periods, student-initiated interactions, and private teacher-student interactions. The observation system focused on dyadic interactions or occasions in which the teacher interacted with a single student. Interactions in which the teacher addressed comments to a group of students or to the class were not recorded. Recordings of interactions included: (1) who initiated the interaction; (2) the type of interaction initiated; (3) the type of response the student gave the teacher; (4) the type of feedback the student received from the teacher; and (5) whether the interaction was public and monitored by the class or was a private interaction between the student and the teacher. In addition, all instances of praise, criticism, and statements of causal attributions for performance were coded. Attributions were coded into the following categories: ability or lack of ability, effort or lack of effort, and task ease or difficulty (84% agreement).

Procedure

Trained observers (four females and one male) coded interactions between teachers and individual students during 10 class sessions per class. Coding began after the observers had been in each classroom for three to five sessions familiarizing themselves with the teacher's general style and with the students' names. Observer reliability was assessed for 3 or 4 hours per observer, 1–2 hours taken prior to data collection and 1–2 hours taken approximately halfway through the observational period. The mean percentages of agreement at each day of collection for each observer ranged from 75% to 86% on both an estimate of total agreement and an estimate of the reliability for particular behaviors. Observation was completed in a 2-month period in the spring of 1978.

Questionnaires were administered to both teachers and students in a 2-week period following the observation of each classroom. Student questionnaires were group administered in two 30–40-min sessions. Teachers filled out their questionnaires at home, returning them on a specified date.

Analysis I

RESULTS

Overview of Measures in Analysis I

Thirty-seven classroom interactional variables were created; 28 represent raw frequency counts. These raw frequency scores were converted to the average number of times each type of interaction occurred each class period that the student was present. (A summary of the raw frequency data and tests of differences in these frequencies between groups of males and females and high-expectancy and low-expectancy students can be obtained from the first author.)

Nine of the variables represent proportions of various types of interaction frequencies. Since proportions can be formed only if the student has a score for the denominator frequency, only students who, in fact, interacted with the teacher have scores for these variables. Since the modal frequency for many of the 28 mean frequency scores was zero, the N for some of these analyses is slightly less than half the total sample.

The 37 observation variables were grouped into three categories: behaviors characteristic of teacher style (teacher behaviors under primary control of the teacher); behaviors characteristic of student style (behaviors under primary control of the student); and behaviors dependent on both teacher and student style (behaviors requiring interactive responses of both the teacher and the student). A list of the variables is presented in table 1.

Individual Difference Analyses

To test for sex and teacher-expectancy group differences in interaction patterns at the individual level, analyses of variance with planned paired comparisons were run on each of the 37 interactional variables, on the three student attitudinal variables, and the measure of student's past performance in math. Interactional scores for these analyses are the average number of interactions each student received per class period present. Means for all significant effects are displayed in table 2.

Nine variables yielded main effects for sex. Compared to males, females had lower future expectancies, $F = 5.55$, $p = .019$; believed math was more difficult, $F = 4.10$, $p = .044$; received less total criticism, $F = 8.16$, $p = .005$; work criticism, $F = 6.56$, $p = .011$; and conduct criticism, $F = 6.21$, $p = .013$; had fewer of their response opportunities criticized, $F = 7.00$, $p = .009$; had a smaller proportion of

TABLE 1—Observational Variables with Total Frequencies of Occurrence or Grand Means of Proportions

I. Frequency Variables

Teacher Style Behaviors			Student Style Variables			Joint Style Variables		
Items	Frequency	N^a	Items	Frequency	N	Items	Frequency	N
Teacher-initiated dyadics^b	291	155	Student-initiated procedure questions	221	106	Total response opportunities^c	2,003	309
Direct questions^d	671	224	Student-initiated dyadics	1,491	321	Open questions^e	950	180
Teacher-initiated interactions	1,078	306	Student-initiated questions	969	199	Total dyadics	1,780	349
Response opportunities yielding criticism	672	207				Total interactions	5,034	413
Response opportunities yielding work criticism	18	16				Affirms^f	1,340	275
Conduct criticism	619	189				Negates^g	277	132
Total work criticism	41	34				Student-initiated questions yielding praise	14	12
Total criticism	727	219				Student-initiated questions yielding criticism	7	6
Response opportunities yielding praise	174	92						
Response opportunities yielding work praise	154	86						
Total work praise	295	137						
Total praise	319	141						
Attribution statements	88	64						
Negates with feedback	97	59						
Ask other^h	129	86						
Sustaining feedback^i	263	154						
Negates with sustaining feedback	36	29						

II. Proportional Variables

Teacher Style Behaviors			Joint Style Variables		
Items	Mean Proportion	N	Items	Mean Proportion	N
% criticism on work	6.3%	219	% student-initiated questions yielding praise	1.8%	199
% interactions yielding criticism	13.2%	413	% student-initiated questions yielding criticism	.8%	199
% praise on work	93.0%	141	% response opportunities yielding negates	.13%	309
% interactions yielding praise	6.5%	413	% response opportunities yielding affirms	.64%	309

a N = number of students having nonzero frequencies.

b Dyadics are private one-on-one interactions.

c "Response opportunities" are teacher-initiated questions which can yield right or wrong answer.

d "Direct questions" are teacher questions directed at a student who has not volunteered.

e "Open questions" are teacher questions directed at a student who has raised his or her hand to volunteer.

f "Affirm" is a teacher feedback acknowledging the correctness of an answer.

g "Negate" is a teacher feedback acknowledging the incorrectness of an answer.

h "Ask other" is a teacher feedback in which the teacher turns to another student for the answer following an incorrect response.

i "Sustaining feedback" is a teacher feedback in which the teacher re-asks a question after the student has given a response.

328 Child Development

their total interactions criticized, $F = 6.13$, $p = .014$; and asked more questions, $F = 10.84$, $p = .001$, especially procedural questions, $F = 8.74$, $p = .003$. In comparison to males, then, females, on the average, have lower future expectancies, see math as more difficult, receive less criticism, and ask more questions.

Twelve main effects for teacher-expectancy groups emerged. Relative to low-teacher-expectancy children, high-teacher-expectancy children had done better in math in the past, $F = 69.96$, $p = .0000$; had higher self-concepts of their math ability, $F = 95.29$, $p = .0000$; had

higher future expectations for success, $F = 47.81$, $p = .0000$; saw math as easier, $F = 46.25$, $p = .0000$; received slightly less work praise, $F = 3.66$, $p = .056$, and total praise, $F = 4.37$, $p = .037$; had a higher proportion of their questions praised, $F = 4.00$, $p = .047$; received less conduct criticism, $F = 4.87$, $p = .028$, and less total criticism, $F = 6.22$, $p = .013$; had fewer of their response opportunities criticized, $F = 5.00$, $p = .026$; received fewer teacher-initiated dyadic interactions, $F = 15.61$, $p = .0001$; and fewer total teacher-initiated interactions, $F = 6.91$, $p = .009$. Of these, four

TABLE 2

Mean Proportions for Significant Proportional Interaction Variables, Mean Frequencies per Student per Class Period for Significant Interaction Variables, and Mean Scores for Student Performance and Questionnaire Responses

VARIABLES	OVERALL MEAN	FEMALE		MALE	
		Low Expectancy	High Expectancy	Low Expectancy	High Expectancy
Mean proportions:[a]					
Teacher style variables:					
% interactions yielding criticism[c]	13.2% (413)[b]	11.6% (85)	9.9% (112)	16.6% (101)	14.6% (115)
% interactions yielding praise[d]	6.5% (413)	8.6% (85)	4.3% (112)	6.0% (101)	7.4% (115)
Joint style variables:					
% student-initiated questions yielding praise[e]	1.8% (199)	0% (38)	1.0% (59)	.2% (48)	5.4% (54)
Mean frequencies per child per session present:[a]					
Teacher style variables:					
Teacher-initiated dyadics[d,e]	.08 (426)	.08 (89)	.05 (114)	.13 (103)	.05 (120)
Teacher-initiated interactions[e]	.28 (426)	.31 (89)	.26 (114)	.33 (103)	.23 (120)
Conduct criticism[e,d,e]	.16 (426)	.12 (89)	.12 (114)	.27 (103)	.13 (120)
Total work criticism[e]	.01 (426)	.005 (89)	.006 (114)	.02 (103)	.01 (120)
Total criticism[e,d,e]	.19 (426)	.15 (89)	.14 (114)	.31 (103)	.16 (120)
Response opportunities yielding criticism[e,d,e]	.17 (426)	.13 (89)	.13 (114)	.29 (103)	.15 (120)
Total work praise[e]	.08 (426)	.11 (89)	.06 (114)	.08 (103)	.07 (120)
Total praise[e]	.08 (426)	.11 (89)	.06 (114)	.09 (103)	.07 (120)
Student style variables:					
Student-initiated procedure questions[e]	.06 (426)	.08 (89)	.07 (114)	.04 (103)	.04 (120)
Student-initiated questions[e]	.25 (426)	.29 (89)	.41 (114)	.16 (103)	.16 (120)
Student and teacher questionnaire responses and student past performance: mean response:					
Past performance[e,f]	3.99 (291)	3.58 (69)	4.31 (88)	3.47 (53)	4.32 (81)
Teacher expectancy[e,g]	4.21 (483)	3.22 (106)	5.20 (128)	3.03 (117)	5.10 (132)
Math ability concept[e,h,d]	4.91 (286)	4.33 (60)	5.12 (92)	4.32 (52)	5.47 (82)
Task difficulty concept[e,e,h]	4.47 (285)	5.00 (60)	4.31 (91)	4.84 (52)	4.02 (82)
Future expectancies[e,e,h]	5.09 (323)	4.60 (76)	5.21 (99)	4.70 (60)	5.63 (88)

[a] Based on observations.

[b] N = number of students represented in the proportion or frequency of scale mean.

[c] Significant sex effect, $p < .05$.

[d] Significant teacher-expectancy $\times$ sex interaction effect, $p < .05$.

[e] Significant teacher-expectancy effect, $p < .05$.

[f] Based on standardized summary score of past grades and performance on standardized tests.

[g] Based on teacher's rating of each student.

[h] Based on student's self-rating on student questionnaire.

variables (conduct criticism, total criticism, response opportunities criticized, and teacher-initiated dyadic interactions) yielded a significant expectancy group × sex interaction, indicating that the expectancy group effect was significant only for males. In comparison to low-expectancy children, then, high-expectancy children have done better in the past, have higher self-concepts of their ability, see math as easier, receive less total praise but have a higher proportion of their questions praised, and have fewer teacher-initiated interactions.

Six teacher-expectancy group × sex interactions were significant. Both high-teacher-expectancy and low-teacher-expectancy males and low-teacher-expectancy females had a higher proportion of their interactions praised than did high-teacher-expectancy females, $F = 4.86$, $p = .028$. Females in the high-teacher-expectancy group had a lower self-concept of their math ability than did males in the same expectancy group, $F = 3.19$, $p = .075$. Low-expectancy males received more conduct criticism, $F = 4.69$, $p = .031$; more total criticism, $F = 4.48$, $p = .035$; more teacher-initiated dyadics, $F = 5.36$, $p = .02$; and had more of their response opportunities criticized, $F = 4.4$, $p = .037$, than all other groups. Thus, high-expectancy females have lower self-concepts of their ability than high-expectancy males; high-expectancy females have the smallest proportion of their interactions praised; and low-expectancy males receive the most criticism and the most teacher-initiated dyadics.

Since the present sample was predominantly seventh and ninth graders and the sample in Dweck et al. (1978) consisted of fourth and fifth graders, we ran additional ANOVAs for the fifth and sixth graders on the variables derived from the Dweck et al. (1978) hypotheses. None of these were significant. As was true in the total sample, fifth- and sixth-grade boys received more total criticism than girls, $F = 4.93$, $p = .01$, but the discriminant quality (i.e., the proportion associated with the academic content of a student's work rather than conduct or form) of both criticism and praise was equivalent across the sexes.

Relations between Interactional Variables and Student Attitudes

Correlations were used to assess relations between (1) observation variables and the students' self-concept, (2) observation variables and the students' perceptions of their teacher's expectancy for them, and (3) observation variables and the teacher's actual expectancy for the students.

Correlations across the sexes and within each sex were used as the initial step in assessing relations between each of the 36 interaction variables and the student self-concept measures. Very few significant correlations emerged. The significant relations are summarized in table 3. The general pattern of relations is similar for boys and girls: high self-concepts of math ability, low ratings of task difficulty, and high future expectancies were related most strongly to the teachers' written expectations even when the effects of past performance were partialed out (partialed r of teacher expectancy to students' self-concept of ability = .43, $p < .01$; to students' rating of task difficulty = $-.26$, $p < .01$; and to students' future expectations = .26, $p < .01$).

Among the observation variables, work criticism had the strongest and most consistent effect on student attitudes. For both girls and boys high levels of work criticism in public response opportunities and high proportions of criticism associated with academic work were related to high self-concepts of ability, low estimates of difficulty, and high future expectancies. The total amount of criticism received was related to low estimates of difficulty only for girls.

The relation between praise and student attitudes was less clear. A relation between praise and a low estimate of math difficulty was found for all students, but a high amount of praise was related to a high ability concept only for boys. In addition, the proportion of praise focused on work was positively related to ability concept and future expectancies only for boys.

The use and interpretation of student-initiated questions also distinguished girls and boys. Among boys the number of questions they asked related positively to how hard they thought math was, while the number of questions girls asked was unrelated to their estimates of difficulty. A high number of student-initiated questions criticized related to low-ability concept and low expectancies for all students.

To provide additional light on these relationships, we asked the students to give us their estimate of their teachers' expectations for them. If teachers' influences on students' self-concepts are mediated by inferential processes, then there ought to be a relation between the interactional variables and the students' perceptions of their teachers' expectations for them. Significant correlations testing these relations

TABLE 3

Zero-Order Correlation Matrix: Observational Variables and Teacher Expectancy × Student Attitudinal Measures

	Total			Female			Male		
	Math Ability Concept	Child's Future Expectancy	Task Difficulty Concept	Math Ability Concept	Child's Future Expectancy	Task Difficulty Concept	Math Ability Concept	Child's Future Expectancy	Task Difficulty Concept
Teacher expectancy	.54**	.39**	-.36**	.46**	.33**	-.32**	.64**	.48**	-.40**
Response opportunities yielding work criticism	.16*	.17**	-.16*	.15	.16	-.17*	.17	.17	-.15
Total criticism	.01	.04	-.12	.06	.02	-.21*	-.06	.01	.00
% criticism on work	.15	.14	-.19*	.17	.13	-.22	.15	.17	-.16
Response opportunities yielding praise	.06	.01	-.16*	.00	-.03	-.13	.14	.03	-.21*
Response opportunities yielding work praise	.09	.01	-.17**	.01	-.02	-.14	.19*	.07	-.22*
Total work praise	.11	.02	-.15*	.02	-.05	-.13	.21*	.11	-.16
Negates with feedback	-.16*	-.11	.13*	-.13	-.09	.14	-.20*	-.16	.13
% praise on work	.19*	-.11	-.06	-.03	-.03	-.00	.36*	.27*	-.12
Student-initiated question	-.06	-.04	.03	-.02	.00	.13	-.14	-.05	.20*
Student-initiated questions yielding criticism	-.25**	-.19*	.05	-.31**	-.24**	.04	-.21*	-.15	.06
% Student-initiated questions yielding criticism	-.33**	-.28**	.05	-.39**	-.32**	.04	-.26*	-.19	.06

* $p < .05$.

** $p < .01$.

are presented in table 4. For both boys and girls, frequency of direct questions and teacher-initiated interactions were positively related to perceptions of teachers' expectancies while the percentage of student questions yielding praise was positively related to perceptions of teachers' expectations for girls and negatively for boys. In addition, total work praise and total praise were both positively related to perceptions of teacher's expectancies for boys only. Interestingly, it is only these last two relations that coincide with the relations existing between the interactive variables and the students' self-concept of ability: praise was related to self-concept of ability for boys only.

The variables relating to students' perceptions of teacher expectancy were not the same variables that related to actual teacher expectancies. For all students, teachers' expectancies were related negatively to the number of teacher-initiated dyadics and to the amount of criticism given. There was no relation between teacher praise and teachers' expectancies.

Since we are most interested in the biasing effect of teacher-student interactions, the variables identified above were entered with past performance into stepwise regression analyses. Past performance, as the control variable, was entered into the analyses at the first step, allowing for the assessment of the magnitude of the effects of teacher-student interaction patterns on each of the three criteria measures over and above the effect of the child's past history of

performance in math. Because the sample size and membership fluctuated so markedly as the various proportional variables were added to the analyses, only the mean frequency data items and the two proportional items on which there were data for 90% of the sample were used in these analyses. The independent effects of the other proportional items with significant zero-order effects were tested with partial correlations. In each set of analyses, regressions were run on samples composed of both sexes as well as on samples composed of each sex separately. However, since the frequencies and variance of some of the variables differed in the male and female sample and since the psychological meaning of any of these interaction variables is a function of one's total interactional pattern, no attempt was made to either compare the correlations for males and females directly or to interpret differences in the size of the various correlations. The results of the multiple-regression analyses are presented in table 5.

With regard to self-concept of ability, past performance accounts for the largest share of the variance for both boys and girls. For girls the number of student-initiated questions yielding criticism is negatively related to self-concept; while for boys the number of negates with feedback is negatively related and both the amount of total praise and number of response opportunities yielding work criticism are positively related to boys' self-concept. For the pop-

TABLE 4

Zero-Order Correlation Matrix: Observational Variables × Child's Perception of Teacher Expectancy and Teacher's Actual Expectancy for the Child

	Total		Female		Male	
	Child's Perception of Teacher Expectancy	Teacher Expectancy for Child	Child's Perception of Teacher Expectancy	Teacher Expectancy for Child	Child's Perception of Teacher Expectancy	Teacher Expectancy for Child
Teacher-initiated dyadics.............	.07	−.24**	.16	−.11	−.01	−.32**
Direct questions.....................	.20**	.13**	.18*	.10	.22*	.14
Teacher-initiated interactions.........	.20**	−.01	.20*	.07	.20*	−.09
Total criticism......................	.07	−.25**	.11	−.13*	.05	−.32**
Total work praise....................	.14*	−.05	.09	−.04	.19*	−.06
Total praise........................	.14*	−.06	.09	−.03	.19*	−.09
% praise on work....................	.01	.09	.02	−.19	.00	.23*
% interactions yielding criticism......	−.12	−.19**	−.18*	−.19**	−.07	−.17*
% student-initiated questions yielding praise...........................	−.19*	.09	.19	.03	−.28*	.14
% student-initiated questions yielding criticism........................	−.08	−.10	−.04	−.12	−.20	−.17

* $p < .05$.
** $p < .01$.

TABLE 5

SUMMARY OF STEPWISE REGRESSION ANALYSES

	TOTAL SAMPLE (N = 236)			FEMALES (N = 127)			MALES (N = 109)		
	Variable[a]	Beta[b]	R²[c]	Variable	Beta	R²	Variable	Beta	R²
Math Ability Concept									
1. Past performance		.35	.16	Past performance	.23	.09	Past performance	.48	.27
2. Student-initiated questions yielding criticism		−.18	.19	Student-initiated questions yielding criticism	−.24	.14	Negates with feedback	−.26	.30
3. Response opportunities yielding work criticism		.23	.22				Total praise	.21	.34
4. Negates with feedback		−.17	.25				Response opportunities yielding work criticism	.18	.37
5. % interactions yielding praise		.14	.27						
Future Expectancies									
1. Past performance		.28	.10	Past performance	.22	.07	Past performance	.38	.16
2. Response opportunities yielding work criticism		.23	.13	Student-initiated questions yielding criticism	−.18	.10	Response opportunities yielding work criticism	.21	.19
3. Student-initiated questions yielding criticism		−.14	.15				Negates with feedback	−.17	.22
4. Negates with feedback		−.13	.17						
Task Difficulty Concept									
1. Past performance		−.29	.08	Past performance	−.23	.04	Past performance	−.38	.14
2. Total praise		−.20	.11	% interactions yielding praise	−.23	.08			
3. % interactions yielding criticism		−.14	.13	Total praise	−.19	.12			
4. Negates with feedback		.20	.16						
5. Response opportunity yielding work criticism		−.20	.19						

[a] Listed in order of appearance by step.
[b] Significant at $p < .05$.
[c] Cumulative R^2.

ulation as a whole, high self-concept is predicted by high past performance, relatively high proportions of interactions yielding praise, relatively high incidence of work criticism, low incidence of public feedback following a public error, and low incidence of criticism following a student-initiated question. (We include the qualifier of "relatively" because actual incidence rates of both praise and criticism are quite low. Consequently, it would be misleading to suggest that absolutely defined high levels of praise or criticism would produce similar effects.) In combination, past performance and the interactional variables accounted for a higher proportion of the variance in self-concept for boys than for girls.

Mirroring the results obtained for self-concept of ability, high future expectancies are predicted by high past performance, high levels of work criticism in response opportunities, low levels of teacher criticism in response to student-initiated questions, and feedback following public errors. Again these variables accounted for more variance among the boys than among the girls.

With regard to beliefs about task difficulty, past performance again accounts for a large share of the predicted variance for both boys and girls. Both percent of interactions yielding criticism and total praise are negatively related to girls' rating of the difficulty of math. For the population as a whole, the belief that math is a difficult subject is predicted by low past performance, low proportion of interactions yielding criticism, low levels of work criticism and total praise, and relatively high levels of public feedback following an error.

It has been suggested in previous research that the sex difference in proportion of variance accounted is a consequence of a sex difference in the amount of variance on either the predictor or criterion variables. F tests were used to ascertain whether this hypothesis might be a viable explanation for the sex differences we found in the proportion of variance accounted for on the three criterion measures. There were no significant differences in amount of variance on any of the relevant variables.

The partial correlation analyses revealed four additional significant effects when past performance was partialed out. Self-concept of ability was related positively to the proportion of a student's questions yielding praise for girls only, partialed $r = .26$, $p < .05$, and negatively to the proportion of student questions yielding criticism for the sample as a whole,

partialed $r = -.22$, $p < .05$. Similarly, for the sample as a whole, future expectancy was related negatively to the proportion of a student's questions yielding criticism, partialed $r = -.194$, $p < .05$, and the belief that math is difficult was related negatively to the proportion of a student's criticism that was focused on work, partialed $r = -.196$, $p < .05$.

DISCUSSION

Relations of Teacher and Student Characteristics to Classroom Interaction

Student sex was related to student-teacher interaction patterns but not in the manner predicted by Dweck et al. (1978). The nature of the sex differences that emerged largely replicated the findings reported by Brophy and Good (1974): girls as a whole received less criticism than low-teacher-expectancy boys; high-teacher-expectancy girls, in particular, received less praise than other groups. In addition, girls asked more questions than did boys. Low-teacher-expectancy boys got a disproportionate amount of criticism and teacher-initiated dyadic interactions. Other than these few differences, boys and girls were treated similarly. Unlike other studies (e.g., Brophy & Good 1974; Fennema, in press), on the average, the boys and girls in this sample participated equally; low-expectancy boys were slightly more likely to engage in private interactions and girls were slightly more likely to engage in public interactions. But these differences were small.

Teacher-expectancy group effects were also minimal. Teacher-expectancy grouping was related most strongly to both the children's past performance and the children's attitudes: high-teacher-expectancy children had done the best in their past math courses and were confident of their math abilities both in the present and for the future. These results probably reflect the congruence of teacher expectations with a student's past performance rather than the effects of teacher expectations on student attitudes.

While teachers appeared to be treating these two groups of students fairly similarly, when they discriminated they did so primarily between the high- and low-expectancy boys. In support of the prediction derived from the work of Cooper (1979) and Brophy and Good (1974), low-expectancy children, especially boys, received more criticism and had fewer of their student-initiated questions praised than high-expectancy children. Low-expectancy boys

334   Child Development

received more teacher-initiated dyadics, as was predicted by Cooper (1979), while low-expectancy females received more praise especially in response to teacher-controlled questioning. Apparently teachers use different control strategies for low-expectancy boys and girls. Teachers act as though they are trying to draw low-expectancy females into public class participation and low-expectancy males into private interactions. But, as noted above, these differences were small.

Relations between the Interaction Variables and the Student Attitudinal Variables

Again there was no support for the hypotheses proposed by Dweck et al. (1978). In fact, contrary to what Dweck et al. (1978) had suggested, it was the absolute level of praise and criticism and not their discriminative use (i.e., proportion of criticism and praise directed toward work rather than conduct and form) that was important: higher absolute levels of both praise and criticism directed to the academic quality of one's work were positively related to the self-concept of ability of boys. In the only marginally significant relation between the Dweck et al. (1978) feedback variables and student attitudes, high discriminative use of criticism for work was predictive of the belief that math is easy. Thus, if anything, one would have to conclude that the discriminative use of criticism for academic work has a positive rather than a negative effect on students' beliefs. This conclusion is bolstered by the positive relation between work criticism and self-concept of ability. Together these results lend support to the prediction derived from the attributional perspective (e.g., criticism for work conveys a message of high teacher expectations). However, the low frequency of work criticism must be noted. Our results may be true only when work criticism is used sparingly. As Dweck et al. (1978) had suggested, criticism may have its effect only when it is made more salient by its infrequent and discriminant use. But rather than having the negative effect associated with punishment, as proposed by Dweck et al. (1978), it appears that it is the inferential value of the criticism that is made salient by this pattern of administration.

The positive relation between boys' self-concept of ability and teacher praise supports, in part, the predictions based on the work of Brophy and Good and on the role of reinforcements. Praise, however, was not predictive of girls' self-concepts of ability; instead it was predictive of their belief that math is easy. This variation in the effect of praise on boys' and girls'

mathematics attitudes could result from several factors. Teachers may be using praise differently for boys and girls; for example, teacher praise for boys may be associated with teacher expectancies, while for girls it may be administered more randomly. If this were the case, then praise would be a reliable cue of teacher expectancies for boys but not for girls. Data to be discussed in the Analysis II section provide some support for this hypothesis.

Teachers may praise different work behaviors for boys and girls; for example, girls may be praised for easy answers while boys are praised for difficult answers. We have no data to test this hypothesis. Alternatively, teachers may use praise similarly but boys and girls may assimilate this information to different cognitive schema; for example, girls may use praise to infer task ease while boys use it to infer ability. Attributional differences between males and females make this a viable hypothesis. The fact that work praise is unrelated to girls' perceptions of teachers' expectancies but is related to boys' perceptions of teachers' expectancies provides additional support.

Contrary to the predictions based on Brophy and Good (1974), neither frequency of interactions nor encouragement to continue responding (as measured by sustaining feedback and feedback following incorrect response) were related to students' attitudes. In fact, the frequency of feedback following an incorrect response was negatively related to self-concept of ability for boys. Boys in this sample do not appear to respond favorably to feedback following an error.

The effect of teacher's use of praise and criticism on students' self-concept-related attitudes is of particular interest. Use of praise and criticism is under the teacher's control. Teachers use praise and criticism quite selectively, and these data suggest that it is the use of praise and criticism rather than other interactional variables which influence students' self-concepts: praise having a reinforcing effect and work criticism serving as a cue to teachers' expectations. Other variables that are under more mutual control of students and teachers, such as number of response opportunities and whether an answer is correct or incorrect, were not significant predictors of student attitudes.

Analysis II

To explore the possibility that some classrooms might have especially debilitating effects on females' achievement-related expectancies and self-concepts, we compared the expectancies of boys and girls within each of two types of classrooms. There was a significant sex difference in expectations in only five of the classrooms (one ninth-grade and four seventh-grade classrooms). The other classrooms varied in the magnitude of the nonsignificant sex differences. The five classrooms (three ninth-grade and two seventh-grade classrooms) with the least sex difference in student expectancies were selected for comparison. Sex of teacher was not included in the analysis since the number of classrooms was so small. Both male and female teachers, however, were represented in each of the two class types.

RESULTS

Two $\times$ 2 $\times$ 2 (sex of student $\times$ classroom type $\times$ teacher expectancy) ANOVAs with planned comparisons were run on each of the 36 interactional variables, on the student attitudinal variables, and on the measure of the student's past performance. Only those interactions which included classroom type were explored in these analyses. As was true for the previous analyses, most variables did not yield significant differences. Neither the past performance measures nor the variables predicted by Dweck's model yielded classroom-type effects. Those differences that were significant are summarized in tables 6 and 7.

Table 6 summarizes the effects for classroom type and the interaction of classroom type with student sex. The sex differences in expectancy in the high-difference classrooms were a function of the girls' expectancies: girls' expectancies were lower in the high-difference classrooms, while boys' expectancies were equivalent in the two classroom types. In addition, these classroom types differed in the dynamics observed. Teachers in high-sex-differentiated classrooms used more criticism and praise, were more likely to rely on public response opportunities, were less likely to rely on more private dyadic interactions, and made more use of student volunteers for answers (open questions) than teachers in low-sex-differentiated classrooms.

The relation between student sex and classroom interactions varied as a function of classroom type. In comparison to boys, girls interacted more and received more praise in the low-sex-differentiated classrooms ($p < .05$ using Tukey HSD test for pairwise comparisons). Boys, on the other hand, interacted more and received more praise than girls in the high-sex-differentiated classrooms.

We next divided the sample into two additional groups: those students for whom the teacher had high expectations and those students for whom the teacher had low expecta-

TABLE 6

SEX $\times$ CLASSROOM TYPE: MEAN FREQUENCY PER CHILD PER CLASS PERIOD

	CLASS TYPE			
	Low Difference		High Difference	
BEHAVIOR	Females	Males	Females	Males
Teacher style behaviors:				
Response opportunities yielding praise[a,b]	.043	.013[c]	.045	.085[e,d]
Total work praise[b]	.099	.032[c]	.066	.121[e,d]
Conduct criticism[a]	.089	.141	.179[d]	.274[d]
Teacher-initiated dyadics[a]	.094	.092	.035	.046
Total criticism[a]	.110	.164	.196	.334
Student style behaviors:				
Student-initiated interaction[b,e]	1.51	.61[c]	1.01	1.23[d]
Student-initiated dyadics[a]	.590	.375	.277	.329
Expectancies[f]	5.08	5.17	4.41[d]	5.24[c]
Joint style behaviors:				
Total response opportunities[a,b]	.536	.188[c]	.471	.842[e,d]
Total dyadics[a]	.684	.467[c]	.312[d]	.375[d]
Open questions[a,b]	.314	.017[c]	.271	.499[e,d]
Total interaction[b]	1.76	.80	1.20[d]	1.52[d]

[a] Class-type main effect significant: $p < .05$.
[b] Sex $\times$ class-type interaction significant: $p < .05$.
[c] Sex differences within classroom type significant: $p < .05$.
[d] Classroom-type effect within sex grouping significant: $p < .05$.
[e] Sex main effect significant: $p < .05$.
[f] Scored on a seven point scale with 7 = highest expectancies.

336 Child Development

tions. The effects of this division on the relations between student sex and classroom type are tested with the three-way interaction term from the $2 \times 2 \times 2$ ANOVAs described above. Tukey's HSD test was used for pairwise comparisons of interactional variables for which the three-way interactive term was significant. Student t tests were used to test for differences between a select set of pairs of future expectancy scores since predictions regarding these differences were made a priori. The results of these analyses are summarized in table 7. In general both high-expectancy males and high-expectancy females were treated differently in each of the two classroom types. High-expectancy girls interacted the most, initiated more interactions, and received more work praise in the low sex-differentiated classrooms. High-expectancy girls received less praise and interacted less than either the high-expectancy boys or the low-expectancy girls in the high sex-differentiated classrooms. In contrast in low-differences classrooms, boys and girls were treated similarly but the high-expectancy boys initiated significantly fewer interactions than the high-expectancy girls.

Discussion

The sex × teacher expectancy interactions are particularly interesting in the high-difference classrooms where the teacher-expectancy effects follow the predicted pattern for boys only. High-expectancy girls in these classrooms are not treated in the manner predicted by the teacher-expectancy literature. Furthermore, the praise given to the low-expectancy girls in these classrooms does not appear to have the facilitative effect on their future expectation one would expect, even though they are participating more than the other girls. These data suggest that being in a classroom in which praise is used differently for boys and girls has a detrimental effect on all of the girls but not the boys. It is only the girls' expectations that differ across these two classroom types. In the low-difference classrooms, while boys are getting less praise than the girls, the pattern of its distribution across high- and low-teacher-expectancy children is equivalent for the two sexes. In this social climate, there is no sex difference in expectancies despite the fact that the girls are both getting more praise and interacting more than the boys. One cannot infer from these data that praise itself is responsible for the expectancy differences in the two classrooms. Rather, it appears that it is the pattern of distribution

of praise across the various subgroups that is critical. Boys and girls have equivalent expectancies when the relative distribution of praise and criticism across high- and low-expectancy groups is similar for both sexes.

General Discussion

The data from both Analyses I and II taken together clearly indicate that, unlike the old adage, a praise is not a praise is not a praise, and a criticism is not a criticism is not a criticism. The meaning of each appears to be situationally specific and dependent on its communicative meaning. To suggest that teachers should avoid criticism or give praise more freely overlooks the power of the context in determining the meaning of any message. A well-chosen criticism can convey as much positive information as a praise; abundant or indiscriminate praise can be meaningless; insincere praise which does not covary with the teachers' expectations for the students can have a detrimental effect on many students. Praise was positively related to self-concept of ability only in the group (in this case, boys) in which it, in fact, conveys information about the teacher's expectations. Among girls, a group for which the teacher's use of praise did not covary with the teacher expectations, praise was related neither to students' self-concept of ability nor to perceptions of the teachers' expectations. Thus, contrary to what Dweck et al. (1978) suggested, it is not the discriminativeness of praise to one's work that is critical; almost all praise is directed to work. Instead it is the informative value of praise with regard to the teacher's expectations that is critical. If the amount of praise is considered by the students to be a good indicator of the teacher's expectations, then the amount of praise one gets is related to one's self-concept of ability. When it is not a good indicator of teacher expectations, it has no direct relation to one's self-concept.

What role, then, do teachers play in perpetuating sex differences in expectancies? These data suggest that differential treatment is a key factor. The girls had lower expectancies in those classrooms in which they were treated in a qualitatively different manner than the boys; in particular, in those classrooms in which high-teacher-expectancy girls were not praised while high-teacher-expectancy boys were. Further, cross class-type comparisons suggest that providing relatively high levels of praise to the high-expectancy females facilitates the expectations of both high-expectancy and low-expec-

TABLE 7

SEX × CLASSROOM TYPE × TEACHER EXPECTANCIES[a]

	LOW-DIFFERENCE CLASSROOMS				HIGH-DIFFERENCE CLASSROOMS				GRAND MEAN
	Low Teacher Expectancy		High Teacher Expectancy		Low Teacher Expectancy		High Teacher Expectancy		
	Females	Males	Females	Males	Females	Males	Females	Males	
Teacher style behaviors:									
Praise during response opportunity	.03	.02x	.05	.01x	.11Y	.02x	.01x,y	.12x	.05
Total praise for work	.08	.02x	.12	.04x	.14	.05	.02x	.17x	.08
Student style behaviors:									
Student-initiated procedure questions	.05x	.02x	.09x	.04x	.24x	.02x	.03x	.05x	.07
Student-initiated interactions	1.0	.69x	1.9x	.56x,y	1.6Y	.88x	.61x,y	1.4	1.1
Expectancy[b]	4.95N	4.98	5.28M	5.53	3.4a	4.48N	4.70m	5.58M	...
Joint style behaviors:									
Open questions	.15	.03x	.48	.01x	.42	.28	.16	.63x	.27
Response opportunities	.32x	.24x	.75	.15x	.75	.50	.29x	1.1x	.51
Total interactions	1.23	1.00x	2.15x	.67x,y	1.85Y	1.15	.76x,y	1.75x	1.33

NOTE.—X,Y; x,y: within each row a capital letter signifies a mean which is significantly greater than all means superscripted with a corresponding lowercase letter; significant differences were determined using Tukey's HSD, $p < .01$.

[a] All three-way interaction terms significant at $p < .01$.

[b] Student questionnaire item; scale 1–7, 7 = highest; M,N and m,n: significant differences were determined using a priori t tests at $p < .03$.

338 Child Development

tancy girls. Whether this is a causal relation or not remains to be tested.

In concluding, it is important to stress six additional points. First, the frequency rates of all these interactive variables, especially the use of praise and criticism, are quite low. The meaning of any of these variables is undoubtedly tied to the frequency with which it occurs. Changing frequencies markedly may well change the nature of the relation uncovered in this study.

A second, and related, conclusion regarding the potential impact of teachers on children's expectancies needs to be made. Many variables that one would predict as important mediators of teacher effects did not emerge as significant primarily due to their low frequency. We did not see teachers making attributions, stressing the significance of math for one's future, or actually involving children in the more enjoyable aspects of math. Casserly (Note 3) has documented the importance of these last two variables in creating a more positive attitude toward math. Dweck (1975) demonstrated the potential impact of attributional retraining on children's expectancies. Thus, while our data suggest that teachers are not having a big effect on girls' achievement attitudes, they might well have a positive effect if they included these strategies in their teaching styles.

Third, the interactional variables are not as predictive of students' self- and task concepts as are other variables we measured (e.g., students' past performance and teachers' expectancies). As has been argued by Brophy and Good (1974) and others, the interactional patterns do not have big effects on student outcome measures. Much of what is going on is noise. But teachers' expectations do have an effect independent of the students' past grades. These effects must be mediated by processes more subtle than the interactional variables we observed.

Fourth, the variables we chose to study account for less variance in girls' self-concepts of ability than boys'. In part this may be a function of the lower information value of teacher behaviors for girls. But in part it is also a function of the lower predictive value of past performance. Why this might be true is not apparent in our data. But it is clear that we need additional studies to identify the factors that do determine girls' expectations and self-concepts. Our findings do not support the suggestion that girls' expectancies, while lower than boys', are more accurate than boys' (cf. Cran-

dall 1969; Fennema, in press). They are, instead, more unpredictable.

Fifth, the effects of classroom type may be mediated by the general social climate in the classroom rather than by the direct effects of one-to-one teacher-student interactions. Social climate is a function of both the teacher and the set of students in each particular class. Consequently, while classroom interactions may be having an effect on children's expectancies, the effects are not large and are, in part at least, a function of the children as well as the teacher.

Sixth and finally, if these data tell us nothing else, they highlight the necessity of assessing hypotheses regarding teacher effects on students' expectancies in the classroom as well as in the laboratory. Causal relations which emerge with clarity in the laboratory (e.g., Dweck et al. 1978) do not necessarily hold in the hustle and bustle of real classroom life. And intervention procedures designed on sound laboratory-based reasoning may backfire in the schools.

Reference Notes

1. Parsons, J.; Adler, T.; Futterman, R.; Goff, S.; Kaczala, C.; Meece, J.; & Midgley, C. Self-perceptions, task perceptions, and academic choice: origins and change. Final Report to the National Institute of Education, Washington, D.C., 1979. (ERIC Document Reproduction No. ED 186 477)
2. Brophy, J. E., & Good, T. L. Teacher-child dyadic interaction: a manual for coding classroom behavior. Report Series No. 43. Research and Development Center for Teacher Education, University of Texas at Austin, 1969.
3. Casserly, P. Factors related to young women's persistence and achievement in mathematics, with special focus on the sequence leading to and through advanced placement math. Final Report to the National Institute of Education, Washington, D.C., 1979. (ERIC Document Reproduction No. ED 186 477)

References

Brophy, J. E., & Good, T. *Teacher-student relationships: causes and consequences.* New York: Holt, Rinehart & Winston, 1974.
Cooper, H. Pygmalion grows up: a model for teacher expectation communication and performance influence. *Review of Educational Research,* 1979, **49,** 389–410.
Crandall, V. C. Sex differences in expectancy of intellectual and academic reinforcement. In

C. P. Smith (Ed.), *Achievement-related be-haviors in children.* New York: Russell Sage, 1969.

Dweck, C. S. The role of expectations and attributions in the alleviation of learned helplessness. *Journal of Personality and Social Psychology*, 1975, **31**, 674–685.

Dweck, C. S., & Bush, E. Sex differences in learned helplessness: I. Differential debilitation with peer and adult evaluations. *Developmental Psychology*, 1976, **12**, 147–156.

Dweck, C. S.; Davidson, W.; Nelson, S.; & Enna, B. I. Sex differences in learned helplessness. II. The contingencies of evaluative feedback in the classroom. III. An experimental analysis. *Developmental Psychology*, 1978, **14**, 268–276.

Fennema, E. Attribution theory and achievement in mathematics. In S. R. Yussen (Ed.), *The development of reflection.* New York: Academic Press, in press.

Hearn, J. C., & Moos, R. H. Subject matter and classroom climate: a test of Holland's environmental propositions. *American Educational Research Journal*, 1978, **15**, 111–124.

Heller, K. A., & Parsons, J. E. Sex differences in teachers' evaluative feedback and students' expectancies for success in mathematics. *Child Development*, 1981, **52**(3), 1015–1019.

Joreskog, K. G., & Sorbom, D. *EFAP-II: exploratory factor analysis program, a Fortran IV program. User's guide.* Chicago: National Educational Resources, 1978.

Parsons, J. E.; Adler, T. F.; Futterman, R.; Goff, S.; Kaczala, C. M.; Meece, J. L.; & Midgley, C. Expectancies, value and academic choice: origins and change. In J. Spence (Ed.), *Assessing achievement.* San Francisco: W. H. Freeman, in press.

Parsons, J. E.; Ruble, D. N.; Hodges, K. L.; & Small, A. W. Cognitive-developmental factors in emerging sex differences in achievement-related expectancies. *Journal of Social Issues*, 1976, **32**, 47–61.

[23]

REVISIONS/REPORTS

Social Forces Shape Math Attitudes and Performance

Jacquelynne S. Eccles and Janis E. Jacobs

Debate has continued throughout the last decade over the existence and possible causes of differences between males' and females' mathematical skills. Several observations recur as the focus of this controversy. First, adolescent boys have been found to score higher than girls on standardized mathematics achievement tests.[1] Second, males are more likely than females to engage in a variety of optional activities related to mathematics, from technical hobbies to careers in which math skills play an important role.[2] Third, adolescent males typically perform better than their female

We would like to thank Carol Midgley, Carol Kaczala, David E. Meyer, Judith Meece, D. Bruce Carter, Toby Jayaratne, Diane Gromala, and Terry Adler for their assistance in preparing and reviewing this article. This research was funded by National Institute of Mental Health grant 1-RO1-MH-31724-0 to Jacquelynne Eccles.

1. See, e.g., Lynn Fox, Linda A. Brody, and Dianne Tobin, eds., *Women and the Mathematical Mystique* (Baltimore, Md.: Johns Hopkins University Press, 1980).

2. See, e.g., Lucy Sells, "The Mathematics Filter and the Education of Women and Minorities," and Dianne Tobin and Lynn Fox, "Career Interests and Career Education: A Key to Change," in Fox, Brody, and Tobin, eds., pp. 66–75, and 179–92, respectively; George Dunteman, Joseph A. Wisenbaker, and Mary Ellen Taylor, *Race and Sex Differences in College Science Program Participation* (Research Triangle Park, N.C.: Research Triangle Institute, 1979).

[*Signs: Journal of Women in Culture and Society* 1986, vol. 11, no. 2]

counterparts on spatial-visualization tests.[3] Researchers have attributed these differences to a variety of hereditary and environmental factors without reaching a consensus about their origins.

A significant addition to this controversy came in a 1980 *Science* article by Camilla Benbow and Julian Stanley. Within a sample of highly gifted seventh- and eighth-grade children, the authors found that, on the average, boys scored higher than girls on the College Board's Scholastic Aptitude Test for Mathematics (SAT-M).[4] This difference was especially marked at the extreme upper end of the distribution. These data extend a pattern of commonly found sex differences to a select population of junior high-school students and thus are neither surprising nor particularly novel.[5] What is novel, however, is Benbow and Stanley's interpretation of their data. They argue that "superior male mathematical ability" is the best explanation for the sex differences, since the boys and girls in their sample had essentially identical mathematics training prior to the seventh grade. Furthermore, they suggest that "superior male mathematical ability" is the probable cause of general sex differences in both mathematical achievement and attitudes toward math. These conclusions have sparked renewed controversy in the scientific community and a disturbing response in the mass media. This article questions Benbow and Stanley's underlying assumptions and presents data counter to their conclusions.

Benbow and Stanley base their argument on the following suppositions: (*a*) students' scores on the SAT-M are primarily a measure of their mathematical aptitude; (*b*) students who have taken similar formal educational courses in mathematics have had similar experiences with the discipline; and (*c*) a demonstrated sex difference in mathematical reasoning supports the conclusion that "less well-developed mathematical reasoning contributes to girls' taking fewer mathematics courses and achieving less than boys."[6] In her rebuttal to Benbow and Stanley, Alice Schafer concluded that taking the SAT-M as a measure of mathematical aptitude is unjustifiable. Moreover, Warner Slack and Douglas Porter and Rex Jackson have pointed out that the SAT measures acquired intellec-

3. See, e.g., Michelle Wittig and Anne Peterson, eds., *Sex-related Differences in Cognitive Functioning* (New York: Academic Press, 1979).
4. Camilla P. Benbow and Julian C. Stanley, "Sex Differences in Mathematical Ability: Fact or Artifact?" *Science*, no. 210 (December 1980), pp. 1262–64, esp. p. 1262.
5. Portions of these results have been reported in other sources. See, e.g., Lynn Fox and Sanford Cohn, "Sex Differences in the Development of Precocious Mathematical Talent," in Fox, Brody, and Tobin, eds., pp. 94–112, esp. p. 94; Lynn Fox and Daniel Keating, eds., *Intellectual Talent: Research and Development* (Baltimore, Md.: Johns Hopkins University Press, 1976). The reported pattern of sex differences, in fact, forms part of the collection of results researchers are now seeking to explain.
6. Benbow and Stanley, pp. 1264, 1262.

tual skills.[7] Thus, one must question Benbow and Stanley's assumption that the SAT-M measures mathematical aptitude. Furthermore, performance on timed tests is influenced by a wide variety of motivational and affective factors such as test anxiety, risk-taking preferences, cognitive style, and confidence in one's abilities. Since males and females differ on some of these factors, it is quite possible that the sex differences reported by Benbow and Stanley reflect these noncognitive differences rather than, or in addition to, true aptitudinal differences.

The authors' assumption that the boys and girls in their sample had equivalent mathematical experiences is also problematic. Assessing students' mathematical experiences is extremely difficult. Counting the number of mathematics courses the children have taken is only one possible method, feasible only if the sample is in secondary school. The fact that all the children in Benbow and Stanley's sample had completed the sixth grade does not support the inference that these students had equivalent formal educational experiences with mathematics. Concluding that their informal experiences were equivalent is even more suspect.

To justify such inferences one would need to develop appropriate measures of the quantity and quality of elementary school children's mathematical experiences and then test for sex differences on these measures. Using one such strategy, Gaea Leinhardt, Andria Seewald, and Mary Engel observed the formal teaching practices of thirty-three second-grade teachers and found that teachers spent relatively more time teaching mathematics to boys than to girls. Based on their results, in fact, boys may receive as much as thirty-six more hours of formal mathematics instruction than do girls by the time the children reach the seventh grade. Both Helen Astin and Lynn Fox and her colleagues have investigated participation in less formal activities related to mathematics. According to their studies, boys are more likely than girls to have informal, mathematically related experiences such as playing with scientific toys, participating in mathematical games, and reading mathematics books.[8] Thus, Benbow and Stanley's assumption that their boys and girls have had equivalent

7. Alice Schafer, "Sex and Mathematics," *Science*, no. 211 (January 1981), p. 392; Warner Slack and Douglas Porter, "Training, Validity, and the Issue of Aptitude: A Reply to Jackson," *Harvard Educational Review* 50, no. 3 (1980): 392–401; Rex Jackson, "The Scholastic Aptitude Test: A Response to Slack and Porter's 'Critical Appraisal,'" ibid., 50, no. 3 (1980): 382–91, esp. 382.

8. Gaea Leinhardt, Andria Seewald, and Mary Engel, "Learning What's Taught: Sex Differences in Instruction," *Journal of Educational Psychology* 71, no. 3 (1979): 432–39, esp. 432; Helene Astin, "Sex Differences in Mathematical and Scientific Precocity," in *Mathematical Talent: Discovery, Description, and Development*, ed. Julian Stanley, Daniel Keating, and Lynn Fox (Baltimore, Md.: Johns Hopkins University Press, 1974), pp. 70–86, esp. p. 70; Fox and Cohn, p. 94.

mathematical experiences is questionable, precluding definitive conclusions regarding the origin of observed differences on SAT-M scores.[9]

Benbow and Stanley's assumption that their data contribute new insights into the origins of sex differences in mathematical achievement and attitudes is also suspect. The authors in no way establish the power of SAT-M scores to predict a student's subsequent achievement in, attitudes toward, or course enrollment in mathematics. Other investigators have suggested that the link, if any, is weak. For example, Slack and Porter concluded that the SAT-M score is a poorer predictor of a student's mathematics achievement in college than either high school grades or a score on the SAT Mathematical Achievement test. In addition, in a follow-up of the 1976 cohort of Benbow and Stanley's sample, Lynn Fox and Sanford Cohn found no relation between the girls' SAT-M scores and their subsequent educational acceleration. Finally, Laurie Steel and Lori Wise found that although mathematical ability is a significant predictor of subsequent mathematics achievement and course enrollment, it does not account for the sex differences in either high school seniors' mathematics grades or their high school mathematics enrollment patterns.[10] Apparently variations in mathematical reasoning ability contribute little to variations in subsequent course-taking patterns among either the group of gifted girls studied by Benbow and Stanley or more representative samples of mathematically competent high school students.

Predictors of Math Achievement and Math Participation

What does predict the course-taking plans and achievement patterns of mathematically competent (as distinguished from gifted) junior high school students? Contrary to Benbow and Stanley's conclusion, our data suggest that social and attitudinal factors have a greater influence on junior and senior high school students' grades and enrollment in mathematics courses than do variations in mathematical aptitude. Further, our data suggest that sex differences in mathematical achievement and attitudes are largely due to sex differences in math anxiety; the gender-stereotyped beliefs of parents, especially mothers; and the value students attach to mathematics.

9. It is possible that sex differences in innate mathematical aptitude account for boys' greater interest in mathematically related activities. But it is impossible to discern the cause and effect relations among innate aptitude, interest, and subsequent skill without extensive longitudinal testing. Our critical point here is that one cannot assume equivalent mathematical experiences in a population of seventh-grade girls and boys.

10. Slack and Porter; Fox and Cohn, p. 94; Laurie Steel and Lori Wise, "Origins of Sex Differences in High School Math Achievement and Participation" (paper presented at the American Educational Research Association, San Francisco, March 1979).

Signs *Winter 1986* *371*

Our conclusions are based on a two-year longitudinal study of 250 average and above-average students in the seventh through ninth grades, their parents, and their mathematics teachers. We gave questionnaires to the students in two successive years and examined their mathematics course grades and scores on a standardized achievement test (either the Michigan Educational Assessment Program or the California Achievement Test) for each year of the study. We also gathered questionnaire data from both parents and teachers.

We created our scales by applying exploratory factor analysis to the information in the student and parent questionnaires. Factor analysis is a statistical procedure whereby items are grouped together according to the similarity of respondents' answers. For example, because mothers and fathers gave similar estimates of their children's mathematical abilities, we grouped all questions regarding these estimates in one scale rather than analyzing those questions individually.[11]

Four parent factors emerged: mothers' estimates of the difficulty of mathematics for their children, fathers' estimates of the difficulty of mathematics for their children, both parents' estimates of their children's mathematical abilities, and both parents' estimates of the importance of enrolling in mathematics courses. Three student factors emerged: students' estimates of their own mathematical abilities, their estimates of the difficulty of mathematics, and their rating of the value of mathematics courses. We created three additional scales: one reflecting teachers' estimates of each student's mathematical ability, one reflecting each student's math anxiety, and one reflecting mathematical aptitude/achievement based on each student's previous year's mathematics grade and most recent score on a standardized test of math achievement.

We assume, based on arguments by Slack and Porter and others,[12] that the latter composite score is at least as good an estimate of mathematical aptitude as is the SAT-M score. To the extent that mathematics achievement scores reflect mathematical aptitude, this measure provides an estimate of individual differences in mathematical aptitude. Moreover, given that this score summarizes the performance information provided to students, parents, and teachers, it is also an indicator of the objective performance differences on which children, parents, and teachers base their estimates of an individual student's math potential and ability.

We entered each of these scores, along with the student's sex, into a multiple regression, recursive path analysis (see fig. 1). The total sample

11. See Karl Joreskog and Dan Sorbon, eds., *Advances in Factor Analyses and Structural Equation Models* (Cambridge, Mass.: ABT Books, 1979). Factor loadings can be obtained from the authors.
12. Slack and Porter, p. 392.

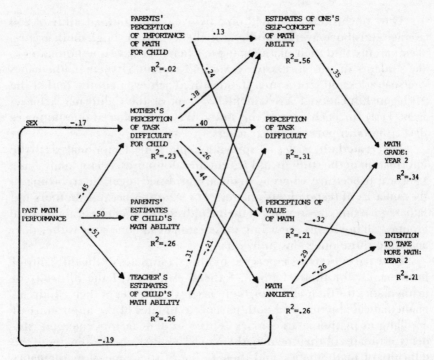

FIG. 1.—Longitudinal influences on students' mathematics course grades and future course enrollment plans.

size was 164 students, their parents, and their mathematics teachers. Path analysis is a statistical procedure used to assess the direct and indirect relations among a set of scales or variables. It allows us to estimate how strong the influence of one variable is on other variables. For example, it enables an estimate of the extent to which students' grades in sixth-grade mathematics courses influence their parents' estimates of their children's mathematical ability one year later. Path analysis also allows us to test predictions that students' grades in mathematics have an indirect, rather than direct, effect on their confidence in their own abilities and that parents' interpretations of the students' grades mediate this indirect effect.

Recursive path analysis estimates the direction of effects in only one direction; in figure 1, this direction is always left to right.[13] Only statistically significant paths are depicted in this chart. To make it easier to interpret the direction of impact of these paths, we placed our scales in

13. We did not test for effects in the reverse direction, and we did not test for relationships between variables within a given column. We believe such effects exist but did not test for them in this analysis.

Signs   *Winter 1986*   *373*

four columns, left to right, representing the chronological sequence in which we collected the data. Variables in the column on the far left reflect scales of students' mathematical performance prior to entry into our study, as well as their sex. Variables in the second column are parent and teacher scales gathered in the first year of our study.[14] With the exception of math anxiety, the variables in the third column are student attitudinal scales based on questionnaires distributed in the first year of our research; math anxiety is a student belief scale gathered in the second year. Variables in the fourth column on the far right represent students' grades and course-taking plans gathered during the study's second year. We estimated all possible paths across columns.[15]

Standardized column-wise multiple regression equation procedures were used to estimate path coefficients. At each step, each of the variables in one column was regressed on the set of all variables in the columns to the left. This procedure yields standardized path coefficients, reflecting the relative predictive power of each variable in comparison to all other variables. These coefficients, printed on each path, can vary from -1 to $+1$.

A high path coefficient (either positive or negative) reflects a relatively strong relationship. A positive path coefficient means that high scores on the variable to the left predict high scores on the variable to the right. Conversely, a negative path coefficient means that low scores on the variable to the left predict high scores on the variable to the right. We entered sex as a dummy variable, with females equal to 1 and males equal to 2. Thus, the two weak negative path coefficients on the paths leading from the sex variable indicate that females have slightly higher scores on the two related variables; that is, females have slightly higher math anxiety scores, and girls' mothers rate mathematics as slightly more difficult for their children than do boys' mothers.[16]

We used t-tests to calculate the significance of each path coefficient. The R^2 value printed below each scale represents the percent of variance in a measure that is explained by the variables to its left. A large R^2 value

14. Fathers' estimates of the difficulty of mathematics for their children did not contribute to the prediction of students' mathematics achievement or their course enrollment plans. Including these estimates in the analysis reduced the sample size considerably. Thus this variable is omitted from all our analyses reported here. Fathers' effects in this data set appear to be redundant with, but less powerful than, mothers' effects.

15. Using variables from different years strengthens our conclusions about the direction in which the variables in the columns affect each other but does not rule out the possibility that effects can occur in the opposite direction as well.

16. Specification of the path model, i.e., assignment of variables to particular columns, was based on the theoretical model in Jacquelynne Eccles (Parsons) et al., "Expectations, Values, and Academic Behaviors," in *Achievement and Achievement Motivation*, ed. Janet Spence (San Francisco: W. H. Freeman & Co., 1983), pp. 75–146.

indicates that we can predict more about that variable using the variables to its left than we can predict about variables with lower R^2 values.

Grades and plans to continue taking mathematics are predicted most directly by the students' beliefs listed in the third column: their estimates of their mathematical abilities, their perceptions of the value of mathematics courses, and their levels of math anxiety. These student beliefs, in turn, are related most strongly to the students' mothers' beliefs concerning the difficulty of mathematics for their children. Parents' estimates of the importance of mathematics courses for their children and teachers' estimates of each student's mathematical ability also predict some of the students' beliefs.

What does this analysis tell us about boys' and girls' attitudes toward mathematics and their enrollment decisions? To answer this question we need to consider the results of the path analysis in conjunction with the pattern of correlations between the important variables. A correlation is a statistical coefficient (signified by an r value) that indicates the strength of the relationship between two variables; it does not take into account any other variables or possible mediating effects. Like standardized path coefficients, correlation coefficients can range from -1 to $+1$; the higher the number (either positive or negative), the stronger the relationship between the two variables. The closer the coefficient is to zero, the weaker the relationship. A correlation coefficient of zero indicates no relationship between the two variables. In the discussion that follows, we will include the relevant correlation coefficients whenever they aid the interpretation of the path analysis and enhance our understanding of boys' and girls' attitudes toward mathematics.

The path analysis suggests that a student's performance in mathematics has an indirect effect on that student's attitudes toward mathematics and subsequent mathematics grades. While past mathematics aptitude/achievement scores are related both to a child's subsequent mathematics grades ($r = .40$) and course enrollment plans ($r = .17$), these relationships appear to be mediated by mothers' and teachers' beliefs, by students' estimates of their mathematical abilities, and by students' beliefs about the value of mathematics. Thus, students' grades appear to affect subsequent mathematics performance and course-taking plans only to the extent that these grades influence both parents' confidence in their children's ability to learn mathematics and students' own beliefs, motivation, and math anxiety. Furthermore, the influence of past grades on students' beliefs appears to be mediated by the parents' interpretation of these grades. Finally, when one compares the correlations between girls' and boys' estimates of the value of mathematics and objective indicators of their mathematical ability, an interesting difference emerges. Boys' estimates of the value of mathematics are related to their past performance in

Signs *Winter 1986* 375

mathematics (r = .33) and to both their teachers' and parents' estimates of their mathematical ability (r = .33, r = .28). In contrast, girls' estimates of the value of mathematics are not related to any of these measures (r = .06, r = .03, and r = .06, respectively). Thus, a student's mathematical aptitude, as measured in this study, can serve only as an indirect predictor of that child's attitudes toward mathematics, future mathematics achievement, and course-enrollment plans. Social and attitudinal factors appear to have much stronger direct effects on these beliefs and plans, especially among girls.

Math anxiety also appears to be an important predictor of both subsequent mathematics grades and course-taking plans, and girls report higher levels of this anxiety than do boys. These results are especially interesting in light of three additional relations. First, in this sample of mathematically competent students, math anxiety is only weakly related to the students' previous performance in mathematics (r = −.17). Consequently, the individual variations in math anxiety are not primarily a consequence of objective differences in performance. Second, math anxiety has a stronger and more direct relation to mathematics grades and to students' future plans for taking math courses than does our mathematical aptitude/achievement score. Third, math anxiety is directly and strongly influenced by social factors, in particular by mothers' beliefs about the difficulty of the subject for their children. Thus, math anxiety appears to be a key social/attitudinal variable that might account for sex differences in achievement and enrollment in mathematics courses. Furthermore, given the common finding that anxiety has a debilitating effect on children's scores on standardized achievement tests,[17] one must ask whether the sex differences in math anxiety are strong enough to explain most of the variance in the SAT-M scores that Benbow and Stanley attribute to superior male mathematical ability.

The results of our path analysis also point out parents' importance as critical socializers of sex differences in mathematical achievement and attitudes. While teachers' beliefs are predictive of students' beliefs, teachers in our study estimated that boys and girls had similar mathematical ability. In addition, the impact of teachers' beliefs is not as large as that of parents' beliefs and does not have a direct effect on students' plans to continue taking mathematics. These data suggest that parents' gender-stereotyped beliefs are a key cause of sex differences in students' attitudes toward mathematics.

17. Kennedy Hill, "The Relation of Evaluative Practices to Test Anxiety and Achievement Motivation," *Educator* 19, no. 15 (1977): 15–22; Diane Ruble and Anne Boggiano, "Optimizing Motivation in an Achievement Context," in *Advances in Special Education*, ed. Barbara Keogh (Greenwich, Conn.: JAI Press, 1980), pp. 183–238.

Although it could be argued that parents' gender-stereotyped beliefs about the difficulty of mathematics for their children are veridical, reflecting a real sex difference in children's behaviors, the following additional results suggest that this is not the case. First, girls and boys in this sample had equivalent mathematics grades and standardized math test scores at the start of the study. Second, when asked how much math homework they do, the boys and girls reported equivalent amounts. Third, the teachers' estimates of these girls' and boys' mathematical abilities did not differ. And finally, mothers who endorsed the gender stereotype that boys do better than girls in advanced high school mathematics courses thought that math was harder for their daughters than did the mothers who believed that girls and boys can do equally well in advanced math courses. Thus, the gender stereotypes evident in mothers' and fathers' beliefs do not appear to be grounded in reality. The extent to which they reflect a "real" sex difference in mathematical aptitude remains to be demonstrated.

Thus, Benbow and Stanley's conclusion that sex differences in attitudes toward and achievement in mathematics may result from "superior male mathematical ability" is premature at best. Although the authors may favor a biological explanation, their data do not provide a test of that hypothesis.

Further, one must be concerned about the effect their conclusion may have on girls' future mathematical achievement and attitudes. This concern is especially justified given the distortion of Benbow and Stanley's findings by the popular media (see fig. 2) and the strong influence parental beliefs about mathematical ability have in shaping girls' attitudes toward math and their actual achievement. This is not to say that we should rule out the possibility of biological influences on mathematics competence. Biological processes may be important. But the nature, the magnitude, and the malleability of those factors are not yet understood. Our data suggest that, at present, social factors are a major cause of sex differences in both mathematics performance and attitudes toward math in the population at large. And, as noted above, the extensive and biased coverage of the Benbow and Stanley article in the mass media may have provided yet one more social force discouraging female participation in mathematics-related courses and career fields. This is the issue we will now address.

Impact of Media Coverage

Since we were in the midst of a longitudinal study of the socialization of girls' and boys' attitudes toward math when the Benbow and Stanley story broke, we were in a unique position to assess the impact of the media

Do Males Have a Math Gene?

Can girls do math as well as boys? All sorts of recent tests have shown that they cannot. Most educators and feminists

tude Test normally given to high-school seniors. In the results on the math portion of the SAT—there was no appreciable dif-

Newsweek, Dec. 15, 1980

The Gender Factor in Math

A new study says males may be naturally abler than females

Until about the seventh grade, boys and girls do equally well at math. In early high school, when the emphasis

Julian C. Stanley of Johns University, males inherently have more mathematical ability than females

Time, Dec. 15, 1980

Male superiority

Are boys born superior to girls in mathematical ability? The answer is probably Yes, say Camilla Persson Benbow and Julian C. Stanley, researchers in the department of psychology at the Johns

The Chronicle of
Higher Education,
December, 1980

Are Boys Better At Math?

New York Times,
Dec. 7, 1980

BOYS HAVE SUPERIOR MATH ABILITY, STUDY SAYS

Boys are inherently better at math than girls, according to an eight-year study of 10,000 gifted students. Coun-

Education U.S.A.,
Dec. 15, 1980

SEX + MATH = ?

Why do boys traditionally do better than girls in math? Many say it's because boys are encouraged to pursue

Family Weekly,
Jan. 25, 1981

Study suggests boys may be better at math

WASHINGTON (UPI) — Two psychologists said Friday boys are better than girls in math reasoning, and they urged educators to accept the fact that something more than social factors is re-

Ann Arbor News,
Dec. 6, 1980

FIG. 2.—News report headlines of Benbow and Stanley's *Science* article

campaign on parents' stereotypes and beliefs regarding their children's mathematical ability.[18]

We sent the parents in our sample a questionnaire similar to our original one about three months after the research report appeared in *Science*. We added a question, placed on the last page of the form, which described the media coverage of the research and asked if parents had heard about it. Approximately one-quarter of the responding parents (57 out of 200) said yes. While most of these had read about the study in either a magazine or a newspaper, many indicated that they had heard about the report from several sources. We compared the responses of parents who had read the media reports (referred to as the misinformed group) to the responses of those who had not (referred to as the uninformed group).[19]

We first assessed the impact of the media exposure on parents' attitudes about their children's mathematical abilities. The result was different for mothers and fathers. Compared to estimates made by uninformed mothers of girls, responses by misinformed mothers of girls indicated that they felt their daughters had less mathematical ability, would have less success in future math courses, would find mathematics more difficult, and would have to work harder in order to do well in math courses. In addition, the misinformed mothers of girls thought that mathematics was much more difficult for their daughters than did the misinformed mothers of boys. In contrast, uninformed mothers of both girls and boys had similar beliefs about their children's mathematical abilities.

Fathers responded quite differently. Generally, the fathers of girls felt that their daughters had slightly less mathematical ability than did the fathers of sons. However, misinformed fathers of girls were more positive about their daughters' mathematical abilities after reading the media coverage than they had been before reading the reports. In contrast, uninformed fathers of girls had come to feel that their daughters had less mathematical ability than they had estimated one year earlier.

We next assessed the impact of the media reports on parents' stereotypes regarding the utility of mathematics for boys and girls in general. We also asked parents how useful they felt the study of mathematics was for their child. In response to the first question, both misinformed and uninformed mothers felt that math was more useful for males than for females, regardless of the sex of their child. In addition,

18. For more details, see Janis Jacobs and Jacquelynne Eccles, "Gender Differences in Math Ability: The Impact of Media Reports on Parents," *Educational Researcher* 14, no. 3 (1985): 20–25.

19. In order to test the hypothesis that parents in the misinformed group and those in the uninformed group may have had significant differences unrelated to their media exposure, analyses of variance were performed on all pretest variables including the two groups' demographic and attitudinal variables. The parents were similar on all of these measures.

Signs   Winter 1986   379

the mothers' beliefs had become more gender-stereotyped in the year following our first survey. They now rated math as even more useful for males in their adult lives than they had earlier.

A slightly different pattern emerged for fathers. When fathers were talking about their own children, fathers of sons rated mathematics as more useful for their child than fathers of daughters. In addition, misinformed fathers of sons felt that math was more useful for their sons than did the uninformed fathers of sons. When asked about the usefulness of math for males in general, the misinformed fathers of sons stood out from the other parent groups even more distinctly; they thought mathematics was *much* more important for males than for females. It appears that exposure to the media coverage increased the gender-stereotyped attitudes of fathers of sons.

In summary, media reports of the Benbow and Stanley article did appear to change parents' attitudes. The effect, however, depended on both the sex of the parent and the sex of the child. Misinformed mothers had their gender-stereotypic beliefs confirmed regarding the difficulty of math for females and its comparative ease for males. In contrast, misinformed fathers of girls became more confident in their daughters' mathematical abilities. Unfortunately, while the misinformed fathers of girls came to the defense of their daughters' math abilities, misinformed fathers of boys responded quite differently. They became even more convinced than their uninformed counterparts of the validity of the broader gender stereotypes regarding mathematics abilities. They felt that females in general do not perform as well as males in advanced math classes and that mathematics is more useful to males than to females.

These findings are not surprising. We know that the salience of any event determines how it will be interpreted and remembered. We would expect parents of mathematically able daughters to interpret the news of superior male mathematical ability very differently from parents with sons, and mothers to interpret it differently from fathers. In this case, it appears that exposure to media reports confirmed mothers' beliefs that their daughters are not as able in mathematics as are their sons, while it put fathers of girls in a position of challenging the "evidence" on behalf of their daughters. For fathers the opposite happened for variables measuring general gender-stereotyped beliefs. Fathers of sons had their gender-stereotyped beliefs confirmed and strengthened although their beliefs about their own children did not change.

Conclusions

Our research suggests that sex differences in students' attitudes toward mathematics and in plans to continue taking math courses are influenced substantially by their parents' perceptions of the difficulty of mathematics for their child and by their own attitudes about the value of mathematics. Furthermore, parents' beliefs, especially mothers' beliefs, appear to have a greater influence on students' attitudes than do students' mathematics grades. Doris Entwisle and D. P. Baker recently reported a similar result for children in grades one through three.[20] Although the girls and boys in their study had received similar grades in mathematics and similar scores on a math aptitude measure, the boys had higher expectations for their mathematics performance than did the girls. This sex difference seemed to stem from the different expectations parents held for their sons and for their daughters. Finally, our results suggest that media reports attributing sex differences in mathematics to innate or biological factors have a negative impact on mothers' confidence in their daughters' math abilities.

Even though parents in general held stereotypic beliefs, many parents of daughters spoke of the need to change stereotypic views of women and mathematics. One mother summed up this position succinctly when she said, "For whatever reason, boys in general *seem* to pick up math concepts with more ease and less methodical study. There are exceptions, however, and I would not want *my* daughter to feel she could not do equally well in math as her brothers." She continued, "Perhaps society has encouraged boys in math more than girls. I hope it is changing."

We too hope it will change but fear that change will be very slow, especially given the prevailing biases that influence what is spotlighted and what is ignored in national news coverage. In the meantime, we, as feminists, parents, and teachers, need to do all we can to support and encourage girls in their efforts to develop interests in math and science. In this area, passive nondiscrimination is simply not an adequate intervention strategy.

Department of Psychology
University of Michigan

20. Doris Entwisle and D. P. Baker, "Gender and Young Children's Expectations for Performance," *Developmental Psychology* 19, no. 2 (1983): 200–214, esp. 200.

Part III
Socialization

Part III
Socialization

Psychological Bulletin
1991. Vol. 109. No. 2, 267-296

Parents' Differential Socialization of Boys and Girls: A Meta-Analysis

Hugh Lytton and David M. Romney
University of Calgary, Calgary, Alberta, Canada

A meta-analysis of 172 studies attempted to resolve the conflict between previous narrative reviews on whether parents make systematic differences in their rearing of boys and girls. Most effect sizes were found to be nonsignificant and small. In North American studies, the only socialization area of 19 to display a significant effect for both parents is encouragement of sex-typed activities. In other Western countries, physical punishment is applied significantly more to boys. Fathers tend to differentiate more than mothers between boys and girls. Over all socialization areas. effect size is not related to sample size or year of publication. Effect size decreases with child's age and increases with higher quality. No grouping by any of these variables changes a nonsignificant effect to a significant effect. Because little differential socialization for social behavior or abilities can be found, other factors that may explain the genesis of documented sex differences are discussed.

To what extent parents make a systematic difference between boys and girls in their socialization practices is an important question because it takes us to the heart of the issue of the origins of the behavioral differences known or suspected to exist between males and females. Indeed the theory that sex-typed behavior is brought about through "shaping" by parents is a widely held view among social scientists as well as the general public. Both Block (1983) and Huston (1983), for instance, made this theory a central theme in their expositions. Maccoby and Jacklin (1974) summarized earlier theorizing as follows: "The role of direct socialization appears to be crucial, then, not only in its own right but also in establishing the foundation upon which later self-socialization is based" (p. 303). The existence and importance of such shaping behavior are in accord with social-learning theory, which explains the acquisition of sex differences in behavior and attitudes by the same mechanisms that apply to all kinds of behavior, viz., reinforcement and modeling. The home environment will, of course, be the first and perhaps most salient agent of such reinforcement, but others, particularly peers and teachers, will also play a role. On the other hand, the notion of parental reinforcement is not crucial to cognitive-developmental theory, which asserts that children imitate same-sex models and engage in sex-typed behavior preferentially because acts conventionally thought appropriate for their sex are consonant with their self-concept and

sexual self-identity (cf. Kohlberg, 1966). We discuss here some evidence that presents some difficulty for this theory.[1]

Maccoby and Jacklin's (1974) classic work dealt extensively with studies of parents' sex-differentiated socialization practices. They reviewed research in this area by counting the studies that revealed sex-differentiated practices in one direction or the other and those that did not (the vote-counting method), and then based their qualitative summary largely on these counts. They concluded that parents do indeed reinforce sex-typed behavior, narrowly defined (e.g., they reward traditionally sex-typed play activities and toy choices), but that apart from this "the reinforcement contingencies for the two sexes appear to be remarkably similar" (p. 342).

This conclusion was criticized particularly by Block in several thoughtful articles (1976, 1978, 1983). Block argued that Maccoby and Jacklin had underestimated the extent to which parents do apply differential-socialization practices to the two sexes, and she attributed these, in her opinion, misconceived conclusions to various shortcomings of the Maccoby and Jacklin review.

Five criticisms concern us here. First, fathers are underrepresented in the studies surveyed. Second, the investigations are mainly concerned with young children: 77% of studies of socialization practices included deal with children under 6 years of age. Both points, in Block's view, may lead to an underestimate of sex-differentiated socialization practices. Third, on a more theoretical level, parental socialization emphases are dynamic and will accommodate themselves to the emerging capabilities and needs of a maturing child. Hence, parents are likely

This research was supported by grants from the Social Sciences and Humanities Research Council of Canada and from the University of Calgary. We thank Eugene Edgington and Walter Zwirner for statistical advice. We are also grateful to Mark Atkinson for assistance with the literature search and to John Begoray, Gisela Engels, Ken Gerke, and, above all, John Beames for help with the computer analysis and computer programming.

Correspondence concerning this article should be addressed to Hugh Lytton, Department of Educational Psychology, University of Calgary, Calgary, Alberta, Canada T2N 1N4.

[1] Some authors use the term *sex* to refer to biological aspects of behavior and *gender* to indicate psychological-cultural aspects of behavior. However, which behaviors are biologically based and which are molded mainly by psychological-cultural influences is still an unresolved question, and its resolution cannot be anticipated by the use of a particular terminology.

to make greater differences at later ages; yet the review did not take account of age of child. Fourth, inclusion criteria for the behavioral categories that they established are too heterogeneous. Fifth, the authors gave the same weight in their interpretation to each study regardless of its quality or sample size.

Let us comment on these points of criticism. As for the first two, Maccoby and Jacklin themselves recognized these limitations of their review, which, however, were essentially limitations of the data base they had to work with. We discuss the third point later in this article, but note here that Block had some fragmentary evidence to support it at the time. The last two points represent the most fundamental and important criticisms. In arguing the fourth criticism, Block illustrated the miscellaneous character of the variables included in a particular summary category by showing that achievement pressure embraced expectations for household help, anxious intrusions into the child's problem-solving attempts, and demands on the child during discussions in which consensus must be reached, as well as other variables. It should be noted that to form superordinate categories from a vast diversity of measures used by the authors of primary studies is a procrustean task that may sometimes produce conformity by rather arbitrary means. No universal agreement can be expected on any such classification: ipso facto any categorization whatsoever will represent subjective judgment and will be open to criticism. Nevertheless, we should note also that our subjective judgment agrees with Block's in the case of achievement pressure and our classification decisions here differed from Maccoby and Jacklin's (see later discussion). However, one cannot aspire to elevate one's subjective judgment to an absolute standard.

In a more general vein, Block (1978) also stated that lumping conceptually distinct behaviors into one large category tends to level differences that would otherwise be seen, and she illustrated this with the behaviors subsumed under the category of dependency. She claimed that if parents' responses to help seeking and to clinging (both categorized as responses to dependency) were studied separately, differences would have an opportunity to emerge. She may be right, but this has not yet been proved. In any case, a review—narrative or quantitative—has to bring together and to bridge diverse measurements of what the reviewer considers the "same" construct precisely to provide an overall view of the research regarding a given construct, and this is also one of its benefits (cf. Nurius & Yeaton, 1987). Concepts such as dependency are multidimensional and diverse indicators are, in fact, desirable to capture all their aspects. For a more detailed discussion of what has often been called the "apples and oranges problem" in meta-analysis, see Glass (1977).

As for Block's fifth point, it is possible to weight studies in different ways. In a quantitative review, it is desirable to weight study effect by sample size or inverse of the variance, and it can be enlightening to analyze outcomes by moderator variables, including a quality rating, or to weight studies by this (see later discussion), but it must be recognized that quality ratings also represent subjective judgments that are open to debate.

The qualitative reviews, discussed previously here, agreed that parents make differences between boys and girls in some areas of socialization, but disagreed in which areas important

differences occur or what the extent of the differential treatment is. Their disagreements arose from finely shaded nuances of interpretation of essentially the same studies.

Primary studies published since the appearance of these reviews have continued to generate conflicting evidence on the extent to which parents treat boys and girls differently. Take as an example the acceptance of children's dependent behavior. Most studies report no difference in parents' reactions to young boys' and young girls' proximity or comfort seeking. However, Fagot (1978) found that such behavior was more accepted for toddler girls than toddler boys. On the other hand, a twin study reported that mothers encouraged dependency and provided nurturance more for young boys than young girls (Goshen-Gottstein, 1981). A cross-sex effect in this area had been noted earlier by Rothbart and Maccoby (1966): in reactions to taped voices of a boy and a girl, not their own children, mothers were more accepting of boys' comfort seeking and fathers more of that from girls. Differences between the treatment of boys and girls that Block (1978) had expected to be noticeable, when these behaviors were analyzed separately, did indeed emerge in these studies, but in opposite directions.

It seems to us that a quantitative review of the area, although this too has its limitations, provides a partial way out of the dilemma of conflicting studies and conflicting reviews. It does so mainly because quantitative or meta-analytic methods inject some objectivity into the reviewing process that constrains generalizations within certain limits (cf. Eagly, 1987). However, a detailed justification for meta-analytic procedures seems no longer needed.

Meta-analyses of sex differences exist in a variety of areas (e.g., verbal ability [Hyde & Linn, 1988], helping behavior [Eagly & Crowley, 1986], spatial ability [Linn & Petersen, 1985]), and some of them have been brought together in one book (Hyde & Linn, 1986). No quantitative review of studies of sex-differentiated socialization has, however, to our knowledge appeared, and this is the gap that our study attempts to fill. Such a meta-analysis at this time is able to take note of the many studies in this domain published since Maccoby and Jacklin's (1974) book, and it can also benefit from and take account of the criticisms of the review noted previously here.

Such a meta-analysis by itself will not allow us to decide whether any differential practices found are a reaction to differences in boys' and girls' preexisting dispositions (the hypothesis of evocative genotype → environment influences suggested by Scarr & McCartney, 1983) or, alternatively, whether they are an expression of the parents' stereotypical values and preoccupations. However, in areas where no differential treatment is found, parental treatment should not be invoked as a cause of possible differences in male and female characteristics, although this judgment must be seen in light of the literature available for summarizing.

In view of the previous conflicting reviews in the area, it seems important from a theoretical point of view to know more precisely in which areas, at which ages, and to what extent mother or father, or both, treat their sons and daughters differentially. From a practical point of view, knowing where differential treatment occurs may suggest ways of modifying undesirable socialization emphases, as Block (1978) suggested. Null

PARENTS' DIFFERENTIAL SOCIALIZATION 269

results would stimulate the theoretical and empirical search for other possible influences that may account for behavioral differences between the sexes.

The Current Study

The current meta-analysis was designed to answer clearly three questions. First, in which areas of socialization do mothers and fathers (analyzed separately where possible) treat sons and daughters differentially, and what is the extent of the differences they make? Second, do fathers make greater differences between sons and daughters than mothers do, as narrative reviews have suggested? Third, are there any moderating factors (e.g., age of child, design of study, or year of publication) that affect the size of the difference?

We formulated the following hypotheses regarding the effects of these moderator variables. First, differential treatment of boys and girls (i.e., the effect size) will, in general, increase with age. This was based on Block's (1978) hypothesis and prior evidence (e.g., Newson & Newson, 1976). Second, effect sizes will be larger when data were obtained from observation or experiment rather than from parent interview. This followed from the theoretical expectation that parents will minimize any actual differences they make in interview/questionnaire responses. Third, effect sizes will be larger in published than in unpublished studies (cf. Glass, McGaw, & Smith, 1981; Light & Pillemer, 1984), a phenomenon thought to be due to publication bias in favor of significant effects. Fourth, effect sizes will be larger in earlier than in more recently published studies. This followed from the theoretical expectation that the more egalitarian climate of recent times would be reflected in less sex-differentiated child-rearing strategies.

To answer the second question just presented, we calculated separate effect sizes for mothers and fathers, where possible, in addition to an overall effect size for parents combined. Thus, the differences between mothers and fathers in their differential treatment of the sexes are reported, and the magnitude of these differences was tested for significance. In view of the complexity of this meta-analysis, we did not attempt to analyze the contrast between same-sex effects (i.e., mother favoring daughter, father favoring son) and cross-sex effects (i.e., mother favoring son and so on). Nor did we analyze the differences between the associations of parental treatment with boys' and girls' characteristics, respectively (e.g., the correlations between parental restrictiveness and boys' vs. girls' independence). Although this is an important topic, it exceeded the scope of the present investigation.

Method

Literature search. We obtained items from Maccoby's (1966), Maccoby and Jacklin's (1974), and Block's (1978) references, as well as from other review articles and lists supplied by researchers in the field. The main sources of material were the computerized data bases of PsycINFO (1974 to early 1987), entered with the descriptors *parent–child relations* or *socialization* (or equivalents) and *human sex differences*, and *Dissertation Abstracts* (1980–1987). A supplementary manual search of *Psychological Abstracts* from 1973 to 1986 was also performed. We studied at least the abstracts, and often the full text, of about 1,250 articles. The criterion for including an item in the data base was that it examined the treatment of sons and daughters by mothers or fathers, or both, and that it contained quantitative data on the level of this treatment for sons versus daughters.

Through successive screening procedures, 172 studies were identified that contained usable quantitative information, which translates into a hit rate of about 14%. (Only 42 of about 100 studies on socialization practices, listed in Maccoby and Jacklin, 1974, contained sufficient quantitative data for a meta-analysis.) One hundred fifty-eight studies were from North America, and 17 from other Western countries, including Australia (some overlapped two continents). The studies spanned the years 1952 to 1987. Because many studies had data on more than one socialization area (see later discussion) there were 376 comparisons to be evaluated. The total number of subjects was 27,836, ranging from 11 to 3,750 per study.

Many studies, no doubt, exist that have investigated some other topic, but that in passing examined sex-related differential socialization, and then concluded with a bald statement such as "No significant differences due to sex of child were found." This information is insufficient for the calculation of an effect size. Many of the studies that we used for one or more socialization areas contained statements such as this for other socialization areas. We identified an additional 28 studies that only contained such a statement; they were not included in the data base proper, but were segregated for use in a secondary analysis (see later discussion). We probably missed many more such studies, but their inclusion would only have further diluted the effect sizes that we did find.

Classification of socialization variables in studies. Socialization was defined as parental treatment of and attitudes toward boys and girls. Perceptions were included only for the area of sex-typed characteristics. Our conceptual model posited that the differences in socialization pressures between boys and girls would vary in different domains, and we therefore adopted the principle that outcomes should be aggregated only when they represent the same construct (cf. Bangert-Drowns, 1986). Hence, we established separate categories for different socialization areas, considered as constructs, each of which was submitted to a separate meta-analysis. This was a major task, and some of the problems inherent in such a classification have already been discussed here. The socialization areas are listed in Table 1 and the decision rules for inclusion in the various socialization areas are shown in Appendix A.

We started from Maccoby and Jacklin's (1974, chapter 9) classification, but we changed their categorization when we thought a certain critique was justified, as in the case of achievement pressure, discussed earlier here. Our category system also accommodated itself to conceptualizations found in the literature (i.e., it was kept flexible, particularly in the early stages of this process). For instance, we added the category clarity communication/reasoning and later abandoned some categories, first established, when we did not find sufficient instances of them in the literature. Thus, responsiveness, first a separate category, was combined with warmth, nurturance for analysis purposes. A tentative category, permissiveness of sexual activity/talk, was later abandoned altogether.

By the nature of a meta-analysis, the categories had to be applicable to a number of studies, and therefore some novel measure or construct that appeared in only one or two studies could not be used, but most measures could be fitted to our category system.

We established eight major socialization areas for which meta-analyses were run and effects of moderator variables were tested. Some of these were broken down into subareas, and these, together with some smaller socialization areas, were submitted to meta-analytic runs but not to moderator analyses. The breakdown into smaller units was necessary to test the claim of critics (cf. Block, 1978) that lumping conceptually distinct behaviors into one broad category would obscure existing differences, and that significant effects might emerge in more nar-

270   HUGH LYTTON AND DAVID M. ROMNEY

Table 1
Socialization Areas

Number	Socialization area
10S	*Amount of interaction*
10	Interaction: undifferentiated
11	Verbal interaction
12	Stimulation of motor behavior
13	Joint play
20S	*Total achievement encouragement*
20	Achievement encouragement: general
21	Achievement encouragement in mathematics
30	*Warmth, nurturance, responsiveness (including praise)*
33	*Material reward*
40	*Encouragement of dependency*
50	*Restrictiveness/low encouragement of independence*
60S	*Disciplinary strictness*
60	Discipline: undifferentiated
61	Nonphysical disciplinary strictness, firm control
62	Physical punishment
70	*Discouragement of aggression*
80	*Encouragement of sex-typed activities, sex-typed perception*
82	Encouragement of sex-typed activities in boys more than in girls
100	*Clarity of communication/use of reasoning.*

Note. Socialization areas (major areas for which moderator analyses were performed) in italics. Indented socialization areas are subsidiary areas summed in the major area above them.

rowly defined areas. There also were reasons for expecting the subareas to show differential effects in different directions (e.g., slightly more verbal interaction for girls and more motor stimulation for boys [cf. Maccoby & Jacklin, 1974]). When several subareas occurred in the same study, the effect sizes were analyzed separately and also averaged for the major area.

To fit the diverse labels and measures for parental behavior that authors use to our categories, we used the authors' own categorization, as indicated by their interpretation of a variable, whenever possible. Thus, noncontingent help giving for young children was included in the category of encouragement of dependence, as the author (Rothbart, 1971) related it to dependence. The longer definition of a measure, often contained in an article, rather than the brief label in a table served as a guide for classification. However, consistency of classification was all important to ensure homogeneity of meaning for each category across studies. We also had to be sensitive to the differing contexts in which similarly labeled behavior occurred; thus, helping with school work, as opposed to the help giving for young children, noted previously, was classified as encouragement of achievement.

One difficult problem for classification was the measure for demands for help in the house or for orderliness, which we classified as restrictiveness in keeping with the intention of a number of authors as well as with Maccoby and Jacklin's (1974) classification, although we could understand the argument for counting this as encouragement of mature behavior. We performed a special trial analysis of the seven studies that contained this description of parental practice and found that the weighted mean difference was .06 (i.e., smaller than the effect size for restrictiveness and no different in direction). The measure was therefore kept in the restrictiveness category. However, demands for mature behavior at the toddler stage was categorized as encouragement of achievement because authors generally considered it as such.

Nine studies, comprising 22 comparisons, were categorized independently by each of the two authors, and we achieved 86% agreement on

these. The rest of the studies were categorized by the first author alone, but doubtful cases were decided by consultation.

There is bound to be some element of subjectivity in such classification decisions. The justification for this particular categorization system is that it is rational, based on an informed view of the literature, and mostly in keeping with authors' own categorizations. Other experts in the area will, no doubt, disagree with one or the other specific decision, but then their categorizations may also be disputed, because no universally agreed classification system of socialization practices exists. The basis for the decisions, at any rate, are in the public domain.

Coding study characteristics. We coded various aspects that characterized a given study and that could represent "moderator variables," which might explain variability in study outcomes. The following were coded whenever the information was available in the primary studies: social class or education level of parents, birth order, ethnicity, and age of children, but only age of children was used as a moderator variable. Data-collection method (see the scale later), source of study (journal, book, dissertation, and so on), year of publication, sex of first author, sample size, and number of boys and girls were also coded. Intercoder agreement ranged from 78% to 100% on these variables (median: of 89%).

Quality of the study was rated by us on the basis of our judgment of the internal validity of the study's procedures. The overall quality rating was the average of five subratings on a scale of 1 to 5:

1. Appropriateness of operationalization of constructs.
2. Carefulness of data collection (including reliability of measures).
3. Appropriateness of statistical analysis.
4. Degree of reporting of statistical information.
5. Soft–hard scale of data-collection method (from low to high): report by child, interview/questionnaire for parent, reaction to video/story, observation/experiment (counted as one level). The agreement on quality rating between the two coauthors, who rated nine studies independently, was 89%. Country of study was noted, and this determined which accumulation of studies the given study was assigned to, because we analyzed separately for North America and other Western countries. The characteristics of the sample of studies are shown in Table 2.

Statistical analysis. After reviewing several approaches to meta-analysis, we decided to adopt the one proposed by Hunter, Schmidt, and Jackson (1982) because this appears to take into account all sources of variance. This approach seeks to answer the question: What is the true or population effect of the independent variable? Statistics such as effect size d and effect strength r are averaged across studies to estimate the corresponding population parameters delta and rho. However, the effects found in different studies are, as we have seen, often inconsistent. Part if not all of the variability among studies will be unsystematic (i.e., because of a combination of sampling and measurement error). Once the error variance is removed from the variation among study effects, the variation remaining may be negligible. On the other hand, should the residual variation be relatively large, it would permit a search for moderator variables.

The effect size was d, the mean difference between boys' and girls' treatment divided by the pooled standard deviation. We adopted the working convention of considering a difference in the male direction as positive and a difference in the female direction as negative. When a study measured what could be considered the same socialization area by different methods, to avoid redundant effect sizes we either chose one set of measures as the one more closely resembling our categories or, when possible, we combined data from the two methods (e.g., an experiment and a home observation). When a construct was assessed by several measures within one study, the effect sizes were averaged to form a composite. Different statistics reported in the studies were converted to d following procedures developed by Hedges and Becker (1986) and Rosenthal (1984).

Table 2

Characteristics of Sample of Studies (N = 172)

Characteristic	No. of studies
Sample size	
≤50	70
51–150	60
>150	42
Parent sex	
Mother only	60
Father only	11
Both parents	101
Age of children	
0–5 years	95
6–12 years	44
13–adulthood	25
Not stated, mixed	11
Data-collection method	
Report by child	34
Interview/questionnaire for parent	56
Reaction to video/story	8
Observation/experiment	76
Source of study	
Published (journal, book)	140
Unpublished (dissertation, and so on)	32
Year of publication	
≤1973	42
1974–1980	59
>1980	71
Sex of first author	
Male	80
Female	92
Quality rating	
Low (2 and 3)	67
High (4 and 5)	105

The conceptualization and scoring of encouragement of sex-typed activities differed from those of the other socialization areas and need some comment. The question asked here was "To what extent do parents encourage conventionally sex-typed play or other activities in their children?" Hence, the effect size here is not simply the treatment of boys minus the treatment of girls, but it represents the extent of the difference parents make between boys and girls, each time in the stereotypical direction. For example, how much more do parents encourage boys than girls, say, to play with hammers and expect them to shovel the sidewalk, and how much more do they encourage girls than boys, say, to play with dolls and expect them to dust furniture? Each of these differences would be in the expected direction and therefore would be scored as positive.

In averaging several component effect sizes to form one composite for a socialization area in a given study, we encountered the following problem: Often a study provided statistics for one measure of a given socialization area (even if it was only $p < .05$) and proceeded to state for quite a number of other measures of the same socialization construct that they showed no significant difference for sex without giving any further statistic. If one simply ignores the nonsignificant measures and calculates an effect size from the (significant) statistic provided, one gives an inflated impression of the real sex difference found in this study. If, alternatively, one interprets the insufficient information as indicating precisely no sex difference and, therefore, counts a p value of .5 for each of these measures in the pooled effect size for this socialization area, one unduly minimizes the sex difference found. When the direction of the difference was reported in such cases, we used a compromise procedure that involved taking the average between the significant p value reported (typically .05) and a p value of .5 (i.e., a p

value of .275 for each such measure) and then including these p values in the averaged effect size for the given construct (E. S. Edgington, personal communication, April 1988). When no significant difference was reported for a socialization area as a whole, we used the procedure of assuming a p value of .5 (i.e., a difference of exactly zero) in a secondary analysis as others have done (cf. Eagly & Crowley, 1986).

Overall meta-analytic statistics (i.e., average effect size for each socialization area, variance, and error variance [cf. Hunter et al., 1982]), were calculated by an adaptation of Program K (Mullen & Rosenthal, 1985) on the Macintosh computer. The calculations of effect sizes and overall meta-analytic statistics were performed by a research assistant and were checked by both coauthors.

We weighted the average effect size by the sample sizes of the studies, because the frequency-weighted effect size yields a more accurate representation of the overall effect than the unweighted average (Hunter et al., 1982), provided sample size is uncorrelated with the magnitude of the effect. The correlation between these two variables across all socialization areas was −.03. To guard against the possibility of results being distorted by the excessive weight of some very large studies, we performed secondary analyses, omitting studies with very large sample sizes (see later discussion).

According to Hunter et al.'s (1982) guidelines, as adapted by Peters, Hartke, and Pohlmann (1985), if the sampling error variance alone is removed (which was the case in our study) and this sampling error does not exceed 60% of the total variance, it is appropriate to test whether certain moderator variables account for the variability in effect sizes. Because this figure was not exceeded for any of our major socialization areas, we tested the hypotheses regarding moderator variables by linear contrasts between groups (e.g., three separate age groups) by a procedure proposed by Rosenthal and Rubin (1982) by means of a program adapted from Mullen and Rosenthal (1985). We also tested for linear contrasts for quality, author sex, and sample size, because their influence on effect size is of interest. Correlations of moderator variables with effect sizes would have been misleading, because effects were positive when in the male direction and negative when in the female direction. A negative correlation between, say, age and effect size, therefore, could have several interpretations: It might mean that effect sizes in the male direction decrease over age, that effect sizes in the female direction become stronger over age, or else it might indicate a change in direction of effect size from male to female with increasing age. For this reason we did not correlate moderator variables with effect size, but instead report group means.

Results

Mean effect sizes. Table 3 shows the studies included in the sample. For each study, the socialization areas for which effect sizes could be computed, the sample size, and the study's characteristics are provided. The effect size (d) shown is the one for the highest level of aggregation for which it could be calculated (i.e., if data are reported for mother [or father] only, the effect size applies to mother [or father]). If the study reported data on both parents separately, we kept the data for mother and father separate for the overall meta-analytic calculations, but the effect size in Table 3 refers to the parents combined, and is based either on combined data reported in the study or on our averaging of data for mother and for father. Studies that dealt with our topic, but did not provide sufficient information for the computation of an effect size, are not included here. Bibliographical details for all studies, including the latter category, are shown in Appendix B.

(text continues on page 282)

Table 3
Effect Sizes by Study and Socialization Area

Study	N	Age (years)	Data-collection method	Sex of first author	Country	Parent[a]	d
			Interaction: undifferentiated				
Barnett, Howard, King, & Dino (1980)	72	6–12	Report by child	Male	No. America	PC	−.50
Barrett Fields (1981)	353	6–12	Report by child	Male	No. America	Mother	−.21
Bronfenbrenner (1961)	192	>12	Report by child	Male	No. America	PC	−.19
Easterbrooks & Goldberg (1984)	75	0–5	IQP	Female	No. America	Father	.42
Fagot (1974)	12	0–5	Observation, experiment	Female	No. America	PC	−1.71
Fagot (1978)	24	0–5	Observation, experiment	Female	No. America	PC	−1.32
Hanson (1975)	110	0–12	IQP	Male	No. America	PC	.13
Minton, Kagan, & Levine (1971)	90	0–5	Observation, experiment	Female	No. America	Mother	.45
Noller (1978)	87	0–5	Observation, experiment	Female	Other Western Country	PC	−.39
Power (1980)	24	0–5	Observation, experiment	Male	No. America	PC	−1.00
Radin (1974)	52	0–5	Observation, experiment	Female	No. America	Mother	−.16
Reinhardt (1985)	50	0–5	IQP	Female	No. America	PC	.87
Rothbarth (1971)	56	0–5	Observation, experiment	Female	No. America	Mother	−.35
Sacks (1981)	32	0–5	Observation, experiment	Female	No. America	PC	.51
Siegelman (1965)	212	6–12	Report by child	Male	No. America	PC	.12
Smart & Smart (1976)	269	6–12	Report by child	Male	Other Western country	PC	−.08
Stinnett, Farris, & Walters (1974)	499	>12	Report by child	Male	No. America	Mother	−.11
Tasch (1952)	160	NSM	IQP	Female	No. America	Father	−.18
Weinstein & Geisel (1960)	410	NSM	IQP	Male	No. America	Mother	−.18
Yarrow et al. (1984)	68	0–5	Observation, experiment	Male	No. America	PC	−.03
Yarrow, Rubenstein, & Pederson (1975)	41	0–5	Observation, experiment	Male	No. America	Mother	.76
			Verbal interaction				
Arco, DeMeis, Self, & Guttrecht (1984)	48	0–5	Observation, experiment	Female	No. America	Mother	.25
Barnes (1986)	16	0–5	Observation, experiment	Female	No. America	PC	1.40
Baumrind (1988)	164	6–12	Observation, experiment	Female	No. America	PC	−.20
Brown et al. (1975)	45	0–5	Observation, experiment	Male	No. America	Mother	.80
Cherry & Lewis (1976)	12	0–5	Observation, experiment	Female	No. America	Mother	−1.26
Cicirelli (1978)	80	6–12	Observation, experiment	Male	No. America	Mother	.54
Clevenger Bright & Stockdale (1984)	29	0–5	Observation, experiment	Female	No. America	PC	.00
Dolins (1980)	40	0–5	Observation, experiment	Female	No. America	Mother	.48
Fried Weitzman (1983)	40	0–5	Observation, experiment	Female	No. America	Mother	.75
Gaines (1981)	16	0–5	Observation, experiment	Female	No. America	Father	−.15
Goldberg & Lewis (1969)	64	0–5	Observation, experiment	Female	No. America	Mother	−.90
Halverson & Waldrop (1970)	42	0–5	Observation, experiment	Male	No. America	Mother	−1.18
Hanson (1975)	110	0–12	IQP	Male	No. America	PC	.09
Kuczynski (1984)	64	0–5	Observation, experiment	Male	No. America	Mother	.61

Table 3 (*continued*)

Study	N	Age (years)	Data-collection method	Sex of first author	Country	Parent[a]	d
			Verbal interaction (*continued*)				
Lamb (1977)	20	0–5	Observation, experiment	Male	No. America	PC	.60
Landerholm (1984)	17	0–5	Observation, experiment	Female	No. America	Mother	−.35
Landerholm & Scriven (1981)	22	0–5	Observation, experiment	Female	No. America	PC	.53
Lewis (1972)	32	0–5	Observation, experiment	Male	No. America	Mother	−.74
Lewis & Cherry (1977)	12	0–5	Observation, experiment	Male	No. America	Mother	−1.61
Michnick Golinkoff & Johnson Ames (1979)	12	0–5	Observation, experiment	Female	No. America	PC	.98
Moss (1967)	25	0–5	Observation, experiment	Male	No. America	Mother	−.73
Moss (1974)	44	0–5	Observation, experiment	Male	No. America	PC	−.52
Palkovitz (1984)	40	0–5	Observation, experiment	Male	No. America	Father	−.66
Pepi (1981)	20	0–5	Observation, experiment	Female	No. America	PC	.59
Rosenthal (1983)	63	0–5	Observation, experiment	Female	Other Western country	Mother	−.28
Schaffer & Crook (1980)	24	0–5	Observation, experiment	Male	Other Western country	Mother	−1.48
Stoneman & Brody (1981)	18	0–5	Observation, experiment	Female	No. America	PC	−.65
Thoman, Leiderman, & Olson (1972)	40	0–5	Observation, experiment	Female	No. America	Mother	−.74
Wasserman & Lewis (1985)	60	0–5	Observation, experiment	Female	No. America	Mother	−.50
Weinraub & Lewis (1977)	50	0–5	Observation, experiment	Female	No. America	Mother	−.18
Weston (1982)	41	0–5	Observation, experiment	Female	No. America	PC	−.68
Wolkin (1983)	23	0–5	Observation, experiment	Female	No. America	Mother	.53
			Stimulation of motor behavior				
Arco et al. (1984)	48	0–5	Observation, experiment	Female	No. America	Mother	−.41
Brown et al. (1975)	45	0–5	Observation, experiment	Male	No. America	Mother	.84
Goldberg & Lewis (1969)	64	0–5	Observation, experiment	Female	No. America	Mother	−.51
Landerholm (1984)	17	0–5	Observation, experiment	Female	No. America	Mother	.12
Landerholm & Scriven (1981)	22	0–5	Observation, experiment	Female	No. America	PC	.77
Lewis (1972)	32	0–5	Observation, experiment	Male	No. America	Mother	.47
Ling & Ling (1974)	48	0–5	Observation, experiment	Male	No. America	Mother	1.44
Maccoby, Snow, & Jacklin (1984)	57	0–5	Observation, experiment	Female	No. America	Mother	.54
Moss (1967)	25	0–5	Observation, experiment	Male	No. America	Mother	.65
Pepi (1981)	20	0–5	Observation, experiment	Female	No. America	PC	.58
Smith & Lloyd (1978)	32	0–5	Observation, experiment	Female	Other Western country	Mother	1.14
Thoman et al. (1972)	40	0–5	Observation, experiment	Female	No. America	Mother	−.26

(*table continues*)

Table 3 (*continued*)

Study	N	Age (years)	Data-collection method	Sex of first author	Country	Parent[a]	d
			Joint play				
Clevenger Bright & Stockdale (1984)	29	0–5	Observation, experiment	Female	No. America	PC	.30
Fagot (1974)	12	0–5	Observation, experiment	Female	No. America	PC	.94
Fagot (1978)	24	0–5	Observation, experiment	Female	No. America	PC	.94
Fried Weitzman (1983)	40	0–5	Observation, experiment	Female	No. America	Mother	−.52
Kotelchuck (1976)	144	0–5	IQP	Male	No. America	Father	.44
Landerholm (1984)	17	0–5	Observation, experiment	Female	No. America	Mother	−.43
Landerholm & Scriven (1981)	22	0–5	Observation, experiment	Female	No. America	PC	−1.11
Lewis (1972)	32	0–5	Observation, experiment	Male	No. America	Mother	−.08
MacDonald & Parke (1986)	700	NSM	IQP	Male	No. America	PC	−.02
Pepi (1981)	20	0–5	Observation, experiment	Female	No. America	PC	−.98
Rendina & Dickerscheid (1976)	40	0–5	Observation, experiment	Female	No. America	Father	.57
Tauber (1979)	145	6–12	Observation, experiment	Female	No. America	PC	−.01
Tudiver (1980)	24	0–5	Observation, experiment	Female	No. America	PC	−.56
Weinraub & Lewis (1977)	50	0–5	Observation, experiment	Female	No. America	Mother	.10
			Achievement encouragement: general				
Anderson & Evans (1976)	102	>12	Report by child	Male	No. America	PC	.20
Block (1978)	569	0–>12	IQP	Female	No. America	PC	.15
Block (1978)	128	6–12	IQP	Female	Other Western country	PC	.12
Block, Block, & Harrington (1974)	117	0–5	Observation, experiment	Female	No. America	PC	.18
Bronfenbrenner (1961)	192	>12	Report by child	Male	No. America	PC	.38
Brook, Whiteman, Lukoff, & Scorell Gordon (1979)	175	>12	IQP	Female	No. America	Mother	.33
Buck & Austrin (1971)	100	>12	IQP	Female	No. America	Mother	.15
Hanson (1975)	110	0–12	IQP	Male	No. America	PC	.06
Hatfield, Ferguson, & Alpert (1967)	40	0–5	Observation, experiment	Male	No. America	Mother	.06
Kavanagh (1986)	82	0–5	IQP	Female	No. America	PC	−.13
Kelly & Worell (1976)	481	>12	Report by child	Male	No. America	PC	−.06
Lynn & Sawrey (1962)	76	6–12	IQP	Male	Other Western country	Mother	.46
Marcus & Corsini (1978)	40	0–5	IQP	Male	No. America	PC	−.27
Mirkin Schwartz (1982)	92	0–5	IQP	Female	No. America	Mother	.32
Raymond & Persson Benbow (1986)	411	>12	Report by child	Female	No. America	PC	−.06
Rothbart (1971)	56	0–5	Observation, experiment	Female	No. America	Mother	−.19
Russell (1983)	2,689	>12	Report by child	Female	No. America	PC	−.11
Russell (1983)	877	>12	Report by child	Female	Other Western country	PC	−.52
Sears, Maccoby, & Levin (1957)	379	0–5	IQP	Male	No. America	Mother	.19
Siegelman (1965)	212	6–12	Report by child	Male	No. America	PC	.11
Smart & Smart (1976)	269	6–12	Report by child	Male	Other Western country	PC	.08
Spitalnik (1981)	27	0–5	IQP	Female	No. America	PC	−.24
Tasch (1952)	160	NSM	IQP	Female	No. America	Father	.11
Tudiver (1980)	24	0–5	Observation, experiment	Female	No. America	PC	.43

Table 3 (*continued*)

Study	N	Age (years)	Data-collection method	Sex of first author	Country	Parent[a]	d
Achievement encouragement in math							
Parsons Eccles, Adler, & Kaczala (1982)	1,108	>12	IQP	Female	No. America	PC	.08
Raymond & Persson Benbow (1986)	411	>12	Report by child	Female	No. America	PC	.00
Schneider (1984)	225	>12	IQP	Female	No. America	PC	−.12
Warmth, nurturance, responsiveness							
Armentrout (1975)	126	>12	Report by child	Male	No. America	PC	−.02
Armentrout & Burger (1972)	635	6–12	Report by child	Male	No. America	PC	−.19
Barnes (1986)	16	0–5	Observation, experiment	Female	No. America	PC	−1.80
Barnett et al. (1980)	72	6–12	Report by child	Male	No. America	PC	−.56
Baumrind (1971)	149	0–5	Observation, experiment	Female	No. America	PC	−.08
Baumrind (1988)	164	6–12	Observation, experiment	Female	No. America	PC	−.14
Bledsoe & Wiggins (1974)	100	NSM	Report by child	Male	No. America	PC	−.41
Block (1978)	569	0–>12	IQP	Female	No. America	PC	−.07
Block (1978)	128	6–12	IQP	Female	Other Western country	PC	.07
Breckenridge (1982)	181	0–5	Observation, experiment	Male	No. America	Mother	−.25
Bronfenbrenner (1961)	192	>12	Report by child	Male	No. America	PC	−.15
Buriel (1981)	112	6–12	Report by child	Male	No. America	PC	.07
Burke & Weir (1978)	274	>12	Report by child	Male	No. America	PC	−.03
Burton, Maccoby, & Allinsmith (1961)	77	0–5	IQP	Male	No. America	Mother	−.26
Carlson (1963)	43	6–12	IQP	Male	No. America	PC	.44
Clevenger Bright & Stockdale (1984)	29	0–5	Observation, experiment	Female	No. America	PC	.02
Clingempeel, Levoli, & Brand (1984)	32	6–12	IQP	Male	No. America	PC	.34
Corter & Bow (1976)	24	0–5	Observation, experiment	Male	No. America	Mother	.93
Droppleman & Schaefer (1963)	165	>12	Report by child	Male	No. America	PC	−.21
Elder, Nguyen, & Caspi (1985)	121	6–12	IQP	Male	No. America	Father	.30
Emmerich (1962)	225	6–12	IQP	Male	No. America	PC	−.23
Fagot (1974)	12	0–5	Observation, experiment	Female	No. America	PC	−.27
Fagot (1978)	24	0–5	Observation, experiment	Female	No. America	PC	−.08
Falender & Heber (1975)	30	0–5	Observation, experiment	Female	No. America	Mother	−.20
Frankel & Rollins (1983)	36	6–12	Observation, experiment	Male	No. America	PC	.27
Gaines (1981)	16	0–5	Observation, experiment	Female	No. America	Father	−.27
Gill & Spilka (1962)	60	>12	IQP	Female	No. America	Mother	.20
Gjerde (1986)	44	>12	Observation, experiment	Male	No. America	Father	−.66
Gordon (1983)	74	0–5	Observation, experiment	Female	No. America	Mother	.76
Hanson Moore (1984)	257	0–5	IQP	Female	No. America	PC	−.07
Hunter & Youniss (1982)	120	NSM	Report by child	Male	No. America	PC	.24
Jeyaraj (1982)	72	NSM	Report by child	Male	No. America	PC	−.30
Johnson (1981)	24	0–5	Observation, experiment	Male	No. America	PC	−.18
Kavanagh (1986)	82	0–5	IQP	Female	No. America	PC	.29
Kelly & Worell (1976)	481	>12	Report by child	Male	No. America	Mother	.10
Kroger (1983)	123	>12	Report by child	Female	Other Western country	PC	−.07

(*table continues*)

276   HUGH LYTTON AND DAVID M. ROMNEY

Table 3 *(continued)*

Study	N	Age (years)	Data-collection method	Sex of first author	Country	Parent[a]	d
			Warmth, nurturance, responsiveness *(continued)*				
Landerholm (1984)	17	0–5	Observation, experiment	Female	No. America	Mother	.64
Landerholm & Scriven (1981)	22	0–5	Observation, experiment	Female	No. America	PC	.43
Last & Klein (1984)	76	>12	Report by child	Male	Other Western country	PC	−.25
Lawson & Fitzgerald Slaughter (1977)	480	NSM	Report by child	Female	No. America	PC	.00
Lefkowitz (1962)	616	6–12	IQP	Male	No. America	PC	.05
Lewis (1972)	32	0–5	Observation, experiment	Male	No. America	Mother	.34
Maccoby & Jacklin (1987)	73	6–12	Observation, experiment	Female	No. America	PC	.09
Maccoby et al. (1984)	57	0–5	Observation, experiment	Female	No. America	Mother	−.45
MacDonald & Parke (1986)	700	NSM	IQP	Male	No. America	PC	−.15
Margolin & Patterson (1975)	28	6–12	Observation, experiment	Female	No. America	PC	.84
Moss (1967)	25	0–5	Observation, experiment	Male	No. America	Mother	.12
Moss (1974)	44	0–5	Observation, experiment	Male	No. America	PC	−.76
Mussen & Rutherford (1963)	103	6–12	Report by child	Male	No. America	PC	.11
Newson & Newson (1976)	697	6–12	IQP	Male	Other Western country	Mother	−.09
Noller (1978)	87	0–5	Observation, experiment	Female	Other Western country	PC	−.13
Paivio (1964)	294	6–12	IQP	Male	No. America	PC	−.14
Pepi (1981)	20	0–5	Observation, experiment	Female	No. America	PC	−.15
Peters & Stewart (1981)	253	0–5	Observation, experiment	Male	No. America	Father	−.31
Radin (1974)	52	0–5	Observation, experiment	Female	No. America	Mother	−.47
Ribas (1982)	32	6–12	Report by child	Male	No. America	PC	.26
Robin (1982)	42	0–5	Observation, experiment	Female	Other Western country	Mother	−.96
Rosenthal (1983)	63	0–5	Observation, experiment	Female	Other Western country	Mother	−.12
Rothbart (1971)	56	0–5	Observation, experiment	Female	No. America	Mother	.01
Schaefer (1980)	72	6–12	IQP	Female	No. America	Mother	−.16
Sears et al. (1957)	379	0–5	IQP	Male	No. America	Mother	−.06
Sears, Whiting, Nowlis, & Sears (1953)	40	0–5	IQP	Male	No. America	Mother	.31
Sheehan (1982)	95	6–12	Observation, experiment	Female	No. America	PC	−.02
Siegelman (1965)	212	6–12	Report by child	Male	No. America	PC	.07
Smart & Smart (1976)	269	6–12	Report by child	Male	Other Western country	PC	−.24
Stayton, Hogan, & Ainsworth (1971)	25	0–5	Observation, experiment	Female	No. America	Mother	.40
Stinnett et al. (1974)	499	>12	Report by child	Male	No. America	PC	−.10
Tudiver (1980)	24	0–5	Observation, experiment	Female	No. America	PC	−.08
Wasserman & Lewis (1985)	60	0–5	Observation, experiment	Female	No. America	Mother	.13
Will, Self, & Datan (1976)	11	0–5	Observation, experiment	Female	No. America	Mother	−.84
Wyer (1965)	827	>12	IQP	Male	No. America	PC	−.12

Table 3 (*continued*)

Study	N	Age (years)	Data-collection method	Sex of first author	Country	Parent[a]	d
			Material reward				
Flynn (1979)	62	0–5	IQP	Male	No. America	PC	−.49
Hanson Moore (1984)	257	0–5	IQP	Female	No. America	PC	−.08
Poag Longeway (1983)	40	6–12	Observation, experiment	Female	No. America	Mother	−.52
			Encouragement of dependency				
Antell (1982)	48	6–12	Observation, experiment	Female	No. America	PC	−.91
Barrett Fields (1981)	353	6–12	Report by child	Male	No. America	Mother	−.28
Baumrind (1971)	149	0–5	Observation, experiment	Female	No. America	PC	−.17
Block (1978)	569	0–>12	IQP	Female	No. America	PC	−.06
Block (1978)	128	6–12	IQP	Female	Other Western country	PC	−.07
Buriel (1981)	112	6–12	Report by child	Male	No. America	PC	.01
Droppleman & Schaefer (1963)	165	>12	Report by child	Male	No. America	PC	−.10
Fagot (1978)	24	0–5	Observation, experiment	Female	No. America	PC	−.55
Gill & Spilka (1962)	60	>12	IQP	Female	No. America	Mother	−.21
Goshen-Gottstein (1981)	22	0–5	Observation, experiment	Female	Other Western country	Mother	.92
Hatfield et al. (1967)	40	0–5	Observation, experiment	Male	No. America	Mother	−.09
Kagan & Freeman (1963)	50	NSM	Observation, experiment	Male	No. America	Mother	.59
Kavanagh (1986)	82	0–5	IQP	Female	No. America	PC	.00
Kroger (1983)	123	>12	Report by child	Female	Other Western country	PC	−.25
Lambert, Yackley, & Hein (1971)	73	6–12	RVS	Male	No. America	PC	−.23
Last & Klein (1984)	76	>12	Report by child	Male	Other Western country	PC	−.36
Rothbart (1971)	56	0–5	Observation, experiment	Female	No. America	Mother	−.66
Rothbart & Maccoby (1966)	130	0–5	RVS	Female	No. America	PC	.27
Sears et al. (1957)	379	0–5	IQP	Male	No. America	Mother	−.08
Siegelman (1965)	212	6–12	Report by child	Male	No. America	PC	.15
			Restrictiveness/low encouragement of independence				
Anderson & Evans (1976)	102	>12	Report by child	Male	No. America	PC	.67
Armentrout (1975)	126	>12	Report by child	Male	No. America	PC	.06
Armentrout & Burger (1972)	635	6–12	Report by child	Male	No. America	PC	.30
Baumrind (1971)	149	0–5	Observation, experiment	Female	No. America	PC	.23
Baumrind (1988)	164	6–12	Observation, experiment	Female	No. America	PC	.07
Bee, Mitchell, Barnard, Eyres, & Hammond (1984)	169	0–5	IQP	Female	No. America	Mother	.04
Block (1978)	569	0–>12	IQP	Female	No. America	PC	−.04
Block (1978)	128	6–12	IQP	Female	Other Western country	PC	−.04
Buriel (1981)	112	6–12	Report by child	Male	No. America	PC	.22
Burton et al. (1961)	77	0–5	IQP	Male	No. America	Mother	−.29
Clevenger Bright & Stockdale (1984)	29	0–5	Observation, experiment	Female	No. America	PC	.39
Dean Callard (1968)	80	0–5	IQP	Female	No. America	Mother	.82
Devereux, Bronfenbrenner, & Suci (1963)	72	6–12	Report by child	Male	No. America	PC	.22

(*table continues*)

Table 3 *(continued)*

Study	N	Age (years)	Data-collection method	Sex of first author	Country	Parent[a]	d
	Restrictiveness/low encouragement of independence *(continued)*
Devereux et al. (1963)	72	6–12	Report by child	Male	Other Western country	PC	−.22
Droppleman & Schaefer (1963)	165	>12	Report by child	Male	No. America	PC	.14
Fagot (1978)	24	0–5	Observation, experiment	Female	No. America	PC	.79
Frankel & Rollins (1983)	36	6–12	Observation, experiment	Male	No. America	PC	.45
Goshen-Gottstein (1981)	22	0–5	Observation, experiment	Female	Other Western country	Mother	−1.04
Hanson (1975)	110	0–12	IQP	Male	No. America	PC	−.10
Hatfield et al. (1967)	40	0–5	Observation, experiment	Male	No. America	Mother	.04
Hawkes, Burchinal, & Gardner (1957)	256	6–12	Report by child	Male	No. America	PC	−.21
Johnson (1981)	24	0–5	Observation, experiment	Male	No. America	PC	.10
Jurich, Bollman, & Moxley (1976)	39	>12	Report by child, IQP	Male	No. America	PC	−.86
Kagan & Freeman (1963)	50	NSM	Observation, experiment	Male	No. America	Mother	.59
Kavanagh (1986)	82	0–5	IQP	Female	No. America	PC	.09
Kell & Aldous (1960)	50	>12	Report by child	Female	No. America	Mother	−.41
Kroger (1983)	123	>12	Report by child	Female	Other Western country	PC	.06
Kronsberg, Schmaling, & Fagot (1985)	63	0–5	RVS	Female	No. America	PC	.19
Last & Klein (1984)	76	>12	Report by child	Male	Other Western country	PC	−.02
Maccoby & Jacklin (1987)	73	6–12	Observation, experiment	Female	No. America	PC	.09
Minton et al. (1971)	90	0–5	Observation, experiment	Female	No. America	Mother	.17
Newson & Newson (1976)	697	6–12	IQP	Male	Other Western country	Mother	−.16
Power (1980)	24	0–5	Observation, experiment	Male	No. America	PC	−.43
Radin (1974)	52	0–5	Observation, experiment	Female	No. America	Mother	.59
Ribas (1982)	32	6–12	Report by child	Male	No. America	PC	−.34
Rothbart & Maccoby (1966)	130	0–5	RVS	Female	No. America	PC	−.22
Russell (1983)	2,689	>12	Report by child	Female	No. America	PC	.09
Russell (1983)	877	>12	Report by child	Female	Other Western country	PC	.01
Schab (1982)	751	>12	Report by child	Male	No. America	PC	.04
Schaffer & Crook (1980)	24	0–5	Observation, experiment	Male	Other Western country	Mother	−1.15
Sears et al. (1953)	40	0–5	IQP	Male	No. America	Mother	−.41
Sears et al. (1957)	379	0–5	IQP	Male	No. America	Mother	.00
Sheehan (1982)	95	6–12	Observation, experiment	Female	No. America	PC	−.09
Siegelman (1965)	212	6–12	Report by child	Male	No. America	PC	.08
Smart & Smart (1976)	269	6–12	Report by child	Male	Other Western country	PC	.21
Spitalnik (1981)	27	0–5	IQP	Female	No. America	PC	.02
Stayton et al. (1971)	25	0–5	Observation, experiment	Female	No. America	Mother	−.06
Tasch (1952)	160	NSM	IQP	Female	No. America	Father	.08
Tudiver (1980)	24	0–5	Observation, experiment	Female	No. America	PC	.13
Whyte (1983)	284	6–12	Report by child	Female	Other Western country	PC	.21

Table 3 (*continued*)

Study	N	Age (years)	Data-collection method	Sex of first author	Country	Parent[a]	d
			Discipline: undifferentiated				
Block (1978)	569	0->12	IQP	Female	No. America	PC	.08
Block (1978)	128	6–12	IQP	Female	Other Western country	PC	.05
Buriel (1981)	112	6–12	Report by child	Male	No. America	PC	.43
Paivio (1964)	294	6–12	IQP	Male	No. America	PC	−.13
Roberts (1983)	30	0–5	Observation, experiment	Male	No. America	PC	.69
Sears et al. (1953)	40	0–5	IQP	Male	No. America	Mother	.06
			Nonphysical disciplinary strictness				
Adams & LaVoie (1975)	197	6–12	RVS	Male	No. America	PC	−.29
Armentrout & Burger (1972)	635	6–12	Report by child	Male	No. America	PC	−.01
Armentrout (1975)	126	>12	Report by child	Male	No. America	PC	−.18
Bartz & Levine (1978)	80	6–12	IQP	Female	No. America	PC	.54
Baumrind (1971)	149	0–5	Observation, experiment	Female	No. America	PC	.35
Block (1978)	569	0->12	IQP	Female	No. America	PC	.11
Block (1978)	128	6–12	IQP	Female	Other Western country	PC	.27
Britain & Abad (1974)	72	>12	Report by child	Female	No. America	PC	−.77
Burton et al. (1961)	77	0–5	IQP	Male	No. America	Mother	−.05
Devereux et al. (1963)	72	6–12	Report by child	Male	No. America	PC	.26
Devereux et al. (1963)	72	6–12	Report by child	Male	Other Western country	PC	.41
Domash & Balter (1976)	92	0–5	IQP	Female	No. America	Mother	.18
Droppleman & Schaefer (1963)	165	>12	Report by child	Male	No. America	PC	.36
Flynn (1979)	62	0–5	IQP	Male	No. America	PC	−.58
Hanson Moore (1984)	257	0–5	IQP	Female	No. America	PC	−.04
Hunter (1984)	180	>12	Report by child	Male	No. America	PC	.31
Jasper Crase. Foss. & Karal Colbert (1981)	172	6–12	Report by child	Female	No. America	PC	.28
Jurich, Bollman, & Moxley (1976)	39	>12	Report by child. IQP	Male	No. America	PC	−1.19
Kagan & Freeman (1963)	50	NSM	Observation, experiment	Male	No. America	Mother	.59
Kavanagh (1986)	82	0–5	IQP	Female	No. America	PC	−.08
Kohn (1959)	313	6–12	IQP	Male	No. America	Mother	.06
Kroger (1983)	123	>12	Report by child	Female	Other Western country	PC	.16
Kuczynski (1984)	64	0–5	Observation, experiment	Male	No. America	Mother	.54
Lambert et al. (1971)	73	6–12	RVS	Male	No. America	PC	.32
Last & Klein (1984)	76	>12	Report by child	Male	Other Western country	PC	−.54
Lawson & Fitzgerald Slaughter (1977)	480	NSM	Report by child	Female	No. America	PC	−.14
Levy-Shiff (1982)	179	0–5	IQP	Female	Other Western country	Mother	−.30
McLaughlin, Schutz, & White (1980)	24	0–5	Observation, experiment	Male	No. America	PC	.43
Mussen & Rutherford (1963)	103	6–12	Report by child	Male	No. America	PC	−1.89
Newson & Newson (1976)	697	6–12	IQP	Male	Other Western country	Mother	−.05
Poag Longeway (1983)	40	6–12	Observation, experiment	Female	No. America	Mother	.27
Ribas (1982)	32	6–12	Report by child	Male	No. America	PC	.32
Schaefer (1980)	72	6–12	IQP	Female	No. America	Mother	.41
Sears et al. (1957)	379	0–5	IQP	Male	No. America	Mother	−.08
Siegelman (1965)	212	6–12	Report by child	Male	No. America	PC	.14
Smart & Smart (1976)	269	6–12	Report by child	Male	Other Western country	PC	−.40

(*table continues*)

280 HUGH LYTTON AND DAVID M. ROMNEY

Table 3 (*continued*)

Study	N	Age (years)	Data-collection method	Sex of first author	Country	Parent[a]	d
			Nonphysical disciplinary strictness (*continued*)				
Smith & Daglish (1977)	32	0–5	Observation, experiment	Male	Other Western country	PC	.77
Snow et al. (1983)	107	0–5	Observation, experiment	Female	No. America	Father	.68
Stayton et al. (1971)	25	0–5	Observation, experiment	Female	No. America	Mother	.28
Weinstein & Geisel (1960)	410	NSM	IQP	Male	No. America	Mother	.31
Zussman (1978)	44	6–12	IQP	Male	No. America	Mother	.62
			Physical punishment				
Block (1978)	569	0–>12	IQP	Female	No. America	PC	.07
Block (1978)	128	6–12	IQP	Female	Other Western country	PC	.19
Bronfenbrenner (1961)	192	>12	Report by child	Male	No. America	PC	.24
Burton et al. (1961)	77	0–5	IQP	Male	No. America	Mother	.37
Devereux et al. (1963)	72	6–12	Report by child	Male	No. America	PC	.01
Devereux et al. (1963)	72	6–12	Report by child	Male	Other Western country	PC	.34
Falender & Heber (1975)	30	0–5	Observation, experiment	Female	No. America	Mother	.60
Gordon (1983)	74	0–5	Observation, experiment	Female	No. America	Mother	.51
Hanson Moore (1984)	257	0–5	IQP	Female	No. America	PC	.03
Jeyaraj (1982)	72	NSM	Report by child	Male	No. America	PC	.72
Jurich et al. (1976)	39	>12	Report by child, IQP	Male	No. America	PC	.40
Kavanagh (1986)	82	0–5	IQP	Female	No. America	PC	−.09
Kohn (1959)	313	6–12	IQP	Male	No. America	PC	.05
Minton et al. (1971)	90	0–5	Observation, experiment	Female	No. America	Mother	.37
Newson & Newson (1976)	697	6–12	IQP	Male	Other Western country	Mother	.37
Sears et al. (1957)	379	0–5	IQP	Male	No. America	Mother	.22
Siegelman (1965)	212	6–12	Report by child	Male	No. America	PC	.42
Smart & Smart (1976)	269	6–12	Report by child	Male	Other Western country	PC	.45
Weinstein & Geisel (1960)	410	NSM	IQP	Male	No. America	Mother	.14
			Discouragement of aggression				
Block (1978)	569	0–>12	IQP	Female	No. America	PC	−.07
Block (1978)	128	6–12	IQP	Female	Other Western country	PC	.00
Droppleman & Schaefer (1963)	165	>12	Report by child	Male	No. America	PC	−.21
Eron, Walder, Toigo, & Lefkowitz (1963)	451	6–12	IQP	Male	No. America	PC	.07
Gates (1982)	79	6–12	RVS	Male	No. America	PC	−.99
Kavanagh (1986)	82	0–5	IQP	Female	No. America	PC	−.11
Rothbart & Maccoby (1966)	130	0–5	RVS	Female	No. America	PC	.13
Sears et al. (1957)	379	0–5	IQP	Male	No. America	Mother	−.15
Sears et al. (1953)	40	0–5	IQP	Male	No. America	Mother	.18
Stern (1984)	60	0–5	RVS	Female	No. America	PC	−2.05
Wenger, Berg-Cross, & Berg-Cross (1980)	160	NSM	RVS	Female	No. America	PC	.02
			Encouragement of sex-typed activities, sex-typed perception				
Atkinson & Endsley (1976)	40	0–5	IQP	Female	No. America	PC	.60
Bell & Carver (1980)	30	0–5	IQP	Female	No. America	Mother	.06
Birnbaum & Croll (1984)	58	0–5	IQP	Female	No. America	PC	1.23
Boyce Fauls & Smith (1956)	38	0–5	Report by child	Female	No. America	PC	.93

Table 3 (*continued*)

Study	N	Age (years)	Data-collection method	Sex of first author	Country	Parent[a]	d
			Encouragement of sex-typed activities, sex-typed perception (*continued*)				
Costos (1986)	120	NSM	Report by child	Male	No. America	PC	.35
Dino, Barnett, & Howard (1984)	76	6–12	Report by child	Male	No. America	PC	.32
Duncan, Schuman, & Duncan (1973)	1,880	>12	IQP	Male	No. America	Mother	.34
Eisenberg, Wolchik, Hernandez, & Pasternack (1985)	20	0–5	Observation, experiment	Female	No. America	PC	.68
Fagot (1978)	24	0–5	Observation, experiment	Female	No. America	PC	.81
Fried Weitzman (1983)	40	0–5	Observation, experiment	Female	No. America	Mother	.44
Gendler (1984)	200	6–12	IQP	Female	No. America	PC	.28
Jacklin, DiPietro, & Maccoby (1984)	54	0–5	Observation, experiment	Female	No. America	PC	.79
Langlois & Downs (1980)	96	0–5	Observation, experiment	Female	No. America	PC	.38
Mirkin Schwartz (1982)	92	0–5	IQP	Female	No. America	Mother	1.37
Reinhardt (1985)	50	0–5	IQP	Female	No. America	PC	.40
Rheingold & Cook (1975)	96	0–5	IQP	Female	No. America	PC	.71
Rubin, Provenzang, & Luvin (1974)	30	0–5	IQP	Male	No. America	PC	.56
Smith & Lloyd (1978)	32	0–5	Observation, experiment	Female	Other Western country	Mother	.78
Snow et al. (1983)	107	0–5	Observation, experiment	Female	No. America	Father	.44
Will et al. (1976)	11	0–5	Observation, experiment	Female	No. America	Mother	1.12
Wiltshire Goodenough (1957)	40	0–5	IQP	Female	No. America	PC	.89
			Encouragement of sex-typed activities in boys more than girls				
Block (1978)	569	0–>12	IQP	Female	No. America	PC	.01
Block (1978)	128	6–12	IQP	Female	Other Western country	PC	−.16
Domash & Balter (1976)	92	0–5	IQP	Female	No. America	Mother	.26
Fling & Manosevitz (1972)	29	0–5	IQP	Female	No. America	PC	1.02
Hanson (1975)	110	0–12	IQP	Male	No. America	PC	.01
Katz & Boswell (1986)	134	NSM	IQP	Female	No. America	PC	.46
Lambert et al. (1971)	73	6–12	RVS	Male	No. America	PC	.23
Lansky (1967)	98	0–5	IQP	Male	No. America	PC	.60
Power (1980)	24	0–5	Observation, experiment	Male	No. America	PC	1.08
			Clarity of communication/use of reasoning				
Baumrind (1971)	149	0–5	Observation, experiment	Female	No. America	PC	−.03
Bearison (1979)	65	6–12	IQP	Male	No. America	PC	.28
Block (1978)	569	0–>12	IQP	Female	No. America	PC	−.10
Block (1978)	128	6–12	IQP	Female	Other Western country	PC	.00
Burton et al. (1961)	77	0–5	IQP	Male	No. America	Mother	.25
Flake-Hobson, Robinson, & Skeen (1981)	76	0–5	IQP	Female	No. America	PC	−.38
Grusec, Dix, & Mills (1982)	20	6–12	RVS	Female	No. America	Mother	−.29
Hanson Moore (1984)	257	0–5	IQP	Female	No. America	PC	−.05
Hoppe et al. (1977)	32	6–12	Observation, experiment	Female	No. America	Mother	.93
Minton et al. (1971)	90	0–5	Observation, experiment	Female	No. America	Mother	−.12

(*table continues*)

Table 3 *(continued)*

Study	N	Age (years)	Data-collection method	Sex of first author	Country	Parent[a]	d
			Clarity of communication/use of reasoning *(continued)*				
Schab (1982)	751	>12	Report by child	Male	No. America	PC	−.09
Siegelman (1965)	212	6–12	Report by child	Male	No. America	PC	.24
Smart & Smart (1976)	269	6–12	Report by child	Male	Other Western country	PC	−.08
Tudiver (1980)	24	0–5	Observation, experiment	Female	No. America	PC	−.20
Zussman (1978)	44	6–12	IQP	Male	No. America	Mother	−.64

Note. Bibliographical details of studies are listed in Appendix B.   IQP = interview/questionnaire for parent; PC = parents combined; NSM = not stated, mixed; RVS = reaction to video/story.
[a] This column shows highest level of aggregation in study; *d* refers to this level.

Tables 4 and 5 display the mean effect sizes, weighted by sample size, for the major and the subsidiary socialization areas, respectively, and lists them for mother, father, and parents combined. Some studies reported only data for parents, undifferentiated by sex, and could therefore be included only in the parents combined column. The Tables also show the 95% confidence intervals, established on the basis of the sampling error variance, and the number of comparisons on which each mean effect size is based. Where a cell is empty, fewer than three comparisons were available.

We first discuss the findings from the major socialization areas. When the confidence interval includes zero the effect size is nonsignificant, and it can be seen that this is the case for almost all socialization areas; effect sizes are also generally of very small magnitude. The direction of the differences is of some interest, although in the absence of a significant effect size this must not be overinterpreted. In North American stud-

ies encouragement of achievement, restrictiveness, and disciplinary strictness (including physical punishment) are applied slightly more to boys and warmth and encouragement of dependence slightly more to girls. The counts of positive and negative effect sizes (Table 6) show that these are not consistent weak effects for all studies; rather studies fluctuate in direction, with the majority being in the same direction as the overall effect. In other words, there is considerable variability in the effects. The preponderance for encouragement of dependence in the female direction, however, is notable, although the average effect is nonsignificant. Differences are also generally rather small in the primary studies. For instance, only 2 of 22 effect sizes for encouragement of achievement are significant, one in each direction, and 7 of 40 in the area of restrictiveness. Hence, one cannot speak of parents making any consistent difference in these areas. These findings are consonant with the cautious conclusions of Maccoby and Jacklin (1974).

Table 4
Mean Effect Size by Socialization Area: Major Socialization Areas

Area	Mothers			Fathers			Parents combined		
	d	95% CI	N	d	95% CI	N	d	95% CI	N
	North American studies								
Interaction	−.06	−.57/.45	47	.06	−.44/.56	16	−.03	−.51/.46	74
Encourage achievement	.05	−.19/.29	15	.11	−.13/.35	12	.02	−.20/.23	22
Warmth	−.07	−.38/.24	42	.00	−.30/.30	31	−.07	−.38/.25	63
Encourage dependency	−.06	−.35/.23	12	−.02	−.33/.28	6	−.10	−.41/.22	16
Restrictiveness	.07	−.28/.42	28	.16	−.18/.50	18	.08	−.20/.36	40
Discipline	.07	−.28/.41	37	.19	−.14/.52	21	.08	−.27/.44	53
Encourage sex-typed activities	.34	.08/.61	11	.49	.05/.93	7	.43	.11/.75	20
Clarity/reasoning	.01	−.34/.36	10	.01	−.29/.31	5	−.05	−.34/.25	13
	Studies from other Western countries								
Interaction	−.45	−1.03/.13	4				−.25	−.65/.16	5
Encourage achievement	.19	−.12/.50	3				−.29	−.50/−.07	4
Warmth	−.23	−.52/.05	7	−.16	−.52/.19	5	−.22	−.51/.07	8
Encourage dependency	−.01	−.43/.41	4	−.31	−.69/.06	3	−.14	−.56/.28	4
Restrictiveness	−.09	−.38/.19	7	.12	−.20/.44	4	−.03	−.27/.22	10
Discipline	−.02	−.34/.30	10	.26	−.16/.69	7	.09	−.26/.45	13

Note. CI = confidence interval: low/high; *N* = number of comparisons.

Table 5
Mean Effect Size by Socialization Area: Subsidiary Socialization Areas

	Mothers			Fathers			Parents combined		
Area	*d*	95% CI	*N*	*d*	95% CI	*N*	*d*	95% CI	*N*
				North American studies					
General interaction	−.08	−.35/.19	8	.14	−.22/.50	4	−.08	−.42/.26	19
Verbal interaction	−.14	−.73/.45	22	−.22	−.77/.32	6	−.09	−.70/.52	30
Motor stimulation	.32	−.31/.95	10				.33	−.31/.97	11
Joint play	−.20	−.91/.51	7	.18	−.37/.72	5	.02	−.39/.43	14
Encourage achievement: general	.10	−.18/.37	13	.09	−.19/.37	10	.01	−.22/.23	20
Encourage achievement: mathematics	−.05	−.21/.12	3	.12	−.05/.28	3	.04	−.13/.20	3
Material reward							−.20	−.56/.16	3
Nonphysical discipline	.02	−.26/.31	23	.17	−.11/.45	14	.05	−.26/.35	33
Physical discipline	.15	−.12/.42	11	.27	−.04/.57	5	.17	−.12/.45	15
Discourage aggression	−.12	−.39/.16	9	−.19	−.48/.11	7	−.13	−.40/.14	10
Encourage sex typed (boys > girls)	.13	−.15/.41	4	.20	−.10/.49	3	.20	−.13/.53	8
				Studies from other Western countries					
Nonphysical discipline	−.17	−.42/.08	6	.16	−.16/.48	4	−.04	−.32/.23	8
Physical punishment	.32	.11/.52	3	.51	.23/.79	2	.37	.14/.60	4

Note. CI = confidence interval: low/high; *N* = number of comparisons.

The one socialization area in North American studies where a clearly significant sex difference emerges is encouragement of sex-typed activities and perceptions of sex-stereotyped characteristics, hereinafter referred to as ESTA, with father making somewhat larger differences than mother does. Even so, the magnitudes of the effects range from one third to one half a standard deviation (i.e., they are fairly modest). This finding echoes similar findings of the earlier narrative reviews (Block, 1978; Huston, 1983; Maccoby & Jacklin, 1974).

As a result of the scoring conventions for ESTA, a negative effect size for this area could arise in a study only if parents on average encouraged cross-sex-typed behavior more than same-sex-typed behavior, an unlikely set of circumstances that in fact never arose in any study. We are not saying that the significant sex difference in this area is therefore illusory, but we wish to draw attention to the particular features of this socialization area, which must be borne in mind in its interpretation.

From the studies in other Western countries, there appears one rather incongruous, significant sex difference, suggesting that parents as a whole encourage achievement more in girls than in boys. It is based on only four studies, and we later discuss what happens when we remove one large study from this set.

In turning to the subsidiary socialization areas (see Table 5), we note that in North American studies effect sizes are nonsignificant and generally very small; the only exception is the rather large sex difference in favor of boys for stimulation of motor behavior, an effect size that, because of its large variability, is nonsignificant. We should comment here that ESTA for boys more than girls was coded separately where the study measure was appropriate, and scored as the treatment of boys minus the treatment of girls. The difference, though nonsignificant, is in the male direction (all eight North American studies are in this direction) and larger for fathers, as might be expected from others' tentative conclusions (e.g., Huston, 1983; Maccoby &

Jacklin, 1974). The discouragement of aggression is directed slightly more toward girls, although this difference too is far from significant.

In studies from other Western countries, there are significant effect sizes for physical punishment, which both mothers and fathers inflict more on boys than on girls. The result should be treated with some reservation, because the number of studies on which it is based was small.

We ran contrast analyses for mothers' versus fathers' treatment, but only restrictiveness turned out to be significant ($p <$ .05). However, considering all socialization areas, there seems to be a general tendency, although nonsignificant, for fathers to make larger differences, where the effect is larger for boys. For joint play and for interaction in general, a slight same-sex parent effect appears, with fathers interacting more with boys and mothers more with girls, although again the effect is not significant.

Table 6
Number of Positive and Negative Effect Sizes

	Number of comparisons with:		
Socialization area	Positive *d*	Negative *d*	χ^2
Amount of interaction	35	39	.22
Encouragement of achievement	14	8	1.64
Warmth	27	36	1.29
Encouragement of dependency	3	13	6.25*
Restrictiveness	27	13	4.90*
Disciplinary strictness	38	15	9.98**
Encouragement of sex-typed activities	20	0	20.00***
Clarity of communication	4	9	1.92

* $p < .05$.   ** $p < .01$.   *** $p < .001$.

Effects of weighting by sample size: Unweighted effect sizes. Despite the low, nonsignificant correlation for sample size across all socialization areas reported earlier, we thought it prudent to compare weighted with unweighted effect sizes; hence, the latter were also calculated (not shown). They appear to be a little higher (mean across all socialization areas: .06) than the weighted effect sizes (mean across all socialization areas: .03). This implies that studies with larger samples may have somewhat lower effect sizes. However, when we examined the unweighted values for parents combined in North American studies, the only socialization area for which unweighting created a significant effect not present with weighted values was ESTA for boys more than for girls ($d = .46$; confidence interval: .12/.79). One study (Block, 1978) with a fairly large sample (569 in North America) had a very small d for this area, and this had a minimizing effect on the weighted mean d not present in the unweighted d.

The linear-trend analysis, outlined previously here, was performed for the major socialization areas; studies were collapsed into three sample-size groups (see Table 8). The trend across all socialization areas is not significant, and only one suggestive finding for individual areas emerged; for disciplinary strictness there is a near-significant tendency for effect size to diminish with increasing sample size. Thus, sample size overall seems to have practically no effect on the magnitude of effects.

Effects of weighting by sample size: Large samples. When we weight effects by sample size, studies with large samples may exert an excessive influence on the mean effect size that results in a distorted picture of the relationships found in most studies. To test the robustness of our findings, we therefore performed a second analysis, removing studies with a sample size larger than 800 from all the socialization areas where they occurred. None of the nonsignificant effects became significant. The results for the significant findings are shown in Table 7.

Table 7 also presents the results of a third analysis in which we added to the analysis of previously significant effects all the findings that simply stated for a given socialization area that no significant difference by sex was found and for which we therefore had to assume a difference of exactly zero, or a p value of .5. These findings came from studies where effect sizes could be calculated for other socialization areas as well as from studies that contained no usable quantitative information at all. The addition of these (assumed) zero differences will always reduce the mean effect size found and the inclusion of all available reports thus tests the robustness of the original finding.

A study by Duncan, Schuman, and Duncan (1973) asked mothers about their expectations of sex-appropriate household chores (classified as ESTA) and had a sample size of 1,880. Once this study was removed, the effect for mothers was no longer significant, but it remained significant for parents combined, because among the greater number of studies the influence of this one large study was no longer as pronounced. When we added in the studies with a p value of .5, the effects for ESTA remained significant. Thus, this effect was quite robust for parents combined.

In studies from Western countries, the effect for physical punishment remained significant when one study with a p value of .5 was added, and it thus demonstrated some robustness, although the number of studies was small.

Table 7
Significant Effect Sizes

Socialization area	Parent	Studies with known effect sizes	Studies of $N < 800$	Studies with $p = .5$ added
North America				
Encourage sex-typed activities	Mother	.34* (11)	.37 (10)	.31* (13)
	Father	.49* (7)		
	PC	.43* (20)	.58* (19)	.37* (23)
Western countries				
Physical punishment	Mother	.32* (3)		
	Father	.51* (2)		
	PC	.37* (4)		.24* (5)
Encourage achievement	PC	−.28* (4)	.15 (3)	−.19 (6)

Note. Figures in parentheses are number of studies included. PC = parents combined.
* $p < .05$.

The significant difference in the female direction for encouragement of achievement in Western countries can be attributed to one study (Russell, 1983) that contributed 877 subjects to the weighted effect size and was in fact the only study of the four that showed a difference in the female direction. The data of this investigation—a dissertation—were based on a questionnaire administered to high school students in Great Britain as well as in the United States (where the difference in this study, although not as strong, was in the female direction too). This investigation seems anomalous, and it also had some statistical problems. Once this study is removed, the effect size points in the direction of greater encouragement for boys, but it is nonsignificant (the same result as was found in North American studies). When findings with a p value of .5 are added, the effect for this area is also reduced to nonsignificance. This example illustrates how important it is in the interpretation of a meta-analysis to be aware of the nature of the studies that constitute the sample.

Effects of moderator variables. We tested the hypotheses that we had formulated about the effects of certain characteristics of the studies—the "moderator variables"—by linear-trend analysis in North American studies. Table 8 reports all the results for the summed socialization areas overall. To test whether the effect sizes of these aggregated data are significantly different from zero is not meaningful, and such tests were therefore not performed, but the trends were tested for significance. For individual socialization areas, only significant trends are presented to avoid swamping the reader with data.

The hypothesis that differential treatment of boys and girls would increase with age was not supported. In fact, a trend in the opposite direction emerges for socialization areas overall, as well as in significant trends in the individual socialization areas of disciplinary strictness and ESTA. This trend suggests that parents treat older children less differentially than younger children. However, very few studies of children older than 5 years were found for ESTA and hence this result must be treated with caution.

Table 8
Contrasts (Linear Trends) for Effect Sizes by Moderator Variables: North American Studies

Socialization area	Overall		Interaction			Warmth			Encourage dependency			Restrictiveness			Discipline			Encourage sex-typed activities			Clarity		
	M	N	M	95% CI	N	M	95% CI	N	M	95% CI	N	M	95% CI	N	M	95% CI	N	M	95% CI	N	M	95% CI	N
Sample size																							
≤50	.09	123													.34	−.36/1.04	11						
51–150	.10	111													.09	−.36/.55	21						
>150	.01	90													.06*	−.21/.33	21						
Age (years)																							
0–5	.08	179													.16	−.26/.59	23	.71	.15/1.28	16			
6–12	.01	69													.01	−.34/.36	21	.29	−.05/.62	2			
>12	.03***	40													.09***	−.28/.47	10	(.34)***	N/A	1			
Data collection																							
Interview	.03	184										.07	−.16/.30	25	.04	−.30/.37	42						
Observation/experiment	.06	140										.18**	−.33/.69	15	.48***	−.03/.98	11						
Source of data																							
Published	.04	255				−.06	−.36/.23	49	−.08	−.37/.21	14												
Unpublished	−.01**	69				−.11**	−.55/.32	14	−.34**	−.83/.15	2												
Year of publication																							
<1974	.05	107	−.16	−.59/.27	16				.10	−.22/.42	10				.07	−.26/.39	23				.10	−.24/.45	4
1974–1980	.02	99	.07	−.45/.59	27				−.08	−.31/.15	2				−.03	−.39/.33	16				−.06	−.38/.26	5
>1980	.02	118	−.01***	−.51/.48	31				−.24**	−.56/.08	4				.31***	−.11/.74	14				−.11**	−.34/.13	4
Author sex																							
Male	.03	151							−.08	−.37/.22	8							.34	.17/.51	4			
Female	.04*	173							−.12**	−.43/.20	8							.63**	.12/1.14	16			
Quality																							
Low	.00	127										.04	−.16/.24	15	.04	−.30/.38	31				−.10	−.33/.13	7
High	.10***	19										.17**	−.22/.57	25	.16***	−.22/.54	22				.13**	−.30/.55	9

Note. For socialization areas overall, no significance tests of effect sizes were performed. For individual socialization areas, only significant contrasts are shown. Encouragement of achievement is omitted, because no breakdown showed a significant trend. N = number of comparisons; CI = confidence interval: low/high.
* $p < .10$, one-tailed, for linear trends. ** $p < .05$, one-tailed, for linear trends. *** $p < .01$, one-tailed, for linear trends.

For method of data collection, we contrasted report by child, interview/questionnaire, and reaction to video or story by parent on the one hand with observation or experiment on the other. The majority of studies in the first group were interview/questionnaire studies. The hypothesis that interview or questionnaire would yield smaller effect sizes than observation or experiment received some tentative support by the nonsignificant trend in this direction for socialization areas overall. However, there were individually significant trends (to be treated as tentative findings) in the same direction for restrictiveness and disciplinary strictness. Thus, it appears that methods that give more direct access to parental behaviors may reveal larger differences in the treatment of boys and girls than do interview or questionnaire methods, which allow parents to minimize such differences. However, even the observational/experimental studies did not produce significant effects for these domains. We should note also that the ratio of interview studies to observational/experimental studies was 1 to 2 for studies of children younger than age 6, but was about 3 to 1 or more for studies of older children. However, this did not translate into larger effect sizes for the younger age group, as we have seen.

For source of items we contrasted published material (i.e., journal articles and books or book chapters) with unpublished material (i.e., dissertations, conference reports, and unpublished manuscripts). The hypothesis of smaller effect sizes arising from unpublished material seemed to be supported by a significant trend for socialization areas overall in keeping with previous findings (e.g., Glass et al., 1981). However, it should be realized that a decrease in positive effect size overall may be brought about by an increase in negative effect sizes in some constituent socialization areas. In this contrast, in fact, the only significant trends for individual socialization areas are toward larger effect sizes in the negative direction in unpublished material for warmth and encouragement of dependence contrary to the hypothesis. These effect sizes themselves remain nonsignificant. Other nonsignificant trends vary in direction. The publication bias, claimed to be the reason for the finding of larger effects in published studies reported in earlier writings, does not seem to be operating so clearly in this domain. Possibly editorial bias against the reporting of nonsignificant findings for gender differences may have declined in recent years because of the controversy over Maccoby and Jacklin's (1974) findings, as Hyde and Linn (1988) suggested.

The hypothesis that parenting has become less sex differentiated in more recent times was not supported. The nonsignificant trend in this direction overall masks a variety of changes: Individually significant trends (to be treated with caution) show both increasing and decreasing tendencies or a change from the male to the female direction. The variations in effect size by year of publication across the different socialization areas thus seem to reflect almost random fluctuations.

We tested the effects of certain other characteristics for which we had not formed any hypotheses, but which might account for variability in effect sizes. Sex of first author, it can be seen, has some effect. Overall there is a near-significant tendency for female authors to generate somewhat larger effect sizes, and this trend is significant for encouragement of dependence, where the trend is in the negative direction, and ESTA, where it is in the positive direction.

The contrast between low-quality ratings (2 and 3) and high-quality ratings (4 and 5) reveals a significant tendency for effect sizes to increase with higher quality across all socialization areas. This overall increase is made up of generally higher positive effect sizes (trend significant for restrictiveness and disciplinary strictness) as well as some lower negative effect sizes. Because of the possibility that weighting by quality might produce significant effects where weighting by sample size does not, we experimentally weighted effect sizes by quality. When this was done, the only socialization area that changed from nonsignificance to significance was ESTA for boys more than for girls, as it did when we used unweighted effect sizes. In view of this last fact, the significance of the quality-weighted result very likely is simply due to the data not being weighted by sample size. Even in the higher quality studies, no significant difference emerged, where there was none for all studies. Hence, the possible argument that lack of effects overall may be caused by poor design or execution of studies loses its force.

The effect sizes were also analyzed by a social class/education index, but no additional significant effect sizes or findings of special interest emerged, and this analysis will therefore not be reported on further.

It must be stressed that no grouping by any moderator variable reduced variability to such an extent that a previously nonsignificant effect became significant.

Discussion

We summarize the results as follows:

1. The effect sizes for most socialization areas are nonsignificant and generally very small, fluctuating in direction across studies.

2. In North American studies the only socialization area that displays a significant effect is encouragement of sex-typed activities for mother, father, and parents combined. The effect remains robust for parents combined when studies with a sample size larger than 800 are omitted and when studies with a *p* value of .5 are added.

3. Studies from other Western countries show a significant sex difference for physical punishment, with more being meted out to boys. This effect also is robust for parents combined, but it is based on a small number of studies. The significant effect for encouragement of achievement (more for girls), however, is shown to be unstable and attributable to one anomalous large-sample study.

4. Fathers generally tend to make greater differences between sons and daughters than mothers do when the treatment effect is in the male direction, but the difference between mothers and fathers is significant only for restrictiveness.

5. The outcomes for the hypotheses regarding the moderator variables are as follows. First, contrary to the hypothesis, differential treatment decreases over age overall and specifically in disciplinary strictness and ESTA. Second, the hypothesis that observation or experiment would produce larger effect sizes receives some limited support. Third, the hypothesis that published studies would generate larger effect sizes is, on detailed examination, not supported. Fourth, the hypothesis that sex differentiation may have been greater in "unenlightened" earlier times is not corroborated at least for the period from the

1950s on. The effect sizes in different socialization areas over the years seem to fluctuate almost randomly.

6. Sample size in general is not related to effect size. Unweighted effect sizes essentially do not differ from weighted ones, except for the significant finding for unweighted values of ESTA more for boys than girls.

7. Higher quality of study tends to go with larger effect size. Grouping studies by quality—or any other moderator variable—however, did not produce any additional significant effect sizes.

From the finding that parents emphasize sex stereotypes in play activities and household chores, we may conclude that parents in this way shape the child's sex-stereotypical behavior in an important area. It must be borne in mind, however, that such encouragement may build on the child's already existing preferences, and that it is the child's genotype that may evoke differential responses from others (the so-called evocative genotype → environment effect; cf. Scarr & McCartney, 1983). There is, indeed, some evidence that supports such an interpretation: Snow, Jacklin, and Maccoby (1983) reported that fathers were less likely to give dolls to 1-year-old boys than girls, but boys also played less with dolls when given them than girls did. Caldera, Huston, and O'Brien (1989) discovered that 18-month-old boys and girls already showed greater involvement when playing with toys conventionally associated with their sex, although parents did not overtly promote play with same-sex-typed toys.

Moreover, it has been shown that girls who have been exposed to heightened levels of masculinizing hormones prenatally (congenital adrenal hyperplasia) show greater preferences for male sex-typed toys in childhood (Berenbaum & Hines, 1989; Money & Ehrhardt, 1968), and also that levels of prenatal testosterone (ascertained through amniocentesis) are related to block building in boys at age 4 (Finegan, Bartleman, Zacher, & Mervyn, 1989). Thus, some biological substrate may exist even for same-sex toy preferences, and parents therefore may simply reinforce these preferences rather than create them.

The finding that parents in Western countries inflict physical punishment more on boys suggests there is a cultural difference here that leads parents in Western countries outside North America to feel that physical punishment is more appropriate for boys, whereas North American parents apply it in a relatively egalitarian manner to both sexes. The sex difference in North American studies is in the same direction, although nonsignificant. However, greater resort to physical punishment for boys may also be a reaction to boys' more defiant or disobedient behavior (cf. Anderson, Lytton, & Romney, 1986). It should be stressed that our data do not provide any information on whether parents outside North America use physical punishment more or less than North American parents do.

Recent meta-analyses indicate that the magnitude of observed sex differences in cognitive or social characteristics is smaller than had previously been found or has been declining in recent years (cf. Hyde & Linn, 1988, for verbal ability; Feingold, 1988, for mathematical and other abilities; Hyde, 1984, for aggression). The evidence presented here suggests that sex differences that remain (e.g., in high mathematical reasoning ability or aggression) are not due to parents directly and systematically reinforcing stereotypical behavior or abilities in their chil-

dren. This confirms not only Maccoby and Jacklin's (1974) conclusions, but also more recent findings such as those by Raymond and Benbow (1986) on the equal parental encouragement of extremely high mathematical ability in boys and girls.

We must, however, not underestimate the importance of ESTA by parents because this may have larger ramifications for other behavioral differences. Whiting and Edwards (1975), cited in Block (1978), observed in different cultures that girls are more frequently assigned domestic and child-care chores, whereas boys are more often assigned chores that take them from the vicinity of the house (e.g., feeding and herding animals). Hence, girls tend to interact more with adults and infants, and boys more with peers. Younger girls in all cultures were found to be significantly more nurturant and responsible than boys. In later childhood, girls were still more nurturant, but boys also came to show responsibility after they began to herd animals. Whiting and Edwards attributed these behavioral differences to girls being exposed to different tasks and persons than are boys; eventually "we become the company we keep."

Block (1983) further suggested that boys' toys provide more opportunity for manipulation and inventiveness, and that girls' preferred play activities contribute to a more structured world that elicits less creativity and more compliance. Moreover, masculine sex-typed play may also afford an opportunity for practicing visuospatial skills. Parental encouragement of certain play activities will thus have far-reaching implications, but it must be remembered, in view of the evidence for a biological substrate for toy and play preferences, that parents may simply play a reinforcing and amplifying role, a possibility that Block (1983) acknowledged.

It may be argued that for many of the areas studied there is little reason to expect differential socialization, although many theorists have hypothesized that it exists. Perhaps one should search for differential socialization in domains where sex differences have been demonstrated. For sex-typed play and activities, we did, of course, find differential encouragement. For aggression, we found none, nor did we find any for mathematics skills. However, there were only three studies for this last area and none for spatial ability, measured directly (but note the possible influence from masculine sex-typed play discussed previously). Also some of the clearest sex differences in adolescence and adulthood seem to occur in domains such as occupational choice and interests. It is reasonable to ask how socialization practices affect these differences. Yet there were almost no studies of ESTA beyond the preschool age. Clearly there is a lack of studies of parental pressures in some of the domains in which consistent sex differences appear.

Having presented the meta-analytic results, we might stop here. However, so as not to leave these findings dangling in an atheoretical vacuum, we believe it is incumbent on us to discuss their broader implications for the origins of existing sex differences, although our remarks from here on must inevitably be more speculative. First, it should be acknowledged that although differences were nonsignificant in most socialization areas, the direction of these differences (e.g., more prohibition of aggression for girls, more warmth for girls) were in the expected direction, and indicate some slight differential treatment that may amplify children's existing behavioral tendencies. Such differential treatment may indeed result in greater inhibition of aggression or greater nurturance in girls. Second, there may be some subtle forms of parental treatment that were not captured by our categories and that might conceivably show some differences by sex. We did not include, for instance, contingent responding to emotion expressions by infants in our analysis because only one study (Malatesta & Haviland, 1982) reported sex differences for this. (Categories, such as encouragement of dependence, discouragement of independence, or discouragement of aggression do denote contingent reactions, but the measures constituting these categories were not reactions to emotion expressions, like joy or anger, that Malatesta & Haviland analyzed.) We could not include complexity of language or elaborativeness of play in the meta-analysis, nor could we analyze the effects of maternal employment as a moderator variable. The reason for all these omissions was the fact that very few studies reported on such variables in relation to differential parental treatment. However, the subdivision of the major socialization areas into more homogeneous categories did not produce significant effects and, hence, we are doubtful whether other divisions, even if feasible, would do so.

Third, even if parents do not differentiate reliably between sons and daughters in the amount of, say, warmth or independence they accord each sex, the same parental treatment may affect boys and girls differently. Baumrind (1989), for instance, suggested that parental abrasiveness may be more beneficial for girls. We could not examine such effects. However, are such possible differential effects not due to the two sexes' differential responsiveness and amenability to influence? That is, are they not effects inherent in the child rather than being due to environmental forces?

Fourth, children derive sex-role schemas or sex stereotypes from the observation of models appropriate for their sex, a process that Maccoby (1988) called "cognitive categorizing," and this, no doubt, is a powerful force impelling children toward the adoption of sex-typed behaviors. Parents as well as other adults and especially peers can serve as models, as can television. The social stereotypes from which children thus acquire sex-typed behavior may, however, also have a basis in biological reality. Imitation on the basis of the sex appropriateness of the actions rather than of the sex of the model has been demonstrated after age 6 (Barkley, Ullman, Lori, & Brecht, 1977). However, in imitating sex-typed behaviors or showing sex-typed play preferences, do 2- or 3-year-old children attempt to match their behavior to sex-role stereotypes, or do they prefer these types of actions for other reasons? Perry, White, and Perry (1984) first elicited toy preferences and then assessed knowledge of stereotypes in 2- to 5-year-old children. Their findings indicate that boys' development of sex-typed preferences preceded their acquisition of sex-role stereotypes by about 1 year, whereas with girls the order was not clear. Other research (e.g., Blakemore, LaRue, & Olejnik, 1979) has produced similar findings. Thus, knowledge of sex stereotypes and categories is not a necessary prerequisite for sex-appropriate play preferences, and findings such as these are at variance with cognitive-developmental explanations of the development of sex typing (cf. Grusec & Lytton, 1988). Social-learning theory can account for such results by pointing to the possible early influence of ESTA, but potential biological underpinnings

cannot be ignored. Fifth, peers are generally acknowledged to be a potent force in socializing children in sex-typed ways, and there is evidence for peers' influence from preschool age up (e.g., Fagot & Patterson, 1969). Here too it is a moot point whether peers are a primary influence or rather reinforce and amplify existing tendencies (cf. Fagot, 1985).

The finding of relative uniformity in the treatment of sons and daughters by parents does not by itself allow us to decide between various environmental and biological explanations of existing sex differences. All the mechanisms cited previously here are quite likely partial explanations of such differences. They are overtly environmental in nature, and many may consider this interpretation sufficient. However, we adduced other evidence to show that the last three points may also (but need not) be seen as effects arising from the child.

In view of all the evidence, we cannot close our eyes to the possibility of biological predispositions providing a part of the explanation for existing sex differences. Aggression is a behavioral area where the influence of biological factors has been shown most clearly (cf. Maccoby & Jacklin, 1980). Evidence also suggests that asymmetries in brain organization may differ between males and females (e.g., Witelson, 1988), and this may be related to the large male preponderance for extremely high ability in mathematics, which has survived meta-analytic aggregation, although mathematics performance in the general population does not seem to display a significant sex difference (Hyde, Fennema, & Lamon, 1990). Because environmental explanations do not by themselves entirely account for this phenomenon, Benbow (1988) examined evidence for physiological correlates of high mathematics ability (e.g., left-handedness, allergies, myopia). The relationships among brain lateralization, sex, and cognition are quite complex, and interpretation must be guarded. Nevertheless, the evidence overall is suggestive of brain–behavior relationships and of a possible biological basis for high mathematical reasoning ability in addition to environmental factors. (See the commentaries following Benbow's article for a detailed debate on these complexities.)

The influence of simple biological sex dimorphism will, of course, be modified in actual characteristics by personal individuality (variation within the sexes is generally larger than between the sexes). Above all, biological factors will interact with, and be reinforced by, parents' influences and other societal, environmental forces that we listed previously here. Bidirectional processes will be operating in parent–child interactions, and phenotypic characteristics will be influenced by these.

The present meta-analysis has demonstrated a virtual absence of sex-distinctive parental socialization pressures, except in one area, at least as far as these have been captured by existing measures and reported in English-language publications. We realize that for many social scientists such findings are difficult to accept. We therefore conclude with a few comments on the capabilities and limitations of a meta-analysis.

A quantitative review that surveys systematically, and with statistical safeguards, a large number of studies—the existing literature—is a powerful tool for testing hypotheses and can produce clearer answers than a single study can. It can show overall trends in relationships and, by relating effect sizes to certain characteristics of the primary studies, it can trace the influence of, and the patterns arising from, these characteristics, or the absence thereof. It is something like a satellite picture of the earth, with its advantages and also with its limitations.

Meta-analyses, by their nature, do seem to produce a washout effect, as the regular findings in recent meta-analytic studies of smaller sex differences than had previously been supposed indicate. What looms large in one study often appears as the odd case from a more general perspective. Strong and replicable effects will, however, show up even in a meta-analysis (e.g., a d of .73 for spatial ability in mental rotation tests [Linn & Petersen, 1985] or a d of .50 in aggression [Hyde, 1984]).

A possible obstacle to the acceptance of a finding of essentially no significant effects for a set of studies is the presence of great variability among studies. If there is great variability in both the positive and negative direction among studies, this will produce a low average or nonsignificant effect size. However, in this case, the meta-analysis may simply reflect the state of research in the area and clearly reveal the stark truth, namely that no reliable results in any direction are available. If a breakdown by moderator variables still does not yield reliable effects, then the null finding will become quite firmly grounded.

As for the limitations of a meta-analysis, it is true that the reviewer is restricted by the knowledge base we have (i.e., by the topics and constructs that primary researchers have chosen to study). The subtle aspects of parental socializing practices, noted earlier, as well as Baumrind's "authoritative" and "authoritarian" parenting styles appeared in only one or two studies that assessed differential treatment and thus slipped through the net of the analysis. There were also few studies of parents' contingent reactions in some domains that are clearly sex differentiated. The limitations of the existing literature are, of course, also ever present with narrative reviews, but meta-analyses make the problem more visible.

It is also true that the reviewer cannot remedy the flaws and limitations of the primary literature, and if all the primary studies are weak, the meta-analysis will be built on sand. If this was indeed the case in any given area, and provided the meta-analysis had sampled the literature appropriately, the only conclusion one could draw would be that one does not and cannot know anything scientifically about that topic, because there is no other research to fall back on. In our case, however, even confining ourselves to the higher quality studies in our data base did not change the findings. (The one additional significant effect was due to the effect sizes not being frequency weighted.)

Some people, despite the evidence of this quantitative review, may be convinced that sex-related differences in parental treatment exist, but may argue that a meta-analysis, because of the need to aggregate data over studies, cannot capture these more subtle differences. They might then be willing to concede that scientifically speaking practically no differences can be detected, but might fall back on intuitive knowledge—a mode of knowing that is distinct from scientific knowledge—as a basis for asserting their existence. It must be said, however, that intuitive knowledge gives rise to metaphors that may throw an illuminating shaft of light on a problem and are often compelling, but such metaphors are ambiguous and private and, by virtue of expressing a very personal point of view, they may also distort.

We believe that the finding of very few differences in paren-

tal treatment of boys and girls represents the best evidence we have on the topic at this time. We cannot say whether a replication of this meta-analysis would present a different picture. Our reading of the literature certainly suggests that meta-analyses, like primary studies, can benefit from replication. In any case, the broader implications of this research for the origins of sex differences are indeed open to further debate.

References

Anderson, K. E., Lytton, H., & Romney, D. M. (1986). Mothers' interactions with normal and conduct-disordered boys: Who affects whom? *Developmental Psychology, 22,* 604–609.

Bangert-Drowns, R. J. (1986). Review of developments in meta-analytic method. *Psychological Bulletin, 99,* 388–399.

Barkley, R. G., Ullman, D. B., Lori, O., & Brecht, J. M. (1977). The effects of sex typing and sex appropriateness of modeled behavior on children's imitation. *Child Development, 48,* 721–725.

Baumrind, D. (1989, April). *Sex-differentiated socialization effects in childhood and adolescence.* Paper presented at the biennial meeting of the Society for Research in Child Development, Kansas City, MO.

Benbow, C. P. (1988). Sex differences in mathematical reasoning ability in intellectually talented preadolescents: Their nature, effects, and possible causes. *Behavioral and Brain Sciences, 11,* 169–183.

Berenbaum, S. A., & Hines, M. (1989, April). *Hormonal influences on sex-typed toy preferences.* Paper presented at the biennial meeting of the Society for Research in Child Development, Kansas City, MO.

Blakemore, J. E. O., LaRue, A. A., & Olejnik, A. B. (1979). Sex-appropriate toy preference and the ability to conceptualize toys as sex-role related. *Developmental Psychology, 15,* 339–340.

Block, J. H. (1976). Issues, problems, and pitfalls in assessing sex differences: A critical review of "The psychology of sex differences." *Merrill-Palmer Quarterly, 22,* 283–308.

Block, J. H. (1978). Another look at sex differentiation in the socialization behaviors of mothers and fathers. In J. A. Sherman & F. L. Denmark (Eds.), *The psychology of women: Future directions in research* (pp. 29–87). New York: Psychological Dimensions.

Block, J. H. (1983). Differential premises arising from differential socialization of the sexes: Some conjectures. *Child Development, 54,* 1335–1354.

Caldera, Y. M., Huston, A. C., & O'Brien, M. (1989). Social interactions and play patterns of parents and toddlers with feminine, masculine and neutral toys. *Child Development, 60,* 70–76.

Duncan, O. D., Schuman, H., & Duncan, B. (1973). *Social change in a metropolitan community.* New York: Russell Sage.

Eagly, A. H. (1987). On taking research findings seriously. *Contemporary Psychology, 32,* 759–760.

Eagly, A. H., & Crowley, M. (1986). Gender and helping behavior: A meta-analytic review of the social psychological literature. *Psychological Bulletin, 100,* 283–308.

Fagot, B. I. (1978). The influence of sex of child on parental reactions to toddler children. *Child Development, 49,* 459–465.

Fagot, B. I. (1985). Beyond the reinforcement principle: Another step toward understanding sex role development. *Developmental Psychology, 21,* 1097–1104.

Fagot, B. I., & Patterson, G. R. (1969). An in vivo analysis of reinforcing contingencies for sex-role behaviors in the preschool child. *Developmental Psychology, 1,* 563–568.

Feingold, A. (1988). Cognitive gender differences are disappearing. *American Psychologist, 43,* 95–103.

Finegan, J. A., Bartleman, B., Zacher, J., & Mervyn, J. (1989, April). *Prenatal testosterone and development at age 4 years.* Paper presented at the biennial meeting of the Society for Research in Child Development, Kansas City, MO.

Glass, G. V. (1977). Integrating findings: The meta-analysis of research. *Review of Research in Education, 5*, 351–379.

Glass, G. V., McGaw, B., & Smith, M. L. (1981). *Meta-analysis in social research.* Beverly Hills, CA: Sage.

Goshen-Gottstein, E. R. (1981). Differential maternal socialization of opposite-sexed twins, triplets, and quadruplets. *Child Development, 52,* 1255–1264.

Grusec, J. E., & Lytton, H. (1988). *Social development: History, theory and research.* New York: Springer-Verlag.

Hedges, L. V., & Becker, B. J. (1986). Statistical methods in the meta-analysis of research on gender differences. In J. S. Hyde & M. C. Linn (Eds.), *The psychology of gender: Advances through meta-analysis* (pp. 14–50). Baltimore, MD: John Hopkins University Press.

Hunter, J. E., Schmidt, F. L., & Jackson, G. B. (1982). *Meta-analysis: Cumulating research findings across studies.* Beverly Hills, CA: Sage.

Huston, A. C. (1983). Sex typing. In E. M. Hetherington (Ed.), *Handbook of child psychology: Vol. 4. Socialization, personality and social development* (pp. 387–467). New York: Wiley.

Hyde, J. S. (1984). How large are gender differences in aggression? A developmental meta-analysis. *Developmental Psychology, 20,* 722–732.

Hyde, J. S., Fenneman, E., & Lamon, S. J. (1990). Gender differences in mathematics performance: A meta-analysis. *Psychological Bulletin, 107,* 139–155.

Hyde, J. S., & Linn, M. C. (Eds.). (1986). *The psychology of gender.* Baltimore, MD: Johns Hopkins University Press.

Hyde, J. S., & Linn, M. C. (1988). Gender differences in verbal ability: A meta-analysis. *Psychological Bulletin, 104,* 53–69.

Kohlberg, L. (1966). A cognitive-developmental analysis of children's sex-role concepts and attitudes. In E. E. Maccoby (Ed.), *The development of sex differences.* (pp. 82–173). Stanford, CA: Stanford University Press.

Light, R. J., & Pillemer, D. B. (1984). *Summing up: The science of reviewing research.* Cambridge, MA: Harvard University Press.

Linn, M. C., & Petersen, A. C. (1985). Emergence and characterization of sex differences in spatial ability: A meta-analysis. *Child Development, 56,* 1479–1498.

Maccoby, E. E. (Ed.). (1966). *The development of sex differences.* Stanford, CA: Stanford University Press.

Maccoby, E. E. (1988). Gender as a social category. *Developmental Psychology, 24,* 755–765.

Maccoby, E. E., & Jacklin, C. N. (1974). *The psychology of sex differences.* Stanford, CA: Stanford University Press.

Maccoby, E. E., & Jacklin, C. N. (1980). Sex differences in aggression: A rejoinder and a reprise. *Child Development, 51,* 964–980.

Malatesta, C. Z., & Haviland, J. M. (1982). Learning display rules: The socialization of emotion expression in infancy. *Child Development, 53,* 991–1003.

Money, J., & Ehrhardt, A. A. (1968). Prenatal hormonal exposure: Possible effects on behavior in man. In R. P. Michael (Ed.), *Endocrinology and human behavior* (pp. 32–48). Oxford, England: Oxford University Press.

Mullen, B., & Rosenthal, R. (1985). *BASIC meta-analysis: Procedures and programs.* Hillsdale, NJ: Erlbaum.

Newson, J., & Newson, E. (1976). *Seven years old in the home environment.* London: Allen & Unwin.

Nurius, P. S., & Yeaton, W. H. (1987). Research synthesis reviews: An illustrated critique of "hidden" judgments, choices and compromises. *Clinical Psychology Review, 7,* 695–714.

Perry, D. G., White, A. J., & Perry, L. C. (1984). Does early sex typing result from children's attempts to match their behavior to sex role stereotypes? *Child Development, 55,* 2114–2121.

Peters, L. H., Hartke, D. D., & Pohlmann, J. T. (1985). Fiedler's contingency theory of leadership: An application of the meta-analysis procedures of Schmidt and Hunter. *Psychological Bulletin, 97,* 274–285.

Raymond, C. L., & Persson Benbow, C. (1986). Gender differences in mathematics: A function of parental support and student sex typing? *Developmental Psychology, 22,* 808–819.

Rosenthal, R. (1984). *Meta-analytic procedures for social and behavioral research.* Beverly Hills, CA: Sage.

Rosenthal, R., & Rubin, D. B. (1982). Comparing effect sizes of independent studies. *Psychological Bulletin, 92,* 500–504.

Rothbart, M. K. (1971). Birth order and mother-child interaction in an achievement situation. *Journal of Personality and Social Psychology, 17,* 113–120.

Rothbart, M. K., & Maccoby, E. E. (1966). Parent's differential reaction to sons and daughters. *Journal of Personality and Social Psychology, 4,* 237–243.

Russell, C. M. (1983). Achievement and socialization in British and American adolescents. *Dissertation Abstracts International, 44,* 2900. (University Microfilms No. 83-28685)

Scarr, S., & McCartney, K. (1983). How people make their own environments: A theory of genotype-environment effects. *Child Development, 54,* 424–435.

Snow, M. E., Jacklin, C. N., & Maccoby, E. E. (1983). Sex-of-child differences in father-child interaction at one year of age. *Child Development, 54,* 227–232.

Whiting, B., & Edwards, C. P. (1975). A cross-cultural analysis of sex differences in the behavior of children age three through eleven. In S. Chess & A. Thomas (Eds.), *Annual progress in child psychiatry and child development, 1974* (pp. 32–49). New York: Brunner/Mazel.

Witelson, S. F. (1988). Neuroanatomical sex differences: Of no consequence for cognition? *Behavioral and Brain Sciences, 11,* 215–217.

Appendix A

Inclusion Rules for Classification of Socialization Areas

No.	Area
10	Interaction: undifferentiated: "involvement" with infants
11	Verbal interaction; social stimulation
12	Stimulation motor behavior; stimulate, arouse infant; touch, hold, rock
13	Joint play
10S	Total amount of interaction (total of 10, 11, 12, 13)
20	Encouragement and pressure for achievement, verbal and general; early maturity demands; help with school work; instruct; teach; educational expectations
21	Encouragement of achievement: mathematics
20S	Total achievement encouragement (total of 20 and 21)
30	Warmth, love, nurturance; responsiveness; praise; positive affect, involvement; supporting; smile to infant; acceptance of child; approval in teaching interaction; 30 reversed: negative affect; disapproval in teaching situation; rejection; hostility
33	Material rewards
40	Encouragement of dependency; noncontingent helping behavior at early ages; "anxious intrusion"; possessiveness; hold/proximity in context of dependence
50	Restrictiveness/low encouragement of independence; nonpermissiveness; demandingness; control–autonomy; punishment of independence; demands for help around house for keeping things in order; concern with neatness, cleaning up; prescription of responsibility; "directive" in teaching interaction; prohibition; intrusiveness; 50 reversed: acceptance of individuation; independence granting; autonomy
60	Discipline: undifferentiated
61	Nonphysical disciplinary strictness; firm control; enforcement; tell to stop, threaten; consistency; affective punishment; love withdrawal; isolate child; 61 reversed: inconsistent, lax discipline
62	Physical punishment
60S	Disciplinary strictness (total of 60, 61, 62)
70	Discouragement of aggression; punishment of aggression
80	Encouragement of sex-typed activities, play, toy choices, household chores; perception of sex-typed characteristics
82	Encouragement of sex-typed activities in boys more than girls
100	Clarity of communication/use of reasoning; give reasons, encourage verbal give and take; discussion of feelings; empathy training; respect child's opinions, take child's preferences into account

Appendix B

Studies Used in the Meta-Analysis

Adams, G. R., & LaVoie, J. C. (1975). Parental expectations of educational and personal-social performance and childrearing patterns as a function of attractiveness, sex, and conduct of the child. *Child Development, 5,* 125–142.

Allaman, J. D., Joyce, C. S., & Crandal, V. C. (1972). The antecedents of social desirability response tendencies of children and young adults. *Child Development, 43,* 1135–i160.

Anderson, J. G., & Evans, F. B. (1976). Family socialization and educational achievement in two cultures: Mexican-American and Anglo-American. *Sociometry, 39,* 209–222.

Antell, P. A. (1982). Parent-child interactional styles: A look at second-order effects (Doctoral dissertation, Northern Illinois University, 1982). *Dissertation Abstracts International, 43,* 2366B.

Arco, C. M. B., DeMeis, D. K., Self, P. A., & Gutrecht, N. (1984). Interrelationships among maternal and infant characteristics during the neonatal period. *Journal of Pediatric Psychology, 9,* 131–147.

Armentrout, J. A. (1975). Repression-sensitization and MMPI correlates of retrospective reports of parental child-rearing behaviors. *Journal of Clinical Psychology, 31,* 444–448.

Armentrout, J. A., & Burger, G. K. (1972). Children's reports of parental child-rearing behavior at five grade levels. *Developmental Psychology, 7,* 44–48.

Atkinson, J., & Endsley, R. C. (1976). Influence of sex of child and parent on parental reactions to hypothetical parent-child situations. *Genetic Psychology Monographs, 94,* 131–147.

Barnes, C. L. (1986). Comparison of fathers' and mothers' speech to their preschool children. *Dissertation Abstracts International, 47,* 1752B. (University Microfilms No. 86-13270)

Barnett, M. A., Howard, J. A., King, L. M., & Dino, G. A. (1980). Antecedents of empathy: Retrospective accounts of early socialization. *Personality and Social Psychology Bulletin, 6,* 361–365.

Barrett Fields, A. (1981). Perceived parent behavior and the self-evaluations of lower-class black male and female children. *Adolescence, 16,* 919–934.

Bartz, K. W., & Levine, E. S. (1978). Childrearing by black parents: A description and comparison to Anglo and Chicano parents. *Journal of Marriage and the Family, 40,* 709–719.

Baumrind, D. (1971). Current patterns of parental authority. *Developmental Psychology Monograph, 1*(4, Pt. 2).

Baumrind, D. (1988). *Familial antecedents of social competence in middle childhood.* Unpublished manuscript.

Bearison, D. J. (1979). Sex-linked patterns of socialization. *Sex Roles, 5,* 11–18.

Bee, H. L., Mitchell, S. K., Barnard, K. E., Eyres, S. J., & Hammond, M. A. (1984). Predicting intellectual outcomes: Sex differences in response to early environmental stimulation. *Sex Roles, 10,* 783–803.

Bee, H. L., Van Egeren, L. F., Streissguth, A. P., Nyman, B. A., & Leckie, M. S. (1969). Social class differences in maternal teaching strategies and speech patterns. *Developmental Psychology, 1,* 726–734.

Bell, N. J., & Carver, W. (1980). A reevaluation of gender label effects: Expectant mothers' responses to infants. *Child Development, 51,* 925–927.

Belsky, J., Gilstrap, B., & Rovine, M. (1984). The Pennsylvania infant and Family Development Project, I: Stability and change in mother-infant and father-infant interaction in a family setting at one, three, and nine months. *Child Development, 55,* 692–705.

Birnbaum, D. W., & Croll, W. L. (1984). The etiology of children's stereotypes about sex differences in emotionality. *Sex Roles, 10,* 677–691.

Bledsoe, J. C., & Wiggins, R. G. (1974). Self-concepts and academic aspirations of "understood" and "misunderstood" boys and girls in ninth grade. *Psychological Reports, 35,* 57–58.

Blehar, M., Lieberman, A., & Ainsworth, M. (1977). Early face-to-face interaction and its relations to later infant-mother attachment. *Child Development, 48,* 182–194.

Block, J. H. (1978). Another look at sex differentiation in the socialization behaviors of mothers and fathers. In J. A. Sherman & F. L. Denmark (Eds.), *The psychology of women: Future directions in research* (pp. 29–87). New York: Psychological Dimensions.

Block, J. H., Block, J., & Harrington, D. (1974, April). *The relationship of parental teaching strategies to ego-resiliency in pre-school children.* Paper presented at the meeting of the Western Psychological Association, San Francisco, CA.

Boyce Fauls, L., & Smith, W. D. (1956). Sex-role learning of five-year-olds. *Journal of Genetic Psychology, 89,* 105–117.

Breckenridge, J. N. (1982). A confluence model of mother-infant interaction. *Dissertation Abstracts International, 43,* 892B. (University Microfilms No. 82-17210)

Britain, S. D., & Abad, M. (1974). Field-independence: A function of sex and socialization in a Cuban and an American group. *Personality and Social Psychology Bulletin, 1,* 319–320.

Bronfenbrenner, U. (1961). Some familial antecedents of responsibility and leadership in adolescents. In L. Petrullo & B. M. Bass (Eds.), *Leadership and interpersonal behavior* (pp. 239–270). New York: Holt, Rinehart & Winston.

Brook, J. S., Whiteman, M., Lukoff, I. F., & Scovell Gordon, A. (1979). Maternal and adolescent expectations and aspirations as related to sex, ethnicity, and socioeconomic status. *The Journal of Genetic Psychology, 135,* 209–216.

Brown, J. V., Bakeman, R., Snyder, P. A., Frederickson, T. W., Morgan, S. T., & Helper, R. (1975). Interactions of black inner-city mothers with their newborn infants. *Child Development, 46,* 677–686.

Buck, M. R., & Austrin, H. R. (1971). Factors relating to school achievement in an economically disadvantaged group. *Child Development, 42,* 1813–1826.

Buriel, R. (1981). The relation of Anglo- and Mexican American children's locus of control beliefs to parents' and teachers' socialization practices. *Child Development, 52,* 104–113.

Burke, R. J., & Weir, T. (1978). Sex differences in adolescent life stress, social support, and well-being. *The Journal of Psychology, 98,* 277–288.

Burton, R. V., Maccoby, E. E., & Allinsmith, W. (1961). Antecedents of resistance to temptation in four-year-old children. *Child Development, 32,* 689–710.

Carlson, R. (1963). Identification and personality structure in preadolescents. *Journal of Abnormal and Social Psychology, 67,* 566–573.

Cherry, L., & Lewis, M. (1976). Mothers and two-year-olds: A study of sex-differentiated aspects of verbal interaction. *Developmental Psychology, 12,* 278–282.

Cicirelli, V. G. (1978). Effect of sibling presence on mother-child interaction. *Developmental Psychology, 14,* 315–316.

Clarke-Stewart, K. A. (1973). Interactions between mothers and their young children: Characteristics and consequences. *Monographs of*

the Society for Research in Child Development, 38, (6–7, Serial No. 153).

Clevenger Bright, M., & Stockdale, D. F. (1984). Mothers', fathers', and preschool children's interactive behaviors in a play setting. *The Journal of Genetic Psychology, 144,* 219–232.

Clingempeel, W. G., Levoli, R., & Brand, E. (1984). Structural complexity and the quality of stepfather-stepchild relationships. *Family Process, 23,* 547–560.

Copeland, A. P. (1984). An early look at divorce: Mother-child interactions in the first post-separation year. *Journal of Divorce, 8,* 17–30.

Corter, C., & Bow, J. (1976). The mother's response to separation as a function of her infant's sex and vocal distress. *Child Development, 47,* 872–876.

Costos, D. (1986). Sex role identity in young adults: Its parental antecedents and relation to ego development. *Journal of Personality and Social Psychology, 50,* 602–611.

Crawley, S., Rogers, P., Friedman, S., Iacobbo, M., Critics, A., Richardson, L., & Thompson, M. (1978). Developmental changes in the structure of mother-infant play. *Developmental Psychology, 14,* 30–36.

Dean Callard, E. (1968). Achievement motive of four-year-olds and maternal achievement expectancies. *Journal of Experimental Education, 36,* 14–23.

Devereux, E. C., Jr., Bronfenbrenner, U., & Suci, G. J. (1963). Patterns of parental behavior in the United States of America and the Federal Republic of Germany: A cross-national comparison. *International Social Science Journal, 14,* 488–506.

Devereux, E. C., Shouval, R., Bronfenbrenner, U., Rodgers, R. R., Kav-Venaki, S., Kiely, E., & Karson, E. (1974). Socialization practices of parents, teachers, and peers in Israel: The kibbutz versus the city. *Child Development, 45,* 269–281.

Dino, G. A., Barnett, M. A., & Howard, J. A. (1984). Children's expectations of sex differences in parents' responses to sons and daughters encountering interpersonal problems. *Sex Roles, 11,* 709–717.

Dolins, M. T. (1980). Effects of child's sex and ordinal position on mother-child dialogue (Doctoral dissertation, Yeshiva University, 1980). *Dissertation Abstracts International, 41,* 1535B.

Domash, L., & Balter, L. (1976). Sex and psychological differentiation in preschoolers. *The Journal of Genetic Psychology, 128,* 77–84.

Donate-Bartfield, E., & Passman, R. H. (1985). Attentiveness of mothers and fathers to their baby's cries. *Infant Behavior & Development, 8,* 385–393.

Droppleman, L. F., & Schaefer, E. S. (1963). Boys' and girls' reports of maternal and paternal behavior. *Journal of Abnormal and Social Psychology, 67,* 648–654.

Duncan, O. D., Schuman, H., & Duncan, B. (1973). *Social change in a metropolitan community.* New York: Russell Sage.

Easterbrooks, M. A., & Goldberg, W. A. (1984). Toddler development in the family: Impact of father involvement and parenting characteristics. *Child Development, 55,* 740–752.

Eisenberg, N., Wolchik, S. A., Hernandez, R., & Pasternack, J. F. (1985). Parent socialization of young children's play: A short-term longitudinal study. *Child Development, 56,* 1506–1513.

Elder, G. H., Jr., Nguyen, T. V., & Caspi, A. (1985). Linking family hardship to children's lives. *Child Development, 56,* 361–375.

Emmerich, W. (1962). Variations in the parent role as a function of the parent's sex and the child's sex and age. *Merrill-Palmer Quarterly, 8,* 1–11.

Eron, L. D., Walder, L. O., Toigo, R., & Lefkowitz, M. M. (1963). Social class, parental punishment for aggression, and child aggression. *Child Development, 34,* 849–867.

Fagot, B. I. (1974). Sex differences in toddlers' behavior and parental reaction. *Developmental Psychology, 10,* 554–558.

Fagot, B. I. (1978). The influence of sex of child on parental reactions to toddler children. *Child Development, 49,* 459–465.

Falender, C. A., & Heber, R. (1975). Mother-child interaction and participation in a longitudinal intervention program. *Developmental Psychology, 11,* 830–836.

Field, T. (1978). Interaction patterns of primary verse secondary caretaker fathers. *Developmental Psychology, 14,* 183–185.

Flake-Hobson, C., Robinson, B. E., & Skeen, P. (1981). Relationship between parental androgyny and early child-rearing ideals and practices. *Psychological Reports, 49,* 667–675.

Fling, S., & Manosevitz, M. (1972). Sex typing in nursery school children's play interests. *Developmental Psychology, 7,* 146–152.

Flynn, T. M. (1979). Parental attitudes and the preschool child's self-concept. *Child Study Journal, 9,* 69–79.

Frankel, M. T., & Rollins, H. A., Jr. (1983). Does mother know best? Mothers and fathers interaction with preschool sons and daughters. *Developmental Psychology, 19,* 694–702.

Fraser, C., & Roberts, N. (1973). Mothers' speech to children of four different ages. *Journal of Psycholinguistic Research, 4,* 9–16.

Fried Weitzman, N. (1983). Traditional and non-traditional mothers' communication with their daughters and sons (Doctoral dissertation, State University of New York at Stony Brook, 1983). *Dissertation Abstracts International, 44,* 649B.

Frodi, A. M., Lamb, M. E., Frodi, M., Hwang, C.-P., Forsstrom, B., & Corry, T. (1982). Stability and change in parental attitudes following infant's birth into traditional and nontraditional Swedish families. *Scandinavian Journal of Psychology, 23,* 53–62.

Gaines, L. (1981). Sex-differentiated aspects of father-child verbal interaction (Doctoral dissertation, New York University, 1981). *Dissertation Abstracts International, 42,* 685A.

Gates, F. L. (1982). Socialization of sex differences in aggression: Peer and parental influences. *Dissertation Abstracts International, 43,* 272B. (University Microfilms No. 82-27304)

Gendler, N. K. (1984). Children's sex-trait and sex-role stereotypes: Development and relationship to parent's stereotypes. *Dissertation Abstracts International, 46,* 325B. (University Microfilms No. 85-03427)

Gill, L. J., & Spilka, B. (1962). Some nonintellectual correlates of academic achievement among Mexican-American secondary school students. *Journal of Educational Psychology, 53,* 144–149.

Gjerde, P. F. (1986). The interpersonal structure of family interaction settings: Parent-adolescent relations in dyads and triads. *Developmental Psychology, 22,* 297–304.

Goldberg, S., & Lewis, M. (1969). Play behavior in the year old infant: Early sex differences. *Child Development, 40,* 21–32.

Gordon, J. E., & Smith, E. (1965). Children's aggression, parental attitudes, and the effects of an affiliation-arousing story. *Journal of Personality and Social Psychology, 1,* 654–659.

Gordon, N. B. (1983). Maternal perception of child temperament and observed mother-child interaction. *Child Psychiatry and Human Development, 13,* 153–167.

Goshen-Gottstein, E. R. (1981). Differential maternal socialization of opposite-sexed twins, triplets, and quadruplets. *Child Development, 52,* 1255–1264.

Greenglass, E. R. (1971). A cross-cultural comparison of maternal communication. *Child Development, 42,* 685–692.

Grusec, J. E., Dix, T., & Mills, R. (1982). The effects of type, severity, and victim of children's transgressions on maternal discipline. *Canadian Journal of Behavioral Science, 14,* 276–289.

Grusec, J. E., & Kuczynski, L. (1980). Direction of effect in socialization: A comparison of the parent's versus the child's behavior as determinants of disciplinary techniques. *Developmental Psychology, 16,* 1–9.

Halverson, C. F., Jr., & Waldrop, M. F. (1970). Maternal behavior toward own and other preschool children: The problem of "ownness." *Child Development, 41,* 839–845.

Hanson, R. A. (1975). Consistency and stability of home environmental measures related to IQ. *Child Development, 46,* 470–480.

Hanson Moore, M. L. (1984). Parental perceptions of 2, 3, and 4-year-old children: 1963–1983 (Doctoral dissertation, University of North Carolina at Greensboro, 1984). *Dissertation Abstracts International, 46,* 494B.

Hatfield, J. S., Ferguson, L. R., & Alpert, R. (1967). Mother-child interaction and the socialization process. *Child Development, 38,* 365–414.

Hawkes, G. R., Burchinal, L. G., & Gardner, B. (1957). Measurement of pre-adolescents' views of family control of behavior. *Child Development, 28,* 387–392.

Hilton, I. (1967). Differences in the behavior of mothers towards first- and later-born children. *Journal of Personality and Social Psychology, 7,* 282–290.

Hoppe, C. M., Kagan, S. M., & Zahn, G. L. (1977). Conflict resolution among field-independent and field-dependent Anglo-American and Mexican-American children and their mothers. *Developmental Psychology, 13,* 591–598.

Hunter, F. T. (1984). Socializing procedures in parent-child and friendship relations during adolescence. *Developmental Psychology, 20,* 1092–1099.

Hunter, F. T., & Youniss, J. (1982). Changes in functions of three relations during adolescence. *Developmental Psychology, 18,* 806–811.

Jacklin, C. N., DiPietro, J. A., & Maccoby, E. E. (1984). Sex-typing behavior and sex-typing pressure in child/parent interaction. *Archives of Sexual Behavior, 13,* 413–425.

Jacklin, C. N., Maccoby, E. E., & Dick, A. E. (1973). Barrier behavior and toy preference: Sex differences (and their absence) in the year-old child. *Child Development, 44,* 196–200.

Jasper Crase, S., Foss, C. J., & Karal Colbert, K. (1981). Children's self-concept and perception of parents' behavior. *The Journal of Psychology, 108,* 297–303.

Jeyaraj, M. (1982). Male-female behavioral differences of religious secondary school principals as related to their childhood experiences. *Dissertation Abstracts International, 43,* 607A. (University Microfilms No. 82-17131)

Johnson, D. M. (1981). Some characteristics of mothers and fathers in parent-child play (Doctoral dissertation, University of Maryland, 1981). *Dissertation Abstracts International, 42,* 3428A.

Jurich, A. P., Bollman, S. R., & Moxley, V. M. (1976). Families of hospitalized adolescents: Sex differences. *Psychological Reports, 38,* 883–886.

Kagan, J., & Freeman, M. (1963). Relation of childhood intelligence, maternal behaviors, and social class to behavior during adolescence. *Child Development, 34,* 899–911.

Katz, P. A., & Boswell, S. (1986). Flexibility and traditionality in children's gender roles. *Genetic, Social, and General Psychological Monographs, 112,* 105–147.

Kavanagh, K. (1986). Socialization processes and determinants with two year olds. *Dissertation Abstracts International, 47,* 3136B. (University Microfilms No. 86-22504)

Kell, L., & Aldous, J. (1960). The relations between mother's child-rearing ideologies and their children's perception of maternal control. *Child Development, 31,* 145–156.

Kelly, J. A., & Worell, L. (1976). Parent behaviors related to masculine, feminine, and androgynous sex role orientations. *Journal of Consulting and Clinical Psychology, 44,* 843–851.

Kendrick, C., & Dunn, J. (1980). Caring for a second baby: Effects on interaction between mother and firstborn. *Developmental Psychology, 16,* 303–311.

Klein, P. S. (1984). Behavior of Israeli mothers toward infants in relation to infants' perceived temperament. *Child Development, 55,* 1212–1218.

Kohn, M. L. (1959). Social class and the exercise of parental authority. *American Sociological Review, 24,* 352–366.

Kotelchuck, M. (1976). The infant's relationship to the father: Experimental evidence. In M. E. Lamb (Ed.), *The role of the father in child development* (pp. 329–344). New York: Wiley.

Kroger, J. (1983). University students' perceptions of their parents' child-rearing behavior. *New Zealand Journal of Educational Studies, 18,* 115–125.

Kronsberg, S., Schmaling, K., & Fagot, B. I. (1985). Risk in a parent's eyes: Effects of gender and parenting experience. *Sex Roles, 13,* 329–341.

Kuczynski, L. (1984). Socialization goals and mother-child interaction: Strategies for long-term and short-term compliance. *Developmental Psychology, 20,* 1061–1073.

Lamb, M. E. (1977). The development of mother-infant and father-infant attachments in the second year of life. *Developmental Psychology, 13,* 637–648.

Lambert, W. E., Yackley, A., & Hein, R. N. (1971). Child training values of English Canadian and French Canadian parents. *Canadian Journal of Behavioral Sciences, 3,* 217–236.

Landerholm, E. (1984). Teenage parenting skills. *Early Child Development and Care, 13,* 351–364.

Landerholm, E. J., & Scriven, G. (1981). A comparison of mother and father interaction with their six-month-old male and female infants. *Early Child Development and Care, 7,* 317–328.

Langlois, J. H., & Downs, A. C. (1980). Mothers, fathers, and peers as socialization agents of sex-typed play behaviors in young children. *Child Development, 51,* 1217–1247.

Lansky, L. M. (1967). The family structure also affects the model: Sex-role attitudes in parents of preschool children. *Merrill-Palmer Quarterly, 13,* 139–150.

Last, U., & Klein, H. (1984). Impact of parental holocaust traumatization on offsprings' reports of parental child-rearing practices. *Journal of Youth and Adolescence, 13,* 267–283.

Lawson, E. D., & Fitzgerald Slaughter, M. (1977). Reward and punishment patterns in rural and town school children. *Child Study Journal, 7,* 145–158.

Lefkowitz, M. M. (1962). Some relationships between sex role preference of children and other parent and child variables. *Psychological Reports, 10,* 43–53.

Levy-Shiff, R. (1982). The effects of father absence on young children in mother-headed families. *Child Development, 53,* 1400–1405.

Lewis, M. (1972). State as an infant-environment interaction: An analysis of mother-infant interaction as a function of sex. *Merrill-Palmer Quarterly, 18,* 95–121.

Lewis, M., & Cherry, L. (1977). Social behavior and language acquisition. In M. Lewis & L. Rosenblum (Eds.), *Interaction, conversation, and the development of language: The origins of behavior* (Vol. 2, pp. 227–246). New York: Plenum.

Ling, D., & Ling, A. H. (1974). Communication development in the first three years of life. *Journal of Speech and Hearing Research, 17,* 146–158.

Londerville, S., & Main, M. (1981). Security of attachment, compliance, and maternal training methods in the second year of life. *Developmental Psychology, 17,* 289–299.

Lynn, D. B., & Sawrey, W. L. (1962). Sex differences in the personality development of Norwegian children. *Journal of Genetic Psychology, 101,* 367–374.

Maccoby, E. E., & Jacklin, C. N. (1987). *Parent-child interaction in dyads and triads, at age 6½ years.* Unpublished manuscript.

Maccoby, E. E., Snow, M. E., & Jacklin, C. N. (1984). Children's dispositions and mother-child interaction at 12 and 18 months: A short-term lonitudinal study. *Developmental Psychology, 20,* 459–472.

MacDonald, K., & Parke, R. D. (1986). Parent-child physical play: The effects of sex and age of children and parents. *Sex Roles, 15,* 367–378.

Marcus, T. L., & Corsini, D. A. (1978). Parental expectations of preschool children as related to child gender and socioeconomic status. *Child Development, 49,* 243–246.

Margolin, G., & Patterson, G. R. (1975). Differential consequences provided by mothers and fathers for their sons and daughters. *Developmental Psychology, 11,* 537–538.

McLaughlin, B. (1983). Child compliance to parental control techniques. *Developmental Psychology, 19,* 667–673.

McLaughlin, B., Schutz, C., & White, D. (1980). Parental speech to five-year-old children in a game-playing situation. *Child Development, 51,* 580–582.

Michnick Golinkoff, R., & Johnson Ames, G. (1979). A comparison of fathers' and mothers' speech with their young children. *Child Development, 50,* 28–32.

Minton, C., Kagan, J., & Levine, J. A. (1971). Maternal control and obedience in the two-year-old. *Child Development, 42,* 1873–1894.

Mirkin Schwartz, M. (1982). Effects of maternal sex-role attitudes on certain aspects of preschoolers' behavior (Doctoral dissertation, Fordham University, 1982). *Dissertation Abstracts International, 43,* 123A.

Moss, H. (1967). Sex, age and state as determinants of mother-infant interaction. *Merrill-Palmer Quarterly, 13,* 19–36.

Moss, H. A. (1974). Early sex differences and mother-infant interaction. In R. C. Friedman, R. M. Richart, & R. L. Van de Wiele (Eds.), *Sex differences in behavior* (pp. 149–163). New York: Wiley.

Mussen, P., & Rutherford, E. (1963). Parent-child relations and parental personality in relation to young children's sex-role preferences. *Child Development, 34,* 589–607.

Newson, J., & Newson, E. (1976). *Seven years old in the home environment.* London: Allen & Unwin.

Noller, P. (1978). Sex differences in the socialization of affectionate expression. *Developmental Psychology, 14,* 317–319.

Paivio, A. (1964). Childrearing antecedents of audience sensitivity. *Child Development, 35,* 397–416.

Palkovitz, R. (1984). Parental attitudes and fathers' interactions with their 5-month-old infants. *Developmental Psychology, 20,* 1054–1060.

Parsons Eccles, J., Adler. T. F., & Kaczala, C. (1982). Socialization of achievement attitudes and beliefs: Parental influences. *Child Development, 53,* 310–321.

Pepi, J. S. (1981). Father-infant and mother-infant interactions in the first three months of the infant's life (Doctoral dissertation, The University of Chicago, 1981). *Dissertation Abstracts International, 42,* 1154B.

Peters, D. L., & Stewart, R. B., Jr. (1981). Father-child interactions in a shopping mall: A naturalistic study of father role behavior. *The Journal of Genetic Psychology, 138,* 269–278.

Phillips, J. R. (1973). Syntax and vocabulary of mothers' speech to young children: Age and sex comparisons. *Child Development, 44,* 182–185.

Poag Longeway, K. (1983). The effects of divorce on maternal affect and disciplinary practices (Doctoral disseration, University of Wisconsin-Milwaukee, 1983). *Dissertation Abstracts International, 45,* 357B.

Power, T. G. (1980). Patterns of early infant socialization: A descriptive analysis of mother- and father-infant interaction in the home. *Dissertation Abstracts International, 41,* 4287B. (University Microfilms No. 81-08631)

Radin, N. (1974). Observed maternal behavior with four-year-old boys and girls in lower-class families. *Child Development, 45,* 1126–1131.

Raymond, C. L., & Persson Benbow, C. (1986). Gender differences in mathematics: A function of parental support and student sex typing? *Developmental Psychology, 22,* 808–819.

Rebelsky, F., & Hanks, C. (1971). Father's verbal interaction with infants in the first three months of life. *Child Development, 42,* 63–68.

Reinhardt, C. I. (1985). Maternal and paternal perceptions of infant development: Their effect on scores of the Kent Infant Development Scale (Doctoral dissertation, Kent State University, 1985). *Dissertation Abstracts International, 47,* 388B.

Rendina, I., & Dickerscheid, J. O. (1976). Father involvement with first-born infants. *Family Coordinator, 25,* 373–379.

Rheingold, H. L., & Cook, K. V. (1975). The contents of boys' and girls' rooms as an index of parents' behavior. *Child Development, 46,* 459–463.

Ribas, M. A. (1982). Parenting behavior as perceived by Chicano children during late childhood with implications for family therapy. *Dissertation Abstracts International, 44,* 323B. (University Microfilms No. 83-11132)

Roberts, W. L. (1983). Family interactions and child competence in a preschool setting (Doctoral dissertation, Simon Fraser University, British Columbia, 1983). *Dissertation Abstracts International, 46,* 685B.

Robin, M. (1982). Neonate-mother interaction: Tactile contacts in the days following birth. *Early Child Development and Care, 9,* 221–236.

Rosen, B. C., & Aneshensel, C. S. (1978). Sex differences in the educational-occupational expectation process. *Social Forces, 57,* 164–186.

Rosenthal, M. K. (1983). State variation in the newborn and mother-infant interaction during breast feeding: Some sex differences. *Developmental Psychology, 19,* 740–745.

Rosenthal, M. K. (1984). Sex differences in mother-infant interaction during breast-feeding in the neonatal period. *The Southern Psychologist, 2,* 3–7.

Rothbart, M. K. (1971). Birth order and mother-child interaction in an achievement situation. *Journal of Personality and Social Psychology, 17,* 113–120.

Rothbart, M. K., & Maccoby, E. E. (1966). Parent's differential reaction to sons and daughters. *Journal of Personality and Social Psychology, 4,* 237–243.

Rowe, D. C. (1981). Environmental and genetic influences on dimensions of perceived parenting: A twin study. *Developmental Psychology, 17,* 203–208.

Rubin, J., Provenzano, F., & Lurin, Z. (1974). The eye of the beholder: Parents' views on sex of newborns. *American Journal of Orthopsychiatry, 44,* 512–519.

Russell, C. M. (1983). Achievement and socialization in British and American adolescents. *Dissertation Abstracts International, 44,* 2900. (University Microfilms No. 83-28685)

Sacks, J. A. Y. (1981). Father-child interaction as a function of age and gender of the child (Doctoral dissertation, The City University of New York, 1981). *Dissertation Abstracts International, 42,* 2103B.

Schab, F. (1982). Early adolescence in the south: Attitudes regarding the home and religion. *Adolescence, 17,* 605–612.

Schaefer, R. A. (1980). Maternal choice of child-rearing strategy and birth order of child (Doctoral dissertation, Duke University, 1980). *Dissertation Abstracts International, 41,* 1125B.

Schaffer, R. H., & Crook, C. K. (1980). Child compliance and maternal control techniques. *Developmental Psychology, 16,* 54–61.

Schneider, D. (1984). The influence of parental beliefs, encouragement, and expectations on their children's mathematical needs, values, and plans (Doctoral dissertation, Fordham University, 1984). *Dissertation Abstracts International, 45,* 133A.

Sears, R. R., Maccoby, E. E., & Levin, H. (1957). *Patterns of child rearing.* Evanston, IL: Row, Peterson.

Sears, R. R., Whiting, J., Nowlis, V., & Sears, P. S. (1953). Some child rearing antecedents of aggression and dependency in young children. *Genetic Psychology Monographs, 47,* 135–236.

Sheehan, T. D. (1982). Children's originality and dependence and their relation to parental control and affect. (Doctoral dissertation, University of Waterloo, 1982). *Dissertation Abstracts International, 43,* 1600B.

Siegelman, M. (1965). Evaluation of Bronfenbrenner's Questionnaire for children concerning parental behavior. *Child Development, 36,* 163–174.

Smart, R. C., & Smart, M. S. (1976). Preadolescents' perceptions of parents and their relations to a test of responses to moral dilemmas. *Social Behavior and Personality, 4,* 297–308.

Smith, C., & Lloyd, B. (1978). Maternal behavior and perceived sex of infant: Revisited. *Child Development, 49,* 1263–1265.

Smith, P. K., & Daglish, L. (1977). Sex differences in parent and infant behavior in the home. *Child Development, 48,* 1250–1254.

Snow, M. E., Jacklin, C. N., & Maccoby, E. E. (1983). Sex-of-child differences in father-child interaction at one year of age. *Child Development, 54,* 227–232.

Spitalnik, D. M. (1981). Independence training: Parental expectations for independent functioning of pre-school children with phenylketonuria (PKU) and pre-school children without interferences in their development (Doctoral dissertation, Temple University, 1981). *Dissertation Abstracts International, 43,* 265B.

Stayton, D. J., Hogan, R., & Ainsworth, M. D. S. (1971). Infant obedience and maternal behavior: The origins of socialization reconsidered. *Child Development, 42,* 1057–1069.

Stern, A. (1984). Sex-typed expectations of aggression: An investigation of parents and their preschool children (Doctoral dissertation, Temple University, 1984). *Dissertation Abstracts International, 45,* 1043B.

Stinnett, N., Farris, J. A., & Walters, J. (1974). Parent-child relationships of male and female high school students. *The Journal of Genetic Psychology, 125,* 99–106.

Stoneman, Z., & Brody, G. H. (1981). Two's company, three makes a difference: An examination of mothers' and fathers' speech to their young children. *Child Development, 52,* 705–707.

Tasch, R. J. (1952). The role of the father in the family. *Journal of Experimental Education, 20,* 319–361.

Tauber, M. A. (1979). Sex differences in parent-child interaction styles during a free-play session. *Child Development, 50,* 981–988.

Thoman, E. B., Leiderman, P. H., & Olson, J. P. (1972). Neonate-mother interaction during breast feeding. *Developmental Psychology, 6,* 110–118.

Tudiver, J. G. (1980). Parents and the sex role development of the child (Doctoral dissertation, University of Western Ontario, 1980). *Dissertation Abstracts International, 41,* 4646B.

Uddenberg, N., & Englesson, I. (1980). Perception of mother in four-and-a-half-year-old children: A comparison with the mother's social and emotional history. *International Journal of Behavioral Development, 3,* 27–45.

Wasserman, G. A., & Lewis, M. (1985). Infant sex differences: Ecological effects. *Sex Roles, 12,* 665–675.

Weinraub, M., & Lewis, M. (1977). The determinants of children's responses to separation. *Monographs of the Society for Research in Child Development, 42*(4, Serial No. 172).

Weinstein, E. A., & Geisel, P. N. (1960). An analysis of sex differences in adjustment. *Child Development, 31,* 721–728.

Wenger, S., Berg-Cross, L., & Berg-Cross, G. (1980). Parents' judgments of children's aggressive behavior. *Merrill-Palmer Quarterly, 26,* 161–169.

Weston, M. (1982). The effects of gender, sex role type, and temperament on the play behavior of parents and infants (Doctoral dissertation, New York University, 1982). *Dissertation Abstracts International, 43,* 3755B.

Whyte, J. (1983). Control and supervision of urban 12-year-olds within and outside Northern Ireland: A pilot study. *The Irish Journal of Psychology, 1,* 37–45.

Will, J. A., Self, P. A., & Datan, N. (1976). Maternal behavior and perceived sex of infant. *American Journal of Orthopsychiatry, 46,* 135–139.

Wiltshire Goodenough, E. (1957). Interest in persons as an aspect of sex difference in the early years. *Genetic Psychology Monographs, 55,* 287–323.

Wolkin, L. (1983). A descriptive analysis of cognitive-linguistic aspects of interactions between mothers and their three year-olds (Doctoral dissertation, Fordham University, 1983). *Dissertation Abstracts International, 43,* 3859A.

Wyer, R. S., Jr. (1965). Self-acceptance, discrepancy between parents' perceptions of their children, and goal-seeking effectiveness. *Journal of Personality and Social Psychology, 2,* 311–316.

Yarrow, L. J., MacTurk, R. H., Vietze, P. M., McCarthy, M. E., Klein, R. P., & McQuiston, S. (1984). Developmental course of parental stimulation and its relationship to mastery motivation during infancy. *Developmental Psychology, 20,* 492–503.

Yarrow, L. J., Rubenstein, J. L., & Pedersen, F. A. (1975). *Infant and environment: Early cognitive and motivational development.* New York: Halsted.

Zegiob, L. E., & Forehand, R. (1975). Maternal interactive behavior as a function of race, socioeconomic status, and sex of the child. *Child Development, 46,* 564–568.

Zussman, J. U. (1978). Relationship of demographic factors to parental discipline techniques. *Developmental Psychology, 14,* 685–686.

Received July 5, 1989
Revision received May 7, 1990
Accepted June 12, 1990 ▪

[25]

Sex Roles, Vol. 8, No. 11, 1982

Sex Differences in Parental Directives to Young Children[1]

David C. Bellinger and Jean Berko Gleason
Boston University

This study investigated how children learn sex-associated strategies for requesting action. We compared the directives which mothers and fathers address to their 2 1/2- to 5-year-old children. Ten children, 5 boys and 5 girls, engaged separately with each parent in a construction task. Fathers produced more directives than mothers and tended to phrase them as imperatives (e.g., Put the screw in*) or as highly indirect "hints" (e.g.,* The wheel's going to fall off*) more often than mothers, who relied more on relatively transparent indirect forms (e.g.,* Can you put the screw in?*). There were no differences in the form of the directives addressed to girls and boys, nor were there any cross-sex effects. Parental modeling. rather than differential socialization of girls and boys, appears to be the mechanism by which children learn to request action in sex-associated ways.*

A competent speaker can express the same information in several ways depending on the interests and abilities of the addressee and a variety of situational factors such as time and channel constraints. Alternation rules govern the selection of the appropriate form in which to phrase a message under different circumstances (Ervin-Tripp, 1968). Although the possible forms may be equivalent referentially, they often differ substantially in the social meaning they convey. Hence, a speaker's choice may reveal the way he feels about himself, his addressee, their relationship, and the task at hand. The study of alternation rules thus provides a window on the intersection of linguistic and social structure.

[1] This research was supported by grant BNS 75-21909 A01 from the National Science Foundation and by Public Health Service Research Fellowship F32-MH07094. We wish to thank Dr. Julia Matthews-Bellinger, Dr. Esther Blank Greif, and Rivka Perlman for helpful discussion; Rivka Perlmann and David Alderton for their aid in coding; and Nobi Yonekura for helping to prepare the manuscript.
[2] Correspondence should be sent to David Bellinger, Children's Hospital Medical Center, Enders Building, 300 Longwood Avenue, Boston, Massachusetts 02115.

The speech act most studied in terms of its social components is the directive. Ervin-Tripp (1976, 1977) has shown that the surface form which a speaker chooses varies systematically with social features of the situation. For instance, she has found that, in English, the imperative form (e.g., *Shut the window*) is generally addressed to those lower in rank than the speaker or to one of equal rank with whom the speaker is very familiar. The indirect forms (e.g., *Can you shut the window? Would you be willing to shut the window?*), on the other hand, tend to be addressed to those of higher rank than the speaker, to those of equal rank with whom the speaker is unfamiliar, or to addressees whose compliance with the request would entail some sacrifice. Usually, the social features that characterize an interaction specify a range of forms appropriate for requesting action. Not surprisingly, the details of these form-context relationships are somewhat culture specific (e.g., see Hollos & Beeman, 1978, for a comparison of Norwegian and Hungarian). Various studies have shown that by age 3 or 4, children are aware of at least some aspects of these relationships (e.g., James, 1978; Shatz & Gelman, 1973; Hollos & Beeman, 1978; Gleason, 1973; Andersen & Johnson, 1973; Sachs & Devin, 1976).

Gleason (1975), Lakoff (1973), Key (1975) and others have proposed that men and women may differ in the way they request other people to do things. Specifically, these authors suggest that primarily men use the imperative, while women tend to opt for forms which are indirect (i.e., nonimperative). Although it has only anecdotal support, this hypothesis is consistent with the growing evidence that women's speech is less assertive and more polite than men's (e.g., Crosby & Nyquist, 1977; Haas, 1979; Thorne & Henley, 1975). Nevertheless, sex of speaker is a social variable whose role in the alternation rules that govern choice of directive form has not been well studied except insofar as it is often confounded with rank.

Whether these differences between men and women actually exist, they are part of the stereotypic view about the characteristics of "male" and "female" speech. Kramer (1977) presents strong evidence that high school and college students of both sexes tend to perceive male speech as "blunt," "forceful," and "straight to the point," and women's speech as "polite," "gentle," and "friendly." The evidence available suggests that children share these perceptions. In a study of the development of these stereotypes, Edelsky (1977) found that sixth-grade children showed high consensus in judging the indirect directive frame *Won't you please...* to be a female form and, furthermore, considered the imperative to be a male form, though with low consensus among judges. Andersen (Note 1) found that, when playing the role of "father," 4-year-old children phrased directives in imperative form; but when playing "mother," they tended to choose indirect forms. Thus, from a rather early age, children associate the more direct way of requesting action with males and the more indirect ways with females.

How children might acquire these stereotypes is an important developmental question. We examined parent-child interaction for clues. In the most general terms, there are two basic theoretical views about the role that parents play in their children's acquisition of the stereotypes described above: One emphasizes differences in the speech of mothers and fathers as parents' primary input to this process (see Hypothesis 1 below), and one emphasizes differences in the speech that parents address to boys and girls (see Hypotheses 2 and 3 below). It should be emphasized that the outcome of the socialization process is not at question, rather the mechanism by which parents socialize their children with regard to this aspect of linguistic behavior. The hypotheses about how this socialization takes place are as follows:

Hypothesis 1. Parental modeling is the important process involved in children's acquisition of sex-associated ways to request action. This hypothesis leads us to predict that fathers use the imperative form more frequently than mothers, who, in turn, make relatively more frequent use of indirect forms. Previous studies have generally shown that imperatives account for a greater percentage of males' than females' utterances to young children across a variety of settings (Gleason, 1975; Kriedberg, Note 2; Weintraub, Note 3; Rondal, Note 4). However, all of these studies examined only directives that were imperative in syntactic form. None examined the full range of forms which can be used directively. To date, there has been no comparison of the relative frequencies with which fathers and mothers use the alternative forms. Golinkoff and Ames (1979) compared fathers' and mothers' use of explicit (i.e., imperative) versus implicit directives, but considered only a narrow range of forms to be "implicit" directives, (viz., those phrased interrogatively). Therefore, it is unclear how to interpret their finding that the mothers and fathers of 19-month-old girls and boys did not differ in the frequencies with which they used explicit and implicit directives.

Hypothesis 2. Parents use different forms to boys and girls, who, in turn, learn to speak as they have been spoken to. This phenomenon has been noted in the use of kinship terms in some Arabic-speaking cultures, where, for instance, a grandfather might address his grandson as *Grandfather* (Ferguson, personal communication). If this process is at work in the present case, we should find that boys are exposed to more directives in the form of imperatives than girls, and girls exposed to more indirect forms than boys. Gleason (1975) noted in a pilot study that fathers tended to use more imperatives when speaking to sons than daughters and suggested that, early in life, boys, unlike girls, become used to giving and receiving orders. Similarly, Cherry and Lewis (1976) reported that mothers addressed a greater number of directives (regardless of their surface form) to 2-year-old boys than girls, although the difference fell just short of significance.

Hypothesis 3. The directive forms that parents address to young girls and boys reflect the ultimate status that males and females have in our society. If this is correct, we should, as above, expect the sex of a child to be an important influence on the parent's choice of directive form. However, in this case, boys, who are the future favored citizens, should receive more indirect (i.e., deferential) forms than girls, who, in turn, should receive more imperatives than boys. Greif (Note 5) found that parents interrupt preschool girls more frequently than they interrupt preschool boys, giving support to this nonintuitive idea that young boys might be treated with greater degerence than young girls. Blount (1972), in a study of Luo and Samoan, observed that adult speech to a girl contained a higher percentage of imperatives than the speech to two boys of a similar age. However, this sample was very small and, as in the studies cited under Hypothesis 1, the relative frequencies of the various alternative directive forms in parents' speech to boys and girls were not compared.

In Summary, the predictions which derive from the three hypotheses are as follows:

Hypothesis 1. Parental modeling of the various directive forms is the critical process, so that fathers should use relatively more imperative directives than mothers, who should use relatively more indirect forms.

Hypothesis 2. Children learn to speak as they are spoken to. Therefore, boys should be the recipients of relatively more imperative directives and girls the recipients of relatively more indirect forms.

Hypothesis 3. The way a child is addressed reflects the child's future status. Therefore, parents should request action from boys via the more polite indirect forms, and from girls via the imperative directive.

Note that only Hypotheses 2 and 3 are incompatible. It would be quite possible for the data to support Hypotheses 1 and 2 or Hypotheses 1 and 3.

METHODS

Sample

We obtained the samples of parental speech during two visits by each family to a laboratory playroom. On each visit, the child was recorded and videotaped for 30 minutes with one parent. The parent was asked to divide the time equally among three activities: reading a book which had no words, playing with a Playskool "take apart" car, and playing store using a toy cash register and a variety of food items. A previous study (Weintraub, Note 3) had shown that the car situation tended to elicit the most controlling speech from the parents, as the frequency of imperatives in their speech in this situation was about twice as high as in either of the other two. Therefore, in our analyses, we focused on the utterances that the parents produced during the car episode. (One might expect that since this task is more a "masculine" task than a "feminine" activity, its use as a data base might introduce bias. While we cannot rule out this possibility, there did not appear to be any difference in the enthusiasm with which mothers, as opposed to fathers, and daughters, as opposed to sons, tackled the problem.)

Because we were interested in parental differences in the use of different types of directives, it was important that the parents produce enough directives to permit a distributional analysis. Therefore, as a criterion for inclusion in the study, both parents in a family had to produce at least 15 directives during the period in which they and their child played with the car. We had access to a sample of 23 middle- to upper-middle-class families participating in a study of children's acquisition of communicative competence. Of these 23 sets of parents, 10 satisfied the criterion. In 5 of these families, the child was a male; in the remaining 5 a female. All children were first-born. The mean ages of the girls and boys were not significantly different (girls: 3; 11, range 3; 0-4; 11, boys: 3; 7, range 2; 6-4; 4, $t(8) = .71$).

These 10 families were select in terms of educational background. Eight of the fathers and 5 of the mothers had earned graduate degrees. However, they were fairly traditonal in terms of the way child-care responsibilities were divided in that only 1 mother worked full-time. Another 5 worked part-time for periods ranging from 6 to 27 hours per week. In all 10 families, the mother's estimate of average daily contact with the child was greater than the father's.

Each family was also given the Parent Awareness Measure, an instrument designed to assess both a child's language development and his or her parents' knowledge of the child's status. In essence, this is done by determining how accurately each parent can predict their child's response to a variety of test items. A detailed description of this instrument is given in Gleason, Greif, Weintraub, and Fardella (Note 6).

All play sessions were videotaped using a camera operated frm a camouflaged booth in the playroom. Audiotapes were also made to facilitate the preparation and verification of the transcripts. On both the videotapes and the transcripts, utterances which seemed to function as requests for action were identified and assigned to one of the three form classes discussed below. The directives produced by the children during this same period were also classified in order to compare parents' and children's relative use of the alternative directive forms.

Because of this use of videotapes, the coder was not blind to the sex of either the child or parent. The alternative of coding parents' intent solely from transcripts from which all references to parent and child sex had been eliminated was deemed even less satisfactory, since transcripts do not contain much of the information that is criticial to the judgment of speaker intent.

Directives

A directive was defined as any request for action, regardless of the syntactic form in which the request was phrased. Directives were coded into the three following categories: conventional imperatives, conventionalized indirect directives, and implied direct directives.

Conventional Imperatives. These include directives of the following forms: (a) *Do X* (e.g., *Pick that up*). (b) *You do X* (e.g., *You pick that up*). (c) *Let's do X* (if it was clear from the context of delivery that the child was to be the sole actor; e.g., *Let's go to the bathroom*). (d) Sentence fragments (usually manner adverbials) which follow conventional imperatives and/or are spoken with imperative intonation; for example, (2) and (3) in the following sequence: (1) *Turn the screw to the right.* (2) *To the right.* (3) *More.*

Conventionalized Indirect Directives. Here, the act being requested and the child as proposed agent of that act are identified explicitly in the utterance, by nonverbal cues provided by the speaker, or by the recent history of the interaction. The directives considered to be conventionalized indirect took a variety of interrogative and declarative forms such as the following: (a) *Can you . . . ?* (b) *You can . . .* (c) *Do you want to . . . ?* (d) *Are you going to . . . ?* (e) *Do you know how to . . . ?* (f) *This one goes here.* (g) *Would you . . . ?* (h) *You need to . . .* (i) *You have to . . .* (j) *Why don't you . . . ?* (k) *How about . . . ?*

Most directives of this sort are generally considered ritualized, almost idiomatic. Unlike true indirect speech acts, they do not require the addressee to compute the speaker's intention on the basis of complex conversational principles or postulates (e.g., Bates, 1976; Ervin-Tripp, 1977). Rather, such a form appears to function more as a routine (i.e., an unanalyzed unit) and is consistently used to communicate a certain intention (e.g., directive) despite the apparent discrepancy between the speaker's intention and the mood of the form.

Implied Indirect Directives. Unlike imperative and conventionalized indirect directives, these fail to make explicit the act that the child is being directed to perform or even the fact that he or she is being asked to do anything. Instead, implied indirect directives correspond to arguments, phrased either interrogatively or declaratively, for why an act should or should not be performed. Only by engaging in a process of logical inference is it possible to interpret these directives properly (see Bellinger, 1979, for a discussion of the logical status of these directives). For example, to a boy who was trying to place one of the wheels on the "take apart" car, a father said *It's going to fall off* in an attempt to get the boy to tighten the wheel a bit more, yet the father chose to do so by referring only to the consequence of failing to tighten the wheel. This forced the child to recognize that to allow the wheel to fall off would be counterproductive and, furthermore, to deduce from his own knowledge of cause-effect relationships the action that would prevent this.

Reliability. Reliability in identifying directives and classifying them by form was checked by having two individuals code the interaction between a father and his son. The rate at which this father produced directives was typical of that the other fathers, but the car episode lasted a particularly long time for this pair. The father produced 318 utterances, of which 75 were directives. This represents 11% of the total number of directives on which the following analyses are based.

Coders reached 92.8% agreement in indentifying utterances intended as directives. Agreement in classifying the directives on which there was consensus into form classes was 96.9%.

RESULTS

Unless otherwise noted, the data were analyzed by two-way analyses of variance with one between-subjects factor (Sex of Child) and one within-subjects factor (Sex of Parent).

Parents' Directives

Number of Utterances and Frequency of Directives. There were no significant differences in the total number of utterances produced by the fathers and mothers during the "take apart" car segment of the interaction (overall $\bar{X}$ = 187 utterances), suggesting equal engagement in the task. There was, however, a significant effect for Sex of Parent (at least in this sample of parents who met the criterion of producing at least 15 directives) in terms of the percentage of utterances which were judged to be directive in intent (regardless of the form in which this intent was realized). The frequency of directives in fathers' speech was higher than the frequency in mothers' speech (28.1% vs. 19.0%), $F(1, 8) =$ 8.08, $p < .025$. Directives were addressed to girls and boys with very nearly the same frequency (22.8% vs. 24.3% of all utterances, respectively).

Form Class Frequencies. The percentage of fathers' and mothers' directives which fell into the three form classes (i.e., imperative, conventionalized indirect, and implied indirect) in speech to boys and girls are presented in Tables I-III.[3] The rank ordering of the three types of directives in terms of frequency of use

---

[3] An ANOVA was performed on the group percentages of each form class. Two problems are associated with this strategy. First, since the three percentages for any parent must sum to 100, the three ANOVAs are not independent of one another and are subject to the problems of interpretation which arise when one performs multiple tests of significance on a single set of data. While interpreting the meaning of a group difference which reaches significance under these circumstances would be problematic, the failure of a group difference to reach significance may be taken as strong evidence that a true difference between the group means is unlikely. Second, the test of Hypothesis 1 involves the comparison of the speech of 10 fathers and 10 mothers. The tests of Hypotheses 2 and 3 involve the comparison of parents' speech to 5 girls and 5 boys. Hence, the power of the significance test for hypothesis 1 is greater than for Hypotheses 2 and 3.

Table I. Percentage of Parents' Directives in Imperative Form[a]

	Sex of parent		
	Father	Mother	Combined
Sex of child			
Boy	62.3 (22.3)	54.1 (14.5)	58.3
Girl	70.9 (12.1)	58.4 (12.1)	64.6
Combined	66.6	56.3	

[a] The numbers in parentheses are standard deviations.

Table II. Percentage of Parents' Directives in Conventionalized Indirect Form[a]

	Sex of parent		
	Father	Mother	Combined
Sex of child			
Boy	30.1 (18.0)	43.1 (14.4)	36.6
Girl	22.3 (10.5)	37.0 (9.4)	29.6
Combined	26.2	40.1	

[a] The numbers in parentheses are standard deviations.

was the same for fathers and mothers: imperative, conventionalized indirect, and implied indirect. However, the relative frequencies with which fathers and mothers used these different forms were not the same. A greater percentage of fathers' directives were implied indirect, $F(1, 8) = 6.10$, $p < .025$, while a greater percentage of mothers' directives were phrased in one of the conventionalized indirect frames, $F(1, 8) = 7.70$, $p < .025$. Furthermore, fathers showed

Table III. Percentage of Parents' Directives in Implied Indirect Form[a]

	Sex of parent		
	Father	Mother	Combined
Sex of child			
Boy	7.7 (6.2)	2.8 (2.8)	5.2
Girl	6.8 (5.9)	4.5 (3.2)	5.6
Combined	7.2	3.7	

[a] The numbers in parentheses are standard deviations.

a nonsignificant tendency to phrase a greater percentage of their directives in imperative form, $F(1, 8) = 3.66, p < .10$.

Neither Sex of Child nor the interaction effect even approached significance for any of the three types of directive, indicating that the directives which parents addressed to boys were not phrased differently from the directives addressed to girls.

To sharpen our view of parental differences in use of the various directive forms (and to avoid the problem of intertest dependence associated with the ANOVAs), we tested the hypothesis that the father and mother in a particular family show the following pattern in the frequencies with which their directives fall into the three form classes: Imperative and implied indirect forms account for a greater percentage of the father's directives than the mother's, and conventionalized indirect forms account for a greater percentage of the mother's than the father's. Five of the 10 couples displayed this pattern. Since there are 6 possible patterns that a couple could show, the probability that 5 or more couples out of 10 would show this pattern by chance alone is .015.[4] Therefore, within couples, fathers appear to produce more imperative and implied indirect directives than mothers. Mothers, in turn, tend to employ conventionalized indirect forms more often than fathers.

Children's Directives

Since the children tended to produce relatively few directives in the car episode (only 3 of the 10 children produced 15 or more, the criterion for including parents in the sample), we pooled the data within child sex (thus precluding the possibility of testing the significance of group differences). Table IV indicates the relative frequencies with which boys' and girls' directives to fathers and mothers were assigned to the various form classes. The

[4] Actually, there are 8 theoretically possible patterns:

	Imperative	Indirect	Implied
(1)	F > M	F > M	F > M
(2)	F > M	F > M	M > F
(3)	F > M	M > F	F > M
(4)	F > M	M > F	M > F
(5)	M > F	M > F	M > F
(6)	M > F	M > F	F > M
(7)	M > F	F > M	M > F
(8)	M > F	F > M	F > M

However, because the data are percentages, which must sum to 100 for each member of a couple, it is impossible for the percentages of one parent to exceed the percentages of the other for all three form classes. Therefore, no couple could follow pattern (1) or (5).

Table IV. Percentage of Children's Directives in the Three Form Classes

	Father			Mother		
	Imperative	Conventionalized indirect	Implied indirect	Imperative	Conventionalized indirect	Implied indirect
Boys	72.7	13.6	13.6	73.1	26.9	0
Girls	61.4	38.6	0	58.8	35.3	5.9

Table V. Percentage of Directives in the Three Form Classes:
Children Versus Parents

	Imperative	Conventionalized indirect	Implied indirect
Children			
Boys	72.9	20.8	6.3
Girls	60.2	37.2	2.6
Parents			
Fathers	66.6	26.2	7.2
Mothers	56.3	40.1	3.7

differences between girls and boys are in the same direction and of approximately the same magnitude as those between mothers and fathers (see Table V). That is, the boys produced more imperative and implied indirect directives, while the girls produced more of the conventionalized indirect forms. Furthermore, just as the sex of a child did not influence the frequency with which the parents used the alternative forms, the sex of the parent did not appear to influence the children's choice of form. These data must be interpreted with caution because of the small numbers of directives which the children produced.

Parents' Perceptions of Their Children's Linguistic Abilities

Mothers and fathers did not differ significantly in the accuracy with which they were able to predict their children's responses to the items comprising the "linguistic comprehension" and "linguistic production" scales of the Parent Awareness Measure (fathers: $\bar{X}$ = 51.8; mothers: $\bar{X}$ = 54.7, t = 1.03, df = 9, $p > .20$). Moreover, the scores for spouses were significantly correlated (r = .81, df = 8, $p < .01$), indicating that the mothers and fathers tended to have highly similar perceptions of their children's language skills. Together, these findings suggest that the differences noted in mothers' and fathers' use of the various directive forms are probably not due to differences in their perceptions of the children's linguistic abilities.

DISCUSSION

We know from previous studies that more of fathers' than mothers' utterances are imperatives (Gleason, 1975; Kriedberg, Note 2; Weintraub, Note 3; Rondal, Note 4). The present study demonstrates that this is part of a broader phenomenon in that fathers not only produce more imperatives than mothers but more directive speech acts in general. However, we found that mothers and fathers select differently from among the forms which can be used to express directive intent. Fathers relied on imperatives and implied indirect forms more often than mothers, who tended to employ conventionalized indirect forms more often than fathers. No other group differences reached significance. Hence, only Hypothesis 1 was confirmed: Parental modeling is the strongest candidate for the mechanism by which children learn to use the sex-associated strategies for requesting action. Parents' use of politeness routines follows the same pattern (Gleason & Greif, Note 7). Fathers and mothers prompt girls and boys to produce the routines *Thank you* and *Goodbye* with equal frequency, but mothers themselves use more of these politeness formulas than do fathers in their own speech.

There was little evidence that parents request action differently when speaking to boys and girls and thus little support for the notion that differential treatment of girls and boys is important in this aspect of social development. One cannot prove the null hypothesis, and this conclusion is based on a relatively small number of children. However, these data indicate that there was no striking difference in the types of directives addressed to girls and boys. Furthermore, this is consistent with the findings of Maccoby and Jacklin (1974), who, after an exhaustive review of the literature, concluded that little consistent evidence indicates that parents directly "shape" sex-appropriate behaviors in their children apart from supplying them with sex-typed clothing and toys and, perhaps, putting greater "socialization pressure" on boys than girls.

We should note a few characteristics of the families studied and the setting employed which bear on the generalizability of these findings. First, to obtain a reliable estimate of directive form preferences, it was necessary to select only parents who were relatively "directive" in this situation. Parents who issue fewer directives may exhibit different form preferences. (There was a significant positive correlation between the percentage of a parent's utterances that were directive and the percentage of directives that were conventional imperatives; $r = .53, df = 18, p < .02$). However, parents who met our criterion of 15 directives did not differ from those who did not in terms of level of education, the partitioning of child care responsibilities, the frequency of maternal employment outside the home, the MLU of speech to the child in the car episode, or the age of the child. There was a nonsignificant tendency for the parents included in the sample to be more talkative in the car episode. (The excluded mothers produced 27% fewer utterances than the included mothers; the excluded fathers 16% fewer utterances than the included fathers). Thus, differences in loquacity, rather than in some personality variable relating to "authoritarianism," may have been partly responsible for the fact that one parent satisfied the criterion and another did not. Second, sex of parent and role in the family were confounded in this study. In every family, the mother was the child's primary caretaker. Therefore, the differences noted could equally well be considered differences between primary and secondary caretakers, or between the individuals playing the nurturant/expressive versus authoritarian/instrumental roles in the family. However, while the nature of a speaker's role may influence his choice of directive form, the effect of sex of speaker apparently persists even over changes in role. Gleason (1975) studied a natural experiment in which the separate effects of sex and role could be observed, viz., a day-care center which employed male as well as female caregivers. Despite their sex, the male caregivers were in a primarily nurturant role, similar to that played by mothers in families with the traditional division of labors. Caregivers of both sexes produced many fewer imperative directives than either mothers or fathers in the home; but the male caregivers produced many more than the female caregivers, just as fathers tend to produce more than mothers. There appears to be a tendency for males to produce more imperatives than females, even when role is held as constant as this type of natural experiment permits. However, role does exert a tremendous influence on the absolute frequency with which speakers of either sex produce this type of directive.

The unavoidably artificial setting of the laboratory "playroom" in which the families were observed may have led the parents to suppress any inclination to take different tacks in requesting action from girls and boys. This seems unlikely, however, since several studies of the same sample of families in the same setting have found marked effects for Sex of Child on many aspects of parental behavior (and also many cross-sex effects) (e.g., Masur, Note 8; Masur & Gleason, Note 9; Weintraub, Note 3; Greif, Note 5). We are currently analyzing parent-child interaction in the home (for the same sample) to see whether the father-mother differences noted in the laboratory are accentuated in this more natural setting, where parental roles are more clearly defined. We may also see effects for the sex of the child on parental directives, since children may be treated differently in the home and laboratory (Gleason, 1975). In all likelihood, we studied a rather select group of directives (i.e., those issued under relatively congenial, cooperative circumstances). The directives that parents issue when disciplining or prohibiting their children's behavior may take quite different forms. For instance, there are undoubtedly situations in which urgency overrides politeness as a determinant of directive form and the imperative is the form most likely to be used. On these occasions, the differences between fathers and mothers in choice of form may disappear. On the other hand, there may be circumstances in which the sex of child is a more potent influence on parents' choice of form than it was in the setting we used. Only by examining the directives which parents use under widely differing circumstances can we establish the generality of the findings reported here.

Lakoff (1973) has speculated that since little boys generally spend most of their early years with their mothers, they probably use "female" speech until about age 10, when the extensive same-sex peer group interaction characteristic of middle and late childhood finally leads them to begin using the "masculine" tongue. Similarly, Edelsky (1976) comments that while acquisition of phonology, syntax. and other strictly grammatical aspects of language occurs during the early childhood years, only much later do children acquire stereotypes about "male" and "female" speech. The limited evidence gathered in this study regarding children's strategies for requesting action from their parents suggests that the situation may be quite otherwise. By the age of 4 or so, the children were already using the alternative directive forms with frequencies very similar to those of their same-sex parent. Thus, learning about the linguistic habits that go along with being "male" or "female" may begin earlier than late childhood. This possibility would be consistent with the evidence that, by age 4, children's speech reveals considerable knowledge of form-context relationships (see introduction).

It is curious that fathers tended to phrase their directives in both the most and least explicit forms more often than the mothers. Since the imperative form is usually directed downward in rank, this pattern may simply be a linguistic reflection of fathers' usual position as family authoritarian or at least highest-status member. But why did the fathers phrase their directives in implied indirect form more often than mothers? Ervin-Tripp (1977) argues that this form is used when speaker and addressee share a rich network of knowledge and assumptions, so that only a few well-chosen words are sufficient to communicate a complex message. It follows that implied indirect directives are likely to be more difficult to understand than either imperative or conventionalized indirect forms. An easy explanation for fathers' more frequent use of such forms would be that since they spend much less time than mothers with their children, fathers are less sensitive to their children's comprehension skills and are more likely to produce messages that are beyond their children's understanding.

Two pieces of information suggest that this is not the case. First, the fathers were as accurate as the mothers in predicting their children's answers on the Parent Awareness Measure, suggesting that fathers do not have a less detailed knowledge of their children's communication skills. Second, there is evidence that children who are 4 years old are fairly capable of both interpreting and producing speech acts of the type we considered implied indirect directives (e.g., Leonard, Wilcox, Fulmer, & Davis, 1978; Garvey, 1975; Hollos & Beeman, 1978). Indeed, our impression was that the children did not have more trouble responding to the implied indirect directives than either of the other types. The interpretation we favor rests on the observation that an implied indirect directive not only can serve as an oblique way to establish a request between two individuals who share a rich network of knowledge but also can serve the didactic function of fostering the development of this network in the less experienced person. Teachers often use indirect speech acts of this sort to stimulate logical reasoning by their students (e.g., see Mishler, 1972). When a parent answers a child's question *Where does this piece go?* with the information *It has straight edges,* the child is forced to bring to bear a general principle of problem solving (e.g., "Pieces with straight edges go around the outside of a puzzle"). The parent hopes that this principle, in conjunction with the information offered by the parent, will lead the child to answer his own question (i.e., "Therefore, this piece goes around the outside of the puzzle") Fathers' more frequent use of implied indirect directives may reflect a greater tendency for them to pose logical challenges of this sort for children (c.f. Gleason's 1975 discussion of fathers as "bridges" between children and the outside world). This may, in turn, be the result of greater expectations regarding children's ability to reason logically or a greater desire that they learn to do so. This is all consistent with the findings of Masur and Gleason (Note 9), who noted that fathers generally are avid testers and consolidators of children's knowledge. They also found that fathers take more opportunities to deepen children's knowledge by providing relevant new and often more complex information on the same topic.

These data suggest that not all indirect directives are equivalent pragmatically. The contrast highlighted in this study was "conventionalized" (e.g., *Could you remove your hat please?*) versus implied indirect forms (e.g., *Your hat is blocking my view*). The principal difference between these forms, the requirement for logical inference, may be meaningful, since the forms were distributed in a consistently different manner in the speech of mothers and fathers. If this distinction had been ignored and both types of indirect directives lumped together, there would not have been a significant difference between fathers and mothers in the frequencies with which their directives were "indirect" as opposed to "imperative" in form. (This finding is reported by Golinkoff & Ames, 1979, who did not make this distinction). Hence, the categorization "direct" versus "indirect" may be too gross to capture certain subtle aspects of registral variation.

REFERENCE NOTES

1. Andersen, E. *Register variation in young children's role-play speech.* Paper presented at the biennial meeting of the Society for Research in Child Development, San Francisco, March 1979.
2. Kriedberg, G. *Hail to the chief.* Unpublished paper, Boston University, 1975.
3. Weintraub, S. *Parent's speech to children: some situational and sex differences.* Unpublished doctoral dissertation, Boston University, 1978.
4. Rondal, J. *Father's speech and mother's speech in early language development.* Paper presented at the First International Congress for the Study of Child Language, Tokyo, August 1978.
5. Greif, E. *Sex differences in parent-child conversations: Who interrupts whom?* Paper presented at the biennial meeting of the Society for Research in Child Development, San Francisco, March 1979.
6. Gleason, J., Greif, E., Weintraub, S., & Fardella, J. *Father doesn't know best: Parents' awareness of their children's linguistic, cognitive, and affective development.* Paper presented at the biennial meeting of the Society for Research in Child Development, New Orleans, March 1977.
7. Gleason, J., & Greif, E. *Hi, thanks, and goodbye: More routine information.* Paper presented at the 11th Annual Stanford Child Language Research Forum, Stanford, April 1979.

8. Masur, E. *Clues, strategies, rules and plans: Cognitive functions of parents' questions and directives.* Paper presented at the 11th Annual Stanford Child Language Research Forum, Stanford, April 1979.
9. Masur, E., & Gleason, J. *Parent-child interaction and the acquisiton of lexical information during play.* Paper presented at the biennial meeting of the Society for Research in Child Development, San Francisco, March 1979.

REFERENCES

Andersen, E., & Johnson, C. Modifications in the speech of an eight year old as a reflection of age of listener. *Stanford Occasional Papers in Linguistics, 1973, 3,* 149-160.

Bates, E. *Language and context: The acquisition of pragmatics.* New York: Academic Press, 1976.

Bellinger, D. Changes in the explicitness of mothers' directives as children age. *Journal of Child Language, 1979, 6,* 443-458.

Blount, B. Parental speech and language acquisition: Some Luo and Samoan examples. *Anthropological Linguistics, 1972, 14,* 119-130.

Cherry, L., & Lewis, M. Mothers and two-year-olds: A study of sex-differentiated aspects of verbal interaction. *Developmental Psychology, 1976, 12,* 278-282.

Crosby, F., & Nyquist, L. The female register: An empirical study of Lakoff's hypotheses. *Language in Society, 1977, 6,* 313-322.

Edelsky, C. The acquisiton of communicative competence: Recognition of linguistic correlates of sex roles. *Merrill-Palmer Quarterly, 1976, 22,* 47-59.

Edelsky, C. Acquisition of an aspect of communicative competence: Learning what it means to talk like a lady. In S. Ervin-Tripp & C. Mitchell-Kernan (Eds.), *Child discourse.* New York: Academic Press, 1977.

Ervin-Tripp, S. Sociolinguistics. In L. Berkowitz (Ed.), *Advances in experimental social psychology* (Vol. 4). New York: Academic Press, 1968.

Ervin-Tripp, S. Is Sybil there? The structure of some American English directives. *Language in Society, 1976, 5,* 25-66.

Ervin-Tripp, S. Wait for me roller skate. In S. Ervin-Tripp & C. Mitchell-Kernan (Eds.), *Child discourse.* New York: Academic Press, 1977.

Garvey, C. Requests and responses in children's speech. *Journal of Child Language, 1975, 2,* 41-63.

Gleason, J. B. Code-switching in children's language. In T. Moore (Ed.), *Cognitive development and the acquisition of language.* New York: Academic Press, 1973.

Gleason, J. B. Fathers and other strangers: Men's speech to young children. In D. Dato (Ed.), *Georgetown University Round Table on Languages and Linguistics, 1975.* Washington, D.C.: Georgetown University Press, 1975. Pp. 289-297.

Golinkoff, R., & Ames, G. A comparison of fathers' and mothers' speech with their young children. *Child Development, 1979, 50,* 28-32.

Haas, A. Male and female spoken language differences: Stereotypes and evidence. *Psychological Bulletin, 1979, 86,* 616-626.

Hollos, M., & Beeman, W. The development of directives among Norwegian and Hungarian children: An example of communicative style in culture. *Language in Society, 1978, 7,* 345-355.

James, S. Effect of listener age and situation on the politeness of children's directives. *Journal of Psycholinguistic Research, 1978, 7,* 307-317.

Key, M. *Male/female language.* Metuchen, N.J.: Scarecrow Press, 1975.

Kramer, C. Perceptions of female and male speech. *Language and Speech, 1977, 20,* 151-161.

Lakoff, R. Language and woman's place. *Language in Society, 1973, 2,* 45-80.

Leonard, L., Wilcox, M., Fulmer, K., & Davis, G. Understanding indirect speech requests: An investigation of children's comprehension of pragmatic meanings. *Journal of Speech and Hearing Research, 1978, 21,* 528-537.

Parental Directives   1139

Maccoby, E., & Jacklin, C. *The psychology of sex differences.* Stanford: Stanford University Press, 1974.

Mishler, E. Implications of teacher strategies for language and cognition: Observations in first grade classrooms. In C. Cazden, V. John, & D. Hymes (Eds.), *Functions of language in the classroom.* New York: Teachers College Press, 1972.

Sachs, J., & Devin, J. Young children's use of age-appropriate speech styles in social interaction and role-playing. *Journal of Child Language, 1976, 3,* 81-98.

Shatz, M., & Gelman, R. The development of communication skills: Modifications in the speech of young children as a function of listener. *Monographs of the Society for Research in Child Development, 1973, 38*(5, Serial No. 152).

Thorne, B., & Henley, N. (Eds.). *Language and sex: Difference and dominance.* Rowley, Mass.: Newbury House, 1975.

[26]

Women's Studies Int. Quart., 1980, Vol. 3, pp. 253–258
Pergamon Press, Ltd.   Printed in Great Britain

SEX DIFFERENCES IN PARENT–CHILD CONVERSATIONS[1]

ESTHER BLANK GREIF

Department of Psychology, Boston University, 64 Cummington Street, Boston, MA 02215, U.S.A.

(*Accepted November* 1979)

Synopsis—The current study examined sex differences in the use of two conversational management techniques, interruptions and simultaneous speech, during conversations between parents
and pre-school children. Participants were 16 children, ages 2 to 5, and both their parents. Each
parent–child pair engaged in semi-structured play for 30 minutes. There were no significant
differences between boys and girls in the use of these two conversational techniques. However,
fathers interrupted more and spoke simultaneously more than mothers did. Further, both
parents were more likely to interrupt their daughters and to speak simultaneously with their
daughters. Results were discussed in relation to the power differences between men and
women, and in reference to the socialization of children into gender roles.

Language is one of the major tools used in the process of gender socialization. Messages
about gender are conveyed to children from actual content of speech, as well as from the
style of speech (e.g. which words are emphasized, etc.) and from nonverbal behaviors which
accompany speech (e.g. smiling). The current study looks at conversational management, to
see who regulates the conversation when parents and children are talking. Specifically, this
study examines two management techniques—interrupting and speaking simultaneously—
and looks at their use in conversations between parents and their pre-school children.

Recent studies of language have found that males and females use language differently
(Bodine, 1975; Haas, 1979). Lakoff (1973), in a paper titled 'Language and woman's place',
suggests that women's speech is more polite and less forceful than the speech of men. She
argues that women are socialized to their special style, and are discouraged from using the
male style. It has also been suggested (Henley, 1975) that women are more sensitive to
nonverbal cues of other people than men are, and are therefore more polite speakers. Both
interrupting someone and speaking at the same time as someone can show impoliteness,
inattention, and manipulation of one speaker by another.

In our society, children are usually taught not to interrupt a person who is talking. Yet
many adults themselves interrupt others. For instance, individuals in high status positions
may interrupt people of lower status (cf. Henley, 1977). Further, if interruptions can be used
to demonstrate power and status, then one might predict that men would interrupt more
than women. In fact, there is evidence that this is the case. Zimmerman and West (1975)
compared the naturalistic conversations of male–female adult pairs with conversations of
male–male and female–female pairs. They found that there were many more interruptions

[1] The research reported in this paper was supported by Grant No. BNS 75-21909 A01 from the National
Science Foundation. An earlier version of this paper was presented at the meeting of the Society for Research
in Child Development, San Francisco, Calif., March 1979.
   The author wishes to thank David Alderton for his invaluable assistance with data coding. Thanks also to
David Bellinger and Jean Berko Gleason for their helpful comments on an earlier version of this paper.
Finally, I would like to thank the families and staff from the Old South Pre-school for their cooperation with
this study.

in the opposite sex pairs than in same-sex pairs. Even more striking was their finding that males were more likely to interrupt the speech of women than vice versa. Using a college population, Natale *et al.* (1979) also found that males interrupt more than females. One aim of the current study was to examine interruptions of parents during interactions with their pre-school children, to determine if fathers interrupt children more than mothers.

A second aim of the study was to examine the incidence of simultaneous speech. Typically in a conversation both people obey rules of turn-taking which are designed to reduce the likelihood of speakers talking at the same time (cf. Sacks *et al.*, 1974). But simultaneous speech still does occur. When it does, adults may smile at each other, recognizing the turn-taking or transition error, and then one person gives up the floor. Even though simultaneous speech seems more accidental than interruptions, one speaker can take advantage of the situation to maintain or gain control. If fathers are using simultaneous speech as a conversational management technique, possibly a result of their socialization into male language patterns, then fathers may engage in more simultaneous speech with their children than mothers.

Finally, this study looks at the effect of a child's sex on parents' tendencies to interrupt and speak simultaneously. Parents may interact differently with boys and girls, for a variety of reasons (e.g. cues from the child; parents' expectations; etc.). If so, we might find differences in conversations with boys and girls. For example, parents may be more polite with sons than with daughters.

To sum, then, there were three major aims of the current study:

(1) to see if there are differences between mothers and fathers in the use of interruptions;

(2) to see if there are differences between mothers and fathers in the incidence of simultaneous speech; and,

(3) to see if either of these features differs in the speech of parents to girls and boys.

METHOD

Participants

Sixteen middle-class children, eight girls and eight boys, and both their parents participated in the study. Children ranged in age from 2 to 5 years, with a mean age of 3½ years.

Procedure

Each child visited a laboratory playroom twice, once with each parent. During each visit, the parent–child pair was asked to engage in three activities during a 30-minute play session. The activities included reading a book which had no words, playing with a toy car that had removable parts, and using food items and a cash register to play pretend store. All play sessions were videotaped, conversations were transcribed, and utterances were marked.

Coding

Instances of interruptions by parents and children were recorded, as well as occurrences of simultaneous speech. Interruptions were coded when one person began to talk while the other person was already speaking. For example, if during the play store situation a child started to say 'I'm going to buy some . . .' and the parent at that point said 'Why don't you buy some peanut butter?', an interruption would be coded. Simultaneous speech was coded when both speakers began to speak at the same time.

RESULTS

For each family, all instances of interruptions and simultaneous speech were converted to percentages based on (a) total number of parent utterances; (b) total number of child utterances; or (c) total number of utterances of parent and child combined.

Table 1 provides descriptive information about the mean number of utterances used during the 30-minute play sessions. As one can see, parents spoke more than their children.

Table 1. Mean number of utterances during 30-minute play session for mothers, fathers, and children

Parent		Child		Total utterances (parent and child)
Mother with son	551·25 (117·56)	Son with mother	291·00 (66·55)	842·25
Mother with daughter	545·75 (77·44)	Daughter with mother	293·00 (88·58)	838·75
Father with son	528·00 (109·72)	Son with father	277·38 (70·78)	805·38
Father with daughter	528·13 (135·47)	Daughter with father	354·00 (112·82)	882·13

Standard deviations are in parentheses.

There were no significant differences in the number of utterances used by mothers vs fathers, or in the number of utterances used by parents to girls vs boys.

The mean number of interruptions by parents and children, and mean number of instances of simultaneous speech, are contained in Table 2. From inspection, one can see

Table 2. Mean number of instances of interruptions and simultaneous speech during 30-minute play sessions

Parent	Interruptions	Child		Total per dyad	Simultaneous speech	
Mothers to sons	5·50 (3·82)	Sons to mothers	5·13 (3·52)	10·63	Mother–son	13·13 (8·2)
Mothers to daughters	9·0 (7·73)	Daughters to mothers	4·50 (4·57)	13·50	Mother–daughter	20·13 (11·27)
Fathers to sons	7·0 (5·55)	Sons to fathers	5·25 (2·19)	12·25	Father–son	17·25 (11·91)
Fathers to daughters	9·75 (6·25)	Daughters to fathers	4·13 (3·09)	13·88	Father–daughter	26·63 (10·57)

Standard deviations are in parentheses.

that there were more instances of simultaneous speech than of interruptions. Further, parents tended to interrupt their children 7·8 times per play session. The range of number of interruptions by parents to children was 1 to 25. The range of instances of simultaneous speech was 5 to 45.

All statistical analyses of interruptions were performed using percentages based on the number of each child's utterances. For interruptions, differences between number of interruptions by mothers vs fathers was just short of significance, with fathers interrupting more (Wilcoxon W_s (16) = 41, $p < 0.088$). Comparison of speech to boys vs girls showed that parents were more likely to interrupt girls (U (8, 8) = 58, $p < 0.09$). Thus, there was a tendency for fathers to interrupt more than mothers, and for both parents to interrupt girls more than boys.

Analyses of simultaneous speech were performed using percentages based on the total number of utterances of parent and child combined. Differences in the percentages of simultaneous speech between mothers and children vs fathers and children were highly significant (W_s (16) = 8, $p < 0.01$). Father–child pairs were more likely than mother–child pairs to speak at the same time. Further, both parents were more likely to engage in simultaneous speech with their daughters than with their sons (U (8, 8) = 52, $p < 0.052$).

Since simultaneous speech involves both speakers, either the child or the parent could use the occurrence of simultaneous speech to maintain or gain control of the conversation. To determine who continued to speak, instances of simultaneous speech were analyzed. Results are presented in Table 3. Parents were significantly more likely to continue talking than

Table 3. Analysis of instances of simultaneous speech

	Speech continued by		
	Parent (%)	Child (%)	Both (%)
Mother with son	49	23	28
Mother with daughter	40	30	30
Father with son	50	26	24
Father with daughter	45	30	25
Total mean	46	27	27

were children (45 per cent vs 27 per cent for mothers and children; W_s (16) = 22·5, $p < 0.02$; 48 per cent vs 28 per cent for fathers and children; W_s (15) = 13, $p < 0.01$). About 25 per cent of the instances of simultaneous speech resulted in both the parent and child continuing to speak. Thus, parents do not gain conversational control every time simultaneous speech occurs, but they do gain or keep control more often than their children do. There were no mother–father differences.

An analysis of children's interruptions of their parents showed no significant differences between boys and girls, although there was a trend for boys to interrupt both mothers and fathers more than girls (X for boys = 5·19; X for girls = 4·32). Further, there was no relationship between the number of times the child interrupted the parents and the number of times the child was interrupted by the parent.

Correlations were computed between the frequency of interruptions and simultaneous speech, to see if parents who interrupt a lot also engage in a lot of simultaneous speech. For mothers and fathers, $r = 0·61$ ($p < 0.005$). Thus, parents seem to be consistent. Correlations were also computed to see if there was any consistency in the use of interruptions and simultaneous speech within families. Correlations between number of interruptions for mothers and fathers was 0·50 ($p < 0.05$). For simultaneous speech, $r = 0·48$ ($p < 0.05$). Thus, there does seem to be a family pattern.

DISCUSSION

To summarize the findings, it seems that fathers interrupt their children more than mothers do, and that both parents interrupt daughters more than sons. Also, fathers engage in simultaneous speech with their children more than mothers, and both parents exhibit more simultaneous speech with daughters. Further, parents were consistent in being either high or low on interruptions and simultaneous speech. Also, within families, mothers and fathers were similar in their styles.

If the use of interruptions and simultaneous speech is considered to be a sign of impoliteness to the other speaker, and a way of controlling conversations, then these results suggest that fathers are less sensitive to their children and are more controlling than mothers, and that both mothers and fathers are less sensitive to daughters than to sons. Why might fathers be less polite and more controlling than mothers? Perhaps they are behaving in accordance with prescriptions for the male role. Males are typically socialized to be dominant and to take charge of situations. Therefore fathers may demonstrate their high status and show their children who is in charge by controlling the conversations with their children, and interrupting and speaking simultaneously are two ways of doing this. Since men seem to interrupt more than women in adult conversations, it is not surprising that this occurs with parent–child conversations. By interrupting, one can change topics, introduce new ideas, and so on; that is, one has control. Further, by interrupting, fathers are showing their children who is more powerful.

The next question that arises is why mothers and fathers seem more dominant toward daughters. Perhaps parents are using conversational techniques to teach their sons and daughters about their status or place in society. The message to girls is that they are more interruptible, which suggests, in a subtle way, that they are also not very important, or at least less so than boys. Also, adult men and women are used to interrupting women more than men (Natale *et al.*, 1979; Zimmerman and West, 1975), and this may extend to their interactions with their children.

What effects might this differential treatment have on the development of boys and girls? Children are learning from observations that males and females behave differently, and that males are more dominant. Children also may be acquiring 'appropriate' gender patterns; after all, modeling is a powerful teaching tool (cf. Bandura, 1969). Thus, children may learn about their overall status or roles from the way they are treated; and, they may learn how to behave by modeling appropriate adults.

The finding that parents are consistent among themselves in style shows that children are getting the same message from the parent; either the child is interruptible, or not. Further, the family pattern suggests that children are getting relatively consistent treatment within a family. It is important to remember that the results reported here are mean differences. Not all families followed the pattern of treating girls and boys differently.

In sum, then, this paper looked at conversational management and found that fathers are more likely than mothers to interrupt and engage in simultaneous speech with their preschool children, and that both mothers and fathers are more likely to interrupt and speak simultaneously with daughters than with sons. I suggested that fathers may use these techniques to control conversations with their children and that both parents may be more controlling with girls. Further research on parent–child conversations needs to be done to clarify the effects of situational factors, age differences, social class, and so on. Further analysis of subtle conversational management techniques, like the ones studied here, as well as patterns of pauses, and intonation, may reveal a variety of ways in which adult men and women speak differently, and ways in which they speak differently to boys and girls. Knowledge of these differences can give us insight into the processes of gender socialization and can provide us with the tools for social change.

REFERENCES

Bandura, Albert. 1969. Social-learning theory of identificatory processes. In David Goslin (ed.), *Handbook of socialization theory and research*. Rand McNally, Chicago.

Bodine, Ann. 1975. Sex differentiation in language. In Barrie Thorne and Nancy Henley (eds.), *Language and sex: Difference and dominance*. Newbury House, Rowley, Mass.

Haas, Adelaide. 1979. Male and female spoken language differences: Stereotypes and evidence. *Psychological Bull.* 86 (3), 616–626.

Henley, Nancy. 1975. Power sex and nonverbal communication. In Barrie Thorne and Nancy Henley (eds.), *Language and sex: Difference and dominance*. Newbury House, Rowley, Mass.

Henley, Nancy. 1977. *Body politics*. Prentice–Hall, Englewood Cliffs, NJ.

Lakoff, Robin. 1973. Language and woman's place. *Language in Society* 2, 145–179.

Natale, Michael, Elliot Entin and Joseph Jaffe. 1979. Vocal interruptions in dyadic communication as a function of speech and social anxiety. *Journal of Personality and Social Psychology* 37 (6), 865–878.

Sacks, Harvey, Emmanuel Schegloff and Gail Jefferson. 1974. A simplest systematics for the organization of turn-taking for conversation. *Language* 50, 696–735.

Zimmerman, Don and Candace West. 1975. Sex roles, interruptions, and silences in conversations. In Barrie Thorne and Nancy Henley (eds.), *Language and sex: Difference and dominance*. Newbury House, Rowley, Mass.

Journal of Personality and Social Psychology
1984, Vol. 47, No. 6, 1292–1302

Influence of Gender Constancy and Social Power on Sex-Linked Modeling

Kay Bussey
Macquarie University
New South Wales, Australia

Albert Bandura
Stanford University

Competing predictions derived from cognitive–developmental theory and social learning theory concerning sex-linked modeling were tested. In cognitive–developmental theory, gender constancy is considered a necessary prerequisite for the emulation of same-sex models, whereas according to social learning theory, sex-role development is promoted through a vast system of social influences with modeling serving as a major conveyor of sex role information. In accord with social learning theory, even children at a lower level of gender conception emulated same-sex models in preference to opposite-sex ones. Level of gender constancy was associated with higher emulation of both male and female models rather than operating as a selective determinant of modeling. This finding corroborates modeling as a basic mechanism in the sex-typing process. In a second experiment we explored the limits of same-sex modeling by pitting social power against the force of collective modeling of different patterns of behavior by male and female models. Social power over activities and rewarding resources produced cross-sex modeling in boys, but not in girls. This unexpected pattern of cross-sex modeling is explained by the differential sex-typing pressures that exist for boys and girls and socialization experiences that heighten the attractiveness of social power for boys.

Most theories of sex role development assign a major role to modeling as a basic mechanism of sex role learning (Bandura, 1969; Kagan, 1964; Mischel, 1970; Sears, Rau & Alpert, 1965). Maccoby and Jacklin (1974) have questioned whether social practices or modeling processes are influential in the development of sex-linked roles. They point to findings that in laboratory situations children do not consistently pattern their

This research was supported by Research Grant No. M-5162-21 from the National Institute of Mental Health, U.S. Public Health Services, and by the Lewis S. Haas Child Development Research Fund, Stanford University. We thank Martin Curland, Brad Carpenter, Brent Shaphren, Deborah Skriba, Erin Dignam, and Pamela Minet for serving as models. We are indebted to Marilyn Waterman for filming and editing the videotape modeling sequence, to Eileen Lynch and Sara Buxton, who acted as experimenters, and to Nancy Adams, who assisted in collecting the data. Finally, we also thank the staff and children from Bing Nursery School, Stanford University.

Requests for reprints should be sent to either Kay Bussey, School of Behavioral Sciences, Macquarie University, North Ryde, Australia, 2113, or to Albert Bandura, Department of Psychology, Stanford University, Building 420 Jordan Hall, Stanford, California 94305.

behavior after same-sex models. However, these studies typically include only one model of each sex. In a recent series of studies, Bussey and Perry (1982; Perry & Bussey, 1979) have used multiple modeling as more closely related to how modeling influences operate in everyday life. When exposed to multiple models the propensity of children to pattern their performances after same-sex models increases as the percentage of same-sex models displaying the same preferences increases.

The preceding research lends support to the view that same-sex modeling can promote same-sex differentiated patterns of behavior. It remains an open question, however, concerning the extent to which modeling plays an important role in the development of sex-typed behavior in younger children. Models may simply serve to activate the already developed sex-typedness of children.

Cognitive–developmental theory holds that sex typing is simply one outgrowth of children's cognitive development. From this viewpoint, the most important consideration of the child's sex role development is the child's cognitive capacity. According to Kohlberg (1966), it is not until about age six that a child understands that a person's gender remains constant regardless of appearance changes. Recognition of gender constancy is achieved during the same stage in which Piagetian conservation is attained. After children achieve a clear conception of themselves as a "boy" or "girl," they automatically value and strive to behave in ways appropriate for their sex. Therefore, in this view, it is as a result of having attained the concept of gender constancy that children will seek behavior appropriate for their own sex. Furthermore, consistency between the child's gender, self-categorization, and appropriate behaviors and values is thought to sustain the child's self-esteem. Sex-typed behavior is considered to be motivated by the child's desire to behave in a way consistent with his or her sexual label.

According to cognitive–developmental theory, children imitate same-sex models because they perceive them as similar to themselves. Such selective imitation fosters emotional ties to same-sex models. Children's differentiation of gender roles and their perception of themselves as more similar to same-sex models precedes, rather than follows, identification. That is, sex typing is not viewed as a product of identification, but rather as an antecedent of it.

One of the problems for Kohlberg's (1966) theory has been that children show preferences for sex-typed objects earlier than gender constancy normally develops (Maccoby & Jacklin, 1974). Although stable gender identity is not attained until about 4 to 6 years of age, Thompson (1975) found that 24-month-olds did quite well when asked to sort pictures of feminine and masculine toys, articles of clothing, tools, and appliances in terms of their stereotypical sex relatedness.

Social learning theorists (Bandura, 1969; Mischel, 1966, 1970) view sex role development as promoted through a vast system of social influences. These involve differential gender labeling and the structuring of activities in ways that teach the sex roles traditionally favored by the culture. Modeling serves as a major conveyor of sex role information (Bandura, in press). Children are continuously exposed to models of sex-typed behavior in the home, in schools, and in televised representations of society. On the basis of these multiple sources of sex role information, young children learn the behaviors appropriate for their own sex. Social sanctions make outcomes partly dependent on the sex-appropriateness of actions. Observed consequences to others also convey role knowledge. On the basis of direct and vicarious experiences, children learn to use sex-typing information as a guide for action. Other things being equal, children are, therefore, more inclined to pattern their behavior after a same-sex model than an opposite-sex model.

Kohlberg (1966) postulates attainment of gender constancy as a necessary prerequisite for children's identification with same-sex models. Social learning theorists, however, view gender constancy as a product rather than an antecedent of the emulation of same-sex models. To explore these contrasting predictions, we selected children for study on the basis of their level of gender constancy as measured by the procedure devised by Slaby and Frey (1975). This measure distinguishes between gender identity (knowledge of self and other's gender), gender stability (knowledge that gender remains invariant across time), and gender consistency (knowledge that gender remains invariant across situations). Children at three levels of gender constancy were selected: low, medium, and high. Those in the low group had not achieved gender identity. The medium gender constancy group had attained gender identity, but neither gender stability nor consistency. Finally, the high group had attained both gender identity and gender stability and some displayed gender consistency as well. Children from these three levels of gender constancy were exposed to multiple male and female models exhibiting differential patterns of behavior, whereupon the children's acquisition and spontaneous emulation of the modeled patterns was measured.

Experiment 1

Method

Subjects. Subjects were 18 boys and 18 girls enrolled in the Stanford University Nursery School. They ranged in age from 29 to 68 months, with mean age of 44.5 months. Models were three men and three women, all of whom had prior acting experience. Two female experimenters conducted the study.

Design. The subjects were assigned randomly to a modeling group and a control group of 18 subjects each. Within each group, equal numbers of boys and girls were selected as either low, medium, or high on the Slaby and Frey (1975) gender constancy interview.

Assessment of gender constancy. The tester administered the gender constancy interview (Slaby & Frey, 1975) to each child individually. On the basis of the children's responses, equal numbers of boys and girls were selected at the low, medium, and high levels of gender constancy.

Sex-linked modeling. Approximately 3 days after the test of sex constancy, the same experimenter brought each child individually to the experimental room and asked the child if he or she wanted to watch television. The child was seated in front of the television set and the experimenter sat in front of and with her back to the child. This seating arrangement prevented the experimenter from inadvertently communicating to the child any reactions to the modeled displays. Half of the children saw a modeling videotape and the other half a cartoon; both were in color. The modeling display depicted three men and three women playing a game, *Find the Surprise,* in which all the men exhibited the same behavior patterns but differed from the women, who also acted like each other.

Two modeling tapes were produced to counterbalance sex of models and the set of behaviors they modeled. For the second videotape, the men and women displayed the set of behaviors and verbalizations performed by the opposite-sex models in the first tape. Half the subjects in the modeling condition saw one videotape and the remainder saw the other one. The modeling display opened with a woman inviting three men and three women seated on chairs beside her to play a game, *Find the Surprise.* She explained that she would hide a picture sticker in one of two boxes and the object of the game was to guess which box contained the sticker. They would take turns playing this guessing game. The sticker game served as a cover task for modeling a varied array of stylistic behaviors, preferences, and novel utterances.

The models were then invited to select a "thinking cap." All the men chose a green Mickey Mouse cap and placed it with the Mickey Mouse photograph to the front of their head. The women chose a blue Mickey Mouse cap and placed the cap on their head with the Mickey Mouse photograph to the back. The experimenter then hid the picture sticker in one of the two boxes. Each model individually had a chance to find a sticker. When a female model approached one of the boxes she said, "Forward march," and began marching slowly towards Box A repeating, "March, march, march." When she reached Box A she said, "Jump, jump," as she made a koala bear jump from the lid of the box. She opened the box and exclaimed, "Bingo," took the sticker from the box and walked to the paper hanging on the wall behind the boxes and said, "Lickit-stickit," as she pressed the picture sticker with her thumb, in the upper-right quadrant of the paper, with the comment "Up there." She then placed the koala bear on the lid of the box facing sideways and said, "Look at the door," walked back to her chair with her arms folded and said, "There." Each female model displayed the same patterns of behavior.

The men in their turn each stood up and said, "Get set, go," and walked stiffly towards the boxes repeating, "Left, right, left, right." When the male model reached Box B he said, "Fly, fly" as he made the koala bear fly from the lid of the box. He opened the box and exclaimed, "A stickeroo," took the sticker from the box and walked to the paper hanging on the wall behind the boxes and said, "Weto-smacko" as he slapped the picture sticker with his open hand, in the lower left quadrant of the paper, and said, "Down there." He then placed the koala bear on the lid of the box and said, "Lay down," and walked back to his chair with his hands behind his back and sat down with the comment, "That's it."

At the completion of the game, the male models said, "Off with think caps," walked to Box A and placed their hats inside the box and said, "In there." The female models said, "No more think caps," walked to Box B and placed their hats on top of the box and said, "On top." Each model exhibited the appropriate behavior pattern twice. In the other version of the modeling videotape, the behavior patterns of the male and female models were reversed.

Test for modeled behavior. The modeling videotape and cartoon were of approximately 11 min duration. After the two sets of models had selected their Mickey Mouse caps, the experimenter turned off the television and informed the child that another woman at the nursery school was playing a game with children. The experimenter returned with the second experimenter who was unaware of the experimental condition to which the children were assigned. The first experimenter exited and the second experimenter asked the child to select a Mickey Mouse cap. The children were free to perform any or none of the behaviors they had seen modeled in the videotape.

After the test for modeled behavior, the first experimenter showed the children a further segment of the videotape in which the two sets of models had a chance to find a sticker. The first experimenter exited again and the second experimenter administered seven trials on the sticker task. The children then watched the remainder of the videotape, after which they performed the sticker task for a further eight trials. A picture sticker was hidden 12 out of the total 15 trials for each child. Children in the control condition were exposed to the cartoon for the same length of time as children in the modeling condition. The same procedure of interspersing tests for imitation between segments of television viewing was also used. Televised exposure and test trials were interspersed to sustain children's attention.

The child's spontaneous imitative behavior was recorded by an observer who watched the test sessions through a one-way mirror. The observer was provided with a checklist of responses exhibited by the models in the videotape and the observer simply checked any of the responses performed by each child on each trial. The observer was unaware of the child's experimental assignment. A second observer independently scored the performance of five children. The product–moment correlation ($r = .99$) revealed virtually perfect interrater agreement.

Acquisition test. Children in the modeling condition were administered a test of acquisition at the conclusion of the experiment. They were asked to demonstrate how the men and women behaved. The order in which they reenacted the behavior of each sex was counterbalanced. Standard prompts were used to direct the children's attention to different aspects of the modeled events. For example, the experimenter asked, "How did the boys (girls) walk to the box?" Following the acquisition test, the children responded to questions designed to check the effectiveness of the experimental manipulations.

Results

Modeled behavior. A $2 \times 3 \times 2 \times 2$ (Sex of Subject $\times$ Level of Gender Constancy: High, Medium, Low $\times$ Condition: Modeling, Control $\times$ Sex of Models/Within-Subjects Factor) analysis of variance (ANOVA) was performed on the scores for modeled behavior. These scores were obtained by summing the frequency of the stylistic responses (postural, verbal, and motor) and preferences that matched those of either the male or female models. This analysis yielded a significant main effect for gender constancy level, $F(2, 24) = 3.41, p < .05$. Children of low gender constancy reproduced fewer of the modeled behaviors than children of either medium

gender constancy, $t(24) = 2.48, p < .05$, or high gender constancy, $t(24) = 1.97, p < .06$, who did not differ from each other. The main effect for modeling is also significant, $F(1, 24) = 49.40, p < .0001$. Children exposed to modeling performed substantially more of the behaviors exemplified by the models than children in the control condition.

A significant interaction emerged between sex of model and sex of subject, $F(1, 24) = 11.22, p < .005$. This interaction was qualified, however, by a three-way interaction involving sex of model, sex of subject, and condition, $F(1, 24) = 16.20, p < .0005$. This interaction is depicted graphically in Figure 1. We examined the nature of this interaction by performing t tests on the subgroup means. In the modeling condition, boys spontaneously performed those behaviors displayed by the male models in preference to those displayed by the female models, $t(24) = 5.06, p < .001$, and conversely the girls spontaneously performed behaviors exhibited by the female models over those displayed by the

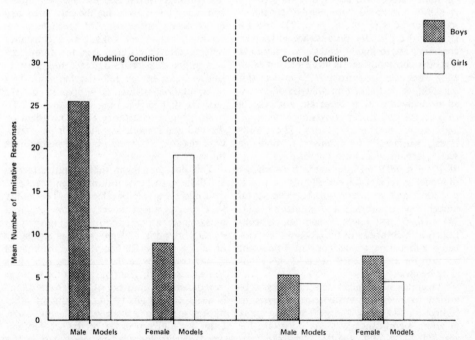

Figure 1. Mean imitative performance scores of boys and girls exposed to male and female models as a function of condition (Experiment 1).

male models, $t(24) = 2.71$, $p < .02$. Children in the control condition, who had no exposure to the modeled behavior, evidenced few matching responses in either of the two modeled sets of performances. The latter finding demonstrates the efficacy of the modeling influence and also reveals the neutrality of the modeled responses. The sex-linked modeling provides strong support for the same-sex modeling hypothesis regardless of gender constancy level.

Acquisition of modeled behavior patterns. Children in the modeling condition were asked to reenact the various behaviors displayed by the male and female models, respectively. In the ANOVA performed on these scores the only effect to attain significance was gender constancy level, $F(2, 12) = 4.40$, $p < .05$. Children of low gender constancy ($M = 3.67$) recalled fewer modeled responses than did children of either medium ($M = 7.67$) or high ($M = 9.50$) gender constancy, whose scores did not differ from each other.

Relation between age and gender constancy level. Children who achieve higher gender constancy scores are also older. Indeed, age is highly correlated with gender constancy scores for boys ($r = .76$, $p < .01$) and for girls ($r = .82$, $p < .01$). Because age and gender constancy are so highly related, we might ask if gender constancy exerts any effect on modeling when age is controlled? To answer this question we performed an analysis of covariance, using age as a covariate and sex of subject, level of gender constancy, condition, and sex of models as factors. The results reveal, as in the previous analyses of modeling scores, a main effect for modeling, $F(1, 23) = 48.70$, $p < .001$; an interaction between sex of model and sex of subject, $F(1, 24) = 11.22$, $p < .005$; and an interaction between sex of model, sex of subject, and modeling, $F(1, 24) = 16.20$, $p < .0005$. When age is controlled as a covariate in the analysis of spontaneous modeling, gender constancy does not account for any variance in children's modeling behavior.

The children's acquisition scores were submitted to a similar covariance analysis to control for the effect of age. The only effect to attain significance was the covariate for age, $F(1, 11) = 5.99$, $p < .05$. Therefore, gender constancy is no longer a significant determinant of modeling when age is controlled.

Discussion

Results of this experiment document the prevalence of same-sex modeling. When children observe that same-sex models collectively exhibit stylistic behaviors that diverge from those displayed by opposite-sex models under the same circumstances, children are far more likely to pattern their behavior after same-sex models. The same-sex modeling occurs irrespective of children's level of gender constancy.

Children with low levels of gender constancy, in this case, those who had not even achieved gender identity on Slaby and Frey's (1975) gender constancy scale, adopted more behaviors displayed by same-sex than opposite-sex models. Although the total amount of modeling behavior increased with the children's level of gender constancy, they adopted more behaviors displayed by same-sex than opposite-sex models irrespective of their gender constancy level. Because age and gender constancy levels were highly correlated and low gender identity did not preclude same-sex modeling, it seems that gender constancy reflects children's overall cognitive competencies rather than operating as a uniquely selective factor in sex role development. This interpretation is further supported by the analysis that shows that when age is controlled, gender constancy exerts no effect on the children's modeling behavior. A stereotypic sex role conception is not a prerequisite for same-sex modeling.

This does not mean that cognitive factors are thought to be of minimal significance in the child's sex role development. The ability to selectively adopt these behaviors displayed by same-sex models requires cognitive skills in categorization and judgment of similarity of self to others. Rather, the specific role of gender constancy in the sex-typing process is being questioned. There is little in the findings to indicate that mastery of gender constancy is necessary for sex-typing. Results of other studies are also consistent with this view. Large sex differences in preference for sex-typed objects and play patterns exist in the toddler and nursery school child long before a fully matured gender constancy is established (Blakemore, La Rue, & Olejnik, 1979; Masters & Wilkinson, 1976; Thompson, 1975). Children as young as 2 and 3 years possess remarkable awareness of sex role stereotypes and sex differences (Kuhn, Nash, & Brucken, 1978; Marcus & Overton, 1978).

Same-sex modeling seems to involve relying on classifying males and females into distinct groups, recognizing personal similarity to one group of models, and tagging that group's behavior patterns in memory as the ones to be used as a guide to behavior. Even very young children give evidence of classificatory capabilities involving social stimuli. By the time infants are 6 months old, they are capable of treating infant faces as a category different from adult faces, and female faces as different from male faces (Fagan & Singer, 1979). Sex labeling and differential structuring of social experiences teach children to use the sex of the model as a guide for action (Huston, 1983).

It is thus possible to explain same-sex modeling even in young children on the basis of their having cognitively abstracted activities stereotypical for each sex and judging that behaviors displayed by same-sex models are the appropriate ones for them to adopt, without requiring a conception of gender constancy. Both the gender classificatory basis of same-sex modeling and the impact of social factors on this process accord with Spence's (1984) formulation. She posits that sexual identity facilitates adoption of prototypic gender-congruent attributes, but interacting social and personal factors determine what particular constellations of gender-related characteristics are developed. Thus people within each sex can develop heterogeneous patterns of gender-related attributes while retaining a confirmed personal sense of masculinity and femininity.

Results of the acquisition test cast further doubt on mastery of gender constancy as the selective mechanism of sex role learning. Children's level of gender conception was related to acquisition of modeled patterns, but not selectively according to the model's sex. The higher the gender conception was, the more children learned the behavior of both types of models. The measure of gender conception may serve more as a proxy measure of skill in cognitive processing than a unique determinant of sex role learning. The older the children are, the more they learn the behavior of both male and female models. Thus when age is controlled, children of all gender constancy levels learn equally from the models.

Gender-schema theory also suggests that children's readiness to classify objects and people in gender-related terms may well develop before a conception of gender constancy is achieved (Bem, 1981; Markus, Crane, Bernstein, & Siladi, 1982). Children learn to encode, organize, and retrieve information about themselves and others in terms of a developing gender schema. Results of the acquisition test, however, reveal that same-sex modeling is not due to differential gender-schematic processing and retention of the behavior patterns exhibited by the male and female models. Rather, gender self-knowledge seems to be operating more on selective retrieval and enactment of what has been learned observationally from both sexes. These findings underscore the importance of including measures of observational learning as well as of spontaneous performance in testing theories about gender-role development. Children observe and learn extensively from models of both sexes, but they are selective in what they express behaviorally.

Experiment 2

The purpose of the second experiment was to test the power of model sex on same-sex modeling when countervailing social influences come into play. Do children always choose a same-sex model over an opposite-sex one, or is this proclivity readily altered by social factors? Sex roles reflect, in part, power relations in a society. Social power can exert a strong impact on modeling (Bandura, Ross, & Ross, 1963). It is, therefore, of considerable interest to clarify what happens in the course of modeling when social power is pitted against the force of collective modeling. In most societies, men typically wield more social power than do women. Of special interest is the impact of cross-sex social power on cross-sex modeling.

To clarify these issues, we varied the power of one group of models over the other group. In one condition, three male models were depicted as the powerful controllers of rewarding resources and three female models occupied a subordinate role. In a second condition, the male and female power positions were reversed so that the female models were the powerful members of the group and the male models the subordinate ones. Social power was manifested in several ways: ownership of play materials, command over play activities, and the dispensation of food and soft drinks.

After children observed on videotape either the men or the women exercising power, they were then exposed to the same collective modeling used in the previous experiment. Children assigned to a condition in which power of the models was not varied watched a cartoon in place of the power induction videotape and then the videotape of collective modeling of behavior patterns. Children in the control condition, who were exposed neither to power nor modeling displays, saw two cartoons. If social power is an influential determinant of model selection, cross-sex modeling would be expected in those conditions in which models of the opposite sex are portrayed as the wielders of social power.

Method

Subjects. Subjects were 16 boys and 16 girls enrolled in the Stanford Nursery School. They ranged in age from 3 years to 5 years and 10 months, with a mean age of 4 years and 8 months, and all were catagorized as high scorers on the Slaby and Frey (1975) gender constancy measure (i.e., 72% had attained at least gender identity and gender stability, and 28% has also attained gender consistency).

Design. Children were assigned randomly to conditions in a 2 × 4 design involving sex of child (boys, girls) and treatment condition (men in power, women in power, no power, control).

Procedure. The procedure used in this experiment was virtually identical to that described in Experiment 1. The main difference was the portrayal of social power before the collective modeling.

The two videotapes for the power induction were identical, except that in one videotape the male models were in power and in the other the female models exercised power. The females-in-power movie opened with a narrative about three girls who owned a playroom. The girls are seen in their playroom unpacking their large collection of toys and having much fun playing with them. As they were playing with their toys, three boys

walk by and hear the fun and laughter emanating from the room. One of the boys peeks through the ajar door to see what is happening inside. He quickly exclaims to the other boys that there are some girls in there who are playing with some "really neat" toys. The boys ask the girls if they too could play with some of their toys. After some deliberation, the girls allow the boys into the playroom, but initially only to watch them play. The girls play with even more interesting games, a Mickey Mouse dip game, a wind-up dog, musical instruments, and other exciting playthings. Finally, the girls who are the controllers of these resources, allow the boys to play with one of their toys. The boys express much joy at being able to play with the girls' toys. The boys are given other playthings.

The girls further exemplify their controller status by telling the boys that they recently had $50 to spend, so they went to San Francisco and bought a pinball machine. After taking turns playing the pinball machine, the girls announce, "It's time for treats," whereupon they set out cans of soda, cookies, candy, chocolates, and make popcorn in their popcorn machine. The girls shared their goodies with the boys. The end of the session is heralded by the boys, at the girls' request, packing away the toys for the day. Before leaving the playroom, one of the girls announces that she had located a "really neat" department store in San Francisco that sells lots of things suitable for their playroom. The girls count their money and then peruse the department store's catalogue. They consider buying roller skates and computer games, but finally settle on a color television set: "Let's buy a color T.V. set for our room. We can keep it in our room. Then we can come to our room and watch any program we like."

When the boys were in power, the sequence of events and activities were the same except that the boys rather than the girls exercised the control over resources and activities. The participants in the power-induction videotape appear as the models in the collective modeling videotape.

At the completion of the power induction or exposure to the cartoon, children in the experimental condition observed the collective modeling on the television monitor, the children in the control condition saw another cartoon. The tests for acquisition and spontaneous adoption of modeled behavior were identical to those followed in Experiment 1. Similarly, the test procedures were identical, with the tester having no knowledge of the conditions to which the children were assigned.

Results

Modeled behavior. A 2 × 4 × 2 (Sex of Subject × Treatment Condition × Sex of Models/Within-Subject Factor) ANOVA was performed on the scores of modeled behavior. There was a strong main effect of modeling, $F(3, 24) = 12.14$, $p < .001$, with children in the modeling conditions displaying more modeled behavior than children not exposed to the models. A significant interaction between sex of subject and sex of model, $F(1, 24) = 10.58$, $p < .005$, also emerged. We ex-

Table 1

Modeled Behavior Means for Interaction of Sex of Subject and Sex of Model (Experiment 2)

Sex of subject	Sex of models	
	Males	Females
Boys	18.88	9.81
Girls	12.19	15.19

amined the nature of this interaction by performing *t* tests on the means in Table 1. Both boys and girls patterned their behavior more after same-sex models than opposite-sex models. This effect was highly statistically significant for boys, $t(24) = 3.49$, $p < .01$, but the difference fell short of significance for girls, $t(24) = 1.15$, $p > .10$.

The three-way interaction involving all three factors (sex of subject, power treatment, and sex of model) was also significant, $F(3, 24) = 3.30$, $p < .05$. This interaction is depicted graphically in Figure 2. In contrast to

boys and girls in the control condition, children in the treatment conditions were influenced by the power displays. First, it is of interest to note that in the no-power condition, same-sex modeling predominates, an effect that is stronger for boys, $t(24) = 4.38$, $p < .001$, than for girls, $t(24) = 1.59$, $p = .12$.

The portrayal of the models as powerful produced different results depending on the sex of the models and the sex of the observer. Boys emulated many of the behaviors of the male models irrespective of whether they were powerful or not, enacting an average of 20, 22, and 29 imitative responses in the males-in-power, females-in-power, and no-power conditions, respectively. However, the boys did not show an equal propensity to imitate the female models irrespective of power. The boys' mean imitative scores of the female models for the males-in-power and no-power conditions, were 8 and 6, respectively. When the female models were in power, however, a different result emerged. The boys emulated the female models ($M = 18$) almost

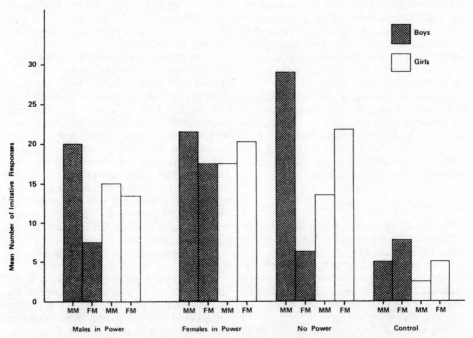

Figure 2. Mean imitative performance scores of boys and girls exposed to male and female models as a function of condition (Experiment 2; MM = male models, FM = female models).

to the same extent as the male models ($M =$ 21), $t(24) = 0.72$, $p > .10$, and this was significantly greater than their imitation of female models who lacked power $t(24) =$ 1.98, $p < .06$, or for whom power relations were left undefined, $t(24) = 2.20$, $p < .05$. Their emulation of female models in power was equal to that of the male models in power, $t(24) = 0.43$, $p > .10$, but less than their imitation of the male models for whom power relations were left undefined, $t(24) =$ 2.11, $p < .05$. Same-sex modeling is thus a robust phenomenon in boys. Emulation of female models is relatively infrequent in boys, unless the female models command power; under such conditions the boys' same-sex imitation preference is attenuated so that male and female models are emulated equally.

In all conditions the girls were influenced by both male and female models. When power differentials were not exhibited girls tended to favor same-sex models. When female models exercised power, girls adopted significant amounts of both the female and male models' behavior, although they revealed a slight preference for the female models over the male models, $t(24) = 0.48$, $p > .10$. For girls, seeing women command rewarding power equalized sex-linked modeling; seeing males exercise power attenuated but did not completely override the influence of the same-sex models, $t(24) = 0.24$, $p > .10$.

Acquisition of modeled pattern. Analysis of variance of the acquisition scores yielded no significant differences as a function of sex status and power differentials. The latter factors clearly exert their effects on spontaneous performance of modeled patterns of behavior rather than on their acquisition.

Discussion

Results of the second experiment further corroborate the prevalence of same-sex modeling, although the effect was much stronger for boys than for girls. Interestingly, powerful female models were effective in producing cross-sex imitation in boys. This readiness to emulate a powerful opposite-sex model was not so apparent for the girls.

The results of this study, along with those of others (Bussey, 1979; Bussey & Perry, 1980; Bussey & Perry, 1982; Perry & Bussey,

1979), underscore the efficacy of models in the sex-typing process. They further support the two-process model of sex-typing proposed by Bussey and Perry (1982), for boys. The stronger same-sex modeling shown by boys in many of the modeling studies presumably stems from boys' desire to adopt masculine behavior, and, simultaneously, to reject feminine behavior. Girls also adopt same-sex behavior, but not at the expense of rejecting behavior patterns modeled by the opposite sex.

A surprising finding of this research is that cross-sex modeling was more pronounced in boys than for girls. This finding would seem to contradict the common view that boys show a more rigid adherence to the masculine role than girls show for the feminine role (Brown, 1956; Hartup & Moore, 1963; Hetherington, 1967; Kleinke & Nicholson, 1979; Marcus & Overton, 1978; Nadelman, 1974). For example, boys are less likely to imitate cross-sex behavior or to develop egalitarian conceptions of sex roles when pressured to do so (Abramovitch & Grusec, 1978; Flerx, Fidler, & Rogers, 1976; Grusec & Brinker, 1972; Wolf, 1973, 1975). Why then was cross-sex modeling so effective, in this study, for boys but not girls?

For boys, cross-sex modeling resulted when female models commanded power, which in this instance involved controlling rewarding resources and the activities of others. This form of interpersonal power may conform more closely to the sex role that boys have been socialized to play. If the type of power exercised in this study is more in keeping with the male sex role, the results become understandable. Boys may be prone to emulate models whose style of behavior is consistent with the male sex role stereotype, regardless of the models' sex. Similar cross-sex modeling may well occur for girls if, for example, a factor such as nurturance, which is more consistent with the female sex role stereotype, was varied instead of power.

An alternative explanation is that girls are less constrained in their modeling by the sex of the model. Girls, typically, do not reject opposite-sex models to the same extent as boys do (Bussey & Perry, 1982). In the condition that did not include power differentials girls tended to imitate male models more than the boys imitated female ones. Because boys tend to adopt the behavior patterns of same-sex models and reject the behavior patterns of opposite-sex models, they generally engaged in minimal cross-sex imitation. If, however, the opposite-sex models command power, which may appeal to boys, then the boys not only cease rejecting the behavior patterns of the opposite-sex models, but actively adopt them.

In contrast to the boys, the girls exhibited greater consistency, across all three modeling conditions, in their degree of cross-sex modeling, whereas the boys engaged in highly specific cross-sex modeling confined predominantly to the condition in which the female models had social power. For girls, cross-sex modeling was thus not as dramatic as for boys, because it occurred to a lesser extent under ordinary conditions. The same inhibition for cross-sex models does not exist for girls in the way it does for boys, so that unless the behavior is particularly unattractive to girls, they are likely to demonstrate some cross-sex imitation, at least more than is characteristic of boys. Boys, in contrast, are unlikely to show much cross-sex modeling at all in the absence of strong vicarious instigators.

General Discussion

The results of our studies support and extend previous research (Bussey & Perry, 1982; Perry & Bussey, 1979) in demonstrating the viabililty of same-sex modeling as a mechanism of sex role development. The results demonstrate this impact on diverse behavior patterns in children as young as 3 years of age, who have not even achieved gender identity. This finding is at variance with the assumption in cognitive–developmental theory (Kohlberg, 1966) that the attainment of gender constancy is a necessary antecedent of same-sex modeling. Instead, this research shows that children pattern their behavior after members of their sex long before they grasp gender constancy.

Another noteworthy feature of this research is the dramatic cross-sex modeling effect for boys. There are few reports of successful cross-sex modeling effects for boys, but many for girls. The finding of this study departs

from these typical findings in that the reverse was true: Cross-sex modeling was more successful and dramatic in boys than girls. One reason for this lies in the nature of the factor pitted against sex of the model, namely, the powerfulness of the models. Boys emulated powerful female models almost to the same extent as male models. Because power is a valued male behavior, the boys were prepared to emulate models assuming power, regardless of their sex. The girls, in contrast, were less affected by the power manipulation. There are two possible explanations for this finding. First, girls displayed more generalized adoption of cross-sex behavior across the various modeling conditions and hence it was more difficult to demonstrate a cross-sex modeling effect for girls than boys. Second, power is much more consistent with the male role and hence the girls were less likely to construe the male models as appropriate models for themselves. Had the male models behaved in a way more consistent with the female sex role, the reverse result might have been obtained.

References

Abramovitch, R., & Grusec, J. E. (1978). Peer imitation in a natural setting. *Child Development, 49*, 60–65.

Bandura, A. (1969). Social-learning theory of identificatory processes. In D. A. Goslin (Ed.), *Handbook of socialization theory and research* (pp. 213–262). Chicago: Rand McNally.

Bandura, A. (in press). *Social foundations of thought and action.* Englewood Cliffs, NJ: Prentice-Hall.

Bandura, A., Ross, D., & Ross, S. A. (1963). A comparative test of the status envy, social power, and secondary reinforcement theories of identificatory learning. *Journal of Abnormal and Social Psychology, 67*, 527–534.

Bem, S. L. (1981). Gender schema theory: A cognitive account of sex typing. *Psychological Review, 88*, 354–364.

Blakemore, J. E. O., La Rue, A. A., & Olejnik, A. B. (1979). Sex-appropriate toy preference and the ability to conceptualize toys as sex-role related. *Developmental Psychology, 15*, 339–340.

Brown, D. G. (1956). Sex role preference in young children. *Psychological Monographs, 70*, (14, Whole No. 421).

Bussey, K. (1979). *Same-sex imitation: Fact or fiction?* Unpublished doctoral dissertation, University of Queensland, Brisbane, Australia.

Bussey, K., & Perry, D. G. (1980). *Model's sex role as a determinant of children's imitation.* Unpublished manuscript.

Bussey, K., & Perry, D. G. (1982). Same-sex imitation: The avoidance of cross-sex models or the acceptance of same-sex models? *Sex Roles, 8*, 773–784.

1302   KAY BUSSEY AND ALBERT BANDURA

Fagan, J. F., & Singer, L. T. (1979). The role of simple feature differences in infants' recognition of faces. *Infant Behavior and Development, 2*, 39–45.

Flerx, V. C., Fidler, D. S., & Rogers, R. W. (1976). Sex role stereotypes: Developmental aspects and early intervention. *Child Development, 47*, 998–1007.

Grusec, J. E., & Brinker, D. B. (1972). Reinforcement for imitation as a social learning determinant with implications for sex-role development. *Journal of Personality and Social Psychology, 21*, 149–158.

Hartup, W. W., & Moore, S. G. (1963). Avoidance of inappropriate sex-typing by young children. *Journal of Consulting Psychology, 27*, 467–473.

Hetherington, E. M. (1967). The effects of familial variables on sex typing, on parent-child similarity, and on imitation in children. In J. P. Hill (Ed.), *Minnesota symposia on child psychology* (Vol. 1, pp. 82–107). Minneapolis: University of Minnesota Press.

Huston, A. C. (1983). Sex typing. In P. H. Mussen (Ed.), *Handbook of child psychology* (4th ed., Vol. 4, pp. 387–467). New York: Wiley.

Kagan, J. (1964). Acquisition and significance of sex typing and sex role identity. In M. L. Hoffman & L. W. Hoffman (Eds.), *Review of child development research* (Vol. 1, pp. 137–167). New York: Sage.

Kleinke, C. L., & Nicholson, T. A. (1979). Black and white children's awareness of de facto race and sex difference. *Developmental Psychology, 15*, 84–86.

Kohlberg, L. (1966). A cognitive–developmental analysis of children's sex-role concepts and attitudes. In E. E. Maccoby (Ed.), *The development of sex differences* (pp. 82–173). Stanford, CA: Stanford University Press.

Kuhn, D., Nash, S. C., & Brucken, L. (1978). Sex role concepts of two- and three-year-olds. *Child Development, 49*, 445–451.

Maccoby, E. E., & Jacklin, C. N. (1974). *The psychology of sex differences.* Stanford, CA: Stanford University Press.

Marcus, D. E., & Overton, W. F. (1978). The development of cognitive gender constancy and sex role preferences. *Child Development, 49*, 434–444.

Markus, H., Crane, M., Bernstein, S., & Siladi, M.

(1982). Self-schemas and gender. *Journal of Personality and Social Psychology, 42*, 38–50.

Masters, J. C., & Wilkinson, A. (1976). Consensual and discriminative stereotypy of sex-type judgments by parents and children. *Child Development, 47*, 208–217.

Mischel, W. (1966). A social learning view of sex differences in behavior. In E. E. Maccoby (Ed.), *The development of sex differences* (pp. 56–81). Stanford, CA: Stanford University Press.

Mischel, W. (1970). Sex-typing and socialization. In P. H. Mussen (Ed.), *Carmichael's manual of child psychology* (Vol. 2, pp. 3–72). New York: Wiley.

Nadelman, L. (1974). Sex identity in American children: Memory, knowledge, and preference tests. *Developmental Psychology, 10*, 413–417.

Perry, D. G., & Bussey, K. (1979). The social learning theory of sex differences: Imitation is alive and well. *Journal of Personality and Social Psychology, 37*, 1699–1712.

Sears, R. R., Rau, L., & Alpert, R. (1965). *Identifications and child rearing.* Stanford, CA: Stanford University Press.

Slaby, R. G., & Frey, K. S. (1975). Development of gender constancy and selective attention to same-sex models. *Child Development, 46*, 849–856.

Spence, J. T. (1984). Gender identity and its implications for concepts of masculinity and femininity. In *Nebraska symposium on motivation.* Lincoln: University of Nebraska Press.

Thompson, S. K. (1975). Gender labels and early sex role development. *Child Development, 46*, 339–347.

Wolf, T. M. (1973). Effects of live modeled sex-inappropriate play behavior in a naturalistic setting. *Developmental Psychology, 9*, 120–123.

Wolf, T. M. (1975). Response consequences to televised modeled sex-inappropriate play behavior. *Journal of Genetic Psychology, 127*, 35–44.

Received September 21, 1983
Revision received March 9, 1984 ■

[28]

Journal of Personality and Social Psychology
1979, Vol. 37, No. 10, 1699–1712

The Social Learning Theory of Sex Differences: Imitation is Alive and Well

David G. Perry
University of Alberta, Edmonton, Canada

Kay Bussey
Stanford University

The hypothesis that sex role development depends in part upon children's tendencies to imitate same-sex individuals more than opposite-sex models is central to most theories of sex typing. Yet Maccoby and Jacklin, in an influential recent review of the literature, conclude that the hypothesis has been disconfirmed. In the present article, it is argued that the research on which Maccoby and Jacklin based their conclusion is weak both methodologically and conceptually. This article presents a modified social learning theory account of the contribution of imitation to sex role development. It is suggested that children learn which behaviors are appropriate to each sex by observing differences in the frequencies with which male and female models as groups perform various responses in given situations. Furthermore, children employ these abstractions of what constitutes male-appropriate and female-appropriate behavior as models for their imitative performance. A first experiment confirmed that children engage in these processes. A second experiment extended the validity of the formulation by showing how it accounts for children's imitation of individual adult models. Specifically, it was shown that a child's imitation of an adult is strongly influenced by the degree to which the child believes that the adult usually displays behaviors that are appropriate to the child's sex (that is, behaviors that occur with greater frequency among individuals of the child's sex than among opposite-sex persons). In sum, the present research reinstates same-sex imitation as a viable mechanism of sex role development.

Sex role development, or sex typing, is the process by which children come to adopt the attitudes, feelings, behaviors, and motives that are culturally defined as appropriate [1] for their sex (Hetherington, 1967; Mischel, 1970). Virtually every leading theory of sex typing assigns a prominent place to imitation in the process. Psychoanalytic theory (Freud, 1949), cognitive-developmental theory (Kohlberg, 1969), cognitive consistency theory (Kagan, 1964), and social learning theory (Bandura & Walters, 1963; Mischel, 1966, 1970) all suggest that psychological differences between the sexes are at least in part perpetuated by the fact that boys and girls as groups are more inclined to imitate responses displayed by same-sex models than they are to imitate opposite-sex models. Furthermore, within each sex, individual differ-

---

[1] The question of whether a given response is more "appropriate" to one or the other sex can be determined in any of a number of ways. These include consensus by a panel of judges, empirical determination of the relative frequency with which the response is performed by the two sexes, and differences in the consequences boys and girls receive for performing a given response. Regardless of the manner in which one chooses to operationalize sex-appropriateness of behavior, however, the processes through which sex role learning is effected are likely to be similar, and it is with process that the present article is concerned.

This research was supported by an Australian Research Grant to the first author and an Australian Commonwealth Postgraduate Scholarship to the second author. The authors thank Judy Leah, Louise Perry, and Ray Pike for commenting on an earlier draft and the Department of Education, Brisbane, for providing a subject pool.

Requests for reprints should be sent to David G. Perry, Department of Psychology, University of Alberta, Edmonton, Alberta, Canada T6G 2E9.

ences in children's masculinity and femininity (or the degree to which a child displays responses appropriate, respectively, to the male or female sex) are believed to stem in part from the strength of children's tendencies to prefer imitation of one sex model over the other.

Recently, the validity of the hypothesis that psychological differences between the sexes are due in any significant degree to differential imitation of same-sex models has come under serious attack, notably by Maccoby and Jacklin (1974). These authors argue forcefully in their influential volume that the research to date fails to support the idea that differential imitation of like-sex models is probably a mechanism through which sex differences eventuate.

In arriving at their conclusion, Maccoby and Jacklin (1974) reviewed more than 20 imitation studies in which both sex of subject and sex of model had been included as factors in the research design, and they discovered that the vast majority of such studies failed to find a significant interaction of sex of observer and sex of model on children's imitation. A more recent review (Barkley, Ullman, Otto, & Brecht, 1977) included more than 80 studies and reached essentially the same conclusion. Furthermore, the same null result holds regardless of whether the modeled behavior is traditionally sex-typed or not and of whether the models are strange adults or familiar persons such as the child's own parents. Maccoby and Jacklin therefore concluded that it is necessary to search for factors other than same-sex imitation (e.g., biological determinants or direct elicitation and reinforcement of sex-appropriate behavior) to account for sex typing. If accepted, the Maccoby and Jacklin conclusion would constitute a devastating blow to most psychologists' understanding of the sex-typing process since, as has been pointed out, most theories assign a prominent role to the imitation of same-sex models.

We believe that it is premature to abandon the same-sex imitation hypothesis altogether. The results of these literature reviews suggest, however, that if the same-sex imitation hypothesis is to be retained, then a reconceptual-ization of the way in which same-sex imitation contributes to sex role development may be in order.

It is our contention that the typical investigation designed to explore same-sex imitation has employed an experimental paradigm that is conceptually remote from how imitation actually contributes to sex role development and therefore that the null results of much of the previous research on same-sex imitation constitute an inappropriate base for rejecting the same-sex imitation hypothesis. In the typical investigation, children are exposed to a single (often unfamiliar) male and/or female performing (often novel) responses and are then tested for imitation of the models' responses. The same-sex imitation hypothesis, in its usual form, predicts that children will view the actions of the single same-sex model as a better guide for their own behavior than the actions of the opposite-sex model and will thus imitate the former model more. This is actually quite unlike the way in which children use the responses of same- and cross-sex models as guides to their own behavior in naturalistic settings. In the real course of development, children discern what behaviors are appropriate for each sex by watching the behavior of *many* male and female models and by noticing differences between the sexes in the frequency with which certain behaviors are performed in certain situations. They then use these abstractions of sex-appropriate behavior as "models" for their own imitative performance. This is quite a different view from assuming that children develop such widely generalized tendencies to imitate same-sex models that they readily take the behavior of a single same-sex model as a more reliable guide to their own behavior than the behavior of an opposite-sex model, even when the same-sex model is unfamiliar or displays novel responses, or when the child has no idea about whether the model's behavior is likely to be consensually validated by others of the model's sex.

When conceptualizing the contribution of imitation to sex-role development, we find it useful to draw on the distinction made by social learning theorists between the observational learning and performance of modeled behavior (Bandura, 1965, 1977; Mischel, 1970). According to social learning theory, through the observation of the behavior of models of both sexes, children cognitively acquire the potential to perform a vast repertoire of social behaviors that includes not only behaviors appropriate to the child's own sex but also (at least most of) the behaviors appropriate to the opposite sex. This is accomplished through such observational learning strategies as attending to the models' actions, coding the models' responses into covert imaginal or symbolic representations, and mentally rehearsing the models' actions. We propose that an additional and crucial (for sex typing) aspect of the observational learning process involves children's coding, or organizing in memory, of various responses as male-appropriate or female-appropriate on the basis of their having witnessed different proportions of available male and female models performing the responses. For example, if children observe that 80% of available male models perform a particular response in a given situation but only 5% of female models perform it, they are likely to code the response as male-appropriate or masculine.

Not everything learned is performed, however. Thus, although most boys know how to put on a dress, apply makeup, and primp in front of a mirror, few boys actually choose to perform these behaviors. Children are most likely to perform behaviors they have coded as appropriate for their own sex. According to social learning theory, which responses children select to perform from their repertoires depends primarily on the response consequences the children anticipate. Children should prefer to perform behaviors exhibited by same-sex models, because they have more often been rewarded and less often criticized for imitating same-sex models and because they gradually learn that the social environment holds similar expectations and imposes similar reinforcement contingencies on them and others of their sex (Bandura, 1969; Bussey & Perry, 1976; Mischel, 1970). In sum, although children acquire, via observational learning, behaviors that are appropriate to both sexes and label certain responses as

same-sex-appropriate and others as opposite-sex-appropriate, they prefer spontaneously to imitate actions coded as same-sex-appropriate. This is because they infer that what is expected or permissible behavior for others of their sex is also likely to be appropriate behavior for them.

Our first experiment constitutes a laboratory analog study of how we hypothesize same-sex imitation to operate in naturalistic settings. In real life, male and female models as groups frequently diverge in the responses they display in a given situation. When confronted with a similar situation and the option to perform one of the responses they have seen male and female models exhibit, children should be inclined to choose an option they recognize as same-sex appropriate. Consider, for example, a 10-year-old boy who has recently transferred to a new school. In his first days, he observes that during recess the majority of girls play hopscotch, whereas most of the boys play baseball; that during library periods, most boys check out a Hardy Boys mystery, whereas most of the girls read Nancy Drew; that when given a choice of technical electives, boys choose woodwork, whereas girls choose sewing. Even if the boy has not previously observed sex differences in the performance of these various responses, he is now likely to code the responses as masculine or feminine and to use these codings as guides to his own response selection. Experiment 1 was designed to determine whether these suggestions are tenable.

Experiment 1

Method

Overview. Boys and girls were assigned to one of three modeling conditions or to a no-model control condition. In all the modeling conditions, children viewed 8 adult models (4 male, 4 female) individually and indicated their preferences on a series of two-choice preference tasks. In a first experimental condition, on every trial all the male models chose one of the items and all of the women chose the other item. In a second condition, on every trial 3 of the men and 1 of the women chose one item and the remaining man and women chose the other item. In a third condition, on every trial 2 of the men and 2 of the women chose one item and the other 2 men and 2 women chose the other item. Subjects in the no-model condition skipped this phase. Subsequently, children in all groups were asked to indicate their own preferences for each item pair. The hypothesis was that children's endorsement of an item would be a function of the difference in the frequency with which same- and opposite-sex models had displayed a similar preference—the greater the difference, the more likely same-sex imitation was hypothesized to be.

Participants. Subjects were 96 8- and 9-year-old children, half boys and half girls, who attended a public school in a middle-class suburb of Brisbane, Australia. Models were four men and four women, all in their twenties. The experimenter was a female in her early twenties.

Stimuli. The preference task involved 16 pairs of objects. Within each pair the items belonged to the same class (e.g., a banana and an apple; a small plastic cow and a small plastic horse). Models were shown (on a black and white video monitor) making their choices from among the actual items, which were presented to them by an adult female (not the experimenter). The preference task was presented to subjects by showing them 16 color slides, each depicting one item pair. We deliberately selected responses as modeling stimuli that did not have clearly established histories of being more appropriate for one sex than the other. This was because our major goal was to demonstrate in the laboratory a major process through which previously sex-neutral responses *become* sex-linked. Furthermore, the use of already sex-typed responses could introduce potentially troublesome and irrelevant factors (e.g., the relative interest value of masculine and feminine behaviors) that might render unambiguous interpretations of the results in terms of cause and effect relations quite difficult.

Procedure. Each child was brought individually by the experimenter to a spare room on the school premises and, if assigned to a modeling condition, was seated before the video monitor. To modeling subjects, the experimenter explained that they would watch some people telling which things they "like better." In all modeling groups, the children saw, on the video monitor, the experimenter place the first item pair on a table before the eight models, individually solicit a preference from each model, and then continue to the next item pair until all 16 trials were completed. The models, who were asked for their preferences in a different order on every trial, always indicated their preference by pointing to the item of their choice and saying, "I like the (item) better." On each trial, four models always chose one item and the other four the remaining item. This equated for all groups the number of models endorsing a given item. Twelve boys and 12 girls were randomly assigned to each of three modeling conditions or to a no-model control condition which were run concurrently in a randomized blocks procedure.

In the first modeling condition, or *high (100%) within-sex consensus* modeling condition, for every

item pair all the men chose one item and all the women chose the other item. Two modeling tapes were made for this condition, with half the subjects seeing one tape and the remainder seeing the other. The tapes were designed to counterbalance for the sex of model displaying a given item preference. For the first tape, determination of whether the men or the women chose a given item was determined randomly for each trial. On the second tape, the sex of the models choosing a given item was opposite to the sex of the models who had chosen that item on the first tape.

In the second modeling condition, or *moderate (75%) within-sex consensus* modeling condition, on every trial three men and one woman chose one item and the remaining three women and one man chose the other item. The identity of the man who chose as did the majority of the women and of the woman who chose as did the majority of the men changed from trial to trial, with each model serving four times as the "odd person out" for his or her sex. Half of the subjects watched a tape in which the items preferred by the three male models were identical to those preferred by all the men in the first tape used in the high within-sex consensus condition; the remaining subjects saw a tape in which the items preferred by the three male models were those that had been preferred by all the men in the second tape used in the high within-sex consensus condition.

In the third modeling condition, or *low (50%) within-sex consensus* modeling condition, on each trial two of the men and two of the women chose one item, whereas the remaining models chose the other item. Again, two tapes were used, with half the subjects viewing each. In the first tape, two men and two women were randomly drawn, for each trial, to make the same item choices as those made by all the men for that trial on the first tape used in the high within-sex consensus condition. The remaining models chose the other item. In the second tape, the two men and the two women who had been drawn for a given trial made the choice for that trial that had been made by all the male models in the second tape of the high within-sex consensus condition.

The remaining 12 boys and 12 girls were assigned to a no-model condition and proceeded directly to the imitation test after arrival at the experimental room. Children in the modeling groups proceeded to the imitation test immediately after the models had made their choices for the 16th item pair and the video equipment had been shut off.

In the *test for imitative performance,* children were shown the 16 slides depicting the item pairs and were told to indicate for each slide (verbally as well as by using a pointer) which item they preferred.

Subjects in the three modeling conditions were then given a *recall test.* The experimenter once again displayed the 16 slides, pointed to one of the two items for each slide, and instructed the child to tell if more of the men had liked that item, if more of the women had liked it, or if an equal number of men and women had liked it. Children were promised a token (exchangeable for small prizes) for each correct answer.

Children in all groups were told they had performed very well and were awarded little prizes that were distributed when testing was completed.

Results

Imitative performance. An imitation score was derived for every child in the study by counting the number of the child's choices that matched the choices that had been unanimously *displayed by the male models in the high within-sex consensus modeling condition*. These scores of course could vary from 0 to 16 for a given child. The reasoning behind choosing imitation of the responses displayed by the male models in the high within-sex consensus condition as the datum to be compared across treatments is the following. According to the hypothesis of the research, boys' imitation of these responses should be highest in the high within-sex consensus condition and girls' imitation should be lowest in this condition. This follows from the prediction that children's endorsement of an item will be a function of the percentage of same-sex models who had displayed the preference. In this condition, 100% of the male and 0% of the female models endorsed these items. To see how changes in the percentage of same- and opposite-sex models endorsing an item alter imitation, it is necessary to examine imitation of the *same responses* but under conditions where the percentages of same- and opposite-sex models endorsing them have changed. This is most easily done by maintaining imitation of the male models' responses from the high within-sex consensus condition as the dependent variable across treatment conditions. As we move from examining children's imitation of these responses in the high within-sex consensus condition to the moderate and then the low within-sex consensus conditions, boys' scores should steadily decrease, and girls' should steadily increase. This is because the percentage of male models endorsing the preferences exhibited by the male models in the high within-sex consensus condition decreases as one moves to the moderate and then the low

conditions, whereas the percentage of female models endorsing these responses increases as we move in this direction.

Recall that within each of the three modeling conditions, two modeling tapes were used (in order to counterbalance the models' choices), with half the children in each condition viewing one tape and the other half seeing the other tape. This affected computation of children's imitation scores in two ways. First, imitation scores for subjects in each modeling condition who viewed the first modeling tape for their condition (described in the method section) were computed by counting the number of the children's choices that matched the choices unanimously made by the male models in the first modeling tape of the high within-sex consensus modeling condition; imitation scores for subjects in each condition who viewed the second tape for their condition were computed by counting the children's choices that matched the choices unanimously made by the male models in the second modeling tape of the high within-sex consensus modeling condition. Second, imitation scores for subjects in the no-model group were calculated as follows: For a random half of the subjects, scores were taken as the number of choices that matched those of the male in the first modeling tape of the high within-sex consensus modeling condition; for the remaining no-model subjects, scores were taken as the number of choices that matched those of the male models in the second modeling tape of the high within-sex consensus modeling condition.

The mean imitation scores are presented separately for boys and girls for each treatment condition in Table 1. It may be seen that the data lend strong support to the hypothesis that children's imitation of a response increases as the percentage of same-sex models displaying the response increases. It is interesting to note that essentially identical results were achieved for girls. The fact that girls imitated, on the average, only 2.8 of the males' responses in the high within-sex consensus condition of course means that they were imitating 13.2 of the choices that 100% of the female models had made. As the percentage of female models endorsing these re-

Table 1
Imitative Performance Means of Boys and Girls in Each Treatment Condition (Experiment 1)

	Treatment condition			
Child	High (100%) within-sex consensus	Moderate (75%) within-sex consensus	Low (50%) within-sex consensus	No-model control
Boys	13.9$_e$	11.6$_d$	8.7$_e$	8.5$_e$
Girls	2.8$_a$	5.8$_b$	8.5$_e$	8.2$_e$

Note. For all treatment conditions, a subject's imitation score was the number of his or her preferences that matched those made by the male models in the high within-sex consensus condition. A subject's score could range from 0 to 16. Each mean is based on scores of 12 subjects. Cells not sharing a common subscript differ significantly from each other ($p < .05$) by a two-tailed t test.

sponses declined, so too did the girls' imitation of them. It can be seen, then, that the imitative performance of both boys and girls is strongly affected by changes in the frequency with which same- and opposite-sex models display the behavior.

An analysis of variance was performed on the means in Table 1, with sex of child and treatment condition as factors. There was a strong main effect of sex of child, $F(1, 88) = 162.87$, $p < .001$, as well as a significant interaction of sex of child and treatment condition, $F(3, 88) = 58.50$, $p < .001$. The sex main effect is, of course, due to the fact that imitation scores were determined by children's imitation of preferences given by the male models in the high within-sex consensus condition. If imitation of the preferences given by the female models in this condition had arbitrarily been chosen as the dependent variable, then of course a highly significant main effect of sex in the opposite direction would have been obtained. The significant interaction effect and its pattern clearly substantiate the conclusions reached above.

A final comment on the performance results is in order. When children skipped the modeling phase and therefore had no information about the sex-appropriateness of the responses, their imitation of the responses was not markedly different from when they observed equal numbers of male and female models display them (as in the low within-sex consensus condition). In fact, within each of the two rows of Table 1, all pairwise comparisons between means are significant (by two-tailed t tests) at $p < .05$, except for the

comparison between the mean of the low within-sex condition and that of the no-model control condition.

Recall. Children in each modeling condition were asked, for each item choice displayed by the male models in the high within-sex consensus condition, whether more of the men, more of the women, or equal numbers of men and women had chosen it. The number of correct answers the children gave were analyzed in a 2×3 analysis of variance with sex of subject and modeling treatment condition as factors. The only significant effect was the main effect of treatment condition, $F(2, 66) = 7.78$, $p < .002$. Mean correct responses for the high, moderate, and low within-sex consensus conditions, respectively, were 14.4, 12.6, and 11.9. Clearly, the more consensus in choices there is among models of a given sex, the better able children are to remember whether and how the behavior is sex-typed. Boys and girls do not seem to differ in their propensities to do this.

Discussion

The research clearly supports our revised version of the same-sex imitation hypothesis. It is quite clear that when children observe same-sex models as a group exhibiting a response that diverges from the response made collectively by opposite-sex models under the same circumstances, the children are far more likely to imitate the response made by same-sex models. Obviously, the research restores same-sex imitation as a plausible mechanism of sex role development and reverses the Maccoby and Jacklin (1974) decision. However, the study suggests that the same-sex model for a child's imitation is the child's abstracted definition of appropriate behavior for the child's sex based on the child's observation of multiple examples of each sex behaving in a particular situation.

Experiment 2

Previous research on the same-sex imitation hypothesis has been guided by the assumption that children develop strongly generalized tendencies to imitate same-sex models. Recent reformulations of social learning theory (Bandura, 1977; Bandura & Barab, 1971; Mischel, 1968, 1973), however, stress the discriminating nature of children's selection of responses and models from among the vast array available to them. The negative results of research on the same-sex imitation hypothesis suggest that children do not automatically assume that a strange same-sex adult is a more appropriate role model for them than an opposite-sex model. Children probably learn quite early that individual differences exist among male and female models in terms of their masculinity and femininity and thus their suitability as models. Children should imitate a model when they believe the model's behavior is appropriate for them, too, but in order to conclude that a same-sex model is an especially reliable guide for their own behavior, the children must have some fairly unambiguous indication that the model is behaving typically for his or her sex (and is therefore an appropriate model). Experiment 2 tested this possibility.

Method

Overview. In an initial phase, children observed 8 adult models, 4 male and 4 female, indicating their preferences on a series of two-choice preference tasks. On each trial, 3 of the men and 1 woman chose one item, whereas the other man and the remaining women chose the other item. Across the trials, it was always the same man who chose as the 3 women did, and it was always the same woman who chose as the 3 men did. Thus, it was expected that over the trials children would learn that 3 of the men consistently concurred in their choices and thus were behaving sex-appropriately, whereas 1 of the men consistently chose with the majority of the women

and thus was behaving sex-inappropriately. Similarly, children were expected to learn that the behavior of 3 of the women was sex-appropriate but that that of the fourth was sex-inappropriate. Some children (assigned to a no-premodeling control group) skipped this first phase and proceeded straight to the second phase.

In a second phase, children viewed 1 of the 8 models making choices alone on a new series of preference trials. For half of the children who had participated in the first phase, this model was one of those who had behaved appropriately for his or her sex during the first phase; for the other half of the children who had participated in the first phase, the model was one who had behaved sex-inappropriately in the first phase. Children who skipped the first phase (no-premodeling control subjects) also saw one of the models from the first phase, but of course they had no idea of the degree to which the model's behavior had previously agreed or disagreed with that of other members of his or her sex. Half of the children in each of these three groups saw a male model and the other half a female model.

In a third phase, children were tested for imitation of the preferences the single model had displayed in the second phase. It was predicted, first, that same-sex imitation effects would not occur for children assigned to the no-premodeling control group because these children (as in most previous studies) would not know whether the model was behaving appropriately or inappropriately for his or her sex. Second, it was predicted that same-sex imitation effects would be extremely powerful among children exposed to a same-sex model whose behavior the children knew had a history of concurrence with other same-sex models.

Participants and design. Subjects were 84 8-year-olds, half boys and half girls, enrolled at a school in a middle-class suburb of Brisbane. Six boys and six girls were assigned to cells in a 2 × 3 × 2 design involving Sex of Child × Sex-Appropriateness of the Single Model Seen in Phase 2 (appropriate, inappropriate, or no-premodeling control) × Sex of Model. An additional six boys and six girls were assigned to a no-model control condition. These children skipped the first two phases (that is, both modeling phases) but were asked for their own preferences during the third phase just as the other children were. Children had an equal chance of being assigned to any of the experimental design groups or to the no-model group, which were run concurrently in a randomized blocks procedure. The models and the female experimenter were the same as in the first experiment.

Stimuli. Stimuli used to solicit models' preferences during the first, multiple-modeling phase were different from but similar to those used in the first experiment. Again, there were 16 item pairs. The same set of 16 item pairs was used during the second, single-modeling phase as had been used in Experiment 1. Models in both phases were shown making choices from the actual items on a black-and-white video monitor. Children were asked for their own preferences in the third phase and were shown the 16 color slides used in Experiment 1.

Procedure. Subjects were tested individually in a spare room at the school. Subjects participating in the first phase (multiple modeling) viewed the eight models making their choices, as in Experiment 1, on the video monitor. Three of the men always chose one item and three of the women always chose the other item; the remaining man and woman (inappropriate models) always chose as the majority of the opposite-sex models did. It should be clear that this treatment was identical to that received by subjecs in the moderate within-sex consensus condition of Experiment 1, with the exception that in the present experiment the identity of the odd model out for his or her sex remained constant across trials. No-premodeling control children and no-model control children skipped this phase.

Children who had participated in the first phase or who were assigned to the no-premodeling control group participated in a second phase (single modeling). Children saw one of the male or one of the female models from the multiple modeling video tape indicate his or her preferences on a series of 16 new item choices. This modeling sequence was also presented on videotape. For children who had participated in the first, multiple-modeling phase, this model was one whom they had previously seen behave either appropriately or inappropriately for his or her sex. Children in the no-premodeling control condition observed one of the same models that children who had participated in the multiple-modeling phase saw, but as noted, they had no basis for knowing whether the model had a history of behaving appropriately or inappropriately for his or her sex.

To minimize contamination of the results by idiosyncratic attributes of the particular model that children viewed during this second, single-modeling phase, different models served as appropriate and inappropriate models for different groups of children. To have given each of the eight models a chance at participating in each of the various roles he or she could have assumed would have necessitated making a prohibitively large number of modeling tapes. As a compromise, the following procedure was used. Two multiple-modeling tapes were made for use in the first phase. Half the subjects participating in this phase saw one tape and the other half saw the other tape. For each of the two tapes, a different male or female model served as the model who made inappropriate choices for his or her sex. Children who were assigned to see an inappropriate model in the second phase of course viewed whichever model had served as the inappropriate model in the tape they had seen in the first phase (with half seeing the male and half seeing the female model). Children who were assigned to see an appropriate model in the second phase, however, viewed whichever model had served as the inappropriate model in the tape they had *not* seen (but who, of course, had served as one of the

three appropriate models in the tape they *had* seen). For children assigned to the no-premodeling control condition, half viewed one of the two male models who had served as either an appropriate or an inappropriate model for children in the other conditions, and the other half viewed one of the two female models who had served in one of these roles for the other children. These procedures equated the frequency across conditions with which children viewed a particular model in the second phase as well as permitted more than one of the male and one of the female models to play the sex-inappropriate role.

In this study all the models made the same choices in the second phase. Extra tapes depicting the models making opposite choices were not used because examination of the data from Experiment 1 indicated that similar results were obtained regardless of the models' actual choices. The model's choices in the present experiment were the same as the choices seen by the children who saw the first tape in the high within-sex consensus modeling condition of the last experiment.

All children, including those assigned to a no-model control condition, were then shown the 16 slides depicting the item pairs used in the second phase and were told to give their own preferences, as in Experiment 1.

Children in the modeling conditions were asked to recall the choices the model had made in the second phase and were promised rewards for doing so. Finally, children were asked to respond on 7-point scales to the questions, "How much do you like (the model)?", "How much are you like (the model)?" "Do you think that most people would like (the model)?", and "How good is (the model) at making choices?" Children received small prizes for participating and were returned to the classroom.

Results

Imitative performance. A $2 \times 3 \times 2$ analysis of variance with sex of child, sex-appropriateness of the model, and sex of model as factors was performed on imitation scores of all the children except those assigned to the no-model control condition. Significant effects included sex of subject, $F(1, 60) = 9.32$, $p < .005$; sex-appropriateness of model, $F(2, 60) = 19.55$, $p < .001$; the interaction of sex of subject and sex of model, $F(1, 60) = 9.92$, $p < .005$; and sex of model with sex-appropriateness of model, $F(2, 60) = 3.27$, $p < .05$. However, the three-way interaction among all the variables was also highly reliable, $F(2, 60) = 41.15$, $p < .001$. The means for this analysis are given in Table 2. The least significant difference required for

Table 2

Imitative Performance Means for Interaction of Sex of Subject, Sex-Appropriateness of Model, and Sex of Model (Experiment 2)

	Sex-appropriateness of model		
Subject and model	Appropriate	Inappropriate	No-premodeling control
Boys			
Male model	14.7_f	4.3_a	13.2_{def}
Female model	3.5_a	9.3_{bc}	12.0_{de}
Girls			
Male model	8.2_b	11.2_{cd}	12.7_{def}
Female model	14.3_{ef}	8.3_b	12.8_{def}

Note. Each mean is based on six subjects' scores. Cells not sharing the same subscript are significantly different from one another ($p < .05$) by a two-tailed t test.

any two means in this table to be reliably different from one another at $p < .05$ by a two-tailed t test is 2.62.

The results confirm the hypotheses. First, examine the data for children assigned to the no-premodeling control condition by glancing down the third column in Table 2. None of the means in the column is significantly different from any other mean in the column. This substantiates the prediction that when children do not know how the behavior of a model compares with that of other members of the model's sex, the same-sex imitation hypothesis is not confirmed. Also note that the means in this column are all relatively high. This suggests the possibility of a ceiling effect. When children see only one model displaying item preferences in an experimental setting and they do not know whether the model is a "good" or "bad" example for his or her sex, they may assume that the model—regardless of sex— is likely to be a relatively safe example to follow in that setting. That the high scores in the no-premodeling groups are in fact due to imitation is apparent from the fact that children assigned to the no-model control condition made choices that matched the models' at a substantially and significantly ($p < .05$) lower rate (M for boys in no-model group = 8.0; M for girls = 8.2).

The second hypothesis was that same-sex imitation effects would occur when the children were exposed to a model whose behavior, they had learned, was typical of others of the model's sex. It is evident, by

glancing down the first column of Table 2, that this hypothesis received strong support, especially for boys. Note how boys who saw a sex-appropriate female model actually chose fewer of the model's responses than they did when they had not seen any model perform at all ($p < .05$).

Two other features of the pattern of means are noteworthy. First, glance down the middle column of means in Table 2, where data are presented for children's imitation of a model whom they had previously seen behave sex-inappropriately. Apparently, when children know an opposite-sex model is a more reliable indicator of behavior appropriate to the child's own sex than a same-sex model, they are more likely to imitate the opposite-sex model. Interestingly, cross-sex imitation is really evident only among girls, because the imitation scores displayed by girls exposed to an inappropriate male model ($M = 11.2$) were significantly ($p < .05$) higher than the imitation scores of no-model control girls ($M = 8.2$). In contrast, boys' imitation scores were not significantly higher with an inappropriate female ($M = 9.3$) than in the no-model control condition ($M = 8.0$). Boys may ignore rather than imitate females who behave masculinely.

A second point is that boys more actively inhibited imitation of sex-inappropriate behavior than girls. Imitation scores of boys who saw either an inappropriate male model ($M = 4.3$) or an appropriate female model ($M = 3.5$) were lower ($p < .05$ in each case) than those of no-model control boys. In contrast, girls did not inhibit imitation of male-appropriate behavior, when it was displayed by either a male ($M = 8.2$) or a female ($M = 8.3$) model.

Recall. Correctly recalled choices of the model were subjected to a similar $2 \times 3 \times 2$ analysis of variance. No effect attained significance (Grand $M = 15.1$).

Questionnaire data. Children's responses to the four postexperimental questions were subjected to similar three-way analyses of variance. No significant effects were obtained on the first question, which asked children to indicate their attraction to the model. For the second question, which asked children to rate their similarity to the model, several effects were significant, but they were all subsumed by a significant highest order interaction, $F(2, 60) = 14.03$, $p < .001$. The means indicated that when children saw a sex-appropriate model, there was stronger perceived similarity to a same-sex model for both boys and girls; when children saw a sex-inappropriate model, boys actually expressed greater similarity to the female model than the male model (no parallel result occurred for girls); among children in the no-premodeling conditions, there were no differences in perceived similarity to the model. It is, of course, important to remember that these data were collected after the subjects' imitation test and may thus have been influenced by their imitative performance. On the third question, which asked children to tell whether most people would like the model, there were no significant effects. On the final question, which asked children to indicate how good they thought the model was at making choices, there was a significant three-way interaction, $F(2, 60) = 3.97$, $p < .05$. It appeared that the only major contributor to this interaction was the fact that boys in the no-premodeling control condition perceived the female model as more competent than the male at making choices. Why this result emerged is unknown. However, in sum it appears that neither perceptions of the model's competence nor attraction to the model can account for the imitation results. On the other hand, perceived similarity to the model does appear as an influential possibility.

General Discussion

The major contribution of the present research is to reinstate same-sex imitation as a viable mechanism of sex role development. Maccoby and Jacklin's (1974) conclusion that differential imitation of same-sex models contributes negligibly to sex role development was based on the results of studies that lacked an adequately developed conceptual framework of how imitation contributes to the social learning of sex differences. The present article demonstrates quite clearly that children discern behaviors appropriate to the two sexes by observing differences between the sexes in the frequency with which they perform various responses in a given situation and, furthermore, that children use these abstractions concerning sex-appropriate behaviors as guides to their own performance in similar situations.

The research also demonstrates that a child's imitation of a single model is in part governed by the degree to which the child has come to believe that the model's behavior is ordinarily appropriate or inappropriate to the child's sex. In other words, children are most likely to imitate persons whom they perceive to be good examples of their sex role. It is of interest that some previous research has shown that girls are especially likely to imitate a warm or nurturant model, whereas boys are particularly likely to imitate a dominant model (Hetherington, 1967). This may be in part because children usually perceive warmth as indicative of femininity and dominance as reflective of masculinity (Best, Williams, Cloud, Davis, Robertson, Edwards, Giles, & Fowles, 1977; Rothbaum, 1977; Williams, Bennett, & Best, 1975). Clearly, then, children judge the likely appropriateness of an individual model's behavior by recalling how well that person's attitudes and behaviors usually match up with others of his or her sex.

According to social learning theory, children acquire (via observational learning) responses appropriate to both sexes but prefer to perform responses exhibited by same-sex models. In other words, model sex affects performance more than observational learning. Results of the second study are quite in line with this proposition. In this experiment, there were no significant effects of the experimental variables upon children's recall of the model's behavior, although the same factors strongly affected children's imitative performance. These results mesh with those of Williams et al. (1975), who found that boys and girls do not differ in their knowledge of cultural stereotypes for male and female behavior which, we could argue, are primarily learned via observational learning. We do not wish to overstate the case, however. Several studies do show that children sometimes attend more closely to, as well as learn more about, the behavior of models consistent with their own sex role (Grusec & Brinker, 1972; Maccoby & Wilson, 1957; Maccoby, Wilson, & Burton, 1958; Perry & Perry, 1975; Slaby & Frey, 1975). Nadelman (1974) also found that children were able to identify correctly the sex-appropriateness of items appropriate for their own sex better than they were able to identify the sex-appropriateness of items traditionally associated with the opposite sex. Thus, although the preference for performing same-sex behaviors may well be stronger than the preference for learning same-sex behavior, it is not as though the latter phenomenon is nonexistent.

Our analysis of same-sex imitation in sex role development suggests that children must master certain cognitive achievements before their sex typing can to any significant degree be influenced by imitation of like-sex models. Before children will encode responses they see performed more often by members of a given sex as male- or female-appropriate, they must realize that human beings are divided into males and females. Before they will prefer to perform responses coded as same-sex-appropriate, they must realize that not only do they belong to one of these sexes, but they are subject to a similar set of expectations and reinforcement contingencies as others of their sex. Children may learn that other people are divided into males and females before they establish their own gender identities (Thompson, 1975). Thus children may proceed through an initial stage in which they acquire some knowledge of male- and female-appropriate behavior (via

observational learning) but, not realizing they belong to one of these sexes, may fail to display a preference for imitating same-sex-appropriate behavior. Such a possibility should be tested. Once children attain gender constancy they do attend more to same-sex models (Slaby & Frey, 1975). However, developmental research that tracks the emergence of children's gender identities and their beliefs that they are expected to behave similarly to members of a particular sex and relates these variables to children's imitation of same- and cross-sex models is needed.

Because the present formulation emphasizes that children imitate responses that they abstract as appropriate for their sex as a group, it clearly assigns less importance to children's imitation of particular individuals (e.g., the like-sex parent) than do more traditional theories, especially Freudian theory (1949) or various other views that hold that children achieve sex typing via imitation of a warm and/or socially powerful parental figure (Hetherington, 1967; Mussen & Distler, 1959; Parsons, 1955; Sears, Rau, & Alpert, 1965). Although this is true, we do not mean to imply that children's sex typing is never influenced by their especially strong imitation of "significant others," for it undoubtedly is. However, we would expect that children who initially adopt responses by imitating a highly nurturant and/or dominant same-sex parent would ultimately drop the responses from their active repertoires if they eventually realize that no other same-sex individuals perform the responses but that many opposite-sex persons do.

Although in the first experiment boys and girls did not differ in their propensities to imitate abstracted same-sex-appropriate behavior, there was clear evidence in the second experiment that boys were more concerned than girls with matching their behavior to a model known to exemplify sex-typical behavior. This concurs with previous findings that a variety of socializing agents, including parents and peers, enforce stronger sanctions on boys than on girls for conforming to culturally defined sex-role prescriptions (Fagot, 1977; Fling & Manosevitz, 1972) and that boys are more likely to conform to peer pressure than are girls (Maccoby &

Jacklin, 1974). It may indeed be the case, as Lynn (1969) suggests, that boys become sex-typed through "masculine role identification" by acquiring and imitating cultural stereotypes of male-appropriate behavior learned by observing a variety of male figures both within and beyond the home. Girls, on the other hand, are less concerned with conforming to abstract standards.

Although this research indicates that imitation of abstracted sex-appropriate behavior is a plausible mechanism of sex role development, it is not implied that other factors (e.g., genetics, direct elicitation, and shaping of sex-typed behavior) are unimportant. The present formulation is probably a weak or inadequate explanation of early sex differences, say, those occurring in the first year or two of life. As early as age 1, there are sex differences in children's toy preferences, though the exact qualities of the toys (e.g., softness, faceness, number of moving parts, manipulability) responsible for the differences have yet to be isolated (Jacklin, Maccoby, & Dick, 1973). It seems unlikely that such early differences are due to abstracted differences about sex-appropriate behavior learned from observation of multiple models. The cognitive capacities required to notice that the sexes differ in their frequency of performing certain behaviors, to register the information in memory as male- or female-appropriate, and to learn that one is expected to conform to sex-appropriate role behavior take time to develop. Obviously, other factors must be involved in early sex differences.

One might wish to level the criticism against the present research that results are attributable to "demand characteristics" of the experimental procedures. In particular, it might be argued that using multiple models and testing the child in the presence of an experimenter who knew how the models had responded placed stronger demands on the child to display same-sex imitation than would exist under more natural circumstances and therefore that the results are artifactual. We would argue that many sex-typed behaviors are indeed public, with people in a position to view a performer's behavior just as aware as the performer of the sex-appro-

priateness of various response options in the situation. Consequently, it is entirely appropriate to examine imitation of sex-appropriate and -inappropriate behavior in the laboratory under circumstances similar to those that exist outside of it (i.e., in the presence of an observer—here, the experimenter). Moreover, the results of a third experiment conducted by the authors indicate that same-sex imitation does occur even in the absence of the experimenter.[2]

In the procedures used in the present study, endorsement of a choice preferred by the majority of one sex of model was confounded with rejection of the choice preferred by the majority of opposite-sex models. To illustrate, consider the models' choices in the high within-sex consensus condition of the first experiment. The endorsement by 100% of the male models of a particular item was, of course, coupled with implicit rejection of the item unanimously chosen by the female models. In any two-item forced-choice situation, endorsement of one item implies rejection of the other. In the present research, it is not possible to determine, for example, if a boy's imitation of responses endorsed by male models was a function of an active desire to emulate the male models or a wish not to display a choice indicated

---

[2] To examine the generality of some of the findings from the first two experiments reported, the authors conducted a third experiment. The design was identical to that of Experiment 2 of the present report. However, the procedure was altered in three major ways. First, peers instead of adults were used as models. Second, although the first, multiple-modeling phase of the study was conducted exactly as in Experiment 2 (with models indicating their preferences from among item pairs), the second modeling phase involved the modeling of novel action and verbal sequences rather than the modeling of additional item preferences. Third, the test for imitation involved leaving the child alone with the objects the model had used in displaying the action and verbal responses in the second phase, with instructions to "see if you can do some interesting things with them" while the experimenter was gone. Children's imitation of responses displayed by the model in the second phase was assessed by a time-sampling technique while the child was observed through a one-way vision screen for a 4-minute period. Results were virtually identical to those obtained in Experiment 2.

by the female models. In real-life settings, of course, many choice situations do exemplify the two-pronged situation facing children in our study where one choice was masculine and the other feminine. For theoretical reasons however, it would be interesting to develop a methodology that permits separate manipulation and assessment of a propensity to accept same-sex models' behavior, on the one hand, and a tendency to reject opposite-sex models' behavior, on the other. For instance, the stronger same-sex imitation shown by boys in the present research may stem from simultaneous desires to accept masculine behavior and to reject feminine behavior. Perhaps girls are also prone to accept same-sex behavior but are less repulsed by the thought of displaying cross-sex behavior.

Conclusion

The present research restores the same-sex imitation hypothesis as a plausible mechanism of social learning of sex differences, though in a modified conceptual context. Many important questions remain, however. These include the nature of the processes accounting for sex differences in the early years; the exact roles played by parents, peers, unfamiliar adults, and other classes of social models in the process; the sequencing of such cognitive accomplishments as children's realization that the social world is divided into males and females, that they belong to one of these groups, that they and others of their sex are subject to a similar set of expectations and reinforcing contingencies from the social environment; the relationship of these factors to children's observational learning and performance of sex-type behavior; and whether acceptance of same-sex behavior and rejection of opposite-sex behavior contribute equally to same-sex imitation in children of both sexes.

References

Bandura, A. Influence of models' reinforcement contingencies on the acquisition of imitative responses. *Journal of Personality and Social Psychology,* 1965, *1,* 589–595.

Bandura, A. Social-learning theory of identificatory processes. In D. A. Goslin (Ed.), *Handbook of socialization theory and research.* Chicago: Rand McNally, 1969.

Bandura, A. *Social learning theory.* Englewood Cliffs, N.J.: Prentice-Hall, 1977.

Bandura, A., & Barab, P. G. Conditions governing nonreinforced imitation. *Developmental Psychology,* 1971, *5,* 244–255.

Bandura, A., & Walters, R. H. *Social learning and personality development.* New York: Holt, Rinehart & Winston, 1963.

Barkley, R. A., Ullman, D. G., Otto, L., & Brecht, J. M. The effects of sex typing and sex appropriateness of modeled behavior on children's imitation. *Child Development,* 1977, *48,* 721–725.

Best, D. L., Williams, J. E., Cloud, J. M., Davis, S. W., Robertson, L. S., Edwards, J. R., Giles, H., & Fowles, J. Development of sex-trait stereotypes among young children in the United States, England, and Ireland. *Child Development,* 1977, *48,* 1375–1384.

Bussey, K., & Perry, D. G. Sharing reinforcement contingencies with a model: A social-learning analysis of similarity effects in imitation research. *Journal of Personality and Social Psychology,* 1976, *84,* 1168–1176.

Fagot, B. I. Consequences of moderate cross-gender behavior in preschool children. *Child Development,* 1977, *48,* 902–907.

Fling, S., Manosevitz, M. Sex typing in nursery school children's play interests. *Developmental Psychology,* 1972, *7,* 146–152.

Freud, S. *An outline of psychoanalysis.* (1st ed., 1940). New York: Norton, 1949.

Grusec, J. E., & Brinker, D. B., Jr. Reinforcement for imitation as a social learning determinant with implications for sex-role development. *Journal of Personality and Social Psychology,* 1972, *21,* 149–158.

Hetherington, E. M. The effects of familial variables on sex typing, on parent–child similarity and on imitation in children. In J. P. Hill (Ed.), *Minnesota symposia on child psychology* (Vol. 1). Minneapolis: University of Minnesota Press, 1967.

Jacklin, C. N., Maccoby, E. E., & Dick, A. E. Barrier behavior and toy preference: Sex differences (and their absence) in the year-old child. *Child Development,* 1973, *44,* 196–200.

Kagan, J. Acquisition and significance of sex typing and sex role identity. In M. L. Hoffman and L. W. Hoffman (Eds.), *Review of child development research* (Vol. 1). New York: Russell Sage Foundation, 1964.

Kohlberg, L. Stage and sequence: The cognitive-developmental approach to socialization. In D. A. Goslin (Ed.), *Handbook of socialization theory and research.* Chicago: Rand McNally, 1969.

Lynn, D. B. *Parental and se x-role identification: A theoretical formulation.* Berkeley, Calif.: McCutchan, 1969.

Maccoby, E. E., & Jacklin, C. N. *The psychology*

of sex differences. Stanford, Calif.: Stanford University Press, 1974.

Maccoby, E. G., & Wilson, W. C. Identification and observational learning from films. *Journal of Abnormal and Social Psychology*, 1957, *55*, 76–87.

Maccoby, E. G., Wilson, W. C., & Burton, R. V. Differential movie-viewing behavior of male and female viewers. *Journal of Personality*, 1958, *26*, 259–267.

Mischel, W. A social-learning view of sex differences in behavior. In E. E. Maccoby (Ed.), *The development of sex differences*. Stanford, Calif.: Stanford University Press, 1966.

Mischel, W. *Personality and assessment*. New York: Wiley, 1968.

Mischel, W. Sex-typing and socialization. In P. H. Mussen (Ed.), *Carmichael's manual of child psychology*. New York: Wiley, 1970.

Mischel, W. Toward a cognitive social learning reconceptualization of personality. *Psychological Review*, 1973, *80*, 252–283.

Mussen, P. H., & Distler, L. Masculinity, identification, and father–son relationship. *Journal of Abnormal and Social Psychology*, 1959, *59*, 350–356.

Nadelman, L. Sex identity in American children: Memory, knowledge, and preference tests. *Developmental Psychology*, 1974, *10*, 413–417.

Parsons, T. Family structure and the socialization of the child. In T. Parsons & R. F. Bales (Eds.), *Family socialization and interaction process*. Glencoe, Ill.: Free Press, 1955.

Perry, D. G., & Perry, L. C. Observational learning in children: Effects of sex of model and subject's sex role behavior. *Journal of Personality and Social Psychology*, 1975, *31*, 1083–1988.

Rothbaum, F. Developmental and gender differences in the sex stereotyping of nurturance and dominance. *Developmental Psychology*, 1977, *13*, 531–532.

Sears, R. R., Rau, L., & Alpert, R. *Identification and childrearing*. Stanford, Calif.: Stanford University Press, 1965.

Slaby, R. G., & Frey, K. S. Development of gender constancy and selective attention to same-sex models. *Child Development*, 1975, *46*, 849–856.

Thompson, S. K. Gender labels and early sex role development. *Child Development*, 1975, *46*, 339–347.

Williams, J. E., Bennett, S. M., & Best, D. L. Awareness and expression of sex stereotypes in young children. *Developmental Psychology*, 1975, 635–642.

Received October 5, 1978 ∎

[29]

DEVELOPMENTAL REVIEW, 5, 83–98 (1985)

Changes in Thinking about Early Sex Role Development

BEVERLY I. FAGOT

University of Oregon and Oregon Social Learning Center

How do we learn to recognize ourselves and to live as beings endowed with gender? This paper discusses changes in our answer to this question over the last 15 years. As our methods of study have changed, we have been forced to see the development of sex role as an increasingly complicated process. This paper documents two studies that were attempts to bring together two methodologies: cognitive development and social learning. In the first study, 180 children were tested using the R. G. Slaby and K. S. Frey (1975, Child Development, 46, 849–856) gender identification interview. The findings documented that children's gender understanding followed the sequence predicted by L. Kohlberg (1966, in E. Maccoby (Ed.), *The development of sex differences*. Stanford, CA: Stanford Univ. Press): identity, stability, and constancy. However, the child's level of gender understanding was unrelated to the adoption of sex-typed behaviors. In the second study, a second group of 64 children, 20 to 30 months of age, were tested for understanding of gender labels, gender identity, and sex-typed behaviors. Sex of playmates and boys' play with feminine toys were related to understanding of verbal gender labels. Reasons for continuing problems of interpretation in the sex role area are discussed. © 1985 Academic Press, Inc.

In science and out, a good question has consequences as well as answers. It stings us to thought as we try to loose the knot of its particular mystery, but it also changes the way we think about other questions and, sometimes, the way we lead our lives. *How do we learn to recognize ourselves and to live as beings endowed with gender?* When do we begin? At five? At three? At one? Who is the master/mistress of this art? Who teaches us? The family we inherit? The language we assume? The body we are born to? What is the cost if we stumble in this learning, or if we are tripped? Who must pay then? Who will pick us up when we fall? Clearly, the constant fact of gender and the inescapable consequences of that fact pose a very good question. What have we done with this question we have been given? Often we have ignored it, pretending that we could study personality without some understanding of sex role development, even though these roles are founded deep in the grammar with which we

Data analyses were supported by BRSG Grant RR07980 awarded by the Biomedical Research Support Grant Program, Division of Research Resources, National Institutes of Health. The final writeup was completed on a postdoctoral fellowship (Grant 1 T32 MH 16955-01) through the Oregon Social Learning Center. All correspondence and reprint requests should be sent to Beverly I. Fagot, Department of Psychology, University of Oregon, Eugene, OR 97403.

83

announce ourselves to the world. We study a neutered kind of cognition or social development, even though boys and girls obviously are not neuters and live in different worlds in which the same behaviors may have different consequences according to the perceived sex of the child.

When I first began to study sex differences, I started with the social learning viewpoint then current. I assumed that if I could understand the types of reinforcers received by children for sex-typed behaviors, I would understand sex role development. My early work concentrated on 4- and 5-year-old boys and girls, for it was fairly well accepted in the literature prior to 1961 that sex differences in children below the age of 4 were unstable. Freudians speculated that the identification process took place between 4 and 5, when we were too old for the crib, too young for the couch, but just the right age to remember (with a practitioner's help, of course). Two more modern approaches, modified learning theory and cognitive theory, led to the same opinion. Working within the terms of the former approach, Sears (1965) held that the child of either sex matched behaviors with the mother until such time as the father took a more active role with the boy, and then, at about 5, the male child could start matching behaviors with the father. Working within the latter approach, Kohlberg (1966) also suggested that real sex differences would emerge at around 5 years of age as a function of the cognitive understanding of gender identity. And where the theorists led the metricists followed, for the technique of measurement used in many of these early studies—the It test (Brown, 1956)—also led to the conclusion that a stable estimate of sex differences was not really obtained until the subject was about 5.

Today, we can see that there were three serious shortcomings in this early research. First, the children were too old. Second, it tended to subordinate investigation to theory and in the process to create a kind of Ptolemaic psychology dedicated to saving the appearances and the sanctity of the laboratory. Third, it tended to substitute for the complex reality of a single organic process—a child coming to know its sex—the simpler ideology of Developmental Psychology or of Cognitive Psychology or of Social Learning. Obviously, these failings are not without connection, so in working to correct one, we inevitably work on all. For example, it is now generally accepted that 3- and probably 2-year-old children show well-developed sex differences in their behavior. Have children suddenly become more sophisticated than they used to be? No, the indication is that children have not changed much at all. Data collected in 1963 on 3-year-olds are very similar to data collected in the 1970s (Fagot, 1977), but what has changed is the way the data are collected. More flexible theoretical approaches in social learning and in ethology have led to children being observed as they play in their natural environments. At first, findings from this research indicated that sex differences were present from age 3 (Clark, Wyon, & Richards, 1969; Fagot & Patterson, 1969). Then studies using similar techniques found stable sex differences as early as 18 months (Blurton-Jones, 1972; Etaugh, Collins, & Gerson, 1975). The earlier negative and inconsistent findings were due to the difficulties of obtaining reliable verbal responses to testing rather than to the lack of real sex differences in the younger children.

What are some of these differences and why do they merit study? Block (1983) grouped sex-related differences in each child into seven conceptual domains: aggression, activity, impulsivity, susceptibility to anxiety, achievement-related behaviors, self-concept, and social relationships. These categories can help us explain why there is so much evidence that boys and girls are at risk in different areas of their development and at different ages. Baumrind (1979), for example, pointed out that male insufficiencies in development are apparent by the age of 4 in the guise of less developed prosocial behaviors, so that boys are more aggressive, work less well at tasks, and often lack control over their impulses. Girls seem to show insufficiencies at a later age, displaying in their early teens lower self-esteem, a more diffuse self-concept, and an unwillingness to break away from dependent relationships. Similarly, Eme (1979) noted that sex differences are present in psychopathology from a very early age, and basically show a pattern of undercontrol of impulses for males and overdependency for females, and that boys run into difficulties at a much earlier age than girls.

The study of sex role development has been hindered by vocabularies that are only approximately shared, which leads to a coarsening of discriminations and can yield downright confusion. A careful distinction must be made between the development of cognitive categories concerning sex and the expectancy of one's sex. Money and Ekhardt (1972) made an important distinction between gender identity (as a private understanding) and gender role (as a public expression of this private understanding). We must not allow these two terms to blur, for it appears that gender identity is learned very early, and is extremely difficult to change, while gender role behaviors often change as a function of age (Maccoby & Jacklin, 1974), of particular stages of life, or of movement across cultures (Block, 1973). Huston (1983) carefully delineated the dimensions of sex role in terms of content and private and public expressions of such constructs. Her schema suggested that different investigators often give the same names to quite different content areas and constructs, and this should help us understand why results in the area often appear contradictory. In particular, self-perception, beliefs, and behavioral enactment are often simply subsumed under a label of sex typing, despite the fact that they may all be quite uncorrelated. We know something about the socialization of gender role behaviors or behavioral adoptions by family and peer groups, for these processes are highly visible and easy to study; we do not know how these variables affect gender identity, or even if they do.

Sex differences in child behavior do not begin to appear with any regularity until about the first birthday, and even then the differences are few in comparison with the similarities observed between such young boys and girls. Nor are all differences, once found, found again. One widely quoted study (Goldberg & Lewis, 1969) found several sex differences in the behavior of 1-year-olds when they were individually observed with their mothers during a "free play" situation. The infants' behavior corresponded to sex stereotypes of parents and to observations of sex differences in older children's behavior. However, most replication studies with children of this age have not found such extensive sex differences in style of play or behavior toward the mothers (Brookes & Lewis, 1974; Clarke-Stewart, 1973; Jacklin, Maccoby, & Dick, 1973). While sex differences in the behavior of infant boys and girls are minimal, by the time children approach their second birthday, there is substantial evidence for consistent differences that would appear to be an extension of those occasionally observed during the first year of life. For example, a frequent finding involves differences in the toy preferences of toddler girls and boys observed during play at home. Girls tend to play with soft toys and dolls, they dress up and dance, while boys tend to play with transportation toys and blocks, to manipulate objects actively, and to play more often with toys and household items forbidden by parents (Fagot, 1974, 1978; Fein, Johnson, Kosson, Stork, & Wasserman, 1975; Smith & Daglish, 1977). Also consistent with the expected or stereotyped social expressive orientation of girls and the object orientation of boys, girls tend to begin to talk earlier than boys (Schachter, Shore, Hodapp, R., Chalfin, & Bundy, 1978) and to use this ability to their advantage in problem situations such as the barrier frustration task (Feiring & Lewis, 1979).

Information provided by the child's environment is not always consistent and there may be fairly long intervals between presentations of similar events, yet children develop categories or gender schemata which allow them to classify behaviors, attitudes, and themselves as male or female. Parental interventions and environmental factors may punctuate the process of growth, but the child, too, must be studied in terms of its own developing capabilities so far as this is possible. The most popular technique during the 1970s was to focus upon the sequence in which the child comes to recognize gender. According to Eaton and Von Burgen's (1981) summary, *gender understanding* consists of four components that enter a child's cognitive repertoire in the following order: (1) *labeling* of self, then others as "boy" or "girl," (2) *stability,* the recognition that gender is permanent over time, (3) *motive,* knowledge that gender cannot change even if one wants it to, and (4) *constancy,* knowledge that gender (one's own and that of others) is invariant despite changes in activity, appearance, attire, and so on. Much of the work done so far has concentrated upon looking at whether this sequence of understanding holds true.

The work by Martin and Halverson (1981) and Bem (1981) is an attempt to apply information process theory to the child's understanding of gender. Both researchers suggest that understanding of gender is an attempt by the child to organize and structure social information. Both approaches suggest that children will develop a very differentiated schema for their own sex and a much less differentiated schema for the opposite sex. Carter and Patterson (1982) found that conception of gender, like understanding of other social conventions, became more flexible with age. They also suggested that gender is merely one aspect of the development of social–conventional thought. Cognitive research on sex role in the 1980s has attempted to look at sex role through more conventional information-processing approaches, while social learning and ethological research have concentrated upon the child's performance in the natural environment. It is now time to bring the two systems of research together to develop a more complete understanding of the child's attempt to understand the complexities of gender.

A normative study of cognitive gender understanding in children from 18 months to 5 years of age is presented in this paper. Several normative studies have been completed but the results have been somewhat contradictory as to age-related developments, because each has covered very small age ranges (Kuhn, Nash, & Brucken, 1978; Marcus & Overton, 1978; Slaby & Frey, 1975). In the longitudinal study presented in this paper, the development of gender constructs was examined to determine whether it follows the predicted sequences. A major purpose of the study was to examine the relationship between the child's construction of gender identity and the adoption of sex role behavior.

STUDY 1

Method

Subjects

The total sample for this study consisted of 180 children, 90 boys and 90 girls, whose ages ranged from 18 to 54 months old at the beginning of the study. The broad age range of the sample allowed observation of change at several levels of gender understanding and development. Subjects were blocked into 6-month age intervals for statistical treatment of the group data. There were 15 children of each sex within each 6-month age interval. One hundred seventeen of these children were also observed in play groups while the testing took place, and were followed up and retested every 3 months for a period of 1 year.

The 117 children (59 boys, 58 girls) who were observed in play groups and followed for 1 year all attended play groups in the psychology department at the University of Oregon. The additional children attended child day-care centers which had a population of parents very similar to the psychology department groups. The socioeconomic background of the children was varied, from professional to welfare families. Approximately one half of the mothers in this sample were employed or attended school, but this was not related to the social class of the family. Approximately half of the children were in various kinds of alternative care for 5 or more hours per day. The children were all Caucasian (white); 10 minority children were tested but not included in the results.

Behavior Checklist[1]

A list of 34 child behaviors and 15 teacher and peer reactions were used for this study. The child behaviors included activities such as rough-and-tumble play, build with small blocks, and dance, while the reactions included categories of behaviors such as hug and give physical affection, parallel play, and continue alone. The child behavior was always recorded first, then the reactor (if there was one), and then the reaction. For each observation there were always separate child behaviors and reactions.

Psychology Department Play Group Setting

The play groups consisted of 12 to 15 children, with an approximately equal number of boys and girls in each class. Two undergraduate students served as teachers throughout each term in each class. The large study has been in progress for 6 years, with each year divided into three 10-week terms corresponding to the university school year. The children for this study were observed during their first two terms of attendance in the project, with approximately 15 children observed each year. There were no consistent differences in play behaviors or in teacher or peer consequences among the different cohorts, so the children were combined into a single sample. The playroom was approximately 20 × 25 ft, equipped with standard preschool toys such as blocks, dolls, books, and transportation toys. Teachers were instructed to let the children choose their own activities and to interfere only when a child was obviously disturbed. The teachers did provide varied activities each day by placing toys on the tables or the floor for the children to choose, but no attempt was made to have each child sample all activities.

[1] A coding manual for the behavior checklist can be obtained from the author.

Observations

Observers were first trained using videotapes from children engaged in the play groups in previous terms. The tapes were precoded so that over the 2 years of the study all observers were checked against criterion tapes. None of the videotaped interactions are included as data in this study. Throughout each term of data collection, reliability spot checks were run at least once a week and sometimes three times a week. There was an average of 12 reliability checks in a term of data collection, with a range of 10 to 15.

The observers had to give exactly the same code number on each observation to be considered in agreement. Each spot check lasted approximately 15 min, which gave the observers time to code all children in the room three different times so that each set of coders working at the same time shared 120 or more observations. The pairs of observers all exceeded 90% agreement for the child behaviors (range = 91 to 98%) and 75% for the reactions (range 78 to 92%).

Procedures

Observers were in an observation room with a separate entrance and observed the children through a one-way mirror. Two hours of observation were completed during each play session. All children were observed each session using a scan sampling technique. Each child was observed in a predetermined order for 2–5 s, and the child's behavior, the reactors, and the reaction were coded. Using this technique, each child in the play group was observed 12 times per hour for a total of 480 to 720 observations during the term. This technique gives a picture of the types of activities favored by the children in the group, and gives a pattern of peer and teacher reaction within the group.

Gender Constancy Task

The child was administered the gender constancy interview of Slaby and Frey (1975) with minimal changes. The interview consisted of a set of 14 questions. We also added the question used by Emmrich that combined motivation and a belief in the constancy of gender (If I had a magic wand, could I change you into a [child of the opposite sex])?

Definition of Male, Female, and Neutral Behaviors

Behaviors were categorized as male, female, or neutral in a previous study (Fagot, 1984), in which tests for sex differences in behavior were made for a separate sample of 180 children. At least 12 and as many as 80 h of observation per child were coded using the behavior checklist described above. Eight play activities showed significant sex differences

90 BEVERLY I. FAGOT

TABLE 1
GENDER STAGE PASSED AT EACH AGE LEVEL

Age (months)	Total N	Own identity		Gender identity		Stability		Constancy	
		n	%	n	%	n	%	n	%
				Boys					
18–24	14	2	13	2	13	1	7	0	
25–30	15	7	47	4	27	0		0	
31–36	15	10	67	10	67	0		1	7
37–42	15	15	100	15	100	3	20	4	27
43–48	15	15	100	15	100	4	27	8	53
49–54	15	15	100	12	80	12	80	12	80
				Girls					
18–24	15	1	6	2	13	0		0	
25–30	15	2	13	2	13	1	7	0	
31–36	15	8	53	8	53	2	13	0	
37–42	15	11	73	11	73	4	27	4	27
43–48	15	15	100	15	100	6	40	6	40
49–54	15	15	100	15	100	15	100	15	100

(i.e., were more likely to be engaged in by one sex or the other as de-termined by t tests significant at the .01 level). Male-typical activities included rough-and-tumble play, transportation toys, large blocks, and carpentry play. Female-typical activities were doll play, dress up, art activities, and dance. The 10 following behaviors showed no significant sex differences and were designated as neutral behaviors: play in wagon, climb and slide, play with clay, play with design boards and puzzles, play with small blocks, play with puppets, play ball or frisbee, fantasy play, sing or listen to records, and look at books. This system was used to classify the behavior observed in the present study, so that scores for the play behavior categories were combined to yield male-typical, female-typical, and neutral behavior scores for each child.

Results

Gender Constancy

The percentage of boys and girls who answered both the question and its reverse correctly for each stage in the gender constancy task during their first interview are presented in Table 1. As can be seen, there was an age-related trend, with gender identity questions answered earlier than stability, and stability earlier than constancy. There were no sex differ-ences in the number of boys and girls passing the items at each age category (sign test). The results replicate those by Slaby and Frey (1975) and Marcus and Overton (1978), who used slightly older samples, and Kuhn, Nash, and Brucken (1978).

TABLE 2
NUMBER OF CHILDREN IN EACH TYPE OF SEQUENCE OVER 1 YEAR

	Boys	Girls
Predicted sequence	37	40
– + – –	0	1
+ + – +	3	1
– – + –	0	1
None (no stage passed successfully)	19	15
Total	59	58

Longitudinal Results

Children were retested once a term during their attendance in the play groups so that their development over a time span could be plotted. The data from the longitudinal sample also fit the cognitive development predictions. Table 2 presents the results of children who received the gender constancy test over at least three different terms. Only six children, three boys and three girls, differed from the predicted sequence.

Relationship between Sex Preference and Gender Constancy

Sex role scores were the proportion of time spent in each sex-typed category normalized using arc sine transformations. The correlations between gender constancy scores and sex role scores were computed with age partialed out. There were no significant relationships for either boys or girls between sex role preference and gender constancy (girls, .10; boys, –.01). In other words, there was no linear relationship between the sex role score and the child's gender understanding. However, Kohlberg's (1966) theory predicts a curvilinear relationship. Children should start to show more sex-typed behavior once gender identity is established, and then should become increasingly sex typed as sex role is organized. However, once constancy is achieved, then the child should begin to try out different behaviors and could become less stereotyped.

When we look at children who achieve constancy, we see no change in their behavior. Those who were very stereotyped continue so, while those less stereotyped continue in their mode. Neither the group data nor the individual data help us to understand the relationship between the cognitive category and the adoption of behaviors. The nature of Slaby and Frey's task may contribute to these findings. First, they make verbal responses—though minimal—necessary. Second, the interview itself is confusing. For each discrimination, the child must produce the correct response and then negate the incorrect one. For example, in the attempt to avoid random and perseverative correct answers, the child is asked, "Is this a girl?" If the answer is "Yes," she/he is asked of the same figure, "Is this a boy?" Such questioning may disconcert young children, and perhaps lead them to think their first answer was wrong. Finally, the child is considered to have mastered a level only when *all* of the questions at that level are answered correctly; such stringent criteria may easily mask the beginnings of competence. While it appears likely that findings with regard to sequence in the acquisition of gender constancy are valid, the beginnings of the process are not illuminated by this line of work.

STUDY 2

Although there was no relationship between sex role behavior and gender constancy tasks in the first study, it still seemed reasonable that a child's understanding of "boy" and "girl" might influence the way she/he organizes his or her play behaviors. The Slaby–Frey interview is built to ensure that a child understands the concept under confusing conditions. In other words, the Piagetian model of pushing to the limits is used. Perhaps the organization is done earlier at a much simpler level.

Thompson (1975) included a nonverbal gender discrimination task in his investigation of gender labeling and sex role development in preschool children: subjects could identify pictures according to the label paired boy–girl, man–woman, man–lady, father–mother, mommy–daddy, brother–sister, he–she, him–her, and his–hers. At 24 months, children were correct on 61% of the noun pairs and 51% of the pronoun pairs; by 36 months these figures were 90 and 88%, respectively. In addition, subjects sorted pictures of children, including photographs of themselves, into spearate containers: 24-month-olds classified their own pictures correctly 50% of the time, 36-month-olds 88%. Except for the brother–sister pairs, which elicited the most errors, it is not clear whether children responded differentially to pictures of adults and children, nor whether the discrimination task included reinforcement for correct responses (i.e., trained, rather than just assessed the ability in question). Some children may have begun to make gender discriminations regarding other people by the age of 2, but their ability to identify themselves as male or female was not evident. However, the beginning of this ability may develop before the child is able to communicate such knowledge and may even precede any conscious awareness of sex differences.

In the next study, the relationship among the child's ability to give gender labels and the adoption of sex-typed play and same-sexed friends is examined.

Method

Subjects

Sixty-four children, half boys and half girls, from 20 to 30 months of age were included in this study. Except that the mean age was younger, they did not differ from the children in the first study.

Procedure

The children were observed while participating in peer play groups. Scan samples were done in each group over a period of 4 weeks during which each child was observed. A very simple checklist of play with male and female toys (defined from previous study) and play with peer male, female, or both sexes was constructed. Each child was scanned 10 times on four different occasions for a total of 40 observations. From these observations it was possible to determine whether the children adopted behaviors typical to their sex (sex-typical behaviors), and their playmate choice. Two different measures of the child's understanding of sex and sex role were given to the child. One was similar to a task derived from Thompson (1975), where the child was asked to point to pictures as either a male or female (gender label). The second task was the interview devised by Slaby and Frey (1975) designed to test the child's understanding of gender identity, stability, and constancy. For this study, only the gender identity questions of the Slaby–Frey is examined. The children fall into three different groups. One group correctly identified 75% of the pictures (gave the appropriate gender label) and showed gender identity on the Slaby–Frey interview. Another group identified the pictures (gave the appropriate gender labels) but did not answer gender identity questions correctly. A third group answered neither gender labels above chance levels nor gender identity questions correctly. The mean age of the three groups was the same.

Results

The first question is, are there any differences among the three groups in the amount of time spent with same- and opposite-sex peers? Children of both sexes who answered the gender label questions correctly spent an average of 80% of their time in same-sex groups, while children who answered the gender label questions below that level spent about 50% of their time in same-sex groups (see Table 3). If playing with a member of the same sex is an attempt to match your behavior to someone you perceive as like you, then it appears that understanding of gender labels predicts playmate choices. The second question is, does the understanding of gender labels predict the choosing of sex-typical behaviors? Here the answer is more complicated. For girls, there was no difference

TABLE 3
STUDY 2: COMPARISON OF PLAY GROUPS' PLAY BEHAVIORS FOR
THREE GROUPS OF CHILDREN

Play behavior	No gender understanding		Gender labels		Gender labels and identity	
	Boys	Girls	Boys	Girls	Boys	Girls
Percentage of peer play with same-sex peers	55	49	82	78	78	80
Percentage all toys same-sex toys	11	9	13	10	14	15
Percentage all toys opposite-sex toys	10	10	4	9	5	8

among the three groups in the amount of time spent with male-typical and female-typical toys. For boys, there was no significant difference in amount of time spent with male-typical toys, but boys who did not have gender labels spent more time with female-typical toys than boys who did have such labels. In particular, boys without gender labels or gender identity played with dolls at about equal rates as girls, but this behavior was almost nonexistent in boys who showed some knowledge of gender labels.

DISCUSSION

The work in sex role development has diverged in two directions over the past 6 or 7 years. One group of researchers examined the construction of gender categories. There has been good progress made in understanding the different stages of cognitive understanding of gender. Cohen and Strauss (1979), for instance, have adapted the habituation paradigm to study the development of gender categories in children under a year. Martin and Halverson (1981) have employed a schematic processing model to explain the prevalence of sex stereotyping in young children. Work in social learning has documented just how prevalent sex-typed socialization is in the environment. Fagot (1978) demonstrated differential socialization of boys and girls in the home. Lamb and his colleagues (Lamb, Easterbrooks, & Holden, 1980; Lamb & Roopnarine, 1979) have shown how peer groups teach boys and girls different ways of behaving. Bem (1981, 1983) suggested that, while children do actively attempt to develop a gender schema during the first 3 years of life, parents should make every attempt to help them not overgeneralize such a schema.

However, just how the cognitive development of understanding of gender and the social information received interact is not clear. The two studies presented in this paper were an attempt to understand that relationship. While the first study gave fairly clear evidence that there is a consistent sequence of cognitive development, it did not help illuminate the relationship between that cognitive development and the adoption of sex role behaviors. It is my belief that this is because the measurement instrument was not developed to tap into the beginnings of gender understanding. The second study used a simplified procedure to measure the beginnings of gender understanding. By studying the beginnings of gender understanding, we began to see how adoption of sex role behaviors is related.

Perry and Bussey (1979) presented a modified social learning theory view of how imitation contributes to sex role development. They proposed that the child observes the different frequencies at which each sex performs certain behaviors in different situations. The child then employs the different frequencies as abstractions of what constitutes male-appropriate and female-appropriate behavior as models for imitative performance. It would seem reasonable to hypothesize that children also abstract information from the differential frequencies of reinforcement they receive for performance of different types of behavior. However, children also react to the category of respondent, so it is necessary to assume that the child has some concept of gender that would lend greater value to some individuals than others.

Why did not we see relationships between gender understanding and adoption of sex role behaviors in our earlier studies? I would like to argue that sex role behavior after very early awareness is a particularly good example of what Langer (1978) calls "automatic behavior" or "non-thinking behavior." This refers to behavior which is so overlearned that one does not have to "think" about what one is doing. The behavior occurs when one has overlearned the script, which is then enacted without engaging the rational thought processes. Most of what has been studied about sex role has dealt with subjects who have already invoked such "automatic processes." After behaviors are so overlearned and have become automatic, then relationships between cognitive variables and behavioral performance may be poor. However, in the period up until 3 years of age, when children are actively engaged in the construction of gender categories, we should see them attempting to behave in ways congruent with those categories. In our attempts to study such relationships in the first study, most children were beyond this construction phase. It is now my belief, still to be fully tested, that stronger relationships between behavioral adoption and categorization will take place between 12 and 36 months of age because children are actively trying out behaviors to match their developing gender categories.

In our lab we have developed a discrimination task (Leinbach, 1983) which allows is to examine children from 16 months of age concerning their knowledge of gender labels. I believe that when the child is con-

96   BEVERLY I. FAGOT

structing gender categories, all kinds of attempts to categorize the world
by gender will be made. For instance, children who show the ability to
categorize boys and girls, are more likely to choose same-sex playmates
than children who do not yet have such knowledge (Fagot, 1983). In the
Fagot study, techniques developed from the cognitive approach and observational technology developed from social learning were used to help
understand an old finding, that of the rapid gender segregation we find
in preschool-aged children.

However, there is still one aspect of sex role development which needs
to be incorporated; that is, how does the process become so important
to the child, or to put it in another way, how does the category of one's
gender become so affect laden? With recent attempts to study the inter-
face between cognition and affect, new methods are being developed
which should help us study all aspects of sex role development rather
than splitting our studies into artificial domains.

REFERENCES

Baumrind, D. (1979). *Sex related socialization effects*. Paper presented at the meetings of
the Society for Research in Child Development, San Francisco.

Bem, S. L. (1981). Gender schema theory: A cognitive account of sex typing. *Psychological
Review*, 88, 354–364.

Bem, S. L. (1983). Gender schema theory and its implications of child development: Raising
gender-aschematic children in a gender-schematic society. *Signs*, 8, 598–616.

Block, J. H. (1973). Conceptions of sex role: Some cross-cultural and longitudinal perspectives. *American Psychologist*, 28, 512–526.

Block, J. H. (1979). Socialization influences on personality development in males and females. In M. H. Parks (Ed.), *APA Master lecture series on issues of sex and gender*.
Washington, DC: American Psychological Association.

Block, J. H. (1983). Differential premises arising from differential socialization of the sexes:
Some conjectures. *Child Development*, 54, 1335–1354.

Blurton-Jones, N. (Ed.). (1972). *Ethological studies of child behavior*. Cambridge: Cambridge Univ. Press.

Brookes, J., & Lewis, M. (1974). Attachment behavior in thirteen-month-old opposite sex
twins. *Child Development*, 45, 243–247.

Brown, D. C. (1956). Sex role preference in young children. *Psychological Monographs*,
70(14, Whole No. 421).

Carter, D. B., & Patterson, C. (1982). Sex roles as social conventions: The development
of children's conceptions of sex role stereotypes. *Developmental Psychology*, 18, 812–
824.

Clark, A. H., Wyon, S. M., & Richards, M. P. M. (1969). Freeplay in nursery school children. *Journal of Child Psychology and Psychiatry*, 10, 205–216.

Clarke-Stewart, K. A. (1973). Interactions between mothers and their young children: Characteristics and consequences. *Monographs of the Society for Research in Child Development*, 38(6–7, Serial No. 153).

Cohen, L. B., & Strauss, M. S. (1979). Concept acquisition in the human infant. *Child
Development*, 50, 419–424.

Eaton, W. O., & Van Burgen, D. (1981). Asynchronous development of gender understanding in preschool children. *Child Development*, 52, 1020–1027.

Eme, R. F. (1979). Sex differences in childhood psychopathology: A review. *Psychological Bulletin*, 86, 574–595.

Etaugh, C., Collins, G., & Gerson, A. (1975). Reinforcement of sex-typed behaviors of two-year-old children in a nursery school setting. *Developmental Psychology*, 11, 255.

Fagot, B. I. (1974). Sex differences in toddlers' behavior and parental reaction. *Developmental Psychology*, 10, 554–558.

Fagot, B. I. (1977). Consequences of moderate cross-gender behavior in preschool children. *Child Development*, 48, 902–907.

Fagot, B. I. (1978). The influence of sex of child on parental reactions to toddler children. *Child Development*, 49, 459–465.

Fagot, B. I. (1983, April 21–24). Recognition of gender and playmate choice. In L. Serbin (Chair), *A cognitive–developmental approach to affiliation patterns: Children's awareness of and use of gender language and body type as social dimensions*. Symposium presented at Biennial Conference for Society for Research in Child Development, Detroit, MI.

Fagot, B. I. (1984). Teacher and peer reactions to boys' and girls' play styles. *Sex Roles*, 11, 691–762.

Fagot, B. I., & Patterson, G. R. (1969). An in vivo analysis of reinforcing contingencies for sex-role behaviors in the preschool child. *Developmental Psychology*, 1, 563–568.

Fein, G., Johnson, D., Kosson, N., Stork, L., & Wasserman, L. (1975). Sex stereotypes and preferences in the toy choices of 20-month-old boys and girls. *Developmental Psychology*, 11, 527–528.

Feiring, C., & Lewis, M. (1979). Sex and age differences in young children's reactions to frustration: A further look at the Goldberg and Lewis subjects. *Child Development*, 50, 848–853.

Goldberg, S., & Lewis, M. (1969). Play behavior in the year-old infant: Early sex differences. *Child Development*, 40, 21–31.

Huston, A. C. (1983). Sex typing. In P. H. Mussen (Ed.), *Handbook of child psychology: Vol. 4. Socialization, personality, and social development*. New York: Wiley.

Jacklin, C., Maccoby, E., & Dick, A. (1973). Barrier behavior and toy preferences: Sex differences (and their absence) in the year-old child. *Child Development*, 44, 196–200.

Kohlberg, L. (1966). A cognitive-developmental analysis of children's sex-role concepts and attitudes. In E. Maccoby (Ed.), *The development of sex differences*. Stanford, CA: Stanford Univ. Press.

Kuhn, D., Nash, S. C., & Brucken, L. (1978). Sex role concepts of two- and three-year olds. *Child Development*, 49, 445–451.

Lamb, M. E., Easterbrooks, M. A., & Holden, G. A. (1980). Reinforcement and punishment among preschoolers: Characteristics, effects and correlates. *Child Development*, 51, 1230–1236.

Lamb, M. E., & Roopnarine, J. (1979). Peer influences on sex role development in preschoolers. *Child Development*, 50, 1219–1222.

Langer, E. J. (1978). Rethinking the role of thought in social interaction. In J. Harves, W. Ickes, & R. Kidd (Eds.), *New directions in attribution theory* (Vol. 2). Hillsdale, NJ: Erlbaum.

Leinbach, M. D. (1983, April 21–24). *Gender discrimination in toddler's identifying pictures of male and female children and adults*. Paper presented at biennial conference for Society for Research in Child Development, Detroit, MI.

Maccoby, E. E., & Jacklin, C. N. (1974). *The psychology of sex differences*. Stanford, CA: Stanford Univ. Press.

Marcus, D. E., & Overton, W. F. (1978). The development of cognitive gender constancy and sex role preferences. *Child Development*, 49, 434–444.

98   BEVERLY I. FAGOT

Martin, C. L., & Halverson, C. F. (1981). A schematic processing model of sex typing and stereotyping in children. *Child Development*, 52, 1119–1134.

Money, J., & Ekhardt, A. A. (1972). *Man and woman, boy and girl*. Baltimore: Johns Hopkins Univ. Press.

Perry, D. G., & Bussey, K. (1979). The social learning theory of sex differences: Imitation is alive and well. *Journal of Personality and Social Psychology*, 37, 1699–1712.

Sears, R. R. (1965). Development of gender role. In F. A. Beach, *Sex and behavior*. New York: Wiley.

Schachter, F. F., Shore, E., Hodapp, R., Chalfin, S., & Bundy, C. (1978). Do girls talk earlier?: Mean length of utterance in toddlers. *Developmental Psychology*, 14, 388–392.

Slaby, R. G., & Frey, K. S. (1975). Development of gender constancy and elective attention to same-sex models. *Child Development*, 46, 849–856.

Smith, P. K., & Daglish, L. (1977). Sex differences in parent and infant behavior. *Child Development*, 48, 1250–1254.

Thompson, S. K. (1975). Gender labels and early sex-role development. *Child Development*, 46, 339–347.

RECEIVED: August 29, 1983; REVISED: February 24, 1984.

Psychological Review
1981, Vol. 88, No. 4, 354-364

Gender Schema Theory: A Cognitive Account of Sex Typing

Sandra Lipsitz Bem
Cornell University

Gender schema theory proposes that the phenomenon of sex typing derives, in part, from gender-based schematic processing, from a generalized readiness to process information on the basis of the sex-linked associations that constitute the gender schema. In particular, the theory proposes that sex typing results from the fact that the self-concept itself gets assimilated to the gender schema. Several studies are described which demonstrate that sex-typed individuals do, in fact, have a greater readiness to process information—including information about the self—in terms of the gender schema. It is speculated that such gender-based schematic processing derives, in part, from the society's ubiquitous insistence on the functional importance of the gender dichotomy. The political implications of gender schema theory are discussed, as is the relationship of the theory to the concept of androgyny.

The distinction between male and female serves as a basic organizing principle for every human culture. Although societies differ in the specific tasks they assign to the two sexes, all societies allocate adult roles on the basis of sex and anticipate this allocation in the socialization of their children. Not only are boys and girls expected to acquire sex-specific skills, they are also expected to have or to acquire sex-specific self-concepts and personality attributes, to be masculine or feminine as defined by that particular culture (Barry, Bacon, & Child, 1957). The process by which a society thus transmutes male and female into masculine and feminine is known as the process of sex typing.

The universality and importance of this process is reflected in the prominence it receives in psychological theories of development, which seek to elucidate how the developing child learns the appropriate repertoire. Psychoanalytic theory empha-

Preparation of this article was supported in part by National Science Foundation Grant BNS-78-22637 to Sandra Lipsitz Bem and in part by a small seed grant from the Center for Research on Women at Stanford University. The author would like to express her thanks to Daryl J. Bem and Lee D. Ross for critical comments on the manuscript and to Nancy Van Derveer and Mary Milne for computer programming.

Requests for reprints should be sent to Sandra Lipsitz Bem, Department of Psychology, Uris Hall, Cornell University, Ithaca, New York 14853.

sizes the importance of identification with the same-sex parent (e.g., Sears, Rau, & Alpert, 1965); social learning theory emphasizes the explicit rewards and punishments for behaving in sex-appropriate ways as well as the vicarious learning that observation and modeling can provide (e.g., Mischel, 1970); cognitive-developmental theory emphasizes the ways in which children socialize themselves once they have firmly labeled themselves as male or female (Kohlberg, 1966). (See Maccoby & Jacklin, 1974, and Mussen, 1969, for reviews of these theories.)

But what is it that is learned? Clearly the developing child is learning content-specific information, the particular behaviors and attributes that are to be linked with sex. In most societies, this is a diverse and sprawling network of associations encompassing not only those features directly related to male and female persons, such as anatomy, reproductive function, division of labor, and personality attributes, but also features more remotely or metaphorically related to sex, such as the angularity or roundedness of an abstract shape and the periodicity of the moon. Indeed, there appears to be no other dichotomy in human experience with as many entities assimilated to it as the distinction between male and female.

But there is more. It is proposed here that in addition to learning such content-specific information, the child is also learning to invoke this heterogeneous network of sex-related associations in order to evaluate and assimilate new information. The child, in short, learns to process information in terms of an evolving gender *schema*, and it is this gender-based schematic processing that constitutes the heart of the present account of sex typing.

The Gender Schema

A schema is a cognitive structure, a network of associations that organizes and guides an individual's perception. A schema functions as an anticipatory structure, a readiness to search for and to assimilate incoming information in schema-relevant terms. Schematic processing is thus highly selective and enables the individual to impose structure and meaning onto the vast array of incoming stimuli. Schema theory—if it can be called a theory—construes perception as a constructive process wherein what is perceived is a product of the interaction between the incoming information and the perceiver's preexisting schema (Neisser, 1976; Taylor & Crocker, in press). The readiness with which an individual invokes one schema rather than another is referred to as the *cognitive availability* of the schema (Nisbett & Ross, 1980; Tversky & Kahneman, 1973, 1974).

Schematic processing can manifest itself in a number of ways. For example, individuals who have a generalized readiness to process information in terms of a particular schema should be able to encode schema-consistent information quickly; they should organize information in schema-relevant categories; they should make highly differentiated judgments along schema-relevant dimensions; and when given a choice, they should spontaneously choose to make discriminations along those same dimensions. In general, their perceptions and actions should reflect the kinds of biases that schema-directed selectivity would produce (Nisbett & Ross, 1980; Taylor & Crocker, in press).

What gender schema theory proposes, then, is that the phenomenon of sex typing derives, in part, from gender-based schematic processing, from a generalized readiness to process information on the basis of the sex-linked associations that constitute the gender schema. In particular, the theory proposes that sex typing results, in part, from the fact that the self-concept itself gets assimilated into the gender schema. As children learn the contents of the society's gender schema, they learn which attributes are to be linked with their own sex and, hence, with themselves. This does not simply entail learning where each sex is supposed to stand on each dimension or attribute—that boys are to be strong and girls weak, for example—but involves the deeper lesson that the dimensions themselves are differentially applicable to the two sexes. Thus the strong–weak dimension itself is absent from the schema that is to be applied to girls just as the dimension of nurturance is implicitly omitted from the schema that is to be applied to boys. Adults in the child's world rarely notice or remark upon how strong a little girl is becoming or how nurturant a little boy is becoming, despite their readiness to note precisely these attributes in the "appropriate" sex. The child learns to apply this same schematic selectivity to the self, to choose from among the many possible dimensions of human personality only that subset defined as applicable to his or her own sex and thereby eligible for organizing the diverse contents of the self-concept. Thus do self-concepts become sex typed, and thus do the two sexes become, in their own eyes, not only different in degree but different in kind.

Simultaneously, the child also learns to evaluate his or her adequacy as a person in terms of the gender schema, to match his or her preferences, attitudes, behaviors, and personal attributes against the prototypes stored within it. The gender schema becomes a prescriptive standard or guide (Kagan, 1964; Kohlberg, 1966), and self-esteem becomes its hostage. Here, then, enters an internalized motivational factor that prompts the individual to regulate his or her behavior so that it conforms to the culture's definitions of maleness and femaleness. And that sex-typed behavior, in turn, further reinforces the gender-based differentiation of the self-concept through the individual's observation of his or her own behavior (cf. Bem, 1972). Thus do cultural myths become self-fulfilling prophecies, and thus do we arrive at the phenomenon known as sex typing.

It is important to note that gender schema theory is a theory of process, not content. Because sex-typed individuals are seen as processing information in terms of and conforming to whatever definitions of masculinity and femininity the culture happens to provide, it is the process of partitioning the world into two equivalence classes on the basis of the gender schema, not the contents of the equivalence classes, that is central to the theory. Accordingly, sex-typed individuals are seen as differing from other individuals not primarily in terms of how much masculinity or femininity they possess, but in terms of whether or not their self-concepts and behaviors are organized on the basis of gender. Many non-sex-typed individuals may describe themselves as, say, dominant or nurturant without implicating the concepts of masculinity or femininity. When sex-typed individuals so describe themselves, however, it is precisely the gender connotations of the attributes or behaviors that are presumed to be salient for them (cf. Bem & Allen, 1974).

As a recent review by Taylor and Crocker (in press) points out, the schema concept has been a heuristically valuable, if ill-defined, concept within psychology. The gender schema is currently at a comparable level of conceptual maturity. For example, although it is likely that much of the information in the gender schema consists of "fuzzy sets" organized around male and female prototypes (e.g., Cantor & Mischel, 1979; Rosch, 1975), the theory does not explicitly commit itself with respect to the exact nature or structure of the gender schema. The intent of this article is not to specify the precise structural representation of gender knowledge nor even to establish that the gender schema satisfies some well-defined set of necessary and sufficient conditions for calling it a schema. Rather, the purpose is to provide a new perspective on the process of sex typing and to test a set of empirical propositions deriving from that perspective.

The Gender-Based Schematic Processing of the Sex-Typed Individual

As noted earlier, schematic processing can manifest itself in a number of ways, and cognitive psychologists have found studies of memory a fruitful way of probing schema-like structures. For example, if an individual is spontaneously inclined to encode and organize information on the basis of some underlying schema or network of associations, then thinking of one schema-related item should enhance the probability of thinking of another. Thus, if the individual has been given a number of items to memorize and is then asked to recall them in whatever order they happen to come to mind, the sequence of recall should reveal runs or clusters of items that were linked in memory via the schema (Bousfield & Bousfield, 1966; Hamilton, Katz, & Leirer, 1980). In the following study, we used this clustering paradigm to provide a first test of gender schema theory. If sex-typed individuals do, in fact, organize information in terms of the gender schema, then they should show more clustering of gender-relevant items in free recall than non-sex-typed individuals.

Study 1: Gender Clustering in Free Recall[1]

Method. Forty-eight male and 48 female Stanford undergraduates were preselected for this study on the basis of their scores on the Bem Sex Role Inventory (BSRI; Bem, 1974), an instrument that identifies sex-typed individuals on the basis of their self-concepts or self-ratings of their personal attributes. The BSRI asks the respondent to indicate on a 7-point scale how well each of 60 attributes describes himself or herself. Although it is not apparent to the respondent, 20 of the attributes reflect the culture's definition of masculinity (e.g., *assertive*) and 20 reflect its definition of femininity (e.g., *tender*), with the remaining attributes serving as filler. Each respondent receives both a masculinity and a femininity score, and those who score above the median on the sex-congruent scale and below the median on the sex-incongruent scale are defined as sex typed. Those who show the reverse pattern are designated as cross-sex typed; those who score above the median on both scales are designated as androgynous; and those who score below the median on both scales are designated as undifferentiated.[2]

---

[1] This study was conducted as part of a senior honors thesis at Stanford University by Rachel Moran.

[2] The BSRI was chosen as the selection instrument because it has a number of features that make it especially appropriate for identifying sex-typed individuals. Most importantly, previous research has indicated that individuals classified as sex typed by the BSRI are sex typed in their behavior (Bem, 1975; Bem, Martyna, & Watson, 1976) and are motivated to select sex-typed activities (Bem & Lenney, 1976). In addition, the masculine and feminine items on the BSRI were specifically

In the experimental session, subjects were presented with a sequence of 61 words in random order. These words included 16 proper names, 15 animal names, 15 verbs, and 15 articles of clothing. Half of the proper names were male and half were female. One third of the items within each of the other semantic categories had been consistently rated by undergraduate judges as masculine (e.g., *gorilla, hurling, trousers*), one third as feminine (e.g., *butterfly, blushing, bikini*), and one third as neutral (e.g., *ant, stepping, sweater*). The words were presented on slides at 3-sec intervals, and subjects were told that their recall would later be tested. Three seconds after the presentation of the last word, they were given a period of 8 min to write down on a sheet of paper as many words as they could, in any order.

Results. It will be noted that subjects could cluster words in recall both according to the semantic categories and according to gender. The particular list of words recalled by each subject was scored for gender clustering by counting the number of sequential pairs that belonged to the same gender. Intrusions—words "recalled" that had not been on the stimulus list—were categorized by two independent judges and included in the clustering computation. Two types of sequential pairs were counted: gender clustering within semantic category (e.g., *gorilla/eagle* or *bikini/nylons*) and gender clustering across semantic categories (e.g., *hurling/Daniel* or *butterfly/dress*). In order to control for the total number of items recalled as well as for the extent of an individual's category clustering, the amount of gender clustering within and across semantic categories was expressed as the percentage of category and noncategory pairs, respectively, that were clustered on the basis of gender. The mean of these two percentages defined the total amount of an individual's gender clustering.

The hypothesis that sex-typed individuals would show the most gender clustering was tested by means of a planned comparison

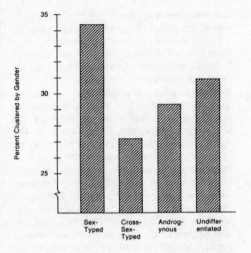

Figure 1. Mean percentage of sequential pairs within and across categories clustered on the basis of gender by sex-typed, cross-sex-typed, androgynous, and undifferentiated subjects.

contrasting the gender clustering of sex-typed subjects with the gender clustering of cross-sex-typed, androgynous, and undifferentiated subjects combined. Additional planned comparisons tested whether cross-sex-typed subjects differed significantly from androgynous and undifferentiated subjects combined and whether androgynous and undifferentiated subjects differed significantly from one another. The results are presented in Figure 1. Because there were no main effects or interactions on this measure involving sex, the results for male and female subjects have been combined.

As can be seen in Figure 1, sex-typed subjects clustered a significantly higher percentage of words on the basis of gender than the other three groups, $t(88) = 2.01$, $p < .025$, one-tailed. There were no significant differences among the groups in the amount of category clustering, $F(3, 88) < 1$, *ns*. As can also be seen in Figure 1, cross-sex-typed subjects did not differ significantly from androgynous or undifferentiated subjects, $t(88) = 1.07$, *ns*; and androgynous and undifferentiated subjects did not differ significantly from one another, $t(88) < 1$, *ns*. Although there were no sex differences in the total amount of gender clustering, sex-typed males differed from other males primarily in the amount of gender clustering

selected so as to reflect the definitions of sex appropriateness held by American society at large (Bem, 1974, 1979). In principle, however, sex-typed individuals could have been selected by means of any instrument or procedure that assesses the extent to which one's self-concept and/or behavior matches the culture's definitions of masculinity and femininity, and studies using other selection procedures will be described below. Similarly, the BSRI itself can be scored in several alternate ways (e.g., Bem, 1977; Orlofsky, Aslin, & Ginsburg, 1977). For research purposes in which group data are analyzed, it seems unlikely that the differences among the various scoring systems would be of much consequence.

within semantic category, male $t(88) = 2.51$, $p < .01$, one-tailed; female $t(88) < 1$, ns; whereas sex-typed females differed from other females primarily in the amount of gender clustering across semantic categories, female $t(88) = 2.30$, $p < .025$, one-tailed; male $t(88) < 1$, ns.

In addition to this clustering study, there are a number of other memory studies already in the literature that are also consistent with gender schema theory's major proposition that sex-typed individuals engage in gender-based schematic processing more than do non-sex-typed individuals. In one such study, for example, Kail and Levine (1976) selected 7- and 10-year-old girls who had been identified as sex-typed or non-sex-typed on the basis of toy preferences and asked them to recall words that had been presented to them immediately before a brief distractor task. This procedure was repeated over several trials. Previous research in short-term memory has demonstrated that recall declines over trials if all of the stimulus words are members of a single category (e.g., all color names or all spelled-out numbers) but that recall improves again following a shift from one category to another—a phenomenon known as release from proactive inhibition (Wickens, 1972). This improvement in performance is taken as evidence that the individual has, correspondingly, shifted his or her encoding categories for the stimulus words. Kail and Levine reasoned that sex-typed individuals should show this effect when stimulus words shifted from masculine to feminine or vice versa, whereas non-sex-typed individuals should be relatively less sensitive to this shift in gender connotation and hence should fail to show as much release from proactive inhibition. Their results supported this hypothesis.

In a second memory study with children, Liben and Signorella (1980) found that 6-, 7-, and 8-year-old children with highly stereotyped views of sex-appropriate behavior were significantly more likely than less stereotyped children to remember pictures that were consistent with the culture's gender stereotypes. And, in a study with college students using the BSRI, Taylor (in press) found that when sex-typed subjects were asked to recall and identify "who said what"

after listening to a group discussion, they were more likely than androgynous subjects to make within-sex rather than cross-sex errors, that is, to confuse women with women and men with men.

Studies using other paradigms have also yielded supporting results. For example, it was suggested earlier than an individual who engages in schematic processing should make highly differentiated judgments along schema-relevant dimensions and when given the opportunity should spontaneously choose to make discriminations along these same dimensions. In another study with college students using the BSRI, sex-typed subjects made significantly more differentiated judgments of masculinity–femininity than did androgynous subjects when rating handwriting samples, and they also weighted the dimension of masculinity–femininity more heavily than did androgynous subjects when making similarity judgments of these samples (Lippa, 1977). And finally, subjects identified as sex-typed on the BSRI differentiated between male and female stimulus persons significantly more than did androgynous subjects when asked to segment each person's videotaped sequence of behaviors into units that seemed natural and meaningful to them (Deaux & Major, 1977).

Although these several studies support the proposition that sex-typed individuals process gender-relevant information in terms of a gender schema, they do not address the critical issue of whether the self-concept itself gets assimilated to the schema. Accordingly, the following study was designed to demonstrate that sex-typed individuals organize their self-concepts in terms of the sex-linked associations that constitute the gender schema.

Study 2: Gender-Schematic Processing of the Self-Concept[3]

When describing themselves on the BSRI, sex-typed individuals by definition rate sex-congruent attributes as more self-descriptive than sex-incongruent attributes. But what

[3] This study was completed as part of a doctoral dissertation at Stanford University by Brenda Girvin. The assistance of Virginia Coles, Colombus Cooper, Tim Reagan, and Michael Wilkins is gratefully acknowledged.

process do sex-typed individuals go through when deciding that a particular attribute is or is not self-descriptive? Gender schema theory implies that they may simply "look up" the attribute in the gender schema and answer in the affirmative if the attribute is sex-congruent; that is, they do not go through the time-consuming process of recruiting behavioral evidence from memory and then judging whether the evidence warrants an affirmative answer. This implies that sex-typed individuals ought to be faster than non-sex-typed individuals when they make schema-consistent judgments, such as, that a sex-congruent attribute is self-descriptive or that a sex-incongruent attribute is not. Conversely, sex-typed individuals ought to be slower than non-sex-typed individuals in those few instances when they make schema-inconsistent judgments, such as, that a sex-congruent attribute is not self-descriptive or that a sex-incongruent attribute is (Markus, 1977; Taylor & Crocker, in press).

This reasoning was tested in a doctoral dissertation on self-schemata by Girvin (1978), who sought the same kind of evidence for the schematic processing of "self" information on the gender dimension that had previously been found on the independence–dependence dimension by Markus (1977). The measure most directly relevant here was the individual's response latency when asked to make a dichotomous *me/not me* judgment about each of the 60 attributes on the BSRI itself.[4]

Method. Forty-eight male and 48 female Stanford undergraduates were preselected on the basis of a median split on the BSRI as sex typed, cross-sex typed, androgynous, or undifferentiated. During an individual experimental session, the 60 attributes from the BSRI were projected on a screen one at a time and the subject was requested to push one of two buttons, "ME" or "NOT ME," to indicate whether the attribute was self-descriptive. The subject's response latency was recorded for each judgment.

Results. For purposes of this discussion, two measures of gender-schematic processing were computed for each subject, the mean latency of schema-consistent judgments (sex-congruent ME and sex-incongruent NOT ME) and the mean latency of schema-inconsistent judgments (sex-congruent NOT ME and sex-incongruent ME). In order to control for individual differences in general response latency, both measures

were expressed as difference scores between these schema-relevant latencies and the subject's mean latency for the sex-neutral attributes on the BSRI. There were no overall differences among the sex types in their response latencies to the neutral attributes themselves, $F(3, 88) < 1$, *ns*.

The hypothesis that sex-typed subjects would show the most gender-schematic processing was tested by means of a planned comparison contrasting sex-typed subjects with cross-sex-typed, androgynous, and undifferentiated subjects combined. Additional orthogonal planned comparisons tested whether cross-sex-typed subjects differed significantly from androgynous and undifferentiated subjects combined and also whether androgynous and undifferentiated subjects differed significantly from one another. The results for both schema-consistent and schema-inconsistent judgments are presented in Figure 2. Positive scores signify faster responding for schema-relevant than for neutral judgments; negative scores signify slower responding. Because there were no main effects or interactions involving sex, the results for male and female subjects have been combined.

As can be seen, sex-typed subjects were, in fact, significantly faster than the other three groups when making schema-consistent judgments about themselves, $t(88) = 5.13$, $p < .001$, one-tailed; and they were also significantly slower than the others when making schema-inconsistent judgments, $t(83) = 2.97$, $p < .005$, one-tailed. These results support the central hypothesis of gender schema theory that sex typing is accompanied by a readiness to process information about the self in terms of the gender schema, and they indicate that the attributes on the BSRI are themselves processed in this fashion.[5]

_____

[4] More recently, Markus and her colleagues have themselves begun to investigate the schematic processing of "self" information related to gender (Markus, Crane, Bernstein, & Salidi, in press). Their preliminary findings appear to be consistent with gender schema theory in many respects.

[5] The same pattern of significant results is obtained when the schema-consistent and schema-inconsistent judgments themselves are analyzed before converting them into difference scores. Moreover, the main effect of sex type is significant in a two-way analysis of variance, using either the judgments themselves or the dif-

360   SANDRA LIPSITZ BEM

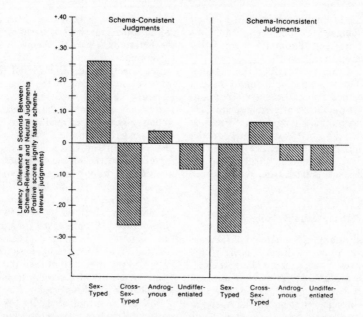

Figure 2. Gender-schematic processing in response latencies for schema-consistent and schema-inconsistent judgments by sex-typed, cross-sex-typed, androgynous, and undifferentiated subjects.

The data in Figure 2 also explicitly raise a question about cross-sex-typed individuals. Like sex-typed subjects, cross-sex-typed subjects partition the attributes on the BSRI into gender categories, but they rate the sex-incongruent set as more self-descriptive. Do they invoke a gender schema to process self-relevant information or not? If they do, then their results should be the mirror image of the sex-typed subjects' results. That is, they should reach their judgments slowly in those few instances when they decide that sex-congruent attributes are self-descriptive or that sex-incongruent attributes are not (the schema-consistent judgments), and conversely, they should reach their judgments quickly in these modal instances when they decide that sex-congruent attributes are not

self-descriptive or that sex-incongruent attributes are (the schema-inconsistent judgments). Unfortunately the data in Figure 2 are mixed. In the orthogonal planned comparison, cross-sex-typed subjects are significantly different from androgynous and undifferentiated subjects when making schema-consistent judgments about the self, $t(88) = 3.17$, $p < .01$, two-tailed, but not when making schema-inconsistent judgments, $t(83) = 1.64$, *ns*. The question thus remains unanswered, although it should be recalled that in the clustering study, cross-sex-typed subjects displayed the least amount of gender clustering of all the groups, implying that they are not inclined to process information in terms of a gender schema.

Finally, as can also be seen in Figure 2, there were no significant differences between androgynous and undifferentiated subjects either in their latencies for schema-consistent judgments, $t(88) = 1.40$, *ns.*, or in their latencies for schema-inconsistent judgments, $t(83) < 1$, *ns*. This null result indicates that androgynous and undifferentiated subjects are similarly disinclined to process information about themselves in terms of the gen-

ference scores. And finally, although ME judgments have shorter latencies overall than NOT ME judgments for all subjects, this difference is not artifactually producing either the short latencies of sex-typed subjects when they make schema-consistent judgments nor the long latencies when they make schema-inconsistent judgments. In fact, the obtained differences among the groups in their proportions of ME and NOT ME judgments work against the hypothesis.

der schema, as might be predicted by their both endorsing approximately equal amounts of masculinity and femininity when rating themselves on the BSRI.

Taken together, the results of these studies indicate that sex-typed individuals have a greater readiness than cross-sex-typed, androgynous, or undifferentiated individuals to process information—including information about the self—in terms of the gender schema, and hence support the major contention of gender schema theory that sex typing is derived, in part, from gender-based schematic processing.

The Heterosexuality Subschema

Although the specific contents of the gender schema are not of direct concern to the account of sex typing proposed here, the sex-related associations involving heterosexuality have a distinctive status that warrants special treatment. First of all, the phenomenon of heterosexual attraction seems likely itself to have fostered the development of gender-based schematic processing in many young adults by facilitating the generalization that the two sexes are—and are supposed to be—quite different from each other. Certainly the motto *vive la difference* derives both its sense and its punch from the common experience of being attracted to members of the other sex and wanting to do what one can both to preserve and to facilitate that heterosexual attraction.

In addition, many societies, including our own, treat an exclusively heterosexual orientation as the sine qua non of adequate masculinity and femininity. Regardless of how closely an individual's attributes and behavior match the male or female prototypes stored within the gender schema, violation of the prescription to be exclusively heterosexual is sufficient by itself to call into question the individual's adequacy as a man or a woman. The society thus attaches strong affect to this portion of the gender schema, thereby motivating many individuals to be expecially vigilant with respect to their heterosexuality. Partly in the service of highlighting the fact that they are exclusively heterosexual, such individuals may develop a generalized readiness to encode all cross-sex interactions in sexual terms and all members of the opposite sex in terms of sexual attractiveness, in short, a readiness to invoke the heterosexuality subschema in social interaction.[6]

Because they are predisposed to process information in terms of the gender schema generally, it is proposed here that sex-typed individuals are among those who are likely to have a generalized readiness to invoke the heterosexuality subschema in their social interactions and, in particular, to respond differentially to the physical attractiveness of members of the opposite sex with whom they are interacting. This hypothesis was tested as part of a study by Andersen and Bem (in press) in which sex-typed and androgynous subjects of both sexes engaged in getting-acquainted telephone conversations with four different partners. The subjects were led to believe that each of their partners was either physically attractive or physically unattractive, a belief manipulated by means of a Polaroid snapshot allegedly taken of the partner a few moments before. Each subject conversed with two allegedly attractive and unattractive partners of his or her own sex as well as with two allegedly attractive and unattractive partners of the opposite sex. The partners in this study were all naive, not confederates, and all were strangers to the subjects with whom they conversed. Each conversation lasted approximately 8 min. and was totally uncontrived.

Three independent judges—all blind with respect to the subject's BSRI category as well as the partner's sex and alleged physical attractiveness—listened to the subject's half

---

[6] Indeed, this is the basis of the feminist objection to the ubiquitous sexual coloring of so many cross-sex interactions. The objection is not to sexuality per se but to the promiscuous availability of the gender schema—and the heterosexuality subschema in particular—in situational contexts where other schemata should have priority. The objection is to individuals whose heterosexuality subschemata have such low activation thresholds that they code all cross-sex interactions in sexual terms and all members of the other sex in terms of sexual attractiveness rather than in terms of other dimensions that are more individuating or more relevant to the situational context. There is no implication here that individuals for whom the heterosexuality subschema is readily available are necessarily higher in sexual motivation per se than other individuals, although it is plausible that enhanced sexual motivation might be one factor that would increase anyone's readiness to process information in sexual terms.

of each conversation and rated him or her on a number of dimensions. Among other things, the results indicated that sex-typed subjects were more likely than androgynous subjects to behave differentially toward attractive and unattractive members of the opposite sex, displaying greater animation, enthusiasm, and interest toward those they thought more attractive. It appears, then, that the sex-typed individual may have a generalized readiness to code members of the opposite sex in terms of sexual attractiveness and that this readiness may be powerful enough to influence his or her social behavior in spontaneous social interaction.

The Antecedents of Gender-Based Schematic Processing: Some Speculations

What prompts so many individuals to organize information in general, and their self-concepts in particular, in terms of gender? Why the prevalence of gender-based schematic processing? The answer would seem to derive, in part, from the society's ubiquitous insistence on the functional importance of the gender dichotomy, from its insistence that an individual's sex makes a difference in virtually every domain of human experience. The typical American child cannot help but observe, for example, that what parents, teachers, and peers consider to be appropriate behavior varies as a function of sex; that toys, clothing, occupations, hobbies, domestic chores—even pronouns—all vary as a function of sex.

Society thus teaches the developing child two things about gender. First, as noted earlier, it teaches the substantive network of sex-related associations that can come to serve as a cognitive schema. Second, it teaches that the dichotomy between male and female has extensive and intensive relevance to virtually every aspect of life.

It is this latter knowledge, moreover, that is here presumed to transform a passive network of associations into an active and readily available schema for interpreting reality. Children will learn many associative networks of concepts throughout life, many potential cognitive schemata, but it is the learned centrality or alleged functional importance of particular categories and distinctions that animates their associated networks and gives these schemata priority and availability over others. In the case of the gender schema in particular, it may also be that sex has evolved to be a basic category of perception for our species and that the gender schema thereby has a biologically based priority over many other schemata. Be that as it may, however, society's ubiquitous insistence on the functional importance of the gender dichotomy cannot help but render the gender schema even more cognitively available—and in more remotely relevant contexts—than it would be otherwise. Not everyone becomes equally sex typed, of course, and individual differences presumably derive from the extent to which one's particular socialization history has stressed the functional importance of the gender dichotomy.

Is There a Feminist Moral to Gender Schema Theory?

The central figure in gender schema theory has been the sex-typed individual. This represents a shift of focus from my earlier work in which it was the non-sex-typed individual, the androgynous individual in particular, who commanded center stage. That earlier focus reflected both theoretical and political concerns.

At the theoretical level, the recent debate within personality psychology over the cross-situational consistency of behavior has challenged the common practice of dismissing individuals who are not consistent as merely sources of uninteresting error variance. In the arena of sex role research, this practice prevented the androgynous individual, the individual who is flexibly masculine or feminine as circumstances warrant, from even being conceptualized. Although we routinely see such individuals among our colleagues, our lovers, and presumably our subjects, they were strangely absent from our theories and our journals—until the concept of androgyny brought them into focus.

Politically, of course, androgyny was a concept whose time had come, a concept that appeared to provide a liberated and more humane alternative to the traditional, sex-biased standards of mental health. And it is true that the concept of androgyny can be applied equally to both men and women and that it encourages individuals to embrace both the masculine and the feminine within themselves. But the concept of androgyny can also be seen as replacing a prescription to be masculine *or* feminine with the doubly incarcerating prescription to be masculine *and* feminine. The individual now has not one but two potential sources of inadequacy to contend with (cf. Sampson, 1977).

Even more importantly, however, the concept of androgyny is insufficiently radical from a feminist perspective because it continues to presuppose that there is a masculine and a feminine within us all, that is, that the concepts of masculinity and femininity have an independent and palpable reality rather that being themselves cognitive constructs derived from gender-based schematic processing. A focus on the concept of androgyny thus fails to prompt serious examination of the extent to which gender organizes both our perceptions and our social world.

In contrast, the concept of gender-based schematic processing has the potential for "raising our consciousness" in precisely this way. It can lead us, for example, to notice how the male–female distinction is insinuated in totally gratuitous ways into the society's curriculum for the developing child. In elementary schools, for example, boys and girls line up separately or alternately; they learn songs in which the fingers are "ladies" and thumbs are "men"; they see boy and girl paper doll silhouettes alternately placed on the days of the month in order to learn about the calendar. Children, it will be noted, are not lined up separately or alternately as blacks and whites; fingers are not "whites" and thumbs "blacks"; black and white dolls do not alternately mark the days of the calendar. The irony is that even though our society has become sensitized to negative sex stereotypes and has begun to expunge them from the media and from children's literature, it remains blind to its gratuitous emphasis on the gender dichotomy itself. Our society seeks to deemphasize racial distinctions but continues to exaggerate sexual distinctions.

Thus, to the extent that gender schema theory contains a feminist moral, it is that the network of associations that constitutes the gender schema ought to become more limited in scope and that society ought to temper its insistence upon the ubiquitous functional importance of the gender dichotomy. In short, human behaviors and personality attributes should cease to have gender, and society should stop projecting gender into situations irrelevant to genitalia.

Were this to occur, we might then come to accept as a given the fact that we are male or female as un-self-consciously as we now accept as a given the fact that we are human. Our maleness or femaleness would be self-evident and nonproblematic; rarely would we be prompted to ponder it, to assert that it is true, to fear that it might be in jeopardy, or to wish that it were otherwise. The gender distinctions that remained would still be perceived—perhaps even cherished—but they would not function as imperialistic schemata for organizing everything else, and the artificial constraints of gender on the individual's unique blend of temperament and behavior would be eliminated. The feminist prescription, then, is not that the individual be androgynous, but that the society be aschematic.

References

Andersen, S. M., & Bem, S. L. Sex typing and androgyny in dyadic interaction: Individual differences in responsiveness to physical attractiveness. *Journal of Personality and Social Psychology*, 1981, *41*, 74–86.

Barry, H., Bacon, M. K., & Child, I. L. A cross-cultural survey of some sex differences in socialization. *Journal of Abnormal and Social Psychology*, 1957, *55*, 327–332.

Bem, D. J. Self-perception theory. In L. Berkowitz (Ed.), *Advances in experimental social psychology* (Vol. 6). New York: Academic Press, 1972.

Bem, D. J., & Allen, A. On predicting some of the people some of the time: The search for cross-situational consistencies in behavior. *Psychological Review*, 1974, *81*, 506–520.

Bem, S. L. The measurement of psychological androgyny. *Journal of Consulting and Clinical Psychology*, 1974, *42*, 155–162.

Bem, S. L. Sex role adaptability: One consequence of psychological androgyny. *Journal of Personality and Social Psychology*, 1975, *31*, 634–643.

Bem, S. L. On the utility of alternative procedures for assessing psychological androgyny. *Journal of Consulting and Clinical Psychology*, 1977, *45*, 196–205.

Bem, S. L. Theory and measurement of androgyny: A reply to the Pedhazur-Tetenbaum and Locksley-Colten critiques. *Journal of Personality and Social Psychology*, 1979, *37*, 1047–1054.

Bem, S. L., & Lenney, E. Sex typing and the avoidance

of cross-sex behavior. *Journal of Personality and Social Psychology*, 1976, *33*, 48–54.

Bem, S. L., Martyna, W., & Watson, C. Sex typing and androgyny: Further explorations of the expressive domain. *Journal of Personality and Social Psychology*, 1976, *34*, 1016–1023.

Bousfield, A. K., & Bousfield, W. A. Measurement of clustering and of sequential constancies in repeated free recall. *Psychological Reports*, 1966, *19*, 935–942.

Cantor, N., & Mischel, W. Prototypes in person perception. In L. Berkowitz (Ed.), *Advances in experimental social psychology* (Vol. 12). New York: Academic Press, 1979.

Deaux, K., & Major, B. Sex-related patterns in the unit of perception. *Personality and Social Psychology Bulletin*, 1977, *3*, 297–300.

Girvin, B. *The nature of being schematic: Sex-role self-schemas and differential processing of masculine and feminine information.* Unpublished doctoral dissertation, Stanford University, 1978.

Hamilton, D. L., Katz, L. B., & Leirer, V. O. Organizational processes in impression formation. In R. Hastie, T. Ostrom, E. Ebbesen, R. Wyer, D. Hamilton, & R. Carlston (Eds.), *Person memory: The cognitive basis of social perception.* Hillsdale, N.J.: Erlbaum, 1980.

Kagan, J. Acquisition and significance of sex-typing and sex role identity. In M. L. Hoffman & L. W. Hoffman (Eds.), *Review of child development research* (Vol. 1). New York: Russell Sage Foundation, 1964.

Kail, R. V., & Levine, L. E. Encoding processes and sex-role preferences. *Journal of Experimental Child Psychology*, 1976, *21*, 256–263.

Kohlberg, L. A cognitive-developmental analysis of children's sex-role concepts and attitudes. In E. E. Maccoby (Ed.), *The development of sex differences.* Stanford, Calif.: Stanford University Press, 1966.

Liben, L. S., & Signorella, M. L. Gender-related schemata and constructive memory in children. *Child Development*, 1980, *51*, 11–18.

Lippa, R. Androgyny, sex typing, and the perception of masculinity–femininity in handwriting. *Journal of Research in Personality*, 1977, *11*, 21–37.

Maccoby, E. E., & Jacklin, C. N. *The psychology of sex differences.* Stanford, Calif.: Stanford University Press, 1974.

Markus, H. Self-schemata and processing information about the self. *Journal of Personality and Social Psychology*, 1977, *35*, 63–78.

Markus, H., Crane, M., Bernstein, S., & Siladi, M. Self-schemas and gender. *Journal of Personality and Social Psychology*, in press.

Mischel, W. Sex-typing and socialization. In P. H. Mussen (Ed.), *Carmichael's manual of child psychology* (Vol. 2). New York: Wiley, 1970.

Mussen, P. H. Early sex-role development. In D. A. Goslin (Ed.), *Handbook of socialization theory and research.* Chicago: Rand McNally, 1969.

Neisser, U. *Cognition and reality.* San Francisco: Freeman, 1976.

Nisbett, R. E., & Ross, L. *Human inference: Strategies and shortcomings of social judgement.* Englewood Cliffs, N.J.: Prentice-Hall, 1980.

Orlofsky, J., Aslin, A. L., & Ginsburg, S. D. Differential effectiveness of two classification procedures on the Bem Sex Role Inventory. *Journal of Personality Assessment*, 1977, *41*, 414–416.

Rosch, E. Cognitive reference points. *Cognitive Psychology*, 1975, *1*, 532–547.

Sampson, E. E. Psychology and the American ideal. *Journal of Personality and Social Psychology*, 1977, *35*, 767–782.

Sears, R. R., Rau, L., & Alpert, R. *Identification and child rearing.* Stanford, Calif.: Stanford University Press, 1965.

Taylor, S. E. A categorization approach to sterotyping. In D. L. Hamilton (Ed.), *Cognitive processes in stereotyping and intergroup behavior.* Hillsdale, N.J.: Erlbaum, in press.

Taylor, S. E., & Crocker, J. Schematic bases of social information processing. In E. T. Higgins, P. Hermann, & M. P. Zanna (Eds.), *The Ontario Symposium on Personality and Social Psychology* (Vol. 1). Hillsdale, N.J.: Erlbaum, in press.

Tversky, A., & Kahneman, D. Availability: A heuristic for judging frequency and probability. *Cognitive Psychology*, 1973, *5*, 207–232.

Tversky, A., & Kahneman, D. Judgment under uncertainty: Heuristics and biases. *Science*, 1974, *185*, 1124–1131.

Wickens, D. D. Characteristics of word encoding. In A. W. Melton & E. Martin (Eds.), *Coding processes in human memory.* New York: Wiley, 1972.

Received June 23, 1980 ■

[31]

Gender Schema Theory and Its Implications for Child Development: Raising Gender-aschematic Children in a Gender-schematic Society

Sandra Lipsitz Bem

As every parent, teacher, and developmental psychologist knows, male and female children become "masculine" and "feminine," respectively, at a very early age. By the time they are four or five, for example, girls and boys have typically come to prefer activities defined by the culture as appropriate for their sex and also to prefer same-sex peers. The acquisition of sex-appropriate preferences, skills, personality attributes, behaviors, and self-concepts is typically referred to within psychology as the process of sex typing.

The universality and importance of this process is reflected in the prominence it has received in psychological theories of development, which seek to elucidate how the developing child comes to match the template defined as sex appropriate by his or her culture. Three theories of sex typing have been especially influential: psychoanalytic theory, social learning theory, and cognitive-developmental theory. More recently, a fourth theory of sex typing has been introduced into the psychological literature—gender schema theory.

This article is designed to introduce gender schema theory to feminist scholars outside the discipline of psychology. In order to provide a background for the conceptual issues that have given rise to gender schema theory, I will begin with a discussion of the three theories of sex typing that have been dominant within psychology to date.

Psychoanalytic Theory

The first psychologist to ask how male and female are transmuted into masculine and feminine was Freud. Accordingly, in the past virtually

[*Signs: Journal of Women in Culture and Society* 1983, vol. 8, no. 4]

Signs Summer 1983 599

every major source book in developmental psychology began its discussion of sex typing with a review of psychoanalytic theory.[1]

Psychoanalytic theory emphasizes the child's identification with the same-sex parent as the primary mechanism whereby children become sex typed, an identification that results from the child's discovery of genital sex differences, from the penis envy and castration anxiety that this discovery produces in females and males, respectively, and from the successful resolution of the Oedipus conflict.[2] Although a number of feminist scholars have found it fruitful in recent years to work within a psychoanalytic framework,[3] the theory's "anatomy is destiny" view has been associated historically with quite conservative conclusions regarding the inevitability of sex typing.

Of the three dominant theories of sex typing, psychoanalytic theory is almost certainly the best known outside the discipline of psychology, although it is no longer especially popular among research psychologists. In part, this is because the theory is difficult to test empirically. An even more important reason, however, is that the empirical evidence simply does not justify emphasizing either the child's discovery of genital sex differences in particular[4] or the child's identification with his or her same-sex parent[5] as a crucial determinant of sex typing.

Social Learning Theory

In contrast to psychoanalytic theory, social learning theory emphasizes the rewards and punishments that children receive for sex-appropriate and sex-inappropriate behaviors, as well as the vicarious

1. See, e.g., Paul H. Mussen, "Early Sex-Role Development," in *Handbook of Socialization Theory and Research*, ed. David A. Goslin (Chicago: Rand McNally & Co., 1969), pp. 707–31. For a more recent review that does not even mention psychoanalytic theory, see Aletha C. Huston, "Sex-Typing," to appear in *Carmichael's Manual of Child Psychology*, ed. Paul H. Mussen, 4th ed. (New York: John Wiley & Sons, in press).

2. Urie Bronfenbrenner, "Freudian Theories of Identification with Their Derivatives," *Child Development* 31, no. 1 (March 1960): 15–40; Sigmund Freud, "Some Psychological Consequences of the Anatomical Distinction between the Sexes (1925)," in *Collected Papers of Sigmund Freud*, ed. Ernest Jones, 5 vols. (New York: Basic Books, 1959), 5:186–97; Sigmund Freud, "The Passing of the Oedipus Complex (1924)," ibid., 2: 269–76.

3. E.g., Nancy Chodorow, *The Reproduction of Mothering: Psychoanalysis and the Sociology of Gender* (Berkeley: University of California Press, 1978); Gayle Rubin, "The Traffic in Women: Notes on the 'Political Economy' of Sex," in *Toward an Anthropology of Women*, ed. Rayna Reiter (New York: Monthly Review Press, 1975), pp. 157–210.

4. Lawrence Kohlberg, "A Cognitive-Developmental Analysis of Children's Sex-Role Concepts and Attitudes," in *The Development of Sex Differences*, ed. Eleanor E. Maccoby (Stanford, Calif.: Stanford University Press, 1966), pp. 82–173; Maureen J. McConaghy, "Gender Permanence and the Genital Basis of Gender: Stages in the Development of Constancy of Gender Identity," *Child Development* 50, no. 4 (December 1979): 1223–26.

5. Eleanor E. Maccoby and Carol N. Jacklin, *The Psychology of Sex Differences* (Stanford, Calif.: Stanford University Press, 1974).

learning that observation and modeling can provide.[6] Social learning theory thus locates the source of sex typing in the sex-differentiated practices of the socializing community.

Perhaps the major virtue of social learning theory for psychologists is that it applies to the development of psychological femaleness and maleness the very same general principles of learning that are already known to account for the development of a multitude of other behaviors. Thus, as far as the formal theory is concerned, gender does not demand special consideration; that is, no special psychological mechanisms or processes must be postulated in order to explain how children become sex typed beyond those already used to explain how children learn other socialized behaviors.

Interestingly, the theory's generality also constitutes the basis of its appeal to feminist psychologists in particular. If there is nothing special about gender, then the phenomenon of sex typing itself is neither inevitable nor unmodifiable. Children become sex typed because sex happens to be the basis of differential socialization in their culture. In principle, however, any category could be made the basis for differential socialization.

Although social learning theory can account for the young child's acquiring a number of particular behaviors that are stereotyped by the culture as sex appropriate, it treats the child as the relatively passive recipient of environmental forces rather than as an active agent striving to organize and thereby to comprehend the social world. This view of the passive child is inconsistent with the common observation that children themselves frequently construct and enforce their own version of society's gender rules. It is also inconsistent with the fact that the flexibility with which children interpret society's gender rules varies predictably with age. In one study, for example, 73 percent of the four-year-olds and 80 percent of the nine-year-olds believed—quite flexibly—that there should be no sexual restrictions on one's choice of occupation. Between those ages, however, children held more rigid opinions, with the middle children being the least flexible of all. Thus, only 33 percent of the five-year-olds, 10 percent of the six-year-olds, 11 percent of the seven-year-olds, and 44 percent of the eight-year-olds believed there should be no sexual restrictions on one's choice of occupation.[7]

This particular developmental pattern is not unique to the child's interpretation of gender rules. Even in a domain as far removed from gender as syntax, children first learn certain correct grammatical forms through reinforcement and modeling. As they get a bit older, however, they begin to construct their own grammatical rules on the basis of what they hear spoken around them, and they are able only later still to allow

6. Walter Mischel, "Sex-Typing and Socialization," in *Carmichael's Manual of Child Psychology*, ed. Paul H. Mussen, 2 vols. (New York: John Wiley & Sons, 1970), 2:3–72.

7. William Damon, *The Social World of the Child* (San Francisco: Jossey-Bass, 1977).

Signs   Summer 1983   601

for exceptions to those rules. Thus, only the youngest and the oldest children say "ran"; children in between say "runned."[8] What all of this implies, of course, is that the child is passive in neither domain. Rather, she or he is actively constructing rules to organize—and thereby to comprehend—the vast array of information in his or her world.

Cognitive-Developmental Theory

Unlike social learning theory, cognitive-developmental theory focuses almost exclusively on the child as the primary agent of his or her own sex-role socialization, a focus reflecting the theory's basic assumption that sex typing follows naturally and inevitably from universal principles of cognitive development. As children work actively to comprehend their social world, they inevitably "label themselves—call it alpha—and determine that there are alphas and betas in the environment. Given the cognitive-motivational properties of the self, . . . the child moves toward other alphas and away from betas. That is, it is the child who realizes what gender he or she is, and in what behaviors he or she should engage."[9] In essence, then, cognitive-developmental theory postulates that, because of the child's need for cognitive consistency, self-categorization as female or male motivates her or him to value that which is seen as similar to the self in terms of gender. This gender-based value system, in turn, motivates the child to engage in gender-congruent activities, to strive for gender-congruent attributes, and to prefer gender-congruent peers. "Basic self-categorizations determine basic valuings. Once the boy has stably identified himself as male, he then values positively those objects and acts consistent with his gender identity."[10]

The cognitive-developmental account of sex typing has been so influential since its introduction into the literature in 1966 that many psychologists now seem to accept almost as a given that the young child will spontaneously develop both a gender-based self-concept and a gender-based value system even in the absence of external pressure to behave in a sex-stereotyped manner. Despite its popularity, however, the theory fails to explicate why sex will have primacy over other potential categories of the self such as race, religion, or even eye color. Interestingly, the formal theory itself does not dictate that any particular category should have such primacy. Moreover, most cognitive-developmental theorists do not explicitly ponder the "why sex" question nor do they even raise the possibility that other categories could fit the general theory just as well. To the extent that cognitive-developmental

8. Courtney B. Cazden, "The Acquisition of Noun and Verb Inflections," *Child Development* 39, no. 2 (June 1968): 433–48; Herbert H. Clark and Eve V. Clark, *Psychology and Language: An Introduction to Psycholinguistics* (New York: Harcourt Brace Jovanovich, 1977).

9. Michael Lewis and Jeanne Brooks-Gunn, *Social Cognition and the Acquisition of Self* (New York: Plenum Publishing Corp., 1979), p. 270.

10. Kohlberg, p. 89.

psychologists address this question at all, they seem to emphasize the perceptual salience to the child of the observable differences between the sexes, particularly biologically produced differences such as size and strength.[11]

The implicit assumption here that sex differences are naturally and inevitably more perceptually salient to children than other differences may not have cross-cultural validity. Although it may be true that our culture does not construct any distinctions between people that we perceive to be as compelling as sex, other cultures do construct such distinctions, for example, distinctions between those who are high caste and those who are low caste, between those who are inhabited by spirits and those who are not, between those who are divine and those who are mortal, between those who are wet and those who are dry, or between those who are open and those who are closed.[12] Given such cross-cultural diversity, it is ironic that a theory emphasizing the child's active striving to comprehend the social world should not be more open to the possibility that a distinction other than sex might be more perceptually salient in another cultural context. What appears to have happened is that the universality and inevitability that the theory claims for the child's cognitive processes have been implicitly and gratuitously transferred to one of the many substantive domains upon which those processes operate: the domain of gender.

This is not to say, of course, that cognitive-developmental theory is necessarily wrong in its implicit assumption that all children have a built-in readiness to organize their perceptions of the social world on the basis of sex. Perhaps evolution has given sex a biologically based priority over many other categories. The important point, however, is that the question of whether and why sex has cognitive primacy is not included within the bounds of cognitive-developmental theory. To understand why children become *sex* typed rather than, say, race or caste typed, we still need a theory that explicitly addresses the question of how and why children come to utilize sex in particular as a cognitive organizing principle.

Gender Schema Theory

Gender schema theory[13] contains features of both the cognitive-

11. Kohlberg; Lewis and Brooks-Gunn; Dorothy Z. Ullian, "The Child's Construction of Gender: Anatomy as Destiny," in *Cognitive and Affective Growth: Developmental Interaction*, ed. Edna K. Shapiro and Evelyn Weber (Hillsdale, N.J.: Lawrence Erlbaum Associates, 1981), pp. 171–85.

12. For a discussion of the wet-dry distinction, see Anna S. Meigs, "Male Pregnancy and the Reduction of Sexual Opposition in a New Guinea Highlands Society," *Ethnology* 15, no. 4 (1976): 393–407; for a discussion of the open-closed distinction, see Sally Falk Moore, "The Secret of the Men: A Fiction of Chagga Initiation and Its Relation to the Logic of Chagga Symbolism," *Africa* 46, no. 4 (1976): 357–70.

13. Sandra L. Bem, "Gender Schema Theory: A Cognitive Account of Sex Typing,"

developmental and the social learning accounts of sex typing. In particular, gender schema theory proposes that sex typing derives in large measure from gender-schematic processing, from a generalized readiness on the part of the child to encode and to organize information—including information about the self—according to the culture's definitions of maleness and femaleness. Like cognitive-developmental theory, then, gender schema theory proposes that sex typing is mediated by the child's own cognitive processing. However, gender schema theory further proposes that gender-schematic processing is itself derived from the sex-differentiated practices of the social community. Thus, like social learning theory, gender schema theory assumes that sex typing is a learned phenomenon and, hence, that it is neither inevitable nor unmodifiable. In this discussion, I shall first consider in some detail what gender-schematic processing is and how it mediates sex typing; I shall then explore the conditions that produce gender-schematic processing, thereby providing an explicit account of why sex comes to have cognitive primacy over other social categories.

Gender-schematic Processing

Gender schema theory begins with the observation that the developing child invariably learns his or her society's cultural definitions of femaleness and maleness. In most societies, these definitions comprise a diverse and sprawling network of sex-linked associations encompassing not only those features directly related to female and male persons—such as anatomy, reproductive function, division of labor, and personality attributes—but also features more remotely or metaphorically related to sex, such as the angularity or roundedness of an abstract shape and the periodicity of the moon. Indeed, no other dichotomy in human experience appears to have as many entities linked to it as does the distinction between female and male.

But there is more. Gender schema theory proposes that, in addition to learning such content-specific information about gender, the child also learns to invoke this heterogeneous network of sex-related associations in order to evaluate and assimilate new information. The child, in short, learns to encode and to organize information in terms of an evolving gender schema.

A schema is a cognitive structure, a network of associations that organizes and guides an individual's perception. A schema functions as an anticipatory structure, a readiness to search for and to assimilate incoming information in schema-relevant terms. Schematic information

Psychological Review 88, no. 4 (July 1981): 354–64; and "Gender Schema Theory and Self-Schema Theory Compared: A Comment on Markus, Crane, Bernstein, and Siladi's 'Self-Schemas and Gender,' " *Journal of Personality and Social Psychology* 43, no. 6 (December 1982): 1192–94.

processing is thus highly selective and enables the individual to impose structure and meaning onto a vast array of incoming stimuli. More specifically, schematic information processing entails a readiness to sort information into categories on the basis of some particular dimension, despite the existence of other dimensions that could serve equally well in this regard. Gender-schematic processing in particular thus involves spontaneously sorting attributes and behaviors into masculine and feminine categories or "equivalence classes," regardless of their differences on a variety of dimensions unrelated to gender, for example, spontaneously placing items like "tender" and "nightingale" into a feminine category and items like "assertive" and "eagle" into a masculine category. Like schema theories generally,[14] gender schema theory thus construes perception as a constructive process in which the interaction between incoming information and an individual's preexisting schema determines what is perceived.

What gender schema theory proposes, then, is that the phenomenon of sex typing derives, in part, from gender-schematic processing, from an individual's generalized readiness to process information on the basis of the sex-linked associations that constitute the gender schema. Specifically, the theory proposes that sex typing results, in part, from the assimilation of the self-concept itself to the gender schema. As children learn the contents of their society's gender schema, they learn which attributes are to be linked with their own sex and, hence, with themselves. This does not simply entail learning the defined relationship between each sex and each dimension or attribute—that boys are to be strong and girls weak, for example—but involves the deeper lesson that the dimensions themselves are differentially applicable to the two sexes. Thus the strong-weak dimension itself is absent from the schema to be applied to girls just as the dimension of nurturance is implicitly omitted from the schema to be applied to boys. Adults in the child's world rarely notice or remark upon how strong a little girl is becoming or how nurturant a little boy is becoming, despite their readiness to note precisely these attributes in the "appropriate" sex. The child learns to apply this same schematic selectivity to the self, to choose from among the many possible dimensions of human personality only that subset defined as applicable to his or her own sex and thereby eligible for organizing the diverse contents of the self-concept. Thus do children's self-concepts become sex typed, and thus do the two sexes become, in their own eyes, not only different in degree, but different in kind.

Simultaneously, the child also learns to evaluate his or her adequacy as a person according to the gender schema, to match his or her prefer-

14. Ulric Neisser, *Cognition and Reality* (San Francisco: W. H. Freeman & Co., 1976); Shelley E. Taylor and Jennifer Crocker, "Schematic Bases of Social Information Processing," in *Social Cognition, the Ontario Symposium,* ed. E. Tory Higgins, C. Peter Herman, and Mark P. Zanna (Hillsdale, N.J.: Lawrence Erlbaum Associates, 1981), 1:89–135.

Signs   *Summer 1983*   605

ences, attitudes, behaviors, and personal attributes against the prototypes stored within it. The gender schema becomes a prescriptive
standard or guide,[15] and self-esteem becomes its hostage. Here, then,
enters an internalized motivational factor that prompts an individual to
regulate his or her behavior so that it conforms to cultural definitions of
femaleness and maleness. Thus do cultural myths become self-fulfilling
prophecies, and thus, according to gender schema theory, do we arrive
at the phenomenon known as sex typing.

It is important to note that gender schema theory is a theory of
process, not content. Because sex-typed individuals are seen as processing information and regulating their behavior according to whatever
definitions of femininity and masculinity their culture happens to provide, the process of dividing the world into feminine and masculine
categories—and not the contents of the categories—is central to the
theory. Accordingly, sex-typed individuals are seen to differ from other
individuals not primarily in the degree of femininity or masculinity they
possess, but in the extent to which their self-concepts and behaviors are
organized on the basis of gender rather than on the basis of some other
dimension. Many non-sex-typed individuals may describe themselves as,
say, nurturant or dominant without implicating the concepts of femininity or masculinity. When sex-typed individuals so describe themselves, however, it is precisely the gender connotations of the attributes
or behaviors that are presumed to be salient for them.

Empirical Research on Gender-schematic Processing

Recent empirical research supports gender schema theory's basic
contention that sex typing is derived from gender-schematic processing.
In a variety of studies using different subject populations and different
paradigms, female and male sex-typed individuals have been found to
be significantly more likely than non-sex-typed individuals to process
information—including information about the self—in terms of gender.[16]

15. Jerome Kagan, "Acquisition and Significance of Sex Typing and Sex Role Iden-
tity," in *Review of Child Development Research,* ed. Martin L. Hoffman and Lois W. Hoffman
(New York: Russell Sage Foundation, 1964), 1:137–67.
16. Susan M. Andersen and Sandra L. Bem, "Sex Typing and Androgyny in Dyadic
Interaction: Individual Differences in Responsiveness to Physical Attractiveness," *Journal
of Personality and Social Psychology* 41, no. 1 (July 1981): 74–86; Bem, "Gender Schema
Theory"; Kay Deaux and Brenda Major, "Sex-related Patterns in the Unit of Perception,"
Personality and Social Psychology Bulletin 3, no. 2 (Spring 1977): 297–300; Brenda Girvin,
"The Nature of Being Schematic: Sex-Role Self-Schemas and Differential Processing of
Masculine and Feminine Information" (Ph.D. diss., Stanford University, 1978); Robert V.
Kail and Laura E. Levine, "Encoding Processes and Sex-Role Preferences," *Journal of
Experimental Child Psychology* 21, no. 2 (April 1976): 256–63; Lynn S. Liben and Margaret L.
Signorella, "Gender-related Schemata and Constructive Memory in Children," *Child Devel-*

One study, for example, used a memory task to determine whether gender connotations are, in fact, more "cognitively available" to sex-typed individuals than to non-sex-typed individuals, as gender schema theory claims.[17] The subjects in this study were forty-eight male and forty-eight female undergraduates who had described themselves as either sex typed or non–sex typed on the Bem Sex Role Inventory (BSRI).[18]

During the experimental session, subjects were presented with a randomly ordered sequence of sixty-one words that included proper names, animal names, verbs, and articles of clothing. Half of the proper names were female, half were male; one-third of the items within each of the other semantic categories had been consistently rated by undergraduate judges as feminine (e.g., butterfly, blushing, bikini), one-third as masculine (e.g., gorilla, hurling, trousers), and one-third as neutral (e.g., ant, stepping, sweater). The words were presented on slides at three-second intervals, and subjects were told that their recall would later be tested. Three seconds after the presentation of the last word, they were given a period of eight minutes to write down as many words as they could, in whatever order they happened to come to mind.

As expected, the results indicated that although sex-typed and non-sex-typed individuals recalled equal numbers of items overall, the order in which they recalled the items was different. Once having recalled a

---

opment 51, no. 1 (March 1980): 11–18; Richard Lippa, "Androgyny, Sex Typing, and the Perception of Masculinity-Femininity in Handwriting," *Journal of Research in Personality* 11, no. 1 (March 1977): 21–37; Hazel Markus et al., "Self-Schemas and Gender," *Journal of Personality and Social Psychology* 42, no. 1 (January 1982): 38–50; Shelley E. Taylor and Hsiao-Ti Falcone, "Cognitive Bases of Stereotyping: The Relationship between Categorization and Prejudice," *Personality and Social Psychology Bulletin* 8, no. 3 (September 1982): 426–32.

17. Bem, "Gender Schema Theory," pp. 356–58.

18. The Bem Sex Role Inventory, or BSRI, is an instrument that identifies sex-typed individuals on the basis of their self-concepts or self-ratings of their personal attributes. The BSRI asks the respondent to indicate on a seven-point scale how well each of sixty attributes describes himself or herself. Although it is not apparent to the respondent, twenty of the attributes reflect the culture's definition of masculinity (e.g., assertive), and twenty reflect its definition of femininity (e.g., tender), with the remaining attributes serving as filler. Each respondent receives both a masculinity and a femininity score, and those who score above the median on the sex-congruent scale and below the median on the sex-incongruent scale are defined as sex typed. That is, men who score high in masculinity and low in femininity are defined as sex typed, as are women who score high in femininity and low in masculinity. The BSRI is described in detail in the following articles: Sandra L. Bem, "The Measurement of Psychological Androgyny," *Journal of Consulting and Clinical Psychology* 42, no. 2 (April 1974): 155–62; "On the Utility of Alternative Procedures for Assessing Psychological Androgyny," *Journal of Clinical and Consulting Psychology* 45, no. 2 (April 1977): 196–205; "The Theory and Measurement of Androgyny: A Reply to the Pedhazur-Tetenbaum and Locksley-Colten Critiques," *Journal of Personality and Social Psychology* 37, no. 6 (June 1979): 1047–54; and *A Manual for the Bem Sex Role Inventory* (Palo Alto, Calif.: Consulting Psychologists Press, 1981).

Signs   *Summer 1983*   607

feminine item, sex-typed individuals were more likely than non-sex-typed individuals to recall another feminine item next rather than a masculine or a neutral item. The same was true for masculine items. In other words, the sequence of recall for sex-typed individuals revealed significantly more runs or clusters of feminine items and of masculine items than the sequence of recall for non-sex-typed individuals. Thinking of one feminine (or masculine) item could enhance the probability of thinking of another feminine (or masculine) item in this way only if the individual spontaneously encodes both items as feminine (or masculine), and the gender schema thereby links the two items in memory. These results thus confirm gender schema theory's claim that sex-typed individuals have a greater readiness than do non-sex-typed individuals to encode information in terms of the sex-linked associations that constitute the gender schema.

A second study tested the hypothesis that sex-typed individuals have a readiness to decide on the basis of gender which personal attributes are to be associated with their self-concepts and which are to be dissociated from their self-concepts.[19] The subjects in this second study were another set of forty-eight male and forty-eight female undergraduates who had also described themselves as sex typed or non–sex typed on the Bem Sex Role Inventory. During each of the individual experimental sessions, the sixty attributes from the BSRI were projected on a screen one at a time, and the subject was requested to push one of two buttons, "Me" or "Not Me," to indicate whether the attribute was or was not self-descriptive. Of interest in this study was the subject's response latency, that is, how long it took the subject to make a decision about each attribute.

Gender schema theory predicts and the results of this study confirm that sex-typed subjects are significantly faster than non-sex-typed subjects when endorsing sex-appropriate attributes and when rejecting sex-inappropriate attributes. These results suggest that when deciding whether a particular attribute is or is not self-descriptive, sex-typed individuals do not bother to go through a time-consuming process of recruiting behavioral evidence from memory and judging whether the evidence warrants an affirmative answer—which is presumably what non-sex-typed individuals do. Rather, sex-typed individuals "look up" the attribute in the gender schema. If the attribute is sex appropriate, they quickly say yes; if the attribute is sex inappropriate, they quickly say no. Occasionally, of course, even sex-typed individuals must admit to possessing an attribute that is sex inappropriate or to lacking an attribute that is sex appropriate. On these occasions, they are significantly slower than non-sex-typed individuals. This pattern of rapid delivery of gender-consistent self-descriptions and slow delivery of gender-

19. Bem, "Gender Schema Theory," pp. 358–61.

inconsistent self-descriptions confirms gender schema theory's contention that sex-typed individuals spontaneously sort information into categories on the basis of gender, despite the existence of other dimensions that could serve equally well as a basis for categorization.

Antecedents of Gender-schematic Processing

But how and why do sex-typed individuals develop a readiness to organize information in general, and their self-concepts in particular, in terms of gender? Because gender-schematic processing is considered a special case of schematic processing, this specific question is superseded by the more general question of how and why individuals come to organize information in terms of any social category, that is, how and why a social category becomes transformed into a cognitive schema.

Gender schema theory proposes that the transformation of a given social category into the nucleus of a highly available cognitive schema depends on the nature of the social context within which the category is embedded, not on the intrinsic nature of the category itself. Given the proper social context, then, even a category like eye color could become a cognitive schema. More specifically, gender schema theory proposes that a category will become a schema if: (a) the social context makes it the nucleus of a large associative network, that is, if the ideology and/or the practices of the culture construct an association between that category and a wide range of other attributes, behaviors, concepts, and categories; and (b) the social context assigns the category broad functional significance, that is, if a broad array of social institutions, norms, and taboos distinguishes between persons, behaviors, and attributes on the basis of this category.

This latter condition is most critical, for gender schema theory presumes that the culture's insistence on the functional importance of the social category is what transforms a passive network of associations into an active and readily available schema for interpreting reality. We all learn many associative networks of concepts throughout life, many potential cognitive schemata, but the centrality or functional importance assigned by society to particular categories and distinctions animates their associated networks and gives these schemata priority and availability over others.

From the perspective of gender schema theory, then, gender has come to have cognitive primacy over many other social categories because the culture has made it so. Nearly all societies teach the developing child two crucial things about gender: first, as noted earlier, they teach the substantive network of sex-related associations that can come to serve as a cognitive schema; second, they teach that the dichotomy between male and female has intensive and extensive relevance to virtually every domain of human experience. The typical American child cannot help observing, for example, that what parents, teachers, and peers consider to be appropriate behavior varies as a function of sex; that toys, clothing, occupations, hobbies, the domestic division of labor—even pronouns—all vary as a function of sex.

Gender schema theory thus implies that children would be far less likely to become gender schematic and hence sex typed if the society were to limit the associative network linked to sex and to temper its insistence on the functional importance of the gender dichotomy. Ironically, even though our society has become sensitive to negative sex stereotypes and has begun to expunge them from the media and from children's literature, it remains blind to its gratuitous emphasis on the gender dichotomy itself. In elementary schools, for example, boys and girls line up separately or alternately; they learn songs in which the fingers are "ladies" and the thumbs are "men"; they see boy and girl paper-doll silhouettes alternately placed on the days of the month in order to learn about the calendar. Children, it will be noted, are not lined up separately or alternately as blacks and whites; fingers are not "whites" and thumbs "blacks"; black and white dolls do not alternately mark the days of the calendar. Our society seeks to deemphasize racial distinctions but continues to exaggerate sexual distinctions.

Because of the role that sex plays in reproduction, perhaps no society could ever be as indifferent to sex in its cultural arrangements as it could be to, say, eye color, thereby giving the gender schema a sociologically based priority over many other categories. For the same reason, it may even be, as noted earlier, that sex has evolved to be a basic category of perception for our species, thereby giving the gender schema a biologically based priority as well. Be that as it may, however, gender schema theory claims that society's ubiquitous insistence on the functional importance of the gender dichotomy must necessarily render it even more cognitively available—and available in more remotely relevant contexts—than it would be otherwise.

It should be noted that gender schema theory's claims about the antecedents of gender-schematic processing have not yet been tested empirically. Hence it is not possible at this point to state whether individual differences in gender-schematic processing do, in fact, derive from differences in the emphasis placed on gender dichotomy in individuals' socialization histories, or to describe concretely the particular kinds of socialization histories that enhance or diminish gender-schematic processing. Nevertheless, I should like to set forth a number of plausible strategies that are consistent with gender schema theory for raising a gender-aschematic child in the midst of a gender-schematic society.

This discussion will, by necessity, be highly speculative. Even so, it will serve to clarify gender schema theory's view of exactly how gender-schematic processing is learned and how something else might be learned in its place. As we shall see, many of the particular strategies recommended for raising gender-aschematic children are strategies that have already been adopted by feminist parents trying to create what is typically called a nonsexist or a gender-liberated form of child rearing. In these cases, what gender schema theory provides is a new theoretical framework for thinking about the psychological impact of various child-rearing practices. Sprinkled throughout the discussion will be examples taken from my own home. These are meant to be illustrations and not systematic evidence that such strategies actually decrease gender-schematic processing.

Raising Gender-aschematic Children

Feminist parents who wish to raise gender-aschematic children in a gender-schematic world are like any parents who wish to inculcate their children with beliefs and values that deviate from those of the dominant culture. Their major option is to try to undermine the dominant ideology before it can undermine theirs. Feminist parents are thus in a difficult situation. They cannot simply ignore gender in their child rearing as they might prefer to do, because the society will then have free rein to teach their children the lessons about gender that it teaches all other children. Rather, they must manage somehow to inoculate their children against gender-schematic processing.

Two strategies are suggested here. First, parents can enable their children to learn about sex differences initially without their also learning the culture's sex-linked associative network by simultaneously retarding their children's knowledge of sex's cultural correlates and advancing their children's knowledge of sex's biological correlates. Second, parents can provide alternative or "subversive" schemata that their children can use to interpret the culture's sex-linked associative network when they do learn it. This step is essential if children are not simply to learn gender-schematic processing somewhat later than their counterparts from more traditional homes. Whether one is a child or an adult, such alternative schemata "build up one's resistance" to the lessons of the dominant culture and thereby enable one to remain gender-aschematic even while living in a gender-schematic society.

Teaching Children about Sex Differences

Cultural correlates of sex.—Children typically learn that gender is a sprawling associative network with ubiquitous functional importance through their observation of the many cultural correlates of sex existing in their society. Accordingly, the first step parents can take to retard the development of gender-schematic processing is to retard the child's knowledge of these cultural messages about gender. Less crudely put, parents can attempt to attenuate sex-linked correlations within the child's social environment, thereby altering the basic data upon which the child will construct his or her own concepts of maleness and femaleness.

In part, parents can do this by eliminating sex stereotyping from their own behavior and from the alternatives that they provide for their children, just as many feminist parents are already doing. Among other things, for example, they can take turns making dinner, bathing the children, and driving the car; they can ensure that all their children—regardless of sex—have both trucks and dolls, both pink and blue clothing, and both male and female playmates; and they can arrange for their children to see women and men in nontraditional occupations.

When children are quite young, parents can further inhibit cultural messages about gender by actually censoring books and television programs whose explicit or implicit message is that the sexes differ on nonbiological dimensions. At present, this tactic will eliminate many children's books and most television programming. Ironically, it will also temporarily eliminate a number of feminist books designed to overcome sex stereotypes; even a book which insists that it is wrong for William not to be allowed to have a doll by implication teaches a child who has not yet learned the associative network that boys and dolls do not normally go together.

To compensate for this censorship, parents will need to seek out—and to create—materials that do not teach sex stereotypes. With our own children, my husband and I got into the habit of doctoring books whenever possible so as to remove all sex-linked correlations. We did this, among other ways, by changing the sex of the main character; by drawing longer hair and the outline of breasts onto illustrations of previously male truck drivers, physicians, pilots, and the like; and by deleting or altering sections of the text that described females or males in a sex-stereotyped manner. When reading children's picture books aloud, we also chose pronouns that avoided the ubiquitous implication that all characters without dresses or pink bows must necessarily be male: "And what is this little piggy doing? Why, he or she seems to be building a bridge."

All of these practices are designed to permit very young children to dwell temporarily in a social environment where, if the parents are lucky, the cultural correlations with sex will be attenuated from, say, .96 to .43. According to gender schema theory, this attenuation should retard the formation of the sex-linked associative network that will itself form the basis of the gender schema. By themselves, however, these practices teach children only what sex is not. But children must also be taught what sex is.

Biological correlates of sex.—What remains when all of the cultural correlates of sex are attenuated or eliminated, of course, are two of the undisputed biological correlates of sex: anatomy and reproduction. Accordingly, parents can make these the definitional attributes of femaleness and maleness. By teaching their children that the genitalia constitute the definitive attributes of females and males, parents help them to apprehend the merely probabilistic nature of sex's cultural correlates and thereby restrict sex's associative sprawl. By teaching their children that whether one is female or male makes a difference only in the context of reproduction, parents limit sex's functional significance and thereby retard gender-schematic processing. Because children taught these lessons have been provided with an explicit and clear-cut rule about what sex is and when sex matters, they should be predisposed to construct their own concepts of femaleness and maleness based on biology, rather than on the cultural correlates to which they have been exposed. And to the extent that young children tend to interpret rules and categories rigidly rather than flexibly, this tendency will serve to enhance their belief that sex is to be narrowly defined in terms of anatomy and reproduction rather than to enhance a traditional belief that every arbitrary gender rule must be strictly obeyed and enforced. Thus there may be an irony, but there is no inconsistency, in the fact that an emphasis on the biological differences between the sexes should here be advocated as the basis for feminist child rearing.

The liberation that comes from having an unambiguous genital definition of sex and the imprisonment that comes from not having such a definition are nicely illustrated by the story of what happened to our son Jeremy, then age four, the day he decided to wear barrettes to nursery school. Several times that day, another little boy told Jeremy that he, Jeremy, must be a girl because "only girls wear barrettes." After trying to explain to this child that "wearing barrettes doesn't matter" and that "being a boy means having a penis and testicles," Jeremy finally pulled down his pants as a way of making his point more convincingly. The other child was not impressed. He simply said, "Everybody has a penis; only girls wear barrettes."

In the American context, children do not typically learn to define sex in terms of anatomy and reproduction until quite late, and, as a result, they—like the child in the example above—mistakenly treat many of the cultural correlates of sex as definitional. This confusion is facilitated, of course, by the fact that the genitalia themselves are not usually visible and hence cannot be relied on as a way of identifying someone's sex.

Accordingly, when our children asked whether someone was male or female, we frequently denied certain knowledge of the person's sex, emphasizing that without being able to see whether there was a penis or a vagina under the person's clothes, we had no definitive information. Moreover, when our children themselves began to utilize nonbiological markers as a way of identifying sex, we gently teased them about that

Signs   *Summer 1983   613*

strategy to remind them that the genitalia—and only the genitalia—consitute the definition of sex: "What do you mean that you can tell Chris is a girl because Chris has long hair? Does Chris's hair have a vagina?"

We found Stephanie Waxman's picture book *What Is a Girl? What Is a Boy?* to be a superb teaching aid in this context.[20] Each page displays a vivid and attractive photograph of a boy or a girl engaged in some behavior stereotyped as more typical of or more appropriate for the other sex. The accompanying text says such things as, "Some people say a girl is someone with jewelry, but Barry is wearing a necklace and he's a boy." The book ends with nude photographs of both children and adults, and it explicitly defines sex in terms of anatomy.

These particular lessons about what sex is, what sex is not, and when sex matters are designed to make young children far more naive than their peers about the cultural aspects of gender and far more sophisticated than their peers about the biological aspects of sex. Eventually, of course, their naiveté will begin to fade, and they too will begin to learn the culture's sprawling network of sex-linked associations. At that point, parents must take steps to prevent that associative network from itself becoming a cognitive schema.

Providing Alternative Schemata

Let us presume that the feminist parent has successfully produced a child who defines sex in terms of anatomy and reproduction. How is such a child to understand the many sex-linked correlations that will inevitably begin to intrude upon his or her awareness? What alternative schemata can substitute for the gender schema in helping the child to organize and to assimilate gender-related information?

Individual differences schema.—The first alternative schema is simply a child's version of the time-honored liberal truism used to counter stereotypic thinking in general, namely, that there is remarkable variability of individuals within groups as compared with the small mean differences between groups. To the child who says that girls do not like to play baseball, the feminist parent can thus point out that although it is true that some girls do not like to play baseball, it is also true that some girls do (e.g., your Aunt Beverly and Alissa who lives across the street) and that some boys do not (e.g., your dad and Alissa's brother Jimmy). It is, of course, useful for parents to supply themselves with a long list of counterexamples well in advance of such occasions.

This individual differences schema is designed to prevent children from interpreting individual differences as sex differences, from as-

20. Stephanie Waxman, *What Is a Girl? What Is a Boy?* (Culver City, Calif.: Peace Press, 1976).

similating perceived differences among people to a gender schema. Simultaneously, it should also encourage children to treat as a given that the sexes are basically similar to one another and, hence, to view all glib assertions about sex differences as inherently suspect. And it is with this skepticism that feminist consciousness begins.

Cultural relativism schema.—As the child's knowledge and awareness grow, he or she will gradually begin to realize that his or her family's beliefs and attitudes about gender are at variance with those of the dominant culture. Accordingly, the child needs some rationale for not simply accepting the majority view as the more valid. One possible rationale is cultural relativism, the notion that "different people believe different things" and that the coexistence of even contradictory beliefs is the rule in society rather than the exception.

Children can (and should) be introduced to the schema of cultural relativism long before it is pertinent to the domain of gender. For example, our children needed the rationale that "different people believe different things" in order to understand why they, but not the children next door, had to wear seat belts; why our family, but not the family next door, was casual about nudity in the home. The general principle that contradictory beliefs frequently coexist seems now to have become a readily available schema for our children, a schema that permits them to accept with relative equanimity that they have different beliefs from many of their peers with respect to gender.

Finally, the cultural relativism schema can solve one of the primary dilemmas of the liberal feminist parent: how to give one's children access to the riches of classical literature—as well as to the lesser riches of the mass media—without abandoning them to the forces that promote gender-schematic processing. Happily, the censorship of sex-stereotyped materials that is necessary to retard the initial growth of the sex-linked associative network when children are young can end once children have learned the critical lesson that cultural messages reflect the beliefs and attitudes of the person or persons who created those messages.

Accordingly, before we read our daughter her first volume of fairy tales, we discussed with her the cultural beliefs and attitudes about men and women that the tales would reflect, and while reading the tales, we frequently made such comments as, "Isn't it interesting that the person who wrote this story seems to think that girls always need to be rescued?" If such discussions are not too heavy-handed, they can provide a background of understanding against which the child can thoroughly enjoy the stories themselves, while still learning to discount the sex stereotypes within them as irrelevant both to their own beliefs and to truth. The cultural relativism schema thus brings children an awareness that fairy tales are fairy tales in more than one sense.

Sexism schema.—Cultural relativism is fine in its place, but feminist

Signs   *Summer 1983*   615

parents will not and should not be satisfied to pretend that they think all ideas—particularly those about gender—are equally valid. At some point, they will feel compelled to declare that the view of women and men conveyed by fairy tales, by the mass media—and by the next-door neighbors—is not only different, but wrong. It is time to teach one's children about sexism.

Moreover, it is only by giving children a sexism schema, a coherent and organized understanding of the historical roots and the contemporaneous consequences of sex discrimination, that they will truly be able to comprehend why the sexes appear to be so different in our society: why, for example, there has never been a female president of the United States; why fathers do not stay home with their children; and why so many people believe these sex differences to be the natural consequence of biology. The child who has developed a readiness to encode and to organize information in terms of an evolving sexism schema is a child who is prepared to oppose actively the gender-related constraints that those with a gender schema will inevitably seek to impose.

The development of a sexism schema is nicely illustrated by our daughter Emily's response to Norma Klein's book *Girls Can Be Anything*.[21] One of the characters is Adam Sobel, who insists that "girls are always nurses and boys are always doctors" and that "girls can't be pilots, . . . they have to be stewardesses." After reading this book, our daughter, then age four, spontaneously began to label with contempt anyone who voiced stereotyped beliefs about gender an "Adam Sobel." Adam Sobel thus became for her the nucleus of an envolving sexism schema, a schema that enables her now to perceive—and also to become morally outraged by and to oppose—whatever sex discrimination she meets in daily life.

As feminist parents, we wish it could have been possible to raise our children with neither a gender schema nor a sexism schema. At this historical moment, however, that is not an option. Rather we must choose either to have our children become gender schematic and hence sex typed, or to have our children become sexism schematic and hence feminists. We have chosen the latter.

A Comment on Psychological Androgyny

The central figure in gender schema theory is the sex-typed individual, a shift in focus from my earlier work in which the non-sex-typed individual—the androgynous individual in particular—commanded center stage.[22] In the early 1970s, androgyny seemed to me and to many

21. Norma Klein, *Girls Can Be Anything* (New York: E. P. Dutton, 1973).
22. Sandra L. Bem, "Sex-Role Adaptability: One Consequence of Psychological Androgyny," *Journal of Personality and Social Psychology* 31, no. 4 (April 1975): 634–43; Sandra

others a liberated and more humane alternative to the traditional, sex-biased standards of mental health. And it is true that this concept can be applied equally to both women and men, and that it encourages individuals to embrace both the feminine and the masculine within themselves. But advocating the concept of androgyny can also be seen as replacing a prescription to be masculine or feminine with the doubly incarcerating prescription to be masculine and feminine. The individual now has not one but two potential sources of inadequacy with which to contend. Even more important, however, the concept of androgyny is problematic from the perspective of gender schema theory because it is based on the presupposition that there is a feminine and a masculine within us all, that is, that "femininity" and "masculinity" have an independent and palpable reality and are not cognitive constructs derived from gender-schematic processing. Focusing on androgyny thus fails to prompt serious examination of the extent to which gender organizes both our perceptions and our social world.

In contrast, the concept of gender-schematic processing directs our attention to the promiscuous availability of the gender schema in contexts where other schemata ought to have priority. Thus, if gender schema theory has a political message, it is not that the individual should be androgynous. Rather, it is that the network of associations constituting the gender schema ought to become more limited in scope and that society ought to temper its insistence on the ubiquitous functional importance of the gender dichotomy. In short, human behaviors and personality attributes should no longer be linked with gender, and society should stop projecting gender into situations irrelevant to genitalia.

Department of Psychology and the Women's Studies Program
Cornell University

L. Bem, Wendy Martyna, and Carol Watson, "Sex-Typing and Androgyny: Further Explorations of the Expressive Domain," *Journal of Personality and Social Psychology* 34, no. 5 (November 1976): 1016–23; Sandra L. Bem, "Beyond Androgyny: Some Presumptuous Prescriptions for a Liberated Sexual Identity," in *The Future of Women: Issues in Psychology*, ed. Julia Sherman and Florence Denmark (New York: Psychological Dimensions, Inc., 1978), pp. 1–23; Sandra L. Bem and Ellen Lenney, "Sex-Typing and the Avoidance of Cross-Sex Behavior," *Journal of Personality and Social Psychology* 33, no. 1 (January 1976): 48–54.

[32]

Sex Roles, Vol. 11, Nos. 7/8, 1984

Sex Differences in the Relationship of Height to Children's Actual and Attributed Social and Cognitive Competencies[1]

Nancy Eisenberg,[2] Karlsson Roth,
Karyl A. Bryniarski, and Edward Murray

In three studies, the relationship of children's height to both (a) adults' attributions regarding the children and (b) preschoolers' social and cognitive competencies were examined. Sex differences were consistent with stereotypic conceptions. In the first two studies, mothers of preschool children rated photographs of toddlers varying in height on a variety of social and cognitive abilities. The mothers also assigned punishment to the children for hypothetical transgressions. In Experiment 1, mothers rated the large boys as more competent than the average-sized and small boys (even when effects of mothers' perceptions of the children's ages were covaried). In Experiment 2, involving female stimuli, mothers rated small girls as being less able (especially less independent) than average-sized or tall girls. While the effect of height on mothers' attributions was still evident when the effects of perceived age of the children were covaried, the pattern of results was less clear. Mothers assigned more punishment to tall girls (but not tall boys) than to small girls regardless of perceptions of age. In Experiment 3, height was associated with boys', but not girls', competence on tasks of logical ability and boys' sociometric nominations of whom they prefer to play with (significant for girls, marginally significant for boys). Height was not highly correlated with peers' perceptions of competence. The implications of the research for the socialization process are discussed.

[1]The authors wish to express their gratitude to the parents, teachers, and children at the Child Study Laboratory, Students' Child Center, Palo Alto Preschools, and Tempe Preschool. The authors would also like to thank Michael Gunzelman, Michelle White, Julie Mankowski, Marsha Kaplan, and Melissa Rook for their able assistance in data collection.
[2]Correspondence should be sent to Nancy Eisenberg, Department of Psychology, Arizona State University, Tempe, Arizona 85287.

It is widely believed by both social scientists and laymen that gross aspects of physique and appearance including height, weight, muscular strength, and facial attractiveness affect the individual's behavior and personality (Barker, Wright, & Gonick, 1946; Meyerson, 1963). This effect is likely to be both direct and indirect. According to Meyerson (1963), one's physique is a social stimulus which (a) arouses expectations for behavior, (b) is one of the criteria for assigning a person to a social role, and (c) influences the individual's perception of himself/herself both directly, through comparison with others, and indirectly, through the processing of others' expectations.

If people differing in structure and appearance do elicit differential expectations and attributions from others — expectations which are likely to influence the individual's behavior and self-perception — it is important to determine the nature of these reactions and when and under what circumstances they occur. One important variable that may mediate the strength of others' reactions to an individual's physical size is sex of the individual. According to traditional, stereotypic conceptions, masculine males are big and feminine females are petite. Apparently, large size for males is associated with dominance and/or competence, while small structure for women is interpreted as an index of stereotypic femininity (i.e., submissiveness and/or dependency).

At least for men, some empirical evidence supports the view that an individual's size influences how he is perceived by others. According to the limited research, tall males frequently are more successful than their shorter counterparts in their occupations (Gowin, 1927). Furthermore, dominant, high status persons are perceived as being taller than less powerful, lower status people (Dannenmaier & Thurmin, 1964; Wilson, 1968). For children, Prieto (1975) found that peers' and teachers perceptions of male junior high school students' heights were positively related to their evaluations of the students' academic and/or social performance, and to the students' perceptions of their capacities. Actual height — which was highly correlated with peers', teachers', and the child's own estimates of his height — was related to only the child's perception of his own academic performance. Although cause and effect are unclear, perceptions of height, actual height, and attributions regarding adult and adolescent males' performance appear closely related.

Research on the relationship between others' attributions and young children's height is virtually nonexistent, as are data on actual competence of children varying in size. Based on the research conducted with older males, one would expect tall boys to be viewed more positively than smaller boys. Since the young child is in the early phases of developing cognitive and social skills, young boys' skills, as well as their emerging self-esteem, might be especially vulnerable to interpersonal reactions elicited by the child's stature (Meyerson, 1963; Wylie, 1961).

Much of the research on the relationship between height and attributions regarding competence has been conducted in noncontrolled settings or in experimental situations which manipulated competence or status, not height. In studies in real-life settings, cause and effect are unclear; performance (and/or perceptions of performance) may influence perceptions of height, or height (and/or perceptions of height) may affect performance (or perceptions thereof). Thus, to determine how height influences attributions regarding performance, research is needed in which height (not performance) is manipulated.

The first two experiments described in the present article implement such a manipulation. Using photography, heights of preschool children were manipulated so that a given child, in three different photographs, appeared taller, smaller, or equivalent in size to a peer. Parents of preschool children then were asked to rate one of the children in one photograph on a number of cognitive and social capacities that should be developing in the toddler years. Since differential expectations for performance based on height could influence adults' assignment of punishment for wrongdoing, the parents also were asked to prescribe punishment for a hypothetical transgression committed by the same child that they rated.

EXPERIMENT 1

Subjects

Participants were 100 mothers, all of whom had preschool children in four preschools located in the same suburb. The mothers were predominantly Caucasian and middle class.

Materials

The height manipulation was achieved with three photographs, each containing the same two boys. These boys were both 19 months old and resembled one another in both height and general appearance. With the aid of props (sweaters to conceal bodily features and blocks to stand on), Child 1 appeared taller than Child 2 in one picture; Child 2 appeared taller in another photograph; and the children were the same height in the third picture. The sweaters hid the children's waistlines (so that a child standing on a block did not look out of proportion); the "taller" child stood on a cement block while being photographed. Thus, each child served as a tall, average, and small stimulus in different pictures.

Perceptions of competency, assignment of punishment, and estimates of the children's ages were assessed with a questionnaire. One section of the instrument contained 17 questions regarding various competencies followed by 6-point rating scales ranging from "extremely capable" to "extremely incapable." The subjects were instructed to indicate their "personal reactions" to one of the two children in only one picture via these questions (by indicating how capable the child would be at a variety of skills). The first 5 items were included merely to accustom the mothers to use the extreme ends of the rating scale; that is, they were asked how capable the child would be at very simple or very hard skills (e.g., walking, math). The next 12 items (which are presented in Table I) assessed parental expectations regarding social and cognitive skills which should be in various stages of development during the preschool years. The items were chosen to reflect a range of skills relevant to toddlers' social and cognitive functioning.

To assess assignment of punishment for wrongdoing, the mothers were asked to recommend punishment for the transgression in the following story: "The boy in the picture has been told many times not to push or hit the baby that lives next door. Despite numerous warnings, he has continued to push and hit the neighbor's baby. His mother and father decided that the boy should be punished by staying in his room. How long should he have to stay in his room?" The mothers indicated how much punishment should be assigned with a rating scale including the following punishments: no time, 2, 5, 10, 15, 20, 30, 40, 50, or more than 50 minutes.

Finally, a third section of the questionnaire contained several demographic questions and the following question, "How old do you think the child in the picture was?"

Procedures

Each mother was approached by one of three female experimenters when either arriving at or leaving her child's day-care center. The experimenter told the mother that she was conducting a study on parents' reactions to children, and asked if the mother would be willing to fill out a questionnaire. If the mother agreed (most did at one time or another when their hands were not full), she was randomly assigned to one of the three photographs and, by means of numbers on the questionnaires (which were alternated), she was assigned to one of the two children. Each parent rated only one child in one picture. Approximately half the mothers in each condition responded to the questions regarding competencies prior to responding to the punishment question; the remainder received these sections in reverse order. For half the subjects, demographic and age questions were presented last; for the remaining mothers, these questions were situated between the punishment and competency questions.

Results

The data were analyzed with 2 (child) X 3 (height: small, average, tall) multivariate and univariate analyses. For the 12 competency items, the multivariate F (Wilks' lambda) for the main effect of height was significant, $F(24, 166) = 2.34, p < .001$, as was the multivariate F for the height X child interaction, $F(24, 166) = 1.81, p < .02$.

According to univariate analyses, the main effect of height was significant for 10 of the 12 items. To determine which height groups differed from the others, tests of simple effects were then computed. There was a significant difference between the ratings for the tall and average-sized groups for 9 of the 10 items. Furthermore, according to tests contrasting the ratings for tall and small boys, 9 of the 10 comparisons were significant at the .05 level of significance; the tenth was significant at the .10 level. Finally, there was a significant difference between ratings of small and average boys for only 1 item. In all cases, the larger boys were perceived as being more competent. Information on the specific items is presented in Table I.

According to additional univariate analyses, the height X child interaction was marginally significant for only 2 of the 12 items: "getting along and playing with other children," $F(2, 94) = 2.74, p < .07$, and "doing well in school," $F(2, 94) = 2.78, p < .07$. According to tests of simple effects (height within each child) for these items, the interaction was due to an effect of height for one child, $F(2, 94) = 8.60$ and $4.41, ps < .05$, respectively for the two items; but not for the other child, $F(2, 94) = 1.16$ and 2.03, respectively for the two items. Nevertheless, the means were in the expected direction for both children. Thus, for two items, the main effect of height was somewhat more apparent for one child than the other. However, since the univariate analyses for the height X child interactions were marginally significant while the analogous univariate analyses for the main effect of height were highly significant, the two height X child interaction effects do little to diminish the strong pattern of data indicating a main effect of height across many items.

According to two additional univariate analyses of variance, the mothers did not assign different punishment or ages in the various conditions. The mothers thought a moderate punishment was appropriate for the hypothetical transgression ($M = 5$ minutes), and that the children were somewhat older than their real age ($M = 2.90$ years). Furthermore,

Table I. Experiment 1 Competence Ratings[a]

Item	Univariate F	Means[b]			Simple effects F		
		Tall	Average	Small	Tall vs. Small	Tall vs. Average	Average vs. small
1. Obeying rules or instructions (e.g., doing what parents say at home)	3.09[c] (2.66[f])	2.32	2.81	2.76	3.85[e] (4.10[e])	5.16[e] (4.12[e])	
2. Getting along and playing with other children	7.14[c] (7.16[c])	2.29	2.62	3.16	13.90[c] (14.07[c])		
3. Understanding another person's point of view (how another person feels and thinks)	10.66[c] (9.79[c])	2.94	4.09	3.70	8.47[d] (10.25[d])	20.67[c] (18.18[c])	5.76[e] (6.16[e])
4. Being independent (rather than dependent and seeking help from adults)	5.05[d] (5.03[d])	2.97	3.84	3.46	2.83[f] (3.57[f])	10.16[c] (10.17[c])	
5. Not crying when frustrated	5.70[d] (5.94[d])	3.39	4.03	4.27	10.63[d] (10.59[d])	5.32[e] (6.62[e])	
6. Doing well in school	3.62[e] (3.33[e])	2.58	3.16	3.14	5.14[e] (5.04[e])	5.51[e] (4.87[e])	

Table I. Experiment 1 Competence Ratings[a] Continued

					—	—
7. Taking care of his own needs, like getting himself water and picking up his toys	4.02* (4.99e)	2.52	3.06	3.14	6.80d (9.36e)	4.97* (4.49*)
8. Minding teachers at school	2.13 (2.00)	2.48	2.91	2.76	—	—
9. Being able to ask for something he wants rather than just taking it impulsively	4.62d (4.47d)	2.55	3.16	3.11	6.14d (7.01d)	7.39d (6.52d)
10. Being able to get along with the desires of others, being able to agree to do what the group wants even if he doesn't want to	6.37d (5.69d)	2.97	3.84	3.51	4.42c (3.97c)	12.63c (11.47c)
11. Being able to concentrate on a boring task	1.76 (1.72)	3.90	4.31	4.35	—	—
12. Being able to do chores when told to do so, (e.g., picking up toys)	2.96f (3.01f)	2.61	3.06	3.03	3.93c (4.73c)	4.75c (4.46c)

[a]Numbers in parentheses represent F values with the effects of perceived age covaried.
[b]Low values indicate higher levels of competence.
[c]$p < .001$.
[d]$p < .01$.
[e]$p < .05$.
[f]$p < .10$.

when the effects of mothers' perceptions of age on attributions regarding performance were controlled by treating estimates of age as a covariate in the multivariate and univariate analyses, the pattern of results was generally unaltered (see Table I).

To summarize, mothers' attributions regarding the children's competence were directly related to child size, with bigger children being perceived as more able. There was a marginally significant height X child interaction for only two items. Assignment of punishment and perceptions of age were not affected by size of the child.

EXPERIMENT 2

Nearly all of the research on the effects of height on people's attributions of competence has involved male stimuli. Thus, it is not known whether females' heights influence others' evaluations. However, since large size is not viewed as an especially positive characteristic for females, one would not expect tall girls to be viewed more positively than smaller girls. Experiment 2 was conducted to determine if mothers' attributions regarding preschool girls' competence are influenced by height in a manner analogous to their perceptions of boys.

Subjects

Participants were 108 mothers whose children attended five pre-schools in the same surburban area. Most of the women were Caucasian and from middle-class families.

Materials and Procedures

The materials and procedures used in Experiment 2 were the same as those in Experiment 1 with the following exceptions: (a) The three photographs were of two girls, aged 19 and 20 months, who were similar in height; (b) the items on the questionnaires were altered to refer to a female rather than a male.

Results

As in Experiment 1, the data were analyzed with multivariate and univariate analyses of variance. For the 12 performance items, only the multivariate F for the effect of height was marginally significant, $F(24, 182)$

= 1.53, $p < .07$. Five of the 12 univariate analyses were significant at the .05 level of significance or higher.

According to tests of simple effects, mothers rated the tall children as different from small children on 4 of the 5 items, and the average-sized girls as different from small girls on all 5 items (at the .07 level of significance or better). In all cases, the small girls were viewed as less competent than the tall or average girls (see Table II). Tall and average-sized girls were not rated differently on any items. The items that differentiated small girls tended to concern independent versus dependent behavior (specifically items 4, 5, and 7, but not items 3 or 11) rather than degree of compliance with adults' wishes or quality of peer interactions. This pattern of results is consistent with the stereotype of the small girls as being helpless and dependent, but not especially noncompliant or inept in social relationships.

Unlike the results obtained for boys in Experiment 1, the mothers' estimates of the girls' ages were related to size of the girls, $F(2, 102) = 4.10$, $p < .02$. According to tests of simple effects, mothers thought that small girls were significantly younger ($M = 2.33$ years) than average-sized girls ($M = 2.89$ years); $F(2, 102) = 8.22, p < .005$. Estimates of age for the tall girls ($M = 2.53$ years) did not differ from estimates for either the small or average girls.

To determine if the pattern of results for the attribution data was due to the fact that mothers believed the small girls to be younger than the tall or average-sized girls, the attributional data were reanalyzed using perceived age as a covariate. While the pattern of results was weaker when age was treated as a covariate, the multivariate F for the main effect of height was still marginally significant, $F(24, 180) = 1.49$, $p < .08$, as were several univariate analyses (see Table II). Thus, the mothers' perceptions of small girls were not due solely to perceptions of age differences.

According to an additional analysis of variance, height of the child (but not which child) affected mothers' assignments of punishment for wrongdoing, $F(2, 102) = 3.68$, $p < .03$. Small girls were assigned less punishment than tall or average girls, $F(1, 102) = 5.03$ and $3.12, p < .02$, and .08, respectively. Mean assignments of punishment were 11.95, 10.75, and 6.50 minutes for tall, average, and small girls, respectively. When the effects of perceived age of the child were covaried, the main effect of height was still marginally significant, $F(2, 101) = 2.74, p < .07$. Mothers assigned more punishment to the tall children than the small children, $F(1, 101) = 4.36, p < .04$. None of the other comparisons between height groups was significant.

EXPERIMENT 3

The results of Experiments 1 and 2 are consistent with the conclusion that mothers have different expectations for children, especially boys, based

Table II. Experiment 2 Competence Ratings[a]

Item	Univariate F	Means[b]			Simple effects F[c]	
		Tall	Average	Small	Tall vs. small	Average vs. small
3. Understanding another person's point of view (how another person feels and thinks)	6.58[d] (5.53[d])	3.55	3.15	4.09	4.77[c] (4.36[c])	12.20[c] (10.10[d])
4. Being independent (rather than dependent and seeking help from adults)	5.06[d] (5.14[d])	3.16	3.00	3.72	5.24[c] (5.43[c])	7.56[d] (7.76[d])
5. Not crying when frustrated	3.13[c] (2.42[f])	3.66	3.70	4.23	4.45[c] (3.76[c])	3.46[f]
7. Taking care of her own needs, like getting herself water and picking up her toys	3.41[c] (2.20)	2.82	2.60	3.14	3.46[f] (2.76[f])	7.95[f] (5.13[f])
11. Being able to concentrate on a boring task	3.66[d] (2.48[f])	4.13	3.85	4.56		6.05[d] (3.83[d])

[a]Numbers in parentheses represent F values with the effects of perceived age covaried.
[b]Low values indicate higher levels of competence. There were no simple effects F for tall vs. average.
[c]$p < .001$.
[d]$p < .01$.
[e]$p < .05$.
[f]$p < .10$.

on child size—expectations that might influence level of parental demands for competence and mature functioning and, consequently, subsequent social and cognitive development. Experiment 3 was designed to see if preschoolers varying in size differ in terms of cognitive capacities (performance on Piagetian tasks), peer acceptance, and peer evaluations of competence. Based on the literature reviewed, and the fact that maternal attributions of competence were more strongly related to height for boys than girls, tall preschool boys were expected to be more cognitively and socially competent than smaller boys, and the relationship between size and competence was expected to be greater for boys than for girls.

Subjects

The participants were 27 girls (mean age = 57 months) and 36 boys (mean age = 60 months) in four preschool classes for 4-5-year-olds. All children except 4 were Caucasian, and all came from a middle-class suburban area.

Procedure

The procedure included three parts: measurement of size, assessment of Piagetian logical skills, and participation in a sociometric task.

All children were measured (to the nearest quarter inch) and weighed (to the nearest pound). To assess logical development, the children were administered (with wooden beads) a Piagetian one-to-one correspondence task and two conservation-of-number tasks. Wording of the questioning across the two conservation-of-number tasks was counterbalanced. The experimenter was unaware of any specific hypotheses when administering the tasks.

Sociometric evaluations were obtained from all but 1 child, who refused to participate. With the use of photographs of all the children in class, children were asked to indicate who was good at playing games, good at making art projects, and who was smart. The children were asked to indicate their first three choices. Finally, with the use of the sociometric measure of popularity developed by Asher, Singleton, Tinsley, and Hymel (1979), the children were asked to indicate by sorting pictures of their classmates into three piles how much they liked to play with their peers.

Coding and Interrater Reliability

Children's performance on the Piagetian tasks was coded according to a 4-point scale (1 = the child could do none of the tasks, 4 = the child could do all three tasks). Interrater reliability for scoring of tasks performance was 98%.

Each child received three scores for each sociometric question—the mean rating assigned to the child by female classmates, mean rating assigned by male classmates, and mean rating for the combined sample of classmates. For the items involving three choices, the scoring system was as follows: 3 for a first-choice nomination, 2 for a second choice, and 1 for a third choice. The Asher *et al.* sociometric measure of popularity was also scored on a 3-point system. Sociometric scores were standardized within each class (standard Z scores) for analyses.

RESULTS

Piagetian Measures. Since both weight and age covary with height, the relationship between height and performance on the Piagetian tasks was assessed with correlations partialing out the effects of both age (in months) and weight. According to the partial correlation coefficients, tallness was significantly related to higher performance on the logical tasks for boys, partial $r(32) = .46$, $p < .004$, but not for girls, partial $r(23) = -.10$. As might be expected, the partial correlations were slightly more positive when the effects of age were not controlled.

Sociometric Evaluations. The relationships between height and peer sociometric evaluations were assessed by computing partial correlation coefficients controlling for the effects of age and weight. There were relatively few relationships between height and peer evaluations of competence. Small boys were viewed by boys (and the combined sample of peers of both sexes) as more able at art projects than tall boys, $r(32) = -.36$ and $-.39$, respectively, $p < .05$. Tall boys were perceived by female classmates as smarter than smaller boys, $r(32) = .42$, $p < .015$. Height was unrelated to peer evaluations of girls' competence.

Popularity (as measured by peer evaluations) was related to height for both sexes. Tall boys tended to be better liked by boys (but not girls) than were smaller boys, $r(32) = .31$, $p < .07$ (controlling for age and height). Similarly, large girls were better liked by boys than smaller girls, $r(32) = .48$, $p < .02$. The patterns of correlations for the sociometric and popularity measures were virtually unchanged when the effects of age were not partialed out.

DISCUSSION

According to the data in Experiments 1 and 2, mothers of preschool children hold different expectations for children of different heights (especially boys), even when the effects of perceived age are controlled. According to the data in Experiment 3, boys' size is related to their logical capacities, and taller boys and girls are preferred as playmates by male classmates. Height was not highly related to peer evaluations of competence, although tall boys were rated as smarter than smaller boys by female classmates (but as less able at art projects).

The data concerning height in Experiment 3 (in terms of both the direction of most of the findings and the sex differences in the strength of the data) are consistent with the finding in Experiments 1 and 2 that mothers of toddlers attributed more competence to larger than smaller toddlers, and attributed fewer differences in competence to girls of varying heights than to boys. If adults expect a larger child to be more competent than a smaller child, they may provide differential reinforcement and express different expectations for children varying in height. These expectations would be likely to influence boys' social and cognitive behaviors by age 4, and might be reinforced by others' reactions to the child. In brief, since tall toddlers, especially boys, seem to elicit more positive attributions than smaller children, it is not surprising that tall preschoolers are at an advantage in terms of social (popularity) and cognitive (logical ability) competence.

The pattern of relationships between preschoolers' height and peer judgments of competence in Experiment 3 is less clear than the data concerning competence on logical tasks and assessments of peer preference for play. Tall boys, in comparison to smaller boys, were perceived as smarter (by female classmates), but as less competent at doing art projects (by boys and the combined sample of classmates). None of the relationships was significant for girls. This pattern makes sense if one considers the fact that art projects such as drawing and painting typically are performed more frequently by females during the preschool years (Connor & Serbin, 1977). What could be occurring is that peers view tall boys as being more masculine (a type of competence) and as less likely to "make good art projects." If this were true, the pattern of findings relating to peer assessments of competence would be consistent with the overall pattern of data indicating that tall children, especially boys, are viewed as more competent, and behave more competently, than smaller children. However, it is unclear if peer assessments of competence reflect genuine differences in behavior or are merely an early manifestation of the attributional bias in favor of taller children noted in Experiments 1 and 2.

It is not entirely clear why the dimension of height influenced mothers' attributions regarding boys more than mothers' attributions of girls. Nor is it clear why the effect of height on adults' attributions was more pronounced for *tall* boys and *small* girls. Perhaps, because of a cultural emphasis on males', but not females', strength and size, large boys stand out more than large girls and are particularly likely to be viewed as "special." Furthermore, the association between size (particularly large size) and competence may be stronger for males because of the greater concern for male competence and dominance in Western culture (most of the research on the relationship between height and either achievement or others' attributions has been conducted with male stimuli). While tallness is viewed as an asset for men and would tend to be associated with positive attributes, tall women frequently are at a social disadvantage in our culture (consider the common expectation that females should date someone as tall or taller than themselves).

The fact that the effect of height on adult attributions is more pronounced for small than tall girls (small girls differed from average-sized as well as tall girls, while average-sized and tall girls did not differ) also may be due to cultural stereotypes. In our culture, small girls are frequently seen as being especially feminine (i.e., as being dainty, cute, defenseless, and dependent). In other words, small girls are stereotypically "feminine," just as large boys are stereotypically "masculine." Thus, it is not surprising that small, not tall, girls were most likely to be seen as different from other girls. Furthermore, if one considers dependence and "helplessness" as desirable traits for females, the mothers' view of the small girls was not especially negative (particularly when the effects of perceived age were controlled). Rather, the small girls, like the tall boys, were viewed in ways consistent with sex-role stereotypes (e.g., the small girls were seen as being relatively dependent and likely to cry when frustrated).

The relationship of height to boys', but not girls', logical abilities (Experiment 3) also may be due, in part, to prevailing sex-role stereotypes. It is a common stereotype that it is more important for men than women to be intellectually competent, and some data suggest that parents are more active in their attempts to shape their sons' cognitive skills than their daughters' (e.g., Block, Block, & Harrington, Note 1). Thus, it seems logical to assume that adults' expectations regarding cognitive competencies would be more likely to be communicated to boys than girls and, consequently, would be more likely to differentially influence boys' than girls' cognitive development (depending on their size).

It seems reasonable to assume that socializers' attributions regarding the competence of children varying in size cause behavioral differences such as those noted in Experiment 3, rather than reflect actual early behavioral differences. It is possible that cause and effect are reversed; that is, large children (especially boys) are biologically more competent than smaller children, and both adults' attributions and the children's actual behaviors reflect this reality. For example, one could argue that large children, like animals (Jerrison, 1973), have larger brains than smaller children and, thus, are more competent. However, IQ appears to be unrelated to size among young children (Bayley, 1956). Furthermore, if larger children possessed a biological advantage, one would expect tall girls (like tall boys) to be much more competent than smaller girls on behavioral, attributional, and sociometric measures, and heavier children (whose brains could be heavier) to outperform children who are less heavy. Since these patterns of results generally did not occur, it is unlikely that tall children have an innate advantage over smaller children; their superior cognitive performance and somewhat greater popularity is more likely due to feedback from their social environment. It is also likely that the mothers in Experiments 1 and 2 attributed more competence to tall preschool children due to (a) the fact that our culture values tallness, and/or (b) a perceived association between size and competence for older children and adults (real or not).

For girls, but not for boys, there was an effect of size of a child on adults' assignment of punishment for a hypothetical transgression. This difference probably was due, in part, to the fact that small girls (but not small boys) were perceived as being the youngest children. Since younger children generally are held less responsible for wrongdoing and frequently are punished less harshly than are older children, it is logical that mothers would recommend less punishment for children who they believed to be especially young. However, since mothers assigned marginally more punishment to tall than small girls even when the effects of age were covaried, it appears that more than size alone contributed to maternal choice of punishment. While the reason for this finding is not entirely clear, it is likely that mothers simply expect large girls to be more capable of controlling their behavior than smaller girls and, thus, punish large girls' deviations more harshly. However, there is no simple explanation of why this would not also hold true for boys.

In summary, the data from the present studies are consistent with the conclusion that early differences in children's physical size influence adults' expectations of toddlers' competencies and are associated with actual differences in behavior by the preschool years. While there currently are no data bearing directly on the issue of cause and effect, adults' attributions based on children's size probably have some effect on children's social and cognitive development. This is an issue which needs to be addressed by researchers.

REFERENCES

Asher, S., Singleton, L., Tinsley, B., & Hymel, S. A reliable sociometric measure for preschool children. *Developmental Psychology,* 1979, *15,* 443-444.

Barker, R. G., Wright, B. A., & Gonick, M. R. *Adjustment to physical handicap and illness: A survey of the social psychology of physique and disability.* New York: Social Science Research Council, 1946.

Bayley, N. Individual patterns of development. *Child Development,* 1956, *27,* 45-74.

Connor, V. M., & Serbin, L. A. Behaviorally based masculine and feminine-activity preference scales for preschoolers: Correlates with other classroom behaviors and cognitive tests. *Child Development,* 1977, *48,* 1411-1416.

Dannenmaier, W. D., & Thurmin, F. J. Authority status as a factor in perceptual distortion of size. *Journal of Social Psychology,* 1964, *63,* 361-365.

Gowin, E. B. *The executive and his control of men.* New York: Macmillan, 1972.

Jerrison, J. J. Evolution of brain and intelligence. New York: Academic Press, 1973.

Meyerson, L. Somatopsychology of physical disability. In W. Cruickshank (Ed.), *Psychology of exceptional children.* Englewood Cliffs, N.J.: Prentice-Hall, 1963.

Prieto, A. G. Junior high school students' height and its relationship to academic and social performance (Doctoral dissertation, University of Missouri, Columbia, 1974). *Dissertation Abstracts International,* 1975, *36,* 222A (University Microfilms No. 75-10, 638).

Wilson, P. R. Perceptual distortion of height as a function of ascribed academic status. *Journal of Social Psychology,* 1968, *74,* 97-102.

Wylie, R. C. *The self-concept: A critical survey of pertinent research literature.* Lincoln: University of Nebraska Press, 1961.

[33]

Gender-related Schemata and Constructive Memory in Children

Lynn S. Liben and Margaret L. Signorella

Pennsylvania State University

LIBEN, LYNN S., and SIGNORELLA, MARGARET L. *Gender-related Schemata and Constructive Memory in Children.* CHILD DEVELOPMENT, 1980, **51**, 11–18. To examine the relationship between children's gender attitudes and memories, 57 first and second graders were shown pictures of people in various occupations and activities and were tested for recognition memory. Of the original 60 pictures, 20 were traditional (e.g., female secretary), 20 nontraditional (e.g., male secretary), and 20 neutral (e.g., man reading a newspaper). Children were given a recognition task with 30 of the original pictures and 30 new pictures, in which the sex of the actor had been reversed. A stereotyping measure was also given to classify children as having high or low gender stereotypes. Results showed that on new items, the low number of false recognitions precluded meaningful subject or task effects. On old items, children with relatively highly stereotyped gender attitudes recognized significantly more traditional than nontraditional pictures when the actor was male. Children with low gender stereotypes did not show this differential responding. Results suggest that children's memories are affected by their own gender attitudes and by the differential evaluation of men and women engaged in nontraditional activities.

Gender identity is a pervasive social classification that is established early in childhood (Kohlberg 1966; Marcus & Overton 1978) and is an important aspect of the self system (Money & Ehrhardt 1972; Sherif 1976). Children as young as kindergartners have demonstrated extensive knowledge of gender stereotypes (e.g., Williams, Bennett, & Best 1975). Although many researchers have examined the effect of gender and related attitudes on occupational choice (e.g., Bacon & Lerner 1975; Looft 1971; Papalia & Tennent 1975); verbal, mathematical, and spatial skills (e.g., Connor & Serbin 1977; Dwyer 1974); and school achievement (e.g., Fitzpatrick 1978), relatively few investigators have examined the association between these attitudes and memory. The research described here was focused on the latter relationship.

The theoretical context for the present work is derived from the constructive view of memory proposed by Bartlett (1932). Bartlett suggested that an individual's reproduction of verbal or graphic material is controlled not only by the characteristics of the original stimulus but by the subject's own attitudes and knowledge (schemata) as well. In his early work, Bartlett showed that adults had difficulty recalling ideas that were culturally foreign to them, and that, when reproducing stories and pictures, they tended to modify the original stimulus to fit their own cultural knowledge and attitudes.

Recent research on adults has expanded and refined Bartlett's original notion of schemata. Cognitive psychologists have formulated a variety of schema theories (e.g., see Bobrow & Norman 1975; Neisser 1976; Rumelhart 1975), studying the effects of schemata on cognitive processes, including the initial recognition of stimuli (e.g., Minsky 1975) and the retention of prose (e.g., Bransford & Franks 1971; Sulin & Dooling 1974; Thorndyke 1977). Social psychologists have also been interested in cognitive schemata and their role in encoding and remembering social material (e.g.,

Order of authorship was determined by a coin toss: This paper represents a completely collaborative effort. Portions of this research were presented at the meetings of the Association for Women in Psychology, Pittsburgh, March 1978. We thank the students, teachers, and staff at Elm Grove School, Peters Township School District, McMurray, Pennsylvania, for their cooperation; Wesley Jamison and Maria E. Vegega for their assistance in data analysis; and Richard M. Lerner, Carolyn W. Sherif, and anonymous reviewers for their comments on the manuscript. Requests for reprints should be addressed to Lynn S. Liben, College of Human Development, Division of Individual and Family Studies, Pennsylvania State University, University Park, Pa. 16802.

12   Child Development

Cantor & Mischel 1977; Tsujimoto, Wilde, & Robertson 1978). Consistent with Bartlett's theory, subjects show better memory for self-related material (e.g., Markus 1977; Rogers, Kuiper, & Kirker 1977; Rogers, Rogers, & Kuiper 1979).

Recent investigations of children's memory have also been conducted within the constructive perspective, but in most of this work children's memories have been studied as a function of cognitive skills and knowledge rather than as a function of attitudes and beliefs (e.g., see reviews by Kail [1979]; Liben [1977]; Ornstein [1978]; Paris & Lindauer [1977]). Although children's memory and gender attitudes have not been studied in the context of the constructive theory of memory, some empirical data on the relationship between memory and gender-related material have been reported. Nadelman (1970, 1974), for example, asked children in Britain and the United States to recall pictures of sex-typed activities (e.g., ironing, fixing a car) and to indicate preferences among these activities. In general, children gave predominantly same-sex preferences and recalled more same-sex than opposite-sex items.

In a later study, Kail and Levine (1976) used Wicken's release from proactive inhibition (PI) paradigm and demonstrated that 7–10-year-old children with same-sex preferences in the Nadelman preference task showed release from PI upon a change from masculine to feminine words (or vice versa). In contrast, children with cross-sex preferences did not show release from PI under the same conditions. These results suggest that children who are strongly identified with their own sex (as measured by activity preference) encode words in memory along a masculine-feminine dimension.

Two recent studies have examined children's memory for verbal stories as a function of the sex appropriateness of the characters' activities and traits. Jennings (1975) told stories to groups of 4- and 5-year-old children. The main characters in these stories followed either usual or unusual behaviors for their sex. Significantly more children preferred the story with the usual sex-role behavior, but recall of themes was better from the story with unusual sex-role behavior. The findings from this study are difficult to interpret, however, because of various procedural difficulties (see Koblinsky, Cruse, & Sugawara 1978). In the most recent study relating gender stereotyping to memory, Koblinsky et al. (1978) gave fifth-grade children a series of stories, each with a major boy and girl character who exhibited both stereotypic and reverse-stereotypic activities and traits. Subjects remembered more of the stereotypic than nonstereotypic activities and traits, a finding consistent with the constructive theory of memory cited above.

The present research draws on and extends the work reviewed above in several ways. First, with respect to the constructive theory of memory, children's memories are studied here as a function of attitudinal schemata. As noted above, this contrasts with earlier developmental work derived from constructive theory in which children's memories have been examined as a function of cognitive schemes such as logical abilities (e.g., Liben & Posnansky 1977) or world knowledge (e.g., Brown, Smiley, Day, Townsend, & Lawton 1977).

The present investigation also extends past work on the relation between gender stereotypes and memory in several ways. Most critically, we assessed individual children's attitudes with respect to gender stereotypes and tested their memory for traditional and nontraditional stimuli. Our approach contrasts with early investigators who had either compared memory for traditional versus nontraditional material without a measure of individual children's attitudes (namely, Jennings 1975; Koblinsky et al. 1978) or had assessed individuals' attitudes but had not included stimuli that could be considered nontraditional (namely, Kail & Levine 1976; Nadelman 1970, 1974). Furthermore, of those investigators who did assess attitudes, Nadelman (1970, 1974) could not relate memory to individual children's activity preferences because virtually every child expressed a same-sex preference, while Kail and Levine (1976) examined preferences in relation to the use of a masculine-feminine dimension for encoding words but did not study retention over longer intervals.

The present study was, therefore, designed to investigate the issue raised by Bartlett (1932), namely, whether children would remember stimuli that are congruent with their attitudes better than they remember stimuli that are incongruent with their attitudes. More specifically, it was hypothesized that children with highly stereotyped gender-related attitudes would have greater difficulty remembering pictures that violate cultural gender stereotypes than remembering pictures consonant with cultural stereotypes. Furthermore, it was hypothesized that if some of the nontraditional pictures were replaced by traditional pictures on a recognition test, children with highly stereotyped attitudes would falsely recognize the traditional substitutions more often than substitutions of nontraditional for traditional pictures. In contrast, no differential stimulus effects were expected in children with relatively unstereotyped attitudes.

Stimulus materials were pictures of men and women engaged in various activities. Traditional items showed males engaged in "masculine" activities and females engaged in "feminine" activities, while nontraditional items showed males engaged in "feminine" activities and females in "masculine" activities. Males and females were also shown in gender-neutral activities to determine if absolute levels of memory were comparable in children who had high and low gender stereotypes.

Method

Subjects and Procedural Overview

The subjects were 36 first graders (19 boys and 17 girls) and 24 second graders (13 boys and 11 girls) from a predominantly white, middle-class school near Pittsburgh, Pennsylvania. The mean age of the first graders was 7-0 (range = 6-2 to 7-11) and of the second graders was 8-2 (range = 7-5 to 9-0).

Each child was seen individually by Signorella in a single session which lasted approximately 30 min. All children were given the memory task and the stereotyping measure described below. The stereotyping measure was given last to prevent it from alerting children to the gender dimensions of the memory stimuli.

Memory Task

Materials.—In the traditional pictures used in the present study, the sex of the person ("actor") performing an activity or occupation was the same as the sex traditionally associated with that activity or occupation; in the nontraditional pictures, the sex of the person was opposite that usually associated with the activity or profession. To determine empirically which activities are considered masculine, feminine, or neutral in this culture, a list of 131 activities and occupations was compiled from articles about stereotyping in children's books, from data about the sex composition of occupations, and from common classroom books and materials. This list was given to 43 male and female college students who were asked to rate each item according to whether most people would consider it masculine, feminine, or neutral. Ratings were consistent with pre-

vious stereotype research with both children and adults (e.g., Garrett, Ein, & Tremaine 1977; Koblinsky et al. 1978; Shinar 1975). On the basis of consistent ratings ($M = 84\%$ agreement; range $= 70\%-100\%$) and availability of pictures, 20 judged masculine, 20 judged feminine, and 20 judged neutral activities and occupations were chosen for use in the present study. Included, for example, were the following items: fire fighter, directing traffic (masculine); nurse, sewing (feminine); singer, reading a book (neutral). A complete list of items used may be obtained from the authors.

Stimuli were simple black-and-white line drawings (adapted from a variety of sources, e.g., classroom materials on occupations, the Peabody Picture Vocabulary Test) on 4 × 6-inch (10.2 × 15.2-cm) cards. Two decks of 60 cards each were prepared, one an acquisition deck and the second a recognition deck. The acquisition deck contained 20 traditional items (10 male actors engaged in masculine activities; 10 female actors engaged in feminine activities), 20 nontraditional items (10 male actors engaged in feminine activities; 10 female actors engaged in masculine activities), and 20 neutral items (10 with male actors and 10 with female actors).

The recognition deck contained 30 old pictures that were identical to those in the acquisition deck in all respects (10 traditional, 10 nontraditional, 10 neutral) and 30 new pictures which had been altered by changing the sex of the actor in the picture. Thus, there were 10 new traditional pictures which had previously been nontraditional, 10 new nontraditional pictures which had previously been traditional, and 10 neutral pictures which had previously been neutral, but with a person of the other sex.

Procedure.—After establishing rapport, the experimenter explained that she was trying to understand more about how children remember, and she would ask the child to remember some pictures. If the child agreed to participate (all children whose parents consented to their participation also agreed to participate), the experimenter took out the acquisition deck and told the child to look very carefully at the pictures because he or she would be asked about them later on. The experimenter then showed each card, one at a time, at the rate of 1 per sec. After the entire deck of 60 cards had been presented, the child and experimenter played a block-stacking game ("Blockhead") to fill a 5-min delay interval.

14   Child Development

Following the 5-min delay, the recognition deck was taken out and the experimenter said, "I have some pictures over here. Some of these pictures are *exactly* like the ones you saw before, and some are different. I'd like you to look at each picture and say 'yes' if it's *exactly* like the one you saw before, and 'no' if it's different. Okay?" The child was then shown the pictures in the recognition deck one at a time, and the child responded yes or no to each one. A break was taken (another game of Blockhead) halfway through the recognition deck to prevent fatigue.

The order of presentation of the pictures in both decks was randomized for each subject.

Stereotyping Measure

Materials and procedure.—The stereotyping measure was a modification of a measure developed by Flerx, Fidler, and Rogers (1976) to assess children's attitudes about what activities can be done by men and women. A list of 35 activities and occupations was chosen from items used by Flerx et al. (1976), Nadelman (1970), and from those items rated by adults for the present study. Included were 14 stereotypically masculine and 14 stereotypically feminine items, along with seven neutral items used as fillers. Of these, eight had also been included as items on the memory task.

Three cardboard stands containing black-and-white line drawings of people—one of two men, one of two women, and one of a man and a woman—were placed in front of the child. The position of the pairs of figures was varied for each child. Children were told, "I've got a list of activities here, and I'd like you to tell me whether you think these things can be done by men [pointing to the pair of men], by women [pointing to the pair of women], or by both men and women [pointing to the male-female pair]. Let's practice on a few. Can you show me who can be a Daddy? Show me who can be a Mommy? Show me who has two legs." The child was then asked about each of the 35 items, prefaced by "Show me who can. . . ." The list was presented in a different random order for every child.

Scoring.—The stereotyping score was the total number of "both men and women" responses given to the stereotyped (masculine and feminine) items. Those who gave at or below the median number (7) of "both" answers were classified as highly stereotyped in their attitudes, while those who gave above the median number of "both" answers were classi-

fied as low in stereotypic attitudes. This median score was based on the total group of children (i.e., boys and girls combined), which resulted in approximately equal numbers of boys ($N = 16$) and girls ($N = 13$) being classified as highly stereotyped. (Medians derived for each sex separately were virtually identical: 7 for boys and 8 for girls.) Kuder-Richardson reliability for the measure was .83.

Results

Three boys (one first grader and two second graders) who claimed to recognize virtually every item (between 92% and 97% of both old and new items) were excluded from analysis.

As explained earlier, neutral items had been included in the memory task as a check on the comparability of memory across subject groups when gender appropriateness was not at issue. Recall of neutral items was, therefore, examined in a preliminary analysis. This analysis showed that performance was comparable across groups. Therefore, neutral items were eliminated from subsequent analyses and are not discussed further. Other preliminary analyses also revealed no differences between first- and second-grade children, and thus subjects were pooled across grades in the remaining analyses.

Because recognition responses to old items represent correct responses, whereas recognition responses to new items represent incorrect responses (i.e., false recognitions), the recognition scores for the old and new items were analyzed separately (see Lindauer & Paris 1976). In one analysis, however, the old and new items were combined in order to ascertain that old items were recognized significantly more often than new items. For this analysis, the number of items identified as "old" served as the dependent variable in a five-way, unweighted means analysis of variance, specifically a 2 (sex of subject) × 2 (subject's stereotyping level: high, low) × 2 (old versus new) × 2 (picture type: traditional, nontraditional) × 2 (sex of actor in picture) ANOVA. In this design, the first two factors were between subjects, and the last three were within subjects. Means for each measure are given, by group, in table 1. Of major interest from this analysis was the significant effect of old-new, $F(1,53) = 118.80$, $p < .001$, showing that the old pictures ($M = 3.4$) were recognized significantly more often than the new pictures ($M = 1.7$). As explained above, other effects are more meaningfully examined in the separate analyses of old and new items which are described below.

Old Pictures

The analysis of the old items revealed a significant stereotyping × picture type × sex of actor interaction, $F(1,53) = 4.15$, $p < .05$, displayed in figure 1. Newman-Keuls post hoc

analyses showed that among the subjects with low stereotyping scores (those who have a large number of "both" responses), there were no significant differences in the number recognized as a function of picture type or sex of the actor in the picture. Among the highly stereotyped subjects, however, traditional pictures with a male actor were recognized sig-

TABLE 1

MEAN NUMBER OF RECOGNITIONS BY SUBJECT GROUP AND PICTURE CHARACTERISTICS

| | OLD PICTURES | | | | NEW PICTURES | | | |
| | Traditional | | Nontraditional | | Traditional | | Nontraditional | |
GROUP	Male	Female	Male	Female	Male	Female	Male	Female
High stereotype:								
Boys ($N=16$)	4.4	3.0	3.2	3.1	2.0	1.6	1.5	1.9
	(.9)	(1.2)	(1.2)	(1.3)	(.8)	(1.3)	(1.5)	(1.5)
Girls ($N=13$)	4.2	3.7	2.8	3.9	1.8	1.9	1.5	2.1
	(1.2)	(1.0)	(1.2)	(.9)	(1.1)	(1.2)	(1.2)	(1.8)
Low stereotype:								
Boys ($N=13$)	3.8	3.4	3.2	3.5	2.0	1.5	1.4	1.5
	(1.1)	(1.4)	(1.4)	(.8)	(.8)	(1.3)	(1.2)	(1.6)
Girls ($N=15$)	3.5	3.1	3.2	2.9	1.7	1.3	1.6	1.4
	(1.7)	(1.2)	(1.1)	(1.3)	(1.3)	(1.2)	(1.2)	(1.1)

NOTE.—Numbers in parentheses are SDs.

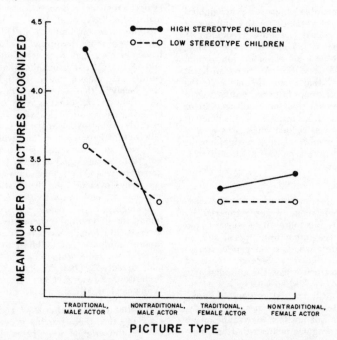

FIG. 1.—Mean number of pictures recognized as a function of subject's stereotyping and picture characteristics.

16 Child Development

nificantly more often than nontraditional pictures with a male actor ($p < .05$). No differences were evident in these subjects when the actor in the picture was female.

Also significant was the three-way sex of actor × sex of subject × stereotyping interaction, $F(1,53) = 5.14$, $p < .05$. Newman-Keuls post hoc analyses ($p < .05$) showed that boys with highly stereotyped attitudes remembered more items with male actors than with female actors ($M = 3.8$ vs. 3.0), whereas boys with low stereotyping scores did not remember these items differentially ($M = 3.5$ vs. 3.4). For girls, items with female actors were remembered significantly more often by girls with highly stereotyped attitudes than by girls with low stereotypes ($M = 3.8$ vs. 3.0), while items with male actors were not remembered differentially by the two groups ($M = 3.5$ vs. 3.4).

Subsumed by these three-way interactions were a significant two-way interaction of picture type × sex of actor, $F(1,53) = 13.38$, $p < .001$, and a significant main effect of picture type, $F(1,53) = 9.08$, $p < .01$.

New Pictures

The comparable four-way unweighted means analysis of variance on the number of new items recognized (i.e., false recognitions) revealed only one significant effect, specifically, a picture type × sex of actor interaction, $F(1,53) = 5.65$, $p < .05$. A Newman-Keuls analysis showed that when the actor in the picture was male, more false recognitions were given on traditional than nontraditional items ($M = 1.9$ and 1.5, respectively), whereas when the actor was female, there was no difference in the number of false recognitions as a function of picture type ($M = 1.6$ and 1.7).

Discussion

The hypotheses derived from the constructive theory of memory were supported by the pattern of results found in responses to old items on the recognition test. Specifically, as predicted, children who had low gender stereotype scores did not show different levels of memory performance across the different picture types, whereas children with highly stereotyped gender attitudes did respond differentially to the different picture types. Specifically, boys with high, but not low, stereotypes were more likely to recognize pictures that had male actors than female actors. Even more important, highly stereotyped children responded

differently to traditional and nontraditional pictures. Specifically, these children remembered fewer of the pictures that violated gender stereotypes of this culture than pictures that were consistent with gender stereotypes, although only on those items with a male actor (as shown by the significant stereotyping × picture type × sex of actor interaction). Interestingly, this result was *not* further modified by the sex of the subject. These findings suggest that both boys and girls find that males in feminine activities are more incongruent than are females in masculine activities. The finding that there were more false recognitions of traditional than nontraditional items with a male but not with a female actor is consistent with this conclusion.

Koblinsky et al. (1978) reported a similar effect in their study of fifth-grade children's memories for behaviors and traits of male and female story characters. They found that subjects were particularly poor at remembering the feminine traits of male characters. The finding that the violation of male stereotypes has a greater effect on children's memories than the violation of female stereotypes might reflect stronger prohibitions in this culture against cross-sex behaviors for males than females (Koblinsky et al. 1978). Consistent with this interpretation, Feinman (1974) found that adults were more disapproving of cross-sex behavior in boys than in girls. Similarly, Taynor and Deaux (1975) concluded that men in our culture may have a smaller latitude of acceptable behavior than do women on the basis of their data showing that women who did well in a masculine situation were judged to be more deserving of reward than were men who did well in the same situation, while men who did well in a feminine situation were not judged to be deserving of reward. It should be noted, however, that some investigators have not found evidence for devaluation of males engaged in feminine activities (e.g., O'Leary & Donoghue 1978). Another possible explanation of the differential response to the violation of male and female stereotypes found in the present study is that children in the United States learn male stereotypes earlier than female stereotypes (Best, Williams, Cloud, Davis, Robertson, Edwards, Giles, & Fowles 1977; Williams et al. 1975).

Although the patterns of recognitions of old items did, then, provide general confirmation of the original hypotheses derived from the constructive theory of memory, the data from the new items did not conform to predictions. On the basis of constructive theory, memory distortions were predicted such that highly stereotyped children were expected to show differential patterns of false recognitions across items, whereas the children with low stereotypes were not expected to respond differentially. More specifically, children with high stereotypes would be expected to make false recognitions of pictures that were originally nontraditional but which had been changed to traditional on the recognition task. The stimulus change from nontraditional to traditional should parallel the process thought to occur when attitudes distort memories. The failure to find differential responding to new items as a function of stereotyping is probably attributable to the generally good performance on the new items, since subjects successfully rejected most new items. Perhaps the number of false recognitions could be increased by lengthening the delay interval, by making the pictures more complex, or by changing subjects' response criteria through directions that emphasize the importance of not missing any old items. Alternatively, since picture recognition is notoriously good (e.g., Brown & Scott 1971), another more sensitive technique that could be used to tap memory distortions would be to use reproduction tasks rather than recognition tasks. It must be realized, however, that reproduction tasks with complex material are likely to present procedural difficulties with young children.

In sum, it appears that children's memories are distorted by their gender-related attitudes. This finding supports interpretations which view the self system as a set of cognitive schemata or interrelated attitudes which may affect the evaluation and processing of incoming information (cf. Markus 1977; Rogers et al. 1977; Sherif & Sherif 1969). In addition, the effects observed in the present study were consistent with Bartlett's constructive theory, although additional research is needed to determine more precisely the boundary conditions of these effects. It should also be noted that, although the present investigation was focused on the effects of attitudinal schemata on memory, these schemata may also affect the initial interpretation of stimuli. For example, a picture intended to depict a male secretary may instead be interpreted by the viewer as a picture of a typewriter repairman. (Reinterpretations of this kind would serve to reduce differences in performance between traditional and nontraditional items since so-called nontraditional items would actually be processed

as traditional by the highly stereotyped viewer.) If, indeed, knowledge (via encoding and/or storage) depends not only on characteristics of the stimuli but also on attitudinal schemata of the viewer, both must be taken into account if intervention programs (e.g., those aimed at encouraging occupational choices unrestricted by gender) are to prove successful.

References

Bacon, C., & Lerner, R. M. Effects of maternal employment status on the development of vocational-role perception in females. *Journal of Genetic Psychology*, 1975, **126**, 187–193.

Bartlett, F. C. *Remembering*. Cambridge: Cambridge University Press, 1932.

Best, D. L.; Williams, J. E.; Cloud, J. M.; Davis, S. W.; Robertson, L. S.; Edwards, J. R.; Giles, H.; & Fowles, J. Development of sex-trait stereotypes among young children in the United States, England, and Ireland. *Child Development*, 1977, **48**, 1375–1384.

Bobrow, D. G., & Norman, D. A. Some principles of memory schemata. In D. G. Bobrow & A. Collins (Eds.), *Representation and understanding*. New York: Academic Press, 1975.

Bransford, J. D., & Franks, J. J. The abstraction of linguistic ideas. *Cognitive Psychology*, 1971, **2**, 331–350.

Brown, A. L., & Scott, M. S. Recognition memory for pictures in preschool children. *Journal of Experimental Child Psychology*, 1971, **11**, 401–412.

Brown, A. L.; Smiley, S. S.; Day, J. D.; Townsend, M. A.; & Lawton, S. C. Intrusion of a thematic idea in children's comprehension and retention of stories. *Child Development*, 1977, **48**, 1454–1466.

Cantor, N., & Mischel, W. Traits as prototypes: effects on recognition memory. *Journal of Personality and Social Psychology*, 1977, **35**, 38–48.

Connor, J. M., & Serbin, L. A. Behaviorally based masculine- and feminine-activity-preference scales for preschoolers: correlates with other classroom behaviors and cognitive tests. *Child Development*, 1977, **48**, 1411–1415.

Dwyer, C. A. Influence of children's sex role standards on reading and arithmetic achievement. *Journal of Educational Psychology*, 1974, **66**, 811–816.

Feinman, S. Approval of cross-sex-role behavior. *Psychological Reports*, 1974, **35**, 643–648.

Fitzpatrick, J. L. Academic underachievement, other-direction, and attitudes toward women's roles in bright adolescent females. *Journal of Educational Psychology*, 1978, **70**, 645–650.

18 Child Development

Flerx, V. C.; Fidler, D. S.; & Rogers, R. W. Sex role stereotypes: developmental aspects and early intervention. *Child Development,* 1976, **47,** 998–1007.

Garrett, C. S.; Ein, P. L.; & Tremaine, L. The development of gender stereotyping of adult occupations in elementary school children. *Child Development,* 1977, **48,** 507–512.

Jennings, S. A. Effects of sex typing in children's stories on preference and recall. *Child Development,* 1975, **46,** 220–223.

Kail, R. V. *The development of memory in children.* San Francisco: W. H. Freeman, 1979.

Kail, R. V., & Levine, L. E. Encoding processes and sex-role preferences. *Journal of Experimental Child Psychology,* 1976, **21,** 256–263.

Koblinsky, S. G.; Cruse, D. F.; & Sugawara, A. I. Sex-role stereotypes and children's memory for story content. *Child Development,* 1978, **49,** 452–458.

Kohlberg, L. A. A cognitive-developmental analysis of children's sex-role concepts and attitudes. In E. E. Maccoby (Ed.), *The development of sex differences.* Stanford, Calif.: Stanford University, 1966.

Liben, L. S. Memory from a cognitive-developmental perspective: a theoretical and empirical review. In W. Overton & J. Gallagher (Eds.), *Knowledge and development.* Vol. 1. *Advances in research and theory.* New York: Plenum, 1977.

Liben, L. S., & Posnansky, C. J. Inferences on inference: the effects of age, transitive ability, memory load, and lexical factors. *Child Development,* 1977, **48,** 1490–1497.

Lindauer, B. K., & Paris, S. G. Problems with a false recognition paradigm for developmental memory research. *Journal of Experimental Child Psychology,* 1976, **22,** 319–330.

Looft, W. R. Sex differences in the expression of vocational aspiration by elementary school children. *Developmental Psychology,* 1971, **5,** 366.

Marcus, D. E., & Overton, W. F. The development of cognitive gender constancy and sex role preferences. *Child Development,* 1978, **49,** 434–444.

Markus, H. Self-schemata and processing information about the self. *Journal of Personality and Social Psychology,* 1977, **35,** 63–78.

Minsky, M. A framework for representing knowledge. In P. Winston (Ed.), *The psychology of computer vision.* New York: McGraw-Hill, 1975.

Money, J., & Ehrhardt, A. A. *Man and woman, boy and girl.* Baltimore: Johns Hopkins University Press, 1972.

Nadelman, L. Sex identity in London children: memory, knowledge and preference tests. *Human Development,* 1970, **13,** 28–42.

Nadelman, L. Sex identity in American children: memory, knowledge and preference tests. *Developmental Psychology,* 1974, **10,** 413–417.

Neisser, U. *Cognition and reality.* San Francisco: W. H. Freeman, 1976.

O'Leary, V. E., & Donoghue, J. M. Latitudes of masculinity: reactions to sex-role deviance in men. *Journal of Social Issues,* 1978, **34**(1), 17–28.

Ornstein, P. *Memory development in children.* Hillsdale, N.J.: Erlbaum, 1978.

Papalia, D. E., & Tennent, S. S. Vocational aspirations in preschoolers: a manifestation of early sex-role stereotyping. *Sex Roles,* 1975, **1,** 197–199.

Paris, S. G., & Lindauer, B. K. Constructive aspects of children's comprehension and memory. In R. V. Kail, Jr., & J. W. Hagen (Eds.), *Perspectives on the development of memory and cognition.* Hillsdale, N. J.: Erlbaum, 1977.

Rogers, T. B.; Kuiper, N. A.; & Kirker, W. S. Self-reference and the encoding of personal information. *Journal of Personality and Social Psychology,* 1977, **35,** 677–688.

Rogers, T. B.; Rogers, P. J.; & Kuiper, N. A. Evidence for the self as a cognitive prototype: the "false alarms effect." *Personality and Social Psychology Bulletin,* 1979, **5,** 53–56.

Rumelhart, D. E. Notes on a schema for stories. In D. G. Bobrow & A. Collins (Eds.), *Representation and understanding.* New York: Academic Press, 1975.

Sherif, C. W. *Orientation in social psychology.* New York: Harper & Row, 1976.

Sherif, M., & Sherif, C. W. *Social psychology.* New York: Harper & Row, 1969.

Shinar, E. H. Sexual stereotypes of occupations. *Journal of Vocational Behavior,* 1975, **7,** 99–111.

Sulin, R. A., & Dooling, D. J. Intrusion of a thematic idea in retention of prose. *Journal of Experimental Psychology,* 1974, **103,** 255–262.

Taynor, J., & Deaux, K. Equity and perceived sex differences: role behavior as defined by the task, the mode, and the actor. *Journal of Personality and Social Psychology,* 1975, **32,** 381–390.

Thorndyke, P. W. Cognitive structures in comprehension and memory of narrative discourse. *Cognitive Psychology,* 1977, **9,** 77–110.

Tsujimoto, R. N.; Wilde, J.; & Robertson, D. R. Distorted memory for exemplars of a social structure: evidence for schematic memory processes. *Journal of Personality and Social Psychology,* 1978, **36,** 1402–1414.

Williams, J. E.; Bennett, S. M.; & Best, D. L. Awareness and expression of sex stereotypes in young children. *Developmental Psychology,* 1975, **11,** 635–642.

[34]

A Schematic Processing Model of Sex Typing and Stereotyping in Children

Carol Lynn Martin and Charles F. Halverson, Jr.
University of Georgia

MARTIN, CAROL LYNN, and HALVERSON, CHARLES F., JR. *A Schematic Processing Model of Sex Typing and Stereotyping in Children.* CHILD DEVELOPMENT, 1981, **52**, 1119–1134. The thesis of the present paper is that sex stereotyping is a normal cognitive process and is best examined in terms of information-processing constructs. A model is proposed in which stereotypes are assumed to function as schemas that serve to organize and structure information. The particular schemas involved in stereotyping are described, and the functions and biases associated with these schemas are elaborated. Both the development and maintenance of stereotypes are explained using the schematic processing model. The schematic model is found to be useful for explaining many of the results from sex-typing and stereotyping studies, as well as indicating areas needing further investigation. To describe the relation between sex schemas and other types of schemas, a typology is proposed which divides schemas according to whether they are potentially self-defining and according to their salience or availability. Using the typology, stereotyping and sex stereotyping are said to occur because the schemas involved are self-defining and salient. The role of salience in mediating the use of schemas is discussed.

Introduction

Sex typing and stereotyping have been studied in both children and adults. For adults, social psychologists have emphasized process—how such stereotypes influence behavior, cognition, and perception. In contrast, developmental psychologists have tended to ignore process considerations and have instead focused on the acquisition of sex-typing and sex role information. This is not surprising, since both cognitive developmental theory (Kohlberg 1966) and social learning theory (Mischel 1966, 1970) emphasize acquisition. Consequently, little effort has been directed toward a description of how or why sex typing is maintained so tenaciously throughout childhood, and little is known about how sex stereotypes affect children's perceptions, cognitions, and behaviors. In the present paper, we propose a model of sex stereotyping in children that attempts to explain how such stereotypes are acquired, how and why they are maintained, and how they influence behavior, cognition, and perception.

First, to understand the basis for the proposed model, it is necessary to consider how stereotyping has been approached in the past. Until recently, the prevailing view has been that the stereotyping process in both children and adults was different from normal cognitive operations (Cauthen, Robinson, & Krauss, Note 1). The difference was thought to be that stereotyping was faulty or dysfunctional (Lippman 1922). Stereotyping has also been considered the result of inferior judgmental processes (Edwards 1940; Fishman 1956), a kind of pathological thinking (see McCauley, Stitt, & Segal 1980), overgeneralizations, or a function of prejudice (Vinacke 1957). Brown (1958) argued that, "from the writings of social scientists it is clear that they have a poor opinion of . . . stereotypes—they think they are irrational and probably wicked to subscribe to them" (p. 364).

In the literature on sex stereotyping in children and adults, it has been hypothesized that sex stereotypes are detrimental because they oversimplify perceptions of reality and re-

Order of authorship was arbitrarily determined: This paper represents a completely collaborative effort. The authors wish to thank the following persons for helpful comments on an earlier version of this paper: Jack Balswick, Richard C. Endsley, William Graziano, Delroy Paulhus, Abraham Tesser, James Walters, and Karen Wampler. We would particularly like to acknowledge the trenchant critiques of two anonymous reviewers who provided important conceptual clarification of many of the points in the paper. Requests for reprints should be sent to either author, Department of Child and Family Development, Dawson Hall, University of Georgia, Athens, Georgia 30602.

[*Child Development*, 1981, **52**, 1119–1134. © 1981 by the Society for Research in Child Development, Inc. 0009-3920/81/5204-0002$01.00]

1120   Child Development

strict life options (Bem 1974; Block 1976; Bradbard & Endsley, in press; Saario, Jacklin, & Tittle 1973; Weitzman, Eifler, Hokada, & Ross 1972). The assumption has been made that once people learn the stereotypical roles for women and men, their behavior and thinking are impoverished by being confined to sex-appropriate ways of operating.

In recent years, the research focus has been changing. There is a movement toward viewing stereotyping as a normal cognitive process. This trend has been fostered by the recognition that the faulty-processing view of stereotyping has limited understanding of how stereotypes function (Cauthen et al., Note 1) and by the rediscovery that there are many similarities between the characteristics of stereotyping and of other types of information processing that were actually proposed much earlier by such theorists as Allport (1954), and Bruner and others (e.g., Bruner, Goodnow, & Austin 1956). For example, Mischel (1970) argued that the criticism that stereotypes are overgeneralizations is not appropriate because ". . . people do generalize and categorize events pervasively, and it is hard to imagine life without this ability to group and subsume many events into fewer units" (p. 8). With the limitations of perceptual (Broadbent 1958) and memory systems (Miller 1956), the categorization of information into fewer and simpler units allows for efficient information processing. Because stereotyping involves the categorization of social information into simpler units, it seems appropriate to consider stereotyping as one example of information processing.

THE SCHEMATIC PROCESSING MODEL OF SEX TYPING AND STEREOTYPING

The information processing model adopted in this paper is based on the schema construct and the types of processing associated with schemas. Recently, Taylor and Crocker (1979) reviewed the literature on schemas and described how they function in the processing of social information. In the present paper, we elaborate the general characteristics of schematic processing into a model of sex stereotyping in young children.

In discussing the model, it is important to clarify the way "stereotyping" will be used. Sex stereotypes have been typically defined as

a constellation of traits and roles generally attributed to men and women (Williams, Bennett, & Best 1975). This definition is untenable for use in studies investigating development of sex typing in young children. Research has shown that children are not aware of the more subtle personality traits associated with each of the sexes until 10 or 11 years of age (Williams et al. 1975). Very young children do know, however, many of the behaviors, objects, and roles appropriate to each sex (Edelbrock & Sugawara 1978). For this reason, the concept of stereotyping in this paper has been expanded to include considerations of how children perceive and behave toward both the animate and the inanimate environment—that is, sex typing (Kagan 1964).

Overview of the Model

The basic unit of the schematic processing model of stereotyping is the schema. Schemas are naive theories that guide information processing by structuring experiences, regulating behavior, and providing bases for making inferences and interpretations. Models based on the schema construct have been described as involving "theory-driven" processing (Neisser 1976) or "top-down" processing (Bobrow & Norman 1973).

To understand how schemas function in sex typing, a few specific examples of schematic processing will be considered. In figure 1, the schematic processing model is summarized. According to the schematic model, a young girl when presented with an object would make several decisions based on her sex-typing schemas that will influence if or how she will interact with the object. For example, when presented with a doll, she will decide first that dolls are self-relevant; second, that dolls are "for girls" and "I am a girl," which means "dolls are for me."[1] The results of these decisions are that the girl will approach the doll, explore it, ask questions about it, and play with it to obtain further information about it. This information will be elaborated and remembered. In contrast, the same girl presented with a truck will decide that the truck is schema relevant in the sense that trucks are "for boys" and "I am a girl." This decision leads to the concept "trucks are not for me." The result will be avoidance of the truck. No further information about the truck will be seen as important and none will be acquired beyond the information "for boys, not for me."

---

[1] The labels "for boys" and "for girls" could be supplied by others (e.g., adults, peers, mass media).

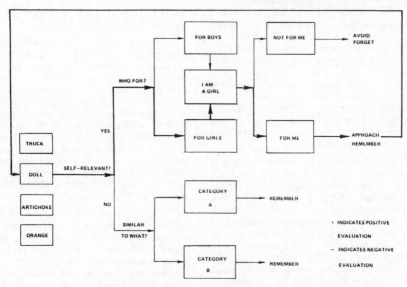

Fig. 1.—The schematic-processing model of sex role stereotyping

If asked later about these toys, the girl's memory would be consistent with her sex-typing schemas—she would remember more about the sex-appropriate toys than about the sex-inappropriate toys. Generally, her behavior and cognition will be made to be schema consistent.

TYPES OF SEX-RELATED SCHEMAS

What schemas are involved in sex typing and sex role learning? We propose two: First, an overall, "in-group-out-group" schema consisting of all the general information children need to categorize objects, behavior, traits, and roles as being either for males or for females; and second, an "own-sex" schema, a narrower, more detailed and specific version of the first, consisting of the information children have about the objects, behavior, traits, and roles that characterize their own sex.

To understand the differences in the types of information contained in each schema, consider how these two schemas might guide behavior. The overall schema guides behavior by giving information at the level of labels (e.g., for boys) about what kinds of things should be approached because they are sex inappropriate. This schema is similar in function to the operation of sex role standards as originally discussed by Kagan (1964). Children need information about what is appropriate for both sexes (Hartup, Moore, &

Sager 1963) and the overall schema contains this information. A boy can rely on his overall schema to obtain the information that "boys play with trucks" and "girls play with dolls." Both bits of information are necessary so the boy can act consistently with his own sex by playing with trucks and not by playing with dolls. At a very young age children have considerable knowledge about the things to approach and the things to avoid (Kuhn, Nash, & Brucken 1978).

The own-sex schema consists of detailed scripts and plans of action necessary to carry out sex-appropriate behaviors. For example, a girl may know from her overall schema that "girls sew." To act consistently with her own sex, however, she will need to learn how to sew. The action patterns involved in sewing then become part of her own-sex schema. In contrast, the same girl may know that "boys fix cars" by referring to her overall schema. Because fixing cars is not sex appropriate, however, she will probably lack the motivation to learn anything else about the subject, and such action patterns will not become part of her own-sex schema.

Functions of Schemas

How do schemas function in the processing of sex-related information?

Regulating behavior.—Schemas regulate behavior by providing the basis for anticipating

1122   Child Development

the future, setting goals, making plans, and developing behavioral routines to implement the plans (Bandura 1977; Taylor & Crocker 1979). They allow the perceiver to set goals and to select appropriate behavioral sequences to reach those goals. Used in this way schemas have been called "scripts" (Schank & Abelson 1977) or "frames" (Goffman 1959). They are useful in that they define the sequence of actions to be performed in well-known situations and give the perceiver knowledge of the situation in advance.

There is considerable evidence that sex-typing schemas function to regulate children's behavior. The research literature supports the contention that sex-typing schemas direct both play and nonplay activity, as well as children's preferences in many situations. Children as young as two years old tend to play with sex-appropriate toys and prefer same-sex peers (Jacklin & Maccoby 1978; Maccoby & Jacklin 1974). Other studies, using toy-preference measures, have found that young children consistently prefer objects appropriate for their own sex (De Lucia 1963; Nadelman 1974) and prefer stories where the characters were engaged in sex-appropriate rather than sex-inappropriate behaviors (Jaudon & Halverson, in press; Jennings 1975).

The schematic processing model predicts that children's behavior is guided toward sex-appropriate activities and objects by labels that define the overall schema of in-group and out-group. Thompson (1975) found that by 36 months of age, gender labels led children to to choose objects labeled as being for their own sex. Liebert, McCall, and Hanratty (1971) supported the hypothesis that young children's toy preferences were altered by knowledge of the usual preferences of their own sex. Bradbard and Endsley's (in press) study demonstrated how sex-typed labels influence exploration. Specifically, children touched and explored novel objects labeled as sex appropriate and sex neutral significantly more often than objects labeled as sex inappropriate.

Sex-typed labeling of activities has also been found to affect performance. Montemayor (1974) found that children's performance was highest when a game was labeled sex appropriate, intermediate when labeled sex neutral, and lowest when labeled sex inappropriate. Stein, Pohly, and Mueller (1971) found that achievement behavior in children was related to the sex-typed label of the task. Boys were

found to spend most of their time working at tasks labeled as sex appropriate.

Most researchers have focused on the role sex-appropriate labels play in approaching sex-appropriate activities. The schematic processing model also predicts that the overall schema guides behavior by providing information about which things should be avoided. This function of the overall sex-typing schema is supported by both White (1978) and Hartup (Hartup et al., 1963) who found children of both sexes avoiding sex-inappropriate objects. Similarly, Ross and Ross (1972) found that when a teacher suggested opposite-sex toys to children, both boys and girls resisted playing with the suggested toy.

Clearly, young children play with and prefer sex-appropriate objects. Labels function to provide information about the sex typing of objects which, in turn, leads to behavior consistent with the sex-typing schemas. When materials already have sex-typed labels (e.g., dolls, trucks), children will use their overall schema (for girls, for boys) to guide their actions into sex-appropriate patterns. With novel materials that have no previous sex typing associated with them, children will rely on sex-typing information provided by adults or peers to guide their behavior.

By taking a schematic view of sex typing, several additional research areas concerning regulating and guiding behavior are apparent. Previous research on schematic processing has shown that adults with highly developed schemas are more likely to behave in schema-consistent patterns than are people with less well-developed schemas (Tesser & Leone 1977). For sex stereotypes, it is expected that children who have well-developed overall schemas would be more likely to approach sex-appropriate toys and activities and to avoid those that are sex inappropriate more than children with less well-developed schemas. It also follows that children with well-developed overall schemas are more likely to elaborate their own-sex schemas by learning how to perform sex-consistent behaviors.

Organizing and attending to information. —Schemas structure experience by providing the organization by which information is processed (Taylor & Crocker 1979). Through the use of schemas, schema-consistent information is made salient, while schema-inconsistent information is ignored (Tesser 1978). In this way, schemas influence the kind of information that is attended to, encoded, and recalled. The evidence from social psychological research on adults supports the organizational function of schemas in that information consistent with schemas is remembered better than information that is not (Rothbart, Evans, & Fulero 1979; Snyder & Cantor 1979; Snyder & Uranowitz 1978; Zadny & Gerard 1974).

Not all studies, however, have found improved recall for consistent information. Some show that distinctive (Hamilton & Gifford 1976) or schema-inconsistent (Hastie & Kumar 1979) information is also well remembered. Theories such as cognitive dissonance (Festinger 1957) are based on the idea that inconsistent information is more salient to the perceiver than consistent information. Whether consistent or inconsistent information is remembered better probably depends on salience (Mandler 1978) and the time between presentation of information and memory testing (Hastie & Kumar 1979). In either case, the construct of schema is important for understanding how information is organized in experience.

Without appropriate schemas, some information will never be encoded.[2] The importance of schemas in encoding information has been demonstrated in a variety of experiments concerning the comprehension and retention of prose (Ausubel 1960; Bartlett 1932; Bransford & Franks 1972; Bransford & Johnson 1972; Christie & Schumacher 1975; Dooling & Lachman 1971). The consistent conclusion from such studies has been that information is not encoded in memory unless an organizing structure is presented prior to the prose passage. The organizing structure, or schema, allows for the information from the passage to be subsumed, acting to "incorporate the unfamiliar into the familiar . . ." (Brown, Smiley, Day, Townsend, & Lawton 1977, p. 1454).

Little research has focused on how sex-typing schemas affect processing and retention of sex-related information. The findings from the few studies that have examined sex-stereotyping influences on children's memory are consistent with the predictions from the schematic model. Selective recall of sex-appropriate information over sex-inappropriate information has been shown. For example, Nadelman (1974) found that boys recalled more masculine items than feminine items, while girls showed the opposite pattern. Bradbard and Endsley (in press) found that children remembered the names of novel objects labeled sex

appropriate, and Liben and Signorella (1980) also documented the influence of sex-typed schemas on recall for young children.

Some evidence, however, is not consistent with the model. Jennings (1975) studied the effects of the sex-typing of children's stories on preference and recall. Using an immediate recall task, children recalled more information from reversed sex role stories than for the usual sex role stories. Jennings argued that because reverse sex role information is novel, it is remembered better. It has been suggested, however, that short-term recall is influenced by novelty, but that long-term recall would be transformed to be schema consistent (Hastie & Kumar 1979).

Several other memory studies demonstrate how the overall schema affects recall of information. Koblinsky, Cruse, and Sugawara (1978) presented fifth graders with stories where a male and female character displayed stereotypic and reversed stereotypic behaviors. In a recognition test, sex-consistent information was remembered better than sex-inconsistent information. In a later study, Koblinsky and Cruse (Note 2) found that children demonstrated selective memory for content consistent with advanced descriptions. They provided children with stereotypic (e.g., Mary would rather play with girls than boys) or reverse-stereotypic (e.g., Bill would rather play with girls than boys) descriptions prior to the presentation of stories about the characters. A recognition test for memory of sex-related story content revealed that the prior presentation of sex-stereotypic descriptions produced better memory for stereotypic content, and reverse-stereotypic descriptions led to better memory for reverse-stereotypic content. As well as providing evidence for schematic processing of sex-related information, this study demonstrated that children also formed schemas about reversed stereotypes that influenced recall.

An exception to the prediction that information tends to be encoded and remembered when it is schema consistent and ignored or forgotten when it is inconsistent is that children should remember the sex typing of objects, even when the objects are sex inappropriate. Such information is important because children also need to remember what to avoid. For example, Bradbard and Endsley (in press) found that children remembered the sex-typed labels (for boys, for girls) of both sex-appro-

[2] The inability to encode information when appropriate schemas are lacking is the basis for Piaget's theory of intellectual development.

1124   Child Development

priate and sex-inappropriate novel objects, but remembered only the names of sex-appropriate objects.

Are the differential effects of sex-typing schemas related to encoding processes, retrieval processes, or both? There is evidence that sex-related information is encoded during learning. In a release from proactive inhibition task, Kail and Levine (Note 3) demonstrated that sex-typed information was encoded with object names and influenced recall of these names. From the adult social psychological research, there is support for the idea that the selective effects of schemas operate at the encoding stage (Rothbart et al. 1979; Zadny & Gerard 1974), and the retrieval stage (Snyder & Uranowitz 1978). Further research is necessary to discover how and when sex-typed information is encoded with other information and to discover the influence of the coding of this information.

Structuring of inference and interpretation.—When information is deficient or ambiguous, schemas allow the perceiver to supply what is missing by relying on information already contained in the schemas (Taylor & Crocker 1979; Tesser 1978). Also, schemas serve an inferential function in familiar, easily assimilated situations. We do not attend to all the details of familiar experiences—information is often filled in by the schema itself rather than by actual perception (Mandler 1978; Nisbett & Wilson 1977). This has been termed "default processing," meaning that the most expected (default) value of a variable is used to aid in filling in the details of experiences (Bobrow & Norman 1973; Mandler 1978; Tesser 1978). The inferential function of schemas has been demonstrated in research on prose comprehension with both adults (Bransford, Barclay, & Franks 1972) and children (Paris & Upton 1976), but this function has not been investigated directly for sex-typing schemas in children. From the schematic processing model we would expect that, in either typical or information-deficient situations, children would supply information by relying on their sex-typing schemas. For example, if children are given the information that a fire fighter would be visiting the school, they should infer from their in-group-out-group schema that the fire fighter would be a male (schema consistent) rather than a female (schema inconsistent). While many researchers discuss the inferential function of sex-typing schemas (e.g., Ashmore & Del Boca 1979; Mischel 1970; Taylor & Crocker 1979), little research has been done.

Liabilities of Schematic Processing

Schematic processing is considered to be efficient and generally accurate. However, since schematic processing involves selective attention, encoding, representation, and retrieval, information loss and distortion also occur (Taylor & Crocker 1979). It is this tendency for information to be "made to fit" the schema that results in both the efficiency and the distortions associated with schematic processing. Typically, schematic processing results in accurate information because our cognitive structures, for the most part, tend to fit the world well (Mandler 1978). At other times, however, the selectivity associated with schematic processing results in an inaccurate view of the world. Keeping the relations between functions and biases in schematic processing in mind, the more significant biases and their importance for sex typing will be examined.

Inappropriate schemas.—When an inappropriate schema is used, the default or "best guess" options of that inappropriate schema result in faulty interpretations of situations. Consider a child who has the schema that another child is a "sissy" when, in fact, that child is just as sex consistent as the first child. By maintaining this inappropriate schema, the perceiver's view will be biased—certain behaviors will not be noticed or they will be misinterpreted, while others will be more salient—all interpretations being consistent with the sissy schema. No research has been found on the effects of applying inappropriate sex-typing schemas on social interactions of children.

Illusory data bases.—Taylor and Crocker (1979) define an illusory data base as "inferences, or bits of information which are not actually present in the stimulus configuration which the perceiver encounters, but which rather constitute the contribution the schema makes to the stimulus configuration" (p. 38). For the perceiver, the inferences supplied by the schema and the actual information in the environment are indistinguishable. This illusory data base leads to faulty interpretation of the situations being perceived or remembered.

There are several ways an illusory data base can develop. In one case, faulty data result from a lack of information in the stimulus configuration; the missing information being supplied by default options of the schema. These intrusions, while not accurate, may be recalled as having actually occurred, thereby providing additional confirmation of the validity of the schema (Taylor & Crocker 1979). Evidence for this comes from studies of prose comprehension where thematic intrusion errors are quite common. Brown et al. (1977) found that young children showed the same basic patterns previously found with adults. Children tended to remember information congruent with the theme of a story even though the information was not contained in the story.

An illusory data base also can operate in situations where information is complete. Taylor & Crocker (1979) refer to this tendency as the application of the correct schema "too enthusiastically." Relying on schemas when it is unnecessary may be related to the strength of the schema, that is, how well-developed or important the schema is to the perceiver.

In sex stereotyping, the tendency to apply schemas enthusiastically may result in affirming the content of the stereotype. Since most young children have well-developed sex-typing schemas (Edelbrock & Sugawara 1978), we could expect that such schemas will often be applied too enthusiastically, leading to the formation of faulty data bases. Most children will say that "fathers drive," even though they often see both their mothers and fathers driving. Despite information to the contrary, children will maintain that driving is a masculine activity. Although no studies have been found that investigated this phenomenon, the formation of illusory data bases in children should be studied, since faulty data appear to support such thinking about sex-typed activities.

Type I errors.—When we accept information as schema consistent, when in fact it is inconsistent or neutral, we have distorted the information. These distortions are called type I errors (Taylor & Crocker 1979). For sex stereotypes, the implications of type I errors are far-reaching. Children can confirm their schemas by distorting neutral and sex-inconsistent information into sex-consistent information. There are two ways that sex-inconsistent information can be converted into sex-consistent information. Consider the case of children observing a boy cooking with a stove. Since a boy who is cooking would be sex inconsistent, this information can be converted in memory to be schema consistent by either changing the sex of the person cooking or by changing the way in which the activity is construed. The children could make the information congruent with the schema by changing the sex of the actor and remember seeing a girl cooking, or they could move toward schematic consistency by changing the nature of the activity and remember seeing a boy fixing the stove.

There is only one study that demonstrates distortion in the direction of consistency with sex-typing schemas. Cordua, McGraw, and Drabman (1979) presented young children with videotapes of males and females portraying stereotypic and reversed stereotypic occupations. The children tended to distort reversed occupations into sex-appropriate ones, for example, children shown a female doctor relabeled her as a nurse. Recently, Liben and Signorella (1980) attempted to demonstrate distortion based on changing the sex of the observed person. Children shown pictures of people in various occupations and activities and then given an immediate recognition test for these pictures, as well as similar pictures with the sex of the actor reversed, showed no evidence of sex reversals. Giving an immediate recognition test may account for lack of significant results. Distortion effects are more likely to occur after a delay between presentation and testing (Sulin & Dooling 1974). Recent research using a 1-week delay between presentation and testing did find that children tended to make sex reversals so that actors and activities were sex consistent (Martin & Halverson, Note 4).

When information that could be used to change sex-typing schemas is distorted to support preexisting schemas, these schemas will be maintained tenaciously despite disconfirming evidence. Investigation of the extent that such distortion occurs will provide information on the maintenance of sex-typing schemas. Such research may also suggest ways that inconsistent information can be presented so that it is encoded in memory without distortion.

Illusory correlations.—When we misjudge the degree of covariation between two categories of events we have the bias of the "illusory correlation." Chapman (1967) discussed this concept as referring to "the report of observers of a correlation between two classes of events which, in reality, (a) are not correlated, or (b) are correlated to a lesser extent than reported" (p. 151).

Most research on illusory correlations has concentrated on how erroneous correlations between patient symptoms and psychodiagnostic test performance occur (e.g., Chapman & Chapman 1967, 1969). Recently, researchers have begun to examine the role of illusory correlations in making stereotypic judgments about people in group situations (e.g., Hamilton & Gifford 1976).

How do illusory correlations form if they

1126   Child Development

do not represent actual covariation of events? Illusory correlations can result from schemas making certain types of information more salient, while other types of information are selectively ignored (Hamilton 1979; Taylor & Crocker 1979). For instance, there is evidence that the frequency of distinctive or uncommon events occurring in minority-group members is overestimated (Hamilton & Gifford 1976). Biasing factors in information processing lead to the differential attributions about members of different groups. True differences between groups, however, are not necessary for making illusory correlations. Recent research indicates that cognitive factors alone are sufficient to produce differential perceptions of social groups (Hamilton & Gifford 1976).

No research on illusory correlations in children's sex stereotyping have been located. From the schematic processing model, illusory correlations would be expected to account for much of the covariation in judgments children make about characteristics that typify the sexes. Further, such covariation may be much overestimated, resulting in over-generalizations about what males and females are like. The study of the influence of illusory correlations on the development and maintenance of sex-typing schemas in children needs further investigation.

All the above biases in schematic processing tend to distort information toward schema consistency and lead to misinterpretations of situations, faulty recall of events, and faulty judgments. These liabilities are also those characteristics that lead many researchers to conclude that stereotyping is faulty. As McCauley et al. (1980) suggest, "what is wrong with stereotyping is no more and no less than what is wrong with human conceptual behavior generally" (p. 195). By focusing on the negative aspects, the usefulness of stereotypic or schematic thinking has been largely ignored. Schemas about people also serve to stabilize the social environment by making it more predictable and manageable. These functions need further investigation as well.

Sex-typing Schemas and Their Relation to Other Types of Schemas

Several different classifications of schemas have been proposed (e.g., Greenwald 1980; Markus 1977; Taylor & Crocker 1979). The classification proposed here is based on two considerations: first, whether schemas are potentially self-defining and, second, how salient or available they are to the perceiver. This classification makes it possible to understand how schemas associated with sex typing compare with the many other types of schemas currently discussed in the literature.

The first consideration is whether schemas are potentially self-defining. Examples of self-defining schemas are those that include physical descriptions (e.g., blue eyes, brown hair), psychological descriptions (e.g., independent, assertive), and role descriptions (e.g., mother, mayor). Each schema provides some information about self-definition, in that the self is a member of the schema. At the same time, it must be noted that many schemas are not generally relevant to self-definition. Such schemas include those used in perceiving and classifying objects and events, for example, a "shape" schema used to classify objects.

The second consideration, salience, refers to the extent that schemas are available for encoding information about both the self and objects in the world. For example, a person may have a creativity schema which organizes information about self and others, while another person may not use such a schema. Many individual and situational differences concerning which self-schemas are generally salient, and those that are not have been documented (Bem & Allen 1974; Markus 1977).

There are many ways that schemas become salient. In the development of self-definition, a person makes many self/nonself differentiations that eventuate in a set of elaborated schemas of central importance. Epstein (1973) and Kelly (1955) have discussed how people formulate central self-concepts around what the person sees as a core of similarity about the self. Salience may also be affected by others' attributions. Consider the case of sex-typing schemas. A girl may find a consistent pattern in her own behavior that she comes to label "feminine." The salience of such a schema, however, also depends on other individuals who may also define, label, and interpret her behavior using a sex-typing schema. Even a girl who does not define herself as feminine may find many other people applying that label to her behavior and expecting her to conform to the "femininity" schema. Other person's sex-stereotypic expectations may lead to an increase in salience for sex stereotypes through behavioral confirmation of those expectations (see Rosenthal & Jacobson 1968; Snyder, Tanke, & Berscheid 1977) or through acceptance of others' attributions.

Salience of schemas clearly depends on the obvious physical characteristics of events or objects. Some types of information, particularly gender and race, are effective for distinguishing people. Consider gender classifications. Gender is an obvious and stable human characteristic. Other types of self-defining groupings such as national origin are not so apparent. Because sex is an obvious physical category, it is quite easy for a perceiver to make in-group and out-group discriminations. Unlike many other types of self-defining categories, gender categories are also dichotomous. Information about either group can be used in defining the self. Girls can acquire stereotypes by learning those things that are feminine (to approach them) or by learning what things are masculine (to avoid them).

Factual information can also influence salience and the elaboration of schemas. For example, almost all studies show a mean difference in aggression, with boys on the average being more aggressive than girls (Maccoby & Jacklin 1974). Further, there is probably a relatively small group of boys who operate at a high level of aggression that is practically never seen in girls. This behavior comes to be labeled as "boylike" even though it does not characterize a majority of boys. When it does occur, it is highly diagnostic and differentiating.[3] Thus, the sex stereotype is based on a real behavioral distinction, a "kernel of truth," that may lead to schema adoption even when the schema does not predict behavior effectively.

Some self-schemas may become salient only in certain instances. For example, a person's "personality" may not be self-defined according to eye color, yet eye color is important for self-definition when applying for a driver's license. There are also a wide range of schemas that do not define the self and yet are salient in certain situations or for certain time periods. For instance, a schema for "Japanese cars" is not self-defining, but it may be salient when considering buying a car.

Salience of schemas can be experimentally manipulated. Subjects who have been told that the picture they are about to see is a certain object (e.g., eyeglasses) or a certain situation (e.g., a burglary), will remember and distort information to be consistent with that schema (Carmichael, Hogan, & Walter 1932; Zadny & Gerard 1974). Schemas can also be made salient through prior experience. When a certain solution has been found effective in problem solving, people tend to maintain that solution (develop a "set"), even when an easier solution can be used (e.g., Luchins & Luchins 1959).

According to the proposed classification system, sex-typing schemas are self-defining schemas that vary in their salience for different individuals. For children, sex-typing schemas are generally quite salient. For adults, the salience of these schemas appears to vary. Some individuals frequently process information in sex-typed ways, while other individuals do not (Bem & Allen 1974).

Self-schemas are both self-defining and salient and provide information about similarities and differences between the individual and others. For example, having a self-schema that you are "independent" means that you believe you are independent in most, if not all, of life's circumstances. You process your behavior, as well as that of others, in terms of independence and see yourself as like others who are independent and different from others who are dependent. Someone who does not have this schema will not consider independence or dependence as a predictive descriptor of the self and will, therefore, be less able to make judgments about the self and others in these terms (Markus 1977). Self-schemas also appear to be characterized by evaluation. The group to which the self belongs usually will be positively evaluated, and other groups not involving the self will be negatively evaluated (e.g., Kuhn et al. 1978).

Do schemas about the self function differently from other types of schemas? Specifically, does self-involvement in schematic processing increase cognitive bias (Greenwald 1980)? Our contention is that processing is essentially the same for all types of schemas. Once they are invoked, all schemas function basically in the same way. The issue is whether self schemas differ in availability or salience from nonself schemas. In most social situations, there is a greater likelihood that a salient self-schema will be invoked than a nonself schema. When a person sees an object in a fog, and the only information available is that it is an inanimate object with four legs, schemas like "chair" or "table" are likely to be used. If no additional information is forthcoming, the chance of the chair schema being used is equal to that of the table schema.

---

[3] The authors are grateful to the anonymous reviewer for this suggestion.

1128   Child Development

In contrast, consider a person who labels herself as independent. In a situation where the person is asked to interpret an ambiguous behavior (not clearly independent or dependent), the person is more likely to use the "independence" schema to define the situation than any other type of schema. We can say, therefore, that people have a set about how to interpret their own behavior and the behavior of others (Epstein 1973). This highly available set involves self-schemas rather than nonself schemas. Salience, therefore, influences when schemas are used rather than how processing occurs.

Is Stereotyping a Normal Cognitive Operation?

Our premise is that sex stereotyping is a normal cognitive operation. When sex schemas are compared to other types of schemas, it is apparent that stereotyping is just one type of schematic processing associated with self-defining, salient schemas. One aspect of stereotyping—the in-group-out-group distinction—may, however, still lead to the belief that stereotypes are unique. In fact, some research has pointed to this as the unique feature of stereotypes. The typical finding is that when people have been categorized on even a relatively arbitrary dimension, persons in the perceiver's group (the in-group) are evaluated positively, while persons in the out-group are evaluated negatively (e.g., Allen & Wilder 1975; Billig & Tajfel 1973; Tajfel & Billig 1974; Wilder & Allen 1974). For sex-stereotypes, Kuhn et al. (1978) found selective evaluations of sex-typed information for children as young as 3 years of age.

Even though the in-group-out-group nature of stereotyping often leads to erroneous evaluations of others, is the underlying processing in stereotyping truly different—does the content of the material short-circuit normal processing (Taylor, Fiske, Etcoff, & Ruderman 1978)? To investigate this problem, we need to consider whether in-groups and out-groups characterize only stereotypic thinking and not other kinds of thinking.

It can be argued that in-groups and out-groups characterize other self-relevant schemas, even though they are seldom recognized as such. For the self-schema of independence, one can argue that all people falling within a certain range of perceived independence are the "in-group," and others are the "out-group." Once in-groups and out-groups are distin-

guished, evaluations of the groups can then occur. Evaluation, however, is not a necessary result of schematic processing, rather, it can and often does occur once groups are defined. Membership in a group does not automatically lead to in-group-out-group distinctions, but group membership in a salient group can lead to distinguishing and evaluating members of the in-group and out-group. For sex stereotypes, people are members of either the male or female group. When this distinction is salient, in-group-out-group designations and consequent evaluation can occur. People who belong to the group "blue eyed" have a reference group, but unless eye color is salient in a particular situation, in-groups and out-groups will not be distinguished. Thus, even though only the highly salient self-defining schemas of stereotyping (e.g., sex, racial, ethnic) are usually discussed in terms of in-groups and out-groups, any salient schema can be used to make such classifications. Stereotypes are distinctive because in-group and out-group designations are made, and concomitant evaluations are associated with these groups. This evaluational aspect of stereotyping, however, does not necessarily imply that a different type of processing has occurred.

Development of Sex-typing Schemas

To explain how sex typing develops in children, one basic assumption must be made—children have a tendency to group information. Such grouping serves two purposes: First, it allows large amounts of information to be processed in an efficient manner and second, it assists the child in establishing self-identity. Since gender is a stable and easily discriminable natural dichotomy, the developing tendency to classify by gender is certainly understandable (Lewis & Brooks-Gunn 1979; Mischel 1970; Thompson 1975). Part of the self-definitional process, then, is classification by sex.

To classify by sex, children must be able to identify people accurately as either male or female. For this gender-grouping process to result in sex typing, gender groups must be salient. Since gender groupings are useful for self-monitoring, predicting the behavior of others, and understanding the social expectations linked to sex, they are salient (Maccoby 1980).

There has been some discussion about the level of gender understanding necessary for the development of sex typing. Some theorists

(Emmerich, Goldman, Kirsh, & Sharabany 1977; Kohlberg 1966; Marcus & Overton 1978; Slaby & Frey 1975) have argued that children must not only understand their gender identity, but also that gender is stable over time and constant across situations (gender constancy) before sex typing occurs. Others feel that it is sufficient simply to identify self and others by sex (Constantinople 1979; Martin & Halverson, in press). While the research data are not clear, it may be that children do not need to understand gender constancy in order to adopt sex-typed modes of behavior—gender identity may be sufficient. By assuming that only gender identity is necessary for self-socialization, it is possible to explain why some sex-appropriate behaviors are seen in children who do not understand gender constancy. Children who cannot identify gender, however, would not be expected to act according to schemas that have yet to be formed. Conceivably, children could show some sex typing of behavior before the age at which the schemas are present (e.g., Jacklin & Maccoby [1978] found some preference for same-sex peers at 33 months of age). Such possibilities would need to be explained by resorting to explanations involving biological proclivities and/or our inability to assess information-processing strategies in very young children. This interesting issue is, however, beyond the scope of the present paper.

In any case, when children can identify gender and reliably place themselves in the salient gender category, they recognize that they belong to one group (in-group) and not the other (out-group).[4] For young children, evaluation follows in that the in-group is positively evaluated and the out-group is negatively evaluated. Evaluation motivates children to be like one's own group and be different from the out-group and leads to the acquisition of the information in the overall schema. Information about the self is acquired by watching members of both gender groups. By observing same-sex models, children learn about what members of the in-group do, thereby learning what things are sex appro-priate (Slaby & Frey 1975). By observing opposite-sex models, children learn about what members of the in-group do not do, thereby learning what things are sex inappropriate (see Perry & Bussey [1979] for empirical support of this assertion).

The acquisition of information in the overall schema leads to the elaboration of the own-sex schema and the lack of development of the opposite-sex schema. As children grow older, they will tend to increase their knowledge of the things "for me" (own-sex schema) by learning the sex-appropriate plans of action. They will not learn as much about sex-inappropriate plans of action. The own-sex schema, then, is elaborated by increasing the number and complexity of plans of action (e.g., the number of things boys can do). Overall schemas develop only through an increase in the number of things associated with each sex. Further, there is evidence suggesting a developmental progression in the kinds of sex-related knowledge children acquire. First they acquire information about behaviors and activities and later acquire information about the more subtle psychological traits associated with sex roles (Kohlberg & Ullian 1979; Williams et al. 1975).

Cognitive level is also an important factor in the development and use of sex schemas. Young children's preoperational structures of thought limit their ability to form and reason with hierarchical classes, because they fail to understand the various ways in which people can be classified on social characteristics. They focus on one aspect of classification and do not deal effectively with multiple classifications (Flavell 1977). Since sex-role categories are so obvious, children may tend to use this classification system rather than more complex ones.

Once sex schemas are adopted by children, the information processing associated with schemas increases the likelihood that these schemas will be maintained. Sex stereotypes become almost self-perpetuating because only sex-consistent information is perceived and/or

---

[4] We have assumed here that, when children can reliably distinguish the two sexes, they also classify the self as "same as the other" or "different from the other." Our anonymous reviewer suggested a cogent alternative. The matching of two categories (as same or different) may be cognitively more complex than simply identifying category membership (man or woman). In concept formation studies, very young children can identify and label colors but cannot sort an array by colors. We cannot assume that, just because children can do better than chance identifying self and others by sex, they are using this information as a basis of matching themselves to others as same or different. This point is important in considering the developmental course of the sex-typing process outlined here and needs research.

1130   Child Development

remembered (Kohlberg 1966). Further, sex schemas are maintained by making inconsistent and neutral information congruent with schemas. Since schemas resist disconfirmation, information that is incongruent will, at most, cause increasing differentiation rather than cause the schema to be discarded.

Although it is beyond the scope of this paper, there may be a relation between how rigidly sex-typing schemas are maintained and children's perceptions of "good" and "bad." The bases for children's evaluations of good and bad undergo developmental changes. For example, Damon (1977) found that young children (approximately ages 2–4 years) evaluate good and bad egocentrically—"what I'm doing is good and for me (and my sex)." Children from about 5 to 7 years view good and bad in terms of rule violations—"I know what's good for me and my sex because there is a rule that boys do this and girls do not." At later ages (7–10 years), the basis for evaluation shifts to a concern with social sanctions—"what's good for me is what others will not laugh at." This developmental progression certainly has implications for children's evaluation of sex-typed material. At the present time, however, little is known about how children's changing concepts of good and bad affect sex-typed processing about self and others.

In conclusion, sex schemas develop as part of the child's self-socialization. That is, sex-typing information is acquired through a process of the child defining the self and defining the relationship of the self to others. The combination of the motivation to define the self and the way in which people process information leads to the acquisition and maintenance of sex-typing schemas. Sex-typing schemas can be considered the result of normal cognitive processes, developing with little effort, and requiring only minimal socialization input.

IMPLICATIONS FOR CHANGING SEX-ROLE ORIENTATIONS

Given the way human beings process information and the type of society in which we live, it is not surprising that children are highly sex stereotyped by age 4 and that these stereotypes are maintained throughout childhood and often into adulthood. What does seem surprising, however, is that research indicates there are individuals who apparently are not highly sex stereotyped (Bem 1974).

Under what circumstances does unwarranted processing change? Clearly, none of us has the same sex stereotypes we had as children; personal experiences do somehow change our views over time. While a detailed examination of the requisites for such change is beyond the scope of the present paper, a few comments on such change are appropriate.

The androgynous person (Bem 1974) is considered to be "sex-role flexible," since both masculine and feminine behavior patterns are included in their behavioral repertoire. For persons to become androgynous, therefore, they would have learned plans of action for both "appropriate" and "inappropriate" behaviors. This view is supported by social learning theory. Mischel (1966) argued that children know how to perform both appropriate and inappropriate behaviors—but since environmental supports (reinforcements) for the performance of inappropriate behaviors are not present, they are not performed. In contrast, the schematic model posits that the problem is not performance, but rather competence—lack of complete knowledge about how to perform the inappropriate behaviors. Flexibility, therefore, can only occur after the individual has learned how to perform inappropriate behaviors. Further, the schematic model also predicts that sex stereotyping may not be easily changed through mere exposure to new or contradictory evidence. It is not that new or contradictory evidence will never produce change, only that it will produce less change than would be expected from a rational information-processing model (Ross 1977).

We can only speculate how sex stereotyping may become more flexible. Schemas may become more flexible by changing their evaluations. How might this take place? As schemas become more differentiated there will be more overlap between "male" and "female" things and, consequently, less evaluation will be associated with being consistent with the own-sex schema. Evaluation may also lessen as the number of groups in which one is self-involved increases. Young children with limited cognitive capacity may perceive themselves in relation to the environment solely through reliance on highly salient sex schemas. As children cognitively mature, there may be more types of groups that are used to define the self. An older child may think in terms of: "I am a girl," "I like music," and "I am a good student." Only the first of these groups involves sex; the others cut across gender groups. Once children or adults can define themselves according to many different groups and roles, not all of them sex-related, sex and sex roles may then become relatively less evaluative and central in their thinking.

Also, by eliminating the in-group-out-group aspect of stereotyping, the differential evaluation of such a distinction would be attenuated, and the motivation to act consistently with the own-sex schema would be lessened. This could occur by redefining one's group as "people" rather than male or female. People could then increase their knowledge of the things previously considered sex inappropriate and off limits.

Given the concreteness of young children's thinking and the attendant limitations on information processing, it is unlikely that children's sex stereotyping can be made flexible with much success. The view taken here is that flexibility in sex typing can only occur after a certain level of cognitive development has been reached. Then it is possible that the individual can change the evaluations associated with sex typing and/or redefine group membership, and develop a more flexible sex-typing orientation.

Summary and Conclusions

The proposed schematic model is similar to other cognitive views of sex stereotyping, particularly models proposed by Kohlberg (Kohlberg 1966; Kohlberg & Ullian 1979) and Maccoby and Jacklin (1974). The model, however, goes beyond these theories by explaining other aspects of the stereotyping process and elaborating the consequences of learning sex-related information. While earlier theory focused on the inputs to the stereotyping system, the present model considers both the inputs to and the outcomes of stereotyping. By using the schematic model, the process of how and why stereotypes are maintained tenaciously throughout childhood can also be understood.

The schematic model is also similar to many other theories of stereotyping that emphasize normal information processing (Ashmore & Del Boca 1979; Constantinople 1979; McCauley et al. 1980; Mischel 1970; Perry & Bussey 1979; Vinacke 1957). These theories treat stereotypes as generalizations, rules, concepts, or categories, and stereotyping is not viewed as necessarily negative in either content or process. As McCauley et al. (1980) state, "Stereotypes are not necessarily incorrect, illogical, or rigid—at least not by definition" (p.

196). These models stress the usefulness of stereotypes—how they simplify the environmental input by structuring and restricting information. Rather than concentrate on the negative aspects of stereotyping, attention is directed to how stereotypes organize perceptions, memory, and behavior.

The schematic model differs from many other theories in that attention is shifted from categories of "male things" and "female things" to thinking about "things for me" and "things not for me." Although subtle, this distinction is of major importance because it captures both the categorization aspects and the selective effects of stereotyping that result from the perceiver being a member of one of the social categories. Conceptualizing stereotypes in this manner ties together many of the loose ends in the literature on stereotyping, while also affirming the parallels between stereotyping and other cognitive operations. Another advantage of using an information-processing model based on schemas is that it is heuristic in that many areas needing further investigation are described.

It is beyond the scope of this paper to compare in detail the schematic model with existing models of stereotyping. Our purpose has been to elaborate a theory based on a construct which appears to clarify the stereotyping process. Since schematic models are being used by social psychologists to describe and explain other areas of social information processing, there is considerable evidence to support the functions and liabilities of schemas in adults, but little evidence of these processes in children. Our hope is that many of the approaches used in understanding social information processing at a general level will be applied to the specific type of social information processing involved in children's sex typing.

Reference Notes

1. Cauthen, N. R.; Robinson, I. E.; & Krauss, H. H. The psychological reality of stereotypes (Research Report No. 10). Unpublished manuscript, University of Calgary, 1973.
2. Koblinsky, J. A., & Cruse, D. F. The role of frameworks in children's retention of sex-related story content. Paper presented at the Biennial Meeting of the Society for Research in Child Development, San Francisco, 1970.
3. Kail, R. V., & Levine, L. Encoding processes and sex-role preferences. Paper presented at the Biennial Meeting of the Society for Research in Child Development, Denver, 1975.

1132   Child Development

4.   Martin, C. L., & Halverson, C. F. The influence of sex-stereotypes on children's memory. Unpublished manuscript, University of Georgia, 1980.

References

Allen, V. L., & Wilder, D. A. Categorization, belief similarity, and intergroup discrimination. *Journal of Personality and Social Psychology*, 1975, **32**, 971–977.

Allport, G. W. *The nature of prejudice.* Cambridge, Mass.: Addison-Wesley, 1954.

Ashmore, R. D., & Del Boca, F. K. Sex stereotypes and implicit personality theory: toward a cognitive-social psychological conceptualization. *Sex Roles*, 1979, **5**, 219–248.

Ausubel, D. P. The use of advanced organizers in the learning and retention of meaningful verbal material. *Journal of Educational Psychology*, 1960, **51**, 267–272.

Bandura, A. *Social learning theory.* Englewood Cliffs, N.J.: Prentice-Hall, 1977.

Bartlett, F. C. *Remembering.* Cambridge: Cambridge University Press, 1932.

Bem, S. L. The measurement of psychological androgyny. *Journal of Consulting and Clinical Psychology*, 1974, **42**, 155–162.

Bem, D. J., & Allen, A. On predicting some of the people some of the time: the search for cross-situational consistencies in behavior. *Psychological Review*, 1974, **81**, 506–520.

Billig, M., & Tajfel, H. Social categorization and similarity in intergroup behavior. *European Journal of Social Psychology*, 1973, **3**, 27–52.

Block, J. H. Conceptions of sex role: some cross-cultural and longitudinal perspectives. In A. G. Kaplan & J. P. Bean (Eds.), *Beyond sex-role stereotypes: readings toward a psychology of androgyny.* Boston: Little, Brown, 1976.

Bobrow, D. G., & Norman, D. A. Some principles of memory schemata. In D. G. Bobrow & A. M. Collins (Eds.), *Representation and understanding studies in cognitive science.* New York: Academic Press, 1973.

Bradbard, M. R., & Endsley, R. C. The effects of sex-typed labeling on children's information-seeking and retention. *Sex Roles*, in press.

Bransford, J. D.; Barclay, J. R.; & Franks, J. J. Sentence memory: a constructive versus interpretible approach. *Cognitive Psychology*, 1972, **3**, 193–209.

Bransford, J. D., & Franks, J. J. The abstraction of linguistic ideas. *Cognitive Psychology*, 1972, **2**, 331–350.

Bransford, J. D., & Johnson, M. K. Contextual prerequisites for understanding: some investigations of comprehension and recall. *Journal of*

Verbal Learning and Verbal Behavior, 1972, **11**, 717–726.

Broadbent, D. *Perception and communication.* New York: Pergamon, 1958.

Brown, A. L.; Smiley, S. S.; Day, J. D.; Townsend, M. A. R.; & Lawton, S. C. Intrusion of a thematic idea in children's comprehension and retention of stories. *Child Development*, 1977, **48**, 1454–1466.

Brown, R. *Words and things.* Glencoe, Ill.: Free Press, 1958.

Bruner, J. S.; Goodnow, J. J.; & Austin, G. *A study of thinking.* New York: Wiley, 1956.

Carmichael, L.; Hogan, H. P.; & Walter, A. A. An experimental study of the effect of language on the reproduction of visually perceived form. *Journal of Experimental Psychology*, 1932, **15**, 73–86.

Chapman, L. J. Illusory correlation in observational report. *Journal of Verbal Learning and Verbal Behavior*, 1967, **6**, 151–155.

Chapman, L. J., & Chapman, J. P. Illusory correlation as an obstacle to the use of valid psychodiagnostic signs. *Journal of Abnormal Psychology*, 1969, **74**, 193–204.

Chapman, L. J., & Chapman, J. P. Genesis of popular but erroneous diagnostic observations. *Journal of Abnormal Psychology*, 1967, **72**, 193–204.

Christie, D. J., & Schumacher, G. M. Developmental trends in the abstraction and recall of relevant versus irrelevant thematic information from connected verbal materials. *Child Development*, 1975, **46**, 598–602.

Constantinople, A. Sex-role acquisition: in search of the elephant. *Sex Roles*, 1979, **5**, 121–133.

Cordua, G. D.; McGraw, K. O.; & Drabman, R. S. Doctor or nurse: children's perception of sex typed occupations. *Child Development*, 1979, **50**, 590–593.

Damon, W. *The social world of the child.* San Francisco: Jossey-Bass, 1977.

DeLucia, L. A. The toy preference test: a measure of sex role identification. *Child Development*, 1963, **34**, 107–117.

Dooling, D. J., & Lachman, R. Effects of comprehension on retention of prose. *Journal of Experimental Psychology*, 1971, **88**, 216–222.

Edelbrock, C., & Sugawara, A. I. Acquisition of sex-typed preferences in preschool children. *Developmental Psychology*, 1978, **14**, 614–623.

Edwards, A. L. Four dimensions in political stereotypes. *Journal of Abnormal and Social Psychology*, 1940, **35**, 566–572.

Emmerich, W.; Goldman, K. S.; Kirsch, B.; & Sharabany, R. Evidence for a transitional phase in the development of gender constancy. *Child Development*, 1977, **48**, 930–936.

Epstein, S. The self-concept revisited or a theory of a theory. *American Psychologist*, 1973, **28**, 404–416.

Festinger, L. *A theory of cognitive dissonance*. Evanston, Ill.: Row, Peterson, 1957.

Fishman, J. A. An examination of the process and function of social stereotyping. *Journal of Social Psychology*, 1956, **43**, 27–64.

Flavell, J. H. *Cognitive development*. Englewood Cliffs, N.J.: Prentice-Hall, 1977.

Goffman, E. *The presentation of self in everyday life*. New York: Anchor Books, 1959.

Greenwald, A. G. The totalitarian ego: fabrication and revision of personal history. *American Psychologist*, 1980, **35**, 603–618.

Hamilton, D. L. A cognitive-attributional analysis of stereotyping. In L. Berkowitz (Ed.), *Advances in experimental social psychology*. Vol. **12**. New York: Academic Press, 1979.

Hamilton, D. L., & Gifford, R. K. Illusory correlation in interpersonal perception: a cognitive basis of stereotypic judgments. *Journal of Experimental Social Psychology*, 1976, **12**, 392–407.

Hartup, W. W.; Moore, S. G.; & Sager, G. Avoidance of inappropriate sex-typing by young children. *Journal of Consulting Psychology*, 1963, **27**, 467–473.

Hastie, R., & Kumar, P. A. Person memory: personality traits as organizing principles in memory for behaviors. *Journal of Personality and Social Psychology*, 1979, **37**, 25–38.

Jacklin, C. N., & Maccoby, E. E. Social behavior at 33 months in same-sex and mixed-sex dyads. *Child Development*, 1978, **49**, 557–569.

Jaudon, J. E., & Halverson, C. F. Preschool children's preferences and recall for stereotyped versus non-stereotyped stories. *Sex Roles*, in press.

Jennings, S. A. Effects of sex-typing in children's stories on preference and recall. *Child Development*, 1975, **46**, 220–223.

Kagan, J. Acquisition and significance of sex typing and sex-role identity. In M. Hoffman & L. Hoffman (Eds.), *Review of child development research*. Vol. **1**. New York: Russell Sage, 1964.

Kelly, G. A. *The psychology of personal constructs*. Vol. **1**. *A theory of personality*. New York: W. W. Norton, 1955.

Koblinsky, S.; Cruse, D. F.; & Sugawara, A. I. Sex role stereotypes and children's memory for story content. *Child Development*, 1978, **49**, 452–458.

Kohlberg, L. A cognitive-developmental analysis of children's sex-role concepts and attitudes. In E. E. Maccoby (Ed.), *The development of sex differences*. Stanford, Calif.: Stanford University Press, 1966.

Kohlberg, L., & Ullian, D. Z. Stages in the development of psychosexual concepts and attitudes. In R. C. Friedman, R. M. Richart, & R. L. Vande Wicke (Eds.), *Sex differences in behavior*. New York: Wiley, 1979.

Kuhn, D.; Nash, S.; & Brucken, L. Sex role concepts of two- and three-year-olds. *Child Development*, 1978, **49**, 445–451.

Lewis, M., & Brooks-Gunn, J. *Social cognition and the acquisition of self*. New York: Plenum, 1979.

Liben, L. S., & Signorella, M. L. Gender-related schemata and constructive memory in children. *Child Development*, 1980, **51**, 11–18.

Liebert, R. M.; McCall, R. B.; & Hanratty, M. S. Effects of sex-typed information on children's toy preferences. *Journal of Genetic Psychology*, 1971, **119**, 133–136.

Lippman, W. *Public opinion*. New York: Harcourt Brace, 1922.

Luchins, A. S., & Luchins, E. H. *Rigidity of behavior: a variational approach to the effect of Einstellung*. Eugene: University of Oregon Books, 1959.

McCauley, C.; Stitt, C. L.; & Segal, M. Stereotyping: from prejudice to prediction. *Psychological Bulletin*, 1980, **87**, 195–208.

Maccoby, E. E. *Social development: psychological growth and the parent-child relationship*. New York: Harcourt Brace Jovanovich, 1980.

Maccoby, E. E., & Jacklin, C. N. *The psychology of sex differences*. Stanford, Calif.: Stanford University Press, 1974.

Mandler, J. M. Categorical and schematic organization in memory. In C. R. Puff (Ed.), *Memory, organization, and structure*. New York: Academic Press, 1978.

Marcus, D. E., & Overton, W. F. The development of cognitive gender constancy and sex role preferences. *Child Development*, 1978, **49**, 434–444.

Markus, H. Self-schemata and processing information about the self. *Journal of Personality and Social Psychology*, 1977, **35**, 63–78.

Martin, C. L., & Halverson, C. F. Gender constancy: a methodological and theoretical analysis. *Sex Roles*, in press.

Miller, G. The magical number seven, plus or minus two: some limits on our capacity for processing information. *Psychological Review*, 1956, **63**, 81–97.

Mischel, W. A social learning view of sex differences in behavior. In E. E. Maccoby (Ed.), *The development of sex differences*. Stanford, Calif.: Stanford University Press, 1966.

1134   Child Development

Mischel, W. Sex-typing and socialization. In P. H. Mussen (Ed.), *Carmichael's manual of child psychology*. Vol. 1. New York: Wiley, 1970.

Montemayor, R. Children's performance in a game and their attraction to it as a function of sex-typed labels. *Child Development*, 1974, **45**, 152–156.

Nadelman, L. Sex identity in American children: memory, knowledge, and preference tests. *Developmental Psychology*, 1974, **10**, 413-417.

Neisser, U. *Cognition and reality*. San Francisco: Freeman, 1976.

Nisbett, R. E., & Wilson, T. D. The halo effect: evidence for unconscious alterations of judgments. *Journal of Personality and Social Psychology*, 1977, **35**, 250–256.

Paris, S. G., & Upton, L. R. Children's memory for inferential relationships in prose. *Child Development*, 1976, **47**, 660–668.

Perry, D. G., & Bussey, K. The social learning theory of sex differences: imitation is alive and well. *Journal of Personality and Social Psychology*, 1979, **37**, 1699–1712.

Rosenthal, R., & Jacobson, L. *Pygmalion in the classroom: teacher expectation and pupils' intellectual development*. New York: Holt, Rinehart & Wilson, 1968.

Ross, D. M., & Ross, S. A. Resistance by preschool boys to sex-inappropriate behavior. *Journal of Educational Psychology*, 1972, **63**, 342–346.

Ross, L. The intuitive psychologist and his shortcomings: distortions in the attribution process. In L. Berkowitz (Ed.), *Advances in experimental social psychology*. Vol. 10. New York: Academic Press, 1977.

Rothbart, M.; Evans, M.; & Fulero, S. Recall for confirming events: memory processes and the maintenance of social stereotypes. *Journal of Experimental Social Psychology*, 1979, **15**, 343–355.

Saario, T. N.; Jacklin, C. N.; & Tittle, C. K. Sex role stereotyping in the public schools. *Harvard Educational Review*, 1973, **43**, 386–414.

Schank, R. C., & Abelson, R. P. *Scripts, plans, goals, and understanding*. Hillsdale, N.J.: Erlbaum, 1977.

Slaby, R. G., & Frey, K. S. Development of gender constancy and selective attention to same-sex models. *Child Development*, 1975, **46**, 849–856.

Snyder, M., & Cantor, N. Testing hypotheses about other people: the use of historical knowledge. *Journal of Experimental Social Psychology*, 1979, **15**, 330–342.

Snyder, M.; Tanke, E. D.; & Berscheid, E. Social perception and interpersonal behavior: on the self-fulfilling nature of social stereotypes. *Journal of Personality and Social Psychology*, 1977, **35**, 656–666.

Snyder, M., & Uranowitz, S. W. Reconstructing the past: some cognitive consequences of person perception. *Journal of Personality and Social Psychology*, 1978, **36**, 941–950.

Stein, A.; Pohly, S.; & Mueller, E. The influence of masculine, feminine, and neutral tasks on children's achievement behavior, expectancies of success, and attainment values. *Child Development*, 1971, **42**, 195–207.

Sulin, R. A., & Dooling, D. J. Intrusion of a thematic idea in retention of prose. *Journal of Experimental Psychology*, 1974, **103**, 255–262.

Tajfel, H., & Billig, M. Familiarity and categorization in intergroup behavior. *Journal of Experimental Social Psychology*, 1974, **10**, 159–170.

Taylor, S. E., & Crocker, J. Schematic bases of social information processing. In E. T. Higgins, P. Herman, & M. P. Zanna (Eds.), *The Ontario symposium in personality and social psychology*. Vol. 1. Hillsdale, N.J.: Erlbaum, 1979.

Taylor, S. E.; Fiske, S. T.; Etcoff, N. L.; & Ruderman, A. J. Categorical and contextual bases of person memory and stereotyping. *Journal of Personality and Social Psychology*, 1978, **36**, 778–793.

Tesser, A. Self-generated, attitude change. In L. Berkowitz (Ed.), *Advances in experimental social psychology*. Vol. 11. New York: Academic Press, 1978.

Tesser, A., & Leone, C. Cognitive schemas and thought as determinants of attitude change. *Journal of Experimental Social Psychology*, 1977, **13**, 340–356.

Thompson, S. K. Gender labels and early sex role development. *Child Development*, 1975, **46**, 339–347.

Vinacke, W. E. Stereotypes as social concepts. *Journal of Social Psychology*, 1957, **46**, 229–243.

Weitzman, L. J.; Eifler, D.; Hokada, E.; & Ross, C. Sex-role socialization in picture books for preschool children. *American Journal of Sociology*, 1972, **77**, 1125–1150.

Wilder, D., & Allen, W. Effects of social categorization and belief similarity upon intergroup behavior. *Personality and Social Psychology Bulletin*, 1974, **1**, 281–283.

Williams, J. E.; Bennett, S. M.; & Best, D. L. Awareness of expression of sex stereotypes in young children. *Developmental Psychology*, 1975, **11**, 635–642.

White, D. G. Effects of sex-typed labels and their sources on the imitative performance of young children. *Child Development*, 1978, **49**, 1266–1269.

Zadny, J., & Gerard, H. B. Attributed intentions and informational selectivity. *Journal of Experimental Social Psychology*, 1974, **10**, 34–52.

[35]

The Effects of Sex-typing Schemas on Young Children's Memory

Carol Lynn Martin
University of British Columbia

Charles F. Halverson, Jr.
University of Georgia

MARTIN, CAROL LYNN, and HALVERSON, CHARLES F., JR. *The Effects of Sex-typing Schemas on Young Children's Memory.* CHILD DEVELOPMENT, 54, 1983, 563–574. Children 5–6 years of age were shown pictures depicting males and females performing sex-consistent and sex-inconsistent activities. 1 week later, memory for activities and for sex of actor performing activities was tested using a variety of memory measures. Level of stereotyping and perceived similarity to actors were also assessed. As predicted, children tended to distort information by changing the sex of the actor in sex-inconsistent pictures and not by changing the sex of actor on sex-consistent pictures. Children were also more confident of memory for pictures remembered as sex consistent (whether distorted or not) than for inconsistent pictures. Children's ratings of perceived similarity followed gender of actor and did not influence memory or distortion. Results were discussed in terms of a schematic processing model of sex stereotyping and in terms of the influence sex reversals could have on the development and maintenance of sex stereotypes.

Most research concerning sex stereotyping in children has focused on how sex-related information and behavior are acquired. Little is known, however, about how sex stereotypes influence children's cognition. One way to conceptualize the extent of influence of sex stereotypes on cognition is to consider stereotypes as information-processing structures. Recently, Martin and Halverson (1981) proposed an information-processing model of sex stereotyping with the basic idea that stereotypes are "schemas," or naive theories that are relevant to the self, and function to organize and structure experience by telling the perceiver the kinds of information to look for in the environment and how to interpret such information.

On the basis of this model, two predictions can be made about how sex stereotypes should influence memory. The first prediction is that stereotypes will be used to organize memory. This organizational function is supported by two findings in the literature on memory for sex-related information. When memory for sex-consistent information has been compared to memory for sex-inconsistent information, children tend to show selective remembering of sex-consistent information. For example, children remember toys and objects that are sex-typed for their own sex better than those sex-typed for the opposite sex (Bradbard & Endsley, in press; Nadelman, 1974). Also, stereotypic information about both sexes is better remembered than reversed stereotypic information (Koblinsky, Cruse, & Sugawara, 1978).

The second prediction is that schemas will influence memory through distortion of information. Distortions occur when information is seen as consistent with a schema when it is, in fact, inconsistent or neutral (Taylor & Crocker, 1979). Sex-inconsistent information can be distorted into sex-consistent information in two ways. Consider the

This paper is based on a doctoral dissertation by the first author under the direction of the second author and submitted to the Graduate School of the University of Georgia, Athens. Portions of this paper were presented at the biennial meeting of the Society for Research in Child Development, Boston, 1981. We gratefully acknowledge the helpful comments of Richard C. Endsley, William G. Graziano, Delroy Paulhus, Abraham Tesser, and James C. Walters on an earlier draft of this paper. We would like to thank the directors, teacher, and students of the McPhaul Center, the Young World of Learning, and the Jack and Jill Day Care Center for their help. Requests for reprints should be sent to Carol Lynn Martin, Department of Family Science, School of Home Economics, University of British Columbia, Vancouver, British Columbia, Canada V6T 1W5.

[*Child Development*, 1983, 54, 563–574. © 1983 by the Society for Research in Child Development, Inc.
All rights reserved. 0009-3920/83/5403-0006$01.00]

564   Child Development

case of a child observing a boy cooking at a stove. Since the person and activity are sex inconsistent, this information may be converted to be consistent with the stereotypes either by changing the sex of the person (remembering a *girl* cooking rather than a *boy*) or by construing the activity differently (remembering a boy *fixing* the stove rather than a boy *cooking*).

Only two recent studies could be found that examined distortion in the direction of consistency with sex stereotypes. Cordua, McGraw, and Drabman (1979) presented children with videotapes of males and females portraying stereotypic and reverse-stereotypic roles. Children tended to convert reversed roles into stereotypic roles (e.g., when shown a female doctor they relabeled her as a nurse). Liben and Signorella (1980) attempted to demonstrate distortion based on changing the sex of the observed person. Children were shown pictures of people in various occupations and activities and then were given an immediate recognition test for the previously seen pictures and for pictures similar to those previously seen except that the sex of the actor in the pictures was reversed. However, sex reversals were not found, probably because of the way memory was assessed (see Liben & Signorella, 1980, and Discussion section of this article).

Three questions have not been addressed completely in the few studies on children's distortion of sex-related information: (*a*) What methods are most sensitive for detecting distortion? (*b*) When does distortion occur? and (*c*) Do other self-relevant schemas besides sex-typing produce distortion?

First, what methods of memory assessment are most sensitive in detecting distortion? Since simple tasks may result in nearly perfect memory performance (e.g., Brown & Scott, 1971), a relatively difficult task is needed so that chances of perfectly accurate memory are small (e.g., the time between presentation and testing may need to be relatively long and/or the stimulus pictures may need to be complex). Further, detection of memory distortions may depend on how memory is assessed. In adults, distortion is typically assessed by a memory-reproduction task (e.g., Bartlett, 1932) where the unstructured nature of the task is conducive to finding distortions. For children, such tasks are so difficult that most researchers have used structured recognition formats where

pictures are shown and children are asked to decide if the pictures had been presented before (e.g., Liben & Signorella, 1980). A problem in using recognition formats to detect distortion is that children's recognition memory for pictures is extremely good (Brown & Scott, 1971).

A compromise used in the present study was to use a task more structured than free recall and yet less structured than the standard recognition task. Specifically, we used a structured recall task (e.g., "did I show you a picture of a boy sewing before?") rather than actually showing the child the stimulus material and asking if they remembered seeing it. Further, we used another memory measure that may be sensitive to memory distortion—children's ratings of how confident they were that they had seen what they said they had. Since there is evidence that information abstracted or inferred from a stimulus array is indistinguishable from the information in the original stimulus array (e.g., Bransford & Franks, 1971), it might be expected that distortions of sex-related information would be perceived as being as "real" in memory as nondistorted information. Specifically, when queried about how confident they were that they saw an actor or activity before, children should be as confident of distorted information as nondistorted information.

Second, when does distortion occur? Based on the adult literature (Taylor & Crocker, 1979), we believe that there are at least two points at which distortion can occur. Children may inaccurately perceive information when it is being presented (distort during encoding) or they may inaccurately recall information after it has been accurately encoded (distort during retrieval). An attempt was made to examine distortion at both points in the present study.

Third, do other self-relevant schemas besides sex-typing produce distortion? According to our view (Martin & Halverson, 1981), children may use self-relevant schemas other than sex stereotypes to organize memory. For example, when shown pictures of actors performing various activities, children may perceive themselves to be like the actors in the pictures based on dress, hair, etc. This perceived similarity may lead to an increase in memory for certain pictures independent of the stereotyping of the actor or activity. Since research has shown that adults have better memory for self-relevant than for non-self-relevant information (e.g., Markus, 1977; Martin & Paulhus, Note 1; Rogers, Kuiper, & Kirker, 1977), children's perceived similarity to actors in stimulus pictures was assessed in the present study. The similarity assessment provided information concerning whether other kinds of self-relevant schemas influenced memory.

Taking the above three questions into consideration, the present study was designed to investigate memory and distortion of sex-related information. In an incidental memory task, children were shown a series of pictures depicting males and females performing a variety of sex-consistent and sex-inconsistent activities. One week later, children were asked to remember the activities they had seen before and the sex of the actors performing the activities. Memory was assessed using free-recall and probed-recall procedures. Children's confidence in their memory was also assessed. Two measures were used to assess individual differences in level of stereotyping. One measured general *knowledge* about the traditional roles for males and females, while the other measured *preference* for roles and objects sex-typed for the same sex over roles and objects sex-typed for the opposite sex. Our major interest was in the sex-role preference measures, since we wanted to divide children on the basis of how sex stereotypes influenced their *own* behavior rather than how well they had learned the traditional sex-role stereotypes. Level of stereotyping was included as a moderating variable, since there is evidence to indicate that people with well-developed schemas are more likely to make distortion errors than people with less well-developed schemas (Tesser & Leone, 1977).

It was predicted that children who have well-developed sex-stereotyping schemas would be more likely to remember seeing an activity before and be more confident of that memory if the activity was presented in a sex-consistent context (e.g., girl cooking) rather than a sex-inconsistent context (e.g., boy cooking). In comparison to children who are less sex stereotyped, highly stereotyped children were also expected to be more likely to distort information inconsistent with their stereotypes into sex-consistent information and to be more confident of their recall when the sex of the actor was consistent rather than inconsistent with the sex-typing of the activity.

Method

Subjects

Subjects were 48 children (24 males and 24 females) ranging in age from 5 to 6 years ($M = 5.7$). They were predominately white and middle class and were enrolled in day-care centers in kindergartens.

Materials

The Sex Role Learning Inventory (SERLI) (Edelbrock & Sugawara, 1978) was used to assess each child's sex-role preference (SRP) score and their sex-role discrimination score (SRD). The SRP score refers to the extent to which children's preferences adhere to adult standards of sex-role stereotyping. The SRD score refers to what children know about traditional sex roles for females and males.

A set of 72 black-and-white line drawings was assembled to be used for assessing memory. Thirty-six pictures depicted traditionally masculine activities and 36 pictures depicted traditionally feminine activities. From this set of pictures, three subsets of pictures were selected so that every activity was presented equally often with a male actor, a female actor, or was used as a new activity. The pictures used were a subset of the SERLI pictures (Edelbrock & Sugawara, 1978) and several items from Brown's (1957) sex-role test.

For the memory task, each child was presented with one subset of 16 pictures on the first day. Of the 16 pictures, eight of the pictures showed activities consistent for the actor in the picture (e.g., boy playing with a train) and eight of the pictures showed activities inconsistent for the actor in the picture (e.g., girl sawing wood). Eight activities not shown on the first day were included during the memory testing session. These new items were used to investigate response bias (see Results section for an explanation of this procedure).

Children were asked to give ratings on several dimensions during both the presentation of the pictures and during memory testing. To obtain the ratings, a series of four blocks were used. The blocks were made of yellow poster board and were arranged from largest to smallest on a strip of orange poster board. The blocks ranged in size from 10.3 cm to 2.5 cm square.

Procedure

Each child was tested individually on both the memory task and on the SERLI. The

566 Child Development

SERLI was given 1–2 weeks following the recognition task.

Presentation of pictures.—Children were individually presented with 16 pictures, one at a time, for a duration of approximately 10 sec per picture. The female experimenter instructed the children to look at the pictures and identify the sex and age of each actor in the picture (man, woman, boy, or girl). Gender identifications were recorded by the experimenter, and any mistakes in identifying the sex or age of the actor in the picture were corrected immediately. For each picture, the children were also asked to rate how much they were "like [the man, woman, girl, boy] in the picture." Ratings were obtained by asking the children to point to the block that corresponded with how much they were like the person. The largest block was used to indicate "very much like," the next largest block indicated "pretty much like," the next block "a little bit like," and the smallest block "not at all like." After the rating, the experimenter asked the children to explain their reasons for the judgments. The presentation of the pictures was randomized and no memory instructions were given.

Memory testing.—One week later, memory for the previously shown pictures was assessed. Children were first asked to try to remember any of the pictures using a free-recall procedure. These responses were recorded verbatim. A probed-recall procedure for activities immediately followed. The children were asked about all the activities they were shown in pictures previously and about eight activities not shown before. The order of the activities was randomized. For each activity, they were asked, "do you remember seeing a picture of someone doing [activity] in the pictures I showed you last week?" For remembered activities, children were asked to rate how confident they were of having seen that activity before by pointing to the block that represented their confidence. Selecting the largest block indicated that they were "very sure" of having seen someone doing that activity before, the next largest indicated "pretty sure," the next size indicated "fairly sure," and the smallest indicated "not sure at all."

After the ratings, a probed-recall procedure for sex of actor was done. The children were asked whether they remembered seeing a girl, a boy, a man, or a woman performing each activity in the pictures shown the week before. Confidence ratings for memory of the sex of each actor performing each activity were also obtained using the same four-point scale. Children were asked to point to the box that indicated how sure they were that their responses about the sex of the persons in the picture were correct. All responses were recorded verbatim by the experimenter.

SERLI task.—The parts of the Sex Role Learning Inventory (Edelbrock & Sugawara, 1978) were administered in a separate session.

Scoring
Gender identification during presentation.—Gender identification for the actors in the pictures was scored as correct or incorrect. Scores were summed over inconsistent and consistent pictures.

Recall measures.—Scoring responses on free recall involved assessing whether the activity was actually seen before and whether the sex of the actor corresponded to the previously shown picture. For probed recall of activities, children were given a score of 1 if an activity was remembered and a 0 if it was not. For probed recall of sex of actors, for those activities in previously shown pictures, children were given a score of 1 if they named the opposite sex than originally presented (a sex reversal) and a 0 if they named the same sex as originally presented. For new activities, children's responses were scored according to whether the sex of actor corresponded with the sex-typing of the activity. When sex of actor and sex-typing of the activity were consistent, a score of 1 was given. When sex of actor and the sex-typing of the activity were inconsistent, a score of 0 was given.

Stereotyping measure.—The SERLI was scored using the system developed by Edelbrock and Sugawara (1978). The parts of the SERLI concerning sex-role preference (SRP) for child and adult activities were summed for each child. Children whose summed SRP scores fell below the median were classified as low in stereotypic preferences, while those whose scores were above the median were classified as high in stereotypic preferences. The median score was based on the total group of children and resulted in approximately equal numbers of boys and girls being classified as highly stereotyped.

Results

Probed recall of activities.—To assess recognition accurately, children's response tendency to answer "yes" indiscriminately had to be considered. To do this, the number of "yes" responses to the items not previously seen was examined. A relatively large number of positive responses were given on these new items ($M = 1.87$), signifying that some children had a general tendency to say they had seen these activities before, even though they were not in the original memory stimuli. Because of this response tendency, a new score was devised to correct for the bias. For all possible groupings of pictures, the new scores were the number of old activities remembered divided by the number of new activities falsely remembered plus 1. Scores could range from 0 to 4.0.

The corrected probed-recall score served as the dependent variable in a repeated-measures analysis of variance on the previously presented items. A $2 \times 2 \times 2 \times 2$ unweighted means analysis of variance with two between-subjects factors (sex of subject, male and female; level of stereotyping, high and low) and two within-subjects factors (sex of actor in picture, male and female; picture type, consistent and inconsistent) was used to analyze probed-recall scores.

The analysis of probed-recall scores revealed a significant picture type × sex of actor interaction, $F(1,44) = 5.31$, $p < .03$, $\Omega^2 = .11$. These data are summarized in Figure 1. Post hoc analyses for simple effects showed that for the pictures where the actor and activity were consistent, children said they remembered the activities performed by female actors ($M = .79$) more often than those performed by male actors ($M = .65$). For the pictures where the actor and activity were inconsistent, the reverse pattern was found. Children said they remembered the activities performed by male actors ($M = .78$) more often than those performed by female actors ($M = .69$).

There was also a picture type × sex of subject × level of stereotyping interaction, $F(1,44) = 4.01$, $p < .05$, $\Omega^2 = .08$. Post hoc analyses revealed that the picture type × level of stereotyping interactions were not significant for either sex. Subsumed by the three-way interaction was the marginal main effect of level of stereotyping, $F(1,44) = 3.60$, $p < .07$, $\Omega^2 = .08$, indicating that both boys

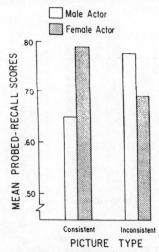

FIG. 1.—Mean probed-recall scores for activities by picture type.

and girls who were highly stereotyped remembered more activities than those children who were not highly stereotyped.

Confidence ratings for activities.—Children's confidence about memory for the activities was also assessed with a $2 \times 2 \times 2 \times 2$ unweighted means repeated-measures analysis of variance. The dependent measure was the mean confidence rating from the remembered old activities for each group of pictures (e.g., female actor–inconsistent activity). Scores ranged from 0 to 4.

The analysis revealed a significant picture type × set of actor × set of subject interaction, $F(1,35) = 7.33$, $p < .01$, $\Omega^2 = .17$. Post hoc analyses revealed the nature of the interaction illustrated in Figure 2. For boys, but not girls, a significant picture type × sex of actor interaction was found. Further analyses revealed that for consistent pictures, boys were more confident of memory for activities performed by male actors ($M = 3.37$) than female actors ($M = 2.54$). The reverse was found for inconsistent pictures. When the actor was performing a sex-inconsistent activity, boys were more confident of memory for activities performed by female actors ($M = 3.20$) than by male actors ($M = 2.55$).

Sex reversals during probed recall.—A $2 \times 2 \times 2 \times 2$ unweighted means repeated-measures analysis of variance was used to analyze children's memory for sex of actors.

568   Child Development

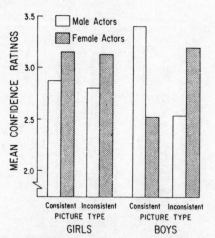

FIG. 2.—Mean confidence ratings for activities by sex of actor and sex of subject.

TABLE 1

PROPORTIONS OF HIGH AND LOW CONFIDENCE RATINGS GIVEN ON CONSISTENT AND INCONSISTENT PICTURES WHEN SEX ASSIGNMENTS WERE CORRECT AND INCORRECT

	CONFIDENCE	
	Low	High
Correct sex assignments:		
Sex remembered as consistent with activity.........	.20	.45
Sex remembered as inconsistent with activity.......	.08	.27
Incorrect sex assignments:		
Sex distorted to be consistent with activity.........	.27	.49
Sex distorted to be inconsistent with activity.........	.11	.13

NOTE.—Proportions for correct sex assignments based on total frequency = 290. Proportions for incorrect sex assignments based on total frequency = 183.

The dependent measure for distortion was the number of sex reversals occurring for the activities remembered from each picture grouping. For example, a child may have remembered three out of four of the originally presented activities in female-inconsistent pictures. If the child then reversed the sex of the actor on two pictures, the sex-reversal score for that picture grouping would be .67, indicating that on two-thirds of the recognized pictures distortion of sex occurred. Since the sex-reversal scores were proportions, heterogeneity of variance was minimized by using Winer's (1971) arcsin correction for proportions.

The analysis revealed a significant main effect for picture type, $F(1,36) = 31.55$, $p < .001$, $\Omega^2 = .47$. Regardless of level of stereotyping, both boys and girls were more likely to make sex reversals on inconsistent pictures ($M = 1.64$) than on consistent pictures ($M = .56$).

Confidence ratings for sex-of-actor judgments.—Confidence ratings were analyzed separately for correct and incorrect sex assignments. As illustrated in Table 1, both analyses involved a comparison of scores on consistent and inconsistent pictures. Confidence ratings were collapsed into two groups—high confidence (scores of 3 and 4) and low confidence (scores of 1 and 2). The frequency of high and low confidence scores was divided by the total number of responses given. The resulting proportions were compared using McNemar's test (Winer, 1971). Analyses revealed that boys and girls were more often

confident of sex assignments when assignments matched the sex-typing of the activity (consistent) rather than when they did not (inconsistent). Interestingly, the same pattern of confidence scores resulted when children were incorrect as well as when they were correct on sex assignments. That is, the children were just as confident of their judgments when the actors and activities were remembered as consistent, even if they were, in fact, wrong in their recall.

Sex reversals during free recall.—Before the recognition test, children were asked to try to remember the pictures they were shown before. For each activity correctly recalled, the sex assignment for the actor was analyzed by examining the proportions of correct and incorrect sex assignments for consistent and inconsistent pictures. While few pictures were recalled, there were significantly ($p < .05$) more sex reversals on inconsistent pictures (6 out of 20, 30%) than on consistent pictures (2 out of 24, 8%).

Sex reversals during picture presentation.—Children were asked to identify sex of the actors in each picture as they were being presented. Few errors occurred during picture presentation (31), but out of those that did occur, 84% occurred on pictures where the actor was performing a sex-inconsistent activity, and only 16% occurred on pictures where the actor was performing a sex-consistent activity. Further analyses revealed that most errors occurred on the following pictures: boy holding doll (5), man holding purse (4), and girl holding hammer (3).

Perceived Similarity Judgments

Ratings of perceived "likeness" to actors were assessed to discover the characteristics of pictures children used to make such judgments.

A $2 \times 2 \times 2 \times 2$ unweighted means analysis of variance was used to analyze children's ratings of perceived similarity to actors. A significant two-way interaction of sex of actor × sex of subject was found, $F(1,44) = 35.32$, $p < .001$, $\Omega^2 = .45$. As can be seen in Figure 3, boys rated themselves more "like" male actors ($M = 10.21$) than female actors ($M = 8.42$), and girls rated themselves more like female actors ($M = 11.17$) than male actors ($M = 6.99$). Subsumed in the two-way interaction was a significant main effect for sex of actor, $F(1,44) = 6.55$, $p < .02$, $\Omega^2 = .13$. Female actors ($M = 9.79$) were given higher similarity ratings than male actors ($M = 8.60$).

To investigate whether children's ratings of similarity influenced memory, comparisons were made between similarity ratings and probed-recall scores. Neither the correlation for pictures with female actors, $r(48) = .03$, nor the pictures with male actors, $r(48) = -.15$, were significant, indicating that perceived similarity with actors did not improve recall. Ratings of similarity were also compared to distortion scores. The correlations for pictures with female actors, $r(44) = .10$, and for pictures with male actors, $r(44) = .09$, were low, suggesting that perceived similarity did not influence the occurrence of sex reversals.

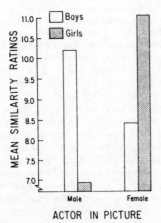

Fig. 3.—Mean similarity ratings by sex of actor and sex of subject.

Discussion

Distortion of Gender Information

The predictions concerning distortion of sex toward consistency with stereotypes were supported. Consistent with the schematic processing model (Martin & Halverson, 1981), children tended to change sex-inconsistent information into sex-consistent information by changing the sex of the actors. Specifically, the same pattern of sex reversals was found in probed recall, free recall, and during the presentation of the pictures. The stereotyping schema influenced memory by causing sex-of-actor information to be remembered if it was consistent with the sex-typing of the activity, and by causing sex-of-actor information to be changed if it was inconsistent with the sex-typing of the activity.

It might be argued that these results demonstrate, not true distortion, but some kind of response bias. That is, when they could not recall the sex of an actor, children simply guessed based on knowledge about which sex typically performs each activity. In this case, the bias should be called a stereotyping response bias since it is based on what children believe about sex stereotypes. There are several factors that strongly suggest that such a bias did not occur.

First, during memory testing children were admonished to "remember the pictures I showed you before." These instructions made it clear that children should try to remember the actual pictures rather than guess. Second, children were given the option of saying they did not remember the sex of the actor. Since this option was virtually never used, children appeared to believe they were not guessing. Third, if children were guessing rather than remembering, we would expect the confidence ratings to reflect lack of confidence in memory. Instead, the confidence ratings indicated that children were extremely confident about those memory distortions that were consistent with stereotypes. In fact, they were just as confident in those cases as when they were correct. Fourth, if this bias was occurring, we would expect it to be evident even on false alarms. That is, children occasionally falsely remembered some of the activities they were not shown before, and in those cases, they also "remembered" the sex of the actor. So, if the bias was occurring, then children's scores for "stereotyping bias" on the original inconsistent pictures (where a high sex-reversal score indicated that sex of actor was made consistent with activity) should posi-

570   Child Development

tively correlate with "stereotyping bias" on falsely remembered new pictures. In fact, the correlations between the scores on new and old activities were not significant (inconsistent pictures, $r[34] = -.06$, consistent pictures, $r[34] = -.12$), again suggesting that response bias was not a factor.

In sum, the pattern of errors indicates true distortion and is consistent with a reconstructionist or substitution theory of memory (e.g., Loftus & Loftus, 1980). A stereotyping response bias could not account for distortion in the present study. Further research examining stereotyping response biases is necessary to discover whether they contribute at all to distortions in memory.

Contrary to prediction, level of stereotyping did not interact with distortion. Regardless of level of stereotyping, some distortion of sex-inconsistent information occurred. Level of stereotyping probably did not influence distortion because there was a narrow range in stereotyping, with most children being moderately to highly stereotyped. Or, it may be that only a minimal level of stereotyping is necessary to cause distortions to occur.

Children's confidence ratings also indicated the importance of being consistent with stereotypes. Children were confident of their memory for pictures where actor and activity were consistent. Interestingly, they were as confident about pictures they distorted to be consistent as they were about consistent pictures correctly remembered. Apparently, distorted information that is consistent with stereotypes is as "real" to these children as nondistorted information. In contrast, children lacked confidence of their memory of information if it was distorted to be inconsistent with stereotypes.

These findings are congruent with research on prose memory. Bransford and Franks (1971) demonstrated that subjects were extremely confident about memory for thematically consistent information even when it was not actually presented in the story. Schemas function as "illusory data bases" supplying missing information (Martin & Halverson, 1981; Taylor & Crocker, 1979) indistinguishable in memory from actual information. In the present study, only distorted information consistent with the stereotype received high confidence ratings and implies that consistency with schemas is crucial for information to appear real in memory.

Even though the mean level of free recall was extremely low, these data also provided support for the distortion hypothesis in that more sex reversals occurred on inconsistent pictures than on consistent pictures. Also, the few sex reversals made when the pictures were originally presented were mostly in the direction of making the actor's sex consistent with the sex-typing of the activity; this suggests that some sex reversals toward consistency with the stereotype occur while encoding information.

The idea that stereotyping schemas influence both the encoding and retrieval of information in memory is consistent with previous research of schematic processing models in adults (Rothbart, Evans, & Fulero, 1979; Snyder & Uranowitz, 1978; Zadny & Gerard, 1974). One study with children examined the encoding of sex-typed information. Kail and Levine (Note 2) demonstrated that sex-typed information is encoded with object names and influenced recall of these names.

The findings from the present study provide support for stereotyping schemas operating at both the encoding and retrieval stages. Since children sometimes erred in identifying the sex of the actor during picture presentation, it appears that stereotyping schemas affect the encoding of information. It might even be argued that distortions observed at retrieval merely reflected earlier encoding distortions. For several reasons, this argument cannot be sustained. First, all errors in identifying sex during picture presentation were immediately corrected. Indeed, these corrections appeared to be effective in ensuring that the information was encoded correctly. In the cases where sex of actor was incorrectly identified during presentation, most were later remembered with the correct sex of actor (52%), few were remembered with the incorrect sex of actor (13%), and some were not remembered at all (35%). Second, it is unlikely that mistakes in identifying sex accounted for later sex reversals, since many more sex reversals occurred during the probed-recall task than during picture presentation. Evidently, some information is distorted during encoding, but most of the distortion appears to occur during retrieval of information. Further investigations of the effect of stereotypes on distortion are necessary to clarify the extent to which stereotyping influences encoding and retrieval processes.

The present results suggest that children often distort inconsistent information by changing the sex of the actor. Earlier research, however, demonstrated that children redefined activities to match the sex of the actor (Cordua et al., 1979). Possibly, sex reversals will occur when the activity is made salient (as in the present study), and activity redefinition will occur when the actor is made salient, as in the Cordua et al. (1979) study.

Further research is also necessary to discover what variables affect distortion. For example, in a recent study by Liben and Signorella (1980), sex reversals were not found. Several factors may have operated in their study to minimize sex distortions. First, distortion may only occur when there has been a delay between presentation and recall of information (Sulin & Dooling, 1974; see discussion by Hastie & Kumar, 1979). Liben and Signorella (1980) used an immediate-recognition task and did not find sex reversals. In the present study, a 1-week delay was used, and sex reversals were found. Second, the standard recognition format used by Liben and Signorella (1980) was so easy that perfect recall occurred. Even very young children have extremely good memory for pictures (Brown & Scott, 1971). In contrast, the free-recall procedure used in the present study was very difficult for young children, while the probed-recall procedure produced the best evidence for sex reversals.

Memory for Activities

The second major hypothesis from the schematic processing model was that stereotyping schemas would organize memory such that children would remember more activities from pictures where the actors were engaged in sex-consistent activities rather than in sex-inconsistent activities. This hypothesis was only partially supported.

For pictures with female actors, those activities consistent with the stereotype were more often remembered than inconsistent activities, while for pictures with male actors, those activities inconsistent with the stereotype were remembered better than consistent. Possibly the violation of male stereotypes was so novel that such information became extremely salient and was remembered. In contrast, the violation of female stereotypes may not have been as novel. There is research to support the idea that novel information is well remembered. In some cases, schema-inconsistent (Hastie & Kumar, 1979) or distinctive (Hamilton & Gifford, 1976) informa-

tion is remembered better than nondistinctive information. For example, Jennings (1975) found that children remembered sex-inconsistent information better than sex-consistent information.

Another way to interpret these findings is to categorize the activities into those generally performed by either males or females regardless of consistency of actor and activity. When considered this way, children generally remembered more feminine activities than male activities, regardless of sex of actor. Given the types of activities portrayed in the pictures, such a result is not surprising. Most of the feminine activities are those that children probably see frequently, such as cooking, ironing, sewing, and dishwashing, while the masculine activities are probably less often seen (e.g., boxing, digging, sawing wood, and firefighting). Children of both sexes may remember more of the feminine activities than masculine activities because they are more often exposed to feminine activities.

Additional insight concerning the memory-for-activity results can be obtained by examining confidence ratings where confidence in memories varied depending on sex of the child making the judgment. Girls were equally confident of memory for activities regardless of whether or not the sex of the actor performing the activity was consistent wth the sex-typing of the activity. Boys, however, were more confident of memory of masculine activities than for feminine activities, regardless of sex of actor. Boys were most confident of memories consistent with male stereotypes, even though they remembered few of these activities, and less confident of the many activities they remembered from male-inconsistent pictures. It does appear that consistency with sex stereotypes influenced memory in the case of boys' confidence ratings.

Children were expected to remember more activities from consistent pictures and be more confident about memory for activities from consistent pictures. The results provided only partial support for this hypothesis, as the confidence ratings and probed-recall memory did not coincide for either boys or girls. Apparently, what children remember and how sure they are about remembering are somehow different. Further research is necessary to clarify the similarities and differences between remembering an activity and confidence about that memory.

572 Child Development

The findings concerning memory for activities in the present study are very different than those found by Liben and Signorella (1980), who also investigated children's memory as a function of their stereotypic attitudes. They found the predicted memory differences between consistent and inconsistent pictures when the actor was male. In the present study, the predicted difference was found for pictures when the actor was female. Liben and Signorella (1980) found that only highly stereotyped children showed differences between consistent and inconsistent pictures, while in the present study, level of stereotyping related to the general level of recall rather than being related to selective memory effects.

Despite the conceptual similarity between the two studies, three methodological differences are worth noting, as they may account for the discrepancies in results. First, the present study used a 1-week delay between presentation and testing, while Liben and Signorella (1980) used immediate memory testing. Second, using a probed-recall task (present study) may produce different results than a recognition task (Liben & Signorella, 1980). The probed-recall task was designed to test memory for activities separately from memory for sex of actor, in contrast to a recognition task that tests memory for actors and activities simultaneously. The probed-recall task was used to make the analysis of sex reversals clearer by separating memory for actor and activity and to increase the likelihood of obtaining sex reversals by using a task more difficult than recognition. Also, memory for activities was correct for response biases in the present study and not in the Liben and Signorella (1980) study.

The third difference between the two studies concerns how level of stereotyping was assessed. In the present study, the score used was one part of the SERLI (Edelbrock & Sugawara, 1978) that measured that extent to which children's preferences for activities and occupations conformed to adult standards of stereotyping. Liben and Signorella (1980) measured stereotyping by showing children pictures of sex-typed activities and asking whether each activity was most often done by men, women, or both men and women. Those children who gave few "both" responses were considered low in stereotyping. Certainly asking children their preferences for activities (as in the present study) is quite different from asking what activities can be performed by each sex (as in the Liben & Signorella study).

So that direct comparisons could be made between the two studies, we attempted to score our data to be as similar as possible to those used by Liben and Signorella. To begin, we examined part of the SERLI data that were not originally used—the sex-role discrimination scores (SRD). To obtain the SRD scores, children were asked to sort sex-typed objects according to "who would use [object]? boys? girls? or both boys and girls?" By adding each child's number of both responses, we had a stereotyping score virtually identical to the knowledge scores used by Liben and Signorella. The memory scores were more difficult. Since this study was under way before the Liben and Signorella study was published, we were unable to include a memory measure exactly comparable to the one used by Liben and Signorella. For this reason, the closest we could come to having a similar measure was by recomputing the memory scores. To recompute the memory scores, we considered "correct" responses as those cases where the activity was recognized and the actor's sex was correctly remembered. So, rather than using activity scores separately, responses concerning activity and actor were considered together.

To examine whether the discrepancy in results was due to the way stereotyping was measured, an analysis was done using the original memory scores and the new stereotyping scores. This resulted in a pattern fairly similar to the original findings. For male actors in consistent pictures, highly stereotyped children remembered slightly more ($M = .67$) than children not highly stereotyped ($M = .59$). For male actors in inconsistent pictures, the same pattern was found, with high-stereotyped children ($M = .86$) remembering slightly more pictures than low-stereotyped children ($M = .74$). For female actors in consistent pictures, high-stereotyped children ($M = .92$) showed better memory than low-stereotyped children ($M = .67$). For female actors in inconsistent pictures, high-stereotyped children ($M = .79$) also showed better memory than low-stereotyped children ($M = .56$).

To discover whether the differences in the way memory was measured accounted for the discrepancy in results, an analysis was done using the original stereotyping scores and the new memory scores. This resulted in a pattern of results similar to those found by Liben and Signorella. For male actors in consistent pictures, high-stereotyped children ($M = 2.40$) showed better memory than low-stereotyped children ($M = 1.18$). For male actors in inconsistent pictures, the differences in recall between high-stereotyped children ($M = .18$) and low-stereotyped children ($M = .47$) were smaller. For female actors in consistent pictures, high-stereotyped children ($M = 2.65$) showed better memory than low-stereotyped children ($M = 2.33$). For female actors in inconsistent pictures, the differences were quite small (high-stereotyped $M = 2.22$, low-stereotyped $M = 2.09$).

Since the results were more similar to the Liben and Signorella pattern of results when the new memory scores were used to reanalyze the data, it appears that the major factor accounting for the discrepancy between the studies was how memory was measured. The differences in the ways stereotyping was assessed also played a role in the discrepancy, but a much more minor role. Despite attempts to construct a memory score similar to the Liben and Signorella score, the new score was still quite dissimilar. These post-hoc analyses do, however, suggest that the discrepancy is due to whether actor and activity information is analyzed as a whole or as separate components rather than resulting from either time delay or using picture recognition versus verbal recall tasks.

In conclusion, it appears that the way memory is assessed can have a dramatic influence on patterns of results. While we cannot immediately suggest a mechanism for these differences, it is clear that future studies must take some care in selecting a measure of recall.

Similarity Judgments

The findings indicated that children judged similarity with actors based solely on the sex of the actor. Boys rated themselves as like male actors; girls rated themselves as like female actors. Ratings of similarity were not affected by the type of activity in which the actor was engaged or by the relation between the sex of the actor and the sex-typing of the activity. Since the question concerning similarity was focused on the actor, it is not surprising that sex was the determining characteristic. Sex is an obvious and easily distinguishable physical category to use for judging similarity (Thompson, 1975). Grouping people by gender similarity may also help children organize their environment by providing separate groups of "people

like me" and "people not like me" (Lewis & Brooks-Gunn, 1979; Martin & Halverson, 1981).

For adults, there is evidence to indicate that schemas that are salient to a person influence thinking and memory (e.g., Markus, 1977). In the present study, the expectation was that memory would be influenced by perceived similarity with actors, so that memory for the activity performed by that actor and remembering the actor's sex would be enhanced. This prediction was not supported. Children did not better remember sex of actors or the activities performed by actors who were perceived to be similar to themselves. Distortion of sex of actor occurred regardless of how similar children perceived actors to be with themselves. Perceived similarity may not have influenced memory for several reasons. It may be that young children can make these similarity ratings, and yet the schema for similarity may not be used to structure memory because it is not salient. Also, the design of the study made it difficult to examine the relation between similarity and memory. Children were not shown the original pictures during testing; they were asked to remember without using the stimulus pictures. Perhaps similarity would affect memory if the actual pictures were used in memory testing.

Further research is necessary to define the situations where stereotypes will influence memory. Schematic processing models of stereotyping appear to be useful in predicting the influence that stereotypes may have in the processing of social information. Of particular interest is discovering more about how and why children make distortions of sex-related information, since the consequences of these distortions are far-reaching. Every time that sex-inconsistent information is converted into sex-consistent information, the child is confirming the stereotype rather than using this information to disconfirm it. Further investigation of sex-related distortion may be useful in discovering how sex stereotypes are maintained and possibly how these distortions can be minimized. Such information would be useful for intervention programs attempting to teach children more equalitarian sex-role orientations.

Reference Notes

1.   Martin, C. L., & Paulhus, D. L. *Bipolar biasing effects of self and gender structures on*

574 Child Development

memory for traits. Manuscript submitted for publication, 1981.

2. Kail, R. V., & Levine, L. *Encoding processes and sex-role preferences.* Paper presented at the biennial meeting of the Society for Research in Child Development, Denver, 1975.

References

Bartlett, F. C. *Remembering.* Cambridge, Mass.: Harvard University Press, 1932.

Bradbard, M. R., & Endsley, R. C. The effects of sex-typed labeling on children's information seeking and retention. *Sex Roles,* in press.

Bransford, J. D., & Franks, J. J. The abstraction of linguistic ideas. *Cognitive Psychology,* 1971, **2,** 331–350.

Brown, A. L., & Scott, M. S. Recognition memory for pictures in preschool children. *Journal of Experimental Child Psychology,* 1971, **11,** 401–412.

Brown, D. G. Masculinity-femininity development in children. *Journal of Consulting Psychology,* 1957, **21,** 197–202.

Cordua, G. D., McGraw, K. O., & Drabman, R. S. Doctor or nurse: Children's perception of sex-typed occupations. *Child Development,* 1979, **50,** 590–593.

Edelbrock, C., & Sugawara, A. I. Acquisition of sex-typed preferences in preschool children. *Developmental Psychology,* 1978, **14,** 614–623.

Hamilton, D. L., & Gifford, R. K. Illusory correlation in interpersonal perception: A cognitive basis of stereotypic judgments. *Journal of Experimental Social Psychology,* 1976, **12,** 392–407.

Hastie, R., & Kumar, P. A. Person memory: Personality traits as organizing principles in memory for behaviors. *Journal of Personality and Social Psychology,* 1979, **37,** 25–38.

Jennings, S. A. Effects of sex-typing in children's stories on preference and recall. *Child Development,* 1975, **46,** 220–223.

Koblinsky, S., Cruse, D. F., & Sugawara, A. I. Sex-role stereotypes and children's memory for story content. *Child Development,* 1978, **49,** 452–458.

Lewis, M., & Brooks-Gunn, J. *Social cognition and the acquisition of the self.* New York: Plenum, 1979.

Liben, L. S., & Signorella, M. L. Gender-related

schemata and constructive memory in children. *Child Development,* 1980, **51,** 11–18.

Loftus, E. F., & Loftus, G. R. On the permanence of stored information in the human brain. *American Psychologist,* 1980, **35,** 409–420.

Markus, H. Self-schemata and processing information about the self. *Journal of Personality and Social Psychology,* 1977, **35,** 63–78.

Martin, C. L., & Halverson, C. F. A schematic processing model of sex-typing and stereotyping in children. *Child Development,* 1981, **52,** 1119–1134.

Nadelman, L. Sex identity in American children: Memory, knowledge, and preference tests. *Developmental Psychology,* 1974, **10,** 413–417.

Rogers, T. B., Kuiper, N. A., & Kirker, W. S. Self-reference and the encoding of personal information. *Journal of Personality and Social Psychology,* 1977, **35,** 677–688.

Rothbart, M., Evans, M., & Fulero, S. Recall for confirming events: Memory processes and the maintenance of social stereotypes. *Journal of Experimental Social Psychology,* 1979, **15,** 343–355.

Snyder, M., & Uranowitz, S. W. Reconstructing the past: Some cognitive consequences of person perception. *Journal of Personality and Social Psychology,* 1978, **36,** 941–950.

Sulin, R. A., & Dooling, D. J. Intrusion of a thematic idea in a retention of prose. *Journal of Experimental Psychology,* 1974, **103,** 255–262.

Taylor, S. E., & Crocker, J. Schematic bases of social information processing. In E. T. Higgins, P. Herman, & M. P. Zanna (Eds.), *The Ontario symposium in personality and social psychology* (Vol. 1). Hillsdale, N.J.: Erlbaum, 1979.

Tesser, A., & Leone, C. Cognitive schemas and thought as determinants of attitude change. *Journal of Experimental Psychology,* 1977, **13,** 340–356.

Thompson, S. K. Gender labels and early sex-role development. *Child Development,* 1975, **46,** 339–347.

Winer, B. J. *Statistical principles in experimental design.* New York: McGraw-Hill, 1971.

Zadny, J., & Gerard, H. B. Attributed intentions and informational selectivity. *Journal of Experimental Social Psychology,* 1974, **10,** 34–52.

Part IV
Moral Development

[36]

In a Different Voice: Women's Conceptions of Self and of Morality

CAROL GILLIGAN
Harvard University

As theories of developmental psychology continue to define educational goals and practice, it has become imperative for educators and researchers to scrutinize not only the underlying assumptions of such theories but also the model of adulthood toward which they point. Carol Gilligan examines the limitations of several theories, most notably Kohlberg's stage theory of moral development, and concludes that developmental theory has not given adequate expression to the concerns and experience of women. Through a review of psychological and literary sources, she illustrates the feminine construction of reality. From her own research data, interviews with women contemplating abortion, she then derives an alternative sequence for the development of women's moral judgments. Finally, she argues for an expanded conception of adulthood that would result from the integration of the "feminine voice" into developmental theory.

The arc of developmental theory leads from infantile dependence to adult autonomy, tracing a path characterized by an increasing differentiation of self from other and a progressive freeing of thought from contextual constraints. The vision of Luther, journeying from the rejection of a self defined by others to the assertive boldness of "Here I stand" and the image of Plato's allegorical man in the cave, separating at last the shadows from the sun, have taken powerful hold on the psychological understanding of what constitutes development. Thus, the individual, meeting fully the developmental challenges of adolescence as set for him by Piaget, Erikson, and Kohlberg, thinks formally, proceeding from theory to fact, and defines both the self and the moral autonomously, that is, apart from the identification and conventions that had comprised the particulars of his childhood world. So

The research reported here was partially supported by a grant from the Spencer Foundation. I wish to thank Mary Belenky for her collaboration and colleagueship in the abortion decision study and Michael Murphy for his comments and help in preparing this manuscript.

Harvard Educational Review Vol. 47 No. 4 November 1977

equipped, he is presumed ready to live as an adult, to love and work in a way that is both intimate and generative, to develop an ethical sense of caring and a genital mode of relating in which giving and taking fuse in the ultimate reconciliation of the tension between self and other.

Yet the men whose theories have largely informed this understanding of development have all been plagued by the same problem, the problem of women, whose sexuality remains more diffuse, whose perception of self is so much more tenaciously embedded in relationships with others and whose moral dilemmas hold them in a mode of judgment that is insistently contextual. The solution has been to consider women as either deviant or deficient in their development.

That there is a discrepancy between concepts of womanhood and adulthood is nowhere more clearly evident than in the series of studies on sex-role stereotypes reported by Broverman, Vogel, Broverman, Clarkson, and Rosenkrantz (1972). The repeated finding of these studies is that the qualities deemed necessary for adulthood—the capacity for autonomous thinking, clear decision making, and responsible action—are those associated with masculinity but considered undesirable as attributes of the feminine self. The stereotypes suggest a splitting of love and work that relegates the expressive capacities requisite for the former to women while the instrumental abilities necessary for the latter reside in the masculine domain. Yet, looked at from a different perspective, these stereotypes reflect a conception of adulthood that is itself out of balance, favoring the separateness of the individual self over its connection to others and leaning more toward an autonomous life of work than toward the interdependence of love and care.

This difference in point of view is the subject of this essay, which seeks to identify in the feminine experience and construction of social reality a distinctive voice, recognizable in the different perspective it brings to bear on the construction and resolution of moral problems. The first section begins with the repeated observation of difference in women's concepts of self and of morality. This difference is identified in previous psychological descriptions of women's moral judgments and described as it again appears in current research data. Examples drawn from interviews with women in and around a university community are used to illustrate the characteristics of the feminine voice. The relational bias in women's thinking that has, in the past, been seen to compromise their moral judgment and impede their development now begins to emerge in a new developmental light. Instead of being seen as a developmental deficiency, this bias appears to reflect a different social and moral understanding.

This alternative conception is enlarged in the second section through consideration of research interviews with women facing the moral dilemma of whether to continue or abort a pregnancy. Since the research design allowed women to define as well as resolve the moral problem, developmental distinctions could be derived directly from the categories of women's thought. The responses of women to structured interview questions regarding the pregnancy decision formed the basis for describing a developmental sequence that traces progressive differentiations in their understanding and judgment of conflicts between self and other. While the sequence of women's moral development follows the three-level progression of all

In a Different Voice
CAROL GILLIGAN

social developmental theory, from an egocentric through a societal to a universal perspective, this progression takes place within a distinct moral conception. This conception differs from that derived by Kohlberg from his all-male longitudinal research data.

This difference then becomes the basis in the third section for challenging the current assessement of women's moral judgment at the same time that it brings to bear a new perspective on developmental assessment in general. The inclusion in the overall conception of development of those categories derived from the study of women's moral judgment enlarges developmental understanding, enabling it to encompass better the thinking of both sexes. This is particularly true with respect to the construction and resolution of the dilemmas of adult life. Since the conception of adulthood retrospectively shapes the theoretical understanding of the development that precedes it, the changes in that conception that follow from the more central inclusion of women's judgments recast developmental understanding and lead to a reconsideration of the substance of social and moral development.

Characteristics of the Feminine Voice

The revolutionary contribution of Piaget's work is the experimental confirmation and refinement of Kant's assertion that knowledge is actively constructed rather than passively received. Time, space, self, and other, as well as the categories of developmental theory, all arise out of the active interchange between the individual and the physical and social world in which he lives and of which he strives to make sense. The development of cognition is the process of reappropriating reality at progressively more complex levels of apprehension, as the structures of thinking expand to encompass the increasing richness and intricacy of experience.

Moral development, in the work of Piaget and Kohlberg, refers specifically to the expanding conception of the social world as it is reflected in the understanding and resolution of the inevitable conflicts that arise in the relations between self and others. The moral judgment is a statement of priority, an attempt at rational resolution in a situation where, from a different point of view, the choice itself seems to do violence to justice.

Kohlberg (1969), in his extension of the early work of Piaget, discovered six stages of moral judgment, which he claimed formed an invariant sequence, each successive stage representing a more adequate construction of the moral problem, which in turn provides the basis for its more just resolution. The stages divide into three levels, each of which denotes a significant expansion of the moral point of view from an egocentric through a societal to a universal ethical conception. With this expansion in perspective comes the capacity to free moral judgment from the individual needs and social conventions with which it had earlier been confused and anchor it instead in principles of justice that are universal in application. These principles provide criteria upon which both individual and societal claims can be impartially assessed. In Kohlberg's view, at the highest stages of development morality is freed from both psychological and historical constraints, and the individual can judge independently of his own particular needs and of the values of those around him.

That the moral sensibility of women differs from that of men was noted by Freud (1925/1961) in the following by now well-quoted statement:

> I cannot evade the notion (though I hesitate to give it expression) that for women the level of what is ethically normal is different from what it is in man. Their superego is never so inexorable, so impersonal, so independent of its emotional origins as we require it to be in men. Character-traits which critics of every epoch have brought up against women—that they show less sense of justice than men, that they are less ready to submit to the great exigencies of life, that they are more often influenced in their judgments by feelings of affection or hostility—all these would be amply accounted for by the modification in the formation of their super-ego which we have inferred above. (pp. 257–258)

While Freud's explanation lies in the deviation of female from male development around the construction and resolution of the Oedipal problem, the same observations about the nature of morality in women emerge from the work of Piaget and Kohlberg. Piaget (1932/1965), in his study of the rules of children's games, observed that, in the games they played, girls were "less explicit about agreement [than boys] and less concerned with legal elaboration" (p. 93). In contrast to the boys' interest in the codification of rules, the girls adopted a more pragmatic attitude, regarding "a rule as good so long as the game repays it" (p. 83). As a result, in comparison to boys, girls were found to be "more tolerant and more easily reconciled to innovations" (p. 52).

Kohlberg (1971) also identifies a strong interpersonal bias in the moral judgments of women, which leads them to be considered as typically at the third of his six-stage developmental sequence. At that stage, the good is identified with "what pleases or helps others and is approved of by them" (p. 164). This mode of judgment is conventional in its conformity to generally held notions of the good but also psychological in its concern with intention and consequence as the basis for judging the morality of action.

That women fall largely into this level of moral judgment is hardly surprising when we read from the Broverman et al. (1972) list that prominent among the twelve attributes considered to be desirable for women are tact, gentleness, awareness of the feelings of others, strong need for security, and easy expression of tender feelings. And yet, herein lies the paradox, for the very traits that have traditionally defined the "goodness" of women, their care for and sensitivity to the needs of others, are those that mark them as deficient in moral development. The infusion of feeling into their judgments keeps them from developing a more independent and abstract ethical conception in which concern for others derives from principles of justice rather than from compassion and care. Kohlberg, however, is less pessimistic than Freud in his assessment, for he sees the development of women as extending beyond the interpersonal level, following the same path toward independent, principled judgment that he discovered in the research on men from which his stages were derived. In Kohlberg's view, women's development will proceed beyond Stage Three when they are challenged to solve moral problems that

In a Different Voice
CAROL GILLIGAN

require them to see beyond the relationships that have in the past generally bound their moral experience.

What then do women say when asked to construct the moral domain; how do we identify the characteristically "feminine" voice? A Radcliffe undergraduate, responding to the question, "If you had to say what morality meant to you, how would you sum it up?," replies:

> When I think of the word morality, I think of obligations. I usually think of it as conflicts between personal desires and social things, social considerations, or personal desires of yourself versus personal desires of another person or people or whatever. Morality is that whole realm of how you decide these conflicts. A moral person is one who would decide, like by placing themselves more often than not as equals, a truly moral person would always consider another person as their equal . . . in a situation of social interaction, something is morally wrong where the individual ends up screwing a lot of people. And it is morally right when everyone comes out better of.[1]

Yet when asked if she can think of someone whom she would consider a genuinely moral person, she replies, "Well, immediately I think of Albert Schweitzer because he has obviously given his life to help others." Obligation and sacrifice override the ideal of equality, setting up a basic contradiction in her thinking.

Another undergraduate responds to the question, "What does it mean to say something is morally right or wrong?," by also speaking first of responsibilities and obligations:

> Just that it has to do with responsibilties and obligations and values, mainly values. . . . In my life situation I relate morality with interpersonal relationships that have to do with respect for the other person and myself. [Why respect other people?] Because they have a consciousness or feelings that can be hurt, an awareness that can be hurt.

The concern about hurting others persists as a major theme in the responses of two other Radcliffe students:

> [Why be moral?] Millions of people have to live together peacefully. I personally don't want to hurt other people. That's a real criterion, a main criterion for me. It underlies my sense of justice. It isn't nice to inflict pain. I empathize with anyone in pain. Not hurting others is important in my own private morals. Years ago, I would have jumped out of a window not to hurt my boyfriend. That was pathological. Even today though, I want approval and love and I don't want enemies. Maybe that's why there is morality—so people can win approval, love and friendship.

> My main moral principle is not hurting other people as long as you aren't going against your own conscience and as long as you remain true to yourself. . . . There are many moral issues such as abortion, the draft, killing, stealing, monogamy, etc. If something is a controversial issue like these, then I always say it is up to the individual. The individual has to decide and then follow his own con-

---

1 The Radcliffe women whose responses are cited were interviewed as part of a pilot study on undergraduate moral development conducted by the author in 1970.

science. There are no moral absolutes. . . . Laws are pragmatic instruments, but
they are not absolutes. A viable society can't make exceptions all the time, but I
would personally. . . . I'm afraid I'm heading for some big crisis with my boyfriend someday, and someone will get hurt, and he'll get more hurt than I will.
I feel an obligation to not hurt him, but also an obligation to not lie. I don't
know if it is possible to not lie and not hurt.

The common thread that runs through these statements, the wish not to hurt
others and the hope that in morality lies a way of solving conflicts so that no one
will get hurt, is striking in that it is independently introduced by each of the four
women as the most specific item in their response to a most general question. The
moral person is one who helps others; goodness is service, meeting one's obligations
and responsibilities to others, if possible, without sacrificing oneself. While the first
of the four women ends by denying the conflict she initially introduced, the last
woman anticipates a conflict between remaining true to herself and adhering to her
principle of not hurting others. The dilemma that would test the limits of this
judgment would be one where helping others is seen to be at the price of hurting
the self.

The reticence about taking stands on "controversial issues," the willingness to
"make exceptions all the time" expressed in the final example above, is echoed
repeatedly by other Radcliffe students, as in the following two examples:

I never feel that I can condemn anyone else. I have a very relativistic position.
The basic idea that I cling to is the sanctity of human life. I am inhibited about
impressing my beliefs on others.

I could never argue that my belief on a moral question is anything that another
person should accept. I don't believe in absolutes. . . . If there is an absolute for
moral decisions, it is human life.

Or as a thirty-one-year-old Wellesley graduate says, in explaining why she would
find it difficult to steal a drug to save her own life despite her belief that it would
be right to steal for another: "It's just very hard to defend yourself against the
rules. I mean, we live by consensus, and you take an action simply for yourself, by
yourself, there's no consensus there, and that is relatively indefensible in this society
now."

What begins to emerge is a sense of vulnerability that impedes these women from
taking a stand, what George Eliot (1860/1965) regards as the girl's "susceptibility"
to adverse judgments of others, which stems from her lack of power and consequent
inability to do something in the world. While relativism in men, the unwillingness
to make moral judgments that Kohlberg and Kramer (1969) and Kohlberg and
Gilligan (1971) have associated with the adolescent crisis of identity and belief,
takes the form of calling into question the concept of morality itself, the women's
reluctance to judge stems rather from their uncertainty about their right to make
moral statements or, perhaps, the price for them that such judgment seems to entail. This contrast echoes that made by Matina Horner (1972), who differentiated
the ideological fear of success expressed by men from the personal conflicts about
succeeding that riddled the women's responses to stories of competitive achievement.

486

In a Different Voice
CAROL GILLIGAN

Most of the men who responded with the expectation of negative consequences because of success were not concerned about their masculinity but were instead likely to have expressed existential concerns about finding a "non-materialistic happiness and satisfaction in life." These concerns, which reflect changing attitudes toward traditional kinds of success or achievement in our society, played little, if any, part in the female stories. Most of the women who were high in fear of success imagery continued to be concerned about the discrepancy between success in the situation described and feminine identity. (pp. 163–164)

When women feel excluded from direct participation in society, they see themselves as subject to a consensus or judgment made and enforced by the men on whose protection and support they depend and by whose names they are known. A divorced middle-aged woman, mother of adolescent daughters, resident of a sophisticated university community, tells the story as follows:

As a woman, I feel I never understood that I was a person, that I can make decisions and I have a right to make decisions. I always felt that that belonged to my father or my husband in some way or church which was always represented by a male clergyman. They were the three men in my life: father, husband, and clergyman, and they had much more to say about what I should or shouldn't do. They were really authority figures which I accepted. I didn't rebel against that. It only has lately occurred to me that I never even rebelled against it, and my girls are much more conscious of this, not in the militant sense, but just in the recognizing sense. . . . I still let things happen to me rather than make them happen, than to make choices, although I know all about choices. I know the procedures and the steps and all. [Do you have any clues about why this might be true?] Well, I think in one sense, there is less responsibility involved. Because if you make a dumb decision, you have to take the rap. If it happens to you, well, you can complain about it. I think that if you don't grow up feeling that you ever had any choices, you don't either have the sense that you have emotional responsibility. With this sense of choice comes this sense of responsibility.

The essence of the moral decision is the exercise of choice and the willingness to accept responsibility for that choice. To the extent that women perceive themselves as having no choice, they correspondingly excuse themselves from the responsibility that decision entails. Childlike in the vulnerability of their dependence and consequent fear of abandonment, they claim to wish only to please but in return for their goodness they expect to be loved and cared for. This, then, is an "altruism" always at risk, for it presupposes an innocence constantly in danger of being compromised by an awareness of the trade-off that has been made. Asked to describe herself, a Radcliffe senior responds:

I have heard of the onion skin theory. I see myself as an onion, as a block of different layers, the external layers for people that I don't know that well, the agreeable, the social, and as you go inward there are more sides for people I know that I show. I am not sure about the innermost, whether there is a core, or whether I have just picked up everything as I was growing up, these different influences. I think I have a neutral attitude towards myself, but I do think in terms of good and bad. . . . Good—I try to be considerate and thoughtful of other people and I try to be fair in situations and be tolerant. I use the words but I try and work them out practically. . . . Bad things—I am not sure if they are bad, if they are altruistic or I am doing them basically for approval of other people. [Which things are these?] The values I have when I try to act them out. They deal mostly with interpersonal type relations. . . . If I were doing it for approval, it would be a very tenuous thing. If I didn't get the right feedback, there might go all my values.

Ibsen's play, *A Doll House* (1879/1965), depicts the explosion of just such a world through the eruption of a moral dilemma that calls into question the notion of goodness that lies at its center. Nora, the "squirrel wife," living with her husband as she had lived with her father, puts into action this conception of goodness as sacrifice and, with the best of intentions, takes the law into her own hands. The crisis that ensues, most painfully for her in the repudiation of that goodness by the very person who was its recipient and beneficiary, causes her to reject the suicide that she had initially seen as its ultimate expression and chose instead to seek new and firmer answers to the adolescent questions of identity and belief.

The availability of choice and with it the onus of responsibility has now invaded the most private sector of the woman's domain and threatens a similar explosion. For centuries, women's sexuality anchored them in passivity, in a receptive rather than active stance, where the events of conception and childbirth could be controlled only by a withholding in which their own sexual needs were either denied or sacrificed. That such a sacrifice entailed a cost to their intelligence as well was seen by Freud (1908/1959) when he tied the "undoubted intellectual inferiority of so many women" to "the inhibition of thought necessitated by sexual suppression" (p. 199). The strategies of withholding and denial that women have employed in the politics of sexual relations appear similar to their evasion or withholding of judgment in the moral realm. The hesitance expressed in the previous examples to impose even a belief in the value of human life on others, like the reluctance to claim one's sexuality, bespeaks a self uncertain of its strength, unwilling to deal with consequence, and thus avoiding confrontation.

Thus women have traditionally deferred to the judgment of men, although often while intimating a sensibility of their own which is at variance with that judgment. Maggie Tulliver, in *The Mill on the Floss* (Eliot, 1860/1965) responds to the accusations that ensue from the discovery of her secretly continued relationship with Phillip Wakeham by acceding to her brother's moral judgment while at the same time asserting a different set of standards by which she attests her own superiority:

> I don't want to defend myself. . . . I know I've been wrong—often continually. But yet, sometimes when I have done wrong, it has been because I have feelings that you would be the better for if you had them. If *you* were in fault ever, if you had done anything very wrong, I should be sorry for the pain it brought you; I should not want punishment to be heaped on you. (p. 188)

An eloquent defense, Kohlberg would argue, of a Stage Three moral position, an assertion of the age-old split between thinking and feeling, justice and mercy, that underlies many of the clichés and stereotypes concerning the difference between the sexes. But considered from another point of view, it is a moment of con-

In a Different Voice
CAROL GILLIGAN

frontation, replacing a former evasion, between two modes of judging, two differing constructions of the moral domain—one traditionally associated with masculinity and the public world of social power, the other with femininity and the privacy of domestic interchange. While the developmental ordering of these two points of view has been to consider the masculine as the more adequate and thus as replacing the feminine as the individual moves toward higher stages, their reconciliation remains unclear.

The Development of Women's Moral Judgment

Recent evidence for a divergence in moral development between men and women comes from the research of Haan (Note 1) and Holstein (1976) whose findings lead them to question the possibility of a "sex-related bias" in Kolhberg's scoring system. This system is based on Kohlberg's six-stage description of moral development. Kohlberg's stages divide into three levels, which he designates as preconventional, conventional, and postconventional, thus denoting the major shifts in moral perspective around a center of moral understanding that equates justice with the maintenance of existing social systems. While the preconventional conception of justice is based on the needs of the self, the conventional judgment derives from an understanding of society. This understanding is in turn superseded by a postconventional or principled conception of justice where the good is formulated in universal terms. The quarrel with Kohlberg's stage scoring does not pertain to the structural differentiation of his levels but rather to questions of stage and sequence. Kohlberg's stages begin with an obedience and punishment orientation (Stage One), and go from there in invariant order to instrumental hedonism (Stage Two), interpersonal concordance (Stage Three), law and order (Stage Four), social contract (Stage Five), and universal ethical principles (Stage Six).

The bias that Haan and Holstein question in this scoring system has to do with the subordination of the interpersonal to the societal definition of the good in the transition from Stage Three to Stage Four. This is the transition that has repeatedly been found to be problematic for women. In 1969, Kohlberg and Kramer identified Stage Three as the characteristic mode of women's moral judgments, claiming that, since women's lives were interpersonally based, this stage was not only "functional" for them but also adequate for resolving the moral conflicts that they faced. Turiel (1973) reported that while girls reached Stage Three sooner than did boys, their judgments tended to remain at that stage while the boys' development continued further along Kohlberg's scale. Gilligan, Kohlberg, Lerner, and Belenky (1971) found a similar association between sex and moral-judgment stage in a study of high-school students, with the girls' responses being scored predominantly at Stage Three while the boys' responses were more often scored at Stage Four.

This repeated finding of developmental inferiority in women may, however, have more to do with the standard by which development has been measured than with the quality of women's thinking per se. Haan's data (Note 1) on the Berkeley Free Speech Movement and Holstein's (1976) three-year longitudinal study of

489

adolescents and their parents indicate that the moral judgments of women differ from those of men in the greater extent to which women's judgments are tied to feelings of empathy and compassion and are concerned more with the resolution of "real-life" as opposed to hypothetical dilemmas (Note 1, p. 34). However, as long as the categories by which development is assessed are derived within a male perspective from male research data, divergence from the masculine standard can be seen only as a failure of development. As a result, the thinking of women is often classified with that of children. The systematic exclusion from consideration of alternative criteria that might better encompass the development of women indicates not only the limitations of a theory framed by men and validated by research samples disproportionately male and adolescent but also the effects of the diffidence prevalent among women, their reluctance to speak publicly in their own voice, given the constraints imposed on them by the politics of differential power between the sexes.

In order to go beyond the question, "How much like men do women think, how capable are they of engaging in the abstract and hypothetical construction of reality?" it is necessary to identify and define in formal terms developmental criteria that encompass the categories of women's thinking. Such criteria would include the progressive differentiations, comprehensiveness, and adequacy that characterize higher-stage resolution of the "more frequently occurring, real-life moral dilemmas of interpersonal, empathic, fellow-feeling concerns" (Haan, Note 1, p. 34), which have long been the center of women's moral judgments and experience. To ascertain whether the feminine construction of the moral domain relies on a language different from that of men, but one which deserves equal credence in the definition of what constitutes development, it is necessary first to find the places where women have the power to choose and thus are willing to speak in their own voice.

When birth control and abortion provide women with effective means for controlling their fertility, the dilemma of choice enters the center of women's lives. Then the relationships that have traditionally defined women's identities and framed their moral judgments no longer flow inevitably from their reproductive capacity but become matters of decision over which they have control. Released from the passivity and reticence of a sexuality that binds them in dependence, it becomes possible for women to question with Freud what it is that they want and to assert their own answers to that question. However, while society may affirm publicly the woman's right to choose for herself, the exercise of such choice brings her privately into conflict with the conventions of femininity, particularly the moral equation of goodness with self-sacrifice. While independent assertion in judgment and action is considered the hallmark of adulthood and constitutes as well the standard of masculine development, it is rather in their care and concern for others that women have both judged themselves and been judged.

The conflict between self and other thus constitutes the central moral problem for women, posing a dilemma whose resolution requires a reconciliation between femininity and adulthood. In the absence of such a reconciliation, the moral prob-

In a Different Voice
CAROL GILLIGAN

lem cannot be resolved. The "good woman" masks assertion in evasion, denying responsibility by claiming only to meet the needs of others, while the "bad woman" forgoes or renounces the commitments that bind her in self-deception and betrayal. It is precisely this dilemma—the conflict between compassion and autonomy, between virtue and power—which the feminine voice struggles to resolve in its effort to reclaim the self and to solve the moral problem in such a way that no one is hurt.

When a woman considers whether to continue or abort a pregnancy, she contemplates a decision that affects both self and others and engages directly the critical moral issue of hurting. Since the choice is ultimately hers and therefore one for which she is responsible, it raises precisely those questions of judgment that have been most problematic for women. Now she is asked whether she wishes to interrupt that stream of life which has for centuries immersed her in the passivity of dependence while at the same time imposing on her the responsibility for care. Thus the abortion decision brings to the core of feminine apprehension, to what Joan Didion (1972) calls "the irreconcilable difference of it—that sense of living one's deepest life underwater, that dark involvement with blood and birth and death" (p. 14), the adult questions of responsibility and choice.

How women deal with such choices has been the subject of my research, designed to clarify, through considering the ways in which women construct and resolve the abortion decision, the nature and development of women's moral judgment. Twenty-nine women, diverse in age, race, and social class, were referred by abortion and pregnancy counseling services and participated in the study for a variety of reasons. Some came to gain further clarification with respect to a decision about which they were in conflict, some in response to a counselor's concern about repeated abortions, and others out of an interest in and/or willingness to contribute to ongoing research. Although the pregnancies occurred under a variety of circumstances in the lives of these women, certain commonalities could be discerned. The adolescents often failed to use birth control because they denied or discredited their capacity to bear children. Some of the older women attributed the pregnancy to the omission of contraceptive measures in circumstances where intercourse had not been anticipated. Since the pregnancies often coincided with efforts on the part of the women to end a relationship, they may be seen as a manifestation of ambivalence or as a way of putting the relationship to the ultimate test of commitment. For these women, the pregnancy appeared to be a way of testing truth, making the baby an ally in the search for male support and protection or, that failing, a companion victim of his rejection. There were, finally, some women who became pregnant either as a result of a failure of birth control or intentionally as part of a joint decision that later was reconsidered. Of the twenty-nine women, four decided to have the baby, one miscarried, twenty-one chose abortion, and three remained in doubt about the decision.

In the initial part of the interview, the women were asked to discuss the decision that confronted them, how they were dealing with it, the alternatives they were considering, their reasons for and against each option, the people involved, the conflicts entailed, and the ways in which making this decision affected their self-concepts and their relationships with others. Then, in the second part of the interview, moral judgment was assessed in the hypothetical mode by presenting for resolution three of Kohlberg's standard research dilemmas.

While the structural progression from a preconventional through a conventional to a postconventional moral perspective can readily be discerned in the women's responses to both actual and hypothetical dilemmas, the conventions that shape women's moral judgments differ from those that apply to men. The construction of the abortion dilemma, in particular, reveals the existence of a distinct moral language whose evolution informs the sequence of women's development. This is the language of selfishness and responsibility, which defines the moral problem as one of obligation to exercise care and avoid hurt. The infliction of hurt is considered selfish and immoral in its reflection of unconcern, while the expression of care is seen as the fulfillment of moral responsibility. The reiterative use of the language of selfishness and responsibility and the underlying moral orientation it reflects sets the women apart from the men whom Kohlberg studied and may be seen as the critical reason for their failure to develop within the constraints of his system.

In the developmental sequence that follows, women's moral judgments proceed from an initial focus on the self at the *first level* to the discovery, in the transition to the *second level,* of the concept of responsibility as the basis for a new equilibrium between self and others. The elaboration of this concept of responsibility and its fusion with a maternal concept of morality, which seeks to ensure protection for the dependent and unequal, characterizes the *second level* of judgment. At this level the good is equated with caring for others. However, when the conventions of feminine goodness legitimize only others as the recipients of moral care, the logical inequality between self and other and the psychological violence that it engenders create the disequilibrium that initiates the *second* transition. The relationship between self and others is then reconsidered in an effort to sort out the confusion between conformity and care inherent in the conventional definition of feminine goodness and to establish a new equilibrium, which dissipates the tension between selfishness and responsibility. At the *third level,* the self becomes the arbiter of an independent judgment that now subsumes both conventions and individual needs under the moral principle of nonviolence. Judgment remains psychological in its concern with the intention and consequences of action, but it now becomes universal in its condemnation of exploitation and hurt.

Level I: Orientation to Individual Survival

In its initial and simplest construction, the abortion decision centers on the self. The concern is pragmatic, and the issue is individual survival. At this level, "should" is undifferentiated from "would," and others influence the decision only through their power to affect its consequences. An eighteen-year-old, asked what she thought when she found herself pregnant, replies: "I really didn't think anything except that I didn't want it. [Why was that?] I didn't want it, I wasn't ready for it, and next year will be my last year and I want to go to school."

Asked if there was a right decision, she says, "There is no right decision. [Why?]

In a Different Voice
CAROL GILLIGAN

I didn't want it." For her the question of right decision would emerge only if her own needs were in conflict; then she would have to decide which needs should take precedence. This was the dilemma of another eighteen-year-old, who saw having a baby as a way of increasing her freedom by providing "the perfect chance to get married and move away from home," but also as restricting her freedom "to do a lot of things."

At this first level, the self, which is the sole object of concern, is constrained by lack of power; the wish "to do a lot of things" is constantly belied by the limitations of what, in fact, is being done. Relationships are, for the most part, disappointing: "The only thing you are ever going to get out of going with a guy is to get hurt." As a result, women may in some instances deliberately choose isolation to protect themselves against hurt. When asked how she would describe herself to herself, a nineteen-year-old, who held herself responsible for the accidental death of a younger brother, answers as follows:

> I really don't know. I never thought about it. I don't know. I know basically the outline of a character. I am very independent. I don't really want to have to ask anybody for anything and I am a loner in life. I prefer to be by myself than around anybody else. I manage to keep my friends at a limited number with the point that I have very few friends. I don't know what else there is. I am a loner and I enjoy it. Here today and gone tomorrow.

The primacy of the concern with survival is explicitly acknowledged by a sixteen-year-old delinquent in response to Kohlberg's Heinz dilemma, which asks if it is right for a desperate husband to steal an outrageously overpriced drug to save the life of his dying wife:

> I think survival is one of the first things in life and that people fight for. I think it is the most important thing, more important than stealing. Stealing might be wrong, but if you have to steal to survive yourself or even kill, that is what you should do. . . . Preservation of oneself, I think, is the most important thing; it comes before anything in life.

The First Transition: From Selfishness to Responsibility

In the transition which follows and criticizes this level of judgment, the words selfishness and responsibility first appear. Their reference initially is to the self in a redefinition of the self-interest which has thus far served as the basis for judgment. The transitional issue is one of attachment or connection to others. The pregnancy catches up the issue not only by representing an immediate, literal connection, but also by affirming, in the most concrete and physical way, the capacity to assume adult feminine roles. However, while having a baby seems at first to offer respite from the loneliness of adolescence and to solve conflicts over dependence and independence, in reality the continuation of an adolescent pregnancy generally compounds these problems, increasing social isolation and precluding further steps toward independence.

To be a mother in the societal as well as the physical sense requires the assumption of parental responsibility for the care and protection of a child. However, in order to be able to care for another, one must first be able to care responsibly for oneself. The growth from childhood to adulthood, conceived as a move from selfishness to responsibility, is articulated explicitly in these terms by a seventeen-year-old who describes her response to her pregnancy as follows:

> I started feeling really good about being pregnant instead of feeling really bad, because I wasn't looking at the situation realistically. I was looking at it from my own sort of selfish needs because I was lonely and felt lonely and stuff. . . . Things weren't really going good for me, so I was looking at it that I could have a baby that I could take care of or something that was part of me, and that made me feel good . . . but I wasn't looking at the realistic side . . . about the responsibility I would have to take on . . . I came to this decision that I was going to have an abortion [because] I realized how much responsibility goes with having a child. Like you have to be there, you can't be out of the house all the time which is one thing I like to do . . . and I decided that I have to take on responsibility for myself and I have to work out a lot of things.

Stating her former mode of judgment, the wish to have a baby as a way of combating loneliness and feeling connected, she now criticizes that judgment as both "selfish" and "unrealistic." The contradiction between wishes for a baby and for the freedom to be "out of the house all the time"—that is, for connection and also for independence—is resolved in terms of a new priority, as the criterion for judgment changes. The dilemma now assumes moral definition as the emergent conflict between wish and necessity is seen as a disparity between "would" and "should." In this construction the "selfishness" of willful decision is counterposed to the "responsibility" of moral choice:

> What I want to do is to have the baby, but what I feel I should do which is what I need to do, is have an abortion right now, because sometimes what you want isn't right. Sometimes what is necessary comes before what you want, because it might not always lead to the right thing.

While the pregnancy itself confirms femininity—"I started feeling really good; it sort of made me feel, like being pregnant, I started feeling like a woman"—the abortion decision becomes an opportunity for the adult exercise of responsible choice.

> [How would you describe yourself to yourself?] I am looking at myself differently in the way that I have had a really heavy decision put upon me, and I have never really had too many hard decisions in my life, and I have made it. It has taken some responsibility to do this. I have changed in that way, that I have made a hard decision. And that has been good. Because before, I would not have looked at it realistically, in my opinion. I would have gone by what I wanted to do, and I wanted it, and even if it wasn't right. So I see myself as I'm becoming more mature in ways of making decisions and taking care of myself, doing something for myself. I think it is going to help me in other ways, if I have other decisions to make put upon me, which would take some responsibility. And I would know that I could make them.

In the epiphany of this cognitive reconstruction, the old becomes transformed in

In a Different Voice
CAROL GILLIGAN

terms of the new. The wish to "do something for myself" remains, but the terms of its fulfillment change as the decision affirms both femininity and adulthood in its integration of responsibility and care. Morality, says another adolescent, "is the way you think about yourself . . . sooner or later you have to make up your mind to start taking care of yourself. Abortion, if you do it for the right reasons, is helping yourself to start over and do different things."

Since this transition signals an enhancement in self-worth, it requires a conception of self which includes the possibility for doing "the right thing," the ability to see in oneself the potential for social acceptance. When such confidence is seriously in doubt, the transitional questions may be raised but development is impeded. The failure to make this first transition, despite an understanding of the issues involved, is illustrated by a woman in her late twenties Her struggle with the conflict between selfishness and responsibility pervades but fails to resolve her dilemma of whether or not to have a third abortion.

> I think you have to think about the people who are involved, including yourself. You have responsibilities to yourself . . . and to make a right, whatever that is, decision in this depends on your knowledge and awareness of the responsibilities that you have and whether you can survive with a child and what it will do to your relationship with the father or how it will affect him emotionally.

Rejecting the idea of selling the baby and making "a lot of money in a black market kind of thing . . . because mostly I operate on principles and it would just rub me the wrong way to think I would be selling my own child," she struggles with a concept of responsibility which repeatedly turns back on the question of her own survival. Transition seems blocked by a self-image which is insistently contradictory:

> [How would you describe yourself to yourself?] I see myself as impulsive, practical—that is a contradiction—and moral and amoral, a contradiction. Actually the only thing that is consistent and not contradictory is the fact that I am very lazy which everyone has always told me is really a symptom of something else which I have never been able to put my finger on exactly. It has taken me a long time to like myself. In fact there are times when I don't, which I think is healthy to a point and sometimes I think I like myself too much and I probably evade myself too much, which avoids responsibility to myself and to other people who like me. I am pretty unfaithful to myself. . . I have a hard time even thinking that I am a human being, simply because so much rotten stuff goes on and people are so crummy and insensitive.

Seeing herself as avoiding responsibility, she can find no basis upon which to resolve the pregnancy dilemma. Instead, her inability to arrive at any clear sense of decision only contributes further to her overall sense of failure. Criticizing her parents for having betrayed her during adolescence by coercing her to have an abortion she did not want, she now betrays herself and criticizes that as well. In this light, it is less surprising that she considered selling her child, since she felt herself to have, in effect, been sold by her parents for the sake of maintaining their social status.

The Second Level: Goodness as Self-Sacrifice

The transition from selfishness to responsibility is a move toward social participation. Whereas at the first level, morality is seen as a matter of sanctions imposed by a society of which one is more subject than citizen, at the second level, moral judgment comes to rely on shared norms and expectations. The woman at this level validates her claim to social membership through the adoption of societal values. Consensual judgment becomes paramount and goodness the overriding concern as survival is now seen to depend on acceptance by others.

Here the conventional feminine voice emerges with great clarity, defining the self and proclaiming its worth on the basis of the ability to care for and protect others. The woman now constructs the world perfused with the assumptions about feminine goodness reflected in the stereotypes of the Broverman et al. (1972) studies. There the attributes considered desirable for women all presume an other, a recipient of the "tact, gentleness and easy expression of feeling" which allow the woman to respond sensitively while evoking in return the care which meets her own "very strong need for security" (p. 63). The strength of this position lies in its capacity for caring; its limitation is the restriction it imposes on direct expression. Both qualities are elucidated by a nineteen-year-old who contrasts her reluctance to criticize with her boyfriend's straightforwardness:

> I never want to hurt anyone, and I tell them in a very nice way, and I have respect for their own opinions, and they can do the things the way that they want, and he usually tells people right off the bat. . . . He does a lot of things out in public which I do in private. . . . it is better, the other [his way], but I just could never do it.

While her judgment clearly exists, it is not expressed, at least not in public. Concern for the feelings of others imposes a deference which she nevertheless criticizes in an awareness that, under the name of consideration, a vulnerability and a duplicity are concealed.

At the second level of judgment, it is specifically over the issue of hurting that conflict arises with respect to the abortion decision. When no option exists that can be construed as being in the best interest of everyone, when responsibilities conflict and decision entails the sacrifice of somebody's needs, then the woman confronts the seemingly impossible task of choosing the victim. A nineteen-year-old, fearing the consequences for herself of a second abortion but facing the opposition of both her family and her lover to the continuation of the pregnancy, describes the dilemma as follows:

> I don't know what choices are open to me; it is either to have it or the abortion; these are the choices open to me. It is just that either way I don't . . . I think what confuses me is it is a choice of either hurting myself or hurting other people around me. What is more important? If there could be a happy medium, it would be fine, but there isn't. It is either hurting someone on this side or hurting myself.

While the feminine identification of goodness with self-sacrifice seems clearly to dictate the "right" resolution of this dilemma, the stakes may be high for the

In a Different Voice
CAROL GILLIGAN

woman herself, and the sacrifice of the fetus, in any event, compromises the altruism of an abortion motivated by a concern for others. Since femininity itself is in conflict in an abortion intended as an expression of love and care, this is a resolution which readily explodes in its own contradiction.

"I don't think anyone should have to choose between two things that they love," says a twenty-five-year-old woman who assumed responsibility not only for her lover but also for his wife and children in having an abortion she did not want:

> I just wanted the child and I really don't believe in abortions. Who can say when life begins. I think that life begins at conception and . . . I felt like there were changes happening in my body and I felt very protective . . . [but] I felt a responsibility, my responsibility if anything ever happened to her [his wife]. He made me feel that I had to make a choice and there was only one choice to make and that was to have an abortion and I could always have children another time and he made me feel if I didn't have it that it would drive us apart.

The abortion decision was, in her mind, a choice not to choose with respect to the pregnancy—"That was my choice, I had to do it." Instead, it was a decision to subordinate the pregnancy to the continuation of a relationship that she saw as encompassing her life—"Since I met him, he has been my life. I do everything for him; my life sort of revolves around him." Since she wanted to have the baby and also to continue the relationship, either choice could be construed as selfish. Furthermore, since both alternatives entailed hurting someone, neither could be considered moral. Faced with a decision which, in her own terms, was untenable, she sought to avoid responsibility for the choice she made, construing the decision as a sacrifice of her own needs to those of her lover. However, this public sacrifice in the name of responsibility engendered a private resentment that erupted in anger, compromising the very relationship that it had been intended to sustain.

> Afterwards we went through a bad time because I hate to say it and I was wrong, but I blamed him. I gave in to him. But when it came down to it, I made the decision. I could have said, 'I am going to have this child whether you want me to or not,' and I just didn't do it.

Pregnant again by the same man, she recognizes in retrospect that the choice in fact had been hers, as she returns once again to what now appears to have been a missed opportunity for growth. Seeking, this time, to make rather than abdicate the decision, she sees the issue as one of "strength" as she struggles to free herself from the powerlessness of her own dependence:

> I think that right now I think of myself as someone who can become a lot stronger. Because of the circumstances, I just go along like with the tide. I never really had anything of my own before . . . [this time] I hope to come on strong and make a big decision, whether it is right or wrong.

Because the morality of self-sacrifice had justified the previous abortion, she now must suspend that judgment if she is to claim her own voice and accept responsibility for choice.

She thereby calls into question the underlying assumption of Level Two, which leads the woman to consider herself responsible for the actions of others, while holding others responsible for the choices she makes. This notion of reciprocity, backwards in its assumptions about control, disguises assertion as response. By reversing responsibility, it generates a series of indirect actions, which leave everyone feeling manipulated and betrayed. The logic of this position is confused in that the morality of mutual care is embedded in the psychology of dependence. Assertion becomes personally dangerous in its risk of criticism and abandonment, as well as potentially immoral in its power to hurt. This confusion is captured by Kohlberg's (1969) definition of Stage Three moral judgment, which joins the need for approval with the wish to care for and help others.

When thus caught between the passivity of dependence and the activity of care, the woman becomes suspended in an immobility of both judgment and action. "If I were drowning, I couldn't reach out a hand to save myself, so unwilling am I to set myself up against fate" (p. 7), begins the central character of Margaret Drabble's novel, *The Waterfall* (1971), in an effort to absolve herself of responsibility as she at the same time relinquishes control. Facing the same moral conflict which George Eliot depicted in *The Mill on the Floss*, Drabble's heroine proceeds to relive Maggie Tulliver's dilemma but turns inward in her search for the way in which to retell that story. What is initially suspended and then called into question is the judgment which "had in the past made it seem better to renounce myself than them" (Drabble, p. 50).

The Second Transition: From Goodness to Truth

The second transition begins with the reconsideration of the relationship between self and other, as the woman starts to scrutinize the logic of self-sacrifice in the service of a morality of care. In the interview data, this transition is announced by the reappearance of the word selfish. Retrieving the judgmental initiative, the woman begins to ask whether it is selfish or responsible, moral or immoral, to include her own needs within the compass of her care and concern. This question leads her to reexamine the concept of responsibility, juxtaposing the outward concern with what other people think with a new inner judgment.

In separating the voice of the self from those of others, the woman asks if it is possible to be responsible to herself as well as to others and thus to reconcile the disparity between hurt and care. The exercise of such responsibility, however, requires a new kind of judgment whose first demand is for honesty. To be responsible, it is necessary first to acknowledge what it is that one is doing. The criterion for judgment thus shifts from "goodness" to "truth" as the morality of action comes to be assessed not on the basis of its appearance in the eyes of others, but in terms of the realities of its intention and consequence.

A twenty-four-year-old married Catholic woman, pregnant again two months following the birth of her first child, identifies her dilemma as one of choice: "You have to now decide; because it is now available, you have to make a decision. And if it wasn't available, there was no choice open; you just do what you have to do." In the absence of legal abortion, a morality of self-sacrifice was necessary in order to

In a Different Voice
CAROL GILLIGAN

insure protection and care for the dependent child. However, when such sacrifice becomes optional, the entire problem is recast.

The abortion decision is framed by this woman first in terms of her responsibilities to others: having a second child at this time would be contrary to medical advice and would strain both the emotional and financial resources of the family. However, there is, she says, a third reason for having an abortion, "sort of an emotional reason. I don't know if it is selfish or not, but it would really be tying myself down and right now I am not ready to be tied down with two."

Against this combination of selfish and responsible reasons for abortion is her Catholic belief that

> . . . it is taking a life, and it is. Even though it is not formed, it is the potential, and to me it is still taking a life. But I have to think of mine, my son's and my husband's, to think about, and at first I think that I thought it was for selfish reasons, but it is not. I believe that too, some of it is selfish. I don't want another one right now; I am not ready for it.

The dilemma arises over the issue of justification for taking a life: "I can't cover it over, because I believe this and if I do try to cover it over, I know that I am going to be in a mess. It will be denying what I am really doing." Asking "Am I doing the right thing; is it moral?," she counterposes to her belief against abortion her concern with the consequences of continuing the pregnancy. While concluding that "I can't be so morally strict as to hurt three other people with a decision just because of my moral beliefs," the issue of goodness still remains critical to her resolution of the dilemma:

> The moral factor is there. To me it is taking a life, and I am going to take that upon myself, that decision upon myself and I have feelings about it, and talked to a priest . . . but he said it is there and it will be from now on, and it is up to the person if they can live with the idea and still believe they are good.

The criteria for goodness, however, move inward as the ability to have an abortion and still consider herself good comes to hinge on the issue of selfishness with which she struggles to come to terms. Asked if acting morally is acting according to what is best for the self or whether it is a matter of self-sacrifice, she replies:

> I don't know if I really understand the question. . . . Like in my situation where I want to have the abortion and if I didn't it would be self-sacrificing, I am really in the middle of both those ways . . . but I think that my morality is strong and if these reasons—financial, physical reality and also for the whole family involved—were not here, that I wouldn't have to do it, and then it would be a self-sacrifice.

The importance of clarifying her own participation in the decision is evident in her attempt to ascertain her feelings in order to determine whether or not she was "putting them under" in deciding to end the pregnancy. Whereas in the first transition, from selfishness to responsibility, women made lists in order to bring to their consideration needs other than their own; now, in the second transition, it is the needs of the self which have to be deliberately uncovered. Confronting the reality of her own wish for an abortion, she now must deal with the problem of selfishness and the qualification that she feels it imposes on the "goodness" of her decision. The primacy of this concern is apparent in her description of herself:

> I think in a way I am selfish for one thing, and very emotional, very . . . and I think that I am a very real person and an understanding person and I can handle life situations fairly well, so I am basing a lot of it on my ability to do the things that I feel are right and best for me and whoever I am involved with. I think I was very fair to myself about the decision, and I really think that I have been truthful, not hiding anything, bringing out all the feelings involved. I feel it is a good decision and an honest one, a real decision.

Thus she strives to encompass the needs of both self and others, to be responsible to others and thus to be "good" but also to be responsible to herself and thus to be "honest" and "real."

While from one point of view, attention to one's own needs is considered selfish, when looked at from a different perspective, it is a matter of honesty and fairness. This is the essence of the transitional shift toward a new conception of goodness which turns inward in an acknowledgement of the self and an acceptance of responsibility for decision. While outward justification, the concern with "good reasons," remains critical for this particular woman: "I still think abortion is wrong, and it will be unless the situation can justify what you are doing." But the search for justification has produced a change in her thinking, "not drastically, but a little bit." She realizes that in continuing the pregnancy she would punish not only herself but also her husband, toward whom she had begun to feel "turned off and irritated." This leads her to consider the consequences self-sacrifice can have both for the self and for others. "God," she says, "can punish, but He can also forgive." What remains in question is whether her claim to forgiveness is compromised by a decision that not only meets the needs of others but that also is "right and best for me."

The concern with selfishness and its equation with immorality recur in an interview with another Catholic woman whose arrival for an abortion was punctuated by the statement, "I have always thought abortion was a fancy word for murder." Initially explaining this murder as one of lesser degree—"I am doing it because I have to do it. I am not doing it the least bit because I want to," she judges it "not quite as bad. You can rationalize that it is not quite the same." Since "keeping the child for lots and lots of reasons was just sort of impractical and out," she considers her options to be either abortion or adoption. However, having previously given up one child for adoption, she says: "I knew that psychologically there was no way that I could hack another adoption. It took me about four-and-a-half years to get my head on straight; there was just no way I was going to go through it again." The decision thus reduces in her eyes to a choice between murdering the fetus or damaging herself. The choice is further complicated by the fact that by continuing the pregnancy she would hurt not only herself but also her parents, with whom she lived. In the face of these manifold moral contradictions, the psychological demand for honesty that arises in counseling finally allows decision:

In a Different Voice
CAROL GILLIGAN

> On my own, I was doing it not so much for myself; I was doing it for my parents. I was doing it because the doctor told me to do it, but I had never resolved in my mind that I was doing it for me. Because it goes right back to the fact that I never believed in abortions. . . . Actually, I had to sit down and admit, no, I really don't want to go the mother route now. I honestly don't feel that I want to be a mother, and that is not really such a bad thing to say after all. But that is not how I felt up until talking to Maureen [her counselor]. It was just a horrible way to feel, so I just wasn't going to feel it, and I just blocked it right out.

As long as her consideration remains "moral," abortion can be justified only as an act of sacrifice, a submission to necessity where the absence of choice precludes responsibility. In this way, she can avoid self-condemnation, since, "When you get into moral stuff then you are getting into self-respect and that stuff, and at least if I do something that I feel is morally wrong, then I tend to lose some of my self-respect as a person." Her evasion of responsibility, critical to maintaining the innocence necessary for self-respect, contradicts the reality of her own participation in the abortion decision. The dishonesty in her plea of victimization creates the conflict that generates the need for a more inclusive understanding. She must now resolve the emerging contradiction in her thinking between two uses of the term right: "I am saying that abortion is morally wrong, but the situation is right, and I am going to do it. But the thing is that eventually they are going to have to go together, and I am going to have to put them together somehow." Asked how this could be done, she replies:

> I would have to change morally wrong to morally right. [How?] I have no idea. I don't think you can take something that you feel is morally wrong because the situation makes it right and put the two together. They are not together, they are opposite. They don't go together. Something is wrong, but all of a sudden because you are doing it, it is right.

This discrepancy recalls a similar conflict she faced over the question of euthanasia, also considered by her to be morally wrong until she "took care of a couple of patients who had flat EEGs and saw the job that it was doing on their families." Recalling that experience, she says:

> You really don't know your black and whites until you really get into them and are being confronted with it. If you stop and think about my feelings on euthanasia until I got into it, and then my feelings about abortion until I got into it, I thought both of them were murder. Right and wrong and no middle but there is a gray.

In discovering the gray and questioning the moral judgments which formerly she considered to be absolute, she confronts the moral crisis of the second transition. Now the conventions which in the past had guided her moral judgment become subject to a new criticism, as she questions not only the justification for hurting others in the name of morality but also the "rightness" of hurting herself. However, to sustain such criticism in the face of conventions that equate goodness with self-sacrifice, the woman must verify her capacity for independent judgment and the legitimacy of her own point of view.

Once again transition hinges on self-concept. When uncertainty about her own worth prevents a woman from claiming equality, self-assertion falls prey to the old criticism of selfishness. Then the morality that condones self-destruction in the name of responsible care is not repudiated as inadequate but rather is abandoned in the face of its threat to survival. Moral obligation, rather than expanding to include the self, is rejected completely as the failure of conventional reciprocity leaves the woman unwilling any longer to protect others at what is now seen to be her own expense. In the absence of morality, survival, however "selfish" or "immoral," returns as the paramount concern.

A musician in her late twenties illustrates this transitional impasse. Having led an independent life which centered on her work, she considered herself "fairly strong-willed, fairly in control, fairly rational and objective" until she became involved in an intense love affair and discovered in her capacity to love "an entirely new dimension" in herself. Admitting in retrospect to "tremendous naiveté and idealism," she had entertained "some vague ideas that some day I would like a child to concretize our relationship . . . having always associated having a child with all the creative aspects of my life." Abjuring, with her lover, the use of contraceptives because, "as the relationship was sort of an ideal relationship in our minds, we liked the idea of not using foreign objects or anything artificial," she saw herself as having relinquished control, becoming instead "just simply vague and allowing events to just carry me along." Just as she began in her own thinking to confront "the realities of that situation"—the possibility of pregnancy and the fact that her lover was married—she found herself pregnant. "Caught" between her wish to end a relationship that "seemed more and more defeating" and her wish for a baby, which "would be a connection that would last a long time," she is paralyzed by her inability to resolve the dilemma which her ambivalence creates.

The pregnancy poses a conflict between her "moral" belief that "once a certain life has begun, it shouldn't be stopped artificially" and her "amazing" discovery that to have the baby she would "need much more [support] than I thought." Despite her moral conviction that she "should" have the child, she doubts that she could psychologically deal with "having the child alone and taking the responsibility for it." Thus a conflict erupts between what she considers to be her moral obligation to protect life and her inability to do so under the circumstances of this pregnancy. Seeing it as "my decision and my responsibility for making the decision whether to have or have not the child," she struggles to find a viable basis on which to resolve the dilemma.

Capable of arguing either for or against abortion "with a philosophical logic," she says, on the one hand, that in an overpopulated world one should have children only under ideal conditions for care but, on the other, that one should end a life only when it is impossible to sustain it. She describes her impasse in response to the question of whether there is a difference between what she wants to do and what she thinks she should do:

In a Different Voice
CAROL GILLIGAN

Yes, and there always has. I have always been confronted with that precise situation in a lot of my choices, and I have been trying to figure out what are the things that make me believe that these are things I should do as opposed to what I feel I want to do. [In this situation?] It is not that clear cut. I both want the child and feel I should have it, and I also think I should have the abortion and want it, but I would say it is my stronger feeling, and that I don't have enough confidence in my work yet and that is really where it is all hinged, I think . . . [the abortion] would solve the problem and I know I can't handle the pregnancy.

Characterizing this solution as "emotional and pragmatic" and attributing it to her lack of confidence in her work, she contrasts it with the "better thought out and more logical and more correct" resolution of her lover who thinks that she should have the child and raise it without either his presence or financial support. Confronted with this reflected image of herself as ultimately giving and good, as self-sustaining in her own creativity and thus able to meet the needs of others while imposing no demands of her own in return, she questions not the image itself but her own adequacy in filling it. Concluding that she is not yet capable of doing so, she is reduced in her own eyes to what she sees as a selfish and highly compromised fight

for my survival. But in one way or another, I am going to suffer. Maybe I am going to suffer mentally and emotionally having the abortion, or I would suffer what I think is possibly something worse. So I suppose it is the lesser of two evils. I think it is a matter of choosing which one I know that I can survive through. It is really. I think it is selfish, I suppose, because it does have to do with that. I just realized that. I guess it does have to do with whether I would survive or not. [Why is this selfish?] Well, you know, it is. Because I am concerned with my survival first, as opposed to the survival of the relationship or the survival of the child, another human being . . . I guess I am setting priorities, and I guess I am setting my needs to survive first. . . . I guess I see it in negative terms a lot . . . but I do think of other positive things; that I am still going to have some life left, maybe. I don't know.

In the face of this failure of reciprocity of care, in the disappointment of abandonment where connection was sought, survival is seen to hinge on her work which is "where I derive the meaning of what I am. That's the known factor." While uncertainty about her work makes this survival precarious, the choice for abortion is also distressing in that she considers it to be "highly introverted—that in this one respect, having an abortion would be going a step backward; going outside to love someone else and having a child would be a step forward." The sense of retrenchment that the severing of connection signifies is apparent in her anticipation of the cost which abortion would entail:

Probably what I will do is I will cut off my feelings, and when they will return or what would happen to them after that, I don't know. So that I don't feel anything at all, and I would probably just be very cold and go through it very coldly. . . . The more you do that to yourself, the more difficult it becomes to love again or to trust again or to feel again. . . . Each time I move away from that, it

becomes easier, not more difficult, but easier to avoid committing myself to a relationship. And I am really concerned about cutting off that whole feeling aspect.

Caught between selfishness and responsibility, unable to find in the circumstances of this choice a way of caring which does not at the same time destroy, she
confronts a dilemma which reduces to a conflict between morality and survival.
Adulthood and femininity fly apart in the failure of this attempt at integration as
the choice to work becomes a decision not only to renounce this particular relationship and child but also to obliterate the vulnerability that love and care
engender.

The Third Level: The Morality of Nonviolence

In contrast, a twenty-five-year-old woman, facing a similar disappointment, finds
a way to reconcile the initially disparate concepts of selfishness and responsibility
through a transformed understanding of self and a corresponding redefinition of
morality. Examining the assumptions underlying the conventions of feminine self-
abnegation and moral self-sacrifice, she comes to reject these conventions as immoral in their power to hurt. By elevating nonviolence—the injunction against
hurting—to a principle governing all moral judgment and action, she is able to
assert a moral equality between self and other. Care then becomes a universal
obligation, the self-chosen ethic of a postconventional judgment that reconstructs
the dilemma in a way that allows the assumption of responsibility for choice.

In this woman's life, the current pregnancy brings to the surface the unfinished
business of an earlier pregnancy and of the relationship in which both pregnancies
occurred. The first pregnancy was discovered after her lover had left and was
terminated by an abortion experienced as a purging expression of her anger at
having been rejected. Remembering the abortion only as a relief, she nevertheless
describes that time in her life as one in which she "hit rock bottom." Having hoped
then to "take control of my life," she instead resumed the relationship when the
man reappeared. Now, two years later, having once again "left my diaphragm in
the drawer," she again becomes pregnant. Although initially "ecstatic" at the
news, her elation dissipates when her lover tells her that he will leave if she chooses
to have the child. Under these circumstances, she considers a second abortion but
is unable to keep the repeated appointments she makes because of her reluctance
to accept the responsibility for that choice. While the first abortion seemed an
"honest mistake," she says that a second would make her feel "like a walking
slaughter-house." Since she would need financial support to raise the child, her
initial strategy was to take the matter to "the welfare people" in the hope that they
would refuse to provide the necessary funds and thus resolve her dilemma:

> In that way, you know, the responsibility would be off my shoulders, and I could
> say, it's not my fault, you know, the state denied me the money that I would need
> to do it. But it turned out that it was possible to do it, and so I was, you know,
> right back where I started. And I had an appointment for an abortion, and I kept
> calling and cancelling it and then remaking the appointment and cancelling it,
> and I just couldn't make up my mind.

In a Different Voice
CAROL GILLIGAN

Confronting the need to choose between the two evils of hurting herself or ending the incipient life of the child, she finds, in a reconstruction of the dilemma itself, a basis for a new priority that allows decision. In doing so, she comes to see the conflict as arising from a faulty construction of reality. Her thinking recapitulates the developmental sequence, as she considers but rejects as inadequate the components of earlier-stage resolutions. An expanded conception of responsibility now reshapes moral judgment and guides resolution of the dilemma, whose pros and cons she considers as follows:

> Well, the pros for having the baby are all the admiration that you would get from, you know, being a single woman, alone, martyr, struggling, having the adoring love of this beautiful Gerber baby . . . just more of a home life than I have had in a long time, and that basically was it, which is pretty fantasyland; it is not very realistic. . . . Cons against having the baby: it was going to hasten what is looking to be the inevitable end of the relationship with the man I am presently with. . . . I was going to have to go on welfare, my parents were going to hate me for the rest of my life, I was going to lose a really good job that I have, I would lose a lot of independence . . . solitude . . . and I would have to be put in a position of asking help from a lot of people a lot of the time. Cons against having the abortion is having to face up to the guilt . . . and pros for having the abortion are I would be able to handle my deteriorating relation with S. with a lot more capability and a lot more responsibility for him and for myself . . . and I would not have to go through the realization that for the next twenty-five years of my life I would be punishing myself for being foolish enough to get pregnant again and forcing myself to bring up a kid just because I did this. Having to face the guilt of a second abortion seemed like, not exactly, well, exactly the lesser of the two evils but also the one that would pay off for me personally in the long run because by looking at why I am pregnant again and subsequently have decided to have a second abortion, I have to face up to some things about myself.

Although she doesn't "feel good about having a second abortion," she nevertheless concludes,

> I would not be doing myself or the child or the world any kind of favor having this child. . . . I don't need to pay off my imaginary debts to the world through this child, and I don't think that it is right to bring a child into the world and use it for that purpose.

Asked to describe herself, she indicates how closely her transformed moral understanding is tied to a changing self-concept:

> I have been thinking about that a lot lately, and it comes up different than what my usual subconscious perception of myself is. Usually paying off some sort of debt, going around serving people who are not really worthy of my attentions because somewhere in my life I think I got the impression that my needs are really secondary to other people's, and that if I feel, if I make any demands on other people to fulfill my needs, I'd feel guilty for it and submerge my own in favor of other people's, which later backfires on me, and I feel a great deal of resentment for other people that I am doing things for, which causes friction and the eventual

deterioration of the relationship. And then I start all over again. How would I describe myself to myself? Pretty frustrated and a lot angrier than I admit, a lot more aggressive than I admit.

Reflecting on the virtues which comprise the conventional definition of the feminine self, a definition which she hears articulated in her mother's voice, she says, "I am beginning to think that all these virtues are really not getting me anywhere. I have begun to notice." Tied to this recognition is an acknowledgement of her power and worth, both previously excluded from the image she projected:

> I am suddenly beginning to realize that the things that I like to do, the things I am interested in, and the things that I believe and the kind of person I am is not so bad that I have to constantly be sitting on the shelf and letting it gather dust. I am a lot more worthwhile than what my past actions have led other people to believe.

Her notion of a "good person," which previously was limited to her mother's example of hard work, patience and self-sacrifice, now changes to include the value that she herself places on directness and honesty. Although she believes that this new self-assertion will lead her "to feel a lot better about myself" she recognizes that it will also expose her to criticism:

> Other people may say, 'Boy, she's aggressive, and I don't like that,' but at least, you know, they will know that they don't like that. They are not going to say, 'I like the way she manipulates herself to fit right around me.' . . . What I want to do is just be a more self-determined person and a more singular person.

While within her old framework abortion had seemed a way of "copping out" instead of being a "responsible person [who] pays for his mistakes and pays and pays and is always there when she says she will be there and even when she doesn't say she will be there is there," now, her "conception of what I think is right for myself and my conception of self-worth is changing." She can consider this emergent self "also a good person," as her concept of goodness expands to encompass "the feeling of self-worth; you are not going to sell yourself short and you are not going to make yourself do things that, you know, are really stupid and that you don't want to do." This reorientation centers on the awareness that:

> I have a responsibility to myself, and you know, for once I am beginning to realize that that really matters to me . . . instead of doing what I want for myself and feeling guilty over how selfish I am, you realize that that is a very usual way for people to live . . . doing what you want to do because you feel that your wants and your needs are important, if to no one else, then to you, and that's reason enough to do something that you want to do.

Once obligation extends to include the self as well as others, the disparity between selfishness and responsibility is reconciled. Although the conflict between self and other remains, the moral problem is restructured in an awareness that the occurrence of the dilemma itself precludes non-violent resolution. The abortion decision is now seen to be a "serious" choice affecting both self and others: "This is a life that I have taken, a conscious decision to terminate, and that is just very

In a Different Voice
CAROL GILLIGAN

heavy, a very heavy thing." While accepting the necessity of abortion as a highly compromised resolution, she turns her attention to the pregnancy itself, which she now considers to denote a failure of responsibility, a failure to care for and protect both self and other.

As in the first transition, although now in different terms, the conflict precipitated by the pregnancy catches up the issues critical to development. These issues now concern the worth of the self in relation to others, the claiming of the power to choose, and the acceptance of responsibility for choice. By provoking a confrontation with these issues, the crisis can become "a very auspicious time; you can use the pregnancy as sort of a learning, teeing-off point, which makes it useful in a way." This possibility for growth inherent in a crisis which allows confrontation with a construction of reality whose acceptance previously had impeded development was first identified by Coles (1964) in his study of the children of Little Rock. This same sense of possibility is expressed by the women who see, in their resolution of the abortion dilemma, a reconstructed understanding which creates the opportunity for "a new beginning," a chance "to take control of my life."

For this woman, the first step in taking control was to end the relationship in which she had considered herself "reduced to a nonentity," but to do so in a responsible way. Recognizing hurt as the inevitable concomitant of rejection, she strives to minimize that hurt "by dealing with [his] needs as best I can without compromising my own . . . that's a big point for me, because the thing in my life to this point has been always compromising, and I am not willing to do that any more." Instead, she seeks to act in a "decent, human kind of way . . . one that leaves maybe a slightly shook but not totally destroyed person." Thus the "nonentity" confronts her power to destroy which formerly had impeded any assertion, as she consider the possibility for a new kind of action that leaves both self and other intact.

The moral concern remains a concern with hurting as she considers Kohlberg's Heinz dilemma in terms of the question, "who is going to be hurt more, the druggist who loses some money or the person who loses their life?" The right to property and right to life are weighed not in the abstract, in terms of their logical priority, but rather in the particular, in terms of the actual consequences that the violation of these rights would have in the lives of the people involved. Thinking remains contextual and admixed with feelings of care, as the moral imperative to avoid hurt begins to be informed by a psychological understanding of the meaning of nonviolence.

Thus, release from the intimidation of inequality finally allows the expression of a judgment that previously had been withheld. What women then enunciate is not a new morality, but a moral conception disentangled from the constraints that formerly had confused its perception and impeded its articulation. The willingness to express and take responsibility for judgment stems from the recognition of the psychological and moral necessity for an equation of worth between self and other. Responsibility for care then includes both self and other, and the obligation not to hurt, freed from conventional constraints, is reconstructed as a universal guide to moral choice.

The reality of hurt centers the judgment of a twenty-nine-year-old woman, married and the mother of a preschool child, as she struggles with the dilemma posed by a second pregnancy whose timing conflicts with her completion of an advanced degree. Saying that "I cannot deliberately do something that is bad or would hurt another person because I can't live with having done that," she nevertheless confronts a situation in which hurt has become inevitable. Seeking that solution which would best protect both herself and others, she indicates, in her definition of morality, the ineluctable sense of connection which infuses and colors all of her thinking:

> [Morality is] doing what is appropriate and what is just within your circumstances, but ideally it is not going to affect—I was going to say, ideally it wouldn't negatively affect another person, but that is ridiculous, because decisions are always going to affect another person. But you see, what I am trying to say is that it is the person that is the center of the decision making, of that decision making about what's right and what's wrong.

The person who is the center of this decision making begins by denying, but then goes on to acknowledge, the conflicting nature both of her own needs and of her various responsibilities. Seeing the pregnancy as a manifestation of the inner conflict between her wish, on the one hand, "to be a college president" and, on the other, "to be making pottery and flowers and having kids and staying at home," she struggles with contradiction between femininity and adulthood. Considering abortion as the "better" choice—because "in the end, meaning this time next year or this time two weeks from now, it will be less of a personal strain on us individually and on us as a family for me not to be pregnant at this time," she concludes that the decision has

> got to be, first of all, something that the woman can live with—a decision that the woman can live with, one way or another, or at least try to live with, and that it be based on where she is at and other people, significant people in her life, are at.

At the beginning of the interview she had presented the dilemma in its conventional feminine construction, as a conflict between her own wish to have a baby and the wish of others for her to complete her education. On the basis of this construction she deemed it "selfish" to continue the pregnancy because it was something "I want to do." However, as she begins to examine her thinking, she comes to abandon as false this conceptualization of the problem, acknowledging the truth of her own internal conflict and elaborating the tension which she feels between her femininity and the adulthood of her work life. She describes herself as "going in two directions" and values that part of herself which is "incredibly passionate and sensitive"—her capacity to recognize and meet, often with anticipation, the needs of others. Seeing her "compassion" as "something I don't want to lose" she regards it as endangered by her pursuit of professional advancement. Thus the self-deception of her initial presentation, its attempt to sustain the fiction of her own innocence, stems from her fear that to say that *she* does not want to have another baby at this time would be

> an acknowledgement to me that I am an ambitious person and that I want to

In a Different Voice
CAROL GILLIGAN

have power and responsibility for others and that I want to live a life that extends from 9 to 5 every day and into the evenings and on weekends, because that is what the power and responsibility means. It means that my family would necessarily come second . . . there would be such an incredible conflict about which is tops, and I don't want that for myself.

Asked about her concept of "an ambitious person" she says that to be ambitious means to be

power hungry [and] insensitive. [Why insensitive?] Because people are stomped on in the process. A person on the way up stomps on people, whether it is family or other colleagues or clientele, on the way up. [Inevitably?] Not always, but I have seen it so often in my limited years of working that it is scary to me. It is scary because I don't want to change like that.

Because the acquisition of adult power is seen to entail the loss of feminine sensitivity and compassion, the conflict between femininity and adulthood becomes construed as a moral problem. The discovery of the principle of nonviolence begins to direct attention to the moral dilemma itself and initiates the search for a resolution that can encompass both femininity and adulthood.

Developmental Theory Reconsidered

The developmental conception delineated at the outset, which has so consistently found the development of women to be either aberrant or incomplete, has been limited insofar as it has been predominantly a male conception, giving lip-service, a place on the chart, to the interdependence of intimacy and care but constantly stressing, at their expense, the importance and value of autonomous judgment and action. To admit to this conception the truth of the feminine perspective is to recognize for both sexes the central importance in adult life of the connection between self and other, the universality of the need for compassion and care. The concept of the separate self and of the moral principle uncompromised by the constraints of reality is an adolescent ideal, the elaborately wrought philosophy of a Stephen Daedalus, whose flight we know to be in jeopardy. Erikson (1964), in contrasting the ideological morality of the adolescent with the ethics of adult care, attempts to grapple with this problem of integration, but is impeded by the limitations of his own previous developmental conception. When his developmental stages chart a path where the sole precursor to the intimacy of adult relationships is the trust established in infancy and all intervening experience is marked only as steps toward greater independence, then separation itself becomes the model and the measure of growth. The observation that for women, identity has as much to do with connection as with separation led Erikson into trouble largely because of his failure to integrate this insight into the mainstream of his developmental theory (Erikson, 1968).

The morality of responsibility which women describe stands apart from the morality of rights which underlies Kohlberg's conception of the highest stages of moral judgment. Kohlberg (Note 3) sees the progression toward these stages as

509

resulting from the generalization of the self-centered adolescent rejection of societal morality into a principled conception of individual natural rights. To illustrate this progression, he cites as an example of integrated Stage Five judgment, "possibly moving to Stage Six," the following response of a twenty-five-year-old subject from his male longitudinal sample:

> [What does the word morality mean to you?] Nobody in the world knows the answer. I think it is recognizing the right of the individual, the rights of other individuals, not interfering with those rights. Act as fairly as you would have them treat you. I think it is basically to preserve the human being's right to existence. I think that is the most important. Secondly, the human being's right to do as he pleases, again without interfering with somebody else's rights. (p. 29)

Another version of the same conception is evident in the following interview response of a male college senior whose moral judgment also was scored by Kohlberg (Note 4) as at Stage Five or Six:

> [Morality] is a prescription, it is a thing to follow, and the idea of having a concept of morality is to try to figure out what it is that people can do in order to make life with each other livable, make for a kind of balance, a kind of equilibrium, a harmony in which everybody feels he has a place and an equal share in things, and it's doing that—doing that is kind of contributing to a state of affairs that go beyond the individual in the absence of which, the individual has no chance for self-fulfillment of any kind. Fairness; morality is kind of essential, it seems to me, for creating the kind of environment, interaction between people, that is prerequisite to this fulfillment of most individual goals and so on. If you want other people to not interfere with your pursuit of whatever you are into, you have to play the game.

In contrast, a woman in her late twenties responds to a similar question by defining a morality not of rights but of responsibility:

> [What makes something a moral issue?] Some sense of trying to uncover a right path in which to live, and always in my mind is that the world is full of real and recognizable trouble, and is it heading for some sort of doom and is it right to bring children into this world when we currently have an overpopulation problem, and is it right to spend money on a pair of shoes when I have a pair of shoes and other people are shoeless. . . . It is part of a self-critical view, part of saying, how am I spending my time and in what sense am I working? I think I have a real drive to, I have a real maternal drive to take care of someone. To take care of my mother, to take care of children, to take care of other people's children, to take care of my own children, to take care of the world. I think that goes back to your other question, and when I am dealing with moral issues, I am sort of saying to myself constantly, are you taking care of all the things that you think are important and in what ways are you wasting yourself and wasting those issues?

While the postconventional nature of this woman's perspective seems clear, her judgments of Kohlberg's hypothetical moral dilemmas do not meet his criteria for scoring at the principled level. Kohlberg regards this as a disparity between normative and metaethical judgments which he sees as indicative of the transition

In a Different Voice
CAROL GILLIGAN

between conventional and principled thinking. From another perspective, how-ever, this judgment represents a different moral conception, disentangled from so-cietal conventions and raised to the principled level. In this conception, moral judg-ment is oriented toward issues of responsibility. The way in which the responsibility orientation guides moral decision at the postconventional level is described by the following woman in her thirties:

> [Is there a right way to make moral decisions?] The only way I know is to try to be as awake as possible, to try to know the range of what you feel, to try to consider all that's involved, to be as aware as you can be to what's going on, as conscious as you can of where you're walking. [Are there principles that guide you?] The principle would have something to do with responsibility, responsibility and car-ing about yourself and others. . . . But it's not that on the one hand you choose to be responsible and on the other hand you choose to be irresponsible—both ways you can be responsible. That's why there's not just a principle that once you take hold of you settle—the principle put into practice here is still going to leave you with conflict.

The moral imperative that emerges repeatedly in the women's interviews is an injunction to care, a responsibility to discern and alleviate the "real and recog-nizable trouble" of this world. For the men Kohlberg studied, the moral impera-tive appeared rather as an injunction to respect the rights of others and thus to protect from interference the right to life and self-fulfillment. Women's insistence on care is at first self-critical rather than self-protective, while men initially con-ceive obligation to others negatively in terms of noninterference. Development for both sexes then would seem to entail an integration of rights and responsibilities through the discovery of the complementarity of these disparate views. For the women I have studied, this integration between rights and responsibilities appears to take place through a principled understanding of equity and reciprocity. This understanding tempers the self-destructive potential of a self-critical morality by asserting the equal right of all persons to care. For the men in Kohlberg's sample as well as for those in a longitudinal study of Harvard undergraduates (Gilligan & Murphy, Note 5) it appears to be the recognition through experience of the need for a more active responsibility in taking care that corrects the potential indiffer-ence of a morality of noninterference and turns attention from the logic to the consequences of choice. In the development of a postconventional ethic under-standing, women come to see the violence generated by inequitable relationships, while men come to realize the limitations of a conception of justice blinded to the real inequities of human life.

Kohlberg's dilemmas, in the hypothetical abstraction of their presentation, divest the moral actors from the history and psychology of their individual lives and separate the moral problem from the social contingencies of its possible occur-rence. In doing so, the dilemmas are useful for the distillation and refinement of the "objective principles of justice" toward which Kohlberg's stages strive. How-ever, the reconstruction of the dilemma in its contextual particularity allows the understanding of cause and consequence which engages the compassion and toler-ance considered by previous theorists to qualify the feminine sense of justice. Only when substance is given to the skeletal lives of hypothetical people is it possible to consider the social injustices which their moral problems may reflect and to imagine the individual suffering their occurrence may signify or their resolution engender.

The proclivity of women to reconstruct hypothetical dilemmas in terms of the real, to request or supply the information missing about the nature of the people and the places where they live, shifts their judgment away from the hierarchical ordering of principles and the formal procedures of decision making that are critical for scoring at Kohlberg's highest stages. This insistence on the particular signifies an orientation to the dilemma and to moral problems in general that differs from any of Kohlberg's stage descriptions. Given the constraints of Kohlberg's system and the biases in his research sample, this different orientation can only be construed as a failure in development. While several of the women in the research sample clearly articulated what Kohlberg regarded as a postconventional metaethical position, none of them were considered by Kohlberg to be principled in their normative moral judgments of his hypothetical moral dilemmas (Note 4). Instead, the women's judgments pointed toward an identification of the violence inherent in the dilemma itself which was seen to compromise the justice of any of its possible resolutions. This construction of the dilemma led the women to recast the moral judgment from a consideration of the good to a choice between evils.

The woman whose judgment of the abortion dilemma concluded the developmental sequence presented in the preceding section saw Kohlberg's Heinz dilemma in these terms and judged Heinz's action in terms of a choice between selfishness and sacrifice. For Heinz to steal the drug, given the circumstances of his life (which she inferred from his inability to pay two thousand dollars), he would have "to do something which is not in his best interest, in that he is going to get sent away, and that is a supreme sacrifice, a sacrifice which I would say a person truly in love might be willing to make." However, not to steal the drug "would be selfish on his part . . . he would just have to feel guilty about not allowing her a chance to live longer." Heinz's decision to steal is considered not in terms of the logical priority of life over property which justifies its rightness, but rather in terms of the actual consequences that stealing would have for a man of limited means and little social power.

Considered in the light of its probable outcomes—his wife dead, or Heinz in jail, brutalized by the violence of that experience and his life compromised by a record of felony—the dilemma itself changes. Its resolution has less to do with the relative weights of life and property in an abstract moral conception than with the collision it has produced between two lives, formerly conjoined but now in opposition, where the continuation of one life can now occur only at the expense of the other. Given this construction, it becomes clear why consideration revolves around the issue of sacrifice and why guilt becomes the inevitable concomitant of either resolution.

Demonstrating the reticence noted in the first section about making moral judgments, this woman explains her reluctance to judge in terms of her belief

In a Different Voice
CAROL GILLIGAN

that everybody's existence is so different that I kind of say to myself, that might be something that I wouldn't do, but I can't say that it is right or wrong for that person. I can only deal with what is appropriate for me to do when I am faced with specific problems.

Asked if she would apply to others her own injunction against hurting, she says:

See, I can't say that it is wrong. I can't say that it is right or that it's wrong because I don't know what the person did that the other person did something to hurt him . . . so it is not right that the person got hurt, but it is right that the person who just lost the job has got to get that anger up and out. It doesn't put any bread on his table, but it is released. I don't mean to be copping out. I really am trying to see how to answer these questions for you.

Her difficulty in answering Kohlberg's questions, her sense of strain with the construction which they impose on the dilemma, stems from their divergence from her own frame of reference:

I don't even think I use the words right and wrong anymore, and I know I don't use the word moral, because I am not sure I know what it means. . . . We are talking about an unjust society, we are talking about a whole lot of things that are not right, that are truly wrong, to use the word that I don't use very often, and I have no control to change that. If I could change it, I certainly would, but I can only make my small contribution from day to day, and if I don't intentionally hurt somebody, that is my contribution to a better society. And so a chunk of that contribution is also not to pass judgment on other people, particularly when I don't know the circumstances of why they are doing certain things.

The reluctance to judge remains a reluctance to hurt, but one that stems now not from a sense of personal vulnerability but rather from a recognition of the limitations of judgment itself. The deference of the conventional feminine perspective can thus be seen to continue at the postconventional level, not as moral relativism but rather as part of a reconstructed moral understanding. Moral judgment is renounced in an awareness of the psychological and social determinism of all human behavior at the same time as moral concern is reaffirmed in recognition of the reality of human pain and suffering.

I have a real thing about hurting people and always have, and that gets a little complicated at times, because, for example, you don't want to hurt your child. I don't want to hurt my child but if I don't hurt her sometimes, then that's hurting her more, you see, and so that was a terrible dilemma for me.

Moral dilemmas are terrible in that they entail hurt; she sees Heinz's decision as "the result of anguish, who am I hurting, why do I have to hurt them." While the morality of Heinz's theft is not in question, given the circumstances which necessitated it, what is at issue is his willingness to substitute himself for his wife and become, in her stead, the victim of exploitation by a society which breeds and legitimizes the druggist's irresponsibility and whose injustice is thus manifest in the very occurrence of the dilemma.

The same sense that the wrong questions are being asked is evident in the response of another woman who justified Heinz's action on a similar basis, saying
"I don't think that exploitation should really be a right." When women begin to
make direct moral statements, the issues they repeatedly address are those of
exploitation and hurt. In doing so, they raise the issue of nonviolence in precisely
the same psychological context that brought Erikson (1969) to pause in his consideration of the truth of Gandhi's life.

In the pivotal letter, around which the judgment of his book turns, Erikson
confronts the contradiction between the philosophy of nonviolence that informed
Gandhi's dealing with the British and the psychology of violence that marred his
relationships with his family and with the children of the ashram. It was this contradiction, Erikson confesses,

> which almost brought *me* to the point where I felt unable to continue writing
> *this* book because I seemed to sense the presence of a kind of untruth in the very
> protestation of truth; of something unclean when all the words spelled out an
> unreal purity; and, above all, of displaced violence where nonviolence was the
> professed issue. (p. 231)

In an effort to untangle the relationship between the spiritual truth of Satyagraha and the truth of his own psychoanalytic understanding, Erikson reminds
Gandhi that "Truth, you once said, 'excludes the use of violence because man is
not capable of knowing the absolute truth and therefore is not competent to
punish' " (p. 241). The affinity between Satyagraha and psychoanalysis lies in
their shared commitment to seeing life as an "experiment in truth," in their being

> somehow joined in a universal "therapeutics," committed to the Hippocratic
> principle that one can test truth (or the healing power inherent in a sick situation)
> only by action which avoids harm—or better, by action which maximizes mutuality
> and minimizes the violence caused by unilateral coercion or threat. (p. 247)

Erikson takes Gandhi to task for his failure to acknowledge the relativity of truth.
This failure is manifest in the coercion of Gandhi's claim to exclusive possession
of the truth, his "unwillingness to learn from *anybody anything* except what was
approved by the 'inner voice' " (p. 236). This claim led Gandhi, in the guise of
love, to impose his truth on others without awareness or regard for the extent to
which he thereby did violence to their integrity.

The moral dilemma, arising inevitably out of a conflict of truths, is by definition a "sick situation" in that its either/or formulation leaves no room for an
outcome that does not do violence. The resolution of such dilemmas, however,
lies not in the self-deception of rationalized violence—"I was" said Gandhi, "a
cruelly kind husband. I regarded myself as her teacher and so harassed her out of
my blind love for her" (p. 233)—but rather in the replacement of the underlying
antagonism with a mutuality of respect and care.

Gandhi, whom Kohlberg has mentioned as exemplifying Stage Six moral judgment and whom Erikson sought as a model of an adult ethical sensibility, instead
is criticized by a judgment that refuses to look away from or condone the infliction of harm. In denying the validity of his wife's reluctance to open her home to

514

In a Different Voice
CAROL GILLIGAN

strangers and in his blindness to the different reality of adolescent sexuality and temptation, Gandhi compromised in his everyday life the ethic of nonviolence to which in principle and in public he was so steadfastly committed.

The blind willingness to sacrifice people to truth, however, has always been the danger of an ethics abstracted from life. This willingness links Gandhi to the biblical Abraham, who prepared to sacrifice the life of his son in order to demonstrate the integrity and supremacy of his faith. Both men, in the limitations of their fatherhood, stand in implicit contrast to the woman who comes before Solomon and verifies her motherhood by relinquishing truth in order to save the life of her child. It is the ethics of an adulthood that has become principled at the expense of care that Erikson comes to criticize in his assessment of Gandhi's life.

This same criticism is dramatized explicitly as a contrast between the sexes in *The Merchant of Venice* (1598/1912), where Shakespeare goes through an extraordinary complication of sexual identity (dressing a male actor as a female character who in turn poses as a male judge) in order to bring into the masculine citadel of justice the feminine plea for mercy. The limitation of the contractual conception of justice is illustrated through the absurdity of its literal execution, while the "need to make exceptions all the time" is demonstrated contrapuntally in the matter of the rings. Portia, in calling for mercy, argues for that resolution in which no one is hurt, and as the men are forgiven for their failure to keep both their rings and their word, Antonio in turn foregoes his "right" to ruin Shylock.

The research findings that have been reported in this essay suggest that women impose a distinctive construction on moral problems, seeing moral dilemmas in terms of conflicting responsibilities. This construction was found to develop through a sequence of three levels and two transitions, each level representing a more complex understanding of the relationship between self and other and each transition involving a critical reinterpretation of the moral conflict between selfishness and responsibility. The development of women's moral judgment appears to proceed from an initial concern with survival, to a focus on goodness, and finally to a principled understanding of nonviolence as the most adequate guide to the just resolution of moral conflicts.

In counterposing to Kohlberg's longitudinal research on the development of hypothetical moral judgment in men a cross-sectional study of women's responses to actual dilemmas of moral conflict and choice, this essay precludes the possibility of generalization in either direction and leaves to further research the task of sorting out the different variables of occasion and sex. Longitudinal studies of women's moral judgments are necessary in order to validate the claims of stage and sequence presented here. Similarly, the contrast drawn between the moral judgments of men and women awaits for its confirmation a more systematic comparison of the responses of both sexes. Kohlberg's research on moral development has confounded the variables of age, sex, type of decision, and type of dilemma by presenting a single configuration (the responses of adolescent males to hypothetical dilemmas of conflicting rights) as the basis for a universal stage sequence. This paper underscores the need for systematic treatment of these variables and points toward their study as a critical task for future moral development research.

For the present, my aim has been to demonstrate the centrality of the concepts of responsibility and care in women's constructions of the moral domain, to indicate the close tie in women's thinking between conceptions of the self and conceptions of morality, and, finally, to argue the need for an expanded developmental theory that would include, rather than rule out from developmental consideration, the difference in the feminine voice. Such an inclusion seems essential, not only for explaining the development of women but also for understanding in both sexes the characteristics and precursors of an adult moral conception.

Reference Notes

1. Haan, N. *Activism as moral protest: Moral judgments of hypothetical dilemmas and an actual situation of civil disobedience.* Unpublished manuscript, University of California at Berkeley, 1971.
2. Turiel, E. *A comparative analysis of moral knowledge and moral judgment in males and females.* Unpublished manuscript, Harvard University, 1973.
3. Kohlberg, L. *Continuities and discontinuities in childhood and adult moral development revisited.* Unpublished paper, Harvard University, 1973.
4. Kohlberg, L. Personal communication, August, 1976.
5. Gilligan, C., & Murphy, M. *The philosopher and the "dilemma of the fact": Moral development in late adolescence and adulthood.* Unpublished manuscript, Harvard University, 1977.

References

Broverman, I., Vogel, S., Broverman, D., Clarkson, F., & Rosenkrantz, P. Sex-role stereotypes: A current appraisal. *Journal of Social Issues*, 1972, 28, 59–78.
Coles, R. *Children of crisis.* Boston: Little, Brown, 1964.
Didion, J. The women's movement. *New York Times Book Review*, July 30, 1972, pp. 1–2; 14.
Drabble, M. *The waterfall.* Hammondsworth, Eng.: Penguin Books, 1969.
Eliot, G. *The mill on the floss.* New York: New American Library, 1965. (Originally published, 1860.)
Erikson, E. H. *Insight and responsibility.* New York: W. W. Norton, 1964.
Erikson, E. H. *Identity: Youth and crisis.* New York: W. W. Norton, 1968.
Erikson, E. H. *Gandhi's truth.* New York: W. W. Norton, 1969.
Freud, S. "Civilized" sexual morality and modern nervous illness. In J. Strachey (Ed.), *The standard edition of the complete psychological works of Sigmund Freud* (Vol. 9). London: Hogarth Press, 1959. (Originally published, 1908.)
Freud, S. Some psychical consequences of the anatomical distinction between the sexes. In J. Strachey (Ed.), *The standard edition of the complete psychological works of Sigmund Freud* (Vol. 19). London: Hogarth Press, 1961. (Originally published, 1925.)
Gilligan, C., Kohlberg, L., Lerner, J., & Belenky, M. Moral reasoning about sexual dilemmas: The development of an interview and scoring system. *Technical Report of the President's Commission on Obscenity and Pornography* (Vol. 1) [415 060–137]. Washington, D.C.: U.S. Government Printing Office, 1971.
Haan, N. Hypothetical and actual moral reasoning in a situation of civil disobedience. *Journal of Personality and Social Psychology*, 1975, 32, 255–270.
Holstein, C. Development of moral judgment: A longitudinal study of males and females. *Child Development*, 1976, 47, 51–61.

In a Different Voice
CAROL GILLIGAN

Horner, M. Toward an understanding of achievement-related conflicts in women. *Journal of Social Issues*, 1972, 29, 157–174.

Ibsen, H. *A doll's house*. In *Ibsen plays*. Hammondsworth, Eng.: Penguin Books, 1965. (Originally published, 1879.)

Kohlberg, L. From is to ought: How to commit the naturalistic fallacy and get away with it in the study of moral development. In T. Mischel (Ed.), *Cognitive development and epistemology*. New York: Academic Press, 1971.

Kohlberg, L., & Gilligan, C. The adolescent as a philosopher: The discovery of the self in a postconventional world. *Daedalus*, 1971, 100, 1051–1056.

Kohlberg, L., & Kramer, R. Continuities and discontinuities in childhood and adult moral development. *Human Development*, 1969, 12, 93–120.

Piaget, J. *The moral judgment of the child*. New York: The Free Press, 1965. (Originally published, 1932.)

Shakespeare, W. *The merchant of Venice*. In *The comedies of Shakespeare*. London: Oxford University Press, 1912. (Originally published, 1598.)

[37]

Merrill-Palmer Quarterly, Vol. 34, No. 3

Two Moral Orientations:
Gender Differences and Similarities

Carol Gilligan and Jane Attanucci
Harvard University

Recent discussions of sex differences in moral development equate moral stage in Kohlberg's justice framework with moral orientation—the distinction between justice and care perspectives. The present study of real-life dilemmas from 46 men and 34 women, primarily adolescents and young adults, shows that: (a) Concerns about both justice and care are represented in people's thinking about real-life moral dilemmas, but people tend to focus on one set of concerns and minimally represent the other. And (b) There is an association between moral orientation and gender such that men and women use both orientations, but Care Focus dilemmas are most likely to be presented by women and Justice Focus dilemmas by men. Consideration of moral orientation transforms the debate over sex differences in moral reasoning into serious questions about moral perspectives that are open to empirical study.

Recent discussions of sex differences in moral development have equated moral stage in Kohlberg's justice framework with moral orientation—the distinction between justice and care perspectives. Kohlberg (1984), Walker (1984, 1986), Baumrind (1986), and Haan (1985) address the question of whether women and men score differently on the Kohlberg scale of justice reasoning, and report contradictory findings. In the present study, evidence of two moral perspectives in people's discussions of actual moral conflicts is examined. Also considered is whether there is an association between moral orientation and gender.

The research was supported by grants from the NIE, the Picker Foundation, and the Blake School, Minneapolis, MN. The authors acknowledge the generous support of the Mailman Foundation and Mrs. Marilyn Brachman Hoffman, thank the participants in these studies for their time and thoughtful responses, and also thank the interviewers and the coders. Diana Baumrind's detailed commentary on earlier drafts was immensely helpful. The authors are also indebted to Terry Tivnan, for his statistical assistance, and to their colleagues at the Center for the Study of Gender, Education, and Human Development. Correspondence should be sent to Jane Attanucci, Graduate School of Education, Harvard University, Roy E. Larsen Hall, Appian Way, Cambridge, MA 02138.

Merrill-Palmer Quarterly, July 1988, Vol. 34, No. 3, pp. 223–237.

The distinction between justice and care perspectives was made in the course of studying the relationship between judgment and action. These studies (Gilligan, 1977; Gilligan & Belenky, 1980; Gilligan & Murphy, 1979) of college students describing experiences of moral conflict and choice and pregnant women considering abortion, shifted the focus from people's thinking about hypothetical dilemmas to their construction of real-life choices. With this change in approach, it became possible to see how people describe moral problems in their lives and to explore the relationship between the understanding of moral problems and the strategies used in resolving them.

For example, some men who scored at the highest level of the Kohlberg scale and defined moral conflicts in their lives as problems of justice, described themselves as not acting on principles of justice because they considered just solutions to be morally problematic (Gilligan & Murphy, 1979). It was also observed that some women, especially when describing their own experiences of moral conflict and choice, often defined and resolved moral problems in a way that differed from those described in established theories of moral development and in the measures for its assessment.

Previous interpretations of individual, cultural, and sex differences in moral reasoning have been constrained by the assumption that there is a single moral perspective, that of justice. The analysis of women's moral judgments clarified an alternative approach to moral decision making which was designated the *care perspective* (Gilligan, 1982).

The language of the public abortion debate, for example, reveals a justice perspective. Whether the abortion dilemma is cast as a conflict of rights or in terms of respect for human life, the claims of the fetus and the pregnant woman are balanced or placed in opposition. The morality of abortion decisions thus considered hinges on the question of whether the fetus is a person, and, if so, whether its claims take precedence over those of the pregnant woman. Framed as a problem of care, the dilemma posed by abortion shifts. The connection between the fetus and the pregnant woman becomes the focus and the question becomes whether it is responsible or irresponsible, caring or careless, to extend or to end this connection. To ask what actions constitute care or are more caring directs attention to the parameters of connection and the costs of detachment, which become subjects of moral concern.

The distinction made here between a justice orientation and a care orientation pertains to the ways in which moral problems are conceived and reflects different dimensions of human relationships that give rise to moral concern. A justice perspective draws attention

to problems of inequality and oppression and holds up an ideal of reciprocal rights and equal respect for individuals. A care perspective
draws attention to problems of detachment or abandonment and
holds up an ideal of attention and response to need.

Two moral injunctions, not to treat others unfairly and not to turn
away from someone in need, capture these different concerns. From
a developmental standpoint, both inequality and attachment are universal human experiences: All children are born into a situation of inequality and no child survives in the absence of some kind of adult attachment. These two intersecting dimensions of equality and
attachment characterize all forms of human relationship. All relationships can be described in both sets of terms: as unequal or equal and
as attached or detached. Because everyone has been vulnerable both
to oppression and to abandonment, two moral visions—one of justice
and one of care—recur in human experience.

Psychologists studying moral development have equated morality with justice, characterized the parent-child relationships as a relationship of inequality, and contrasted it with the equality of peer relations. Previous discussions of "two moralities" (Haan, 1978; Youniss,
1980) have been cast in terms of inequality and equality, following
the Piaget (1932/1965) equation of moral development with the development of the idea of justice and his distinction between relationships of constraint and relationships of cooperation.

Although the dimensions of constraint and cooperation represent
the opposite poles of inequality and equality in relationships, neither
addresses the dimension of attachment and detachment, responsiveness and failures to respond, in those relationships. The present discussion of two moral orientations refers instead to the dimensions of
attachment and equality in all relationships and considers moral development in terms of both changes in the understanding of what fairness means and in terms of changes in the understanding of what
constitutes care. Because problems of inequality and problems of detachment arise throughout human life and in both public and private
realms, it would be expected that equality and attachment would persist as moral concerns.

The present paper is a report of the results of three studies undertaken to investigate the two moral orientations and to determine
to what extent men and women differentially raise concerns about
justice and care in discussing moral conflicts in their lives. The examples presented in Table 1, drawn from discussions of real-life dilemmas, illustrate the concept of moral orientation. Each pair of dilemmas
reveals how a problem is seen from a justice perspective and from a
care perspective. In each pair of examples, the justice construction is

Table 1. Examples of Justice Care Perspectives in
Real-Life Moral Domain Data

Justice	Care
1J [If people were taking drugs and I was the only one who wasn't I would feel it was stupid, I know for me what is right is right and what's wrong is wrong . . . it's like a set of standards I have.] (*High School Student*)	*1C* [If there was one person it would be a lot easier to say no, I could talk to her, because there wouldn't be seven others to think about. I do think about them, you know, and wonder what they say about me and what it will mean . . . I made the right decision not to because my real friends accepted my decision.] (*High School Student*)
2J [The conflict was that by all rights she should have been turned into the honor board for violation of the alcohol policy.] [I liked her very much.] [She is extremely embarrassed and upset. She was contrite, she wished she had never done it. She had all the proper levels of contriteness and guilt and] [I was supposed to turn her in and didn't.] (*Medical Student*)	*2C* [It might just be his business if he wants to get drunk every week or it might be something that is really a problem and that should be dealt with professionally; and to be concerned about someone without antagonizing them or making their life more difficult than it had to be; maybe there was just no problem there.] [I guess in something like a personal relationship with a proctor you don't want to just go right out there and antagonize people, because that person will go away and if you destroy any relationship you have, I think you have lost any chance of doing anything for a person.] (*Medical Student*)
3J [I have moral dilemmas all the time, but I have no problem solving them usually. I usually resolve them according to my internal morality . . . the more important publicly your office is, to me the more important it is that you *play by the rules* because society hangs together by these rules and in my view, if you cheat on them, even for a laudatory purpose, eventually you break the rules down, because it is impossible to draw any fine lines.] (*Lawyer*)	*3C* [I have to preside over these decisions and try to make them as nondisastrous as possible for the people who are most vulnerable. The fewer games you play the better, because you are really dealing with issues that are the very basis to people's day-to-day well-being, and it is people's feelings, people's potential for growth, and you should do everything in your power to smooth it.] (*Lawyer*)

the more familiar one, capturing the way such problems are usually defined from a moral standpoint.

In 1J, a peer pressure dilemma is presented in terms of how to uphold one's moral standards and how to withstand the pressure from one's friends to deviate from what one knows for oneself to be right. In 1C, a similar decision (not to smoke) is cast in terms of how to respond both to one's friends and to oneself. The rightness of the decision not to smoke is established in terms of the fact that it did not break relationships: "My real friends accepted my decision." Attention to one's friends, to what they say and how choices affect the friendship, is presented as a moral concern.

In the second pair of examples, the dilemma of whether to report someone who has violated the medical school's alcohol policy is posed differently from the justice and care perspectives. The decision not to tell is reasoned in different ways. A clear example of justice tempered by mercy is presented in 2J. The student believes that the violator should be turned in ("I was supposed to turn her in") and justifies not doing so on the grounds that she deserved mercy because "She had all the proper level of contriteness" that was appropriate for the situation.

In 2C, a student decides not to turn a proctor in for drinking because it would "destroy any relationship you have" and therefore would "hurt any chance of doing anything for that person." In this construction, turning in the person is seen as impeding efforts to help. The concern about maintaining the relationship in order to be able to help is not mentioned in 2J. Similarly, the concern about maintaining the honor board policy is not mentioned in 2C.

A further illustration of how justice and care perspectives restructure moral understanding can be seen by observing that in 2J the student justifies not turning in the violator because of questions about the rightness of the alcohol policy itself. But in 2C the student considers whether what was deemed a problem was really a problem for the other person. The case of 2C illustrates what is meant by striving to see the other person in his or her own particular terms. It also exemplifies the contrast between this endeavor and the effort to establish, independently of persons, the legitimacy of existing rules and standards.

The third pair of examples further illustrates the distinction between establishing and maintaining existing rules and universal impartial standards (3J) and attending to people in their particular circumstances and minimizing the damaging effects of legal decisions (3C). In 3J, the lawyer affirms the value of the American legal system, dismissing the "impossible . . . fine lines." In 3C, the lawyer struggles with those same fine lines in order to protect those personally vulnerable to society's "game." These interpretations of the same legal system differ; neither is entirely wrong or naive. In 3J, the lawyer asserts the necessity of our legal system to hold society together. But in 3C, the lawyer appeals to the injunction not to abandon those in need.

It is important to emphasize that these examples were selected to highlight the contrast between a justice perspective and a care perspective. It must be stressed, however, that most people who participated in this research used considerations of both justice and care in discussing a moral conflict they faced.

In the present study two questions were posed: (a) In the evidence of justice and care orientations in people's discussion of real-life moral conflict, do people represent both orientations equally or do they tend to focus on one and minimally represent the other? And (b) Is there a relationship between moral orientation and gender?

METHOD

Subjects

Subjects were drawn from three research studies. In each study, the subjects were asked to describe a real-life moral dilemma. All three samples consisted of men and women who were matched for levels of education; the adults were matched for professional occupations. See Table 2 for the distribution of subjects, by sample, in age and gender categories.

Study 1. The design matched participants for high levels of education and professional occupations to examine the variables of age, gender, and type of dilemma. The adolescents and adults included were 11 women and 10 men. The racial composition (19 white and 2 minority) was not statistically random, as race was not a focal variable of the study.

Study 2. First-year students were randomly selected from two prestigious northeastern medical schools to be interviewed as part of a longitudinal study of stress and adaptation in physicians.[1] The 26 men and 13 women students represented the proportions of each gender in the class at large. The 19 white and 20 minority students (Black, Hispanic and Asian Americans) were selected to balance the

---

[1]Nineteen other medical students who could not (two would not) describe a situation of moral conflict are not in the present study. We acknowledge the bias created by such attrition. Their response may reflect the pressures on first-year medical students in a context which discourages the uncertainty about knowing what is the right thing to do. Generalizations about physicians from this specific study would be unwarranted, however, as several physicians who participated in Study 1 provided both care and justice perspectives on their experiences of conflict and choice.

Table 2. Gender and Age of Subjects By Study

	15–22 Years	23–34 Years	35–77 Years	n
Study 1				
Women	4	2	5	11
Men	4	1	5	10
Study 2				
Women	9	4	0	13
Men	12	14	0	26
Study 3				
Women	10	0	0	10
Men	10	0	0	10

sample's racial composition (the only sample in the present study with such a design). The students ranged in age from 21 to 27 years.

Study 3. The 10 female and 10 male participants were randomly selected from a coeducational private school in a midwestern city. The 19 white and 1 minority student ranged in age from 14 to 18 years.

Research Interview

All participants were asked the following series of questions about their personal experience of moral conflict and choice:

1. Have you ever been in a situation of moral conflict where you had to make a decision but weren't sure what was the right thing to do?
2. Could you describe the situation?
3. What were the conflicts for you in that situation?
4. What did you do?
5. Do you think it was the right thing to do?
6. How do you know?

The interviewer asked questions to encourage the participants to clarify and elaborate their responses. For example, participants were asked what they meant by words like *responsibility, obligation, moral, fair, selfish,* and *caring.* The interviewers followed the participants' logic in presenting the moral problem, most commonly querying, "Anything else?"

The interviews were conducted individually, tape recorded, and later transcribed. The moral conflict questions were one segment of an interview which included questions about morality and identity (Gilligan et al., 1982). The interviews lasted about 2 hours.

Data Analysis

The real-life moral dilemmas were analyzed by using methods described in Lyons's *Manual for Coding Real-Life Dilemmas* (1982). The Lyons procedure[2] is a content analysis which identifies moral considerations. The unit of analysis is the *consideration*, defined as each idea the participant presents in discussing a moral problem. The units are designated in Table 1 with brackets.

To reach an acceptable level of reliability in identifying considerations required extensive training. The three coders trained by Lyons were blind to the gender, age, and race of the participants and achieved high levels of intercoder reliability (a range of 67% to 95%, and a mean of 80% agreement, across samples of randomly selected cases). Typically, a real-life moral dilemma consisted of 7 considerations, with a range of 4 to 17. A minimum of four considerations was required for the present analysis. When only four considerations were present, in all but one case, the four considerations were in one orientation. The coder classified these considerations as either justice or care.

The Lyons score was simply the predominant, most frequent, mode of moral reasoning (justice or care). For the present study, *predominance* was redefined so that a real-life moral dilemma consisting of only care or justice considerations was labeled *Care Only* or *Justice Only*. A dilemma consisting of 75% or more care or justice considerations was labeled *Care Focus* or *Justice Focus*, respectively. A dilemma in which less than 75% of the total number of considerations were care or justice was placed in the *Care Justice* category.

---

[2]Lyons's coding sheet (Lyons, 1983) specifies five categories that establish whether the consideration is assigned to justice or care. Intercoder reliability is computed across categories. In the present study, most of the considerations coded fit Categories 2 and 3 under justice and care. When we ran our analysis using only these categories, some subjects were lost due to an insufficient number of considerations, but the direction of the findings as reported in the results section (with all categories included) remained. This fact is significant because Categories 2 and 3 under justice and care best capture our distinction between justice and care: concern with fulfilling obligations, duty or commitments, or maintaining standards or principles of fairness (justice), and concern with maintaining or restoring relationships, or with responding to the weal and woe of others (care). Lyons's Categories 1, 4, and 5 under justice and care are consistent with her focus on the perspective taken toward others. Yet Categories 1, 4, and 5 can readily be confused with a conception of justice and care as bi-polar opposites of a single dimension of moral reasoning or as mirror image conceptions where justice is egoistic and uncaring and caring is altruistic and unjust. Because these categories were rarely evident in the current data, these questions, although important for other researchers to consider, are only marginally relevant to the present discussion.

Table 3. Number of Participants by Moral Orientation Category

	Care Only	Care Focus	Care Justice	Justice Focus	Justice Only
Observed	5	8	27	20	20
Expected	.64	4	70	4	.64

RESULTS

The real-life dilemma data are summarized from three studies with comparable designs. That is, samples with male and female subjects are matched for high socioeconomic status. Frequencies and statistical tests are presented across samples. The statistical comparison of samples on moral orientation is not significant ($\chi^2(4, N = 80) = 9.21$ n.s.). Parallel tests have been performed for each sample and discrepancies from the overall pattern are reported and discussed.

Two observations can be made from the data in Table 3. First, the majority of people represent both moral orientations; 69% compared to the 31% who use Care or Justice Only. Second, two thirds of the dilemmas are in the Focus categories (Care Only, Care Focus, Justice Only, Justice Focus), and only one third are in the Care Justice category. The question addressed by Table 3 is, Do people tend to focus their discussion of a moral problem in one or the other orientation?

For the typical case, the ratio of care to justice considerations is Care Only 7:0; Care Focus 6:1; Care Justice 5:2, 4:3, 3:4, 2:5; Justice Focus 1:6; and Justice Only 0:7. Using a binomial model, if an equal probability of care and justice considerations in an account of a real-life moral dilemma ($p = .5$) is assumed, then a random sampling of moral considerations (typically $N = 7$) over 80 trials (80 participants' single dilemmas) would result in an expected binomial distribution. To test whether the distribution of scores fit the expected distribution, the χ^2 goodness of fit test is applied. The observed distribution differs significantly from the expected, $\chi^2(4, N = 80) = 133.8$, $p < .001$, and provides supporting evidence for the contention that an individual's moral considerations are not random but tend to be focused in either the care or justice orientation.

In Table 4 the distribution of moral orientations for each gender is presented. The statistical test of gender differences is based on a combination of Care Only and Care Focus, as well as a combination of Justice Only and Justice Focus in order to have expected values greater than 5: $\chi^2(2, N = 80) = 18.33$, $p < .001$. This test demonstrates the relationship between moral orientation and gender in which both men and women present dilemmas in the Care Justice category, but Care Focus is much more likely in the moral dilemma of a woman and Justice Focus more likely in the dilemma of a man. In

Table 4. Frequency of Moral Orientation Categories by Gender of Participants

	Care Only	Care Focus	Care Justice	Justice Focus	Justice Only
Women	5	7	12	6	4
Men	0	1	15	14	16

fact, if women were excluded from a study of moral reasoning, Care Focus could easily be overlooked.

The relationship between moral orientation and age was not tested because the majority of participants were adolescents and young adults, providing little age range. Furthermore, in the present study, age was confounded with sample (i.e., the young adults were the medical students), making interpretation difficult.

The medical student data (Study 2) raised further questions of interpretation which bear on the issues addressed in this analysis. First, the dilemmas from the medical students, when tested separately, do not show the same relationship between gender and moral orientation, $\chi^2(2, n = 39) = 4.36$, n.s. However, consistent with the overall findings, the two Care Focus dilemmas were presented by women.

As for the pattern of difference in this racially diverse sample, the Care Focus dilemmas were presented by one white woman and one minority woman. The relationship between moral orientation and race for both men and women was that the dilemmas presented by white students were more likely to fall in the Care Justice category and dilemmas of minority students in the Justice Focus category (Fisher's Exact $p = .045$ for women, and $p = .0082$ for men).

DISCUSSION

The present exploration of moral orientation has demonstrated that: (a) Concerns about justice and care are both represented in people's thinking about real-life moral dilemmas, but people tend to focus on one set of concerns and minimally represent the other. And (b) there is an association between moral orientation and gender such that both men and women use both orientations, but Care Focus dilemmas are more likely to be presented by women and Justice Focus dilemmas by men.

Analysis of care and justice as distinct moral orientations that address different moral concerns leads to a consideration of both perspectives as constituitive of mature moral thinking. The tension between these perspectives is suggested by the fact that detachment, which is the mark of mature moral judgment in the justice perspective, becomes the moral problem in the care perspective, that is, the failure to attend to need. Conversely, attention to the particular needs and circumstances of individuals, the mark of mature moral judgment in the care perspective, becomes the moral problem in the justice perspective, that is, failure to treat others fairly, as equals. Care Focus and Justice Focus reasoning suggest a tendency to lose sight of one perspective in arriving at moral decision. That the focus phenomenon was demonstrated by two thirds of both men and women in the present study suggests that this liability is shared by both sexes.

This finding provides an empirical explanation for the equation of morality with justice in the theories of moral development that are derived from all-male research samples (Kohlberg, 1969, 1984; Piaget, 1932/1965). If women were eliminated from the present study, the focus on care would virtually disappear. Given the presence of justice concerns, most of the dilemmas described by women could be analyzed for justice considerations without reference to care considerations.

In addition, the Care Focus dilemmas presented by women offer an explanation for the fact that within a justice conception of morality, moral judgments of girls and women have appeared anomalous and difficult to interpret; Piaget (1932/1965) cites this explanation as the reason for studying boys. Furthermore, finding Care Focus mainly among women indicates why the analysis of women's moral thinking elucidated the care perspective as a distinct moral orientation and why the considerations of care that has been noted in dilemmas presented by men did not seem fully elaborated (Gilligan & Murphy, 1979).

The evidence of orientation focus as an observable characteristic of moral judgment does not justify the conclusion that focus is a desirable attribute of moral decision. However, careful attention to women's articulation of the care perspective has led to a different conception of the moral domain and to a different way of analyzing the moral judgment of both men and women.

The category Care Justice in our findings raises important questions that merit investigation in future research. Dilemmas in this "bifocal" category were equally likely among men and women in our study. It is possible that interviews involving more dilemmas and further questioning might reveal the focus phenomenon to be more common. But it is also possible that such studies might find and elucidate further an ability to sustain two moral perspectives, an ability, which according to the present data, seems equally characteristic of men and women.

The findings presented here suggest that people know and use both moral orientations. Although Care Focus dilemmas are raised by women, it is important to emphasize that the focus phenomenon in two moral orientations is replicated in an all-female sample of students in a private girls' high school. The moral dilemmas of these 48 adolescent girls are distributed as follows: Care Focus, 22; Care Justice, 17; and Justice Focus, 9. This distribution differs significantly from the expected binomial distribution, as well. The statistical test is based on a combination of Care Only and Care Focus, as well as a combination of Justice Only and Justice Focus in order to have expected values greater than 5: $\chi^2(2, N = 48) = 154.4, p < .001$).

Further evidence is provided in a study by Johnston (1985) who created a standard method for studying spontaneous orientation and orientation preference. She found in a sample of 60 11- and 15-year-olds from a middle-class suburban community that most children could understand and use the logic of both orientations. She also found sex differences in spontaneous and preferred orientation. Her findings underscore our contention that moral orientation must be considered a variable in moral judgment research.

If people know both moral orientations, as our theory and data suggest, researchers can cue perception in one or the other direction in a real-life dilemma by the questions they raise or by their failure to ask questions. The context of the research study as well as the interview itself must be considered for its influence on the likelihood of eliciting care or justice reasoning. In the case of the medical student data (Study 2) presented in this paper, the findings raise just such contextual questions.

In this large-scale study of stress and adaptation which included extensive standard, evaluative inventories, as well as the clinical interview, is it possible that the first-year medical students might have been reluctant to admit uncertainty? Some could not or would not describe a situation in which they were not sure what the right thing to do was. Also, is it possible that the focus on justice represents efforts by the students to align themselves with the perceived values of the prestigious institution they are entering rather than with the values inherent in a caring profession. The focus on justice by minority students is of particular interest because it counters the suggestion that a care orientation is the perspective of social subordinates or people of lower social power and status.

Evidence that moral orientation organizes moral judgment as well as the discovery of the focus phenomenon has led us to make the following changes in our research interview, which we offer as suggestions for other researchers:

1. That interviewers proceed on the assumption that people can adopt both a justice and a care perspective and that they encourage participants to generate different perspectives on a moral problem

("Is there another way to think about this problem?") and to examine the relationship between them.

2. That interviewers seek to determine the conception of justice and care that organizes the moral thinking in the discussion of a particular dilemma. The Kohlberg stages describe the development of justice reasoning. The description by Gilligan (1977, 1982) of the different ways that women think about care and of changes in care reasoning over time offers a guide to thinking about developmental transitions in the care perspective. These empirical efforts are necessary prior to any further discussion of the relationship between stage and orientation.

3. That interviewers should attend to where the self stands with respect to the two moral orientations. In our present research we included the question, "What is at stake for you in the conflict?" to encourage subjects to reveal where they see themselves in the dilemmas they describe and how they align themselves with different perspectives on the problem.

The evidence of two moral perspectives suggests that the choice of moral standpoint, whether implicit or explicit, may indicate a preferred way of seeing. If so, the implications of the preference need to be explored. Orientation preference may be a dimension of identity or self-definition, especially when moral decision becomes more reflective or "postconventional" and the choice of moral standpoint becomes correspondingly more self-conscious.

The evidence accumulated, using the Lyons procedure, has lead to the interview changes just outlined and to insights that necessitate new coding procedures (Brown et al., 1987). Although some moral considerations can be assigned to mutually exclusive categories of justice and care, other considerations can be seen as both justice and care concerns. Awareness of both perspectives highlights the issue of interpretation. The entire research endeavor is thereby rendered more self-conscious. Researchers must ask not only the moral standpoint of participants but simultaneously address the question of their own perspectives on the interview. As Mishler (1986) has argued, the interview becomes a jointly constructed understanding rather than a participant's response to standard research questions.

The promise of approaching moral development in terms of moral orientation lies in its potential to transform debates over sex differences in moral reasoning into serious questions about moral perspectives that are open to empirical study. If moral maturity consists in the ability to sustain concerns about justice and care and if the focus phenomenon indicates a tendency to lose sight of one set of concerns, then the encounter with orientation difference can tend to offset errors in moral perception. Like the moment when the ambiguous figure shifts from a vase to two faces, the recognition that there is another way to look at a problem may expand moral understanding.

REFERENCES

BAUMRIND, D. (1986). Sex differences in moral reasoning: Response to Walker's (1984) conclusion that there are none. *Child Development, 57,* 511–521.

BROWN, L., ARGYRIS, D., ATTANUCCI, J., BARDIGE, B., GILLIGAN, C., JOHNSTON, K., MILLER, B., OSBORNE, R., WARD, J., WIGGINS, G., & WILCOX, D. (1987). A guide to reading narratives of moral conflict and choice for self and moral voice. In L. Brown (Ed.), *Mapping the moral domain: A method of inquiry* (pp. 35–140). Monograph #1. Cambridge, MA: The Center for the Study of Gender, Education, and Human Development, Harvard University.

GILLIGAN, C. (1977). In a different voice: Women's conception of self and morality. *Harvard Educational Review, 47* (4), 481–517.

GILLIGAN, C. (1982). *In a different voice: Psychological theory and women's development.* Cambridge, MA: Harvard University Press.

GILLIGAN, C., & BELENKY, M. (1980). A naturalistic study of abortion decision. In R. Selman & R. Yando (Eds.), *Clinical-developmental psychology* (pp. 69–90). San Francisco: Jossey-Bass.

GILLIGAN, C., LANGDALE, C., LYONS, N., & MURPHY, M. (1982). *The contribution of women's thought to developmental theory.* Final report submitted to National Institute of Education.

GILLIGAN, C., & MURPHY, J. (1979). Development from adolescence to adulthood: The philosopher and the dilemma of the fact. In D. Kuhn (Ed.), *Intellectual development beyond childhood* (pp. 85–99). San Francisco: Jossey-Bass.

HAAN, N. (1978). Two moralities in action contexts: Relationships to thought, ego regulation and development. *Journal of Personality and Social Psychology, 36,* 286–305.

HAAN, N. (1985). *Gender differences in moral development.* Paper presented at the American Psychological Association meetings, Los Angeles, CA.

JOHNSTON, K. (1985). *Two moral orientations—Two problem-solving strategies: Adolescents' solutions to dilemmas in fables.* Unpublished doctoral dissertation, Harvard University, Cambridge, MA.

KOHLBERG, L. (1969). Stage and sequence: The cognitive-developmental approach to socialization. In D. A. Goslin (Ed.), *Handbook of socialization theory and research* (pp. 347–480). Chicago: Rand McNally.

KOHLBERG, L. (1984). *The psychology of moral development, Vol. 2.* San Francisco: Harper & Row.

LYONS, N. (1982). *Conceptions of self and morality and modes of moral choice: Identifying justice and care in judgments of actual moral dilemmas.* Unpublished doctoral dissertation, Harvard University, Cambridge, MA.

LYONS, N. (1983). Two perspectives: On self, relationships, and morality. *Harvard Educational Review, 53,* 125–145.

MISHLER, E. (1986). *Research interviewing: Context and narrative.* Cambridge, MA: Harvard University Press.

PIAGET, J. (1965). *The moral judgment of the child.* New York: Free Press. (Original work published 1932)

WALKER, L. J. (1984). Sex differences in the development of moral reasoning: A critical review. *Child Development, 55,* 677–691.

WALKER, L. J. (1986). Sex differences in the development of moral reasoning: A rejoinder to Baumrind. *Child Development, 57,* 522–526.

YOUNISS, J. (1980). *Parents and peers in social development.* Chicago: University of Chicago Press.

[38]

THE FEMALE WORLD OF CARDS AND HOLIDAYS: WOMEN, FAMILIES, AND THE WORK OF KINSHIP[1]

MICAELA DI LEONARDO

Why is it that the married women of America are supposed to write all the letters and send all the cards to their husbands' families? My old man is a much better writer than I am, yet he expects me to correspond with his whole family. If I asked him to correspond with mine, he would blow a gasket. [LETTER TO ANN LANDERS]

Women's place in man's life cycle has been that of nurturer, caretaker, and helpmate, the weaver of those networks of relationships on which she in turn relies. [CAROL GILLIGAN, *In a Different Voice*][2]

Feminist scholars in the past fifteen years have made great strides in formulating new understandings of the relations among gender, kinship,

Many thanks to Cynthia Costello, Rayna Rapp, Roberta Spalter-Roth, John Willoughby, and Barbara Gelpi, Susan Johnson, and Sylvia Yanagisako of *Signs* for their help with this article. I wish in particular to acknowledge the influence of Rayna Rapp's work on my ideas.

[1] Acknowledgment and gratitude to Carroll Smith-Rosenberg for my paraphrase of her title, "The Female World of Love and Ritual: Relations between Women in Nineteenth-Century America," *Signs: Journal of Women in Culture and Society* 1, no. 1 (Autumn 1975): 1–29.

[2] Ann Landers letter printed in *Washington Post* (April 15, 1983); Carol Gilligan, *In a Different Voice* (Cambridge, Mass.: Harvard University Press, 1982), 17.

[*Signs: Journal of Women in Culture and Society* 1987, vol. 12, no. 3]

Spring 1987 / **SIGNS**

and the larger economy. As a result of this pioneering research, women are newly visible and audible, no longer submerged within their families. We see households as loci of political struggle, inseparable parts of the larger society and economy, rather than as havens from the heartless world of industrial capitalism.[3] And historical and cultural variations in kinship and family forms have become clearer with the maturation of feminist historical and social-scientific scholarship.

Two theoretical trends have been key to this reinterpretation of women's work and family domain. The first is the elevation to visibility of women's nonmarket activities—housework, child care, the servicing of men, and the care of the elderly—and the definition of all these activities as *labor*, to be enumerated alongside and counted as part of overall social reproduction. The second theoretical trend is the nonpejorative focus on women's domestic or kin-centered networks. We now see them as the products of conscious strategy, as crucial to the functioning of kinship systems, as sources of women's autonomous power and possible primary sites of emotional fulfillment, and, at times, as the vehicles for actual survival and/or political resistance.[4]

Recently, however, a division has developed between feminist inter- preters of the "labor" and the "network" perspectives on women's lives. Those who focus on women's work tend to envision women as sentient, goal-oriented actors, while those who concern themselves with women's ties to others tend to perceive women primarily in terms of nurturance, other-orientation—altruism. The most celebrated recent example of this

---

[3] Heidi I. Hartmann, "The Family as the Locus of Gender, Class, and Political Struggle: The Example of Housework," *Signs* 6, no. 3 (Spring 1981): 366–94; and Christopher Lasch, *Haven in a Heartless World: The Family Besieged* (New York: Basic Books, 1977).

[4] Representative examples of the first trend include Joann Vanek, "Time Spent on Housework," *Scientific American* 231 (November 1974): 116–20; Ruth Schwartz Cowan, "A Case Study of Technological and Social Change: The Washing Machine and the Working Wife," in *Clio's Consciousness Raised*, ed. Mary Hartmann and Lois Banner (New York: Harper & Row, 1974), 245–53; Ann Oakley, *Women's Work: The Housewife, Past and Present* (New York: Vintage, 1974); Hartmann; and Susan Strasser, *Never Done: A History of American Housework* (New York: Pantheon Books, 1982). Key contributions to the second trend include Louise Lamphere, "Strategies, Cooperation and Conflict among Women in Domestic Groups," in *Women, Culture and Society*, ed. Michelle Zimbalist Rosaldo and Louise Lamphere (Stanford, Calif.: Stanford University Press, 1974), 97–112; Mina Davis Caulfield, "Imperialism, the Family and the Cultures of Resistance," *Socialist Revolution* 20 (October 1974): 67–85; Smith-Rosenberg; Sylvia Junko Yanagisako, "Women-centered Kin Networks and Urban Bilateral Kinship," *American Ethnologist* 4, no. 2 (1977): 207–26; Jane Humphries, "The Working Class Family, Women's Liberation and Class Struggle: The Case of Nineteenth Century British History," *Review of Radical Political Economics* 9 (Fall 1977): 25–41; Blanche Weisen Cook, "Female Support Networks and Political Activism: Lillian Wald, Crystal Eastman, Emma Goldman," in *A Heritage of Her Own*, ed. Nancy F. Cott and Elizabeth H. Pleck (New York: Simon & Schuster, 1979); Temma Kaplan, "Female Con- sciousness and Collective Action: The Case of Barcelona, 1910–1918," *Signs* 7, no. 3 (Spring 1982): 545–66.

division is the opposing testimony of historians Alice Kessler-Harris and Rosalind Rosenberg in the Equal Employment Opportunity Commission's sex discrimination case against Sears Roebuck and Company. Kessler-Harris argued that American women historically have actively sought higher-paying jobs and have been prevented from gaining them because of sex discrimination by employers. Rosenberg argued that American women in the nineteenth century created among themselves, through their domestic networks, a "women's culture" that emphasized the nurturance of children and others and the maintenance of family life and that discouraged women from competition over or heavy emotional investment in demanding, high-paid employment.[5]

I shall not here address this specific debate but, instead, shall consider its theoretical background and implications. I shall argue that we need to fuse, rather than to oppose, the domestic network and labor perspectives. In what follows, I introduce a new concept, the work of kinship, both to aid empirical feminist research on women, work, and family and to help advance feminist theory in this arena. I believe that the boundary-crossing nature of the concept helps to confound the self-interest/altruism dichotomy, forcing us from an either-or stance to a position that includes both perspectives. I hope in this way to contribute to a more critical feminist vision of women's lives and the meaning of family in the industrial West.

In my recent field research among Italian-Americans in Northern California, I found myself considering the relations between women's kinship and economic lives. As an anthropologist, I was concerned with people's kin lives beyond conventional American nuclear family or household boundaries. To this end, I collected individual and family life histories, asking about all kin and close friends and their activities. I was also very interested in women's labor. As I sat with women and listened to their accounts of their past and present lives, I began to realize that they were involved in three types of work: housework and child care, work in the labor market, and the work of kinship.[6]

By kin work I refer to the conception, maintenance, and ritual celebration of cross-household kin ties, including visits, letters, telephone calls, presents, and cards to kin; the organization of holiday gatherings; the creation and maintenance of quasi-kin relations; decisions to neglect or to

[5] On this debate, see Jon Weiner, "Women's History on Trial," *Nation* 241, no. 6 (September 7, 1985): 161, 176, 178–80; Karen J. Winkler, "Two Scholars' Conflict in Sears Sex-Bias Case Sets Off War in Women's History," *Chronicle of Higher Education* (February 5, 1986), 1, 8; Rosalind Rosenberg, "What Harms Women in the Workplace," *New York Times* (February 27, 1986); Alice Kessler-Harris, "Equal Employment Opportunity Commission vs. Sears Roebuck and Company: A Personal Account," *Radical History Review* 35 (April 1986): 57–79.

[6] Portions of the following analysis are reported in Micaela di Leonardo, *The Varieties of Ethnic Experience: Kinship, Class and Gender among California Italian-Americans* (Ithaca, N.Y.: Cornell University Press, 1984), chap. 6.

Spring 1987 / **SIGNS**

intensify particular ties; the mental work of reflection about all these
activities; and the creation and communication of altering images of family
and kin vis-à-vis the images of others, both folk and mass media. Kin work
is a key element that has been missing in the synthesis of the "household
labor" and "domestic network" perspectives. In our emphasis on individual women's responsibilities within households and on the job, we
reflect the common picture of households as nuclear units, tied perhaps to
the larger social and economic system, but not to *each other*. We miss the
point of telephone and soft drink advertising, of women's magazines'
holiday issues, of commentators' confused nostalgia for the mythical American extended family: it is kinship contact *across households*, as much as
women's work within them, that fulfills our cultural expectation of satis-
fying family life.

Maintaining these contacts, this sense of family, takes time, intention,
and skill. We tend to think of human social and kin networks as the
epiphenomena of production and reproduction: the social traces created by
our material lives. Or, in the neoclassical tradition, we see them as part of
leisure activities, outside an economic purview except insofar as they
involve consumption behavior. But the creation and maintenance of kin
and quasi-kin networks in advanced industrial societies is *work*; and,
moreover, it is largely women's work.

The kin-work lens brought into focus new perspectives on my informants' family lives. First, life histories revealed that often the very existence of kin contact and holiday celebration depended on the presence of
an adult woman in the household. When couples divorced or mothers
died, the work of kinship was left undone; when women entered into
sanctioned sexual or marital relationships with men in these situations,
they reconstituted the men's kinship networks and organized gatherings
and holiday celebrations. Middle-aged businessman Al Bertini, for example, recalled the death of his mother in his early adolescence: "I think that's
probably one of the biggest losses in losing a family—yeah, I remember as a
child when my Mom was alive . . . the holidays were treated with enthusiasm and love . . . after she died the attempt was there but it just didn't
materialize." Later in life, when Al Bertini and his wife separated, his own
and his son Jim's participation in extended-family contact decreased rapidly. But when Jim began a relationship with Jane Bateman, she and he
moved in with Al, and Jim and Jane began to invite his kin over for
holidays. Jane single-handedly planned and cooked the holiday feasts.

Kin work, then, is like housework and child care: men in the aggregate
do not do it. It differs from these forms of labor in that it is harder for men to
substitute hired labor to accomplish these tasks in the absence of kinswomen. Second, I found that women, as the workers in this arena, generally had much greater kin knowledge than did their husbands, often
including more accurate and extensive knowledge of their husbands' fami-

lies. This was true both of middle-aged and younger couples and surfaced as a phenomenon in my interviews in the form of humorous arguments and in wives' detailed additions to husbands' narratives. Nick Meraviglia, a middle-aged professional, discussed his Italian antecedents in the presence of his wife, Pina:

> *Nick:* My grandfather was a very outspoken man, and it was reported he took off for the hills when he found out that Mussolini was in power.
> *Pina:* And he was a very tall man; he used to have to bow his head to get inside doors.
> *Nick:* No, that was my uncle.
> *Pina:* Your grandfather too, I've heard your mother say.
> *Nick:* My mother has a sister and a brother.
> *Pina: Two* sisters!
> *Nick:* You're right!
> *Pina:* Maria and Angelina.

Women were also much more willing to discuss family feuds and crises and their own roles in them; men tended to repeat formulaic statements asserting family unity and respectability. (This was much less true for younger men.) Joe and Cetta Longhinotti's statements illustrate these tendencies. Joe responded to my question about kin relations: "We all get along. As a rule, relatives, you got nothing but trouble." Cetta, instead, discussed her relations with each of her grown children, their wives, her in-laws, and her own blood kin in detail. She did not hide the fact that relations were strained in several cases; she was eager to discuss the evolution of problems and to seek my opinions of her actions. Similarly, Pina Meraviglia told the following story of her fight with one of her brothers with hysterical laughter: "There was some biting and hair pulling and choking . . . it was terrible! I shouldn't even tell you. . . ." Nick, meanwhile, was concerned about maintaining an image of family unity and respectability.

Also, men waxed fluent while women were quite inarticulate in discussing their past and present occupations. When asked about their work lives, Joe Longhinotti and Nick Meraviglia, union baker and professional, respectively, gave detailed narratives of their work careers. Cetta Longhinotti and Pina Meraviglia, clerical and former clerical, respectively, offered only short descriptions focusing on factors of ambience, such as the "lovely things" sold by Cetta's firm.

These patterns are not repeated in the younger generation, especially among younger women, such as Jane Bateman, who have managed to acquire training and jobs with some prospect of mobility. These younger

Spring 1987 / **SIGNS**

women, though, have *added* a professional and detailed interest in their jobs to a felt responsibility for the work of kinship.[7]

Although men rarely took on any kin-work tasks, family histories and accounts of contemporary life revealed that kinswomen often negotiated among themselves, alternating hosting, food-preparation, and gift-buying responsibilities—or sometimes ceding entire task clusters to one woman. Taking on or ceding tasks was clearly related to acquiring or divesting oneself of power within kin networks, but women varied in their interpretation of the meaning of this power. Cetta Longhinotti, for example, relied on the "family Christmas dinner" as a symbol of her central kinship role and was involved in painful negotiations with her daughter-in-law over the issue: "Last year she insisted—this is touchy. She doesn't want to spend the holiday dinner together. So last year we went there. But I still had my dinner the next day . . . I made a big dinner on Christmas Day, regardless of who's coming—candles on the table, the whole routine. I decorate the house myself too . . . well, I just feel that the time will come when maybe I won't feel like cooking a big dinner—she should take advantage of the fact that I feel like doing it now." Pina Meraviglia, in contrast, was saddened by the centripetal force of the developmental cycle but was unworried about the power dynamics involved in her negotiations with daughters- and mother-in-law over holiday celebrations.

Kin work is not just a matter of power among women but also of the mediation of power represented by household units.[8] Women often choose to minimize status claims in their kin work and to include numbers of households under the rubric of family. Cetta Longhinotti's sister Anna, for example, is married to a professional man whose parents have considerable economic resources, while Joe and Cetta have low incomes and no other well-off kin. Cetta and Anna remain close, talk on the phone several times a week, and assist their adult children, divided by distance and economic status, in remaining united as cousins.

Finally, women perceived housework, child care, market labor, the care of the elderly, and the work of kinship as competing responsibilities. Kin work was a unique category, however, because it was unlabeled and because women felt they could either cede some tasks to kinswomen and/or could cut them back severely. Women variously cited the pressures of market labor, the needs of the elderly, and their own desires for freedom

---

[7] Clearly, many women do, in fact, discuss their paid labor with willingness and clarity. The point here is that there are opposing gender tendencies in an identical interview situation, tendencies that are explicable in terms of both the material realities and current cultural constructions of gender.

[8] Papanek has rightly focused on women's unacknowledged family status production, but what is conceived of as "family" shifts and varies (Hanna Papanek, "Family Status Production: The 'Work' and 'Non-Work' of Women," *Signs* 4, no. 4 [Summer 1979]: 775–81).

and job enrichment as reasons for cutting back Christmas card lists, organized holiday gatherings, multifamily dinners, letters, visits, and phone
calls. They expressed guilt and defensiveness about this cutback process
and, particularly, about their failures to keep families close through constant contact and about their failures to create perfect holiday celebrations.
Cetta Longhinotti, during the period when she was visiting her elderly
mother every weekend in addition to working a full-time job, said of her
grown children, "I'd have the whole gang here once a month, but I've been
so busy that I haven't done that for about six months." And Pina Meraviglia
lamented her insufficient work on family Christmases, "I wish I had really
made it traditional . . . like my sister-in-law has special stories."

Kin work, then, takes place in an arena characterized simultaneously
by cooperation and competition, by guilt and gratification. Like housework
and child care, it is women's work, with the same lack of clear-cut agreement concerning its proper components: How often should sheets be
changed? When should children be toilet trained? Should an aunt send a
niece a birthday present? Unlike housework and child care, however, kin
work, taking place across the boundaries of normative households, is as yet
unlabeled and has no retinue of experts prescribing its correct forms.
Neither home economists nor child psychologists have much to say about
nieces' birthday presents. Kin work is thus more easily cut back without
social interference. On the other hand, the results of kin work—frequent
kin contact and feelings of intimacy—are the subject of considerable cultural manipulation as indicators of family happiness. Thus, women in
general are subject to the guilt my informants expressed over cutting back
kin-work activities.

Although many of my informants referred to the results of women's kin
work—cross-household kin contacts and attendant ritual gatherings—as
particularly Italian-American, I suggest that in fact this phenomenon is
broadly characteristic of American kinship. We think of kin-work tasks such
as the preparation of ritual feasts, responsibility for holiday card lists, and
gift buying as extensions of women's domestic responsibilities for cooking,
consumption, and nurturance. American men in general do not take on
these tasks any more than they do housework and child care—and probably
less, as these tasks have not yet been the subject of intense public debate.
And my informants' gender breakdown in relative articulateness on kinship
and workplace themes reflects the still prevalent occupational segregation—most women cannot find jobs that provide enough pay, status, or
promotion possibilities to make them worth focusing on—as well as
women's perceived power within kinship networks. The common recognition of that power is reflected in Selma Greenberg's book on nonsexist child
rearing. Greenberg calls mothers "press agents" who sponsor relations
between their own children and other relatives; she advises a mother

whose relatives treat her disrespectfully to deny those kin access to her children.[9]

Kin work is a salient concept in other parts of the developed world as well. Larissa Adler Lomnitz and Marisol Pérez Lizaur have found that "centralizing women" are responsible for these tasks and for communicating "family ideology" among upper-class families in Mexico City. Matthews Hamabata, in his study of upper-class families in Japan, has found that women's kin work involves key financial transactions. Sylvia Junko Yanagisako discovered that, among rural Japanese migrants to the United States, the maintenance of kin networks was assigned to women as the migrants adopted the American ideology of the independent nuclear family household. Maila Stivens notes that urban Australian housewives' kin ties and kin ideology "transcend women's isolation in domestic units."[10]

This is not to say that cultural conceptions of appropriate kin work do not vary, even within the United States. Carol B. Stack documents institutionalized fictive kinship and concomitant reciprocity networks among impoverished black American women. Women in populations characterized by intense feelings of ethnic identity may feel bound to emphasize particular occasions—Saint Patrick's or Columbus Day—with organized family feasts. These constructs may be mediated by religious affiliation, as in the differing emphases on Friday or Sunday family dinners among Jews and Christians. Thus the personnel involved and the amount and kind of labor considered necessary for the satisfactory performance of particular kin-work tasks are likely to be culturally constructed.[11] But while the kin and quasi-kin universes and the ritual calendar may vary among women according to race or ethnicity, their general responsibility for maintaining kin links and ritual observances does not.

As kin work is not an ethnic or racial phenomenon, neither is it linked

[9] Selma Greenberg, *Right from the Start: A Guide to Nonsexist Child Rearing* (Boston: Houghton Mifflin Co., 1978), 147. Another example of indirect support for kin work's gendered existence is a recent study of university math students, which found that a major reason for women's failure to pursue careers in mathematics was the pressure of family involvement. Compare David Maines et al., *Social Processes of Sex Differentiation in Mathematics* (Washington, D.C.: National Institute of Education, 1981).

[10] Larissa Adler Lomnitz and Marisol Pérez Lizaur, "The History of a Mexican Urban Family," *Journal of Family History* 3, no. 4 (1978): 392–409, esp. 398; Matthews Hamabata, *For Love and Power: Family Business in Japan* (Chicago: University of Chicago Press, in press); Sylvia Junko Yanagisako, "Two Processes of Change in Japanese-American Kinship," *Journal of Anthropological Research* 31 (1975): 196–224; Maila Stivens, "Women and Their Kin: Kin, Class and Solidarity in a Middle-Class Suburb of Sydney, Australia," in *Women United, Women Divided*, ed. Patricia Caplan and Janet M. Bujra (Bloomington: Indiana University Press, 1979), 157–84.

[11] Carol B. Stack, *All Our Kin: Strategies for Survival in a Black Community* (New York: Harper & Row, 1974). These cultural constructions may, however, vary within ethnic/racial populations as well.

only to one social class. Some commentators on American family life still reflect the influence of work done in England in the 1950s and 1960s (by Elizabeth Bott and by Peter Willmott and Michael Young) in their assumption that working-class families are close and extended, while the middle class substitutes friends (or anomie) for family. Others reflect the prevalent family pessimism in their presumption that neither working- nor middle-class families have extended kin contact.[12] Insofar as kin contact depends on residential proximity, the larger economy's shifts will influence particular groups' experiences. Factory workers, close to kin or not, are likely to disperse when plants shut down or relocate. Small businesspeople or independent professionals may, however, remain resident in particular areas—and thus maintain proximity to kin—for generations, while professional employees of large firms relocate at their firms' behest. This pattern obtained among my informants.

In any event, cross-household kin contact can be and is effected at long distance through letters, cards, phone calls, and holiday and vacation visits. The form and functions of contact, however, vary according to economic resources. Stack and Brett Williams offer rich accounts of kin networks among poor blacks and migrant Chicano farmworkers functioning to provide emotional support, labor, commodity, and cash exchange—a funeral visit, help with laundry, the gift of a dress or piece of furniture.[13] Far different in degree are exchanges such as the loan of a vacation home, a multifamily boating trip, or the provision of free professional services—examples from the kin networks of my wealthier informants. The point is that households, as labor- and income-pooling units, whatever their relative wealth, are somewhat porous in relation to others with whose members they share kin or quasi-kin ties. We do not really know how class differences operate in this realm; it is possible that they do so largely in terms of ideology. It may be, as David Schneider and Raymond T. Smith suggest, that the affluent and the very poor are more open in recognizing

[12] Elizabeth Bott, *Family and Social Network*, 2d ed. (New York: Free Press, 1971); Michael Young and Peter Willmott, *Family and Kinship in East London* (London: Routledge & Kegan Paul, 1957), and *Family and Class in a London Suburb* (London: Routledge & Kegan Paul, 1960). Classic studies that presume this class difference are Herbert Gans, *The Urban Villagers: Group and Class in the Life of Italian-Americans* (New York: Free Press, 1962); and Mirra Komarovsky, *Blue-Collar Marriage* (New York: Random House, 1962). A recent example is Ilene Philipson, "Heterosexual Antagonisms and the Politics of Mothering," *Socialist Review* 12, no. 6 (November–December 1982): 55–77. Edward Shorter, *The Making of the Modern Family* (New York: Basic Books, 1975), epitomizes the pessimism of the "family sentiments" school. See also Mary Lyndon Shanley, "The History of the Family in Modern England: Review Essay," *Signs* 4, no. 4 (Summer 1979): 740–50.

[13] Stack; and Brett Williams, "The Trip Takes Us: Chicano Migrants to the Prairie" (Ph.D. diss., University of Illinois at Urbana-Champaign, 1975).

necessary economic ties to kin than are those who identify themselves as middle class.[14]

Recognizing that kin work is gender rather than class based allows us to see women's kin networks among all groups, not just among working-class and impoverished women in industrialized societies. This recognition in turn clarifies our understanding of the privileges and limits of women's varying access to economic resources. Affluent women can "buy out" of housework, child care—and even some kin-work responsibilities. But they, like all women, are ultimately responsible, and subject to both guilt and blame, as the administrators of home, children, and kin network. Even the wealthiest women must negotiate the timing and venue of holidays and other family rituals with their kinswomen. It may be that kin work is the core women's work category in which all women cooperate, while women's perceptions of the appropriateness of cooperation for housework, child care, and the care of the elderly varies by race, class, region, and generation.

But kin work is not necessarily an appropriate category of labor, much less gendered labor, in all societies. In many small-scale societies, kinship is the major organizing principle of all social life, and all contacts are by definition kin contacts.[15] One cannot, therefore, speak of labor that does not involve kin. In the United States, kin work as a separable category of gendered labor perhaps arose historically in concert with the ideological and material constructs of the moral mother/cult of domesticity and the privatized family during the course of industrialization in the eighteenth and nineteenth centuries. These phenomena are connected to the increase in the ubiquity of productive occupations *for men* that are not organized through kinship. This includes the demise of the family farm with the capitalization of agriculture and rural-urban migration; the decline of family recruitment in factories as firms grew, ended child labor, and began to assert bureaucratized forms of control; the decline of artisanal labor and of small entrepreneurial enterprises as large firms took greater and greater shares of the commodity market; the decline of the family firm as corporations—and their managerial work forces—grew beyond the capacities of individual families to provision them; and, finally, the rise of civil service bureaucracies and public pressure against nepotism.[16]

---

[14] David Schneider and Raymond T. Smith, *Class Differences and Sex Roles in American Kinship and Family Structure* (Englewood Cliffs, N.J.: Prentice-Hall, Inc., 1973), esp. 27.

[15] See Nelson Graburn, ed., *Readings in Kinship and Social Structure* (New York: Harper & Row, 1971), esp. 3–4.

[16] The moral mother/cult of domesticity is analyzed in Barbara Welter, "The Cult of True Womanhood, 1820–1860," *American Quarterly* 18, no. 2 (Summer 1966): 151–74; Nancy Cott, *The Bonds of Womanhood: "Women's Sphere" in New England, 1780–1835* (New

di Leonardo / THE WORK OF KINSHIP

As men increasingly worked alongside of non-kin, and as the ideology of separate spheres was increasingly accepted, perhaps the responsibility for kin maintenance, like that for child rearing, became gender-focused. Ryan points out that "built into the updated family economy . . . was a new measure of voluntarism." This voluntarism, though, "perceived as the shift from patriarchal authority to domestic affection," also signaled the rise of women's moral responsibility for family life. Just as the "idea of fatherhood itself seemed almost to wither away" so did male involvement in the responsibility for kindred lapse.[17]

With postbellum economic growth and geographic movement, women's new kin burden involved increasing amounts of time and labor. The ubiquity of lengthy visits and of frequent letter-writing among nineteenth-century women attests to this. And for visitors and for those who were residentially proximate, the continuing commonalities of women's domestic labor allowed for kinds of work sharing—nursing, child-keeping, cooking, cleaning—that men, with their increasingly differentiated and controlled activities, probably could not maintain. This is not to say that some kin-related male productive work did not continue; my own data, for instance, show kin involvement among small businessmen in the present. It is, instead, to suggest a general trend in material life and a cultural shift that influenced even those whose productive and kin lives remained commingled. Yanagisako has distinguished between the realms of domestic and public kinship in order to draw attention to anthropology's relatively "thin descriptions" of the domestic (female) domain. Using her typology, we might say that kin work as gendered labor comes into existence within the domestic domain with the relative erasure of the domain of public, male kinship.[18]

Haven, Conn.: Yale University Press, 1977); and Ruth Bloch, "American Feminine Ideals in Transition: The Rise of the Moral Mother, 1785–1815," *Feminist Studies* 4, no. 2 (June 1978): 101–26. The description of the general political-economic shift in the United States is based on Harry Braverman, *Labor and Monopoly Capital: The Degradation of Work in the Twentieth Century* (New York: Monthly Review Press, 1974); Peter Dobkin Hall, "Family Structure and Economic Organization: Massachusetts Merchants, 1700–1850," in *Family and Kin in Urban Communities, 1700–1950*, ed. Tamara K. Hareven (New York: New Viewpoints, 1977), 38–61; Michael Anderson, "Family, Household and the Industrial Revolution," in *The American Family in Social-Historical Perspective*, ed. Michael Gordon (New York: St. Martin's Press, 1978), 38–50; Tamara K. Hareven, *Amoskeag: Life and Work in an American Factory City* (New York: Pantheon Books, 1978); Richard Edwards, *Contested Terrain: The Transformation of the Workplace in the Twentieth Century* (New York: Basic Books, 1979); Mary Ryan, *The Cradle of the Middle Class: The Family in Oneida County, New York, 1790–1865* (Cambridge: Cambridge University Press, 1981); Alice Kessler-Harris, *Out to Work: A History of Wage-earning Women in the United States* (New York: Oxford University Press, 1982).

[17] Ryan, 231–32.

[18] Sylvia Junko Yanagisako, "Family and Household: The Analysis of Domestic Groups," *Annual Review of Anthropology* 8 (1979): 161–205.

Spring 1987 / **SIGNS**

Whether or not this proposed historical model bears up under further research, the question remains, Why do women do kin work? However material factors may shape activities, they do not determine how individuals may perceive them. And in considering issues of motivation, of intention, of the cultural construction of kin work, we return to the altruism versus self-interest dichotomy in recent feminist theory. Consider the epigraphs to this article. Are women kin workers the nurturant weavers of the Gilligan quotation, or victims, like the fed-up woman who writes to complain to Ann Landers? That is, are we to see kin work as yet another example of "women's culture" that takes the care of others as its primary desideratum? Or are we to see kin work as another way in which men, the economy, and the state extract labor from women without a fair return? And how do women themselves see their kin work and its place in their lives?

As I have indicated above, I believe that it is the creation of the self-interest/altruism dichotomy that is itself the problem here. My women informants, like most American women, accepted their primary responsibility for housework and the care of dependent children. Despite two major waves of feminist activism in this century, the gendering of certain categories of unpaid labor is still largely unaltered. These work responsibilities clearly interfere with some women's labor force commitments at certain life-cycle stages; but, more important, women are simply discriminated against in the labor market and rarely are able to achieve wage and status parity with men of the same age, race, class, and educational background.[19]

Thus for my women informants, as for most American women, the domestic domain is not only an arena in which much unpaid labor must be undertaken but also a realm in which one may attempt to gain human satisfactions—and power—not available in the labor market. Anthropologists Jane Collier and Louise Lamphere have written compellingly on the ways in which varying kinship and economic structures may shape women's competition or cooperation with one another in domestic domains.[20] Feminists considering Western women and families have looked at the issue of power primarily in terms of husband-wife relations or psychological relations between parents and children. If we adopt Collier and Lamphere's broader canvas, though, we see that kin work is not only women's labor from which men and children benefit but also labor that women undertake in order to create obligations in men and children and to gain power over one another. Thus Cetta Longhinotti's struggle with her daughter-in-law over the venue of Christmas dinner is not just about a

---

[19] See Donald J. Treiman and Heidi I. Hartmann, eds., *Women, Work and Wages: Equal Pay for Jobs of Equal Value* (Washington, D.C.: National Academy Press, 1981).

[20] Lamphere (n. 4 above); Jane Fishburne Collier, "Women in Politics," in Rosaldo and Lamphere, eds. (n. 4 above), 89–96.

competition over altruism, it is also about the creation of future obligations. And thus Cetta's and Anna's sponsorship of their children's friendship with each other is both an act of nurturance and a cooperative means of gaining power over those children.

Although this was not a clear-cut distinction, those of my informants who were more explicitly antifeminist tended to be most invested in kin work. Given the overwhelming historical shift toward greater autonomy for younger generations and the withering of children's financial and labor obligations to their parents, this investment was in most cases tragically doomed. Cetta Longhinotti, for example, had repaid her own mother's devotion with extensive home nursing during the mother's last years. Given Cetta's general failure to direct her adult children in work, marital choice, religious worship, or even frequency of visits, she is unlikely to receive such care from them when she is older.

The kin-work lens thus reveals the close relations between altruism and self-interest in women's actions. As economists Nancy Folbre and Heidi Hartmann point out, we have inherited a Western intellectual tradition that both dichotomizes the domestic and public domains and associates them on exclusive axes such that we find it difficult to see self-interest in the home and altruism in the workplace.[21] But why, in fact, have women fought for better jobs if not, in part, to support their children? These dichotomies are Procrustean beds that warp our understanding of women's lives both at home and at work. "Altruism" and "self-interest" are cultural constructions that are not necessarily mutually exclusive, and we forget this to our peril.

The concept of kin work helps to bring into focus a heretofore unacknowledged array of tasks that is culturally assigned to women in industrialized societies. At the same time, this concept, embodying notions of both love and work and crossing the boundaries of households, helps us to reflect on current feminist debates on women's work, family, and community. We newly see both the interrelations of these phenomena and women's roles in creating and maintaining those interrelations. Revealing the actual labor embodied in what we culturally conceive as love and considering the political uses of this labor helps to deconstruct the self-interest/altruism dichotomy and to connect more closely women's domestic and labor-force lives.

The true value of the concept, however, remains to be tested through further historical and contemporary research on gender, kinship, and labor. We need to assess the suggestion that gendered kin work emerges in concert with the capitalist development process; to probe the historical record for women's and men's varying and changing conceptions of it; and

[21] Nancy Folbre and Heidi I. Hartmann, "The Rhetoric of Self-Interest: Selfishness, Altruism, and Gender in Economic Theory," in *The Consequences of Economic Rhetoric*, ed. Arjo Klamer and Donald McCloskey (New York: Cambridge University Press, forthcoming).

Spring 1987 / **SIGNS**

to research the current range of its cultural constructions and material realities. We know that household boundaries are more porous than we had thought—but they are undoubtedly differentially porous, and this is what we need to specify. We need, in particular, to assess the relations of changing labor processes, residential patterns, and the use of technology to changing kin work.

Altering the values attached to this particular set of women's tasks will be as difficult as are the housework, child-care, and occupational-segregation struggles. But just as feminist research in these latter areas is complementary and cumulative, so researching kin work should help us to piece together the home, work, and public-life landscape—to see the female world of cards and holidays as it is constructed and lived within the changing political economy. How female that world is to remain, and what it would look like if it were not sex-segregated, are questions we cannot yet answer.

Department of Anthropology
Yale University

[39]

DEVELOPMENTAL REVIEW 6, 165–180 (1986)

Estimating Gender Differences in the Comprehension and Preference of Moral Issues

STEPHEN J. THOMA

University of Minnesota

The claim of a gender bias is considered on measures of moral judgment focusing on concepts of justice. Both meta-analyses and secondary analyses on 56 samples of over 6000 male and female subjects are used to estimate the magnitude of gender effects. Inconsistent with current expectations, the results indicate that overall, and at every age/educational level, females score significantly higher than males. Second, the magnitude of this difference is small, both in comparison with age/education effects and in relation to conventional interpretations of the measures employed. Several possible interpretations of these results are discussed especially with regard to C. Gilligan's (1977, Harvard Educational Review, 47, 481–517) recent criticism of Kohlberg's theory. © 1986 Academic Press, Inc.

The issue of a gender bias on Kohlbergian derived measures of moral reasoning has been a persistent controversy within the morality domain (Brabeck, 1983; Gilligan, 1977, 1979, 1982; Holstein, 1976; Kohlberg, Levine, & Hewer, 1983; Rest, 1979a; Walker, 1984). Critics state that when female moral reasoning is assessed by measures derived from a Kohlbergian definition of morality as concepts of justice, a systematic gender bias emerges with the result that "the thinking of women is often classified with that of children" (Gilligan, 1977, p. 490). This paper is an attempt to address this increasingly common assertion that the study of moral judgment in terms of concepts of justice is inherently gender biased in favor of males.

The claim of a gender bias within a justice defined theory of morality has primarily centered around the procedures by which Kohlberg's theory was developed and subsequently refined. Critics point out that the norming sample used by Kohlberg for these purposes consists entirely of males, a procedure which violates traditional views concerning theory building and measurement construction. Under more traditional guidelines, it is considered essential to construct a representative norming sample from the population to which the theory and measurement device are intended.

This work was supported in part by a Doctoral Dissertation Fellowship and the University of Minnesota Computer Center. The author thanks James Rest and Mark Davison for commenting on an earlier draft of this paper. Requests for reprints should be sent to the author, Department of Educational Psychology, University of Minnesota, 178 Pillsbury Drive S.E., Minneapolis, MN 55455.

166   STEPHEN J. THOMA

While a justice oriented conceptualization of morality has been applied
to other more representative samples with theoretically meaningful results (Gibbs & Widaman, 1982; Nisan & Kohlberg, 1982; Rest, 1979a;
Snarey, Reimer, & Kohlberg, 1985), a recent paper by Gilligan (1977)
calls into question the assumption that a morality of justice is equally
valid for women. Arguing in part from interview data supplied by women
discussing their own abortion decisions, Gilligan questioned whether a
morality of justice was equally sensitive to the traditionally feminine concerns of responsibility and care. In Gilligan's view, by relying on a male
norming sample, Kohlberg's theory and related measurement systems
routinely fail to recognize the principled nature of these female concerns
with the result that such reasoning is considered less competent. In response to these perceived discrepancies between theory and data, Gilligan proposed significant modifications in the conception and measurement of moral reasoning. Specifically, she claimed (a) there exist two
distinct moral systems, a morality of care and of justice; (b) these
systems are gender related; (c) hypothetical moral dilemmas, adequate
for measuring abstract concepts of justice, are inappropriate for the assessment of a more context-sensitive care orientation. In the place of
hypothetical dilemmas, Gilligan suggests the use of real-life dilemmas,
spontaneously produced by subjects within the interview session. Taken
together, Gilligan claims that the differential validity by gender of a morality of justice places women at a disadvantage when assessed by a
moral system framed by and validated on men. She writes:

> While Kohlberg claims universality for his stage sequence and considers his con-
> ception of justice as fairness to have been naturalistically derived, those groups not
> included in his original sample rarely reach his higher stages (Edwards, 1975; Gil-
> ligan, 1977). Prominent among those found to be deficient in moral development
> when measured by Kohlberg's scale are women. (1979, p. 441; see also Holstein,
> 1976, pp. 60–61)

Thus Gilligan and others have implied a gender bias in the study of concepts of justice.

Two previous reviews have considered the question of a gender bias on
moral systems defined by concepts of justice. Rest (1979a) compiled 17
studies with 20 independent comparisons of males and females on his
Defining Issues Test (DIT), an objective measure of comprehension and
preference of moral issues based on Kohlberg's system. He found only
two significant gender differences, both favoring females. Walker (1984)
reviewed 108 independent samples from 79 studies using Kohlberg's production measure of moral reasoning. Like the DIT, Kohlberg's measure
defines maturity of moral thinking in terms of concepts of justice, yet as a
production task, it taps aspects of moral development that are separate

from the comprehension and preference information supplied by the DIT (Colby, Kohlberg, Gibbs, & Lieberman, 1983, Rest, 1979). On Kohlberg's measure, Walker found few and inconsistent patterns'of significant differences, leading him to suspect these findings could best be attributed to factors external to the theory and measurement device, such as differences in prerequisite and role-taking skills. In support of these conclusions Walker reported a meta-analytic summary of his data. Using the Stouffer method (cf. Rosenthal, 1978) for combining significance levels, Walker found a nonsignificant tendency to favor males ($Z = .73$, $p = .23$), which agrees with his claim that males and females respond similarly on production measures of moral reasoning.

Taken together, both the Rest and Walker reviews suggest gender differences are not a large contributor to the variance on measures of moral reasoning. However, neither study has convincingly ruled out a more reasonable expectation of moderate gender effects. The Rest review used a small pool of samples and relied on patterns of individual study significance levels to determine the existence of a gender effect. This method, often labeled the vote counting method (Light & Smith, 1971), has been shown to be insensitive to moderate effects (Hedges & Olkin, 1980; Hunter, Schmidt, & Jackson, 1983).

Walker (1984) supplemented his vote counting results with an overall statistical test of gender differences across studies. While a significant improvement on the Rest review, the utility of this index is severely reduced by Walker's decision to insert the exact finding of no difference ($p = .50$) for what he describes as the many studies claiming nonsignificant gender differences yet failing to report a test statistic. This decision increases the probability of a false no difference conclusion (Type II error).

Perhaps a more serious difficulty in interpreting Walker's summary index is due to his failure to test the homogeneity assumption of an overall estimate, namely that each study estimates the same underlying effect. In describing his results, Walker notes gender effects in younger subjects tend to favor females, whereas in older populations this tendency reverses to favor males. It is conceivable, therefore, that an overall estimate of gender differences is artificially low due to summing across studies actually assessing multiple population effects of a different direction.

Further, Walker's overall test of gender differences that aggregates data from different studies is difficult to interpret because of the many conceptual and procedural revisions to Kohlberg's theory occurring during the period covered by his review. These revisions involved substantial changes—for instance, scoring the same data by an earlier scoring system correlated only .39 with the same data scored with a more

168   STEPHEN J. THOMA

recent system (Kohlberg, Colby, & Damon, 1978). Walker addresses this issue by suggesting gender differences may interact with different scoring systems. Earlier studies using outdated scoring rules, Walker claims, are associated with the majority of significant gender differences. This suggestion of an interaction between study characteristics and gender differences again questions the validity of a single overall estimate of gender differences and, further, does not exclude the possibility of moderate gender differences on more recent versions of production measures of moral reasoning.

The goals of this study, therefore, are three-fold. Given the suggestion of moderate gender effects on constructs theoretically related to moral development, e.g., altruism, decoding of visual and auditory emotional cues, and affective arousal (Hall, 1978; Hoffman, 1977; Krebs, 1975); this study is a more systematic examination of gender differences using a methodology sensitive to moderate effects. Second, in addition to providing statistical tests of gender differences, the more informative magnitude of the effect is described. Finally, to ensure comparability across studies, the focus of this study is on the comprehension and preference of justice concepts as measured by the DIT.

METHOD

Dependent Measure

Since all of the studies to be reviewed used the DIT the following brief description of this measure is included.

The DIT is an objective measure of moral reasoning as concepts of justice (Rest, 1979a, 1979b). This measure is composed of six hypothetical dilemmas describing situations which highlight competing social claims. Following each story, subjects are asked to decide on an appropriate solution to the dilemma, then rate 12 issues in accordance with that decision. Finally, subjects are asked to rank the four most important issues. The majority of these issues are stage typed to Kohlberg's (1969) stages of moral development. The remaining issues are designed as reliability checks. It is important to note that the DIT's items and format have remained unchanged since the test's construction in the early 1970s.

The DIT provides two indices of moral reasoning, the P and D score. The P score utilizes the ranking data and is defined as the weighted sum of the ranked principled issues (moral stages 5, 6). A transformed version of this score, percentage P, ranges from 0 to 95 and is the most common index currently in use.

The D score, a newer index, uses the rating data and represents the ratings of principled items in relation to preconventional (Moral Stage 2) and conventional (Stages 3, 4) items. The benefit of this index is that it utilizes responses to all items.

Studies investigating the reliability of the DIT have shown it to have better than average psychometric properties for measures in this domain. Internal consistency coefficients for P and D scores range from the high .70s to low .80s (Davison & Robbins, 1977). Test–retest reliability coefficients also range from the high .70s to low .80s in age heterogeneous samples. For age homogeneous samples these correlations drop to the high .60s and low .70s.

Statistical Analyses

When statistically summarizing the results of studies using an identical dependent measure it is usually possible to perform a secondary analysis. In these cases, statistical procedures are applied to an aggregate sample consisting of data obtained from different independent samples. In the present case it was not possible to rely fully on a secondary analysis. First, researchers described their results using the two different summary indices described above. In studies where both %P and D scores were provided, the more common %P score was selected; however, in some instances only the D score was reported. While %P and D scores are related, they are not identical, differing both conceptually and statistically. Therefore simple aggregation of these scores is meaningless. Second, in many studies the use of raw P or the transformed %P scores was left unreported. Aggregating over raw and transformed values would also be problematic. Given these difficulties and a concern for maintaining a broad and diverse population of studies, it was decided to employ meta-analytic procedures (Glass, McGaw, & Smith, 1981).

Two measures were chosen to express the magnitude of gender effects in each study; effect size d (Cohen, 1969; Glass et al., 1981); and ω^2 (Fleiss, 1969; Hays, 1963). Effect size d is hereafter defined as the difference between the mean DIT scores for males and the mean DIT scores for females divided by the weighted average of the two groups' standard deviation, or the within-group standard deviation. The general formula is

$$d = (\overline{X}_1 - \overline{X}_2)/\overline{s}$$

where $\overline{X}_1$ and $\overline{X}_2$ are the mean DIT scores for each gender and $\overline{s}$, the within-group standard deviation. This ratio expresses the difference between means in standard score form, therefore $d = .30$ would indicate the two means differed by three-tenths of a standard deviation. Cohen (1969) offers a generic interpretation of the magnitude of effect size estimates suggesting d's of 0.2, 0.5 and 0.8 be considered small, medium, and large, respectively.

The sign of d was set to be positive if the study's findings were consistent with the hypothesis that males outperform females on the DIT. Therefore, a negative d would signify females have higher scores than males. Statistical treatment of the independent effect sizes followed the procedure outlined by Kraemer (1983).

The second statistic measuring the magnitude of gender effects is $\hat{\omega}^2$. In the present case $\hat{\omega}^2$ is defined as an estimate of the proportion of variance in DIT scores accounted for by gender differences. $\hat{\omega}^2$ can be obtained by a simple conversion of the sample statistic (usually t or F) provided in the individual report (Fleiss, 1969). In those studies where the t or F statistic is <1.0, the estimate of $\hat{\omega}^2$ becomes negative, which, unlike the d statistic, is a meaningless occurrence. In such cases convention holds that $\hat{\omega}^2$ be set equal to zero (Hays, 1963, p. 383).

Finally, to ensure statistical independence, only one estimate of the gender effect was computed for each independent sample contained in a study. In studies which included multiple assessments of their subjects, as in a preassessment–postassessment design; the initial testing was selected to represent the sample.

Selection of Studies

The studies analyzed below were obtained from two sources: published journal articles and the files of Minnesota Moral Research Projects housed at the University of Minnesota. This latter source has been compiled by the developer of the DIT, James Rest, who requests users of the DIT to send reports of their findings.

Following Glass (Glass et al., 1981), no effort was made to limit the data selection to studies meeting some predetermined quality criterion, such as selecting only those articles published in refereed journals. Included in the initial pool of samples, therefore, were studies of all types: published papers, unpublished dissertations and master's theses, unpublished research reports, and in some cases unpublished data. This initial pool of samples was then reduced by eliminating studies with the following characteristics: (a) studies whose authors requested their data not be released; (b) studies which compared non-North American subjects; (c) samples which did not include comparable age ranges of both sexes (for example, a study comparing mothers' moral reasoning scores to their sons' scores would not be included); (d) studies with disparate group sample sizes, more precisely, the proportion of one sex, p, had to fall within the range $.3 \le P \le .7$ of the total sample; and (e) studies with sample sizes of a gender grouping less than 10, therefore studies with sample sizes less than 20 were deleted. These last two conditions were included to ensure a statistically stable estimate of gender effects (cf.

Kraemer, 1983). The 56 independent samples that met the above criteria are summarized in Table 1.

RESULTS

The results of the meta-analysis are presented in Table 2. As well as contributing to overall estimates, each study is summarized in one of five groups. The first four groups correspond to major age/education levels, and the fifth consists of those studies which present subject data at more than one age/educational level. It should be noted that the fifth, or mixed, group is overly represented by older subjects.

Of particular interest in Table 2 is the consistent pattern of negative *d* values. As mentioned earlier, a negative *d* suggests that gender differences favor women. In addition, each effect size shown in this table, while statistically different from zero, is small, according to Cohen's criterion mentioned earlier. Moreover, gender accounts for no more than 0.9% of the variance in DIT scores. Overall, less than ½ of 1% of the variance can be accounted for by gender differences.

A second question that can be asked of the data presented in Table 2 is whether the effect size estimates are homogeneous across studies. That is, do the data suggest an overall estimate of gender differences is warranted, or are the studies providing estimates of multiple population effect sizes? This question has an additional importance with respect to subsequent analyses, because only in the latter case does it become appropriate to assess whether variations in effect sizes can be explained by potential moderator variables such as age of subjects, study quality, or sex of investigator (see Hunter et al., 1982). Following Kraemer (1983) the homogeneity of effect sizes was tested. The resulting χ^2 statistic is nonsignificant ($\chi^2_{(52, N = 53)} = 54.85, p > .30$), suggesting the variability in effect sizes is due to sampling error about a single population gender effect.

We can conclude from Table 2 that there exists a stable gender effect which consistently favors women across the lifespan. The magnitude of this effect is small by Cohen's (1969) criteria.

To help interpret the relative magnitude of the observed gender effect, one can supplement Cohen's generic recommendation with a more informative approach where gender is directly compared to another variable of interest. In Table 3 a comparison of gender and age/educational effects is presented. Specifically, Table 3 provides the descriptive statistics for a subset of the total collection of studies described in the previous table. This subset consists of those studies which both included the necessary descriptive data and unambiguously reported the summary index. The

TABLE 1

DISTRIBUTION OF SAMPLES BY DATA SOURCE AND AGE/EDUCATIONAL LEVELS

	Jr. high school	High school	College	Adult/graduate students	Mixed age/educational samples	Totals
Journal articles	2	2	5	1	1	11
Doctoral dissertations	2	5	4	2	3	16
Master's theses	0	6	0	1	1	8
Unpublished manuscripts	2	3	7	0	4	16
Unpublished data	2	0	3	0	0	5
Totals	8	16	19	4	9	56

TABLE 2

SUMMARY OF THE META-ANALYSES

	Jr. high school	High school	College	Adult/graduate students	Mixed	Total group
$\bar{d}$	−.152	−.167	−.213	−.279	−.238	−.207
95% C.I.	$(-.27 \leq \delta \leq -.04)$	$(-.29 \leq \delta \leq -.05)$	$(-.32 \leq \delta \leq -.11)$	$(-.50 \leq \delta \leq -.07)$	$(-.32 \leq \delta \leq -.16)$	$(-.26 \leq \delta \leq -.16)$
Mdn ω^2	.001	<.001	.004	.007	.009	.003
Range[b]	.014	.090	.150	.107	.029	.150
Number of samples	8	16(14)[a]	19(18)[a]	4	9	56(53)[a]
Number of subjects	1255	1249(1107)[a]	1539(1468)[a]	370	2450	6863(6650)[a]

[a] Three samples left unreported the direction of gender differences. In these cases ω^2 was the only measure computed.
[b] Range = (highest value − lowest value).

resulting sample size of 2791 represents 42% of the total number of subjects across the original 56 independent samples.

Given the information presented in Table 3 it is possible to directly compare the variance due to gender differences with the variance accounted for by age/education level. A comparison of this sort holds gender effects against the most powerful demographic correlate of moral reasoning as measured by the DIT (Rest, 1979a).

An unweighted means ANOVA was performed on the data in Table 3, yielding an estimate of the gender, age/education, and interaction term effects. Given the large sample sizes, statistically significant results were expected and confirmed for both main effects (sex $F(1, 2718) = 12.606, p < .001$; age/ed. $F(2, 2718) = 1571.705, p < .001$). The interaction term was nonsignificant ($F(2, 2718) = 0.77, p = $ NS). $\hat{\omega}^2$s were computed from the ANOVA results for both main effects (cf. Fleiss, 1969, Formulas 9, 10). The $\hat{\omega}^2$ corresponding to the gender effect is .002; for the age/educational effect $\hat{\omega}^2 = .525$. Thus our best estimate is that age/education effects through the college years are over 250 times more powerful than gender differences in accounting for the variance in DIT scores.

DISCUSSION

Critics who assert a gender bias in Kohlbergian approaches to morality raise two primary issues. First, moral systems defined by concepts of justice are insensitive to, and downgrade, female moral thinking. The second claim, made by Gilligan (1977), is there are two distinct gender-related moral orientations (justice vs care). It is unfortunate that the current debate over whether or not females perform as well on justice measures has obscured Gilligan's primary criticism of justice reasoning. For Gilligan, justice morality, at minimum, does not fully capture subject responses to a type of moral dilemma (e.g., self-produced) for a specific group of people (e.g., females). Thus Gilligan is primarily questioning Kohlberg's claim that justice reasoning is the universal foundation of moral development.

It is important to note that these two criticisms of the Kohlbergian system are independent. That is, when the research focus is on self-produced moral dilemmas, the suggestion of gender differences on alternative moral orientations does not demand gender differences on justice measures. Females may respond to justice defined measures of moral reasoning much the same way as males, yet prefer the care orientation in discussing their own spontaneously produced moral dilemmas.

Gilligan (1977) originally combined both claims by using those studies indicating a male advantage on justice measures to promote a strong version of her theory. This version suggests that the different moral orientations lead not only to gender differences in the spontaneous production of

174   STEPHEN J. THOMA

TABLE 3
DESCRIPTIVE STATISTICS FOR THE MAJOR AGE/EDUCATIONAL LEVELS

	Jr. high school	High school	College	Graduate school[a]	Adult[a]
Males					
$\bar{x}$	19.068	28.685	44.106	60.97	42.78
SD	6.229	11.770	12.212	14.04	11.77
N	528	424	449	52	90
Females					
$\bar{x}$	19.789	30.361	45.875	62.97	46.04
SD	6.332	10.851	12.190	10.87	12.85
N	519	436	436	42	183
Number of samples	8	12	14	2	2

[a] The descriptive data for these groups were not included in the secondary analysis due to their relatively small sample sizes.

moral issues, but to a female bias on justice reasoning as well. A weaker version of Gilligan's theory which maintains the distinction between the two claims mentioned earlier is at present equally possible. This second version would allow for similar male and female responses to justice measures while suggesting differences on self-produced real-life dilemmas.

The data presented above appropriately address the first criticism, and in so doing test whether Gilligan's strong theory is plausible. In these data we find no support for the claim that females are at a disadvantage when measured by the DIT. Not only are gender differences a very minor contributor to the variance in DIT scores, it is also the case that females consistently outperform their male peers across the life span. Together with the Walker (1984) review there is now little to suggest that mean scores of male and female groups differ on justice oriented measures of moral development.

Complementing these findings at the group level, two longitudinal studies reported in Colby et al. (1983) indicate that female subjects follow the same justice oriented developmental sequence as their male peers. In both studies there were no significant differences in the rate of males and females failing to conform to the theoretical pattern of development. If justice measures were differentially valid for females, then we would have expected a higher rate of failures to conform with the specified developmental sequence. Taken together, these data make a convincing case for rejecting the notion that females are less capable of using justice concepts in their moral thinking and further fail to support Gilligan's strong theory, where male and female orientations lead to gender differences on both real-life and hypothetical justice oriented dilemmas.

As discussed above, a rejection of Gilligan's strong theory does not remove the possibility that gender differences exist on alternative moral systems such as the care orientation. Unfortunately, given the lack of pertinent data it is not possible to determine whether moral development is best viewed as a gender-specific or universal system. In fact, given its popularity, the absence of empirical evidence supporting a gender-specific theory of moral development is surprising. At present there are few empirical studies which address the question of gender differences on the care orientation (cf. Lyons, 1983) and no evidence that a morality of care has the developmental properties necessary to be considered a rival stage theory (e.g., empirical confirmation that there are distinct care orientations; that the development of care is sequential; the demonstration that care measures are related to moral decision making and behavior). In addition, there have been no attempts to generalize Kohlberg's system to real-life dilemmas. Studies of this type are necessary to assess whether response to these dilemmas can be appropriately measured within a justice orientation.

176   STEPHEN J. THOMA

While future research may clarify the merits of a gender-blind or gender-specific theory of morality, it should be noted that here has been a considerable interest in integrating Gilligan's position within a broader view of morality. For instance, Kohlberg (1982; Kohlberg & Candee, 1981) suggests Gilligan's context sensitive care orientation and associated judgments of responsibility may be a mediating factor between the more abstract justice reasoning and moral actions. Brabeck (1983) has argued on similar lines, viewing responsibility judgments as a motivating force operating in interaction with concepts of justice to increase the likelihood of a moral decision.

One final point deserves mention, namely the findings of a significant female advantage in the comprehension and preference of moral issues. Interpreting this finding must be somewhat speculative given the lack of corroborating data. However, two possibilities seem plausible. First, the direction of gender differences on the DIT is congruent with those found on constructs theoretically related to moral judgment, including altruism (Krebs, 1975), affective arousal (Hoffman, 1977), and the decoding of visual and auditory emotional cues (Hall, 1978). While at least two reviews have questioned the scope of these related trends (Eisenberg & Lennon, 1983; Shantz, 1983), taken together such findings are suggestive of a female advantage in this general domain.

Second, the DIT as a paper-and-pencil measure is sensitive to reading and verbal skills. The observed gender differences may therefore be a reflection of the often noted verbal superiority of females (Maccoby & Jacklin, 1974; Hyde, 1981). On both the moral reasoning and verbal ability measures, gender effects are small, with moral reasoning differences in the smaller of the two. This pattern would be expected if verbal ability differences were influencing DIT score variability. Admittedly, a verbal ability explanation for the obtained gender differences weakens in the older, more educated subgroups.

In summary, the present study clarifies previously conflicting interpretations of gender differences on moral judgment measures assessing concepts of justice. It was determined that a gender difference in the comprehension and preference of moral issues does exist, however, unlike current expectations, females consistently scored higher than males. While this finding is of theoretical interest, it should be emphasized that the observed difference is very small both as suggested in a direct comparison with age/educational effects, and in terms of Cohen's interpretive guidelines. There is now considerable evidence to suggest that justice defined measures of moral reasoning are not biased against females. Further, there is little support for the notion that males are better able to reason about hypothetical dilemmas, or that justice reasoning is in some way a male domain. While these findings suggest that the strong version of Gilligan's (1977) theory is incorrect, the possibility of gender differences on alternative moral orientations focusing on the discussion of self-produced moral dilemmas remains unclear.

REFERENCES

Bainer, D. L. (1982). *The influence of school philosophy and religious background on student's socio-moral development and environmental ethics.* Unpublished master's thesis, Ohio State University, Columbus.*

Bidwell, S. Y. (1982). *Attitudes of caregivers towards grief: A cognitive-developmental investigation.* Unpublished master's thesis, University of Minnesota, Minneapolis.*

Bilbro, T., Boni, M., Johnson, B., & Roe, S. (1979). *The relationship of parental acceptance/rejection to the development of moral reasoning.* Unpublished manuscript, University of Connecticut, Storrs.*

Blackner, G. L. (1975). *Moral development of young adults involved in weekday religious education and self-concept relationships.* Unpublished doctoral dissertation, Brigham Young University, Provo, UT.*

Bloomberg, M. (1974). On the relationship between internal–external control and morality. *Psychological Reports, 35,* 1077–1078.*

Boland, M. L. (1980). *The effect of classroom discussion of moral dilemmas on junior high student's level of principled moral judgment.* Unpublished manuscript, Spalding College, Louisville, KY.*

Brabeck, M. (1983). Moral judgment: Theory and research on differences between males and females. *Developmental Review, 3,* 274–291.

Bransford, C. (1973). *Moral development in college students.* Unpublished manuscript, St. Olaf College, Northfield, MN.*

Bredemeier, B. J., & Shields, D. L. (1982). *The utility of moral stage analysis in the prediction of athletic aggression.* Unpublished manuscript.*

Cain, T. (1982). *The moral and ego development of high school subcultures.* Unpublished master's thesis, University of Minnesota, MN.*

Cauble, M. A. (1976). Formal operations, ego identity, and principled morality: are they related? *Developmental Psychology, 12,* 363–364.*

Cistone, D. (1980). *Levels of moral reasoning compared with demographic data among teachers, administrators, and pupil personnel employees enrolled in graduate school.* Unpublished doctoral dissertation, University of Southern California, Los Angeles.*

Clark, G. (1979). *Discussion of moral dilemmas in the development of moral reasoning.* Unpublished manuscript, Spartanburg Day School, Spartanburg, SC.*

Clouse, B. (1979). *Moral reasoning of teacher education students as related to sex, politics, and religion.* Unpublished manuscript, Indiana State University, Terre Haute, IN.*

Coder, R. (1975). *Moral judgment in adults.* Unpublished doctoral dissertation, University of Minnesota, Minneapolis.*

Cohen, J. (1969). *Statistical power analysis for the behavioral sciences.* New York: Academic Press.

Colby, A., Kohlberg, L., Gibbs, J., & Lieberman, M. (1983). A longitudinal study of moral judgment. *Monographs of the Society for Research in Child Development, 48*(1–2, Serial No. 200).

Crowder, J. W. (1978). *The Defining Issues Test and correlates of moral judgment.* Unpublished master's thesis, University of Maryland, College Park.*

Davison, M. L., & Robbins, S. (1978). The reliability and validity of objective indices of moral development. *Applied Psychological Measurement, 2*(3), 391–403.

Edwards, C. P. (1975). Societal complexity and moral development: A Kenyan study. *Ethos, 3,* 505–527.

* An asterisk following a reference indicates the study was used in the meta-analysis.

178   STEPHEN J. THOMA

Eisenberg, N., & Lennon, R. (1983). Sex differences in empathy and related capacities. *Psychology Bulletin,* 94(1), 100–131.

Fielding, G. (1980). *A comparison of an inquiry-oriented and a direct instruction approach to teaching legal problem solving to secondary school students.* Unpublished doctral dissertation, University of Oregon, Eugene.*

Finn, E. (1978). *The effect of parental influence and peer influence on the morals of suburban 9th grade students.* Unpublished doctoral dissertation, St. John's University, Jamaica, NY.*

Fleiss, J. L. (1969). Estimating the magnitude of experimental effects. *Psychological Bulletin,* 72(4), 273–276.

French, M. D. (1977). *A study of Kohlbergian moral development and selected behaviors among high school students in classes using values clarification and other teaching methods.* Unpublished doctoral dissertation, Auburn University, Auburn, GA.*

Garwood, S. G., Levine, D. W., & Ewing, L. (1980). Effect of protagonist's sex on assessing gender differences in moral reasoning. *Developmental Psychology,* 16(6), 677–698.*

Gfellner, B. (1980). *Moral development, ego development, and sex role differences in adolescence.* Unpublished doctoral dissertation, University of Manitoba, Winnipeg.*

Gibbs, J. C., & Widaman, K. F. (1982). *Social intelligence: Measuring the development of sociomoral reflection.* Englewood Cliffs, NJ: Prentice–Hall.

Gilligan, C. (1977). In a different voice: Women's conceptions of the self and morality. *Harvard Educational Review,* 47, 481–517.

Gilligan, C. (1979). Women's place in man's life cycle. *Harvard Educational Review,* 49, 431–446.

Gilligan, C. (1982). *In a different voice: Psychological theory and women's development.* Cambridge, MA: Harvard Univ. Press.

Glass, G. V., McGaw, B., & Smith, M. L. (1981). *Meta-analysis in social research.* Beverly Hills: Sage.

Guttenberg, R. (1975). *Videotaped moral dilemmas: Altering the presentation of the stimuli in the Defining Issues Test.* Unpublished manuscript, Brown University, Providence, RI.*

Hains, A. A., & Miller, D. J. (1978). (Defining Issues Test scores). Unpublished raw data.*

Hall, J. A. (1978). Gender effects in decoding nonverbal cues. *Psychological Bulletin,* 85, 845–858.

Hay, J. A. (1982). *A study of principled moral reasoning within a sample of conscientious objectors.* Unpublished doctoral dissertation, Temple University, Philadelphia.*

Hays, W. L. (1963). *Statistics for psychologists.* New York: Holt, Rinehart & Winston.

Hedges, L. V., & Olkin, I. (1980). Vote counting methods in research synthesis. *Psychological Bulletin,* 88, 359–369.

Hoffman, M. L. (1977). Sex differences in empathy and related behaviors. *Psychological Bulletin,* 84, 712–722.

Holstein, C. B. (1976). Irreversible, stepwise sequence in the development of moral judgment: A longitudinal study of males and females. *Child Development,* 47, 51–61.

Hunter, J. E., Schmidt, F. L., & Jackson, G. B. (1982). *Meta-analysis: Cumulating research findings across studies.* Beverly Hills: Sage.

Hurt, B. L. (1974). *Psychological education for college students: A cognitive-developmental curriculum.* Unpublished doctoral dissertation, University of Minnesota, Minneapolis.*

Hyde, J. S. (1981). How large are cognitive gender differences? A meta-analysis using $\hat{\omega}^2$ and *d. American Psychologist,* 36(8), 892–901.

Jacobson, L. T. (1977). *A study of relationships among mother, student, and teacher levels* *of moral reasoning in a department of defense middle school.* Unpublished doctoral dissertation, Michigan State University, East Lansing.*

Johnson, M. A. (1974). *A study of relationships between religious knowledge, moral judgment and personal religious orientations.* Unpublished manuscript, Temple University, Philadelphia.*

Kenvin, W. A. (1981). *A study of the effect of systematic value instruction on level of moral judgment.* Unpublished doctoral dissertation, Rutgers University, New Brunswick, NJ.*

Kitchener, K., King, P., Davison, M., & Parker, C. (1982). *Moral and ego development.* Paper presented to the American College Personnel Association Annual Meeting, Detroit, MI.*

Kohlberg, L. (1969). Stage and sequence: The cognitive developmental approach to socialization. In D. A. Goslin (Ed.), *Handbook of socialization theory and research.* Chicago: Rand McNally.

Kohlberg, L. (1982). A reply to Owen Hanagan and some comments on the Puka-Goodpaster exchange. *Ethics,* 92, 513–528.

Kohlberg, L., & Candee D. (1981, December 17–19). *The relationship of moral judgment to moral action.* Paper presented at the Florida International University Conference on morality and moral development, Miami Beach.

Kohlberg, L., Colby, A., & Damon, W. (1978). *Assessment of moral judgment in childhood and youth.* Grant proposed to the National Institutes of Health.

Kohlberg, L., Levine, C., & Hewer, A. (1983). Moral stages: A current formulation and a response to critics. In J. Meacham (Ed.), *Contributions to human development* (Vol. 10). Basel, Switzerland: S. Karger.

Kraemer, H. C. (1983). Theory of estimation and testing of effect sizes: Use in meta-analysis. *Journal of Educational Statistics,* 8(2), 93–101.

Krebs, D. (1975). Empathy and altruism. *Journal of Personality and Social Psychology,* 32, 1124–1146.

Leahy, R. L. (1981). Parental practices and the development of moral judgment and self-image disparity during adolescence. *Developmental Psychology,* 17, 580–594.*

Leahy, R. L., & Eiter, M. (1980). Moral judgment and the development of real and ideal androgynous self-image during adolescence and young adulthood. *Developmental Psychology,* 16, 362–370.*

Light, R. J., & Smith, P. V. (1971). Accumulating evidence: Procedures for resolving contradictions among different studies. *Harvard Educational Review,* 41, 429–471.

Loesch, L. S. (1980). *Field dependence–independence, locus of control, and moral reasoning.* Unpublished paper, The College of Wooster, Wooster, OH.*

Lyons, N. P. (1983). Two perspectives: On self, relationships and morality. *Harvard Educational Review,* 53, 125–145.

Maccoby, E. E., & Jacklin, C. N. (1974). *The psychology of sex differences.* Stanford, CA: Stanford Univ. Press.

Mahler, I. (1981). (Defining Issues Test scores.) Unpublished raw data.*

Marayama, M., & Schweinberger, B. (1981). *The effects of legal education and moral judgment.* Unpublished manuscript, University of California, Berkeley.*

Medairy, A. L. (1976). *Moral judgment and locus of control in college freshmen and seniors.* Unpublished manuscript, Whitman College, Walla Walla, WA.*

Miller, B. M. (1980). *Kohlberg's moral development theory: Effect of grade, sex, and Catholic high school environment.* Available from author, 408 Waring Rd, Elkins Park, PA 19117.*

Miller, D. G. (1979). *A cross-cultural study of moral development in Mexican and American adolescents.* Unpublished master's thesis, Universidad de la Americas, Mexico.*

Mitchell, H. R. (1982). *Moral development and sexual orientation.* Unpublished doctoral dissertation, University of California, Berkeley.*

180   STEPHEN J. THOMA

Nisan, M., & Kohlberg, L. (1982). Universality and cross-cultural variation in moral devel-
    opment: A longitudinal and cross-sectional study in Turkey. *Child Development, 53,*
    865–876.
Olson, A. A. (1982). *Effects of leadership training and experience on student development.*
    Unpublished doctoral dissertation. Seattle University, Seattle, WA.*
Orchowsky, S. J., & Jenkins, L. R. (1979). Sex biases in the measurement of moral judg-
    ment. *Psychological Reports, 44,* 1040.*
Prawat, R. (1976). Mapping the affective domain in young adolescents. *Journal of Educa-
    tional Psychology, 68*(5), 566–572.*
Preston, D. (1979). *A moral education program conducted in the health and physical educa-
    tion curriculum.* Unpublished doctoral dissertation, University of Georgia, Athens.*
Reck, C. (1978). *A study of the relationship between participants in school services and
    moral development.* Unpublished doctoral dissertation, St. Louis University, St.
    Louis.*
Redman, G. (1981). (Defining Issues Test scores). Unpublished raw data, Hamline Univer-
    sity, St. Paul, MN.*
Rest, J. R. (1979a). *Development in judging moral issues.* Minneapolis: Univ. of Minnesota
    Press.
Rest, J. R. (1979b). *Manual for the Defining Issues Test.* Available from author, 330 Burton
    Hall, University of Minnesota, Minneapolis, MN 55455.
Rest, J. R. (1983). Morality. In J. Flavell & E. Markman (Eds.), *Cognitive development,*
    Vol. IV, P. Mussen (General Ed.), *Manual of child psychology.* New York: Wiley.
Rosenthal, R. (1978). Combining results of independent studies. *Psychological Bulletin, 85,*
    185–193.
Russell, M. J., & Budd, L. S. (1981). *Moral development issues in choice of parenthood:
    Implications for counseling.* Unpublished manuscript, University of Minnesota, Minne-
    apolis.*
Schneeweis, T. G. (1974). *The relationship between the Allport–Vernon–Lindzey study of
    values and an objective measure of moral judgment.* Unpublished master's thesis,
    Moorhead State College, Moorhead, MN.*
Schomberg, S. F., & Baulkum, E. (1976). *Evaluation of two instructional approaches in
    teaching ethics.* Unpublished manuscript, University of Minnesota, Minneapolis.*
Shanteau, J. (1982). *The effects of teacher's moral reasoning on the student's attitude and
    performance.* Unpublished master's thesis, California State College, Hayward, CA.*
Shantz, C. U. (1983). Social cognition. In J. H. Flavell & Markham (Eds.), *Charmichael's
    manual of child psychology* (4th ed.) New York: Wiley.
Snarey, J. C., Reimer, J., & Kohlberg, L. (1985). The development of social–moral rea-
    soning among Kibbutz adolescents: A longitudinal cross-cultural study. *Developmental
    Psychology, 21*(1), 3–17.
Thoma, S. J. (1983). (Defining Issues Test scores). Unpublished raw data.*
Thoma, S. J., & Davison, M. L. (1983). Moral reasoning development and graduate educa-
    tion. *Journal of Applied Developmental Psychology, 4,* 227–238.*
Wahrman, I. (1980). *A study of the relationship of dogmatic religious group membership
    and moral judgment development.* Unpublished doctoral dissertation, New York Uni-
    versity, New York.*
Walker, L. (1984). Sex differences in the development of moral reasoning: A critical review.
    Child Development, 55, 677–691.
Warren, B. (1982). *Social interest and social–moral reasoning in high school student basic
    education and special education classes.* Unpublished master's thesis, Bryn Mawr Col-
    lege, PA.*
Whitely, J. et al. (1982). *Character development in college students, Volume I: The
    freshman year.* New York: Character Research.*

RECEIVED: January 21, 1985; REVISED: May 19, 1985.

Journal of Personality and Social Psychology
1986, Vol. 50, No. 4, 777–783

Gender Differences in Moral Reasoning: A Comparison of the Use of Justice and Care Orientations

Maureen Rose Ford
University of Kentucky

Carol Rotter Lowery
Lexington, Kentucky

The present study examines the adequacy of Lawrence Kohlberg's cognitive-developmental model as a representation of female moral reasoning. Specifically, this study examines the claims of Gilligan (1982) that there are two different conceptions of morality—one described as a morality of justice, on which Kohlberg's scheme is based, and one described as a morality of care, seen by Gilligan as more representative of female thinking about moral conflict. A sample of 202 college students (M age = 19 years) filled out a self-report questionnaire on moral dilemmas they had experienced. They then rated their use of both justice and care orientations in resolving those dilemmas. The use of the two orientations was examined in relationship to subject gender, sex role, and perceptions of the two orientations. Few significant differences were obtained except that female subjects were more consistent in their use of a care orientation, and that male subjects were more consistent in their use of a justice orientation, and more feminine males were more likely to report the use of a care orientation than less feminine males. Male and female reasoning about moral conflict is examined in the light of these two perspectives and the relationship of sex roles to endorsement of each perspective is investigated.

In 1932, Piaget published his first major work on moral development, *The Moral Judgment of the Child.* In it he outlines a three-step process in which there is a basic progression from an external to an internal locus for evaluating "right" and from a more concrete to a more abstract mode of reasoning. The basic moral structure is seen to parallel the development of logical reasoning, and advancements in the latter are seen as necessary for advancements in the former. This is the structural approach to moral development on which Kohlberg built his cognitive-developmental model.

When discussing the first stage of moral development, Piaget commented:

> The relations between parents and children are certainly not only those of constraint. There is a spontaneous mutual affection, which from the first prompts the child to acts of generosity and even self-sacrifice, to very touching demonstrations which are in no way prescribed. And here no doubt is the starting point for the morality of good which we shall see developing alongside of the morality of right or duty, and which in some persons completely replaces it. (1932, pp. 193–194)

Thus, in 1932, Piaget noted the existence of two different types of morality, a morality of good and a morality of right or duty. Yet, the work of Carol Gilligan has raised this as an empirical question 50 years later. To understand the 50-year gap, one need only look a few pages further in Piaget's original work. He goes on to say that though

> The affective aspect of cooperation and reciprocity eludes interrogation, there is one notion, probably the most rational of moral notions, which seems to be the direct result of cooperation and of which the analysis can be attempted without encountering too much

difficulty—we mean the notion of justice. It will therefore be on this point that most of our efforts will be directed. (p. 195)

And thus, the "morality of good" drops out of Piaget's analysis of moral development.

Almost a quarter of a century later, Lawrence Kohlberg began a longitudinal study of the moral development of adolescent males. Working with Piaget's theory, he sought and found evidence for a structural developmental model of the type described by Piaget. He proposed his universal, invariant sequence, six-stage model of moral development wherein each stage reflects a more advanced social perspective and logical structure—a structure which parallels Piaget's logical stages and is "best formulated as a justice structure" (Kohlberg, 1971, p. 195).

Kohlberg argued that justice is "the basic moral principle" (1971, p. 220). Kohlberg noted that "the only general principle of content, other than justice, seriously advanced by (moral) philosophers, has been the principle variously termed utility or benevolence." Although admitting that, like justice, benevolence can be universalized, he nevertheless saw benevolence as insufficient because "it cannot resolve a conflict of welfares" (p. 220).

With his dismissal of benevolence as being inadequate for solving dilemmas, Kohlberg nevertheless acknowledged that without such a moral attitude, moral conflict is not even experienced. It is on this point that much of the criticism against Kohlberg turns. Peters (1971), for example, discusses the importance of other issues besides knowledge of justice in the moral development of the child. The child, he says, "might know what justice is, but not care about it overmuch. . . . How do children come to care? This seems to be the most important question in moral education; but no clear answer to it can be found in Kohlberg's writings" (p. 262).

Many other writers and researchers have taken issue with Kohlberg's model as to its sufficiency in explaining moral development (e.g., Holstein, 1976; Simpson, 1974). The particular

Correspondence concerning this article should be addressed to Carol Rotter Lowery, Family Psychology Services, 1708 Liberty Road, Lexington, Kentucky 40505.

criticism of Kohlberg's failure to include the concept of care along with the concept of justice is receiving more attention in the psychological literature recently, principally because of the work of Carol Gilligan. Her interest is the issue that in choosing to focus on an ethic of justice, Kohlberg creates a model of adult moral development whose focus on autonomy, separation, and individuation leaves women at a distinct disadvantage. Traditional female qualities, such as a sense of responsibility to and for others, are qualities almost exclusively relegated to Stage 3 in Kohlberg's model, the stage just above the egocentric concerns of the pre-conventional stage. It is an "unfair paradox," as Gilligan says, "that the very traits that have traditionally defined the 'goodness' of women, are those that mark them as deficient in moral development" (Gilligan, 1982, p. 18).

The question of whether men and women do differ in stages of moral reasoning has been extensively debated in the literature. Langdale (1980) cites many studies which found that women did not score as high on Kohlberg's scale as did men. Several studies (e.g., Bussey & Manghan, 1982; Poppen, 1974) suggest that Stage 3 is the modal stage for women, and that Stage 4 is the modal stage for men. Given the findings that many adults never make it past this conventional level of moral development (Kuhn, Langer, Kohlberg, & Haan, 1977), the issue of whether Stages 3 and 4 are sex-typed and possibly alternate conventional stages is an important one in terms of their use in indicating degree of moral development.

Gilligan, however, objects to the whole process of trying to fit women into models that were developed on men and that in her view, do not adequately represent the development of the female person. In order to construct models of development which represent the "voices" of women, Gilligan believes we must return to the source, much as Piaget did, and listen to women's discourse as they struggle to make decisions about moral conflicts in their lives (1982, p. 20).

Using an open-ended interview, Gilligan asked women considering whether to continue or abort a pregnancy questions regarding how they were thinking about the decision (Gilligan, 1977). Her subjects were 29 women, ranging in age from 15 to 33, diverse in ethnic background and social class. What Gilligan found as she listened to these women was that their moral language was replete with words like selfishness, responsibility, care and avoiding hurt and that their decisions were weighed in light of their relationships with others. Using Kohlberg's and Piaget's preconventional, conventional, and postconventional scheme, she traces a developmental path of a morality of care. But unlike Kohlberg's scheme, which ties the development of morality as justice to the changing understanding of equality and reciprocity, the development of morality as care is tied to a changing understanding of responsibility and relationships.

Having "found" this second conception of morality, a morality centered on issues of care, Gilligan and her colleagues sought to investigate its prevalence (Gilligan, Langdale, Lyons, & Murphy, 1982). They used a cross-sectional sample of men and women matched for age, educational experience, and social class. Subjects were asked to describe a personal, real-life experience of moral conflict, and they were then asked a series of standard follow-up questions inquiring into how the subject constructed, resolved, and evaluated the conflict. The results reported were that 75% (12) of the women used a predominantly care orientation,

whereas only 25% (4) of the women used a predominantly justice orientation. For men, 79% (11) used a predominantly justice orientation and 14% (2) used a predominantly care orientation, with 7% (1) using both equally. There were no women who failed to present a consideration of care, and no men who failed to present a consideration of rights. However, 36% (6) of the women failed to present any consideration of justice, and 36% (6) of the men failed to present any consideration of care. The author's conclusion was that "in real-life moral conflict, individuals call upon and think about considerations predominantly within one mode which is related to, but not defined by, a person's gender" (Gilligan et al., 1982).

The purpose of the present study was to investigate further these findings of differential use by men and women of the justice and care orientations to moral conflict. Given the observation that these orientations are not completely gender specific, a measure of psychological sex roles was included to investigate whether sex role may be more predictive than gender for the use of either orientation. One study (Pratt & Royer, 1982) has found this to be the case. The present study stays with Gilligan's suggestion that moral decisions should be studied in the context of subjects' real-life dilemmas. However, when Gilligan used a derivative methodology in her second study, she trained raters to code the language used by subjects. To avoid the potential confound of gender-related differences in the semantics of expressing moral decisions rather than in the moral reasoning process itself, the present study uses a more direct methodology. The present study also controls for bias that may be introduced by having subjects report their own dilemmas due to possible gender-related differences in self-disclosure that are incidental to moral judgment.

Method

Subjects

Subjects were 101 male and 101 female undergraduates from introductory psychology classes who volunteered to participate. The average age of subjects was 19 years, with a range of 18 to 29 years. They had no known prior exposure to the concepts or theories addressed by the study.

Procedure

Subjects were asked to describe three important moral conflicts in their lives. After each, they were asked to rate the importance of the conflict in their life at that time and the degree of difficulty they experienced in making their decision about what to do. Both ratings were done on 7-point Likert scales.

After describing and rating all three conflicts, subjects read summary descriptions of the justice and care orientations to moral conflict. Each summary consisted of a five-sentence description of the orientation; both had been previewed by Gilligan's colleagues (N. P. Lyons, personal communication, October 1982) and designated as accurate representations of the two orientations. They were then asked to rate, on 7-point Likert scales, the degree to which each orientation was a part of their own thinking about each of the conflicts they described.

Subjects completed two additional measures: the Interpersonal Disposition Inventory (IDI) and selected items from the Semantic Differential.

The IDI is an 85-item scale developed by Berzins, Welling, and Wetter (1977) to measure psychological sex roles. Scores are obtained on masculinity and femininity subscales, and median splits on these subscale scores are used to divide subjects into high and low masculinity and femininity groups, and into four sex role categories (masculine, feminine, androgynous, and indeterminate).

The Semantic Differential is a standardized procedure for measuring the connotation of a concept for an individual (Osgood, Suci, & Tannenbaum, 1957). Factorial analyses of the original set of 50 scales revealed that concepts are judged on three major independent dimensions: Evaluative, Potency, and Activity factors. Three sets of adjectives from each of these factors (a total of 9 pairs) made up the differential used in this study. The adjective pairs chosen were those that had relatively high loadings on the factor in question and relatively low loadings on the other two factors. In order to evaluate the connotation of each orientation, the two paragraphs summarizing the justice and care orientations were presented separately and subjects completed a differential on each, thus yielding ratings of both on all nine bipolar scales.

The entire procedure took about 2 hr, with subjects working in small groups and reporting their responses on forms provided.

Fifty subjects were asked to complete the justice and care ratings on their conflicts again, 3 to 4 weeks later. These ratings were used as a measure of the reliability of the rating procedure.

In a post hoc procedure, 50 subjects' protocols (25 men and 25 women) were selected at random and their first moral conflicts submitted to a content analysis. This was done to assess the extent to which the issues as presented in the subjects' dilemmas were embedded in relationship and justice contexts. These ratings were done on 7-point Likert scales by two independent judges trained to be familiar with the care and justice concepts as presented in this study. These ratings focused on the content of the dilemmas only, not on their construction or evaluation. These ratings were thus quite distinct from the subjects' ratings of the extent to which these concepts had been a part of their thinking about the dilemmas.

Results

Because subjects were generating their own conflicts, direct between-subjects comparisons of the ratings of the two conceptions of morality were not possible without some preliminary analyses. Results to be considered first are the reliability of the moral conflict ratings and the relationship of the importance and difficulty ratings to gender and use of moral orientation.

The reliability of the justice and care ratings was assessed by retesting a subset of 50 subjects.

Reliability coefficients were calculated separately for men and women, with interesting results. Again summed across all three dilemmas, the correlations obtained were men, $r = .76, p < .001$, on justice ratings, $r = .39, p < .12$, on care ratings; women, $r = .17, p < .34$, on justice ratings, $r = .70, p < .001$, on care ratings. Fisher's r to z transformation showed that men were significantly more consistent in their use of the justice orientation than women (Fisher's $z = 4.88$, $p < .05$) and that women were significantly more consistent than men in the use of the care orientation (Fisher's $z = 2.69$, $p < .05$).

The pattern of results shown in Table 1 indicated that only the ratings of the first conflicts were moderately reliable measures of the justice and care orientations for both men and women. Thus, between-subjects comparisons on the justice and care ratings were made only on the first set of ratings.

Importance and Difficulty as Covariates

In order to assess how properties of the content of the subjects' dilemmas may have been related to their preference for one or

Table 1

Test–Retest Correlations of Justice and Care Ratings for the Three Conflict Situations

Situation	Men		Women		Combined	
	r	p	r	p	r	p
			Justice			
Conflict 1	.61	.009	.40	.023	.41	.003
Conflict 2	.43	.086	.13	.489	.21	.149
Conflict 3	.57	.018	.17	.350	.27	.061
Overall	.76	.001	.17	.340	.31	.030
			Care			
Conflict 1	.59	.013	.51	.003	.51	.001
Conflict 2	.20	.433	.65	.001	.52	.001
Conflict 3	.35	.168	.53	.001	.47	.001
Overall	.39	.120	.70	.001	.57	.001

Note. In the justice and care orientations, $N = 17$ for men, $N = 33$ for women, and $N = 50$ combined.

the other moral orientations, subjects were asked to rate the importance and difficulty of each conflict. The correlation between importance and difficulty for the first dilemma was $r = .53, p < .001$. Though statistically significant, the correlation was too weak to justify combining importance and difficulty as a single measure of "significance," so both were retained as separate measures. Subjects' ratings of the importance and difficulty of their first conflicts were compared with their ratings of their use of the care and justice orientations. These correlations are given for men and women, combined and separately, in Table 2. Both measures of significance were more highly correlated with care ratings than with justice ratings.

A one-way analysis of variance (ANOVA) on importance by sex yielded a significant sex difference, $F(1, 200) = 4.86, p < .05$. The same analysis on difficulty ratings yielded a marginally significant result, $F(1, 200) = 2.95, p < .08$. In both cases, female mean scores were higher than the male means scores (see Table 3). These results indicate that men and women may have been providing themselves with different stimuli; that is, women rated their self-reported conflicts as significantly more important in their lives and their decisions as more difficult to make.

To test whether men and women would differ in their use of the justice and care orientations, the effects of importance and difficulty just noted needed to be controlled. Therefore, a multivariate analysis of covariance (MANCOVA) was used (see Table 3). Analyzing justice and care ratings by sex, with importance and difficulty as covariates, yielded nonsignificant sex differences, $F(2, 197) = .398, p < .67$.

To evaluate whether psychological sex role may be a mediating variable in man/woman use of the different conceptions of morality, subjects were divided into high and low masculinity, and into high and low femininity categories (Berzins et al., 1977). Analyses were also performed with subjects classified into the four sex role categories: masculine (high MASCUL, low FEMIN), feminine (high FEMIN, low MASCUL), androgynous (high MASCUL, high FEMIN) and indeterminate (low MASCUL, low FEMIN).

A 2×2 MANCOVA on the justice and care ratings, using sex

Table 2

Conflict Situation 1: Pearson Correlations of Importance and Difficulty Ratings With Justice and Care Ratings

Rating	Men	Women	Combined
Difficulty w/Justice	.18	−.17	.001
Difficulty w/Care	.30**	.22*	.27**
Importance w/Justice	−.003	−.006	−.01
Importance w/Care	.13	.41**	.27**

* $p < .05$. ** $p < .01$.

and high/low masculinity as the between-subjects variables, and importance and difficulty as covariates, showed no multivariate effects for sex or masculinity classification and no interaction. The same analysis with high/low femininity as the between-subjects variable yielded a significant multivariate effect for femininity classification, $F(2, 195) = 3.00$, $p < .05$, and a trend toward significance for the interaction of sex and femininity classification, $F(2, 195) = 2.31$, $p < .10$.

The significant effects of the latter MANCOVA were subsequently analyzed by univariate ANOVAs. For care ratings, there was a significant main effect for femininity classification, $F(1, 196) = 6.0$, $p < .02$, moderated by a significant sex by femininity classification interaction, $F(1, 196) = 4.56$, $p < .03$. Mean comparisons were conducted using the Tukey HSD procedure (Wike, 1971) and indicated that men classified as high femininity had higher care ratings than men classified as low femininity. Univariate ANOVAs on justice ratings showed no significant effects for femininity classification or the interaction of sex and femininity classification. In summary, masculinity classification did not significantly affect justice or care ratings. Femininity classification affected only care ratings and only for men. Mean justice and care ratings by sex and high/low masculinity and femininity are listed in Table 4.

Analyses were also performed by the four sex role categories, because the four categories reflect all possible combinations of scores on gender orientation. A 2 × 4 MANCOVA on the justice and care ratings, using sex and sex role as the between-subjects variables, with importance and difficulty as covariates, showed nonsignificant differences between sex role categories, no significant main effect for sex, and a nonsignificant interaction between sex and sex role.

Table 3

Mean Importance, Difficulty, Care, and Justice Ratings For the Three Conflict Situations

	Importance		Difficulty		Care		Justice	
Situation	Men	Women	Men	Women	Men	Women	Men	Women
Conflict 1								
M	5.27	5.75	4.79	5.22	5.29	5.58	4.69	4.57
SD	1.62	1.51	1.75	1.78	1.68	1.52	1.66	1.73

In all situations, $N = 101$.

Table 4

Mean Justice and Care Ratings by Sex and High/Low Masculinity and Femininity Classification

	Men			Women		
Rating	M	SD	n	M	SD	n
Justice						
High Masculinity	4.52	1.73	65	4.39	1.95	38
Low Masculinity	5.0	1.49	36	4.68	1.59	63
High Femininity	4.86	1.65	37	4.56	1.72	69
Low Femininity	4.59	1.67	64	4.59	1.79	32
Care						
High Masculinity	5.37	1.66	65	5.60	1.62	38
Low Masculinity	5.14	1.72	36	5.57	1.48	63
High Femininity	5.92[a]	1.32	37	5.57	1.53	59
Low Femininity	4.92[b]	1.77	64	5.63	1.54	32

[a,b] Means a and b differ at the $p < .05$ level.

Semantic Differential

Subjects rated the justice and care paragraphs on a 7-point differential made up of three independent semantic dimensions: Evaluative, Potency, and Activity factors. Mean dimension ratings for each orientation are listed in Table 5. Because Osgood's dimensions are orthogonal, a repeated measures ANOVA was used. This mixed design ANOVA, using gender as the between-subjects factor, and moral orientation and the three semantic dimensions as the within-subjects factors, showed a significant main effect for the semantic dimensions, $F(2, 394) = 484.95$, $p < .001$, a significant interaction between the dimensions and the two orientations, $F(2, 394) = 21.67$, $p < .001$, and a significant sex by dimensions interaction, $F(2, 394) = 6.63$, $p < .001$.

The interactions noted were further evaluated by the Bonferroni t post hoc comparison procedure (Wike, 1971). The care and justice orientations differed significantly on the potency factor, $t(201) = 6.17$, $p < .01$, with the justice orientation being rated as more potent than the care orientation. The two orientations were not significantly different on the evaluative and activity factors, which were seen as equally good and active approaches to moral conflict. Investigation of the sex by dimensions interaction indicated nonsignificant differences between men and women in their ratings on the three dimensions. Mean ratings of the two orientations on the potency scale are shown in Table 6.

Content Analysis

Fifty subjects' first dilemmas were rated by two independent judges to assess the extent to which the content of the dilemmas was imbedded in care and justice contexts. Interrater reliability was computed by the Pearson formula and found to be adequate for research purposes: for care ratings, $r = .72$, $p < .01$, and for justice ratings, $r = .79$, $p < .01$. The mean ratings across the two raters on justice and care for men, and justice for women, were identical ($M = 4.56$). The mean rating for women on care was somewhat higher ($M = 4.94$), but not significantly different from the justice ratings for women (as evaluated with a t test). These

Table 5
Mean Semantic Dimension Ratings for the Justice and Care Orientations[a]

	Justice			Care		
Rating	Men	Women	Combined	Men	Women	Combined
Evaluative						
M	2.12	2.03	2.08	2.28	1.99	2.14
SD	1.08	1.05	1.06	1.07	1.01	1.05
Potency						
M	3.55	3.71	3.63	4.13	4.44	4.29
SD	1.01	1.17	1.10	.99	1.10	1.05
Activity						
M	3.96	3.85	3.91	3.87	3.72	3.80
SD	.90	.81	.86	.78	.85	.81

Note. In the justice and care orientations for men and women, $N = 101$; $N = 202$ in the justice and care orientations combined.
[a] The semantic differential is constructed in such a way that *lower* scores indicate higher evaluation, potency, and activity ratings.

results suggest that the contents of male and female dilemmas did not substantially differ in the extent to which they were embedded in contexts of care and justice.

Discussion

One of the purposes of this study was to examine whether the gender differences Gilligan reported in her research could be found across a set of conflicts. Gilligan's conclusions were based on single conflict investigations (Gilligan, 1982; Gilligan et al., 1982). Generalizations of her findings across three conflict situations would provide stronger support for her claim that men and women approach moral conflicts from basically different orientations. Unfortunately, such direct comparisons could not be made, as test–retest coefficients showed the ratings to be unreliable measures of the justice and care orientations for all but the first conflict. However, the finding that there were very different reliability patterns for men and women on the justice and care ratings provides indirect support for Gilligan's assertions. For women, the care ratings of the three conflicts were significantly more stable from one time to the next than were the justice ratings. Exactly the reverse was true for men. It would seem, then, that despite findings of differences or similarities in actual ratings of the two orientations for a given conflict, the care orientation is a consistent consideration for women, and the justice orientation is a consistent consideration for men.

Worell and Worell (1965), in a study of personality conflict, suggest such intraindividual variability can be viewed as lawfully produced. Highly variable responses to the same stimuli are seen as indications of competing response tendencies. In a situation where none of the responses are clearly dominant, the subjects respond with any one of their closely competing responses. In contrast, the person with a dominant response is less conflicted and will tend to repeat the response in similar situations and thus show less variability. In terms of this study, this perspective would suggest that for women, considerations of care are consistent dominant responses. Thus their sense of the role care

plays in their moral dilemmas is nonconflicted and therefore their ratings of the care orientation less variable from one time to the next. In contrast, considerations of justice are less dominant for women, and their sense of the role of justice in their moral dilemmas less clear and more conflicted. This leads to greater variability in justice ratings in response to the same stimulus, and thus lower coefficients of reliability. For men, the justice perspective would be the dominant response tendency and thus shows less variability. The care orientation would reflect more competing response tendencies and thus be more variable.

The decision to allow subjects to generate and rate their own conflicts rather than respond to standardized dilemmas made it necessary to evaluate in some manner the relative meaning or significance of the conflicts in their lives. This was necessary so that any differences along this dimension could be controlled when assessing differences in the justice and care orientations. Differences in the importance and difficulty of the conflicts were also of interest relative to the use of the different orientations.

The results showed that the importance of the conflict in the subject's life and the difficulty of the decision were in fact significantly associated with care ratings but not with justice ratings. It seems, then, that for both men and women, the more important and more difficult moral decisions they have made up to this point in their lives are more related to issues of care than to issues of justice. Recalling that Kohlberg's dilemmas are constructed as abstract problems of opposition—competing rights, competing values—it is worth noting that such abstract issues were not at the heart of the important moral conflicts for the subjects in this sample.

The correlations between care and importance help in clarifying a possible confounding variable in this study, which is that women generally rated their conflicts as more important and more difficult than men did. This suggests that the two groups of subjects were providing themselves with different stimuli. Because all subjects were asked to describe the most significant conflicts they had faced up to that point in time, an obvious observation is that women perceived themselves as having had to make more important and difficult moral decisions than men did. Given the relationship between importance, difficulty, and

Table 6
Mean Ratings of the Justice and Care Orientations on the Three Potency Scales

	Justice		Care	
Scale	Men	Women	Men	Women
Severe-lenient				
M	3.99	3.72	4.28	4.34
SD	1.52	1.59	1.43	1.56
Masculine-feminine				
M	3.24	3.80	3.96	4.33
SD	1.11	1.19	1.26	1.13
Hard-soft				
M	3.41	3.60	4.16	4.65
SD	1.44	1.59	1.53	1.58

Note. In the justice and care orientations, $N = 101$.

care already mentioned, it would seem possible that the reason women rated their conflicts as more important and difficult was because the conflicts they wrote about were those in which issues of care were the central concern, more so than in the conflicts of male subjects. There is support in the literature for such a speculation (Block, 1973; Maccoby & Jacklin, 1974); however, a post hoc content analysis of a sample of subjects' dilemmas did not suggest that this was the case. Though females' dilemmas were rated as presenting issues somewhat more embedded in care or relationship contexts than were males' dilemmas for the sample selected, this difference was not statistically significant.

The question addressed in part by this content analysis is whether women select and report dilemmas defined by relationship issues out of a pool of dilemmas similar to the pool that men experience, or whether women in actuality experience more relationship dilemmas because of their social context. Kohlberg believed the second hypothesis was true and that that was why women gravitated toward Stage 3. He felt women would progress to higher levels of moral development if they experienced more varied contexts (Kohlberg & Kramer, 1969). Gilligan believes the first is true, that women identify relationship issues in their conflicts more than men.

Turning to the major purpose of this study, it was expected that men would show greater usage of the justice orientation than women, and women greater usage of the care orientation than men. Additionally, it was expected that psychological sex role would mediate the relationship somewhat, with high femininity being more associated with the use of care and high masculinity being more associated with the use of justice. Men and women showed a tendency to differ in the predicted directions in the use of justice and care, but the differences were very small and statistically nonsignificant. Both sexes apparently considered questions of relationship, care, and responsibility, as well as questions of fairness, justice, and rights, and they considered them fairly equally. In accounting for these results in light of the very different retest patterns already mentioned, one might speculate as to whether subjects could have a primary orientation but, when presented with the other, see it as a reasonable and valuable approach and rate their conflicts in that light. Regardless, this pattern of results differs considerably from the more extreme findings of Gilligan and her colleagues. In their studies, subjects' descriptions of their conflicts were coded by the researchers for considerations of justice and care. The researchers, in essence, were coding the language used by the subjects to describe their conflicts. It is possible that the language used by the subjects in their own descriptions truly differed and was not tapped by the methodology of this study. However, Gilligan may have encountered the same confound that was a concern in this study: women were perhaps presenting somewhat different dilemmas than men, and ones in which the nature of the dilemma pulled more for one orientation than the other. The content analysis in this study did not indicate significant differences in the extent to which the contents of male and female dilemmas were embedded in contexts of care and justice. However, it is difficult to guarantee the equivalence of subject generated dilemmas; an equivalence that would be necessary to address this question. To sort out the influence of the content of the dilemmas, and concentrate on the issue of subject identification of care or justice issues, it would

seem necessary to present standardized dilemmas that are equated or balanced for the extent to which the content is embedded in justice or care contexts.

Moving from gender to sex roles, levels of femininity proved an important influence on considerations of care issues. High scorers on the IDI femininity scale have been characterized as nurturant, affiliative, and self-subordinating (Berzins et al., 1977). It was not surprising, therefore, to find that persons with high levels of femininity rated considerations of care more highly than persons with low levels of femininity. It was interesting, however, that this was true almost exclusively for men, with women high and low on femininity rating considerations of care about the same. Levels of masculinity did not significantly influence care ratings for men or women.

In regard to justice ratings, levels of masculinity did not prove to be an important influence on use of the justice orientation. In understanding this result, we need to return to the definition of the masculinity construct as defined for the IDI. High scorers on the masculinity scale have been described as dominant, instrumental, autonomous, and oriented toward physical risk. Though the characteristic of autonomy can be viewed as part of the noncontextual, removed-in-judgment approach to moral conflict described as the justice orientation, characteristics such as dominance and orientation toward risk are less theoretically related to the justice orientation than the construct of femininity is to the care orientation.

The semantic differential was used in this study to examine the meaning of the justice and care orientations to men and women. The first question of interest was whether the subjects would indicate one orientation to be clearly "better" than the other on any of these dimensions. Examination of the three factors indicates that both orientations were seen as highly positive and of average activity by both women and men. The only significant difference was on the potency factor with the justice orientation being seen as more potent than the care orientation. The three pairs of adjectives that made up this dimension were severe–lenient, masculine–feminine, hard–soft, a very sex role stereotypic set of adjectives. A check of the mean scores revealed that the justice orientation was clearly seen as more masculine and the care orientation as more feminine. Thus, though both orientations were equally valued, one was perceived as a masculine response and one as a feminine response.

Taken together, the findings from this study suggest some gender differences in use of the justice and care orientations but raise questions about the strength and nature of these differences. The complex pattern of findings also raises the question of whether women reported more relationship concerns because they generally cast the conflicts they encounter in those terms' or whether their social context means they experience more conflicts dealing with issues of care than men do.

In the only study in which Gilligan and her colleagues directly compared males and females (Gilligan et al., 1982), subjects' dilemmas were coded for considerations of response and rights but were not equated for content. Thus her conclusions about differences in orientation between males and females may also be largely reflective of the kinds of conflicts her male and female subjects chose to discuss. That female conflicts reflected more considerations of care, and male conflicts reflected more considerations of rights is a significant finding, and should not be minimized, but it may be no more than a reflection of the different arenas and self-definitions out of which the majority of males and females operate. It does not directly address the question of whether, in a given conflict situation, females would focus on issues of relationship, responsibility, and care, and males would focus on issues of rights, rules, and justice. Again, to get at this latter question it seems necessary to return to a standardized dilemma format.

This study provides some support for Gilligan's assertions that females are more attuned to issues of care in moral conflicts and males more attuned to issues of justice. However, it also supports the conclusion that the realm of care is not an exclusively female realm nor justice an exclusively male realm. Brabeck (1983), after surveying the literature on moral reasoning, empathy and altruism, concludes that sex differences in morality are at best minimal and are not consistently found. She raises the question as to why so many people find Gilligan's claims intuitively appealing and believe they speak to an essential truth, even when there is no clear empirical support, or in the case of moral reasoning, there is evidence which contradicts her claims. Her answer is that we may be dealing with a mythic truth rather than an empirical truth. Mentioning studies that found boys and girls to be perceived differently in their helping behaviors when behaving very much the same (Shigetomi, Hartmann, & Gilford, 1981), she suggests we may have some need to perceive males and females as morally different. Indeed, in the present study, males and females did not significantly differ in their use of the two orientations, yet they rated the justice orientation as masculine and the care orientation as feminine. Brabeck suggests this myth meets our emotional and cultural needs.

> There is an essential tension between autonomy and interdependence, between the requirements of justice and the demands of mercy, between absolute moral principles and situation specific moral action, between reason and affect. To resolve this tension by assigning half to males and half to females when evidence does not support that division is to reduce the complexity of morality, to cloud truth with myth, to do an injustice to the capacities of both sexes and to lose an opportunity to revise and modify our theories of morality. (Brabeck, 1983, p. 287)

Though this study indicates there may in fact be some differences in the moral orientations of men and women, the investigator agrees with Brabeck that Gilligan's significant contribution may not be in suggesting that men and women differ in their orientations to moral conflict, but in broadening our definition of what constitutes an adequate description of the moral reasoning process.

References

Berzins, J., Welling, M., & Wetter, R. (1977, July). *The PRF-ANDRO scale users manual-revised.* Unpublished materials, University of Kentucky.

Block, J. H. (1973). Conceptions of sex role: Some cross-cultural, longitudinal perspectives. *American Psychologist, 28*(6), 512–526.

Brabeck, M. (1983). Moral judgment: Theory and research on differences between males and females. *Developmental Review, 3,* 274–291.

Bussey, K., & Maughan, B. (1982). Gender differences in moral reasoning. *Journal of Personality and Social Psychology, 42,* 701–706.

Gilligan, C. (1977). In a different voice: Women's conception of the self and morality. *Harvard Education Review, 47*(4), 481–517.

Gilligan, C. (1982). *In a different voice.* Cambridge, MA: Harvard University Press.

Gilligan, C., Langdale, S., Lyons, N., & Murphy, M. (1982). The contribution of women's thought to developmental theory: The elimination of sex bias in moral development research and education. Final Report: *National Institute of Education.*

Holstein, C. B. (1976). Irreversible, stepwise sequence in the development of moral judgment: A longitudinal study of males and females. *Child Development, 47,* 51–61.

Kohlberg, L. (1971). From is to ought: How to commit the naturalistic fallacy and get away with it in the study of moral development. In T. Mischel (Ed.), *Cognitive development and epistemology.* New York: Academic Press.

Kohlberg, L. (1976). Moral stages and moralization: The cognitive developmental approach. In T. Lickona (Ed.), *Moral development and behavior: Theory, research, and social issues.* New York: Holt, Rinehart & Winston.

Kohlberg, L., & Kramer, R. (1969). Continuities and discontinuities in childhood and adult moral development. *Human Development, 12,* 92–120.

Kuhn, D., Langer, J., Kohlberg, L., & Haan, N. (1977). The development of formal operations in logical and moral judgment. *Genetic Psychology Monographs, 95,* 97–188.

Langdale, S. (1980). Conceptions of morality in developmental psychology: Is there more than justice? Unpublished manuscript, Harvard University.

Maccoby, E., & Jacklin, C. (1974). *The psychology of sex differences.* Stanford: Stanford University Press.

Osgood, C., Suci, G., & Tannenbaum, P. (1957). *The measurement of meaning.* Urbana: University of Illinois Press.

Peters, R. G. (1971). Moral development: A plea for pluralism. In T. Mischel (Ed.), *Cognitive development and epistemology.* New York: Academic Press.

Piaget, J. (1932). *The moral judgment of the child* (M. Gabain, Trans.). New York: Harcourt, Brace and Company.

Poppen, P. J. (1974). The development of sex differences in moral judgment for college males and females. *Dissertation Abstracts International, 35*(2-B), 1108.

Pratt, M. W., & Royer, J. M. (1982). When rights and responsibilities don't mix: Sex and sex-role patterns in moral judgment orientation. *Canadian Journal of Behavioral Science, 14,* 190–214.

Shigetomi, C. C., Hartmann, D. P., & Gilford, D. M. (1981). Sex differences in children's altruistic behavior and reputations for helpfulness. *Developmental Psychology, 17*(4), 434–437.

Simpson, E. L. (1974). Moral development research: A case of scientific cultural bias. *Human Development, 17,* 81–106.

Wike, E. L. (1971). *Data analysis.* Chicago: Aldine-Atherton.

Worell, J., & Worell, L. (1965). Personality conflict, originality of response, and recall. *Journal of Consulting Psychology, 29*(1), 55–62.

Received March 19, 1985
Revision received August 6, 1985 ■

[41]

INTERPERSONAL RELATIONS AND GROUP PROCESSES

Gender, Life Experiences, and Moral Judgment Development: A Process-Oriented Approach

Janet P. Boldizar and Kenneth L. Wilson
Department of Sociology and Social Psychology,
Florida Atlantic University

Deborah Kay Deemer
Office of Research and Evaluation,
Alverno College

The purpose of this study was to reexamine the issue of gender differences in moral development from a process-oriented perspective. We hypothesized that life experiences and value orientations toward those experiences would exert differential influences on the processes (but not necessarily the outcomes) of moral development for women and men. Ss were 52 men and 50 women (mean adult age = 26.8 years) who were tested over a 10-year period spanning from high school (1973) to young adulthood (1983). We used path analysis (using ordinary least squares regression) to estimate the effects of education experiences, occupational experiences, and marriage on Ss' moral judgment development (assessed using Rest's, 1979, Defining Issues Test). Although we found no significant outcome differences between women's and men's adult levels of moral development, education, or occupational attainment, we did find that the processes linking education, occupation, and marriage to adult moral development differed for men and women. We interpreted these results as reflecting the influence of contemporary patterns of sex role socialization on adult processes of moral development.

A critical issue in the area of moral development research was raised by Gilligan's (1977, 1982) claims of gender bias in Kohlberg's theory and measurement of moral development (e.g., 1969, 1976). These charges were based on earlier studies that reported a sex difference favoring men over women in moral reasoning scores (Haan, Langer, & Kohlberg, 1976; Holstein, 1976; Kohlberg & Kramer, 1969). It was argued that, because existing (Kohlbergian) measures of moral judgment focused solely on the male-oriented justice perspective, the female-oriented care perspective of moral judgment was downgraded in the scoring system, resulting in the appearance of female inferiority in moral development.

Despite the intuitive appeal of these claims, their empirical support has been difficult to establish (Brabeck, 1983). Comprehensive reviews of moral development literature have revealed few consistent gender differences in modal stage scores using Kohlberg's production measure of moral judgment (Lifton, 1985; Walker, 1984, 1986b) or in eventual attainment of

principled moral reasoning using Rest's Defining Issues Test (DIT), a comprehension/preference measure of moral judgment based on Kohlberg's theory (Rest, 1979, 1986; Thoma, 1986). Similarly inconclusive results have been reported in tests of differences in moral orientation (Ford & Lowery, 1986; Gibbs, Arnold, & Burkhart, 1984; Rothbart, Hanley, & Albert, 1986; Walker, de Vries, & Trevethan, 1987). Although differences have been reported in the consistency of men's and women's respective use of justice and care orientations, both orientations have been found to characterize both men's and women's thinking about moral issues.

Thus, despite more than a decade of empirical studies that have attempted to demonstrate gender differences in moral judgment development, few reliable differences have been reported. This lack of significant findings may simply mean that there are, in fact, no differences in women's and men's moral development. Alternatively, past research may not have looked in the right places. In the present study, we propose an alternative approach to the study of the relation between gender and moral judgment development that is not dependent on gender differences in moral development outcomes that are static representations of an individual's current reasoning. Rather, our approach is an attempt to view moral development as a dynamic social process that may be differentially affected by the socialization and life experiences of the individual. We propose to explore gender differences in the ways in which different life

We are grateful to James Rest for his generous assistance in obtaining the data used in this study. We also extend our thanks to Harry Reis and the anonymous reviewers for their helpful comments on earlier versions of this article.

Correspondence concerning this article should be addressed to Janet P. Boldizar, who is now at the Department of Psychology, University of Alabama, UAB Station, Birmingham, Alabama 35294.

Journal of Personality and Social Psychology. 1989. Vol. 57, No. 2, 229–238
Copyright 1989 by the American Psychological Association, Inc. 0022-3514/89/$00.75

experiences contribute to, or detract from, men's and women's moral judgment development.[1]

This approach is consistent with Deaux's (1984) analysis of gender research in the past decade. She noted that approaches focusing on sex as a subject or personality variable have made important, but limited, contributions to researchers' understanding of the relation between gender and social behavior. Furthermore, Deaux concluded that advances in this area would require a conceptual shift away from static views of gender and toward a process-oriented approach that treats gender-related phenomena as part of the larger social interactional context in which they occur.

The idea that different types of life experiences can affect the process of moral development is not new. Kohlberg (1969) initially proposed that role taking and conceptual conflict in interpersonal settings formed the basis of sociomoral experiences that made important contributions to the development of moral reasoning. Subsequent studies have confirmed the link between life experiences such as education and occupation and rate of moral development (e.g., Colby, Kohlberg, Gibbs, & Lieberman, 1983; Rest, 1979, 1986; Walker, 1986a). Further research into the nature of the effects of these variables found that global value orientations toward both education and occupation were significant predictors of moral judgment development (Deemer, 1986; Rest, 1986).

In the present study, we used path analysis (using ordinary least squares regression) to estimate the effects of educational experiences, occupational experiences, and marriage on women's and men's moral judgment development over a 10-year period between high school and early adulthood. We hypothesized that, to the extent that behavioral and psychological expectancies associated with the interpersonal life experiences of women and men are influenced by gender stereotypes and reinforced by traditional patterns of sex role socialization (cf. Deaux, 1984), these experiences would differ in the contributions they would make to male and female models of moral judgment development. In the following sections, we suggest ways in which women and men might differ in the process of moral judgment development in each of these three life experiences.

Education

The fact that formal education plays a substantial role in moral judgment development is well-documented (Colby et al., 1983; Rest, 1986) and has been theoretically linked to general intellectual stimulation as well as to exposure to and reflection on social and moral issues in formal and informal interpersonal settings (Rest & Thoma, 1985). Colby et al. (1983) also pointed out that the effects of education cannot be explained as simple reflections of IQ or socioeconomic status, because the correlation between education and moral judgment (in their longitudinal sample at age 28) was still significant with both IQ and socioeconomic status partialed out.

Walker (1986a) has reported that, although education was a significant predictor for both sexes, it was more strongly correlated with men's moral development than with women's moral development. In addition, Baumrind (1986) found that, among those who earned graduate degrees, men used significantly more postconventional reasoning than did women. In contrast,

among those who did not pursue higher education, men scored lower in moral reasoning than did women with similarly low levels of education. These findings led us to predict that educational experiences would have a stronger effect on men's moral development than they would on women's moral development.

Occupation

A second major focus in the life experiences of young adults is work. Because higher status occupations are often characterized by increased autonomy that may afford opportunities to participate in decision making and conflict resolution, they may be more likely than lower status occupations to facilitate the development of higher justice perspectives. That is, taking into consideration the rights and welfare of diverse groups of individuals who may be affected by one's judgments could be conducive to the development of higher sociomoral perspectives characteristic of principled moral reasoning. A moderate relation has, in fact, been reported between occupational status and moral development (Colby et al., 1983). We expected, however, that the effects of status on moral judgment would be mediated by the extent to which subjects identified with and were involved in the work experience. Those subjects whose careers provided a sense of identity and personal fulfillment were expected to reap the greatest benefits (in terms of moral development) from the work experience.

Although no studies to date have examined whether there are gender differences in the impact of occupational experiences on moral development, research into the relation between work experiences and psychological functioning has revealed some gender differences relevant to our study. Mortimer, Finch, and Maruyama (1988) found that, among young adults (aged 20–33 years), the stability of women's income and work experiences (i.e., the likelihood of working for the same employer), assessed longitudinally over a 4-year period (between 1973–1977), was lower than men's. These findings suggest that occupational experiences may be less central to the life experiences of younger women and thus would have a weaker impact on women's moral judgment development than on men's.

Marriage

The final aspect of the life experiences of young adults that we chose to include in our model was marriage. Although this factor has not been examined in previous studies, there are sound theoretical reasons for including it in the present study. Because of the intimate interpersonal nature of the marriage relationship, marriage can be expected to afford many unique opportunities for role taking and conflict resolution in situa-

---

[1] The distinction we make between outcomes and processes of moral development is not intended to parallel the content/structure distinction that has been a controversial focus of much moral development research (cf. Nisan, 1984). Rather, we use these terms to call attention to the fact that whereas outcomes are static measurements that differentiate between levels of adult development at a single point in time, processes are the unique configurations of dynamic social and psychological experiences that underlie these differences (or similarities) in developmental endpoints.

tions of joint decision making (requiring the adoption of perspectives of other family members to arrive at just solutions to family problems) that would be expected to exert an influence on the process of moral development. Moreover, marriage is an experience that is particularly relevant to the issue of how stereotypic expectancies about sex roles may contribute to gender differences in the process of moral development. Many studies have reported that husbands generally have greater power in the marital relationship than wives (although this pattern seems to be somewhat moderated in relationships in which husbands and wives approach equality in earning power; Blumstein & Schwartz, 1983; Duncan & Duncan, 1978; England & Farkas, 1986) and that wives typically perform the majority of routine household chores regardless of whether they also work outside of the home (Nyquist, Slivkin, Spence, & Helmreich, 1985; Pleck, 1985). These findings suggest that married women (especially those who work outside the home) might not only have less time and opportunity to explore new roles and pursue personal development, but also may experience marriage as a state of reduced autonomy in which their opportunities to engage in joint decision making and conflict resolution are to some degree suppressed within the relationship. We therefore predicted that marriage would contribute less to women's moral development than it would to men's moral development.

Theoretical Model

Our theoretical model of moral judgment development is diagrammed in Figure 1. The model includes variables that measure education-related experiences (high school academic orientation, dedication to educational goals, and educational attainment), variables that measured occupation-related experiences (dedication to career goals, occupational attainment, and career fulfillment), and marriage. The model also includes a measure of high school moral judgment, which provided a baseline for estimating the contributions of prior moral judgment development to the life experiences and attitudes of young adulthood and allowed us to be able to separate these effects from those hypothesized to exist between the variables of interest and moral judgment development a decade after high school. The specification of the structural model was based on a logical reconstruction of the life processes measured by the model that took into account the meaning and approximate timing of the variables.

On the basis of reports of significant levels of stability in individual differences in moral reasoning between the mid- to late-teen years and the late twenties (Colby et al., 1983), we predicted that moral judgment in adolescence (P1) would exert a moderate direct influence on moral judgment in young adulthood (P2). We also expected to find a correlation between P1 and high school academic orientation because earlier studies have reported a moderate but significant relation between school achievement measures and the DIT (Rest, 1979). The path linking educational experiences to adult moral judgment development began with high school academic orientation. We predicted that those who were academically involved in high school would be more likely to be dedicated to the pursuit of higher education. Dedication and hard work in college were expected to predict educational attainment, which was hypothe

sized to make a direct contribution to moral judgment development in adulthood. The path linking occupational experiences to adult moral judgment development began with dedication to career goals and educational attainment, which were expected to predict occupational attainment. We did not, however, expect to find a direct path between occupational attainment and moral judgment development; rather, we predicted that occupational status effects would be indirectly linked to moral development through career fulfillment, a measure of meaningful involvement in one's work. Finally, we predicted that the opportunities for role taking and conflict resolution within the intimate interpersonal settings afforded by the marriage relationship would exert a direct influence on moral judgment development.

This general model served as a guide in our separate analyses of the male and female models. These models were expected to differ in accordance with the gender hypotheses described earlier. In general, we expected that moral judgment development would be more strongly determined by all three life experiences—education, occupation, and marriage—in the male model than they would be in the female model.

Method

Subjects

The 102 participants in this study were a subsample of Rest's (1979) longitudinal sample drawn from a mixture of urban and rural midwestern communities. The original sample consisted of 237 individuals, of whom approximately half were men and half were women. The severe reduction in sample size over the 10-year period occurred for a number of reasons: Identification numbers could not be linked with the name of the participant or high school testing data was unusable (53 cases), the participant could not be located (60 cases), a mutually agreeable interview time could not be arranged (10 cases), or the person declined to participate (12 cases). At the time of the initial contact, individuals were offered either $25 or a selection of books, which they received on completion of all testing materials.

The 52 men and 50 women in our study were first tested as high school students in the years 1972–1974 and were recontacted in 1983. They represented a roughly even distribution of gender across a diversity of educational backgrounds: 10 had no formal education beyond high school (5 men, 5 women), 17 attended technical school (9 men, 8 women), 22 completed fewer than 2 years of college (10 men, 12 women), 11 completed 2 or more years of college (5 men, 6 women), 28 were college graduates (15 men, 13 women), and 14 attended graduate school (8 men, 6 women). Forty-nine individuals were currently married (29 men, 20 women); 5 of these were remarried following an earlier divorce (2 men, 3 women). Of those who were classified as unmarried, 6 were divorced (4 men, 2 women).

Procedure

Participants were contacted by phone. If they agreed to participate they were sent a letter that explained the rationale and procedures of the experiment and a formal consent form. Before they were to be interviewed, participants were also mailed a packet of materials to complete and return to the interviewer. The packet included the DIT (Rest, 1979; see the next section for a description of this questionnaire) and a complete time-line questionnaire requesting information about influential individuals, living arrangements, and major life events throughout the period between 1972–1974 and 1983. They then participated in an ex

232 J. BOLDIZAR, K. WILSON, AND D. DEEMER

tensive, structured interview concerning major life experiences from the time of high school through young adulthood.

The interviewers (one woman, one man) were blind to any hypotheses about sex and to the participants' DIT scores. The interview was guided by an interview script that had been pilot-tested on 4 men and 4 women with diverse educational backgrounds (2 graduate students, 3 college seniors, 2 individuals with fewer than 2 years of college, and 1 individual who did not continue in formal education beyond high school).

We developed a coding manual with detailed descriptions of codes for the variables to be rated. Deborah Kay Deemer was primarily responsible for transcribing and coding the interviews. To establish reliability, a female college student who was blind to all hypotheses and to the participants' DIT scores was asked to independently score 24 transcribed interviews. These interviews were randomly selected from the total sample and then previewed by one of the authors to ensure that they included an adequate range of levels-of-experience codes and DIT scores, as well as a balanced demographic representation of the sample. No changes in the randomly drawn sample were necessary to ensure this diversity. We used two indexes for assessing agreement in coding: raw interrater percent agreement and Cohen's kappa. For the variables of high school academic orientation, dedication to education/career, and career fulfillment the interrater agreements were 90%, 79%, and 88%, respectively; Cohen's kappas were .85, .67, and .80, respectively.

Measurement of Variables

Moral judgment measurement: P1 and P2. The DIT was developed by Rest (1979) as an objective measure of moral judgment. This instrument is based on Kohlberg's (1969) cognitive developmental theory of moral development and consists of six hypothetical dilemmas. The subject is asked first to decide on an appropriate solution to the dilemma and then to rate the importance of 12 issue statements in resolving the dilemma. The majority of these statements represent Kohlberg's six stages of moral development; the remainder serve as reliability checks. Finally, the subject is asked to rank the 4 most important statements. The DIT score used in the present research is the P-score, which is the weighted sum of the ranked principled (i.e., Stage 5 or 6) choices made by the subject across the six DIT dilemmas. Alternative ways to combine the data from the six dilemmas have been examined with hundreds of data sets. The weighted sum of principled choices was found to be most generalizable across data sets. Rest (1979) reported internal con-

sistency and test–retest reliabilities for the DIT in the high 0.70s and low 0.80s. P1 was the DIT P-score assessed in the first interview wave (1972–1974); P2 was the DIT P-score assessed in 1983. P1 scores ranged from 4 to 40; P2 scores ranged from 6 to 48.

Career fulfillment. This variable reflected a judgment about the extent to which subjects were invested in meaningful work that provided a sense of career identity. *Career identity* was defined as "awareness of one's capabilities and interests, and movement toward the utilization of these in the career" (Deemer, 1986, p. 22). Responses were coded on a scale ranging from 5 to 1, on which

> 5 = individuals who had identified a career that they found challenging and meaningful; their career meant something to them that was part of their identity.
>
> 4 = individuals who had made a commitment to a career field but were currently in transition between school and work or still in school.
>
> 3 = individuals who had no career identity, never planned to have a career, or were unable to succeed in their field; they worked to earn a living but were not invested in or did not identify with their work.
>
> 2 = individuals who suffered from job insecurity characterized by prolonged unemployment or work in fields that were constantly under the threat of layoffs.
>
> 1 = individuals who did no meaningful work or who had no independent income.

Occupational attainment. This was a measure of the participant's 1983 occupation, scaled according to the Duncan Socioeconomic Index.

Educational attainment. This variable was scored on a six-item scale representing the highest level of education attained by 1983. Values were assigned as follows: 6 = graduate school, 5 = college graduate, 4 = 2 or more years of college, 3 = fewer than 2 years of college, 2 = technical school, 1 = no formal education beyond high school.

Dedication to education/career. This variable focused on the years after high school and was a combination of two scored interview items, "educational orientation" for college students only and "career orientation" for those who did not attend college and who were just beginning their occupational careers. The two items were not available separately for this research. In both interview questions, participants were asked

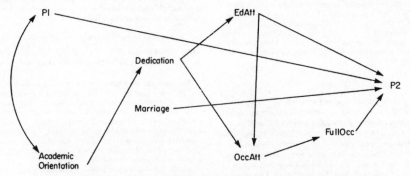

Figure 1. General theoretical model of moral judgment development. (P1 = moral judgment in adolescence, EdAtt = educational attainment, OccAtt = occupational attainment, FullOcc = fulfilling career, P2 = moral judgment in young adulthood.)

how actively they were involved in pursuing their work or educational goals. College students were asked how much time and effort they devoted to educational pursuits. Those who did not attend college were asked how strongly motivated they were to do well in their work. Both items were measured and were rated on a scale ranging from 3 to 1, on which

> 3 = individuals who worked hard at their studies or career goals, professed a desire to learn or advance in a career, and chose friends who were serious students or who were career oriented.
>
> 2 = individuals who were less involved in the pursuit of educational or career goals and chose more modest goals that did not reflect a strong desire for advancement.
>
> 1 = individuals who were confused about educational or career goals, were not invested in developing a career or in the academic side of college life, and chose friends that reflected these values.

Academic orientation. This was an interview item that asked to what extent the person was invested in the academic aspects of high school. The concept behind this question was similar to that for dedication but was measured for the high school years. The item was scored on a 3-point scale, on which

> 3 = individuals who got good grades, studied hard, cared about school, and enjoyed reading.
>
> 2 = individuals who did their school work and were satisfied with average grades, but for whom academics took a backseat to athletics, a job, or social activities.
>
> 1 = individuals who reported little or no concern for academics in high school, made below average grades, disliked reading, and were only interested in jobs, athletics, and parties.

Statistical Procedures

We performed a basic simultaneous equations analysis (path analysis) using ordinary least squares regression. The analysis was conducted in two stages: (a) estimation of the theoretical model and (b) subsequent empirical testing of postulated theoretical relations in the manner suggested by Heise (1969) and Reis (1982).

For overidentified models, as is the case here, testing is done in two steps: (a) postulated paths are tested for significance, and (b) omitted paths are tested for nonsignificance. The latter test is based on the implicit assertion that every omitted path between an endogenous variable and a causally prior variable is mediated by the other variables in the system. The accuracy of such assertions can be tested for each endogenous variable by simply comparing the R^2s of the theoretically specified model with those produced by reentering omitted paths. Those variables that significantly increase the R^2 must be represented in the final model with direct paths. We report the final models, along with the direct and indirect effects estimated using Wolfe and Ethington's (1985) GEMINI program.[2]

Results

Means, standard deviations, and zero-order correlations for both subsamples are reported in Table 1. Although we present this information primarily as background for the main analyses, there were some gender differences worth noting. The means of the two high school variables, moral judgment development (P1) and academic orientation, were significantly lower for women than for men. The P1 mean for women was more than 3 points lower than that for men, $t(100) = 1.98$, $p < .05$ (two-tailed), and the mean academic orientation for women was less than half of that for men, $t(100) = 2.55$, $p < .02$ (two-tailed).

These differences are especially interesting in light of the fact that there were no gender differences in the educational, occupational, or moral judgment attainments assessed in 1983, and men and women did not differ significantly in any of the global value orientations or in marital status.

Table 2 presents the standardized direct and indirect coefficients for the female and male models. Those coefficients that made a significant contribution to either model are included. The *t* test for significant subsample differences is reported in Wilson (1980). All tests for significant differences between subsamples were conducted with the metric coefficients.[3] They are not included in the table because the standardized coefficients are more readily interpretable and reflect all the differences found with metric coefficients.

An examination of the coefficients of determination confirms our general expectation that the female model of moral judgment development would be less determined than the male model. The female model explains 46% of the variation in P2, whereas the male model explains 52%; omitting P1 (which was included primarily as a baseline referent) from the equation leaves R^2s of .41 and .50 for women and men, respectively. Although these results are in the predicted direction, they are not significantly different.

We did, however, find evidence that the life experiences of men and women differ significantly in their effects on moral judgment development. The total number of estimated direct effects was 15, and 6 of the effects in the female and male models differed at $p < .05$, with another 4 effects differing at $p < .10$. Thus, two thirds of the effects in the two models were different. The differences in the direct effects also produced several significantly different indirect effects. The processes linking education, occupation, and marriage to moral development are illustrated in Figures 2 and 3, which present the final models for women and men, respectively. In these models we have excised the insignificant effects that were included in Table 2 for purposes of statistical comparison of the two subsamples. Thus, this final reestimation of coefficients included only those effects that were significant within each model, rather than across the two models. We decided to include those paths in the models that were significant at the $p < .10$ level because of the relatively small sample sizes. In the following sections, we discuss each of the three processes as they relate to each model.

Education and Moral Judgment Development

Our model predicted that P1 would be correlated with academic orientation in high school and that academic orientation

---

[2] The magnitude of indirect effects is estimated by multiplying the coefficients of an indirect causal chain (such as x-a-b-y) and adding that result to the results of similar multiplications for any other alternative causal sequences (such as x-a-c-y). The result is the total indirect effect, and adding that amount to the direct effect yields the "total" effect. The examination of indirect effects focuses our attention on the "systemic" quality of our theorizing and on the interrelations or processes existing between variables as a complementary perspective to a focus on the final outcome, the dependent variable.

[3] Interpretations of subsample differences should usually be made using the metric coefficients, as the standardized coefficients are subject to bias resulting from any significant differences in variable variances across populations.

J. BOLDIZAR, K. WILSON, AND D. DEEMER

Table 1

Means, Standard Deviations, and Zero-Order Correlations for Female (Above the Diagonal) and Male (Below the Diagonal) Subsamples

Variables	1	2	3	4	5	6	7	8	M	SD
1. P1	—	.310	.133	−.187	.407	.332	.203	.550	19.6	9.10
2. Academic orientation	.232	—	.070	−.383	.244	.090	.002	.361	0.180	.388
3. Dedication	.296	.541	—	.122	.139	.260	.300	.254	1.9	.678
4. Marriage	.181	−.056	.005	—	−.232	.039	.159	−.320	0.400	.495
5. Educational attainment	.196	.363	.552	−.147	—	.572	.375	.491	3.64	1.56
6. Occupational attainment	.388	.243	.383	.088	.378	—	.577	.411	506	248
7. Fulfilling career	.189	.457	.527	.149	.365	.273	—	.278	3.72	1.07
8. P2	.342	.341	.543	.073	.527	.352	.607	—	25.7	9.05
M	22.8	0.404	2.135	0.558	3.75	516	3.38	26.6		
SD	7.37	0.495	0.817	0.502	1.63	190	1.22	8.63		

Note. P1 = moral judgment in adolescence, P2 = moral judgment in young adulthood.

would influence a sense of dedication to educational goals. Dedication was expected to promote educational attainment, which was expected to make a significant contribution to adult moral judgment development. The male model conformed nicely to these predictions. P1 and academic orientation were correlated, and both were significant predictors of dedication (although the latter variable was by far the stronger of the two). P1 also had a direct effect on men's P2 scores. Dedication was subsequently

Table 2

Standardized Direct and Indirect Effects for Model of Moral Judgment Development by Gender

Dependent variables and gender	Independent variables							
	P1	Academic orientation	Dedication	Marriage	Educational attainment	Occupational attainment	Full career	R²
Dedication								
Female	.124	.032 ⎤						.019
Male	.180*	.478*** ⎦						.324
Marriage								
Female	−.075 ⎤	−.359*** ⎤						.151
Male	.205 ⎦	−.104 ⎦						.043
Educational attainment								
Female	.395*** ⎤		.086					.173
Male	.036 ⎦		.541*** ⎦					.324
(indirect)								
Female	.011	.003						
Male	.098*	.270*** ⎦						
Occupational attainment								
Female	.103		.176*		.506*** ⎤			.369
Male	.293**		.172		.226 ⎦			.265
(indirect)								
Female	.227** ⎤	.007 ⎤	.044					
Male	.061 ⎦	.147** ⎦	.122*					
Fulfilling career								
Female		−.011 ⎤	.148	.116		.535*** ⎤		.372
Male		.253** ⎦	.368***	.156*		.057 ⎦		.349
(indirect)								
Female	.186**	−.033 ⎤	.118*		.271*** ⎤			
Male	.118*	.176** ⎦	.017		.013 ⎦			
P2								
Female	.371***	.171*		−.237** ⎤	.221		.106 ⎤	.461
Male	.170*	.125		.023 ⎦	.281**		.403*** ⎦	.521
(indirect)								
Female	.149**	.086* ⎤	.047 ⎤	.012	.029	.057		
Male	.112*	.309*** ⎦	.307*** ⎦	.063	.005	.023		

Note. P1 = moral judgment development in adolescence, P2 = moral judgment development in young adulthood. Brackets denote coefficients that differ significantly between the two subsamples beyond $p < .10$ level.
* $p < .10$. ** $p < .05$. *** $p < .01$.

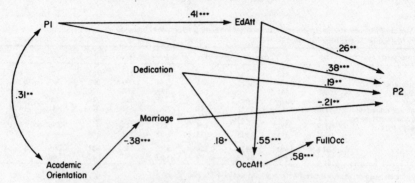

Figure 2. Final model of women's moral judgment development. (PI = moral judgment in adolescence, EdAtt = educational attainment, OccAtt = occupational attainment, FullOcc = fullfilling career, P2 = moral judgment in young adulthood. *p < .10. **p < .05. ***p < .01.)

a strong determinant of men's educational attainment, and educational attainment made a significant contribution to their moral development. Thus, dedication to goals played an important indirect role in men's moral judgment development through educational attainment (as well as through career fulfillment).

In the female model, PI was also correlated with academic orientation, but the latter variable failed to produce any significant influence on either dedication to educational goals or educational attainment. However, PI did exert a strong direct effect on women's educational attainment, as well as the most powerful direct effect on P2 in the female model. In addition, dedication was not significantly related to education in the female model and was not determined by high school academic orientation. It was, however, a direct predictor of women's moral judgment development. Thus, although educational at-

tainment and PI played a similar direct role in women's and men's moral judgment development, there were large significant differences favoring men in the direct effects of academic orientation on dedication to goals and of dedication to goals on educational attainment. Furthermore, the indirect effects of high school academic orientation and dedication on P2 were also significantly higher for men.

Occupation and Moral Judgment Development

We expected both educational attainment and dedication to the pursuit of career goals to contribute to occupational attainment. Attaining higher status in one's career was expected to afford more opportunities to find meaning and fulfillment in one's work experiences that would lead to moral judgment development. Although educational attainment had a significant

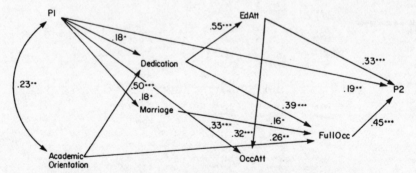

Figure 3. Final model of men's moral judgment development. (PI = moral judgment in adolescence, EdAtt = educational attainment, OccAtt = occupational attainment, FullOcc = fulfilling career, P2 = moral judgment in young adulthood. *p < .10. **p < .05. ***p < .01.)

effect on both men's and women's occupational attainment, this relation was significantly stronger for women. Having a fulfilling career also operated in an entirely different manner for women and men. For women, career dedication did predict occupational attainment, which led to career fulfillment, but neither occupational attainment nor career fulfillment was linked to women's moral judgment development. For men, dedication to career goals did not affect their occupational attainment, but it did have a direct effect on their career fulfillment (along with academic orientation and marriage). More important, having a meaningful career did produce the expected strong effect on P2 in the male model. In sum, although career issues were not directly related to women's moral judgment development, having a fulfilling career was the most powerful predictor of men's moral judgment development.

Marriage and Moral Judgment Development

The final major prediction in the model was that marriage would exert a direct influence on moral judgment development. We found, however, that women with a strong high school academic orientation were less likely to marry, and that marriage exerted a significant negative effect on women's P2 scores even after controlling for the effects of P1, dedication, educational attainment, occupational attainment, and fulfilling career. In contrast, marriage had no appreciable effect on men's moral judgment development.

Discussion

These findings clearly indicate that, although women and men did not differ in adult levels of moral judgment development, they nevertheless differed substantially in the processes that determined moral judgment development in adulthood. Specifically, we found that educational attainment was a predictor of moral development for both sexes, but that dedication to educational goals and high school academic orientation were important determinants of educational attainment only for men. Dedication and academic orientation were unrelated to educational attainment for women, but dedication had a direct effect on their moral judgment development. Although career fulfillment was the most powerful predictor of moral development in the male model, neither occupational attainment nor career fulfillment was related to women's moral development. Finally, whereas marriage detracted from women's moral judgment development and women with high academic orientations were less likely to marry, marriage had an insignificant effect on men's moral judgment development. We address each of these findings in the following paragraphs.

The first major difference involves the processes that worked through education to determine moral judgment development. Our prediction that educational attainment would exert a stronger influence on men's moral development than it would on women's was not supported. One possible reason why we failed to replicate earlier studies' findings of a gender difference is that subjects in those studies were from older cohorts than were our subjects. (The median ages for the Baumrind, 1986, sample were 38 years for women and 41 years for men; the mean age of the Walker, 1986a, sample was 39 years and ranged from 23 to 84 years of age.) Because of changes in traditional patterns of gender segregation in higher education that have taken place during the decade over which our cohort was studied (Wilson & Boldizar, in press), the women and men in our sample may have had greater opportunities for equal participation and representation in all aspects of the educational experience than did earlier cohorts, thus explaining the lack of a significant gender difference in the impact of educational attainment on moral judgment development.

However, the subjective value orientations toward education did reveal several gender differences. For example, the extent to which men reported that they were involved in and dedicated to educational goals had an indirect effect on their moral judgment development (primarily through their educational attainment and career fulfillment), whereas women's reported dedication to goals had a direct effect on their moral judgment development but bore no relation at all to their educational attainment. This configuration of results suggests that men's subjective academic orientations toward educational experiences afforded them opportunities for advancement within institutional settings, and these gains made important contributions to men's moral development. On the other hand, the process of women's moral development appears to have been a direct function of hard work and involvement in educational and career goals, independent of any opportunities for advancement these values might have afforded.

The second major difference is found in the processes linking occupational experiences to moral judgment development. As hypothesized, occupational attainment was not directly related to moral development in either model. Also as expected, the extent to which men were identified with, and found meaning and fulfillment in, their occupation was the most powerful direct predictor of their moral development. However, contrary to expectations, career fulfillment was not dependent on occupational status for men, and dedication was the strongest predictor of men's career fulfillment. For women, dedication and hard work predicted occupational status, which in turn led to career fulfillment; however, unlike men, finding meaning and fulfillment in their career did not lead to moral development.

We have no ready explanation for the lack of a relation between occupational attainment and career fulfillment in the male model. However, our hypothesis that younger women's higher levels of job instability (perhaps due to young women's attempts to balance work with home, family responsibilities, or both) would lead to weaker effects of work on women's moral judgment development was generally confirmed. The different configuration of results in the two models indicates that, although women and men may not differ in objective measures of work experiences, the subjective factors that contribute to men's and women's perceptions of career fulfillment hold different meanings (with different implications for moral judgment development) for men and women. Future research will need to focus on more specific work-value indicators to explain these gender differences in the role of occupational experiences in moral development.

One problem in the interpretation of these results is that our measures of work experiences and moral development were assessed concurrently. Although the model hypothesizes that occupational experiences predict moral development, it is also quite possible that moral development leads to more opportunities for career advancement or to the choice of more meaningful or fulfilling careers. Our data indicate that high school moral development (P1) did have a significant impact on occupational attainment, but occupational attainment was not related to adult moral development (P2) in either model. On the other hand, whereas P1 and career fulfillment were only weakly related (in both models), the relation between career fulfillment and P2 was extremely powerful in the male model. It therefore seems likely that it was the perceived level of career fulfillment that affected men's adult moral judgment development rather than the reverse. Kohn and Schooler (1983) have also addressed the issue of reciprocal effects between various job characteristics (e.g., substantive complexity and occupational self-direction) and personality measures (e.g., authoritarian conservatism and self-esteem). They found that the effects of jobs on personality were more likely to be contemporaneous, whereas personality effects on job situations were more likely to be long-term consequences (i.e., lagged effects over a 10-year period). These findings suggest that, in our relatively young adult sample, the more reasonable causal direction is from work experiences to moral development; however, in an older, more work-experienced sample, a reciprocal influence may also be found. This hypothesis will be interesting to test in future longitudinal studies that include older working adults.

Finally, the third major difference between the male and female models of development is in the relation between marriage and moral judgment development. Our data indicate that although marriage did not affect men's moral development, it had a direct negative effect on women's moral development. It is noteworthy that marriage did not detract from women's educational attainment, lower their occupational attainment, or serve as an obstacle to finding a fulfilling career. We also found that women who had a strong academic orientation in high school were less likely to marry. Although the latter finding was not surprising, and is consistent with the stereotype that achievement-oriented women are less likely to pursue traditional female roles associated with early marriage, the former findings were not what we expected.

Clearly, a great deal more research is needed to pinpoint the exact mechanisms through which marriage detracts from women's moral judgment development. Given the relatively youthful age of our sample, age of marriage is one possibility that should be explored. Because the average marriage age of women in our sample was 21.3 years (and 21.6 years for men, both ages below the 1980 averages of 22.1 years for women and 24.6 years for men; Hacker, 1983), the married women in our sample may have had relatively limited opportunities to independently establish their own identities and life-styles before they became immersed in the gender role expectations of the marital relationship. Thus, the extent to which women have independently experienced a variety of social roles in which they have opportunities to engage in joint decision making and role taking prior to marrying may determine whether marriage detracts from the process of their moral judgment development. This hypothesis is consistent with Haan, Smith, and Block's (1968) finding that living independently, rather than with parents or in residences, in conjunction with higher levels of political and social activity,

were significantly correlated with college students' moral reasoning scores.

Another issue related to sex role expectancies within the marriage relationship is that of bearing and raising children. Approximately 65% of the married women in our sample were mothers (and 59% of the married men were fathers). Research suggests that wives are expected to take primary responsibility for child rearing associated with this period in the family cycle (England & Farkas, 1986). Domestic power typically becomes more patriarchal with parenthood (Cowan, 1978; especially as women are more likely to be financially dependent on their husbands at this time), and even the most egalitarian couples tend to revert to traditional gender roles on the arrival of the first child (LaRossa & LaRossa, 1981). The fact that women are expected to take major responsibility for caring for children (in addition to other traditional duties) can also contribute to lower levels of involvement in social and career roles outside of the family (Rossi, 1983).

Because the majority of first marriages occur during the time span examined in our study, early adulthood appears to be a period of particular vulnerability for married women's potential moral judgment development. Indeed, it is notable that some of the most convincing examples of gender differences in modal stage scores of moral development have exclusively examined intact married couples (e.g., Baumrind, 1986; Haan et al., 1976; Holstein, 1976). The models developed in this study point to at least one reason why the differences reported in these studies should not be dismissed.

We have emphasized the strong probability that the age of our sample, as well as the relatively small sample size, restricts the generalizability of specific findings. It is also important to interpret these results in light of the fact that we used Rest's (1979) DIT as our measure of moral judgment. Although its reliability and validity are well established, the DIT is a comprehension/preference measure, in contrast to Kohlberg's production (interview) measure of moral judgment. This difference has been related to a pattern of gender differences on the DIT that, although weak, has consistently favored women (Thoma, 1986). This may have limited the probability that we would find support for a gender bias in moral judgment outcomes that favored men. On the other hand, if we therefore consider the DIT a more conservative means of assessing gender differences in moral judgment development, our finding that marriage significantly detracted from women's development takes on even greater importance.

Despite these caveats, we believe that the process-oriented approach to the study of gender differences in moral judgment development provides a means of resolving some of the controversy that has surrounded this issue. Although we did not test for gender differences in the process of developing a care orientation to moral dilemmas, our findings support Gilligan's (1982) general contention that developmental theories must work to understand and incorporate the life experiences and perspectives of women as well as those of men. At the same time, we also found support for the positions of Rest (1986) and Walker (1984)—among others—who have argued that women's moral development can be adequately assessed on a Kohlbergian-derived measure. We demonstrated that, although women are not morally inferior to men when assessed on these measures, their experiences make contributions to their development that are very different from those of men. It is perhaps those specific experiences that make negative contributions to women's development on Kohlbergian-derived measures (such as marriage) that may be more amenable to measurement on a care-oriented Gilligan-derived measure.

References

Baumrind, D. (1986). Sex differences in moral reasoning: Response to Walker's (1984) conclusion that there are none. *Child Development, 57*, 511–521.

Blumstein, P., & Schwartz, P. (1983). *American couples.* New York: William Morrow.

Brabeck, M. (1983). Moral judgment: Theory and research of differences between males and females. *Developmental Review, 3,* 274–291.

Colby, A., Kohlberg, L., Gibbs, J., & Lieberman, M. (1983). A longitudinal study of moral judgment. *Monographs of the Society for Research in Child Development, 48*(1, Serial No. 200).

Cowan, C. P. (1978). Becoming a family: The impact of a first child's birth on the couple's relationship. In W. B. Miller & L. F. Newman (Eds.), *The first child and family formation.* Chapel Hill: University of North Carolina, Carolina Population Center.

Deaux, K. (1984). From individual differences to social categories: Analysis of a decade's research on gender. *American Psychologist, 39,* 105–116.

Deemer, D. K. (1986). *Life experiences and moral judgment development.* Unpublished doctoral dissertation. University of Minnesota, Minneapolis.

Duncan, B., & Duncan, O. D. (1978). *Sex typing and social roles: A research report.* New York: Academic Press.

England, P., & Farkas, G. (1986). *Households, employment, and gender: A social, economic, and demographic view.* New York: Aldine.

Ford, M. R., & Lowery, C. R. (1986). Gender differences in moral reasoning: A comparison of the use of justice and care orientations. *Journal of Personality and Social Psychology, 50,* 777–783.

Gibbs, J. C., Arnold, K. D., & Burkhart, J. E. (1984). Sex differences in the expression of moral judgment. *Child Development, 55,* 1040–1043.

Gilligan, C. (1977). In a different voice: Women's conception of the self and of morality. *Harvard Educational Review, 47,* 481–517.

Gilligan, C. (1982). *In a different voice: Psychological theory and women's development.* Cambridge, MA: Harvard University Press.

Haan, N., Langer, J., & Kohlberg, L. (1976). Family patterns of moral reasoning. *Child Development, 47,* 1204–1206.

Haan, N., Smith, M. B., & Block, J. (1968). Moral reasoning of young adults: Political-social behavior, family background, and personality correlates. *Journal of Personality and Social Psychology, 10,* 183–201.

Hacker, A. (1983). *U/S: A statistical portrait of the American people.* New York: Viking Press.

Heise, D. R. (1969). Problems in path analysis and causal inference. In E. F. Borgatta & G. W. Bohrnstedt (Eds.), *Sociological methodology 1969* (pp. 37–73). San Francisco: Jossey-Bass.

Holstein, C. B. (1976). Irreversible, stepwise sequence in the development of moral judgment: A longitudinal study of males and females. *Child Development, 47,* 51–61.

Kohlberg, L. (1969). Stage and sequence: The cognitive-developmental approach to socialization. In D. A. Goslin (Ed.), *Handbook of socialization theory and research* (pp. 347–480). Chicago: Rand McNally.

Kohlberg, L. (1976). Moral stages and moralization: The cognitive-developmental approach. In T. Lickona (Ed.), *Moral development and behavior: Theory, research, and social issues.* New York: Holt, Rinehart & Winston.

Kohlberg, L., & Kramer, R. (1969). Continuities and discontinuities in childhood and adult moral development. *Human Development, 12,* 93–120.

Kohn, M. L., & Schooler, C. (1983). Job conditions and personality: A longitudinal assessment of their reciprocal effects. In M. L. Kohn & C. Schooler (Eds.), *Work and personality: An inquiry into the impact of social stratification* (pp. 125–153). Norwood, NJ: Ablex Publishing.

LaRossa, R., & LaRossa, M. M. (1981). *Transition to parenthood: How infants change families.* Beverly Hills, CA: Sage.

Lifton, P. D. (1985). Individual differences in moral development: The relation of sex, gender, and personality to morality. *Journal of Personality, 53,* 306–334.

Mortimer, J. T., Finch, M. D., & Maruyama, G. (1988). Work experience and job satisfaction: Variation by age and gender. In J. T. Mortimer & K. M. Borman (Eds.), *Work experience and psychological development through the life span* (pp. 109–156). Boulder, CO: Westview Press.

Nisan, M. (1984). Content and structure in moral judgment: An integrative view. In W. M. Kurtines & J. L. Gewirtz (Eds.) *Morality, moral behavior, and moral development* (pp. 208–224). New York: Wiley.

Nyquist, L., Slivkin, K., Spence, J. T., & Helmreich, R. (1985). Household responsibilities in middle-class couples: The contribution of demographic and personality variables. *Sex Roles, 12,* 15–34.

Pleck, J. H. (1985). *Working wives/working husbands.* Beverly Hills, CA: Sage.

Reis, H. T. (1982). An introduction to the use of structural equations: Prospects and problems. In L. Wheeler (Ed.), *Review of personality and social psychology: 3* (pp. 258–284). Beverly Hills, CA: Sage.

Rest, J. R. (1979). *Development in judging moral issues.* Minneapolis: University of Minnesota Press.

Rest, J. R. (1986). *Moral development: Advances in research and theory.* New York: Praeger.

Rest, J. R., & Thoma, S. J. (1985). Relation of moral judgment development to formal education. *Developmental Psychology, 21,* 709–714.

Rossi, A. S. (1983). Transition to parenthood. In A. S. Skolnick & J. H. Skolnick (Eds.), *Family in transition.* Boston: Little, Brown.

Rothbart, M. K., Hanley, D., & Albert, M. (1986). Gender differences in moral reasoning. *Sex Roles, 15,* 645–653.

Thoma, S. J. (1986). Estimating gender differences in the comprehension and preference of moral issues. *Developmental Review, 6,* 165–180.

Walker, L. J. (1984). Sex differences in the development of moral reasoning: A critical review. *Child Development, 55,* 677–691.

Walker, L. J. (1986a). Experiential and cognitive sources of moral development in adulthood. *Human Development, 29,* 113–124.

Walker, L. J. (1986b). Sex differences in the development of moral reasoning: A rejoinder to Baumrind. *Child Development, 57,* 522–526.

Walker, L. J., de Vries, B., & Trevethan, S. D. (1987). Moral stages and moral orientations in real-life and hypothetical dilemmas. *Child Development, 58,* 842–858.

Wilson, K. L. (1980). On the practical value of causal modeling: I. Estimating contextual effects. *The Journal of Applied Behavioral Science, 16,* 107–114.

Wilson, K. L., & Boldizar, J. B. (in press). Tradition and change: Influences of aspirations, mathematics achievement, and income on gender segregation in higher education. *Sociology of Education.*

Wolfe, L. M., & Ethington, C. A. (1985). GEMINI: Program for analysis of structural equations with standard errors of indirect effects. *Behavioral Research Methods, Instruments, and Computers, 17,* 581–584.

Received April 11, 1988
Revision received February 28, 1989
Accepted March 3, 1989 ∎

[42]

VIEWPOINT

On *In a Different Voice:*
An Interdisciplinary Forum

Linda K. Kerber, Catherine G. Greeno and Eleanor E. Maccoby, Zella Luria, Carol B. Stack, and Carol Gilligan

Some Cautionary Words for Historians

Linda K. Kerber

In a Different Voice is a study of psychological theory written by psychologist Carol Gilligan. It makes only a single, brief reference to women's history. Nevertheless, the book has been widely read and often acclaimed by historians, some of whom now seem to be attempting to integrate its findings and suggestions into their own scholarship. Since most of this

---

EDITOR'S NOTE: *Often* Signs *creates a cross-disciplinary dialogue among feminists simply by publishing articles from a variety of disciplines on adjoining pages. This symposium, however, is an example of a more truly interdisciplinary exchange, as it allows the perspective and knowledge of scholars from a range of fields to bring into focus different aspects of the same issues. Here, too, this meeting of ideas generates real controversy: are there meaningful sex differences in female and male moral development? Interesting as well is a related question: does the style of this forum itself represent a new academic "voice," a break from the male-dominated tradition of confrontational debate? The reader will have to decide.—* CAROL NAGY JACKLIN

[Signs: Journal of Women in Culture and Society 1986, vol. 11, no. 2]

work is at the prepublication stage, appearing at present in working papers and discussed in professional conversations, the following remarks are intended to encourage second thoughts and a more careful reading of Gilligan's work.

Like feminist historians, Gilligan criticizes the long-established pattern in academic research of establishing norms based on men's experience alone. Building on the theories of Nancy Chodorow and other ego psychologists, Gilligan stresses the necessarily different early experiences of girls, who understand at a very young age that they are like their mothers, and boys, whose first psychic task is to learn that they are not and can never grow up to be like their mothers. The socializing effects of this contrast create gender differences: for boys, "a self defined through separation"; for girls, "a self delineated through connection."[1] The tasks of adolescents are therefore markedly different as well. Adolescent boys need to learn to manage relationships despite their basic and central sense of separation and individuality while girls must struggle to establish a separate identity while maintaining relationships. Ultimately, Gilligan argues, men and women claim different moral imperatives: women feel "a responsibility to discern and alleviate the 'real and recognizable trouble' of this world" while men's moral imperative "appears rather as an injunction to respect the rights of others" (p. 100).

Although Gilligan calls for studies of other ethical dilemmas (p. 126) and reminds her readers that we should all seek an ethics both of justice and of care (pp. 62–63), the primary research on which the book rests is a study of women—and only women—confronting a decision about abortion. But it cannot be surprising that themes of responsibility and care emerge in women's articulation of their concerns about abortion. Gilligan alleges that the tendency to see "moral dilemmas in terms of conflicting responsibilities" (p. 105) is a distinct characteristic of women's decision making, but conflicting responsibilities—to oneself, to the fetus, to its father, to one's own parents and family—are necessarily embedded in a decision on abortion. The theme of care is equally present; if a pregnancy is chosen, the child's need for care will transform the mother's life. The conclusions that Gilligan reports are implicit in the central question of the project itself.

Meanwhile, we are given no accompanying study of men's responses to a similar challenge. Do not men also in some circumstances find themselves similarly stretched on the rack between selfishness and responsibility? Were we to listen to men during their process of decision on, say, draft resistance, might we not also hear similarly anguished contem-

---

1. Carol Gilligan, *In a Different Voice: Psychological Theory and Women's Development* (Cambridge, Mass.: Harvard University Press, 1982), p. 35; hereafter cited in parentheses in the text.

plation of their responsibility to their families, to the needs of those who depend on them for care?

Despite Gilligan's occasional explicit warnings that her work is preliminary and the implicit warning that broad generalization is dangerous from experimental work done on such a small scale—one quite interesting study of self-concept includes only five women and nine men (pp. 158 ff.)—the argument that women define themselves through relationships with others, through a web of relationships of intimacy and care rather than through a hierarchy based on separation and self-fulfillment, runs as a leitmotif through the book, giving it much of its structure and much of its attractiveness.

In a Different Voice is part of a major feminist redefinition of social vocabulary. What was once dismissed as gossip can now be appreciated as the maintenance of oral tradition; what was once devalued as mere housewifery can be understood as social reproduction and a major contribution to the gross national product. Gilligan is invigorating in her insistence that behavior once denigrated as waffling, indecisive, and demeaningly "effeminate" ought rather to be valued as complex, constructive, and humane. Yet this historian, at least, is haunted by the sense that we have heard this argument before, vested in different language. Some variants of it are as old as Western civilization itself; central to the traditions of our culture has been the ascription of reason to men and feeling to women. This bifurcated view of reality can easily be traced at least to classical Greece, where men were understood to realize themselves best in the public sector, the polis, and women in domesticity. Ancient tradition has long been reinforced by explicit socialization that arrogated public power to men and relegated women to domestic concerns, a socialization sometimes defended by argument from expediency, sometimes by argument from biology. Although now Gilligan appears to be adding argument from psychology, her study infers at times that gendered behavior is biologically determined and at others that it, too, is learned, albeit at an earlier stage of socialization than previous analysts had assumed.

A more recent version of this dualism, prevalent in the nineteenth and early twentieth centuries, is the doctrine of "separate spheres." Nearly twenty years ago, Barbara Welter pointed to a pervasive descriptive language by which women were measured, "the cult of true womanhood." This language located woman's "proper sphere" in the home and associated with it the cardinal virtues of domesticity, piety, purity, and submissiveness. Women were understood to realize themselves through care for their families and through nurturance of relationships within them. Such rigid role definition may also have been a mode by which middle-class women maintained their upwardly mobile state. "It is no accident," Gerda Lerner wrote in 1969, "that the slogan 'woman's place is in the home' took on a certain aggressiveness and shrillness precisely at the time when increasing numbers of poorer women *left* their homes to become factory workers."[2]

Ten years ago, Carroll Smith-Rosenberg gave a new understanding to this separation of spheres when she argued that it had made possible psychologically sustaining relationships among women and had been congruent with strong bonds of female friendship, affection, and love.[3] As interpreted by Smith-Rosenberg, and many historians who wrote after her, the separation of spheres could offer advantages as well as the disadvantages emphasized by Welter. It could sustain a distinctive women's culture which embraced creativity in the domestic arts, distinctive forms of labor, and particular patterns of nurturing relationships. For the last decade a rich literature and a lively debate among historians have explored the nuances of this nineteenth-century ideology: Was it constraining to women? Should it be understood as a way in which a culture coped defensively with social change and the transformation of the Industrial Revolution? Ought the "separate female sphere" be understood as a source of strength for women, a psychic room of their own?

Although she makes no mention of it, Gilligan actually enters the dialogue about the separation of spheres. Her formulations suggest that what was once called a separate sphere of nurture and self-sacrifice was in fact personality called into existence by women's distinctive psychological development rather than a result of explicit socialization. Her conclusion that women "define their identity through relationships of intimacy and care" (p. 164) is congruent with claims made in the nineteenth century in defense of a separate sphere for women.

In her single use of historical argument, Gilligan suggests that when Mary Wollstonecraft and Elizabeth Cady Stanton called for self-development and self-respect they were in effect saying that the search for identity through relationships of intimacy and care had gone far enough; that is, they were directly attacking the doctrine of separate spheres on the grounds of the psychological damage it had done. In effect, critics of Wollstonecraft and Stanton were right in complaining that both claimed for women a male psychological style. But Gilligan does not explore the psychological limitations of the female "voice" that she identifies, and the effect of her argument is to encourage the conclusion that women really are more nurturant than men, less likely to dominate, more likely to negotiate than are men—just as Gilligan's women and girls

2. Barbara Welter, "The Cult of True Womanhood: 1820–1860," *American Quarterly* 18 (Summer 1966): 151–74; Gerda Lerner, "The Lady and the Mill Girl: Changes in the Status of Women in the Age of Jackson," *Midcontinent American Studies Journal* 10 (Spring 1969): 5–15.

3. Carroll Smith-Rosenberg, "The Female World of Love and Ritual: Relations between Women in Nineteenth-Century America," *Signs: Journal of Women in Culture and Society* 1, no. 1 (Autumn 1975): 1–29.

do when considering the Heinz dilemma, the classic case in which a man named Heinz must decide whether or not to steal a drug needed by his dying wife. Perhaps there was—and is—something in the separation of spheres that is more than mere socialization. Perhaps when Victorians claimed that women were intrinsically more peaceable than men, they knew something that Gilligan has just rediscovered. Perhaps.

But the reification of separate spheres, now freshly buttressed by Gilligan's study of psychological development, poses major dangers of oversimplification. As Ellen DuBois warned five years ago, single-minded focus on women's own culture brings with it the risk of ignoring "the larger social and historical developments of which it was a part" and does not "address the limitations of the values of women's culture," the ways that they restrained and confined women. A rigid dualism makes no room for analysis of the sort offered by Estelle Freedman in her important 1979 essay, "Separatism as Strategy," in which she contends that distinctive female institutions like schools, clubs, and settlement houses can be thought of as a public version of the female separate sphere that has "helped mobilize women and [been used by them to gain] political lever-age in the larger society." Freedman argues that women have been most effective politically when they have reserved for themselves a territory free of contamination by male aggressiveness from which they might operate as critics of culture. When she calls for continued support of separate female institutions, Freedman explains, she does so "not because the values, culture, and politics of the two sexes are biologically, irrevers-ibly, distinct, but rather because the historical and contemporary experi-ences that have created a unique female culture remain both salient for and compatible with the goal of sexual equality."[4]

* * *

What, then, are the risks of relying on women's allegedly "different voice"? One danger, I think, is a familiar variety of feminist self-righteousness. Historically the rhetoric of feminism has spoken with two voices: one that claimed for women the natural rights of all human beings, and one that claimed that women were different from—and, usually, better than—men. One major wing of suffragist feminism, for example, relied heavily on a rhetoric which grew out of the separation of spheres and maintained that women were more law-abiding, more peace-loving, more charitable than men. Give women the vote, the argument went, and the streets would be clean, child labor would be eliminated, war would be

4. Ellen DuBois, "Politics and Culture in Women's History," *Feminist Studies* 6, no. 1 (Spring 1980): 28–36, esp. 31; Estelle Freedman, "Separation as Strategy: Female Institu-tion Building and American Feminism, 1870–1930," *Feminist Studies* 5, no. 3 (Fall 1979): 512–29, esp. 513, 523, 525.

at an end. One antisuffragist, Annie Nathan Meyer of New York, thinking of spread-eagle politics, called this wishful thinking "spreadhenism."
Suffragists were right in expecting that support for peace movements and
progressive legislation would come from newly enfranchised women, but
they were wrong to predict that most women would support a political
agenda drawn up from the concerns central to women's sphere. Newly
enfranchised women voted as the interests of their race and class dictated,
just as our own contemporaries have recently done. It is no surprise that
the more extensive promises to usher in a new world made by suffragists
could not be fulfilled.[5]

I agree with Gilligan that our culture has long undervalued nurturance and that when we measure ethical development by norms more
attainable by boys than by girls our definition of norms is probably biased.
But by emphasizing the biological basis of distinctive behavior (departing
here from Chodorow, who emphasizes learning), Gilligan permits her
readers to conclude that women's alleged affinity for "relationships of
care" is both biologically natural and a good thing.

The other risk is one of romantic oversimplification. If women can be
counted on to care for others, how are we to deal with self-interest,
selfishness, and meanness of spirit which women surely display as much as
do men? If we let the cycle of historical revisionism come full circle, are we
not back once again in the world of the angel in the house? And if we
permit that, how are we to deal with the occasions when women's supposed ethic of relationship and care does not seem to have been an
adequate moral imperative for all men or all women? Even Elizabeth
Cady Stanton was not above making a racist appeal to white men that they
choose white women for enfranchisement before black men. A recent
book of essays on women in Weimar and Nazi Germany gives evidence of
the attraction of housewives' organizations to fascism, the desertion of
Jewish members by the German feminist movement, and the support for
Nazi eugenics by the organization of German Women Doctors which
quickly moved to expel its own Jewish members.[6]

It seems well established that little boys face a psychic task of separation that little girls do not. But let us not be in haste to conclude that most
or all of what have been called the characteristics of separate spheres
emerge naturally from women's own distinctive psychology, biologically

5. See Aileen Kraditor, *The Ideas of the Woman Suffrage Movement, 1890–1920* (New
York: Columbia University Press, 1965), pp. 49–50; Annie Nathan Meyer, letters to the *New
York Tribune* (March 30, 1908; January 16, 1938). For the ease with which suffragism's
emphasis on women's special virtue could cooperate with white supremacy arguments, see
Kraditor, pp. 140–70.

6. Renate Bridenthal, Atina Grossmann, and Marion Kaplan, *When Biology Became
Destiny: Women in Weimar and Nazi Germany* (New York: Monthly Review Press, 1984).

rooted in patterns of maturation. Much, perhaps most, of it may well be rooted in the distinctive socialization of young girls in a culture which has always rested on the sexual division of labor, which has long ascribed some social tasks to men and others to women, and which has served as a mechanism by which a patriarchal society excludes one segment of the population from certain roles and therefore makes easier the task of producing hegemonic consensus. Gilligan describes how women make lemonade out of the lemons they have inherited. She does not tell how to transform the lemons into chocolate.

Department of History
University of Iowa

How Different Is the "Different Voice"?

Catherine G. Greeno and Eleanor E. Maccoby

Gilligan's book *In a Different Voice* was intended to right a wrong. In 1965 Jean Piaget wrote, "The most superficial observation is sufficient to show that in the main the legal sense is far less developed in little girls than in boys." Several studies using Lawrence Kohlberg's moral development scale also reported sex differences (and male superiority) in the level of moral reasoning employed in response to hypothetical moral dilemmas.[7] Gilligan argues that these supposed deficiencies of female development result from an injustice inherent in the research. She notes that the research paradigm, and the analyses of moral "levels," have been based primarily on the study of male subjects. As a result, psychologists have fallen into an observational bias; by "implicitly adopting the male life as the norm, they have tried to fashion women out of a masculine cloth" (p. 6), and women's particular moral development "falls through the sieve" (p. 31) of an androcentric research tradition. Gilligan's view is that with a less biased approach to moral thinking, one would find that women's thinking was somewhat different from men's, but not less mature. Psychologists have erred, not in believing that women are different from men, but that they are inferior to men; because women develop along a moral path that is distinct from that followed by men, existing research paradigms have failed them.

Because Gilligan addresses Kohlberg's paradigm primarily, it is well

7. Jean Piaget, *The Moral Judgment of the Child* (New York: Free Press, 1965), p. 77; Henry Alker and Paul J. Poppen, "Ideology in University Students," *Journal of Personality* 41, no. 4 (December 1973): 653–71.

Signs   Winter 1986   311

to be aware of certain features of his work, as well as some of the recent advances in theory, method, and findings.[8] The major goal of Kohlberg and his colleagues has been to trace developmental change in moral reasoning. While Kohlberg originally thought he could distinguish six such levels, more recent work indicates that there are four that can be applied to the large majority of children and adults. These four levels form a clear developmental progression. That is, individuals move from one to the next as they grow older, and there is evidence for the claim that the four levels have validity for individuals from a variety of cultural backgrounds. The transition from level 3 to level 4 is of the greatest interest for our purposes. Level 3 is considered to be the first stage of adult reasoning. Some studies using Kohlberg's rating system found that women tended to remain scored there, while men more consistently matured to level 4.[9] Level 3 reasoning involves a concern with maintaining bonds of trust with others. The individual strives to be—and to be seen by others as—a "good" or "nice" person. The "good" or "right" action is that which will not hurt those with whom one has valued relationships. Shared feelings and agreements take priority over individual interests. The move to level 4 involves what might be called a move to a societal level of thought, where moral issues are considered in terms of a system of law or justice that must be maintained for the good of society. The higher level does not supersede or supplant the lower—persons who can think in societal terms about moral issues also can continue to think about the effects of their actions on other persons with whom they have relationships—but a new progression in thought has occurred. There can be no doubt that level 4 considerations do appear in an individual's thinking later than level 3 considerations. In this sense, the societal level is more mature.

Here Gilligan makes her primary departure from the work that precedes her. She argues that although the androcentric coding system used for Kohlberg's dilemmas shows women remaining at level 3 more often than do men, women are not in fact fixed at this relatively immature level but progress along a path different from that followed by men. Specifically, she believes that women move from an exclusive orientation toward serving others' interests to a greater emphasis on self-

8. Lawrence Kohlberg, *The Philosophy of Moral Development: Moral Stages and the Idea of Justice* (New York: Harper & Row, 1981); Anne Colby et al., "A Longitudinal Study of Moral Judgment," *Monographs for the Society for Research in Child Development* 48, nos. 1–2, whole no. 200 (Chicago: University of Chicago Press, 1983).

9. James Fishkin, Kenneth Keniston, and Catharine MacKinnon, "Moral Reasoning and Political Ideology," *Journal of Personality and Social Psychology* 27, no. 1 (July 1973): 109–19; Norma Haan, M. Brewster Smith, and Jeanne Block, "Moral Reasoning of Young Adults: Political-social Behavior, Family Background, and Personality Correlates," *Journal of Personality and Social Psychology* 10, no. 3 (November 1968): 183–201.

actualization. Thus the "different construction of the moral problem by women may be seen as the reason for their failure to develop within the constraints of Kohlberg's system" (p. 19).

Current work reveals, however, that Gilligan has been attacking a straw man. In a comprehensive review paper, Lawrence Walker considers sixty-one studies in which the Kohlberg paradigm is used to score moral reasoning for subjects of both sexes. These show that in childhood and adolescence, there is no trend whatever for males to score at higher levels than females on Kohlberg's scales. In adulthood, the large majority of comparisons reveal no sex differences. In the studies that do show sex differences, the women were less well educated than the men, and it appears that education, not gender, accounts for women's seeming lesser maturity. Throughout this large body of research, there is no indication whatever that the two sexes take different developmental paths with respect to moral thought about abstract, hypothetical issues.[10]

Because Gilligan's own writings do not include data on how girls and women change their moral thinking as they grow older, we do not know whether a different scoring system, based on Gilligan's formulations, would show differences in the sequence of developmental steps. For two reasons we think it highly doubtful that such differences will emerge if and when the necessary comparisons are made: (1) the number of men and the number of women who reach the different Kohlberg levels at successive ages are highly similar, which suggests that the sexes follow the same developmental path; and (2) thinking about moral issues is closely linked to, though not identical with, general cognitive development, and we know that the sexes do not differ in the average rate at which they climb the ladder of cognitive growth.

Of course, thinking about hypothetical moral issues is not all there is to morality. In retrospect, it is unfortunate that Gilligan focused her attack primarily on the Kohlberg paradigm. Gilligan has other points to make about morality, and in the long run, her greatest contribution may be her work on these other aspects of moral decision making. Women, Gilligan believes, are bound into a network of intimate interpersonal ties. Compared with men, they are more empathic and compassionate, more concerned lest they fail to respond to others' needs, and made more anxious by the threat of separation from their loved ones. All these things could be true even if the sexes did not differ in their thinking about abstract moral issues.

Gilligan is not the only writer to point to sex differences in the capacity for intimate interpersonal relationships. The claim that women are more oriented toward interpersonal relations has a well-established

10. Lawrence Walker, "Sex Differences in the Development of Moral Reasoning: A Critical Review," *Child Development* 55, no. 3 (June 1984): 667–91.

Signs   *Winter 1986*   *313*

history in many forums of discussion. Women's predominance in the nurturance and care of young children is an accepted and cross-culturally universal fact. Theorists have used women's presumably greater interpersonal orientation to "explain" a wide variety of sex-linked phenomena, ranging from differences in mathematical or spatial ability to differences in the nature of the roles assigned to women in most societies. Talcott Parsons and R. F. Bales's distinction between the instrumental (masculine) and the expressive (feminine) functions in family organization provides an early example. The more recent work of Sandra Bem and of Janet Spence, Robert Helmreich, and Joy Stapp makes similar distinctions.[11]

Research has indicated that there are indeed some robust sex differences that relate to Gilligan's concerns. For example, empathy and altruism have been frequently examined for sex differences.[12] Self-report scores on these qualities are particularly striking: in each of the sixteen self-report studies reported by Nancy Eisenberg and Roger Lennon, women rate themselves as more empathic than do men. These sex differences are sometimes very large statistically. Also, it has been found that when observers, such as teachers or peers, are asked to rate qualities of people they know, females are rated as more empathic and altruistic than males.[13] The stereotype of women's greater empathy and altruism is very strong, and, as Martin Hoffman points out in his review of empathy, "The relevant theorizing in the literature is in essential agreement with this stereotype. . . . There appear to have been no theorists who contradict [it]."[14]

It is clear that women have a greater *reputation* for altruism and empathy than do men, and that women accept its validity. Whether the reputation is deserved is a more complicated question. There are many studies in which people are unobtrusively observed while confronting an opportunity to help others. In general, these studies do not show that women are any more likely than men to offer help. However, most of these studies involve situations in which the person to be helped is a

11. Talcott Parsons and Robert F. Bales, *Family, Socialization and Interaction Process* (Glencoe, Ill.: Free Press, 1955); Sandra L. Bem, "The Measurement of Psychological Androgyny," *Journal of Consulting and Clinical Psychology* 42, no. 2 (April 1974): 155–62; Janet T. Spence, Robert Helmreich, and Joy Stapp, "Ratings of Self and Peers on Sex Role Attributes and Their Relation to Self-Esteem and Conceptions of Masculinity and Femininity," *Journal of Personality and Social Psychology* 32, no. 1 (July 1975): 29–39.

12. For a useful review, see Nancy Eisenberg and Roger Lennon, "Sex Differences in Empathy and Related Capacities," *Psychological Bulletin* 94, no. 1 (July 1983): 100–131.

13. Douglas B. Sawin et al., "Empathy and Altruism" (Department of Psychology, University of Texas at Austin, 1979, mimeographed).

14. Martin L. Hoffman, "Sex Differences in Empathy and Related Behaviors," *Psychological Bulletin* 84, no. 4 (July 1977): 712–22.

stranger. It has become clear that an individual's helpfulness to strangers depends on a complex set of factors that may or may not be related to gender. Thus, a person's readiness to offer help depends on the sex of the person in need, on perceived risks entailed in helping, and on the helper's beliefs about whether he or she has the skills needed to be an effective resource (e.g., a man is more likely to offer to change a tire, a woman, to soothe a child). It should be noted that in real life most altruistic acts are performed for the benefit of persons close to us. We suspect that if a real sex difference in altruism emerges, it will be found with respect to helpful acts directed toward friends and intimates, not toward strangers. But this work remains to be done; so far a sex difference can be neither confirmed nor refuted.

Recent work on children's play groups indicates that even at a very early age males and females show decidedly different styles in social interactions.[15] This research provides some evidence supporting an "agentive/expressive" distinction, similar to the one proposed by Parsons and Bales, but at a preadult phase of development. Girls' groups are smaller, most often a dyad or triad of "best friends" whose interactions are based on shared confidences. Boys' groups are larger and more task-oriented; that is, play tends to center on some goal-directed game or activity. These differences appear fairly early in childhood and are persistent. It is possible that some of the gender differences postulated in areas such as empathy and altruism stem from these early tendencies and preferences. An interesting parallel is, in fact, found in the literature on intimacy among adults. Women's relationships tend to focus on self-disclosure, and "liking" among women is highly correlated to the amount of self-disclosure that goes on in a relationship. For men the correlation between liking and self-disclosure is very low.[16] Self-disclosure tends to be a feature of intimacy and may be connected to the kind of network of interpersonal ties that Gilligan perceives. A great deal of work is left to be done on the exact nature of intimate relationships and possible gender differences therein.

When we read Gilligan, it is easy to be impressed by the elegance of her style and by the historical, philosophical depth of what she has to say. In these respects, her writing is very refreshing compared to the dry fact citing of much of social science. It seems almost philistine to challenge the nature of her evidence. Many women readers find that the comments by

15. For a review, see Eleanor Maccoby, "Social Groupings in Childhood: Their Relationship to Prosocial and Antisocial Behavior in Boys and Girls," in *Development of Antisocial and Prosocial Behavior: Theories, Research and Issues*, ed. Dan Olwens, Jack Block, and Marian Radke-Yarrow (San Diego: Academic Press, 1985).

16. Zick Rubin and Stephen Schenker, "Friendship, Proximity, and Self-Disclosure," *Journal of Personality* 46, no. 1 (March 1978): 1–22.

women quoted in Gilligan's book resonate so thoroughly with their own experience that they do not need any further demonstration of the truth of what is being said. The fact remains, however, that Gilligan claims that the views expressed by women in her book represent a *different* voice— different, that is, from men. This assertion demands quantitative, as well as qualitative, research. There is no sphere of human thought, action, or feeling in which the two sexes are entirely distinct. Reproductive activity is the area in which behaviors come closest to being truly dimorphic, but apart from this, the male and female distributions overlap greatly, and in most respects, men and women are more alike than they are different. A claim that the two sexes speak in different voices amounts to a claim that there are more women than men who think, feel, or behave in a given way. Simply quoting how some women feel is not enough proof. We need to know whether what is being said is distinctively *female*, or simply human. We believe that no researcher who makes assertions such as Gilligan's can escape the obligation to demonstrate a quantitative difference in the proportion of the two sexes who show the characteristic in question. Here, Gilligan's research, as cited in the book, is unsatisfying. One study on abortion decisions was understandably confined to women subjects, and we consequently cannot compare how women and men think about this issue. Another study by Susan Pollak and Gilligan, after comparing the responses of men and women to a set of pictured scenes, maintained that women are made more anxious than men by the isolation that is involved in achievement, while men are made anxious by intimacy. However, a recent attempt to replicate that study raises serious questions about the way the pictures were classified to elicit the sex differences. Other classification systems reveal no tendency for the sexes to differ in their anxiety about intimacy or separation.[17] Finally, Gilligan has not yet provided any evidence that boys and girls follow different developmental courses in their thinking about morality. The book's only evidence concerning children's responses to moral issues consists of quotations from two eight-year-olds and two eleven-year-olds. These quotations fit our stereotypes about boys and girls, and intuitively we may feel that Gilligan must be right. But can we remain satisfied with this level of evidence?

We can only sound a warning: women have been trapped for generations by people's willingness to accept their own intuitions about the truth of gender stereotypes. To us, there seems no alternative to the slow,

---

17. Susan Pollak and Carol Gilligan, "Images of Violence in Thematic Apperception Test Stories," *Journal of Personality and Social Psychology* 42, no. 1 (January 1982): 159–67; Kay Bussey and Betty Maugham, "Gender Differences in Moral Reasoning," ibid., 42, no. 4 (April 1982): 701–6; Cynthia J. Benton et al., "Is Hostility Linked with Affiliation among Males and with Achievement in Females? A Critique of Pollak and Gilligan," ibid., 45, no. 5 (November 1983): 1167–71.

painful, and sometimes dull accumulation of quantitative data to show whether the almost infinite variations in the way human beings think, feel, and act are actually linked to gender. Let us hasten to say that we are not arguing that the sexes do not differ in important respects. We only urge that claims about what these differences are should be subjected to the empirical tests that are the basis of social science.

Department of Psychology
Stanford University

A Methodological Critique

Zella Luria

In a Different Voice has had a predictably wide audience among women. Indeed the six story-filled essays have an intuitive fit with how many women see themselves, especially in relation to men. Given the potential influence of this work in characterizing women's thinking, it becomes imperative to scrutinize the bases of its arguments and to ask whether the evidence is yet sufficient to warrant Gilligan's conclusions. If the evidence is found insufficient, what further research might be needed for a more rigorous test of the book's intriguing assertions?

Gilligan's work demonstrates her immersion in the field of adolescent development and the influence on her of psychoanalytic theory. In research (as well as in popular thought) on the psychology of adolescence, Sigmund Freud and Erik Erikson are critical figures; the theories and methodologies of both turn up repeatedly in all of Gilligan's writing here and elsewhere. The weaving of literary examples (presumably as metaphors), theoretical proposal, and loosely defined empirical research can be a winning but seductive design; occasionally Gilligan does not draw a clear line between theoretical speculation and discussion of data and slips from hunch, example, or metaphor to "proven fact." The structure of her work, to use a metaphor myself, is built of solid bricks intermixed with some of cardboard.

In Gilligan's interview work, for instance, the nature of the evidence is sometimes unclear. Although psychological work on adolescents has been criticized for relying too heavily on the single method of the semi-structured interview that is favored by Gilligan, that method *can* be a useful technique if certain requirements of rigorous research are fulfilled. First, good samples must be carefully characterized by age, social class, education, and method of recruitment so that readers can securely apply the findings to similar groups. In general, Gilligan's sample specification is inadequate to justify her group characterizations. For example, eight males and eight females at different ages do not make up a number sufficient to characterize all males and females. Then, too, samples drawn from classes on moral development at Harvard University are dubious exemplars of students generally. Questionable, moreover, is the match within this sample itself between male and female students. Such matching does not occur in the central study of attitudes toward abortion. Twenty-nine women considering abortions in Boston may provide an important example of decision making, but they cannot provide data on how men and women differ in such thinking.[18] None of this rules out the possibility that adequate, well-specified samples for interview could be studied. Gilligan, however, has not yet done it.

Second, interviews that yield discursive data such as explanations, personal histories, and discussion of abstract questions require objective rules that categorize the respondents' texts. The rules for categorizing—X is a caring answer, Y is a rationalization and is also an abstract answer, Z is an abstract answer with caring, and so on—must be specified to ensure that all investigators make the same decisions about what particular responses mean, regardless of the theory under study. If the measuring system is reliable, investigators who may not share biases or views should, by careful rule application, agree nonetheless on the categorization of interview answers. Since the group working with Kohlberg on the studies of moral development central to Gilligan's critique has had three coding schemes and since Gilligan tells little of her own, no reader can know if this second requirement—the reliable objective scoring system—has been met. Thus the reader cannot make a personal judgment on the author's understanding of a particular answer or on the way in which answers are classified.

Third, Gilligan's juxtapositions of disparate samples pose problems about combination rules. Even if all subjects were asked about Kohlberg's dilemma on Heinz and the pharmacist, what was the rationale for considering abortion candidates and Harvard students as combined sources for data on two gender voices? The interviews of the twenty-nine pregnant women in the abortion study covered many questions necessarily absent from the Harvard students' interviews. After all, the family planning agency from which Gilligan recruited subjects expected her to talk about more than Heinz and the Kohlberg moral dilemmas. One is left with the sense that the combination of the data does not conform to the usual rules of psychological procedure—shared sampling, shared procedure, shared scoring—but is the result of a somewhat impressionistic

18. This sample is also unlike one of women who refuse to consider abortion, as can be seen in Kristin Luker's *Abortion and the Politics of Motherhood* (Berkeley and Los Angeles: University of California Press, 1984).

grouping of the stories Gilligan's subjects told. Obviously no psychologist would object to such a technique for deriving hypotheses, but Gilligan seems, at least, to be proferring it as a basis for proof.

It is highly likely that Gilligan is concerned with these issues of methodology. However, the book lacks any careful statement on them. One is left with the knowledge that there were some studies involving women and sometimes men and that women were somehow sampled and somehow interviewed on some issues as well as on the Kohlberg stories. Somehow the data were sifted and somehow yielded a clear impression that women could be powerfully characterized as caring and interrelated. This is an exceedingly intriguing proposal but it is not yet substantiated as a research conclusion. The interesting answers to queries liberally sprinkled along with the case studies through the volume cannot substitute for objectively derived data.

Gilligan's hypothesis, moreover, gives rise to another question, Does she truly believe that we need one psychology for women and another for men? At the 1983 meeting of the Society for Research in Child Development, her response was no, but her book suggests that her answer is yes. She gives no evidence of the extent of overlap between male and female responses to the Kohlberg moral dilemmas, as if the data consist of two virtually nonoverlapping curves. If there is one statement to be clearly and loudly stated to the public by students of sex differences, it is that overlap of scores by males and females is always far greater than the differences in those scores, particularly on psychological measures. We are not two species; we are two sexes.

It appears, then, that to yield so strong a theory as that which structures *In a Different Voice*, Gilligan has to some degree oversimplified the case and overinterpreted the data. Yet we might still ask whether her conclusions seem plausible when placed in the context of overall evidence. The lead review by Lawrence Walker in the June 1984 issue of *Child Development* details the evidence on sex differences found in studies using the Kohlberg moral reasoning measure. No sex differences that can be measured in replicable, developmentally orderly, and statistically significant ways are cited in the review. Of the nineteen adult studies reported there, fourteen yield no significant sex differences and five find men ahead in measures of moral reasoning. When usual summary techniques are applied to add all the studies together, the data do not support any finding of a statistically significant sex difference. In the review's last table, however, there is a footnote citing results by Gilligan et al. in an unpublished 1982 manuscript. Four samples of sixteen subjects—made up, one gathers, of eight men and eight women in each of four different age groups—were tested and showed no difference in average scores of men and women. A footnote suggests that "more men than women displayed at least one instance of postconventional (a higher stage) reasoning."[19] Are thirty-two men and thirty-two women the data base for Gilligan's different voices?

A recent doctoral thesis by Betsy Speicher-Dubin helps us to understand why some interpretations of sex differences may have been derived from older data. When social class is truly controlled, that is, by determining a married woman's class by her own education and work history rather than by her spouse's, sex differences do not appear. Results from the University of California Institute of Human Development at Berkeley based on archival data from the Oakland study—whose design was described by Harold Jones in 1939 and whose results relevant to this discussion were described by Speicher-Dubin in 1982[20]—showed women coming out slightly ahead on the Kohlberg measure. As the match between male and female class and education becomes more equitable, it might be reasonable to expect that male and female scores may not be very different. The relevant literature is replete with instances of presumed sex differences (we call some of them stereotypes) that disappear when better controls are used. On the other hand, if one wants to find sex differences, as Gilligan apparently does, one can get them simply by not controlling for class and education. One further related point: a 1979 review of work on a Kohlberg-like test—the Defining Issues Test developed by J. R. Rest—concluded that sex differences are rarely significant among students at the junior high, senior high, college, or graduate level or among adults. It is not even true, therefore, that at one stage in life one sex has an advantage which the other assumes at a later stage.[21] This evidence has not since been disputed.

Curiously, all of this discussion began just as Kohlberg and his colleagues took a new scoring manual to press. A previous publication by that group includes an example in an appendix of how responses demonstrating care of others can be coded at all stages.[22] Still, we cannot know whether Gilligan used such a method because her book contains no statement describing her interview and scoring criteria. Another recent review concludes that Gilligan's theory has been given wide scholarly

19. Carol Gilligan et al., "The Contribution of Women's Thought to Developmental Theory: The Elimination of Sex Bias in Moral Development Research and Education," cited in Walker (n. 10 above), p. 686.

20. Harold E. Jones, "The Adolescent Growth Study, I. Principles and Methods," and "The Adolescent Growth Study, II. Procedures," *Journal of Consulting Psychology* 3 (1939): 157–59, 177–80; Betsy Speicher-Dubin, "Relationships between Parent Moral Judgment, Child Moral Judgment, and Family Interaction: A Correlational Study" (Ph.D. diss., Harvard Graduate School of Education, 1982).

21. Mary Brabeck, "Moral Judgment: Theory and Research on Differences between Males and Females," *Developmental Review* 3, no. 3 (September 1983): 274–91.

22. Anne Colby et al., *Assessing Moral Stages: A Manual* (New York: Cambridge University Press, 1984); Colby et al. (n. 8 above).

attention, but "empirical evidence in support of her assertions is less available."[23] I welcome the research that will test those assertions.

* * *

What is it that we want today as women and as feminists? That is not a question about evidence but about goals. Do we truly gain by returning to a modern cult of true womanhood? Do we gain by the assertion that women think or reason in one voice and men in another? Gilligan's view focuses on characteristics of the person; the situation is only a vehicle for the expression of the reasoning personality, whether that be caring or abstract. The same rationale has often been used to shunt people into the "appropriate" job. Social psychologists during the last decade have been struggling to free psychology of these views of personality produced in the 1950s for the good reason that people are not, in fact, all that predictable in different circumstances. People differ in how they size up situations and then in their behavioral responses.[24] Actually, Gilligan's tie to the Kohlberg method does not give her—or Kohlberg—a sound basis for talking about people's behavior, only for analyzing what they say, alas!

A reasonable goal seems to me to make women—and men—able to choose when to be caring and related and when to be concerned with abstract issues. (While I do not view abstraction and ability to care as opposites, for the sake of the argument let us assume that they are nonoverlapping ways of thinking or behaving.) Modern women will need *not* to be always caring and interrelated, if indeed they ever were constantly so. And they are also in situations where being abstract and rights oriented is a necessity. My purpose as a feminist is to train women to choose their actions sensibly and flexibly depending on the situations they confront.

Some of my students are frightened. All around them are striving women. Many of my students are feminists but are also somewhat timid, traditionally feminine, and unsure of their ability to manage the real overload of work and family. They are horrified by real life competition for graduate school, for jobs, for men. How can we help such women deal with society today while trying to change it in productive ways? That seems to me to be the task. The world will not stop to let off those caring

23. Brabeck, pp. 275, 277.

24. Daryl Bem and David C. Funder, "Predicting More of the People More of the Time: Assessing the Personality of Situations," *Psychology Review* 85 (1978): 485–501; Jack Block and Jeanne H. Block, "Studying Situational Dimensions: A Grand Perspective and Some Limited Empiricism," in *The Situation: An Interactional Perspective*, ed. David Magnusson (Hillsdale, N.J.: Lawrence Erlbaum Associates, 1980); David Magnusson and Norman S. Endler, eds., *Personality at the Crossroads: Current Issues in Interactional Psychology* (Hillsdale, N.J.: Lawrence Erlbaum Associates, 1977).

women whose fears and repugnance keep them from learning new choices. Surely Gilligan and I want one voice that allows both men and women a variety of differentiated responses. Anything else is a step backward.

Department of Psychology
Tufts University

The Culture of Gender: Women and Men of Color[25]

Carol B. Stack

Gilligan's assertion that there is a female model for moral development, and that this model appeals to responsibilities rather than to rights, echoes similar developments in feminist anthropological thinking of the 1970s. Anthropological research published in that decade uncovered a set of oppositions between maleness and femaleness primarily derived from studies of non-class-based societies. For example, Sherry Ortner and Harriet Whitehead, in their introduction to *Sexual Meanings*, emphasize that women in the societies described by the book's contributors tend to be more involved with private and particularistic concerns, with relationships, and with the welfare of their own families than they are with the more general social good. Men, on the other hand, are more universalistic and have a concern for the welfare of the whole. Their suggestion—in full agreement with the earlier assumptions of Michelle Rosaldo and Louise Lamphere on the universal distinction between the public domain and the domestic domain—is that these notions are nearly universal.[26] Until the last few years, these gender-based principles of opposition and dualism were recognized as the premises underlying feminist theory's heritage from anthropology.

Gilligan, in keeping with other feminist theorists studying the construction of gender, discovered enduring self-images that guide women through their lives—images set in contrast to the thoughts and actions of men. In Gilligan's model, women are more inclined to link morality to responsibility and relationships and to their ability to maintain ongoing

25. I would like to thank Sandra Morgen, Margery Wolf, and Brackette Williams for their lively interest in this work and their valuable suggestions.

26. Sherry B. Ortner and Harriet Whitehead, eds., *Sexual Meanings: The Cultural Construction of Gender and Sexuality* (New York: Cambridge University Press, 1981); Michelle Zimbalist Rosaldo and Louise Lamphere, eds., *Woman, Culture, and Society* (Stanford, Calif.: Stanford University Press, 1974).

social ties than are men. They achieve power and prestige through caring for others, and, Gilligan argues, their embeddedness in relationships should not be considered a developmental liability. Male development is linked to morality, fairness, rights, and rules, and to the social good; men forge their identities in relation to the external world and strive for personal autonomy.

Within the academic fields of psychology, sociology, anthropology, and history and in a variety of theoretical feminist models, several assumptions seemingly shared by Gilligan as well as influenced by her theory constitute the current dogma: (1) Men and women differ significantly in their construction of themselves in relationship to others. (2) Women and men experience issues of dependency differently. (3) Women and men experience class differently. (4) Women's work is perceived differently from men's work. (5) Boys and girls experience relationships differently. (6) There is a male and a female model for moral development. Feminist thinking across the disciplines links the construction of gender to these differences or oppositions.[27]

Preliminary analysis of data from my ongoing research with Black return migrants to the rural South reveals inconsistencies between this accepted feminist theory and findings derived from interviews. Returnees' discussions of the dilemmas of adulthood, the meaning of social ties, and the shared visions of maturity, as well as the principles that they set forth as they consider these topics, confirm Gilligan's own observation that the cross-cultural construction of gender remains unexplored.

Data from my study of return migration confirm my deeply held conviction from earlier studies that the caste and economic system within rural southern communities creates a setting in which Black women and men have a very similar experience of class, that is, a similar relationship to production, employment, and material and economic rewards.[28] Intriguing hypotheses arise from this insight. The data suggest that under conditions of economic deprivation there is a convergence between

27. Relevant sources for these assumptions, in addition to Gilligan, include Rosalind Petchesky, "Reproduction and Class Divisions among Women," in *Class, Race, and Sex: The Dynamics of Control*, ed. Amy Swerdlow and Hanna Lessinger (Boston: G. K. Hall & Co., 1983), pp. 157–243; Micaela di Leonardo, *The Varieties of Ethnic Experience: Kinship, Class, and Gender among California Italian-Americans* (Ithaca, N.Y.: Cornell University Press, 1984); Naomi Quinn, "Occupational Segregation and Cultural Beliefs about Women" (paper prepared for the National Academy of Sciences Committee on Women's Employment and Related Issues, Washington, D.C., 1982); and Jean Baker Miller, *Toward a New Psychology of Women* (Boston: Beacon Press, 1976).

28. See especially Carol Stack, *All Our Kin: Strategies for Survival in a Black Community* (New York: Harper & Row, 1974); Carol B. Stack and Robert L. Hall, eds., *Holding On to the Land and the Lord: Kinship, Ritual, Land Tenure, and Social Policy in the Rural South* (Athens: University of Georgia Press, 1982).

women and men in their construction of themselves in relationship to others, and that these conditions produce a convergence also in women's and men's vocabulary of rights, morality, and the social good. I view Black women's and men's contextualization of morality and the meaning of social ties as a cultural alternative to Gilligan's model of moral development, with a different configuration of gender differences and similarities.

Gender consciousness emerges from a negotiation between material conditions and cultural ideologies, from a negotiation between what is out there (historical conditions, class- and race-specific experiences, age and generation, the ecology of life course) and what we see with (the assumptions and interpretations that we have in our minds, our shared models of the world, our visions and dilemmas of adulthood). While it is extremely difficult to create a theory that makes it possible to negotiate between these two models, my aim is to demonstrate the importance of bringing race, class, consciousness, and generation to theory building and the construction of gender.[29]

My previous study, *All Our Kin*, examined the cultural strategies of Black women within the network of family relationships in urban communities, never making explicit questions concerning male and female adult development. My current research focuses on the return migration of Black women, men, and children from the urban Northeast to the rural South, exploring the meaning of social ties and the dilemmas of adulthood within the context of their migration experience. Between 1975 and 1980, the Black population in the South grew by 2 million, the largest decennial increase for Blacks in any census region in history.[30] Changing migration patterns reflect a new social movement that forecasts a dramatic spatial reorganization of population, and the restructuring of the social, cultural, and material conditions of migrants' lives, including the set of arrangements for organizing the gender system within family networks.

In the detailed life histories of return migrants, both women and men describe with force and conviction the strength of their kinship ties to their rural southern families and the nature of these ties that bind. For many of the Black men and women I interviewed, the relation to a home place has been and is the lodestar that provides place and context, meaning, continuity, and identity. As urban migrants, they with their families were satellites to home places, magnetized to the core. Their rural kin ties somberly represent spirit and purpose, fate, circumstance, and obliga-

29. Bonnie Thornton Dill, "'On the Hem of Life': Race, Class, and the Prospects for Sisterhood," in Swerdlow and Lessinger, eds. (n. 27 above), pp. 173–88.
30. Joint Center for Political Studies, *Blacks on the Move: A Decade of Demographic Change* (Washington, D.C.: Joint Center for Political Studies, 1982).

tion. A collective social conscience among these migrants manifests itself in several cultural strategies: concern for reciprocity, commitment to kin and community, and belief in the morality of responsibility.

The data I have analyzed from this return migration study reveal an African-American model of moral development. Men and women alike redefine and recontextualize moral dilemmas and the principles they use to think about them. These women's and men's voices, in unison with one another, appear to be very different from those on which Gilligan and Kohlberg based their models of relatedness and moral reasoning. However, the data used to generate this preliminary critique of gender-related theories of moral development were collected for a different purpose and were based on a different methodology from that used by moral development theorists. The life histories and the discussions of people's thoughts about migration choices, however, provide a starting point for placing Gilligan's theory in the context of culture and class. In future interviews with male and female return migrants, I will be using some of Gilligan's methods, slightly modified, in order to generate more precisely comparable data.

Gilligan's theory of women's moral development has taken root in native soil. It is a powerful and persuasive theory that derives a female model of moral development from the moral reasoning of primarily white, middle-class women in the United States. The model fits the data, and it fits the conceptualizations of many feminist researchers. However, as Black and Third World feminist researchers have emphasized, gender is a construct shaped by the experience of race, class, culture, caste, and consciousness.[31] Future research must contribute another dimension to the construction of feminist theory: it should provide a critical framework for analyzing gender consciousness and a cautionary reminder to those theorists who think that gender construction is the same in all societies.

Institute of Policy Sciences and Public Affairs
Duke University

Reply by Carol Gilligan

Among his many astute observations, William James noted that when a new idea is introduced, the first response is to say that it is so obviously false, it is hard to see how anyone could believe it; the second is to say that

---

31. See Dill; Bell Hooks, *Ain't I a Woman: Black Women and Feminism* (Cambridge, Mass.: South End Press, 1981); Gloria T. Hull, Patricia Bell Scott, and Barbara Smith, eds., *But Some of Us Are Brave: Black Women's Studies* (Old Westbury, N.Y.: Feminist Press, 1982).

Signs   Winter 1986   325

it is not original, and everyone has always known it to be true.[32] My critics are making both statements, but in doing so they introduce a central confusion. I am saying that the study of women calls attention to a different way of constituting the self and morality; they are focusing on the issue of sex differences as measured by standards derived from one sex only. In other words, my critics take the ideas of self and morality for granted as these ideas have been defined in the patriarchal or male-dominated tradition. I call these concepts in question by giving examples of women who constitute these ideas differently and hence tell a different story about human experience. My critics say that this story seems "intuitively" right to many women but is at odds with the findings of psychological research. This is precisely the point I am making and exactly the difference I was exploring: the dissonance between psychological theory and women's experience.

The sex difference issue was raised in a curiously unacknowledged way by those psychologists who chose all-male research samples, since the choice of a single-sex sample reflects an implicit premise of gender difference. But a sex-difference hypothesis cannot be tested adequately unless the standards of assessment are derived from studies of women as well as from studies of men. Otherwise, the questions being asked are, How much are women like men? Or, how much do women deviate from a male-defined standard?

It was in an effort to ask a different question that I wrote the book under discussion, seeking to discover whether something had been missed by the practice of leaving out girls and women at the theory-building stage of research in developmental psychology—that is, whether Piaget's and Kohlberg's descriptions of moral development, Erikson's description of identity development, Offer's description of adolescent development, Levinson's and Vaillant's descriptions of adult development, as well as more general accounts of human personality and motivation, contained a consistent conceptual and observational bias, reflected in and extended by their choice of all-male research samples.[33]

---

32. William James, *Pragmatism* (New York: New American Library, 1907), p. 131.

33. Piaget (n. 7 above); Lawrence Kohlberg, "Stage and Sequence: The Cognitive-Developmental Approach to Socialization," in *Handbook of Socialization*, ed. David A. Goslin (New York: Rand McNally, 1909). Erikson began his work on identity with returning war veterans in the 1950s and advanced it further in *Young Man Luther* (New York: W. W. Norton & Co., 1958). Daniel Offer, *The Psychological World of the Teenager: A Study of 175 Boys* (New York: Basic Books, 1969); Daniel Levinson, *The Seasons of a Man's Life* (New York: Ballantine Books, 1978); George Vaillant, *Adaptation to Life* (Boston: Little, Brown & Co., 1977). For a discussion of psychological norms based on studies of males, see David McClelland, *Power: The Inner Experience* (New York: Irvington, Halsted-Wiley, 1975); Joseph Adelson, ed., *Handbook of Adolescent Psychology* (New York: John Wiley & Sons, 1980), esp. Joseph Adelson and Margery Doehrman, "The Psychodynamic Approach to Adolescence."

The "different voice" hypothesis was an answer to this question. What had been missed by leaving out women was a different way of constituting the idea of the self and the idea of what is moral. Rather than seeing to what extent women exemplify what generally is taken to be self and morality, I saw in women's thinking the lines of a different conception, grounded in different images of relationship and implying a different interpretive framework. Attention to women's thinking thus raised a new set of questions about both male and female development and explained a series of observations that previously had not made sense. Discrepant data on girls and women, commonly interpreted as evidence of female deficiency, pointed instead to a problem in psychological theory.

That this problem affected women differently from the way it affected men seemed clear. Since women's voices were heard though a filter that rendered them confused and incoherent, it was difficult for men to understand women and for women to listen to themselves. In my book, I sought to clarify two related sets of problems, put forth in my subtitle: problems in psychological theory and problems in women's development. The argument was not statistical—that is, not based on the representativeness of the women studied or on the generality of the data presented to a larger population of women or men. Rather, the argument was interpretive and hinged on the demonstration that the examples presented illustrated a different way of seeing.

In defining a shift in perspective that changes the meaning of the key terms of moral discourse—such as the concept of self, the idea of relationship, and the notion of responsibility—I described an ethic of care and response that I contrasted with an ethic of justice and rights. I also cited as an empirical observation the prominence of the care perspective in women's moral thinking and used literary examples to amplify and extend the voices in my interview texts. My critics cannot make up their minds whether it is naive or self-serving to think of women as caring or whether this is a fact so obvious that it does not need repeating. But as they elaborate these contentions, it becomes increasingly apparent that the book they are discussing is different from the book which I have written.

They speak of the nineteenth-century ideal of pure womanhood and the romanticizing of female care: I portray twentieth-century women choosing to have abortions, as well as women college students, lawyers, and physicians reconsidering what is meant by care in light of their recognition that acts inspired by conventions of selfless feminine care have led to hurt, betrayal, and isolation. My critics equate care with feelings, which they oppose to thought, and imagine caring as passive or confined to some separate sphere. I describe care and justice as two moral perspectives that organize both thinking and feelings and empower the self to take different kinds of action in public as well as private life. Thus,

Signs   Winter 1986   327

in contrast to the paralyzing image of the "angel in the house," I describe a critical ethical perspective that calls into question the traditional equation of care with self-sacrifice.

The title of my book was deliberate; it reads, "in a *different* voice," not "in a *woman's* voice." In my introduction, I explain that this voice is identified not by gender but by theme. Noting as an empirical observation the association of this voice with women, I caution the reader that "this association is not absolute, and the contrasts between male and female voices are presented here to highlight a distinction between two modes of thought and to focus a problem of interpretation rather than to represent a generalization about either sex." In tracing development, I "point to the interplay of these voices within each sex and suggest that their convergence marks times of crisis and change." No claims, I state, are made about the origins of these voices or their distribution in a wider population, across cultures or time (p. 2). Thus, the care perspective in my rendition is neither biologically determined nor unique to women. It is, however, a moral perspective different from that currently embedded in psychological theories and measures, and it is a perspective that was defined by listening to both women and men describe their own experience.

The most puzzling aspect of my critics' position is their dissociation of women's experience from women's thinking—as if experiences common to women leave no psychological trace. Thus Greeno and Maccoby cite examples of sex differences in their references to "women's predominance in the nurturance and care of young children [as] an accepted and cross-culturally universal fact" (p. 313 above); to recent research indicating "that even at a very early age males and females show decidedly different styles in social interactions" (p. 314); and to findings of sex differences "in the literature on intimacy among adults" (p. 314). Kerber observes that "it seems well established that little boys face a psychic task of separation that little girls do not" (p. 309 above). Yet in endorsing the position of no sex differences, they appear to believe that nothing of significance for moral or self development is learned from these activities and experiences. The burden of proof would seem to rest with my critics to give a psychologically coherent explanation of why the sex differences they mention make no difference to moral development or self-concept. To say that social class and education contribute to moral development while experiences typically associated with gender are essentially irrelevant may say more about the way development is being measured than it does about morality or gender.

In replying to my critics, I wish to address three issues they raise: the issue of method, the issue of theory or interpretation, and the issue of goals or education. The first question is what constitutes data and what data are sufficient to support the claims I have made. To claim that there is a voice different from those which psychologists have represented, I need only one example—one voice whose coherence is not recognized within existing interpretive schemes. To claim that common themes recur in women's conceptions of self and morality, I need a series of illustrations. In counterposing women's conceptions of self and morality to the conceptions embedded in psychological theories, I assume that a psychology literature filled with men's voices exemplifies men's experience. Therefore, in listening to women, I sought to separate their descriptions of their experience from standard forms of psychological interpretation and to rely on a close textual analysis of language and logic to define the terms of women's thinking.

Like all psychological research, my work is limited by the nature and context of my observations and reflects my own interpretive frame. There are no data independent of theory, no observations not made from a perspective. Data alone do not tell us anything; they do not speak, but are interpreted by people. I chose to listen to women's descriptions of experiences of moral conflict and choice, to attend to the ways that women describe themselves in relation to others, and to observe changes in thinking over time. On the basis of these observations and my reading of psychology, I made a series of inferences about the nature of sex differences, about women's development, about the concept of self, and about the nature of moral experience.

Seizing on the Walker article recently published in *Child Development*, my critics claim that there are no sex differences in moral development because there are no sex differences on the Kohlberg scale.[34] Thus they completely miss my point. My work focuses on the difference between two moral orientations—a justice and a care perspective rather than on the question of whether women and men differ on Kohlberg's stages of justice reasoning. On two occasions, I have reported no sex differences on Kohlberg's measure.[35] But the fact that educated women are capable of high levels of justice reasoning has no bearing on the question of whether they would spontaneously choose to frame moral problems in this way. My interest in the way people *define* moral problems is reflected in my research methods, which have centered on first-person accounts of moral conflict.[36]

34. Walker (n. 10 above).

35. John Michael Murphy and Carol Gilligan, "Moral Development in Late Adolescence and Adulthood," *Human Development* 23, no. 2 (1980): 77–104; Gilligan et al. (n. 19 above).

36. Carol Gilligan and John Michael Murphy, "Development from Adolescence to Adulthood: The Philosopher and 'The Dilemma of the Fact,'" in *Intellectual Development beyond Childhood*, ed. Deanna Kuhn (San Francisco: Jossey-Bass, 1979), pp. 85–99; Carol Gilligan and Mary Belenky, "A Naturalistic Study of Abortion Decisions," in *Clinical-Developmental Psychology*, ed. Robert L. Selman and Regina Yando (San Francisco: Jossey-Bass, 1980), pp. 69–90.

Signs   Winter 1986   329

My critics are unaware that Walker's conclusions and use of statistics have been seriously challenged by two of the researchers on whose findings he most heavily relies. In replies submitted to *Child Development*, Norma Haan reports significant sex differences on the Kohlberg test, even when controlling for social class and education and using the new scoring method; Diana Baumrind notes that the most highly educated women in her sample were less likely than other women or men to score at Kohlberg's postconventional stages because they were less likely to frame moral problems in terms of abstract principles of justice.[37] Thus lower scores on the Kohlberg measure do not necessarily reflect lower levels of moral development but may signify a shift in moral perspective or orientation.

The example in my book of eleven-year-old Amy illustrates how a care perspective is rendered incomprehensible by the Kohlberg frame. This point is extended by interviews conducted with Amy and Jake when they were fifteen. At fifteen, both children introduce both moral perspectives in thinking about the Heinz dilemma, although the order of introduction is not the same. Amy's ability to solve the problem within the justice framework leads her to advance a full stage on Kohlberg's scale, but Jake's introduction of the care perspective signifies no advance in moral development, according to Kohlberg's measure. The Kohlberg test, in its equation of moral development with justice reasoning, does not adequately represent either Amy's or Jake's moral thinking. Amy's own terms remain at fifteen the terms of the care perspective, and from this standpoint she sees moral problems in the justice construction. To equate her moral development with her ability to reason within this framework is to ignore her perceptions; but it is also to encourage her, in the name of development, to accept a construction of reality and morality that she identifies as problematic. For Jake, the equation of moral judgment with the logic of justice reasoning encourages him to take the position that anyone disagreeing with his judgment has "the wrong set of priorities." He takes this stand at first when asked about the druggist's refusal to relinquish his profit but then abandons it in the recognition that there is another way to think about this problem. At eleven, Jake saw the Heinz dilemma as "sort of like a math problem with humans"; at fifteen he recasts it as a story about two people whose actions can be interpreted differently, depending on the constraints of their situation, and whose feelings, when elaborated, evoke understanding and compassion. What

37. For a more extensive discussion of Amy's and Jake's moral reasoning at age fifteen, see Carol Gilligan, "Remapping Development: The Power of Divergent Data," in *Value Presuppositions in Theories of Human Development*, ed. Leonard Cirillo and Seymour Wapner (Hillside, N. J.: Lawrence Erlbaum Associates, in press).

had seemed a simple exercise in moral logic thus becomes a more complex moral problem.[38]

If my critics had pursued their questions about method and evidence, they would have discovered that in 1983 Nona Lyons reported a systematic procedure for identifying justice and care considerations in people's descriptions of real life dilemmas, and Sharry Langdale, in a doctoral dissertation, demonstrated that Lyons's method could be adapted for coding responses to hypothetical dilemmas.[39] With a cross-sectional, life-cycle sample of 144 males and females who were matched for social class and education, Langdale found significant sex differences in the use of justice and care considerations. My critics also could have learned that Kay Johnston, in a recently completed dissertation, created a standard method (using Aesop's fables) for assessing moral orientation use and preference. Johnston demonstrated that sixty eleven- and fifteen-year-old girls and boys from a middle-class suburban community were able to understand the logic of both the justice and care orientations, to use both strategies of reasoning in solving the problems posed by the fables, and to explain why one or the other orientation provided a better solution. She also found consistent sex differences in orientation use and preference, as well as variation across fables.[40]

These studies and others confirm and refine the "different voice" hypothesis by demonstrating that (1) the justice and care perspectives are distinct orientations that organize people's thinking about moral problems in different ways; (2) boys and men who resemble those most studied by developmental psychologists tend to define and resolve moral problems within the justice framework, although they introduce considerations of care; and (3) the focus on care in moral reasoning, although not characteristic of all women, is characteristically a female phenomenon in the advantaged populations that have been studied. These findings provide an empirical explanation for the equation of moral judgment with

38. Norma Haan, "With Regard to Walker (1984) on Sex 'Differences' in Moral Reasoning" (University of California, Berkeley, Institute of Human Development, 1985, mimeographed); Diana Baumrind, "Sex Differences in Moral Reasoning: Response to Walker's (1984) Conclusion That There Are None," *Child Development* (in press).

39. Nona Lyons, "Two Perspectives: On Self, Relationships, and Morality," *Harvard Education Review* 53, no. 2 (1983): 125–46, and "Conceptions of Self and Morality and Modes of Moral Choice: Identifying Justice and Care in Judgments of Actual Moral Dilemmas" (Ed.D. diss., Harvard Graduate School of Education, 1982); Sharry Langdale, "Moral Orientations and Moral Development: The Analysis of Care and Justice Reasoning across Different Dilemmas in Females and Males from Childhood through Adulthood" (Ed.D. diss., Harvard Graduate School of Education, 1983).

40. Kay Johnston, "Two Moral Orientations—Two Problem-solving Strategies: Adolescents' Solutions to Dilemmas in Fables" (Ed.D. diss., Harvard Graduate School of Education, 1985).

justice reasoning in theories derived from studies of males; but they also explain why the study of women's moral thinking changes the definition of the moral domain.

My critics' readiness to dismiss findings of sex differences is evident as well in the fact that they cite the Benton et al. critique of Susan Pollak's and my study of images of violence but overlook the three articles that followed in its wake: our reply, "Differing about Differences"; their response, "Compounding the Error"; and our rejoinder, "Killing the Messenger."[41] Pollak and I agree with Benton et al. that a priori classification of Thematic Apperception Test (TAT) pictures poses a serious problem in motivation research, but we see no exception to this problem in the classification they propose. Our study, however, relied on a content analysis of the violent stories written by women and men, an analysis that our critics ignore. This analysis revealed that, within the texts of the stories written (considered independently of the pictures), violence was associated with intimacy in stories written by men and with isolation in stories written by women. The report by Benton and her associates of sex differences in the incidence and location of violence are not inconsistent with our conclusions; however, their failure to conduct a content analysis suggests that their study was not a serious attempt at replication.[42]

If the Walker article implies that questions about sex differences in moral development can be reduced to an issue of Kohlberg test scores, the Benton et al. critique suggests that questions about sex differences in violent fantasies can be reduced to an issue of picture classification. Given that researchers repeatedly find significant sex differences in the incidence of both violent fantasies and violent behavior, the rush to dismiss the exploration of these differences on the basis of picture classification seems like an attempt to paper over a huge social problem with a methodological quibble. My critics are concerned about stereotypes that portray women as lacking in anger and aggression; but they do not consider the lower incidence of violence in women's fantasies and behavior to be a sex difference worth exploring. Thus my critics essentially accept the psychology I call into question—the psychology that has equated male with human in defining human nature and thus has construed evidence of sex differences as a sign of female deficiency, a psychology that, for all the talk about research design and methods, has failed to see all-male research samples as a methodological problem.

41. Pollak and Gilligan (n. 17 above); Benton et al. (n. 17 above); Susan Pollak and Carol Gilligan, "Differences about Differences: The Interpretation of Violent Fantasies in Women and Men," *Journal of Personality and Social Psychology* 45, no. 5 (1983): 1172–75; Bernard Weiner et al., "Compounding the Error: A Reply to Pollak and Gilligan," ibid., pp. 1176–78; Susan Pollak and Carol Gilligan, "Killing the Messenger," ibid. 48, no. 2 (1985): 374–75.

42. Pollak and Gilligan, "Killing the Messenger," pp. 374–75.

My work offers a different perspective, on psychology and on women. It calls into question the values placed on detachment and separation in developmental theories and measures, values that create a false sense of objectivity and render female development problematic. My studies of women locate the problem in female development not in the values of care and connection or in the relational definition of self, but in the tendency for women, in the name of virtue, to give care only to others and to consider it "selfish" to care for themselves. The inclusion of women's experience dispels the view of care as selfless and passive and reveals the activities that constitute care and lead to responsiveness in human relationships. In studies conducted by myself and my students, women who defined themselves in their own terms—as indicated by the use of active, first-person constructions—generally articulated the value of care and affirmed their own relational concerns. In thinking about choices in their lives, these women were able to adopt a critical perspective on societal values of separation and independence and to reject confusing images of women, such as "supermother" or "superwoman," that are at odds with women's knowledge about relationships and about themselves. Women's ability to act on this knowledge was associated in several doctoral dissertations with invulnerability to eating disorders, recovery from depression, and the absence of depressive symptoms in mothers of young children.[43] But if my characterization is accurate, there is no question that this knowledge brings women into conflict with current societal arrangements and often confronts them with painful and difficult choices.

My critics and I share a common concern about the education of our women students, as well as, I assume, a more general concern about the future of life on this planet. In light of these considerations, how best might we approach the education of both women and men students? To label women's concerns about conflicts between achievement and care as a sign of weakness is to render women frightened and fearful. This approach only reinforces the impression that women's fears are groundless. Women need to engage the problems created by the overload of work and family because these conflicts fall most heavily on women. But it is a disservice to both women and men to imply that these are women's problems.

43. Catherine Steiner-Adair, "The Body Politic: Normal Female Adolescent Development and the Development of Eating Disorders" (Ed.D. diss., Harvard Graduate School of Education, 1984); Dana Crowley Jack, "Clinical Depression in Women: Cognitive Schemas of Self, Care, and Relationships in a Longitudinal Study" (Ed.D. diss., Harvard Graduate School of Education, 1984); Ann Kinsella Willard, "Self, Situation and Script: A Psychological Study of Decisions about Employment in Mothers of One Year Olds" (Ed.D. diss., Harvard Graduate School of Education, 1985). See also Jane Stoodt Attanucci, "Mothers in Their Own Terms: A Developmental Perspective on Self and Role" (Ed.D. diss., Harvard Graduate School of Education, 1984).

Signs   *Winter 1986*   *333*

That developmental psychology has been built largely from the study of men's lives is not my invention. While we may disagree about the particular nature of the problems in this representation, as women we do ourselves an immense disservice to say that there is no problem. Since morality is closely tied to the problem of aggression—an area where sex differences are uncontested—it may be of particular interest at this time for both sexes to explore whether women's experience illuminates the psychology of nonviolent strategies for resolving conflicts. I am well aware that reports of sex differences can be used to rationalize oppression, and I deplore any use of my work for this purpose. But I do not see it as empowering to encourage women to put aside their own concerns and perceptions and to rely on a psychology largely defined by men's perceptions in thinking about what is of value and what constitutes human development.[44]

Graduate School of Education
Harvard University

44. The research described in this paper was supported by a generous gift from Marilyn Brachman Hoffman, and by grants from the William F. Milton Fund, the small grants section of NIMH, the Spencer Foundation grants to Harvard junior faculty, the National Institute of Education, and the Carnegie Corporation and the Bunting Institute of Radcliffe College. I owe a particular debt of gratitude to Jane Attanucci, Lyn Mikel Brown, Kay Johnston, and Bernard Kaplan.

Name Index